REDBOOK

New York
Civil Practice Law and
Rules

2010 Edition

CPLR
with Judicial Conference Notes and Statutory Cross References
CPLR TIMETABLE
UNIFORM CIVIL RULES FOR SUPREME AND COUNTY COURTS
SELECTED PRACTICE PROVISIONS
COURT DIRECTORY
REVISED INDEX

As amended by the 2009 Regular Legislative Session (current through Laws of 2009, Chapters 1 through 488, excluding Chapter 15)

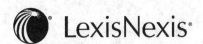

QUESTIONS ABOUT THIS PUBLICATION?

For questions about the **Editorial Content** appearing in these volumes or reprint permission, please call:

Robert R. Faszczewski at .... 1-800-526-4902 Ext. 8786
Email: .... robert.faszczewski@lexisnexis.com
Jacqueline M. Morris J.D. at .... 1-800-252-9257 Ext. 673-1528
Email: .... Jacqueline.M.Morris@lexisnexis.com

For assistance with replacement pages, shipments, billing or other customer service matters, please call:

Customer Services Department at . . . . (800)833-9844
Outside the United States and Canada, please call . . . . (518)487-3000
Fax Number . . . . (518)487-3584
Customer Service Website . . . . http://www.lexisnexis.com/custserv/
For information on other Matthew Bender publications, please call

Your account manager or . . . . (800)223-1940
Outside the United States and Canada, please call . . . . (518)487-3000

Library of Congress Card Number: 1547-2795

ISBN: 978-1-4224-7524-9

Editorial Offices
121 Chanlon Rd., New Providence, NJ 07974 (908) 464-6800
201 Mission St., San Francisco, CA 94105-1831 (415) 908-3200
www.lexisnexis.com

MATTHEW⬥BENDER

(2009–Pub.076)

Table of Contents

CIVIL PRACTICE LAW AND RULES

Table of Contents

Table of Contents

Table of Contents

UNIFORM CIVIL RULES FOR SUPREME AND COUNTY COURTS   PART 202

General Synopsis

Table of Contents

Table of Contents

Table of Contents

APPENDIX
SELECTED PRACTICE PROVISIONS

Table of Contents

COURT DIRECTORY

TABLE OF 2009 CPLR AMENDMENTS

CPLR Section or Rule	Amendment	Effective Date
105	Amended to extend until June 30, 2014 (at which time it will be automatically repealed) the provisions of the section which define "sheriff" and which confer on New York city marshals the same functions, powers and duties as sheriffs with respect to money judgments.	07/11/09
306-a	Amended to extend until September 1, 2011 sections of CPLR 306-a which were scheduled to expire on September 1, 2009.	04/07/09
312-a(d)	Amended to eliminate the requirement that members of the armed services include their serial number in an acknowledgment of the receipt of a summons and complaint, summons and notice, or notice of petition and petition by mail.	07/14/09
1101	Amended to extend the expiration dates of subd. (d) and (f) to Sept. 1, 2011.	04/07/09
2103	Amended to eliminate the requirement of consent to filing of certain papers by electronic means under certain circumstances, but subject to certain rights to opt out, and to eliminate the expiration date of CPLR 2103(b)(7). *See* enacting chapter—L. 2009, Ch. 416.	09/01/09
5205	Amended subdivision (l) and added subdivision (o) to provide that personal property that is otherwise exempt from application for satisfaction of a debt, may be applied to a debt to the state or its political subdivisions, or if the debt is for child support, spousal support, alimony or maintenance.	05/04/09
5222(k)	Added to provide that personal property that is otherwise exempt from application for satisfaction of a debt, may be applied to a debt to the state or its political subdivisions, or if the debt is for child support, spousal support, alimony or maintenance.	05/04/09

CPLR Section or Rule	Amendment	Effective Date
5222-a	Amended subdivisions (a), (b) and (c) and added subd. (i) to provide that personal property that is otherwise exempt from application for satisfaction of a debt, may be applied to a debt to the state or its political subdivisions, or if the debt is for child support, spousal support, alimony or maintenance.	05/04/09
5230(a)	Amended to provide that personal property that is otherwise exempt from application for satisfaction of a debt, may be applied to a debt to the state or its political subdivisions, or if the debt is for child support, spousal support, alimony or maintenance.	05/04/09
5232	Amended subd. (e) and added subd. (h) to provide that personal property that is otherwise exempt from application for satisfaction of a debt, may be applied to a debt to the state or its political subdivisions, or if the debt is for child support, spousal support, alimony or maintenance.	05/04/09
5241	Amended subdivisions (b) and (h) to amend the priority for deductions via an income execution; part of more comprehensive bill also amending the family court act and the domestic relations law.	10/9/09
8007	Amended to provide that certain newspapers in Richmond County may charge the regularly established classified advertising rate for publication of certain legal notices in such newspapers.	09/16/09
8012(b) (4)	Amended, effective August 5, 2008, to grant poundage to the sheriff upon a settlement, when a property execution has been issued and the property has been levied against; providing omitted language which should have been included in 2008 amendment.	08/05/08
8023	Amended, effective September 1, 2009, to eliminate the scheduled repeal date of the section.	09/01/09

TABLE OF 2008 CPLR AMENDMENTS

CPLR Section or Rule	Amendment	Effective Date
205(a)	Amended to require that when a dismissal is one for neglect to prosecute an action the judge must set forth on the record the specific conduct constituting the neglect. The conduct specified must demonstrate a general pattern of delay in proceeding with the action.	07/07/08
214-b	Amended to enlarge the period of inclusion of the provision so that it effectively begins on February 28, 1961; and to once again extend the time period for commencing an action under CPLR 214-b until June 16, 2010.	06/30/08
302(d)	Added to protect journalists and authors by declaring foreign defamation judgments unenforceable in New York unless the New York court determines that the foreign court's defamation law provides at least as much free speech protections (including freedom of the press) guaranteed under the New York and United States Constitutions.	04/28/08
3001	Amended to permit a claimant in a personal injury or wrongful death case to commence a declaratory judgment action directly against the defendant's insurer, as provided under Insurance Law § 3420(a)(6) (that is, where the insurer's denial of coverage is based on the insured's failure to provide timely notice and neither the insured nor the insurer has previously commenced a declaratory judgment action within 60 days of the disclaimer, naming the injured person or other claimant as a party).	01/17/09

CPLR Section or Rule	Amendment	Effective Date
R 3408	Added to provide that in a residential foreclosure action (where the defendant resides on the property) involving a high cost loan consummated between 1/1/03 and 9/1/08 or a subprime or non-traditional home loan, the court is required to schedule a settlement conference within 60 days after the filing of proof of service of the complaint. The amendment provides details of what is to transpire at such a conference. This is part of a more comprehensive amendment.	08/05/08
5205(l), (M), and (N)	Added to establish a procedure for claiming exemption of certain income from levy to execution by judgment debtors; provides that certain accounts shall be exempt from execution.	01/01/09
5222(b), (c), (d), and (e)	Amended to establish a procedure for claiming exemption of certain income from levy to execution by judgment debtors; provides that certain accounts shall be exempt from execution.	01/01/09
5222(h), (i), and (j)	Added to establish a procedure for claiming exemption of certain income from levy to execution by judgment debtors; provides that certain accounts shall be exempt from execution.	01/01/09
5222-a	Added to establish a procedure for claiming exemption of certain income from levy to execution by judgment debtors; provides that certain accounts shall be exempt from execution.	01/01/09
5230(a)	Amended to establish a procedure for claiming exemption of certain income from levy to execution by judgment debtors; provides that certain accounts shall be exempt from execution.	01/01/09
5231(b)	Amended to establish a procedure for claiming exemption of certain income from levy to execution by judgment debtors; provides that certain accounts shall be exempt from execution.	01/01/09
5232(e), (f), and (g)	Added to establish a procedure for claiming exemption of certain income from levy to execution by judgment debtors; provides that certain accounts shall be exempt from execution.	01/01/09

CPLR Section or Rule	Amendment	Effective Date
5241(e)	Amended to require that, where an income execution is issued, applications to assert a mistake of fact in Supreme Court be made by order to show cause or motion on notice to the creditor in the same action in which the order or judgment sought to be enforced was entered.	05/27/08
5304(b)(8)	Added to prohibit enforcement in New York of a foreign defamation judgment unless the New York court determines that the foreign court's defamation law provides at least as much free speech protections (including freedom of the press) guaranteed under the New York and United States Constitutions.	04/28/08
8012(b)(2), (3)	Amended to provide that where a settlement is made (1) after a levy by service of an execution (CPLR 8012(b)(2)) or (2) either before or after judgment, after levy by service of an order of attachment (CPLR 8012(b)(3)), the Sheriff is entitled to poundage fees on the judgment or settlement amount, whichever is less.	08/05/08
8012(b)(4), (5)	Added to provide that: (a) where a settlement occurs after service of an income or property execution on the debtor (as per CPLR 5231(d)) or upon a garnishee under CPLR 5231(e), the Sheriff is entitled to receive poundage fees on the judgment or settlement amount, whichever is less; (b) if after levy, an income or property execution is set aside or vacated, the Sheriff is entitled to poundage fees upon the value of the levied property, not to exceed the amount set forth in the execution, and the court can order the liable party to pay the Sheriff; (c) if the Sheriff brings an action to collect the poundage fees, the court can also award attorneys' fees and costs.	08/05/08
8019(f)	Amended to cover the actual costs for copies of any record on file in a format other than paper in accordance with Public Officers Law §87(1)(c), as amended.	08/06/08

CPLR Section or Rule	Amendment	Effective Date
8021(a)(4)(a)	Amended to allow county governments, at local option, to increase the fee for recording, entering, indexing and endorsing a certificate on any instrument from $5 to $20 and to increase the per-page fee from $3 per page to $5 per page. The amendment also prohibits a cover page from including social security numbers and/or dates of birth.	07/07/08

CPLR TIMETABLE

Introductory Note: This timetable is arranged in chronological order, following the usual sequence of litigation.

The column on the left lists the act—such as filing or service of papers or giving of notice—that is required of counsel, sheriff or court. The second column indicates the time period available to handle the matter. The third column cites the applicable rule or statute. The fourth column comments on the time period or on the attorney's further tasks or options, or provides further references.

Generally, the Civil Practice Law and Rules are cited, but other relevant provisions are indicated, including the New York Codes, Rules and Regulations regarding appellate proceedings and proceedings in the Supreme and County Courts. In the section on Appeals, after the first reference to 22 NYCRR, only the rule number is provided. The timetable does not include statutes or rules specific to Family Court proceedings, real property actions and proceedings, criminal matters, or Surrogate's Court proceedings. In addition, there are limited references to statutes applicable to inferior courts of jurisdiction.

This timetable is intended as a handy reference guide only and is not a substitute for thorough research. Counsel should refer directly to each statute and rule cited for further details and should see the applicable text in Weinstein, Korn & Miller, New York Civil Practice—CPLR (Matthew Bender) for discussion thereof.

CONTENTS

Timetable

I. STATUTES OF LIMITATION AND CONDITIONS

Act To Be Performed	Time Period Available	Statute or Rule	Comments
Action on a bond	Within 20 years of accrual	CPLR 211(a)	
Action to enforce money judgment	Within 20 years of docketing	CPLR 211(b)	Presumption of payment and satisfaction; not strictly speaking a statute of limitations.
Action for recovery of real property by state or grantee of state	Within 20 years of accrual	CPLR 211(c), (d)	
Action for support, alimony or maintenance	Within 20 years of accrual	CPLR 211(e)	
Action for recovery of real property	Within 10 years of seizing or possession of property by plaintiff or plaintiff's predecessor in interest	CPLR 212(a)	See RPAPL § 311.

Act To Be Performed	Time Period Available	Statute or Rule	Comments
Action to annul letters patent or grant of real property	Within 10 years after determination of voidness	CPLR 212(b)	
Action to redeem from a mortgage	Within 10 years of breach of condition of mortgage or date of recording of deed	CPLR 212(c)	
Action against licensed engineers, architects, land surveyors or landscape architects		CPLR 214-d	Notice must be given 90 days before commencement of action based upon professional performance, conduct or omission occurring more than 10 years prior to the date of the claim.

Act To Be Performed	Time Period Available	Statute or Rule	Comments
Civil action by crime victim for damages	Within seven years of crime	CPLR 213-b	*Exception*: 10 years for crimes specified in Executive Law § 632-a(1)(e); *See also* CPLR 215(8) (one year, discussed below).
Action for which there is no prescribed limitation	Six years	CPLR 213(1)	For common law causes of action. For statutory causes of action, see CPLR 214(2)–3 years.

Act To Be Performed	Time Period Available	Statute or Rule	Comments
Action on contractual obligation or liability	Six years	CPLR 213(2)	*Exception: See* CPLR 213-a; *see* UCC Art. 2 sales; *see* UCC § 2-725 (normally four years). *below*; actions based on breach of home sale warranty (*see* General Business Law Article 36-B) generally within one year after the warranty period or within four years of the warranty period, or within four years of the warranty date, whichever is later.
Action on a sealed instrument	Six years	CPLR 213(3)	
Action on a bond or note secured by mortgage on real property	Six years	CPLR 213(4)	

Act To Be Performed	Time Period Available	Statute or Rule	Comments
Action by state for spoliation or misappropriation of public property	Six years	CPLR 213(5)	Computed from discovery of facts by state.
Action based on mistake	Six years	CPLR 213(6)	
Shareholders' derivative action	Six years	CPLR 213(7)	
Action based on fraud	Six years	CPLR 213(8)	Actual fraud: later of six years from fraud or two years from time plaintiff discovers fraud or could with reasonable diligence have discovered fraud. Constructive fraud: six years from fraud (no discovery rule).

Act To Be Performed	Time Period Available	Statute or Rule	Comments
Forfeiture action to recover proceeds of crime or instrumentality of crime	Within five years of commission of crime	CPLR 1311(1)	
Action for divorce or separation	Five years	DRL §§ 170, 200, 210	See DRL § 210(a) for exceptions.
Civil Action for rape and certain sexual related crimes	Five years	CPLR 213-c	See also CPLR 215(8)(b) regarding further extension where there is criminal proceeding.
Action for breach of contract for sale	Four years after cause of action has accrued (tender of delivery unless warranty extends to future performance).	UCC § 2-725	By written agreement, the parties may shorten the period (Exception: contract for sale of goods may not reduce period to less than one year. UCC § 2-725.) but may not extend it. See also CPLR 203(f).

Act To Be Performed	Time Period Available	Statute or Rule	Comments
Action on residential rent overcharge	Four years	CPLR 213-a	Challenge must be made within four years of the first alleged overcharge.
Action against enforcement officer for nonpayment of money collected on an execution	Three years	CPLR 214(1)	
Action for statutory liability, penalty or forfeiture	Three years	CPLR 214(2)	*Exceptions: See* CPLR 213 (six years) and CPLR 215 (one year).
Replevin action	Three years	CPLR 214(3)	
Property damage action	Three years	CPLR 214(4)	*Exception: See* CPLR 214-c.

Act To Be Performed	Time Period Available	Statute or Rule	Comments
Personal injury action	Three years	CPLR 214(5)	*Exceptions: See* CPLR 214-b ("Agent Orange," two years), 214-c, and 215(3) (intentional torts, i.e., assault, battery, false imprisonment, one year).
Tort actions	Three years	CPLR 214	*Exceptions: See, e.g.,* CPLR 215 (3) (Intentional torts) tort action against certain governmental entities; CPLR 214-b ("Agent Orange," two years); CPLR 214-c (certain toxic torts); wrongful death (2 years).

Act To Be Performed	Time Period Available	Statute or Rule	Comments
Malpractice, other than medical, dental or podiatric	Three years	CPLR 214(6)	Whether the underlying theory is based in contract or tort. *See* CPLR 214-d regarding notice in particular actions against engineers and architects. *See also* CPLR 214-a regarding medical, dental or podiatric malpractice (2 ½ years), and CPLR 214(5) regarding negligence (three years).

Act To Be Performed	Time Period Available	Statute or Rule	Comments
Action against licensed engineers and architects			Notice must be given 90 days before commencement of action based upon professional performance, conduct or omission occurring more than 10 years prior to the date of the claim. CPLR 214-d. Does not affect statute of limitations (3 years). *See also* CPLR 3211(h) and 3212(i) re heightened burden placed on plaintiff.
Annulment on ground of fraud	Three years	CPLR 214(7)	Computed from discovery by spouse whose consent was obtained by fraud.

Act To Be Performed	Time Period Available	Statute or Rule	Comments
Action to recover for exposure to latent toxic substances	Three years	CPLR 214-c	Computed from date of discovery or date discovery should have occurred, with reasonable diligence. *See* CPLR 214-c(4) regarding applicable period when discovery of cause of injury is alleged to have occurred less than five years after the discovery of injury; *see also* uncodified revival provisions in sections 4 and 5 of L. 1986, ch. 682. *See* CPLR 214-c(6) regarding dates of acts or omissions to which the statute applies.

Act To Be Performed	Time Period Available	Statute or Rule	Comments
Medical, dental or podiatric malpractice	Two and one-half years	CPLR 214-a	Computed from act or omission or from last treatment if continuous treatment. *Exception:* foreign object in body, one year from discovery or discovery of facts which would reasonably lead to discovery, whichever is earlier. *See* CPLR 214(6) regarding malpractice, other than medical, dental or podiatric, and CPLR 214(5) regarding negligence (three years).

Act To Be Performed	Time Period Available	Statute or Rule	Comments
Action to recover for "Agent Orange" (phenoxy herbicides) injury	Two years; but extension provided to 6/16/10 to commence action.	CPLR 214-b	Computed from date of discovery or date discovery should have occurred, with reasonable diligence. Restricted to member of armed forces serving in Indo-China from 2/28/61–5/7/75.
Wrongful death action	Two years, or at least one year from termination of criminal action against same defendant with respect to same event or occurrence.	EPTL § 5-4.1	
Contract action against village	18 months	CPLR 9802	
Tort action against municipality	Notice of claim; within 90 days	GML § 50-e	Written verified claim within one year.

Act To Be Performed	Time Period Available	Statute or Rule	Comments
	Actions must be commenced within one year and 90 days of accrual	GML § 50-i	*Exception:* Wrongful death, two years to commence action.
Tort actions against NYCTA	Notice of claim within 90 days; action must be commenced within one year and 90 days of accrual	Public Authority Law § 1212(2)	*Exception:* Wrongful death, two years to commence action. *See* Title 11 of Article 9 of PAL (PAL §§ 2980, 2981).
Tort actions against NYC Health and Hospitals	Notice of intention to commence action within 90 days; action must be commenced within one year and 90 days of accrual	Unconsolidated Law § 7401	*Exception:* Wrongful death, two years to commence action. *See* Title 11 of Article 9 of PAL (PAL §§ 2980, 2981).
Tort actions against Port Authority	Notice of claim must be served at least 60 days before suit; action must be commenced within one year of accrual	Unconsolidated Law § 7107	

Act To Be Performed	Time Period Available	Statute or Rule	Comments
Tort actions against MTA	Notice of claim within 90 days; action must be commenced within one year of accrual	Public Authority Law § 1276(2)	*Exception:* Wrongful death, two years to commence action. *See* Title 11 of Article 9 of PAL (PAL §§ 2980, 2981).
Tort actions against TBTA	Notice of intention to commence action within six months; action must be commenced within one year of accrual	Public Authority Law § 569-a	*Exception:* Wrongful death, two years to commence action. *See* Title 11 of Article 9 of PAL (PAL §§ 2980, 2981).
Action for intentional tort	One year	CPLR 215(3)	
Action against sheriff, coroner, constable for official act or omission	One year	CPLR 215(1)	
Action on arbitration award	One year	CPLR 215(5)	*See also* CPLR 7510.

Act To Be Performed	Time Period Available	Statute or Rule	Comments
Action to enforce penalty or forfeiture created by statute	One year if commenced by a private person	CPLR 215(4)	If not commenced within one year, may be commenced within three years on behalf of the state.
Action against officer for escape of civil prisoner	One year	CPLR 215(2)	
Action to recover or enforce penalty for interest overcharge	One year	CPLR 215(6)	
Action by tenant against landlord for retaliation	One year	CPLR 215(7)	See RPL § 223-b(3).
Civil action against specific crime victim	One year from termination of criminal action	CPLR 215(8)	Compare CPLR 213-b (seven-year statute of limitations).

Act To Be Performed	Time Period Available	Statute or Rule	Comments
Proceeding to set aside judicial sale	Within one year after sale	CPLR 2003	Does not apply to judicial sales made pursuant to UCC Art. 9.
Article 78 proceeding; actions complaining about conduct that would constitute a union's breach of its duty of fair representation	Four months, but may be shorter	CPLR 217	Consult relevant statute authorizing proceeding. *Exception*: With leave of court, if petitioner was under statutorily defined disability, two years.
Notice of appeal/ motion for permission	Served and filed within 30 days of service of the order or judgment (appealed from) with notice of entry	CPLR 5513(a)	*See* CPLR 2221(d) regarding motion to reargue (similar 30-day period).
Tort actions against certain municipalities, public corporations or authorities	File notice of claim within 90 days.	GML §§ 50-e; 50-i; PAL §§ 1212(2), 1276(2), 2980, 2981	

Act To Be Performed	Time Period Available	Statute or Rule	Comments
Tort (unintentional) actions against New York State	Claim must be filed and served within 90 days after accrual, unless claimant files notice of intention within 90 days, in which case two years to file claim.	Ct. of Claims § 10(3-a)	*See* Ct. of Claims § 10(3-b) regarding intentional torts.

II. OTHER TIMING ISSUES

Act To Be Performed	Time Period Available	Statute or Rule	Comments
A. SERVICE OF SUMMONS AND COMPLAINT			
Service of summons and complaint, summons with notice, third-party summons and complaint and notice of petition or order to show and petition	Within 120 days of proper filings except proceeding/action with statute of limitations of four months or less, then not later than 15 days after the expiration of the statute of limitations	CPLR 306-b, 304, 203(c).	*Exception:* Proceeding commenced under the election law; if service not effected, action dismissed without prejudice unless court extends time "upon good cause shown or in the interest of justice." A similar but not identical requirement (120 days) has been adopted in the New York City Civil Court, the District Courts and the City Courts, establishing commencement by filing in those courts. *See* NYCCA § 411, UDCA § 411, UCCA § 411.

Act To Be Performed	Time Period Available	Statute or Rule	Comments
			See also amendments to CPLR 105, 304, 306-a and 2102 (L. 2007, ch. 125) concerning filing with the clerk in the Supreme and County Court (effective 1/1/08 for all actions or proceedings commenced after that date) and to CPLR 2001 (L. 2007, ch. 529, eff. 8/15/07) re: court's ability to correct mistakes in the method of filing.
Filing of proof of service by delivery to person of suitable age and discretion at defendant's actual place of business, dwelling place or usual place of abode within the state and mailing to last known residence or to actual place of business (as provided in CPLR 308(2)), within 20 days of each other	Within 20 days of delivery or mailing, whichever occurs later	CPLR 308(2)	Service is complete 10 days after such filing, except in matrimonial actions where such service is made pursuant to order in accordance with DRL § 232(a).

Act To Be Performed	Time Period Available	Statute or Rule	Comments
Filing of proof of service by nailing to door at defendant's actual place of business, dwelling place, or usual place of abode within the State and mailing to last known residence or to actual place of business, as provided in CPLR 308(4), within 20 days of each other.	Within 20 days of nailing or mailing, whichever occurs later	CPLR 308(4)	Service is complete 10 days after such filing, except in matrimonial actions where such service is made pursuant to order in accordance with DRL § 232(a).
Filing of proof of service on unauthorized foreign corporation via the Secretary of State	Within 30 days (i) after service, where process by personal service (ii) of receipt of return receipt signed by the foreign corporation, or other official proof of delivery or of the original envelope mailed	BCL § 307	Proof of service requires affidavit of compliance (one copy of pleadings served on Secretary of State, one on defendant); *see also* BCL § 306 regarding service on domestic corporation or authorized foreign corporation (two copies served on Secretary of State).

Act To Be Performed	Time Period Available	Statute or Rule	Comments
Filing of proof of service via Secretary of State on out-of-state defendant in motor vehicle accident case	Within 30 days after plaintiff receives return receipt or other affidavit of proof of delivery or the original envelope bearing a notation of refusal	VTL §§ 253, 254	Proof of service requires affidavit of compliance; applies also to residents who depart from state and remain absent for at least 30 days continuously (VTL § 254).
Notice by mailing copy of summons prior to entry of default judgment in non-payment action	At least 20 days prior to entry	CPLR 3215(g)(3)	
Service of summons by publication	At least once in each of four successive weeks	CPLR 316(a)	*Exception*: In matrimonial action, at least once in each of three successive weeks. Consult CPLR 316(a).
			Pleading, order and papers to be filed on or before first day of publication. *See* CPLR 316(a). In matrimonial actions, copy of summons to be mailed on or before first day of publication. *See* CPLR 316(b).

Act To Be Performed	Time Period Available	Statute or Rule	Comments
Time of publication	First publication required within 30 days after order	CPLR 316(c)	Service is complete on 28th day after first publication, except in matrimonial action, complete on 21st day. Service is complete earlier if defendant appears during period of publication of summons against him. *See also* CPLR 2402.
Service of complaint where summons served without complaint	(1) Defendant may serve written demand for complaint or notice of appearance within 20 days after service if served by personal delivery in New York or within 30 days if service of summons was other than by personal delivery in New York.	CPLR 3012(b)	Service of demand extends time for defendant to appear to within 20 days after service of complaint. Summons must contain proper notice; bare summons is jurisdictionally defective.
	(2) Complaint shall be served within 20 days after defendant makes demand for same (in demand or in notice).		

Act To Be Performed	Time Period Available	Statute or Rule	Comments
Service when summons is delivered to sheriff (outside of NYC) or county clerk (in NYC)	**Applicable to commencement by service courts.** Thus, for actions in the supreme court or the county courts, CPLR 203(c), 306-a, and 306-b obviate the need to deliver the summons to a sheriff or clerk for service; actions in those courts are commenced for statute of limitations and other purposes by filing the summons with notice or summons and complaint with the clerk and securing an index number ($210 fee), with service generally within 120 days thereafter. *See* CPLR 203(c), 304, 306-a and 306-b. Because commencement by filing has now been adopted in most courts, CPLR 203 (b)(5) has very limited applicability (*see* comments).	CPLR 203(b)(5)	Required to timely interpose claim in complaint. Note that commencement by filing (similar but not identical to the Supreme Court system) has been adopted in three inferior courts: the NYC Civil Court, District Court and City Court. See NYC Civil Court Act §§ 400, 409, 411; Uniform District Court Act §§ 400, 409, 411; Uniform City Court Act §§ 400, 409, 411. Town and Village Courts remain commencement by service courts. *See* CPLR 203 (b)(6), which contains provisions similar to CPLR 203(b)(5), but which is applicable to "a court not of record".

Act To Be Performed	Time Period Available	Statute or Rule	Comments
	Service must be made personally on defendant within 60 days after period of limitation would have expired but for this provision or;		
	First publication must be made within 60 days after period of limitation would have expired, but for this provision, and publication is completed subsequently or;		
	If defendant dies within 60-day period, and before service or publication completed, service must be made upon executor or administrator within 60 days after letters are issued.		

Act To Be Performed	Time Period Available	Statute or Rule	Comments
B. AMENDED AND SUPPLEMENTAL PLEADINGS			
Service of amended pleading if motion to correct is granted	Within 10 days after service of notice of entry order	CPLR 3024(c)	
Amendment of pleadings without leave of court	Within 20 days after service, or at any time before period for responding to it expires, or within 20 days after service of responsive pleading	CPLR 3025(a)	
Amendments and supplemental pleadings by leave	At any time by leave of court or by stipulation of all parties	CPLR 3025(b)	
Service of answer or reply to amended or supplemental pleadings	Within 20 days after service	CPLR 3025(d)	

Act To Be Performed	Time Period Available	Statute or Rule	Comments
Addition of parties to action	At any stage of the action by leave of court or by stipulation of all parties who have appeared. Without leave of court, once as of right, within 20 days after service of the original summons or before the time to respond to the summons has expired, or within 20 days after service of a pleading responding to it.	CPLR 1003	
Amendment of complaint to assert claim against third-party defendant without leave of court	Within 20 days after service of the answer to the third-party complaint on plaintiff's attorney	CPLR 1009	Does not deal with statute of limitation issues.
Extension of time where paper is served by regular mail	Five days	CPLR 2103(b)(2)	

Act To Be Performed	Time Period Available	Statute or Rule	Comments

C. DEFENSE OF ACTION

Answer or Appearance

Act To Be Performed	Time Period Available	Statute or Rule	Comments
Defendant's appearance by answer, notice of appearance, demand for complaint, or motion having effect of extending time to answer	Within 20 days after service, if service of summons was made on defendant by personal delivery in New York	CPLR 320(a), 3012(a)	If summons served without complaint, time to appear is extended until 20 days after service of complaint pursuant to defendant's demand or notice of appearance. *See* CPLR 3012(b).
	Within 30 days after service complete, if service of summons was other than by personal delivery in New York	CPLR 320(a), 3012(a)	Includes service on attorney as agent, delivery to person of suitable age and discretion and mailing, service pursuant to court order. *See* CPLR 303, 308(2)–(5), 313, 314, 315. *See also*, BCL §§ 306, 307 (service on corporations via the Secretary of State); and VTL §§ 253 and 254 (service via Secretary of State on out-of-state defendant in motor vehicle accident case).

Act To Be Performed	Time Period Available	Statute or Rule	Comments
			If summons served without complaint, time to appear is extended until 20 days after service of complaint pursuant to defendant's demand. *See* CPLR 3012(b).
Defendant's answer where service is by mail	Within 20 days after signed acknowledgment of receipt is mailed or delivered to sender	CPLR 312-a	
Service of copy of written authority by attorney for non-resident defendant or service of notice of filing same	Within 20 days after appearing or making a motion	CPLR 322(b)	
Service of answer or reply, generally	Within 20 days after service of pleading to which it responds	CPLR 3012(a)	
Defense of action by person served other than by personal delivery or personal delivery to agent who does not appear	Within one year after obtaining knowledge of entry of judgment but not more than five years after entry	CPLR 317	Court must make finding defendant did not receive summons in time to defend and that defendant had a meritorious defense. *See also* CPLR 5015.

Act To Be Performed	Time Period Available	Statute or Rule	Comments
D. VENUE			
Service of defendant's demand for change of place of trial on ground of improper venue	With answer or before answer served	CPLR 511(a)	
Defendant's motion to change place of trial	Within 15 days after service of demand, unless within five days plaintiff serves written consent	CPLR 511(b)	
Motion for change of place of trial on other ground	Within a "reasonable time after commencement of the action"	CPLR 511(a)	

Act To Be Performed	Time Period Available	Statute or Rule	Comments
E. BILL OF PARTICULARS			
Service of bill of particulars	Within 30 days after demand	CPLR 3042(a)	Including objections.
Amendment of bill of particulars as of course, in an action in which a note of issue is required to be filed	Once, before trial, prior to filing note of issue	CPLR 3042(b)	
Service of supplemental bill of particulars without leave	Not less than 30 days prior to trial	CPLR 3043(b)	In personal injury actions with respect to claims of continuing special damages and disabilities.

Act To Be Performed	Time Period Available	Statute or Rule	Comments
F. DISCLOSURE			
Objection to discovery, inspection or examination	Within 20 days of service of a notice or subpoena duces tecum under CPLR 3120 or CPLR 3121	CPLR 3122	Party or person to whom notice or subpoena is directed must state the reasons for the objection with "reasonable particularity"; included within response.
Service of subpoena duces tecum upon hospital, department, or bureau of a municipal corporation or of the state	At least three days before time fixed for production of records, unless court otherwise orders	CPLR 2306(a)	Where subpoena requires production of patient records, transcript certified by head of hospital, department, bureau (or by assistant), or officer.
Service of subpoena duces tecum upon library, department, or bureau of a municipal corporation or of the state	At least 24 hours before time fixed for production of records, unless court otherwise orders	CPLR 2307	Where subpoena requires production of books, papers, or other things.

Act To Be Performed	Time Period Available	Statute or Rule	Comments
Service of subpoena on non-party witness, or employee or officer of a party	At least 20 days before examination	CPLR 3106(b)	
Notification that a different deponent will be produced	At least 10 days prior to scheduled deposition	CPLR 3106(d)	
Review of proceeding where witness fails to comply with subpoena and has been committed to jail	Within 90 days	CPLR 2308(c)	Periodic review after not more than 90 days.

Act To Be Performed	Time Period Available	Statute or Rule	Comments
Service of notice of taking oral deposition	On 20 days' notice, unless court directs otherwise	CPLR 3107	A party to be examined may serve notice of at least 10 days for examination of another party, his agent or employee, at same time and place. For videotaped deposition, *see* 22NYCRR § 202.15. *See also,* amendment effective January 1, 2005 regarding stipulation to take deposition by telephone or other remote electronic means. CPLR 3113(d). *See also* Uniform Rules, 22 NYCRR § 221, effective 10/1/06, confirming limitation on objections at deposition and to prevent "talking objections."
Service of written cross-questions	Within 15 days after service of written questions and notice	CPLR 3109(a)	
Service of written redirect questions	Within seven days after service of written cross-question	CPLR 3109(a)	

Act To Be Performed	Time Period Available	Statute or Rule	Comments
Service of written recross questions	Within five days after service of written redirect questions	CPLR 3109(a)	
Service of written objection to errors in notice for taking deposition	At least three days before time for taking deposition	CPLR 3112	Otherwise, errors and irregularities are waived.
Service of written objection to form of written questions	Within time allowed for serving succeeding questions or within three days after service	CPLR 3115(e)	Otherwise, objections are waived.
Compliance with demand for address of party	Within 10 days of service of demand	CPLR 3118	
Exchange of medical information in personal injury and wrongful death actions			*See* 22 NYCRR § 202.17.

Act To Be Performed	Time Period Available	Statute or Rule	Comments
Service of written request for admission as to matters of fact, papers, documents and photographs	At any time after service of answer or after expiration of 20 days from service of summons, whichever is sooner, but not later than 20 days before trial	CPLR 3123(a)	Deemed admitted unless within 20 days after service or as court allows, adverse party serves sworn statement of denial or explanation. *See* CPLR 3123(a).
Service of written interrogatories	After commencement of the action but not before the defendant's time to serve a responsive pleading has expired, except by leave of court	CPLR 3132	
Service of answers or objections to interrogatories	Within 20 days after service of interrogatories	CPLR 3133	A party who objects to answering an interrogatory need not move for an order to strike, but may instead set forth the objection in the response.
Motion for review of order of referee supervising disclosure	Within five days after order is made	CPLR 3104(d)	

Act To Be Performed	Time Period Available	Statute or Rule	Comments
Exchange and filing of statements of net worth in actions and proceedings involving alimony, maintenance, support and equitable distribution	Within 20 days after receipt of written demand or if not demanded, it shall be filed by each party within 10 days after joinder of issue	DRL § 236(B), Fam. Ct. Act § 464, 22 NYCRR § 202.16.	
Exchange and filing of proposed disposition in actions and proceedings involving alimony, maintenance, support, and equitable distribution			*See* 22 NYCRR § 202.16(h)(1)-(3), which provides that the statement of proposed disposition be filed with the note of issue (§ 202.21) and that the other party shall file such statement within 20 days "of such service."
Amendment or supplementation of responses to discovery	Whenever the responding party subsequently learns that a response was incorrect or incomplete when given, or when the responding party learns that a response, though correct and complete when made, no longer is correct and complete	CPLR 3101(h)	The duty to amend or supplement a previous response arises when the failure to act would be materially misleading.

Act To Be Performed	Time Period Available	Statute or Rule	Comments
Signature and return of deposition; changes made to deposition	Within 60 days after submission of the deposition to the witness for examination	CPLR 3116(a)	If the witness fails to return the deposition, it may be used as fully as though signed. No changes may be made to the deposition more than 60 days after submission to the witness for examination.

Act To Be Performed	Time Period Available	Statute or Rule	Comments
G. PRE-TRIAL MOTIONS			
Service of notice of motion and supporting affidavits	If served by hand, at least eight days before return date; motion on at least 16 days' notice gets additional answering time and a reply	CPLR 2214(b)	Add five days for service by regular mail. CPLR 2103(b)(2); one business day if by overnight delivery. CPLR 2103(b)(6). *See* amendment to CPLR 2214/2215 which permits seven-day demand to apply also to any cross motion (L. 2007, ch. 185, eff. 7/3/07) and discussion *below*.
Service of answering affidavits	At least two days before return date; but at least seven days before return date if notice of motion served at least 16 days before return date so demands	CPLR 2214(b)	
Service of reply affidavits	At least one day before return date if notice of motion was served at least 16 days before return date and demanded answering papers at least seven days before return date.	CPLR 2214(b)	No reply permitted on eight day notice of motion.

Act To Be Performed	Time Period Available	Statute or Rule	Comments
Service of notice of cross-motion	If served by hand, at least seven days before return date where the original motion is served at least 16 days before the return date and the notice of motion expressly demands service of cross motions at least seven days before the return date; otherwise at least three days before return date.	CPLR 2215	Add three days (not five days as with notice of motion, *see above*) if served by regular mail; one day if by overnight delivery. CPLR 2215 (L. 2007, ch. 185, eff. 7/3/07).
Furnishing papers to court and adverse party	At hearing	CPLR 2214(c)	Check Uniform Rules and local court/judge rules.
Service of subpoena duces tecum upon a hospital or a department or a bureau of a municipal corporation or of the state regarding records relating to condition or treatment of a patient	At least three days before return date	CPLR 2306(a)	

Act To Be Performed	Time Period Available	Statute or Rule	Comments
Motion for subpoena duces tecum upon library, a department or bureau of a municipal corporation or of the state regarding producing documents	At least one day's notice	CPLR 2307	
Time for taking procedural steps where parties will be substituted	Extended until 15 days after substitution	CPLR 1022	Includes time for making motion for new trial, taking appeal, or making motion for permission to appeal. *See also* CPLR 1021.
Service of notice of motion to correct pleadings	Within 20 days after service of challenged pleading	CPLR 3024(c)	If motion is denied, responsive pleading must be served within 10 days after service of notice of entry of the order. If motion is granted, amended pleading complying with order must be served within 10 days after service of notice of entry of the order.

Act To Be Performed	Time Period Available	Statute or Rule	Comments
Service of notice of motion for order directing settlement of statement terms and determination of controversy under New York Simplified Procedure for Court Determination of Disputes	Eight days' notice or as court deems appropriate	CPLR 3034(1), (2)	
Order determining a motion relating to a provisional remedy	Within 20 days after submission of motion	CPLR 2219	
Order determining any other motion	Within 60 days after submission of motion	CPLR 2219	*See* 22 N.Y.C.R.R. § 202.8(h) re reports of Chief Administrator or designee regarding motions undecided 60 days after final submission.
Motion for order to determine whether action will be maintained as class action	Within 60 days after time to serve a responsive pleading has expired for all named defendants	CPLR 902	

Act To Be Performed	Time Period Available	Statute or Rule	Comments
H. ACCELERATED JUDGMENT			
Motion to dismiss for improper service where objecting party raises the objection in the answer	Within 60 days after service of the answer containing the objection	CPLR 3211(e)	Failure to move for dismissal will result in waiver of the objection. The court may extend the time on the ground of "undue hardship."
Extension of time to serve pleading where motion to dismiss cause of action [CPLR 3211(a)] or to dismiss defense [CPLR 3211(b)] is made before service of pleading responsive to cause of action or defense	Until 10 days after service of notice of entry of order determining motion	CPLR 3211(f)	

Act To Be Performed	Time Period Available	Statute or Rule	Comments
Motion for summary judgment	Any time after issue has been joined but no later than 120 days after filing the note of issue	CPLR 3212(a)	However, the court may set a date by which any such motion shall be made, which must be no earlier than 30 days after filing the note for issue. The court may extend either date upon a showing of good cause. Some courts have rules setting time of less than 120 days. Note also rules for Commercial Division of the Supreme Court, 22 NYCRR § 202.70 (Rule 19-a), providing that the court *may* require a statement of material facts to be submitted by moving party.
Notice of motion for summary judgment in lieu of complaint	Hearing date must be minimum of 20 days after service of summons if personal delivery in New York or 30 days if other than personal delivery in New York	CPLR 3213, 320(a)	If hearing date is later than minimum time, plaintiff may require defendant to serve copy of answering papers within extended period of time, not exceeding 10 days prior to hearing date. CPLR 3213.

Act To Be Performed	Time Period Available	Statute or Rule	Comments
Default Judgment			
Plaintiff's application for default judgment (claim for sum certain)	Within one year after default	CPLR 3215(a)	If plaintiff fails to comply, court shall dismiss complaint. *See* CPLR 3215(c). *See also* CPLR 1203.
Defendant's application for judgment for costs	Within one year after default	CPLR 3215(a)	
Notice of application for default judgment to be provided to defendant who has appeared	At least five days	CPLR 3215(g)(1)	If application is made to court, unless otherwise provided in specific action.
Notice of default motion to be provided to defendant who has not appeared	If more than one year has elapsed since default, at least five days' notice	CPLR 3215(g)(1)	Unless court orders otherwise.
Notice, to be given to defendant, of reference or assessment by jury	At least five days	CPLR 3215(g)(2)	If defendant who has not appeared serves demand for notice, before motion for judgment is heard.

Act To Be Performed	Time Period Available	Statute or Rule	Comments
Additional notice required to take a default judgment against a natural person based upon nonpayment of a contractual obligation	At least 20 days before entry of judgment	CPLR 3215(g)(3)	Does not apply to small claims part of any court or to any summary proceeding to recover possession of real property or to actions affecting title to real property, except residential mortgage foreclosure actions. (L. 2007, ch. 458, eff. 8/1/07).
Additional notice required to take a default judgment against a domestic or authorized foreign corporation served pursuant to BCL § 306(b)	At least 20 days before entry of judgment	CPLR 3215(g)(4)	Does not apply to small claims part or commercial claims part of any court, or to any summary proceeding to recover possession of real property, or to actions affecting title to real property.
Motion to dismiss for want of prosecution	At least one year must have elapsed since joinder of issue	CPLR 3216(b)	See CPLR 3216 for other requirements, including written demand for service and filing note of issue within 90 days after receipt.

Act To Be Performed	Time Period Available	Statute or Rule	Comments
Motion to relieve party from judgment or order, on ground of excusable default	Within one year after service of copy of judgment or order with written notice of entry, upon moving party, or if entered by moving party, within one year after such entry	CPLR 5015(a)(1)	*See also* CPLR 2006, 3012(d) concerning delay or default resulting from law office failure. *See* CPLR 317 regarding defense by person to whom summons not personally delivered.
Motion to reargue	Within 30 days after service of a copy of the order determining the prior motion and written notice of entry	CPLR 2221(d)	Good practice would be to serve and file notice of appeal simultaneously. Note conflict as to whether pre-codification case law permitting later filing (i.e., before appeal has been submitted, or, at the latest, determined) survives.

Act To Be Performed	Time Period Available	Statute or Rule	Comments
Voluntary Discontinuance			
Service of notice of discontinuance	At any time before a responsive pleading is served or within 20 days after service of pleading asserting the claim, whichever is earlier	CPLR 3217(a)(1)	See CPLR 3217 for other methods of discontinuance. See also 22 NYCRR § 202.28, regarding filing stipulation to discontinue action within 20 days of discontinuance. Note: 7/14/03 amendment requires all notices, stipulations or certificates regarding voluntary discontinuance to be filed with county clerk by defendant. Also note $35 filing fee. See CPLR 8020(d).
Judgment by Confession			
Filing of defendant's affidavit by confession	Within three years after execution	CPLR 3218(b)	May not be entered after defendant's death.

Act To Be Performed	Time Period Available	Statute or Rule	Comments
I. SETTLEMENT			
Deposit of payment with court clerk and service upon claimant of written tender of payment	Not later than 10 days before trial	CPLR 3219	In contract action, by party against whom a separate judgment may be taken. Claimant may withdraw funds within 10 days.
Offer to liquidate damages conditionally	Not later than 10 days before trial	CPLR 3220	In contract action.
Offer to compromise	Not later than 10 days before trial	CPLR 3221	In any action except matrimonial action.

Act To Be Performed	Time Period Available	Statute or Rule	Comments
J. SUBMISSION OF ORDERS, JUDGMENTS AND DECREES–SUPREME AND COUNTY COURTS			
Submission of proposed order or judgment for signature (with proof of service) where order or judgment is directed to be settled or submitted for signature	Within 60 days after signing and filing of decision directing that order be settled or submitted	22 NYCRR § 202.48	
Service of copy of proposed order or judgment with notice of settlement where settlement is directed by court	If by personal service, not less than 5 days before date of settlement	22 NYCRR § 202.48	
	If by mail, not less than 10 days before date of settlement		

Act To Be Performed	Time Period Available	Statute or Rule	Comments
Service of proposed counter-order or judgment	If by personal service, not less than 2 days before date of settlement If by mail, not less than 7 days before date of settlement	22 NYCRR § 202.48	A counter-order or counter-judgment should be submitted with a "copy clearly marked to delineate each proposed change to the order or judgment to which objection is made."

Act To Be Performed	Time Period Available	Statute or Rule	Comments
K. CALENDAR PRACTICE			
Placing case on calendar--filing note of issue and certificate of readiness	At any time after issue is joined, or at least 40 days after completion of service of summons	CPLR 3402(a)	File within 10 days after service of note of issue. *See also* 22 NY-CRR § 202.21.
Service of note of issue upon new party	Within five days	CPLR 3402(b)	
Filing statement with clerk on bringing in new party	Within five days	CPLR 3402(b)	
Service of notice of motion for preference	With note of issue, by party serving note of issue, or 10 days after such service by any other party (or thereafter during pendency of action by party who reaches age 70 or is terminally ill)	CPLR 3403(b)	

Act To Be Performed	Time Period Available	Statute or Rule	Comments
Abandonment of case in Supreme Court or County Court marked "Off" or struck from calendar or unanswered on calendar roll	If not restored within one year	CPLR 3404	Case shall be dismissed without necessity for order.
Notice of dental, medical, or podiatric malpractice actions	Within 60 days after issue is joined or after the time for a defaulting party to appear, answer or move with respect to a pleading has expired.	CPLR 3406, 22 NYCRR § 202.56	The notice is to be in the form specified by the Chief Administrator. *See* 22 NYCRR § 202.56(a). Notice must be filed with other documents.
Filing of demand for trial by jury	If not in note of issue, within 15 days after service of note of issue	CPLR 4102(a)	File with proof of service upon each party. If trial by jury has been demanded of only some of the issues, any other party within 10 days after service of demand may serve and file demand for trial by jury of any other issues triable by jury. CPLR 4102(b). *See also* 22 NYCRR § 202.21(c).

Act To Be Performed	Time Period Available	Statute or Rule	Comments
Motion for trial by referee or advisory jury	Within 20 days after note of issue is filed	CPLR 4015	*Exceptions*: Where issue to be tried arises on a motion or pursuant to a judgment.
Motion to strike case from calendar	Within 20 days after service of note of issue and certificate of readiness (does not apply to tax assessment review proceedings)	22 NYCRR § 202.21	After the 20-day period, no motion shall be allowed except for good cause shown.

Act To Be Performed	Time Period Available	Statute or Rule	Comments
L. TRIAL			
Decision of court	Within 60 days after final submission of cause or matter or within 60 days after motion for new trial or to confirm or reject (CPLR 4403), whichever is later	CPLR 4213(c)	
First hearing by referee	Within 20 days after date of order of reference	CPLR 4313	
Filing of referee's decision	Within 30 days after final submission of cause or matter	CPLR 4319	If not timely filed, court may grant new trial.
Filing of referee's report, findings of fact, and conclusions of law	Within 30 days after final submission of cause or matter	CPLR 4320(b)	Transcript to be filed with report, unless otherwise stipulated.

Act To Be Performed	Time Period Available	Statute or Rule	Comments
Motion to confirm or reject judicial hearing officer's or referee's report	Plaintiff shall move on notice within 15 days after notice of filing was given. If plaintiff fails to make motion, defendant shall make motion within 30 days after notice of filing.	22 NYCRR § 202.44	

Act To Be Performed	Time Period Available	Statute or Rule	Comments
M. POST-TRIAL MOTIONS			
Motion for new trial or to confirm or reject verdict of advisory jury or report of referee to report	Within 15 days after verdict or filing of referee's report and prior to further trial	CPLR 4403	
Post-trial motion for judgment and new trial	Within 15 days after decision, verdict or discharge of jury	CPLR 4405	
Petition for remission or mitigation of forfeiture of proceeds of crime	Within one year of entry of judgment of forfeiture	CPLR 1311(7)	

N. ENFORCEMENT OF JUDGMENTS

Act To Be Performed	Time Period Available	Statute or Rule	Comments
Mailing of copy of satisfaction-piece to judgment debtor	Within 10 days after date of filing	CPLR 5020(a)	
Execution of satisfaction-piece by attorney for judgment creditor	Within 10 days after entry of judgment	CPLR 5020(b)	
Civil penalty for failure of judgment creditor to execute and file satisfaction piece	On failure to comply with CPLR 5020(a) or (d) within 20 days after receiving full satisfaction	CPLR 5020(c)	If the City of New York is the judgment creditor, written demand is first required.
Entry upon return of execution arising out of small claims action	Within 90 days after receipt of judgment by sheriff	CPLR 5021(b)	

Act To Be Performed	Time Period Available	Statute or Rule	Comments
Leave to issue execution to levy upon real property after death of party against whom order awarding possession was obtained	Upon 20 days' notice to occupants of real property and to heirs or devisees	CPLR 5102	
Expiration of judgment lien existing against real property at time of judgment debtor's death	Two years thereafter or 10 years after filing of judgment-roll, whichever is later	CPLR 5208	

Act To Be Performed	Time Period Available	Statute or Rule	Comments
Service of restraining notice	If notice to judgment debtor or obligor [CPLR 5222(e)] has not been given to judgment debtor or obligor within one year before service of restraining notice, copy of restraining notice and notice to judgment debtor or obligor shall be mailed by first class mail or personally delivered to each judgment debtor or obligor who is a natural person within four days of service of restraining notice.	CPLR 5222(d)	In 2008, the New York State Legislature passed sweeping amendments to Article 52 of the CPLR in connection with restraining bank accounts, levy procedures and exempt property. The legislation amended 5222 (b), (c), (d) and (e), 5230 (a), 5231 (b) and adds 5205 (l), (m) and (n), 5222 (h) (i), and (j), 5222-a, and 5232 (e), (f) and (g). The broad purpose of the amendments was to enable judgment debtors to more easily access exempt funds in accounts in banks which have been served with restraining notices by judgment creditors.

Act To Be Performed	Time Period Available	Statute or Rule	Comments
Return of answers to information subpoena	Within seven days after receipt	CPLR 5222(a)(4), 5224(a)(3)	An information subpoena served by judgment creditor (other than where the state, a municipality or an agency or officer of the state or a municipality is the judgment creditor) must contain certification that party served "has in their possession information about the debtor that will assist the creditor in collecting the judgment." CPLR 5224(a)(3).
Deposition or examination of books and papers	Not less than 10 days' notice, unless court orders shorter notice	CPLR 5224(c)	
Subsequent examination	Within one year, requires leave of court	CPLR 5224(f)	
Return of execution to court clerk or to support collection unit	Within 60 days after issuance unless served in accordance with CPLR 5231 or 5232(a)	CPLR 5230(c), 5231, 5232(a)	May be extended in writing by judgment creditor's attorney or by the support collection unit, for not more than 60 additional days.

Act To Be Performed	Time Period Available	Statute or Rule	Comments
Service of income execution upon debtor	Within 20 days after delivery to sheriff	CPLR 5231(d)	
Levy upon default or failure to serve debtor	After 20 days	CPLR 5231(e)	
Accounting by sheriff of monies collected	At least once every 90 days from the time a levy is made	CPLR 5231(k)	
Voidness of levy	At expiration of 90 days after service of execution, or as provided by court	CPLR 5232(a)	*Exceptions*: As to debts paid to sheriff or support collection unit or as to which proceeding under CPLR 5225 or CPLR 5227 has been brought.
Service by sheriff or support collection unit of copy of execution, and notice to judgment debtor or obligor	Within four days after service of execution upon garnishee	CPLR 5232(c)	

Timetable

Act To Be Performed	Time Period Available	Statute or Rule	Comments
Priority of other judgment creditors	For 60 days after order is filed, unless otherwise specified or unless extended by order within the 60 days	*See* CPLR 5234(c)	If order is filed before property or debt is levied upon.
Levy upon real property	10 years after filing of judgment roll	CPLR 5235	
Sale of real property levied upon	Between 56th and 63rd day after first publication of copy of notice of sale	CPLR 5236(a)	As to notice of sale, *see* CPLR 5236(c).
Sheriff's delivery to purchaser, of proofs regarding sale, and deed	Within 10 days after sale	CPLR 5236(f)	
Foreign judgments			
Filing of foreign judgment	Within 90 days of date of authentication	CPLR 5402(a)	

Act To Be Performed	Time Period Available	Statute or Rule	Comments
Mailing of notice of filing	Within 30 days after filing of judgment	CPLR 5403	Proceeds shall not be distributed earlier than 30 days after filing proof of service.

Act To Be Performed	Time Period Available	Statute or Rule	Comments
O. APPEALS			
Appeals generally			
Taking of appeal as of right, or moving for permission to appeal	Within 30 days after service of copy of judgment or order and notice of entry	CPLR 5513(a), (b)	If attorney dies within 30-day period, extended to 60 days from date of death. CPLR 5514(b).
Taking of cross-appeal	Same as above, or within 10 days after service of notice of appeal or motion for permission to appeal, whichever is longer	CPLR 5513(c)	

Act To Be Performed	Time Period Available	Statute or Rule	Comments

NOTE THAT EFFECTIVE SEPTEMBER 1, 2005 THE NEW YORK STATE COURT OF APPEALS RESCINDED IN ITS ENTIRETY 22 NYCRR PART 500 AND APPROVED A NEW PART 500 ENTITLED "THE RULES OF PRACTICE OF THE COURT OF APPEALS".

Court of Appeals

Act To Be Performed	Time Period Available	Statute or Rule	Comments
Filing and service of appellant's preliminary appeal statement with attachments and proof of service.	Within 10 days from time appeal is taken	22 NYCRR § 500.9	**This is a new type of required document.** If party will assert that a statute is unconstitutional, written notice to attorney general must be given before filing preliminary appeal statement. *See* § 500.9(b).

Act To Be Performed	Time Period Available	Statute or Rule	Comments
Sua sponte examination of merits (alternative review procedure for selected appeals) - Appellant's service and submission to Court, including original and two copies of letter containing arguments	Within 25 days of clerk's letter initiating review	§ 500.11(c)	Appellant may request review in its preliminary appeal statement. § 500.11(a).
Sua sponte examination of merits - Respondent's service and filing of submission	20 days after receipt of appellant's submission	§ 500.11(d)	Respondent may request review within 5 days after appeal taken. § 500.11(a).
Filing and service of appellant's record materials and brief (original and 24 copies of brief with proof of service of 3 copies on every party)	Within 60 days from taking the appeal unless another due date has been set by the clerk in the scheduling letter.	§ 500.12(b),	Appeal will be dismissed for failure of appellant to file and serve required papers. § 500.16. *See* § 500.13 re content and form of briefs in normal course appeals. The clerk is authorized to grant, for good cause shown, a reasonable extension of time for filing papers on an appeal. § 500.15.

Act To Be Performed	Time Period Available	Statute or Rule	Comments
Filing and service of respondent's brief and supplementary appendix, if any (original and 24 copies of brief with 3 copies on every party)	Within 45 days of service of appellant's papers unless another date has been set by the clerk in the scheduling letter	§ 500.12(c)	*See* § 500.13 re content and form of briefs in normal course appeals. The clerk is authorized to grant, for good cause shown, a reasonable extension of time for filing papers on an appeal. § 500.15.
Filing and service of reply brief (original and 24 copies of brief with 3 copies on every party)	Within 15 days of receipt of respondent's brief, if no scheduling letter is issued	§ 500.12(d)	*See* § 500.13 re content and form of briefs in normal course appeals. The clerk is authorized to grant, for good cause shown, a reasonable extension of time for filing papers on an appeal. § 500.15.
Motions to Court of Appeals	On at least eight days' notice if personally served or by fax (13 if service by mail; 9 days if by overnight mail)	§ 500.21(b)	*See* § 500.21 generally re motions; no oral argument unless Court directs otherwise. *See* § 500.22 re motion for permission to appeal in civil cases.
Service of notice of motion for reargument	Within 30 days after appeal, certified question or motion decided, unless otherwise permitted by Court	§ 500.24(b)	

Act To Be Performed	Time Period Available	Statute or Rule	Comments
Withdrawal of appeal or motion	With respect to appeal, at any time prior to argument or submission	§ 500.8(a)	By stipulation signed by counsel for all parties to the appeal and by all self-represented litigants (and in criminal appeals, by defendant additionally); after those dates submission to Court is necessary
	With respect to motion, at any time before return date	§ 500.8(b)	Upon receipt by the clerk of a written notice of withdrawal signed by counsel for the moving party, with proof of service; after return date, request must be submitted to Court for determination and supported by stipulation of withdrawal signed by counsel for all parties to motion and by all self-represented litigants.
Dismissal of appeal	If appellant or respondent fails to file and serve papers timely then the clerk shall enter an order.	§ 500.16	

Act To Be Performed	Time Period Available	Statute or Rule	Comments
Oral argument of Appeals	30 minutes per party unless otherwise permitted by Court	§ 500.18	Counsel should presume Court's familiarity with facts, procedural history and legal issues
	Appellant may orally request specific number of minutes rebuttal time *before* argument begins		Only one counsel may argue per party, unless permitted by Court. Any rebuttal time is deducted from total time assigned to appellant.
Disclosure statement	All papers filed on behalf of a corporation or other business entity	§ 500.1(f)	
Certified questions		§ 500.27	Discretionary proceedings to review certified questions from federal courts and other courts of last resort.
Appellate Divisions			
Supplementary Documents to be filed with Notice of Appeal or Order Granting Permission	1st Dep't: Pre-Argument Statement	22 NYCRR § 600.17	

Act To Be Performed	Time Period Available	Statute or Rule	Comments
	2d Dep't: Request for Appellate Division Intervention	22 NYCRR § 670.3	
	3d Dep't: Pre-Calender Statement	22 NYCRR § 800.24-a	
Filing of record (appendix system)	1st Dep't: Within 30 days after settlement of transcript or statement in lieu of transcript	§ 600.5(a)(1)	*See* CPLR 5525, 5526, 5528(a)(5).
	2d Dep't: Appellant shall subpoena from the clerk of the court from which the appeal is taken all papers constituting the record on appeal and cause them to be filed with the clerk of this court prior to the filing of the appendix.	§ 670.9(b)	*See* CPLR 5525, 5528(a)(5), 5532.
	3d Dep't: *See* §§ 800.4(b), 800.7(b) and consult court clerk.		

Act To Be Performed	Time Period Available	Statute or Rule	Comments
	4th Dep't: Party shall file and serve at the same time that party serves and files a brief.	§ 1000.2(g)	
Filing of original record, stipulated and settled	4th Dep't: Within 60 days of serving notice of appeal.	§§ 1000.2(b), 1000.3(b)	
Filing of agreed statement in lieu of record	1st Dep't: Within 30 days after approval	§ 600.5(b)(2).	*See* CPLR 5527.
	2d Dep't: *See* § 670.10 and CPLR 5531.	§ 670.9(c)	
	3d Dep't: *See* CPLR 5531.	§ 800.4(d)	
	4th Dep't: Within 20 days after notice of appeal has been filed and served	§ 1000.4(c)	See CPLR 5527, 5531.
Filing of optional full record	1st Dep't: Within 30 days after settlement of transcript or statement in lieu of transcript.	§ 600.5(c)	*See* CPLR 5526, 5528(a)(5).

Act To Be Performed	Time Period Available	Statute or Rule	Comments
	2d Dep't: *See* § 670.10.1 and § 670.10.2.	§ 670.9(a)	
Filing of records in case where record does not involve settlement or approval	1st Dep't: Within 30 days after taking notice of appeal.	§ 600.5(d)	
	2d Dep't: Together with the brief.	§ 670.9(b)(3)	Where transcript or statement not involved.

Placing appeal on calendar

Act To Be Performed	Time Period Available	Statute or Rule	Comments
1st Dep't: By filing note of issue with proof of service	Within 20 days after filing record on appeal, statement in lieu of record or papers in transferred Art. 78 proceeding and at least 57 days before first day of term.	§ 600.11(a)(1), (b); *see* § 600.4	*Exception:* Submission of controversy is placed on calendar at time of filing agreed statement of facts. Papers and briefs must be filed within nine months of date of notice of appeal (in Art. 78 proceeding, from date of order of transfer to App. Div.). *See* § 600.11(a)(3).
2d Dep't: Same as above	*See* § 670.9	§ 670.8(a)	
3d Dep't: Not specified	Not specified by Rule or CPLR		Similarly, *see* § 800.12.

Act To Be Performed	Time Period Available	Statute or Rule	Comments
4th Dep't: *See* § 1000.10. *See also* §§ 1000.8, 1000.9	Not specified by Rule or CPLR		After appellant has perfected the appeal.
Appellant's filing main brief	2d Dep't: *See* § 670.9.	§ 670.8(a)	File with record.
	3d Dep't: Generally, within 60 days after service of notice of appeal.	§ 800.9(a)	
Filing of answering (respondent's) brief	1st Dep't: At least 27 days before first day of term.	§ 600.11(c)	
	2d Dep't: Within 30 days after service of appellant's brief.	§ 670.8(b)	
	3d Dep't: Within 45 days from the date clerk sends scheduling memorandum after acceptance of appellant's brief and record, or within such shorter time as the memorandum may direct.	§ 800.9(b)	

Act To Be Performed	Time Period Available	Statute or Rule	Comments
	4th Dep't: Within 30 days after service of appellant's brief.	§ 1000.2(d)	
Filing of reply brief	1st Dep't: Within nine days after service of answering brief.	§ 600.11(c)	
	2d Dep't: Within 10 days of service of respondent's brief.	§ 670.8(b)	
	3d Dep't: Within 10 days of service of respondent's brief.	§ 800.9(c)	
	4th Dep't: Within 10 days of service of respondent's brief.	§ 1000.2(e)	
Cross appeals			
Filing by respondent/cross appellant	1st Dep't: Within 30 days after perfection of appellant's appeal	§ 600.11(d)	
	2d Dep't: 30 days after service of appellant's main brief.	§ 670.8(c)(3)	Filing and service of adverse party's answering brief.

Act To Be Performed	Time Period Available	Statute or Rule	Comments
	3d Dep't: Within 30 days after service of first brief.	§ 800.9(e)	Filing and service of answering brief and appendix.
	4th Dep't: Within 30 days of service of main brief.	§ 1000.2(d)	Filing and service of answering brief (or brief and appendix).
Filing of reply by first appellant	2d Dep't: Within 30 days after service of answering brief.	§ 670.8(c)(3)	
	3d Dep't: Within 10 days after service of answering brief.	§ 800.9(e)	
	4th Dep't: Within 10 days of service of answering brief.	§ 1000.2(e), (f)	
Filing of reply brief to cross-appeal	1st Dep't: Within nine days after reply to the answering brief filed.	§ 600.11(d)	
	2d Dep't: Within 10 days after service of appellant's reply to brief.	§ 670.8(c)(3)	

Act To Be Performed	Time Period Available	Statute or Rule	Comments
	3d Dep't: Within 10 days after service of appellant's reply to brief.	§ 800.9(e)	
	4th Dep't: Within 10 days of service of reply to answering brief.	§ 1000.2(f)	
Written notification to clerk of time desired for argument	1st Dep't: On or before the court's scheduled date in that particular term.	§ 600.11(f)(1)	
Request for change of date of argument	3d Dep't: At least 14 days prior to commencement of term.	§ 800.11	
Filing of stipulation of adjournment	1st Dep't: Not later than 26 days before first day of term for which appeal has been noticed.	§ 600.11(g)	
Motion for reargument	1st Dep't: Within 30 days after appeal has been decided.	§ 600.14(a)	

Act To Be Performed	Time Period Available	Statute or Rule	Comments
Other provisions relating to appeals		CPLR 5530(a), 5519(c), 5525(c)(1), (d), 5527	2d Dep't: *See* §§ 670.9(b), 670.10(c), 670.12, 670.13, 670.14, 670.18. 3d Dep't: *See* §§ 800.8(c), 800.13, 800.18–800.22. 4th Dep't: *See* §§ 1000.2–100.5, 1000.7.
Appeals Under NYS Human Rights Law			See §§ 600.7(c), (1st Dep't), 670.17 (2d Dep't), 800.20 (3d Dep't), 1000.5(j) (4th Dep't).

Act To Be Performed	Time Period Available	Statute or Rule	Comments
P. PROVISIONAL REMEDIES			
Election of remedy	May be required by court on motion for provisional remedy	CPLR 6001	Applies to seizure of chattel as well as attachment, injunction, receivership, and notice of pendency.
Interposition of claim in complaint when order for provisional remedy is granted	Summons served on defendant within 30 days or published pursuant to an order and publication completed. If defendant dies within 30 days after the order and before summons served or publication completed, summons served on executor/administrator within 60 days after letters are issued.	CPLR 203(b)(3)	Provisional remedy excludes attachment but includes seizure of chattel.

Act To Be Performed	Time Period Available	Statute or Rule	Comments
Injunction			
Application for preliminary injunction or temporary restraining order	No time constraints	CPLR 6301, 6313	TRO may be granted pending hearing for preliminary injunction, where immediate and irreparable injury would otherwise result. *See* new rule effective 10/1/06 limiting ex parte relief to situation where there is an "affirmation demonstrating there will be significant prejudice to the party seeking the restraining order by giving the notice." Otherwise, there must be a showing of good faith to notify the adversary. 22 NYCRR § 202.7(f). *See also* 22 NYCRR § 202.70, Rule 20 (Rules of the Commercial Division of the Supreme Court).
Service of notice of motion for preliminary injunction	With summons or at any time thereafter and prior to judgment	CPLR 6311(1)	

Act To Be Performed	Time Period Available	Statute or Rule	Comments
Posting of undertaking by plaintiff seeking preliminary injunction	Required prior to granting of preliminary injunction	CPLR 6312(b)	*Exceptions*: Does not apply to state, municipal corporation, village, or certain public officers. *See* CPLR 2512, 4110-a, 2505.
Attachment			
Posting of undertaking	On motion for order of attachment	CPLR 6212(b)	
Granting of order of attachment without notice	Before or after service of summons and at any time prior to judgment	CPLR 6211(a)	On grounds for attachment, *see* CPLR 6201.
Granting of temporary restraining order prohibiting transfer of assets by garnishee	Permitted upon motion on notice for order of attachment	CPLR 6210	
Plaintiff's filing of order of attachment and supporting papers, summons and complaint	Within 10 days after granting of order	CPLR 6212(c)	

Act To Be Performed	Time Period Available	Statute or Rule	Comments
Action is commenced by filing summons and complaint and securing index number pursuant to CPLR 304 and CPLR 306-a. *See also* CPLR 203(c) and 306-b.	Within 60 days after order of attachment is granted. Application may be made for extension of time, prior to expiration of time	CPLR 6213	Required to make order of attachment valid. If defendant dies prior to service or publication within the 60-day period, summons must be served upon executor within 60 days after letters are issued. CPLR 6213.
Levy by sheriff pursuant to order of attachment	At any time prior to final judgment	CPLR 6211(a)	Levy upon personal property made by service of order of attachment, normally valid for 90 days. CPLR 6214(e). *See also* CPLR 6214(d). *Compare* CPLR 6215 (levy by seizure), 6216 (levy upon real property). As to attachment or levy upon a security or share, *see* UCC § 8-317.
Sheriff's filing of inventory of property seized	Within 15 days after service of order of attachment or "forthwith" after such order has been vacated or annulled	CPLR 6218(b)	

Act To Be Performed	Time Period Available	Statute or Rule	Comments
Garnishee's service upon sheriff of statement specifying debts to defendant	Within 10 days after service of order of attachment or sooner if court directs	CPLR 6219	
Plaintiff's motion for order confirming order of attachment	Within five days after levy	CPLR 6211(b)	
Defendant's demand for papers	At any time after levy	CPLR 6212(d)	
Plaintiff's service of papers upon defendant's demand	Not more than one day after service of demand for same	CPLR 6212(d)	
Motion to vacate or modify order of attachment	Prior to application of property or debt to the satisfaction of judgment	CPLR 6223	By defendant, garnishee or any person having an interest in the property or debt.

Act To Be Performed	Time Period Available	Statute or Rule	Comments
Receivership			
Appointment of temporary receiver	Before or after service of summons and at any time prior to judgment, or during the pendency of an appeal	CPLR 6401(a)	Motion made by person not already a party constitutes an appearance in the action. *See also* CPLR 5228.
Duration of temporary receivership	Does not continue after final judgment, unless otherwise directed by court	CPLR 6401(c)	
Removal of receiver	At any time by court upon motion of any party or on its own initiative	CPLR 6405	
Notice of Pendency			
Filing notice of pendency	Before or after service of summons and at any time prior to judgment	CPLR 6511(a)	Unless complaint has already been filed in county where property is situated, complaint shall be filed with the notice of pendency.

Act To Be Performed	Time Period Available	Statute or Rule	Comments
Effectiveness of notice of pendency filed before an action is commenced	Only if: Summons is served on defendant within 30 days after filing of notice of penalty; or First publication of summons is made pursuant to order and is completed subsequently within 30 days after filing of notice of pendency; or If defendant dies before service of summons or publication is completed, within 30-day period, summons must be served on executor or administrator within 60 days after letters are issued.	CPLR 6512	

Act To Be Performed	Time Period Available	Statute or Rule	Comments
Duration of notice of pendency	Three years from date of filing	CPLR 6513	Extension may be granted, upon motion, before expiration of prior period. Pursuant to a 2005 amendment adding CPLR 6516, successive notices of pendency can be filed in certain foreclosure actions (e.g. mortgage) even though a previously filed notice of such action or previous foreclosure action has expired under CPLR 6513 or become ineffective because service of a summons had not been completed within the time provided by CPLR 6512.
Cancellation by stipulation or by plaintiff	At any time prior to judgment	CPLR 6514(d),(e)	*See* CPLR 6514(a),(b) (mandatory cancellation, discretionary cancellation by court); *See also* CPLR 6515 (filing of undertaking to cancel a notice of pendency and plaintiff's failure to provide undertaking).

Act To Be Performed	Time Period Available	Statute or Rule	Comments
Seizure of Chattel			
Plaintiff's motion for order confirming ex parte order of seizure	Within five days after seizure	CPLR 7102(d)(4)	
Sheriff's retention of custody of chattel	For 10 days after seizure pursuant to order granted on notice and until served with an order of confirmation where seizure is pursuant to ex parte order	CPLR 7102(f)	
Sheriff's delivery of chattel to plaintiff	After 10-day period if sheriff not served with notice of exception to plaintiff's surety, notice of motion for an impounding or returning order, or the necessary papers to reclaim the chattel	CPLR 7102(f).	As to reclaiming chattel, *see* CPLR 7103.
Sheriff's filing of return	Within 20 days after delivery of chattel	CPLR 7107	

Act To Be Performed	Time Period Available	Statute or Rule	Comments
Notice of motion to punish sheriff for contempt for not filing return before hearing on contempt	At least 10 days' notice to sheriff	CPLR 7107	

Act To Be Performed	Time Period Available	Statute or Rule	Comments
Q. ARBITRATION			
Arbitration of damages in medical, dental or podiatric malpractice action	Upon a concession of liability by defendant, defendant may demand that plaintiff elect whether to consent to arbitration of damages. Demand may be made at any time after service of bill of particulars but no later than 60 days after filing notice of medical, podiatric or dental malpractice	CPLR 3045	Within 20 days after receipt of demand, plaintiff shall elect whether to arbitrate damages; if defendant serves a concession of liability within 20 days of such election, issue of damages shall be subject to arbitration under CPLR Article 75-A.
Application to stay arbitration	Within 20 days after service of demand for arbitration or notice of intention to arbitrate	CPLR 7503(c)	As to compulsory arbitration in civil actions for sum of money, *see* 22 NYCRR § 28.2. As to grievance arbitration involving public employers and recognized or certified employee organizations, *see* 4 NYCRR § 207.4 and Civ. Serv. L. Art. 14.

Act To Be Performed	Time Period Available	Statute or Rule	Comments
Notice of arbitration hearing	At least eight days' notice	CPLR 7506(b)	
Making of award by confession	At any time within 3 months after statement is verified	CPLR 7508(b)	
Written application for modification of award to arbitrator	Within 20 days after delivery of award to applicant	CPLR 7509	
Service of written objection to modification of arbitrator's award	Within 10 days of receipt of notice of application for modification	CPLR 7509	
Disposition, by arbitrators, of application	Within 30 days	CPLR 7509	
Application for confirmation of award	Within one year after delivery of award to applicant	CPLR 7510	Unless award is vacated or modified; see CPLR 7510, 7511.

Act To Be Performed	Time Period Available	Statute or Rule	Comments
Application to court to vacate or modify arbitration award	Within 90 days after delivery of award	CPLR 7511(a)	

Act To Be Performed	Time Period Available	Statute or Rule	Comments
R. SPECIAL PROCEEDINGS/ ARTICLE 78 PROCEEDINGS			
Service of notice of petition, petition and affidavits	At least eight days before noticed to be heard; if provide at least 12 days' notice, get additional answering and reply time	CPLR 403(b)	Court may grant order to show cause to be served in lieu of notice of petition at a time and in a manner specified therein. CPLR 403(d). Proceeding commenced by filing of petition and securing an index number ($210 fee) pursuant to CPLR 203(c), CPLR 304, and CPLR 306-a followed by service of notice of petition or order to show cause and petition as required by CPLR 306-b. The 2005 amendments to the NYC Civil Court Act, the Uniform District Court Act and the Uniform City Court Act, require that the notice of petition or order to show cause and the petition be filed in order to commence the action in those designated inferior courts.

Act To Be Performed	Time Period Available	Statute or Rule	Comments
			See NYCCA § 400, UDCA § 400, UCCA § 400. *See* CPLR 203(c), 217, 304, 306-a, 306-b. *See also* amendments to CPLR 105, 304, 306-a and 2102 (L. 2007, ch. 125) concerning filing with the clerk in the Supreme and County Court (effective 1/1/08 for all actions or proceedings commenced after that date) and to CPLR 2001 (L. 2007, ch. 529, eff. 8/15/07) re: court's ability to correct mistakes in the method of filing.
Service of answer and any supporting affidavits	At least two days before petition is noticed to be heard; but if notice of petition is served at least 12 days before return date and so demands, answer must be served at least seven days before return date.	CPLR 403(b)	

Act To Be Performed	Time Period Available	Statute or Rule	Comments
Service of reply and any supporting affidavits	At or before hearing date; but if answer was served at least seven days before return date in compliance with demand in notice of petition served at least 12 days before return date, reply must be served at least one day before hearing date.	CPLR 403(b)	
Respondent's raising objection in point of law	In answer or by motion to dismiss petition, upon notice within the time allowed for answer	CPLR 404(a)	
Respondent's time to serve and file answer if motion to dismiss petition is denied.	Unless otherwise specified by order, within five days after service of order with notice of entry	CPLR 404(a)	
Re-notice, by petitioner, for hearing	Two days' notice	CPLR 404(a)	Petitioner may object in point of law to new matter, in reply or by motion to strike on hearing day. CPLR 404(b).

Act To Be Performed	Time Period Available	Statute or Rule	Comments
Re-notice, by respondent, for hearing	Upon service of the answer upon seven days' notice	CPLR 404(a)	
Motion to correct defects	Within time allowed for responsive pleading	CPLR 405(b)	By serving notice of motion or order to show cause.
Service of responsive pleading after service of amended pleading	Within five days	CPLR 405(b)	Where party cannot serve responsive pleading until papers are corrected, and court so orders.
Service of responsive pleading if motion to correct is denied	Within two days after service of order denying motion with notice of entry, unless order specifies otherwise	CPLR 405(b)	Where time to serve responsive pleading has been extended.
Re-notice for hearing after motion to correct	Two days' notice	CPLR 405(b)	
Petitioner's motion to correct	In reply or by motion on hearing or re-hearing date	CPLR 405(c)	

Act To Be Performed	Time Period Available	Statute or Rule	Comments
Motion in special proceeding, made before petition noticed to be heard	Shall be noticed to be heard at return date of petition	CPLR 406	
Severance of claim or party	At any time, by court	CPLR 407	
Service of notice to admit	Not later than three days before return date of petition	CPLR 408	Does not apply to Surrogate's Court proceedings or to proceedings relating to express trusts (CPLR Art. 77); *see* CPLR Art. 31.
Service of statement denying or setting forth reasons for failing to admit or deny	Not later than one day before return date of petition, unless otherwise ordered by court on ex parte motion	CPLR 408	Does not apply to Surrogate's Court proceedings or to proceedings relating to express trusts (CPLR Art. 77); *see* CPLR Art. 31.
Furnishing of papers	At hearing	CPLR 409(a)	

Act To Be Performed	Time Period Available	Statute or Rule	Comments
Habeas Corpus			
Filing of return to writ of habeas corpus	At time specified in writ, or, if returnable forthwith, within 24 hours after service	CPLR 7008(a)	
Service of written notice of habeas corpus hearing, where detention is by virtue of a mandate	By personal service, eight days before hearing, or as court directs	CPLR 7009(a)	

Act To Be Performed	Time Period Available	Statute or Rule	Comments
Article 78 Proceeding			
Service of notice of petition, petition and affidavits	At least 20 days before CPLR 7804(c) petition noticed to be heard	CPLR 7804(c)	Unless court signs order to show cause in lieu of notice of petition (setting its own schedule). Proceeding commenced by filing of petition and paying index number fee ($210). CPLR 304, 8018(a). Service of the petition and notice of petition or order to show cause must be effected within 15 days of the expiration of the applicable statute of limitations, except proceedings commenced under the Election Law. The 2005 amendments to the NYC Civil Court Act, the Uniform District Court Act and the Uniform City Court Act, require that the notice of petition or order to show cause and the petition be filed in order to commence the action in those designated inferior courts.

Act To Be Performed	Time Period Available	Statute or Rule	Comments
			See NYCCA § 400, UDCA § 400, UCCA § 400. *See* CPLR 203(c), 217, 304, 306-a, 306-b. *See also* amendments to CPLR 105, 304, 306-a and 2102 (L. 2007, ch. 125) concerning filing with the clerk in the Supreme and County Court (effective 1/1/08 for all actions or proceedings commenced after that date) and to CPLR 2001 (L. 2007, ch. 529, eff. 8/15/07) re: court's ability to correct mistakes in the method of filing.
Service of answer and supporting affidavits	At least five days before petition is noticed to be heard	CPLR 7803(c)	
Service of reply and any supporting affidavits	At least one day before petition is noticed to be heard	CPLR 7804(c)	
Service and filing of respondent's answer following denial of motion to dismiss petition	Within five days after service of order with notice of entry	CPLR 7804(f)	*See* CPLR 7804(f) regarding objections in point of law.

Act To Be Performed	Time Period Available	Statute or Rule	Comments
Re-notice, by petitioner, for hearing	Two days' notice	CPLR 7804(f)	Petitioner may object in point of law to new matter, in reply or on day of hearing.
Re-notice, by respondent, for hearing	Upon service of the answer upon seven days' notice	CPLR 7804(f)	

Act To Be Performed	Time Period Available	Statute or Rule	Comments
S. TAXATION OF COSTS			
Taxation on notice	Five days' notice	CPLR 8402	
Notice of retaxation	Five days' notice	CPLR 8403	Service within five days after service of bill of costs without notice.

Act To Be Performed	Time Period Available	Statute or Rule	Comments
T. SECURITY FOR COSTS			
Plaintiff's giving security for costs by undertaking	Within 30 days from date of court order	CPLR 8502	If not timely given, court may dismiss complaint upon motion and may award costs to defendant. *See* CPLR 8503.

Act To Be Performed	Time Period Available	Statute or Rule	Comments
U. UNDERTAKINGS			
Exception to surety	Within 10 days after receipt of a copy of the undertaking	CPLR 2506	May only be taken where a certificate of qualification (Ins. L. § 1111(b), (c) and (d) is not filed with the undertaking.
Surety's motion to justify	Within 10 days after service of notice of exception	CPLR 2507(a)	If motion to justify is not timely made, the undertaking is without effect except that surety remains liable until new undertaking is allowed. *See* CPLR 2507(b). Motion can also be made by person on whose behalf the undertaking was given.
Surety's motion on notice to be discharged from liabilitY for act or omission of fiduciary	Subsequent to court order or the time when new undertaking satisfactory to court is filed	CPLR 2510	Court may restrain fiduciary from acting pending order discharging surety.
Account of fiduciary following surety's motion for discharge	Within such time as court orders but not exceeding 20 days	CPLR 2510(a)	

NEW YORK COURT STRUCTURE (AS OF CALENDAR YEAR 2007)

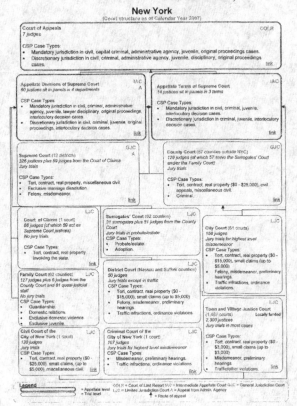

Source: Court Statistics Project, State Court Caseload Statistics, 2007 (National Center for State Courts 2008). Reprinted with permission.

CIVIL PRACTICE LAW AND RULES

As amended by the 2009 Regular Legislative Session

An Act in relation to civil practice and prescribing rules of civil procedure governing generally the civil procedure in the courts of the state of New York and before the judges thereof, constituting chapter eight of the consolidated laws.

Article 1

SHORT TITLE; APPLICABILITY AND DEFINITIONS

CPLR

    (r)   Place where action triable.

    (s)   Real property.

  (s-1)   The sheriff.

    (t)   Type size requirement.

    (u)   Verified pleading.

§ 106.   Civil and criminal prosecutions not merged.

§ 107.   Appendix of official forms.

§ 101. Short title; application.

This chapter shall be known as the civil practice law and rules, and may be cited as "CPLR." The civil practice law and rules shall govern the procedure in civil judicial proceedings in all courts of the state and before all judges, except where the procedure is regulated by inconsistent statute. The civil practice law and rules shall succeed the civil practice act and rules of civil practice and shall be deemed substituted therefor throughout the statutes and rules of the state. Reference to a provision in the civil practice law and rules may, except when such provision is being enacted or amended, be made without indicating whether it is a rule or section.

1964 AMENDMENTS

L. 1964, ch. 252, eff. Sept. 1, 1964, added the last sentence.

§ 102. Amendment, rescission or adoption of rules.

The civil practice rules are herein designated "rule." Any rule in this chapter may be amended, or rescinded, or additional civil practice rules may be adopted, not inconsistent with the constitution, by act of the legislature. No rule so amended, rescinded or adopted shall abridge or enlarge the substantive rights of any party.

CROSS REFERENCES

Judiciary Law § 229, referred to in this section, was repealed by L. 1978, ch. 156, eff. May 19, 1978. **Judiciary Law § 215,** which replaced former § 229, does not refer to the power of the judicial conference to change the rules of the CPLR.

1986 AMENDMENTS

L. 1986, ch. 334, eff. July 17, 1986, deleted the reference to **Judiciary Law § 229(3).**

§ 103. Form of civil judicial proceedings.

(a) One form of action. There is only one form of civil action. The distinctions between actions at law and suits in equity, and the forms of those actions and suits, have been abolished.

(b) Action or special proceeding. All civil judicial proceedings shall be prosecuted in the form of an action, except where prosecution in the form of a special proceeding is authorized. Except where otherwise prescribed by law, procedure in special proceedings shall be the same as in actions, and the provisions of the civil practice law and rules applicable to actions shall be applicable to special proceedings.

(c) Improper form. If a court has obtained jurisdiction over the parties, a civil judicial proceeding shall not be dismissed solely because it is not brought in the proper form, but the court shall make whatever order is required for its proper prosecution. If the court finds it appropriate in the interests of justice, it may convert a motion into a special proceeding, or vice-versa, upon such terms as may be just, including the payment of fees and costs.

2002 AMENDMENTS

L. 2002, ch. 593, § 1, eff. Jan.1, 2003, amended subdivision (c).

§ 104. Construction.

The civil practice law and rules shall be liberally construed to secure the just, speedy and inexpensive determination of every civil judicial proceeding.

§ 105. Definitions.

(a) Applicability. Unless the context requires otherwise, the definitions in this section apply to the civil practice law and rules.

(b) Action and special proceeding. The word "action" includes a special proceeding; the words "plaintiff" and "defendant" include the petitioner and the respondent, respectively, in a special proceeding; and the words "summons" and "complaint" include the notice of petition and the petition, respectively, in a special proceeding.

(c) Attorney. The word "attorney" includes a party prosecuting or defending an action in person.

(d) Civil judicial proceeding. A "civil judicial proceeding" is a prosecution, other than a criminal action, of an independent application to a court for relief.

(e) Clerk. The word "clerk," as used in any provision respecting an action or any proceedings therein, means the clerk of the court in which the action is triable. In supreme and county court, the word "clerk" shall mean the clerk of the county.

(f) Consumer credit transaction. The term "consumer credit transaction" means a transaction wherein credit is extended to an individual and the money, property, or service which is the subject of the transaction is primarily for personal, family or household purposes.

(g) Court and judge. The word "court," as used in any provision concerning a motion, order or special proceeding, includes a judge thereof authorized to act out of court with respect to such motion, order or special proceeding.

(h) Domestic and foreign corporation. A "domestic corporation" is a corporation created by or under the laws of the state, or a corporation located in the state and created by or under the laws of the United States, or a corporation created by or pursuant to the laws in force in the colony of New York before April nineteenth, seventeen hundred seventy-five. Every other corporation is a "foreign corporation."

(i) Garnishee. A "garnishee" is a person who owes a debt to a judgment debtor, or a person other than the judgment debtor who has property in his possession or custody in which a judgment debtor has an interest.

(j) Infant, infancy. The word "infant," as used in this chapter, means a person who has not attained the age of eighteen years. The word "infancy" means the state of being an infant.

(k) Judgment. The word "judgment" means a final or interlocutory judgment.

(l) Judgment creditor. A "judgment creditor" is a person in whose favor a money judgment is entered or a person who becomes entitled to enforce it.

(m) Judgment debtor. A "judgment debtor" is a person, other than a defendant not summoned in the action, against whom a money judgment is entered.

(n) Judicial hearing officer. A "judicial hearing officer" means a person so designated pursuant to provisions of article twenty-two of the judiciary law.

(o) Law. The word "law" means any statute or any civil practice rule.

(p) Matrimonial action. The term "matrimonial action" includes actions for a separation, for an annulment or dissolution of a marriage, for a divorce, for a declaration of the nullity of a void marriage, for a declaration of the validity or nullity of a foreign judgment of divorce and for a declaration of the validity or nullity of a marriage.

(q) Money judgment. A "money judgment" is a judgment, or any part thereof, for a sum of money or directing the payment of a sum of money.

(r) Place where action triable. The place where an action is "triable" means the place where the action is pending; or, if no action has been commenced, any proper place of trial or any proper place to commence the action; or, after entry of judgment, the place where the judgment was entered.

(s) Real property. "Real property" includes chattels real.

(s-1) The sheriff. [*Effective until June 30, 2014*] The term "the sheriff", as used in this chapter, means the county sheriff as defined in subdivision (a) of section thirteen of article thirteen of the constitution and in counties in the city of New York, the city sheriff as defined in section fifteen hundred twenty-six of chapter fifty-eight of the New York City charter. For the purposes of article fifty-two of this chapter relating to the enforcement of money judgments and for the purposes of any provision of law which in effect applies any such provision of article fifty-two of this chapter, such term shall also mean any "city marshal" as defined in article sixteen of the New York city civil court act, except that city marshals shall have no power to levy upon or sell real property and city marshals shall have no power of arrest.

(t) Type size requirement. Whenever a requirement relating to size of type is stated in point size, the type size requirement shall be deemed met if the x-height of the type is a minimum of forty-five percent of the

CPLR

specified point size. each point shall be measured as.351 millimeter. The x-height size shall be measured as it appears on the page. The x-height is the height of the lower case letters, exclusive of ascenders or descenders.

(u) Verified pleading. A "verified pleading" may be utilized as an affidavit whenever the latter is required.

2009 AMENDMENTS

L. 2009, ch.103, § 1, eff. July 11, 2009, extending the automatic repeal of subdivision (s-1) from June 30, 2009 to June 30, 2014.

2007 AMENDMENTS

L. 2007, ch.125, § 1, eff. Jan. 1, 2008, amending subdivision (e), to clearly spell out that in supreme and county court, the clerk of the court is the clerk of the county.

2004 AMENDMENTS

L. 2004, ch.128, § 1, eff. June 29, 2004, extending the automatic repeal of subdivision (s-1) from June 30, 2004 to June 30, 2009.

1999 AMENDMENTS

L. 1999, ch. 71, § 1, eff. June 18, 1999, extending the automatic repeal of subdivision (s-1) from June 30, 1999 to June 30, 2004.

1998 AMENDMENTS

L. 1998, ch. 80, § 3, eff. June 2, 1998, deemed in full force and effect on and after Aug. 26, 1997, amended subdivision (s-1) by providing that city marshals shall not have the power to levy upon or sell real property and shall have no power of arrest. This subdivision will be deemed repealed on June 30, 1999, pursuant to L. 1997, ch. 455.

1997 AMENDMENTS

L. 1997, ch. 455, § 2, eff. Aug. 26, 1997, added a new subdivision (s-1) defining "sheriff," incorporating the definitions of county and city sheriffs and extending the power to enforce judgments to N.Y.C. marshals as well as sheriffs. This subdivision will be repealed on June 30, 1999.

1994 AMENDMENTS

L. 1994, ch. 100, eff. May 16, 1994, amended CPLR 105 by relettering former subdivision (t) as subdivision (u) and adding a new subdivision (t) pertaining to type size requirements.

1983 AMENDMENTS

L. 1983, ch. 840, eff. April 1, 1983, relettered subdivisions (n) through (s) to be (o) through (t) and added a new subdivision (n).

1974 AMENDMENTS

L. 1974, ch. 924, eff. Sept. 1, 1974, added a new subdivision (j) defining the words "infant" and "infancy," and relettered accordingly.

1973 AMENDMENTS

L. 1973, ch. 238, eff. Sept. 1, 1973, added a new subdivision (f) defining "consumer credit transaction," and relettered accordingly.

§ 106.   Civil and criminal prosecutions not merged.

Where the violation of a right admits of both a civil and criminal prosecution, the one is not merged in the other.

§ 107.   Appendix of official forms.

The state administrator shall have the power to adopt, amend and rescind an appendix of forms. Forms adopted pursuant to this section shall be sufficient under the civil practice law and rules and shall illustrate the simplicity and brevity of statement which the civil practice law and rules contemplate.

CROSS REFERENCES

L. 1978, ch. 156, eff. May 19, 1978, replaced the "state administrator" with a "chief administrator of the courts." See **Judiciary Law Article 7-A.**

1974 AMENDMENTS

L. 1974, ch. 615, eff. May 30, 1974, transferred the power to adopt, amend and rescind an appendix of official forms from the judicial conference to the state administrator.

1967 AMENDMENTS

L. 1967, ch. 646, effective Sept. 1, 1967, added Section 107, authorizing the Judicial Conference to promulgate an appendix of official CPLR forms.

CPLR

Article 2

LIMITATIONS OF TIME

_____

SUMMARY OF ARTICLE

CPLR

CPLR

§ 201. Application of article.

An action, including one brought in the name or for the benefit of the state, must be commenced within the time specified in this article unless a different time is prescribed by law or a shorter time is prescribed by written agreement. No court shall extend the time limited by law for the commencement of an action.

CROSS REFERENCES

See **General Obligations Law §§ 17-101 and 17-103**, in Appendix, *below*, as to agreements waiving the statute of limitations.

§ 202. Cause of action accruing without the state.

An action based upon a cause of action accruing without the state cannot be commenced after the expiration of the time limited by the laws of either the state or the place without the state where the cause of action accrued, except that where the cause of action accrued in favor of a resident of the state the time limited by the laws of the state shall apply.

§ 203. Method of computing periods of limitation generally.

(a) Accrual of cause of action and interposition of claim. The time within which an action must be commenced, except as otherwise expressly prescribed, shall be computed from the time the cause of action accrued to the time the claim is interposed.

(b) Claim in complaint where action commenced by service. In an action which is commenced by service, a claim asserted in the complaint is interposed against the defendant or a co-defendant united in interest with such defendant when:

1. the summons is served upon the defendant; or

2. first publication of the summons against the defendant is made pursuant to an order, and publication is subsequently completed; or

3. an order for a provisional remedy other than attachment is granted, if, within thirty days thereafter, the summons is served upon the defendant or first publication of the summons against the defendant is made pursuant to an order and publication is subsequently completed, or, where the defendant dies within thirty days after the order is granted and before the summons is served upon the defendant or publication is completed, if the summons is served upon the defendant's executor or administrator within sixty days after letters are issued; for this purpose seizure of a chattel in an action to recover a chattel is a provisional remedy; or

4. an order of attachment is granted, if the summons is served in accordance with the provisions of section 6213; or

5. the summons is delivered to the sheriff of that county outside the city of New York or is filed with the clerk of that county within the city of New York in which the defendant resides, is employed or is doing business, or if none of the foregoing is known to the plaintiff

after reasonable inquiry, then of the county in which the defendant is known to have last resided, been employed or been engaged in business, or in which the cause of action arose; or if the defendant is a corporation, of a county in which it may be served or in which the cause of action arose; provided that:

(i) the summons is served upon the defendant within sixty days after the period of limitation would have expired but for this provision; or

(ii) first publication of the summons against the defendant is made pursuant to an order within sixty days after the period of limitation would have expired but for this provision and publication is subsequently completed; or

(iii) the summons is served upon the defendant's executor or administrator within sixty days after letters are issued, where the defendant dies within sixty days after the period of limitation would have expired but for this provision and before the summons is served upon the defendant or publication is completed.

6. in an action to be commenced in a court not of record, the summons is delivered for service upon the defendant to any officer authorized to serve it in a county, city or town in which the defendant resides, is employed or is doing business, or if none of the foregoing be known to the plaintiff after reasonable inquiry, then in a county, city or town in which defendant is known to have last resided, been employed or been engaged in business, or, where the defendant is a corporation, in a county, city or town in which it may be served, if the summons is served upon the defendant within sixty days after the period of limitation would have expired but for this provision; or, where the defendant dies within sixty days after the period of limitation would have expired but for this provision and before the summons is served upon the defendant, if the summons is served upon his executor or administrator within sixty days after letters are issued.

(c) Claim in complaint where action commenced by filing. In an action which is commenced by filing, a claim asserted in the complaint is interposed against the defendant or a co-defendant united in interest with such defendant when the action is commenced.

CPLR

(d) Defense or counterclaim. A defense or counterclaim is interposed when a pleading containing it is served. A defense or counterclaim is not barred if it was not barred at the time the claims asserted in the complaint were interposed, except that if the defense or counterclaim arose from the transactions, occurrences, or series of transactions or occurrences, upon which a claim asserted in the complaint depends, it is not barred to the extent of the demand in the complaint notwithstanding that it was barred at the time the claims asserted in the complaint were interposed.

(e) Effect upon defense or counterclaim of termination of action because of death or by dismissal or voluntary discontinuance. Where a defendant has served an answer containing a defense or counterclaim and the action is terminated because of the plaintiff's death or by dismissal or voluntary discontinuance, the time which elapsed between the commencement and termination of the action is not a part of the time within which an action must be commenced to recover upon the claim in the defense or counterclaim or the time within which the defense or counterclaim may be interposed in another action brought by the plaintiff or his successor in interest.

(f) Claim in amended pleading. A claim asserted in an amended pleading is deemed to have been interposed at the time the claims in the original pleading were interposed, unless the original pleading does not give notice of the transactions, occurrences, or series of transactions or occurrences, to be proved pursuant to the amended pleading.

(g) Time computed from actual or imputed discovery of facts. Except as provided in article two of the uniform commercial code or in section two hundred fourteen–a of this chapter, where the time within which an action must be commenced is computed from the time when facts were discovered or from the time when facts could with reasonable diligence have been discovered, or from either of such times, the action must be commenced within two years after such actual or imputed discovery or within the period otherwise provided, computed from the time the cause of action accrued, whichever is longer.

CROSS REFERENCES

Reference to **U.C.C. Article 2 in subd. (f),** *above,* refers to U.C.C. § 2-725, which appears in Appendix, *below.*

2002 AMENDMENTS

L. 2002, ch. 334, eff. Nov. 21, 2001, amended subdivision (c) by deleting subparagraph (1) entirely, and deleting subparagraph 2 except for the words "the action is commenced", which now appear at the end of subdivision (c).

1996 AMENDMENTS

L. 1996, ch. 606, eff. Sept. 1, 1997, and applicable to all actions or special proceedings commenced on or after such date, amended subparagraph (c)(1) by deleting the words "with the court."

1992 AMENDMENTS

L. 1992, ch. 216, eff. July 1, 1992, amended CPLR 203 by adding to the catch line of subdivision (b) the words ". . . where action commenced by service. In an action which is commenced by service, . . ."; by deleting the language added by L. 1992, ch. 55, pertaining to the requirement that an index number be obtained pursuant to CPLR 306–a; by deleting the phrase "the summons is filed, an index number obtained, and" at the beginning of subparagraphs (i), (ii), and (iii); by adding as an entirely new provision the present subdivision (c); by renumbering former subdivisions (c), (d), (e), and (f) as subdivisions (d), (e), (f), and (g) respectively; and by replacing the pronoun "him" with "the defendant" throughout the section.

L. 1992, ch. 55, eff. for all actions pending on July 1, 1992, amended CPLR 203(b)(5) by adding the language pertaining to the requirement that an index number be obtained pursuant to CPLR 306–a, and the phrase "the summons is filed, an index number obtained, and" at the beginning of subparagraphs (i), (ii), and (iii). These amendments, however, were superseded by L. 1992, ch. 216, discussed *supra.*

1979 AMENDMENTS

L. 1979, ch. 404, eff. Jan. 1, 1980, amended CPLR 203 subdivision (b) paragraph 5 by repealing the former provision and enacting the statute in its present form.

1977 AMENDMENTS

L. 1977, ch. 494, eff. Sept. 1, 1977, amended paragraph (5) of subd. (b).

1976 AMENDMENTS

L. 1976, ch. 722, eff. Sept. 1, 1976, amended paragraph (5) of subd. (b). 203(b).

1975 AMENDMENTS

L. 1975, ch. 109, eff. July 1, 1975, amended Subd. (f) by adding the phrase "or in section two hundred fourteen-a of this chapter" after the words "the uniform commercial code," thereby excluding medical malpractice actions based on discovery of foreign objects in the body of the patient from the two

CPLR

year computation of CPLR 203(f). The amendment applies to acts of malpractice occurring on or after July 1, 1975.

1970 AMENDMENTS

L. 1970, ch. 397, eff. Sept. 1, 1970, amended subdivision (b)(3) by excluding attachment from the operation of this provision, thereby conforming the section to the provisions of CPLR 6213; added a new subdivision (b)(4); and renumbered accordingly.

1966 AMENDMENTS

L. 1966, ch. 138, eff. Sept. 1, 1966, amended Subd. (f) by inserting after the title the words "Except as provided in article 2 of the uniform commercial code." See U.C.C. § 2-725 in Appendix, *below.*

1965 AMENDMENTS

L. 1965, ch. 112, eff. Sept. 1, 1965, amended Subd. (b)(4) [now (b)(5)].

L. 1965, ch. 113, eff. Sept. 1, 1965, amended Subd. (b)(5) [now (b)(6)].

L. 1965, ch. 196, eff. Sept. 1, 1965, amended Subd. (d).

L. 1965, ch. 56, eff. Sept. 1, 1965, amended Subd. (f). Amendment recommended by the Judicial Conference Feb. 1, 1965, Report to the Legislature: "Two problems are presented by the present provision: (1) to what actions does the alternative formula apply; and (2) how is 'the time the cause of action accrued' ascertained?

"As to the first problem, § 203(f) confines its application to those cases where the time within which an action must be commenced is computed either from actual or imputed discovery. This would seem clearly to include those actions referred to in § 213(6) (by way of § 206(c)), and in § 213(7), as they are presently constituted, since both of these provisions expressly refer to actual or imputed discovery. But what of those provisions which refer solely to 'discovery,' (e.g., §§ 206(a)(1), 206(b), 213(5), 214(7)) and which may be construed to mean only actual discovery? Must the case be one where the statute of limitations turns on actual *or* imputed discovery before the alternative formula of § 203(f) is to apply?

"The Conference perceives no reason in logic or policy why the principle of § 203(f) should be confined to cases where running of the statute is suspended pending actual *or* imputed discovery, but should not apply to cases where running of the statute is suspended until actual discovery. In the ordinary case, the time of actual discovery will be later than that of imputed discovery, and it would be anomalous, to say the least, to put pressure upon a plaintiff to whom discovery is imputed to bring his action expeditiously, while at the same time permitting a plaintiff with actual knowledge to wait out the full statutory period. The Conference therefore proposes to make the alternative formula of § 203(f) generally applicable to all actions where the time of discovery is a factor in computing the statute of limitations.

". . . this proposed change may affect the courts' interpretation of § 214(7) (action to annul a marriage for fraud) as well as of Domestic Relations Law §§ 171 and 200 (actions for divorce or separation based on adultery). . . ."

§ 204. Stay of commencement of action; demand for arbitration.

(a) Stay. Where the commencement of an action has been stayed by a court or by statutory prohibition, the duration of the stay is not a part of the time within which the action must be commenced.

(b) Arbitration. Where it shall have been determined that a party is not obligated to submit a claim to arbitration, the time which elapsed between the demand for arbitration and the final determination that there is no obligation to arbitrate is not a part of the time within which an action upon such claim must be commenced. The time within which the action must be commenced shall not be extended by this provision beyond one year after such final determination.

§ 205. Termination of action.

(a) New action by plaintiff. If an action is timely commenced and is terminated in any other manner than by a voluntary discontinuance, a failure to obtain personal jurisdiction over the defendant, a dismissal of the complaint for neglect to prosecute the action, or a final judgment upon the merits, the plaintiff, or, if the plaintiff dies, and the cause of action survives, his or her executor or administrator, may commence a new action upon the same transaction or occurrence or series of transactions or occurrences within six months after the termination provided that the new action would have been timely commenced at the time of commencement of the prior action and that service upon defendant is effected within such six-month period. Where a dismissal is one for neglect to prosecute the action made pursuant to rule thirty-two hundred sixteen of this chapter or otherwise, the judge shall set forth on the record the specific conduct constituting the neglect, which conduct shall demonstrate a general pattern of delay in proceeding with the litigation.

(b) Defense or counterclaim. Where the defendant has served an answer and the action is terminated in any manner, and a new action upon the same transaction or occurrence or series of transactions or occurrences is commenced by the plaintiff or his successor in interest, the assertion of any cause of action or defense by the defendant in the new action shall be timely if it was timely asserted in the prior action.

(c) Application. This section also applies to a proceeding brought under the workers' compensation law.

2008 AMENDMENTS

L. 2008, ch. 156 § 1, eff. July 7, 2008, amended CPLR 205(a) by establishing a requirement that when a dismissal is one for neglect to prosecute an action the judge must set forth on the record the specific conduct constituting the neglect. The conduct specified must demonstrate a general pattern of delay in proceeding with the action.

1992 AMENDMENTS

L. 1992, ch. 216, eff. July 1, 1992, amended section 205 by adding to subdivision (a) the words "a failure to obtain personal jurisdiction over the defendant," and the words "and that service upon defendant is effected within such six-month period;" and by making the language gender neutral.

1978 AMENDMENTS

L. 1978, ch. 51, eff. April 11, 1978, amended subdivisions (a) and (b) by eliminating language providing that a new action commenced under the section be limited to a suit upon the same "cause of action" and substituting the provision that the new action be based upon the same "transaction or occurrence," provided that the cause would have been timely when the original action was brought.

1965 AMENDMENTS

L. 1965, ch. 233, eff. Sept. 1, 1965, amended section by dividing it into three subdivisions.

§ 206. Computing periods of limitation in particular actions.

(a) Where demand necessary. Except as provided in article 3 of the uniform commercial code, where a demand is necessary to entitle a person to commence an action, the time within which the action must be commenced shall be computed from the time when the right to make the demand is complete, except that

1. where a right grows out of the receipt or detention of money or property by a trustee, agent, attorney or other person acting in a fiduciary capacity, the time within which the action must be commenced shall be computed from the time when the person having the right to make the demand discovered the facts upon which the right depends; and

2. where there was a deposit of money to be repaid only upon a

special demand, or a delivery of personal property not to be returned specifically or in kind at a fixed time or upon a fixed contingency, the time within which the action must be commenced shall be computed from the demand for repayment or return.

(b) Based on misconduct of agent. Where a judgment is entered against a principal in an action based upon an injury resulting from the act or omission of his deputy or agent, the time within which an action by the principal against the deputy or agent to recover damages by reason of such judgment must be commenced shall be computed, from the time when the action against the principal was finally determined. Where an injury results from the representation by a person that he is an agent with authority to execute a contract in behalf of a principal, the time within which an action to recover damages for breach of warranty of authority must be commenced by the person injured against the purported agent shall be computed from the time the person injured discovered the facts constituting lack of authority.

(c) Based on breach of covenant of seizin or against incumbrances. In an action based upon breach of a covenant of seizin or against incumbrances, the time within which the action must be commenced shall be computed from an eviction.

(d) Based on account. In an action based upon a mutual, open and current account, where there have been reciprocal demands between the parties, the time within which the action must be commenced shall be computed from the time of the last transaction in the account on either side.

CROSS REFERENCES

Reference to **U.C.C. Article 3** in subd. (a), *above*, refers to **U.C.C. § 3-122(3)**, which appears in Appendix, *below*.

1966 AMENDMENTS

L. 1966, ch. 138, eff. Sept. 1, 1966, amended Subd. (a) by inserting after the title the words "Except as provided in article 3 of the uniform commercial code, where."

Amendment recommended by the Judicial Conference Feb. 1, 1966, Report to the Legislature: "CPLR 206(a) provides a cause of action on a demand instrument accrues when the 'right to make the demand is complete.' U.C.C. § 3-122(3), however, provides that such a cause of action accrues 'upon demand' and provides further that 'notice of dishonor is a demand.' The bar should be apprised of the existence of this plain inconsistency so as to avoid possible pitfalls."

1965 AMENDMENTS

L. 1965, ch. 248, eff. Sept. 1, 1965, repealed Subd. (c), and relettered Subds. (d) and (e) to (c) and (d), respectively. Former Subd. (c) transferred to and made part of new § 213(9), now § 213(8).

§ 207. Defendant's absence from state or residence under false name.

If, when a cause of action accrues against a person, he is without the state, the time within which the action must be commenced shall be computed from the time he comes into or returns to the state. If, after a cause of action has accrued against a person, that person departs from the state and remains continuously absent therefrom for four months or more, or that person resides within the state under a false name which is unknown to the person entitled to commence the action, the time of his absence or residence within the state under such a false name is not a part of the time within which the action must be commenced. If an action is commenced against a person described above, the time within which service must be made on such person in accordance with subdivisions (a) and (b) of section three hundred six–b of this chapter shall be computed in accordance with this section. This section does not apply:

1. while there is in force a designation, voluntary or involuntary, made pursuant to law, of a person to whom a summons may be delivered within the state with the same effect as if served personally within the state; or

2. while a foreign corporation has one or more officers or other persons in the state on whom a summons against such corporation may be served; or

3. while jurisdiction over the person of the defendant can be obtained without personal delivery of the summons to the defendant within the state.

CROSS REFERENCES

Examples of designation referred to in subd. (1), *above*, may be found in **Vehicle and Traffic Law §§ 253-254** and **Business Corporations Law §§ 304, 306 and 307**. See Appendix, *below*.

1992 AMENDMENTS

L. 1992, ch. 216, eff. July 1, 1992, amended CPLR 207 by adding the next to last sentence to subdivision (a), beginning with the words "If an action is commenced . . ."; and by making the language gender neutral.

§ 208. Infancy, insanity.

If a person entitled to commence an action is under a disability because of infancy or insanity at the time the cause of action accrues, and the time otherwise limited for commencing the action is three years or more and expires no later than three years after the disability ceases, or the person under the disability dies, the time within which the action must be commenced shall be extended to three years after the disability ceases or the person under the disability dies, whichever event first occurs; if the time otherwise limited is less than three years, the time shall be extended by the period of disability. The time within which the action must be commenced shall not be extended by this provision beyond ten years after the cause of action accrues, except, in any action other than for medical, dental or podiatric malpractice, where the person was under a disability due to infancy. This section shall not apply to an action to recover a penalty or forfeiture, or against a sheriff or other officer for an escape.

CPLR

CROSS REFERENCES

As to claims against the State, see **N.Y. Const. Art. 3 § 19** in Appendix, *below.*

1986 AMENDMENTS

L. 1986, ch. 485, eff. July 21, 1986, and applicable to acts, omissions or failures occurring on or after such date, amended the eleventh line of CPLR 208 by inserting the words "or podiatric" after the word "dental."

1985 AMENDMENTS

L. 1985, ch. 760, eff. July 1, 1985 and applicable to any acts, omissions or failures occurring on or after that date, amended the second sentence of CPLR 208 by inserting the words "or dental" between "medical" and "malpractice."

1975 AMENDMENTS

L. 1975, ch. 109, eff. July 1, 1975, amended the second sentence of CPLR 208 by adding the phrase ", in any action other than for medical malpractice," after the word "except," thereby limiting to a maximum of ten years the extended period for commencing an infant's action where the cause of action is for medical malpractice. The amendment applies to acts of malpractice occurring on or after July 1, 1975.

1974 AMENDMENTS

L. 1974, ch. 924, eff. Sept. 1, 1974, amended the first sentence of CPLR 208 by adding the words "under a disability because of infancy or insanity" and by deleting after the phrase "at the time the cause of action accrues" the words "under the age of twenty-one years or insane." The second sentence of the section was amended by inserting the last five words "a disability due to infancy" and deleting the words "the age of twenty-one years." A person is under the disability of infancy if he is under the age of eighteen years. See CPLR 105(j) enacted simultaneously with the amendment to CPLR 208.

1973 AMENDMENTS

L. 1973, ch. 687, eff. Sept. 9, 1973, amended CPLR 208 by deleting from the first sentence "or imprisoned on a criminal charge or conviction for a term less than for life"; and by adding "or" before "insane" in the first sentence.

§ 209. War.

(a) Cause of action accruing in foreign country. Where a cause of action, whether originally accrued in favor of a resident or non-resident of the state, accrued in a foreign country with which the United States or any of its allies were then or subsequently at war, or territory then or subsequently occupied by the government of such foreign country, the time which elapsed between the commencement of the war, or of such occupation, and the termination of hostilities with such country, or of such occupation, is not a part of the time within which the action must be commenced. This section shall neither apply to nor in any manner affect an action brought pursuant to section six hundred twenty-five of the banking law against a banking organization or against the superintendent of banks.

(b) Right of alien. Where a person is unable to commence an action in the courts of the state because any party is an alien subject or citizen of a foreign country at war with the United States or any of its allies, whether the cause of action accrued during or prior to the war, the time which elapsed between the commencement of the war and the termination of hostilities with such country is not a part of the time within which the action must be commenced.

(c) Non-enemy in enemy country or enemy-occupied territory. Where a person entitled to commence an action, other than a person entitled to the benefits of subdivision (b), is a resident of, or a sojourner in, a foreign country with which the United States or any of its allies are at war, or territory occupied by the government of such foreign country, the period of such residence or sojourn during which the war continues or the territory is so occupied is not a part of the time within which the action must be commenced.

§ 210. Death of claimant or person liable; cause of action accruing after death and before grant of letters.

(a) Death of claimant. Where a person entitled to commence an action dies before the expiration of the time within which the action must be commenced and the cause of action survives, an action may be commenced by his representative within one year after his death.

(b) Death of person liable. The period of eighteen months after the death, within or without the state, of a person against whom a cause of action exists is not a part of the time within which the action must be commenced against his executor or administrator.

(c) Cause of action accruing after death and before grant of letters. In an action by an executor or administrator to recover personal property wrongfully taken after the death and before the issuance of letters, or to recover damages for taking, detaining or injuring personal property within that period, the time within which the action must be commenced shall be computed from the time the letters are issued or from three years after the death, whichever event first occurs. Any distributee, next of kin, legatee or creditor who was under a disability prescribed in section 208 at the time the cause of action accrued, may, within two years after the disability ceases, commence an action to recover such damages or the value of such property as he would have received upon a final distribution of the estate if an action had been timely commenced by the executor or administrator.

§ 211. Actions to be commenced within twenty years.

(a) On a bond. An action to recover principal or interest upon a written instrument evidencing an indebtedness of the state of New York or of any person, association or public or private corporation, originally sold by the issuer after publication of an advertisement for bids for the issue in a newspaper of general circulation and secured only by a pledge of the faith and credit of the issuer, regardless of whether a sinking fund is or may be established for its redemption, must be

CPLR

commenced within twenty years after the cause of action accrues. This subdivision does not apply to actions upon written instruments evidencing an indebtedness of any corporation, association or person under the jurisdiction of the public service commission, the commissioner of transportation, the interstate commerce commission, the federal communications commission, the civil aeronautics board, the federal power commission, or any other regulatory commission or board of a state or of the federal government. This subdivision applies to all causes of action, including those barred on April eighteenth, nineteen hundred fifty, by the provisions of the civil practice act then effective.

(b) On a money judgment. A money judgment is presumed to be paid and satisfied after the expiration of twenty years from the time when the party recovering it was first entitled to enforce it. This presumption is conclusive, except as against a person who within the twenty years acknowledges an indebtedness, or makes a payment, of all or part of the amount recovered by the judgment, or his heir or personal representative, or a person whom he otherwise represents. Such an acknowledgment must be in writing and signed by the person to be charged. Property acquired by an enforcement order or by levy upon an execution is a payment, unless the person to be charged shows that it did not include property claimed by him. If such an acknowledgment or payment is made, the judgment is conclusively presumed to be paid and satisfied as against any person after the expiration of twenty years after the last acknowledgment or payment made by him. The presumption created by this subdivision may be availed of under an allegation that the action was not commenced within the time limited.

(c) By state for real property. The state will not sue a person for or with respect to real property, or the rents or profits thereof, by reason of the right or title of the state to the same, unless the cause of action accrued, or the state, or those from whom it claims, have received the rents and profits of the real property or of some part thereof, within twenty years before the commencement of the action.

(d) By grantee of state for real property. An action shall not be commenced for or with respect to real property by a person claiming by virtue of letters patent or a grant from the state, unless it might have been maintained by the state, as prescribed in this section, if the patent or grant had not been issued or made.

(e) For support, alimony or maintenance. An action or proceeding to enforce any temporary order, permanent order or judgment of any court of competent jurisdiction which awards support, alimony or maintenance, regardless of whether or not arrears have been reduced to a money judgment, must be commenced within twenty years from the date of a default in payment. This section shall only apply to orders which have been entered subsequent to the date upon which this section shall become effective.

1987 AMENDMENTS

L. 1987, ch. 815, eff. Aug. 7, 1987, and applicable to any action or proceeding commenced on or after such date, added a new subdivision (e), making a twenty-year limitation period applicable to actions or proceedings to enforce orders or judgments awarding support, alimony or maintenance. Note that as to orders, the section applies only to those entered subsequent to Aug. 7, 1987.

1970 AMENDMENTS

L. 1970, ch. 267, § 7, eff. March 1, 1971, amended Subd. (a) to provide that the subdivision shall not apply to actions upon a written instrument evidencing an indebtedness of any corporation, association or person under the jurisdiction of the Commissioner of Transportation.

1965 AMENDMENTS

L. 1965, ch. 214, eff. Sept. 1, 1965, added new Subd. (d).

§ 212. Actions to be commenced within ten years.

(a) Possession necessary to recover real property. An action to recover real property or its possession cannot be commenced unless the plaintiff, or his predecessor in interest, was seized or possessed of the premises within ten years before the commencement of the action.

(b) Annulment of letters patent. Where letters patent or a grant of real property, issued or made by the state, are declared void on the ground of fraudulent suggestion or concealment, forfeiture, mistake or ignorance of a material fact, wrongful detaining or defective title, an action to recover the premises may be commenced by the state or by a subsequent patentee or grantee, or his successor in interest, within ten years after the determination is made.

(c) To redeem from a mortgage. An action to redeem real property from a mortgage with or without an account of rents and profits may be commenced by the mortgagor or his successors in interest, against the mortgagee in possession, or against the purchaser of the mortgaged premises at a foreclosure sale in an action in which the mortgagor or his successors in interest were not excluded from their interest in the mortgaged premises, or against a successor in interest of either, unless the mortgagee, purchaser or successor was continually possessed of the premises for ten years after the breach or non-fulfillment of a condition or covenant of the mortgage, or the date of recording of the deed of the premises to the purchaser.

(d) To recover under an affidavit of support of an alien. An action under section one hundred twenty-two of the social services law to recover amounts paid to or on behalf of an alien for whom an affidavit of support pursuant to section 213A of the immigration and naturalization act has been signed.

1997 AMENDMENTS

L. 1997, ch. 436, § 1, Part B, § 150, eff. Aug. 20, 1997, added new subdivision (d).

1964 AMENDMENTS

L. 1964, ch. 388, eff. Sept. 1, 1964, made mechanical correction.

§ 213. Actions to be commenced within six years: where not otherwise provided for; on contract; on sealed instrument; on bond or note, and mortgage upon real property; by state based on misappropriation of public property; based on mistake; by corporation against director, officer or stockholder; based on fraud.

The following actions must be commenced within six years:

1. an action for which no limitation is specifically prescribed by law;

2. an action upon a contractual obligation or liability, express or implied, except as provided in section two hundred thirteen-a of this article or article 2 of the uniform commercial code or article 36-B of the general business law;

3. an action upon a sealed instrument;

4. an action upon a bond or note, the payment of which is secured by a mortgage upon real property, or upon a bond or note and

mortgage so secured, or upon a mortgage of real property, or any interest therein;

5. an action by the state based upon the spoliation or other misappropriation of public property; the time within which the action must be commenced shall be computed from discovery by the state of the facts relied upon;

6. an action based upon mistake;

7. an action by or on behalf of a corporation against a present or former director, officer or stockholder for an accounting, or to procure a judgment on the ground of fraud, or to enforce a liability, penalty or forfeiture, or to recover damages for waste or for an injury to property or for an accounting in conjunction therewith;

8. an action based upon fraud; the time within which the action must be commenced shall be the greater of six years from the date the cause of action accrued or two years from the time the plaintiff or the person under whom the plaintiff claims discovered the fraud, or could with reasonable diligence have discovered it.

CROSS REFERENCES

Reference to **U.C.C. Article 2** in subd. (2), *above*, refers to **U.C.C. § 2-725,** which appears in Appendix, *below.*

2004 AMENDMENTS

L. 2004, ch. 403, §1, eff. Aug. 17, 2004, applicable to duration of time an action based upon fraud must be commenced, amended CPLR 213(8).

1988 AMENDMENTS

L. 1988, ch. 709, eff. March 1, 1989, applicable to all new homes for which contracts of sale are entered into on or after the effective date.

1983 AMENDMENTS

L. 1983, ch. 403, eff. April 1, 1984 and applicable to actions and proceedings commencing on and after that date, amended CPLR 213(2) by inserting a reference to CPLR 213-a.

1975 AMENDMENTS

L. 1975, ch. 43, eff. Sept. 1, 1975, upon the recommendation of the Judicial Conference, amended section heading by deleting "to establish a will"; and by repealing Subd. (7), as well as renumbering former Subds. (8) and (9) to Subds. (7) and (8).

The 1975 Judicial Conference Report stated:

CPLR

"Section 213 is a statute of limitations governing actions to be commenced in six years. Subdivision 7 lists an action to establish a will, and contains discovery and imputed discovery provisions where the will has been lost, concealed or destroyed.

"Article 8 (sections 200–204) of the Decedent Estate Law, which provided for an action to establish a will or construe a device was repealed by L. 1966, ch. 952, eff. Sept. 1, 1967, when the new Estates, Powers and Trust Law became effective.

"Thus, the retention of a six year statute of limitations on an action to establish a will in the Supreme Court, when the statutory basis for the action no longer exists, is an anomaly and misleading to lawyers, and the provision should be repealed, as proposed.

"Although there is no statute of limitations on a proceeding to probate a will in Surrogate's Court (see *In re of Canfield*, 165 Misc. 66 (Surr. Ct. Kings Co. 1937)), the proposed repeal would not necessitate the enactment of such a statute. The purpose of such a provision would be to quiet titles (see Uniform Probate Code, Section 3—108) and this purpose is accomplished by EPTL 3—3.8. That provision validates title of a bona fide purchaser of real property from the distributees unless a will containing a different disposition of the property has been admitted to probate within two years after the testator's death. In addition, SCPA 2113 sets forth the procedure for probate of heirship, in order to determine who the distributees are and to create a record of their interests."

1966 AMENDMENTS

L. 1966, ch. 138, eff. Sept. 1, 1966, inserted the words "except as provided in article 2 of the uniform commercial code" before the semicolon in Subd. (2).

Amendment recommended by the Judicial Conference Feb. 1, 1966, Report to the Legislature: "The purpose of this amendment is to put the bar on notice of the provision in U.C.C. § 2-725(1) that the period of limitations on an action for breach of a contract of sale of goods is four years. Where the cause of action is based on breach of warranty of goods sold this four-year period conflicts with CPLR 213(2) (providing a six-year period for contract actions), possibly conflicts with CPLR 213(9) (providing a six-year period for fraud actions), and possibly conflicts with CPLR 214(4) and (5) (providing a three-year period for actions for damages for property and personal injury)."

1965 AMENDMENTS

L. 1965, ch. 248, eff. Sept. 1, 1965, amended Subd. (6) by deleting the words "fraud or," and by adding a new Subd. (9), now Subd. (8), and by changing the catch-line accordingly.

Amendment recommended by the Judicial Conference Feb. 1, 1965, Report to the Legislature: "The apparent breadth of the language of § 206(c) might mislead practitioners to conclude that its discovery rules apply to any action in which fraud or an element of fraud is involved. The intention of the revisers, however, was to confine § 206(c) to actions for actual fraud within the meaning of § 213(6). Moreover, in the area of constructive fraud it has long been the rule that the statute of limitations begins to run upon commission of the fraud rather than upon its discovery. See *Buttles v. Smith*, 281 N.Y. 226, 236, 22 N.E.2d 350, 353 (1939). If § 206(c) were interpreted to alter this rule, vast and revolutionary changes would be wrought in the law of creditors' rights and fraudulent conveyances, changes which the revisers most certainly would have alluded to had they been intended.

"The Conference therefore believes that the substance of the provisions of § 206(c) should be placed in § 213 in a new subdivision, subdivision (9), [now subdivision (8),] thereby making it clear that the discovery provision applies only to actions for actual fraud.

"The proposed amendment to § 213(6) is designed to separate the provisions relating to fraud from those relating to mistake, as to which no change is proposed."

CPLR

§ 213-a. Actions to be commenced within four years; residential rent overcharge.

An action on a residential rent overcharge shall be commenced within four years of the first overcharge alleged and no determination of an overcharge and no award or calculation of an award of the amount of any overcharge may be based upon an overcharge having occurred more than four years before the action is commenced. This section shall preclude examination of the rental history of the housing accommodation prior to the four-year period immediately preceding the commencement of the action.

1997 AMENDMENTS

L. 1997, ch. 116, eff. June 19, 1997, amended section 213-a by providing that a challenge to a residential rent overcharge must be made within four years of the first alleged overcharge and no determination or award of an overcharge may be based upon an overcharge that occurred more than four years before the commencement of the action. This amendment is applicable to any action or proceeding pending in any court or any application, complaint or proceeding before an administrative agency on June 19, 1997, as well as any action or proceeding commenced thereafter.

1983 AMENDMENTS

L. 1983, ch. 403, eff. April 1, 1984, added section 213-a. The section is applicable to actions and proceedings commencing on and after April 1, 1984.

§ 213-b. Action by a victim of a criminal offense.

Notwithstanding any other limitation set forth in this article or in article five of the estates, powers and trusts law, an action by a crime victim, or the representative of a crime victim, as defined in subdivision six of section six hundred twenty-one of the executive law, may be commenced to recover damages from a defendant: (1) convicted of a crime which is the subject of such action, for any injury or loss resulting therefrom within seven years of the date of the crime or (2) convicted of a specified crime as defined in paragraph (e) of subdivision one of section six hundred thirty-two-a of the executive law which is the subject of such action for any injury or loss resulting therefrom within ten years of the date the defendant was convicted of such specified crime.

2001 AMENDMENTS

L. 2001, ch. 62, § 16, eff. June 25, 2001, amended to broaden the applicability of the statute to include specified crimes as defined in Executive Law § 632-a(1)(e), which are the subject of an action for any injury or loss resulting therefrom within 10 years of the date of defendant's conviction of such specified crime. Notwithstanding the expiration of any other statute of limitations, the amendment shall apply to: (i) all judgments originally entered prior to such effective date, regardless whether such judgment is subsequently amended or satisfied on or after such effective date; and (ii) all judgments, obligations, or agreements to pay profits from a crime or funds of a convicted person entered, incurred, or entered into on or after the effective date of this amendment.

1992 AMENDMENTS

L. 1992, ch. 618, eff. July 24, 1992 and applying only to actions commenced on or after the effective date, added CPLR 213-b, providing that a crime victim may commence a civil action for damages against the criminal defendant within seven years of the date of the crime.

§ 213-c Action by victim of conduct constituting certain sexual offenses.

Notwithstanding any other limitation set forth in this article, a civil claim or cause of action to recover from a defendant as hereinafter defined, for physical, psychological or other injury or condition suffered by a person as a result of acts by such defendant of rape in the first degree as defined in section 130.35 of the penal law, or criminal sexual act in the first degree as defined in section 130.50 of the penal law, or aggravated sexual abuse in the first degree as defined in section

130.70 of the penal law, or course of sexual conduct against a child in the first degree as defined in section 130.75 of the penal law may be brought within five years. As used in this section, the term "defendant" shall mean only a person who commits the acts described in this section or who, in a criminal proceeding, could be charged with criminal liability for the commission of such acts pursuant to section 20.00 of the penal law and shall not apply to any related civil claim or cause of action arising from such acts. Nothing in this section shall be construed to require that a criminal charge be brought or a criminal conviction be obtained as a condition of bringing a civil cause of action or receiving a civil judgment pursuant to this section or be construed to require that any of the rules governing a criminal proceeding be applicable to any such civil action.

2006 AMENDMENTS

L. 2006, ch. 3, eff. June 23, 2006, applying to acts committed on and after the effective date as well as acts committed prior thereto, added CPLR 213-c, providing that a victim of the crimes named in the section may commence a civil action for damages against the criminal defendant within five years of the date of the crime.

§ 214. Actions to be commenced within three years: for non-payment of money collected on execution; for penalty created by statute; to recover chattel; for injury to property; for personal injury; for malpractice other than medical, dental or podiatric malpractice; to annul a marriage on the ground of fraud.

The following actions must be commenced within three years:

1. an action against a sheriff, constable or other officer for the non-payment of money collected upon an execution;

2. an action to recover upon a liability, penalty or forfeiture created or imposed by statute except as provided in sections 213 and 215;

3. an action to recover a chattel or damages for the taking or detaining of a chattel;

4. an action to recover damages for an injury to property except as provided in section 214–c;

5. an action to recover damages for a personal injury except as provided in sections 214–b, 214–c and 215;

6. an action to recover damages for malpractice, other than medical, dental or podiatric malpractice, regardless of whether the underlying theory is based in contract or tort; and

7. an action to annul a marriage on the ground of fraud; the time within which the action must be commenced shall be computed from the time the plaintiff discovered the facts constituting the fraud, but if the plaintiff is a person other than the spouse whose consent was obtained by fraud, the time within which the action must be commenced shall be computed from the time, if earlier, that that spouse discovered the facts constituting the fraud.

1996 AMENDMENTS

L. 1996, ch. 623, eff. Sept. 4, 1996, amended subdivision (6) by adding the words "regardless of whether the underlying theory is based in contract or tort."

1994 AMENDMENTS

L. 1994, ch. 88, eff. May 10, 1994, again extended the period for commencing actions set forth in L. 1981, ch. 266, until June 16, 1996. The 1994 legislation also slightly enlarged the period of inclusion of the provision, so that it effectively begins on December 22, 1961, rather than January 1, 1962.

1986 AMENDMENTS

L. 1986, ch. 485, eff. July 21, 1986, and applicable to acts, omissions or failures occurring on or after such date, amended CPLR 214 to exclude actions for podiatric malpractice from those actions which must be commenced within three years; L. 1986, ch. 682, eff. July 30, 1986, and applicable to actions commenced or claims filed on or after such date, amended CPLR 214(4) and (5) by adding references to new section 214–c.

1985 AMENDMENTS

L. 1985, ch. 760, eff. July 1, 1985, and applicable to any acts, omissions or failures occurring on or after that date, amended CPLR 214(6) to exclude actions for dental malpractice.

1981 AMENDMENTS

L. 1981, ch. 266, eff. June 16, 1981, amended CPLR 214(5) to exclude personal injury actions covered by CPLR 214-b from those actions which must be commenced within three years.

1975 AMENDMENTS

L. 1975, ch. 109, eff. July 1, 1975, amended the section to exclude medical malpractice actions from its coverage; such actions are now treated under

§ 214–a, *below.* The amendment applies to acts of malpractice occurring on or after July 1, 1975. The three-year statute of limitations contained in CPLR 214 is still applicable to causes of action for medical malpractice based upon acts occurring before July 1, 1975.

§ 214–a. Action for medical, dental or podiatric malpractice to be commenced within two years and six months; exceptions.

An action for medical, dental or podiatric malpractice must be commenced within two years and six months of the act, omission or failure complained of or last treatment where there is continuous treatment for the same illness, injury or condition which gave rise to the said act, omission or failure; provided, however, that where the action is based upon the discovery of a foreign object in the body of the patient, the action may be commenced within one year of the date of such discovery or of the date of discovery of facts which would reasonably lead to such discovery, whichever is earlier. For the purpose of this section the term "continuous treatment" shall not include examinations undertaken at the request of the patient for the sole purpose of ascertaining the state of the patient's condition. For the purpose of this section the term "foreign object" shall not include a chemical compound, fixation device or prosthetic aid or device.

CPLR

2004 AMENDMENTS

L. 2004, ch. 68, eff. May 4, 2004. Every cause of action for an injury or death caused by contact with or exposure to phenoxy herbicides while serving as a member of the armed forces of the United States in Indo-China from December 22, 1961 through May 7, 1975, which is or would be barred prior to June 16, 1985, because the applicable period of limitation has expired is hereby revived and extended and any action thereon may be commenced and prose- cuted provided such action is commenced not later than June 16, 2006.

1986 AMENDMENTS

L. 1986, ch. 485, eff. July 21, 1986, and applicable to acts, omissions or failures occurring on or after such date, amended CPLR 214–a to apply to actions for podiatric malpractice.

1985 AMENDMENTS

L. 1985, ch. 760, eff. July 1, 1985, and applicable to any acts, omissions or failures occurring on or after that date, amended CPLR 214-a to apply to actions for dental malpractice.

1975 AMENDMENTS

L. 1975, ch. 109, eff. July 1, 1975, added Section 214-a. The amendment applies to acts of malpractice occurring on or after July 1, 1975. The three-year statute of limitations contained in CPLR 214 is still applicable to causes of action for medical malpractice based upon acts occurring before July 1, 1975.

§ 214-b. Action to recover damages for personal injury caused by contact with or exposure to phenoxy herbicides.

Notwithstanding any provision of law to the contrary, an action to recover damages for personal injury caused by contact with or exposure to phenoxy herbicides while serving as a member of the armed forces of the United States in Indo-China from February twenty-eighth, nineteen hundred sixty-one through May seventh, nineteen hundred seventy-five, may be commenced within two years from the date of the discovery of such injury, or within two years from the date when through the exercise of reasonable diligence the cause of such injury should have been discovered, whichever is later.

2008 AMENDMENTS

L. 2008, ch. 143 § 1, eff. June 30, 2008, amended CPLR 214-b to enlarge the period of inclusion of the provision so that it effectively begins on February 28, 1961; and to once again extend the time period for commencing an action under CPLR 214-b until June 16, 2010.

2006 AMENDMENTS

L. 2006, ch. 39 § 1, eff. May 31, 2006, once again extended the time period for commencing an action under CPLR 214-b until June 16, 2008.

2004 AMENDMENTS

L. 2004, ch. 68, § 1, eff. May 4, 2004, once again extended the time period for commencing an action under CPLR 214-b until June 16, 2006.

2002 AMENDMENTS

L. 2002, ch. 88, § 1, eff. June 11, 2002, once again extended the time period for commencing an action under CPLR 214-b until June 16, 2004.

2000 AMENDMENTS

L. 2000, ch. 26, eff. April 18, 2000, once again extended the time period for commencing an action under CPLR 214-b until June 16, 2002.

1998 AMENDMENTS

L. 1998, ch. 98, eff. June 9, 1998, once again extended the time period for commencing an action under CPLR 214-b until June 16, 2000.

1996 AMENDMENTS

L. 1996, ch. 615, eff. Sept. 4, 1996, again extended the period for commencing actions set forth in L. 1981, ch. 266, until June 16, 1998.

1994 AMENDMENTS

L. 1994, ch. 88, eff. May 10, 1994, again extended the period for commencing actions set forth in L. 1981, ch. 266, until June 16, 1996. The 1994 legislation also slightly enlarged the period of inclusion of the provision, so that it effectively begins on Dec. 22, 1961, rather than Jan. 1, 1962.

1992 AMENDMENTS

L. 1992, ch. 251, eff. June 30, 1992, amended L. 1981, ch. 266, § 4, by extending the time limitations for the actions described therein to June 16, 1994.

1990 AMENDMENTS

L. 1990, ch. 227, eff. June 15, 1990, amended L. 1981, ch. 266, § 4 to read as follows:

§ 4. Every cause of action for an injury or death caused by contact with or exposure to phenoxy herbicides while serving as a member of the armed forces of the United States in Indo-China from January 1, 1962 through May 7, 1975, which is or would be barred prior to June 16, 1985, because the applicable period of limitation has expired is hereby revived or extended as the case may be, and an action thereon may be commenced and prosecuted provided such action is commenced not later than June 16, 1992.

1988 AMENDMENTS

L. 1988, ch. 170, eff. June 27, 1988, amended L. 1981, ch. 266, § 4, to read as follows:

§ 4. Every cause of action for an injury or death caused by contact with or exposure to phenoxy herbicides while serving as a member of the armed forces of the United States in Indo-China from January first, nineteen hundred sixty-two through May seventh, nineteen hundred seventy-five, which is or would be barred prior to June sixteenth, nineteen hundred eighty-five, because the applicable period of limitation has expired is hereby revived or extended as the case may be, and an action thereon may be commenced and prosecuted provided such action is commenced not later than June sixteenth, nineteen hundred ninety.

1987 AMENDMENTS

L. 1987, ch. 194, eff. June 29, 1987, amended L. 1981, ch. 266, § 4, to read as follows:

CPLR

§ 4. Every cause of action for an injury or death caused by contact with or exposure to phenoxy herbicides while serving as a member of the armed forces of the United States in Indo-China from January first, nineteen hundred sixty-two through May seventh, nineteen hundred seventy-five, which is or would be barred prior to June sixteenth, nineteen hundred eighty-five, because the applicable period of limitation has expired is hereby revived or extended as the case may be, and an action thereon may be commenced and prosecuted provided such action is commenced not later than June sixteenth, nineteen hundred eighty-eight.

1985 AMENDMENTS

L. 1985, ch. 498, eff. July 24, 1985, amended L. 1981, ch. 266, § 4, to read as follows:

§ 4. Every cause of action for an injury or death caused by contact with or exposure to phenoxy herbicides while serving as a member of the armed forces of the United States in Indo-China from January first, nineteen hundred sixty-two through May seventh, nineteen hundred seventy-five, which is or would be barred prior to June sixteenth, nineteen hundred eighty-five, because the applicable period of limitation has expired is hereby revived or extended as the case may be, and an action thereon may be commenced and prosecuted provided such action is commenced not later than June sixteenth, nineteen hundred eighty-seven.

1983 AMENDMENTS

L. 1983, ch. 358, eff. June 26, 1983, amended L. 1981, ch. 266, § 4 to read as follows:

§ 4. Every cause of action for an injury or death caused by contact with or exposure to phenoxy herbicides while serving as a member of the armed forces of the United States in Indo-China from January first, nineteen hundred sixty-two through May seventh, nineteen hundred seventy-five, which is or would be barred prior to June sixteenth, nineteen hundred eighty-five, because the applicable period of limitation has expired is hereby revived or extended as the case may be, and an action thereon may be commenced and prosecuted provided such action is commenced not later than June sixteenth, nineteen hundred eighty-five.

1982 AMENDMENTS

L. 1982, ch. 153, eff. June 1, 1982, amended CPLR 214-b by deleting the words "March twenty-ninth, nineteen hundred seventy-three" and adding the words "May seventh, nineteen hundred seventy-five." In addition, L. 1981, ch. 266, § 4, was also amended to reflect the same extension of time limitations for personal injury or death caused by contact with or exposure to phenoxy herbicides.

1981 AMENDMENTS

L. 1981, ch. 266, eff. June 16, 1981, added section 214-b. L. 1981, ch. 266, § 4 provides as follows:

§ 4. Every cause of action for an injury or death caused by contact with or exposure to phenoxy herbicides while serving as a member of the armed forces of the United States in Indo-China from January first, nineteen hundred sixty-two through March twenty-ninth, nineteen hundred seventy-three, which is barred as of the effective date of this act because the applicable period of limitation has expired is hereby revived, and an action thereon may be commenced and prosecuted provided such action is commenced within one year of the effective date of this act.

§ 214-c. Certain actions to be commenced within three years of discovery.

1. In this section: "exposure" means direct or indirect exposure by absorption, contact, ingestion, inhalation, implantation or injection.

2. Notwithstanding the provisions of section 214, the three-year period within which an action to recover damages for personal injury or injury to property caused by the latent effects of exposure to any substance or combination of substances, in any form, upon or within the body or upon or within property must be commenced shall be computed from the date of discovery of the injury by the plaintiff or from the date when through the exercise of reasonable diligence such injury should have been discovered by the plaintiff, whichever is earlier.

3. For the purposes of sections fifty-e and fifty-i of the general municipal law, section thirty-eight hundred thirteen of the education law and the provisions of any general, special or local law or charter requiring as a condition precedent to commencement of an action or special proceeding that a notice of claim be filed or presented within a specified period of time after the claim or action accrued, a claim or action for personal injury or injury to property caused by the latent effects of exposure to any substance or combination of substances, in any form, upon or within the body or upon or within property shall be deemed to have accrued on the date of discovery of the injury by the plaintiff or on the date when through the exercise of reasonable diligence the injury should have been discovered, whichever is earlier.

4. Notwithstanding the provisions of subdivisions two and three of this section, where the discovery of the cause of the injury is alleged to

CPLR

have occurred less than five years after discovery of the injury or when with reasonable diligence such injury should have been discovered, whichever is earlier, an action may be commenced or a claim filed within one year of such discovery of the cause of the injury; provided, however, if any such action is commenced or claim filed after the period in which it would otherwise have been authorized pursuant to subdivision two or three of this section the plaintiff or claimant shall be required to allege and prove that technical, scientific or medical knowledge and information sufficient to ascertain the cause of his injury had not been discovered, identified or determined prior to the expiration of the period within which the action or claim would have been authorized and that he has otherwise satisfied the requirements of subdivisions two and three of this section.

5. This section shall not be applicable to any action for medical or dental malpractice.

6. This section shall be applicable to acts, omissions or failures occurring prior to, on or after July first, nineteen hundred eighty-six, except that this section shall not be applicable to any act, omission or failure:

(a) which occurred prior to July first, nineteen hundred eighty-six, and

(b) which caused or contributed to an injury that either was discovered or through the exercise of reasonable diligence should have been discovered prior to such date, and

(c) an action for which was or would have been barred because the applicable period of limitation had expired prior to such date.

1992 AMENDMENTS

L. 1992, ch. 551, eff. July 24, 1992, amended Subdivision (1) by broadening the definition of "exposure" to include exposure by implantation.

1986 AMENDMENTS

L. 1986, ch. 682, eff. July 30, 1986, and applicable to actions commenced or claims filed on or after such date, added new section 214-c, providing for a three-year discovery statute of limitations for cases involving exposure to latent toxic substances. See uncodified revival provisions contained in sections 4 and 5 of ch. 682, applicable to enumerated substances.

§ 214-d. Limitations on certain actions against licensed engineers and architects.

1. Any person asserting a claim for personal injury, wrongful death or property damage, or a cross or third-party claim for contribution or indemnification arising out of an action for personal injury, wrongful death or property damage, against a licensed architect, engineer, land surveyor or landscape architect or against a partnership, professional corporation or limited liability company lawfully practicing architecture, engineering, land surveying or landscape architecture which is based upon the professional performance, conduct or omission by such licensed architect, engineer, land surveyor or landscape architect or such firm occurring more than ten years prior to the date of such claim, shall give written notice of such claim to each such architect, engineer, land surveyor or landscape architect or such firm at least ninety days before the commencement of any action or proceeding against such licensed architect, engineer, land surveyor or landscape architect or such firm including any cross or third-party action or claim. The notice of claim shall identify the performance, conduct or omissions complained of, on information and belief, and shall include a request for general and special damages. Service of such written notice of claim may be made by any of the methods permitted for personal service of a summons upon a natural person, partnership or professional corporation. A notice of claim served in accordance with this section shall be filed, together with proof of service thereof, in any court of this state in which an action, proceeding or cross or third-party claim arising out of such conduct may be commenced or interposed, within thirty days of the service of the notice of claim. Upon the filing of any such notice of claim, a county clerk shall collect an index number fee in accordance with section eight thousand eighteen of this chapter and an index number shall be assigned.

2. In such pleadings as are subsequently filed in any court, each party shall represent that it has fully complied with the provisions of this section.

3. Service of a notice as provided in this section shall toll the applicable statute of limitations to and including a period of one hundred twenty days following such service.

4. From and after the date of service of the notice provided for in

subdivision one of this section, the claimant shall have the right to serve a demand for discovery and production of documents and things for inspection, testing, copying or photographing in accordance with rule three thousand one hundred twenty of this chapter. Such demand shall be governed by the procedures of article thirty-one of this chapter. In addition, the claimant shall have the right to the examination before trial of such licensed architect, engineer, land surveyor or landscape architect or such firm or to serve written interrogatories upon such licensed architect, engineer, land surveyor or landscape architect or such firm after service of and compliance with a demand for production and inspection in accordance with this section. The court may, at any time at its own initiative or on motion of such licensed architect, engineer, land surveyor or landscape architect or such firm deny, limit, condition or restrict such examination before trial or written interrogatories upon a showing that such claimant has failed to establish reasonable necessity for the information sought or failed to establish that the information sought by such examination or interrogatories cannot reasonably be determined from the documents or things provided in response to a demand for production and inspection served in accordance with this section. Such examination before trial or interrogatories shall otherwise be governed by article thirty-one of this chapter.

5. After the expiration of ninety days from service of the notice provided in subdivision one of this section, the claimant may commence or interpose an action, proceeding or cross or third-party claim against such licensed architect, engineer, land surveyor or landscape architect or such firm. The action shall proceed in every respect as if the action were one brought on account of conduct occurring less than ten years prior to the claim described in said action, unless the defendant architect, engineer, land surveyor or landscape architect or such firm shall have made a motion under rule three thousand two hundred eleven or three thousand two hundred twelve of this chapter, in which event the action shall be stayed pending determination of the motion. Such motion shall be granted upon a showing that such claimant has failed to comply with the notice of claim requirements of this section or for the reasons set forth in subdivision (h) of rule three thousand two hundred eleven or subdivision (i) of rule three thousand two hundred twelve of this chapter; provided, however, such motion

shall not be granted if the moving party is in default of any disclosure obligation as set forth in subdivision four of this section.

6. No claim for personal injury, or wrongful death or property damage, or a cross or third-party claim for contribution or indemnification arising out of an action for personal injury, wrongful death or property damage may be asserted against a licensed architect, engineer, land surveyor or landscape architect or such firm arising out of conduct by such licensed architect, engineer, land surveyor or landscape architect or such firm occurring more than ten years prior to the accrual of such claim shall be commenced or interposed against any such licensed architect, engineer, land surveyor or landscape architect or such firm unless it shall appear by and as an allegation in the complaint or necessary moving papers that the claimant has complied with the requirements of this section. Upon the commencement of such a proceeding or action or interposition of such cross or third-party claim, a county clerk shall not be entitled to collect an index number fee and such action, proceeding or cross or third-party claim shall retain the previously assigned index number. Such action, proceeding or cross or third-party claim shall otherwise be governed by the provisions of this chapter.

CPLR

7. The provisions of this section shall apply only to a licensed architect, engineer, land surveyor or landscape architect or such firm practicing architecture, engineering, land surveying or landscape architecture in the state of New York at the time the conduct complained of occurred and shall not apply to any person or entity, including but not limited to corporations, which was not licensed as an architect, engineer, land surveyor or landscape architect or such firm in this state or to a firm not lawfully practicing architecture, engineering, land surveying or landscape architecture at the time the conduct complained of occurred.

8. The provisions of this section shall not be construed to in any way alter or extend any applicable statutes of limitations except as expressly provided herein.

1997 AMENDMENTS

L. 1997, ch. 518, eff. Sept. 3, 1997, amended CPLR 214-d by adding land surveyors to those protected by its provisions.

1996 AMENDMENTS

L. 1996, ch. 682, eff. Oct. 1, 1996, added new section 214-d.

§ 214-e. Action to recover damages for personal injury caused by the infusion of such blood products which result in the contraction of the human immunodeficiency virus (HIV) and/or AIDS.

Notwithstanding any provision of law to the contrary, any cause of action for an injury or death against a proprietary manufacturer of blood products for damages involving the infusion of such blood products which resulted in the contraction of the human immunodeficiency virus (HIV) and/or AIDS which is barred as of the effective date of this section because the applicable period of limitation has expired is hereby revived, and an action thereon may be commenced and prosecuted provided such action is commenced within two years of the effective date of this section. The provisions of this section shall be inapplicable to any civil action governed by the statute of limitations of another jurisdiction.

1997 AMENDMENTS

L. 1997, ch. 682, eff. Dec. 1, 1997, added new section 214-e to allow for an action to recover damages for personal injury caused by the infusion of blood products which resulted in the contraction of HIV and/or AIDS which would otherwise be barred because the applicable statute of limitations had expired. An action arising under this section may now be commenced and prosecuted within two years of the effective, *i.e.,* Dec. 1, 1997.

§ 215. Actions to be commenced within one year: against sheriff, coroner or constable; for escape of prisoner; for assault, battery, false imprisonment, malicious prosecution, libel or slander; for violation of right of privacy; for penalty given to informer; on arbitration award.

The following actions shall be commenced within one year:

1. an action against a sheriff, coroner or constable, upon a liability incurred by him by doing an act in his official capacity or by omission of an official duty, except the non-payment of money collected upon an execution;

2. an action against an officer for the escape of a prisoner arrested or imprisoned by virtue of a civil mandate;

3. an action to recover damages for assault, battery, false

imprisonment, malicious prosecution, libel, slander, false words causing special damages, or a violation of the right of privacy under section fifty-one of the civil rights law;

4. an action to enforce a penalty or forfeiture created by statute and given wholly or partly to any person who will prosecute; if the action is not commenced within the year by a private person, it may be commenced on behalf of the state, within three years after the commission of the offense, by the attorney-general or the district attorney of the county where the offense was committed; and

5. an action upon an arbitration award.

6. an action to recover any overcharge of interest or to enforce a penalty for such overcharge.

7. an action by a tenant pursuant to subdivision three of section two hundred twenty-three-b of the real property law.

8. (a) Whenever it is shown that a criminal action against the same defendant has been commenced with respect to the event or occurrence from which a claim governed by this section arises, the plaintiff shall have at least one year from the termination of the criminal action as defined in section 1.20 of the criminal procedure law in which to commence the civil action, notwithstanding that the time in which to commence such action has already expired or has less than a year remaining.

(b) Whenever it is shown that a criminal action against the same defendant has been commenced with respect to the event or occurrence from which a claim governed by this section arises, and such criminal action is for rape in the first degree as defined in section 130.35 of the penal law, or criminal sexual act in the first degree as defined in section 130.50 of the penal law, or aggravated sexual abuse in the first degree as defined in section 130.70 of the penal law, or course of sexual conduct against a child in the first degree as defined in section 130.75 of the penal law, the plaintiff shall have at least five years from the termination of the criminal action as defined in section 1.20 of the criminal procedure law in which to commence the civil action, notwithstanding that the time in which to commence

CPLR

such action has already expired or has less than a year remaining.

CROSS REFERENCES

Real Prop. Law § 223-b referred to above deals with prohibitions against retaliation by a landlord against a tenant.

2006 AMENDMENTS

L. 2006, ch. 3, § 4, eff. June 23, 2006, amended subdivision (8) to provide that the victim of the crimes named in the section has an additional five years to commence an action against the perpetrator of the crime, even if the original five-year statute of limitations has expired or has less than a year remaining if a criminal proceeding against the same defendant is commenced. This additional five-year period would begin running at the time that the criminal proceeding against the defendant was terminated.

1983 AMENDMENTS

L. 1983, ch. 95, eff. May 17, 1983, and applying to all pending civil and criminal actions, added subdivision (8).

1979 AMENDMENTS

L. 1979, ch. 693, eff. Sept. 1, 1979, amended CPLR 215 by adding subdivision (7).

1969 AMENDMENTS

L. 1969, ch. 1141, eff. July 1, 1969, repealed Subd. (7), dealing with the enforcement of the New York State Truth-in-Lending Act, also repealed in 1969.

1968 AMENDMENTS

L. 1968, ch. 1072, eff. July 1, 1969, added Subds. (6) and (7).

§ 216. Abbreviation of period to one year after notice.

(a) Action to recover money.

1. No action for the recovery of any sum of money due and payable under or on account of a contract, or for any part thereof, shall be commenced by any person who has made claim to the sum, after the expiration of one year from the giving of notice, as hereinafter provided, to the claimant that an action commenced by another person is pending to recover the sum, or any part thereof, exceeding fifty dollars in amount. This limitation shall not be construed to enlarge the time within which the cause of action of the claimant would otherwise be barred.

2. If any person shall make claim for the recovery of any sum of money due and payable under or on account of a contract, and an action has theretofore been, or shall thereafter be, commenced by another person to recover the sum, or any part thereof, exceeding fifty dollars in amount, the defendant in such action may, within twenty days from the date of service upon him of the complaint or from the date of receipt by him of the claim, whichever occurs later, make a motion before the court in which the action is pending for an order permitting the defendant to give notice to the claimant that the action is pending. The court in which the action is pending shall grant the order where it appears that a person not a party to the action has made claim against the defendant for the sum of money, or any part thereof, exceeding fifty dollars in amount; that the action was brought without collusion between the defendant and the plaintiff; and that the claimant cannot, with due diligence, be served with process in such a manner as to obtain jurisdiction over his person. The order shall provide, among such other terms and conditions as justice may require, that notice shall be given to the claimant by sending by registered mail a copy of the summons and complaint in the action and the order and a notice addressed to the claimant at his last known address. In the event that registration of mail directed to any country or part thereof shall be discontinued or suspended, notice to a claimant whose last known address is within such country or part thereof shall be given by ordinary mail, under such terms and conditions as the court may direct. Proof that the notice has been mailed shall be filed within ten days from the date of the order; otherwise the order becomes inoperative. Upon such filing, notice shall be deemed to have been given on the tenth day after the date of such order.

3. Upon proof by affidavit or otherwise, to the satisfaction of the court, that the conditions of this subdivision have been satisfied and that there is no collusion between the claimant and the defendant, the court shall make an order staying further prosecution of the action for a period not to exceed one year from the date when the notice shall have been given to the claimant. At the time of the granting of such order or at any time thereafter, the court, upon the motion of any party, shall, as a condition of the granting of the order or its continuation, impose upon the defendant such terms as justice may

CPLR

require as to the furnishing of an undertaking in an amount to be fixed by the court. The stay shall be vacated and the undertaking, if any has been given, may be discharged or modified, as justice may require, upon proof to the court by any party to the action that the claimant has intervened or has instituted another action in any court of this state to recover the said sum of money, or any part thereof, exceeding fifty dollars.

4. A motion for any relief as prescribed in this subdivision shall be made on notice to all other parties to the action.

5. Whenever claims are made by two or more persons, each claiming to be, to the exclusion of the other, the duly authorized deputy, officer or agent to demand, receive, collect, sue for or recover the same sum of money due and payable under or on account of a contract, or any part thereof, exceeding fifty dollars in amount, for and on behalf of the same person, each person making such a claim shall be deemed an adverse claimant. Notwithstanding that an action has been commenced in the name of or on behalf of the person for whom he claims to be the duly authorized deputy, officer or agent, any such adverse claimant may be notified of the pendency of an action as provided in this subdivision and may intervene in the action and be designated as claiming to be or as the alleged deputy, officer or agent.

6. Whenever an action has been commenced for the recovery of any sum of money exceeding fifty dollars due and payable under or on account of a contract and the records of the defendant show that a person other than the plaintiff has the right, exclusive of other deputies, officers or agents of the plaintiff, to demand, sue for and recover the same sum of money, or any part thereof, exceeding fifty dollars in amount, either in his own name, on his own behalf, or as the authorized deputy, officer or agent for the plaintiff, and the defendant has received no notice of transfer, revocation, or other change in right or authority acceptable to it, the person so appearing on the records shall be deemed to have made an adverse claim to the sum of money and may be treated as an adverse claimant.

(b) Action to recover property. When an action has been commenced to recover specific personal property, including certificates of stocks, bonds, notes or other securities or obligations, exceeding fifty dollars in value, held by the defendant within the state, or to enforce a vested or contingent interest or lien upon such property, and a person not a party to the action asserts a claim to the whole or any part of the same property or to a right, interest or lien upon it which is adverse to the plaintiff's claim, and the court in which the action is pending has no jurisdiction over the adverse claimant to direct the issuance of process or if the same be issued it would be without effect notwithstanding that the action seeks to have declared, enforced, regulated, defined or limited, rights, interests or liens upon specific personal property within the state, the defendant in the action may within twenty days from the date of service upon him of the complaint or within twenty days of the date of the receipt by him of the adverse claim, whichever shall occur later, make a motion before the court for leave to give notice to the adverse claimant of the pending action in the same manner as provided in subdivision (a). Upon the granting of such an order, the provisions of subdivision (a) shall apply insofar as they are compatible with the subject matter of the action.

CPLR

§ 217. Proceeding against body or officer; actions complaining about conduct that would constitute a union's breach of its duty of fair representation; four months.

1. Unless a shorter time is provided in the law authorizing the proceeding, a proceeding against a body or officer must be commenced within four months after the determination to be reviewed becomes final and binding upon the petitioner or the person whom he represents in law or in fact, or after the respondent's refusal, upon the demand of the petitioner or the person whom he represents, to perform its duty; or with leave of the court where the petitioner or the person whom he represents, at the time such determination became final and binding upon him or at the time of such refusal, was under a disability specified in section 208, within two years after such time.

2.   (a) Any action or proceeding against an employee organization subject to article fourteen of the civil service law or article twenty of the labor law which complains that such employee organization has breached its duty of fair representation regarding someone to whom such employee organization has a duty shall be commenced within four months of the date the employee or former employee knew or should have known that the breach has occurred, or within four months of the date the employee or former employee suffers actual

harm, whichever is later.

(b) Any action or proceeding by an employee or former employee against an employer subject to article fourteen of the civil service law or article twenty of the labor law, an essential element of which is that an employee organization breached its duty of fair representation to the person making the complaint, shall be commenced within four months of the date the employee or former employee knew or should have known that the breach has occurred, or within four months of the date the employee or former employee suffers actual harm, whichever is later.

1990 AMENDMENTS

L. 1990, ch. 467, eff. July 11, 1990, adding the words "actions complaining about conduct that would constitute a union's breach of its duty of fair representation;" to the heading; dividing the section into subdivisions; and adding subdivision 2.

§ 218. Transitional provisions.

(a) Actions barred at effective date. Nothing in this article shall authorize any action to be commenced which is barred when this article becomes effective, except insofar as the right to commence the action may be revived by an acknowledgment or payment.

(b) Cause of action accrued and not barred at effective date. Where a cause of action accrued before, and is not barred when this article becomes effective, the time within which an action must be commenced shall be the time which would have been applicable apart from the provisions of this article, or the time which would have been applicable if the provisions of this article had been in effect when the cause of action accrued, whichever is longer.

Article 3

JURISDICTION AND SERVICE, APPEARANCE AND CHOICE OF COURT

SUMMARY OF ARTICLE

CPLR

CPLR

§ 301. Jurisdiction over persons, property or status.

A court may exercise such jurisdiction over persons, property, or status as might have been exercised heretofore.

CROSS REFERENCES

As to subject matter jurisdiction of the courts, generally, see **Constitutional** and **Judiciary Law** provisions in the Appendix, *below.*

§ 302.   Personal jurisdiction by acts of non-domiciliaries.

(a) Acts which are the basis of jurisdiction. As to a cause of action arising from any of the acts enumerated in this section, a court may exercise personal jurisdiction over any non-domiciliary, or his executor or administrator, who in person or through an agent:

    1. transacts any business within the state or contracts anywhere to supply goods or services in the state; or

    2. commits a tortious act within the state, except as to a cause of action for defamation of character arising from the act; or

    3. commits a tortious act without the state causing injury to person or property within the state, except as to a cause of action for defamation of character arising from the act, if he

        (i) regularly does or solicits business, or engages in any other persistent course of conduct, or derives substantial revenue from goods used or consumed or services rendered, in the state, or

        (ii) expects or should reasonably expect the act to have consequences in the state and derives substantial revenue from interstate or international commerce; or

    4. owns, uses or possesses any real property situated within the state.

(b) Personal jurisdiction over non-resident defendant in matrimonial actions or family court proceedings. A court in any matrimonial action or family court proceeding involving a demand for support, alimony, maintenance, distributive awards or special relief in matrimonial actions may exercise personal jurisdiction over the respondent or defendant notwithstanding the fact that he or she no longer is a resident or domiciliary of this state, or over his or her executor or administrator, if the party seeking support is a resident of or domiciled in this state at the time such demand is made, provided that this state was the matrimonial domicile of the parties before their separation, or the defendant abandoned the plaintiff in this state, or the claim for support, alimony, maintenance, distributive awards or special relief in matrimonial actions accrued under the laws of this state or under an agreement executed in this state. The family court may exercise personal jurisdiction over a non-resident respondent to the extent provided in sections one hundred fifty-four and one thousand thirty-six and article five-B of the family court act and article five-A of the domestic relations law.

(c) Effect of appearance. Where personal jurisdiction is based solely upon this section, an appearance does not confer such jurisdiction with respect to causes of action not arising from an act enumerated in this section.

(d) Foreign defamation judgment. The courts of this state shall have personal jurisdiction over any person who obtains a judgment in a defamation proceeding outside the United States against any person who is a resident of New York or is a person or entity amenable to jurisdiction in New York who has assets in New York or may have to take actions in New York to comply with the judgment, for the purposes of rendering declaratory relief with respect to that person's liability for the judgment, and/or for the purpose of determining whether said judgment should be deemed non-recognizable pursuant to section fifty-three hundred four of this chapter, to the fullest extent permitted by the United States constitution, provided:

1. the publication at issue was published in New York, and

2. that resident or person amenable to jurisdiction in New York (i) has assets in New York which might be used to satisfy the foreign defamation judgment, or (ii) may have to take actions in New York to comply with the foreign defamation judgment. The provisions of this subdivision shall apply to persons who obtained judgments in defamation proceedings outside the United States prior to and/or after the effective date of this subdivision.

2008 AMENDMENTS

L. 2008, ch. 66 § 3, eff. April 28, 2008, added CPLR 302(d), which protects journalists and authors by declaring foreign defamation judgments unenforceable in New York unless the New York court determines that the foreign court's defamation law provides at least as much free speech protections (including freedom of the press) guaranteed under the New York and United States Constitutions

2006 AMENDMENTS

L. 2006, ch. 184 § 5, eff. July 26, 2006, amended CPLR 302(b) by adding cross-references to the Uniform Interstate Family Support Act, Article 5-B of the Family Court Act, and the Uniform Child Custody Jurisdiction and

Enforcement Act, Article 5-A of the Domestic Relations Law.

1995 AMENDMENTS

L. 1995, ch. 441, eff. Oct. 31, 1995, amended CPLR 302(b) by deleting the reference to Article 10 of the Family Court Act and by adding the references to sections 154 and 1036 of the Family Court Act.

1991 AMENDMENTS

L. 1991, ch. 69, eff. April 22, 1991, amended CPLR 302(b) by adding the last sentence.

1982 AMENDMENTS

L. 1982, ch. 505, eff. Sept. 1, 1982, amended CPLR 302(b) by deleting the words "obligation to pay" and inserting the words "claim for."

1980 AMENDMENTS

L. 1980, ch. 281, eff. July 19, 1980, amended CPLR 302(b) by adding references to ". . . maintenance, distributive awards or special relief in matrimonial actions. . . ."

1979 AMENDMENTS

L. 1979, ch. 252, eff. Sept. 1, 1979, amended CPLR 302 subd. (a) par. 1, by expanding the "transaction of business" contact to include the situation where one "contracts anywhere to supply goods or services in the state"; and amended subd. (b) by making the catch line clearer and by correcting a printer's error in the body of the provision.

1974 AMENDMENTS

L. 1974, ch. 859, eff. June 7, 1974, added a new subdivision (b) entitled "Personal jurisdiction over non-resident defendant" and relettered former subdivision (b) as subdivision (c).

1966 AMENDMENTS

L. 1966, ch. 590, eff. Sept. 1, 1966, amended Subd. (a).

Amendment recommended by the Judicial Conference Feb. 1, 1966, Report to the Legislature: "The interpretation of CPLR 302(a)(2) by the Court of Appeals in [*Feathers v. McLucas,* 15 N.Y.2d 443, 261 N.Y.S.2d 8, 209 N.E.2d 68 (1965)] has disclosed a serious gap in this provision. . . . It is now settled that CPLR 302(a)(2) reaches a non-resident who commits a tortious act or omission within the state but does not reach a non-resident who causes a tortious injury within the state through an act or omission committed outside the state (unless he can be held to have transacted business within the state within the meaning of CPLR 302(a)(1)). . . . In view of this serious gap in the coverage afforded by CPLR 302(a)(2) the Judicial Conference believes that an amendment is required which will be broad enough to protect New York residents yet not so broad as to burden unfairly non-residents whose connection with the state is remote and who could not reasonably be expected to foresee that their acts outside of New York could have harmful consequences in New York. The line of distinction is subtle and its statutory delineation requires the utmost care. . . .

"It is suggested, therefore, that as a matter of policy, jurisdiction should not be exercised over a person who causes tortious injuries in the state by an act or omission outside the state unless he had other contacts with the state or unless he was engaged in extensive business activities on an interstate or international level and does an act which he should reasonably foresee might have potential consequences within New York State.

"Accordingly, the proposed amendment set forth above cures the gap in CPLR 302(a)(2) reflected in the *Feathers* case by renumbering present paragraph (3) to be paragraph (4) and by adding a new paragraph (3) thereto . . .

"The jurisdiction of the court under proposed CPLR 302(a)(3) over the non-domiciliary who commits a tortious act outside of the state causing injury within the state is limited to a cause of action arising out of such tortious act. However, there is no necessary connection between the 'act' committed without the state and the additional 'acts' of contact mentioned in subparagraph (i) or the deriving of substantial revenue from interstate or international commerce mentioned in subparagraph (ii). Neither is there a necessary connection between the 'act' from which the cause of action arose and the 'act' of foreseeing mentioned in subparagraph (ii) except that the same act which gives rise to the cause of action also causes the consequences within the state which the non-domiciliary expects or should reasonably expect. It should also be noted that the statutory requirement of foreseeability relates to forum consequences generally and not to the specific event which produced injury within the state. For example, using again the facts of the *Feathers* case as illustration, the requirement of reasonable expectation of potential forum consequences would be satisfied if the foreign corporation which manufactured the defective gas tank knew that it was intended for use in New York.

"Finally, in the event that non-resident plaintiffs seek to avail themselves of the expanded 'long-arm' jurisdiction over non-resident defendants, the doctrine of 'forum non conveniens' is available in appropriate cases."

§ 303. Designation of attorney as agent for service.

The commencement of an action in the state by a person not subject to personal jurisdiction is a designation by him of his attorney appearing in the action or of the clerk of the court if no attorney appears, as agent, during the pendency of the action, for service of a summons pursuant to section 308, in any separate action in which such a person is a defendant and another party to the action is a plaintiff if

CPLR

such separate action would have been permitted as a counterclaim had the action been brought in the supreme court.

1972 AMENDMENTS

L. 1972, ch. 487, eff. Sept. 1, 1972, amended CPLR 303 by adding "pursuant to section 308" after "service of a summons."

§ 304. Method of commencing action or special proceeding.

(a) An action is commenced by filing a summons and complaint or summons with notice in accordance with rule twenty-one hundred two of this chapter. A special proceeding is commenced by filing a petition in accordance with rule twenty-one hundred two of this chapter. Where a court finds that circumstances prevent immediate filing, the signing of an order requiring the subsequent filing at a specific time and date not later than five days thereafter shall commence the action.

(b) Notwithstanding any other provision of law, such filing may be accomplished by facsimile transmission or electronic means, as defined in subdivision (f) of rule twenty-one hundred three of this chapter, where and in the manner authorized by the chief administrator of the courts by rule.

(c) For purposes of this section, and for purposes of section two hundred three of this chapter and section three hundred six-a of this article, filing shall mean the delivery of the summons with notice, summons and complaint or petition to the clerk of the court in the county in which the action or special proceeding is brought or any other person designated by the clerk of the court for that purpose. At the time of filing, the filed papers shall be date stamped by the clerk of the court who shall file them and maintain a record of the date of the filing and who shall return forthwith a date stamped copy, together with an index number, to the filing party, except where filing is by electronic means. Such filing shall not be accepted unless any fee required as specified in section eight thousand eighteen of this chapter has been paid. Where filing is by electronic means, any fee required shall be paid in the time and manner authorized by the chief administrator of the court by rule.

(d) Where filing is by facsimile transmission, the clerk of the court need only return a date stamped copy of the first page of the papers initiating the lawsuit, together with the index number.

(e) Where filing is by electronic means, the clerk shall, in accordance with rules promulgated by the chief administrator, forthwith notify the filing party of the index number and the date and time of filing.

(f) A confirmation record produced by the filing party's facsimile machine or computer and an affidavit of filing by the filing party, shall be prima facie evidence that the filing party transmitted documents consistent with the date, time and place appearing on the confirmation record.

CPLR

§ 304. Method of commencing action or special proceeding.

[*Eff. on and after Sept 1, 2009*] An action is commenced by filing a summons and complaint or summons with notice. A special proceeding is commenced by filing a petition. Where a court finds that circumstances prevent immediate filing, the signing of an order requiring the subsequent filing at a specific time and date not later than five days thereafter shall commence the action. For purposes of this section, and for purposes of sections two hundred three and three hundred six-a of this chapter, filing shall mean the delivery of the summons with notice, summons and complaint or petition to the clerk of the court in the county in which the action or special proceeding is brought or any other person designated by the clerk of the court for that purpose together with any fee required as specified in rule twenty-one hundred two of this chapter for filing. At such time of filing, the original and a copy of such papers shall be date stamped by a court clerk who shall file the original and maintain a record of the date of the filing and who shall immediately return the copy to the party who brought the filing.

2007 AMENDMENTS

L. 2007, ch. 125, § 2, eff. Jan. 8, 2008, added subdivisions (a) through (f) to make reference to CPLR 2102, which relates to the filing of papers.

2005 AMENDMENTS

L. 2005, ch. 504, § 1, eff. Aug. 16, 2005, extending the expiration date of the pilot programs permitting the use of facsimile or electronic transmission to commence an action to Sept. 1, 2009 and limiting the rule's applicability to specific counties, including Niagara, Broome, Essex, Onondaga, and Sullivan counties.

2003 AMENDMENTS

L. 2003, ch. 261, § 1, eff. July 29, 2003, extending the expiration date of the pilot programs permitting the use of facsimile or electronic transmission to commence an action to Sept. 1, 2005 and limiting the rule's applicability to specific counties.

2002 AMENDMENTS

L. 2002, ch. 110, § 1, eff. June 28, 2002, extending the expiration date of the pilot programs permitting the use of facsimile or electronic transmission to commence an action to to July 1, 2003 and limiting the rule's applicability to specific counties.

2001 AMENDMENTS

L. 2001, ch. 473, § 1, effective Nov. 21, 2001, and applicable to special proceedings commenced on or after Nov. 21, 2001, amended CPLR 304 by eliminating the requirement that a notice of petition or order to show cause must be filed with a petition in order to commence a special proceeding; a special proceeding is now commenced by filing a petition. The Nov. 21, 2001 amendments to CPLR 304 made by L. 2001, ch. 473, § 1 do not affect the repeal of certain provisions of CPLR 304 pursuant to L. 1999, ch. 367, and these provisions shall be deemed repealed on July 1, 2002, whereupon L. 2001, ch. 473, § 2 shall take effect.

1999 AMENDMENTS

L. 1999, ch. 367, § 1, eff. July 27, 1999, amended to provide for delivery by facsimile or electronic means (as defined in CPLR 2103(f)) as authorized by the chief administrator of the courts; by adding the provisions providing that where filing is by fax, the clerk of the court need only return dated stamped copy of the first page of the initiating papers with the index number and where filing is by electronic means, the clerk shall, pursuant to the rules of the chief administrator of the courts, "forthwith" notify the filing party of the index number and date and time of filing; and by providing that a confirmation record produced by the filing part's fax or computer and an affidavit of filing constitute prima facie evidence that the filing party transmitted the papers consistent with the date, time and place appearing on the confirmation record.

1996 AMENDMENTS

L. 1996, ch. 606, eff. Sept. 1, 1997, and applicable to all actions or special proceedings commenced on or after such date. amended the section by deleting the words "with the clerk of court" from the first two sentences, adding a reference to section 306-a, expanding the definition of "filing" and adding a new last sentence.

1994 AMENDMENTS

L. 1994, ch. 563, eff. July 26, 1994, amended CPLR 304 by inserting the words "and a petition."

R 305. Summons; supplemental summons; amendment.

(a) Summons; supplemental summons. A summons shall specify the basis of the venue designated and if based upon the residence of the plaintiff it shall specify the plaintiff's address, and also shall bear the index number assigned and the date of filing with the clerk of the court. A third-party summons shall also specify the date of filing of the third-party summons with the clerk of the court. The summons in an action arising out of a consumer credit transaction shall prominently display at the top of the summons the words "consumer credit transaction" and, where a purchaser, borrower or debtor is a defendant, shall specify the county of residence of a defendant, if one resides within the state, and the county where the consumer credit transaction took place, if it is within the state. Where, upon order of the court or by stipulation of all parties or as of right pursuant to section 1003, a new party is joined in the action and the joinder is not made upon the new party's motion, a supplemental summons specifying the pleading which the new party must answer shall be filed with the clerk of the court and served upon such party.

(b) Summons and notice. If the complaint is not served with the summons, the summons shall contain or have attached thereto a notice stating the nature of the action and the relief sought, and, except in an action for medical malpractice, the sum of money for which judgment may be taken in case of default.

(c) Amendment. At any time, in its discretion and upon such terms as it deems just, the court may allow any summons or proof of service of a summons to be amended, if a substantial right of a party against whom the summons issued is not prejudiced.

CROSS REFERENCES

As to the summons in a matrimonial action, see **Domestic Relations Law §§ 211 and 232(a),** in Appendix, *below.*

1996 AMENDMENTS

L. 1996, ch. 39, eff. April 2, 1996, amended subdivision (a) by deleting the final sentence and replacing with a new final sentence, which makes reference to § 1003, Nonjoinder and misjoinder of parties.

1992 AMENDMENTS

L. 1992, ch. 216, eff. July 1, 1992, amended subdivision (a) by adding to the first sentence the words ". . . and also shall bear the index number assigned and the date of filing with the clerk of the court. A third-party summons shall also specify the date of filing of the third-party summons with the clerk of the court"; by adding to the final sentence the words "filed with the clerk of the court and"; and by making the language gender neutral.

1978 AMENDMENTS

L. 1978, ch. 528, eff. Jan. 1, 1979, amended subd. (b) so as to require service of notice of the nature of the action whenever the summons is served without a complaint, and, with the exception of medical malpractice suits, to uniformly require inclusion in such notice of the sum for which a default judgment may be taken.

Amendment recommended by the Judicial Conference in its report to the 1978 Legislature, wherein it stated:

"The permissive language now contained in CPLR 305(b) ('the summons may contain . . . .') constitutes a serious trap for the unwary practitioner who is not familiar with the provisions of CPLR 3215(e) governing proof of default. Under that provision, absent proof of service of the summons and complaint, a 305(b) notice is needed to preserve plaintiff's right to obtain a default judgment (*McDermott v. Hoening*, 32 A.D. 2d 838 (2nd Dept. 1969); *see* 1 Weinstein, Korn & Miller, New York Civil Practice - CPLR, ¶ 305.12 (Matthew Bender)). It is not clear whether and how a plaintiff who has served an unaccompanied summons without notice may, on his own initiative, serve the complaint on the defendant who neither appeared nor made a demand for the complaint . . .

"Under the proposed amendment the uncertainty now surrounding default practice under CPLR 305(b) and 3215(c), (e) would be avoided by the mandatory notice provision. That provision would be in harmony with modern notions of notice pleading. It would assure the defendant at least basic information concerning the nature of the plaintiff's claim and the relief sought. In order to accomplish that aim the content of the mandatory notice would be clarified. The language of the rule which now requires a statement of 'the object of the action and the relief sought' would be amended to provide instead for a brief recital of 'the nature of the action and the relief sought.' The present verbiage could be misread as a redundancy denoting merely a requirement to specify the type of relief sought in terms of damages or other remedy. Such misreading led to the downfall of the plaintiff's action in a negligence case where the court voided a summons served without complaint on the ground that it failed to disclose the object of the action, even though it set forth the damages demanded (*Arden v. Loew's Hotels Inc.*, 40 A.D. 2d 894 (3rd Dept. 1972).

"A different kind of technical defect that may render an unaccompanied summons jurisdictionally void for default purposes is typified by *A.J. Eckert Co. v. George A. Fuller Co., Inc.* 51 A.D. 2d 844 (3rd Dept. 1976). In that case an application to the court for judgment by default was denied when the summons stated the object of the action ('claim for the balance due under a contract and damages for breach thereof') but failed to set forth the sum for which judgment would be taken in case of default as required by CPLR 3215(b). To avoid mishaps of that sort the present requirement that 'in an action for a sum certain or for a sum which by computation can be made certain, the notice must state the sum of money for which judgment will be taken' would be expanded to include any kind of action seeking monetary relief, whether liquidated or unliquidated. The sole exception would be an action to recover damages for medical malpractice where CPLR 3017(c) bars the pleader from stating the amount of damages sought. To require a statement of the sum to which the pleader deems himself entitled in the summons would flout the purpose of that statute.

"The proposed amplification of language with respect to the statement of money damages, liquidated or unliquidated, reiterates more compactly the present practice. The language in rule 305(b) proposed to be deleted, which refers to actions for a sum certain, was derived from rule 46 of the former rules of civil practice, which provided for a short form of complaint for enumerated categories of contract actions (*see* 1 Weinstein, Korn & Miller, New York Civil Practice ¶ 305.12 (Matthew Bender)). L. 1965 ch. 749 amended Rule 305(b) to permit service of a notice, contained in the summons or attached to it, stating the object of the action and the relief sought, as well as the original notice where the suit was for a sum certain. Thus, under the present law, a notice may be served in any action. If the action is one involving liquidated damages, the sum certain or able to be made certain by computation must be stated in the 305(b) notice, in order to allow entry of a default judgment by the clerk (CPLR 3215(a)). If the damages are unliquidated, the sum must be stated in the 305(b) notice, under the rubric of 'relief sought' in order to satisfy the requirement of CPLR 3215(b) that the judgment by default 'not exceed in amount or differ in type from that demanded in the complaint or stated in the notice served pursuant to subdivision (b) of rule 305.' The same applies in an equitable proceeding, such as for specific performance or an injunction, where alternative or incidental money damages are demanded. In short, the proposed language serves as a reminder that a statement of the monetary relief sought in a summons served without complaint is always needed in order to protect plaintiff's rights on default.

"Matrimonial actions would be governed by analogous amendments to Domestic Relations Law, sections 211 and 232 . . . .

"Finally, the question may be asked whether a deviation from the notice standards prescribed by rule 305(b), as proposed to be amended, would constitute a jurisdictional defect or a mere irregularity. The complete absence of any notice would certainly constitute a jurisdictional defect when the summons is not accompanied by the complaint (*see McDermott v. Hoenig*, 32 A.D. 2d 838, 302 N.Y.S.2d 280 (2d Dept 1969)). In accordance with present practice, the court would have to determine whether a defective notice is correctable or, under the circumstances of a particular case, renders the summons jurisdictionally void for purposes of a default proceeding."

1973 AMENDMENTS

L. 1973, ch. 238, eff. Sept. 1, 1973, amended CPLR 305(a) by adding a new second sentence setting forth the requirements for a summons in an action arising out of a consumer credit transaction.

1965 AMENDMENTS

L. 1965, ch. 749, eff. Sept. 1, 1965, amended subd. (b). See comments at 1978 amendment notes.

R 306. Proof of service.

(a) Generally. Proof of service shall specify the papers served, the person who was served and the date, time, address, or, in the event there is no address, place and manner of service, and set forth facts showing that the service was made by an authorized person and in an authorized manner.

(b) Personal service. Whenever service is made pursuant to this article by delivery of the summons to an individual, proof of service shall also include, in addition to any other requirement, a description of the person to whom it was so delivered including, but not limited to, sex, color of skin, hair color, approximate age, approximate weight and height, and other identifying features.

(c) Other service. Where service is made pursuant to subdivision four of section three hundred eight of this chapter, proof of service shall also specify the dates, addresses and the times of attempted service pursuant to subdivisions one, two or three of such section.

(d) Form. Proof of service shall be in the form of a certificate if the service is made by a sheriff or other authorized public officer, in the form of an affidavit if made by any other person, or in the form of a signed acknowledgment of receipt of a summons and complaint, or summons and notice or notice of petition as provided for in section 312-a of this article.

(e) Admission of service. A writing admitting service by the person to be served is adequate proof of service.

CROSS REFERENCES

See **General Business Law § 89-c** as to records required to be kept by process servers.

1989 AMENDMENTS

L. 1989, ch. 274, eff. Jan. 1, 1990 until Jan. 1, 1992.

1977 AMENDMENTS

L. 1977, ch. 103, eff. Jan. 1, 1978, amended subd. (b), which formerly required that proof of service upon an individual contain a description of the person served, by further requiring such a description in all instances in which delivery is made to an individual, such as service upon a corporation by delivery to an officer.

1973 AMENDMENTS

L. 1973, ch. 397, eff. Sept. 1, 1973, amended CPLR 306 by adding detailed requirements as to the contents of proof of service; and divided the rule into subdivisions (a) through (e).

CPLR

§ 306-a. Index number in an action or proceeding commenced in supreme or county court.

(a) Upon filing the summons and complaint, summons with notice or petition in an action or proceeding commenced in supreme or county court with the clerk of the county, an index number shall be assigned and the fee required by subdivision (a) of section eight thousand eighteen of this chapter shall be paid. Upon the filing of a summons and complaint against a person not already a party, as permitted under section one thousand seven or rule one thousand eleven of this chapter, the fee required by subdivision (a) of section eight thousand eighteen of this chapter shall be paid, but a separate index number shall not be assigned.

(b) If a person other than the plaintiff or third-party plaintiff who served the summons or third-party summons obtains the index number and pays the fee therefor, the clerk shall issue an order directing the plaintiff or the third-party plaintiff to pay such person the amount of the fee paid. If such fee is not paid within thirty days of service of the order with notice of entry, the person who paid the fee, in addition to any other remedies available at law, may apply to the clerk for an order dismissing the action without prejudice.

2009 AMENDMENTS

L. 2009, ch. 56, eff. April 7, 2009, amending to extend until September 1,

2011 sections of CPLR 306–a which were scheduled to expire on September 1, 2009.

2007 AMENDMENTS

L. 2007, ch. 125, eff. Jan. 1, 2008, amending the title of § 306-a and subd. a.

2005 AMENDMENTS

L. 2005, ch. 56, eff. April 1, 2005.

2003 AMENDMENTS

L. 2003, ch. 16, § 14, eff. March 31, 2003.

2001 AMENDMENTS

L. 2001, ch. 473, eff. Nov. 21, 2001, amending subdivision (a).

1996 AMENDMENTS

L. 1996, ch. 606, eff. Sept. 1, 1997, and applicable to all actions or special proceedings commenced on or after such date, amended subdivision (a) by deleting the words "with the clerk of the court" from the first sentence.

1992 AMENDMENTS

L. 1992, ch. 216, eff. July 1, 1992, repealed prior versions of CPLR 306–a. CPLR 306–a(a) now provides that a party who files in the supreme or county courts a summons and complaint, or summons with notice, must secure an index number at the time of filing. CPLR 306–a(b) provides that if someone other than the plaintiff purchases the index number, that person is entitled to an order from the clerk of the court, requiring reimbursement by the plaintiff (or the third-party plaintiff) within 30 days of service of the order with notice of entry. If the plaintiff fails to comply, the paying individual may apply to the clerk for an order dismissing the action, but without prejudice.

L. 1992, ch. 55, eff. for all actions that were "pending" on July 1, 1992, amended subdivision (a) by deleting the reference to third-party actions. More important, it provided that unless a summons was filed with the clerk and an index number purchased before process was served, service would be ineffective. It also deleted former subdivision (b) and replaced it with the current subdivision (b) dealing with third-party actions, and revised subdivision (c). These amendments, however, were superseded by L. 1992, ch. 216, discussed *above*.

§ 306-b Service of the summons and complaint, summons with notice, third-party summons and complaint, or petition with a notice of petition or order to show cause.

Service of the summons and complaint, summons with notice, third-party summons and complaint, or petition with a notice of petition or order to show cause shall be made within one hundred twenty days after the filing of the summons and complaint, summons with notice, third-party summons and complaint, or petition, provided that in an action or proceeding, except a proceeding commenced under the election law, where the applicable statute of limitations is four months or less, service shall be made not later than fifteen days after the date on which the applicable statute of limitations expires. If service is not made upon a defendant within the time provided in this section, the court, upon motion, shall dismiss the action without prejudice as to that defendant, or upon good cause shown or in the interest of justice, extend the time for service.

2001 AMENDMENTS

L. 2001, ch. 473, eff. Nov. 21, 2001, amending CPLR 306–b and applicable to special proceedings commenced on or after such date.

1997 AMENDMENTS

L. 1997, ch. 476, eff. Jan. 1, 1998 and applicable to all actions commenced on or after Jan. 1, 1998, repealed former version of CPLR 306–b, as originally added by L. 1992, ch. 216 and added new § 306–b.

§ 307.　Personal service upon the state.

1. Personal service upon the state shall be made by delivering the summons to an assistant attorney-general at an office of the attorney-general or to the attorney-general within the state.

2. Personal service on a state officer sued solely in an official capacity or state agency, which shall be required to obtain personal jurisdiction over such an officer or agency, shall be made by (1) delivering the summons to such officer or to the chief executive officer of such agency or to a person designated by such chief executive officer to receive service, or (2) by mailing the summons by certified mail, return receipt requested, to such officer or to the chief executive officer of such agency, and by personal service upon the state in the manner provided by subdivision one of this section. Service by certified mail shall not be complete until the summons is received in a principal office of the agency and until personal service upon the state in the manner provided by subdivision one of this section is completed. For purposes of this subdivision, the term "principal office of the agency" shall mean the location at which the office of the chief executive officer of the agency is generally located. Service by certified mail shall not be

effective unless the front of the envelope bears the legend "URGENT LEGAL MAIL" in capital letters. The chief executive officer of every such agency shall designate at least one person, in addition to himself or herself, to accept personal service on behalf of the agency. For purposes of this subdivision the term state agency shall be deemed to refer to any agency, board, bureau, commission, division, tribunal or other entity which constitutes the state for purposes of service under subdivision one of this section.

1993 AMENDMENTS

L. 1993, ch. 420, eff. Oct. 19, 1993, amended subdivision (2) by replacing the clause that began "In the event any provision of law . . ." with the clause "Personal service on a state officer sued solely in an official capacity or state agency, which shall be required to obtain personal jurisdiction over such an officer or agency."

1992 AMENDMENTS

L. 1992, ch. 44, eff. Jan. 1, 1993, amended subdivision (2) to add a provision authorizing personal service upon specified state agency officers by certified mail, return receipt requested, in an envelope bearing the legend "URGENT LEGAL MAIL."

1985 AMENDMENTS

L. 1985, ch. 290, eff. Nov. 1, 1985, added subdivision (2).

§ 308. Personal service upon a natural person.

Personal service upon a natural person shall be made by any of the following methods:

1. by delivering the summons within the state to the person to be served; or

2. by delivering the summons within the state to a person of suitable age and discretion at the actual place of business, dwelling place or usual place of abode of the person to be served and by either mailing the summons to the person to be served at his or her last known residence or by mailing the summons by first class mail to the person to be served at his or her actual place of business in an envelope bearing the legend "personal and confidential" and not indicating on the outside thereof, by return address or otherwise, that the communication is from an attorney or concerns an action against the person to be served, such delivery and mailing to be effected within twenty days of each other; proof of such service shall be filed

with the clerk of the court designated in the summons within twenty days of either such delivery or mailing, whichever is effected later; service shall be complete ten days after such filing; proof of service shall identify such person of suitable age and discretion and state the date, time and place of service, except in matrimonial actions where service hereunder may be made pursuant to an order made in accordance with the provisions of subdivision a of section two hundred thirty-two of the domestic relations law; or

3. by delivering the summons within the state to the agent for service of the person to be served as designated under rule 318, except in matrimonial actions where service hereunder may be made pursuant to an order made in accordance with the provisions of subdivision a of section two hundred thirty-two of the domestic relations law;

4. where service under paragraphs one and two cannot be made with due diligence, by affixing the summons to the door of either the actual place of business, dwelling place or usual place of abode within the state of the person to be served and by either mailing the summons to such person at his or her last known residence or by mailing the summons by first class mail to the person to be served at his or her actual place of business in an envelope bearing the legend "personal and confidential" and not indicating on the outside thereof, by return address or otherwise, that the communication is from an attorney or concerns an action against the person to be served, such affixing and mailing to be effected within twenty days of each other; proof of such service shall be filed with the clerk of the court designated in the summons within twenty days of either such affixing or mailing, whichever is effected later; service shall be complete ten days after such filing, except in matrimonial actions where service hereunder may be made pursuant to an order made in accordance with the provisions of subdivision a of section two hundred thirty-two of the domestic relations law;

5. in such manner as the court, upon motion without notice, directs, if service is impracticable under paragraphs one, two and four of this section.

6. For purposes of this section, "actual place of business" shall include any location that the defendant, through regular solicitation

or advertisement, has held out as its place of business.

CROSS REFERENCES

D.R.L. § 232, referred to in subds. (2), (3) and (4), *above,* appears in Appendix, *below.*

1994 AMENDMENTS

L. 1994, ch. 131, eff. Jan. 1, 1995, added CPLR 308(6) pertaining to "actual place of business."

1988 AMENDMENTS

L. 1988, ch. 125, eff. Jan. 1, 1989, amended subdivision 2 to require delivery and mailing to be accomplished within 20 days of each other, and subdivision 4 to require affixing and mailing to be accomplished within 20 days of each other; to require proof of service—under both subdivisions—to be filed within 20 days of whichever service is accomplished later; to make statute gender neutral.

1987 AMENDMENTS

L. 1987, ch. 115, eff. July 15, 1987, amended paragraphs two and four by providing alternative means of satisfying mailing requirement of substituted service and "nailing and mailing" procedures.

1986 AMENDMENTS

L. 1986, ch. 77, eff. Jan. 1, 1987, repealed the undesignated paragraph following paragraph (5) of CPLR 308 relating to the additional notice required to take a default judgment in an action against a natural person based upon nonpayment of a contractual obligation. New paragraph (3) of CPLR 3215(f) now governs.

1977 AMENDMENTS

L. 1977, ch. 344, eff. Jan. 1, 1978, amended CPLR 308 by adding a new undesignated paragraph which provides that in an action against a natural person for nonpayment of a contractual obligation additional notice must be given at least 20 days prior to the entry of a default judgment and which describes the procedures for service of such notice.

1974 AMENDMENTS

L. 1974, ch. 765, eff. July 7, 1974, amended paragraphs two, three and four of CPLR 308 by deleting the words "except in matrimonial actions" at the beginning of each paragraph and by adding the clause "except in matrimonial actions where service hereunder may be made pursuant to an order made in accordance with the provisions of subdivision a of section two hundred thirty-two of the domestic relations law."

1971 AMENDMENTS

L. 1971, ch. 176, eff. Sept. 1, 1971, amended CPLR 308.

This amendment was recommended by the Judicial Conference February 1, 1971 Report to the Legislature, wherein it was stated:

"Paragraph 4 would be amended to provide that in order to avail himself of substituted service by 'nailing and mailing,' a party must make diligent attempts at prior service under paragraphs 1 *and* 2, rather than under paragraphs 1, 2 *or* 3, as at present . . .

"In addition, minor verbal improvements would be made in paragraph 4 . . .

"A similar change is proposed in paragraph 5, to allow the use of a special mode of service according to court order where diligent attempts have failed under paragraphs 1, 2 *and* 4, rather than under paragraphs 1, 2, 3 *or* 4, as at present.

"Paragraphs 1 and 2 would be amended to add the disjunctive word 'or' at the end of each, to clarify that paragraphs 1, 2 or 3 offer alternatives for effecting service and that each of the specified modes can be used as a first preference.

"Paragraph 2 would also be made stylistically consistent with paragraph 4 by changing the word 'address' therein to 'residence.' "

1970 AMENDMENTS

L. 1970, ch. 852, eff. Sept. 1, 1970, repealed former CPLR 308 and inserted a new section 308.

1968 AMENDMENTS

L. 1968, ch. 276, eff. Sept. 1, 1968, amended Subd. (3) [now (4)] to require that proof of substituted service be filed within twenty days after such service.

§ 309. Personal service upon an infant, incompetent or conservatee.

(a) Upon an infant. Personal service upon an infant shall be made by personally serving the summons within the state upon a parent or any guardian or any person having legal custody or, if the infant is married, upon an adult spouse with whom the infant resides, or, if none are within the state, upon any other person with whom he resides, or by whom he is employed. If the infant is of the age of fourteen years or over, the summons shall also be personally served upon him within the state.

(b) Upon a person judicially declared to be incompetent. Personal service upon a person judicially declared to be incompetent to manage his affairs and for whom a committee has been appointed shall be made by personally serving the summons within the state upon the committee and upon the incompetent, but the court may dispense with service upon the incompetent.

(c) Upon a conservatee. Personal service on a person for whom a conservator has been appointed shall be made by personally serving the summons within the state upon the conservator and upon the conservatee, but the court may dispense with service upon the conservatee.

CROSS REFERENCES

If defendant is a patient of any hospital, school or alcoholism facility as defined **Mental Hygiene Law § 1.05**; see **14 N.Y.C.R.R. § 22.2** regarding service of process.

1981 AMENDMENTS

L. 1981, ch. 115, eff. May 18, 1981, added a new subdivision (c).

1968 AMENDMENTS

L. 1968, ch. 844, eff. Sept. 1, 1968, amended Subd. (a) by expanding the category of persons upon whom service of a summons must be made in place of an infant.

§ 310. Personal service upon a partnership.

(a) Personal service upon persons conducting a business as a partnership may be made by personally serving the summons upon any one of them.

(b) Personal service upon said partnership may also be made within the state by delivering the summons to the managing or general agent of the partnership or the person in charge of the office of the partnership within the state at such office and by either mailing the summons to the partner thereof intended to be served by first class mail to his last known residence or to the place of business of the partnership. Proof of such service shall be filed within twenty days with the clerk of the court designated in the summons; service shall be complete ten days after such filing; proof of service shall identify the person to whom the summons was so delivered and state the date, time of day and place of service.

(c) Where service under subdivisions (a) and (b) of this section cannot be made with due diligence, it may be made by affixing a copy of the summons to the door of the actual place of business of the partnership within the state and by either mailing the summons by first class mail to the partner intended to be so served to such person to his last known residence or to said person at the office of said partnership within the state. Proof of such service shall be filed within twenty days thereafter with the clerk of the court designated in the summons; service shall be complete ten days after filing.

(d) Personal service on such partnership may also be made by delivering the summons to any other agent or employee of the partnership authorized by appointment to receive service; or to any other person designated by the partnership to receive process in writing, filed in the office of the clerk of the county wherein such partnership is located.

(e) If service is impracticable under subdivisions (a), (b) and (c) of this section, it may be made in such manner as the court, upon motion without notice directs.

CROSS REFERENCES

See also **General Associations Law §§ 12, 13** as to service upon unincorporated associations in Appendix, *below.*

1991 AMENDMENTS

L. 1991, ch. 338, eff. July 15, 1991, relettered as subdivision (a) the first undesignated paragraph and deleted the phrase "within the state" following the word "summons," and added new subdivisions (b), (c), (d) and (e).

§ 310-a. Personal service upon a limited partnership.

(a) Personal service upon any domestic or foreign limited partnership shall be made by delivering a copy personally to any managing or general agent or general partner of the limited partnership in this state, to any other agent or employee of the limited partnership authorized by appointment to receive service or to any other person designated by the limited partnership to receive process, in the manner provided by law for service of summons, as if such person was the defendant. Personal service upon a limited partnership subject to the provisions of article eight-A of the partnership law may also be made pursuant to section 121-109 of such law.

(b) If service is impracticable under subdivision (a) of this section, it may be made in such manner as the court, upon motion without notice, directs.

(c) A limited liability partnership may also be served pursuant to section 121-1505 of the partnership law.

1999 AMENDMENTS

L. 1999, ch. 341, eff. July 27, 1999, added section to provide for personal service upon a limited partnership.

§ 311. Personal service upon a corporation or governmental subdivision.

(a) Personal service upon a corporation or governmental subdivision shall be made by delivering the summons as follows:

1. upon any domestic or foreign corporation, to an officer, director, managing or general agent, or cashier or assistant cashier or to any other agent authorized by appointment or by law to receive service. A business corporation may also be served pursuant to section three hundred six or three hundred seven of the business corporation law. A not-for-profit corporation may also be served pursuant to section three hundred six or three hundred seven of the not-for-profit corporation law;

2. upon the city of New York, to the corporation counsel or to any person designated to receive process in a writing filed in the office of the clerk of New York county;

3. upon any other city, to the mayor, comptroller, treasurer, counsel or clerk; or, if the city lacks such officers, to an officer performing a corresponding function under another name;

4. upon a county, to the chair or clerk of the board of supervisors, clerk, attorney or treasurer;

5. upon a town, to the supervisor or the clerk;

6. upon a village, to the mayor, clerk, or any trustee;

7. upon a school district, to a school officer, as defined in the education law; and

8. upon a park, sewage or other district, to the clerk, any trustee or any member of the board.

(b) If service upon a domestic or foreign corporation within the one hundred twenty days allowed by section three hundred six-b of this article is impracticable under paragraph one of subdivision (a) of this section or any other law, service upon the corporation may be made in such manner, and proof of service may take such form, as the court, upon motion without notice, directs.

CROSS REFERENCES

See **B.C.L. §§ 304, 306 and 307,** in Appendix, *below,* as to service upon secretary of state or other designated agent of corporation.

1999 AMENDMENTS

L. 1999, ch. 341, eff. July 27, 1999, amended by adding the last two sentences providing that a business corporation may also be served pursuant to B.C.L. § 306 or 307 and a not-for-profit corporation may also be served pursuant to the Not-for-Profit Corporation Law § 306 or 307.

1998 AMENDMENTS

L. 1998, ch. 202, eff. July 7, 1998, amended subdivision (b) by replacing "in time to secure and file the proof of service called for by subdivision (a) of" with "within the one hundred twenty days allowed by." In effect, this provides that an application may be made if service cannot be effected within the 120 days allowed by CPLR 306-b.

1996 AMENDMENTS

L. 1996, ch. 337, eff. Jan. 1, 1997, amended the section by numbering the opening paragraph as subdivision (a); adding new subdivision (b) governing situations where service under subdivision (a) is impracticable; and making the section gender neutral.

1977 AMENDMENTS

L. 1977, ch. 17, eff. March 22, 1977, amended paragraph 8 by striking the reference to a "school" district. A 1976 amendment enacted paragraph 7 to govern service upon a school district.

1976 AMENDMENTS

L. 1976, ch. 745, eff. Sept. 1, 1976, added paragraph (7) to CPLR 311 and renumbered accordingly.

Amendment recommended by the Judicial Conference in its Report to the 1976 Legislature, in which it stated:

"The purpose of the proposed amendment is to broaden the category of persons designated by law as persons to whom a summons, and thus a notice of claim, in a Supreme Court action against a school district may be delivered to include those identified in section 2 of the Education Law. By so doing, notice to school officers to whom parents are most likely to give notice will constitute effective notice, thereby avoiding results like that Mr. Justice Bernard S. Meyer felt compelled to reach in *Bayer* v. *Board of Education,* 58 Misc. 2d 259 (Sup. Ct. Nassau Co. 1968). In that case a letter stating a claim was timely served upon the superintendent of schools but the action was dismissed because the superintendent was not one of those identified by statute as a person upon whom service could be made. The recommended change adopts one of the solutions suggested by Mr. Justice Meyer in his decision."

§ 311-a. Personal service on limited liability companies.

(a) Service of process on any domestic or foreign limited liability company shall be made by delivering a copy personally to (i) any member of the limited liability company in this state, if the management of the limited liability company is vested in its members, (ii) any manager of the limited liability company in this state, if the management of the limited liability company is vested in one or more managers, (iii) to any other agent authorized by appointment to receive process, or (iv) to any other person designated by the limited liability company to receive process, in the manner provided by law for service of a summons as if such person was a defendant. Service of process upon a limited liability company may also be made pursuant to article three of the limited liability company law.

(b) if service is impracticable under subdivision (a) of this section, it may be made in such manner as the court, upon motion without notice, directs.

1999 AMENDMENTS

L. 1999, ch. 341, § 1, eff. July 27, 1999, added section to provide for personal service on limited liability companies.

§ 312. Personal service upon a court, board or commission.

Personal service upon a court consisting of three or more judges may be made by delivering the summons to any one of them. Personal service upon a board or commission having a chairman or other presiding officer, secretary or clerk, by whatever official title he is called, may be made by delivering the summons to him. Personal service upon a board or commission of a town or village may also be made by delivering the summons to the clerk of the town or village. Personal service upon any other board or commission shall be made by delivering the summons to any one of the members.

1987 AMENDMENTS

L. 1987, ch. 109, eff. June 8, 1987, added the provision that personal service upon a board of commission of a town or village may also be made by delivering the summons to the clerk of the town or village.

§ 312-a. Personal service by mail.

(a) Service. As an alternative to the methods of personal service authorized by section 307, 308, 310, 311 or 312 of this article, a summons and complaint, or summons and notice, or notice of petition and petition may be served by the plaintiff or any other person by mailing to the person or entity to be served, by first class mail, postage prepaid, a copy of the summons and complaint, or summons and notice or notice of petition and petition, together with two copies of a statement of service by mail and acknowledgment of receipt in the form set forth in subdivision (d) of this section, with a return envelope, postage prepaid, addressed to the sender.

(b) Completion of service and time to answer.

1. The defendant, an authorized employee of the defendant, defendant's attorney or an employee of the attorney must complete the acknowledgement of receipt and mail or deliver one copy of it within thirty (30) days from the date of receipt. Service is complete on the date the signed acknowledgment of receipt is mailed or delivered to the sender. The signed acknowledgment of receipt shall constitute proof of service.

2. Where a complaint or petition is served with the summons or notice of petition, the defendant shall serve an answer within twenty (20) days after the date the signed acknowledgement of receipt is mailed or delivered to the sender.

(c) Affirmation. The acknowledgement of receipt of service shall be subscribed and affirmed as true under penalties of perjury and shall have the same force and effect as an affidavit.

(d) Form. The statement of service by mail and the acknowledgement of receipt of such service shall be in substantially the following form:

Statement of Service by Mail and
Acknowledgment of Receipt by Mail of
Summons and Complaint or Summons and Notice
or Notice of Petition and Petition

A.STATEMENT OF SERVICE
BY MAIL

To: (Insert the name and address of the person or entity to be served.)

The enclosed summons and complaint, or summons and notice, or notice of petition and petition (strike out inapplicable terms) are served pursuant to section 312-a of the Civil Practice Law and Rules.

To avoid being charged with the expense of service upon you, you must sign, date and complete the acknowledgment part of this form and mail or deliver one copy of the completed form to the sender within thirty (30) days from the date you receive it. You should keep a copy for your records or your attorney. If you wish to consult an attorney, you should do so as soon as possible before the thirty (30) days expire.

If you do not complete and return the form to the sender within thirty (30) days, you (or the party on whose behalf you are being served) will be required to pay expenses incurred in serving the summons and complaint, or summons and notice, or notice of petition and petition in any other manner permitted by law, and the cost of such service as permitted by law will be entered as a judgment against you.

If you have received a complaint or petition with this statement, the return of this statement and acknowledgment does not relieve you of the necessity to answer the complaint or petition. The time to answer expires twenty (20) days after the day you mail or deliver this form to the sender. If you wish to consult with an attorney, you should do so as soon as possible before the twenty (20) days expire.

If you are served on behalf of a corporation, unincorporated association, partnership or other entity, you must indicate under your signature your relationship to the entity. If you are served on behalf of another person and you are authorized to receive process, you must indicate under your signature your authority.

It is a crime to forge a signature or to make a false entry on this statement or on the acknowledgment.

ACKNOWLEDGMENT OF RECEIPT OF SUMMONS AND COMPLAINT OR SUMMONS AND NOTICE OR NOTICE OF PETITION AND PETITION

I received a summons and complaint, or summons and notice, or notice of petition and petition (strike out inapplicable terms) in the above-captioned matter at (insert address). PLEASE CHECK ONE OF THE FOLLOWING:

IF 2 IS CHECKED, COMPLETE AS INDICATED:

1. ☐ I am not in military service.

2. ☐ I am in military service, and my rank and branch of service are as follows:

Rank . . . .

Branch of Service . . . .

TO BE COMPLETED REGARDLESS OF MILITARY STATUS:

Date: . . . .
      (Date this Acknowledgment is executed)

I affirm the above as true under penalty of perjury.

. . . .
                                                                Signature
. . . .
                                                                Print name
. . . .
                        Name of Defendant for which acting
Position with Defendant for which acting (i.e., officer, attorney, etc.)

PLEASE COMPLETE ALL BLANKS INCLUDING DATES

(e) Subsequent service. Where a duly executed acknowledgment is not returned, upon the subsequent service of process in another manner permitted by law, the summons or notice of petition or paper served with the summons or notice of petition shall indicate that an attempt previously was made to effect service pursuant to this section.

(f) Disbursements. Where the signed acknowledgment of receipt is not returned within thirty (30) days after receipt of the documents mailed pursuant to subdivision (a) of this section, the reasonable expense of serving process by an alternative method shall be taxed by the court on notice pursuant to section 8402 of this chapter as a disbursement to the party serving process, and the court shall direct immediate judgment in that amount.

2009 AMENDMENTS

L. 2009, ch. 222, eff. July 14, 2009, amended subdivision (d) by eliminating the requirement that members of the armed services include their serial number in an acknowledgment of the receipt of a summons and complaint, summons and notice, or notice of petition and petition by mail.

1996 AMENDMENTS

L. 1996, ch. 368, eff. July 30, 1996, amended subdivision (a) by deleting the phrase ", an authorized employee of the plaintiff, the plaintiff's attorney or an employee of the attorney" and replacing it with the words "or any other person."

1993 AMENDMENTS

L. 1993, ch. 459, eff. Jan. 1, 1994, amended CPLR 312-a by adding the words "an authorized employee of the plaintiff" to subdivision (a); by adding the words "an authorized employee of the defendant" and the number "30" to subdivision (b); by changing "a copy" in subdivision (b) to "one copy"; by adding the number "20" to subdivision (b)(2); by adding the letter "A." before the words "STATEMENT OF SERVICE BY MAIL" in subdivision (d); by adding the words "strike out inapplicable terms" to subdivision (d); by adding the sentence beginning "You should keep a copy..." to subdivision (d); by replacing "may" with "will" immediately preceding "be required to pay expenses incurred in serving the summons..." in subdivision (d); by replacing "may" with "will" immediately preceding "be entered as a judgment against you" in subdivision (d); by deleting lines for the insertion of the signature, printed name, and address immediately following the sentence beginning "It is a crime to..." in subdivision (d); by adding the letter "B." before "ACKNOWLEDGMENT OF RECEIPT..." in subdivision (d); by adding the words "strike out inapplicable terms" to the sentence beginning "I received a summons..." in subdivision (d); by adding the words "TO BE COMPLETED REGARDLESS OF MILITARY STATUS:" in subdivision (d); by replacing the words "Relationship to entity/Authority to Receive Service of Process" in subdivision (d) with the words "Name Of Defendant For Which Acting/Position With Defendant For Which Acting (i.e. Officer, Attorney, etc.)"; by adding the words "Please Complete All Blanks Including Dates" in subdivision (d); by adding to subdivision (f) the words "on notice pursuant to section 8402 of this chapter"; and replacing in subdivision (f) the words "if that party is awarded costs in the action or proceeding" with "and the court shall direct immediate judgment in that amount."

1992 AMENDMENTS

L. 1992, ch. 216, eff. July 1, 1992, amended subdivision (b)(1) by deleting from the beginning of the second sentence the words "An action is commenced and service" and replacing them with the word "Service."

1991 AMENDMENTS

L. 1991, ch. 249, eff. July 1, 1991, deleted the Jan. 1, 1992 repeal date.

1989 AMENDMENTS

L. 1989, ch. 274, eff. Jan. 1, 1990 until Jan.1, 1992, added a trial period for effectuating personal service by mail.

CROSS REFERENCES

Conforming amendments were also enacted to several court acts; *see* **Civil Practice Annual of New York (Matthew Bender):** the Uniform District Court Act, the New York City Civil Court Act, the Uniform City Court Act and the Uniform Justice Court Act, *see also* proof of service amendment to CPLR 306, *above.* Enacting language mandated that the "chief administrator of the courts shall monitor and survey the cost of personal service following the effective date of this act and shall report findings with respect thereto, including appropriate recommendations to the legislature and the governor, on or before April 1, 1991."

CPLR

§ 313. Service without the state giving personal jurisdiction.

A person domiciled in the state or subject to the jurisdiction of the courts of the state under section 301 or 302, or his executor or administrator, may be served with the summons without the state, in the same manner as service is made within the state, by any person authorized to make service within the state who is a resident of the state or by any person authorized to make service by the laws of the state, territory, possession or country in which service is made or by any duly qualified attorney, solicitor, barrister, or equivalent in such jurisdiction.

§ 314. Service without the state not giving personal jurisdiction in certain actions.

Service may be made without the state by any person authorized by section 313 in the same manner as service is made within the state:

   1. in a matrimonial action; or

   2. where a judgment is demanded that the person to be served be excluded from a vested or contingent interest in or lien upon specific real or personal property within the state; or that such an interest or

lien in favor of either party be enforced, regulated, defined or limited; or otherwise affecting the title to such property, including an action of interpleader or defensive interpleader; or

3. where a levy upon property of the person to be served has been made within the state pursuant to an order of attachment or a chattel of such person has been seized in an action to recover a chattel.

§ 315. Service by publication authorized.

The court, upon motion without notice, shall order service of a summons by publication in an action described in section 314 if service cannot be made by another prescribed method with due diligence.

R 316. Service by publication.

(a) Contents of order; form of publication; filing. An order for service of a summons by publication shall direct that the summons be published together with the notice to the defendant, a brief statement of the nature of the action and the relief sought, and, except in an action for medical malpractice, the sum of money for which judgment may be taken in case of default and, if the action is brought to recover a judgment affecting the title to, or the possession, use or enjoyment of, real property, a brief description of the property, in two newspapers, at least one in the English language, designated in the order as most likely to give notice to the person to be served, for a specified time, at least once in each of four successive weeks, except that in a matrimonial action publication in one newspaper in the English language, designated in the order as most likely to give notice to the person to be served, at least once in each of three successive weeks shall be sufficient. The summons, complaint, or summons and notice in an action for divorce or separation, order and papers on which the order was based shall be filed on or before the first day of publication.

(b) Mailing to accompany publication in matrimonial actions. An order for service of a summons by publication in a matrimonial action shall also direct that on or before the first day of publication a copy of the summons be mailed to the person to be served unless a place where such person probably would receive mail cannot with due diligence be ascertained and the court dispenses with such mailing. A notice of publication shall be enclosed.

(c) Time of publication; when service complete. The first publication of the summons shall be made within thirty days after the order is granted. Service by publication is complete on the twenty-eighth day after the day of first publication, except that in a matrimonial action it is complete on the twenty-first day after the day of first publication.

1979 AMENDMENTS

L. 1979, ch. 191, eff. Jan. 1, 1980, amended CPLR 316 subd. (c) by changing the time within which first publication of the summons must be made from 20 to 30 days from the granting of the order.

The Judicial Conference Report on the CPLR to the 1979 Legislature noted that the twenty day period is unduly short and that: ". . . There is some judicial authority to the effect that the present 20 day period is jurisdictional so that if plaintiff makes the first publication on the twenty-first day no jurisdiction will be acquired (*Caton v. Caton,* 72 Misc. 2d 544 (Sup. Ct. Monroe Co. 1972))."

1978 AMENDMENTS

L. 1978, ch. 528, eff. Jan. 1, 1979, amended subd. (a) to conform the notice provisions therein to analogous provisions in CPLR 305(b), as amended. See 1978 amendment note under CPLR 305, *supra,* for detailed Judicial Conference commentary on the amendment.

1972 AMENDMENTS

Proposal No. 1 made by the Judicial Conference Report to the 1972 Legislature amended Subd. (c), eff. Sept. 1, 1972, by adding to the second sentence thereof the clause, "except that in a matrimonial action it is complete on the twenty-first day after the day of first publication."

1970 AMENDMENTS

Proposal No. 1 made by Judicial Conference Jan. 2, 1970 Report to the 1970 Legislature, eff. Sept. 1, 1970: Subd. (a) amended by adding to the first sentence thereof, the clause, "except that in a matrimonial action publication in one newspaper in the English language, designated in the order as most likely to give notice to the person to be served, at least once in each of three successive weeks shall be sufficient."

1969 AMENDMENTS

L. 1969, ch. 274, eff. Sept. 1, 1969, amended Subd. (a) by adding that ". . . summons and notice in an action for divorce or separation" shall be filed on or before the first day of publication.

§ 317. Defense by person to whom summons not personally delivered.

A person served with a summons other than by personal delivery to

CPLR

him or to his agent for service designated under rule 318, within or without the state, who does not appear may be allowed to defend the action within one year after he obtains knowledge of entry of the judgment, but in no event more than five years after such entry, upon a finding of the court that he did not personally receive notice of the summons in time to defend and has a meritorious defense. If the defense is successful, the court may direct and enforce restitution in the same manner and subject to the same conditions as where a judgment is reversed or modified on appeal. This section does not apply to an action for divorce, annulment or partition.

1964 AMENDMENTS

L. 1964, ch. 388, eff. Sept. 1, 1964, substituted "section" in place of "rule" in last sentence.

R 318. Designation of agent for service.

A person may be designated by a natural person, corporation or partnership as an agent for service in a writing, executed and acknowledged in the same manner as a deed, with the consent of the agent endorsed thereon. The writing shall be filed in the office of the clerk of the county in which the principal to be served resides or has its principal office. The designation shall remain in effect for three years from such filing unless it has been revoked by the filing of a revocation, or by the death, judicial declaration of incompetency or legal termination of the agent or principal.

1987 AMENDMENTS

L. 1987, ch. 788, eff. Nov. 5, 1987, and applicable only to designations filed on and after such date, amended CPLR 318 to provide that a writing designating an agent for service be "executed and acknowledged in the same manner as a deed."

§ 319. [Not used.]

R 320. Defendant's appearance.

(a) Requirement of appearance. The defendant appears by serving an answer or a notice of appearance, or by making a motion which has the effect of extending the time to answer. An appearance shall be made within twenty days after service of the summons, except that if the summons was served on the defendant by delivering it to an official of the state authorized to receive service in his behalf or if it was served pursuant to section 303, subdivision two, three, four or five of section 308, or sections 313, 314 or 315, the appearance shall be made within thirty days after service is complete. If the complaint is not served with the summons, the time to appear may be extended as provided in subdivision (b) of section 3012.

(b) When appearance confers personal jurisdiction, generally. Subject to the provisions of subdivision (c), an appearance of the defendant is equivalent to personal service of the summons upon him, unless an objection to jurisdiction under paragraph eight of subdivision (a) of rule 3211 is asserted by motion or in the answer as provided in rule 3211.

(c) When appearance confers personal jurisdiction, in certain actions; limited appearance. When the court's jurisdiction is not based upon personal service on the defendant, an appearance is not equivalent to personal service upon the defendant:

1. in a case specified in subdivision (3) of section 314, if jurisdiction is based solely upon a levy on defendant's property within the state pursuant to an order of attachment; or

2. in any other case specified in section 314 if an objection to jurisdiction under paragraphs eight or nine of subdivision (a) of rule 3211, or both, is asserted by motion or in the answer as provided in rule 3211, unless the defendant proceeds with the defense after asserting the objection to jurisdiction and the objection is not ultimately sustained.

(d) Appearance after first publication. Where the defendant appears during the period of publication of a summons against him, the service by publication shall be deemed completed by the appearance.

1978 AMENDMENTS

L. 1978, ch. 528, eff. Jan. 1, 1979, amended subdivision (a) of CPLR 320 by adding the final sentence making cross-reference to CPLR 3012(b), which, as amended, grants an extension of time to appear to a defendant who makes a timely demand for the complaint. See 1978 amendment note under CPLR 3012, *below,* for detailed Judicial Conference commentary on the amendment.

CPLR

1970 AMENDMENTS

L. 1970, ch. 852, eff. Sept. 1, 1970, amended Subd. (a) by adding reference to CPLR 308(5).

1969 AMENDMENTS

Amendment No. 1 made by Judicial Conference Feb. 1, 1969, Report to the 1969 Legislature, effective Sept. 1, 1969: Subd. (c) amended.

The Judicial Conference Report stated, in part:

". . . subdivision (c) of Rule 320 of the CPLR [is] amended by incorporating therein a provision for a limited appearance in attachment-based cases. The amendment would provide that in cases where jurisdiction is based solely on a levy on defendant's property within the state pursuant to an order of attachment, defendant's appearance is not equivalent to personal service on the defendant. In any other case where the defendant is subject to the court's in rem jurisdiction under CPLR 314, the existing provisions of Rule 320 (c) which prohibit a limited appearance, would remain unchanged. . . .

". . . it should be noted that the proposed amendment of Rule 320 (c) operates automatically. No notice of a limited appearance would be required. The automatic operation of the amendment parallels CPLR 302 (b) [now 302(c)] which, notwithstanding defendant's appearance, automatically restricts a plaintiff to the prosecution of claims covered by the long-arm statute. . . .

"The Committee is fully aware that problems of res judicata (collateral estoppel) are bound to arise as a result of the proposed amendment. It will be the traditional task of the courts to work out these problems on a case by case basis, keeping in mind the general purpose and intent of the proposed amendment."

1965 AMENDMENTS

Amendment No. 2 made by Judicial Conference Feb. 1, 1965, Report to the Legislature, effective Sept. 1, 1965, added the words "as provided in rule 3211" at end of Subd. (b) for the reason: "The present language of subdivision (b) appears to contravene the traditional policy of favoring the disposition of jurisdictional defenses before defenses going to the merits. The consequences may be highly undesirable. The court may be required to determine issues going to the merits, possibly in favor of the plaintiff, even in a case where later jurisdictional objection by the defendant would necessitate dismissal.

"If such later jurisdictional objection were sustained after a ruling on a defense on the merits adverse to the defendant, a serious problem of *res judicata* would be involved in a second action with the same parties based on the same cause. It is far from clear whether or not a re-litigation of the same defense on the merits would be permitted on the ground that the determination thereof in the first action is void because rendered by a court not having jurisdiction.

"A solution to this dilemma is recommended by way of an amendment to 3211(e) [*below*] to which the proposed amendment of 320(b) makes reference and is ancillary."

Amendment No. 3 made by Judicial Conference Feb. 1, 1965, Report to the Legislature, effective Sept. 1, 1965, deleted the words "at the time of appearance" appearing before "by motion or in the answer" and added the words "as provided in rule 3211" after words "by motion or in the answer" in Subd. (c).

See further discussion in 1965 Amendments to Rule 3211, *below.*

1964 AMENDMENTS

Amendment No. 1 made by Judicial Conference Feb. 1, 1964, Report to the Legislature, effective Sept. 1, 1964: Words "at the time of appearance" appearing before "by motion or in the answer" in Subd. (b) deleted for the reason "The requirement that an objection to jurisdiction of the person of the defendant must be asserted 'at the time of appearance' in order to be effective is inconsistent with rule 3211(e) and may prove a trap for the unwary. In order to avoid such an unintended result the proposed change should be made."

§ 321. Attorneys.

(a) Appearance in person or by attorney. A party, other than one specified in section 1201 of this chapter, may prosecute or defend a civil action in person or by attorney, except that a corporation or voluntary association shall appear by attorney, except as otherwise provided in sections 1809 and 1809–A of the New York city civil court act, sections 1809 and 1809–A of the uniform district court act and sections 1809 and 1809–A of the uniform city court act, and except as otherwise provided in section 501 and section 1809 of the uniform justice court act. If a party appears by attorney such party may not act in person in the action except by consent of the court.

(b) Change or withdrawal of attorney.

1. Unless the party is a person specified in section 1201, an attorney of record may be changed by filing with the clerk a consent to the change signed by the retiring attorney and signed and acknowledged by the party. Notice of such change of attorney shall be given to the attorneys for all parties in the action or, if a party appears without an attorney, to the party.

2. An attorney of record may withdraw or be changed by order of the court in which the action is pending, upon motion on such notice to the client of the withdrawing attorney, to the attorneys of all other parties in the action or, if a party appears without an attorney, to the party, and to any other person, as the court may direct.

(c) Death, removal or disability of attorney.   If an attorney dies, becomes physically or mentally incapacitated, or is removed, suspended or otherwise becomes disabled at any time before judgment, no further proceeding shall be taken in the action against the party for whom he appeared, without leave of the court, until thirty days after notice to appoint another attorney has been served upon that party either personally or in such manner as the court directs.

CROSS REFERENCES

New York City Civil Court Act § 1809, referred to in Subd. (a) governing procedures relating to corporations, insurers and assignees in small claims matters, *above,* appears in the Appendix, *below;* § **1809** of **U.D.C.A., U.C.C.A. and U.J.C.A.** is identical to **N.Y.C. Civ. Ct. Act § 1809.** U.J.C.A. § 501, "Appearance by Corporations," was enacted by L. 1987, ch. 653, eff. Jan. 1, 1988.

1991 AMENDMENTS

L. 1991, ch. 236, eff. July 1, 1991, amended subdivision (a) by adding references to sections 1809 and 1809-A of the N.Y.C. Civ. Ct. Act, the U.D.C.A. and the U.C.C.A.

1987 AMENDMENTS

L. 1987, ch. 653, eff. Jan. 1, 1988, amended subdivision (a) to add references to sections 501 and 1809 of the uniform justice court act.

1980 AMENDMENTS

L. 1980, ch. 119, eff. Jan. 1, 1981, amended CPLR 321(b) by adding new paragraph 2 clarifying the procedure for change or withdrawal of an attorney in a pending action and altering the language of paragraph 1 to reflect the change.

In its report to the 1980 Legislature, the Judicial Conference noted that new paragraph 2 ". . . sets forth that the procedure for the change shall be a mere motion, thus clarifying that a special proceeding need not be brought for this purpose. And rather than attempt to set forth whom to notify, the amendment leaves it to the court to determine. It does this by requiring the motion to be 'on such notice to such persons as the court may direct,' i.e., it contemplates the procedure of an order to show cause. This will enable the court to determine, on a case by case basis, who shall be notified, and how. There may be many parties, and the action may have been quiescent for a time. Leaving it to the court to determine whom to notify, and by what method, permits the factors applicable to the individual case to be weighed."

1976 AMENDMENTS

L. 1976, ch. 200, eff. Sept. 1, 1976, amended Subd. (a) of CPLR 321 by eliminating a provision governing appearance of closely held corporations by an officer or shareholder in defense of small claims actions; the act transferred that provision, without change in substance, to § 1809 of the various court acts, with an appropriate cross-reference in CPLR 321 (a).

1975 AMENDMENTS

L. 1975, ch. 176, eff. Sept. 1, 1975, amended Subd. (a) by adding a provision permitting defense of small claims actions by shareholders or officers of certain closely held corporations.

1964 AMENDMENTS

L. 1964, ch. 511, eff. Sept. 1, 1964, added to subdivision (b): "Notice of such change of attorney shall be given to the attorney for all parties in the action or if a party appears without an attorney to the party."

R 322. Authority for appearance of attorney in real property action.

(a) Authority of plaintiff's attorney. Where the defendant in an action affecting real property has not been served with evidence of the authority of the plaintiff's attorney to begin the action, he may move at any time before answering for an order directing the production of such evidence. Any writing by the plaintiff or his agent requesting the attorney to begin the action or ratifying his conduct of the action on behalf of the plaintiff is prima facie evidence of the attorney's authority.

(b) Authority of non-resident defendant's attorney. The attorney for a non-resident defendant in an action affecting real property shall file with the clerk written authority for his appearance, executed and acknowledged in the form required to entitle a deed to be recorded, and shall serve either a copy of such authority or notice of such filing on the plaintiff's attorney within twenty days after appearing or making a motion.

(c) Agencies or wholly-owned corporations of the United States. This rule does not apply to an attorney representing an official, agency or instrumentality of, or corporation wholly owned by, the United States.

§§ 323–324. [Not used.]

§ 325. Grounds for removal.

(a) By supreme court for mistake in choice of the court. Where a mistake was made in the choice of the court in which an action is commenced, the supreme court, upon motion, may remove the action to the proper court, upon such terms as may be just.

(b) From court of limited jurisdiction. Where it appears that the court in which an action is pending does not have jurisdiction to grant the relief to which the parties are entitled, a court having such jurisdiction may remove the action to itself upon motion. A waiver of jury trial in the first court is inoperative after the removal.

(c) On consent to court of limited jurisdiction. Where it appears that the amount of damages sustained are less than demanded, and a lower court would have had jurisdiction of the action but for the amount of damages demanded, the court in which an action is pending may remove it to the lower court upon reduction of the amount of damages demanded to a sum within the jurisdictional limits of the lower court and upon consent of all parties to the action other than a defendant who has interposed no counterclaim and over whom the lower court would have had jurisdiction if the action had originally been commenced there. A waiver of jury trial in the first court is inoperative after the removal.

(d) Without consent to court of limited jurisdiction. The appellate division, if it determines that the calendar conditions in a lower court so permit, may by rule provide that a court in which an action is pending may, in its discretion, remove such action without consent to such lower court where it appears that the amount of damages sustained may be less than demanded, and the lower court would have had jurisdiction but for the amount of damages demanded. If the action is so removed, then the verdict or judgment shall be subject to the limitation of monetary jurisdiction of the court in which the action was originally commenced and shall be lawful to the extent of the amount demanded within such limitation. A waiver of jury trial in the first court is inoperative after the removal.

(e) From supreme court to surrogate's court where decedent's estate affected. Where an action pending in the supreme court affects the administration of a decedent's estate which is within the jurisdiction of the surrogate's court, the supreme court, upon motion, may remove the action to such surrogate's court upon the prior order of the surrogate's court. The right of jury trial shall be preserved in the subsequent proceedings.

(f) To supreme court where county judge incapacitated. Where a county judge is incapable of acting in an action pending in the county court, the supreme court may remove the action to itself. An objection to jurisdiction that might have been taken in the county court may be taken in the supreme court after the removal.

(g) From one local court to another. Where it is unlikely that an action or proceeding pending in a district court, town court, village court or city court will be disposed of within a reasonable period of time because of (i) death, disability or other incapacity or disqualification of all the judges of such court, or (ii) inability of such court to form a jury in such action or proceeding, a judge of the county court of the county in which such lower court is located, may, upon motion of any party to such action or proceeding, order that it be transferred for disposition by the lower court to any other district court, town court, village court or city court in the same or an adjoining county, provided that such other court has jurisdiction of the subject matter of the action or proceeding and jurisdiction over the classes of persons named as parties.

CROSS REFERENCES

See Appendix, *below*, for **Constitutional and Judiciary Law** provisions as to subject matter jurisdiction, generally; note particularly **Section 19** of **Article VI** of the **New York State Constitution** as to transfer of actions and proceedings.

1988 AMENDMENTS

L. 1988, ch. 397, eff. July 1, 1988, added new subdivision (g) permitting removal from one local (*i.e.*, district, town, village, or city) court to another in the same or an adjoining county, when (i) all judges in the transferring court are unavailable, or (ii) a jury cannot be impaneled in the transferring county.

1968 AMENDMENTS

L. 1968, ch. 502, eff. Sept. 1, 1968, added present Subd. (d) and relettered former Subds. (d) and (e) to be Subd. (e) and (f) respectively.

CPLR

1966 AMENDMENTS

L. 1966, ch. 961, amended Subd. (e) by deleting "of the county of Bronx, Kings, Nassau, New York, Queens, Richmond or Westchester" following the phrase "jurisdiction of the surrogate's court" found in the first sentence, effective Sept. 1, 1967, thereby making the provision applicable to all surrogate's courts.

R 326. Procedure on removal.

(a) Stay of proceedings. An order to stay proceedings for the purpose of moving for removal may be made by the court in which the action is pending or the court to which removal is sought.

(b) Order and subsequent proceedings. Where an order of removal is made by a court other than the court in which the action is pending, a certified copy of the order shall be filed with the clerk of the court in which the action is pending. Upon such filing or upon entry of an order of removal by him, the clerk of the court in which an action is pending shall forthwith deliver to the clerk of the court to which it has been ordered removed all papers and records in the action and certified copies of all minutes and entries which shall be filed, entered or recorded, as the case requires, in the office of the latter clerk. Subsequent proceedings shall be had in the court to which it has been ordered removed as if the action had been originally commenced there and no process, provisional remedy or other proceeding taken in the court from which the action was removed shall be invalid as the result of the removal.

(c) Fees and disbursements. If at the time the order of removal is entered any filing, trial, or jury demand fees have been paid, such fees shall be credited against the fees which, for the same purpose, shall be required in the court to which the action has been ordered removed. A party entitled to tax disbursements after the removal may include fees paid by him prior to the time the order of removal is entered.

1964 AMENDMENTS

Amendment No. 2 made by the Judicial Conference Feb. 1, 1964, Report to the Legislature, effective Sept. 1, 1964, rephrased the first sentence of Subd. (c).

R 327. Inconvenient forum.

(a) When the court finds that in the interest of substantial justice the action should be heard in another forum, the court, on the motion of any party, may stay or dismiss the action in whole or in part on any conditions that may be just. The domicile or residence in this state of any party to the action shall not preclude the court from staying or dismissing the action.

(b) Notwithstanding the provisions of subdivision (a) of this rule, the court shall not stay or dismiss any action on the ground of inconvenient forum, where the action arises out of or relates to a contract, agreement or undertaking to which section 5-1402 of the general obligations law applies, and the parties to the contract have agreed that the law of this state shall govern their rights or duties in whole or in part.

CROSS REFERENCES

General Obligations Law § 5-1402, dealing with the enforceability of choice of forum clauses, appears in the Appendix, *below.*

1984 AMENDMENTS

Subdivision (b) was added by L. 1984, ch. 421, eff. July 19, 1984. Subdivision (b) is applicable to contracts entered into after July 19, 1984 and to contracts entered into on or before July 19, 1984 in connection with any action or proceeding commenced on or after that date.

1972 AMENDMENTS

Rule 327 was added to the CPLR by Proposal No. 2 of the Judicial Conference Report to the 1972 Legislature, effective Sept. 1, 1972.

R 328.   Assistance to tribunals and litigants outside the state.

(a) Pursuant to court order.   Upon application by any interested person or in response to letters rogatory issued by a tribunal outside the state, the supreme court or a county court of the state may order service upon any person who is domiciled or can be found within the state of any document issued in connection with a proceeding in a tribunal outside the state. The order shall direct the manner of service.

(b) Without court order.   Service in connection with a proceeding in a tribunal outside the state may be made within the state without an order of court.

(c) Effect.   Service under this rules does not, of itself, require the recognition or enforcement of an order, judgment or decree rendered outside the state.

CROSS REFERENCES

See also **28 U.S.C. § 1696** as to service by order of federal district court of

CPLR

documents issued in connection with proceedings in a foreign country or an international tribunal.

1973 AMENDMENTS

Rule 328 was added to the CPLR by proposal No. 1 of the Judicial Conference Report to the 1973 Legislature, effective Sept. 1, 1973.

The 1973 Judicial Conference Report stated:

"This proposal would adopt section 2.04 of the Uniform Interstate and International Procedure Act as CPLR Rule 328 to provide that the Supreme Court or County Courts could order service of documents originating outside New York State on persons domiciled or found within the state. It would be made clear that this would not prevent such service without court order, and that service made pursuant to the provision would not, without more, entitle out-of-state judgments based on such service to recognition. That the same assistance can be rendered pursuant to 28 U.S.C.A. § 1696 would not render the proposal superfluous, for it would reduce present expense and delay when a foreign request for assistance is addressed to a New York State court.

"Although the cases which have denied such assistance (*In re Letters Rogatory Out of First Civil Court of City of Mexico,* 261 Fed. 652 (S.D.N.Y. 1919); *Matter of Romero,* 56 Misc. 319 (Sup. Ct. N.Y. Co. 1907)) have probably lost whatever authority they once possessed, it is appropriate to dispel any doubt in this regard in view of the increasing importance of interstate and international cooperation in such matters due to the increase of litigation with cosmopolitan aspects."

Article 4

SPECIAL PROCEEDINGS

SUMMARY OF ARTICLE

§ 401. Parties.

The party commencing a special proceeding shall be styled the petitioner and any adverse party the respondent. After a proceeding is commenced, no party shall be joined or interpleaded and no third-party practice or intervention shall be allowed, except by leave of court.

§ 402. Pleadings.

There shall be a petition, which shall comply with the requirements for a complaint in an action, and an answer where there is an adverse party. There shall be a reply to a counterclaim denominated as such and there may be a reply to new matter in the answer in any case. The court may permit such other pleadings as are authorized in an action upon such terms as it may specify. Where there is no adverse party the petition shall state the result of any prior application for similar relief and shall specify the new facts, if any, that were not previously shown.

1965 AMENDMENTS

L. 1965, ch. 773, eff. Sept. 1, 1965, added the words "and shall specify the new facts, if any, that were not previously shown" at the end of the section.

§ 403. Notice of petition; service; order to show cause.

(a) Notice of petition. A notice of petition shall specify the time and place of the hearing on the petition and the supporting affidavits, if any, accompanying the petition.

(b) Time for service of notice of petition and answer. A notice of petition, together with the petition and affidavits specified in the notice, shall be served on any adverse party at least eight days before the time at which the petition is noticed to be heard. An answer and supporting affidavits, if any, shall be served at least two days before such time. A reply, together with supporting affidavits, if any, shall be served at or before such time. An answer shall be served at least seven days before such time if a notice of petition served at least twelve days before such time so demands; whereupon any reply shall be served at least one day before such time.

(c) Manner of service. A notice of petition shall be served in the same manner as a summons in an action.

(d) Order to show cause. The court may grant an order to show cause to be served, in lieu of a notice of petition at a time and in a manner specified therein.

1988 AMENDMENT

L. 1988, ch. 761, eff. Feb. 24, 1989, amended subdivision (b) to increase the time for serving an answer and supporting affidavits from one day to two days, and to increase the time periods contained in the last sentence for service of an answer from five to seven days if a notice of petition served at least twelve days before (formerly ten days) so demands.

§ 404. Objections in point of law.

(a) By respondent. The respondent may raise an objection in point of law by setting it forth in his answer or by a motion to dismiss the petition, made upon notice within the time allowed for answer. If the motion is denied, the court may permit the respondent to answer, upon such terms as may be just; and unless the order specifies otherwise, such answer shall be served and filed within five days after service of the order with notice of entry; and the petitioner may re-notice the matter for hearing upon two days' notice, or the respondent may re-notice the matter for hearing upon service of the answer upon seven days' notice.

(b) By petitioner. The petitioner may raise an objection in point of law to new matter contained in the answer by setting it forth in his reply or by moving to strike such matter on the day the petition is noticed or re-noticed to be heard.

1993 AMENDMENTS

L. 1993, ch. 202, eff. July 6, 1993, amended subdivision (a) by allowing respondents to "re-notice the matter for hearing upon service of the answer upon two days' notice."

§ 405. Correction of defects in papers.

(a) Motion to correct. Either party may move to cure a defect or omission in the record, or to strike scandalous or prejudicial matter unnecessarily inserted in a pleading, or for a more definite statement of a pleading which is so vague or ambiguous that he cannot reasonably be required to frame a response.

(b) Time limits; pleading after disposition. A party shall make a motion under this section by serving a notice of motion or order to show cause within the time allowed for his responsive pleading. Unless the court so orders on motion made without notice on the ground that the party is unable to plead until the papers are corrected, the motion shall not extend the time for such responsive pleading. If the motion is granted, the party who made the motion shall serve and file his responsive pleading within five days after service of the amended pleading. If the motion is denied and the time to serve a responsive pleading has been extended, the party shall serve and file his responsive pleading within two days after service of the order denying the motion with notice of entry, unless the order specifies otherwise. A party may re-notice the matter for hearing upon two days' notice.

(c) Petitioner's motion. The petitioner may raise the objections specified in subdivision (a) in his reply or by motion on the day on which the petition has been noticed or re-noticed to be heard.

R 406. Motions.

Motions in a special proceeding, made before the time at which the petition is noticed to be heard, shall be noticed to be heard at that time.

§ 407. Severance.

The court may at any time order a severance of a particular claim, counterclaim or cross-claim, or as to a particular party, and order that, as to such claim or party, the special proceeding continue as an action or as a separate special proceeding.

§ 408. Disclosure.

Leave of court shall be required for disclosure except for a notice under section 3123. A notice under section 3123 may be served at any time not later than three days before the petition is noticed to be heard and the statement denying or setting forth the reasons for failing to admit or deny shall be served not later than one day before the petition is noticed to be heard, unless the court orders otherwise on motion made without notice. This section shall not be applicable to proceedings in a surrogate's court, nor to proceedings relating to express trusts pursuant to article 77, both of which shall be governed by article 31.

1976 AMENDMENTS

L. 1976, ch. 193, eff. Sept. 1, 1976, amended CPLR 408 to provide that the section shall not apply to proceedings relating to express trusts pursuant to Article 77, and that disclosure in such proceedings shall be governed by the general disclosure provisions of article 31.

CPLR 7701 was amended by the same chapter to provide for examination of trustees in special proceedings relating to express trusts.

Amendment of CPLR 408 and CPLR 7701 was recommended by the Judicial Conference Report to the 1976 Legislature, wherein it stated:

"This bill would conform the practice under the CPLR relating to *inter vivos* trust proceedings to that in Surrogate's Court, thus rectifying a previous legislative oversight.

"At present, by virtue of the general provisions of CPLR 408, a court order is required for disclosure in *inter vivos* trust proceedings, whereas in testamentary trust proceedings, under SCPA 2211, no such order is necessary. SCPA 2211 also provides that in testamentary trust accountings the fiduciary may be examined under oath by any party to the proceeding, either before or after filing objections. There is no comparable provision in Article 77 of the CPLR with respect to *inter vivos* trusts.

"There is no good reason why the procedure in *inter vivos* trust accountings should be different in this respect from testamentary trust accountings. The general provision in CPLR 408, which requires a court order for disclosure in all special proceedings, was originated by the revisers in order to preserve the summary nature of special proceedings. They felt that to allow disclosure on notice before the hearing would almost certainly extend the eight day notice of petition period. However, this general rule should bend to certain exceptions where examination, because of its inherent importance, should be obtainable more conveniently. Such an exception should apply when a fiduciary is making an accounting, so that interested parties may be afforded full protection. This is already the rule in testamentary trust proceedings in Surrogate's Court."

1964 AMENDMENTS

L. 1964, ch. 477, eff. April 10, 1964, added the sentence: "This section shall not be applicable to proceedings in a surrogate's court, which shall be governed by article 31 of this act."

R 409. Hearing.

(a) Furnishing of papers; filing. Upon the hearing, each party shall furnish to the court all papers served by him. The petitioner shall furnish all other papers not already in the possession of the court necessary to the consideration of the questions involved. Where such papers are in the possession of an adverse party, they shall be produced by such party at the hearing on notice served with the petition. The court may require the submission of additional proof. All papers furnished to the court shall be filed unless the court orders otherwise.

(b) Summary determination. The court shall make a summary

determination upon the pleadings, papers and admissions to the extent that no triable issues of fact are raised. The court may make any orders permitted on a motion for summary judgment.

§ 410. Trial.

If triable issues of fact are raised they shall be tried forthwith and the court shall make a final determination thereon. If issues are triable of right by jury, the court shall give the parties an opportunity to demand a jury trial of such issues. Failure to make such demand within the time limited by the court, or, if no such time is limited, before trial begins, shall be deemed a waiver of the right to trial by jury.

R 411. Judgment.

The court shall direct that a judgment be entered determining the rights of the parties to the special proceeding.

Article 5
VENUE

SUMMARY OF ARTICLE

CPLR

§ 501.   Contractual provisions fixing venue.

Subject to the provisions of subdivision two of section 510, written agreement fixing place of trial, made before an action is commenced, shall be enforced upon a motion for change of place of trial.

§ 502.   Conflicting venue provisions.

Where, because of joinder of claims or parties, there is a conflict of provisions under this article, the court, upon motion, shall order as the place of trial one proper under this article as to at least one of the parties or claims.

§ 503.   Venue based on residence.

(a) Generally. Except where otherwise prescribed by law, the place of trial shall be in the county in which one of the parties resided when it was commenced; or, if none of the parties then resided in the state, in any county designated by the plaintiff. A party resident in more than one county shall be deemed a resident of each such county.

(b) Executor, administrator, trustee, committee, conservator, general or testamentary guardian, or receiver. An executor, administrator, trustee, committee, conservator, general or testamentary guardian, or receiver shall be deemed a resident of the county of his appointment as well as the county in which he actually resides.

(c) Corporation. A domestic corporation, or a foreign corporation authorized to transact business in the state, shall be deemed a resident of the county in which its principal office is located; except that such a corporation, if a railroad or other common carrier, shall also be deemed a resident of the county where the cause of the action arose.

(d) Unincorporated association, partnership, or individually-owned business. A president or treasurer of an unincorporated association, suing or being sued on behalf of the association, shall be deemed a resident of any county in which the association has its principal office, as well as the county in which he actually resides. A partnership or an individually-owned business shall be deemed a resident of any county in which it has its principal office, as well as the county in which the partner or individual owner suing or being sued actually resides.

(e) Assignee. In an action for a sum of money only, brought by an assignee other than an assignee for the benefit of creditors or a holder in due course of a negotiable instrument, the assignee's residence shall be deemed the same as that of the original assignor at the time of the original assignment.

(f) Consumer credit transaction. In an action arising out of a consumer credit transaction where a purchaser, borrower or debtor is a defendant, the place of trial shall be the residence of a defendant, if one resides within the state or the county where such transaction took place, if it is within the state, or, in other cases, as set forth in subdivision (a).

1981 AMENDMENTS

L. 1981, ch. 115, eff. May 15, 1981, amended CPLR 503(b) by adding the conservator of a conservatee to those persons whose county of appointment is a basis of venue in addition to the county of their residence.

1973 AMENDMENTS

L. 1973, ch. 238, eff. Sept. 1, 1973, added a new Subd. (f).

1965 AMENDMENTS

L. 1965, ch. 114, eff. Sept. 1, 1965, amended Subd. (e) by inserting the word "original" before the word "assignor" and before the word "assignment" in the last clause.

Amendment recommended by the Judicial Conference Feb. 1, 1965, Report to the Legislature: "This amendment is designed to make it clear that venue rules may not be evaded by the stratagem of consecutive assignments."

§ 504. Actions against counties, cities, towns, villages, school districts and district corporations.

Notwithstanding the provisions of any charter heretofore granted by the state, and subject to the provisions of subdivision (b) of section 506, the place of trial of all actions against counties, cities, towns, villages, school districts and district corporations or any of their officers, boards or departments shall be, for:

    1. a county, in such county;

    2. a city, except the city of New York, town, village, school district

CPLR

or district corporation, in the county in which such city, town, village, school district or district corporation is situated, or if such school district or district corporation is situated in more than one county, in either county; and

3. the city of New York, in the county within the city in which the cause of action arose, or if it arose outside of the city, in the county of New York.

1966 AMENDMENTS

L. 1966, ch. 444, eff. Sept. 1, 1966, added reference to school districts and district corporations.

§ 505.   Actions involving public authorities.

(a) Generally. The place of trial of an action by or against a public authority constituted under the laws of the state shall be in the county in which the authority has its principal office or where it has facilities involved in the action.

(b) Against New York city transit authority. The place of trial of an action against the New York city transit authority shall be in the county within the city of New York in which the cause of action arose, or, if it arose outside of the city, in the county of New York.

§ 506.   Where special proceeding commenced.

(a) Generally. Unless otherwise prescribed in subdivision (b) or in the law authorizing the proceeding, a special proceeding may be commenced in any county within the judicial district where the proceeding is triable.

(b) Proceeding against body or officer. A proceeding against a body or officer shall be commenced in any county within the judicial district where the respondent made the determination complained of or refused to perform the duty specifically enjoined upon him by law, or where the proceedings were brought or taken in the course of which the matter sought to be restrained originated, or where the material events otherwise took place, or where the principal office of the respondent is located, except that

1. a proceeding against a justice of the supreme court or a judge of a county court or the court of general sessions shall be commenced in the appellate division in the judicial department

where the action, in the course of which the matter sought to be enforced or restrained originated, is triable, unless a term of the appellate division in that department is not in session, in which case the proceeding may be commenced in the appellate division in an adjoining judicial department; and

2. a proceeding against the regents of the university of the state of New York, the commissioner of education, the commissioner of taxation and finance, the tax appeals tribunal except as provided in section two thousand sixteen of the tax law, the public service commission, the commissioner or the department of transportation relating to articles three, four, five, six, seven, eight, nine or ten of the transportation law or to the railroad law, the water resources board, the comptroller or the department of agriculture and markets, shall be commenced in the supreme court, Albany county.

3. notwithstanding the provisions of paragraph two of this subdivision, a proceeding against the commissioner of education pursuant to section forty-four hundred four of the education law may be commenced in the supreme court in the county of residence of the petitioner.

4. a proceeding against the New York city tax appeals tribunal established by section one hundred sixty-eight of the New York city charter shall be commenced in the appellate division of the supreme court, first department.

CROSS REFERENCES

Education Law § 4404, referred to in subdivision (b), paragraph 3, *above,* governs the procedure for appealing the decision of a school board's committee on the handicapped regarding the educational placement and plan for a handicapped child.

1992 AMENDMENTS

L. 1992, ch. 47, eff. April 7, 1992, amended Subd. (b)(2) to include the reference to section two thousand sixteen of the tax law, and L. 1992, ch. 808, eff. Oct. 1, 1992, added Subd. (b)(4), providing that a proceeding against the New York City Tax Appeals Tribunal must be commenced in the Appellate Division, First Department.

1988 AMENDMENTS

L. 1988, ch. 41, eff. April 9, 1988, and applicable to all special proceedings commenced on or after April 9, 1988 pursuant to Education Law § 4404.

CPLR

1986 AMENDMENTS

L. 1986, ch. 282, eff. Sept. 1, 1987, amended Subd. (b)(2) to include proceedings against the commissioner of taxation and finance and the tax appeals tribunal. Such amendments are applicable to all proceedings commenced in the division of tax appeals on or after such date and shall apply to all proceedings commenced prior to such date which have not been the subject of a final and irrevocable administrative action as of such effective date, to the extent ch. 282 can be made applicable. Any proceeding for which a hearing has been commenced prior to the effective date shall be subject to automatic review by the tax appeals tribunal which shall render the decision in such proceeding unless there is a prior settlement.

1970 AMENDMENTS

L. 1970, ch. 267, § 8, eff. March 1, 1971, amended Subd. (b)(2) to include a proceeding against the Commissioner of Transportation or the Department of Transportation relating to Articles Three through Ten of the Transportation Law or to the Railroad Law.

§ 507.　Real property actions.

The place of trial of an action in which the judgment demanded would affect the title to, or the possession, use or enjoyment of, real property shall be in the county in which any part of the subject of the action is situated.

§ 508.　Actions to recover a chattel.

The place of trial of an action to recover a chattel may be in the county in which any part of the subject of the action is situated at the time of the commencement of the action.

§ 509.　Venue in county designated.

Notwithstanding any provision of this article, the place of trial of an action shall be in the county designated by the plaintiff, unless the place of trial is changed to another county by order upon motion, or by consent as provided in subdivision (b) of rule 511.

1965 AMENDMENTS

L. 1965, ch. 773, eff. Sept. 1, 1965, added the words "or by consent as provided in subdivision (b) of rule 511" to the end of the section.

§ 510.　Grounds for change of place of trial.

The court, upon motion, may change the place of trial of an action where:

1. the county designated for that purpose is not a proper county; or

2. there is reason to believe that an impartial trial cannot be had in the proper county; or

3. the convenience of material witnesses and the ends of justice will be promoted by the change.

R 511. Change of place of trial.

(a) Time for motion or demand. A demand under subdivision (b) for change of place of trial on the ground that the county designated for that purpose is not a proper county shall be served with the answer or before the answer is served. A motion for change of place of trial on any other ground shall be made within a reasonable time after commencement of the action.

(b) Demand for change of place of trial upon ground of improper venue, where motion made. The defendant shall serve a written demand that the action be tried in a county he specifies as proper. Thereafter the defendant may move to change the place of trial within fifteen days after service of the demand, unless within five days after such service plaintiff serves a written consent to change the place of trial to that specified by the defendant. Defendant may notice such motion to be heard as if the action were pending in the county he specified, unless plaintiff within five days after service of the demand serves an affidavit showing either that the county specified by the defendant is not proper or that the county designated by him is proper.

(c) Stay of proceedings. No order to stay proceedings for the purpose of changing the place of trial shall be granted unless it appears from the papers that the change is sought with due diligence.

(d) Order, subsequent proceedings and appeal. Upon filing of consent by the plaintiff or entry of an order changing the place of trial by the clerk of the county from which it is changed, the clerk shall forthwith deliver to the clerk of the county to which it is changed all papers filed in the action and certified copies of all minutes and entries, which shall be filed, entered or recorded, as the case requires, in the

CPLR

office of the latter clerk. Subsequent proceedings shall be had in the county to which the change is made as if it had been designated originally as the place of trial, except as otherwise directed by the court. An appeal from an order changing the place of trial shall be taken in the department in which the motion for the order was heard and determined.

1965 AMENDMENTS

Amendment No. 4 made by Judicial Conference Feb. 1, 1965, Report to the Legislature, effective Sept. 1, 1965, added the following sentence to the end of paragraph (d): "An appeal from an order changing the place of trial shall be taken in the department in which the motion for the order was heard and determined."

L. 1965, ch. 773, eff. Sept. 1, 1965, added the words "upon ground of improper venue" before the words "where motion is made" in the catch line to Subd. (b).

Amendment recommended by the Judicial Conference Feb. 1, 1965, Report to the Legislature: "Since the demand procedure for change of place of trial is to be used by defendant only where the ground for change is that the county designated is improper, the suggested change in the catch-line of the applicable subdivision, by so specifying, should assist practitioners and help to prevent possible misuse of the demand procedure and its special provisions. Under the demand procedure, if the plaintiff does not consent to defendant's demand to change venue, the defendant may move for such relief in the county specified as proper in the demand unless plaintiff supports his choice by proper affidavit. In contrast, a motion to change venue on other grounds (impartial trial or convenience of material witnesses) must be made in the county designated by the plaintiff or in one of the alternative counties permitted by § 2212(a). The proposed amendment will alert the bar to the limited application of the demand procedure for change of venue."

1964 AMENDMENTS

L. 1964, ch. 388, eff. Sept. 1, 1964, made mechanical corrections in subd. (b).

R 512.　Change of place of trial of action or issue triable without a jury.

The place of trial of an action or any issue triable without a jury may be, in the discretion of the court, in any county within the judicial district in which the action is triable. After the trial, the decision and all other papers relating to the trial shall be filed and the judgment entered in the county where the action is pending.

§ 513.   Misplacement of venue in consumer credit transactions.

(a) In an action arising out of a consumer credit transaction, the clerk shall not accept a summons for filing when it appears upon its face that the proper venue is a county other than the county where such summons is offered for filing.

(b) The clerk shall indicate upon the summons the date of the rejection and shall enter such date in a register maintained by him together with the name of the counties in which the summons may properly be filed.

(c) Notwithstanding subdivisions one and three of section three hundred eight, where a summons has been rejected for filing by virtue of this section, service is complete ten days after such summons is filed in the proper county with proof of service upon the defendant of the summons, together with proof of service upon the defendant by registered or certified mail of a notice setting forth the following:

> 1. the proper county,

> 2. the date of filing of the summons,

> 3. the date within which the answer or notice of appearance is to be filed, and

> 4. the address at which it is to be filed.

1973 AMENDMENTS

L. 1973, ch. 238, eff. Sept. 1, 1973, added new CPLR 513, concerning misplacement of venue in consumer credit transactions.

CPLR

Article 6

JOINDER OF CLAIMS, CONSOLIDATION AND SEVERANCE

§ 601. Joinder of claims.

(a) The plaintiff in a complaint or the defendant in an answer setting forth a counterclaim or cross-claim may join as many claims as he may have against an adverse party. There may be like joinder of claims when there are multiple parties.

(b) Two or more plaintiffs may join no more than five claims in any one action or proceeding against the same defendant arising out of separate consumer credit transactions, provided that the plaintiffs are represented by the same attorney.

1996 AMENDMENTS

L. 1996, ch. 602, eff. Jan. 1, 1997, amended the section by numbering the existing paragraph as (a) and adding a new subdivision (b).

§ 602. Consolidation.

(a) Generally. When actions involving a common question of law or fact are pending before a court, the court, upon motion, may order a joint trial of any or all the matters in issue, may order the actions consolidated, and may make such other orders concerning proceedings therein as may tend to avoid unnecessary costs or delay.

(b) Cases pending in different courts. Where an action is pending in the supreme court it may, upon motion, remove to itself an action pending in another court and consolidate it or have it tried together with that in the supreme court. Where an action is pending in the county court, it may, upon motion, remove to itself an action pending in a city, municipal, district or justice court in the county and consolidate it or have it tried together with that in the county court.

§ 603.   Severance and separate trials.

In furtherance of convenience or to avoid prejudice the court may order a severance of claims, or may order a separate trial of any claim, or of any separate issue. The court may order the trial of any claim or issue prior to the trial of the others.

§ 604.   Change by supreme court of place of trial of action pending in another court.

Upon motion of any party, the supreme court may order that an issue of fact in an action pending in another court, except an action relating to real property pending in a county court, be tried in the supreme court in another county upon such terms as may be just. After the trial, the clerk of the county in which it has taken place shall certify the minutes thereof, which shall be filed with the clerk of the court in which the action is pending. Subsequent proceedings shall be the same as if the issue had been tried in the court in which the action is pending.

Article 9

CLASS ACTIONS

SUMMARY OF ARTICLE

§ 901. Prerequisites to a class action.

a. One or more members of a class may sue or be sued as representative parties on behalf of all if:

1. the class is so numerous that joinder of all members, whether otherwise required or permitted, is impracticable;

2. there are questions of law or fact common to the class which predominate over any questions affecting only individual members;

3. the claims or defenses of the representative parties are typical of the claims or defenses of the class;

4. the representative parties will fairly and adequately protect the interest of the class; and

5. a class action is superior to other available methods for the fair and efficient adjudication of the controversy.

b. Unless a statute creating or imposing a penalty, or a minimum measure or recovery specifically authorizes the recovery thereof in a class action, an action to recover a penalty, or minimum measure of recovery created or imposed by statute may not be maintained as a class action.

CPLR

1975 AMENDMENTS

L. 1975, ch. 207, eff. Sept. 1, 1975, upon the recommendation of the Judicial Conference, added new Article 9 (CPLR 901–909), to govern class actions in lieu of former CPLR 1005.

The 1975 Judicial Conference Report stated, in part:

"The basic changes in New York class action procedure are designed to achieve two major goals:

"1. to set up a flexible, functional scheme whereby class actions could qualify without the present undesirable and socially detrimental restrictions; and

"2. to prescribe basic guidelines for judicial management of class actions.

"The present provision has remained in force without substantial change since the addition of its predecessor to the Field Code (L. 1849, ch. 438). . . . Under the present law, unless the subject matter of the controversy is a limited fund or specific property, or the relief sought is common to the class in the sense that satisfaction of the individual claims before the court also automatically satisfies the claims of all other class members (see 18 N.Y. Jud. Council Rep. 217, 230 (1952)), a class action can qualify only if a bond of 'privity' exists between the multiple parties forming the class. (*Society Milion Athena, Inc. v. National Bank of Greece*, 281 N.Y. 282 (1939)). In the main, class actions in New York are confined to the closely associated relationships growing out of trusts, partnerships, or joint ventures, and ownership of corporate stock. (*Hall v. Coburn Corp. of Amer.*, 26 N.Y. 2d 396, 402 (1970)). . . .

"The basic feature of the proposed bill is the abandonment of the sterile notion of privity which for over 120 years has blocked the effective implementation of the class action device, producing results under which 'class actions were not permitted where they should have been and were allowed where they should not have been.' *see* 2 Weinstein, Korn & Miller, New York Civil Practice - CPLR ¶ 1005.02 (Matthew Bender). For a critical discussion of illustrative cases see 18 Jud. Council Rep. 217 (1952); *see* 2 Weinstein, Korn & Miller, New York Civil Practice - CPLR ¶ 1005.11(Matthew Bender); Homburger, State Class Actions and the Federal Rule (17 Judicial Conference Report (1972), reprinted from 71 Colum. L. Rev. 609, 612–21 (1971)). In place of the amorphous privity concept, the bill would substitute functional criteria which would take into account the practicalities of life and pressing contemporary needs of our society while at the same time assuring adequate judicial control of the remedy. . . .

". . . the proposed bill adopts the general scheme of the Federal Rule, but is simpler in its basic structure and more consistent in its functional orientation. For a detailed explanation of the modifications of the Federal Rule, *see*

Homburger, State Class Actions and the Federal Rule (17 Judicial Conference Report (1972) reprinted from 71 Colum. L. Rev. 609 (1971)). . . .

"Section 901 contains a unitary scheme of prerequisites for all class actions, as opposed to the overlapping and more complex classification scheme of the Federal Rule. The reach of proposed section 901 is co-extensive with Federal Rule 23(a) and (b) (1), (2) and (3). Like the Federal Rule the proposed section states the prerequisites to the class actions in pragmatic and functional terms avoiding any reference to the abstract nature of the substantive rights involved."

§ 902. Order allowing class action.

Within sixty days after the time to serve a responsive pleading has expired for all persons named as defendants in an action brought as a class action, the plaintiff shall move for an order to determine whether it is to be so maintained. An order under this section may be conditional, and may be altered or amended before the decision on the merits on the court's own motion or on motion of the parties. The action may be maintained as a class action only if the court finds that the prerequisites under section 901 have been satisfied. Among the matters which the court shall consider in determining whether the action may proceed as a class action are:

1. the interest of members of the class in individually controlling the prosecution or defense of separate actions;

2. the impracticability or inefficiency of prosecuting or defending separate actions;

3. the extent and nature of any litigation concerning the controversy already commenced by or against members of the class;

4. the desirability or undesirability of concentrating the litigation of the claim in the particular forum;

5. the difficulties likely to be encountered in the management of a class action.

1975 AMENDMENTS

L. 1975, ch. 207, eff. Sept. 1, 1975, upon the recommendation of the Judicial Conference, added new Article 9 (CPLR 901–909), to govern class actions in lieu of former CPLR 1005. See comments to CPLR 901.

The 1975 Judicial Conference Report, covering proposed CPLR 902, modified by the legislature, and further amended by L. 1975, ch. 474, eff. Sept. 1, 1975, stated:

"Proposed section 902 would adopt the federal policy of determining, at least tentatively, the propriety of maintaining a class action in the initial stages of the proceedings. A wide range of discretion would enable the court to vary the order at any time before reaching a decision on the merits. The section lists factors which the court should consider in determining the propriety of maintaining a class action. In contrast to the Federal Rule, these factors would be significant in any class action and the proposed section would expressly include impracticability or inefficiency of prosecuting or defending separate actions among the relevant factors. The list is non-exhaustive. For example, the apparent merits of the claims asserted may have a bearing on the court's determination."

§ 903. Description of class.

The order permitting a class action shall describe the class. When appropriate the court may limit the class to those members who do not request exclusion from the class within a specified time after notice.

1975 AMENDMENTS

L. 1975, ch. 207, eff. Sept. 1, 1975, upon the recommendation of the Judicial Conference, added new Article 9 (CPLR 901–909), to govern class actions in lieu of former CPLR 1005. See comments to CPLR 901.

The 1975 Judicial Conference Report stated:

"In addition to requiring the description of the class by the order permitting the action, the bill would give to the court discretionary power to direct notice to each member that he may request exclusion from the class within a specified time after notification. Presumably the court would exercise its discretion in favor of granting a right to opt-out when representation of the entire class is not needed for a just disposition of the controversy, when the class members have a significant practical interest in individually controlling the litigation, and when individual notice is feasible without imposing a prohibitive economic or administrative burden on the parties."

§ 904. Notice of class action.

(a) In class actions brought primarily for injunctive or declaratory relief, notice of the pendency of the action need not be given to the class unless the court finds that notice is necessary to protect the interests of the represented parties and that the cost of notice will not prevent the action from going forward.

(b) In all other class actions, reasonable notice of the commencement of a class action shall be given to the class in such manner as the court directs.

(c) The content of the notice shall be subject to court approval. In determining the method by which notice is to be given, the court shall consider

i. the cost of giving notice by each method considered

ii. the resources of the parties and

iii. the stake of each represented member of the class, and the likelihood that significant numbers of represented members would desire to exclude themselves from the class or to appear individually, which may be determined, in the court's discretion, by sending notice to a random sample of the class.

(d) i. Preliminary determination of expenses of notification. Unless the court orders otherwise, the plaintiff shall bear the expense of notification. The court may, if justice requires, require that the defendant bear the expense of notification, or may require each of them to bear a part of the expense in proportion to the likelihood that each will prevail upon the merits. The court may hold a preliminary hearing to determine how the costs of notice should be apportioned.

ii. Final determination. Upon termination of the action by order or judgment, the court may, but shall not be required to, allow to the prevailing party the expenses of notification as taxable disbursements under article eighty-three of the civil practice law and rules.

1975 AMENDMENTS

L. 1975, ch. 207, eff. Sept. 1, 1975, upon the recommendation of the Judicial Conference, added new Article 9 (CPLR 901–909), to govern class actions in lieu of former CPLR 1005. See comments to CPLR 901.

The 1975 Judicial Conference Report, covering proposed CPLR 904, substantially expanded by the legislature, stated, in part:

". . . The flexible scheme, proposed in the bill, requires notice in such manner as the court directs, subject however to the court's power to dispense with notice in appropriate cases. The court should grant dispensation sparingly, as, for example, in cases where notice would be burdensome and costly, the interests of the individual member of the class in controlling the litigation minimal, and effective representation of the class interests attainable without notification.

"The bill would round out the notice provisions by allocating the financial and mechanical burden of notification to the plaintiff unless the court orders otherwise, a provision not contained in the federal counterpart. A reallocation of that burden may be appropriate, depending on the relative strength of two competing policies, as viewed in the light of the circumstances of a particular case: protection of the opponent of the class from harassment on the one hand, and the accessibility of the courts to claimants seeking a determination of the merits of the controversy on the other. A flexible rule giving the court a wide range of discretion is needed. Factors bearing on the exercise of the court's discretion include the meritoriousness of the claims asserted on behalf of the class, the financial status of the representative of the class and their opponent, the interest of the latter in obtaining a binding adjudication, and the availability of inexpensive notification facilities to the opponent of the class. . . .

"Finally, the bill contains express provision, also not contained in the Federal Rule, requiring court approval of the content of the notice in order to forestall the transmittal of improper or misleading information to the class member-ship."

§ 905. Judgment.

The judgment in an action maintained as a class action, whether or not favorable to the class, shall include and describe those whom the court finds to be members of the class.

1975 AMENDMENTS

L. 1975, ch. 207, eff. Sept. 1, 1975, upon the recommendation of the Judicial Conference, added new Article 9 (CPLR 901–909), to govern class actions in lieu of former CPLR 1005. See comments to CPLR 901.

The 1975 Judicial Conference Report stated:

"As under the Federal Rule, the judgment under the proposed section would embrace the entire class whether or not it is favorable to the class. The binding effect on a nonappearing member of the class could of course be determined only in a subsequent action to which such member is a party."

§ 906. Actions conducted partially as class actions.

When appropriate,

1. an action may be brought or maintained as a class action with respect to particular issues, or

2. a class may be divided into subclasses and each subclass treated as a class.

The provisions of this article shall then be construed and applied accordingly.

1975 AMENDMENTS

L. 1975, ch. 207, eff. Sept. 1, 1975, upon the recommendation of the Judicial Conference, added new Article 9 (CPLR 901–909), to govern class actions in lieu of former CPLR 1005. See comments to CPLR 901.

The 1975 Judicial Conference Report stated:

"Following the lead of the Federal Rule, the proposed section expressly authorizes class treatment with respect to particular issues and the formation of subclasses."

R 907.   Orders in conduct of class actions.

In the conduct of class actions the court may make appropriate orders:

1. determining the course of proceedings or prescribing measures to prevent undue repetition or complication in the presentation of evidence or argument;

2. requiring, for the protection of the members of the class, or otherwise for the fair conduct of the action, that notice be given in such manner as the court may direct to some or all of the members of any step in the action, or of the proposed extent of the judgment, or of the opportunity of members to signify whether they consider the representation fair and adequate, or to appear and present claims or defenses, or otherwise to come into the action;

3. imposing conditions on the representative parties or on intervenors;

4. requiring that the pleadings be amended to eliminate therefrom allegations as to representation of absent persons, and that the action proceed accordingly;

5. directing that a money judgment favorable to the class be paid either in one sum, whether forthwith or within such period as the court may fix, or in such installments as the court may specify;

6. dealing with similar procedural matters.

The orders may be altered or amended as may be desirable from time to time.

1975 AMENDMENTS

L. 1975, ch. 207, eff. Sept. 1, 1975, upon the recommendation of the Judicial

Conference, added new Article 9 (CPLR 901–909), to govern class actions in lieu of former CPLR 1005. See comments to CPLR 901.

The 1975 Judicial Conference Report stated:

"The proposed rule like the Federal Rule would provide important guidelines that assist the court in the management of the action. Deviating from the Federal Rule, proposed rule 907 authorizes the court in the exercise of its discretion to determine whether represented parties may enter an appearance without first seeking permission to intervene, and to tailor the effect of an appearance to the exigencies of the particular case. There is also a special provision, not found in the federal rule, which would allow the court to set terms for payment of a judgment to a victorious class in accordance with the financial capacity of the defendant so as to avoid harsh economic and social consequences such as loss of employment. The desirability of this change is self-evident."

R 908. Dismissal, discontinuance or compromise.

A class action shall not be dismissed, discontinued, or compromised without the approval of the court. Notice of the proposed dismissal, discontinuance, or compromise shall be given to all members of the class in such manner as the court directs.

1975 AMENDMENTS

L. 1975, ch. 207, eff. Sept. 1, 1975, upon the recommendation of the Judicial Conference, added new Article 9 (CPLR 901–909), to govern class actions in lieu of former CPLR 1005. See comments to CPLR 901.

The Judicial Conference Report stated:

"The proposed provision is stricter than the present law. In addition to court approval, it requires in all cases notice to the members of the class in such manner as the court directs."

R 909. Attorneys' fees.

If a judgment in an action maintained as a class action is rendered in favor of the class, the court in its discretion may award attorneys' fees to the representatives of the class based on the reasonable value of legal services rendered and if justice requires, allow recovery of the amount awarded from the opponent of the class.

1975 AMENDMENTS

L. 1975, ch. 207, eff. Sept. 1, 1975, upon the recommendation of the Judicial Conference, added new Article 9 (CPLR 901–909), to govern class actions in lieu of former CPLR 1005. See comments to CPLR 901.

CPLR 909 was not among the eight proposals of the Judicial Conference for class actions. It was added by the legislature to new Article 9.

CPLR

Article 10
PARTIES GENERALLY

SUMMARY OF ARTICLE

CPLR

§ 1001.   Necessary joinder of parties.

(a) Parties who should be joined. Persons who ought to be parties if complete relief is to be accorded between the persons who are parties to the action or who might be inequitably affected by a judgment in the action shall be made plaintiffs or defendants. When a person who should join as a plaintiff refuses to do so, he may be made a defendant.

(b) When joinder excused. When a person who should be joined under subdivision (a) has not been made a party and is subject to the jurisdiction of the court, the court shall order him summoned. If jurisdiction over him can be obtained only by his consent or appearance, the court, when justice requires, may allow the action to proceed without his being made a party. In determining whether to allow the action to proceed, the court shall consider:

1. whether the plaintiff has another effective remedy in case the action is dismissed on account of the nonjoinder;

2. the prejudice which may accrue from the nonjoinder to the defendant or to the person not joined;

3. whether and by whom prejudice might have been avoided or may in the future be avoided;

4. the feasibility of a protective provision by order of the court or in the judgment; and

5. whether an effective judgment may be rendered in the absence of the person who is not joined.

§ 1002. Permissive joinder of parties.

(a) Plaintiffs. Persons who assert any right to relief jointly, severally, or in the alternative arising out of the same transaction, occurrence, or series of transactions or occurrences, may join in one action as plaintiffs if any common question of law or fact would arise.

(b) Defendants. Persons against whom there is asserted any right to relief jointly, severally, or in the alternative, arising out of the same transaction, occurrence, or series of transactions or occurrences, may be joined in one action as defendants if any common question of law or fact would arise.

(c) Separate relief; separate trials. It shall not be necessary that each plaintiff be interested in obtaining, or each defendant be interested in defending against, all the relief demanded or as to every claim included in an action; but the court may make such orders as will prevent a party from being embarrassed, delayed, or put to expense by the inclusion of a party against whom he asserts no claim and, who asserts no claim against him, and may order separate trials or make other orders to prevent prejudice.

§ 1003. Nonjoinder and misjoinder of parties.

Nonjoinder of a party who should be joined under section 1001 is a ground for dismissal of an action without prejudice unless the court allows the action to proceed without that party under the provisions of that section. Misjoinder of parties is not a ground for dismissal of an action. Parties may be added at any stage of the action by leave of court or by stipulation of all parties who have appeared, or once without

CPLR

leave of court within twenty days after service of the original summons or at anytime before the period for responding to that summons expires or within twenty days after service of a pleading responding to it. Parties may be dropped by the court, on motion of any party or on its own initiative, at any stage of the action and upon such terms as may be just. The court may order any claim against a party severed and proceeded with separately.

1996 AMENDMENTS

L. 1996, ch. 39, eff. April 2, 1996, amended the section to add a new third sentence, beginning with the words, "Parties may be added," and ending with "pleading responding to it" and made the section gender neutral.

1964 AMENDMENTS

L. 1964, ch. 388, eff. Sept. 1, 1964, amended first sentence at the end thereof to change "rule" to "section."

§ 1004. When joinder unnecessary.

Except where otherwise prescribed by order of the court, an executor, administrator, guardian of the property of an infant, committee of the property of a judicially declared incompetent, conservator of the property of a conservatee, trustee of an express trust, insured person who has executed to his insurer either a loan or subrogation receipt, trust agreement or other similar agreement, or person with whom or in whose name a contract has been made for the benefit of another, may sue or be sued without joining with him the person for or against whose interest the action is brought.

1981 AMENDMENTS

L. 1981, ch. 115, eff. May 18, 1981, amended CPLR 1004 by adding the conservator of a conservatee's property as one who may sue or be sued without joining with him the person for or against whom the action is brought.

§ 1005. [Repealed].

§ 1006. Interpleader.

(a) Stakeholder; claimant; action of interpleader. A stakeholder is a person who is or may be exposed to multiple liability as the result of adverse claims. A claimant is a person who has made or may be expected to make such a claim. A stakeholder may commence an action of interpleader against two or more claimants.

(b) Defensive interpleader. A defendant stakeholder may bring in a claimant who is not a party by filing a summons and interpleader complaint. Service of process upon such a claimant shall be by serving upon such claimant a summons and interpleader complaint and all prior pleadings served in the action.

(c) Effect of pendency of another action against stakeholder. If a stakeholder seeks to bring in a claimant pursuant to subdivision (b) and there is pending in a court of the state an action between the claimant and the stakeholder based upon the same claim, the appropriate court, on motion, upon such terms as may be just, may dismiss the interpleader complaint and order consolidation or joint trial of the actions, or may make the claimant a party and stay the pending action until final disposition of the action in which interpleader is so granted, and may make such further order as may be just.

(d) Abolition of former grounds for objection. It is not ground for objection to interpleader that the claims of the several claimants or the titles on which their claims depend do not have a common origin or are not identical but are adverse to and independent of one another, or that the stakeholder avers that he is not liable in whole or in part to any or all of the claimants.

(e) Issue of independent liability. Where the issue of an independent liability of the stakeholder to a claimant is raised by the pleadings or upon motion, the court may dismiss the claim of the appropriate claimant, order severance or separate trials, or require the issue to be tried in the action.

(f) Discharge of stakeholder. After the time for all parties to plead has expired, the stakeholder may move for an order discharging him from liability in whole or in part to any party. The stakeholder shall submit proof by affidavit or otherwise of the allegations in his pleading. The court may grant the motion and require payment into court, delivery to a person designated by the court or retention to the credit of the action, of the subject matter of the action to be disposed of in accordance with further order or the judgment. An order under subdivision (g) shall not discharge the stakeholder from liability to any claimant until an order granted under this subdivision is complied with.

CPLR

The court shall impose such terms relating to payment of expenses, costs and disbursements as may be just and which may be charged against the subject matter of the action. If the court shall determine that a party is entitled to interest, in the absence of an agreement by the stakeholder as to the rate of interest, he shall be liable to such party for interest to the date of discharge at a rate no greater than the lowest discount rate of the Federal Reserve Bank of New York for discounts for, and advances to, member banks in effect from time to time during the period for which, as found by the court, interest should be paid.

(g) Deposit of money as basis for jurisdiction. Where a stakeholder is otherwise entitled to proceed under this section for the determination of a right to, interest in or lien upon a sum of money, whether or not liquidated in amount, payable in the state pursuant to a contract or claimed as damages for unlawful retention of specific real or personal property in the state, he may move, either before or after an action has been commenced against him, for an order permitting him to pay the sum of money or part of it into court or to a designated person or to retain it to the credit of the action. Upon compliance with a court order permitting such deposit or retention, the sum of money shall be deemed specific property within the state within the meaning of paragraph two of section 314.

1994 AMENDMENTS

L. 1994, ch. 563, eff. July 26, 1994, amended CPLR 1006(b) by adding the words "filing a summons and interpleader complaint. Service of process upon such a claimant shall be made by."

§ 1007.   When third-party practice allowed.

After the service of his answer, a defendant may proceed against a person not a party who is or may be liable to that defendant for all or part of the plaintiff's claim against that defendant, by filing pursuant to section three hundred four of this chapter a third-party summons and complaint with the clerk of the court in the county in which the main action is pending, for which a separate index number shall not be issued but a separate index number fee shall be collected. The third-party summons and complaint and all prior pleadings served in the action shall be served upon such person within one hundred twenty days of the filing. A defendant serving a third-party complaint shall be styled a third-party plaintiff and the person so served shall be styled a third-party defendant. The defendant shall also serve a copy of such third-party complaint upon the plaintiff's attorney simultaneously upon issuance for service of the third-party complaint on the third-party defendant.

1992 AMENDMENTS

L. 1992, ch. 216, eff. July 1, 1992, amended CPLR 1007 by deleting from the first sentence the words "serving upon such person a summons and third-party complaint and all prior pleadings served in the action" and by replacing them with the clause that begins with the words "filing pursuant to"; by adding the second sentence; and by making the language gender neutral.

1984 AMENDMENTS

L. 1984, ch. 329, eff. Jan. 1, 1985, amended CPLR 1007 by specifying that the third-party complaint shall be served upon plaintiff's attorney simultaneously with service on the third-party defendant.

§ 1008. Answer of third-party defendant; defenses.

The third-party defendant shall answer the claim asserted against him by serving copies of his answer upon the third-party plaintiff. The third-party defendant may assert against the plaintiff in his answer any defenses which the third-party plaintiff has to the plaintiff's claim. The third-party defendant shall have the rights of a party adverse to the other parties in the action, including the right to counter-claim, cross-claim and appeal.

R 1009. Claim by plaintiff against third-party defendant.

Within twenty days after service of the answer to the third-party complaint upon plaintiff's attorney, the plaintiff may amend his complaint without leave of court to assert against the third-party defendant any claim plaintiff has against the third-party defendant.

1984 AMENDMENTS

L. 1984, ch. 329, eff. Jan. 1, 1985, amended CPLR 1009.

1972 AMENDMENTS

Proposal No. 3 of the Judicial Conference Report to the 1972 Legislature amended CPLR 1009, effective Sept. 1, 1972, ". . . to allow plaintiff to assert any claim he has against the third-party defendant. [Previously, the rule restricted] the plaintiff to any claim he might have asserted if the third-party defendant had been joined originally as a defendant."

R 1010. Dismissal or separate trial of third-party complaint.

The court may dismiss a third-party complaint without prejudice, order a separate trial of the third-party claim or of any separate issue thereof, or make such other order as may be just. In exercising its discretion, the court shall consider whether the controversy between the third-party plaintiff and the third-party defendant will unduly delay the determination of the main action or prejudice the substantial rights of any party.

R 1011. Successive third-party proceedings; counterclaims.

A third-party defendant may proceed pursuant to section 1007 against any person who is or may be liable to him for all or part of the third-party claim. When a counterclaim is asserted against a plaintiff, he may proceed pursuant to section 1007 as if he were a defendant.

§ 1012. Intervention as of right; notice to attorney-general, city, county, town or village where constitutionality in issue.

(a) Intervention as of right. Upon timely motion, any person shall be permitted to intervene in any action:

    1. when a statute of the state confers an absolute right to intervene; or

    2. when the representation of the person's interest by the parties is or may be inadequate and the person is or may be bound by the judgment; or

    3. when the action involves the disposition or distribution of, or the title or a claim for damages for injury to, property and the person may be affected adversely by the judgment.

(b) Notice to attorney-general, city, county, town or village where constitutionality in issue.

    1. When the constitutionality of a statute of the state, or a rule and regulation adopted pursuant thereto is involved in an action to which the state is not a party, the attorney-general, shall be notified and permitted to intervene in support of its constitutionality.

2. When the constitutionality of a local law, ordinance, rule or regulation of a city, county, town or village is involved in an action to which the city, county, town or village that enacted the provision is not a party, such city, county, town or village shall be notified and permitted to intervene in support of its constitutionality.

3. The court having jurisdiction in an action or proceeding in which the constitutionality of a state statute, local law, ordinance, rule or regulation is challenged shall not consider any challenge to the constitutionality of such state statute, local law, ordinance, rule or regulation unless proof of service of the notice required by this subdivision is filed with such court.

(c) Notice to comptroller of the state of New York where public retirement benefits are in issue. Where public retirement benefits, paid, payable, claimed, or sought to be paid by a state retirement system or any other retirement system established for public employees within this state or any subdivision thereof, or the interpretation of any provisions of law or rules governing any such retirement system or the operation thereof, are involved in an action to which the comptroller of the state of New York is not a party, the court shall notify said comptroller, who shall be permitted, in his discretion, to intervene in such action or to file a brief amicus curiae.

2003 AMENDMENTS

L. 2003, ch. 296, § 7, eff. Jan. 1, 2005, amending section title and subd. (b).

1972 AMENDMENTS

L. 1972, ch. 360, eff. Sept. 1, 1972, added Subd. (c).

§ 1013. Intervention by permission.

Upon timely motion, any person may be permitted to intervene in any action when a statute of the state confers a right to intervene in the discretion of the court, or when the person's claim or defense and the main action have a common question of law or fact. In exercising its discretion, the court shall consider whether the intervention will unduly delay the determination of the action or prejudice the substantial rights of any party.

§ 1014. Proposed intervention pleading.

A motion to intervene shall be accompanied by a proposed pleading setting forth the claim or defense for which intervention is sought.

§ 1015. Substitution upon death.

(a) Generally. If a party dies and the claim for or against him is not thereby extinguished the court shall order substitution of the proper parties.

(b) Devolution of rights or liabilities on other parties. Upon the death of one or more of the plaintiffs or defendants in an action in which the right sought to be enforced survives only to the surviving plaintiffs or against the surviving defendants, the action does not abate. The death shall be noted on the record and the action shall proceed.

§ 1016. Substitution of committee or conservator.

If a party is adjudicated incompetent or a conservator has been appointed, the court shall order substitution of his committee or conservator.

1981 AMENDMENTS

L. 1981, ch. 115, eff. May 18, 1981, amended CPLR 1016 by rewording the title and text to designate an incompetent's committee and a conservatee's conservator as the persons to be substituted in their respective places.

§ 1017. Substitution in case of receivership or dissolution of a corporation.

If a receiver is appointed for a party, or a corporate party is dissolved, the court shall order substitution of the proper parties.

§ 1018. Substitution upon transfer of interest.

Upon any transfer of interest, the action may be continued by or against the original parties unless the court directs the person to whom the interest is transferred to be substituted or joined in the action.

§ 1019. Substitution of public officers.

If a person made a party in his capacity as public officer dies or otherwise ceases to hold office, the action may be continued by or against his successor if it is shown to the court that there is need for so continuing it. Before a substitution is made his successor and, unless the court otherwise orders, the party shall be given reasonable notice of the motion and accorded an opportunity to object. When, in accordance with section 1023, an officer is described by his official title and his name is not added, no substitution is necessary.

§ 1020. Substitution of indemnitors for executing or attaching officer.

Where an action is brought against an officer to recover a chattel levied upon by virtue of an execution or order of attachment, or to recover damages for the detention or sale of such a chattel, and an undertaking indemnifying the officer against such acts has been given, the court may order that the indemnitor be substituted for the officer.

§ 1021. Substitution procedure; dismissal for failure to substitute; presentation of appeal.

A motion for substitution may be made by the successors or representatives of a party or by any party. If a person who should be substituted does not appear voluntarily he may be made a party defendant. If the event requiring substitution occurs before final judgment and substitution is not made within a reasonable time, the action may be dismissed as to the party for whom substitution should have been made, however, such dismissal shall not be on the merits unless the court shall so indicate. If the event requiring substitution occurs after final judgment, substitution may be made in either the court from or to which an appeal could be or is taken, or the court of original instance, and if substitution is not made within four months after the event requiring substitution, the court to which the appeal is or could be taken may dismiss the appeal, impose conditions or prevent it from being taken. Whether or not it occurs before or after final judgment, if the event requiring substitution is the death of a party, and timely substitution has not been made, the court, before proceeding further, shall, on such notice as it may in its discretion direct, order the persons interested in the decedent's estate to show cause why the action or appeal should not be dismissed.

1975 AMENDMENTS

L. 1975, ch. 25, eff. March 25, 1975, amended the third sentence of the section by adding thereto: "however, such dismissal shall not be on the merits unless the court shall so indicate."

1970 AMENDMENTS

L. 1970, ch. 93, eff. Sept. 1, 1970, amended the section by adding thereto, "Whether or not it occurs before or after final judgment, if the event requiring substitution is the death of a party, and timely substitution has not been made, the court, before proceeding further, shall, on such notice as it may in its discretion direct, order the persons interested in the decedent's estate to show cause why the action or appeal should not be dismissed."

The amendment was recommended by the Judicial Conference Jan. 2, 1970, Report to the Legislature, wherein it was stated, in part:

"At present, CPLR 1021 allows the court to dismiss an action or appeal for unreasonable failure to substitute parties. Where the event requiring substitution is the death of a party, this provision conflicts with CPLR 5016 (d), which provides that no verdict or decision shall be rendered against a deceased party.

"Under this amendment, the court will be able to dispose of the matter in one proceeding, rather than denying the motion to dismiss without prejudice to renewal after appointment of a representative. . . ." (See § 5016(d).)

§ 1022. Substitution: extension of time for taking procedural steps.

Unless the court orders otherwise, if the time for making a motion for a new trial or for taking an appeal or for making a motion for permission to appeal or for taking any other procedural step in the action has not expired before the occurrence of an event permitting substitution of a party, the period is extended as to all parties until fifteen days after substitution is made, or, in case of dismissal of the action under section 1021, is extended as to all parties until fifteen days after such dismissal.

§ 1023. Public body or officer described by official title.

When a public officer, body, board, commission or other public agency may sue or be sued in its official capacity, it may be designated by its official title, subject to the power of the court to require names to be added.

§ 1024. Unknown parties.

A party who is ignorant, in whole or in part, of the name or identity of a person who may properly be made a party, may proceed against such person as an unknown party by designating so much of his name and identity as is known. If the name or remainder of the name becomes known all subsequent proceedings shall be taken under the true name and all prior proceedings shall be deemed amended accordingly.

§ 1025. Partnerships and unincorporated associations.

Two or more persons conducting a business as a partnership may sue or be sued in the partnership name, and actions may be brought by or against the president or treasurer of an unincorporated association on behalf of the association in accordance with the provisions of the general associations law.

§ 1026. Review of determinations by administrative officers of the unified court system.

In any action or proceeding brought to review a determination of the chief judge of the court of appeals, of the court of appeals or of the administrative board of the courts, made pursuant to the provisions of article seven-A of the judiciary law or section twenty-eight of article six of the constitution, the only proper party to be named therein shall be the chief administrator of the courts, in his representative capacity. No action or proceeding so instituted shall name the chief judge, the court of appeals or any member thereof, or the administrative board or any member thereof as a party.

CPLR

CROSS REFERENCES

Article 7-A of the Judiciary Law, enacted by L. 1978, ch. 156, eff. May 19, 1978, provides for administration of the unified court system. **N.Y. Const. Art. 6, § 28** appears in the Appendix, *below.*

1978 AMENDMENTS

L. 1978, ch. 156, eff. May 19, 1978, added § 1026.

Article 11

POOR PERSONS

SUMMARY OF ARTICLE

§ 1101. Motion for permission to proceed as a poor person; affidavit; certificate; notice; waiver of fee; when motion not required.

(a) Motion; affidavit. Upon motion of any person, the court in which an action is triable, or to which an appeal has been or will be taken, may grant permission to proceed as a poor person. Where a motion for leave to appeal as a poor person is brought to the court in which an appeal has been or will be taken, such court shall hear such motion on the merits and shall not remand such motion to the trial court for consideration. The moving party shall file an affidavit setting forth the amount and sources of his or her income and listing his or her property with its value; that he or she is unable to pay the costs, fees and expenses necessary to prosecute or defend the action or to maintain or respond to the appeal; the nature of the action; sufficient facts so that the merit of the contentions can be ascertained; and whether any other person is beneficially interested in any recovery sought and, if so, whether every such person is unable to pay such costs, fees and expenses. An executor, administrator or other representative may move for permission on behalf of a deceased, infant or incompetent poor person.

(b) Certificate. The court may require the moving party to file with the affidavit a certificate of an attorney stating that the attorney has examined the action and believes there is merit to the moving party's contentions.

(c) Notice. Except as provided in subdivisions (d) and (e) of this section, if an action has already been commenced, notice of the motion shall be served on all parties, and notice shall also be given to the county attorney in the county in which the action is triable or the corporation counsel if the action is triable in the city of New York.

(d) Waiver of fee in certain cases. [*Expires Sept. 1, 2011*] Except as otherwise provided in subdivision (f) of this section, if applicable, a plaintiff may seek to commence his or her action without payment of the fee required by filing the form affidavit, attesting that such plaintiff is unable to pay the costs, fees and expenses necessary to prosecute or defend the action, which shall be available in the clerk's office along with the summons and complaint or summons with notice or third-party summons and complaint. The case will be given an index number, or, in courts other than the supreme or county courts, any necessary filing number and the application will be submitted to a judge of the court. If the court approves the application, the plaintiff will by written order be given notice that all fees and costs relating to the filing and service shall be waived. If the court denies the application the plaintiff will by written order be given notice that the case will be dismissed if the fee is not paid within one hundred twenty days of the date of the order.

(e) When motion not required. Where a party is represented in a civil action by a legal aid society or a legal services or other nonprofit organization, which has as its primary purpose the furnishing of legal services to indigent persons, or by private counsel working on behalf of or under the auspices of such society or organization, all fees and costs relating to the filing and service shall be waived without the necessity of a motion and the case shall be given an index number, or, in a court other than the supreme or county court, an appropriate filing number, provided that a determination has been made by such society, organization or attorney that such party is unable to pay the costs, fees and expenses necessary to prosecute or defend the action, and that an attorney's certification that such determination has been made is filed with the clerk of the court along with the summons and complaint or summons with notice or third-party summons and complaint or otherwise provided to the clerk of the court. Where an attorney certifies, pursuant to section eleven hundred eighteen of the family court act, and in accordance with procedures of the appropriate appellate division, that a party or child who is the subject of an appeal has been represented in the family court by assigned counsel or a law guardian or by a legal aid society or a legal services or other nonprofit organization, which has as its primary purpose the furnishing of legal services to indigent persons, or by private counsel working on behalf of or under the auspices of such society or organization, and, in the case of a counsel assigned to an adult party, that the party continues to be indigent, the party or child shall be presumed eligible for poor person relief pursuant to this section.

(f) Fees for inmates. [*Expires Sept. 1, 2011*]

1. Notwithstanding any other provision of law to the contrary, a federal, state or local inmate under sentence for conviction of a crime may seek to commence his or her action or proceeding by paying a reduced filing fee as provided in paragraph two of this subdivision. Such inmate shall file the form affidavit referred to in subdivision (d) of this section along with the summons and complaint or summons with notice or third-party summons and complaint or petition or notice of petition or order to show cause. As part of such application, the inmate shall indicate the name and mailing address of the facility at which he or she is confined along with the name and mailing address of any other federal, state or local facility at which he or she was confined during the preceding six month period. The case will be given an index number if applicable, or, in courts other than the supreme or county courts, any necessary filing number and the application will be submitted to a judge of the court. Upon receipt of the application, the court shall obtain from the

CPLR

appropriate official of the facility at which the inmate is confined a certified copy of the inmate's trust fund account statement (or institutional equivalent) for the six month period preceding filing of the inmate's application. If the inmate has been confined for less than six months at such facility, the court shall obtain additional information as follows:

(i) in the case of a state inmate who has been transferred from another state correctional facility, the court shall obtain a trust fund account statement for the six month period from the central office of the department of correctional services in Albany; or

(ii) in the case of a state inmate who is newly transferred from a federal or local correctional facility, the court shall obtain any trust fund account statement currently available from such facility. The court may, in its discretion, seek further information from the prior or current facility.

2. If the court determines that the inmate has insufficient means to pay the full filing fee, the court may permit the inmate to pay a reduced filing fee, the minimum of which shall not be less than fifteen dollars and the maximum of which shall not be more than fifty dollars. The court shall require an initial payment of such portion of the reduced filing fee as the inmate can reasonably afford or shall authorize no initial payment of the fee if exceptional circumstances render the inmate unable to pay any fee; provided however, that the difference between the amount of the reduced filing fee and the amount paid by the inmate in the initial partial payment shall be assessed against the inmate as an outstanding obligation to be collected either by the superintendent or the municipal official of the facility at which the inmate is confined, as the case may be, in the same manner that mandatory surcharges are collected as provided for in subdivision five of section 60.35 of the penal law. The court shall notify the superintendent or the municipal official of the facility where the inmate is housed of the amount of the reduced filing fee that was not directed to be paid by the inmate. Thereafter, the superintendent or the municipal official shall forward to the court any fee obligations that have been collected, provided however, that:

(i) in no event shall the filing fee collected exceed the amount of fees required for the commencement of an action or proceeding; and

(ii) in no event shall an inmate be prohibited from proceeding for the reason that the inmate has no assets and no means by which to pay the initial partial filing fee.

3. The institution at which an inmate is confined, or the central office for the department of correctional services, whichever is applicable, shall promptly provide the trust fund account statement to the inmate as required by this subdivision.

4. Whenever any federal, state or local inmate obtains a judgment in connection with any action or proceeding which exceeds the amount of the filing fee, paid in accordance with the provisions of this subdivision for commencing such action or proceeding, the court shall award to the prevailing inmate, as a taxable disbursement, the actual amount of any fee paid to commence the action or proceeding.

5. The provisions of this subdivision shall not apply to a proceeding commenced pursuant to article seventy-eight of this chapter which alleges a failure to correctly award or certify jail time credit due an inmate, in violation of section six hundred-a of the correction law and section 70.30 of the penal law.

2009 AMENDMENTS

L. 2009, ch. 56 (Part U), eff. April 7, 2009, extended the expiration dates of subd. (d) and (f) to Sept. 1, 2011.

2007 AMENDMENTS

L. 2007, ch. 56 § 18 (Part C), eff. March 31, 2007, extended the expiration dates of subd. (d) and (f) to Sept. 1, 2009.

2005 AMENDMENTS

L. 2005, ch. 3, (Part A), eff. December 21, 2005, amended subd. (e). L. 2005, ch. 56 § 18 (Part D), eff. December 21, 2005, extended the expiration dates of subd. (d) and (f) to Sept. 1, 2007.

2003 AMENDMENTS

L. 2003, ch. 16, § 20, eff. March 31, 2003, amended the expiration date of subd. (d) and (f) to Sept. 1, 2005.

2002 AMENDMENTS

L. 2002, ch. 81, Part F, § 1, eff. May 29, 2002, amended to extend the expiration date to commence an action to September 1, 2003.

1999 AMENDMENTS

L. 1999, ch. 412, Part D, eff. Nov. 7, 1999, and deemed repealed on Dec. 31, 2002, amended CPLR § 1101(d) by adding the opening clause; and added new subdivision (f) relating to fees for inmates.

1994 AMENDMENTS

L. 1994, ch. 563, eff. July 26, 1994, amended CPLR 1101(c) by replacing the word "If" with the words "Except as provided in subdivisions (d) and (e) of this section, if."

1992 AMENDMENTS

L. 1992, ch. 216, eff. July 1, 1992, amended CPLR 1101 by inserting into the catchline the words "waiver of fee; when motion not required"; by adding new subdivisions (d) and (e); and by making the language gender neutral.

1987 AMENDMENTS

L. 1987, ch. 312, eff. Oct. 18, 1987, amended Subd. (a) to add the requirement that an appellate court to which a motion for leave to appeal as a poor person has been or will be taken, shall hear such motion on the merits.

1981 AMENDMENTS

L. 1981, ch. 478, eff. July 7, 1981, amended CPLR 1101(c) to substitute the corporation counsel for the commissioner of finance as one upon whom a motion for permission to proceed as a poor person must be served in an action triable in New York City.

1978 AMENDMENTS

L. 1978, ch. 655, eff. July 24, 1978, amended Subd. (c) by substituting "commissioner of finance" for "finance administrator."

1969 AMENDMENTS

L. 1969, ch. 407, eff. May 9, 1969, amended Subd. (c) by substituting "finance administrator" for "director of finance."

1966 AMENDMENTS

L. 1966, ch. 455, eff. Sept. 1, 1966, amended Subd. (c) by adding after the word "parties" the words "and notice shall also be given to the county attorney in the county in which the action is triable or the director of finance if the action is triable in the city of New York."

§ 1102.   Privileges of poor person.

(a) Attorney. The court in its order permitting a person to proceed as a poor person may assign an attorney.

(b) Stenographic transcript. Where a party has been permitted by order to appeal as a poor person, the court clerk, within two days after the filing of said order with him, shall so notify the court stenographer, who, within twenty days of such notification shall make and certify two typewritten transcripts of the stenographic minutes of said trial or hearing, and shall deliver one of said transcripts to the poor person or his attorney, and file the other with the court clerk together with an affidavit of the fact and date of such delivery and filing. The expense of such transcripts shall be a county charge or, in the counties within the city of New York, a city charge, as the case may be, payable to the stenographer out of the court fund upon the certificate of the judge presiding at the trial or hearing. A poor person may be furnished with a stenographic transcript without fee by order of the court in proceedings other than appeal, the fee therefor to be paid by the county or, in the counties within the city of New York by the city, as the case may be, in the same manner as is paid for transcripts on appeal. Notwithstanding this or any other provision of law, fees paid for stenographic transcripts with respect to those proceedings specified in paragraph (a) of subdivision one of section thirty-five of the judiciary law shall be paid by the state in the manner prescribed by subdivision four of section thirty-five of the judiciary law.

(c) Appeals. On an appeal or motion for permission to appeal a poor person may submit typewritten briefs and appendices, furnishing one legible copy for each appellate justice.

(d) Costs and fees. A poor person shall not be liable for the payment of any costs or fees unless a recovery by judgment or by settlement is had in his favor in which event the court may direct him to pay out of the recovery all or part of the costs and fees, a reasonable sum for the services and expenses of his attorney and any sum expended by the county or city under subdivision (b).

1969 AMENDMENTS

L. 1969, ch. 681, eff. Sept. 1, 1969, amended Subd. (b) by adding thereto the last sentence.

1966 AMENDMENTS

L. 1966, ch. 455, eff. Sept. 1, 1966, enacted a new Subd. (b).

1965 AMENDMENTS

L. 1965, ch. 773, eff. Sept. 1, 1965, amended subdivisions (c) and (d).

1964 AMENDMENTS

L. 1964, ch. 576, eff. April 16, 1964, amended Subd. (b).

§ 1103.   Distribution of recovery in favor of poor person.

Any recovery by judgment or by settlement had in favor of a poor person, shall be paid to the clerk of the court in which the order permitting the person to proceed as a poor person was entered, to await distribution pursuant to court order.

Article 12

INFANTS, INCOMPETENTS AND CONSERVATEES

CPLR

§ 1201. Representation of infant, incompetent person or conservatee.

Unless the court appoints a guardian ad litem, an infant shall appear by the guardian of his property or, if there is no such guardian, by a parent having legal custody, or, if there is no such parent, by another person or agency having legal custody, or, if the infant is married, by an adult spouse residing with the infant, a person judicially declared to be incompetent shall appear by the committee of his property, and a conservatee shall appear by the conservator of his property. A person shall appear by his guardian ad litem if he is an infant and has no guardian of his property, parent, or other person or agency having legal custody, or adult spouse with whom he resides, or if he is an infant, person judicially declared to be incompetent or a conservatee as defined in section 77.01 of the Mental Hygiene Law and the court so directs because of a conflict of interest or for other cause, or if he is an adult incapable of adequately prosecuting or defending his rights.

[**Editor's note:** Articles 77 and 78 of the Mental Hygiene Law were replaced by Article 81, eff. April 1, 1993. CPLR § 1201 remains operative for certain parties. *See* L. 1992, ch. 698, eff. April 1, 1993, as amended by L. 1993, ch. 32, eff. April 1, 1993.]

CROSS REFERENCES

See **SCPA Article 17** as to appointment and powers of guardians and custodians of infants' property.

1981 AMENDMENTS

L. 1981, ch. 115, eff. May 18, 1981, amended CPLR 1201 by adding a conservatee as one who shall be represented by another in an action brought by or against him.

1974 AMENDMENTS

L. 1974, ch. 606, eff. May 30, 1974, amended CPLR 1201 by providing for the appearance of an infant by an agency having legal custody.

1968 AMENDMENTS

L. 1968, ch. 844, eff. Sept. 1, 1968, amended CPLR 1201 to read as above by specifying persons who must represent an infant or incompetent in an action or proceeding.

R 1202.　Appointment of guardian ad litem.

(a) By whom motion made.　The court in which an action is triable may appoint a guardian ad litem at any stage in the action upon its own initiative or upon the motion of:

　1. an infant party if he is more than fourteen years of age; or

　2. a relative, friend, a guardian or committee of the property or conservator; or

　3. any other party to the action if a motion has not been made under paragraph one or two within ten days after completion of service.

(b) Notice of motion.　Notice of a motion for appointment of a guardian ad litem for a person shall be served upon the guardian of his property, upon his committee or upon his conservator, or, if he has no such guardian, committee, or conservator, upon the person with whom he resides. Notice shall also be served upon the person who would be represented if he is more than fourteen years of age and has not been judicially declared to be incompetent.

(c) Consent.　No order appointing a guardian ad litem shall be effective until a written consent of the proposed guardian has been submitted to the court together with an affidavit stating facts showing his ability to answer for any damage sustained by his negligence or misconduct.

CROSS REFERENCES

See **SCPA §§ 403 and 404** as to appointment of guardian ad litem in Surrogate's Court.

1981 AMENDMENTS

L. 1981, ch. 115, eff. May 18, 1981, amended CPLR 1202(a) and (b) by adding a conservatee's conservator as one who may move to appoint a guardian ad litem and as one who must be served with notice of such a motion.

§ 1203.　Default judgment.

CPLR

No judgment by default may be entered against an infant or a person judicially declared to be incompetent unless his representative appeared in the action or twenty days have expired since appointment of a guardian ad litem for him. No default judgment may be entered against an adult incapable of adequately protecting his rights for whom a guardian ad litem has been appointed unless twenty days have expired since the appointment.

§ 1204. Compensation of guardian ad litem.

A court may allow a guardian ad litem a reasonable compensation for his services to be paid in whole or part by any other party or from any recovery had on behalf of the person whom such guardian represents or from such person's other property. No order allowing compensation shall be made except on an affidavit of the guardian or his attorney showing the services rendered.

CROSS REFERENCES

See **SCPA § 405** as to compensation of guardian ad litem in Surrogate's Court, and **SCPA § 2307** as to commissioners of fiduciaries generally.

§ 1205. Liability for costs of infant, judicially declared incompetent, or conservatee, or representative.

An infant, a person judicially declared to be incompetent, a conservatee, a person for whom a guardian ad litem has been appointed, or a representative of any such person, shall not be liable for costs unless the court otherwise orders.

1981 AMENDMENTS

L. 1981, ch. 115, eff. May 18, 1981, amended CPLR 1205 by adding conservatees as persons who shall not be liable for costs in an action, unless otherwise ordered by the court.

§ 1206. Disposition of proceeds of claim of infant, judicially declared incompetent or conservatee.

Except as provided in EPTL 7-4.9, any property to which an infant, a person judicially declared to be incompetent or a conservatee is entitled, after deducting any expenses allowed by the court, shall be distributed to the guardian of his property, the committee of his property or conservator to be held for the use and benefit of such infant, incompetent or conservatee except that:

(a) in the case of an infant who is married to and resides with an adult spouse, the court may order that the property be distributed to such adult spouse for the use and benefit of the infant; or

(b) if the value of the property does not exceed ten thousand dollars the court may order the property distributed to a person with whom such infant, incompetent or conservatee resides or who has some interest in his welfare to be held for the use and benefit of such infant, incompetent or conservatee; or

(c) the court may order that money constituting any part of the property be deposited in one or more specified insured banks or trust companies or savings banks or insured state or federal credit unions or be invested in one or more specified accounts in insured savings and loan associations, or it may order that a structured settlement agreement be executed, which shall include any settlement whose terms contain provisions for the payment of funds on an installment basis, provided that with respect to future installment payments, the court may order that each party liable for such payments shall fund such payments, in an amount necessary to assure the future payments, in the form of an annuity contract executed by a qualified insurer and approved by the superintendent of insurance pursuant to articles fifty-A and fifty-B of this chapter. The court may elect that the money be deposited in a high interest yield account such as an insured "savings certificate" or an insured "money market" account. The court may further elect to invest the money in one or more insured or guaranteed United States treasury or municipal bills, notes or bonds. This money is subject to withdrawal only upon order of the court, except that no court order shall be required to pay over to the infant who has attained the age of eighteen years all moneys so held unless the depository is in receipt of an order from a court of competent jurisdiction directing it to withhold such payment beyond the infant's eighteenth birthday. Notwithstanding the preceding sentence, the ability of an infant who has attained the age of eighteen years to accelerate the receipt of future installment payments pursuant to a structured settlement agreement shall be governed by the terms of such agreement. The reference to the age of twenty-one years in any order made pursuant to this subdivision or its predecessor, prior to September first, nineteen hundred seventy-four, directing payment to the infant without further court order when he reaches the age of twenty-one years, shall be deemed to designate the age of eighteen years; or

(d) the court may order that the property be held for the use and benefit of such infant, incompetent or conservatee as provided by subdivision (d) of section 1210.

CROSS REFERENCES

EPTL § 7-4.9 provides that a will or other instrument may authorize distribution to a minor by means of distribution to a custodian.

1995 AMENDMENTS

L. 1995, ch. 205, eff. July 26, 1995, amended CPLR 1206(b) by increasing the value of the property which a court may order distributed from five to ten thousand dollars.

L. 1995, ch. 464, eff. Aug. 2, 1995, amended CPLR 1206(c) to authorize the court to order deposits with savings banks and insured state or federal credit unions.

1988 AMENDMENTS

L. 1988, ch. 635, eff. Oct. 1, 1988, amended subd. (c) to provide for structured settlement agreements and substituted the reference from EPTL 7-4.8 to EPTL 7-4.9 in the first paragraph.

1986 AMENDMENTS

L. 1986, ch. 125, eff. Sept. 1, 1986, amended Subd. (b) of CPLR 1206 by changing the value of the property which a court may order distributed to five thousand dollars.

1982 AMENDMENTS

L. 1982, ch. 177, eff. Sept. 6, 1982, amended CPLR 1206(c) to permit the court to elect to deposit the proceeds of the claim of an infant, incompetent or conservatee in a high interest yield account or in U.S. treasury or municipal bills, notes or bonds.

1981 AMENDMENTS

L. 1981, ch. 73, eff. Sept. 1, 1981, amended CPLR 1206(b) to increase from one to three thousand dollars the limit on the value of property a court may order distributed on behalf of an infant, incompetent or conservatee. It shall apply to the estates of decedents dying on or after the effective date.

L. 1981, ch. 115, eff. May 18, 1981, amended CPLR 1206 and subdivisions (b) and (d) to add a conservatee as one whose property may be disposed of in accordance with its provisions and add the conservator as one to whom such property may be distributed.

1975 AMENDMENTS

L. 1975, ch. 228, eff. Sept. 1, 1975, amended subdivision (c) of CPLR 1206 by deleting a clause which had provided that the court *may direct* that a payout be made to the infant on demand upon reaching the age of eighteen years, without *further* court order, and substituting a provision that the payout may be made on demand, on reaching eighteen years, absent *any* court order, and that an order permitting payment would only be required to countermand an existing order to withhold payment beyond the infant's eighteenth birthday.

The amendment further provided that an order made prior to September 1, 1974 directing payment without further court order when the infant reaches twenty-one years of age shall be deemed to designate the age as eighteen years.

1974 AMENDMENTS

L. 1974, ch. 924, eff. Sept. 1, 1974, amended Subd. (c) providing for the removal of funds from a depository by an infant upon demand "when he reaches the age of eighteen years." Previously the provision applied to an infant "when he reaches the age of twenty-one years."

1973 AMENDMENTS

L. 1973, ch. 455, eff. June 5, 1973, amended the introductory paragraph of CPLR 1206 by adding thereto "Except as provided in EPTL 7-4.8."

1968 AMENDMENTS

L. 1968, ch. 844, eff. Sept. 1, 1968, amended CPLR 1206 by the addition of Subd. (a) and by the addition to Subd. (c) of the final clause in the first sentence, beginning with the word "unless."

§ 1207. Settlement of action or claim by infant, judicially declared incompetent or conservatee, by whom motion made; special proceeding; notice; order of settlement.

Upon motion of a guardian of the property or guardian ad litem of an infant or, if there is no such guardian, then of a parent having legal custody of an infant, or if there is no such parent, by another person having legal custody, or if the infant is married, by an adult spouse residing with the infant, or of the committee of the property of a person judicially declared to be incompetent, or of the conservator of the property of a conservatee, the court may order settlement of any action commenced by or on behalf of the infant, incompetent or conservatee. If no action has been commenced, a special proceeding may be commenced upon petition of such a representative for settlement of any claim by the infant, incompetent or conservatee in any court where an action for the amount of the proposed settlement could have been commenced. Unless otherwise provided by rule of the chief adminis-trator of the courts, if no motion term is being held and there is no justice of the supreme court available in a county where the action or an action on the claim is triable, such a motion may be made, or special proceeding may be commenced, in a county court and the county judge shall act with the same power as a justice of the supreme court even though the amount of the settlement may exceed the jurisdictional limits of the county court. Notice of the motion or petition shall be given as directed by the court. An order on such a motion shall have the effect of a judgment. Such order, or the judgment in a special proceeding, shall be entered without costs and shall approve the fee for the infant's, incompetent's or conservatee's attorney, if any.

1986 AMENDMENTS

L. 1986, ch. 355, eff. July 17, 1986, amended CPLR 1207 by adding "Unless otherwise provided for by rule of the chief administrator of the courts" after the sentence ending "could have been commenced."

1981 AMENDMENTS

L. 1981, ch. 115, eff. May 18, 1981, amended CPLR 1207 to add conservatees as persons whose actions and claims are to be settled according to this section's provisions.

1971 AMENDMENTS

L. 1971, ch. 571, eff. Sept. 1, 1971, amended CPLR 1207 by deleting "resident" from the third sentence, and by adding "available" after the phrase "there is no justice of the supreme court."

1969 AMENDMENTS

L. 1969, ch. 209, eff. Sept. 1, 1969, included within the category of those who may settle an infant's claim, all those representatives mentioned in CPLR 1201.

R 1208. Settlement procedure; papers; representation.

(a) Affidavit of infant's or incompetent's representative. An affidavit of the infant's or incompetent's representative shall be included in the supporting papers and shall state:

1. his name, residence and relationship to the infant or incompe-tent;

2. the name, age and residence of the infant or incompetent;

3. the circumstances giving rise to the action or claim;

4. the nature and extent of the damages sustained by the infant or incompetent, and if the action or claim is for damages for personal injuries to the infant or incompetent, the name of each physician who attended or treated the infant or incompetent or who was consulted, the medical expenses, the period of disability, the amount of wages lost, and the present physical condition of the infant or incompetent;

5. the terms and proposed distribution of the settlement and his approval of both;

6. the facts surrounding any other motion or petition for settlement of the same claim, of an action to recover on the same claim or of the same action;

7. whether reimbursement for medical or other expenses has been received from any source; and

8. whether the infant's or incompetent's representative or any member of the infant's or incompetent's family has made a claim for damages alleged to have been suffered as a result of the same occurrence giving rise to the infant's or incompetent's claim and, if so, the amount paid or to be paid in settlement of such claim or if such claim has not been settled the reasons therefor.

(b) Affidavit of attorney. If the infant or incompetent or his representative is represented by an attorney, an affidavit of the attorney shall be included in the supporting papers and shall state:

1. his reasons for recommending the settlement;

2. that directly or indirectly he has neither become concerned in the settlement at the instance of a party or person opposing, or with interests adverse to, the infant or incompetent nor received nor will receive any compensation from such party, and whether or not he has represented or now represents any other person asserting a claim arising from the same occurrence; and

3. the services rendered by him.

(c) Medical or hospital report. If the action or claim is for damages for personal injuries to the infant or incompetent, one or more medical or hospital reports, which need not be verified, shall be included in the supporting papers.

(d) Appearance before court. On the hearing, the moving party or petitioner, the infant or incompetent, and his attorney shall attend before the court unless attendance is excused for good cause.

(e) Representation. No attorney having or representing any interest conflicting with that of an infant or incompetent may represent the infant or incompetent.

(f) Preparation of papers by attorney for adverse party. If the infant or incompetent is not represented by an attorney the papers may be prepared by the attorney for an adverse party or person and shall state the fact.

CROSS REFERENCES

See **Judiciary Law § 474** as to special requirements for attorney's contingent fee arrangements on infants' claims.

1968 AMENDMENTS

L. 1968, ch. 844, eff. Sept. 1, 1968, amended the caption and text of CPLR 1208 by having it read as above in Subds. (a), (b), (c) and (d) and by repealing Subd. (g).

1967 AMENDMENTS

L. 1967, ch. 578, eff. July 1, 1967, added Subd. (g), (repealed in 1968).

1964 AMENDMENTS

L. 1964, ch. 195, eff. Sept. 1, 1964, deleted words "of each" and "each" in first sentence of Subd. (c), dealing with affidavit of physician. First sentence formerly read: "If the action or claim is for damages for personal injuries to the infant or incompetent, affidavits of each of one or more physicians shall be included in the supporting papers and each shall state: . . ."

§ 1209. Arbitration of controversy involving infant, judicially declared incompetent or conservatee.

A controversy involving an infant, person judicially declared to be incompetent or conservatee shall not be submitted to arbitration except pursuant to a court order made upon application of the representative of such infant, incompetent or conservatee; provided, however, that a claim brought on behalf of an infant pursuant to paragraph one or two of subdivision (f) of section three thousand four hundred twenty of the insurance law may be submitted to arbitration without a court order.

1997 AMENDMENTS

L. 1997, ch. 365, eff. August 5, 1997, amended CPLR 1209 to provide that a claim for uninsured motorist benefits may be submitted to arbitration without a court order.

1981 AMENDMENTS

L. 1981, ch. 115, eff. May 18, 1981, amended CPLR 1209 to add a controversy involving a conservatee to those governed by this section.

R 1210. Guardian of infant.

(a) Petition for appointment; by whom presented; contents. An infant, if of the age of fourteen years or more, or a relative or friend of an infant, may present a petition to the court for appointment of a guardian. The petition shall state the age and residence of the infant, the name and residence of any living parent and of the person proposed as guardian, the relationship, if any, which such person bears to the infant, and the nature, status and value of the infant's estate.

(b) Hearing. The court shall ascertain the age of the infant, the amount of his personal property, the gross amount or value of the rents and profits of his real estate during his minority, and the sufficiency of the security offered by the proposed guardian. If the infant is of the age of fourteen years or more, the court shall examine him as to his voluntary nomination of or preference for a suitable guardian; if he is under the age of fourteen, the court shall select and appoint a suitable guardian.

(c) Undertaking. The court shall make an order requiring or dispensing wholly or partly with an undertaking, in an amount and according to the conditions set forth in section seventeen hundred eight of the surrogate's court procedure act.

(d) Direction as to management of estate. The court in its discretion may direct that the principal of the estate or any part of it be invested in bonds of the state of New York or of the United States, or invested in bonds or other obligations of any county, city, town, village or school district of the state of New York, or deposited with any bank, trust company, insured savings and loan association or insured savings bank or insured state or federal credit union which has been designated as a depository for such fund; or invested in a bond and mortgage on unincumbered and improved property within the state, having a value, to be shown to the satisfaction of the court, of at least double the amount of principal invested, for the benefit of the infant, and may direct that only the interest or income be received by the guardian.

(e) Filing of certified copy of order of appointment. Upon the appointment of a guardian of the person or property, or both, of an infant the guardian shall file a certified copy of the order of his appointment with the clerk of the surrogate's court of the county in which he has been appointed.

CROSS REFERENCES

SCPA § 1708, referred to in Subd. (c), *above,* appears in Appendix, *below.*

1995 AMENDMENTS

L. 1995, ch. 464, eff. Aug. 2, 1995, amended CPLR 1210(d) by adding the words "or insured state or federal credit union."

1983 AMENDMENTS

L. 1983, ch. 37, eff. Sept. 1, 1983, amended Subd. (d) by allowing for investment in county, city, town, village and school district bonds by guardians or infants.

1975 AMENDMENTS

L. 1975, ch. 490, eff. Sept. 1, 1975, amended Subd. (d) by adding insured savings and loan associations and insured savings banks as depositories for funds deposited by guardians of infants.

1969 AMENDMENTS

Amendment made by Judicial Conference Feb. 1, 1969, Report to the 1969 Legislature, eff. Sept 1, 1969, eliminated the word "general" from the term "general guardian" in the catch line and in subdivisions (a) and (e) of Rule 1210 to effect consistency of terminology with the new Surrogate's Court Procedure Act (Art. 17).

1966 AMENDMENTS

L. 1966, ch. 961, added a new Subd. (e), eff. Sept. 1, 1967.

R 1211. Allowance for infant's support.

(a) Petition to supreme court, county court or surrogate's court; contents. A petition to the supreme court, county court or the surrogate's court for the application of an infant's property or a portion thereof to the infant's support, maintenance or education shall set forth in detail:

    1. the amount and nature of the infant's property, where it is situated and how invested, his income from such property or any other source and any claim against the infant;

    2. whether or not the infant's parents are living and, if either of

them is living, all circumstances relative to their ability to support the infant, and if neither of them is living, the names of other persons legally obligated to support the infant and the circumstances relative to their ability to support the infant; and

3. the terms of any previous order made by any court within or without the state for similar relief and the disposition made of any property pursuant thereto.

(b) Notice. Such notice as the court shall direct shall be given to:

1. the guardian of the property of the infant, if the petition is presented by a person other than such guardian;

2. the infant's father if he is living or, if not, then to the infant's mother or, if neither parent is living, then to the person with whom the infant resides; and

3. the infant if he is of the age of fourteen years or more.

1972 AMENDMENTS

L. 1972, ch. 276, eff. Sept. 1, 1972, added "county court" to Subd. (a).

CPLR

Article 13

ACTIONS BY THE STATE

SUMMARY OF ARTICLE

§ 1301. Actions in behalf of the people to be brought in the name of the state.

An action brought in behalf of the people, except an action to recover a penalty or forfeiture expressly given by law to a particular officer, shall be brought in the name of the state.

§ 1302. Action brought on relation of a person.

Where an action is brought by the attorney-general on the relation or information of a person having an interest in the question, the complaint shall allege, and the title of the action shall show, that the action is so brought. As a condition of bringing an action for the benefit of a person having an interest in the question, the attorney-general shall require the relator to give an undertaking to indemnify the state against costs and expenses.

§ 1303. Procedure in action brought by the state.

Except as otherwise specially prescribed by statute or rule the proceedings in an action brought by the state shall be the same as in an action by a private person.

CPLR

Article 13-A

PROCEEDS OF A CRIME—FORFEITURE

CPLR

§ 1310. Definitions.

In this article:

1. "Property" means and includes: real property, personal property, money, negotiable instruments, securities, or any thing of value or any interest in a thing of value.

2. "Proceeds of a crime" means any property obtained through the commission of a felony crime defined in subdivisions five and six hereof, and includes any appreciation in value of such property.

3. "Substituted proceeds of a crime" means any property obtained by the sale or exchange of proceeds of a crime, and any gain realized by such sale or exchange.

4. "Instrumentality of a crime" means any property, other than real property and any buildings, fixtures, appurtenances, and improvements thereon, whose use contributes directly and materially to the commission of a crime defined in subdivisions five and six hereof.

4–a. "Real property instrumentality of a crime" means an interest in real property the use of which contributes directly and materially to the commission of a specified felony offense.

4–b. "Specified felony offense" means:

(a) a conviction of a person for a violation of section 220.18, 220.21, 220.41, or 220.43 of the penal law, or where the accusatory instrument charges one or more of such offenses, conviction upon a plea of guilty to any of the felonies for which such plea is otherwise authorized by law or a conviction of a person for conspiracy to commit a violation of section 220.18, 220.21, 220.41, or 220.43 of the penal law, where the controlled substances which are the object of the conspiracy are located in the real property which is the subject of the forfeiture action; or

(b) on three or more occasions, engaging in conduct constituting a violation of any of the felonies defined in section 220.09, 220.16, 220.18, 220.21, 220.31, 220.34, 220.39, 220.41, 220.43 or 221.55 of the penal law, which violations do not constitute a single criminal offense as defined in subdivision one of section 40.10 of the criminal procedure law, or a single criminal transaction, as defined in paragraph (a) of subdivision two of section 40.10 of the criminal procedure law, and at least one of which resulted in a conviction of such offense, or where the accusatory instrument charges one or more of such felonies, conviction upon a plea of guilty to a felony for which such plea is otherwise authorized by law; or

(c) a conviction of a person for a violation of section 220.09, 220.16, 220.34 or 220.39 of the penal law, or a conviction of a criminal defendant for a violation of section 221.30 of the penal law, or where the accusatory instrument charges any such felony, conviction upon a plea of guilty to a felony for which the plea is otherwise authorized by law, together with evidence which: (i) provides substantial indicia that the defendant used the real property to engage in a continual, ongoing course of conduct involving the unlawful mixing, compounding, manufacturing, warehousing, or packaging of controlled substances or where the conviction is for a violation of section 221.30 of the penal law, marijuana, as part of an illegal trade or business for gain; and (ii) establishes, where the conviction is for possession of a controlled substance or where the conviction is for a violation of section 221.30 of the penal law, marijuana, that such possession was with the intent to sell it.

5. "Post-conviction forfeiture crime" means any felony defined in the penal law or any other chapter of the consolidated laws of the state.

6. "Pre-conviction forfeiture crime" means only a felony defined in article two hundred twenty or section 221.30 or 221.55 of the penal law.

7. "Court" means a superior court.

8. "Defendant" means a person against whom a forfeiture action is commenced and includes a "criminal defendant" and a "non-criminal defendant."

9. "Criminal defendant" means a person who has criminal liability for a crime defined in subdivisions five and six hereof. For purposes of this article, a person has criminal liability when (a) he has been convicted of a post-conviction forfeiture crime, or (b) the claiming authority proves by clear and convincing evidence that such person has committed an act in violation of article two hundred twenty or section 221.30 or 221.55 of the penal law.

10. "Non-criminal defendant" means a person, other than a criminal defendant, who possesses an interest in the proceeds of a crime, the substituted proceeds of a crime or in an instrumentality of a crime.

11. "Claiming authority" means the district attorney having jurisdiction over the offense or the attorney general for purpose of those crimes for which the attorney general has criminal jurisdiction in a case where the underlying criminal charge has been, is being or is about to be brought by the attorney general, or the appropriate corporation counsel or county attorney, provided that the corporation counsel or county attorney may act as a claiming authority only with the consent of the district attorney or the attorney general, as appropriate.

12. "Claiming agent" means and shall include all persons described in subdivision thirty-four of section 1.20 of the criminal procedure law, and sheriffs, undersheriffs and deputy sheriffs of counties within the city of New York.

CPLR

13. "Fair consideration" means fair consideration is given for property, or obligation, (a) when in exchange for such property, or obligation, as a fair equivalent therefor, and in good faith, property is conveyed or an antecedent debt is satisfied, or (b) when such property, or obligation is received in good faith to secure a present advance or antecedent debt in amount not disproportionately small as compared with the value of the property, or obligation obtained.

14. "District attorney" means and shall include all persons described in subdivision thirty-two of section 1.20 of the criminal procedure law and the special assistant district attorney in charge of the office of prosecution, special narcotics courts of the city of New York.

CROSS REFERENCES

Article 220 of the **Penal Law**, referred to in paragraph (6), deals with controlled substances offenses; **Penal Law §§ 221.30 and 221.55** cover the criminal possession and sale of marihuana in the first degree. **Criminal Procedure Law** § 1.20(34), referred to in paragraph 12, lists persons included within the term "police officer."

1990 AMENDMENTS

L. 1990, ch. 655, eff. Nov. 1, 1990, amended CPLR 1310 by adding subdivisions (4–a), defining "real property instrumentality of a crime," and (4–b), defining "specified felony offense," and by amending subdivision (11) by replacing the words "the defendant in the forfeiture action is a person against whom a" with "the underlying."

1986 AMENDMENTS

L. 1986, ch. 8, eff. Nov. 1, 1986, added new subdivision (14) defining "district attorney"; L. 1986, ch. 174, eff. Nov. 1, 1986, amended subdivision (12) to include sheriffs, undersheriffs and deputy sheriffs of counties in the city of New York, within the definition of "claiming agent."

1984 AMENDMENTS

L. 1984, ch. 669, eff. Aug. 1, 1984, repealed former Article 13-A and added a new Article 13-A, comprising CPLR 1310 through CPLR 1352. New Article 13-A is applicable to crimes committed on and after Aug. 1, 1984.

§ 1311. Forfeiture actions.

1. A civil action may be commenced by the appropriate claiming authority against a criminal defendant to recover the property which constitutes the proceeds of a crime, the substituted proceeds of a crime, an instrumentality of a crime or the real property instrumentality of a

crime or to recover a money judgment in an amount equivalent in value to the property which constitutes the proceeds of a crime, the substituted proceeds of a crime, an instrumentality of a crime, or the real property instrumentality of a crime. A civil action may be commenced against a non-criminal defendant to recover the property which constitutes the proceeds of a crime, the substituted proceeds of a crime, an instrumentality of a crime or the real property instrumentality of a crime, provided, however, that a judgment of forfeiture predicated upon clause (A) of subparagraph (iv) of paragraph (b) of subdivision three hereof shall be limited to the amount of the proceeds of the crime. Any action under this article must be commenced within five years of the commission of the crime and shall be civil, remedial, and in personam in nature and shall not be deemed to be a penalty or criminal forfeiture for any purpose. Except as otherwise specially provided by statute, the proceedings under this article shall be governed by this chapter. An action under this article is not a criminal proceeding and may not be deemed to be a previous prosecution under article forty of the criminal procedure law.

(a) Actions relating to post-conviction forfeiture crimes. An action relating to a post-conviction forfeiture crime must be grounded upon a conviction of a felony defined in subdivision five of section one thousand three hundred ten of this article, or upon criminal activity arising from a common scheme or plan of which such a conviction is a part, or upon a count of an indictment or information alleging a felony which was dismissed at the time of a plea of guilty to a felony in satisfaction of such count. A court may not grant forfeiture until such conviction has occurred. However, an action may be commenced, and a court may grant a provisional remedy provided under this article, prior to such conviction having occurred. An action under this paragraph must be dismissed at any time after sixty days of the commencement of the action unless the conviction upon which the action is grounded has occurred, or an indictment or information upon which the asserted conviction is to be based is pending in a superior court. An action under this paragraph shall be stayed during the pendency of a criminal action which is related to it; provided, however, that such stay shall not prevent the granting or continuance of any provisional remedy provided under this article or any other provisions of law.

(b) Actions relating to pre-conviction forfeiture crimes. An action relating to a pre-conviction forfeiture crime need not be grounded upon conviction of a pre-conviction forfeiture crime, provided, however, that if the action is not grounded upon such a conviction, it shall be necessary in the action for the claiming authority to prove the commission of a pre-conviction forfeiture crime by clear and convincing evidence. An action under this paragraph shall be stayed during the pendency of a criminal action which is related to it; provided, that upon motion of a defendant in the forfeiture action or the claiming authority, a court may, in the interest of justice and for good cause, and with the consent of all parties, order that the forfeiture action proceed despite the pending criminal action; and provided that such stay shall not prevent the granting or continuance of any provisional remedy provided under this article or any other provision of law.

2. All defendants in a forfeiture action brought pursuant to this article shall have the right to trial by jury on any issue of fact.

3. In a forfeiture action pursuant to this article the following burdens of proof shall apply:

(a) In a forfeiture action commenced by a claiming authority against a criminal defendant, except for those facts referred to in paragraph (b) of subdivision nine of section one thousand three hundred ten and paragraph (b) of subdivision one of this section which must be proven by clear and convincing evidence, the burden shall be upon the claiming authority to prove by a preponderance of the evidence the facts necessary to establish a claim for forfeiture.

(b) In a forfeiture action commenced by a claiming authority against a non-criminal defendant:

(i) in an action relating to a pre-conviction forfeiture crime, the burden shall be upon the claiming authority to prove by clear and convincing evidence the commission of the crime by a person, provided, however, that it shall not be necessary to prove the identity of such person.

(ii) if the action relates to the proceeds of a crime, except as provided in subparagraph (i) hereof, the burden shall be upon the claiming authority to prove by a preponderance of the evidence the facts necessary to establish a claim for forfeiture and that the non-criminal defendant either (A) knew or should have known that the proceeds were obtained through the commission of a crime, or (B) fraudulently obtained his or her interest in the proceeds to avoid forfeiture.

(iii) if the action relates to the substituted proceeds of a crime, except as provided in subparagraph (i) hereof, the burden shall be upon the claiming authority to prove by a preponderance of the evidence the facts necessary to establish a claim for forfeiture and that the non-criminal defendant either (A) knew that the property sold or exchanged to obtain an interest in the substituted proceeds was obtained through the commission of a crime, or (B) fraudulently obtained his or her interest in the substituted proceeds to avoid forfeiture.

(iv) if the action relates to an instrumentality of a crime, except as provided for in subparagraph (i) hereof, the burden shall be upon the claiming authority to prove by a preponderance of the evidence the facts necessary to establish a claim for forfeiture and that the non-criminal defendant either (A) knew that the instrumentality was or would be used in the commission of a crime or (B) knowingly obtained his or her interest in the instrumentality to avoid forfeiture.

(v) if the action relates to a real property instrumentality of a crime, the burden shall be upon the claiming authority to prove those facts referred to in subdivision four-b of section thirteen hundred ten of this article by clear and convincing evidence. The claiming authority shall also prove by a clear and convincing evidence that the non-criminal defendant knew that such property was or would be used for the commission of specified felony offenses, and either (a) knowingly and unlawfully benefited from such conduct or (b) voluntarily agreed to the use of such property for the commission of such offenses by consent freely given. For purposes of this subparagraph, a non-criminal defendant knowingly and unlawfully benefits from the commission of a specified felony offense when he derives in exchange for permitting the use or occupancy of such real property by a person or persons committing such specified offense a substantial benefit that would

CPLR

otherwise not accrue as a result of the lawful use or occupancy of such real property. "Benefit" means benefit as defined in subdivision seventeen of section 10.00 of the penal law.

(c) In a forfeiture action commenced by a claiming authority against a non-criminal defendant the following rebuttable presumptions shall apply:

(i) a non-criminal defendant who did not pay fair consideration for the proceeds of a crime, the substituted proceeds of a crime or the instrumentality of a crime, shall be presumed to know that such property was the proceeds of a crime, the substituted proceeds of a crime, or an instrumentality of a crime.

(ii) a non-criminal defendant who obtains an interest in the proceeds of a crime, substituted proceeds of a crime or an instrumentality of a crime with knowledge of an order of provisional remedy relating to said property issued pursuant to this article, shall be presumed to know that such property was the proceeds of a crime, substituted proceeds of a crime, or an instrumentality of a crime.

(iii) in an action relating to a post-conviction forfeiture crime, a non-criminal defendant who the claiming authority proves by clear and convincing evidence has criminal liability under section 20.00 of the penal law for the crime of conviction or for criminal activity arising from a common scheme or plan of which such crime is a part and who possesses an interest in the proceeds, the substituted proceeds, or an instrumentality of such criminal activity is presumed to know that such property was the proceeds of a crime, the substituted proceeds of a crime, or an instrumentality of a crime.

(iv) a non-criminal defendant who participated in or was aware of a scheme to conceal or disguise the manner in which said non-criminal obtained his or her interest in the proceeds of a crime, substituted proceeds of a crime, or an instrumentality of a crime is presumed to know that such property was the proceeds of a crime, the substituted proceeds of a crime, or an instrumentality of a crime.

(d) In a forfeiture action commenced by a claiming authority against a defendant, the following rebuttable presumption shall apply: all currency or negotiable instruments payable to the bearer shall be presumed to be the proceeds of a pre-conviction forfeiture crime when such currency or negotiable instruments are (i) found in close proximity to a controlled substance unlawfully possessed by the defendant in an amount sufficient to constitute a violation of section 220.18 or 220.21 of the penal law, or (ii) found in close proximity to any quantity of a controlled substance or marihuana unlawfully possessed by such defendant in a room, other than a public place, under circumstances evincing an intent to unlawfully mix, compound, distribute, package or otherwise prepare for sale such controlled substance or marihuana.

(e) The presumption set forth pursuant to paragraph (d) of this subdivision shall be rebutted by credible and reliable evidence which tends to show that such currency or negotiable instrument payable to the bearer is not the proceeds of a preconviction forfeiture crime. In an action tried before a jury, the jury shall be so instructed. Any sworn testimony of a defendant offered to rebut the presumption and any other evidence which is obtained as a result of such testimony, shall be inadmissible in any subsequent proceeding relating to the forfeiture action, or in any other civil or criminal action, except in a prosecution for a violation of article two hundred ten of the penal law. In an action tried before a jury, at the commencement of the trial, or at such other time as the court reasonably directs, the claiming authority shall provide notice to the court and to the defendant of its intent to request that the court charge such presumption.

3–a. Conviction of a person in a criminal action upon an accusatory instrument which includes one or more of the felonies specified in subdivision four-b of section thirteen hundred ten of this article, of any felony other than such felonies, shall not preclude a defendant, in any subsequent proceeding under this article where that conviction is at issue, from adducing evidence that the conduct underlying the conviction would not establish the elements of any of the felonies specified in such subdivision other than the one to which the criminal defendant pled guilty. If the defendant does adduce such evidence, the burden shall be upon the claiming authority to prove, by clear and convincing evidence, that the conduct underlying the

CPLR

criminal conviction would establish the elements of the felony specified in such subdivision. Nothing contained in this subdivision shall affect the validity of a settlement of any forfeiture action negotiated between the claiming authority and a criminal defendant contemporaneously with the taking of a plea of guilty in a criminal action to any felony defined in article two hundred twenty or section 221.30 or 221.55 of the penal law, or to a felony conspiracy to commit the same.

4. The court in which a forfeiture action is pending may dismiss said action in the interests of justice upon its own motion or upon an application as provided for herein.

(a) At any time during the pendency of a forfeiture action, the claiming authority who instituted the action, or a defendant may (i) apply for an order dismissing the complaint and terminating the forfeiture action in the interest of justice, or (ii) may apply for an order limiting the forfeiture to an amount equivalent in value to the value of property constituting the proceeds or substituted proceeds of a crime in the interest of justice.

(b) Such application for the relief provided in paragraph (a) hereof must be made in writing and upon notice to all parties. The court may, in its discretion, direct that notice be given to any other person having an interest in the property.

(c) An application for the relief provided for in paragraph (a) hereof must be brought exclusively in the superior court in which the forfeiture action is pending.

(d) The court may grant the relief provided in paragraph (a) hereof if it finds that such relief is warranted by the existence of some compelling factor, consideration or circumstance demonstrating that forfeiture of the property of* any part thereof, would not serve the ends of justice. Among the factors, considerations and circumstances the court may consider, among others, are:

(i) the seriousness and circumstances of the crime to which the property is connected relative to the impact of forfeiture of property upon the person who committed the crime; or

(ii) the adverse impact of a forfeiture of property upon innocent persons; or

(iii) the appropriateness of a judgment of forfeiture in an action relating to pre-conviction forfeiture crime where the criminal proceeding based on the crime to which the property is allegedly connected results in an acquittal of the criminal defendant or a dismissal of the accusatory instrument on the merits; or

(iv) in the case of an action relating to an instrumentality, whether the value of the instrumentality substantially exceeds the value of the property constituting the proceeds or substituted proceeds of a crime.

(e) The court must issue a written decision stating the basis for an order issued pursuant to this subdivision.

4–a. (a) The court in which a forfeiture action relating to real property is pending may, upon its own motion or upon the motion of the claiming authority which instituted the action, the defendant, or any other person who has a lawful property interest in such property, enter an order:

(i) appointing an administrator pursuant to section seven hundred seventy-eight of the real property actions and proceedings law when the owner of a dwelling is a defendant in such action, and when persons who are not defendants in such action lawfully occupy one or more units within such dwelling, in order to maintain and preserve the property on behalf of such persons or any other person or entity who has a lawful property interest in such property, or in order to remedy any other condition which is dangerous to life, health or safety; or

(ii) otherwise limiting, modifying or dismissing the forfeiture action in order to preserve or protect the lawful property interest of any non-criminal defendant or any other person who is not a criminal defendant, or the lawful property interest of a defendant which is not subject to forfeiture; or

(iii) where such action involves interest in a residential leasehold or a statutory tenancy, directing that upon entry of a judgment of forfeiture, the lease or statutory tenancy will be modified as a matter of law to terminate only the interest of the defendant or defendants, and to continue the occupancy or

CPLR

tenancy of any other person or persons who lawfully reside in such demised premises, with such rights as such parties would otherwise have had if the defendant's interest had not been forfeited pursuant to this article.

(b) For purposes of this subdivision the term "owner" has the same meaning as prescribed for that term in section seven hundred eighty-one of the real property actions and proceedings law and the term "dwelling" shall mean any building or structure or portion thereof which is principally occupied in whole or part as the home, residence or sleeping place of one or more human beings.

5. An action for forfeiture shall be commenced by service pursuant to this chapter of a summons with notice or summons and verified complaint. No person shall forfeit any right, title, or interest in any property who is not a defendant in the action. The claiming authority shall also file a copy of such papers with the state division of criminal justice services; provided, however, failure to file such papers shall not be grounds for any relief by a defendant in this section.

6. On the motion of any party to the forfeiture action, and for good cause shown, a court may seal any papers, including those pertaining to any provisional remedy, which relate to the forfeiture action until such time as the property which is the subject of the forfeiture action has been levied upon. A motion to seal such papers may be made ex parte and in camera.

7. Remission. In addition to any other relief provided under this chapter, at any time within one year after the entry of a judgment of forfeiture, any person, claiming an interest in the property subject to forfeiture who did not receive actual notice of the forfeiture action may petition the judge before whom the forfeiture action was held for a remission or mitigation of the forfeiture and restoration of the property or the proceeds of any sale resulting from the forfeiture, or such part thereof, as may be claimed by him. The court may restore said property upon such terms and conditions as it deems reasonable and just if (i) the petitioner establishes that he or she was without actual knowledge of the forfeiture action or any related proceeding for a provisional remedy and did not know or should not have known that the forfeited property was connected to a crime or fraudulently conveyed and (ii) the court determines that restoration of the property would serve the ends

of justice.

8. The total amount that may be recovered by the claiming authority against all criminal defendants in a forfeiture action or actions involving the same crime shall not exceed the value of the proceeds of the crime or substituted proceeds of the crime, whichever amount is greater, and, in addition, the value of any forfeited instrumentality used in the crime. Any such recovery against criminal defendants for the value of the proceeds of the crime or substituted proceeds of the crime shall be reduced by an amount which equals the value of the same proceeds of the same crime or the same substituted proceeds of the same crime recovered against all non-criminal defendants. Any such recovery for the value of an instrumentality of a crime shall be reduced by an amount which equals the value of the same instrumentality recovered against any non-criminal defendant.

The total amount that may be recovered against all non-criminal defendants in a forfeiture action or actions involving the same crime shall not exceed the value of the proceeds of the crime or the substituted proceeds of the crime, whichever amount is greater, and, in addition, the value of any forfeited instrumentality used in the crime. Any such recovery against non-criminal defendants for the value of the proceeds of the crime or substituted proceeds of the crime shall be reduced by an amount which equals the value of the proceeds of the crime or substituted proceeds of the crime recovered against all criminal defendants. A judgment against a non-criminal defendant pursuant to clause A of subparagraph (iv) of paragraph (b) of subdivision three of this section shall be limited to the amount of the proceeds of the crime. Any recovery for the value of an instrumentality of the crime shall be reduced by an amount equal to the value of the same instrumentality recovered against any criminal defendant.

9. Any defendant in a forfeiture action who knowingly and intentionally conceals, destroys, dissipates, alters, removes from the jurisdiction, or otherwise disposes of, property specified in a provisional remedy ordered by the court or in a judgment of forfeiture in knowing contempt of said order or judgment shall be subject to criminal liability and sanctions under sections 80.05 and 215.80 of the penal law.

10. The proper venue for trial of an action for forfeiture is:

CPLR

(a) In the case of an action for post-conviction forfeiture commenced after conviction, the county where the conviction occurred.

(b) In all other cases, the county where a criminal prosecution could be commenced under article twenty of the criminal procedure law, or, in the case of an action commenced by the office of prosecution, special narcotics courts of the city of New York, under section one hundred seventy-seven-b of the judiciary law.

11.

(a) Any stipulation or settlement agreement between the parties to a forfeiture action shall be filed with the clerk of the court in which the forfeiture action is pending. No stipulation or settlement agreement shall be accepted for filing unless it is accompanied by an affidavit from the claiming authority that written notice of the stipulation or settlement agreement, including the terms of such, has been given to the state crime victims board, the state division of criminal justice services, and in the case of a forfeiture based on a felony defined in article two hundred twenty or section 221.30 or 221.55 of the penal law, to the state division of substance abuse services.

(b) No judgment or order of forfeiture shall be accepted for filing unless it is accompanied by an affidavit from the claiming authority that written notice of judgment or order, including the terms of such, has been given to the state crime victims board, the state division of criminal justice services, and in the case of a forfeiture based on a felony defined in article two hundred twenty or section 221.30 or 221.55 of the penal law, to the state division of substance abuse services.

(c) Any claiming authority or claiming agent which receives any property pursuant to chapter thirteen of the food and drug laws (21 U.S.C. § 801 *et seq.*) of the United States and/or chapter four of the customs duties laws (19 U.S.C. § 1301 *et seq.*) of the United States and/or chapter 96 of the crimes and criminal procedure laws (18 U.S.C. § 1961 *et seq.*) of the United States shall provide an affidavit to the commissioner of the division of criminal justice services stating the estimated present value of the property received.

12. Property acquired in good faith by an attorney as payment for the

reasonable and bona fide fees of legal services or reimbursement of reasonable and bona fide expenses related to the representation of a defendant in connection with a civil or criminal forfeiture proceeding or a related criminal matter, shall be exempt from a judgment of forfeiture. For purposes of this subdivision and subdivision four of section one thousand three hundred twelve of this article, "bona fide" means that the attorney who acquired such property had no reasonable basis to believe that the fee transaction was a fraudulent or sham transaction designed to shield property from forfeiture, hide its existence from governmental investigative agencies, or was conducted for any purpose other than for legitimate legal representation.

* **[Editor's note:** So in original. Probably should read "or."]

CROSS REFERENCES

Article 40 of the **Criminal Procedure Law**, referred to in paragraph (1), provides for an exemption from prosecution by reason of previous prosecution; **Penal Law** § 20.00, referred to in paragraph (3)(c)(iii), sets forth the basis for criminal liability for conduct of another; **Penal Law** § 215.80, referred to in paragraph (9), makes it a class A misdemeanor for a defendant in an Article 13-A forfeiture action to unlawfully dispose of assets subject to forfeiture; **Penal Law** § 80.05, also referred to in paragraph (9), sets forth the fine for a violation of **Penal Law** § 215.80; Article 20 of the **Criminal Procedure Law**, referred to in paragraph 10(b), sets forth the principles governing the geographical jurisdiction of offenses; **Judiciary Law** § 177-b, also referred to in paragraph 10(b), establishes special narcotics parts within the Supreme Courts of cities with a population of one million or more.

1990 AMENDMENTS

L. 1990, ch. 655, eff. Nov. 1, 1990, amended CPLR 1311(a) by including the real property instrumentality of a crime among the property that may be recovered in a civil forfeiture action against a criminal defendant; adding paragraphs (b)(v), (d) and (e) to subdivision (3); adding subdivision (3–a); adding subdivision (4–a); amending subdivision (5) to mandate that the claiming authority file a copy of a summons with notice or summons and verified complaint with the state division of criminal justice services; and adding subdivisions (11) and (12).

1985 AMENDMENTS

L. 1985, ch. 379, eff. Nov. 1, 1985, amended paragraph 10(b) to provide that in the case of an action commenced by the office of prosecution, venue for trial of a forfeiture action is in the special narcotics courts of New York City.

1984 AMENDMENTS

L. 1984, ch. 669, eff. Aug. 1, 1984, repealed former Article 13-A and added

a new Article 13-A, comprising CPLR 1310 through CPLR 1352. New Article 13-A is applicable to crimes committed on and after the effective date.

§ 1311–a.   Subpoena duces tecum.

1. At any time before an action pursuant to this article is commenced, the claiming authority may, pursuant to the provisions of subdivision two of this section, apply without notice for the issuance of a subpoena duces tecum.

2. An application for a subpoena duces tecum pursuant to this section:

(a) shall be made in the judicial district in which the claiming authority may commence an action pursuant to this article, and shall be made in writing to a justice of the supreme court, or a judge of the county court; and

(b) shall be supported by an affidavit, and such other written documentation as may be submitted which: (i) sets forth the identity of the claiming authority and certifies that the applicant is authorized to make the application on the claiming authority's behalf; (ii) demonstrates reasonable grounds to believe that the execution of the subpoena would be reasonably likely to lead to information about the nature and location of any debt or property against which a forfeiture judgment may be enforced; (iii) states whether any other such subpoena or provisional remedy has been previously sought or obtained with respect to the subject matter of the subpoena or the matter to which it relates; (iv) contains a factual statement which sets forth the basis for the issuance of the subpoena, including a particular description of the nature of the information sought to be obtained; (v) states whether the issuance of the subpoena is sought without notice to any interested party; and (vi) where the application seeks the issuance of the subpoena without notice to any interested party, contains a statement setting forth the factual basis for the claiming authority's belief that providing notice of the application for the issuance of the subpoena may result in any property being destroyed, removed from the jurisdiction of the court, or otherwise being unavailable for forfeiture or to satisfy a money judgment that may be entered in the forfeiture action, and may interfere with law enforcement investigations or judicial proceedings.

3. An application made pursuant to this section may be granted, in the court's discretion, upon a determination that the application meets the requirements set forth in subdivision two of this section; provided, however, that no such subpoena may be issued or directed to an attorney with regard to privileged records or documents or attorney work-product relating to a client. When a subpoena has been issued pursuant to this section, the claiming authority shall have the right to possession of the subpoenaed material. The possession shall be for a period of time, and on such reasonable terms and conditions, as the court may direct. The reasonableness of such possession, time, terms and conditions shall be determined with consideration for, among other things, (a) the good cause shown by the party issuing the subpoena or in whose behalf the subpoena is issued, (b) the rights and legitimate needs of the person subpoenaed and (c) the feasibility and appropriateness of making copies of the subpoenaed material. Where the application seeks a subpoena to compel the production of an original record or document, the court in its discretion may order the production of a certified transcript or certified copy thereof.

4. Upon a determination pursuant to subdivision three of this section that the subpoena should be granted, the court shall issue the subpoena, seal all papers relating thereto, and direct that the recipient shall not, except as otherwise ordered by the court, disclose the fact of issuance or the subject of the subpoena to any person or entity; provided, however, that the court may require that notice be given to any interested party prior to the issuance of the subpoena, or at any time thereafter, when: (a) an order granting a provisional remedy pursuant to this article with respect to the subject matter of the subpoena or the matter to which it relates has been served upon the defendant whose books and records are the subject matter of the subpoena, whether such books and records are in the possession of the defendant or a third party; or (b) the court determines that providing notice of the application (i) will not result in any property being destroyed, removed from the jurisdiction of the court, or otherwise being unavailable for forfeiture or to satisfy a money judgment that may be entered in the forfeiture action and (ii) will not interfere with law enforcement investigations or judicial proceedings. For purposes of this section, "interested party" means any person whom the court determines might have an interest in the property subject to the forfeiture action brought

CPLR

pursuant to this article.

5. Notwithstanding the provisions of subdivision four of this section, where a subpoena duces tecum has been issued pursuant to this section without notice to any interested party, the claiming authority shall serve written notice of the fact and date of the issuance of the subpoena duces tecum, and of the fact that information was obtained thereby, upon any interested party not later than ninety days after the date of compliance with such subpoena, or upon commencement of a forfeiture action, whichever occurs first; provided, however, where the action has not been commenced and upon a showing of good cause, service of the notice required herein may be postponed by order of the court for a reasonable period of time. The court, upon the filing of a motion by any interested party served with such notice, may, in its discretion, make available to such party or the party's counsel for inspection such portions of the information obtained pursuant to the subpoena as the court directs.

6. Nothing contained in this section shall be construed to diminish or impair any right of subpoena or discovery that may otherwise be provided for by law to the claiming authority or to a defendant in a forfeiture action.

1990 AMENDMENTS

L. 1990. ch. 655, eff. Nov. 1, 1990.

§ 1312. Provisional remedies; generally.

1. The provisional remedies of attachment, injunction, receivership and notice of pendency provided for herein, shall be available in all actions to recover property or for a money judgment under this article.

2. On a motion for a provisional remedy, the claiming authority shall state whether any other provisional remedy has previously been sought in the same action against the same defendant. The court may require the claiming authority to elect between those remedies to which it would otherwise be entitled.

3. A court may grant an application for a provisional remedy when it determines that: (a) there is a substantial probability that the claiming authority will prevail on the issue of forfeiture and that failure to enter the order may result in the property being destroyed, removed from the jurisdiction of the court, or otherwise be unavailable for forfeiture; (b)

the need to preserve the availability of the property through the entry of the requested order outweighs the hardship on any party against whom the order may operate; and (c) in an action relating to real property, that entry of the requested order will not substantially diminish, impair, or terminate the lawful property interest in such real property of any person or persons other than the defendant or defendants.

4. Upon motion of any party against whom a provisional remedy granted pursuant to this article is in effect, the court may issue an order modifying or vacating such provisional remedy if necessary to permit the moving party to obtain funds for the payment of reasonable living expenses, other costs or expenses related to the maintenance, operation, or preservation of property which is the subject of any such provisional remedy or reasonable and bona fide attorneys' fees and expenses for the representation of the defendant in the forfeiture proceeding or in a related criminal matter relating thereto, payment for which is not otherwise available from assets of the defendant which are not subject to such provisional remedy. Any such motion shall be supported by an affidavit establishing the unavailability of other assets of the moving party which are not the subject of such provisional remedy for payment of such expenses or fees.

1990 AMENDMENTS

L. 1990, ch. 655, eff. Nov. 1, 1990, amended CPLR 1312 by adding part (c) of subdivision (3), setting forth the basis for granting an application for a provisional remedy in an action relating to real property, and by adding subdivision (4).

1984 AMENDMENTS

L. 1984, ch. 669, eff. Aug. 1, 1984, repealed former Article 13-A and added a new Article 13-A, comprising CPLR 1310 through CPLR 1352. New Article 13-A is applicable to crimes committed on and after Aug. 1, 1984.

§ 1313. Debt or property subject to attachment; proper garnishee.

Any debt or property against which a forfeiture judgment may be enforced as provided under this article is subject to attachment. The proper garnishee of any such property or debt is the person designated as a proper garnishee for purposes of enforcing money judgments in section five thousand two hundred one of this chapter. For the purpose of applying the provisions to attachment, references to a "judgment debtor" in section five thousand two hundred one and in subdivision (i) of section one hundred five of this chapter shall be construed to mean "defendant."

1984 AMENDMENTS

L. 1984, ch. 669, eff. Aug. 1, 1984, repealed former Article 13-A and added a new Article 13-A, comprising CPLR 1310 through CPLR 1352. New Article 13-A is applicable to crimes committed on and after Aug. 1, 1984.

§ 1314. Attaching creditor's rights in personal property.

Where the claiming authority has delivered an order of attachment to a claiming agent, the claiming authority's rights in a debt owed to a defendant or in an interest of a defendant in personal property against which debt or property a judgment may be enforced, are superior to the extent of the amount of the attachment to the rights of any transferee of the debt or property, except:

1. A transferee who acquired the debt or property before it was levied upon for fair consideration and without knowledge of the order of attachment; or

2. A transferee who acquired the debt or property for fair consideration after it was levied upon without knowledge of the levy while it was not in the possession of the claiming agent.

1984 AMENDMENTS

L. 1984, ch. 669, eff. Aug. 1, 1984, repealed former Article 13-A and added a new Article 13-A, comprising CPLR 1310 through CPLR 1352. New Article 13-A is applicable to crimes committed on and after Aug. 1, 1984.

§ 1315. Discharge of garnishee's obligation.

A person who, pursuant to an order of attachment, pays or delivers to the claiming agent money or other personal property in which a defendant has or will have an interest, or so pays a debt he or she owes the defendant, is discharged from his or her obligation to the defendant to the extent of the payment or delivery.

1984 AMENDMENTS

L. 1984, ch. 669, eff. Aug. 1, 1984, repealed former Article 13-A and added a new Article 13-A, comprising CPLR 1310 through CPLR 1352. New Article 13-A is applicable to crimes committed on and after Aug. 1, 1984.

§ 1316. Order of attachment on notice; temporary restraining order; contents.

Upon a motion on notice for an order of attachment, the court may, without notice to the defendant, grant a temporary restraining order prohibiting the transfer of assets by a garnishee as provided in subdivision two of section one thousand three hundred twenty of this article. The contents of the order of attachment granted pursuant to this section shall be as provided in subdivision one of section one thousand three hundred seventeen of this article.

1984 AMENDMENTS

L. 1984, ch. 669, eff. Aug. 1, 1984, repealed former Article 13-A and added a new Article 13-A, comprising CPLR 1310 through CPLR 1352. New Article 13-A is applicable to crimes committed on and after Aug. 1, 1984.

§ 1317. Order of attachment without notice.

1. When granted; contents. An order of attachment may be granted without notice, before or after service of summons and at any time prior to judgment. It shall specify the amount to be secured by the order of attachment including any interest, costs and any claiming agent's fees and expenses, be endorsed with the name and address of the claiming authority and shall be directed to a claiming agent in any county or in the city of New York where any property in which the defendant has an interest is located or where a garnishee may be served. The order shall direct the claiming agent to levy within his or her jurisdiction, at any time before final judgment, upon such property in which the defendant has an interest and upon such debts owing to the defendant as will satisfy the amount specified in the order of attachment.

2. Confirmation of order. An order of attachment granted without notice shall provide that within a period not to exceed five days after levy, the claiming authority shall move, on such notice as the court shall direct to the defendant, the garnishee, if any, and the claiming agent, for an order confirming the order of attachment. If the claiming authority fails to make such motion within the required period, the order of attachment and levy thereunder shall have no further effect and shall be vacated upon motion. Upon the motion to confirm, the provisions of subdivision two of section one thousand three hundred twenty-nine of this article shall apply. An order of attachment granted

without notice may provide that the claiming agent refrain from taking any property levied upon into his actual custody, pending further order of the court.

1984 AMENDMENTS

L. 1984, ch. 669, eff. Aug. 1, 1984, repealed former Article 13-A and added a new Article 13-A, comprising CPLR 1310 through CPLR 1352. New Article 13-A is applicable to crimes committed on and after Aug. 1, 1984.

§ 1318. Motion papers; filing; demand; damages.

1. Affidavit; other papers. On a motion for an order of attachment, or for an order to confirm an order of attachment, the claiming authority shall show, by affidavit and such other written evidence as may be submitted, that there is a cause of action and showing grounds for relief as required by section one thousand three hundred twelve of this article.

2. Filing. Within ten days after the granting of an order of attachment, the claiming authority shall file it and the affidavit and other papers upon which it was based and the summons and complaint or proposed complaint in the action. A court for good cause shown may extend the time for such filing upon application of the claiming authority. Unless the time for filing has been extended, the order shall be invalid if not so filed, except that a person upon whom it is served shall not be liable for acting upon it as if it were valid without knowledge of the invalidity.

3. Demand for papers. At any time after property has been levied upon, the defendant may serve upon the claiming authority a written demand that the papers upon which the order of attachment was granted and the levy made be served upon him or her. As soon as practicable after service of the demand, the claiming authority shall cause the papers demanded to be served by mailing the same to the address specified in the demand. A demand under this subdivision shall not of itself constitute an appearance in the action.

4. Damages. The claiming authority shall be liable to the defendant for all costs and damages, including reasonable attorney's fees, which may be sustained by reason of the attachment if the defendant recovers judgment, or if it is finally decided that the claiming authority was not entitled to an attachment of the defendant's property. In order to establish the claiming authority's liability, the defendant must prove by

a preponderance of the evidence that in obtaining the order of attachment the claiming authority acted without reasonable cause, and not in good faith.

1984 AMENDMENTS

L. 1984, ch. 669, eff. Aug. 1, 1984, repealed former Article 13-A and added a new Article 13-A, comprising CPLR 1310 through CPLR 1352. New Article 13-A is applicable to crimes committed on and after the effective date.

§ 1319.   Service of summons.

An order of attachment granted before service is made on the defendant against whom the attachment is granted is valid only if, within sixty days after the order is granted, a summons is served upon the defendant or first publication of the summons against the defendant is made pursuant to an order and publication is subsequently completed, except that a person upon whom the order of attachment is served shall not be liable for acting upon it as if it were valid without knowledge of the invalidity. If the defendant dies within sixty days after the order is granted and before the summons is served upon him or her or publication is completed, the order is valid only if the summons is served upon his or her executor or administrator within sixty days after letters are issued. Upon such terms as may be just and upon good cause shown the court may extend the time, not exceeding sixty days, within which the summons must be served or publication commenced pursuant to this section, provided that the application for extension is made before the expiration of the time fixed.

1992 AMENDMENTS

L. 1992, ch. 216, eff. July 1, 1992, amended the first sentence of CPLR 1319 by deleting the words "an action is commenced" after the words "attachment granted before" and inserting in their place "service is made on the defendant against whom the attachment is granted."

1984 AMENDMENTS

L. 1984, ch. 669, eff. Aug. 1, 1984, repealed former Article 13-A and added a new Article 13-A, comprising CPLR 1310 through CPLR 1352. New Article 13-A is applicable to crimes committed on and after Aug. 1, 1984.

§ 1320.   Levy upon personal property by service of order.

1. Method of levy. The claiming agent shall levy upon any interest of the defendant in personal property, or upon any debt owed to the

defendant, by serving a copy of the order of attachment upon the garnishee, or upon the defendant if property to be levied upon is in the defendant's possession or custody, in the same manner as a summons except that such service shall not be made by delivery of a copy to a person authorized to receive service of summons solely be* a designation filed pursuant to a provision of law other than rule three hundred eighteen of this chapter.

2. Effect of levy; prohibition of transfer. A levy by service of an order of attachment upon a person other than the defendant is effective only if, at the time of service, such person owes a debt to the defendant or such person is in the possession or custody of property in which such person knows or has reason to believe the defendant has an interest, or if the claiming authority has stated in a notice which shall be served with the order that a specified debt is owed by the person served to the defendant or that the defendant has an interest in specified property in the possession or custody of the person served. All property in which the defendant is known or believed to have an interest then in and thereafter coming into the possession or custody of such a person, including any specified in the notice, and all debts of such person, including any specified in the notice, then due and thereafter coming due to the defendant, shall be subject to the levy. Unless the court orders otherwise, the person served with the order shall forthwith transfer or deliver all such property, and pay all such debts upon maturity, up to the amount specified in order of attachment, to the claiming agent and execute any document necessary to effect the payment, transfer or delivery. After such payment, transfer or delivery, property coming into the possession or custody of the garnishee, or debt incurred by him or her, shall not be subject to the levy. Until such payment, transfer or delivery is made, or until the expiration of ninety days after the service of the order of attachment upon him or her, or of such further time as is provided by any subsequent order of the court served upon him or her, whichever event first occurs, the garnishee is prohibited to make or suffer any sale, assignment or transfer of, or any interference with any such property, or pay over or otherwise dispose of any such debt, to any person other than the claiming agent except upon direction of the claiming agent or pursuant to an order of the court. A garnishee, however, may collect or redeem an instrument received by him or her for such purpose and he or she may sell or

transfer in good faith property held as collateral or otherwise pursuant to pledge thereof or at the direction of any person other than the defendant authorized to direct sale or transfer, provided that the proceeds in which the defendant has an interest be retained subject to the levy. A claiming authority who has specified personal property or debt to be levied upon in a notice served with an order of attachment shall be liable to the owner of the property or the person to whom the debt is owed, if other than the defendant, for any damages sustained by reason of the levy. In order to establish the claiming authority's liability, the owner of the property of** the person to whom the debt is owed must prove by a preponderance of the evidence that, in causing the levy to occur, the claiming authority acted without reasonable cause and not in good faith.

3. Seizure by claiming agent; notice of satisfaction. Where property or debts have been levied upon by service of an order of attachment, the claiming agent shall take into his or her actual custody all such property capable of delivery and shall collect and receive all such debts. When the claiming agent has taken into his or her actual custody property or debts having value sufficient to satisfy the amount specified in the order of attachment, the claiming agent shall notify the defendant and each person upon whom the order of attachment was served that the order of attachment has been fully executed.

4. Proceeding to compel payment or delivery. Where property or debts have been levied upon by service of an order of attachment, the claiming authority may commence a special proceeding against the garnishee served with the order to compel the payment, delivery or transfer to the claiming agent of such property or debts, or to secure a judgment against the garnishee. Notice of petition shall also be served upon the parties to the action and the claiming agent. A garnishee may assert any defense or counterclaim which he or she may have asserted against the defendant. The court may permit any adverse claimant to intervene in the proceeding and may determine his or her rights in accordance with section one thousand three hundred twenty-seven of this article.

5. Failure to proceed. At the expiration of ninety days after a levy is made by service of the order of attachment, or of such further time as the court, upon motion of the claiming authority on notice to the parties

to the action, has provided, the levy shall be void except as to property or debts which the claiming agent has taken into his or her actual custody, collected or received or as to which a proceeding under subdivision four hereof has been commenced.

* [**Editor's note:** So in original. Probably should read "by."]

** [**Editor's note:** So in original. Probably should be "or."]

1984 AMENDMENTS

L. 1984, ch. 669, eff. Aug. 1, 1984, repealed former Article 13-A and added a new Article 13-A, comprising CPLR 1310 through CPLR 1352. New Article 13-A is applicable to crimes committed on and after Aug. 1, 1984.

§ 1321. Levy upon personal property by seizure.

If the claiming authority shall so direct the collecting agent, as an alternative to the method prescribed by section one thousand three hundred twenty of this article, shall levy upon property capable of delivery by taking the property into his actual custody. In cases in which the collecting agent is a sheriff, the sheriff may require that the claiming authority furnish indemnity that is either satisfactory to the sheriff or is fixed by the court. The collecting agent shall within four days serve a copy of the order of attachment in the manner prescribed by subdivision one of section one thousand three hundred twenty of this article upon the person from whose possession or custody the property was taken.

1984 AMENDMENTS

L. 1984, ch. 669, eff. Aug. 1, 1984, repealed former Article 13-A and added a new Article 13-A, comprising CPLR 1310 through CPLR 1352. New Article 13-A is applicable to crimes committed on and after Aug. 1, 1984.

§ 1322. Levy upon real property.

The claiming agent shall levy upon any interest of the defendant in real property by filing with the clerk of the county in which the property is located a notice of attachment endorsed with the name and address of the claiming authority and stating the names of the parties to the action, the amount specified in the order of attachment and a description of the property levied upon. The clerk shall record and index the notice in the same books, in the same manner and with the same effect, as a notice of the pendency of an action.

1984 AMENDMENTS

L. 1984, ch. 669, eff. Aug. 1, 1984, repealed former Article 13-A and added a new Article 13-A, comprising CPLR 1310 through CPLR 1352. New Article 13-A is applicable to crimes committed on and after Aug. 1, 1984.

§ 1323.   Additional undertaking to carrier garnishee.

A garnishee who is a common carrier may transport or deliver property actually loaded on a conveyance, notwithstanding the service upon him or her of an order of attachment, if it was loaded without reason to believe that an order of attachment affecting the property had been granted, unless the claiming authority gives an undertaking in an amount fixed by the court, that the claiming authority shall pay any such carrier all expenses and damages which may be incurred for unloading the property and for detention of the conveyance necessary for that purpose.

CPLR

1984 AMENDMENTS

L. 1984, ch. 669, eff. Aug. 1, 1984, repealed former Article 13-A and added a new Article 13-A, comprising CPLR 1310 through CPLR 1352. New Article 13-A is applicable to crimes committed on and after Aug. 1, 1984.

§ 1324.   Claiming agent's duties after levy.

1. Retention of property. The claiming agent shall hold and safely keep all property or debts paid, delivered, transferred or assigned to him or her or taken into his or her custody to answer any judgment that may be obtained against the defendant in the action, unless otherwise directed by the court or the claiming authority, subject to the payment of the claiming agent's fees and expenses, if any. Any money shall be held for the benefit of the parties to the action in an interest-bearing trust account at a national or state bank or trust company. If the urgency of the case requires, the court may direct sale or other disposition of property, specifying the manner and terms thereof, with notice to the parties to the action and the garnishee who has possession of such property.

2. Inventory. Within fifteen days after service of an order of attachment or forthwith after such order has been vacated or annulled, the claiming agent shall file an inventory of property seized, a description of real property levied upon, the names and addresses of all persons served with the order of attachment, and an estimate of the

value of all property levied upon.

1984 AMENDMENTS

L. 1984, ch. 669, eff. Aug. 1, 1984, repealed former Article 13-A and added a new Article 13-A, comprising CPLR 1310 through CPLR 1352. New Article 13-A is applicable to crimes committed on and after Aug. 1, 1984.

§ 1325. Garnishee's statement.

Within ten days after service upon a garnishee of an order of attachment, or within such shorter time as the court may direct, the garnishee shall serve upon the claiming agent a statement specifying all debts of the garnishee to the defendant, when the debts are due, all property in the possession or custody of the garnishee in which the defendant has an interest, and the amounts and value of the debts and property specified. If the garnishee has money belonging to, or is indebted to, the defendant in at least the amount of the attachment, he or she may limit his or her statement to that fact.

1984 AMENDMENTS

L. 1984, ch. 669, eff. Aug. 1, 1984, repealed former Article 13-A and added a new Article 13-A, comprising CPLR 1310 through CPLR 1352. New Article 13-A is applicable to crimes committed on and after Aug. 1, 1984.

§ 1326. Disclosure.

Upon motion of any interested person, at any time after the granting of an order of attachment and prior to final judgment in the action, upon such notice as the court may direct, the court may order disclosure by any person of information regarding any property in which the defendant has or may have interest, or any debts owed or which may be owed to the defendant.

1984 AMENDMENTS

L. 1984, ch. 669, eff. Aug. 1, 1984, repealed former Article 13-A and added a new Article 13-A, comprising CPLR 1310 through CPLR 1352. New Article 13-A is applicable to crimes committed on and after Aug. 1, 1984.

§ 1327. Proceedings to determine adverse claims.

Prior to the application of property or debt to the satisfaction of a judgment, any person, other than a party to the action, who has an interest in the property subject to forfeiture may commence a special proceeding against the claiming authority to determine the rights of adverse claimants to the property or debt, and in such proceeding shall serve a notice of petition upon the claiming agent and upon each party in the same manner as a notice of motion. The proceeding may be commenced in the county where the property was levied upon, or in the county where the order of attachment is filed. The court may vacate or discharge the attachment, void the levy, direct the disposition of the property or debt, direct that undertakings be provided or released, or direct that damages be awarded. Where there appear to be disputed questions of fact, the court shall order a separate trial, indicating the person who shall have possession of the property pending a decision and the undertaking, if any, which such person shall give. If the court determines that the adverse claim was fraudulent or made without any reasonable basis whatsoever, it may require the claimant to pay the claiming authority the reasonable expenses incurred in the proceeding, including reasonable attorney's fees, and any other damages suffered by reason of the claim. The commencement of the proceeding shall not of itself subject the adverse claimant to personal jurisdiction with respect to any matter other than the claim asserted in the proceeding.

CPLR

1994 AMENDMENTS

L. 1994, ch. 563, eff. July 26, 1994, amended CPLR 1327 by replacing the words "by serving" with the words "and in such proceeding shall serve."

1984 AMENDMENTS

L. 1984, ch. 669, eff. Aug. 1, 1984, repealed former Article 13-A and added a new Article 13-A, comprising CPLR 1310 through CPLR 1352. New Article 13-A is applicable to crimes committed on and after Aug. 1, 1984.

§ 1328. Discharge of attachment.

1. A defendant whose property or debt has been levied upon may move, upon notice to the claiming authority and the claiming agent, for any* order discharging the attachment as to all or part of the property or debt upon payment of the claiming agent's fees and expenses, if any. On such a motion, the defendant shall give an undertaking, in an amount equal to the value of the property or debt sought to be discharged, that the defendant will pay to the claiming authority the amount of any judgment which may be recovered in the action against him or her, not exceeding the amount of the undertaking. Making a motion or giving an undertaking under this section shall not of itself constitute an appearance in the action.

2. When a motion to discharge is made in the case of property levied upon pursuant to a claimed violation of the tax law, the amount of the undertaking required shall be an amount equal to the lesser of:

(a) The amount specified in subdivision one of this section; or

(b) The aggregate amount of all unpaid tax and civil penalties for such violation.

* [**Editor's note:** So in original. Probably should be "an."]

1985 AMENDMENTS

L. 1985, ch. 65, eff. April 17, 1985, added subdivision (2).

1984 AMENDMENTS

L. 1984, ch. 669, eff. Aug. 1, 1984, repealed former Article 13-A and added a new Article 13-A, comprising CPLR 1310 through CPLR 1352. New Article 13-A is applicable to crimes committed on and after Aug. 1, 1984.

§ 1329. Vacating or modifying attachment.

1. Motion to vacate or modify. Prior to the application of property or debt to the satisfaction of a judgment, the defendant, the garnishee or any person having an interest in the property or debt may move, on notice to each party and the claiming agent, for an order vacating or modifying the order of attachment. Upon the motion, the court may give the claiming authority a reasonable opportunity to correct any defect. If, after the defendant has appeared in the action, the court determines that the attachment is unnecessary to the security of the claiming authority, it shall vacate the order of attachment. Such a motion shall not of itself constitute an appearance in the action.

2. Burden of proof. Upon a motion to vacate or modify an order of attachment the claiming authority shall have the burden of establishing the grounds for the attachment, the need for continuing the levy and the probability that he or she will succeed on the merits.

1984 AMENDMENTS

L. 1984, ch. 669, eff. Aug. 1, 1984, repealed former Article 13-A and added a new Article 13-A, comprising CPLR 1310 through CPLR 1352. New Article 13-A is applicable to crimes committed on and after the effective date.

§ 1330. Annulment of attachment.

An order of attachment is annulled when the action in which it was granted abates or is discontinued or a judgment entered therein in favor of the claiming authority is fully satisfied, or a judgment is entered therein in favor of the defendant. In the last specified case a stay of proceedings suspends the effect of the annulment, and a reversal or vacating of the judgment revives the order of attachment.

1984 AMENDMENTS

L. 1984, ch. 669, eff. Aug. 1, 1984, repealed former Article 13-A and added a new article 13-A, comprising CPLR 1310 through CPLR 1352. New Article 13-A is applicable to crimes committed on and after the effective date.

§ 1331. Return of property; directions to clerk and claiming agent.

Upon motion of any interested person, on notice to the claiming agent and each party, the court may direct the clerk of any county to cancel a notice of attachment and may direct the claiming agent to dispose of, account for, assign, return or release any property or debt, or the proceeds thereof, or any undertaking, or to file additional inventories or returns, subject to the payment of the claiming agent's fees, and expenses, if any. The court shall direct that notice of the motion be given to the claiming authority and plaintiffs in other orders of attachment, if any, and to the judgment creditors of executions, if any, affecting any property or debt, or the proceeds thereof, sought to be returned or released.

1984 AMENDMENTS

L. 1984, ch. 669, eff. Aug. 1, 1984, repealed former Article 13-A and added a new Article 13-A, comprising CPLR 1310 through CPLR 1352. New Article 13-A is applicable to crimes committed on and after the effective date.

§ 1332. Disposition of attachment property after execution issued; priority of orders of attachment.

Where an execution is issued upon a judgment entered against the defendant, the claiming agent's duty with respect to custody and disposition of property or debt levied upon pursuant to an order of attachment is the same as if he or she had levied upon it pursuant to the execution. The priority among two or more orders of attachment against the same defendant shall be in the order in which they were delivered to the officer who levied upon the property or debt. The priority between an order of attachment and an execution, or a payment, delivery or receivership order, is set forth in section five thousand two hundred thirty-four of this chapter.

1984 AMENDMENTS

L. 1984, ch. 669, eff. Aug. 1, 1984, repealed former Article 13-A and added a new Article 13-A, comprising CPLR 1310 through CPLR 1352. New Article 13-A is applicable to crimes committed on and after the effective date.

§ 1333. Grounds for preliminary injunction and temporary restraining order.

A preliminary injunction may be granted in any action under this article, whether for money damages or otherwise, where it appears that the defendant threatens or is about to do, or is doing or procuring or suffering to be done, an act in violation of the claiming authority's rights respecting the subject of the action, and thereby tending to render a resulting judgment ineffectual. A temporary restraining order may be granted pending a hearing for a preliminary injunction where it appears that immediate and irreparable injury, loss or damage will result unless the defendant is restrained before the hearing can be had. A preliminary injunction may be granted only upon notice to the defendant. Notice of the motion may be served with the summons or at any time thereafter and prior to judgment.

1984 AMENDMENTS

L. 1984, ch. 669, eff. Aug. 1, 1984, repealed former Article 13-A and added a new Article 13-A, comprising CPLR 1310 through CPLR 1352. New Article 13-A is applicable to crimes committed on and after the effective date.

§ 1334. Motion papers.

Affidavit; other papers. On a motion for a preliminary injunction the claiming authority shall show, by affidavit and such other written evidence as may be submitted, that there is a cause of action and showing grounds for relief as required by section one thousand three hundred twelve of this article.

1984 AMENDMENTS

L. 1984, ch. 669, eff. Aug. 1, 1984, repealed former Article 13-A and added

a new Article 13-A, comprising CPLR 1310 through CPLR 1352. New Article 13-A is applicable to crimes committed on and after the effective date.

§ 1335. Temporary restraining order.

1. Generally. If, on a motion for a preliminary injunction, the claiming authority shall show that immediate and irreparable injury, loss or damages may result unless the defendant is restrained before a hearing can be had, a temporary restraining order may be granted without notice. Upon granting a temporary restraining order, the court shall set the hearing for the preliminary injunction at the earliest possible time.

2. Service. Unless the court orders otherwise, a temporary restraining order together with the papers upon which it was based, and a notice of hearing for the preliminary injunction, shall be personally served in the same manner as a summons.

1984 AMENDMENTS

L. 1984, ch. 669, eff. Aug. 1, 1984, repealed former Article 13-A and added a new Article 13-A, comprising CPLR 1310 through CPLR 1352. New Article 13-A is applicable to crimes committed on and after Aug. 1, 1984.

§ 1336. Vacating or modifying preliminary injunction or temporary restraining order.

A defendant enjoined by a preliminary injunction may move at any time, on notice to the claiming authority, to vacate or modify it. On motion, without notice, made by a defendant enjoined by a temporary restraining order, the judge who granted it, or in his or her absence or disability, another judge, may vacate or modify the order. An order granted without notice and vacating or modifying a temporary restraining order shall be effective when, together with the papers upon which it is based, it is filed with the clerk and served upon the claiming authority. As a condition to granting an order vacating or modifying a preliminary injunction or a temporary restraining order, a court may require the defendant to give an undertaking, in an amount to be fixed by the court, that the defendant shall pay to the claiming authority any loss sustained by reason of the vacating or modifying order.

1984 AMENDMENTS

L. 1984, ch. 669, eff. Aug. 1, 1984, repealed former Article 13-A and added

CPLR

a new Article 13-A, comprising CPLR 1310 through CPLR 1352. New Article 13-A is applicable to crimes committed on and after Aug. 1, 1984.

§ 1337. Ascertaining damages sustained by reason of preliminary injunction or temporary restraining order.

The damages sustained by reason of a preliminary injunction or temporary restraining order may be ascertained upon motion on such notice to all interested persons as the court shall direct. Where the defendant enjoined was an officer of a corporation or joint-stock association or a representative of another person, the damages sustained by such corporation, association or person represented, to the amount of such excess, may also be ascertained. The amount of damages so ascertained is conclusive upon all persons who were served with notice of the motion and such amount may be recovered by the person entitled thereto in a separate action. In order to establish the claiming authority's liability for damages, the person seeking such damages must prove by a preponderance of the evidence that, in causing the temporary restraining order or preliminary injunction to be granted, the claiming authority acted without reasonable cause and not in good faith.

1984 AMENDMENTS

L. 1984, ch. 669, eff. Aug. 1, 1984, repealed former Article 13-A and added a new Article 13-A, comprising CPLR 1310 through CPLR 1352. New Article 13-A is applicable to crimes committed on and after Aug. 1, 1984.

§ 1338. Appointment and powers of temporary receiver.

1. Appointment of temporary receiver; joinder of moving party. Upon motion of the claiming authority on* any other person having an apparent interest in property which is the subject of an action pursuant to this article, a temporary receiver of the property may be appointed, before or after service of summons and at any time prior to judgment, or during the pendency of an appeal, where there is danger that the property will be removed from the state, or lost, materially injured or destroyed. A motion made by a person not already a party to the action constitutes an appearance in the action and the person shall be joined as a party.

2. Powers of temporary receiver. The court appointing a receiver may authorize him or her to take and hold real and personal property,

and sue for, collect and sell debts or claims, upon such conditions and for such purposes as the court shall direct. A receiver shall have no power to employ counsel unless expressly so authorized by order of the court. Upon motion of the receiver or a party, powers granted to a temporary receiver may be extended or limited or the receivership may be extended to another action involving the property.

3. Duration of temporary receivership. A temporary receivership shall not continue after final judgment unless otherwise directed by the court.

* [**Editor's note:** So in original. Probably should be "or."]

1984 AMENDMENTS

L. 1984, ch. 669, eff. Aug. 1, 1984, repealed former Article 13-A and added a new Article 13-A, comprising CPLR 1310 through CPLR 1352. New Article 13-A is applicable to crimes committed on and after Aug. 1, 1984.

§ 1339. Oath.

A temporary receiver, before entering upon his or her duties, shall be sworn faithfully and fairly to discharge the trust committed to him or her. The oath may be administered by any person authorized to take acknowledgments of deeds by the real property law. The oath may be waived upon consent of all parties.

CROSS REFERENCES

See **Real Prop. L.** § 298 *et seq.,* in Appendix, *below,* for provisions authorizing the taking of acknowledgments of deeds.

1984 AMENDMENTS

L. 1984, ch. 669, eff. Aug. 1, 1984, repealed former Article 13-A and added a new Article 13-A, comprising CPLR 1310 through CPLR 1352. New Article 13-A is applicable to crimes committed on and after Aug. 1, 1984.

§ 1340. Undertaking.

A temporary receiver shall give an undertaking in an amount to be fixed by the court making the appointment, that he or she will faithfully discharge his or her duties.

1984 AMENDMENTS

L. 1984, ch. 669, eff. Aug. 1, 1984, repealed former Article 13-A and added a new Article 13-A, comprising CPLR 1310 through CPLR 1352. New

CPLR

Article 13-A is applicable to crimes committed on and after Aug. 1, 1984.

§ 1341. Accounts.

A temporary receiver shall keep written accounts itemizing receipts and expenditures, and describing the property and naming the depository of receivership funds, which shall be open to inspection by any person having an apparent interest in the property. [Upon motion of the receiver or of any person having an apparent interest in the property,]* the court may require the keeping of particular records or direct or limit inspection or require presentation of a temporary receiver's accounts. Notice of a motion for the presentation of a temporary receiver's accounts shall be served upon the sureties on his or her undertaking as well as upon each party.

* [Editor's note: Bracketed material has apparently been omitted due to an oversight.]

1984 AMENDMENTS

L. 1984, ch. 669, eff. Aug. 1, 1984, repealed former Article 13-A and added a new Article 13-A, comprising CPLR 1310 through CPLR 1352. New Article 13-A is applicable to crimes committed on and after Aug. 1, 1984.

§ 1342. Removal.

Upon motion of any party or upon its own initiative, the court which appointed a receiver may remove him or her at any time.

1984 AMENDMENTS

L. 1984, ch. 669, eff. Aug. 1, 1984, repealed former Article 13-A and added a new Article 13-A, comprising CPLR 1310 through CPLR 1352. New Article 13-A is applicable to crimes committed on and after Aug. 1, 1984.

§ 1343. Notice of pendency; constructive notice.

A notice of pendency may be filed in any action brought pursuant to this article in which the judgment demanded would affect the title to, or the possession, use or enjoyment of, real property. The pendency of such an action is constructive notice, from the time of filing of the notice only, to a purchaser from, or incumbrancer against, any defendant named in a notice of pendency indexed in a block index against a block in which property affected is situated or any defendant against whose name a notice of pendency is indexed. A person whose conveyance or incumbrance is recorded after the filing of the notice is bound by all proceedings taken in the action after such filing to the same extent as if he or she were a party.

1984 AMENDMENTS

L. 1984, ch. 669, eff. Aug. 1, 1984, repealed former Article 13-A and added a new Article 13-A, comprising CPLR 1310 through CPLR 1352. New Article 13-A is applicable to crimes committed on and after Aug. 1, 1984.

§ 1344. Filing, content and indexing of notice of pendency.

1. Filing. In a case specified in section one thousand three hundred forty-three of this article the notice of pendency shall be filed in the office of the clerk of any county where property affected is situated, before or after service of a summons and at any time prior to judgment. Unless it has already been filed in that county, the complaint shall be filed with the notice of pendency.

2. Content, designation of index. A notice of pendency shall state the names of the parties to the action, that the action is for forfeiture pursuant to this article and a description of the property affected. A notice of pendency filed with a clerk who maintains a block index shall contain a designation of the number of each block on the land map of a county which is affected by the notice. A notice of pendency filed with a clerk who does not maintain a block index shall contain a designation of the names of each defendant against whom the notice is directed to be indexed.

3. Indexing. Each county clerk with whom a notice of pendency is filed shall immediately record and index it against the blocks or names designated. A county clerk who does not maintain a block index shall index a notice of pendency of an action for partition against the names of each claiming authority and each defendant not designated as wholly fictitious.

1984 AMENDMENTS

L. 1984, ch. 669, eff. Aug. 1, 1984, repealed former Article 13-A and added a new Article 13-A, comprising CPLR 1310 through CPLR 1352. New Article 13-A is applicable to crimes committed on and after Aug. 1, 1984.

§ 1345. Service of summons.

A notice of pendency filed before an action is commenced is effective only if, within thirty days after filing, a summons is served upon the defendant or first publication of the summons against the defendant is made pursuant to an order and publication is subsequently completed. If the defendant dies within thirty days after filing and before the summons served upon him or her or publication is completed, the notice is effective only if the summons is served upon his or her executor or administrator within sixty days after letters are issued.

1984 AMENDMENTS

L. 1984, ch. 669, eff. Aug. 1, 1984, repealed former Article 13-A and added a new Article 13-A, comprising CPLR 1310 through CPLR 1352. New Article 13-A is applicable to crimes committed on and after Aug. 1, 1984.

§ 1346. Duration of notice of pendency.

A notice of pendency shall be effective for a period of three years from the date of filing. Before expiration of a period or extended period, the court, upon motion of the claiming authority and upon such notice as it may require, for good cause shown, may grant an extension for a like additional period. An extension order shall be filed, recorded and indexed before expiration of the prior period.

1984 AMENDMENTS

L. 1984, ch. 669, eff. Aug. 1, 1984, repealed former Article 13-A and added a new Article 13-A, comprising CPLR 1310 through CPLR 1352. New Article 13-A is applicable to crimes committed on and after Aug. 1, 1984.

§ 1347. Motion for cancellation of notice of pendency.

1. Mandatory cancellation. The court, upon motion of any person aggrieved and upon such notice as it may require, shall direct any county clerk to cancel a notice of pendency, if service of a summons has not been completed within the time limited by section one thousand three hundred forty-five of this article; or if the action has been settled, discontinued or abated; or if the time to appeal from a final judgment against the claiming authority has expired.

2. Discretionary cancellation. The court, upon a motion of any person aggrieved and upon such notice as it may require, may direct any county clerk to cancel a notice of pendency, if the claiming authority has not commenced or prosecuted the action in good faith.

3. Costs and expenses. The court, in an order canceling a notice of pendency under this section, may direct the claiming authority to pay any costs and expenses occasioned by the filing and cancellation, in addition to any costs of the action. In order to establish the claiming authority's liability for such costs and expenses, the person seeking such costs and expenses must prove by a preponderance of the evidence that, in causing the notice to pendency to be filed, the claiming authority acted without reasonable cause and not in good faith.

4. Cancellation by stipulation. At any time prior to entry of judgment, a notice of pendency shall be cancelled by the county clerk without an order, on the filing with him or her of:

(a) An affidavit by the claiming authority showing which defendants have been served with process, which defendants are in default in appearing or answering, and which defendants have appeared or answered and by whom; and

(b) A stipulation consenting to the cancellation, signed by the claiming authority and by the attorneys for all the defendants who have appeared or answered including those who have waived all notices, and executed and acknowledged, in the form required to entitle a deed to be recorded, by the defendants who have been served with process and have not appeared but whose time to do so has not expired, and by any defendants who have appeared in person.

5. Cancellation by a claiming authority. At any time prior to the entry of a judgment a notice of pendency of action shall be cancelled by the county clerk without an order on the filing with him or her of an affidavit by the claiming authority showing that there have been no appearances and that the time to appear has expired for all parties.

1984 AMENDMENTS

L. 1984, ch. 669, eff. Aug. 1, 1984, repealed former Article 13-A and added a new Article 13-A, comprising CPLR 1310 through CPLR 1352. New Article 13-A is applicable to crimes committed on and after Aug. 1, 1984.

§ 1348. Undertaking for cancellation of notice of pendency.

The court, upon motion of any person aggrieved and upon such notice of pendency as it may require, may direct any county clerk to cancel a notice of pendency, upon such terms as are just, whether or not the judgment demanded would affect specific real property, if the moving party shall give an undertaking in an amount to be fixed by the court, and if the court finds that adequate relief can be secured to the claiming authority by the giving of such an undertaking.

1984 AMENDMENTS

L. 1984, ch. 669, eff. Aug. 1, 1984, repealed former Article 13-A and added a new Article 13-A, comprising CPLR 1310 through CPLR 1352. New Article 13-A is applicable to crimes committed on and after Aug. 1, 1984.

§ 1349. Disposal of property.

1. Any judgment or order of forfeiture issued pursuant to this article shall include provisions for the disposal of the property found to have been forfeited.

2. If any other provision of law expressly governs the manner of disposition of property subject to the judgment or order of forfeiture, that provision of law shall be controlling. Upon application by a claiming agent for reimbursement of moneys directly expended by a claiming agent in the underlying criminal investigation for the purchase of contraband which were converted into a non-monetary form or which have not been otherwise recovered, the court shall direct such reimbursement from money forfeited pursuant to this article. Upon application of the claiming agent, the court may direct that any vehicles, vessels or aircraft forfeited pursuant to this article be retained by the claiming agent for law enforcement purposes, unless the court determines that such property is subject to a perfected lien, in which case the court may not direct that the property be retained unless all such liens on the property to be retained have been satisfied or pursuant to the court's order will be satisfied. In the absence of an application by the claiming agent, the claiming authority may apply to the court to retain such property for law enforcement purposes. Upon such application, the court may direct that such property be retained by the claiming authority for law enforcement purposes, unless the court determines that such property is subject to a perfected lien. If not so retained, the judgment or order shall direct the claiming authority to sell the property in accordance with article fifty-one of this chapter, and that the proceeds of such sale and any other moneys realized as a consequence of any forfeiture pursuant to this article shall be appor-

tioned and paid in the following descending order of priority:

(a) Amounts ordered to be paid by the court in satisfaction of any lien or claim against property forfeited. A fine imposed pursuant to the penal law shall not be deemed to constitute a lien or claim for purposes of this section;

(b) Amounts ordered to be paid by the defendant in any other action or proceeding as restitution, reparations or damages to a victim of the crime, which crime constitutes the basis upon which forfeiture was effected under this article, to the extent such amounts remain unpaid;

(c) Amounts ordered to be paid by the defendant in any other action or proceeding as restitution, reparations or damages to a victim of any crime committed by the defendant even though such crime did not constitute the basis for forfeiture under this article, to the extent that such amounts remain unpaid;

(d) Amounts actually expended by a claiming authority or claiming agent, which amounts are substantiated by vouchers or other evidence, for the:

(i) Maintenance and operation of real property attached pursuant to this article. Expenditures authorized by this subparagraph are limited to mortgage, tax and other financial obligations imposed by law and those other payments necessary to provide essential services and repairs to real property whose occupants are innocent of the criminal conduct which led to the attachment or forfeiture; and

(ii) proper storage, cleanup and disposal of hazardous substances or other materials, the disposal of which is governed by the environmental conservation law, when such storage, cleanup or disposal is required by circumstances attendant to either the commission of the crime or the forfeiture action, or any order entered pursuant thereto;

(e) In addition to amounts, if any, distributed pursuant to paragraph (d) of this subdivision, fifteen percent of all moneys realized through forfeiture to the claiming authority in satisfaction of actual costs and expenses incurred in the investigation, preparation and litigation of the forfeiture action, including that proportion of the

CPLR

salaries of the attorneys, clerical and investigative personnel devoted thereto, plus all costs and disbursements taxable under the provisions of this chapter;

(f) In addition to amounts, if any, distributed pursuant to paragraph (d) of this subdivision, five percent of all moneys realized through forfeiture to the claiming agent in satisfaction of actual costs incurred for protecting, maintaining and forfeiting the property including that proportion of the salaries of attorneys, clerical and investigative personnel devoted thereto;

(g) Forty percent of all moneys realized through forfeiture which are remaining after distributions pursuant to paragraphs (a) through (f) of this subdivision, to the chemical dependence service fund established pursuant to section ninety-seven-w of the state finance law;

(h) All moneys remaining after distributions pursuant to paragraphs (a) through (g) of this subdivision shall be distributed as follows:

(i) seventy-five percent of such moneys shall be deposited to a law enforcement purposes subaccount of the general fund of the state where the claiming agent is an agency of the state or the political subdivision or public authority of which the claiming agent is a part, to be used for law enforcement use in the investigation of penal law offenses;

(ii) the remaining twenty-five percent of such moneys shall be deposited to a prosecution services subaccount of the general fund of the state where the claiming authority is the attorney general or the political subdivision of which the claiming authority is a part, to be used for the prosecution of penal law offenses.

Where multiple claiming agents participated in the forfeiture action, funds available pursuant to subparagraph (i) of this paragraph shall be disbursed to the appropriate law enforcement purposes subaccounts in accordance with the terms of a written agreement reflecting the participation of each claiming agent entered into by the participating claiming agents.

3. All moneys distributed to the claiming agent and the claiming

authority pursuant to paragraph (h) of subdivision two of this section shall be used to enhance law enforcement efforts and not in supplantation of ordinary budgetary costs including salaries of personnel, and expenses of the claiming authority or claiming agent during the fiscal year in which this section takes effect.

4. The claiming authority shall report the disposal of property and collection of assets pursuant to this section to the state crime victims board, the state division of criminal justice services and the state division of substance abuse services.

2004 AMENDMENTS

L. 2004, ch. 398, §2, eff. Aug. 17, 2004, amending § 1349, subd.(2)(g), by replacing "substance abuse"with "chemical dependence."

1990 AMENDMENTS

L. 1990, ch. 655, eff. Nov. 1, 1990, repealed former § 1349 and added new § 1349.

§ 1350. Rules of procedure; in general.

The civil practice law and rules shall govern the procedure in proceedings and actions commenced under this article, except where the procedure is regulated by any inconsistent provisions herein.

1984 AMENDMENTS

L. 1984, ch. 669, eff. Aug. 1, 1984, repealed former Article 13-A and added a new Article 13-A, comprising CPLR 1310 through CPLR 1352. New Article 13-A is applicable to crimes committed on and after the effective date.

§ 1351. Application of article.

If any provision of this article or the application thereof to any person or circumstances shall be adjudged by any court of competent jurisdiction to be invalid or unconstitutional, such judgment shall not affect, impair or invalidate the remainder thereof, but shall be confined (i) in its operation of the provision, or (ii) in its application to the person or circumstance directly involved in the controversy in which such judgment shall have been rendered.

1984 AMENDMENTS

L. 1984, ch. 669, eff. Aug. 1, 1984, repealed former Article 13-A and added

a new Article 13-A, comprising CPLR 1310 through CPLR 1352. New Article 13-A is applicable to crimes committed on and after the effective date.

§ 1352. Preservation of other rights and remedies.

The remedies provided for in this article are not intended to substitute for or limit or supersede the lawful authority of any public officer or agency or other person to enforce any other right or remedy provided for by law.

1984 AMENDMENTS

L. 1984, ch. 669, eff. Aug. 1, 1984, repealed former Article 13-A and added a new Article 13-A, comprising CPLR 1310 through CPLR 1352. New Article 13-A is applicable to crimes committed on and after the effective date.

Article 13-B

CIVIL REMEDIES; ENTERPRISE CORRUPTION

SUMMARY OF ARTICLE

§ 1353. Civil remedies.

1. Upon or after conviction of a person of any subdivision of section 460.20 of the penal law, the court may, after making due provision for the rights of innocent persons, enjoin future activity by the person so convicted or an enterprise he controls or in whose control he participates upon a showing that injunctive action is necessary to prevent further violation of that section. In such case the court may:

(a) order the defendant to divest himself of any interest in a specified enterprise;

(b) impose reasonable restrictions upon the future activities or investments of the defendant, including prohibiting the defendant from engaging in the same type of endeavor as the enterprise in which he was engaged in violation of section 460.20 of the penal law;

(c) order the dissolution of any enterprise he controls or the reorganization of any enterprise he controls or of which he participates in the control;

(d) order the suspension or revocation of a license, permit or prior approval granted by any agency of the state or any political subdivision thereof to the defendant or to any enterprise controlled by him or in whose control he participates, provided however, that when the court orders such license, permit or approval revoked or suspended for a period of more than two years, the court shall set a period of time within two years of the date of such revocation or suspension after which the defendant or enterprise may petition the

CPLR

court to permit the defendant or enterprise to request restoration or renewal of such license, permit or approval, by the agency or board empowered to grant it, after notice to and hearing of the party who brought the action in which the revocation or suspension was ordered;

(e) order the revocation of the certificate of incorporation of a corporation organized under the laws of the state in which the defendant has a controlling interest or the revocation of authorization for a foreign corporation in which the defendant has a controlling interest to conduct business within the state upon a finding that the board of directors or a high managerial agent acting on behalf of the corporation, in conducting the affairs of the corporation, has authorized or engaged in activity made unlawful by section 460.20 of the penal law and that such action is necessary for the prevention of future criminal activity made unlawful by section 460.20 of the penal law.

2. The attorney general, the deputy attorney general in charge of the statewide organized crime task force, or any district attorney may institute civil proceedings in the supreme court under this section. Any action brought under this article shall constitute a special proceeding. In any action brought under this article, the supreme court shall proceed as soon as practicable to the hearing and determination thereof. Pending final determination, the supreme court may, at any time, enter such injunctions, prohibitions, or restraining orders or take such actions, including the acceptance of satisfactory performance bonds, ordering of disclosure under article thirty-one of this chapter, or other action as the court may deem proper.

1986 AMENDMENTS

L. 1986, ch. 516, eff. Nov. 1, 1986, permits commencement of a civil or criminal action against a person based upon his participation in a pattern of criminal activity beginning before such date only if his participation in the pattern also specifically includes one criminal act which was a felony and which was committed on or after such date; also added new Article 13-B, comprising CPLR 1353 through 1355.

§ 1354. Joinder of a party.

A person or enterprise not convicted of the crime of enterprise corruption may be made a party to a civil action under this article, whenever joinder of such person or enterprise is necessary pursuant to section 1001 of this chapter.

1986 AMENDMENTS

L. 1986, ch. 516, eff. Nov. 1, 1986, permits commencement of a civil or criminal action against a person based upon his participation in a pattern of criminal activity beginning before such date only if his participation in the pattern also specifically includes one criminal act which was a felony and which was committed on or after such date; also added new Article 13-B, comprising CPLR 1353 through 1355.

§ 1355.   Civil actions notice.

Within fifteen days of commencing a civil proceeding pursuant to this article, the prosecutor bringing such action must notify those district attorneys who were affected district attorneys within the meaning of section 460.60 of the penal law in the prior criminal proceeding.

1986 AMENDMENTS

L. 1986, ch. 516, eff. Nov. 1, 1986, permits commencement of a civil or criminal action against a person based upon his participation in a pattern of criminal activity beginning before such date only if his participation in the pattern also specifically includes one criminal act which was a felony and which was committed on or after such date; also added new Article 13-B, comprising CPLR 1353 through 1355.

CPLR

Article 14

CONTRIBUTION

SUMMARY OF ARTICLE

CPLR

§ 1401. Claim for contribution.

Except as provided in sections 15-108 and 18-201 of the general obligations law, sections eleven and twenty-nine of the workers' compensation law, or the workers' compensation law of any other state or the federal government, two or more persons who are subject to liability for damages for the same personal injury, injury to property or wrongful death, may claim contribution among them whether or not an action has been brought or a judgment has been rendered against the person from whom contribution is sought.

CROSS REFERENCES

G.O.L. § 15-108 appears in Appendix, *below.*

1996 AMENDMENTS

L. 1996, ch. 635, eff. Sept. 10, 1996, amended the section to add references to G.O.L. § 18–201, Workers' Compensation Law §§ 11 and 29, and any other state or federal workers' compensation law.

1974 AMENDMENTS

L. 1974, ch. 742, eff. Sept. 1, 1974, upon the recommendation of the Judicial Conference, repealed former Article 14, entitled "Actions Between Joint Tort-Feasors", and enacted a new Article 14, comprising sections 1401-1404, entitled "Contribution".

The 1974 Judicial Conference Report stated:

"The proposals submitted herewith are directed towards two principal goals:

"First, they would codify and clarify the fundamental rule embodied in [*Dole v. Dow Chem. Co.*, 30 N.Y.2d 143 (1972),] and its progeny (1) that there is no longer the requirement of a joint money judgment against tortfeasors if contribution is to be allowed among them; and (2) that the courts are no longer restricted to either apportioning liability for contribution on a *pro rata* basis, if the statutory prerequisites for contribution have been met, or shifting responsibility entirely from one tortfeasor to another under the primary-secondary tortfeasor doctrine of indemnification. Instead, under proposed new article 14, which the Committee recommends, the courts may apportion the shares of the contributing tortfeasors on the basis of their comparative degrees of culpability.

"Second, a proposed amendment of section 15-108 of the General Obligations Law would remove the disincentive to settle which presently exists under *Dole* for a tortfeasor because he remains subject to contribution to other tortfeasors against whom a judgment in favor of the injured party may be rendered. Under the proposed statutory scheme, the settling tortfeasor would no longer be subject to a claim for contribution by other persons who are liable to the injured party; neither could he assert a claim for contribution against them. Rather, under the proposed amendment, the claim of the injured party against other tortfeasors would be reduced by the amount of the settlement or by the amount of the equitable share of the damages attributable to the released tortfeasor, which ever is the greater.

"[Section 1401] is made applicable to persons subject to liability for the same harm. This provision is broader than that ascribed to a rule encompassing only 'joint tortfeasors' as that phrase has sometimes been construed. . . . [It applies] also, where otherwise appropriate, to 'concurrent tortfeasors,' . . . 'successive and independent tortfeasors,' . . . and to alternative tortfeasors. . . .

"The section is not limited to unintentional tortfeasors. . . . The existence of a procedure in new Article 14 for apportioning liability on the basis of relative degrees of culpability permits the use of the Article where one of the tortfeasors is guilty of intentional misconduct or reckless misconduct while another is not, without fear that the intentional wrongdoer will be 'rewarded' by the presence of a non-intentional wrongdoer. . . .

"While it is expected that in the usual situation in which this Article will be applied, each of the wrongdoers will be charged with the commission of a tort, the Article is not so limited. It is the fact of liability to the same person for the same harm rather than the legal theory upon which tort liability is based which controls.

"For instance, this Article applies in those factual situations in which one or more of the wrongdoers is charged with a breach of warranty. . . . Any conceptual problem arising from an attempt to measure comparative fault, when warranty liability is ostensibly not based upon fault, has been solved by the formulation of the applicable standard of comparison set forth in section 1402.

"When liability to the injured person is predicated upon the violation of a statute, difficult questions concerning the appropriateness of applying the proposed Article arise when the violation of the statute gives rise to strict or absolute liability and does not merely constitute negligence per se. . . . It seems clear that in those strict or absolute liability cases in which every person subject to a claim for contribution has violated the statute, the proposed Article should apply, for its application will foster the goal of loss distribution among wrongdoers without interfering with any legislative policy of deterrence which might have been a motivating factor in the passage of the act.

"However, where only one of the wrongdoers is charged with violating a statute imposing absolute liability, and such wrongdoer attempts to assert a claim for contribution against one who is liable only for common law negligence, resolution of the issue is more difficult. It is suggested that courts should apply this Article in such cases unless it is clear that the legislative policy which led to the passage of the statute would be frustrated by the granting of contribution in favor of the person who violated the statute. . . .

"[The] requirement of common liability is considered essential in a contri- bution statute. . . . However, there may be situations in which one party may not be liable to the injured person but should nonetheless be responsible for contribution. For instance, where, at the time he is sued for contribution, the alleged wrongdoer is not subject to suit directly by the injured party because the statute of limitations has run on that claim, it may nonetheless be proper to subject him to a claim for contribution under this Article if all other requirements of this Article are met. . . .

"The proposed statutory language is broad enough to permit contribution in such cases because the person against whom contribution is sought was 'subject to liability' even though he could not be held liable to the injured person directly at the time he was sued for contribution if he chose to assert the defense of the statute of limitations. Similarly, the proposed statute is not intended to change existing law where contribution is presently permitted despite the fact that the one against whom it is sought had a personal defense against the injured party other than the statute of limitations (e.g., in *Dole* the claim against Dole's employer was barred by the Workmen's Compensation Law, yet the employer was required to contribute his share to the recovery obtained against Dow Chemical Co.). . . ."

§ 1402. Amount of contribution.

The amount of contribution to which a person is entitled shall be the excess paid by him over and above his equitable share of the judgment recovered by the injured party; but no person shall be required to contribute an amount greater than his equitable share. The equitable shares shall be determined in accordance with the relative culpability of each person liable for contribution.

1974 AMENDMENTS

Article added by L. 1974, ch. 742, eff. Sept. 1, 1974.

The 1974 Judicial Conference Report stated, in part:

"The phrase 'relative culpability' is used here in lieu of 'relative degrees of negligence' or 'fault' because this Article permits contribution even when one or more of the wrongdoers is not charged with negligence, or is charged only with a breach of warranty, frequently referred to as a 'no-fault' theory of liability. . . . The phrase is designed to make clear that the setting of 'relative responsibility' which *Dole* sought, and which section 1402 permits, can be accomplished even where some of the tortfeasors are not negligent or at fault. . . .

"It is to be expected that when this section is applied, the 'relative degrees of culpability' will be expressed in terms of percentages as is currently done under *Dole* and its progeny. . . .

"While the claim for contribution may be asserted prior to payment of any amount to the injured person, thus assuring expeditious resolution of the issue of whether a right to contribution exists, the proposed section precludes enforcement of those rights until the person seeking to enforce his right of contribution has paid to the injured person more than his equitable share of the damages.

"This rule has been taken, with appropriate modifications, from the former contribution statute (CPLR § 1401) and is consistent with the rule that where a third-party claim for indemnity against loss has been asserted, and a conditional or provisional judgment has been entered, the judgment cannot be enforced until the original defendant has satisfied all or part of the original plaintiff's judgment. . . .

"Taken, with appropriate modifications, from former section 1401, this section provides, in part, that no person is obligated to pay more to a fellow wrongdoer for contribution than the equitable share of the entire damages which has been assessed against him.

"The effect of this rule is to place upon the wrongdoer who pays the judgment the risk that other wrongdoers responsible for contribution are solvent. To illustrate: If P sues A, B and C, and receives a judgment for $12,000 against each, the equitable share of each A, B and C being assessed as 1/3, if A pays the $12,000 to P, and C is insolvent, A can recover only $4,000 from B, not $6,000, and thus A will bear the entire financial loss resulting from the insolvency of C."

§ 1403. How contribution claimed.

A cause of action for contribution may be asserted in a separate action or by cross-claim, counterclaim or third-party claim in a pending action.

1974 AMENDMENTS

Article added by L. 1974, ch. 742, eff. Sept. 1, 1974.

The 1974 Judicial Conference Report stated, in part:

"A separate action may be necessary where the person against whom contribution is sought is not subject to jurisdiction in the court in which the primary action has been brought. It may also be necessary in those cases in which the existence of a wrongdoer who is subject to liability for contribution is not discovered until after the primary action has been completed or is discovered so late that to introduce the claim for contribution into the primary action would unfairly delay the determination of the injured person's claim.

"However, the assertion of a claim for contribution in a separate action should be discouraged, for it adds to the burden of already crowded courts, creates the possibility of inconsistent verdicts in the two actions and makes more difficult the assessment of equitable shares in multi-party situations in which one of three or more wrongdoers is not joined in the initial action. Therefore, it is hoped that separate actions for contribution will not be instituted if it is possible to resolve the issue in the primary action brought by the injured person."

CPLR

§ 1404. Right of persons entitled to damages not affected; rights of indemnity or subrogation preserved.

(a) Nothing contained in this article shall impair the rights of any person entitled to damages under existing law.

(b) Nothing contained in this article shall impair any right of indemnity or subrogation under existing law.

1974 AMENDMENTS

Article added by L. 1974, ch. 742, eff. Sept. 1, 1974.

The 1974 Judicial Conference Report stated, in part:

"The function of subdivision (a) of this section is to assure that this Article is interpreted consistently with the views of the Court of Appeals . . . to the end that the traditional doctrine of joint and several liability among multiple wrongdoers . . . is not changed by the operation of this Article. This section should not be construed, however, as limiting the effect of General Obligations Law § 15-108.

"In keeping with the premise that *Dole* was intended essentially to modify the law of contribution, leaving much of the traditional common law of indemnity unchanged, . . . subdivision (b) of section 1404 states that in those factual situations in which the Court of Appeals would continue to apply the common law rules of indemnity . . . nothing contained in this

Article should be construed to preclude them from so doing.

"In addition, it is to be expected that whenever the existing common law rules of indemnity are applied to shift the entire financial responsibility from one tortfeasor to another, there is to be no subsequent claim for contribution under this Article.

"To the extent that one party possesses rights in accordance with the laws of subrogation and the existence of those rights would not be inconsistent with the purpose and intent of this Article, those rights should continue to be enforceable."

Article 14-A

DAMAGE ACTIONS: EFFECT OF CONTRIBUTORY NEGLIGENCE AND ASSUMPTION OF RISK

SUMMARY OF ARTICLE

§ 1411.   Damages recoverable when contributory negligence or assumption of risk is established.

§ 1412.   Burden of pleading; burden of proof.

§ 1413.   Applicability.

§ 1411. Damages recoverable when contributory negligence or assumption of risk is established.

In any action to recover damages for personal injury, injury to property, or wrongful death, the culpable conduct attributable to the claimant or to the decedent, including contributory negligence or assumption of risk, shall not bar recovery, but the amount of damages otherwise recoverable shall be diminished in the proportion which the culpable conduct attributable to the claimant or decedent bears to the culpable conduct which caused the damages.

1975 AMENDMENTS

L. 1975, ch. 69, eff. Sept. 1, 1975, upon the recommendation of the Judicial Conference, added new Article 14-A (CPLR 1411–1413), providing new rules as to the effect of contributory negligence and assumption of risk in damage actions, aimed at completing the application of the principle of comparative negligence to contribution among joint tortfeasors, commenced by *Dole v. Dow Chemical Co.*, 30 N.Y.2d 143 (1972), by extending that principle to the case-in-chief.

The 1975 Judicial Conference Report stated, in part:

"(a) Because contributory fault is a defense in actions based upon a theory of strict products liability (*Codling v. Paglia*, 32 N.Y.2d 330 (1973)) and those based upon a theory of breach of warranty, [*Velez v. Craine & Clark Lumber Corp.*, 33 N.Y.2d 117 (1973)] and because 'assumption of risk' has been held to be a defense in an action based upon strict products liability (*Bolm v. Triumph Corp.*, 33 N.Y.2d 151, 157 (1973); *accord*, Restatement (Second) of Torts § 402 A, comment N (1965)), this article is applicable not only to negligence actions, but to all actions brought to recover damages for personal injury, injury to property or wrongful death whatever the legal theory upon which the suit is based.

"(b) The phrase 'culpable conduct' is used instead of 'negligent conduct' because this article will apply to cases where the conduct of one or more of the parties will be found to be not negligent, but will nonetheless be a factor in determining the amount of damages. For example, in *Velez* v. *Craine & Clark Lumber Corp.* (33 N.Y.2d 117 (1973)), defendant was found to have breached a warranty but was not chargeable with negligence. Under existing law, the contributory negligence of the plaintiff would be a complete bar to recovery. This article permits the apportionment of damages in cases such as *Velez* in which the plaintiff's negligence may be the only *negligence*, but the defendant's conduct is nonetheless 'culpable' and therefore to be considered in determining damages.

"The phrase is consistent with that used in section 1402 of the CPLR which provides that contribution 'shall be determined in accordance with the relative culpability of each person . . .' and is used in this article for the same reason that led to its adoption in article fourteen of the CPLR. . . .

"(c) This article equates the defenses of contributory negligence and assumption of risk by providing that neither shall continue to serve as a complete defense in actions to which this article applies. This is consistent with the result reached in the vast majority of states that have adopted some form of comparative negligence (*e.g.*, Oregon Laws 1971, ch. 688 ssl; *McConville* v. *State Farm Mutual Automobile Ins. Co.*, 15 Wisc. 2d 374, 113 N.W.2d 14 (1962); *Lyons* v. *Redding Construction Co.*, 83 Wash. 2d 86, 515 P.2d 821 (1973). *But see Dendy* v. *City of Pascagola*, 193 So. 2d 559 (Miss. 1967)). The statute is also consistent with the position taken by the New York courts, which have found that 'there is a borderline where the concept of contributory negligence merges almost imperceptibly into that of acceptance of a risk. . . . Very often the difference is chiefly one of terminology.' *McFarlane* v. *City of Niagara Falls*, 247 N.Y. 340, 349, 160 N.E. 391 (1928) (Cardozo).

". . . Just as there has been a 'general softening of the rigidities of the doctrine of contributory negligence' with 'a tendency to treat it almost always as a question of fact' (*Rossman* v. *La Grega*, 28 N.Y.2d 300, 306 (1971)), as well as a growing recognition that 'the great issue is not liability but the damages recoverable for injuries' (*Andre* v. *Pomeroy*, —N.Y.2d — (1974) (Breitel, dissenting)), it is expected that the courts will treat assumption of risk as a form of culpable conduct under this article.

"In appropriate cases, of course, the finder of fact may determine that the plaintiff's conduct in assuming the risk is the sole culpable conduct, and diminish damages accordingly.

"(d) 'Assumption of risk' and 'contributory negligence' are not the only doctrines that might be included within the phrase 'culpable conduct.' The Court of Appeals has recently determined that 'use of [a] . . . product for other than its normally intended purpose or other than in the manner normally intended' is a form of contributory 'fault' which bars recovery in an action based upon a theory of strict products liability (*Codling* v. *Paglia,* 32 N.Y.2d 330, 343, 298 N.E.2d 622 (1973)); that defense constitutes a form of 'culpable conduct.' So too, the 'patent danger' rule, made applicable in negligence actions in *Campo* v. *Schofield* (301 N.Y. 458, (1950)), and recently applied to strict products liability cases should be considered within the framework of this article as a factor to be weighed by the trier of fact in determining whether to diminish damages. *Bolm* v. *Triumph Corp.*, 33 N.Y.2d 151, 159 (1973) ('the issue . . . presents a question of fact . . .'

"Neither the specific examples of culpable conduct mentioned in the statute nor those used in this comment are necessarily exhaustive of the range of 'culpable conduct' which may properly be considered. Judicial development of the concept of 'culpable conduct' consistent with the goals of this article is not precluded.

"(e) In determining the total 'culpable conduct which caused the damages,' the culpable conduct of the defendant as well as that of the claimant must be considered. The defendant's culpable conduct may include, but is not necessarily limited to, negligence, breach of warranty, a violation of statute giving rise to civil liability, conduct giving rise to liability upon a theory of strict liability, and intentional misconduct.

"(f) In applying this article, not only the culpable conduct of the claimant or decedent is to be considered, but also any culpable conduct which is legally attributable to him though actually committed or performed by another. However, this article is not intended to create vicarious liability or to expand the doctrine of imputed contributory negligence, and should be interpreted in harmony with recent decisional law which severely restricts, if it does not entirely eliminate, the doctrine of imputed of vicarious contributory negligence. *Kalechman* v. *Drew Auto Rental, Inc.*, 33 N.Y.2d 397 (1973).

"(g) This article requires that the culpable conduct attributable to the decedent or claimant be compared with the total culpable conduct which caused the damages. Several specific policy decisions have been incorporated thereby.

(1) *Joint and Several Liability.* It is not intended that this article change the present rule of joint and several liability among tortfeasors (*Barrett* v. *The Third Avenue Ry. Co.*, 45 N.Y. 628 (1871); *Gleich* v. *Volpe*, 32 N.Y.2d 517, 523–524 (1973)), nor is it intended to preclude judicial reconsideration of the rule.

(2) *Causal Culpability.* Only culpable conduct which was a substantial factor in causing the harm for which recovery is sought is to be considered in determining the amount by which damages are to be diminished. . . .

(3) *Culpability of Non-party.* It is possible that a person whose culpable conduct contributed to the damages may not be a party to the action

instituted by the claimant, as where one of several tortfeasors has settled with the claimant, or is unknown, or is not subject to the jurisidiction of the court in which the claimant has filed suit.

In the usual case the requirement that claimant's conduct be compared with the total culpable conduct of all persons, whether or not parties to the action, should not add to the complexity of the trial nor should it impose unfair burdens upon any party to the action. It is included primarily to reflect the compatibility of this article with article fourteen of the CPLR, and section 15–108 of the General Obligations Law. . . .

"If the claimant sues tortfeasor A and not tortfeasor B, the culpable conduct attributable to claimant should be considered in light of the total culpable conduct—that of the claimant, of A, and of B. As under present law (*Barrett* v. *The Third Avenue Ry. Co.*, 45 N.Y.628 (1871)), A will be liable for the full amount of claimant's damages less the percentage found attributable to the claimant. There is, therefore, no incentive for A to demonstrate that B was also culpable. *Cf,* James, *Connecticut's Comparative Negligence Statute:* An Analysis of Some Problems, 6 *Conn. L. Rev.* 207, 219-221 (1974).

"Where B has settled with claimant, however, A will not only wish to demonstrate that claimant was chargeable with culpable conduct, but will also wish to have the finder of fact determine the percentage of culpability attributable to B, since it is possible that judgment will be entered against A only after the damages suffered by claimant have been twice reduced—once to reflect claimant's culpable conduct, and once to reflect B's culpability. *See N.Y. Gen. Obl. Law* section 15-108 . . .; CPLR rule 4533(b).

"(h) . . .Because the New York courts have consistently recognized that where contributory negligence is not claimed as a bar to recovery, the doctrine of last clear chance is not to be applied (*e.g., Polk* v. *New York Central R.R. Co.,* 10 A.D. 2d 703 (1st Dept. 1960); *Jasinski* v. *New York Central R.R. Co.,* 21 A.D. 2d 456 (4th Dept. 1964), it was thought unnecessary to include an express provision in this article abolishing the doctrine. See *Cushman* v. *Perkins*, 245 A.2d 846 (Maine 1968).

"The continued separate existence of the doctrine of last clear chance cannot be justified; the factors which the doctrine took into consideration can more appropriately be considered in determining the 'culpable conduct' and the issue of causation of damages under this article. . . .

"(i) . . . This article permits a finding that while each of the parties is culpable, each is entitled to recover some portion of his damages. For instance, if plaintiff sues for $5,000 and defendant asserts in a counterclaim that he is entitled to $10,000 in damages, the finder of fact could determine that each was negligent, and that the culpability of each party was fifty percent, thus entitling plaintiff to $2500 and defendant to $5,000.

"It is the intent of this proposed legislation that no casualty insurance company, or other insurer, shall apply as a set-off to payment pursuant to a policy of insurance any amount by which a recovery against its insured was diminished by reason of a counterclaim or cross-claim asserted by the insured pursuant to this article. . . .

"Section 3019(d) of the CPLR provides that a separate judgment may not be had for a cause of action contained in a counterclaim or cross-claim unless the court so orders. It appears, therefore, that the normal procedure when such claim is asserted is to try both the claim and counterclaim together, and to enter only a single judgment for the difference between the amounts awarded in each claim. *See* 3 Weinstein, Korn & Miller, New York Civil Practice - CPLR ¶ 3019.02 (Matthew Bender).

"Because there are legitimate policy reasons for preferring that routine use of multiple judgments be avoided (*see e.g., Illinois McGraw Elec. Co. v. John J. Walters, Inc.,* 7 N.Y.2d 874 (1959); *Pease & Elliman, Inc. v. 926 Park Avenue Corp.,* 23 App. Div. 2d 361 (1st Dept. 1965); *Dalminter, Inc. v. Dalmine, S.P.A.,* 28 App. Be N.Y Div. 2d 852 (1st Dept.), *aff'd,* 23 N.Y.2d 653 (1968)), entry of two judgments has not been made mandatory in all cases.

"Confident that the legislative intent will be fulfilled and that existing legislation and procedural rules are adequate to accomplish that result, it was deemed unnecessary to provide a specific prohibition against set-off. (*See, e.g.,* Rhode Island Stat. Ann. Section 9–20–4.1 (1971))."

§ 1412. Burden of pleading; burden of proof.

Culpable conduct claimed in diminution of damages, in accordance with section fourteen hundred eleven, shall be an affirmative defense to be pleaded and proved by the party asserting the defense.

1975 AMENDMENTS

L. 1975, ch. 69, eff. Sept. 1, 1975, upon the recommendation of the Judicial Conference, added new Article 14-A (CPLR 1411–1413), as to the effect of contributory negligence and assumption of risk in damage actions. See comments to CPLR 1411.

The 1975 Judicial Conference Report stated, in part:

"(a) The New York Court of Appeals has noted: 'Although New York has clung to a rule that a living plaintiff must establish his own freedom from negligence, it is the majority rule in this country that in all negligence actions, including those maintained by living persons for injury or property damage, the defendant claiming contributory negligence of the plaintiff has the burden of showing it. . . . And it is likewise the general rule where contributory negligence is an affirmative defense the injured person "is presumed to have used due . . . . care.' " *Rossman* v. *LaGrega,* 28 N.Y.2d 300, 304 (1971). This section brings New York law on the issue into conformity with the majority rule and represents the culmination of the gradual but persistent erosion of the rule that freedom from contributory negligence must be pleaded and proven by the plaintiff. . . . *Wartels* v. *County Asphalt, Inc.*, 29 N.Y.2d 381 (1972) (Unusual facts 'reduced plaintiff's burden of proof close to the vanishing point'); *Codling* v. *Paglia*, 32 N.Y.2d 330, 343 (1973) ('contributory fault of the plaintiff is a *defense* to an action for strict products liability') (emphasis added).

"(b) Because 'they are both manifestations of the same or similar considerations... . . . burden of pleading and burden of proof are usually parallel.' James, Civil Procedure p. 265 (1965). This is generally true in New York (*see* 3 Weinstein, Korn & Miller, New York Civil Practice - CPLR ¶ 3018.14 (Matthew Bender)), and there is no reason to make an exception where one seeks to diminish damages otherwise recoverable by asserting, pursuant to this article, that the claimant's culpable conduct contributed to his harm. This article may be viewed as having created a partial defense, the effect of which is to mitigate damages, and such defenses traditionally must be pleaded affirmatively. *See* 3 Weinstein, Korn & Miller, New York Civil Practice-CPLR ¶ 3018.17 (Matthew Bender); *Cf. Rehill* v. *Rehill*, 306 N.Y. 126 (1953)."

§ 1413. Applicability.

This article shall apply to all causes of action accruing on or after September first, nineteen hundred seventy-five.

1975 AMENDMENTS

L. 1975, ch. 69, eff. Sept. 1, 1975, upon the recommendation of the Judicial Conference, added new Article 14-A (CPLR 1411–1413), as to the effect of contributory negligence and assumption of risk in damage actions. See comments to CPLR 1411.

The 1975 Judicial Conference Report stated, in part:

"(a) A clear majority of states which have passed legislation establishing some form of comparative negligence have specifically provided that the statute should be applied prospectively only, to causes of action that arise after the effective date of the statute (e.g. Texas Law. 1973, ch. 28, ss. 4), while the remaining few provide either that the statute shall be applied to actions filed after the effective date of the statute (Rhode Isl. Stat. Ann. ss9–20–4), or to trials commenced after the effective date of the statute (Minnesota Laws 1969, ch. 624 ss.2). Where the statute has been silent, the courts have uniformly applied the statute only prospectively. *E.g., Joseph* v. *Lowery*, 495 P.2d 273 (Oregon 1972).

"While at least one court has upheld the validity of a statutory provision calling for retroactive application of a comparative negligence statute (*Peterson* v. *City of Minneapolis,* 173 N.W.2d 353 (1969)), the result in New York of litigation challenging such a provision is not free from doubt. . . .

"In order to avoid the uncertainty and confusion which might result from the retroactive application of the statute, and to protect the legitimate expectations of potential litigants and others who placed reliance upon present law, this statute is made applicable only to causes of action which accrue after its effective date.

"(b) The word 'accrue' used in this article should be given the meaning attached to it for purposes of determining the period within which an action must be commenced. CPLR 203(a). It is not unlikely that the rules for the determination of the date of accrual of some causes of action may be subject to changing judicial interpretations (*see e.g., Flanagan* v. *Mt. Eden General Hospital*, 24 N.Y.2d 427 (1969); *compare Mendel* v. *Pittsburgh Plate Glass Co.*, 25 N.Y.2d 340 (1969) with *Rivera* v. *Berkeley Superwash, Inc.*, 44 App. Div. 2d 316 (2d Dept. 1974)), and it is intended that this article be interpreted to reflect any such developments.

"(c) Under present law it is possible that one claimant will pursue two causes of action for the same or similar injury and that each cause of action will have a different accrual date. *Compare Mendel* v. *Pittsburgh Plate Glass Co.*, 25 N.Y.2d 340 (1969), *Schmidt* v. *Merchants Dispatch Transp. Co.*, 270 N.Y. 287 (1936). *Cf. Caffaro* v. *Trayna*, 35 N.Y.2d 245 (1973). In such transitional cases, when appropriate, the court should apply this article to all related causes of action tried together with a claim to which this article does apply."

CPLR

Article 15

ACTIONS AGAINST PERSONS JOINTLY LIABLE

SUMMARY OF ARTICLE

§ 1501.   Actions against persons jointly liable; service of summons; judgment.

§ 1502.   Provisional remedies and defenses in subsequent action against co-obligor.

§ 1501. Actions against persons jointly liable; service of summons; judgment.

Where less than all of the named defendants in an action based upon a joint obligation, contract or liability are served with the summons, the plaintiff may proceed against the defendants served, unless the court otherwise directs, and if the judgment is for the plaintiff it may be taken against all the defendants.

CROSS REFERENCES

See **General Obligations Law § 15-102** in Appendix, *below,* as to effect of judgment upon non-party co-obligor.

§ 1502. Provisional remedies and defenses in subsequent action against co-obligor.

A subsequent action against a co-obligor who was not summoned in the original action must be maintained in order to procure a judgment enforceable against his individually held property for the sum remaining unpaid upon the original judgment, and such action shall be regarded as based upon the same obligation, contract or liability as the original judgment for the purpose of obtaining any provisional remedy. The complaint in the subsequent action shall be verified. The defendant in the subsequent action may raise any defenses or counterclaims that he might have raised in the original action if the summons had been served on him when it was first served on a co-obligor, and may raise objections to the original judgment, and defenses or counterclaims that have arisen since it was entered.

Article 16

LIMITED LIABILITY OF PERSONS JOINTLY LIABLE

SUMMARY OF ARTICLE

§ 1600. Definitions.

As used in this article the term "non-economic loss" includes but is not limited to pain and suffering, mental anguish, loss of consortium or other damages for non-economic loss.

1986 AMENDMENTS

L. 1986, ch. 682, eff. July 30, 1986, and applicable to actions commenced or claims filed on or after such date, except for actions commenced pursuant to § 4 or claims filed pursuant to § 5 of L. 1986, ch. 682 (revival provisions for certain toxic tort actions), added new Article 16 (CPLR 1600–1603).

§ 1601. Limited liability of persons jointly liable.

1. Notwithstanding any other provision of law, when a verdict or decision in an action or claim for personal injury is determined in favor of a claimant in an action involving two or more tortfeasors jointly liable or in a claim against the state and the liability of a defendant is found to be fifty percent or less of the total liability assigned to all persons liable, the liability of such defendant to the claimant for non-economic loss shall not exceed that defendant's equitable share determined in accordance with the relative culpability of each person causing or contributing to the total liability for non-economic loss; provided, however that the culpable conduct of any person not a party to the action shall not be considered in determining any equitable share herein if the claimant proves that with due diligence he or she was unable to obtain jurisdiction over such person in said action (or in a claim against the state, in a court of this state); and further provided

that the culpable conduct of any person shall not be considered in determining any equitable share herein to the extent that action against such person is barred because the claimant has not sustained a "grave injury" as defined in section eleven of the workers' compensation law.

2. Nothing in this section shall be construed to affect or impair any right of a tortfeasor under section 15-108 of the general obligations law.

1996 AMENDMENTS

L. 1996, ch. 635, eff. Sept. 10, 1996, amended subdivision (1) by adding at the end the clause "and further provided . . . section eleven of the workers' compensation law."

1986 AMENDMENTS

L. 1986, ch. 682, eff. July 30, 1986, and applicable to actions commenced or claims filed on or after such date, except for actions commenced pursuant to § 4 or claims filed pursuant to § 5 of L. 1986, ch. 682 (revival provisions for certain toxic tort actions), added new Article 16 (CPLR 1600–1603).

§ 1602. Application.

The limitations set forth in this article shall:

1. apply to any claim for contribution or indemnification, but shall not include:

(a) a claim for indemnification if, prior to the accident or occurrence on which the claim is based, the claimant and the tortfeasor had entered into a written contract in which the tortfeasor had expressly agreed to indemnify the claimant for the type of loss suffered; or

(b) a claim for indemnification by a public employee, including indemnification pursuant to section fifty-k of the general municipal law or section seventeen or eighteen of the public officers law.

2. not be construed to impair, alter, limit, modify, enlarge, abrogate or restrict (i) the limitations set forth in section twenty-a of the court of claims act; (ii) any immunity or right of indemnification available to or conferred upon any defendant for any negligent or wrongful act or omission; (iii) any right on the part of any defendant to plead and prove an affirmative defense as to culpable conduct attributable to a claimant or decedent which is claimed by such defendant in the diminution of damages in any action; and (iv) any

liability arising by reason of a non-delegable duty or by reason of the doctrine of respondeat superior.

3. not apply to administrative proceedings.

4. not apply to claims under the workers' compensation law or to a claim against a defendant where claimant has sustained a 'grave injury' as defined in section eleven of the workers' compensation law to the extent of the equitable share of any person against whom the claimant is barred from asserting a cause of action because of the applicability of the workers' compensation law provided, however, that nothing in this subdivision shall be construed to create, impair, alter, limit, modify, enlarge, abrogate, or restrict any theory of liability upon which any person may be held liable.

5. not apply to actions requiring proof of intent.

6. not apply to any person held liable by reason of his use, operation, or ownership of a motor vehicle or motorcycle, as those terms are defined in sections three hundred eleven and one hundred twenty-five of the vehicle and traffic law.

7. not apply to any person held liable for causing claimant's injury by having acted with reckless disregard for the safety of others.

8. not apply to any person held liable by reason of the applicability of article ten of the labor law.

9. not apply to any person held liable for causing claimant's injury by having unlawfully released into the environment a substance hazardous to public health, safety or the environment, a substance acutely hazardous to public health, safety or the environment or a hazardous waste, as defined in articles thirty-seven and twenty-seven of the environmental conservation law and in violation of article seventy-one of such law; provided, however, that nothing herein shall require that the violation of said article by such person has resulted in a criminal conviction or administrative adjudication of liability.

10. not apply to any person held liable in a product liability action where the manufacturer of the product is not a party to the action and the claimant establishes by a preponderance of the evidence that jurisdiction over the manufacturer could not with due diligence be

CPLR

obtained and that if the manufacturer were a party to the action, liability for claimant's injury would have been imposed upon said manufacturer by reason of the doctrine of strict liability, to the extent of the equitable share of such manufacturer.

11. not apply to any parties found to have acted knowingly or intentionally, and in concert, to cause the acts or failures upon which liability is based; provided, however, that nothing in this subdivision shall be construed to create, impair, alter, limit, modify, enlarge, abrogate, or restrict any theory of liability upon which said parties may be held liable to the claimant.

12. In conjunction with the other provisions of this article not be construed to create or enlarge actions for contribution or indemnity barred because of the applicability of the workers' compensation law of this state, any other state or the federal government, or section 18-201 of the general obligations law.

13. not apply to any person responsible for the disposal or presence of hazardous or dangerous materials that is the result of the unlawful manufacture of methamphetamine, when such person has been convicted of section 220.73, 220.74, 220.75 or 220.76 of the penal law.

2005 AMENDMENTS

L. 2005, ch. 394, § 12, eff. Oct. 1, 2005, added subdivision (13).

1996 AMENDMENTS

L. 1996, ch. 635, eff. Sept. 10, 1996, amended subdivision (4) by deleting the words "such defendant has impleaded a third party"; adding the phrase "claimant has sustained a "grave injury" . . . equitable share of any person"; deleting the words ", to the extent of the equitable share of said third party"; and adding at the end of the subdivision the clause, "provided, however, that nothing . . . any person may be held liable"; added subdivision (12).

1986 AMENDMENTS

L. 1986, ch. 682, eff. July 30, 1986, and applicable to actions commenced or claims filed on or after such date, except for actions commenced pursuant to § 4 or claims filed pursuant to § 5 of L. 1986, ch. 682 (revival provisions for certain toxic tort actions), added new Article 16 (CPLR 1600–1603).

§ 1603.   Burdens of proof.

In any action or claim for damages for personal injury a party asserting that the limitations on liability set forth in this article do not apply shall allege and prove by a preponderance of the evidence that one or more of the exemptions set forth in subdivision one of section sixteen hundred one or section sixteen hundred two applies. A party asserting limited liability pursuant to this article shall have the burden of proving by a preponderance of the evidence its equitable share of the total liability.

1996 AMENDMENTS

L. 1996, ch. 635, eff. Sept. 10, 1996, amended the section to add a reference to § 1601(1).

1986 AMENDMENTS

L. 1986, ch. 682, eff. July 30, 1986, and applicable to actions commenced or claims filed on or after such date except for actions commenced pursuant to § 4 or claims filed pursuant to § 5 of L. 1986, ch. 682 (revival provisions for certain toxic tort actions), added new Article 16 (CPLR 1600–1603).

CPLR

Article 20

MISTAKES, DEFECTS,
IRREGULARITIES AND EXTENSIONS OF TIME

SUMMARY OF ARTICLE

§ 2001.   Mistakes, omissions, defects and irregularities.

At any stage of an action, including the filing of a summons with notice, summons and complaint or petition to commence an action, the court may permit a mistake, omission, defect or irregularity, including the failure to purchase or acquire an index number or other mistake in the filing process, to be corrected, upon such terms as may be just, or, if a substantial right of a party is not prejudiced, the mistake, omission, defect or irregularity shall be disregarded, provided that any applicable fees shall be paid.

2007 AMENDMENTS

L. 2007, ch. 529, eff. Aug. 15, 2007, amended § 2001.

§ 2002.   Error in ruling of court.

An error in a ruling of the court shall be disregarded if a substantial right of a party is not prejudiced.

§ 2003.   Irregularity in judicial sale.

At any time within one year after a sale made pursuant to a judgment or order, but not thereafter, the court, upon such terms as may be just, may set the sale aside for a failure to comply with the requirements of the civil practice law and rules as to the notice, time or manner of such sale, if a substantial right of a party was prejudiced by the defect. This section does not apply to judicial sales made pursuant to article 9 of the uniform commercial code.

1966 AMENDMENTS

L. 1966, ch. 138, eff. Sept. 1, 1966, added the sentence "This section does not apply to judicial sales made pursuant to article 9 of the uniform commercial code."

Amendment recommended by the Judicial Conference Feb. 1, 1966, Report to the Legislature: "CPLR 2003 permits a court, within one year of a judicial sale, to set aside the sale on grounds of any of the irregularities specified. U.C.C. § 9-501(1), however, permits a secured creditor, after default, either to sell the collateral himself or to reduce his claim to a judgment and sale. U.C.C. § 9-504(4) provides that the purchaser at such sale takes good title despite the failure of the creditor to comply with all relevant provisions of the U.C.C. or the requirements 'of any judicial proceedings.' Thus there is a possible conflict between the U.C.C.'s policy respecting sales under secured transactions and the CPLR's policy as to judicial sales generally. The change is proposed in order to place attorneys on notice of the U.C.C. provision."

§ 2004.   Extensions of time generally.

Except where otherwise expressly prescribed by law, the court may extend the time fixed by any statute, rule or order for doing any act, upon such terms as may be just and upon good cause shown, whether the application for extension is made before or after the expiration of the time fixed.

§ 2005.   Excusable delay or default.

Upon an application satisfying the requirements of subdivision (d) of section 3012 or subdivision (a) of rule 5015, the court shall not, as a matter of law, be precluded from exercising its discretion in the interests of justice to excuse delay or default resulting from law office failure.

1983 AMENDMENTS

L. 1983, ch. 318, added CPLR 2005 in relation to excusable default and extension of time. ch. 318, § 3 provides:

§ 3. This act shall take effect immediately and shall be deemed and construed as remedial in nature and application and shall apply in every action and proceeding heretofore commenced and which either: still is pending before a court; or the time for taking of an appeal from any order or judgment in such action has not yet expired, and in all actions and proceedings hereafter commenced.

CPLR

Article 21
PAPERS

SUMMARY OF ARTICLE

R 2101. Form of papers.

(a) Quality, size and legibility. Each paper served or filed shall be durable, white and, except for summonses, subpoenas, notices of appearance, notes of issue, orders of protection, temporary orders of protection and exhibits, shall be eleven by eight and one-half inches in size. The writing shall be legible and in black ink. Beneath each signature shall be printed the name signed. The letters in the summons shall be in clear type of no less than twelve-point in size. Each other printed or typed paper served or filed, except an exhibit, shall be in clear type of no less than ten-point in size.

(b) Language. Each paper served or filed shall be in the English language which, where practicable, shall be of ordinary usage. Where an affidavit or exhibit annexed to a paper served or filed is in a foreign language, it shall be accompanied by an English translation and an affidavit by the translator stating his qualifications and that the translation is accurate.

(c) Caption. Each paper served or filed shall begin with a caption setting forth the name of the court, the venue, the title of the action, the nature of the paper and the index number of the action if one has been assigned. In a summons, a complaint or a judgment the title shall include the names of all parties, but in all other papers it shall be sufficient to state the name of the first named party on each side with an appropriate indication of any omissions.

(d) Indorsement by attorney. Each paper served or filed shall be indorsed with the name, address and telephone number of the attorney for the party serving or filing the paper, or if the party does not appear by attorney, with the name, address and telephone number of the party.

(e) Copies. Except where otherwise specifically prescribed, copies, rather than originals, of all papers, including orders, affidavits and exhibits may be served or filed. Where it is required that the original be served or filed and the original is lost or withheld, the court may authorize a copy to be served or filed.

(f) Defects in form; waiver. A defect in the form of a paper, if a substantial right of a party is not prejudiced, shall be disregarded by the court, and leave to correct shall be freely given. The party on whom a paper is served shall be deemed to have waived objection to any defect in form unless, within two days after the receipt thereof, he returns the paper to the party serving it with a statement of particular objections.

(g) Service by electronic means. Each paper served or filed by electronic means, as defined in subdivision (f) of rule twenty-one hundred three, shall be capable of being reproduced by the receiver so as to comply with the provisions of subdivisions (a) through (d) of this rule.

1999 AMENDMENTS

L. 1999, ch. 367, eff. July 27, 1999, added subdivision (g) to provide for service by electronic means.

1996 AMENDMENTS

L. 1996, ch. 131, eff. June 11, 1996, amended subdivision (a) by adding the words "orders of protection, temporary orders of protection."

1994 AMENDMENTS

L. 1994, ch. 100, eff. Jan. 1, 1995, amended subdivision (a) by adding the final two sentences; by deleting the provision excepting summonses, subpoenas, notices of appearance, notes of issue and exhibits from the general requirement that all papers served or filed must be on eleven-by-eight-and-one-half-inch paper; and by deleting an obsolete provision extending the time during which non-conforming size forms could be used.

1974 AMENDMENTS

CPLR 2101(a) was amended by proposal No. 1 of the Judicial Conference Report to the 1974 Legislature, eff. Sept. 1, 1974, to provide that courts or other public agencies shall have until Sept. 1, 1976 to utilize their present stock of forms larger than eleven by eight and one-half inches.

1973 AMENDMENTS

CPLR 2101(a) was amended by proposal No. 2 of the Judicial Conference Report to the 1973 Legislature, eff. Sept. 1, 1973, to provide that in all actions and proceedings commenced on or after Sept. 1, 1974, all papers served or filed, except for summonses, subpoenas, notices of appearance, notes of issue and exhibits, shall be eleven by eight and one-half inches in size.

1965 AMENDMENTS

L. 1965, ch. 773, eff. Sept. 1, 1965, amended Subd. (d).

1964 AMENDMENTS

L. 1964, ch. 388, eff. Sept. 1, 1964, amended Subd. (e).

R 2102.   Filing of papers.

(a) Except where otherwise prescribed by law or order of court, papers required to be filed shall be filed with the clerk of the court in which the action is triable. In an action or proceeding in supreme or county court and in a proceeding not brought in a court, papers required to be filed shall be filed with the clerk of the county in which the proceeding is brought.

CPLR

(b) A paper filed in accordance with the rules of the chief administrator or any local rule or practice established by the court shall be deemed filed. Where such rules or practice allow for the filing of a paper other than at the office of the clerk of the court, such paper shall be transmitted to the clerk of the court.

(c) A clerk shall not refuse to accept for filing any paper presented for that purpose except where specifically directed to do so by statute or rules promulgated by the chief administrator of the courts, or order of the court.

2007 AMENDMENTS

L. 2007, ch. 529, eff. Jan. 1, 2008, added subds. (a) through (c).

R 2103. Service of papers.

(a) Who can serve. Except where otherwise prescribed by law or order of court, papers may be served by any person not a party of the age of eighteen years or over.

(b) Upon an attorney. Except where otherwise prescribed by law or order of court, papers to be served upon a party in a pending action shall be served upon the party's attorney. Where the same attorney appears for two or more parties, only one copy need be served upon the attorney. Such service upon an attorney shall be made:

    1. by delivering the paper to the attorney personally; or

    2. by mailing the paper to the attorney at the address designated by that attorney for that purpose or, if none is designated, at that attorney's last known address; service by mail shall be complete upon mailing; where a period of time prescribed by law is measured from the service of a paper and service is by mail, five days shall be added to the prescribed period; or

    3. if the attorney's office is open, by leaving the paper with a person in charge, or if no person is in charge, by leaving it in a conspicuous place; or if the attorney's office is not open, by depositing the paper, enclosed in a sealed wrapper directed to the attorney, in the attorney's office letter drop or box; or

    4. by leaving it at the attorney's residence within the state with a person of suitable age and discretion. Service upon an attorney shall

not be made at the attorney's residence unless service at the attorney's office cannot be made; or

5. by transmitting the paper to the attorney by facsimile transmission, provided that a facsimile telephone number is designated by the attorney for that purpose. Service by facsimile transmission shall be complete upon the receipt by the sender of a signal from the equipment of the attorney served indicating that the transmission was received, and the mailing of a copy of the paper to that attorney. The designation of a facsimile telephone number in the address block subscribed on a paper served or filed in the course of an action or proceeding shall constitute consent to service by facsimile transmission in accordance with this subdivision. An attorney may change or rescind a facsimile telephone number by serving a notice on the other parties; or

6. by dispatching the paper to the attorney by overnight delivery service at the address designated by the attorney for that purpose or, if none is designated, at the attorney's last known address. Service by overnight delivery service shall be complete upon deposit of the paper enclosed in a properly addressed wrapper into the custody of the overnight delivery service for overnight delivery, prior to the latest time designated by the overnight delivery service for overnight delivery. Where a period of time prescribed by law is measured from the service of a paper and service is by overnight delivery, one business day shall be added to the prescribed period. "Overnight delivery service" means any delivery service which regularly accepts items for overnight delivery to any address in the state; or

7. by transmitting the paper to the attorney by electronic means where and in the manner authorized by the chief administrator of the courts by rule upon the party's written consent. The subject matter heading for each paper sent by electronic means must indicate that the matter being transmitted electronically is related to a court proceeding.

(c) Upon a party. If a party has not appeared by an attorney or the party's attorney cannot be served, service shall be upon the party by a method specified in paragraph one, two, four, five or six of subdivision (b) of this rule.

(d) Filing. If a paper cannot be served by any of the methods

CPLR

specified in subdivisions (b) and (c), service may be made by filing the paper as if it were a paper required to be filed.

(e) Parties to be served. Each paper served on any party shall be served on every other party who has appeared, except as otherwise may be provided by court order or as provided in section 3012 or in subdivision (f) of section 3215. Upon demand by a party, the plaintiff shall supply that party with a list of those who have appeared and the names and addresses of their attorneys.

(f) Definitions. For the purposes of this rule:

1. "Mailing" means the deposit of a paper enclosed in a first class postpaid wrapper, addressed to the address designated by a person for that purpose or, if none is designated, at that person's last known address, in a post office or official depository under the exclusive care and custody of the United States Postal Service within the state;

2. "Electronic means" means any method of transmission of information between computers or other machines designed for the purpose of sending and receiving such transmissions, and which allows the recipient to reproduce the information transmitted in a tangible medium of expression;

3. "Facsimile transmission" means any method of transmission of documents to a facsimile machine at a remote location which can automatically produce a tangible copy of such documents.

2009 AMENDMENTS

L. 2009, ch. 416, eff. Sept. 1, 2009, amended to eliminate the requirement of consent to filing of certain papers by electronic means under certain circumstances, but subject to certain rights to opt out, and to eliminate the expiration date of CPLR 2103(b)(7).

2005 AMENDMENTS

L. 2005, ch. 504, eff. Aug. 16, 2005, amended to extend the expiration date of the pilot programs permitting the use of facsimile or electronic transmission to commence an action to Sept. 1, 2009 and extending the pilot programs to Niagara, Broome, Essex, Onondaga, and Sullivan counties.

2003 AMENDMENTS

L. 2003, ch. 261, § 1, eff. July 29, 2003, amended to extend the expiration date of the pilot programs permitting the use of facsimile or electronic transmission to commence an action to Sept. 1, 2005.

2002 AMENDMENTS

L. 2002, ch. 110, § 1, eff. June 28, 2002, amended to extend the expiration date of the pilot programs permitting the use of facsimile or electronic transmission to commence an action to July 1, 2003.

1999 AMENDMENTS

L. 1999, ch. 367, eff. July 27, 1999, amended paragraphs (b)(5) and (6) by substituting the words "facsimile transmission" for "electronic means". Service of papers by facsimile transmission is now covered by CPLR § 2103(b)(5). Service by overnight delivery service is covered in CPLR § 2103(b)(6). CPLR § 2103(b)(7) was added and it pertains to transmitting papers by electronic means. CPLR § 2103(f) was amended by amending paragraph (2) and adding paragraph (3) defining "facsimile transmission."

1990 AMENDMENTS

L. 1990, ch. 244, eff. June 15, 1990, renumbering paragraph 5 of CPLR 2103(b) to be paragraph 6; adding a new paragraph 5, designating service by electronic means. as an additional method of service on a party's attorney; and amending CPLR 2103(c) to include reference to paragraph 6.

1989 AMENDMENTS

L. 1989, ch. 478, eff. Jan. 1, 1990, amended CPLR 2103(b)(5) to provide for the use of overnight mail, and it re-enacted subdivision 2 without the change made by Chapter 461.

1982 AMENDMENTS

L. 1982, ch. 20, eff. Jan. 1, 1983, amended CPLR 2103(b)(2) to increase from three to five the number of days for service of a paper by mail.

1971 AMENDMENTS

Amendment No. 1 made by the Judicial Conference February 1, 1971 Report to the 1971 Legislature, eff. Sept. 1, 1971, amended CPLR 2103(e), by providing, *inter alia,* that each paper served on any party shall be served on every other party who has appeared.

R 2103-a. Confidentiality of addresses in civil proceedings.

(a) Notwithstanding any other provision of law, in any civil proceeding, whether or not an order of protection or temporary order of protection is sought or has been sought in the past, the court may, upon its own motion or upon the motion of any party, authorize any party to keep his or her residential and business addresses and telephone numbers confidential from any party in any pleadings or other papers submitted to the court, where the court makes specific findings on the record supporting a conclusion that disclosure of such addresses or

CPLR

telephone numbers would pose an unreasonable risk to the health or safety of a party. Pending such a finding, any such addresses or telephone numbers of the party seeking confidentiality shall be safeguarded and sealed in order to prevent its inadvertent or unauthorized use or disclosure.

(b) Notwithstanding any other provision of law, if a party has resided or resides in a residential program for victims of domestic violence as defined in section four hundred fifty-nine-a of the social services law, the present address of such party and the address of the residential program for victims of domestic violence shall not be revealed by the court or any court personnel who may have access to such information.

(c) Upon such authorization, the court shall designate the clerk of the court or such other disinterested person as it deems appropriate, with consent of such disinterested person, as the agent for service of process for the party whose residential and business addresses or telephone numbers are to remain confidential and shall notify the parties of such designation and the address of the agent in writing. The clerk or disinterested person designated by the court shall, when served with process on behalf of the party whose information is to remain confidential, promptly notify such party whose information is to remain confidential and forward such process to him or her in a manner calculated to be timely received.

(d) In any case in which such confidentiality authorization is made, the party whose information is to remain confidential shall inform the clerk of the court or disinterested person designated by the court of any change in address for purposes of receipt of service of process or any papers.

2004 AMENDMENTS

L. 2004, ch. 111, §2, eff. July 15, 2004, added CPLR 2103-a in relation to civil proceedings and confidentiality of addresses.

R 2104. Stipulations.

An agreement between parties or their attorneys relating to any matter in an action, other than one made between counsel in open court, is not binding upon a party unless it is in a writing subscribed by him or his attorney or reduced to the form of an order and entered. With respect to stipulations of settlement and notwithstanding the form of the stipulation of settlement, the terms of such stipulation shall be filed by the defendant with the county clerk.

2003 AMENDMENTS

L. 2003, ch. 62, Part J, § 28, eff. July 14, 2003, added second sentence.

§ 2105. Certification by attorney.

Where a certified copy of a paper is required by law, an attorney admitted to practice in the courts of the state may certify that it has been compared by him with the original and found to be a true and complete copy. Such a certificate, when subscribed by such attorney, has the same effect as if made by a clerk.

1970 AMENDMENTS

L. 1970, ch. 307, eff. Sept. 1, 1970, amended the section to allow any attorney duly admitted to practice in the state of New York to certify papers under this section.

1964 AMENDMENTS

L. 1964, ch. 349, eff. Sept. 1, 1964. Amendment was recommended by the Judicial Conference Feb. 1, 1964, Report to the Legislature: "In its present form § 2105 could possibly be interpreted to apply not only to members of the New York bar but also to out-of-state attorneys and even to a party not admitted to practice who appears *pro se* (see § 105(c)). Such a result seems unintended and the proposed change is designed to preclude it."

R 2106. Affirmation of truth of statement by attorney, physician, osteopath or dentist.

The statement of an attorney admitted to practice in the courts of the state, or of a physician, osteopath or dentist, authorized by law to practice in the state, who is not a party to an action, when subscribed and affirmed by him to be true under the penalties of perjury, may be served or filed in the action in lieu of and with the same force and effect as an affidavit.

1973 AMENDMENTS

CPLR 2106 was amended by proposal No. 3 of the Judicial Conference Report to the 1973 Legislature, effective Sept. 1, 1973, to provide that non-party physicians, osteopaths and dentists licensed to practice in the state may file in an action a statement affirmed by them in lieu of an affidavit.

CPLR

Article 22

STAY, MOTIONS, ORDERS AND MANDATES

SUMMARY OF ARTICLE

§ 2201. Stay.

Except where otherwise prescribed by law, the court in which an action is pending may grant a stay of proceedings in a proper case, upon such terms as may be just.

§§ 2202–2210. [Not used.]

§ 2211. Application for order; when motion made.

A motion is an application for an order. A motion on notice is made when a notice of the motion or an order to show cause is served.

§ 2212. Where motion made, in supreme court action.

(a) Motions on notice. A motion on notice in an action in the supreme court shall be noticed to be heard in the judicial district where the action is triable or in a county adjoining the county where the action is triable. Unless statute, civil practice rule or local court rule provides otherwise, the motion shall be noticed to be heard before a motion term or, upon order to show cause granted by a justice, before that justice out of court.

(b) Ex parte motions. A motion in an action in the supreme court that may be made without notice may be made at a motion term or to a justice out of court in any county in the state.

(c) Motions before a county court or judge. The chief administrator of the courts may by rule provide for the hearing of motions on notice or ex parte motions in an action or proceeding in the supreme court by a term of the county court or a county judge in the county in which venue is laid during periods in which no supreme court trial or special term is in session in the county.

(d) Rules of the chief administrator of the courts. The chief administrator may by rule exclude motions within a department, district or county from the operation of subdivisions (a), (b) and (c) of this section, provided, however, that the practice in counties within the city of New York shall be uniform.

1986 AMENDMENTS

L. 1986, ch. 355, eff. July 17, 1986, amended Subd. (c) of CPLR 2212 by replacing references to the departments of the appellate division with "chief administrator of the courts;" Subd. (d) of CPLR 2212 was amended by replacing the reference to appellate division rules with "rules of the chief administrator of the courts" and by making other changes, including the addition of a reference to subdivision (c).

1965 AMENDMENTS

L. 1965, ch. 149, eff. Sept. 1, 1965, amended Subd. (c), to make it clear that a county judge may hear a Supreme Court motion if there is no Supreme Court trial or special term in session in the county.

§ 2213.   Where motion made, in county court action.

(a) Ex parte motions. A motion in an action in a county court that may be made without notice may be made before a motion term of the county court or before the county judge out of court in any county in the state.

(b) Motions that may be made before the supreme court or a justice thereof. When no motion term is being held and there is no county judge available within the county, any motion in an action in a county court, whether or not on notice, may be made or noticed to be heard before a motion term of the supreme court or, upon order to show cause granted by a justice of the supreme court, before such justice out of court, in the judicial district where the action is triable or in a county adjoining the county where the action is triable, except a motion under article forty-four or a motion for an order that would dispose of the action, in whole or in part, in any manner other than by settlement under section 1207.

(c) The chief administrator of the courts may by rule exclude motions from the operation of this section within a department, district or county.

CPLR

1986 AMENDMENTS

L. 1986, ch. 355, eff. July 17, 1986, amended CPLR 2213 by adding the word "available" in the second sentence of subdivision (b); by designating last sentence of section as subdivision (c) and by making other changes to subdivision (c), including replacing "appellate division" with "chief administrator of the courts."

R 2214. Motion papers; service; time.

(a) Notice of motion. A notice of motion shall specify the time and place of the hearing on the motion, the supporting papers upon which the motion is based, the relief demanded and the grounds therefor. Relief in the alternative or of several different types may be demanded.

(b) Time for service of notice and affidavits. Time for service of notice and affidavits. A notice of motion and supporting affidavits shall be served at least eight days before the time at which the motion is noticed to be heard. Answering affidavits shall be served at least two days before such time. Answering affidavits and any notice of cross-motion, with supporting papers, if any, shall be served at least seven days before such time if a notice of motion served at least sixteen days before such time so demands; whereupon any reply or responding affidavits shall be served at least one day before such time.

(c) Furnishing papers to the court. Each party shall furnish to the court all papers served by him. The moving party shall furnish at the hearing all other papers not already in the possession of the court necessary to the consideration of the questions involved. Where such papers are in the possession of an adverse party, they shall be produced by him at the hearing on notice served with the motion papers. Only papers served in accordance with the provisions of this rule shall be read in support of, or in opposition to, the motion unless the court for good cause shall otherwise direct.

(d) Order to show cause. The court in a proper case may grant an order to show cause, to be served in lieu of a notice of motion, at a time and in a manner specified therein. An order to show cause against a state body or officers must be served in addition to service upon the defendant or respondent state body or officers upon the attorney general by delivery to an assistant attorney general at an office of the attorney general in the county in which venue of the action is designated or if there is no office of the attorney general in such county, at the office of the attorney general nearest such county.

2007 AMENDMENTS

L. 2007, ch. 185, eff. July 3, 2007, amended CPLR R 2214(b) by including cross-motions in description of answering affidavits.

1984 AMENDMENTS

L. 1984, ch. 177, eff. Aug. 6, 1984, amended CPLR R 2214(b) by increasing the time for service of a notice of motion demanding answering affidavits and for service of the answering affidavits.

1972 AMENDMENTS

L. 1972, ch. 455, eff. May 24, 1972 and ch. 752, eff. May 30, 1972, amended CPLR R 2214(d) by adding new last sentence providing that an order to show cause served on a state body or officers must also be served on the attorney general.

R 2215. Relief demanded by other than moving party.

At least three days prior to the time at which the motion is noticed to be heard, or seven days prior to such time if demand is properly made pursuant to subdivision (b) of rule 2214, a party may serve upon the moving party a notice of cross-motion demanding relief, with or without supporting papers; provided, however, that:

(a) if such notice and any supporting papers are served by mailing, as provided in paragraph two of subdivision (b) of rule 2103, they shall be served three days earlier than as prescribed in this rule; and

(b) if served by overnight delivery, as provided in paragraph six of subdivision (b) of rule 2103, they shall be served one day earlier than as prescribed in this rule. Relief in the alternative or of several different types may be demanded; relief need not be responsive to that demanded by the moving party.

2007 AMENDMENTS

L. 2007, ch. 185, eff. July 3, 2007, amended CPLR R 2215 by adding subdivs. (a) and (b).

1980 AMENDMENTS

L. 1980, ch. 132, eff. Jan. 1, 1981, amended CPLR R 2215 by adding the requirement that a party who has been moved against and who wishes to make his or her own application for relief by way of a cross-motion specifically serve on the movant a notice of cross-motion.

In making its recommendation to the 1980 Legislature, the Judicial Conference Report on the CPLR noted that this was an attempt to prevent a non-moving party's application for affirmative relief from being buried in the other party's papers, an event which takes the moving party by surprise and adds unnecessary chores for the motion judge. The report stated, "The main idea is to have the covering paper clue the reader in to the whole mission of the accompanying papers, and to avoid the situation in which a demand for cross-relief comes up as almost a hidden incident of affidavits opposing the main motion. The inclusion of a general relief clause, with which a notice of motion ordinarily ends in New York practice, will still cover other items of relief reasonably supportable on the papers, and a general relief clause may also be used in the notice of cross-motion. The proposal is intended to clarify the obligations of a cross-movant. It is not intended to place any restriction on the court's powers to grant affirmative relief."

R 2216. [Repealed.]

R 2217. Prior motion; ex parte motion; transfer of motion.

(a) Prior motion. Any motion may be referred to a judge who decided a prior motion in the action.

(b) Affidavit on ex parte motion. An ex parte motion shall be accompanied by an affidavit stating the result of any prior motion for similar relief and specifying the new facts, if any, that were not previously shown.

(c) Transfer of motion. If a motion is made to a judge who is or will be for any reason unable to hear it, it may be transferred by order of such judge or by written stipulation of the parties to any other judge to whom it might originally have been made.

(d) Rules of the chief administrator of the courts. The chief administrator may by rule exclude motions within a department, district or county from the operation of subdivisions (a) and (c) of this rule.

1986 AMENDMENTS

L. 1986, ch. 355, eff. July 17, 1986, amended CPLR 2217 by adding new Subd. (d), "Rules of the chief administrator of the courts."

§ 2218. Trial of issue raised on motion.

The court may order that an issue of fact raised on a motion shall be separately tried by the court or a referee. If the issue is triable of right by jury, the court shall give the parties an opportunity to demand a jury trial of such issue. Failure to make such demand within the time limited by the court, or, if no such time is limited, before trial begins, shall be deemed a waiver of the right to trial by jury. An order under this rule shall specify the issue to be tried.

R 2219. Time and form of order.

(a) Time and form of order determining motion, generally. An order determining a motion relating to a provisional remedy shall be made within twenty days, and an order determining any other motion shall be made within sixty days, after the motion is submitted for decision. The order shall be in writing and shall be the same in form whether made by a court or a judge out of court. An order determining a motion made upon supporting papers shall be signed with the judge's signature or initials by the judge who made it, state the court of which he or she is a judge and the place and date of the signature, recite the papers used on the motion, and give the determination or direction in such detail as the judge deems proper. Except in a town or village court or where otherwise provided by law, upon the request of any party, an order or ruling made by a judge, whether upon written or oral application or sua sponte, shall be reduced to writing or otherwise recorded.

(b) Signature on appellate court order. An order of an appellate court shall be signed by a judge thereof except that, upon written authorization by the presiding judge, it may be signed by the clerk of the court or, in his absence or disability, by a deputy clerk.

1996 AMENDMENTS

L. 1996, ch. 38, eff. January 1, 1996, amended subdivision (a) by adding a new final sentence and making the subdivision gender neutral.

R 2220. Entry and filing of order; service.

(a) Entry and filing. An order determining a motion shall be entered and filed in the office of the clerk of the court where the action is triable, and all papers used on the motion and any opinion or memorandum in writing shall be filed with that clerk unless the order dispenses with such filing. When a statute or civil practice rule requires such filing and entry in a county other than that in which the order was made, the party prevailing on the motion shall file the order and the papers used on the motion with the proper clerk after receiving them. If a party fails to file any papers required to be filed under this subdivision, the order may be vacated as irregular, with costs.

CPLR

(b) Service. Service of an order shall be made by serving a copy of the order.

1964 AMENDMENTS

Amendment No. 3 made by the Judicial Conference Feb. 1, 1964, Report to the Legislature, eff. Sept. 1, 1964, deleted the word "certified" formerly appearing before "copy of the order" in subd. (b).

R 2221. Motion affecting prior order.

(a) A motion for leave to renew or to reargue a prior motion, for leave to appeal from, or to stay, vacate or modify, an order shall be made, on notice, to the judge who signed the order, unless he or she is for any reason unable to hear it, except that:

1. if the order was made upon a default such motion may be made, on notice, to any judge of the court; and

2. if the order was made without notice such motion may be made, without notice, to the judge who signed it, or, on notice, to any other judge of the court.

(b) Rules of the chief administrator of the courts. The chief administrator may by rule exclude motions within a department, district or county from the operation of subdivision (a) of this rule.

(c) A motion made to other than a proper judge under this rule shall be transferred to the proper judge.

(d) A motion for leave to reargue:

1. shall be identified specifically as such;

2. shall be based upon matters of fact or law allegedly overlooked or misapprehended by the court in determining the prior motion, but shall not include any matters of fact not offered on the prior motion; and

3. shall be made within thirty days after service of a copy of the order determining the prior motion and written notice of its entry. This rule shall not apply to motions to reargue a decision made by the appellate division or the court of appeals.

(e) A motion for leave to renew:

1. shall be identified specifically as such;

2. shall be based upon new facts not offered on the prior motion that would change the prior determination or shall demonstrate that there has been a change in the law that would change the prior determination; and

3. shall contain reasonable justification for the failure to present such facts on the prior motion.

(f) A combined motion for leave to reargue and leave to renew shall identify separately and support separately each item of relief sought. The court, in determining a combined motion for leave to reargue and leave to renew, shall decide each part of the motion as if it were separately made. If a motion for leave to reargue or leave to renew is granted, the court may adhere to the determination on the original motion or may alter that determination.

1999 AMENDMENTS

L. 1999, ch. 281, eff. July 20, 1999, amended CPLR § 2221 by labeling the last paragraph as (c), and adding new subdivisions (d), (e) and (f) pertaining to motions for leave to reargue, motions for leave to renew and combined motions for leave to reargue and renew.

1986 AMENDMENTS

L. 1986, ch. 355, eff. July 17, 1986, amended CPLR 2221 by dividing the material following the heading into Subd. (a) and by adding new Subd. (b), "Rules of the chief administrator of the courts."

R 2222.   Docketing order as judgment.

At the request of any party the clerk shall docket as a judgment an order directing the payment of money, including motion costs, or affecting the title to, or the possession, use or enjoyment of, real property, provided, however, that where the clerk maintains a section and block index, an order affecting the title to, or the possession, use or enjoyment of, real property may be entered in such index in lieu thereof.

1970 AMENDMENTS

L. 1970, ch. 661, eff. May 8, 1970, amended the section by adding thereto the following: "provided, however, that where the clerk maintains a section and block index, an order affecting the title to, or the possession, use or enjoyment of, real property may be entered in such index in lieu thereof."

R 2223.   Duties of officer receiving mandate.

CPLR

An officer to whom a mandate is delivered to be executed shall:

1. execute the mandate according to its command;

2. give without compensation to the person delivering the mandate, if requested, a written receipt describing the mandate and specifying the day and hour of receiving it;

3. deliver without compensation to the person served, if requested, a copy of the mandate; and

4. return the mandate together with his return thereon, by delivering or mailing it to the clerk's office.

Article 23

SUBPOENAS, OATHS AND AFFIRMATIONS

CPLR

SUMMARY OF ARTICLE

§ 2310.   **Exclusions from article.**

§ 2301.   Scope of subpoena.

A subpoena requires the attendance of a person to give testimony. A subpoena duces tecum requires production of books, papers and other things. A child support subpoena is a subpoena issued pursuant to section one hundred eleven-p of the social services law by the office of temporary and disability assistance or a local social services district, or its authorized representative, or another state's child support enforcement agency governed by title IV-D of the social security act. A trial subpoena duces tecum shall state on its face that all papers or other items delivered to the court pursuant to such subpoena shall be accompanied by a copy of such subpoena.

2001 AMENDMENTS

L. 2001, ch. 355, eff. Jan. 1, 2002, amended to provide that a trial subpoena duces tecum shall state on its face that all papers or other items delivered to the court pursuant to such subpoena shall be accompanied by a copy of such subpoena.

1997 AMENDMENTS

L. 1997, ch. 398, eff. Jan. 1, 1998, amended CPLR 2301 by defining a child support subpoena.

1964 AMENDMENTS

L. 1964, ch. 388, eff. Sept. 1, 1964, deleted the word "form" from the caption.

§ 2302.   Authority to issue.

(a) Without court order. Subpoenas may be issued without a court order by the clerk of the court, a judge where there is no clerk, the attorney general, an attorney of record for a party to an action, an administrative proceeding or an arbitration, an arbitrator, a referee, or any member of a board, commission or committee authorized by law to hear, try or determine a matter or to do any other act, in an official capacity, in relation to which proof may be taken or the attendance of a person as a witness may be required; provided, however, that a subpoena to compel production of a patient's clinical record maintained pursuant to the provisions of section 33.13 of the mental hygiene law shall be accompanied by a court order. A child support subpoena may be issued by the department, or the child support enforcement unit coordinator or support collection unit supervisor of a social services district, or his or her designee, or another state's child support enforcement agency governed by title IV-D of the social security act.

(b) Issuance by court. A subpoena to compel production of an original record or document where a certified transcript or copy is admissible in evidence, or to compel attendance of any person confined in a penitentiary or jail, shall be issued by the court. Unless the court orders otherwise, a motion for such subpoena shall be made on at least one day's notice to the person having custody of the record, document or person confined. A subpoena to produce a prisoner so confined shall be issued by a judge to whom a petition for habeas corpus could be made under subdivision (b) of section seven thousand two of this chapter or a judge of the court of claims, if the matter is pending before the court of claims, or a judge of the surrogate's court, if the matter is pending before the surrogate's court, or a judge or support magistrate of the family court, if the matter is pending before the family court, or a judge of the New York city civil court, if the matter is pending before the New York city civil court and it has been removed thereto from the supreme court pursuant to subdivision (d) of section three hundred twenty-five of this chapter.

CROSS REFERENCES

See **Judiciary Law § 2-b** in Appendix, *below,* as to power of court to issue subpoenas.

2007 AMENDMENTS

L. 2007, ch. 136, eff. July 3, 2007, amended CPLR 2302(b) by including references to the judge of the New York city civil court.

2004 AMENDMENTS

L. 2004, ch. 336, eff. Nov. 8, 2004, amended 2302(b) by including grammatical changes, and references to the support magistrate of the family court.

1997 AMENDMENTS

L. 1997, ch. 398, eff. Jan. 1, 1998, amended 2302(a) by including reference to issuing a child support subpoena.

1989 AMENDMENTS

L. 1989, ch. 183, eff. Aug. 23, 1989.

1982 AMENDMENTS

L. 1982, ch. 139, eff. June 1, 1982, amended CPLR 2302(b) by adding the words "or a judge of the surrogate's court if the matter is pending before the surrogates court, or a judge of the family court, if the matter is pending before the family court."

1980 AMENDMENTS

L. 1980, ch. 77, eff. Feb. 13, 1980, amended CPLR 2302(b) by adding the words "or a judge of the court of claims, if the matter is pending before the court of claims."

1964 AMENDMENTS

L. 1964, ch. 519, eff. April 10, 1964, inserted in Subd. (a) the words "the attorney general", clarifying his authority to issue subpoenas.

§ 2303. Service of subpoena; payment of fees in advance.

(a) A subpoena requiring attendance or a subpoena duces tecum shall be served in the same manner as a summons, except that where service of such a subpoena is made pursuant to subdivision two or four of section three hundred eight of this chapter, the filing of proof of service shall not be required and service shall be deemed complete upon the later of the delivering or mailing of the subpoena, if made pursuant to subdivision two of section three hundred eight of this chapter, or upon the later of the affixing or mailing of the subpoena, if made pursuant to subdivision four of section three hundred eight of this chapter. Any person subpoenaed shall be paid or tendered in advance authorized traveling expenses and one day's witness fee. A copy of any subpoena duces tecum served in a pending civil judicial proceeding shall also be served, in the manner set forth in rule twenty-one hundred three of this chapter, on each party who has appeared in the civil judicial proceeding so that it is received by such parties promptly after service on the witness and before the production of books, papers or other things.

(b) A child support subpoena issued pursuant to section one hundred eleven-p of the social services law to public utility companies and corporations, including but not limited to cable television, gas, electric, steam, and telephone companies and corporations, as defined in section two of the public service law, may be served by regular mail, or through an automated process where information sought is maintained in an automated data base. All other child support subpoenas issued pursuant to section one hundred eleven-p of the social services law shall be served in accordance with the provisions of subdivision (a) of this section.

2004 AMENDMENTS

L. 2004, ch. 26, §1, eff. Jan. 1, 2004, amended CPLR 2303(a) replacing the term "civil judicial proceeding" for "action."

2003 AMENDMENTS

L. 2003, ch. 547, eff. Jan. 1, 2004, amended CPLR 2303(a) to provide that a copy of a subpoena duces tecum be served on each party appearing in the action.

1997 AMENDMENTS

L. 1997, ch. 398, eff. Jan. 1, 1997, amended CPLR 2303 by adding subdivisions and a new subdivision (b), providing that certain child support subpoenas issued pursuant to S.S.L. § 111-p may be served by mail or through an automated process.

1982 AMENDMENTS

L. 1982, ch. 618, eff. July 22, 1982, amended CPLR 2303 by adding the exception for service of a subpoena pursuant to CPLR 308.

§ 2303-a. Service of a trial subpoena.

Where the attendance at trial of a party or person within the party's control can be compelled by a trial subpoena, that subpoena may be served by delivery in accordance with subdivision (b) of rule 2103 to the party's attorney of record.

2007 AMENDMENTS

L. 2007, ch. 192, eff. Jan. 1, 2008, added CPLR 2303-a.

§ 2304. Motion to quash, fix conditions or modify.

A motion to quash, fix conditions or modify a subpoena shall be made promptly in the court in which the subpoena is returnable. If the subpoena is not returnable in a court, a request to withdraw or modify the subpoena shall first be made to the person who issued it and a motion to quash, fix conditions or modify may thereafter be made in the supreme court; except that such motion with respect to a child support subpoena issued pursuant to section one hundred eleven-p of the social services law shall be made to a judge of the family court or the supreme court. Reasonable conditions may be imposed upon the granting or denial of a motion to quash or modify.

1997 AMENDMENTS

L. 1997, ch. 398, eff. Jan. 1, 1998, amended CPLR 2304 by providing that a motion to quash with respect to a child support subpoena be made to a family court or supreme court judge.

1964 AMENDMENTS

L. 1964, ch. 388, eff. Sept. 1, 1964 inserted "a" before "request" in the second sentence.

§ 2305. Attendance required pursuant to subpoena; possession of books, records, documents or papers.

(a) When person required to attend. A subpoena may provide that the person subpoenaed shall appear on the date stated and any recessed or adjourned date of the trial hearing or examination. If he is given reasonable notice of such recess or adjournment, no further process shall be required to compel his attendance on the adjourned date. At the end of each day's attendance, the person subpoenaed may demand his fee for the next day on which he is to attend. If the fee is not then paid, he shall be deemed discharged.

(b) Subpoena duces tecum; attendance by substitute.

1. A subpoena duces tecum may be joined with a subpoena to testify at a trial, hearing or examination or may be issued separately.

2. Any person may comply with a subpoena duces tecum for a trial, hearing or examination by having the requisite books, documents or things produced by a person able to identify them and testify respecting their origin, purpose and custody.

(c) Inspection, examination and audit of records. Whenever by statute any department or agency of government, or officer thereof, is authorized to issue a subpoena requiring the production of books, records, documents or papers, the issuing party shall have the right to the possession of such material for a period of time, and on terms and conditions, as may reasonably be required for the inspection, examination or audit of the material. The reasonableness of such possession, time, terms, and conditions shall be determined with consideration for, among other things, (i) the good cause shown by the issuing party, (ii) the rights and needs of the person subpoenaed, and (iii) the feasibility and appropriateness of making copies of the material. The cost of reproduction and transportation incident thereto shall be borne by the person or party issuing the subpoena unless the court determines otherwise in the interest of justice.

2002 AMENDMENTS

L. 2002, ch. 575, § 1, eff. Sept. 1, 2003, adding subparagraph (b)(1) and redesignating former subdivision (b) as subparagraph (b)(2).

1977 AMENDMENTS

L. 1977, ch. 451, eff. July 19, 1977, amended CPLR 2305 by adding a new subd. (c) which controls possession of materials subpoenaed by a governmental authority.

§ 2306. Hospital records; medical records of department or bureau of a municipal corporation or of the state.

(a) Transcript or reproduction. Where a subpoena duces tecum is served upon a hospital, or upon a department or bureau of a municipal corporation or of the state, or an officer thereof, requiring the production of records relating to the condition or treatment of a patient, a transcript or a full sized legible reproduction certified as correct by the superintendent or head of the hospital, department or bureau or his assistant, or the officer, may be produced unless otherwise ordered by a court. Such a subpoena shall be served at least three days before the time fixed for the production of the records unless otherwise ordered by a court.

(b) Delivery to clerk. Where a court has designated a clerk to receive records described in subdivision (a), delivery may be made to him at or before the time fixed for their production. The clerk shall give a receipt for the records and notify the person subpoenaed when they are no longer required. The records shall be delivered in a sealed envelope indicating the title of the action, the date fixed for production and the name and address of the attorney appearing on the subpoena. They shall be available for inspection pursuant to the rules or order of the court.

CROSS REFERENCES

Regarding public access to government records, see **Public Officers Law, Article 6** (Freedom of Information Law) in Appendix, *below.*

1986 AMENDMENTS

L. 1986, ch. 4, eff. Jan. 1, 1987, amended CPLR 2306(a) by allowing full size legible reproductions of hospital records in response to a subpoena duces tecum and changing the time for service of a subpoena duces tecum from twenty-four hours to three days before the time fixed for the production of the records.

§ 2307. Books, papers and other things of a library, department or bureau of a municipal corporation or of the state.

Issuance by court. A subpoena duces tecum to be served upon a library, or a department or bureau of a municipal corporation or of the state, or an officer thereof, requiring the production of any books, papers or other things, shall be issued by a justice of the supreme court in the district in which the book, paper or other thing is located or by a judge of the court in which an action for which it is required is triable. Unless the court orders otherwise, a motion for such subpoena shall be made on at least one day's notice to the library, department, bureau or officer having custody of the book, document or other thing and the adverse party. Such subpoena must be served upon such library, or such department or bureau of such municipal corporation or of the state or an officer having custody of the book, document or other thing and the adverse party at least twenty-four hours before the time fixed for the production of such records unless in the case of an emergency the court shall by order dispense with such notice otherwise required. Compliance with a subpoena duces tecum may be made by producing a full-sized legible reproduction of the item or items required to be produced certified as complete and accurate by the person in charge of such library, department or bureau, or a designee of such person, and no personal appearance to certify such item or items shall be required of such person or designee, unless the court shall order otherwise pursuant to subdivision (d) of rule 2214 of this chapter. Where a stipulation would serve the same purpose as production of the book, document or other thing and the subpoena is required because the parties will not stipulate, the judge may impose terms on any party, including the cost of production of the book or document, and require such cost to be paid as an additional fee to the library, department or officer.

CROSS REFERENCES

Regarding public access to government records, see **Public Officers Law, Article 6** (Freedom of Information Law) in Appendix, *below.*

1991 AMENDMENTS

L. 1991, ch. 389, eff. Jan. 1, 1992, removed the designation for Subd. (a), amended the first paragraph to provide that compliance with a subpoena duces tecum could be made by producing a full-sized legible reproduction of the item or items required to be produced, and deleted Subd. (b).

1976 AMENDMENTS

L. 1976, ch. 419, eff. Sept. 1, 1976, amended Subd. (a) to provide that the subpoena must be served upon the custodian and upon the adverse party at least 24 hours before the time fixed for production, unless emergency circumstances exist, in which case the court may dispense with such notice requirements.

§ 2308. Disobedience of subpoena.

(a) Judicial. Failure to comply with a subpoena issued by a judge, clerk or officer of the court shall be punishable as a contempt of court. If the witness is a party the court may also strike his or her pleadings. A subpoenaed person shall also be liable to the person on whose behalf the subpoena was issued for a penalty not exceeding one hundred fifty dollars and damages sustained by reason of the failure to comply. A court may issue a warrant directing a sheriff to bring the witness into court. If a person so subpoenaed attends or is brought into court, but refuses without reasonable cause to be examined, or to answer a legal and pertinent question, or to produce a book, paper or other thing which he or she was directed to produce by the subpoena, or to subscribe his or her deposition after it has been correctly reduced to writing, the court may forthwith issue a warrant directed to the sheriff of the county where the person is, committing him or her to jail, there to remain until he or she submits to do the act which he or she was so required to do or is discharged according to law. Such a warrant of commitment shall specify particularly the cause of the commitment and, if the witness is committed for refusing to answer a question, the question shall be inserted in the warrant.

(b) Non-judicial.

(1) Unless otherwise provided, if a person fails to comply with a subpoena which is not returnable in a court, the issuer or the person on whose behalf the subpoena was issued may move in the supreme court to compel compliance. If the court finds that the subpoena was authorized, it shall order compliance and may impose costs not exceeding fifty dollars. A subpoenaed person shall also be liable to the person on whose behalf the subpoena was issued for a penalty not exceeding fifty dollars and damages sustained by reason of the failure to comply. A court may issue a warrant directing a sheriff to bring the witness before the person or body requiring his appearance. If a person so subpoenaed attends or is brought before such

person or body, but refuses without reasonable cause to be examined, or to answer a legal and pertinent question, or to produce a book, paper or other thing which he was directed to produce by the subpoena, or to subscribe his deposition after it has been correctly reduced to writing, the court, upon proof by affidavit, may issue a warrant directed to the sheriff of the county where the person is, committing him to jail, there to remain until he submits to do the act which he was so required to do or is discharged according to law. Such a warrant of commitment shall specify particularly the cause of the commitment and, if the witness is committed for refusing to answer a question, the question shall be inserted in the warrant.

(2) Notwithstanding the provisions of paragraph one of this subdivision, if a person fails to comply with a subpoena issued pursuant to section one hundred eleven-p of the social services law by the office of temporary and disability assistance or a social services district, or its authorized representative, or another state's child support enforcement agency governed by title IV-D of the social security act, such office or district is authorized to impose a penalty against the subpoenaed person. The amount of the penalty shall be determined by the commissioner of the office of temporary and disability assistance and set forth in regulation, and shall not exceed fifty dollars. Payment of the penalty shall not be required, however, if in response to notification of the imposition of the penalty the subpoenaed person complies immediately with the subpoena.

(c) Review of proceedings. Within ninety days after the offender shall have been committed to jail he shall, if not then discharged by law, be brought, by the sheriff, or other officer, as a matter of course personally before the court issuing the warrant of commitment and a review of the proceedings shall then be held to determine whether the offender shall be discharged from commitment. At periodic intervals of not more than ninety days following such review, the offender, if not then discharged by law from such commitment, shall be brought, by the sheriff, or other officer, personally before the court issuing the warrant of commitment and further reviews of the proceedings shall then be held to determine whether he shall be discharged from commitment. The clerk of the court before which such review of the proceedings shall be held, or the judge or justice of such court in case there be no clerk, shall give reasonable notice in writing of the date, time and place of each such review to each party or his attorney who shall have appeared of record in the proceeding resulting in the issuance of the warrant of commitment, at their last known address.

CROSS REFERENCES

See selected provisions governing procedures to punish for contempt under **Judiciary Law, Article 19,** Appendix, *below.*

2007 AMENDMENTS

L. 2007, ch. 205, eff. Jan. 1, 2008, amended CPLR 2308, subd. a by increasing the penalty for failure to comply with a subpoena compelling attendance in court to $150.00.

L. 2007, ch. 601, eff. Aug. 15 2007, amended CPLR 2308 subd. b(2) by replacing "Department of Social Services" with "office of temporary and disability assistance."

1997 AMENDMENTS

L. 1997, ch. 398, eff. Jan. 1, 1998, amended 2308 by renumbering subdivision (b) as subparagraph (b)(1) and by adding a new subparagraph (b)(2) dealing with the failure to comply with a subpoena issued pursuant to S.S.L. § 111-p.

1977 AMENDMENTS

L. 1977, ch. 25, eff. Sept. 1, 1977, amended the first sentence of subd. (b) by providing that the "person on whose behalf the subpoena was issued" may move in the supreme court to compel compliance with the subpoena. Previously only the "issuer" of the subpoena could so move.

1965 AMENDMENTS

L. 1965, ch. 231, eff. May 17, 1965, added a new subdivision (c).

§ 2309. Oaths and affirmations.

(a) Persons authorized to administer. Unless otherwise provided, an oath or affirmation may be administered by any person authorized to take acknowledgments of deeds by the real property law. Any person authorized by the laws of this state to receive evidence may administer an oath or affirmation for that purpose. An oath to a juror or jurors may be administered by a clerk of court and his deputies. This section shall not apply to an oath of office.

(b) Form. An oath or affirmation shall be administered in a form calculated to awaken the conscience and impress the mind of the person taking it in accordance with his religious or ethical beliefs.

(c) Oaths and affirmations taken without the state. An oath or affirmation taken without the state shall be treated as if taken within the state if it is accompanied by such certificate or certificates as would be required to entitle a deed acknowledged without the state to be recorded within the state if such deed had been acknowledged before the officer who administered the oath or affirmation.

(d) Form of certificate of oath or affirmation administered by officer of the armed forces of the United States. The certificate of an oath or affirmation administered within or without the state or the United States, by an officer of the armed forces of the United States authorized by the real property law to take acknowledgment of deeds, shall state:

1. the rank and serial number of the officer before whom the oath or affirmation is taken and the command to which he is attached;

2. that the person taking the oath or affirmation was, at the time of taking it, a person enlisted or commissioned in or serving in or with the armed forces of the United States or the dependent of such a person, or a person attached to or accompanying the armed forces of the United States; and

3. the serial number of the person who takes, or whose dependent takes the oath or affirmation, if such person is enlisted or commissioned in the armed forces of the United States. The place where such oath or affidavit is taken need not be disclosed.

CROSS REFERENCES

Real Prop. L. provisions authorizing the taking of acknowledgments of deeds, referred to in Subd. (a), *above*, may be found in **Real Prop. L. § 298,** *et seq.*, in Appendix, *below*.

1964 AMENDMENTS

L. 1964, ch. 287, eff. Sept. 1, 1964, added next to last sentence to Subd. (a) and deleted words "or an oath administered to jurors" in last sentence. The last sentence formerly read: "This section shall not apply to an oath of office or an oath administered to jurors."

§ 2310. Exclusions from article.

The provisions of this article shall not apply to subpoenas issued in proceedings before the New York state labor relations board.

Article 24

PUBLICATION

SUMMARY OF ARTICLE

§ 2401. Order when publication cannot be made.

1. Where because of circumstances beyond the control of a party required to publish, publication required by any statute, rule or court order cannot be made or completed in the specified place or newspaper in the required manner, the court may by order require such other publication as will not unduly prejudice any other party.

2. Notwithstanding the provisions of paragraph 1, if publication required by any statute, rule or court order has been commenced and cannot be completed because of the suspension or termination of publication by a newspaper, publication may be completed in any other newspaper which complies with the statute, rule, or order without further court order.

1971 AMENDMENTS

L. 1971, ch. 927, eff. June 25, 1971, amended CPLR 2401 by adding a new paragraph 2.

§ 2402. Computation of time for publication of notice.

The period of publication of a legal notice shall be computed by excluding the first day of publication and including the day on which the act or event of which notice is given is to take place or which completes the full period of publication.

CPLR

Article 25

UNDERTAKINGS

CPLR

SUMMARY OF ARTICLE

§ 2501. Undertaking; definition.

Undertaking includes

    1. Any obligation, whether or not the principal is a party thereto, which contains a covenant by a surety to pay the required amount, as specified therein, if any required condition, as specified therein or as provided in subdivision (c) section 2502, is not fulfilled; and

    2. any deposit, made subject to the required condition, of the required amount in legal tender of the United States or in face value of unregistered bonds of the United States or of the state.

§ 2502. Surety; form of affidavit; two or more undertakings; condition; acknowledgment.

(a) Surety; form of affidavit. Unless the court orders otherwise, surety shall be:

    1. an insurance company authorized to execute the undertaking within the state, or

    2. a natural person, except an attorney, who shall execute with the undertaking his affidavit setting forth his full name and address and that he is domiciled within the state and worth at least the amount specified in the undertaking exclusive of liabilities and of property exempt from application to the satisfaction of a judgment.

(b) Two or more undertakings. Where two or more undertakings are authorized or required to be given, they may be contained in the same instrument.

(c) Condition. Where no condition is specified in an undertaking in an action or proceeding, the condition shall be that the principal shall faithfully and fairly discharge the duties and fulfill the obligations imposed by law, or court order. Where the condition specifies that the undertaking is to be void upon payment of an amount or performance of an act, the undertaking shall be construed in accordance with the provisions of section 7-301 of the general obligations law.

(d) Acknowledgment. The undertaking shall be acknowledged in the form required to entitle a deed to be recorded.

CROSS REFERENCES

G.O.L. § 7-301, referred to in Subd. (c), *above*, appears in Appendix, *below.*

1970 AMENDMENTS

L. 1970, ch. 848, eff. Sept. 1, 1970, amended Subd. (c). The amendment was recommended by the Judicial Conference Jan. 2, 1970, Report to the Legislature wherein it was stated: "This bill would amend CPLR 2502(c) and 2511 to eliminate the last sentence of each provision, which are substantive provisions governing the extent of the surety's liability in judicial and non-judicial proceedings. These sentences would be combined and placed in the General Obligations Law, as new section 7-301, which would make it clear that the scope of the new provision extends to all undertakings in a penal sum. There would be cross-references to this new section in the CPLR provision, which henceforth would apply only to undertakings given in an action or judicial proceeding."

§ 2503. Undertaking of more than one thousand dollars; real property; lien.

(a) Creation of lien. Unless the court orders otherwise, an undertaking in an amount of more than one thousand dollars, which is not a deposit of legal tender of the United States or in face value of unregistered bonds of the United States or of the state, upon which natural persons are surety shall be secured by real property located in the state which shall be worth the amount specified in the undertaking exclusive of all encumbrances. Such undertaking shall create a lien on the real property when recorded in the individual surety bond liens docket in the office of the clerk or register of the county where the real property is located.

(b) Affidavit of surety. The affidavit of the surety shall contain, in addition to the information required by subdivision (a) of section 2502:

    1. a statement that the surety or sureties is or are the sole owner or owners of the real property offered as security;

    2. a description of the property, sufficiently identified to establish the lien of the undertaking;

3. a statement of the total amount of the liens, unpaid taxes, and other encumbrances against each property offered; and

4. a statement of the assessed value of each property offered, its market value, and the value of the equity over and above all encumbrances, liens and unpaid taxes.

(c) Filing of affidavit; recording. A duplicate original of the affidavit required by this rule shall be filed in the office of the clerk or register of the county where the real property is located. The following information shall be entered on the individual surety bond liens docket in the office of the clerk or register of the county where the real property is located;

1. the names of the sureties listed in alphabetical order;

2. the amount of the undertaking;

3. a description of the real property or properties offered as security thereunder, sufficiently identified to clearly establish the lien of the undertaking;

4. the date of such recording;

5. the title of the action, proceeding or estate; and

6. the court in which the papers are filed.

(d) Release of lien. The clerk or register of the county where the property is located shall make an entry, which shall constitute a release of the lien for all purposes and as to all persons, upon

1. the filing of a consent acknowledged by the person for whose benefit the undertaking was given in the form required to entitle a deed to be recorded; or

2. the order of the court, discharging the surety, made upon motion with such notice to other persons as the court may direct.

§ 2504. Waiver of undertaking; removal and change of parties.

(a) Waiver of undertaking. Unless the court orders otherwise, an undertaking may be waived by the written consent of all parties.

(b) Removal and change of parties. The liability on an undertaking shall remain in effect in favor of the party for whose benefit it was given, notwithstanding a removal of the action or a change of parties.

§ 2505. Filing of undertaking; service upon adverse party; time when effective.

An undertaking together with any affidavit required by this article shall be filed with the clerk of the court in which the action is triable, or, upon an appeal, in the office where the judgment or order of the court of original instance is entered, and a copy shall be served upon the adverse party. The undertaking is effective when so served and filed.

1965 AMENDMENTS

L. 1965, ch. 773, eff. Sept. 1, 1965, deleted the word "pending" in the phrase "the court in which the action is pending" in the first sentence of the section and substituted therefor the word "triable."

Amendment recommended by the Judicial Conference Feb. 1, 1965, Report to the Legislature: "Since undertakings are frequently given before service of summons or after judgment, the proposed change is necessary in order to preclude uncertainty as to the proper place for filing undertakings in such situations, where no action is pending."

§ 2506. Exception to surety; allowance where no exception taken.

(a) Exception to surety. If a certificate of qualification issued pursuant to subsections (b), (c) and (d) of section one thousand one hundred eleven of the insurance law is not filed with the undertaking, a party may except to the sufficiency of a surety by written notice of exception served upon the adverse party within ten days after receipt of a copy of the undertaking. Where the undertaking has been served upon a party by the sheriff, the notice of exception shall be served on the sheriff and on the adverse party. Exceptions deemed by the court to have been taken unnecessarily, or for vexation or delay, may, upon notice, be set aside, with costs.

(b) Allowance where no exception taken. Where no exception to sureties is taken within ten days or where exceptions taken are set aside the undertaking is allowed.

1984 AMENDMENTS

L. 1984, ch. 805, eff. Sept. 1, 1984, amended CPLR 2506(a) to conform the references to the recodified Insurance Law.

1976 AMENDMENTS

L. 1976, ch. 314, eff. Sept. 1, 1976, amended Subd. (a) to provide that exception to sufficiency of a surety may only be taken where a certificate of qualification is not filed with the undertaking.

§ 2507. Justification of surety.

(a) Motion to justify. Within ten days after service of notice of exception, the surety excepted to or the person upon whose behalf the undertaking was given shall move to justify, upon notice to the adverse party and to the sheriff if he was served with the undertaking. The surety shall be present upon the hearing of such motion to be examined under oath. If the court find the surety sufficient, it shall make an appropriate indorsement on the undertaking. A certificate of qualification issued pursuant to subsections (b), (c) and (d) of section one thousand one hundred eleven of the insurance law shall be accepted in lieu of a justification.

(b) Failure to justify. If a motion to justify is not made within ten days after the notice of exception is served, the undertaking shall then be without effect, except as provided in this subdivision. Unless otherwise provided by order of court, a surety on an undertaking excepted to and not justified shall remain liable until a new undertaking is given and allowed, but the original undertaking shall be otherwise without effect.

1984 AMENDMENTS

L. 1984, ch. 805, eff. Sept. 1, 1984, amended CPLR 2507(a) to conform the references to the recodified Insurance Law.

§ 2508. Motion for new or additional undertaking.

Upon motion of any interested person, upon notice to the parties and surety, and to the sheriff, where he was required to be served with the undertaking, the court may order a new or additional undertaking, a justification or rejustification of sureties, or new or additional sureties. Unless otherwise provided by order of court, a surety, on the original undertaking shall remain liable until such order is complied with, but the original undertaking shall be otherwise without effect.

§ 2509. Control of assets by agreement with surety.

Any person of whom an undertaking is required may agree with his surety for the deposit of any assets for which his surety may be held responsible with a bank, or safe deposit or trust company, authorized to do business in the state, if such deposit is otherwise proper and in such manner as to prevent withdrawal without the written consent of the surety or an order of court, made on notice to the surety. The agreement shall not affect the liability of the principal or surety as established by the terms of the undertaking.

§ 2510. Discharge of surety on the undertaking of a fiduciary.

(a) Motion; new undertaking; accounting. Surety on the undertaking of any fiduciary may move with notice to the person upon whose behalf the undertaking was given, to be discharged from liability for any act or omission of such fiduciary subsequent to the order of the court or the time when a new undertaking satisfactory to the court is filed. The court may restrain such fiduciary from acting pending the order discharging such surety from liability. Upon the hearing, the court shall order the fiduciary to give a new undertaking and to account, within such time as the court orders but not exceeding twenty days, for all his acts. If a new undertaking is filed the fiduciary shall account for his acts up to and including the date of such filing. Where the fiduciary does not comply with the order to account, the surety may make and file such account with the same effect as though filed by the fiduciary, and may utilize any disclosure device in obtaining information necessary for such an accounting. The court shall make such provisions with respect to commissions, allowances, disbursement and costs as it deems just.

(b) Settlement of account. When such account has been filed, the court, upon sufficient notice, shall order all persons interested in the proceedings to attend a settlement of the account at a time and place specified, and such settlement shall be made and the rights and liabilities of all parties to the proceeding shall be determined and enforced. After settlement of the account, the court shall make an order relieving the surety from any act or omission of the fiduciary subsequent to the date of such order or the time when a new undertaking satisfactory to the court was filed, whichever is earlier. Upon written demand by the fiduciary, the surety shall return any compensation paid for the unexpired portion of such suretyship.

§ 2511. Liability of surety.

CPLR

Where two or more persons are surety on an undertaking in an action or proceeding, they shall be jointly and severally liable. The amount recoverable from a surety shall be determined in accordance with the provisions of section 7-301 of the General Obligations Law.

CROSS REFERENCES

See **G.O.L. § 7-301 in Appendix,** *below.*

1970 AMENDMENTS

L. 1970, ch. 848, eff. Sept. 1, 1970. See Judicial Conference comments under CPLR 2502, 1970 amendments.

§ 2512. Undertaking by the state, municipal corporation or public officer.

1. Any provision of law authorizing or requiring an undertaking to be given by a party shall be construed as excluding the state, a domestic municipal corporation or a public officer in behalf of the state or of such a corporation. Such parties shall, however, be liable for damages as provided in such provision of law in an amount not exceeding an amount which shall be fixed by the court whenever it would require an undertaking of a private party.

2. Where an appeal is taken by any such party, only the court to which the appeal is taken may fix the amount which shall limit the liability for damages pursuant to this section.

1976 AMENDMENTS

L. 1976, ch. 264, eff. Sept. 1, 1976, amended CPLR 2512 to provide that not only municipalities, as previously provided, but also the state, or a public officer, shall be liable for damages in an amount fixed by the court while being exempt from giving undertakings. The amendment also added paragraph (2), providing that where such parties appeal, only the court to which an appeal is taken may fix the maximum liability.

§ 2513. Action on undertaking to a public officer, board or municipal corporation.

A person for whose benefit an undertaking has been given to a public officer, board or municipal corporation of the state may move, on notice to persons interested in the disposition of the proceeds, for leave to bring an action in his own name for breach of a condition.

Article 26
PROPERTY PAID INTO COURT

§ 2601. Payment of money or securities into court.

(a) Discharge of party paying money into court. A party paying money into court pursuant to the direction of the court is discharged thereby from all further liability to the extent of the money so paid in.

(b) Delivery of money and securities to county treasurer; commissioner of finance of city of New York. All moneys and securities paid into court shall be delivered either by the party making the payment into court or when an officer other than the county treasurer first receives them, by that officer, to the county treasurer of the county where the action is triable or to such other county treasurer as the court specially directs. Where money or securities are received by an officer other than the county treasurer, he shall deliver them to the county treasurer within two days after he receives them. The commissioner of finance of the city of New York shall be considered the treasurer of each of the counties included within that city.

(c) Title to funds paid into court. Title for the benefit of interested parties is vested in the county treasurer to whom any security is transferred pursuant to this article. Any security purchased by the county treasurer as an investment of money paid into court shall be purchased in the name of his office. He may bring an action upon or in relation to a security in his official or representative character.

(d) Subsequent control of money or securities paid into court. A court may direct that money or securities in the custody of a county treasurer pursuant to this section be transferred or invested as it deems proper.

1978 AMENDMENTS

L. 1978, ch. 655, eff. July 24, 1978 amended Subd. (b) by substituting "commissioner of finance" wherever "finance administrator" appears.

1969 AMENDMENTS

L. 1969, ch. 407, eff. May 9, 1969, amended Subd. (b) by substituting "finance administrator" wherever "director of finance" appears.

1964 AMENDMENTS

L. 1964, ch. 576, eff. April 16, 1964, in Subd. (b) substituted "director of finance" for "treasurer" of the city of New York, in the caption, and in the last sentence.

§ 2602. Payment into court of property other than money or securities; deposit with warehouse or safe deposit company.

Property paid into court, other than money or securities, shall not be delivered to the county treasurer. The court may direct that such property be deposited in a warehouse or safe deposit company upon the filing of a bond for the cost of such storage by the party paying the property into court or the party who requested such disposition, as the court may provide. It may make such other or subsequent disposition as it deems proper.

§ 2603. Cost of administration of property paid into court.

A party entitled to the income of any property paid into court shall be charged with the expense of administering such property and of receiving and paying over the income thereof.

§ 2604. Calculation of gross sum in lieu of income.

A gross sum payable to a party in lieu of the income of a sum of money paid into court for his benefit shall be calculated according to article four of the real property actions and proceedings law.

CROSS REFERENCES

R.P.A.P.L. Article 4, referred to in CPLR 2604, *above*, relates to the valuation of interests in real property, covering interest rates as well as mortality and other tables.

1966 AMENDMENTS

L. 1966, ch. 233, eff. April 25, 1966, deleted the entire section after the words "shall be calculated according to" and substituted therefor the words "article four of the real property actions and proceedings law."

R 2605. Duties of depositories.

When property paid into court is deposited with any depository, the entry of such deposit in the books of the depository shall contain a short reference to the title of the cause or matter in relation to which the deposit is made and shall specify the time from which any interest or accumulation on the deposit, if any, is to commence. On or before the first day of February in each year, such depository shall transmit to the appellate division of the supreme court in the department in which the depository is situated a statement describing the property in its custody, including interest or accumulation, if any, to the credit of each cause or matter on the last preceding first day of January.

R 2606. Obtaining order for payment out of court.

Unless otherwise directed by the judgment or order under which the property was paid into court, an order for the payment of property out of court shall be made only:

1. on motion with notice to all parties who have appeared or filed a notice of claim to such property; or

2. by special proceeding. In either case the petition shall be accompanied by a copy of the judgment, order or other paper under which the property was paid into court, together with a certificate of

the county treasurer or other depository of the property, showing the present condition and amount thereof, and stating separately, in the case of money, the amount of principal and interest.

1974 AMENDMENTS

L. 1974, ch. 878, eff. Sept. 1, 1974, amended paragraph 2 of CPLR 2606, which previously read "2. by special proceeding; the petition shall be accompanied by . . .," to read "2. by special proceeding. In either case the petition shall be accompanied. . . ."

R 2607. Payment of property paid into court.

No property paid into court, or income from such property, shall be paid out except upon order of the court directing payment to a specified person, except that if the property so paid into court, or the income from such property, inclusive of interest, does not exceed fifty dollars, a county treasurer may pay the same, without a court order, to the person entitled thereto or his authorized attorney. When the whole or remaining balance of all payments of money into court in an action, or the whole or remaining balance of a distributive share thereof, or any security or other property, is directed to be paid out of court, the order must direct the payment of all accrued income belonging to the party to whom such money or distributive share or remaining balance thereof, or security or other property is paid. A certified copy of the order directing payment shall be delivered to the county treasurer or other custodian of the property. The custodian, in the case of money, shall draw a draft payable to the order of the party entitled thereto specifying the title of the cause or matter on account of which the draft is made and the date of the order authorizing the draft. A certified copy of the order, accompanied by a draft in the case of money, shall be delivered to the depository of the property before it shall pay out any property. If an order directs that periodic payments be made, the filing of one copy of the order shall be sufficient to authorize the payment of subsequent drafts in pursuance thereof. Any other provision of law to the contrary notwithstanding, if an order directing payment by the county treasurer is made by the court, the copy of the order to be delivered to the county treasurer and the depository as herein provided shall be certified by the clerk of the court to be a true copy of the original of such order on file in his office.

1971 AMENDMENTS

L. 1971, ch. 154, eff. April 21, 1971, amended CPLR 2607 by adding new last sentence.

§ 2608. Liability of custodian.

No liability shall attach to a custodian of property paid into court because of a payment made by him in good faith in accordance with the direction of an order of the court or as provided in rule 2607.

1964 AMENDMENTS

L. 1964, ch. 388, eff. Sept. 1, 1964, changed reference to "rule 2606" to "rule 2607."

R 2609. Deposit by referee appointed to sell property.

Money received by a referee appointed to sell property shall be deposited forthwith by the referee, in his name as referee, in a bank or trust company authorized to transact business in this state, or with the chief fiscal officer or county treasurer of the county in which the action or proceeding is pending, as the court shall designate. Such moneys when paid to the chief fiscal officer of the county or county treasurer shall not be withdrawn except as directed by the judgment or order under which the deposit is made, or by an order under rule 2606.

1976 AMENDMENTS

L. 1976, ch. 86, eff. March 30, 1976, amended CPLR 2609 by adding county treasurer as an additional proper designee for deposit of money received by a referee appointed to sell property, and by including deposits with the county treasurer under the provision prohibiting withdrawal absent direction by the court.

1974 AMENDMENTS

L. 1974, ch. 90, eff. Sept. 1, 1974, amended the Rule.

CPLR

Article 27

DISPOSITION OF PROPERTY IN LITIGATION

CPLR

SUMMARY OF ARTICLE

§ 2701.   When court may order disposition of property.

§ 2702.   Sale of property.

§ 2703.   Enforcement of order directing disposition of property.

§ 2701. When court may order disposition of property.

The court, upon motion or on its own initiative, with such notice as it deems proper, may order personal property capable of delivery which is the subject of the action, paid into court, or delivered to such person as it may direct, with such security as the court shall direct, and subject to its further direction if:

1. a party has such property in his possession, custody or control as trustee for another party or where it belongs or is due to another party; or

2. a party has such property in his possession, custody or control and it belongs or is due to another party, where special circumstances make it desirable that payment or delivery to such other party should be withheld; or

3. the ownership of such property will depend on the outcome of a pending action and no party is willing to accept possession or custody of it during the pendency of the action.

1964 AMENDMENTS

L. 1964, ch. 422, eff. Sept. 1, 1964. Amendment was recommended by the Judicial Conference Feb. 1, 1964, Report to the Legislature: "Subdivision 1, as presently worded, permits an order for payment of property into court only where the party to whom it belongs would not have the benefit, use or control of it —i.e., if the party is unable to accept delivery because of special circumstances such as residence in a country where confiscation of the property would be effected. Subdivision 2 covers only those cases where an action is pending and no party is willing to accept possession or custody during pendency of the action. Thus, no provision now exists covering the disposition of property belonging to a party who is able to accept delivery or payment. The proposed changes are designed to provide for this presently omitted situation while also preserving the existing provisions. This would be in accord with analogous provisions of the C.P.A., and no change from the C.P.A. was apparently intended."

§ 2702. Sale of property.

On motion of any party, the court may order the sale, in such manner and on such terms as it deems proper, of any personal property capable of delivery which is the subject of the action if it shall appear likely that its value will be substantially decreased during the pendency of the action. Any party to the action may purchase such property at a judicially-directed sale held pursuant to this section without prejudice to his claim.

1965 AMENDMENTS

L. 1965, ch. 773, eff. Sept. 1, 1965, deleted the word "rule" in the last sentence and substituted therefor the word "section."

§ 2703. Enforcement of order directing disposition of property.

Where the court has directed disposition of personal property capable of delivery and the direction is disobeyed, the court by order, in addition to punishing the disobedience as a contempt, may require the sheriff to take and dispose of the property in accordance with its direction.

1964 AMENDMENTS

L. 1964, ch. 262, eff. Sept. 1, 1964, deleted the last sentence of this section and reenacted the same as CPLR § 5107. It read: "The court may require the sheriff to convey real property in conformity with its directions." The change was recommended by the Judicial Conference; see amendment notes to CPLR 5107.

Article 30

REMEDIES AND PLEADING

SUMMARY OF ARTICLE

CPLR

§ 3001. Declaratory judgment.

The supreme court may render a declaratory judgment having the effect of a final judgment as to the rights and other legal relations of the parties to a justiciable controversy whether or not further relief is or could be claimed. If the court declines to render such a judgment it shall state its grounds. A party who has brought a claim for personal injury or wrongful death against another party may maintain a declaratory judgment action directly against the insurer of such other party, as provided in paragraph six of subsection (a) of section three thousand four hundred twenty of the insurance law.

2008 AMENDMENTS

L. 2008, ch. 388 § 1, eff. Jan. 17, 2009, amended CPLR 3001 to permit a claimant in a personal injury or wrongful death case to commence a declaratory judgment action directly against the defendant's insurer, as provided under Insurance Law § 3420(a)(6) (that is, where the insurer's denial of coverage is based on the insured's failure to provide timely notice and neither the insured nor the insurer has previously commenced a declaratory judgment action within 60 days of the disclaimer, naming the injured person or other claimant as a party.).

§ 3002. Actions and relief not barred for inconsistency.

(a) Action against several persons. Where causes of action exist against several persons, the commencement or maintenance of an action against one, or the recovery against one of a judgment which is unsatisfied, shall not be deemed an election of remedies which bars an action against the others.

(b) Action against agent and undisclosed principal. Where causes of action exist against an agent and his undisclosed principal, the commencement or maintenance, after disclosure of the principal, of an action against either, or the recovery of a judgment against either which is unsatisfied, shall not be deemed an election of remedies which bars an action against the other.

(c) Action for conversion and on contract. Where causes of action exist against several persons for the conversion of property and upon express or implied contract, the commencement or maintenance of an action against one, or the recovery against one of a judgment which is unsatisfied, either for the conversion or upon the contract, shall not be deemed an election of remedies which bars an action against the others either for the conversion or upon the contract.

(d) Action on contract and to reform. A judgment denying recovery in an action upon an agreement in writing shall not be deemed to bar an action to reform such agreement and to enforce it as reformed.

(e) Claim for damages and rescission. A claim for damages sustained as a result of fraud or misrepresentation in the inducement of a contract or other transaction, shall not be deemed inconsistent with a claim for rescission or based upon rescission. In an action for rescission or based upon rescission the aggrieved party shall be allowed to obtain complete relief in one action, including rescission, restitution of the benefits, if any, conferred by him as a result of the transaction, and damages to which he is entitled because of such fraud or misrepresentation; but such complete relief shall not include duplication of items of recovery.

(f) Vendee's lien not to depend upon form of action. When relief is sought, in an action or by way of defense or counterclaim, by a vendee under an agreement for the sale or exchange of real property, because of the rescission, failure, invalidity or disaffirmance of such agreement, a vendee's lien upon the property shall not be denied merely because the claim is for rescission, or is based upon the rescission, failure, invalidity or disaffirmance of such agreement.

§ 3003. Action for periodic payments due under pension or retirement contract no bar to action for future installments.

The commencement or maintenance of an action for the recovery of payments which have become due under the terms of a written agreement providing for the payment of a pension or retirement compensation or deferred compensation for a period of years or for life, whether or not such agreement is part of an employment contract,

CPLR

shall not be deemed to bar subsequent actions to recover payments thereafter becoming due under the terms of such agreement.

§ 3004. Where restoration of benefits before judgment unnecessary.

A party who has received benefits by reason of a transaction that is void or voidable because of fraud, misrepresentation, mistake, duress, infancy or incompetency, and who, in an action or by way of defense or counterclaim, seeks rescission, restitution, a declaration or judgment that such transaction is void, or other relief, whether formerly denominated legal or equitable, dependent upon a determination that such transaction was void or voidable, shall not be denied relief because of a failure to tender before judgment restoration of such benefits; but the court may make a tender of restoration a condition of its judgment, and may otherwise in its judgment so adjust the equities between the parties that unjust enrichment is avoided.

§ 3005. Relief against mistake of the law.

When relief against a mistake is sought in an action or by way of defense or counterclaim, relief shall not be denied merely because the mistake is one of law rather than one of fact.

§§ 3006–3010. [Not used.]

§ 3011. Kinds of pleadings.

There shall be a complaint and an answer. An answer may include a counterclaim against a plaintiff and a cross-claim against a defendant. A defendant's pleading against another claimant is an interpleader complaint, or against any other person not already a party is a third-party complaint. There shall be a reply to a counterclaim denominated as such, an answer to an interpleader complaint, or third-party complaint and an answer to a cross-claim that contains a demand for an answer. If no demand is made, the cross-claim shall be deemed denied or avoided. There shall be no other pleading unless the court orders otherwise.

1977 AMENDMENTS

L. 1977, ch. 26, eff. Sept. 1, 1977, amended CPLR 3011 to provide that an answer to a cross-claim is required only where the cross-claim demands an answer. If no demand is made, the cross-claim is deemed denied or avoided.

The Judicial Conference, in recommending the amendment in its 1977 Report to the Legislature, stated in part:

". . . . In cases arising out of the same incident, where there are multiple plaintiffs each suing numerous defendants, as for example under the theory of *Dole* v. *Dow Chemical Company,* 30 N.Y. 2d 143 (1972), the preparation and service of mandatory answers to cross-claims becomes extremely burdensome.

"This bill would mitigate the problem by providing for an answer to a cross-claim only when it contains a demand for an answer . . . . The result will be to require answers to cross-claims when they serve a purpose but not otherwise, thereby serving the convenience of the courts and the parties and eliminating much unnecessary paperwork."

§ 3012. Service of pleadings and demand for complaint.

(a) Service of pleadings. The complaint may be served with the summons. A subsequent pleading asserting new or additional claims for relief shall be served upon a party who has not appeared in the manner provided for service of a summons. In any other case, a pleading shall be served in the manner provided for service of papers generally. Service of an answer or reply shall be made within twenty days after service of the pleading to which it responds.

(b) Service of complaint where summons served without complaint. If the complaint is not served with the summons, the defendant may serve a written demand for the complaint within the time provided in subdivision (a) of rule 320 for an appearance. Service of the complaint shall be made within twenty days after service of the demand. Service of the demand shall extend the time to appear until twenty days after service of the complaint. If no demand is made, the complaint shall be served within twenty days after service of the notice of appearance. The court upon motion may dismiss the action if service of the complaint is not made as provided in this subdivision. A demand or motion under this subdivision does not of itself constitute an appearance in the action.

(c) Additional time to serve answer where summons and complaint not personally delivered to person to be served within the state. If the complaint is served with the summons and the service is made on the defendant by delivering the summons and complaint to an official of the state authorized to receive service in his behalf or if service of the summons and complaint is made pursuant to section 303, paragraphs two, three, four or five of section 308 or sections 313, 314 or 315, service of an answer shall be made within thirty days after service is complete.

(d) Extension of time to appear or plead. Upon the application of a party, the court may extend the time to appear or plead, or compel the acceptance of a pleading untimely served, upon such terms as may be just and upon a showing of reasonable excuse for delay or default.

1983 AMENDMENTS

L. 1983, ch. 318, eff. June 21, 1983, amended CPLR 3012 by adding a new subd. (d) to provide for an extension of time to appear or plead. ch. 318, § 3 provides:

§ 3. This act shall take effect immediately and shall be deemed and construed as remedial in nature and application and shall apply in every action and proceeding heretofore commenced and which either: still is pending before a court; or the time for taking of an appeal from any order or judgment in such action has not yet expired, and in all actions and proceedings hereafter commenced.

1978 AMENDMENTS

L. 1978, ch. 534, eff. Jan. 1, 1979, amended Subd. (b).

1970 AMENDMENTS

L. 1970, ch. 852, eff. Sept. 1, 1970, amended Subd. (c).

1964 AMENDMENTS

L. 1964, ch. 388, eff. Sept. 1, 1964, amended Subd. (c).

§ 3012-a. Certificate of merit in medical, dental and podiatric malpractice actions.

(a) In any action for medical, dental or podiatric malpractice, the complaint shall be accompanied by a certificate, executed by the attorney for the plaintiff, declaring that:

(1) the attorney has reviewed the facts of the case and has consulted with at least one physician in medical malpractice actions, at least one dentist in dental malpractice actions or at least one podiatrist in podiatric malpractice actions who is licensed to practice in this state or any other state and who the attorney reasonably

believes is knowledgeable in the relevant issues involved in the particular action, and that the attorney has concluded on the basis of such review and consultation that there is a reasonable basis for the commencement of such action; or

(2) the attorney was unable to obtain the consultation required by paragraph one of this subdivision because a limitation of time, established by article two of this chapter, would bar the action and that the certificate required by paragraph one of this subdivision could not reasonably be obtained before such time expired. If a certificate is executed pursuant to this subdivision, the certificate required by this section shall be filed within ninety days after service of the complaint; or

(3) the attorney was unable to obtain the consultation required by paragraph one of this subdivision because the attorney had made three separate good faith attempts with three separate physicians, dentists or podiatrists, in accordance with the provisions of paragraph one of this subdivision to obtain such consultation and none of those contacted would agree to such a consultation.

(b) Where a certificate is required pursuant to this section, a single certificate shall be filed for each action, even if more than one defendant has been named in the complaint or is subsequently named.

(c) Where the attorney intends to rely solely on the doctrine of "res ipsa loquitur", this section shall be inapplicable. In such cases, the complaint shall be accompanied by a certificate, executed by the attorney, declaring that the attorney is solely relying on such doctrine and, for that reason, is not filing a certificate required by this section.

(d) If a request by the plaintiff for the records of the plaintiff's medical or dental treatment by the defendants has been made and such records have not been produced, the plaintiff shall not be required to serve the certificate required by this section until ninety days after such records have been produced.

(e) For purposes of this section, and subject to the provisions of section thirty-one hundred one of this chapter, an attorney who submits a certificate as required by paragraph one or two of subdivision (a) of this section and the physician, dentist or podiatrist with whom the attorney consulted shall not be required to disclose the identity of the

CPLR

physician, dentist or podiatrist consulted and the contents of such consultation; provided, however, that when the attorney makes a claim under paragraph three of subdivision (a) of this section that he was unable to obtain the required consultation with the physician, dentist or podiatrist, the court may, upon the request of a defendant made prior to compliance by the plaintiff with the provisions of section thirty-one hundred of this chapter, require the attorney to divulge to the court the names of physicians, dentists or podiatrists refusing such consultation.

(f) The provisions of this section shall not be applicable to a plaintiff who is not represented by an attorney.

(g) The plaintiff may, in lieu of serving the certificate required by this section, provide the defendant or defendants with the information required by paragraph one of subdivision (d) of section thirty-one hundred one of this chapter within the period of time prescribed by this section.

1987 AMENDMENTS

L. 1987, ch. 507, eff. July 30, 1987, and applicable to any acts, omissions or failures occurring on or after such date, amended section to apply to podiatric malpractice actions.

1986 AMENDMENTS

L. 1986, ch. 266, eff. July 8, 1986 and applicable to actions commenced on or after such date, added new section 3012-a, relating to certificates of merit in medical and dental malpractice actions.

§ 3013. Particularity of statements generally.

Statements in a pleading shall be sufficiently particular to give the court and parties notice of the transactions, occurrences, or series of transactions or occurrences, intended to be proved and the material elements of each cause of action or defense.

R 3014. Statements.

Every pleading shall consist of plain and concise statements in consecutively numbered paragraphs. Each paragraph shall contain, as far as practicable, a single allegation. Reference to and incorporation of allegations may subsequently be by number. Prior statements in a pleading shall be deemed repeated or adopted subsequently in the same pleading whenever express repetition or adoption is unnecessary for a clear presentation of the subsequent matters. Separate causes of action or defenses shall be separately stated and numbered and may be stated regardless of consistency. Causes of action or defenses may be stated alternatively or hypothetically. A copy of any writing which is attached to a pleading is a part thereof for all purposes.

R 3015. Particularity as to specific matters.

(a) Conditions precedent. The performance or occurrence of a condition precedent in a contract need not be pleaded. A denial of performance or occurrence shall be made specifically and with particularity. In case of such denial, the party relying upon the performance or occurrence shall be required to prove on the trial only such performance or occurrence as shall have been so specified.

(b) Corporate status. Where any party is a corporation, the complaint shall so state and, where known, it shall specify the state, country or government by or under whose laws the party was created.

(c) Judgment, decision or determination. A judgment, decision or other determination of a court, judicial or quasi-judicial tribunal, or of a board or officer, may be pleaded without stating matter showing jurisdiction to render it.

(d) Signatures. Unless specifically denied in the pleadings each signature on a negotiable instrument is admitted.

(e) License to do business. Where the plaintiff's cause of action against a consumer arises from the plaintiff's conduct of a business which is required by state or local law to be licensed by the department of consumer affairs of the city of New York, the Suffolk county department of consumer affairs, the Westchester county department of consumer affairs/weight-measures, the county of Rockland, the county of Putnam or the Nassau county department of consumer affairs, the complaint shall allege, as part of the cause of action, that plaintiff is duly licensed and shall contain the name and number, if any, of such license and the governmental agency which issued such license; provided, however, that where the plaintiff does not have a license at the commencement of the action the plaintiff may, subject to the provisions of rule thirty hundred twenty-five of this article, amend the complaint with the name and number of an after-acquired license and

CPLR

the name of the governmental agency which issued such license or move for leave to amend the complaint in accordance with such provisions. The failure of the plaintiff to comply with this subdivision will permit the defendant to move for dismissal pursuant to paragraph seven of subdivision (a) of rule thirty-two hundred eleven of this chapter.

1996 AMENDMENTS

L. 1996, ch. 465, eff. August 8, 1996, amended subdivision (e) to add a reference to Putnam county.

1990 AMENDMENTS

L. 1990, ch. 654, eff. July 18, 1990, amended CPLR 3015(e) to apply to a plaintiff licensed by the Westchester county department of consumer affairs/weight-measures.

1986 AMENDMENTS

L. 1986, ch. 26, eff. April 3, 1986, amended CPLR 3015(e) to apply to a plaintiff licensed by the Rockland County Department of Consumer Affairs.

1985 AMENDMENTS

L. 1985, ch. 26, eff. April 2, 1985, amended CPLR 3015(e) to apply to a plaintiff licensed by the Suffolk County Department of Consumer Affairs.

1984 AMENDMENTS

L. 1984, ch. 243, eff. July 19, 1984, amended CPLR 3015(e) to apply to a plaintiff licensed by the Nassau County Department of Consumer Affairs.

1983 AMENDMENTS

L. 1983, ch. 817, eff. July 30, 1983, and applicable to all actions commenced on and after that date, added CPLR 3015(e).

1972 AMENDMENTS

Former Subd. (d) was deleted and former Subd. (e) was relettered Subd. (d) by Proposal No. 4 of the Judicial Conference Report to the 1972 Legislature, eff. Sept. 1, 1972.

The 1972 Judicial Conference Report stated in part:

"Subdivision (d) of Rule 3015, which requires that special damages be itemized in the pleading, would be deleted. The itemization of special damages is a proper function of the bill of particulars which has been retained substantially unchanged from prior law.

"Rule 3015 (d) was originally proposed when the Advisory Committee on Practice and Procedure decided to abolish the bill of particulars (1 Adv. Comm. Rpt. 65-66 (1957)). It was retained by oversight when the Legislature restored the bill of particulars (5th Rpt. Leg. Doc. (1961) No. 15, pp. 422, 437–440. . . .).

"The proposed repeal of Rule 3015 (d) would implement the intent of both the Advisory Committee and the Legislature. Deletion is not intended to change case law requiring the pleading of special damages forming an element of a cause of action, as required by CPLR 3013. Case law requires the pleading of special damages independent of Rule 3015 (d) (see *Keefe* v. *Lee*, 197 N.Y. 68 (1909))."

1964 AMENDMENTS

Amendment No. 4 made by the Judicial Conference Feb. 1, 1964, Report to the Legislature, eff. Sept. 1, 1964, added the new subdivision (e), now Subd. (d). The Judicial Conference stated: "The first sentence of § 3018(a) permits a party to raise by a general denial the question of the authenticity of a signature on a negotiable instrument. Sections 3-307 and 8-105 (2)(a) of the Uniform Commercial Code, however, provide that every signature on a negotiable instrument is admitted unless specifically denied in the proper pleading. In the view of the Judicial Conference the proposed change is not only necessary for the sake of conformity with the Code but is also desirable in itself as a matter of sound pleading procedure."

CPLR

R 3016. Particularity in specific actions.

(a) Libel or slander. In an action for libel or slander, the particular words complained of shall be set forth in the complaint, but their application to the plaintiff may be stated generally.

(b) Fraud or mistake. Where a cause of action or defense is based upon misrepresentation, fraud, mistake, wilful default, breach of trust or undue influence, the circumstances constituting the wrong shall be stated in detail.

(c) Separation or divorce. In an action for separation or divorce, the nature and circumstances of a party's alleged misconduct, if any, and the time and place of each act complained of, if any, shall be specified in the complaint or counterclaim as the case may be.

(d) Judgment. In an action on a judgment, the complaint shall state the extent to which any judgment recovered by the plaintiff against the defendant, or against a person jointly liable with the defendant, on the same cause of action has been satisfied.

(e) Law of foreign country. Where a cause of action or defense is based upon the law of a foreign country or its political subdivision, the substance of the foreign law relied upon shall be stated.

(f) Sale and delivery of goods or performing of labor or services. In an action involving the sale and delivery of goods, or the performing of labor or services, or the furnishing of materials, the plaintiff may set forth and number in his verified complaint the items of his claim and the reasonable value or agreed price of each. Thereupon the defendant by his verified answer shall indicate specifically those items he disputes and whether in respect of delivery or performance, reasonable value or agreed price.

(g) Personal injury. In an action designated in subsection (a) of section five thousand one hundred four of the insurance law, for personal injuries arising out of negligence in the use or operation of a motor vehicle in this state, the complaint shall state that the plaintiff has sustained a serious injury, as defined in subsection (d) of section five thousand one hundred two of the insurance law, or economic loss greater than basic economic loss, as defined in subsection (a) of section five thousand one hundred two of the insurance law.

(h) Gross negligence or intentional infliction of harm by certain directors, officers or trustees of certain corporations, associations, organizations or trusts. In an action or proceeding based upon the conduct of a director, officer or trustee described in section seven hundred twenty-a of the not-for-profit corporation law, or subdivision six of section 20.09 of the arts and cultural affairs law, the complaint shall be verified and shall state whether or not said complaint is based upon gross negligence or intentional infliction of harm.

CROSS REFERENCES

Insurance Law §§ 5102 and 5104, referred to in Subd. (g), *above*, contain essential provisions of the "no fault" automobile insurance act; §§ 5102–5104, § 5108 are included in the Appendix, *below.*

1991 AMENDMENTS

L. 1991, ch. 656, eff. July 26, 1991, amended CPLR 3016(h) to replace a reference to Gen. Mun. L. § 305 with a reference to Arts and Cultural Affairs L. § 20.09.

1990 AMENDMENTS

L. 1990, ch. 904, eff. July 30, 1990, amended CPLR 3016(h) to include actions or proceedings based upon the conduct of a director, officer or trustee as described in subdivision six of section three hundred five of the General Municipal Law.

1986 AMENDMENTS

L. 1986, ch. 220, eff. June 28, 1986 and applicable only to those causes of action arising on or after that date, added new Subd. (h) to CPLR 3016, requiring a verified complaint in actions based upon § 720(a) of the Not-For-Profit Corporation Law, stating whether the complaint is based upon gross negligence or intentional infliction of harm.

1984 AMENDMENTS

L. 1984, ch. 805, eff. Sept. 1, 1984, amended CPLR 3016(g) to conform the references to the recodified Insurance Law.

1976 AMENDMENTS

L. 1976, ch. 87, eff. April 29, 1976, amended Subd. (c).

1974 AMENDMENTS

L. 1974, ch. 575, eff. Sept. 1, 1974, added Subd. (g).

§ 3017.   Demand for relief.

(a) Generally. Except as otherwise provided in subdivision (c) of this section, every complaint, counterclaim, cross-claim, interpleader complaint, and third-party complaint shall contain a demand for the relief to which the pleader deems himself entitled. Relief in the alternative or of several different types may be demanded. Except as provided in section 3215, the court may grant any type of relief within its jurisdiction appropriate to the proof whether or not demanded, imposing such terms as may be just.

(b) Declaratory judgment. In an action for a declaratory judgment, the demand for relief in the complaint shall specify the rights and other legal relations on which a declaration is requested and state whether further or consequential relief is or could be claimed and the nature and extent of any such relief which is claimed.

(c) Personal injury or wrongful death actions. In an action to recover damages for personal injuries or wrongful death, the complaint, counterclaim, cross-claim, interpleader complaint, and third-party complaint shall contain a prayer for general relief but shall not state the amount of damages to which the pleader deems himself entitled. If the action is brought in the supreme court, the pleading shall also state whether or not the amount of damages sought exceeds the jurisdictional limits of all lower courts which would otherwise have jurisdiction. Provided, however, that a party against whom an action to recover damages for personal injuries or wrongful death is brought, may at any time request a supplemental demand setting forth the total damages to which the pleader deems himself entitled. A supplemental demand shall be provided by the party bringing the action within fifteen days of the request. In the event the supplemental demand is not served within fifteen days, the court, on motion, may order that it be served. A supplemental demand served pursuant to this subdivision shall be treated in all respects as a demand made pursuant to subdivision (a) of this section.

2003 AMENDMENTS

L. 2003, ch. 694, eff. Nov. 27, 2003, amended subd. (c) to prohibit any statement reciting the specific amount of damages demanded by the plaintiff for all personal injury or wrongful death actions. Any complaint in a wrongful death action or personal injury action should contain a demand for general relief.

1989 AMENDMENTS

L. 1989, ch. 442, eff. Aug. 15, 1989, added dental malpractice.

1980 AMENDMENTS

L. 1980, ch. 686, eff. June 26, 1981, amended CPLR 3017(c) to include actions against a municipal corporation.

1976 AMENDMENTS

L. 1976, ch. 955, eff. Aug. 26, 1976, added Subd. (c), banning ad damnum clauses in medical malpractice pleadings, and amended Subd. (a) accordingly.

§ 3018.   Responsive pleadings.

(a) Denials. A party shall deny those statements known or believed by him to be untrue. He shall specify those statements as to the truth of which he lacks knowledge or information sufficient to form a belief and this shall have the effect of a denial. All other statements of a pleading are deemed admitted, except that where no responsive pleading is permitted they are deemed denied or avoided.

(b) Affirmative defenses. A party shall plead all matters which if not pleaded would be likely to take the adverse party by surprise or would raise issues of fact not appearing on the face of a prior pleading such as arbitration and award, collateral estoppel, culpable conduct claimed in diminution of damages as set forth in article fourteen A, discharge in bankruptcy, facts showing illegality either by statute or common law, fraud, infancy or other disability of the party defending, payment, release, res judicata, statute of frauds, or statute of limitation. The application of this subdivision shall not be confined to the instances enumerated.

1980 AMENDMENTS

L. 1980, ch. 111, eff. May 7, 1980, as amended by ch. 504, eff. June 24, 1980, amended CPLR 3018(b) by expanding the enumeration of affirmative defenses that must be pleaded under this section to specifically include pleadings relating to contributory negligence.

§ 3019. Counterclaims and cross-claims.

(a) Subject of counterclaims. A counterclaim may be any cause of action in favor of one or more defendants or a person whom a defendant represents against one or more plaintiffs, a person whom a plaintiff represents or a plaintiff and other persons alleged to be liable.

(b) Subject of cross-claims. A cross-claim may be any cause of action in favor of one or more defendants or a person whom a defendant represents against one or more defendants, a person whom a defendant represents or a defendant and other persons alleged to be liable. A cross-claim may include a claim that the party against whom it is asserted is or may be liable to the cross-claimant for all or part of a claim asserted in the action against the cross-claimant.

(c) Counterclaim against trustee or nominal plaintiff. In an action brought by a trustee or in the name of a plaintiff who has no actual interest in the contract upon which it is founded, a claim against the plaintiff shall not be allowed as a counterclaim, but a claim existing against the person beneficially interested shall be allowed as a counterclaim to the extent of the plaintiff's claim, if it might have been so allowed in an action brought by the person beneficially interested.

(d) Cause of action in counterclaim or cross-claim deemed in complaint. A cause of action contained in a counterclaim or a cross-claim shall be treated, as far as practicable, as if it were contained in a complaint, except that separate process, trial or judgment may not be had unless the court so orders. Where a person not a party is alleged to be liable a summons and answer containing the counterclaim or cross-claim shall be filed, whereupon he or she shall become a defendant. Service upon such a defendant shall be by serving a summons and answer containing the counterclaim or cross-claim. Such defendant shall serve a reply or answer as if he or she were originally

CPLR

a party.

1994 AMENDMENTS

L. 1994, ch. 563, eff. July 26, 1994, amended CPLR 3019(d) by replacing the words "he shall be served with a summons and a copy of the answer containing the counterclaim or cross-claim," with the words "a summons and answer containing the counterclaim or cross-claim shall be filed"; by adding the words "or she"; and by adding the words "Service upon such a defendant shall be by serving a summons and answer containing the counterclaim or cross claim. Such defendant."

1966 AMENDMENTS

L. 1966, ch. 182, eff. Sept. 1, 1966, repealed Subd. (c) and Subd. (d), and redesignated Subd. (e) and Subd. (f) as Subd. (c) and Subd. (d) respectively.

Amendment was recommended by the Judicial Conference Feb. 1, 1966, Report to the Legislature: "U.C.C. § 9-318(1) is inconsistent with CPLR 3019(c). The U.C.C. provision makes the rights of an assignee of a contract of sale subject to (a) all the terms of the contract and any defenses or claims arising therefrom, and (b) any other defense or claim of the debtor against the assignor which accrues before the account debtor receives notification of the assignment. On the other hand, CPLR 3019(c) provides that a defendant can assert against the assignee a claim 'existing' against the assignor 'at the time of the assignment' and belonging to the defendant before notification of the assignment. In this respect CPLR 3019(c) has also for four years been in conflict with § 13-105 of the General Obligations Law (formerly § 41 of the Personal Property Law). 'Existing' means 'matured' at the time of assignment. See *James Talcott, Inc. v. Winco Sales Corp.,* 28 Misc. 2d 612 (App. Term 1st Dept. 1960). The U.C.C. permits an account debtor to assert a claim arising out of the same transaction regardless of when it accrued, and any *other* claim if it accrued prior to notification of the assignment.

"CPLR 3019(d), relating to counterclaims against an assignee of a negotiable instrument who is not a holder in due course, is amply covered by U.C.C. § 3-306, dealing with the same matter.

"The U.C.C. establishes the substantive rules of claims and defenses against assignees of secured contracts or negotiable instruments (Sections 9-318(1) and 3-306). The substantive law regulating claims and defenses of an obligor against an assignee in transactions other than those covered by the Uniform Commercial Code is contained in General Obligations Law § 13-105. Accordingly, CPLR 3019(c) and (d) should be eliminated."

§ 3020. Verification.

  (a) Generally. A verification is a statement under oath that the pleading is true to the knowledge of the deponent, except as to matters alleged on information and belief, and that as to those matters he believes it to be true. Unless otherwise specified by law, where a pleading is verified, each subsequent pleading shall also be verified, except the answer of an infant and except as to matter in the pleading concerning which the party would be privileged from testifying as a witness. Where the complaint is not verified, a counterclaim, cross-claim or third-party claim in the answer may be separately verified in the same manner and with the same effect as if it were a separate pleading.

(b) When answer must be verified. An answer shall be verified:

1. when the complaint charges the defendant with having con-fessed or suffered a judgment, executed a conveyance, assignment or other instrument, or transferred or delivered money or personal property with intent to hinder, delay or defraud his creditors, or with being a party or privy to such a transaction by another person with like intent towards the creditors of that person, or with any fraud whatever affecting a right or the property of another; or

2. in an action against a corporation to recover damages for the non-payment of a promissory note or other evidence of debt for the absolute payment of money upon demand or at a particular time.

(c) Defense not involving the merits. A defense which does not involve the merits of the action shall be verified.

(d) By whom verification made. The verification of a pleading shall be made by the affidavit of the party, or, if two or more parties united in interest are pleading together, by at least one of them who is acquainted with the facts, except:

1. if the party is a domestic corporation, the verification shall be made by an officer thereof and shall be deemed a verification by the party;

2. if the party is the state, a governmental subdivision, board, commission, or agency, or a public officer in behalf of any of them, the verification may be made by any person acquainted with the facts; and

3. if the party is a foreign corporation, or is not in the county where the attorney has his office, or if there are two or more parties united in interest and pleading together and none of them acquainted

with the facts is within that county, or if the action or defense is founded upon a written instrument for the payment of money only which is in the possession of an agent or the attorney, or if all the material allegations of the pleading are within the personal knowledge of an agent or the attorney, the verification may be made by such agent or attorney.

1973 AMENDMENTS

L. 1973, ch. 88, eff. Sept. 1, 1973, amended CPLR 3020(d)(2).

1964 AMENDMENTS

L. 1964, ch. 388, eff. Sept. 1, 1964, made mechanical corrections.

R 3021.   Form of affidavit of verification.

The affidavit of verification must be to the effect that the pleading is true to the knowledge of the deponent, except as to the matters therein stated to be alleged on information and belief, and that as to those matters he believes it to be true. If it is made by a person other than the party, he must set forth in the affidavit the grounds of his belief as to all matters not stated upon his knowledge and the reason why it is not made by the party.

R 3022.   Remedy for defective verification.

A defectively verified pleading shall be treated as an unverified pleading. Where a pleading is served without a sufficient verification in a case where the adverse party is entitled to a verified pleading, he may treat it as a nullity, provided he gives notice with due diligence to the attorney of the adverse party that he elects so to do.

R 3023.   Construction of verified pleading.

The allegations or denials in a verified pleading must, in form, be stated to be made by the party pleading. Unless they are stated to be made upon the information and belief of the party, they must be regarded for all purposes, including a criminal prosecution, as having been made upon the knowledge of the person verifying the pleading. An allegation that the party has not sufficient knowledge or information to form a belief with respect to a matter, must, for the same purposes, be regarded as an allegation that the person verifying the pleading has not such knowledge or information.

R 3024. Motion to correct pleadings.

(a) Vague or ambiguous pleadings. If a pleading is so vague or ambiguous that a party cannot reasonably be required to frame a response he may move for a more definite statement.

(b) Scandalous or prejudicial matter. A party may move to strike any scandalous or prejudicial matter unnecessarily inserted in a pleading.

(c) Time limits; pleading after disposition. A notice of motion under this rule shall be served within twenty days after service of the challenged pleading. If the motion is denied, the responsive pleading shall be served within ten days after service of notice of entry of the order and, if it is granted, an amended pleading complying with the order shall be served within that time.

R 3025. Amended and supplemental pleadings.

(a) Amendments without leave. A party may amend his pleading once without leave of court within twenty days after its service, or at any time before the period for responding to it expires, or within twenty days after service of a pleading responding to it.

(b) Amendments and supplemental pleadings by leave. A party may amend his pleading, or supplement it by setting forth additional or subsequent transactions or occurrences, at any time by leave of court or by stipulation of all parties. Leave shall be freely given upon such terms as may be just including the granting of costs and continuances.

(c) Amendment to conform to the evidence. The court may permit pleadings to be amended before or after judgment to conform them to the evidence, upon such terms as may be just including the granting of costs and continuances.

(d) Responses to amended or supplemental pleadings. Except where otherwise prescribed by law or order of the court, there shall be an answer or reply to an amended or supplemental pleading if an answer or reply is required to the pleading being amended or supplemented. Service of such an answer or reply shall be made within twenty days after service of the amended or supplemental pleading to which it responds.

CPLR

§ 3026. Construction.

Pleadings shall be liberally construed. Defects shall be ignored if a substantial right of a party is not prejudiced.

1964 AMENDMENTS

L. 1964, ch. 388, eff. Sept. 1, 1964, made mechanical corrections.

§§ 3027–3030. [Not used.]

§ 3031. Simplified procedure for court determination of disputes—action without pleadings.

An action may be commenced without the service of a summons, or may be continued after the service of a summons, without pleadings, by the filing of a statement, signed and acknowledged by all the parties or signed by their attorneys, specifying plainly and concisely the claims and defenses between the parties and the relief requested. Signing constitutes a certificate that the issues are genuine, and such filing, together with a note of issue, to be filed at the same time, shall constitute the joinder of issues in the action. The procedure in any action commenced under this section shall constitute "the New York Simplified Procedure for Court Determination of Disputes" and it shall be sufficient so to identify the procedure in any contract or other document referring to it. A submission of a controversy under this procedure shall constitute a waiver by the parties of the right to trial by jury.

R 3032. Contents of statement.

The statement required when an action is commenced without summons, or continued after the service of a summons without pleadings, shall set forth plainly and concisely the claims and defenses in dispute between the parties and the relief sought, including the amount of money demanded, if any. With the permission of the court, amended or supplemental statements may be served and filed at any time.

1964 AMENDMENTS

L. 1964, ch. 388, eff. Sept. 1, 1964, made mechanical corrections.

§ 3033. Contracts to submit; enforcement of submission.

1. Any written contract, otherwise valid under the substantive law, to submit any existing or future controversy to the court pursuant to section 3031 is valid and enforceable and shall be construed as an implied consent of the parties to the jurisdiction of the supreme court of this state to enforce it pursuant to the procedures of rule 3036, and to enter judgment thereon, and shall constitute a waiver by the parties of the right to trial by jury.

2. If the parties to a dispute arising under a contract to submit a controversy to the court under section 3031 are unable to agree on a statement of claims and defenses and relief sought pursuant to that section, the court on motion shall settle the terms of the statement. In deciding the motion the court shall consider and determine any questions as to the existence of the contract or its validity or the failure of any party to perform it. If a substantial issue of fact be raised as to the making of the contract or submission or the failure to comply therewith, the court or judge shall proceed to trial of such issue without a jury, unless either party should demand a jury trial.

R 3034. Motion procedure to settle statement terms.

1. A party aggrieved by the failure of another to perform under a contract to submit a controversy, upon filing a statement, signed and acknowledged by the party, specifying the claim and the relief requested, may move for an order directing settlement of the terms of the statement, if necessary, and the determination of the controversy pursuant to the New York Simplified Procedure for Court Determination of Disputes.

2. Eight days notice of the motion, or such other notice as the court shall deem appropriate, shall be served upon the party alleged to be in default, in such a manner as the court shall direct.

3. If there is no substantial question as to the making of the contract or submission, or the failure to comply therewith, the court shall proceed with the determination of the controversy pursuant to the simplified procedure and these rules. If the court shall find that a substantial issue of fact has been raised as to the making of the contract or submission, or the failure to comply therewith, and the motion shall not have been denied as a matter of law, the court shall proceed expeditiously with the trial thereof without a jury, unless either party upon argument of the motion shall have demanded in writing a trial by

CPLR

jury of the issue of the making of the contract or submission, in which event the court shall proceed as promptly as may be practicable with such trial before a jury.

§ 3035.   Simplified procedure authorized.

(a) Implementation and pre-trial. The procedure in any action under the New York simplified procedure for court determination of disputes authorized by sections 3031 and 3033 shall be as provided in rule 3036 adopted to implement the provisions hereof, which is designed to promote the speedy hearing of such actions and to provide for such actions a procedure that is as simple and informal as circumstances will permit. A pre-trial conference may be held relative to the disposition of questions of law which might be conclusive in the action and avoid a trial.

(b) Technical rules of evidence dispensed. The technical rules of evidence shall be dispensed with to the extent specified in such rule 3036.

(c) Practice. The practice under this procedure relating to motions to stay or to transfer pending actions, and relating to venue, assessment of costs, entry of judgment, judgment by default, and the continuance of the action in case of death or incompetency of parties shall be as prescribed in the rules adopted pursuant hereto.

R 3036.   Court determination.

1. Except upon a trial under paragraph three of rule 3034 of the issue of the making of the contract or submission, the rules as to the admissibility of evidence, except as provided by statutes relating to privileged communications, and as to procedure shall be dispensed with unless the court shall otherwise direct, and shall not apply to or exclude, limit, or restrict the taking of any testimony and the adducing of any proof.

2. In any action brought pursuant to the simplified procedure for court determination of disputes in which the court shall be of the opinion that evidence by an impartial expert would be of material aid to the just determination of the action, it may direct that such evidence be obtained. The fee and expenses of such expert shall be paid by the parties as, in its discretion, the court may direct.

3. Any action or proceeding, other than one brought in accordance with the simplified procedure, which presents an issue referable to the court for determination under the simplified procedure may be stayed by the court in which such action or proceeding is pending, or by the supreme court.

4. If the court directs a party to the contract or submission to serve a statement within a given time, and the party fails to do so, or if a party fails to appear upon proper notice, judgment by default may be awarded.

5. At a pre-trial conference, or at any other time on motion of any party or on its own motion, on notice to the parties, and upon such terms and conditions as in its discretion may seem proper, the court may (a) order or allow any party to serve an additional or amended statement of facts; (b) direct pre-trial disclosure of evidence and discovery and inspection of books, records and documents; (c) permit the taking of depositions for use at the hearing; (d) limit or restrict the number of experts to be heard as witnesses; (e) clarify and define the issues to be tried; (f) stay or transfer and consolidate with the action any other civil action or proceeding pending in any court between parties the action; (g) grant summary judgment in favor of any party as in rule 3212 provided.

6. After a statement complying with the requirements of rule 3032 or settled in accordance with rule 3034 has been filed, any party may serve and file a note of issue. Trial of the action shall commence on the date specified in such note of issue or as soon thereafter as may be practicable. Completion of preliminary procedures required by local court rules prior to the placing of a case upon the calendar for trial shall not be required in actions under the New York Simplified Procedure for Court Determination of Disputes.

7. The judgment roll shall consist of the submission or contract; the statement of claims and defenses; each paper submitted to the court upon a motion and each order of the court thereon: a copy of the judgment and of each paper necessarily affecting the judgment.

8. Those provisions of the civil practice law and rules pertaining to venue, entry and enforcement of judgment and the continuance of a civil action in case of the death or incompetency of parties shall apply

CPLR

to actions under the simplified procedure.

9. Costs and disbursements may be awarded by the court in its discretion. If awarded, the amount thereof must be included in the judgment.

1964 AMENDMENTS

L. 1964, ch. 388, eff. Sept. 1, 1964, changed "subdivision 3" in the first sentence of paragraph (1) to read "paragraph three."

§ 3037. Appeal.

An appeal may be taken only from a judgment, or an order determining the making of the contract or submission or the failure to comply therewith. There shall be no appeal from an intermediate order of the court or of a judge in an action under the simplified procedure provisions, except with the permission of the trial or appellate court, but such order or orders may be reviewed on the appeal from a judgment entered under these provisions. A decision of the trial judge on the facts shall be final if there is any substantial evidence to support it.

§§ 3038–3040. [Not used.]

§ 3041. Bill of particulars in any case.

Any party may require any other party to give a bill of particulars of such party's claim, or a copy of the items of the account alleged in a pleading. As used elsewhere in this article, the term "bill of particulars" shall include "copy of the items of an account."

1994 AMENDMENTS

L. 1994, ch. 562, eff. for actions commenced on or after Jan. 1, 1995, amended CPLR 3041 by replacing "his" with "such party's," and by adding the final sentence.

CROSS REFERENCES

Restrictions on the use of written interrogatories in conjunction with a demand for a bill of particulars are dealt with in CPLR § 3130, *below*.

R 3042. Procedure for bill of particulars.

(a) Demand. A demand for a bill of particulars shall be made by serving a written demand stating the items concerning which particulars are desired. Within thirty days of service of a demand for a bill of particulars, the party on whom the demand is made shall serve a bill of particulars complying with each item of the demand, except any item to which the party objects, in which event the reasons for the objection shall be stated with reasonable particularity. The assertion of an objection to one or more of the items in the demand shall not relieve the party on whom the demand is made from the obligation to respond in full within thirty days of service of the demand to the items of the demand to which no objection has been made.

(b) Amendment. In any action or proceeding in a court in which a note of issue is required to be filed, a party may amend the bill of particulars once as of course prior to the filing of a note of issue.

(c) Failure to respond or to comply with a demand. If a party fails to respond to a demand in a timely fashion or fails to comply fully with a demand, the party seeking the bill of particulars may move to compel compliance, or, if such failure is willful, for the imposition of penalties pursuant to subdivision (d) of this rule.

(d) Penalties for refusal to comply. If a party served with a demand for a bill of particulars willfully fails to provide particulars which the court finds ought to have been provided pursuant to this rule, the court may make such final or conditional order with regard to the failure or refusal as is just, including such relief as is set forth in section thirty-one hundred twenty-six of this chapter.

(e) Service of improper or unduly burdensome demands. If the court concludes that the demand for particulars, or a part thereof, is improper or unduly burdensome, in addition to vacating or modifying the demand, the court may make such order with regard to the improper or unduly burdensome demand as is just.

1994 AMENDMENT

L. 1994, ch. 562, eff. for actions commenced on or after Jan. 1, 1995, amended CPLR 3042 by replacing all of subdivision (a); by deleting subdivisions (b), (c), (d), (e) and (f); by relettering subdivision (g) as subdivision (b); and by completely replacing subdivisions (c), (d) and (e).

1984 AMENDMENTS

L. 1984, ch. 294, eff. Sept. 1, 1984, amended CPLR 3042(a) by increasing the time within which a bill of particulars must be served to twenty days after the demand for the bill.

1978 AMENDMENTS

L. 1978, ch. 296, eff. June 19, 1978, added a new subdivision (g), which allowed amendment of a bill of particulars once as a matter of course, and relettered former subdivision (g) as subdivision (h). Subdivision (g) was subsequently amended by L. 1978, ch. 297, eff. June 19, 1978, which added the opening clause pertaining to proceedings in which a note of issue is required to be filed.

1974 AMENDMENTS

CPLR 3042(a) was amended by proposal No. 3 of the Judicial Conference Report to the 1974 Legislature, eff. Sept. 1, 1974, by substituting the term "five days," which appeared in the second sentence, with the term "ten days."

R 3043. Bill of particulars in personal injury actions.

(a) Specified particulars. In actions to recover for personal injuries the following particulars may be required:

(1) The date and approximate time of day of the occurrence;

(2) Its approximate location;

(3) General statement of the acts or omissions constituting the negligence claimed;

(4) Where notice of a condition is a prerequisite, whether actual or constructive notice is claimed;

(5) If actual notice is claimed, a statement of when and to whom it was given;

(6) Statement of the injuries and description of those claimed to be permanent, and in an action designated in subsection (a) of section five thousand one hundred four of the insurance law, for personal injuries arising out of negligence in the use or operation of a motor vehicle in this state, in what respect plaintiff has sustained a serious injury, as defined in subsection (d) of section five thousand one hundred two of the insurance law, or economic loss greater than basic economic loss, as defined in subsection (a) of section five thousand one hundred two of the insurance law;

(7) Length of time confined to bed and to house;

(8) Length of time incapacitated from employment; and

(9) Total amounts claimed as special damages for physicians' services and medical supplies; loss of earnings, with name and

address of the employer; hospital expenses; nurses' services.

(b) Supplemental bill of particulars without leave. A party may serve a supplemental bill of particulars with respect to claims of continuing special damages and disabilities without leave of court at any time, but not less than thirty days prior to trial. Provided however that no new cause of action may be alleged or new injury claimed and that the other party shall upon seven days notice, be entitled to newly exercise any and all rights of discovery but only with respect to such continuing special damages and disabilities.

(c) Discretion of court. Nothing contained in the foregoing shall be deemed to limit the court in denying in a proper case, any one or more of the foregoing particulars, or in a proper case, in granting other, further or different particulars.

CROSS REFERENCES

Insurance Law §§ 5102 and 5104, referred to in paragraph (6) of Subd. (a), *above,* contain essential provisions of the "no fault" automobile insurance act; §§ 5102–5104, and § 5109 are included in the Appendix, *below.*

1984 AMENDMENTS

L. 1984, ch. 805, eff. Sept. 1, 1984, amended CPLR 3043(a)(6) to conform the references to the recodified Insurance Law.

1979 AMENDMENTS

L. 1979, ch. 590, eff. Sept. 1, 1979, amended CPLR 3043 by adding a new subdivision (b), and by relettering the former subdivision (b) subdivision (c).

1974 AMENDMENTS

L. 1974, ch. 575, eff. Sept. 1, 1974, amended CPLR 3043(a)(6) by adding the provisions relating to an action brought pursuant to Insurance Law § 673(1) for personal injuries arising out of negligence in the use or operation of a motor vehicle in the state.

§ 3044.　Verification of bill of particulars.

If a pleading is verified, a subsequent bill of particulars shall also be verified. A bill of particulars of any pleading with respect to a cause of action for negligence shall be verified whether such pleading be verified or not.

1994 AMENDMENTS

L. 1994, ch. 562, eff. for actions commenced on or after Jan. 1, 1995, amended CPLR 3044 by deleting the words "or a copy of the items of account of that pleading."

1964 AMENDMENTS

L. 1964, ch. 291, eff. Sept. 1, 1964, substituted the first sentence for former first sentence which read: "A bill of particulars of a verified pleading or a copy of the items of an account alleged therein, shall be verified."

§ 3045. Arbitration of damages in medical, dental or podiatric malpractice actions.

(a) At any time after service of a bill of particulars but no later than sixty days after filing of the notice of dental, medical or podiatric malpractice action pursuant to rule thirty-four hundred six of this chapter, any defendant in such an action may demand that the plaintiff elect whether to consent to the arbitration of damages upon a concession of liability in accordance with the provisions of this section.

(b) Within twenty days after receipt of such a demand, the plaintiff shall elect whether to arbitrate damages in such an action pursuant to such a concession of liability by the defendant or defendants in the action. If the defendant or defendants serve a concession of liability upon the plaintiff within twenty days after receipt of such an election, the issue of damages, including the proximate cause thereof, shall be subject to arbitration in accordance with the provisions of article seventy-five-A of this chapter. A concession of the liability, made pursuant to this section, shall not be binding on the defendant for any other purpose.

1987 AMENDMENTS

L. 1987, ch. 507, eff. July 30, 1987, and applicable to any acts, omissions or failures occurring on or after such date, amended section to apply to podiatric malpractice actions.

1986 AMENDMENTS

L. 1986, ch. 266, eff. July 8, 1986 and applicable to actions in which notice pursuant to CPLR 3406 has been filed, added new section 3045 providing for arbitration of damages in medical and dental malpractice actions. CPLR 3045 applies to actions in which the notice pursuant to CPLR 3406 is filed on or after July 8, 1986.

Article 31
DISCLOSURE

SUMMARY OF ARTICLE

CPLR

CPLR

§ 3101. Scope of disclosure.

(a) Generally. There shall be full disclosure of all matter material and necessary in the prosecution or defense of an action, regardless of the burden of proof, by:

(1) a party, or the officer, director, member, agent or employee of a party;

(2) a person who possessed a cause of action or defense asserted in the action;

(3) a person about to depart from the state, or without the state, or residing at a greater distance from the place of trial than one hundred miles, or so sick or infirm as to afford reasonable grounds of belief that he or she will not be able to attend the trial, or a person authorized to practice medicine, dentistry or podiatry who has provided medical, dental or podiatric care or diagnosis to the party demanding disclosure, or who has been retained by such party as an expert witness; and

(4) any other person, upon notice stating the circumstances or reasons such disclosure is sought or required.

(b) Privileged matter. Upon objection by a person entitled to assert the privilege, privileged matter shall not be obtainable.

(c) Attorney's work product. The work product of an attorney shall not be obtainable.

(d) Trial preparation.

1. Experts.

(i) Upon request, each party shall identify each person whom the party expects to call as an expert witness at trial and shall disclose in reasonable detail the subject matter on which each expert is expected to testify, the substance of the facts and opinions on which each expert is expected to testify, the qualifications of each expert witness and a summary of the grounds for each expert's opinion. However, where a party for good cause shown retains an expert an insufficient period of time before the commencement of trial to give appropriate notice thereof, the party shall not thereupon be precluded from introducing the expert's testimony at the trial solely on grounds of noncompliance with this paragraph. In that instance, upon motion of any party, made before or at trial, or on its own initiative, the court may make whatever order may be just. In an action for medical, dental or podiatric malpractice, a party, in responding to a request, may omit the names of medical, dental or podiatric experts but shall be required to disclose all other information concerning such experts otherwise required by this paragraph.

(ii) In an action for medical, dental or podiatric malpractice, any party may, by written offer made to and served upon all other parties and filed with the court, offer to disclose the name of, and to make available for examination upon oral deposition, any person the party making the offer expects to call as an expert witness at trial. Within twenty days of service of the offer, a party shall accept or reject the offer by serving a written reply upon all parties and filing a copy thereof with the court. Failure to serve a reply within twenty days of service of the offer shall be deemed a rejection of the offer. If all parties accept the offer, each party shall be required to produce his or her expert witness for examination upon oral deposition upon receipt of a notice to take oral deposition in accordance with rule thirty-one hundred seven of this chapter. If any party, having made or accepted the offer, fails to make that party's expert available for oral deposition, that party shall be precluded from offering expert testimony at the trial of the action.

(iii) Further disclosure concerning the expected testimony of any expert may be obtained only by court order upon a showing of special circumstances and subject to restrictions as to scope and provisions concerning fees and expenses as the court may deem appropriate. However, a party, without court order, may take the testimony of a person authorized to practice medicine, dentistry or podiatry who is the party's treating or retained expert, as described in paragraph three of subdivision (a) of this section, in which event any other party shall be entitled to the full disclosure authorized by this article with respect to that expert without court order.

2. Materials. Subject to the provisions of paragraph one of this subdivision, materials otherwise discoverable under subdivision (a) of this section and prepared in anticipation of litigation or for trial by or for another party, or by or for that other party's representative (including an attorney, consultant, surety, indemnitor, insurer or agent), may be obtained only upon a showing that the party seeking discovery has substantial need of the materials in the preparation of the case and is unable without undue hardship to obtain the substantial equivalent of the materials by other means. In ordering discovery of the materials when the required showing has been made, the court shall protect against disclosure of the mental impressions, conclusions, opinions or legal theories of an attorney or other representative of a party concerning the litigation.

(e) Party's statement. A party may obtain a copy of his own statement.

(f) Contents of insurance agreement. A party may obtain discovery of the existence and contents of any insurance agreement under which any person carrying on an insurance business may be liable to satisfy part or all of a judgment which may be entered in the action or to indemnify or reimburse for payments made to satisfy the judgment. Information concerning the insurance agreement is not by reason of disclosure admissible in evidence at trial. For purpose of this subdivision, an application for insurance shall not be treated as part of an insurance agreement.

(g) Accident reports. Except as is otherwise provided by law, in addition to any other matter which may be subject to disclosure, there shall be full disclosure of any written report of an accident prepared in the regular course of business operations or practices of any person, firm, corporation, association or other public or private entity, unless prepared by a police or peace officer for a criminal investigation or prosecution and disclosure would interfere with a criminal investigation or prosecution.

(h) Amendment or supplementation of responses. A party shall amend or supplement a response previously given to a request for disclosure promptly upon the party's thereafter obtaining information that the response was incorrect or incomplete when made, or that the response, though correct and complete when made, no longer is correct and complete, and the circumstances are such that a failure to amend or supplement the response would be materially misleading. Where a party obtains such information an insufficient period of time before the commencement of trial appropriately to amend or supplement the response, the party shall not thereupon be precluded from introducing evidence at the trial solely on the grounds of noncompliance with this subdivision. In that instance, upon motion of any party, made before or at trial, or on its own initiative, the court may make whatever order may be just. Further amendment or supplementation may be obtained by court order.

(i) In addition to any other matter which may be subject to disclosure, there shall be full disclosure of any films, photographs, video tapes or audio tapes, including transcripts or memoranda thereof, involving a person referred to in paragraph one of subdivision (a) of this section. There shall be disclosure of all portions of such material, including out-takes, rather than only those portions a party intends to use. The provisions of this subdivision shall not apply to materials compiled for law enforcement purposes which are exempt from disclosure under section eighty-seven of the public officers law.

CROSS REFERENCES

See **D.R.L. § 236 Part B(4)** in Appendix, *below*, as to compulsory financial disclosure in matrimonial actions.

1993 AMENDMENTS

L. 1993, ch. 98, eff. Jan. 1, 1994, amended CPLR 3101(a) by making the section applicable to dentistry and podiatry and by making the section gender neutral; amended CPLR 3101(b) by replacing the word "party" with the words "person entitled to assert the privilege"; and added a new subdivision

(h) addressing amendment or supplementation of a response previously given to a disclosure request.

L. 1993, ch. 574, eff. Sept. 1, 1993, added a new subdivision (i) to provide for comprehensive disclosure of all audio-visual materials involving any person designated in CPLR 3101(a)(1).

1991 AMENDMENTS

L. 1991, ch. 165, eff. Oct. 1, 1991, amended CPLR 3101(d)(1)(ii) by deleting the provision allowing a party to condition an offer to disclose an expert witness's name and make him available for deposition on all parties' waiving a hearing of the matter before the malpractice panel, and the provision specifying that if this offer was conditioned upon a waiver of the malpractice panel's hearing of the matter, the panel shall not be utilized. The October 1, 1991 effective date applies only to actions where, as of this date, the medical malpractice panel has not signed and forwarded to all parties a formal written recommendation concerning the question of liability.

1988 AMENDMENTS

L. 1988, ch. 184, eff. July 1, 1988, renumbered subparagraph (ii) as (iii), and added new subparagraph (ii) permitting consensual deposition of expert witnesses, in lieu of malpractice panel in medical, dental and podiatric actions.

1986 AMENDMENTS

L. 1986, ch. 485, eff. July 21, 1986, and applicable to acts, omissions or failures occurring on or after such date, amended CPLR 3101(d)(i) to provide that in actions for podiatric malpractice, a party responding to a request for pretrial disclosure of expert testimony may omit the names of podiatric experts; CPLR 3101(d)(ii) was amended to provide that in podiatric malpractice actions a party may, without court order, take the testimony of a person authorized to practice podiatry who is the party's treating or retained expert.

1985 AMENDMENTS

L. 1985, ch. 294, eff. July 1, 1985, and applicable to any actions commenced on or after that date, deleted former subdivision (d) and added a new subdivision (d).

1984 AMENDMENTS

L. 1984, ch. 294, eff. Sept. 1, 1984, amended CPLR 3101(a)(4) to provide for disclosure by any other person, upon notice stating the circumstances or reasons disclosure is sought.

1980 AMENDMENTS

L. 1980, ch. 283, eff. Sept. 1, 1980, added new subdivision (g).

1979 AMENDMENTS

L. 1979, ch. 268, eff. Jan. 1, 1980, amended CPLR 3101 subd. (a) par. 3 by providing for disclosure by "a person authorized to practice medicine who has provided medical care or diagnosis to the party demanding disclosure, or who has been retained by him as an expert witness."

The Judicial Conference Report to the 1979 Legislature noted that this amendment ". . . would liberalize the 'special circumstances' rule only with respect to the physicians specified. Thus, unavailability or special circumstances would still have to be shown to obtain the deposition of any physician who provided medical care or diagnosis to the adverse party or who has been retained as an expert witness by the adverse party. There is a strong judicial trend toward liberalizing the 'special circumstances' provision of CPLR 3101(a). In Villano v. Conde Nast Publications, Inc., 361 N.Y.S.2d 351, 46 A.D.2d 118 (1st Dept. 1973) the defendant moved to examine the plaintiff's treating physicians in an action for invasion of privacy, claiming 'special circumstances.' The Appellate Division reversed Special Term's denial of the motion, stating that a mere showing by the lawyer that he needs such witnesses' pre-trial depositions to prepare fully for the trial should suffice as a 'special circumstance.' There remains a need for statutory provision clearly permitting a party to take the deposition, without the necessity of showing special circumstances, of a person authorized to practice medicine who has provided medical care or diagnosis to that party, or who has been retained by him as an expert witness. This measure would supply just such a provision and thereby provide an additional and valuable tool for the trial lawyer. It would ease the burden on litigants, lawyers, courts and physicians, especially where shortages of physicians exist. Coupled with CPLR 3117(a)(4), it would reduce the expense of litigation occasioned by physicians personally testifying at trial."

1975 AMENDMENTS

L. 1975, ch. 668, eff. Aug. 6, 1975, amended CPLR 3101 by adding a new Subd. (f), providing for disclosure of the contents of insurance agreements.

§ 3102. Method of obtaining disclosure.

(a) Disclosure devices. Information is obtainable by one or more of the following disclosure devices: depositions upon oral questions or without the state upon written questions, interrogatories, demands for addresses, discovery and inspection of documents or property, physical and mental examinations of persons, and requests for admission.

(b) Stipulation or notice normal method. Unless otherwise provided by the civil practice law and rules, or by the court, disclosure shall be obtained by stipulation or on notice without leave of the court.

(c) Before action commenced. Before an action is commenced, disclosure to aid in bringing an action, to preserve information or to aid in arbitration, may be obtained, but only by court order. The court may appoint a referee to take testimony.

(d) After trial commenced. Except as provided in section 5223, during and after trial, disclosure may be obtained only by order of the trial court on notice.

(e) Action pending in another jurisdiction. When under any mandate, writ or commission issued out of any court of record in any other state, territory, district or foreign jurisdiction, or whenever upon notice or agreement, it is required to take the testimony of a witness in the state, he may be compelled to appear and testify in the same manner and by the same process as may be employed for the purpose of taking testimony in actions pending in the state. The supreme court or a county court shall make any appropriate order in aid of taking such a deposition.

(f) Action to which state is party. In an action in which the state is properly a party, whether as plaintiff, defendant or otherwise, disclosure by the state shall be available as if the state were a private person.

CROSS REFERENCES

As to public access to government records, see **Public Officers Law, Article 6** (Freedom of information law) in Appendix, *below.*

1993 AMENDMENTS

L. 1993, ch. 98, eff. Jan. 1, 1994, amended CPLR 3102(c) to eliminate the requirement that a copy of any deposition that was obtained before an action was commenced, and that was intended for use in an action involving title to realty, be recorded, and amended CPLR 3102(f) by deleting the disclosure exception for interrogatories and requests for admissions.

1984 AMENDMENTS

L. 1984, ch. 294, eff. Sept. 1, 1984, amended CPLR 3102(f) by eliminating the provision that disclosure by the state may be obtained only by order of the court in which the action is pending.

1967 AMENDMENTS

L. 1967, ch. 638, eff. July 1, 1967, amended caption and text of Subd. (f) to permit adverse party to obtain disclosure against state in any action to which state is properly a party, upon court order, excepting interrogatories and requests for admissions. Formerly, Subd. (f) specified that "In an action in the court of claims, disclosure may be obtained only by order of that court."

1964 AMENDMENTS

L. 1964, ch. 388, eff. Sept. 1, 1964, made mechanical corrections.

§ 3103. Protective orders.

(a) Prevention of abuse. The court may at any time on its own initiative, or on motion of any party or of any person from whom discovery is sought, make a protective order denying, limiting, conditioning or regulating the use of any disclosure device. Such order shall be designed to prevent unreasonable annoyance, expense, embarrassment, disadvantage, or other prejudice to any person or the courts.

(b) Suspension of disclosure pending application for protective order. Service of a notice of motion for a protective order shall suspend disclosure of the particular matter in dispute.

(c) Suppression of information improperly obtained. If any disclosure under this article has been improperly or irregularly obtained so that a substantial right of a party is prejudiced, the court, on motion, may make an appropriate order, including an order that the information be suppressed.

1993 AMENDMENTS

L. 1993, ch. 98, eff. Jan. 1, 1994, amended CPLR 3103(a) by replacing the word "witness" with the words "of any person from whom discovery is sought."

§ 3104. Supervision of disclosure.

(a) Motion for, and extent of, supervision of disclosure. Upon the motion of any party or witness on notice to all parties or on its own initiative without notice, the court in which an action is pending may by one of its judges or a referee supervise all or part of any disclosure procedure.

(b) Selection of referee. A judicial hearing officer may be designated as a referee under this section, or the court may permit all of the parties in an action to stipulate that a named attorney may act as referee. In such latter event the stipulation shall provide for payment of his fees which shall, unless otherwise agreed, be taxed as disbursements.

(c) Powers of referee; motions referred to person supervising disclosure. A referee under this section shall have all the powers of the court under this article except the power to relieve himself of his

CPLR

duties, to appoint a successor, or to adjudge any person guilty of contempt. All motions or applications made under this article shall be returnable before the judge or referee, designated under this section and after disposition, if requested by any party, his order shall be filed in the office of the clerk.

(d) Review of order of referee. Any party or witness may apply for review of an order made under this section by a referee. The application shall be by motion made in the court in which the action is pending within five days after the order is made. Service of a notice of motion for review shall suspend disclosure of the particular matter in dispute. If the question raised by the motion may affect the rights of a witness, notice shall be served on him personally or by mail at his last known address. It shall set forth succinctly the order complained of, the reason it is objectionable and the relief demanded.

(e) Payment of expenses of referee. Except where a judicial hearing officer has been designated a referee hereunder, the court may make an appropriate order for the payment of the reasonable expenses of the referee.

1983 AMENDMENTS

L. 1983, ch. 840, eff. April 1, 1983, amended CPLR 3104(b) and (e).

1963 AMENDMENTS

L. 1963, ch. 307, eff. Sept. 1, 1963, amended CPLR 3104(d) by adding: "Service of a notice of motion for review shall suspend disclosure of the particular matter in dispute."

R 3105. Notice to party in default.

When a party is in default for failure to appear, he shall not be entitled to notice or service of any copy required under this article.

R 3106. Priority of depositions; witnesses; prisoners; designation of deponent.

(a) Normal priority. After an action is commenced, any party may take the testimony of any person by deposition upon oral or written questions. Leave of the court, granted on motion, shall be obtained if notice of the taking of the deposition of a party is served by the plaintiff before that party's time for serving a responsive pleading has expired.

(b) Witnesses. Where the person to be examined is not a party or a person who at the time of taking the deposition is an officer, director, member or employee of a party, he shall be served with a subpoena. Unless the court orders otherwise, on motion with or without notice, such subpoena shall be served at least twenty days before the examination. Where a motion for a protective order against such an examination is made, the witness shall be notified by the moving party that the examination is stayed.

(c) Prisoners. The deposition of a person confined under legal process may be taken only by leave of the court.

(d) Designation of deponent. A party desiring to take the deposition of a particular officer, director, member or employee of a person shall include in the notice or subpoena served upon such person the identity, description or title of such individual. Such person shall produce the individual so designated unless they shall have, no later than ten days prior to the scheduled deposition, notified the requesting party that another individual would instead be produced and the identity, description or title of such individual is specified. If timely notification has been so given, such other individual shall instead be produced.

1985 AMENDMENTS

L. 1985, ch. 327, eff. July 11, 1985, amended CPLR 3106(d) to change the first sentence to read "notice or subpoena."

1984 AMENDMENTS

L. 1984, ch. 294, eff. Sept. 1, 1984, amended subdivisions (a) and (b) and added subdivision (d).

R 3107. Notice of taking oral questions.

A party desiring to take the deposition of any person upon oral examination shall give to each party twenty days' notice, unless the court orders otherwise. The notice shall be in writing, stating the time and place for taking the deposition, the name and address of each person to be examined, if known, and, if any name is not known, a general description sufficient to identify him or the particular class or group to which he belongs. The notice need not enumerate the matters upon which the person is to be examined. A party to be examined pursuant to notice served by another party may serve notice of at least ten days for the examination of any other party, his agent or employee, such examination to be noticed for and to follow at the same time and place.

CROSS REFERENCES

Restrictions on the taking of a deposition under this section, together with the service of written interrogatories, are dealt with in **CPLR 3130**, *below.*

1984 AMENDMENTS

L. 1984, ch. 294, eff. Sept. 1, 1984, amended CPLR 3107 by increasing the notice of oral deposition to 20 days and increasing the notice for examination of any other party at the same time and place to 10 days.

1964 AMENDMENTS

L. 1964, ch. 388, eff. Sept. 1, 1964, made mechanical corrections.

R 3108. Written questions; when permitted.

A deposition may be taken on written questions when the examining party and the deponent so stipulate or when the testimony is to be taken without the state. A commission or letters rogatory may be issued where necessary or convenient for the taking of a deposition outside of the state.

R 3109. Notice of taking deposition on written questions.

(a) Notice of taking; service of questions and cross-questions. A party desiring to take the deposition of any person upon written questions shall serve such questions upon each party together with a notice stating the name and address of the person to be examined, if known, and, if the name is not known, a general description sufficient to identify him or the particular class or group to which he belongs, and the name or descriptive title and address of the officer before whom the deposition is to be taken. Within fifteen days thereafter a party so served may serve written cross-questions upon each party. Within seven days thereafter the original party may serve written redirect questions upon each party. Within five days after being served with written redirect questions, a party may serve written recross-questions upon each party.

(b) Officer asking written questions. A copy of the notice and copies of all written questions served shall be delivered by the party taking the deposition to the officer designated in the notice. The officer shall proceed promptly to take the testimony of the witness in response to the written questions and to prepare the deposition.

1984 AMENDMENTS

L. 1984, ch. 294, eff. Sept. 1, 1984, amended CPLR 3107(a) by increasing the time for service of cross-questions, redirect questions and recross-questions.

R 3110. Where the deposition is to be taken within the state.

A deposition within the state on notice shall be taken:

1. when the person to be examined is a party or an officer, director, member or employee of a party, within the county in which he resides or has an office for the regular transaction of business in person or where the action is pending; or

2. when any other person to be examined is a resident, within the county in which he resides, is regularly employed or has an office for the regular transaction of business in person, or if he is not a resident, within the county in which he is served, is regularly employed or has an office for the regular transaction of business in person; or

3. when the party to be examined is a public corporation or any officer, agent or employee thereof, within the county in which the action is pending; the place of such examination shall be the office of any of the attorneys for such a public corporation or any officer, agent or authorized employee thereof unless the parties stipulate otherwise.

For the purpose of this rule New York city shall be considered one county.

1994 AMENDMENTS

L. 1994, ch. 603, eff. Oct. 1, 1994, amended CPLR 3110(3) by deleting the words "in the court in which the action is pending" and replacing them with the words "the office of any of the attorneys for such a public corporation or any officer, agent or authorized employee thereof."

R 3111. Production of things at the examination.

The notice or subpoena may require the production of books, papers and other things in the possession, custody or control of the person to be examined to be marked as exhibits, and used on the examination. The reasonable production expenses of a non-party witness shall be defrayed by the party seeking discovery.

1994 AMENDMENTS

L. 1994, ch. 100, eff. May 16, 1994, amended by adding the final sentence providing for the payment of expenses to a non-party who is required to produce items to be used at an examination.

R 3112.   Errors in notice for taking depositions.

All errors and irregularities in the notice for taking a deposition are waived unless at least three days before the time for taking the deposition written objection is served upon the party giving the notice.

R 3113.   Conduct of the examination.

(a) Persons before whom depositions may be taken. Depositions may be taken before any of the following persons except an attorney, or employee of an attorney, for a party or prospective party and except a person who would be disqualified to act as a juror because of interest in the event of consanguinity or affinity to a party:

1. within the state, a person authorized by the laws of the state to administer oaths;

2. without the state but within the United States or within a territory or possession subject to the jurisdiction of the United States, a person authorized to take acknowledgments of deeds outside of the state by the real property law of the state or to administer oaths by the laws of the United States or of the place where the deposition is taken; and

3. in a foreign country, any diplomatic or consular agent or representative of the United States, appointed or accredited to, and residing within, the country, or a person appointed by commission or under letters rogatory, or an officer of the armed forces authorized to take the acknowledgment of deeds.

Officers may be designated in notices or commissions either by name or descriptive title and letters rogatory may be addressed "To the Appropriate Authority in (here name the state or country)."

(b) Oath of witness; recording of testimony; objections; continuous examination; written questions read by examining officer. The officer before whom the deposition is to be taken shall put the witness on oath and shall personally, or by someone acting under his direction, record the testimony. The testimony shall be recorded by stenographic or other means, subject to such rules as may be adopted by the appellate division in the department where the action is pending. All objections made at the time of the examination to the qualifications of the officer taking the deposition or the person recording it, or to the manner of taking it, or to the testimony presented, or to the conduct of any person, and any other objection to the proceedings, shall be noted by the officer upon the deposition and the deposition shall proceed subject to the right of a person to apply for a protective order. The deposition shall be taken continuously and without unreasonable adjournment, unless the court otherwise orders or the witness and parties present otherwise agree. In lieu of participating in an oral examination, any party served with notice of taking a deposition may transmit written questions to the officer, who shall propound them to the witness and record the answers.

CPLR

(c) Examination and cross-examination.   Examination and cross-examination of deponents shall proceed as permitted in the trial of actions in open court. When the deposition of a party is taken at the instance of an adverse party, the deponent may be cross-examined by his own attorney. Cross-examination need not be limited to the subject matter of the examination in chief.

(d) The parties may stipulate that a deposition be taken by telephone or other remote electronic means and that a party may participate electronically. The stipulation shall designate reasonable provisions to ensure that an accurate record of the deposition is generated, shall specify, if appropriate, reasonable provisions for the use of exhibits at the deposition; shall specify who must and who may physically be present at the deposition; and shall provide for any other provisions appropriate under the circumstances. Unless otherwise stipulated to by the parties, the officer administering the oath shall be physically present at the place of the deposition and the additional costs of conducting the deposition by telephonic or other remote electronic means, such as telephone charges, shall be borne by the party requesting that the deposition be conducted by such means.

CROSS REFERENCES

Real Property Law provisions authorizing the taking of acknowledgments of deeds, referred to in paragraph (2) of Subd. (a), *supra*, may be found in **Real**

Prop. L. § 298, *et seq.*, in Appendix, *below.*

2004 AMENDMENTS

L. 2004, ch. 66, §1, eff. Jan. 1, 2005, amended CPLR 3113 by adding subdivision (d).

1993 AMENDMENTS

L. 1993, ch. 98, eff. Jan. 1, 1994, amended CPLR 3113(a)(2) by replacing the word "dominion" with the word "jurisdiction".

1977 AMENDMENTS

CPLR 3113(b) was amended by proposal No. 1 of the Judicial Conference, in its Report to the 1977 Legislature, eff. Sept. 1, 1977, to provide that recording of testimony at the examination may be by stenographic or other means. As explained by the 1977 Judicial Conference: "This measure would expressly permit testimony to be perpetuated on videotape."

R 3114. Examination of witness who does not understand the English language.

If the witness to be examined does not understand the English language, the examining party must, at his own expense, provide a translation of all questions and answers. Where the court settles questions, it may settle them in the foreign language and in English. It may use the services of one or more experts whose compensation shall be paid by the party seeking the examination and may be taxed as a disbursement.

R 3115. Objections to qualification of person taking deposition; competency; questions and answers.

(a) Objection when deposition offered in evidence. Subject to the other provisions of this rule, objection may be made at the trial or hearing to receiving in evidence any deposition or part thereof for any reason which would require the exclusion of the evidence if the witness were then present and testifying.

(b) Errors which might be obviated if made known promptly. Errors and irregularities occurring at the oral examination in the manner of taking the deposition, in the form of the questions or answers, in the oath or affirmation, or in the conduct of persons, and errors of any kind which might be obviated or removed if objection were promptly presented, are waived unless reasonable objection thereto is made at the taking of the deposition.

(c) Disqualification of person taking deposition. Objection to the taking of a deposition because of disqualification of the person by whom it is to be taken is waived unless made before the taking of the deposition begins or as soon thereafter as the disqualification becomes known or could be discovered with reasonable diligence.

(d) Competency of witnesses or admissibility of testimony. Objections to the competency of a witness or to the admissibility of testimony are not waived by failure to make them before or during the taking of the deposition, unless the ground of the objection is one which might have been obviated or removed if objection had been made at that time.

(e) Form of written questions. Objections to the form of written questions are waived unless served in writing upon the party propounding the questions within the time allowed for serving succeeding questions or within three days after service.

R 3116. Signing deposition; physical preparation; copies.

(a) Signing. The deposition shall be submitted to the witness for examination and shall be read to or by him or her, and any changes in form or substance which the witness desires to make shall be entered at the end of the deposition with a statement of the reasons given by the witness for making them. The deposition shall then be signed by the witness before any officer authorized to administer an oath. If the witness fails to sign and return the deposition within sixty days, it may be used as fully as though signed. No changes to the transcript may be made by the witness more than sixty days after submission to the witness for examination.

(b) Certification and filing by officer. The officer before whom the deposition was taken shall certify on the deposition that the witness was duly sworn by him and that the deposition is a true record of the testimony given by the witness. He shall list all appearances by the parties and attorneys. If the deposition was taken on written questions, he shall attach to it the copy of the notice and written questions received by him. He shall then securely seal the deposition in an envelope endorsed with the title of the action and the index number of the action, if one has been assigned, and marked "Deposition of (here insert name of witness)" and shall promptly file it with, or send it by registered or certified mail to the clerk of the court where the case is to

CPLR

be tried. The deposition shall always be open to the inspection of the parties, each of whom is entitled to make copies thereof. If a copy of the deposition is furnished to each party or if the parties stipulate to waive filing, the officer need not file the original but may deliver it to the party taking the deposition.

(c) Exhibits. Documentary evidence exhibited before the officer or exhibits marked for identification during the examination of the witness shall be annexed to and returned with the deposition. However, if requested by the party producing documentary evidence or an exhibit, the officer shall mark it for identification as an exhibit in the case, give each party an opportunity to copy or inspect it, and return it to the party offering it, and it may then be used in the same manner as if annexed to and returned with the deposition.

(d) Expenses of taking. Unless the court orders otherwise, the party taking the deposition shall bear the expense thereof.

(e) Errors of officer or person transcribing. Errors and irregularities of the officer or the person transcribing the deposition are waived unless a motion to suppress the deposition or some part thereof is made with reasonable promptness after such defect is, or with due diligence might have been, ascertained.

1996 AMENDMENTS

L. 1996, ch. 117, eff. Jan. 1, 1997, amended subdivision (a) to add to the third sentence the phrases "and return" and "within sixty days"; and to add a new final sentence.

1993 AMENDMENTS

L. 1993, ch. 98, eff. Jan. 1, 1994, amended CPLR 3116(a) to simplify and reform the procedure relating to the signing of depositions.

1978 AMENDMENTS

L. 1978, ch. 292, eff. Sept. 1, 1978, amended subdivision (a), setting forth separate requirements as to signing of the deposition when the witness is an adverse party.

The Governor's memorandum of approval stated in part:

"This bill is designed to expedite preparation for trial and to minimize the effect of dilatory practices of an adverse party witness who refuses to sign and return a deposition.

"Specifically, the bill would provide that if a deposition is forwarded to a witness who is an adverse party and that witness is given 30 days written notice to return the deposition signed, if the witness fails to so return the deposition, the deposition may then be used as fully as though signed."

1966 AMENDMENTS

Amendment No. 1, eff. Sept. 1, 1966, made by the Judicial Conference Feb. 1, 1966, Report to the Legislature, amended Subd. (a).

R 3117.   Use of depositions.

(a) Impeachment of witnesses; parties; unavailable witnesses. At the trial or upon the hearing of a motion or an interlocutory proceeding, any part or all of a deposition, so far as admissible under the rules of evidence, may be used in accordance with any of the following provisions:

1. any deposition may be used by any party for the purpose of contradicting or impeaching the testimony of the deponent as a witness;

2. the deposition testimony of a party or of any person who was a party when the testimony was given or of any person who at the time the testimony was given was an officer, director, member, employee or managing or authorized agent of a party, may be used for any purpose by any party who was adversely interested when the deposition testimony was given or who is adversely interested when the deposition testimony is offered in evidence;

3. the deposition of any person may be used by any party for any purpose against any other party who was present or represented at the taking of the deposition or who had the notice required under these rules, provided the court finds:

(i) that the witness is dead; or

(ii) that the witness is at a greater distance than one hundred miles from the place of trial or is out of the state, unless it appears that the absence of the witness was procured by the party offering the deposition; or

(iii) that the witness is unable to attend or testify because of age, sickness, infirmity, or imprisonment; or

(iv) that the party offering the deposition has been unable to procure the attendance of the witness by diligent efforts; or

CPLR

(v) upon motion or notice, that such exceptional circumstances exist as to make its use desirable, in the interest of justice and with due regard to the importance of presenting the testimony of witnesses orally in open court;

4. the deposition of a person authorized to practice medicine may be used by any party without the necessity of showing unavailability or special circumstances, subject to the right of any party to move pursuant to section 3103 to prevent abuse.

(b) Use of part of deposition. If only part of a deposition is read at the trial by a party, any other party may read any other part of the deposition which ought in fairness to be considered in connection with the part read.

(c) Substitution of parties; prior actions. Substitution of parties does not affect the right to use depositions previously taken. When an action has been brought in any court of any state or of the United States and another action involving the same subject matter is afterward brought between the same parties or their representatives or successors in interest all depositions taken in the former action may be used in the latter as if taken therein.

(d) Effect of using deposition. A party shall not be deemed to make a person his own witness for any purpose by taking his deposition. The introduction in evidence of the deposition or any part thereof for any purpose other than that of contradicting or impeaching the deponent makes the deponent the witness of the party introducing the deposition, but this shall not apply to the use of a deposition as described in paragraph two of subdivision (a). At the trial, any party may rebut any relevant evidence contained in a deposition, whether introduced by him or by any other party.

1996 AMENDMENTS

L. 1996, ch. 117, eff. Jan. 1, 1997, amended subparagraph (a)(2) by adding the word "testimony" following "the deposition" at the beginning of the subparagraph; by adding the phrase "or of any person who at the time the testimony was given" following the phrase "of a party"; by replacing the phrase "or any one" to "of any person"; by replacing the phrase "of taking the deposition" with "the testimony was given"; by adding "employee" to the list of persons giving testimony and deleting "or the deposition of an employee of a party produced at the taking of the deposition by that party"; and by deleting the phrase "adversely interested" and adding the phrase "who is adversely interested when the deposition testimony is offered in evidence" at the end of the subparagraph.

1993 AMENDMENTS

L. 1993, ch. 86, eff. June 1, 1993, amended CPLR 3117(a)(2) by adding the words "at the taking of the deposition."

1979 AMENDMENTS

L. 1979, ch. 268, eff. Jan. 1, 1980, amended CPLR 3117 subd. (a) par. 4 by eliminating the words "medical witness" and substituting the phrase "person authorized to practice medicine."

1977 AMENDMENTS

CPLR 3117(a) was amended by proposal No. 2 of the Judicial Conference in its Report to the 1977 Legislature, eff. Sept. 1, 1977, by the addition of paragraph (4), permitting use of a deposition of a medical witness by any party without a showing of unavailability or special circumstances.

The 1977 Judicial Conference noted in part:

"The term 'medical witness' as used in the proposed amendment is intended to apply to a medical witness other than one who is a party to the action, as the context of the subdivision clearly indicates. The rules governing the use of depositions of parties are contained in paragraph 2 of subdivision (a) of this section and would, of course, govern the deposition of a party who also happened to be a medical person."

R 3118. Demand for address of party or of person who possessed an assigned cause of action or defense.

A party may serve on any party a written notice demanding a verified statement setting forth the post office address and residence of the party, of any specified officer or member of the party and of any person who possessed a cause of action or defense asserted in the action which has been assigned. The demand shall be complied with within ten days of its service.

R 3119. [Not used.]

R 3120. Discovery and production of documents and things for inspection, testing, copying or photographing.

1. After commencement of an action, any party may serve on any other party a notice or on any other person a subpoena duces tecum:

(i) to produce and permit the party seeking discovery, or someone acting on his or her behalf, to inspect, copy, test or photograph any designated documents or any things which are in the possession, custody or control of the party or person served; or

(ii) to permit entry upon designated land or other property in the possession, custody or control of the party or person served for the purpose of inspecting, measuring, surveying, sampling, testing, photographing or recording by motion pictures or otherwise the property or any specifically designated object or operation thereon.

2. The notice or subpoena duces tecum shall specify the time, which shall be not less than twenty days after service of the notice or subpoena, and the place and manner of making the inspection, copy, test or photograph, or of the entry upon the land or other property and, in the case of an inspection, copying, testing or photographing, shall set forth the items to be inspected, copied, tested or photographed by individual item or by category, and shall describe each item and category with reasonable particularity.

3. The party issuing a subpoena duces tecum as provided herein-above shall at the same time serve a copy of the subpoena upon all other parties and, within five days of compliance therewith, in whole or in part, give to each party notice that the items produced in response thereto are available for inspection and copying, specifying the time and place thereof.

4. Nothing contained in this section shall be construed to change the requirement of section 2307 that a subpoena duces tecum to be served upon a library or a department or bureau of a municipal corporation, or of the state, or an officer thereof, requires a motion made on notice to the library, department, bureau or officer, and the adverse party, to a justice of the supreme court or a judge of the court in which the action is triable.

CROSS REFERENCES

As to public access to government records, see **Public Officers Law, Article 6** (Freedom of information law) in Appendix, *below.*

2002 AMENDMENTS

L. 2002, Ch. 575, § 2, eff. Sept. 1, 2003, amended subdivisions (1)–(4).

1993 AMENDMENTS

L. 1993, ch. 98, eff. Jan. 1, 1994, amended CPLR 3120(a)(1) by eliminating the requirement that the notice to produce documents specifically identify the documents being requested, and amended 3120(a)(2) to provide that a notice to produce may identify the items sought either individually or by category.

1984 AMENDMENTS

L. 1984, ch. 294, eff. Sept. 1, 1984, amended CPLR 3120(a)(2) by providing that the time to be specified on the notice of inspection shall be not less than 20 days after service of the notice.

1966 AMENDMENTS

Amendment No. 2, eff. Sept. 1, 1966, made by the Judicial Conference Feb. 1, 1966, Report to the Legislature. "The proposed amendment would make it clear that full discovery of documents and things is available against a non-party witness, by court order. This would appear to be in accord with the intent of the revisers. The burden on the non-party witness is minimized by the requirement that the order provide for the defraying of his expenses. As a protection to the non-party the notice of motion would be required to be served in the same manner as a summons."

CPLR

§ 3121. Physical or mental examination.

(a) Notice of examination. After commencement of an action in which the mental or physical condition or the blood relationship of a party, or of an agent, employee or person in the custody or under the legal control of a party, is in controversy, any party may serve notice on another party to submit to a physical, mental or blood examination by a designated physician, or to produce for such examination his agent, employee or the person in his custody or under his legal control. The notice may require duly executed and acknowledged written authorizations permitting all parties to obtain, and make copies of, the records of specified hospitals relating to such mental or physical condition or blood relationship; where a party obtains a copy of a hospital record as a result of the authorization of another party, he shall deliver a duplicate of the copy to such party. A copy of the notice shall be served on the person to be examined. It shall specify the time, which shall be not less than twenty days after service of the notice, and the conditions and scope of the examination.

(b) Copy of report. A copy of a detailed written report of the examining physician setting out his findings and conclusions shall be delivered by the party seeking the examination to any party requesting to exchange therefor a copy of each report in his control of an examination made with respect to the mental or physical condition in controversy.

1984 AMENDMENTS

L. 1984, ch. 294, eff. Sept. 1, 1984, amended CPLR 3121(a) by providing that the time to be specified on the notice of physical or mental examination shall be not less than 20 days after service of the notice.

R 3122. Objection to disclosure, inspection or examination; compliance.

(a) Within twenty days of service of a notice or subpoena duces tecum under rule 3120 or section 3121, the party or person to whom the notice or subpoena duces tecum is directed, if that party or person objects to the disclosure, inspection or examination, shall serve a response which shall state with reasonable particularity the reasons for each objection. If objection is made to part of an item or category, the part shall be specified. A medical provider served with a subpoena duces tecum requesting the production of a patient's medical records pursuant to this rule need not respond or object to the subpoena if the subpoena is not accompanied by a written authorization by the patient.Any subpoena served upon a medical provider requesting the medical records of a patient shall state in conspicuous bold-faced type that the records shall not be provided unless the subpoena is accompanied by a written authorization by the patient. The party seeking disclosure under rule 3120 or section 3121 may move for an order under rule 3124 or section 2308 with respect to any objection to, or other failure to respond to or permit inspection as requested by, the notice or subpoena duces tecum, respectively, or any part thereof.

(b) Whenever a person is required pursuant to such a notice, subpoena duces tecum or order to produce documents for inspection, and where such person withholds one or more documents that appear to be within the category of the documents required by the notice, subpoena duces tecum or order to be produced, such person shall give notice to the party seeking the production and inspection of the documents that one or more such documents are being withheld. This notice shall indicate the legal ground for withholding each such document, and shall provide the following information as to each such document, unless the party withholding the document states that divulgence of such information would cause disclosure of the allegedly privileged information: (1) the type of document; (2) the general subject matter of the document; (3) the date of the document; and (4) such other information as is sufficient to identify the document for a subpoena duces tecum.

(c) Whenever a person is required pursuant to such notice or order to produce documents for inspection, that person shall produce them as they are kept in the regular course of business or shall organize and label them to correspond to the categories in the request.

(d) Unless the subpoena duces tecum directs the production of original documents for inspection and copying at the place where such items are usually maintained, it shall be sufficient for the custodian or other qualified person to deliver complete and accurate copies of the items to be produced. The reasonable production expenses of a non-party witness shall be defrayed by the party seeking discovery.

2002 AMENDMENTS

L. 2002, ch. 575, § 3, eff. Sept. 1, 2003, amended subds. (a) and (b) and added subd. (d).

1998 AMENDMENTS

L. 1998, ch. 295, eff. July 14, 1998, amended CPLR 3122 by adding a new subdivision (c) to provide that when a person is required to produce documents for inspection, they must be produced as they are kept in the regular course of business or else organized and labeled to correspond to the categories in the request.

1993 AMENDMENTS

L. 1993, ch. 98, eff. Jan. 1, 1994, amended CPLR 3122(a) to modify the procedure to be followed by a party who objects to a disclosure request. The time limit within which a party who is served with a disclosure request under CPLR 3120 or CPLR 3121 must raise an objection was increased from 10 to 20 days. Also, the method for raising an objection was fundamentally altered: instead of moving for a protective order, the objecting party need only serve upon the party seeking disclosure a response stating the reasons for each objection with "reasonable particularity." Additionally, 3122(b) was added to set forth the method by which a party who declines to produce some or all of the documents described in a disclosure request must notify the party seeking the disclosure of the basis upon which material has been withheld.

1979 AMENDMENTS

L. 1979, ch. 80, eff. Sept. 1, 1979, amended CPLR 3122 by changing the time within which a party may serve a notice of motion for a protective order from 5 to 10 days from the date of service of notice under CPLR 3120 or 3121.

The Judicial Conference Report on the CPLR to the 1979 Legislature noted that the five day time period was unrealistic and burdensome, and that: ". . . The frequently expressed objection of the bar to the unworkable shortness of the time period of CPLR 3122, and the growing number of judicial decisions granting relaxation thereof, is compelling reason for immediate extension of that time period, as proposed in this bill."

§ R 3122-a.   Certification of business records.

(a) Business records produced pursuant to a subpoena duces tecum under rule 3120 shall be accompanied by a certification, sworn in the form of an affidavit and subscribed by the custodian or other qualified witness charged with responsibility of maintaining the records, stating in substance each of the following:

1. The affiant is the duly authorized custodian or other qualified witness and has authority to make the certification;

2. To the best of the affiant's knowledge, after reasonable inquiry, the records or copies thereof are accurate versions of the documents described in the subpoena duces tecum that are in the possession, custody, or control of the person receiving the subpoena;

3. To the best of the affiant's knowledge, after reasonable inquiry, the records or copies produced represent all the documents described in the subpoena duces tecum, or if they do not represent a complete set of the documents subpoenaed, an explanation of which documents are missing and a reason for their absence is provided; and

4. The records or copies produced were made by the personnel or staff of the business, or persons acting under their control, in the regular course of business, at the time of the act, transaction, occurrence or event recorded therein, or within a reasonable time thereafter, and that it was the regular course of business to make such records.

(b) A certification made in compliance with subdivision (a) is admissible as to the matters set forth therein and as to such matters shall be presumed true. When more than one person has knowledge of the facts, more than one certification may be made.

(c) A party intending to offer at a trial or hearing business records authenticated by certification subscribed pursuant to this rule shall, at least thirty days before the trial or hearing, give notice of such intent and specify the place where such records may be inspected at reasonable times. No later than ten days before the trial or hearing, a party upon whom such notice is served may object to the offer of business records by certification stating the grounds for the objection. Such objection may be asserted in any instance and shall not be subject to imposition of any penalty or sanction. Unless objection is made pursuant to this subdivision, or is made at trial based upon evidence which could not have been discovered by the exercise of due diligence prior to the time for objection otherwise required by this subdivision, business records certified in accordance with this rule shall be deemed to have satisfied the requirements of subdivision (a) of rule 4518. Notwithstanding the issuance of such notice or objection to same, a party may subpoena the custodian to appear and testify and require the production of original business records at the trial or hearing.

2002 AMENDMENTS

L. 2002, ch. 575, § 4, eff. Sept. 1, 2003, added CPLR 3122-a.

§ 3123. Admissions as to matters of fact, papers, documents and photographs.

(a) Notice to admit; admission unless denied or denial excused. At any time after service of the answer or after the expiration of twenty days from service of the summons, whichever is sooner, and not later than twenty days before the trial, a party may serve upon any other party a written request for admission by the latter of the genuineness of any papers or documents, or the correctness or fairness of representation of any photographs, described in and served with the request, or of the truth of any matters of fact set forth in the request, as to which the party requesting the admission reasonably believes there can be no substantial dispute at the trial and which are within the knowledge of such other party or can be ascertained by him upon reasonable inquiry. Copies of the papers, documents or photographs shall be served with the request unless copies have already been furnished. Each of the matters of which an admission is requested shall be deemed admitted unless within twenty days after service thereof or within such further time as the court may allow, the party to whom the request is directed serves upon the party requesting the admission a sworn statement either denying specifically the matters of which an admission is requested or setting forth in detail the reasons why he cannot truthfully either admit or deny those matters. If the matters of which an admission is requested cannot be fairly admitted without some material qualification or explanation, or if the matters constitute a trade secret or such party would be privileged or disqualified from testifying as a witness concerning them, such party may, in lieu of a denial or statement, serve a sworn statement setting forth in detail his claim and, if the claim is that the matters cannot be fairly admitted without some material qualification or explanation, admitting the matters with such qualification or explanation.

(b) Effect of admission. Any admission made, or deemed to be made, by a party pursuant to a request made under this rule is for the purpose of the pending action only and does not constitute an admission by him for any other purpose nor may it be used against him in any other proceeding; and the court, at any time, may allow a party to amend or withdraw any admission on such terms as may be just. Any admission shall be subject to all pertinent objections to admissibility which may be interposed at the trial.

(c) Penalty for unreasonable denial. If a party, after being served with a request under subdivision (a) does not admit and if the party requesting the admission thereafter proves the genuineness of any such paper or document, or the correctness or fairness of representation of any such photograph, or the truth of any such matter of fact, he may move at or immediately following the trial for an order requiring the other party to pay him the reasonable expenses incurred in making such proof, including reasonable attorney's fees. Unless the court finds that there were good reasons for the denial or the refusal otherwise to admit or that the admissions sought were of no substantial importance, the order shall be made irrespective of the result of the action. Upon a trial by jury, the motion for such an order shall be determined by the court outside the presence of the jury.

R 3124. Failure to disclose; motion to compel disclosure.

If a person fails to respond to or comply with any request, notice, interrogatory, demand, question or order under this article, except a notice to admit under section 3123, the party seeking disclosure may move to compel compliance or a response.

1993 AMENDMENTS

L. 1993, ch. 98, eff. Jan. 1, 1994, added this section, replacing former CPLR 3124.

R 3125. Place where motion to compel disclosure made.

Unless otherwise provided by rule of the chief administrator of courts, the county in which a deposition is being taken or an examination or inspection is being sought may be treated by the moving party as the county in which the action is pending for purposes of section 3124.

1986 AMENDMENTS

L. 1986, ch. 355, eff. July 17, 1986, amended CPLR 3125 by adding the phrase "Unless otherwise provided by rule of the chief administrator of the courts" to the beginning of the paragraph.

§ 3126. Penalties for refusal to comply with order or to disclose.

If any party, or a person who at the time a deposition is taken or an examination or inspection is made, is an officer, director, member, employee or agent of a party or otherwise under a party's control, refuses to obey an order for disclosure or wilfully fails to disclose information which the court finds ought to have been disclosed, pursuant to this article, the court may make such orders with regard to the failure or refusal as are just, among them:

1. an order that issues to which the information is relevant shall be deemed resolved for purposes of the action in accordance with the claims of the party obtaining the order; or

2. an order prohibiting the disobedient party from supporting or opposing designated claims or defenses, from producing in evidence designated things or items of testimony, or from introducing any evidence of the physical, mental or blood condition sought to be determined, or from using certain witnesses; or

3. an order striking out pleadings or parts thereof, or staying further proceedings until the order is obeyed, or dismissing the action or any part thereof, or rendering a judgment by default against the disobedient party.

1993 AMENDMENTS

L. 1993, ch. 98, eff. Jan. 1, 1994, replaced the words "notice duly served" with the words "this article" in the opening paragraph of the section.

CPLR

1978 AMENDMENTS

L. 1978, ch. 42, eff. April 4, 1978, amended the opening paragraph by adding the words "pursuant to notice duly served," thus eliminating any ambiguity as to the applicability of the section to those instances where disclosure is sought upon notice, without court order.

§§ 3127–3129.   [Not used.]

§ 3130.   Use of interrogatories.

1. Except as otherwise provided herein, after commencement of an action, any party may serve upon any other party written interrogatories. Except in a matrimonial action, a party may not serve written interrogatories on another party and also demand a bill of particulars of the same party pursuant to section 3041. In the case of an action to recover damages for personal injury, injury to property or wrongful death predicated solely on a cause or causes of action for negligence, a party shall not be permitted to serve interrogatories on and conduct a deposition of the same party pursuant to rule 3107 without leave of court.

2. After the commencement of a matrimonial action or proceeding, upon motion brought by either party, upon such notice to the other party and to the non-party from whom financial disclosure is sought, and given in such manner as the court shall direct, the court may order a non-party to respond under oath to written interrogatories limited to furnishing financial information concerning a party, and further provided such information is both reasonable and necessary in the prosecution or the defense of such matrimonial action or proceeding.

1986 AMENDMENTS

L. 1986, ch. 257, eff. Sept. 1, 1986, amended subdivision (1) to except matrimonial actions from prohibition against service of written interrogatories and demand for bill of particulars upon same party, and L. 1986, ch. 467, eff. Aug. 20, 1986 (which amended CPLR 3130(1) without incorporating changes made by L. 1986, ch. 257), to provide that in actions to recover damages for personal injury, injury to property or wrongful death predicated solely on a cause of action for negligence, parties cannot serve interrogatories on or conduct depositions of the same party pursuant to CPLR 3107 without leave of court.

1983 AMENDMENTS

L. 1983, ch. 275, eff. July 10, 1983, amended CPLR 3130 by designating the opening paragraph subd. (1) and adding a new subd. (2).

1979 AMENDMENTS

L. 1979, ch. 197, eff. Sept. 1, 1979, amended CPLR 3130 ". . . to remo
the prohibition on the use of interrogatories in actions to recover damages f
an injury to property or personal injury resulting from negligence, or i
wrongful death actions. . . . [I]n addition, the bill adds a requirement tha
in an action to recover damages for injury to property or personal injury
resulting from negligence or in a wrongful death action, a party may not
demand both interrogatories and an oral deposition without leave of the
court." For additional information, see Governor's Memorandum filed with
Assembly Bill 555/B.

§ 3131. Scope of interrogatories.

Interrogatories may relate to any matters embraced in the disclosure
requirement of section 3101 and the answers may be used to the same
extent as the depositions of a party. Interrogatories may require copies
of such papers, documents or photographs as are relevant to the
answers required, unless opportunity for this examination and copying
be afforded.

1975 AMENDMENTS

L. 1975, ch. 859, eff. Sept. 8, 1975, amended the second sentence by adding
the word, "papers," prior to the phrase "documents or photographs".

R 3132. Service of interrogatories.

After commencement of an action, any party may serve written
interrogatories upon any other party. Interrogatories may not be served
upon a defendant before that defendant's time for serving a responsive
pleading has expired, except by leave of court granted with or without
notice. A copy of the interrogatories and of any order made under this
rule shall be served on each party.

1993 AMENDMENTS

L. 1993, ch. 98, eff. Jan. 1, 1994, amended CPLR 3132 by modifying the
time limits for serving interrogatories in certain cases. Leave of court is
required when a plaintiff seeks to serve interrogatories upon a defendant
whose time to answer has not expired.

R 3133. Service of answers or objections to interrogatories.

(a) Service of an answer or objection. Within twenty days after
service of interrogatories, the party upon whom they are served shall
serve upon each of the parties a copy of the answer to each

rogatory, except one to which the party objects, in which event the sons for the objection shall be stated with reasonable particularity.

(b) Form of answers and objections to interrogatories. Interrogatories shall be answered in writing under oath by the party served, if an individual, or, if the party served is a corporation, a partnership or a sole proprietorship, by an officer, director, member, agent or employee having the information. Each question shall be answered separately and fully, and each answer shall be preceded by the question to which it responds.

(c) Amended answers. Except with respect to amendment or supplementation of responses pursuant to subdivision (h) of section 3101, answers to interrogatories may be amended or supplemented only by order of the court upon motion.

1993 AMENDMENTS

L. 1993, ch. 98, eff. Jan. 1, 1994, amended CPLR 3133 to extend the time for responding to interrogatories from 10 to 20 days. A party who objects to answering an interrogatory need not move for an order to strike, but may instead simply set forth the objection to the interrogatory in the response.

R 3134. [Repealed.]

§ 3140. Disclosure of appraisals in proceedings for condemnation, appropriation or review of tax assessments.

Notwithstanding the provisions of subdivisions (c) and (d) of section 3101, the chief administrator of the courts shall adopt rules governing the exchange of appraisal reports intended for use at the trial in proceedings for condemnation, appropriation or review of tax assessments.

1993 AMENDMENTS

L. 1993, ch. 98, eff. Jan. 1, 1994, amended CPLR 3140 to correct a typographical error and to replace the words "appellate division in each judicial department" with the words "chief administrator of the courts."

1967 AMENDMENTS

L. 1967, ch. 640, eff. Sept. 1, 1967, added Section 3140 requiring appellate divisions to adopt rules governing the exchange of appraisal reports.

Article 32

ACCELERATED JUDGMENT

SUMMARY OF ARTICLE

CPLR

R 3222.   **Action on submitted facts.**

    (a)   **Commencement.**

    (b)   **Subsequent proceedings.**

§ 3201. Confession of judgment before default on certain installment contracts invalid.

Notwithstanding the provisions of section thirty-two hundred eighteen, no judgment by confession shall be entered on any affidavit which was executed prior to the time a default in the payment of an installment occurs in connection with the purchase of fifteen hundred dollars or less of any commodities for any use other than a commercial or business use upon any plan of deferred payments whereby the price or cost is payable in two or more installments. Any judgment entered in violation of this section is void and unenforceable.

§§ 3202–3210. [Not used.]

R 3211. Motion to dismiss.

(a) Motion to dismiss cause of action. A party may move for judgment dismissing one or more causes of action asserted against him on the ground that:

    1. a defense is founded upon documentary evidence; or

    2. the court has not jurisdiction of the subject matter of the cause of action; or

    3. the party asserting the cause of action has not legal capacity to sue; or

    4. there is another action pending between the same parties for the same cause of action in a court of any state or the United States; the court need not dismiss upon this ground but may make such order as justice requires; or

    5. the cause of action may not be maintained because of arbitration and award, collateral estoppel, discharge in bankruptcy, infancy or other disability of the moving party, payment, release, res judicata, statute of limitations, or statute of frauds; or

    6. with respect to a counterclaim, it may not properly be interposed in the action; or

7. the pleading fails to state a cause of action; or

8. the court has not jurisdiction of the person of the defendant; or

9. the court has not jurisdiction in an action where service was made under section 314 or 315; or

10. the court should not proceed in the absence of a person who should be a party.

11. the party is immune from liability pursuant to section seven hundred twenty-a of the not-for-profit corporation law. Presumptive evidence of the status of the corporation, association, organization or trust under section 501(c)(3) of the internal revenue code may consist of production of a letter from the United States internal revenue service reciting such determination on a preliminary or final basis or production of an official publication of the internal revenue service listing the corporation, association, organization or trust as an organization described in such section, and presumptive evidence of uncompensated status of the defendant may consist of an affidavit of the chief financial officer of the corporation, association, organization or trust. On a motion by a defendant based upon this paragraph the court shall determine whether such defendant is entitled to the benefit of section seven hundred twenty-a of the not-for-profit corporation law or subdivision six of section 20.09 of the arts and cultural affairs law and, if it so finds, whether there is a reasonable probability that the specific conduct of such defendant alleged constitutes gross negligence or was intended to cause the resulting harm. If the court finds that the defendant is entitled to the benefits of that section and does not find reasonable probability of gross negligence or intentional harm, it shall dismiss the cause of action as to such defendant.

(b) Motion to dismiss defense. A party may move for judgment dismissing one or more defenses, on the ground that a defense is not stated or has no merit.

(c) Evidence permitted; immediate trial; motion treated as one for summary judgment. Upon the hearing of a motion made under subdivision (a) or (b), either party may submit any evidence that could properly be considered on a motion for summary judgment. Whether or not issue has been joined, the court, after adequate notice to the parties, may treat the motion as a motion for summary judgment. The court may, when appropriate for the expeditious disposition of the controversy, order immediate trial of the issues raised on the motion.

(d) Facts unavailable to opposing party. Should it appear from affidavits submitted in opposition to a motion made under subdivision (a) or (b) that facts essential to justify opposition may exist but cannot then be stated, the court may deny the motion, allowing the moving party to assert the objection in his responsive pleading, if any, or may order a continuance to permit further affidavits to be obtained or disclosure to be had and may make such other order as may be just.

(e) Number, time and waiver of objections; motion to plead over. At any time before service of the responsive pleading is required, a party may move on one or more of the grounds set forth in subdivision (a), and no more than one such motion shall be permitted. Any objection or defense based upon a ground set forth in paragraphs one, three, four, five and six of subdivision (a) is waived unless raised either by such motion or in the responsive pleading. A motion based upon a ground specified in paragraph two, seven or ten of subdivision (a) may be made at any subsequent time or in a later pleading, if one is permitted; an objection that the summons and complaint, summons with notice, or notice of petition and petition was not properly served is waived if, having raised such an objection in a pleading, the objecting party does not move for judgment on that ground within sixty days after serving the pleading, unless the court extends the time upon the ground of undue hardship. The foregoing sentence shall not apply in any proceeding under subdivision one or two of section seven hundred eleven of the real property actions and proceedings law. The papers in opposition to a motion based on improper service shall contain a copy of the proof of service, whether or not previously filed. An objection based upon a ground specified in paragraph eight or nine of subdivision (a) is waived if a party moves on any of the grounds set forth in subdivision (a) without raising such objection or if, having made no objection under subdivision (a), he or she does not raise such objection in the responsive pleading.

(f) Extension of time to plead. Service of a notice of motion under subdivision (a) or (b) before service of a pleading responsive to the cause of action or defense sought to be dismissed extends the time to serve the pleading until ten days after service of notice of entry of the order.

(g) Standards for motions to dismiss in certain cases involving public petition and participation. A motion to dismiss based on paragraph seven of subdivision (a) of this section, in which the moving party has demonstrated that the action, claim, cross claim or counterclaim subject to the motion is an action involving public petition and participation as defined in paragraph (a) of subdivision one of section seventy-six-a of the civil rights law, shall be granted unless the party responding to the motion demonstrates that the cause of action has a substantial basis in law or is supported by a substantial argument for an extension, modification or reversal of existing law. The court shall grant preference in the hearing of such motion.

(h) Standards for motions to dismiss in certain cases involving licensed architects, engineers, land surveyors or landscape architects. A motion to dismiss based on paragraph seven of subdivision (a) of this rule, in which the moving party has demonstrated that the action, claim, cross claim or counterclaim subject to the motion is an action in which a notice of claim must be served on a licensed architect, engineer, land surveyor or landscape architect pursuant to the provisions of subdivision one of section two hundred fourteen of this chapter, shall be granted unless the party responding to the motion demonstrates that a substantial basis in law exists to believe that the performance, conduct or omission complained of such licensed architect, engineer, land surveyor or landscape architect or such firm as set forth in the notice of claim was negligent and that such performance, conduct or omission was a proximate cause of personal injury, wrongful death or property damage complained of by the claimant or is supported by a substantial argument for an extension, modification or reversal of existing law. The court shall grant a preference in the hearing of such motion.

CROSS REFERENCES

As to subject matter jurisdiction of the courts, generally, see **Constitutional** and **Judiciary Law** provisions in the Appendix, *below.*

2005 AMENDMENTS

L. 2005, ch. 616, eff. Jan 1, 2006, amended subdivision (e) by repealing the requirement that a pleader facing a motion to dismiss must request leave to replead.

1997 AMENDMENTS

L. 1997, ch. 518, eff. Sept. 3, 1997, amended subdivision (h) by adding references to land surveyors.

1996 AMENDMENTS

L. 1996, ch. 501, eff. Jan. 1, 1997, amended subdivision (e) to add a clause which deems an objection of improper service waived, if the objecting party does not move for judgment within 60 days after serving the pleading that raised the objection. This does not apply in any proceeding under RPAPL § 711(1) or (2); L. 1996, ch. 682, eff. Oct. 1, 1996, added new subdivision (h).

1992 AMENDMENTS

L. 1992, ch. 767, eff. Jan. 1, 1993, added subdivision (g), providing the standards for motions to dismiss in certain cases involving public petition and participation.

1991 AMENDMENTS

L. 1991, ch. 656, eff. July 26, 1991, amended CPLR 3211(a)(11) to replace a reference to Gen. Mun. L. § 305 with a reference to Arts and Cultural Affairs L. § 20.09.

1990 AMENDMENTS

L. 1990, ch. 904, eff. July 30, 1990, amended paragraph (11) of subdivision (a) of CPLR 3211 to include the reference to subdivision six of section three hundred five of the general municipal law.

1986 AMENDMENTS

L. 1986, ch. 220, eff. June 28, 1986 and applicable only to those causes of action arising on or after that date, added new paragraph (11) to CPLR 3211(a), providing for a motion to dismiss when a party is immune from liability under § 720(a) of the Not-For-Profit Corporation Law.

1973 AMENDMENTS

CPLR 3211(c) was amended by proposal No. 4 of the Judicial Conference Report to the 1973 Legislature, eff. Sept. 1, 1973, to provide that the court may treat a motion to dismiss as one for summary judgment whether or not issue has been joined, but only upon adequate notice to the parties.

1965 AMENDMENTS

Amendment No. 5 made by Judicial Conference Feb. 1, 1965, Report to the Legislature, eff. Sept. 1, 1965, added the words "or has no merit" at the end of Subd. (b) for the reason: "As the provision is presently worded, a defense raised in the answer which has no merit but which is not invalid on its face may not be the subject of a motion to dismiss, should the provision be interpreted literally. The spirit of the CPLR, and specifically of 3211, is to the contrary, and therefore, the rule should expressly permit the early testing of the merit of a defense."

Amendment No. 6 made by Judicial Conference Feb. 1, 1965, Report to the Legislature, eff. Sept. 1, 1965, inserted the words "paragraphs one, three, four, five and six of" after the phrase "Any objection or defense based upon a ground set forth in" and deleted the words "except that a" after the words "responsive pleading" and inserted the word "A" therein to start a new sentence beginning "A motion based upon a ground specified . . ." and in that same sentence deleted the words "by motion" and immediately following that sentence inserted a new sentence to read "An objection based upon a ground specified in paragraphs eight or nine of subdivision (a) is waived if a party moves on any of the grounds set forth in subdivision (a) without raising such objection or if, having made no objection under subdivision (a), he does not raise such objection in the responsive pleading" and deleted the words "in subdivision (b)" substituting therefor the words "on the ground that a defense is not stated" and after the words "opposing papers and" deleted the words "in them" and substituted therefor the word "may" all in the third sentence and at the end of the third sentence added the final clause "the court may require the party seeking leave to plead again to submit evidence to justify the granting of such leave" all in Subd. (e) for the reason: "This amendment is designed to enable the court to determine any issue of jurisdiction over the person or of jurisdiction *in rem* or *quasi in rem* before it is required to determine any issue reaching the merits of the case [see amendments to CPLR 320(b) and (c) *supra*].

"The present text of R 3211 (e) creates problems for the lawyer who has prepared his pleading with misplaced confidence in its adequacy. If he fails to comply with the present requirement that evidence supporting leave to plead again be set forth in his papers opposing a motion to dismiss, he may find himself not only with a dismissed pleading, but also unable to make a belated request for leave to plead again, and, if he is asserting an affirmative claim, faced with the alternatives of appeal from the order of dismissal or the commencement of a new action. The problem may be acute where the statute of limitations is about to expire.

"On the other hand, the cautious pleader, though satisfied with the adequacy of his pleading, may feel obliged, in order to avoid the foregoing problems, not only to seek leave in his opposing papers to plead again, but also to submit his supporting evidence in those papers, thus indicating to the court a perhaps unwarranted defeatist attitude. If, having done so, he nevertheless succeeds in overcoming the motion to dismiss, he finds not only that his labors were unnecessary but also that he has prematurely laid bare much of his case and much of the evidence upon which he ultimately intends to rely to prove his case.

"This portion of the rule has been subject to much criticism from bench and bar which the Conference feels justified, while at the same time believing that the former practice of granting leave to plead again without any evidentiary showing should not be restored . . . the proposed amendment steers a desirable middle course by dispensing with the present requirement that supporting evidence must be set forth in the papers opposing the motion to dismiss. The proposed amendment would leave to the court's discretion the timing and method for the submission of evidence supporting a request for leave to plead again, while retaining the present requirement that the request for leave to plead again must be stated in the papers opposing the motion to dismiss.

"The proposed change with respect to a motion to dismiss a defense is necessitated by the [change in rule 3211 (b)]."

L. 1965, ch. 773, eff. Sept. 1, 1965, deleted the word "or" in the final phrase of Subd. (d) "or may make such other order as may be just" and substituted therefor the word "and."

Amendment recommended by the Judicial Conference Feb. 1, 1965, Report to the Legislature: "The amendment is proposed to prevent possible misconstruction which would preclude the granting of unspecified just relief as well as the specific relief set forth in this subdivision relating to motions to dismiss."

1964 AMENDMENTS

Amendment No. 6 made by the Judicial Conference Feb. 1, 1964, Report to the Legislature, eff. Sept. 1, 1964, added the words "and award" after the word "arbitration" in paragraph 5 of Subd. (a).

R 3212. Motion for summary judgment.

(a) Time; kind of action. Any party may move for summary judgment in any action, after issue has been joined; provided however, that the court may set a date after which no such motion may be made, such date being no earlier than thirty days after the filing of the note of issue. If no such date is set by the court, such motion shall be made no later than one hundred twenty days after the filing of the note of issue, except with leave of court on good cause shown.

(b) Supporting proof; grounds; relief to either party. A motion for summary judgment shall be supported by affidavit, by a copy of the pleadings and by other available proof, such as depositions and written admissions. The affidavit shall be by a person having knowledge of the facts; it shall recite all the material facts; and it shall show that there is no defense to the cause of action or that the cause of action or defense has no merit. The motion shall be granted if, upon all the papers and proof submitted, the cause of action or defense shall be established sufficiently to warrant the court as a matter of law in directing

CPLR

judgment in favor of any party. Except as provided in subdivision (c) of this rule the motion shall be denied if any party shall show facts sufficient to require a trial of any issue of fact. If it shall appear that any party other than the moving party is entitled to a summary judgment, the court may grant such judgment without the necessity of a cross-motion.

(c) Immediate trial. If it appears that the only triable issues of fact arising on a motion for summary judgment relate to the amount or extent of damages, or if the motion is based on any of the grounds enumerated in subdivision (a) or (b) of rule 3211, the court may, when appropriate for the expeditious disposition of the controversy, order an immediate trial of such issues of fact raised by the motion, before a referee, before the court, or before the court and a jury, whichever may be proper.

(d) [Repealed.]

(e) Partial summary judgment; severance. In a matrimonial action summary judgment may not be granted in favor of the non-moving party. In any other action summary judgment may be granted as to one or more causes of action, or part thereof, in favor of any one or more parties, to the extent warranted, on such terms as may be just. The court may also direct:

1. that the cause of action as to which summary judgment is granted shall be severed from any remaining cause of action; or

2. that the entry of the summary judgment shall be held in abeyance pending the determination of any remaining cause of action.

(f) Facts unavailable to opposing party. Should it appear from affidavits submitted in opposition to the motion that facts essential to justify opposition may exist but cannot then be stated, the court may deny the motion or may order a continuance to permit affidavits to be obtained or disclosure to be had and may make such other order as may be just.

(g) Limitation of issues of fact for trial. If a motion for summary judgment is denied or is granted in part, the court, by examining the papers before it and, in the discretion of the court, by interrogating counsel, shall, if practicable, ascertain what facts are not in dispute or are incontrovertible. It shall thereupon make an order specifying such facts and they shall be deemed established for all purposes in the action. The court may make any order as may aid in the disposition of the action.

(h) Standards for summary judgment in certain cases involving public petition and participation. A motion for summary judgment, in which the moving party has demonstrated that the action, claim, cross claim or counterclaim subject to the motion is an action involving public petition and participation, as defined in paragraph (a) of subdivision one of section seventy-six-a of the civil rights law, shall be granted unless the party responding to the motion demonstrates that the action, claim, cross claim or counterclaim has a substantial basis in fact and law or is supported by a substantial argument for an extension, modification or reversal of existing law. The court shall grant preference in the hearing of such motion.

(i) Standards for summary judgment in certain cases involving licensed architects, engineers, land surveyors or landscape architects. A motion for summary judgment, in which the moving party has demonstrated that the action, claim, cross claim or counterclaim subject to the motion is an action in which a notice of claim must be served on a licensed architect, engineer, land surveyor or landscape architect pursuant to the provisions of subdivision one of section two hundred fourteen of this chapter, shall be granted unless the party responding to the motion demonstrates that a substantial basis in fact and in law exists to believe that the performance, conduct or omission complained of such licensed architect, engineer, land surveyor or landscape architect or such firm as set forth in the notice of claim was negligent and that such performance, conduct or omission was a proximate cause of personal injury, wrongful death or property damage complained of by the claimant or is supported by a substantial argument for an extension, modification or reversal of existing law. The court shall grant a preference in the hearing of such motion.

1997 AMENDMENTS

L. 1997, ch. 518, eff. Sept. 3, 1997, amended subdivision (i) by adding the references to land surveyors.

1996 AMENDMENTS

L. 1996, ch. 492, eff. Jan. 1, 1997, amended subdivision (a) by adding the words beginning, "provided, however . . ." and continuing to the end of the subdivision; L. 1996, Ch. 682, eff. Oct. 1, 1996, added new subdivision (i).

1992 AMENDMENTS

L. 1992, ch. 767, eff. Jan. 1, 1993, added subdivision (h), providing the standards for summary judgment in certain cases involving public petition and participation.

1984 AMENDMENTS

L. 1984, ch. 827, eff. Aug. 5, 1984, amended CPLR 3212(e) by providing that partial summary judgment may not be granted in matrimonial actions. L. 1984, ch. 828, eff. Aug. 5, 1984, provides that the application of ch. 827 shall be determined in accordance with the provisions of CPLR 10003.

1978 AMENDMENTS

L. 1978, ch. 532, eff. Jan. 1, 1979, repealed former subdivision (d) of CPLR 3212, and deleted references thereto in subdivisions (a) and (e). Former subdivision (d) had provided that summary judgment in matrimonial actions was only available to defendants upon documentary evidence or official records establishing a defense, and was not available to plaintiffs at all. The effect of the amendment is to permit the entry of summary judgment for the plaintiff or the defendant in a matrimonial action as in any other action.

1973 AMENDMENTS

CPLR 3212(c) was repealed and a new subdivision (c) was enacted by proposal No. 5 of the Judicial Conference Report to the 1973 Legislature, effective Sept. 1, 1973.

The 1973 Judicial Conference Report stated:

"This proposal would amend subdivision (c) of Rule 3212, which now provides that on a motion for summary judgment the court may order an immediate trial of any issue of fact as to the amount or extent of damages, in order to permit the court to order immediate trial also of any issue of fact which presently can be raised upon a motion to dismiss (see CPLR 3211 (a) (b) (c)).

"The specific defenses enumerated under Rule 3211(a) are of the kind that commonly form the bases for summary judgment, especially when the defense is founded upon documentary evidence (Rule 3211(a) (1)). Furthermore, a motion to dismiss based on failure to state a cause of action (Rule 3211(a) (7)) often raises the same issues as a motion for summary judgment, and when matters outside the pleading are submitted (Rule 3211(c)) the motion is almost indistinguishable from one for summary judgment.

"Despite these substantial similarities, there exists a formal asymmetry in that on a motion to dismiss the court may order immediate trial of the issues raised on the motion (Rule 3211(c)), while on a motion for summary judgment any triable issue other than as to damages requires denial of the motion (Rule 3212(b)).

"Thus, in the light of the foregoing and because Rule 3211(c) permits motions to dismiss to be converted into motions for summary judgment, the proposed amendment clarifying and conforming practice under the two rules should be effected (*see* 4 Weinstein, Korn & Miller, New York Civil Practice - CPLR ¶ 3212.03 (Matthew Bender); see also Ass'n of the Bar of the City of New York, Report of the Committee on State Legislation 190-191 (1961)).

"The proposed amendment would allow the court under the conditions stated to consider other issues of fact, in addition to the sole present category of disputed damages, the resolution of which would be dispositive."

L. 1973, ch. 651, eff. Sept. 1, 1973, amended CPLR 3212(b) by deleting from the penultimate sentence "other than an issue as to the amount or extent of the damages"; and by adding to the penultimate sentence "Except as provided in subdivision (c) of this rule."

1965 AMENDMENTS

L. 1965, ch. 773, eff. Sept. 1, 1965, deleted the words "or" and "is" in the last phrase of Subd. (f) "or may make such other order as is just" and substituted therefor the words "and" and "may be" respectively.

Amendment recommended by the Judicial Conference Feb. 1, 1965, Report to the Legislature: "The change is proposed in order to make 3212(f) consistent with the language of 3211(d). . . ." See amendment and notes to 3211(d), *supra*.

§ 3213.   Motion for summary judgment in lieu of complaint.

When an action is based upon an instrument for the payment of money only or upon any judgment, the plaintiff may serve with the summons a notice of motion for summary judgment and the supporting papers in lieu of a complaint. The summons served with such motion papers shall require the defendant to submit answering papers on the motion within the time provided in the notice of motion. The minimum time such motion shall be noticed to be heard shall be as provided by subdivision (a) of rule 320 for making an appearance, depending upon the method of service. If the plaintiff sets the hearing date of the motion later than the minimum time therefor, he may require the defendant to serve a copy of his answering papers upon him within such extended period of time, not exceeding ten days, prior to such hearing date. No default judgment may be entered pursuant to subdivision (a) of section 3215 prior to the hearing date of the motion. If the motion is denied, the moving and answering papers shall be deemed the complaint and answer, respectively, unless the court orders otherwise.

1969 AMENDMENTS

L. 1969, ch. 210, eff. Sept. 1, 1969, amended the section to reflect intention that summary procedure may be used where action is based on "any judgment."

1967 AMENDMENTS

L. 1967, ch. 377, eff. Sept. 1, 1967, amended section to read as above by adding next to last sentence and by revising wording of section to achieve a greater degree of clarity.

1965 AMENDMENTS

L. 1965, ch. 350, eff. Sept. 1, 1965, deleted the words "returnable at least twenty days after service" at the end of the first sentence, and added the second, third and fourth sentences.

R 3214.   Motions heard by judge supervising disclosure; stay of disclosure.

(a) Judge supervising disclosure. Unless the chief administrator of the courts has, by rule, provided otherwise, if a case has been assigned to a judge to supervise disclosure pursuant to section 3104, all motions preliminary to trial shall be referred to such judge whenever practicable.

(b) Stay of disclosure. Service of a notice of motion under rule 3211, 3212, or section 3213 stays disclosure until determination of the motion unless the court orders otherwise. If the motion is based solely on the defense that the summons and complaint, summons with notice, or notice of petition and petition was not properly served, disclosure shall not be stayed unless the court orders otherwise.

1996 AMENDMENTS

L. 1996, ch. 501, eff. Jan. 1, 1997, amended subdivision (b) to add a new last sentence.

1986 AMENDMENTS

L. 1986, ch. 355, eff. July 17, 1986, amended subdivision (a) by adding the phrase "Unless the chief administrator of the courts has, by rule, provided otherwise," to the beginning of the subdivision, and substituting "such judge" for "him."

§ 3215.   Default judgment.

(a) Default and entry. When a defendant has failed to appear, plead or proceed to trial of an action reached and called for trial, or when the court orders a dismissal for any other neglect to proceed, the plaintiff may seek a default judgment against him. If the plaintiff's claim is for a sum certain or for a sum which can by computation be made certain, application may be made to the clerk within one year after the default. The clerk, upon submission of the requisite proof, shall enter judgment for the amount demanded in the complaint or stated in the notice served pursuant to subdivision (b) of rule 305, plus costs and interest. Upon entering a judgment against less than all defendants, the clerk shall also enter an order severing the action as to them. When a plaintiff has failed to proceed to trial of an action reached and called for trial, or when the court orders a dismissal for any other neglect to proceed, the defendant may make application to the clerk within one year after the default and the clerk, upon submission of the requisite proof, shall enter judgment for costs. Where the case is not one in which the clerk can enter judgment, the plaintiff shall apply to the court for judgment.

(b) Procedure before court. The court, with or without a jury, may make an assessment or take an account or proof, or may direct a reference. When a reference is directed, the court may direct that the report be returned to it for further action or, except where otherwise prescribed by law, that judgment be entered by the clerk in accordance with the report without any further application. Except in a matrimonial action, no finding of fact in writing shall be necessary to the entry of a judgment on default. The judgment shall not exceed in amount or differ in type from that demanded in the complaint or stated in the notice served pursuant to subdivision (b) of rule 305.

(c) Default not entered within one year. If the plaintiff fails to take proceedings for the entry of judgment within one year after the default, the court shall not enter judgment but shall dismiss the complaint as abandoned, without costs, upon its own initiative or on motion, unless sufficient cause is shown why the complaint should not be dismissed. A motion by the defendant under this subdivision does not constitute an appearance in the action.

(d) Multiple defendants. Whenever a defendant has answered and one or more other defendants have failed to appear, plead, or proceed to trial of an action reached and called for trial, notwithstanding the provisions of subdivision (c) of this section, upon application to the court within one year after the default of any such defendant, the court may enter an ex parte order directing that proceedings for the entry of a judgment or the making of an assessment, the taking of an account or proof, or the direction of a reference be conducted at the time of or following the trial or other disposition of the action against the defendant who has answered. Such order shall be served on the defaulting defendant in such manner as shall be directed by the court.

(e) Place of application to court. An application to the court under this section may be made, except where otherwise prescribed by rules of the chief administrator of the courts, by motion at any trial term in which the action is triable or at any special term in which a motion in the action could be made. Any reference shall be had in the county in which the action is triable, unless the court orders otherwise.

(f) Proof. On any application for judgment by default, the applicant shall file proof of service of the summons and the complaint, or a summons and notice served pursuant to subdivision (b) of rule 305 or subdivision (a) of rule 316 of this chapter, and proof of the facts constituting the claim, the default and the amount due by affidavit made by the party, or where the state of New York is the plaintiff, by affidavit made by an attorney from the office of the attorney general who has or obtains knowledge of such facts through review of state records or otherwise. Where a verified complaint has been served, it may be used as the affidavit of the facts constituting the claim and the amount due; in such case, an affidavit as to the default shall be made by the party or the party's attorney. When jurisdiction is based on an attachment of property, the affidavit must state that an order of attachment granted in the action has been levied on the property of the defendant, describe the property and state its value. Proof of mailing the notice required by subdivision (g) of this section, where applicable, shall also be filed.

(g) Notice.

1. Except as otherwise provided with respect to specific actions, whenever application is made to the court or to the clerk, any defendant who has appeared is entitled to at least five days' notice of the time and place of the application, and if more than one year has elapsed since the default any defendant who has not appeared is

entitled to the same notice unless the court orders otherwise. The court may dispense with the requirement of notice when a defendant who has appeared has failed to proceed to trial of an action reached and called for trial.

2. Where an application for judgment must be made to the court, the defendant who has failed to appear may serve on the plaintiff at any time before the motion for judgment is heard a written demand for notice of any reference or assessment by a jury which may be granted on the motion. Such a demand does not constitute an appearance in the action. Thereupon at least five days' notice of the time and place of the reference or assessment by a jury shall be given to the defendant by service on the person whose name is subscribed to the demand, in the manner prescribed for service of papers generally.

3.   (i) When a default judgment based upon nonappearance is sought against a natural person in an action based upon nonpayment of a contractual obligation an affidavit shall be submitted that additional notice has been given by or on behalf of the plaintiff at least twenty days before the entry of such judgment by mailing a copy of the summons by first-class mail to the defendant at his place of residence in an envelope bearing the legend "personal and confidential" and not indicating on the outside of the envelope that the communication is from an attorney or concerns an alleged debt. In the event such mailing is returned as undeliverable by the post office before the entry of a default judgment, or if the place of residence of the defendant is unknown, a copy of the summons shall then be mailed in the same manner to the defendant at the defendant's place of employment if known; if neither the place of residence nor the place of employment of the defendant is known, then the mailing shall be to the defendant at his last known residence.

(ii) The additional notice may be mailed simultaneously with or after service of the summons on the defendant. An affidavit of mailing pursuant to this paragraph shall be executed by the person mailing the notice and shall be filed with the judgment. Where there has been compliance with the requirements of this paragraph, failure of the defendant to receive the additional notice shall not preclude the entry of default judgment.

(iii) This requirement shall not apply to cases in the small claims part of any court, or to any summary proceeding to recover possession of real property, or to actions affecting title to real property, except residential mortgage foreclosure actions.

4.   (i) When a default judgment based upon non-appearance is sought against a domestic or authorized foreign corporation which has been served pursuant to paragraph (b) of section three hundred six of the business corporation law, an affidavit shall be submitted that an additional service of the summons by first class mail has been made upon the defendant corporation at its last known address at least twenty days before the entry of judgment.

(ii) The additional service of the summons by mail may be made simultaneously with or after the service of the summons on the defendant corporation pursuant to paragraph (b) of section three hundred six of the business corporation law, and shall be accompanied by a notice to the corporation that service is being made or has been made pursuant to that provision. An affidavit of mailing pursuant to this paragraph shall be executed by the person mailing the summons and shall be filed with the judgment. Where there has been compliance with the requirements of this paragraph, failure of the defendant corporation to receive the additional service of summons and notice provided for by this paragraph shall not preclude the entry of default judgment.

(iii) This requirement shall not apply to cases in the small claims part or commercial claims part of any court, or to any summary proceeding to recover possession of real property, or to actions affecting title to real property.

(h) Judgment for excess where counterclaim interposed. In an action upon a contract where the complaint demands judgment for a sum of money only, if the answer does not deny the plaintiff's claim but sets up a counterclaim demanding an amount less than the plaintiff's claim, the plaintiff upon filing with the clerk an admission of the counterclaim may take judgment for the excess as upon a default.

(i) Default judgment for failure to comply with stipulation of settlement.

1. Where, after commencement of an action, a stipulation of settlement is made, providing, in the event of failure to comply with the stipulation, for entry without further notice of a judgment in a specified amount with interest, if any, from a date certain, the clerk shall enter judgment on the stipulation and an affidavit as to the failure to comply with the terms thereof, together with a complaint or a concise statement of the facts on which the claim was based.

2. Where, after commencement of an action, a stipulation of settlement is made, providing, in the event of failure to comply with the stipulation, for entry without further notice of a judgment dismissing the action, the clerk shall enter judgment on the stipulation and an affidavit as to the failure to comply with the terms thereof, together with the pleadings or a concise statement of the facts on which the claim and the defense were based.

CPLR

CROSS REFERENCES

As to default in matrimonial actions, see **Domestic Relations Law §§ 211** and **232(a),** in Appendix, *below.*

2007 AMENDMENTS

L. 2007, ch. 458, eff. Aug. 1, 2007, amended CPLR 3215(g)(3)(iii) by adding ,"except residential mortgage foreclosure actions."

2006 AMENDMENTS

L. 2006, ch. 453, § 1, eff. Aug. 16, 2006, amended CPLR 3215(f) to to provide that in applications for judgment by default where the state of New York is the plaintiff to allow for the submission of proof by affidavit by an attorney from the office of the attorney general who obtains knowledge of the facts through review of state records or otherwise.

1994 AMENDMENTS

L. 1994, ch. 100, eff. May 11, 1994, amended the first sentence of CPLR 3215(g)(1) by replacing "if" with "whenever"; replacing "must be" with "is"; by replacing "if judgment is entered by" with "to"; and by replacing "motion" with "application." The second sentence of CPLR 3215(g)(1) was also amended by deleting the word "also" following the words "The court may."

1992 AMENDMENTS

L. 1992, ch. 255, eff. Jan. 1, 1993, added new Subd. (d) and relettered former Subds. (d)–(h) as (e)–(i), respectively.

1990 AMENDMENTS

L. 1990, ch. 584, eff. Aug. 17, 1990, amended CPLR 3215(f)(1) by deleting the opening sentence and adding the words "or if judgment is entered by the clerk;" L. 1990, ch. 419, eff. Jan. 1, 1991, added subdivision (f)(4).

1986 AMENDMENTS

L. 1986, ch. 77, eff. Jan. 1, 1987, added new paragraph (3) to CPLR 3215(f) governing additional notice requirements in actions based upon nonpayment of contractual obligations, superseding repealed provisions of CPLR 308, and amended subdivision (e) to reflect this change.

L. 1986, ch. 355, eff. July 17, 1986, amended Subd. (d) of CPLR 3215 by replacing "local court rules" with "rules of the chief administrator of the courts."

1977 AMENDMENTS

L. 1977, ch. 344, eff. Jan. 1, 1978, amended CPLR 3215(e) by adding a provision requiring the filing of proof of mailing of the summons to defendant prior to entry of a default judgment in those actions where such additional notice is required by CPLR 308.

1968 AMENDMENTS

L. 1968, ch. 720, eff. Sept. 1, 1968, added second sentence to Subd. (f)(1) and added the phrase "who has failed to appear" to the first sentence of Subd. (f)(2).

1967 AMENDMENTS

L. 1967, ch. 31, eff. Sept. 1, 1967, added paragraph (2) to Subd. (h).

1966 AMENDMENTS

L. 1966, ch. 487, eff. Sept. 1, 1966, added a new Subd. (h).

1965 AMENDMENTS

L. 1965, ch. 148, eff. Sept. 1, 1965, amended Subd. (e), by adding the words "or subdivision (a) of rule 316" after the words "pursuant to subdivision (b) of rule 305" in the first sentence.

1964 AMENDMENTS

L. 1964, ch. 290, eff. Sept. 1, 1964, amended Subd. (e) to make it clear that a verified complaint may be used in place of an affidavit of facts.

R 3216.   Want of prosecution.

(a) Where a party unreasonably neglects to proceed generally in an action or otherwise delays in the prosecution thereof against any party who may be liable to a separate judgment, or unreasonably fails to serve and file a note of issue, the court, on its own initiative or upon motion, may dismiss the party's pleading on terms. Unless the order specifies otherwise, the dismissal is not on the merits.

(b) No dismissal shall be directed under any portion of subdivision (a) of this rule and no court initiative shall be taken or motion made thereunder unless the following conditions precedent have been complied with:

(1) Issue must have been joined in the action;

(2) One year must have elapsed since the joinder of issue;

(3) The court or party seeking such relief, as the case may be, shall have served a written demand by registered or certified mail requiring the party against whom such relief is sought to resume prosecution of the action and to serve and file a note of issue within ninety days after receipt of such demand, and further stating that the default by the party upon whom such notice is served in complying with such demand within said day period will serve as a basis for a motion by the party serving said demand for dismissal as against him for unreasonably neglecting to proceed.

(c) In the event that the party upon whom is served the demand specified in subdivision (b)(3) of this rule serves and files a note of issue within such ninety day period, the same shall be deemed sufficient compliance with such demand and diligent prosecution of the action; and in such event, no such court initiative shall be taken and no such motion shall be made, and if taken or made, the court initiative or motion to dismiss shall be denied.

(d) After an action has been placed on the calendar by the service and filing of a note of issue, with or without any such demand, provided, however, if such demand has been served, within the said ninety day period, the action may not be dismissed by reason of any neglect, failure or delay in prosecution of the action prior to the said service and filing of such note of issue.

(e) In the event that the party upon whom is served the demand specified in subdivision (b)(3) of this rule fails to serve and file a note of issue within such ninety day period, the court may take such initiative or grant such motion unless the said party shows justifiable excuse for the delay and a good and meritorious cause of action.

CPLR

(f) The provisions of this rule shall not apply to proceedings within rule thirty-four hundred four.

1978 AMENDMENTS

L. 1978, ch. 4, eff. Sept. 1, 1978, amended subdivisions (b), (c), (d), and (e) by changing the forty-five day period to a ninety day period.

1967 AMENDMENTS

L. 1967, ch. 770, eff. Sept. 1, 1967, repealed former 3216 and added the present rule.

R 3217.   Voluntary discontinuance.

(a) Without an order. Any party asserting a claim may discontinue it without an order.

1. by serving upon all parties to the action a notice of discontinuance at any time before a responsive pleading is served or within twenty days after service of the pleading asserting the claim, whichever is earlier, and filing the notice with proof of service with the clerk of the court; or

2. by filing with the clerk of the court before the case has been submitted to the court or jury a stipulation in writing signed by the attorneys of record for all parties, provided that no party is an infant, incompetent person for whom a committee has been appointed or conservatee and no person not a party has an interest in the subject matter of the action.

3. by filing with the clerk of the court before the case has been submitted to the court or jury a certificate or notice of discontinuance stating that any parcel of land which is the subject matter of the action is to be excluded pursuant to title three of article eleven of the real property tax law.

(b) By order of court. Except as provided in subdivision (a), an action shall not be discontinued by a party asserting a claim except upon order of the court and upon terms and conditions, as the court deems proper. After the cause has been submitted to the court or jury to determine the facts the court may not order an action discontinued except upon the stipulation of all parties appearing in the action.

(c) Effect of discontinuance. Unless otherwise stated in the notice, stipulation or order of discontinuance, the discontinuance is without prejudice, except that a discontinuance by means of notice operates as an adjudication on the merits if the party has once before discontinued by any method an action based on or including the same cause of action in a court of any state or the United States.

(d) All notices, stipulations, or certificates pursuant to this rule shall be filed with the county clerk by the defendant.

CROSS REFERENCES

Provisions requiring leave of court to discontinue an action are contained in **CPLR 908**, as to class actions; **B.C.L. § 626(d)**, as to shareholders' derivative actions; **Environmental Conservation Law § 71-0505**, as to suits involving title to state lands in forest preserve counties; **Condemnation Law §§ 18 and 56**, as to condemnation proceedings.

2003 AMENDMENTS

L. 2003, ch. 62, Part J, § 29, eff. July 14, 2003, adding subd. (d).

1999 AMENDMENTS

L. 1999, ch. 278, eff. July 20, 1999, amended CPLR § 3217 by replacing the reference in subdivision (a), paragraph (3) from RPTL § 1122(2)(e) to RPTL Title 3, Article 11. This amendment corrects a technical error in the current CPLR reference due to legislative amendments and corrects the reference relating to in rem foreclosures, including hazardous waste disposal sites.

1989 AMENDMENTS

L. 1989, ch. 736, eff. July 24, 1989 added paragraph 3 of subdivision (a).

1981 AMENDMENTS

L. 1981, ch. 115, eff. May 18, 1981, amended CPLR 3217(a)(2) by adding a conservatee as a party whose presence in an action will prevent voluntary discontinuance of that action by stipulation without a court order.

§ 3218. Judgment by confession.

(a) Affidavit of defendant. Except as provided in section thirty-two hundred one, a judgment by confession may be entered, without an action, either for money due or to become due, or to secure the plaintiff against a contingent liability in behalf of the defendant, or both, upon an affidavit executed by the defendant;

    1. stating the sum for which judgment may be entered, authorizing the entry of judgment, and stating the county where the defendant resides or, if he is a non-resident, the county in which entry is authorized;

2. if the judgment to be confessed is for money due or to become due, stating concisely the facts out of which the debt arose and showing that the sum confessed is justly due or to become due; and

3. if the judgment to be confessed is for the purpose of securing the plaintiff against a contingent liability, stating concisely the facts constituting the liability and showing that the sum confessed does not exceed the amount of the liability.

(b) Entry of judgment. At any time within three years after the affidavit is executed, it may be filed with the clerk of the county where the defendant stated in his affidavit that he resided when it was executed or, if the defendant was then a non-resident, with the clerk of the county designated in the affidavit. Thereupon the clerk shall enter a judgment in the supreme court for the sum confessed. He shall tax costs to the amount of fifteen dollars, besides disbursements taxable in an action. The judgment may be docketed and enforced in the same manner and with the same effect as a judgment in an action in the supreme court. No judgment by confession may be entered after the defendant's death.

(c) Execution where the judgment is not all due. Where the debt for which the judgment is entered is not all due, execution may be issued only for the sum which has become due. The execution shall be in the form prescribed for an execution upon a judgment for the full amount recovered, except that it shall direct the sheriff to collect only the sum due, stating the amount with interest and the costs of the judgment. Notwithstanding the issuance and collection of such an execution, the judgment shall remain in force as security for the sum or sums to become due after the execution is issued. When further sums become due, further executions may be issued in the same manner.

(d) Confession by joint debtors. One or more joint debtors may confess a judgment for a joint debt due or to become due. Where all the joint debtors do not unite in the confession, the judgment shall be entered and enforced against only those who confessed it and it is not a bar to an action against the other joint debtors upon the same demand.

R 3219. Tender.

At any time not later than ten days before trial, any party against whom a cause of action based upon contract, express or implied, is asserted, and against whom a separate judgment may be taken, may, without court order, deposit with the clerk of the court for safekeeping, an amount deemed by him to be sufficient to satisfy the claim asserted against him, and serve upon the claimant a written tender of payment to satisfy such claim. A copy of the written tender shall be filed with the clerk when the money is so deposited. The clerk shall place money so received in the safe or vault of the court to be provided for the safekeeping thereof, there to be kept by him until withdrawal by claimant or return to the depositor or payment thereof to the county treasurer or commissioner of finance of the city of New York, as hereinafter provided. Within ten days after such deposit the claimant may withdraw the amount deposited upon filing a duly acknowledged statement that the withdrawal is in satisfaction of the claim. The clerk shall thereupon enter judgment dismissing the pleading setting forth the claim, without costs.

Where there is no withdrawal within such ten-day period, the amount deposited shall, upon request, be repaid to the party who deposited it. If the tender is not accepted and the claimant fails to obtain a more favorable judgment, he shall not recover interest or costs from the time of the offer, but shall pay costs for defending against the claim from that time. A tender shall not be made known to the jury.

Money received by the clerk of the court for safekeeping as hereinabove provided and later withdrawn by claimant or repaid to the depositor pursuant to the provisions hereof shall not be deemed paid into court. If the deposit is neither withdrawn by claimant nor returned to the depositor upon his request at the expiration of the ten-day period, the amount of such deposit shall be deemed paid into court as of the day following the expiration of the ten-day period and the clerk shall pay the amount of the deposit to the county treasurer or commissioner of finance of the city of New York, in accordance with section twenty-six hundred one of the civil practice law and rules. Withdrawal of such amount thereafter shall be in accordance with the provisions of rule twenty-six hundred seven. Fees for services rendered therein by a county treasurer or the commissioner of finance of the city of New York are set forth in section eight thousand ten.

CPLR

1978 AMENDMENTS

L. 1978, ch. 655, eff. July 24, 1978, amended CPLR 3219 by substituting "commissioner of finance" wherever "finance administrator" appears.

1969 AMENDMENTS

L. 1969, ch. 407, eff. May 9, 1969, substituted "finance administrator" wherever "director of finance" appears.

1966 AMENDMENTS

L. 1966, ch. 581, eff. June 14, 1966, amended the first and second paragraphs of CPLR 3219 and added the third paragraph.

1965 AMENDMENTS

L. 1965, ch. 773, eff. Sept. 1, 1965, amended the first paragraph of CPLR 3219.

1964 AMENDMENTS

L. 1964, ch. 388, eff. Sept. 1, 1964, substituted the words "acknowledged statement" for the words "authenticated statement" in the fourth sentence of the first paragraph.

R 3220. Offer to liquidate damages conditionally.

At any time not later than ten days before trial, any party against whom a cause of action based upon contract, express or implied, is asserted may serve upon the claimant a written offer to allow judgment to be taken against him for a sum therein specified, with costs then accrued, if the party against whom the claim is asserted fails in his defense. If within ten days thereafter the claimant serves a written notice that he accepts the offer, and damages are awarded to him on the trial, they shall be assessed in the sum specified in the offer. If the offer is not so accepted and the claimant fails to obtain a more favorable judgment he shall pay the expenses necessarily incurred by the party against whom the claim is asserted, for trying the issue of damages from the time of the offer. The expenses shall be ascertained by the judge or referee before whom the case is tried. An offer under this rule shall not be made known to the jury.

R 3221. Offer to compromise.

Except in a matrimonial action, at any time not later than ten days before trial, any party against whom a claim is asserted, and against whom a separate judgment may be taken, may serve upon the claimant a written offer to allow judgment to be taken against him for a sum or property or to the effect therein specified, with costs then accrued. If within ten days thereafter the claimant serves a written notice that he accepts the offer, either party may file the summons, complaint and offer, with proof of acceptance, and thereupon the clerk shall enter judgment accordingly. If the offer is not accepted and the claimant fails to obtain a more favorable judgment, he shall not recover costs from the time of the offer, but shall pay costs from that time. An offer of judgment shall not be made known to the jury.

R 3222. Action on submitted facts.

(a) Commencement. An action, except a matrimonial action, may be commenced by filing with the clerk a submission of the controversy, acknowledged by all parties in the form required to entitle a deed to be recorded. The submission shall consist of a case, containing a statement of the facts upon which the controversy depends, and a statement that the controversy is real and that the submission is made in good faith for the purpose of determining the rights of the parties. If made to the supreme court, the submission shall specify the particular county clerk with whom the papers are to be filed.

(b) Subsequent proceedings. Subsequent proceedings shall be had according to the civil practice law and rules except that:

    1. an order of attachment or a preliminary injunction shall not be granted;

    2. the controversy shall be determined on the case alone;

    3. if the submission is made to the supreme court, it shall be heard and determined either by the court, or by the appellate division, or, with his consent, by a specified judge or referee, as the parties may stipulate;

    4. on such a submission the court, judge or referee may find facts by inference from the facts stipulated; and

    5. if the statement of facts in the case is not sufficient to enable the court to enter judgment the submission shall be dismissed or the court shall allow the filing of an additional statement.

1986 AMENDMENTS

L. 1986, ch. 355, eff. July 17, 1986, amended Subd. (b)(3) of CPLR 3222 to provide that submissions made to the Supreme Court can be heard and

CPLR

determined by that court in addition to the Appellate Division; reference to Special Term was deleted.

1984 AMENDMENTS

L. 1984, ch. 313, eff. July 3, 1984, amended CPLR 3222(b)(1) by deleting the reference to an order of arrest.

Article 34

CALENDAR PRACTICE; TRIAL PREFERENCES

R 3401. Rules for the hearing of causes.

The chief administrator of the courts shall adopt rules regulating the hearing of causes, which may include the filing of notes of issue, the preparation and publication of calendars and the calendar practice for the courts of the unified court system. Insofar as practicable, such rules within the city of New York shall be uniform.

1986 AMENDMENTS

L. 1986, ch. 355, eff. July 17, 1986, amended CPLR 3401, by changing the title to "Rules for the hearing of causes," and making other changes to reflect transfer of rule-making power from appellate divisions to the chief administrator of the courts.

R 3402. Note of issue.

(a) Placing case on calendar. At any time after issue is first joined, or at least forty days after service of a summons has been completed irrespective of joinder of issue, any party may place a case upon the calendar by filing, within ten days after service, with proof of such service two copies of a note of issue with the clerk and such other data as may be required by the applicable rules of the court in which the note is filed. The clerk shall enter the case upon the calendar as of the date of the filing of the note of issue.

(b) New parties. A party who brings in a new party shall within five days thereafter serve him with the note of issue and file a statement with the clerk advising him of the bringing in of such new party and of any change in the title of the action, with proof of service of the note of issue upon the new party, and of such statement upon all parties who have appeared in the action. The case shall retain its place upon the calendar unless the court otherwise directs.

1968 AMENDMENTS

L. 1968, ch. 19, eff. Sept. 1, 1968, increased from "five" to "ten" days the time specified in Subd. (a) within which a party may place a case upon the calendar after service of a note of issue.

R 3403. Trial preferences.

(a) Preferred cases. Civil cases shall be tried in the order in which notes of issue have been filed, but the following shall be entitled to a preference:

1. an action brought by or against the state, or a political subdivision of the state, or an officer or board of officers of the state or a political subdivision of the state, in his or its official capacity, on the application of the state, the political subdivision, or the officer or board of officers;

2. an action where a preference is provided for by statute; and

3. an action in which the interests of justice will be served by an early trial;

4. in any action upon the application of a party who has reached the age of seventy years.

5. an action to recover damages for medical, dental or podiatric malpractice.

6. an action to recover damages for personal injuries where the plaintiff is terminally ill and alleges that such terminal illness is a result of the conduct, culpability or negligence of the defendant.

(b) Obtaining preference. Unless the court otherwise orders, notice of a motion for preference shall be served with the note of issue by the party serving the note of issue, or ten days after such service by any other party; or thereafter during the pendency of the action upon the application of a party who reaches the age of seventy years, or who is terminally ill.

CPLR

CROSS REFERENCES

State Finance Law § 123-c provides that a citizen-taxpayer action shall have preference over all other causes in all courts.

1990 AMENDMENTS

L. 1990, ch. 670, eff. July 22, 1990, amended CPLR 3403 by adding a new paragraph (a)(6), granting trial preference to an action to recover damages for personal injuries where the plaintiff is terminally ill and alleges that the terminal illness is a result of the defendant's conduct, culpability or negligence, and by adding the words "or who is terminally ill" to the end of subdivision (b).

1986 AMENDMENTS

L. 1986, ch. 485, eff. July 21, 1986, and applicable to acts, omissions or failures occurring on or after such date, amended CPLR 3403(a)(5) to apply to podiatric malpractice actions.

1985 AMENDMENTS

L. 1985, ch. 760, eff. July 1, 1985, and applicable to any acts, omissions or failures occurring on or after that date, amended CPLR 3403(a)(5) to provide a trial preference for dental malpractice cases.

1979 AMENDMENTS

L. 1979, ch. 61, eff. April 9, 1979, amended CPLR 3403 subds. (a)(4) and (b) by changing the age requirement for trial preference from seventy five years to seventy years.

1975 AMENDMENTS

L. 1975, ch. 109, eff. July 1, 1975, amended Subd. (a) by adding new paragraph 5, providing a trial preference for medical malpractice cases. The amendment applies to acts of malpractice occurring on or after July 1, 1975.

1970 AMENDMENTS

L. 1970, ch. 907, eff. Sept. 1, 1970, added new subparagraph 4 to Subd. (a).

L. 1970, ch. 907, eff. Sept. 1, 1970, amended Subd. (b) by adding new language beginning with "or thereafter" to the end of the subdivision.

R 3404. Dismissal of abandoned cases.

A case in the supreme court or a county court marked "off" or struck from the calendar or unanswered on a clerk's calendar call, and not restored within one year thereafter, shall be deemed abandoned and shall be dismissed without costs for neglect to prosecute. The clerk shall make an appropriate entry without the necessity of an order.

R 3405. Arbitration of certain claims.

The chief judge of the court of appeals may promulgate rules for the arbitration of claims for the recovery of a sum of money not exceeding six thousand dollars, exclusive of interest, pending in any court or courts except the civil court of the city of New York, and not exceeding ten thousand dollars, exclusive of interest, pending in the civil court of the city of New York. Such rules must permit a jury trial de novo upon demand by any party following the determination of the arbitrators and may require the demander to pay the cost of arbitration; and shall also provide for all procedures necessary to initiate, conduct and determine the arbitration. A judgment may be entered upon the arbitration award. The rules shall further provide for the recruitment and qualifications of the arbitrators and for their compensation; except that such rules may authorize use of judicial hearing officers as arbitrators. All expenses for compensation, reimbursement and administration under this rule shall be a state charge to be paid out of funds appropriated to the administrative office for the courts for that purpose.

1992 AMENDMENTS

L. 1992, ch. 55, eff. April 10, 1992, amended this rule by providing that the rules promulgated by the chief judge of the Court of Appeals for the arbitration of certain claims may authorize use of judicial hearing officers as arbitrators.

1990 AMENDMENTS

L. 1990, ch. 30, eff. May 22, 1990, amended R. 3405, exempting the civil court for the city of New York from the $6,000 limitation and establishing an alternative $10,000 limitation for those courts.

1978 AMENDMENTS

L. 1978, ch. 156, eff. May 19, 1978, added § 3405.

R 3406. Mandatory filing and pre-calendar conference in dental, podiatric and medical malpractice actions.

(a) Mandatory filing. Not more than sixty days after issue is joined, the plaintiff in an action to recover damages for dental, medical or podiatric malpractice shall file with the clerk of the court in which the action is commenced a notice of dental, medical or podiatric malpractice action, on a form to be specified by the chief administrator of the courts. Together with such notice, the plaintiff shall file: (i) proof of service of such notice upon all other parties to the action; (ii) proof that, if demanded, authorizations to obtain medical, dental, podiatric and hospital records have been served upon the defendants in the action; and (iii) such other papers as may be required to be filed by rule of the chief administrator of the courts. The time for filing a notice of dental, medical or podiatric malpractice action may be extended by the court only upon a motion made pursuant to section two thousand four of this chapter.

(b) Pre-calendar conference. The chief administrator of the courts, in accordance with such standards and administrative policies as may be promulgated pursuant to section twenty-eight of article six of the constitution, shall adopt special calendar control rules for actions to recover damages for dental, podiatric or medical malpractice. Such rules shall require a pre-calendar conference in such an action, the purpose of which shall include, but not be limited to, encouraging settlement, simplifying or limiting issues and establishing a timetable for disclosure, establishing a timetable for offers and depositions pursuant to subparagraph (ii) of paragraph one of subdivision (d) of section thirty-one hundred one of this chapter, future conferences, and trial. The timetable for disclosure shall provide for the completion of disclosure not later than twelve months after the notice of dental, podiatric or medical malpractice is filed and shall require that all parties be ready for the trial of the case not later than eighteen months after such notice is filed. The initial pre-calendar conference shall be held after issue is joined in a case but before a note of issue is filed. To the extent feasible, the justice convening the pre-calendar conference shall hear and decide all subsequent pre-trial motions in the case and shall be assigned the trial of the case. The chief administrator of the courts also shall provide for the imposition of costs or other sanctions, including imposition of reasonable attorney's fees, dismissal of an action, claim, cross-claim, counterclaim or defense, or rendering a judgment by default for failure of a party or a party's attorney to comply with these special calendar control rules or any order of a court made thereunder. The chief administrator of the courts, in the exercise of discretion, may provide for exemption from the requirement of a pre-calendar conference in any judicial district or a county where there exists no demonstrated need for such conferences.

CROSS REFERENCES

See **22 N.Y.C.R.R. § 202.56 of the Uniform Rules** for the Supreme Court and County Court as to the form of the notice of medical, dental or podiatric malpractice action, and as to other special rules relevant to such actions.

1991 AMENDMENTS

L. 1991, ch. 165, eff. Oct. 1, 1991, amended CPLR 3406(b) by deleting the requirement that the initial pre-calendar conference be held before a medical malpractice panel hearing is scheduled. The October 1, 1991 effective date applies only to actions where, as of this date, the medical malpractice panel members have not signed and forwarded to all parties a formal written recommendation concerning the question of liability.

1988 AMENDMENTS

L. 1988, ch.184, eff. July 1, 1988, amended subdivision (b) and its heading to add podiatric cases to the scope of the rule; and to add scheduling of reciprocal expert depositions to the scope of the pre-trial conference.

1986 AMENDMENTS

L. 1986, ch. 485, eff. July 21, 1986, and applicable to acts, omissions or failures occurring on or after such date, amended CPLR 3406(a) to apply to podiatric malpractice actions.

1985 AMENDMENTS

L. 1985, ch. 294, eff. July 1, 1985, and applicable to any action for dental or medical malpractice commenced on or after such date, added Rule 3406.

R 3407. Preliminary conference in personal injury actions involving certain terminally ill parties.

(a) Request for conference. At any time, a party to an action who is terminally ill, and who asserts in a pleading in such action that such terminal illness is the result of the culpable conduct of another party to such action, may request an expedited preliminary conference in such action. Such request shall be filed in writing with the clerk of the court, and shall be accompanied by a physician's affidavit stating that the party is terminally ill, the nature of the terminal illness, and the duration of life expectancy of such party, if known. The court shall hold a preliminary conference in such action within twenty days after the filing of such a request.

(b) Preliminary conference.

1. At such preliminary conference, the court shall issue an order establishing a schedule for the completion of all discovery proceedings, to be completed within ninety days after the date of the preliminary conference, unless it can be demonstrated for good cause that a longer period is necessary.

2. At such preliminary conference, the court shall issue an order that a note of issue and certificate of readiness be filed in such action within a period of time specified in the order, that the action receive a preference in trial, and that the trial be commenced within one year from the date of such order. In its discretion, and upon application of any party, the court may advance or adjourn such trial date based on the circumstances of the case.

3. Notwithstanding the provisions of subdivision (b) of rule 3214 of this chapter, the service or pendency of a motion under rule 3211, 3212 or section 3213 of this chapter shall not stay disclosure in an action where a preliminary conference order has been entered pursuant to this rule.

1992 AMENDMENTS

L. 1992, ch. 582, eff. Sept. 1, 1992, added Rule 3407, which governs filings by terminally ill plaintiffs.

R 3408. Mandatory settlement conference in residential foreclosure actions.

(a) In any residential foreclosure action involving a high-cost home loan consummated between January first, two thousand three and September first, two thousand eight, or a subprime or nontraditional home loan, as those terms are defined under section thirteen hundred

CPLR

four of the real property actions and proceedings law, in which the defendant is a resident of the property subject to foreclosure, the court shall hold a mandatory conference within sixty days after the date when proof of service is filed with the county clerk, or on such adjourned date as has been agreed to by the parties, for the purpose of holding settlement discussions pertaining to the relative rights and obligations of the parties under the mortgage loan documents, including, but not limited to determining whether the parties can reach a mutually agreeable resolution to help the defendant avoid losing his or her home, and evaluating the potential for a resolution in which payment schedules or amounts may be modified or other workout options may be agreed to, and for whatever other purposes the court deems appropriate.

(b) At the initial conference held pursuant to this section, any defendant currently appearing pro se, shall be deemed to have made a motion to proceed as a poor person under section eleven hundred one of this chapter. The court shall determine whether such permission shall be granted pursuant to standards set forth in section eleven hundred one of this chapter. If the court appoints defendant counsel pursuant to subdivision (a) of section eleven hundred two of this chapter, it shall adjourn the conference to a date certain for appearance of counsel and settlement discussions pursuant to subdivision (a) of this section, and otherwise shall proceed with the conference.

(c) At any conference held pursuant to this section, the plaintiff shall appear in person or by counsel, and if appearing by counsel, such counsel shall be fully authorized to dispose of the case. The defendant shall appear in person or by counsel. If the defendant is appearing pro se, the court shall advise the defendant of the nature of the action and his or her rights and responsibilities as a defendant. Where appropriate, the court may permit a representative of the plaintiff to attend the settlement conference telephonically or by video-conference.

2008 AMENDMENTS

L. 2008, ch. 472, eff. Aug. 5, 2008, added CPLR R 3408 to provide that in a residential foreclosure action (where the defendant resides in the property) involving a high cost loan consummated between 1/1/03 and 9/1/08 or a subprime or non-traditional home loan, the court is required to schedule a settlement conference within 60 days after the filing of proof of service of the complaint. The amendment provides details of what is to transpire at such a conference. This is part of a more comprehensive amendment.

Article 40
TRIAL GENERALLY

SUMMARY OF ARTICLE

§ 4001. Powers of referees.

A court may appoint a referee to determine an issue, perform an act, or inquire and report in any case where this power was heretofore exercised and as may be hereafter authorized by law.

§§4002–4009. [Not used.]

§ 4010. [Repealed.]

R 4011. Sequence of trial.

The court may determine the sequence in which the issues shall be tried and otherwise regulate the conduct of the trial in order to achieve a speedy and unprejudiced disposition of the matters at issue in a setting of proper decorum.

R 4012. Marked pleadings furnished.

The party who has filed the note of issue shall furnish the judge who is to preside at the trial with copies of each pleading, where they have not been superseded by the pre-trial order, plainly marked to indicate which statements are admitted and which controverted by the responsive pleading.

R 4013. Trial elsewhere than at courthouse.

Upon stipulation of the parties, the judge who is to preside at the trial of an issue may direct trial in whole or in part at a specified place other than the courthouse.

R 4014. Duration of trial.

Notwithstanding the expiration of the term at which it was commenced, a trial shall continue until it is completed.

R 4015. Time for motion for referee or advisory jury.

A motion for trial by a referee or an advisory jury shall be made within twenty days after note of issue is filed, except where the issue to be tried arises on a motion or pursuant to a judgment.

R 4016. Opening and closing statements.

(a) Before any evidence is offered, an attorney for each plaintiff having a separate right, and an attorney for each defendant having a separate right, may make an opening statement. At the close of all the evidence on the issues tried, an attorney for each such party may make a closing statement in inverse order to opening statements.

(b) In any action to recover damages for personal injuries or wrongful death, the attorney for a party shall be permitted to make reference, during closing statement, to a specific dollar amount that the attorney believes to be appropriate compensation for any element of damage that is sought to be recovered in the action. In the event that an attorney makes such a reference in an action being tried by a jury, the court shall, upon the request of any party, during the court's instructions to the jury at the conclusion of all closing statements, instruct the jury that:

(1) the attorney's reference to such specific dollar amount is permitted as argument;

(2) the attorney's reference to a specific dollar amount is not evidence and should not be considered by the jury as evidence; and

(3) the determination of damages is solely for the jury to decide.

2004 AMENDMENTS

L. 2004, ch.372, eff. Aug. 17, 2004, amended subdivision (b) by eliminating the reference to opening statement.

2003 AMENDMENTS

L. 2003, ch. 694, eff. Nov. 27, 2003, amended CPLR R 4016 by redesignating the opening paragraph as subdivision (a) and adding subdivision (b).

§ 4017. Objections.

Formal exceptions to rulings of the court are unnecessary. At the time a ruling or order of the court is requested or made a party shall make known the action which he requests the court to take or, if he has not already indicated it, his objection to the action of the court. Failure to so make known objections, as prescribed in this section or in section 4110-b, may restrict review upon appeal in accordance with paragraphs three and four of subdivision (a) of section 5501.

1973 AMENDMENTS

L. 1973, ch. 233, eff. Sept. 1, 1973, amended CPLR 4017 by deleting the third sentence, and by inserting in the last sentence, "as prescribed in this section or in section 4110-b." See CPLR 4110-b, *below.*

R 4018. Increased damages.

Where increased damages are granted by statute, the decision, report or verdict shall specify the sum awarded as single damages, and judgment shall be entered for the increased amount.

R 4019. Recording in camera interviews of infants.

(a) A court shall not conduct an in camera interview of an infant in any action or proceeding to fix temporary or permanent custody or to modify judgments and orders of custody concerning marital separation, divorce, annulment of marriage and dissolution of marriage unless a stenographic record of such interview is made.

(b) If an appeal is taken to the appellate division from a judgment or order of the court on any such action or proceeding, the stenographic record of any such interview shall be made a part of the record and forwarded under seal to the appellate division.

1985 AMENDMENTS

L. 1985, ch. 785, eff. Aug. 1, 1985, and applicable to actions and proceedings conducted on or after that date, added CPLR 4019.

Article 41

TRIAL BY A JURY

CPLR

§ 4101. Issues triable by a jury revealed before trial.

In the following actions, the issues of fact shall be tried by a jury unless a jury trial is waived or a reference is directed under section 4317, except that equitable defenses and equitable counterclaims shall be tried by the court:

1. an action in which a party demands and sets forth facts which would permit a judgment for a sum of money only;

2. an action of ejectment; for dower; for waste; for abatement of and damages for a nuisance; to recover a chattel; or for determination of a claim to real property under article fifteen of the real property actions and proceedings law; and

3. any other action in which a party is entitled by the constitution or by express provision of law to a trial by jury.

§ 4102. Demand and waiver of trial by jury; specification of issues.

(a) Demand. Any party may demand a trial by jury of any issue of fact triable of right by a jury, by serving upon all other parties and filing a note of issue containing a demand for trial by jury. Any party served with a note of issue not containing such a demand may demand a trial by jury by serving upon each party a demand for a trial by jury and filing such demand in the office where the note of issue was filed within fifteen days after service of the note of issue. A demand shall not be accepted for filing unless a note of issue is filed in the action. If no party shall demand a trial by jury as provided herein, the right to trial by jury shall be deemed waived by all parties. A party may not withdraw a demand for trial by jury without the consent of the other parties, regardless of whether another party previously filed a note of issue without a demand for trial by jury.

(b) Specification of issues.   In his demand a party may specify the issues which he wishes tried by jury; otherwise he shall be deemed to have demanded trial by jury of all issues so triable. If he has demanded trial by jury of only some of the issues, any other party within ten days after service of the demand may serve and file a demand for trial by jury of any other issues in the action so triable.

(c) Waiver.   A party who has demanded the trial of an issue of fact by a jury under this section waives his right by failing to appear at the trial, by filing a written waiver with the clerk or by oral waiver in open court. A waiver does not withdraw a demand for trial by jury without the consent of the other parties. A party shall not be deemed to have waived the right to trial by jury of the issues of fact arising upon a claim, by joining it with another claim with respect to which there is no right to trial by jury and which is based upon a separate transaction; or of the issues of fact arising upon a counterclaim, cross-claim or third party claim, by asserting it in an action in which there is no right to trial by jury.

(d) Local rules.   The chief administrator of the courts may by rule provide that a party shall be deemed to have demanded trial by jury by filing a note of issue not containing an express waiver of trial by jury.

(e) Relief by court.   The court may relieve a party from the effect of failing to comply with this section if no undue prejudice to the rights of another party would result.

1990 AMENDMENTS

L. 1990, ch. 582, eff. Jan. 1, 1991, amended CPLR 4102(a) to provide that one party cannot withdraw a demand for a jury trial unless the other parties consent, even if another party previously filed a note of issue without a demand for a jury trial.

1986 AMENDMENTS

L. 1986, ch. 355, eff. July 17, 1986, amended CPLR 4102(d) to reflect the transfer of rule-making power from the appellate divisions to the chief administrator of the courts.

1968 AMENDMENTS

L. 1968, ch. 19, eff. Sept. 1, 1968, increased from "ten" to "fifteen" days the time specified in Subd. (a) within which a party must file a demand for a trial by jury after receipt of a note of issue not containing such demand.

§ 4103. Issues triable by a jury revealed at trial; demand and waiver of trial by jury.

When it appears in the course of a trial by the court that the relief required, although not originally demanded by a party, entitles the adverse party to a trial by jury of certain issues of fact, the court shall give the adverse party an opportunity to demand a jury trial of such issues. Failure to make such demand within the time limited by the court shall be deemed a waiver of the right to trial by jury. Upon such demand, the court shall order a jury trial of any issues of fact which are required to be tried by jury.

§ 4104. Number of jurors.

A jury shall be composed of six persons.

1972 AMENDMENTS

L. 1972, ch. 185, § 1, eff. May 28, 1972, repealed former Section 4104 and inserted a new Section 4104 in its place.

§ 4105. Persons who constitute the jury.

The first six persons who appear as their names are drawn and called, and are approved as indifferent between the parties, and not discharged or excused, must be sworn and constitute the jury to try the issue.

1972 AMENDMENTS

L. 1972, ch. 185, § 2, eff. May 28, 1972, amended CPLR 4105 by deleting the phrase "The first twelve, or, if a jury of six is demanded" that formerly appeared at the beginning of the Section.

§ 4106. Alternate jurors.

Unless the court, in its discretion, orders otherwise, one or two additional jurors, to be known as "alternate jurors," may be drawn upon the request of a party. Such jurors shall be drawn at the same time, from the same source, in the same manner, and have the same qualifications as the regular jurors, and be subject to the same examinations and challenges. They shall be seated with, take the oath with, and be treated in the same manner as the regular jurors, except that after final submission of the case, the court shall discharge the alternate jurors. If, before the final submission of the case, a regular juror dies, or becomes ill, or for any other reason is unable to perform his duty, the court may order him to be discharged and draw the name of an alternate, who shall replace the discharged juror in the jury box, and be treated as if he had been selected as one of the regular jurors.

1972 AMENDMENTS

L. 1972, ch. 336, eff. Sept. 1, 1972, amended CPLR 4106 by deleting the first sentence of the Section, which read, "The court, in its discretion, may direct the calling of one or two additional jurors, to be known as 'alternate jurors'," and substituting the present first sentence.

R 4107. Judge present at examination of jurors.

On application of any party, a judge shall be present at the examination of the jurors.

1964 AMENDMENTS

Amendment No. 7 made by the Judicial Conference Feb. 1, 1964, Report to the Legislature, effective Sept. 1, 1964, substituted the word "a" in place of "the" before the word "judge" for the reason: "This change is suggested in order to prevent an interpretation that the judge to be present at the voir dire must be 'the judge' assigned to try the case —an interpretation which could cause serious problems if such judge were then sitting at another trial. If this change is made, the specification of the particular judge to be present at voir dire will be left to implementing local court rules.

"The Judicial Conference is aware of the objections to Rule 4107 voiced by some judges who feel that a judge's presence at voir dire should be discretionary. On the other hand, there are situations on voir dire where the presence of a judge is essential in order to prevent serious harm. The Judicial Conference believes that the results of experience under the rule should be awaited before considering the advisability of its repeal. Its present proposal is designed to alleviate at least to some extent the problems which are involved in the courts in metropolitan centers when a judge's presence is required at the examination of jurors."

§ 4108. Challenges generally.

An objection to the qualifications of a juror must be made by a challenge unless the parties stipulate to excuse him. A challenge of a juror, or a challenge to the panel or array of jurors, shall be tried and determined by the court.

§ 4109. Peremptory challenges.

CPLR

The plaintiff or plaintiffs shall have a combined total of three peremptory challenges plus one peremptory challenge for every two alternate jurors. The defendant or defendants (other than any third-party defendant or defendants) shall have a combined total of three peremptory challenges, plus one peremptory challenge for every two alternate jurors. The court, in its discretion before the examination of jurors begins, may grant an equal number of additional challenges to both sides as may be appropriate. In any case where a side has two or more parties, the court, in its discretion, may allocate that side's combined total of peremptory challenges among those parties in such manner as may be appropriate.

1996 AMENDMENTS

L. 1996, ch. 655, eff. Oct. 24, 1996, and applicable only to actions and proceedings in which the examination of jurors begins on or after such effective date, amended the section to equalize the number of peremptory challenges for plaintiffs and defendants and added a new last sentence.

1972 AMENDMENTS

L. 1972, ch. 185, § 3, eff. May 28, 1972, amended CPLR 4109 by substituting "three" for "six" in the first sentence of the Section.

§ 4110. Challenges for cause.

(a) Challenge to the favor. The fact that a juror is in the employ of a party to the action; or if a party to the action is a corporation, that he is a shareholder or a stockholder therein; or, in an action for damages for injuries to person or property, that he is a shareholder, stockholder, director, officer or employee, or in any manner interested, in any insurance company issuing policies for protection against liability for damages for injury to persons or property; shall constitute a ground for a challenge to the favor as to such juror. The fact that a juror is a resident of, or liable to pay taxes in, a city, village, town or county which is a party to the action shall not constitute a ground for challenge to the favor as to such juror.

(b) Disqualification of juror for relationship. Persons shall be disqualified from sitting as jurors if related within the sixth degree by consanguinity or affinity to a party. The party related to the juror must raise the objection before the case is opened; any other party must raise the objection no later than six months after the verdict.

§ 4110-a. Competency of inhabitants as justices or jurors; undertakings not required of village.

In an action brought by or against a village it shall not be an objection against the person acting as justice or juror in such action that he is a resident of the village or subject to taxation therein. It shall not be necessary for the village to give a bond, undertaking or security to appeal or to obtain a provisional remedy, or to take or prevent any other proceeding; or to do or perform any act or thing notwithstanding any provision of any other law to the contrary, but the village shall be liable to the same extent as if it had given the bond, undertaking or security otherwise required by or in pursuance of law.

1972 AMENDMENTS

L. 1972, ch. 890, eff. Sept. 1, 1973, added new CPLR 4110-a.

§ 4110-b. Instructions to jury; objection.

At the close of the evidence or at such earlier time during the trial as the court reasonably directs, any party may file written requests that the court instruct the jury on the law as set forth in the requests. The court, out of the hearing of the jury, shall inform counsel of its proposed action upon the requests prior to their arguments to the jury, but the court shall instruct the jury after the arguments are completed. No party may assign as error the giving or the failure to give an instruction unless he objects thereto before the jury retires to consider its verdict stating the matter to which he objects and the grounds of his objection. Opportunity shall be given to make the objection out of the hearing of the jury.

1973 AMENDMENTS

L. 1973, ch. 233, eff. Sept. 1, 1973, added new CPLR 4110-b.

§ 4110-c. Trial jury; viewing of premises.

1. When during the course of a trial the court is of the opinion that a viewing or observation by the jury of the premises or place where alleged injuries to person or property were sustained in an accident or occurrence claimed to have been the cause thereof or of any other premises or place involved in the case will be helpful to the jury in determining any material factual issue, it may in its discretion, at any time before the commencement of the summations, order that the jury

CPLR

be conducted to such premises or place for such purpose in accordance with the provisions of this section.

2. In such case, the jury must be kept together throughout under the supervision of an appropriate public servant or servants appointed by the court, and the court itself must be present throughout. The parties to the action and counsel for them may as a matter of right be present throughout, but such right may be waived.

3. The purpose of such an inspection is solely to permit visual observation by the jury of the premises or place in question and neither the court, the parties, counsel nor the jurors may engage in discussion or argumentation concerning the significance or implications of anything under observation or concerning any issue in the case.

1982 AMENDMENTS

L. 1982, ch. 116, eff. Sept. 1, 1982, added new CPLR 4110-c.

R 4111. General and special verdicts and written interrogatories.

(a) General and special verdict defined. The court may direct the jury to find either a general verdict or a special verdict. A general verdict is one in which the jury finds in favor of one or more parties. A special verdict is one in which the jury finds the facts only, leaving the court to determine which party is entitled to judgment thereon.

(b) Special verdict. When the court requires a jury to return a special verdict, the court shall submit to the jury written questions susceptible of brief answer or written forms of the several findings which might properly be made or it shall use any other appropriate method of submitting the issues and requiring written findings thereon. The court shall give sufficient instruction to enable the jury to make its findings upon each issue. If the court omits any issue of fact raised by the pleadings or evidence, each party waives his right to a trial by jury of the issue so omitted unless before the jury retires he demands its submission to the jury. As to an issue omitted without demand, the court may make an express finding or shall be deemed to have made a finding in accordance with the judgment.

(c) General verdict accompanied by answers to interrogatories. When the court requires the jury to return a general verdict, it may also require written answers to written interrogatories submitted to the jury upon one or more issues of fact. The court shall give sufficient instruction to enable the jury to render a general verdict and to answer the interrogatories. When the answers are consistent with each other but one or more is inconsistent with the general verdict, the court shall direct the entry of judgment in accordance with the answers, notwithstanding the general verdict, or it shall require the jury to further consider its answers and verdict or it shall order a new trial. When the answers are inconsistent with each other and one or more is inconsistent with the general verdict, the court shall require the jury to further consider its answers and verdict or it shall order a new trial.

(d) Itemized verdict in medical, dental, or podiatric malpractice actions. In all actions seeking damages for medical, dental, or podiatric malpractice, or damages for wrongful death as a result of medical, dental, or podiatric malpractice, the court shall instruct the jury that if the jury finds a verdict awarding damages it shall in its verdict specify the applicable elements of special and general damages upon which the award is based and the amount assigned to each element, including but not limited to medical expenses, dental expenses, podiatric expenses, loss of earnings, impairment of earning ability, and pain and suffering. In all such actions, each element shall be further itemized into amounts intended to compensate for damages which have been incurred prior to the verdict and amounts intended to compensate for damages to be incurred in the future. In itemizing amounts intended to compensate for future wrongful death damages, future loss of services, and future loss of consortium, the jury shall return the total amount of damages for each such item. In itemizing amounts intended to compensate for future pain and suffering, the jury shall return the total amounts of damages for future pain and suffering and shall set forth the period of years over which such amounts are intended to provide compensation. In itemizing amounts intended to compensate for future economic and pecuniary damages other than in wrongful death actions, the jury shall set forth as to each item of damage, (i) the annual amount in current dollars, (ii) the period of years for which such compensation is applicable and the date of commencement for that item of damage, (iii) the growth rate applicable for the period of years for the item of damage, and (iv) a finding of whether the loss or item of damage is permanent. Where the needs change in the future for a particular item of damage, that change shall be submitted to the jury as a separate item

CPLR

of damage commencing at that time. In all such actions other than wrongful death actions, the jury shall be instructed that the findings it makes with reference to future economic damages, shall be used by the court to determine future damages which are payable to the plaintiff over time.

(e) Itemized verdict in certain actions against a public employer for personal injury and wrongful death. In an action against a public employer or a public employee who is subject to indemnification by a public employer with respect to such action or both, as such terms are defined in subdivision (b) of section forty-five hundred forty-five, for personal injury or wrongful death arising out of an injury sustained by a public employee while acting within the scope of his public employment or duties, the court shall instruct the jury that if the jury finds a verdict awarding damages it shall in its verdict specify the applicable elements of special and general damages upon which the award is based and the amount assigned to each element, including but not limited to medical expenses, loss of earnings, impairment of earning ability, and pain and suffering.

(f) Itemized verdict in certain actions. In an action brought to recover damages for personal injury, injury to property or wrongful death, which is not subject to subdivisions (d) and (e) of this rule, the court shall instruct the jury that if the jury finds a verdict awarding damages, it shall in its verdict specify the applicable elements of special and general damages upon which the award is based and the amount assigned to each element including, but not limited to, medical expenses, dental expenses, loss of earnings, impairment of earning ability, and pain and suffering. Each element shall be further itemized into amounts intended to compensate for damages that have been incurred prior to the verdict and amounts intended to compensate for damages to be incurred in the future. In itemizing amounts intended to compensate for future damages, the jury shall set forth the period of years over which such amounts are intended to provide compensation. In actions in which Article Fifty-A or Fifty-B of this chapter applies, in computing said damages, the jury shall be instructed to award the full amount of future damages, as calculated, without reduction to present value.

2003 AMENDMENTS

L. 2003, ch. 86, §§ 1, 4, eff. July 26, 2003, repealing and replacing subd. (d).

1994 AMENDMENTS

L. 1994, ch. 100, eff. May 16, 1994, amended CPLR 4111(d) and (f) by inserting the words "In actions in which Article Fifty-A or Fifty-B of this chapter applies."

1988 AMENDMENTS

L. 1988, ch. 184, eff. July 1, 1988, amended L. 1986, ch. 682, § 12, L. 1985, ch. 294, § 25, and L. 1984, ch. 701, § 5, to make subsections (d), (e), and (f) applicable to all actions in which trial has not begun as of August 1, 1988.

1986 AMENDMENTS

L. 1986, ch. 485, eff. July 21, 1986 and applicable to acts, omissions or failures occurring on or after such date, amended CPLR 4111(d) to apply to podiatric malpractice actions; L. 1986, ch. 682, eff. July 30, 1986, and applicable to actions commenced or claims filed on or after such date, amended CPLR 4111 by adding new Subd. (f) requiring an itemized verdict in certain actions to recover damages for personal injury, injury to property or wrongful death.

1985 AMENDMENTS

L. 1985, ch. 294, eff. July 1, 1985, and applicable to any action for dental or medical malpractice commenced on or after that date, and L. 1985, ch. 760, eff. July 1, 1985, and applicable to any acts, omissions or failures occurring on or after that date, amended subdivision (d) to apply to dental malpractice actions and to provide for further itemization as to past and future damages in medical or dental malpractice actions.

1984 AMENDMENTS

L. 1984, ch. 701, eff. Oct. 1, 1984, and applicable to all actions commenced on or after that date, added subdivision (e).

1976 AMENDMENTS

L. 1976, ch. 955, eff. Aug. 26, 1976, added subd. (d), providing for itemized verdicts in medical malpractice actions.

R 4112.   Entry of verdict.

When the jury renders a verdict, the clerk shall make an entry in his minutes specifying the time and place of the trial, the names of the jurors and witnesses, the general verdict and any answers to written interrogatories, or the questions and answers or other written findings constituting the special verdict and the direction, if any, which the court gives with respect to subsequent proceedings.

§ 4113.   Disagreement by jury.

(a) Unanimous verdict not required.   A verdict may be rendered by not less than five-sixths of the jurors constituting a jury.

(b) Procedure where jurors disagree.   Where five-sixths of the jurors constituting a jury cannot agree after being kept together for as long as is deemed reasonable by the court, the court shall discharge the jury and direct a new trial before another jury.

Article 42

TRIAL BY THE COURT

SUMMARY OF ARTICLE

CPLR

§ 4201. Powers of referees to report.

A referee to inquire and report shall have the power to issue subpoenas, to administer oaths and to direct the parties to engage in and permit such disclosure proceedings as will expedite the disposition of the issues.

R 4211. Issues to be decided by the court.

The court shall decide any issue not required to be tried by a jury unless it is referred to a referee to determine pursuant to section 4317.

1968 AMENDMENTS

Proposal No. 1, eff. Sept. 1, 1968, made by the Judicial Conference Feb. 1, 1968, Report to the Legislature, inserted cross-reference to "section" in place of reference to "rule" as mechanical correction.

R 4212. Advisory jury; referee to report.

Upon the motion of any party as provided in rule 4015 or on its own initiative, the court may submit any issue of fact required to be decided by the court to an advisory jury or upon a showing of some exceptional condition requiring it or in matters of account, to a referee to report. An order under this rule shall specify the issues to be submitted. The procedures to be followed in the use of an advisory jury shall be the same as those for a jury selected under article forty-one. Where no issues remain to be tried, the court shall render decision directing judgment in the action.

§ 4213. Decision of the court.

(a) Requests for findings. Before the case is finally submitted, the court shall afford the parties an opportunity to submit requests for findings of fact. Each request shall be numbered and so phrased that the court may conveniently pass upon it.

(b) Form of decision. The decision of the court may be oral or in writing and shall state the facts it deems essential. In a medical, dental or podiatric malpractice action or in an action against a public employer or a public employee who is subject to indemnification by a public employer with respect to such action or both, as such terms are defined in subdivision (b) of section forty-five hundred forty-five, for personal injury or wrongful death arising out of an injury sustained by a public employee while acting within the scope of his public employment or duties, and in any other action brought to recover damages for personal injury, injury to property, or wrongful death, a decision awarding damages shall specify the applicable elements of special and general damages upon which the award is based and the amount assigned to each element, including but not limited to medical expenses, dental expenses, podiatric expenses, loss of earnings, impairment of earning ability, and pain and suffering. In a medical, dental or podiatric malpractice action, and in any other action brought to recover damages for personal injury, injury to property, or wrongful death, each element shall be further itemized into amounts intended to compensate for damages which have been incurred prior to the decision and amounts intended to compensate for damages to be incurred in the future. In itemizing amounts intended to compensate for future damages, the court shall set forth the period of years over which such amounts are intended to provide compensation. In computing said damages, the court shall award the full amount of future damages, as calculated, without reduction to present value.

(c) Time for decision. The decision of the court shall be rendered within sixty days after the cause or matter is finally submitted or within sixty days after a motion under rule 4403, whichever is later, unless the parties agree to extend the time.

1986 AMENDMENTS

L. 1986, ch. 485, eff. July 21, 1986, and applicable to acts, omissions or failures occurring on or after such date, amended CPLR 4213(b) to apply to podiatric malpractice actions, and L. 1986, ch. 682, eff. July 30, 1986, and applicable to actions commenced or claims filed on or after such date, which amended CPLR 4213(b) without incorporating changes made by L. 1986, ch. 485, to apply to actions involving personal injury, injury to property or wrongful death.

1985 AMENDMENTS

L. 1985, ch. 294, eff. July 1, 1985, and applicable to any action for dental or medical malpractice commenced on or after that date, and L. 1985, ch. 760, eff. July 1, 1985, and applicable to any acts, omissions or failures occurring on or after that date, amended subdivision (b) to provide that a decision awarding damages in a medical or dental malpractice action include dental expenses in its specification of damages and further itemize as to past and future damages.

1984 AMENDMENTS

L. 1984, ch. 701, eff. Oct. 1, 1984, and applicable to all actions commenced on or after that date, amended subdivision (b) to provide that a decision awarding damages in an action against a public employer for personal injury or wrongful death itemize special and general damages constituting the award.

1976 AMENDMENTS

L. 1976, ch. 955, eff. Aug. 26, 1976, amended subd. (b) to provide that a decision awarding damages in a medical malpractice action itemize special and general damages constituting the award.

CPLR

CIVIL PRACTICE LAW AND RULES
Article 43
TRIAL BY A REFEREE

SUMMARY OF ARTICLE

§ 4301. Powers of referee to determine.

A referee to determine an issue or to perform an act shall have all the powers of a court in performing a like function; but he shall have no power to relieve himself of his duties, to appoint a successor or to adjudge any person except a witness before him guilty of contempt. For the purposes of this article the term referee shall be deemed to include judicial hearing officer.

43-1

1983 AMENDMENTS

L. 1983, ch. 840, eff. April 1, 1983, amended CPLR 4301.

1964 AMENDMENTS

L. 1964, ch. 388, eff. Sept. 1, 1964, changed the word "referees" in the caption to read "referee."

§§ 4302–4310.   [Not used.]

R 4311.   Order of reference.

An order of reference shall direct the referee to determine the entire action or specific issues, to report issues, to perform particular acts, or to receive and report evidence only. It may specify or limit the powers of the referee and the time for the filing of his report and may fix a time and place for the hearing.

R 4312.   Number of referees; qualifications.

1. A court may designate either one or three referees; provided, however, a judicial hearing officer may be designated a referee, in which case there shall be only one referee. Except by consent of the parties, no person shall be designated a referee unless he is an attorney admitted to practice in the state and in good standing. Where a referee may be designated by the parties, they may designate any number of referees.

2. Except in matrimonial actions or where the reference is to a judicial hearing officer, a person to whom all the parties object may not be designated as a referee. In matrimonial actions, only a judicial hearing officer or a special referee appointed by the chief administrator of the courts may be designated to determine an issue. In a matrimonial action the court shall not order a reference to a referee nominated by a party.

3. No person shall serve as referee who holds the position of court clerk, or clerk, secretary or stenographer to a judge; or who is the partner or clerk of an attorney for any party to the action or occupies the same office with such attorney except as provided in paragraph five of this rule.

4. A judge shall not serve as a referee in an action brought in a court of which he is a judge except by the written consent of the parties, and,

in that case, he cannot receive any compensation as referee.

5. In uncontested matrimonial actions, a court clerk, law secretary, or any other non-judicial employee of the court, who is an attorney in good standing admitted to practice in the state, may be appointed by an administrative judge to serve without fee as a referee for the purpose of hearing and reporting to the court.

1983 AMENDMENTS

L. 1983, ch. 840, eff. April 1, 1983, amended CPLR 4312(1) and (2).

1980 AMENDMENTS

L. 1980, ch. 187, eff. June 2, 1980, made permanent the changes in CPLR 4312 enacted by the 1976 Legislature and extended by the 1978 Legislature relating to the appointment of referees in uncontested matrimonial actions. See comments at 1976 amendment notes.

1976 AMENDMENTS

L. 1976, ch. 699, eff. Sept. 1, 1976, and to remain in force and effect until August 31, 1978 [extended to August 30, 1980 by L. 1978, ch. 94, eff. April 25, 1978.] added a new paragraph (5) and a cross-reference thereto in paragraph (3).

Amendment recommended by the Judicial Conference in its report to the 1976 Legislature, wherein it stated, in part:

"The statistics of the Tenth Judicial District (Nassau and Suffolk Counties) strikingly indicate the large numbers of uncontested matrimonial processed by the courts. In that District the court disposed of 4,732 uncontested matrimonial actions in 1974 as contrasted with 2,291 in 1971; the statistical estimate is that the present workload of these cases consumes the full time of three judges. The time that a judge spends in these cases can be more effectively utilized and may be conserved by the appointment of a referee to hear and report, with the determination by the court.

"The power of appointment is vested in the administrative judge to facilitate speedy implementation as the need arises, since he is acquainted with local calendar conditions and availability of personnel for immediate assignment without disruption of other functions.

"This amendment is supplementary to, and in no way diminishes or affects the existing power of the Appellate Division, pursuant to CPLR 4312(2) and 4317 to designate special referees, who also may be court personnel such as law assistants, to hear and determine matrimonial actions without fee. It would, however, facilitate references to hear and report in uncontested matrimonial actions by permitting a more flexible use of qualified court personnel by an administrative judge."

R 4313. Notice.

CPLR

Except where the reference is to a judicial hearing officer or a special referee, upon the entry of an order of reference, the clerk shall send a copy of the order to the referee. Unless the order of reference otherwise provides, the referee shall forthwith notify the parties of a time and place for the first hearing to be held within twenty days after the date of the order or shall forthwith notify the court that he declines to serve.

1983 AMENDMENTS

L. 1983, ch. 840, eff. April 1, 1983, amended CPLR 4313.

R 4314.   Successor referee.

Upon being notified that a referee declines or fails to serve, or in case of death, resignation or removal of a referee, or if a new trial is granted after a reference, on motion of any party or on its own initiative, the court may designate a successor referee, unless a stipulation upon which the order of reference is based expressly provides otherwise.

R 4315.   Referee to be sworn.

A referee, other than a judicial hearing officer or a special referee, before entering upon his duties, shall be sworn faithfully and fairly to do such acts and make such determination and report as the order requires. The oath may be administered by any person authorized to take acknowledgments of deeds by the real property law. The oath may be waived upon consent of all parties.

1983 AMENDMENTS

L. 1983, ch. 840, eff. April 1, 1983, amended CPLR 4315.

R 4316.   Procedure where more than one referee.

Where the reference is to more than one referee all must meet together and hear all the allegations and proofs of the parties; but a majority may appoint a time and place for the trial, decide any question which arises upon the trial, sign a report or settle a case. Any of them may administer an oath to a witness; and a majority of those present at a time and place appointed for the trial may adjourn the trial to a future day.

§ 4317. When reference to determine may be used.

(a) Upon consent of the parties. The parties may stipulate that any issue shall be determined by a referee. Upon the filing of the stipulation with the clerk, the clerk shall forthwith enter an order referring the issue for trial to the referee named therein. Where the stipulation does not name a referee, the court shall designate a referee. Leave of court and designation by it of the referee is required for references in matrimonial actions; actions against a corporation to obtain a dissolution, to appoint a receiver of its property, or to distribute its property, unless such action is brought by the attorney-general; or actions where a defendant is an infant.

(b) Without consent of the parties. On motion of any party or on its own initiative, the court may order a reference to determine a cause of action or an issue where the trial will require the examination of a long account, including actions to foreclose mechanic's liens; or to determine an issue of damages separately triable and not requiring a trial by jury; or where otherwise authorized by law.

(c) Transcript. Unless otherwise stipulated, a transcript of the testimony together with the exhibits or copies thereof of the issue heard before the referee shall be provided to all the parties involved upon payment of appropriate fees.

2006 AMENDMENTS

L. 2006, ch. 582, § 1, eff. Aug. 16, 2006, added CPLR 4317(c) providing that, in the context of a Supreme Court order referring an issue or cause of action to a referee to determine pursuant to CPLR 4317, a transcript of the proceedings and exhibits is to be provided to all the parties upon payment of appropriate fees.

§ 4318. Conduct of trial.

Unless otherwise specified in the order of reference, the referee shall conduct the trial in the same manner as a court trying an issue without a jury. The provisions of article forty-four applicable to trial by the court shall apply to a reference pursuant to this article.

1964 AMENDMENTS

L. 1964, ch. 388, eff. Sept. 1, 1964, substituted the word "article" for the word "rule" at the end of the last sentence.

§ 4319. Decision.

CPLR

The decision of a referee shall comply with the requirements for a decision by the court and shall stand as the decision of a court. Unless otherwise specified in the order of reference, the referee shall file his decision within thirty days after the cause or matter is finally submitted. If it is not filed within the required time, upon the motion of a party before it is filed, the court may grant a new trial and, in that event, the referee shall not be entitled to any fees.

§ 4320. Reference to report.

(a) Conduct of trial. A referee to report shall conduct the trial in the same manner as a court trying an issue without a jury.

(b) Report; transcript. The referee shall file his report, setting forth findings of fact and conclusions of law, within thirty days after the cause or matter is finally submitted. Unless otherwise stipulated, a transcript of the testimony together with the exhibits or copies thereof shall be filed with the report.

R 4321. Fees and expenses.

1. An order or a stipulation for a reference shall determine the basis and method of computing the referee's fees and provide for their payment. The court may make an appropriate order for the payment of the reasonable expenses of the referee. Unless the court otherwise orders or the stipulation otherwise provides, such fees and expenses of the referee shall be taxed as costs.

2. This section shall not apply where the reference is to a judicial hearing officer.

1983 AMENDMENTS

L. 1983, ch. 840, eff. April 1, 1983, amended CPLR 4321 by numbering the opening paragraph (1) and adding a new subdivision (2).

Article 44
TRIAL MOTIONS

SUMMARY OF ARTICLE

R 4401. Motion for judgment during trial.

Any party may move for judgment with respect to a cause of action or issue upon the ground that the moving party is entitled to judgment as a matter of law, after the close of the evidence presented by an opposing party with respect to such cause of action or issue, or at any time on the basis of admissions. Grounds for the motion shall be specified. The motion does not waive the right to trial by jury or to present further evidence even where it is made by all parties.

§ 4401-a. Motion for judgment.

A motion for judgment at the end of the plaintiff's case must be granted as to any cause of action for medical malpractice based solely on lack of informed consent if the plaintiff has failed to adduce expert medical testimony in support of the alleged qualitative insufficiency of the consent.

CROSS REFERENCES

See **Public Health Law § 2805-d in Appendix,** *below,* as to limitation of medical malpractice action based upon lack of informed consent.

1975 AMENDMENTS

L. 1975, ch. 109, eff. July 1, 1975, added section 4401–a. The new section applies to acts of malpractice occurring on or after July 1, 1975.

R 4402.   Motion for continuance or new trial during trial.

At any time during the trial, the court, on motion of any party, may order a continuance or a new trial in the interest of justice on such terms as may be just.

R 4403.   Motion for new trial or to confirm or reject or grant other relief after reference to report or verdict of advisory jury.

Upon the motion of any party or on his own initiative, the judge required to decide the issue may confirm or reject, in whole or in part, the verdict of an advisory jury or the report of a referee to report; may make new findings with or without taking additional testimony; and may order a new trial or hearing. The motion shall be made within fifteen days after the verdict or the filing of the report and prior to further trial in the action. Where no issues remain to be tried the court shall render decision directing judgment in the action.

R 4404.   Post-trial motion for judgment and new trial.

(a) Motion after trial where jury required. After a trial of a cause of action or issue triable of right by a jury, upon the motion of any party or on its own initiative, the court may set aside a verdict or any judgment entered thereon and direct that judgment be entered in favor of a party entitled to judgment as a matter of law or it may order a new trial of a cause of action or separable issue where the verdict is contrary to the weight of the evidence, in the interest of justice or where the jury cannot agree after being kept together for as long as is deemed reasonable by the court.

(b) Motion after trial where jury not required. After a trial not triable of right by a jury, upon the motion of any party or on its own initiative, the court may set aside its decision or any judgment entered thereon. It may make new findings of fact or conclusions of law, with or without taking additional testimony, render a new decision and direct entry of judgment, or it may order a new trial of a cause of action or separable issue.

R 4405. Time and judge before whom post-trial motion made.

A motion under this article shall be made before the judge who presided at the trial within fifteen days after decision, verdict or discharge of the jury. The court shall have no power to grant relief after argument or submission of an appeal from the final judgment.

1965 AMENDMENTS

L. 1965, ch. 673, eff. July 2, 1965, deleted the word "rule" and substituted therefor the word "article" in the first sentence.

R 4406. Single post-trial motion.

In addition to motions made orally immediately after decision, verdict or discharge of the jury, there shall be only one motion under this article with respect to any decision by a court, or to a verdict on issues triable of right by a jury; and each party shall raise by the motion or by demand under rule 2215 every ground for post-trial relief then available to him.

CPLR

Article 45

EVIDENCE

CPLR

CPLR

§ 4501. Self-incrimination.

A competent witness shall not be excused from answering a relevant question, on the ground only that the answer may tend to establish that he owes a debt or is otherwise subject to a civil suit. This section does not require a witness to give an answer which will tend to accuse himself of a crime or to expose him to a penalty or forfeiture, nor does it vary any other rule respecting the examination of a witness.

§ 4502. Spouse.

(a) Incompetency where issue adultery. A husband or wife is not competent to testify against the other in an action founded upon adultery, except to prove the marriage, disprove the adultery, or disprove a defense after evidence has been introduced tending to prove such defense.

(b) Confidential communication privileged. A husband or wife shall not be required, or, without consent of the other if living, allowed, to disclose a confidential communication made by one to the other during marriage.

§ 4503. Attorney.

(a) 1. Confidential communication privileged. Unless the client waives the privilege, an attorney or his or her employee, or any person who obtains without the knowledge of the client evidence of a confidential communication made between the attorney or his or her employee and the client in the course of professional employment, shall not disclose, or be allowed to disclose such communication, nor shall the client be compelled to disclose such communication, in any action, disciplinary trial or hearing, or administrative action, proceeding or hearing conducted by or on behalf of any state, municipal or local governmental agency or by the legislature or any committee or body thereof. Evidence of any such communication obtained by any such person, and evidence resulting therefrom, shall not be disclosed by any state, municipal or local governmental agency or by the legislature or any committee or body thereof. The relationship of an attorney and client shall exist between a professional service corporation organized under article fifteen of the business corporation law to practice as an attorney and counselor-at-law and the clients to whom it renders legal services.

2. (A) Personal representatives. For purposes of the attorney-client privilege, if the client is a personal representative and the attorney represents the personal representative in that capacity, in the absence of an agreement between the attorney and the personal representative to the contrary:

(i) No beneficiary of the estate is, or shall be treated as, the client of the attorney solely by reason of his or her status as beneficiary; and

(ii) The existence of a fiduciary relationship between the personal representative and a beneficiary of the estate does not by itself constitute or give rise to any waiver of the privilege for confidential communications made in the course of professional employment between the attorney or his or her employee and the personal representative who is the client.

(B) For purposes of this paragraph, "personal representative" shall mean (i) the administrator, administrator c.t.a., ancillary administrator, executor, preliminary executor, temporary administrator or trustee to whom letters have been issued within the meaning of subdivision thirty-four of section one hundred three of the surrogate's court procedure act, and (ii) the guardian of an incapacitated communicant if and to the extent that the order appointing such guardian under subdivision (c) of section 81.16 of the mental hygiene law or any subsequent order of any court expressly provides that the guardian is to be the personal representative of the incapacitated communicant for purposes of this section; "beneficiary" shall have the meaning set forth in subdivision eight of section one hundred three of the surrogate's court procedure act and "estate" shall have the meaning set forth in subdivision nineteen of section one hundred three of the surrogate's court procedure act.

(b) Wills. In any action involving the probate, validity or construction of a will, an attorney or his employee shall be required to disclose information as to the preparation, execution or revocation of any will or other relevant instrument, but he shall not be allowed to disclose any communication privileged under subdivision (a) which would tend to disgrace the memory of the decedent.

2002 AMENDMENTS

L. 2002, ch. 430, § 1, eff. Aug. 20, 2002, amended subdivision (a) by deleting reference in title of subdivision to "nonjudicial proceedings", making language gender neutral, and renumbering existing subdivision (a) as subparagraph (1), and adding new subparagraph (2) titled "Personal representatives".

1977 AMENDMENTS

L. 1977, ch. 418, eff. July 12, 1977, amended CPLR 4503(a) by adding the last sentence.

§ 4504. Physician, dentist, podiatrist, chiropractor and nurse.

(a) Confidential information privileged. Unless the patient waives the privilege, a person authorized to practice medicine, registered professional nursing, licensed practical nursing, dentistry, podiatry or chiropractic shall not be allowed to disclose any information which he acquired in attending a patient in a professional capacity, and which was necessary to enable him to act in that capacity. The relationship of a physician and patient shall exist between a medical corporation, as defined in article forty-four of the public health law, a professional service corporation organized under article fifteen of the business corporation law to practice medicine, a university faculty practice corporation organized under section fourteen hundred twelve of the not-for-profit corporation law to practice medicine or dentistry, and the patients to whom they respectively render professional medical services.

A patient who, for the purpose of obtaining insurance benefits, authorizes the disclosure of any such privileged communication to any person shall not be deemed to have waived the privilege created by this subdivision. For purposes of this subdivision:

    1. "person" shall mean any individual, insurer or agent thereof, peer review committee, public or private corporation, political subdivision, government agency, department or bureau of the state, municipality, industry, co-partnership, association, firm, trust, estate or any other legal entity whatsoever; and

    2. "insurance benefits" shall include payments under a self-insured plan.

(b) Identification by dentist; crime committed against patient under sixteen. A dentist shall be required to disclose information necessary for identification of a patient. A physician, dentist, podiatrist, chiropractor or nurse shall be required to disclose information indicating that a patient who is under the age of sixteen years has been the victim of a crime.

(c) Mental or physical condition of deceased patient. A physician or nurse shall be required to disclose any information as to the mental or physical condition of a deceased patient privileged under subdivision (a), except information which would tend to disgrace the memory of the decedent, either in the absence of an objection by a party to the litigation or when the privilege has been waived:

    1. by the personal representative, or the surviving spouse, or the next of kin of the decedent; or

    2. in any litigation where the interests of the personal representative are deemed by the trial judge to be adverse to those of the estate of the decedent, by any party in interest; or

    3. if the validity of the will of the decedent is in question, by the executor named in the will, or the surviving spouse or any heir-at-law or any of the next of kin or any other party in interest.

(d) Proof of negligence; unauthorized practice of medicine. In any action for damages for personal injuries or death against a person not authorized to practice medicine under article 131 of the education law for any act or acts constituting the practice of medicine, when such act or acts were a competent producing proximate or contributing cause of such injuries or death, the fact that such person practiced medicine without being so authorized shall be deemed prima facie evidence of negligence.

CROSS REFERENCES

See **Penal Law § 265.25,** which requires that certain wounds be reported to police authorities by the attending physician or hospital representative.

1993 AMENDMENTS

L. 1993, ch. 555, eff. July 28, 1993, amended CPLR 4504(a) to include not-for-profit university faculty practice corporations licensed to practice medicine or dentistry.

1991 AMENDMENTS

L. 1991, ch. 457, eff. July 19, 1991, amended CPLR 4504 by adding the references to "podiatrist" and "podiatry."

1990 AMENDMENTS

L. 1990, ch. 800, eff. July 25, 1990, amended CPLR 4504 by adding the references to "chiropractor" and "chiropractic."

1984 AMENDMENTS

L. 1984, ch. 913, eff. Oct. 5, 1984, amended CPLR 4504(a) to provide that the authorization of disclosure of any privileged communication for the purpose of obtaining insurance benefits shall not be deemed a waiver of the privilege created by the subdivision.

1971 AMENDMENTS

L. 1971, ch. 1139, eff. July 6, 1971, amended CPLR 4504(a) by creating a physician-patient relationship between a medical corporation, as defined in Public Health Law article 44, a professional service corporation organized under Business Corporation Law article 15, and the patients to whom they respectively render professional medical services.

L. 1971, ch. 987, eff. Sept. 1, 1971, amended CPLR 4504 by adding a new subdivision (d).

1966 AMENDMENTS

L. 1966, ch. 252, eff. Sept. 1, 1966, amended Subd. (a) by adding the words "registered professional nursing, licensed practical nursing" after the phrase "a person authorized to practice medicine" and deleted the words "or a registered professional or licensed practical nurse" after the words "or dentistry."

§ 4505. Confidential communication to clergy privileged.

Unless the person confessing or confiding waives the privilege, a clergyman, or other minister of any religion or duly accredited Christian Science practitioner, shall not be allowed to disclose a confession or confidence made to him in his professional character as spiritual advisor.

1965 AMENDMENTS

L. 1965, ch. 520, eff. June 28, 1965, added the words "or confiding," "or duly accredited Christian Science practitioner," and "or confidence" to the section.

§ 4506. Eavesdropping evidence; admissibility; motion to suppress in certain cases.

1. The contents of any overheard or recorded communication, conversation or discussion, or evidence derived therefrom, which has been obtained by conduct constituting the crime of eavesdropping, as defined by section 250.05 of the penal law, may not be received in evidence in any trial, hearing or proceeding before any court or grand jury, or before any legislative committee, department, officer, agency, regulatory body, or other authority of the state, or a political subdivision thereof; provided, however, that such communication, conversation, discussion or evidence, shall be admissible in any civil or criminal trial, hearing or proceeding against a person who has, or is alleged to have, committed such crime of eavesdropping.

2. As used in this section, the term "aggrieved person" means:

(a) A person who was a sender or receiver of a telephonic or telegraphic communication which was intentionally overheard or recorded by a person other than the sender or receiver thereof, without the consent of the sender or receiver, by means of any instrument, device or equipment; or

(b) A party to a conversation or discussion which was intentionally overheard or recorded, without the consent of at least one party thereto, by a person not present thereat, by means of any instrument, device or equipment; or

(c) A person against whom the overhearing or recording described in paragraphs (a) and (b) was directed.

CPLR

3. An aggrieved person who is a party in any civil trial, hearing or proceeding before any court, or before any department, officer, agency, regulatory body, or other authority of the state, or a political subdivision thereof, may move to suppress the contents of any overheard or recorded communication, conversation or discussion or evidence derived therefrom, on the ground that:

(a) The communication, conversation or discussion was unlawfully overheard or recorded; or

(b) The eavesdropping warrant under which it was overheard or recorded is insufficient on its face; or

(c) The eavesdropping was not done in conformity with the eavesdropping warrant.

4. The motion prescribed in subdivision three of this section must be made before the judge or justice who issued the eavesdropping warrant. If no eavesdropping warrant was issued, such motion must be made before a justice of the supreme court of the judicial district in which the trial, hearing or proceeding is pending. The aggrieved person must allege in his motion papers that an overheard or recorded communication, conversation or discussion, or evidence derived therefrom, is subject to suppression under subdivision three of this section, and that such communication, conversation or discussion, or evidence, may be used against him in the civil trial, hearing or proceeding in which he is a party. The motion must be made prior to the commencement of such trial, hearing or proceeding, unless there was no opportunity to make such motion or the aggrieved person was not aware of the grounds of the motion. If the motion is granted, the contents of the overheard or recorded communication, conversation or discussion or evidence derived therefrom, may not be received in evidence in any trial, hearing or proceeding.

1969 AMENDMENTS

L. 1969, ch. 1147, eff. June 25, 1969, repealed section 4506 and added new section 4506.

§ 4507. Psychologist.

The confidential relations and communications between a psychologist registered under the provisions of article one hundred fifty-three of the education law and his client are placed on the same basis as those provided by law between attorney and client, and nothing in such article shall be construed to require any such privileged communications to be disclosed.

A client who, for the purpose of obtaining insurance benefits, authorizes the disclosure of any such privileged communication to any person shall not be deemed to have waived the privilege created by this section. For purposes of this section:

    1. "person" shall mean any individual, insurer or agent thereof, peer review committee, public or private corporation, political subdivision, government agency, department or bureau of the state, municipality, industry, co-partnership, association, firm, trust, estate or any other legal entity whatsoever; and

    2. "insurance benefits" shall include payments under a self-insured plan.

CPLR

1984 AMENDMENTS

L. 1984, ch. 913, eff. Oct. 5, 1984, amended CPLR 4507 to provide that the authorization of disclosure of any privileged communication for the purpose of obtaining insurance benefits shall not be deemed a waiver of the privilege created by the section.

1968 AMENDMENTS

L. 1968, ch. 274, eff. May 14, 1968, added CPLR 4507 and CPLR 4508.

§ 4508. Social worker.

(a) Confidential information privileged. Confidential information privileged. A person licensed as a licensed master social worker or a licensed clinical social worker under the provisions of article one hundred fifty-four of the education law shall not be required to disclose a communication made by a client, or his or her advice given thereon, in the course of his or her professional employment, nor shall any clerk, stenographer or other person working for the same employer as such social worker or for such social worker be allowed to disclose any such communication or advice given thereon; except

    1. that such social worker may disclose such information as the client may authorize;

    2. that such social worker shall not be required to treat as confidential a communication by a client which reveals the contemplation of a crime or harmful act;

3. where the client is a child under the age of sixteen and the information acquired by such social worker indicates that the client has been the victim or subject of a crime, the social worker may be required to testify fully in relation thereto upon any examination, trial or other proceeding in which the commission of such crime is a subject of inquiry;

4. where the client waives the privilege by bringing charges against such social worker and such charges involve confidential communications between the client and the social worker.

(b) Limitations on waiver. A client who, for the purpose of obtaining insurance benefits, authorizes the disclosure of any such privileged communication to any person shall not be deemed to have waived the privilege created by this section. For purposes of this subdivision:

1. "person" shall mean any individual, insurer or agent thereof, peer review committee, public or private corporation, political subdivision, government agency, department, or bureau of the state, municipality, industry, co-partnership, association, firm, trust, estate or any other legal entity whatsoever; and

2. "insurance benefits" shall include payments under a self-insured plan.

2004 AMENDMENTS
L. 2004, ch. 230, §1, eff. July 27, 2004, rewording subd. (a).

1985 AMENDMENTS
L. 1985, ch. 96, eff. July 20, 1985, deleted the cross reference to Education Law § 7707 and added subdivision (b).

1968 AMENDMENTS
L. 1968, ch. 274, eff. May 14, 1968, added CPLR 4508.

§ 4509. Library records.

Library records, which contain names or other personally identifying details regarding the users of public, free association, school, college and university libraries and library systems of this state, including but not limited to records related to the circulation of library materials, computer database searches, interlibrary loan transactions, reference queries, requests for photocopies of library materials, title reserve requests, or the use of audio-visual materials, films or records, shall be confidential and shall not be disclosed except that such records may be disclosed to the extent necessary for the proper operation of such library and shall be disclosed upon request or consent of the user or pursuant to subpoena, court order or where otherwise required by statute.

1988 AMENDMENTS

L. 1988, ch. 112, eff. June 13, 1988, amended § 4509 to eliminate the restriction to "circulation" records, broadening the category of records deemed confidential.

1982 AMENDMENTS

L. 1982, ch. 14, eff. March 10, 1982, added new CPLR 4509.

§ 4510. Rape crisis counselor.

(a) Definitions. When used in this section, the following terms shall have the following meanings:

1. "Rape crisis program" means any office, institution or center which has been approved pursuant to subdivision fifteen of section two hundred six of the public health law, offering counseling and assistance to clients concerning sexual offenses, sexual abuses or incest.

2. "Rape crisis counselor" means any person who has been certified by an approved rape crisis program as having satisfied the training standards specified in subdivision fifteen of section two hundred six of the public health law, and who, regardless of compensation, is acting under the direction and supervision of an approved rape crisis program.

3. "Client" means any person who is seeking or receiving the services of a rape crisis counselor for the purpose of securing counseling or assistance concerning any sexual offenses, sexual abuse, incest or attempts to commit sexual offenses, sexual abuse, or incest, as defined in the penal law.

(b) Confidential information privileged. A rape crisis counselor shall not be required to disclose a communication made by his or her client to him or her, or advice given thereon, in the course of his or her services nor shall any clerk, stenographer or other person working for the same program as the rape crisis counselor or for the rape crisis counselor be allowed to disclose any such communication or advice

CPLR

given thereon nor shall any records made in the course of the services given to the client or recording of any communications made by or to a client be required to be disclosed, nor shall the client be compelled to disclose such communication or records, except:

1. that a rape crisis counselor may disclose such otherwise confidential communication to the extent authorized by the client;

2. that a rape crisis counselor shall not be required to treat as confidential a communication by a client which reveals the intent to commit a crime or harmful act;

3. in a case in which the client waives the privilege by instituting charges against the rape crisis counselor or the rape crisis program and such action or proceeding involves confidential communications between the client and the rape crisis counselor.

(c) Who may waive the privilege. The privilege may only be waived by the client, the personal representative of a deceased client, or, in the case of a client who has been adjudicated incompetent or for whom a conservator has been appointed, the committee or conservator.

(d) Limitation on waiver. A client who, for the purposes of obtaining compensation under article twenty-two of the executive law or insurance benefits, authorizes the disclosure of any privileged communication to an employee of the crime victims board or an insurance representative shall not be deemed to have waived the privilege created by this section.

1993 AMENDMENTS

L. 1993, ch. 432, eff. Jan. 22, 1994, added new CPLR 4510.

R 4511.   Judicial notice of law.

(a) When judicial notice shall be taken without request. Every court shall take judicial notice without request of the common law, constitutions and public statutes of the United States and of every state, territory and jurisdiction of the United States and of the official compilation of codes, rules and regulations of the state except those that relate solely to the organization or internal management of an agency of the state and of all local laws and county acts.

(b) When judicial notice may be taken without request; when it shall be taken on request. Every court may take judicial notice without request of private acts and resolutions of the congress of the United States and of the legislature of the state; ordinances and regulations of officers, agencies or governmental subdivisions of the state or of the United States; and the laws of foreign countries or their political subdivisions. Judicial notice shall be taken of matters specified in this subdivision if a party requests it, furnishes the court sufficient information to enable it to comply with the request, and has given each adverse party notice of his intention to request it. Notice shall be given in the pleadings or prior to the presentation of any evidence at the trial, but a court may require or permit other notice.

(c) Determination by court; review as matter of law. Whether a matter is judicially noticed or proof is taken, every matter specified in this section shall be determined by the judge or referee, and included in his findings or charged to the jury. Such findings or charge shall be subject to review on appeal as a finding or charge on a matter of law.

(d) Evidence to be received on matter to be judicially noticed. In considering whether a matter of law should be judicially noticed and in determining the matter of law to be judicially noticed, the court may consider any testimony, document, information or argument on the subject, whether offered by a party or discovered through its own research. Whether or not judicial notice is taken, a printed copy of a statute or other written law or a proclamation, edict, decree or ordinance by an executive contained in a book or publication, purporting to have been published by a government or commonly admitted as evidence of the existing law in the judicial tribunals of the jurisdiction where it is in force, is prima facie evidence of such law and the unwritten or common law of a jurisdiction may be proved by witnesses or printed reports of cases of the courts of the jurisdiction.

§ 4512. Competency of interested witness or spouse.

Except as otherwise expressly prescribed, a person shall not be excluded or excused from being a witness, by reason of his interest in the event or because he is a party or the spouse of a party.

§ 4513. Competency of person convicted of crime.

A person who has been convicted of a crime is a competent witness; but the conviction may be proved, for the purpose of affecting the weight of his testimony, either by cross-examination, upon which he

CPLR

shall be required to answer any relevant question, or by the record. The party cross-examining is not concluded by such person's answer.

R 4514. Impeachment of witness by prior inconsistent statement.

In addition to impeachment in the manner permitted by common law, any party may introduce proof that any witness has made a prior statement inconsistent with his testimony if the statement was made in a writing subscribed by him or was made under oath.

CROSS REFERENCES

See **Criminal Procedure Law § 60.35,** as to impeachment of own witness in criminal cases by proof of prior contradictory statement.

R 4515. Form of expert opinion.

Unless the court orders otherwise, questions calling for the opinion of an expert witness need not be hypothetical in form, and the witness may state his opinion and reasons without first specifying the data upon which it is based. Upon cross-examination, he may be required to specify the data and other criteria supporting the opinion.

R 4516. Proof of age of child.

Whenever it becomes necessary to determine the age of a child, he may be produced and exhibited to enable the court or jury to determine his age by a personal inspection.

R 4517. Prior testimony in a civil action.

(a) Impeachment of witnesses; parties; unavailable witness. In a civil action, at the trial or upon the hearing of a motion or an interlocutory proceeding, all or any part of the testimony of a witness that was taken at a prior trial in the same action or at a prior trial involving the same parties or their representatives and arising from the same subject matter, so far as admissible under the rules of evidence, may be used in accordance with any of the following provisions:

1. any such testimony may be used by any party for the purpose of contradicting or impeaching the testimony of the same witness;

2. the prior trial testimony of a party or of any person who was a party when the testimony was given or of any person who at the time the testimony was given was an officer, director, member, employee, or managing or authorized agent of a party, may be used for any purpose by any party who is adversely interested when the prior testimony is offered in evidence;

3. the prior trial testimony of any person may be used by any party for any purpose against any other party, provided the court finds:

(i) that the witness is dead; or

(ii) that the witness is at a greater distance than one hundred miles from the place of trial or is out of the state, unless it appears that the absence of the witness was procured by the party offering the testimony; or

(iii) that the witness is unable to attend or testify because of age, sickness, infirmity, or imprisonment; or

(iv) that the party offering the testimony has been unable to procure the attendance of the witness by diligent efforts; or

(v) upon motion on notice, that such exceptional circumstances exist as to make its use desirable, in the interest of justice and with due regard to the importance of presenting the testimony of witnesses orally in open court;

4. the prior trial testimony of a person authorized to practice medicine may be used by any party without the necessity of showing unavailability or special circumstances subject to the right of any party to move for preclusion upon the ground that admission of the prior testimony would be prejudicial under the circumstances.

(b) Use of part of the prior trial testimony of a witness. If only part of the prior trial testimony of a witness is read at the trial by a party, any other party may read any other part of the prior testimony of that witness that ought in fairness to be considered in connection with the part read.

(c) Substitution of parties; prior actions. Substitution of parties does not affect the right to use testimony previously taken at trial.

CPLR

2000 AMENDMENTS

L. 2000, ch. 268, eff. Jan. 1, 2001, repealed and added § 4517.

R 4518. Business records.

(a) Generally. Any writing or record, whether in the form of an entry in a book or otherwise, made as a memorandum or record of any act, transaction, occurrence or event, shall be admissible in evidence in proof of that act, transaction, occurrence or event, if the judge finds that it was made in the regular course of any business and that it was the regular course of such business to make it, at the time of the act, transaction, occurrence or event, or within a reasonable time thereafter. An electronic record, as defined in section three hundred two of the state technology law, used or stored as such a memorandum or record, shall be admissible in a tangible exhibit that is a true and accurate representation of such electronic record. The court may consider the method or manner by which the electronic record was stored, maintained or retrieved in determining whether the exhibit is a true and accurate representation of such electronic record. All other circumstances of the making of the memorandum or record, including lack of personal knowledge by the maker, may be proved to affect its weight, but they shall not affect its admissibility. The term business includes a business, profession, occupation and calling of every kind.

(b) Hospital bills. A hospital bill is admissible in evidence under this rule and is prima facie evidence of the facts contained, provided it bears a certification by the head of the hospital or by a responsible employee in the controller's or accounting office that the bill is correct, that each of the items was necessarily supplied and that the amount charged is reasonable. This subdivision shall not apply to any proceeding in a surrogate's court nor in any action instituted by or on behalf of a hospital to recover payment for accommodations or supplies furnished or for services rendered by or in such hospital, except that in a proceeding pursuant to section one hundred eighty-nine of the lien law to determine the validity and extent of the lien of a hospital, such certified hospital bills are prima facie evidence of the fact of services and of the reasonableness of any charges which do not exceed the comparable charges made by the hospital in the care of workmen's compensation patients.

(c) Other records. All records, writings and other things referred to in sections 2306 and 2307 are admissible in evidence under this rule and are prima facie evidence of the facts contained, provided they bear a certification or authentication by the head of the hospital, laboratory, department or bureau of a municipal corporation or of the state, or by an employee delegated for that purpose or by a qualified physician. Where a hospital record is in the custody of a warehouse, or "warehouseman" as that term is defined by paragraph (h) of subdivision one of section 7-102 of the uniform commercial code, pursuant to a plan approved in writing by the state commissioner of health, admissibility under this subdivision may be established by a certification made by the manager of the warehouse that sets forth (i) the authority by which the record is held, including but not limited to a court order, order of the commissioner, or order or resolution of the governing body or official of the hospital, and (ii) that the record has been in the exclusive custody of such warehouse or warehousemen since its receipt from the hospital or, if another has had access to it, the name and address of such person and the date on which and the circumstances under which such access was had. Any warehouseman providing a certification as required by this subdivision shall have no liability for acts or omissions relating thereto, except for intentional misconduct, and the warehouseman is authorized to assess and collect a reasonable charge for providing the certification described by this subdivision.

(d) Any records or reports relating to the administration and analysis of a genetic marker or DNA test, including records or reports of the costs of such tests, administered pursuant to sections four hundred eighteen and five hundred thirty-two of the family court act or section one hundred eleven-k of the social services law are admissible in evidence under this rule and are prima facie evidence of the facts contained therein provided they bear a certification or authentication by the head of the hospital, laboratory, department or bureau of a municipal corporation or the state or by an employee delegated for that purpose, or by a qualified physician. If such record or report relating to the administration and analysis of a genetic marker test or DNA test or tests administered pursuant to sections four hundred eighteen and five hundred thirty-two of the family court act or section one hundred eleven-k of the social services law indicates at least a ninety-five percent probability of paternity, the admission of such record or report

CPLR

shall create a rebuttable presumption of paternity, and shall, if unrebutted, establish the paternity of and liability for the support of a child pursuant to articles four and five of the family court act.

(e) Notwithstanding any other provision of law, a record or report relating to the administration and analysis of a genetic marker test or DNA test certified in accordance with subdivision (d) of this rule and administered pursuant to sections four hundred eighteen and five hundred thirty-two of the family court act or section one hundred eleven-k of the social services law is admissible in evidence under this rule without the need for foundation testimony or further proof of authenticity or accuracy unless objections to the record or report are made in writing no later than twenty days before a hearing at which the record or report may be introduced into evidence or thirty days after receipt of the test results, whichever is earlier.

(f) Notwithstanding any other provision of law, records or reports of support payments and disbursements maintained pursuant to title six-A of article three of the social services law by the office of temporary and disability assistance or the fiscal agent under contract to the office for the provision of centralized collection and disbursement functions are admissible in evidence under this rule, provided that they bear a certification by an official of a social services district attesting to the accuracy of the content of the record or report of support payments and that in attesting to the accuracy of the record or report such official has received confirmation from the office of temporary and disability assistance or the fiscal agent under contract to the office for the provision of centralized collection and disbursement functions pursuant to section one hundred eleven-h of the social services law that the record or report of support payments reflects the processing of all support payments in the possession of the office or the fiscal agent as of a specified date, and that the document is a record or report of support payments maintained pursuant to title six-A of article three of the social services law. If so certified, such record or report shall be admitted into evidence under this rule without the need for additional foundation testimony. Such records shall be the basis for a permissive inference of the facts contained therein unless the trier of fact finds good cause not to draw such inference.

(g) Pregnancy and childbirth costs. Any hospital bills or records relating to the costs of pregnancy or birth of a child for whom proceedings to establish paternity, pursuant to sections four hundred eighteen and five hundred thirty-two of the family court act or section one hundred eleven-k of the social services law have been or are being undertaken, are admissible in evidence under this rule and are prima facie evidence of the facts contained therein, provided they bear a certification or authentication by the head of the hospital, laboratory, department or bureau of a municipal corporation or the state or by an employee designated for that purpose, or by a qualified physician.

2007 AMENDMENTS

L. 2007, ch. 601, eff. Jan. 1, 2008, amended CPLR R 4518(f) by replacing "Department of Social Services" with "office of temporary and disability assistance."

2005 AMENDMENTS

L. 2005, ch. 741, eff. Oct. 18, 2005, amended subdivision (a) to effect technical corrections reflecting the transfer of the Office for Technology's enabling legislation to the State Technology Law.

2002 AMENDMENTS

L. 2002, ch. 136, § 1, eff. July 23, 2002, amended subdivision (a) by providing for the admissibility of electronic records.

1997 AMENDMENTS

L. 1997, ch. 398, eff. Nov. 11, 1997, amended CPLR 4518 subdivisions (d), (e) by including records or reports of the costs of genetic marker or DNA tests as admissible evidence, by deleting references to "blood" tests and by adding references to S.S.L. § 111-k and by adding new subdivision (g).

1995 AMENDMENTS

L. 1995, ch. 81, § 236, eff. July 1, 1995, added a new subdivision (f) pertaining to social service support records.

1994 AMENDMENTS

L. 1994, ch. 170, eff. June 15, 1994, amended CPLR 4518 by deleting from subdivision (c) the reference to blood genetic marker tests (*cf.* 1984 amendment note, *below*) and by adding new subdivisions (d) and (e) to specifically regulate those tests and the resulting reports.

1992 AMENDMENTS

L. 1992, ch. 381, eff. July 17, 1992, amended Subdivision (c) by adding the language following the sentence ending with the words "qualified physician."

1984 AMENDMENTS

L. 1984, ch. 792, eff. Aug. 5, 1984, and applicable to any action or proceeding pending on or commenced after Aug. 5, 1984, amended CPLR 4518(c) by substituting blood genetic marker test for blood grouping or human leucocyte antigen test.

1983 AMENDMENTS

L. 1983, ch. 311, eff. June 21, 1983, amended CPLR 4518(c) by providing for certification of blood test results by a laboratory or a qualified physician.

1982 AMENDMENTS

L. 1982, ch. 695, eff. July 22, 1982, amended CPLR 4518(c) to include reports of blood tests and HLA tests among those business records which are admissible into evidence.

1970 AMENDMENTS

Amendment No. 2 made by Judicial Conference Jan. 2, 1970, Report to the 1970 Legislature, effective Sept. 1, 1970, amended by adding thereto new Subd. (c).

§ 4519. Personal transaction or communication between witness and decedent or mentally ill person.

Upon the trial of an action or the hearing upon the merits of a special proceeding, a party or a person interested in the event, or a person from, through or under whom such a party or interested person derives his interest or title by assignment or otherwise, shall not be examined as a witness in his own behalf or interest, or in behalf of the party succeeding to his title or interest against the executor, administrator or survivor of a deceased person or the committee of a mentally ill person, or a person deriving his title or interest from, through or under a deceased person or mentally ill person, by assignment or otherwise, concerning a personal transaction or communication between the witness and the deceased person or mentally ill person, except where the executor, administrator, survivor, committee or person so deriving title or interest is examined in his own behalf, or the testimony of a mentally ill person or deceased person is given in evidence, concerning the same transaction or communication. A person shall not be deemed interested for the purposes of this section by reason of being a stockholder or officer of any banking corporation which is a party to the action or proceeding, or interested in the event thereof. No party or person interested in the event, who is otherwise competent to testify, shall be disqualified from testifying by the possible imposition of costs against him or the award of costs to him. A party or person interested in the event or a person from, through or under whom such a party or interested person derives his interest or title by assignment or otherwise, shall not be qualified for the purposes of this section, to testify in his own behalf or interest, or in behalf of the party succeeding to his title or interest, to personal transactions or communications with the donee of a power of appointment in an action or proceeding for the probate of a will, which exercises or attempts to exercise a power of appointment granted by the will of a donor of such power, or in an action or proceeding involving the construction of the will of the donee after its admission to probate.

Nothing contained in this section, however, shall render a person incompetent to testify as to the facts of an accident or the results therefrom where the proceeding, hearing, defense or cause of action involves a claim of negligence or contributory negligence in an action wherein one or more parties is the representative of a deceased or incompetent person based upon, or by reason of, the operation or ownership of a motor vehicle being operated upon the highways of the state, or the operation or ownership of aircraft being operated in the air space over the state, or the operation or ownership of a vessel on any of the lakes, rivers, streams, canals or other waters of this state, but this provision shall not be construed as permitting testimony as to conversations with the deceased.

CPLR

1978 AMENDMENTS

L. 1978, ch. 550, eff. July 24, 1978, amended CPLR 4519 by eliminating use of the term "lunatic" throughout, and replacing it with the term "mentally ill person."

R 4520.   Certificate or affidavit of public officer.

Where a public officer is required or authorized, by special provision of law, to make a certificate or an affidavit to a fact ascertained, or an act performed, by him in the course of his official duty, and to file or deposit it in a public office of the state, the certificate or affidavit so filed or deposited is prima facie evidence of the facts stated.

R 4521.   Lack of record.

A statement signed by an officer or a deputy of an officer having legal custody of specified official records of the United States or of any state, territory or jurisdiction of the United States, or of any court thereof, or kept in any public office thereof, that he has made diligent search of the records and has found no record or entry of a specified nature, is prima facie evidence that the records contain no such record or entry, provided that the statement is accompanied by a certificate that legal custody of the specified official records belongs to such person, which certificate shall be made by a person described in rule 4540.

1964 AMENDMENTS

L. 1964, ch. 388, eff. Sept. 1, 1964, substituted the word "rule" in place of the word "section" before "4540" in the last line.

R 4522.   Ancient filed maps, surveys and records affecting real property.

All maps, surveys and official records affecting real property, which have been on file in the state in the office of the register of any county, any county clerk, any court of record or any department of the city of New York for more than ten years, are prima facie evidence of their contents.

R 4523.   Search by title insurance or abstract company.

A search affecting real property, when made and certified to by a title insurance, abstract or searching company, organized under the laws of this state, may be used in place of, and with the same legal effect as, an official search.

R 4524.   Conveyance of real property without the state.

A record of a conveyance of real property situated within another state, territory or jurisdiction of the United States, recorded therein pursuant to its laws, is prima facie evidence of conveyance and of due execution.

R 4525.   Copies of statements under article nine of the uniform commercial code.

A copy of a statement which is noted or certified by a filing officer pursuant to section 9–523 of the uniform commercial code and which states that the copy is a true copy is prima facie evidence of the facts stated in the notation or certification and that the copy is a true copy of a statement filed in the office of the filing officer.

2001 AMENDMENTS

L. 2001, ch. 84, § 39, eff. July 1, 2001.

1965 AMENDMENTS

L. 1965, ch. 729, eff. July 21, 1965, repealed former Rule 4525 and enacted a new Rule 4525.

R 4526. Marriage certificate.

An original certificate of a marriage made by the person by whom it was solemnized within the state, or the original entry thereof made pursuant to law in the office of the clerk of a city or a town within the state, is prima facie evidence of the marriage.

CPLR

§ 4527. Death or other status of missing person.

(a) Presumed death. A written finding of presumed death, made by any person authorized to make such findings by the federal missing persons act is prima facie evidence of the death, and the date, circumstances and place of disappearance. In the case of a merchant seaman, a written finding of presumed death, made by the maritime war emergency board or by the war shipping administration or the successors or assigns of such board or administration in connection with war risk insurance is prima facie evidence of the death, and the date, circumstances and place of disappearance.

(b) Death, internment, capture and other status. An official written report or record that a person is missing, missing in action, interned in a neutral country, or beleaguered, besieged or captured by an enemy, or is dead, or is alive, made by an officer or employee of the United States authorized by law of the United States to make it is prima facie evidence of such fact.

CROSS REFERENCES

The **Federal Missing Persons Act,** referred to in Subd. (a), *supra,* appears in **5 USCA § 5561,** *et seq.*

R 4528. Weather conditions.

Any record of the observations of the weather, taken under the direction of the United States weather bureau, is prima facie evidence of the facts stated.

R 4529. Inspection certificate issued by United States department of agriculture.

An inspection certificate issued by the authorized agents of the United States department of agriculture on file with the United States secretary of agriculture is prima facie evidence of the facts stated.

§ 4530. Certificate of population.

(a) Prima facie evidence. A certificate of the officer in charge of the census of the United States, attested by the United States secretary of commerce, giving the result of the census is, except as hereinafter provided, prima facie evidence of such result.

(b) Conclusive evidence. Where the population of the state or a subdivision, or a portion of a subdivision of the state is required to be determined according to the federal or state census or enumeration last preceding a particular time, a certificate of the officer in charge of the census of the United States, attested by the United States secretary of commerce, as to such population as shown by such federal census, or a certificate of the secretary of state as to such population as shown by such state enumeration, is conclusive evidence of such population.

R 4531. Affidavit of service or posting notice by person unavailable at trial.

An affidavit by a person who served, posted or affixed a notice, showing such service, posting or affixing is prima facie evidence of the service, posting or affixing if the affiant is dead, mentally ill or cannot be compelled with due diligence to attend at the trial.

1978 AMENDMENTS

L. 1978, ch. 550, eff. July 24, 1978, amended CPLR 4531 by eliminating use of the term "insane" and replacing it with the term "mentally ill."

R 4532. Self-authentication of newspapers and periodicals of general circulation.

Extrinsic evidence of authenticity as a condition precedent to admissibility is not required with respect to printed materials purporting to be newspapers or periodicals of general circulation; provided however, nothing herein shall be deemed to preclude or limit the right of a party to challenge the authenticity of such printed material, by extrinsic evidence or otherwise, prior to admission by the court or to raise the issue of authenticity as an issue of fact.

1986 AMENDMENTS

L. 1986, ch. 89, eff. May 23, 1986, amended CPLR 4532 by allowing for the self-authentication of newspapers and periodicals of general circulation and removing the need for extrinsic evidence of authenticity as a condition precedent to admissibility.

R4532-a. Admissibility of graphic, numerical, symbolic or pictorial representations of medical or diagnostic tests.

A graphic, numerical, symbolic or pictorial representation of the results of a medical or diagnostic procedure or test is admissible in evidence provided:

(1) the name of the injured party, the date when the information constituting the graphic, numerical, symbolic or pictorial represen-tation was taken, and such additional identifying information as is customarily inscribed by the medical practitioner or medical facility is inserted on such graphic, numerical, symbolic or pictorial repre-sentation; and

(2) (a) the representation has been previously received or exam-ined by the party or parties against whom it is being offered; or

(b) (i) at least ten days before the date of trial of the action, the party intending to offer such graphic, numerical, symbolic or pictorial representation as a proposed exhibit serves upon the party or parties against whom said proposed exhibit is to be offered, a notice of intention to offer such proposed exhibit in evidence during the trial and that the same is available for inspection; and

(ii) the notice aforesaid is accompanied by an affidavit or affirmation of such physician identifying such graphic, numeri-cal, symbolic or pictorial representation and attesting to the identifying information inscribed thereon, attesting that the identifying information inscribed thereon is the same as is customarily inscribed by the medical practitioner or facility,

CPLR

and further attesting that, if called as a witness in the action, he or she would so testify.

Nothing contained in this rule, however, shall prohibit the admissibility of a graphic, numerical, symbolic or pictorial representation in evidence where otherwise admissible.

2004 AMENDMENTS

L. 2004, ch. 375, §1, eff. Jan.1, 2005, amending CPLR 4532-a, describing identifying information inscribed by medical practitioners.

2001 AMENDMENTS

L. 2001, ch. 392, eff. Jan. 1, 2002, amending CPLR 4532-a, including a retitling of this section.

1993 AMENDMENTS

L. 1993, ch. 482, eff. July 26, 1993, amended CPLR 4532-a to provide that certain designated medical test results — X-ray, magnetic resonance image, computed axial tomograph, positron emission tomograph, electromyogram, sonogram and fetal heart rate monitor strip — can be admissible evidence.

1979 AMENDMENTS

L. 1979, ch. 124, eff. Sept. 1, 1979, amended CPLR 4532-a subds. (1) and (3) by eliminating the word radiologist and substituting therefor the word physician.

1972 AMENDMENTS

Proposal No. 5 of the Judicial Conference Report to the 1972 Legislature, effective Sept. 1, 1972, amended Subd. (1) by deleting the words "and age" which appeared between "the name" and "of the injured party."

1970 AMENDMENTS

L. 1970, ch. 772, eff. Sept. 1, 1970, added new Rule 4532-a.

R 4533.   Market reports.

A report of a regularly organized stock or commodity market published in a newspaper or periodical of general circulation or in an official publication or trade journal is admissible in evidence to prove the market price or value of any article regularly sold or dealt in on such market. The circumstances of the preparation of such a report may be shown to affect its weight, but they shall not affect its admissibility.

1964 AMENDMENTS

L. 1964, ch. 388, eff. Sept. 1, 1964, substituted "Market" for "Stock market" reports in caption. In the first sentence after the word "circulation" the words "or in an official publication or trade journal" were inserted.

R 4533-a. Prima facie proof of damages.

An itemized bill or invoice, receipted or marked paid, for services or repairs of an amount not in excess of two thousand dollars is admissible in evidence and is prima facie evidence of the reasonable value and necessity of such services or repairs itemized therein in any civil action provided it bears a certification by the person, firm or corporation, or an authorized agent or employee thereof, rendering such services or making such repairs and charging for the same, and contains a verified statement that no part of the payment received therefor will be refunded to the debtor, and that the amounts itemized therein are the usual and customary rates charged for such services or repairs by the affiant or his employer; and provided further that a true copy of such itemized bill or invoice together with a notice of intention to introduce such bill or invoice into evidence pursuant to this rule is served upon each party at least ten days before the trial. No more than one bill or invoice from the same person, firm or corporation to the same debtor shall be admissible in evidence under this rule in the same action.

1988 AMENDMENTS

L. 1988, ch. 249, eff. July 8, 1988, amended 4533-a to increase from fifteen hundred to two thousand dollars the maximum amount of a bill or invoice admissible as prima facie proof of damages.

1981 AMENDMENTS

L. 1981, ch. 355, eff. June 29, 1981, amended CPLR 4533-a by increasing the amount of an itemized bill admissible as prima facie evidence of the value of services or repairs from one thousand to fifteen hundred dollars.

1975 AMENDMENTS

L. 1975, ch. 103, eff. Sept. 1, 1975, substituted the phrase "one thousand" for "five hundred" before the word "dollars" in the first sentence.

1970 AMENDMENTS

Amendment No. 3 made by the Judicial Conference Jan. 2, 1970, Report to the 1970 Legislature, effective Sept. 1, 1970 amended CPLR 4533-a.

The Judicial Conference Report stated, in part: "Enacted in 1966 to facilitate proof of repairs in petty automobile accident cases, CPLR 4533-a has been the target of much criticism as well as praise, some of it aimed at the philosophy of the rule, much of it at its draftsmanship. The rule, as originally conceived, permitted a plaintiff to prove damage to his automobile, in amount less than three hundred dollars, simply by putting his repair bill into evidence. Where the bill exceeded three hundred dollars, the case was regarded as serious enough for the plaintiff to incur the expense of calling the garage mechanic as a witness.

"In 1968, the Judicial Conference, on the advice of the Committee, amended the rule, greatly expanding it. This expansion was undoubtedly sound so far as its basic thrust was concerned. The 1968 amendment provided that bills for any 'professional or other specialized services or repairs' could be offered. However, the scope of the Rule was limited to actions involving 'tortious damages to a person or property.' Most significantly, under the 1968 amendment, a bill in *any* amount could be admitted, although it could not authorize an 'award' of more than three hundred dollars. The possibility of putting large doctors' bills before the jury without calling the doctors as witnesses has disturbed many attorneys. Numerous suggestions for repeal, modification, clarification, expansion and limitation of CPLR 4533-a, many of them contradictory of one another, were received by the Judicial Conference and the Advisory Committee.

"The Judicial Conference, upon the advice of the Committee, commissioned Professor Joseph M. McLaughlin, of the Fordham University Law School, to study the various suggestions received in respect to this Rule and to formulate recommended amendments. . . . The Committee carefully considered Professor McLaughlin's findings and recommendations and, after extensive discussion, arrived at the following conclusions:

"1. The fundamental concept that bills should be admitted as proof of reasonable value of the services performed is sound, at least in small cases. A plaintiff, even in a personal injury action, should not be compelled to spend a few hundred dollars to obtain the testimony of a doctor that the doctor's bill for, say, seventy-five dollars is reasonable and necessary. This, indeed, is the primary philosophy underlying the Rule. It is eminently sound.

"2. The bill, however, should not be evidence of anything but reasonable value and necessity of the services or repairs. If there is an issue as to whether the services were for injuries proximately caused by the defendant, other proof will be required.

"3. The Rule should apply to bills in an amount of less than $500. However, while the procedure would thus be available for bills in a larger amount than at present, the practice of allowing submission of bills in *any* amount could be discontinued. There is merit in the contention voiced by members of the bar that a jury which sees a bill in excess of the amount it may award will nevertheless be unduly influenced thereby in fixing the amount of the verdict.

"4. If the concept of self-proving (in the sense of prima facie proof) bills has validity, which the Committee believes it does in small cases, it should not be confined to tort cases. Accordingly, it is recommended that the new Rule be extended to all civil actions.

"5. The mere service of a bill upon the defendant does not tell him that the plaintiff intends to offer the bill without calling as a witness the person who sent the bill. This is the key point to the procedure authorized by the Rule. Accordingly, it is recommended that the rule include a notice provision to that effect.

"6. To prevent abuse, it is suggested that the Rule contain a limitation that no more than one bill from the same source to the same debtor may be admitted under these provisions.

"In addition to the amendments necessary to implement these conclusions, some simplification of the language of the present rule seems desirable."

1968 AMENDMENTS

Proposal No. 2, effective Sept. 1, 1968, made by the Judicial Conference Feb. 1, 1968, Report to the Legislature, rescinded former rule 4533-a and promulgated a new rule 4533-a.

1966 AMENDMENTS

L. 1966, ch. 263, eff. Sept. 1, 1966, added new rule 4533-a.

R 4533-b.   Proof of payment by joint tortfeasor.

In an action for personal injury, injury to property or for wrongful death, any proof as to payment by or settlement with another joint tortfeasor, or one claimed to be a joint tortfeasor, offered by a defendant in mitigation of damages, shall be taken out of the hearing of the jury. The court shall deduct the proper amount, as determined pursuant to section 15-108 of the general obligations law, from the award made by the jury.

CROSS REFERENCES

See **G.O.L.§ 15-108** in Appendix, *below.*

1974 AMENDMENTS

L. 1974, ch. 742, eff. Sept. 1, 1974, upon the recommendation of the Judicial Conference, amended Rule 4533-b by adding to the first sentence the phrases "or for wrongful death," "or settlement with another" and "or one claimed to be a joint tortfeasor." The second sentence which read "the court shall deduct the amount of such payment . . ." was amended to read "the court shall deduct the proper amount, as determined pursuant to section 15-108 of the general obligations law. . . ."

The 1974 Judicial Conference Report stated:

"(a) In addition to adding 'wrongful death' actions to those included within the scope of this rule, this rule has been amended in order to conform it to the newly revised General Obligations Law § 15-108. In accordance with that section, it is possible that damages may be mitigated by an amount in excess of the payment made by a joint tortfeasor, and this Rule provides that the court shall deduct the 'proper amount' in accordance with General Obligations Law § 15-108.

"(b) While the Rule refers to 'joint tortfeasor' it is intended that the phrase be construed to also include all those who may claim contribution in accordance with Article 14 of the CPLR whether or not they are 'joint tortfeasors', in the technical sense in which that phrase is sometimes used."

1971 AMENDMENTS

L. 1971, ch. 244, eff. Sept. 1, 1971, added new Rule 4533-b.

The Judicial Conference 1971 report to the 1971 Legislature, Feb. 1, 1971, in recommending the adoption of CPLR 4533-b stated:

"The purpose of the proposed amendment is to modify the rule of *Livant* v. *Livant,* 18 A.D. 2d 383 (First Dept., 1963), under which payments made by one of several joint tortfeasors may be alleged and proved in mitigation in the presence of the jury. Henceforth the proof of such payment would be kept from the jury and at the conclusion of the trial, in the event of a verdict in favor of plaintiff, the trial court would deduct the amount of such settlement from the award.

"The principal reason for changing the rule of *Livant* as proposed is the concern that under the present practice the jury will tend to return a nominal verdict where a prior payment is revealed, and if there are multiple defendants, to think that the tortfeasor who settled before was the only wrongdoer merely because he settled. The proposed amendment would continue to allow mitigation of damages in such circumstances but without the very real possibility that the plaintiff will not be made whole. The proposed amendment would encourage settlements by the holdout defendant, who, under the present rule, may prefer to hazard a nominal award by the jury. The proposed amendment represents the rule in a number of jurisdictions (cf. *Livant* (*supra*) at 386), most notably in Illinois (*DeLude* v. *Rimek,* 351 Ill. App. 466; *Jackson* v. *Hursey*, 1 Ill. App. 2d 598; *Ryan* v. *Monson*, 33 Ill. App. 2d 406).

"In New York, the prejudicial effect in a consolidated action of admitting evidence of a settlement by a party who remains in the lawsuit has been recognized (*Bove* v. *Medeo*, 19 A.D. 2d 646 (Second Dept., 1963) and *Burger* v. *L.I.R.R.*, 24 A.D. 2d 509 (Second Dept., 1965)). Yet the rule of *Livant,* with its contrary thrust, continues in authority. In the interest of justice and consistency, that rule should be abrogated as proposed."

R 4534.   Standard of measurement used by surveyor.

An official certificate of any state, county, city, village, or town sealer elected or appointed pursuant to the laws of the state, or the statement under oath of a surveyor, that the chain or measure used by him conformed to the state standard at the time a survey was made is prima facie evidence of conformity, and an official certificate made by any sealer that the implement used in measuring such chain or other measure was the one provided the sealer pursuant to the provisions of the laws of the state is prima facie evidence of that fact.

R 4535. [Repealed.]

R 4536. Proof of writing by comparison of handwriting.

Comparison of a disputed writing with any writing proved to the satisfaction of the court to be the handwriting of the person claimed to have made the disputed writing shall be permitted.

R 4537. Proof of writing subscribed by witness.

Unless a writing requires a subscribing witness for its validity, it may be proved as if there was no subscribing witness.

R 4538. Acknowledged, proved or certified writing; conveyance of real property without the state.

Certification of the acknowledgment or proof of a writing, except a will, in the manner prescribed by law for taking and certifying the acknowledgment or proof of a conveyance of real property within the state is prima facie evidence that it was executed by the person who purported to do so. A conveyance of real property, situated within another state, territory or jurisdiction of the United States, which has been duly authenticated, according to the laws of that state, territory or jurisdiction, so as to be read in evidence in the courts thereof, is admissible in evidence in the state.

R 4539. Reproductions of original.

(a) If any business, institution, or member of a profession or calling, in the regular course of business or activity has made, kept or recorded any writing, entry, print or representation and in the regular course of business has recorded, copied, or reproduced it by any process, including reproduction, which accurately reproduces or forms a du-

CPLR

rable medium for reproducing the original, such reproduction, when satisfactorily identified, is as admissible in evidence as the original, whether the original is in existence or not, and an enlargement or facsimile of such reproduction is admissible in evidence if the original reproduction is in existence and available for inspection under direction of the court. The introduction of a reproduction does not preclude admission of the original.

(b) A reproduction created by any process which stores an image of any writing, entry, print or representation and which does not permit additions, deletions, or changes without leaving a record of such additions, deletions, or changes, when authenticated by competent testimony or affidavit which shall include the manner or method by which tampering or degradation of the reproduction is prevented, shall be as admissible in evidence as the original.

1996 AMENDMENTS

L. 1996, ch. 27, eff. Nov. 1, 1996, numbered the existing paragraph as subdivision (a) and added the phrase "including reproduction" and added a new subdivision (b) dealing with reproduction by a process which stores an image.

R 4540. Authentication of official record of court or government office in the United States.

(a) Copies permitted. An official publication, or a copy attested as correct by an officer or a deputy of an officer having legal custody of an official record of the United States or of any state, territory or jurisdiction of the United States, or of any of its courts, legislature, offices, public bodies or boards is prima facie evidence of such record.

(b) Certificate of officer of the state. Where the copy is attested by an officer of the state, it shall be accompanied by a certificate signed by, or with a facsimile of the signature of, the clerk of a court having legal custody of the record, and, except where the copy is used in the same court or before one of its officers, with the seal of the court affixed; or signed by, or with a facsimile of the signature of, the officer having legal custody of the original, or his deputy or clerk, with his official seal affixed; or signed by, or with a facsimile of the signature of, the presiding officer, secretary or clerk of the public body or board and, except where it is certified by the clerk or secretary of either house of the legislature, with the seal of the body or board affixed. If the certificate is made by a county clerk, the county seal shall be affixed.

(c) Certificate of officer of another jurisdiction. Where the copy is attested by an officer of another jurisdiction, it shall be accompanied by a certificate that such officer has legal custody of the record, and that his signature is believed to be genuine, which certificate shall be made by a judge of a court of record of the district or political subdivision in which the record is kept, with the seal of the court affixed; or by any public officer having a seal of office and having official duties in that district or political subdivision with respect to the subject matter of the record, with the seal of his office affixed.

(d) Printed tariff or classification subject to public service commission, commissioner of transportation or interstate commerce commission. A printed copy of a tariff or classification which shows a public service commission or commissioner of transportation number of this state and an effective date, or a printed copy of a tariff or classification which shows an interstate commerce commission number and an effective date, is admissible in evidence, without certification, and is prima facie evidence of the filed original tariff or classification.

CPLR

1970 AMENDMENTS

L. 1970, ch. 267, § 9, eff. March 1, 1971, amended Subd. (d) to include the Commissioner of Transportation.

R 4541. Proof of proceedings before justice of the peace.

(a) Of the state. A transcript from the docket-book of a justice of the peace of the state, subscribed by him, and authenticated by a certificate signed by the clerk of the county in which the justice resides, with the county seal affixed, to the effect that the person subscribing the transcript is a justice of the peace of that county, is prima facie evidence of any matter stated in the transcript which is required by law to be entered by the justice in his docket-book.

(b) Of another state. A transcript from the docket-book of a justice of the peace of another state, of his minutes of the proceedings in a cause, of a judgment rendered by him, of an execution issued thereon or of the return of an execution, when subscribed by him, and authenticated as prescribed in this subdivision is prima facie evidence of his jurisdiction in the cause and of the matters shown by the transcript. The transcript shall be authenticated by a certificate of the justice to the effect that it is in all respects correct and that he had jurisdiction of the cause; and also by a certificate of the clerk or prothonotary of the county in which the justice resides, with his official seal affixed, to the effect that the person subscribing the certificate attached to the transcript is a justice of the peace of that county.

R 4542. Proof of foreign records and documents.

(a) Foreign record. A foreign official record, or an entry therein, when admissible for any purpose, may be evidenced by an official publication thereof; or a copy thereof, attested by a person authorized to make the attestation, and accompanied by a final certification as to the genuineness of the signature and official position

1. of the attesting person, or

2. of any foreign official whose certificate of genuineness of signature and official position

(i) relates to the attestation, or

(ii) is in a chain of certificates of genuineness of signature and official position relating to the attestation.

(b) Final certification. A final certification may be made by a secretary of an embassy or legation, consul general, consul, vice consul, or consular agent of the United States, or a diplomatic or consular official of the foreign country assigned or accredited to the United States. If reasonable opportunity has been given to all parties to investigate the authenticity and accuracy of the documents, the court may, for good cause shown, admit an attested copy without final certification, or permit the foreign official record to be evidenced by an attested summary with or without a final certification.

(c) Lack of record. A written statement that after diligent search no record or entry of a specified tenor was found to exist in the foreign records designated by the statement, authenticated in compliance with the requirements set forth in subdivisions (a) and (b) for a copy of a foreign record is admissible as evidence that the records contain no such record or entry.

1972 AMENDMENTS

Proposal No. 6 of the Judicial Conference Report to the 1972 Legislature, effective Sept. 1, 1972, amended Subd. (b) by adding the words "agent of the

United States, or a diplomatic or consular" between the words "or consular" and "official of the foreign country."

1969 AMENDMENTS

Amendment by Judicial Conference Feb. 1, 1969, Report to the 1969 Legislature, effective Sept. 1, 1969, repealed rule 4542 and added new rule 4542. "[T]he new rule 4542 . . . is substantially similar to the parallel provision of the Uniform Interstate and International Procedure Act. . . ."

§ 4543.   Proof of facts or writing by methods other than those authorized in this article.

Nothing in this article prevents the proof of a fact or a writing by any method authorized by any applicable statute or by the rules of evidence at common law.

§ 4544.   Contracts in small print.

The portion of any printed contract or agreement involving a consumer transaction or a lease for space to be occupied for residential purposes where the print is not clear and legible or is less than eight points in depth or five and one-half points in depth for upper case type may not be received in evidence in any trial, hearing or proceeding on behalf of the party who printed or prepared such contract or agreement, or who caused said agreement or contract to be printed or prepared. As used in the immediately preceding sentence, the term "consumer transaction" means a transaction wherein the money, property or service which is the subject of the transaction is primarily for personal, family or household purposes. No provision of any contract or agreement waiving the provisions of this section shall be effective. The provisions of this section shall not apply to agreements or contracts entered into prior to the effective date of this section.

1979 AMENDMENTS

L. 1979, ch. 474, eff. Sept. 1, 1979, amended CPLR 4544 to clarify the admissibility of contracts printed in small type. The statute had previously stated that such contracts were inadmissible if they were unclear and if the print was too small. The Legislature deleted the word "and" adding the word "or."

1975 AMENDMENTS

L. 1975, ch. 370, eff. July 1, 1976, added new CPLR 4544.

§ 4545.   Admissibility of collateral source of payment.

(a) Action for medical, dental or podiatric malpractice. In any action for medical, dental or podiatric malpractice where the plaintiff seeks to recover for the cost of medical care, dental care, podiatric care, custodial care or rehabilitation services, loss of earnings or other economic loss, evidence shall be admissible for consideration by the court to establish that any such past or future cost or expense was or will, with reasonable certainty, be replaced or indemnified, in whole or in part, from any collateral source such as insurance (except for life insurance), social security (except those benefits provided under title XVIII of the social security act), workers' compensation or employee benefit programs (except such collateral sources entitled by law to liens against any recovery of the plaintiff). If the court finds that any such cost or expense was or will, with reasonable certainty, be replaced or indemnified from any collateral source, it shall reduce the amount of the award by such finding, minus an amount equal to the premiums paid by the plaintiff for such benefits for the two-year period immediately preceding the accrual of such action and minus an amount equal to the projected future cost to the plaintiff of maintaining such benefits. In order to find that any future cost or expense will, with reasonable certainty, be replaced or indemnified by the collateral source, the court must find that the plaintiff is legally entitled to the continued receipt of such collateral source, pursuant to a contract or otherwise enforceable agreement, subject only to the continued payment of a premium and such other financial obligations as may be required by such agreement.

(b) Certain actions against a public employer for personal injury and wrongful death.

1. In any action against a public employer or a public employee who is subject to indemnification by a public employer with respect to such action or both for personal injury or wrongful death arising out of an injury sustained by a public employee while acting within the scope of his public employment or duties, where the plaintiff seeks to recover for the cost of medical care, custodial care or rehabilitation services, loss of earnings or other economic loss, evidence shall be admissible for consideration by the court to establish that any such cost or expense was replaced or indemnified, in whole or in part, from a collateral source provided or paid for, in whole or in part, by the public employer, including but not limited

to paid sick leave, medical benefits, death benefits, dependent benefits, a disability retirement allowance and social security (except those benefits provided under title XVIII of the social security act) but shall not include those collateral sources entitled by law to liens against any recovery of the plaintiff. If the court finds that any such cost or expense was replaced or indemnified from any such collateral source, it shall reduce the amount of the award by such finding, minus an amount equal to the contributions of the injured public employee for such benefit.

2. As used in this subdivision, the term "public employer" means the state of New York, a county, city, town, village or any other political subdivision of the state, any public authority operating a rapid transit, commuter railroad, omnibus, marine, airport or aviation facility, a school district or any governmental entity operating a public school, college or university and any municipal housing authority. The term "public employee" means any person holding a position by election, appointment or employment in the service of a public employer, while acting within the scope of his public employment or duties, whether or not compensated, or a volunteer expressly authorized to participate in a volunteer program sponsored by a public employer but does not include an independent contractor. The term public employee includes a former employee, his estate or judicially appointed personal representative.

3. For the purposes of this subdivision a certified report of the actuary of the appropriate public employee retirement system shall be admissible evidence of the present value of any death benefit, dependent benefit or disability retirement allowance.

4. The provisions of this subdivision shall not be construed to affect, alter or amend any provisions of the workers' compensation law or to apply to any claims under such law.

(c) Actions for personal injury, injury to property or wrongful death. In any action brought to recover damages for personal injury, injury to property or wrongful death, where the plaintiff seeks to recover for the cost of medical care, dental care, custodial care or rehabilitation services, loss of earnings or other economic loss, evidence shall be admissible for consideration by the court to establish that any such past or future cost or expense was or will, with reasonable certainty, be

CPLR

replaced or indemnified, in whole or in part, from any collateral source such as insurance (except for life insurance), social security (except those benefits provided under title XVIII of the social security act), workers' compensation or employee benefit programs (except such collateral sources entitled by law to liens against any recovery of the plaintiff). If the court finds that any such cost or expense was or will, with reasonable certainty, be replaced or indemnified from any collateral source, it shall reduce the amount of the award by such finding, minus an amount equal to the premiums paid by the plaintiff for such benefits for the two-year period immediately preceding the accrual of such action and minus an amount equal to the projected future cost to the plaintiff of maintaining such benefits. In order to find that any future cost or expense will, with reasonable certainty, be replaced or indemnified by the collateral source, the court must find that the plaintiff is legally entitled to the continued receipt of such collateral source, pursuant to a contract or otherwise enforceable agreement, subject only to the continued payment of a premium and such other financial obligations as may be required by such agreement.

(d) Voluntary charitable contributions excluded as a collateral source of payment. Voluntary charitable contributions received by an injured party shall not be considered to be a collateral source of payment that is admissible in evidence to reduce the amount of any award, judgment or settlement.

2002 AMENDMENTS

L. 2002, ch. 672, eff. Dec. 9, 2002, added subdivision (d).

1986 AMENDMENTS

L. 1986, ch. 220, eff. June 28, 1986, and applicable to actions or proceedings commenced on or after such date, added subdivision (c) providing that specified damages recovered in actions for personal injury, injury to property or wrongful death, may be reduced by recovery from collateral sources. L. 1986, ch. 485, eff. July 21, 1986, and applicable to acts, omissions or failures occurring on or after such date, amended subdivision (a) to apply to podiatric malpractice actions.

1985 AMENDMENTS

L. 1985, ch. 294, eff. July 1, 1985, and applicable to any action for dental or medical malpractice commenced on or after such date, amended subdivision (a) to apply to dental malpractice actions and to provide for the admissibility of collateral sources to payment for future costs.

1984 AMENDMENTS

L. 1984, ch. 701, eff. Oct. 1, 1984, and applicable to actions commenced on or after that date, added CPLR 4545.

§ 4546. Loss of earnings and impairment of earning ability in actions for medical, dental or podiatric malpractice.

1. In any action for medical, dental or podiatric malpractice where the plaintiff seeks to recover damages for loss of earnings or impairment of earning ability, evidence shall be admissible for consideration by the court, outside of the presence of the jury, to establish the federal, state and local personal income taxes which the plaintiff would have been obligated by law to pay.

2. In any such action, the court shall instruct the jury not to deduct federal, state and local personal income taxes in determining the award, if any, for loss of earnings and impairment of earning ability. The court shall further instruct the jury that any reduction for such taxes from any award shall, if warranted, be made by the court.

3. In any such action, the court shall, if warranted by the evidence, reduce any award for loss of earnings or impairment of earning ability by the amount of federal, state and local personal income taxes which the court finds, with reasonable certainty, that the plaintiff would have been obligated by law to pay.

1987 AMENDMENTS

L. 1987, ch. 507, eff. July 30, 1987, and applicable to any acts, omissions or failures occurring on or after such date, amended section to apply to podiatric malpractice actions.

1986 AMENDMENTS

L. 1986, ch. 266, eff. July 8, 1986, and applicable to actions commenced on or after such date, added new CPLR 4546.

§ 4547. Compromise and offers to compromise.

Evidence of (a) furnishing, or offering or promising to furnish, or (b) accepting, or offering or promising to accept, any valuable consideration in compromising or attempting to compromise a claim which is disputed as to either validity or amount of damages, shall be inadmissible as proof of liability for or invalidity of the claim or the amount of damages. Evidence of any conduct or statement made during compromise negotiations shall also be inadmissible. The provisions of this section shall not require the exclusion of any evidence, which is otherwise discoverable, solely because such evidence was presented during the course of compromise negotiations. Furthermore, the exclusion established by this section shall not limit the admissibility of such evidence when it is offered for another purpose, such as proving bias or prejudice of a witness, negating a contention of undue delay or proof of an effort to obstruct a criminal investigation or prosecution.

1998 AMENDMENTS

L. 1998, ch. 317, eff. July 14, 1998 added new CPLR 4547 to preclude from placing into evidence a party's offer, acceptance and statements made during settlement negotiations to compromise a claim which is in good faith disputed as to liability or amount, if the settlement fails and the parties proceed to trial.

§ 4548.   Privileged communications; electronic communication thereof.

No communication privileged under this article shall lose its privileged character for the sole reason that it is communicated by electronic means or because persons necessary for the delivery or facilitation of such electronic communication may have access to the content of the communication.

1999 AMENDMENTS

L. 1999, ch. 56, eff. May 25, 1999, renumbered CPLR § 4547 to CPLR § 4548. This amendment corrects the conflict in numbering the sections as originally enacted in 1998. The 1998 Regular Legislative Session enacted two sections both numbered as CPLR 4547; the other section pertains to the admission of statements made during settlement discussions.

1998 AMENDMENTS

L. 1998, ch. 156, eff. July 7, 1998 added new CPLR 4547 to protect privileged communications that are communicated electronically.

Article 50

JUDGMENTS GENERALLY

———

SUMMARY OF ARTICLE

CPLR

§ 5001. Interest to verdict, report or decision.

(a) Actions in which recoverable. Interest shall be recovered upon a sum awarded because of a breach of performance of a contract, or because of an act or omission depriving or otherwise interfering with title to, or possession or enjoyment of, property, except that in an action of an equitable nature, interest and the rate and date from which it shall be computed shall be in the court's discretion.

(b) Date from which computed. Interest shall be computed from the earliest ascertainable date the cause of action existed, except that interest upon damages incurred thereafter shall be computed from the date incurred. Where such damages were incurred at various times, interest shall be computed upon each item from the date it was incurred or upon all of the damages from a single reasonable intermediate date.

(c) Specifying date; computing interest. The date from which interest is to be computed shall be specified in the verdict, report or decision. If a jury is discharged without specifying the date, the court upon motion shall fix the date, except that where the date is certain and not in dispute, the date may be fixed by the clerk of the court upon affidavit. The amount of interest shall be computed by the clerk of the court, to the date the verdict was rendered or the report or decision was made, and included in the total sum awarded.

1992 AMENDMENTS

L. 1992, ch. 55, eff. April 10, 1992, amended Subd. (a) by expanding the list of actions in which interest is recoverable to include actions based on the imposition of a civil penalty, and amended Subd. (b) to provide the basis for determining the date from which interest is computed in that type of action.

§ 5002. Interest from verdict, report or decision to judgment.

Interest shall be recovered upon the total sum awarded, including interest to verdict, report or decision, in any action, from the date the verdict was rendered or the report or decision was made to the date of entry of final judgment. The amount of interest shall be computed by the clerk of the court and included in the judgment.

§ 5003. Interest upon judgment.

Every money judgment shall bear interest from the date of its entry. Every order directing the payment of money which has been docketed as a judgment shall bear interest from the date of such docketing.

§ 5003–a. Prompt payment following settlement.

(a) When an action to recover damages has been settled, any settling defendant, except those defendants to whom subdivisions (b) and (c) of this section apply, shall pay all sums due to any settling plaintiff within twenty-one days of tender, by the settling plaintiff to the settling defendant, of a duly executed release and a stipulation discontinuing action executed on behalf of the settling plaintiff.

CPLR

(b) When an action to recover damages has been settled and the settling defendant is a municipality or any subdivision thereof, or any public corporation that is not indemnified by the state, it shall pay all sums due to any settling plaintiff within ninety days of tender, by the settling plaintiff to it, of duly executed release and a stipulation discontinuing action executed on behalf of the settling plaintiff. The provisions of this paragraph shall not inure to the benefit of any insurance carrier for a municipality or any subdivision thereof, or any public corporation that is not indemnified by the state. Any such insurance carrier shall pay all sums due to any settling plaintiff in accordance with the provisions of subdivision (a) of this section.

(c) When an action to recover damages has been settled and the settling defendant is the state, an officer or employee of the state entitled to indemnification pursuant to section seventeen of the public officers law, or a public benefit corporation indemnified by the state, payment of all sums due to any settling plaintiff shall be made within ninety days of the comptroller's determination that all papers required to effectuate the settlement have been received by him. The provisions of this paragraph shall not inure to the benefit of any insurance carrier for the state, an officer or employee of the state entitled to indemnification pursuant to section seventeen of the public officers law, or a public benefit corporation indemnified by the state. Any such insurance carrier shall pay all sums due to any settling plaintiff in accordance with the provisions of subdivision (a) of this section.

(d) In an action which requires judicial approval of settlement, other than an action to which subdivision (c) of this section applies, the plaintiff shall also tender a copy of the order approving such settlement with the duly executed release and stipulation discontinuing action executed on behalf of the plaintiff.

(e) In the event that a settling defendant fails to promptly pay all sums as required by subdivisions (a), (b), and (c) of this section, any unpaid plaintiff may enter judgment, without further notice, against such settling defendant who has not paid. The judgment shall be for the amount set forth in the release, together with costs and lawful disbursements, and interest on the amount set forth in the release from the date that the release and stipulation discontinuing action were tendered.

(f) Nothing in this section shall apply to settlements subject to article seventy-four of the insurance law or to future installment payments to be paid pursuant to a structured settlement agreement.

(g) The term "tender", as used herein, shall mean either to personally deliver or to mail, by registered or certified mail, return receipt requested.

1992 AMENDMENTS

L. 1992, ch. 269, eff. June 30, 1992, added this section. L. 1992, ch. 270, eff. June 30, 1992, amended Subd. (f) by adding the words "or to future installment payments to be paid pursuant to a structured settlement agreement."

§ 5004. Rate of interest.

Interest shall be at the rate of nine per centum per annum, except where otherwise provided by statute.

CROSS REFERENCES

See **General Municipal Law § 3–a** as to rate of interest on judgments and accrued claims against municipal corporations.

1981 AMENDMENTS

L. 1981, ch. 258, eff. June 25, 1981, amended CPLR 5004 by increasing the rate of interest on judgments from six to nine percent. In actions in which interest is to be computed from a date prior to the effective date hereof, it shall be computed at six percent until such date and at nine percent thereafter.

1972 AMENDMENTS

L. 1972, ch. 358, eff. Sept. 1, 1972, amended CPLR 5004.

§§ 5005–5010. [Not used.]

§ 5011. Definition and content of judgment.

A judgment is the determination of the rights of the parties in an action or special proceeding and may be either interlocutory or final. A judgment shall refer to, and state the result of, the verdict or decision, or recite the default upon which it is based. A judgment may direct that property be paid into court when the party would not have the benefit or use or control of such property or where special circumstances make it desirable that payment or delivery to the party entitled to it should be withheld. In any case where damages are awarded to an inmate serving a sentence of imprisonment with the state department of correctional

CPLR

services or to a prisoner confined at a local correctional facility, the court shall give prompt written notice to the state crime victims board, and at the same time shall direct that no payment be made to such inmate or prisoner for a period of thirty days following the date of entry of the order containing such direction.

2001 AMENDMENTS

L. 2001, ch. 62, eff. June 25, 2001, amended to provide that where damages are awarded to an inmate, a written notice shall be given to the state crime victims board and no payment shall be made to such inmate for 30 days following the entry of an order containing such direction. Notwithstanding the expiration of any other statute of limitations, this amendment shall apply to: (i) all judgments originally entered prior to such effective date, regardless whether such judgment is subsequently amended or satisfied on or after such effective date; and (ii) all judgments, obligations, or agreements to pay profits from a crime or funds of a convicted person entered, incurred, or entered into on or after the effective date of this amendment.

R 5012.   Judgment upon part of cause of action; upon several causes.

The court, having ordered a severance, may direct judgment upon a part of a cause of action or upon one or more causes of action as to one or more parties.

R 5013.   Effect of judgment dismissing claim.

A judgment dismissing a cause of action before the close of the proponent's evidence is not a dismissal on the merits unless it specifies otherwise, but a judgment dismissing a cause of action after the close of the proponent's evidence is a dismissal on the merits unless it specifies otherwise.

§ 5014.   Action upon judgment.

Except as permitted by section 15-102 of the general obligations law, an action upon a money judgment entered in a court of the state may only be maintained between the original parties to the judgment where:

    1. ten years have elapsed since the first docketing of the judgment; or

2. the judgment was entered against the defendant by default for want of appearance and the summons was served other than by personal delivery to him or to his agent for service designated under rule 318, either within or without the state; or

3. the court in which the action is sought to be brought so orders on motion with such notice to such other persons as the court may direct.

An action may be commenced under subdivision one of this section during the year prior to the expiration of ten years since the first docketing of the judgment. The judgment in such action shall be designated a renewal judgment and shall be so docketed by the clerk. The lien of a renewal judgment shall take effect upon the expiration of ten years from the first docketing of the original judgment.

CPLR

CROSS REFERENCES

See **G.O.L.** § **15-102** in Appendix, *below.*

1986 AMENDMENTS

L. 1986, ch. 123, eff. Sept. 1, 1986, added a new closing paragraph providing for renewal judgments.

1965 AMENDMENTS

L. 1965, ch. 115, eff. April 26, 1965, amended the first paragraph by substituting reference to section "15-102 of the general obligations" law for reference to "two hundred thirty-two of the debtor and creditor" law.

1964 AMENDMENTS

L. 1964, ch. 485, eff. Sept. 1, 1964, amended paragraph 2.

R 5015.   Relief from judgment or order.

(a) On motion. The court which rendered a judgment or order may relieve a party from it upon such terms as may be just, on motion of any interested person with such notice as the court may direct, upon the ground of:

1. excusable default, if such motion is made within one year after service of a copy of the judgment or order with written notice of its entry upon the moving party, or, if the moving party has entered the judgment or order, within one year after such entry; or

2. newly-discovered evidence which, if introduced at the trial,

would probably have produced a different result and which could not have been discovered in time to move for a new trial under section 4404; or

3. fraud, misrepresentation, or other misconduct of an adverse party; or

4. lack of jurisdiction to render the judgment or order; or

5. reversal, modification or vacatur of a prior judgment or order upon which it is based.

(b) On stipulation. The clerk of the court may vacate a default judgment entered pursuant to section 3215 upon the filing with him of a stipulation of consent to such vacatur by the parties personally or by their attorneys.

(c) On application of an administrative judge. An administrative judge, upon a showing that default judgments were obtained by fraud, misrepresentation, illegality, unconscionability, lack of due service, violations of law, or other illegalities or where such default judgments were obtained in cases in which those defendants would be uniformly entitled to interpose a defense predicated upon but not limited to the foregoing defenses, and where such default judgments have been obtained in a number deemed sufficient by him to justify such action as set forth herein, and upon appropriate notice to counsel for the respective parties, or to the parties themselves, may bring a proceeding to relieve a party or parties from them upon such terms as may be just. The disposition of any proceeding so instituted shall be determined by a judge other than the administrative judge.

(d) Restitution. Where a judgment or order is set aside or vacated, the court may direct and enforce restitution in like manner and subject to the same conditions as where a judgment is reversed or modified on appeal.

1978 AMENDMENTS

L. 1978, ch. 156, eff. May 19, 1978, added new subdivision (c) and relettered former subdivision (c) as subdivision (d). The new CPLR 5015(c) replaces former § 217-a of the Judiciary Law, repealed by L. 1978, ch. 156.

1972 AMENDMENTS

Proposal No. 7 of the Judicial Conference Report to the 1972 Legislature, effective Sept. 1, 1972, amended Rule 5015 by inserting a new Subd. (b), by relettering former Subd. (b) as Subd. (c), and by inserting the words "or vacated" in Subd. (c). Subd. (c) was relettered subd. (d) in 1978.

R 5016. Entry of judgment.

(a) What constitutes entry. A judgment is entered when, after it has been signed by the clerk, it is filed by him.

(b) Judgment upon verdict. Judgment upon the general verdict of a jury after a trial by jury as of right shall be entered by the clerk unless the court otherwise directs; if there is a special verdict, the court shall direct entry of an appropriate judgment.

(c) Judgment upon decision. Judgment upon the decision of a court or a referee to determine shall be entered by the clerk as directed therein. When relief other than for money or costs only is granted, the court or referee shall, on motion, determine the form of the judgment.

(d) After death of party. No verdict or decision shall be rendered against a deceased party, but if a party dies before entry of judgment and after a verdict, decision or accepted offer to compromise pursuant to rule 3221, judgment shall be entered in the names of the original parties unless the verdict, decision or offer is set aside. This provision shall not bar dismissal of an action or appeal pursuant to section 1021.

(e) Final judgment after interlocutory judgment. Where an interlocutory judgment has been directed, a party may move for final judgment when he becomes entitled thereto.

1970 AMENDMENTS

L. 1970, ch. 93, eff. Sept. 1, 1970, amended Subd. (d) by adding new last sentence thereto.

The amendment was recommended by the Judicial Conference Jan. 2, 1970 Report to the Legislature, wherein it was stated in part:

"At present, CPLR 1021 allows the court to dismiss an action or appeal for unreasonable failure to substitute parties. Where the event requiring substitution is the death of a party, this provision conflicts with CPLR 5016(d), which provides that no verdict or decision shall be rendered against a deceased party.

"Under this amendment, the court will be able to dispose of the matter in one proceeding, rather than denying the motion to dismiss without prejudice to renewal after appointment of a representative." (See CPLR 1021.)

R 5017. Judgment-roll.

CPLR

(a) Preparation and filing. A judgment-roll shall be prepared by the attorney for the party at whose instance the judgment is entered or by the clerk. It shall be filed by the clerk when he enters judgment, and shall state the date and time of its filing.

(b) Content. The judgment-roll shall contain the summons, pleadings, admissions, each judgment and each order involving the merits or necessarily affecting the final judgment. If the judgment was taken by default, it shall also contain the proof required by subdivision (f) of section 3215 and the result of any assessment, account or reference under subdivision (b) of section 3215. If a trial was had, it shall also contain the verdict or decision, any tender or offer made pursuant to rules 3219, 3220 or 3221, and any transcript of proceedings then on file. If any appeal was taken, it shall also contain the determination and opinion of each appellate court and the papers on which each appeal was heard. In an action to recover a chattel, it shall also contain the sheriff's return. In an action on submitted facts under rule 3222, the judgment-roll shall consist of the case, submission, affidavit, each judgment and each order necessarily affecting the final judgment. The judgment-roll of a judgment by confession under section 3218 shall consist of the affidavit and a copy of the judgment.

1994 AMENDMENTS

L. 1994, ch. 89, eff. May 10, 1994, amended CPLR 5017(b) to change the reference to CPLR 3215(f).

§ 5018. Docketing of judgment.

(a) Docketing by clerk; docketing elsewhere by transcript. Immediately after filing the judgment-roll the clerk shall docket a money judgment, and at the request of any party specifying the particular adverse party or parties against whom docketing shall be made, the clerks shall so docket a judgment affecting the title to real property, provided however, that where the clerk maintains a section and block index, a judgment affecting the title to, or the possession, use or enjoyment of, real property may be entered in such index in lieu thereof. If the judgment is upon a joint liability of two or more persons the words "not summoned" shall be written next to the name of each defendant who was not summoned. Upon the filing of a transcript of the docket of a judgment of a court other than the supreme, county or a family court, the clerk of the county in which the judgment was entered shall docket the judgment. Upon the filing of a transcript of the docket of a judgment which has been docketed in the office of the clerk of the county in which it was entered, the clerk of any other county in the state shall docket the judgment. Whenever a county clerk dockets a judgment by transcript under this subdivision, he shall notify the clerk who issued it, who, upon receiving such notification, shall make an entry on the docket of the judgment in his office indicating where the transcript has been filed. A judgment docketed by transcript under this subdivision shall have the same effect as a docketed judgment entered in the supreme court within the county where it is docketed.

(b) Docketing of judgment of court of United States. A transcript of the judgment of a court of the United States rendered or filed within the state may be filed in the office of the clerk of any county and upon such filing the clerk shall docket the judgment in the same manner and with the same effect as a judgment entered in the supreme court within the county.

(c) Form of docketing. A judgment is docketed by making an entry in the proper docket book as follows:

1. under the surname of the judgment debtor first named in the judgment, the entry shall consist of:

(i) the name and last known address of each judgment debtor and his trade or profession if stated in the judgment;

(ii) the name and last known address of the judgment creditor;

(iii) the sum recovered or directed to be paid in figures;

(iv) the date and time the judgment-roll was filed;

(v) the date and time of docketing;

(vi) the court and county in which judgment was entered; and

(vii) the name and office address of the attorney for the judgment creditor;

2. under the surname of every other judgment debtor, if any, the entry shall consist of his name and last known address and an appropriate cross-reference to the first entry.

If no address is known for the judgment debtor or judgment

CPLR

creditor, an affidavit executed by the party at whose instance the judgment is docketed or his attorney shall be filed stating that the affiant has no knowledge of an address.

(d) A county clerk may adopt a new docketing system utilizing electro-mechanical, electronic or any other method he deems suitable for maintaining the dockets.

1991 AMENDMENTS

L. 1991, ch. 648, eff. July 26, 1991, added subdivision (d).

1970 AMENDMENTS

L. 1970, ch. 661, eff. May 8, 1970, amended Subd. (a) by inserting in the first sentence, "provided, however, that where the clerk maintains a section and block index, a judgment affecting the title to, or the possession, use or enjoyment of, real property may be entered in such index in lieu thereof."

1966 AMENDMENTS

L. 1966, ch. 707, eff. Sept. 1, 1966, amended Subd. (a). Amendment recommended by the Judicial Conference Feb. 1, 1966, Report to the Legislature: "CPLR 2222 provides for permissive docketing as a judgment of an order affecting title, possession, use or enjoyment of real property while CPLR 5018(a) mandates the docketing of a judgment affecting title to real property.

"In these circumstances the Judicial Conference believes that CPLR 5018(a) should be amended to conform to the request procedure for real property docketing provided in CPLR 2222. Mandatory docketing of all judgments affecting title to real property seems an unnecessary burden since in most cases such a judgment will be recorded and docketing will be pointless. It would appear sufficient to provide only for permissive docketing in the unusual case where it is requested by a party to the action who believes it essential to protect his rights. In such a case it seems reasonable to require that the party requesting docketing specify the particular adverse party or parties against whom the judgment is to be docketed."

1965 AMENDMENTS

L. 1965, ch. 773, eff. Sept. 1, 1965, amended subd. (c).

1964 AMENDMENTS

L. 1964, ch. 292, eff. Sept. 1, 1964, amended the first sentence of Subd. (a).

§ 5019.   Validity and correction of judgment or order; amendment of docket.

(a) Validity and correction of judgment or order.   A judgment or order shall not be stayed, impaired or affected by any mistake, defect or irregularity in the papers or procedures in the action not affecting a substantial right of a party. A trial or an appellate court may require the mistake, defect or irregularity to be cured.

(b) Subsequent judgment or order affecting judgment or lien. When a docketed judgment or the lien thereof is affected in any way by a subsequent order or judgment or retaxation of costs, the clerk of the court in which the judgment was entered shall make an appropriate entry on the docket of the judgment. In the case of a judgment of a court other than the supreme, county or a family court which has been docketed by the clerk of the county in which it was entered, such county clerk shall make an appropriate entry on his docket upon the filing of a certified copy of the order or judgment effecting the change or a certificate of the change issued by the clerk of the court in which the judgment was entered. Unless the order or judgment effecting the change otherwise provides, the duration of the judgment lien on real property shall be measured from the filing of the judgment-roll.

(c) Change in judgment creditor. A person other than the party recovering a judgment who becomes entitled to enforce it, shall file in the office of the clerk of the court in which the judgment was entered or, in the case of a judgment of a court other than the supreme, county or a family court which has been docketed by the clerk of the county in which it was entered, in the office of such county clerk, a copy of the instrument on which his authority is based, acknowledged in the form required to entitle a deed to be recorded, or, if his authority is based on a court order, a certified copy of the order. Upon such filing the clerk shall make an appropriate entry on his docket of the judgment.

(d) Certificate of county clerk. Upon the filing of a certificate of change of the docket of any judgment docketed with the clerk of the county in which it was entered, issued by such county clerk, the clerk of any court or county where the judgment has been docketed shall make an appropriate entry on his docket of the judgment.

§ 5020. Satisfaction-piece.

(a) Generally. When a person entitled to enforce a judgment receives satisfaction or partial satisfaction of the judgment, he shall execute and file with the proper clerk pursuant to subdivision (a) of section 5021, a satisfaction-piece or partial satisfaction-piece acknowledged in the form required to entitle a deed to be recorded, which shall set forth the book and page where the judgment is docketed. A copy of the satisfaction-piece or partial satisfaction-piece filed with the clerk shall be mailed to the judgment debtor by the person entitled to enforce the judgment within ten days after the date of filing.

(b) Attorney of record. Within ten years after the entry of a judgment the attorney of record or the attorney named on the docket for the judgment creditor may execute a satisfaction-piece or a partial satisfaction-piece, but if his authority was revoked before it was executed, the judgment may nevertheless be enforced against a person who had actual notice of the revocation before a payment on the judgment was made or a purchase of property bound by it was effected.

(c) When the judgment is fully satisfied, if the person required to execute and file with the proper clerk pursuant to subdivisions (a) and (d) hereof fails or refuses to do so within twenty days after receiving full satisfaction, then the judgment creditor shall be subject to a penalty of one hundred dollars recoverable by the judgment debtor pursuant to Section 7202 of the civil practice law and rules or article eighteen of either the New York City civil court act, uniform district court act or uniform city court act; provided, however, that such penalty shall not be recoverable when a city with a population greater than one million persons is the judgment creditor, unless such judgment creditor shall fail to execute and file a satisfaction–piece with the proper clerk pursuant to subdivisions (a) and (d) hereof within twenty days after having been served by the judgment debtor with a written demand therefor by certified mail, return receipt requested.

(d) Where a transcript of the docket of a judgment has been docketed in any other county of the state pursuant to subdivision (a) of section 5018, the person required to execute and file with the proper clerk pursuant to subdivision (a) hereof shall, upon receiving full satisfaction, file a certificate of the clerk of the county in which the judgment was entered, in accordance with subdivision (c) of section 5021, with the clerks of all other counties in which such judgment has been docketed.

1979 AMENDMENTS

L.1979, ch. 148, eff. June 28, 1979, amended CPLR 5020 subd. (a) by eliminating the requirement that the judgment debtor bear the cost of the filing and mailing of the satisfaction piece.

1977 AMENDMENTS

L. 1977, ch. 41, eff. Sept. 1, 1977, amended subd. (b) by extending from five to ten years the period after the entry of judgment within which an attorney may execute a satisfaction piece or a partial satisfaction piece.

1975 AMENDMENTS

L. 1975, ch. 575, eff. Aug. 1, 1975, amended Subd. (c) by adding a new proviso, barring a recovery of the statutory penalty when a city, having a population of greater than one million, is the judgment creditor, unless such city fails to execute and file a satisfaction-piece pursuant to Subds. (a) and (d), within 20 days after having been served by the judgment debtor with a written demand for a satisfaction-piece.

1974 AMENDMENTS

L. 1974, ch. 601, eff. July 1, 1974, amended CPLR 5020 by adding a new subdivision (d) and amending subds. (a) and (c).

1969 AMENDMENTS

L. 1969, ch. 213, eff. Sept. 1, 1969, amended Subd. (b) by extending to five years the time within which an attorney may execute a satisfaction-piece.

L. 1969, ch. 1051, eff. Sept. 1, 1969, amended Subd. (b) by extending to five years the time within which an attorney may execute a satisfaction-piece and added new Subd. (c).

§ 5020-a. Payment of judgment in certain cases.

When a judgment debtor has shown to the satisfaction of the clerk of the court from which an execution has been issued that a sum of money which satisfies the judgment had been sent to the last known address of the judgment creditor by registered or certified mail, return receipt requested, but was returned as unclaimed or undeliverable by the post office, the judgment debtor may deposit with the clerk of such court a certified check in an amount equal to the sum of money which satisfies the judgment. Upon receipt of such check any additional charges relating to an execution shall cease to accrue against the judgment debtor and the clerk shall forthwith notify each sheriff to whom an execution was issued that such execution is hereby rescinded. Such notice shall not be effective upon the sheriff until its receipt by him from the clerk. Provided, however, no entry of the satisfaction on the docket of the judgment made * be made by the clerk except pursuant to the provisions of section 5021.

* **[Editor's note:** So in original. Probably should read "may."]

CPLR

1981 AMENDMENTS

L. 1981, ch. 274, eff. Sept. 1, 1981, enacted a new section 5020-a.

§ 5021. Entry of satisfaction.

(a) Entry upon satisfaction-piece, court order, deposit into court, discharge of compounding joint debtor. The clerk of the court in which the judgment was entered or, in the case of a judgment of a court other than the supreme, county or a family court which has been docketed by the clerk of the county in which it was entered, such county clerk, shall make an entry of the satisfaction or partial satisfaction on the docket of the judgment upon:

1. the filing of a satisfaction-piece or partial satisfaction-piece; or

2. the order of the court, made upon motion with such notice to other persons as the court may require, when the judgment has been wholly or partially satisfied but the judgment debtor cannot furnish the clerk with a satisfaction-piece or partial satisfaction-piece; or

3. the deposit with the clerk of a sum of money which satisfies or partially satisfies the judgment pursuant to an order of the court, made upon motion with such notice to other persons as the court may require, permitting such deposit; such an order shall not be made unless the court is satisfied that there are no outstanding executions on which sheriff's fees have not been paid; or

4. the filing of an instrument specified in article eight of the debtor and creditor law, executed by a creditor releasing or discharging a compounding joint debtor; in such case, the entry on the docket of the judgment shall state that the judgment is satisfied as to the compounding debtor only.

(b) Entry upon return of execution. A sheriff shall return an execution to the clerk of the court from which the execution issued if such execution is wholly or partially satisfied, and the clerk shall make an appropriate entry on his docket of the judgment. The sheriff shall also deliver to the person making payment, upon request, a certified copy of the execution and of the return of satisfaction or partial satisfaction. Upon the filing of such copy with the clerk of the county where the execution was satisfied, such clerk shall enter satisfaction or partial satisfaction on his docket of the judgment. Provided however that, in addition, a return of execution arising out of an action brought pursuant to article eighteen of the New York city civil court act, article eighteen of the uniform city court act, article eighteen of the uniform district court act or article eighteen of the uniform justice court act shall be made and entered whether wholly or partially satisfied, or unsatisfied, within ninety days after receipt of the judgment by the sheriff and the clerk shall make an appropriate entry on his docket of the judgment.

(c) Entry upon certificate. Upon the filing of a certificate of the clerk of the county in which the judgment was entered, stating that the judgment has been wholly or partially satisfied, the clerk of any court or county where a judgment has been docketed shall make an appropriate entry on his docket of the judgment.

CROSS REFERENCES

Article 8 of the Debtor and Creditor Law, referred to in paragraph (4) of Subd. (a), *above*, was repealed by L. 1963, ch. 664, eff. Sept. 27, 1964; relevant provisions of the former article are now contained in **General Obligations Law § 15-101**, *et seq.*

1976 AMENDMENTS

L. 1976, ch. 156, eff. Sept. 1, 1976, amended Subd. (b) to provide for the return of an unsatisfied execution in actions brought under the small claims provisions of the Uniform Justice Court Act.

1975 AMENDMENTS

L. 1975, ch. 486, eff. Sept. 1, 1975, amended Subd. (b) by adding a new fourth sentence, requiring the making and entry of a return of execution arising out of small claims actions brought under Articles 18 of the N.Y.C. Civ. Ct. Act, U.C.C.A., or U.D.C.A., whether wholly or partially satisfied, or unsatisfied, within 90 days after sheriff's receipt of judgment, with an appropriate entry on judgment docket by the court clerk.

1970 AMENDMENTS

L. 1970, ch. 660, eff. May 8, 1970, amended Subd. (b) by deleting the requirements that the sheriff endorse his return on the execution and that the clerk maintain a record of all returns of executions; and by adding at the end of the first sentence the phrase "and the clerk shall make an appropriate entry on his docket of the judgment." The subdivision as amended requires the clerk of the issuing court to enter on his docket of the judgment whether the execution was returned wholly or partially satisfied.

CPLR

1965 AMENDMENTS

L. 1965, ch. 773, eff. Sept. 1, 1965, amended Subd. (b).

Article 50-A

PERIODIC PAYMENT OF JUDGMENTS IN MEDICAL AND DENTAL MALPRACTICE ACTIONS

SUMMARY OF ARTICLE

§ 5031. Basis for determining judgment to be entered.

In order to determine what judgment is to be entered on a verdict in an action to recover damages for medical, dental, or podiatric malpractice, or damages for wrongful death as a result of medical, dental, or podiatric malpractice, the court shall proceed as follows:

(a) The court shall apply to the findings of past and future damages any applicable rules of law regarding additurs and/or remittiturs, and adjust the verdict accordingly.

(b) Awards for all past damages, all damages for future loss of services, all damages for future loss of consortium, all damages in wrongful death actions, and damages for future pain and suffering of five hundred thousand dollars or less shall be paid in a lump sum. In any case in which all damages are to be paid in lump sums, the judgment shall be entered on the total of the lump sums, without further regard to this section.

(c) As to any award of damages for future pain and suffering in excess of five hundred thousand dollars, the court shall determine the greater of thirty-five percent of such damages or five hundred thousand dollars and such amount shall be paid in a lump sum. The remaining amount of the award for damages for future pain and suffering shall be paid in a stream of payments over the period of time determined by the trier of fact or eight years, whichever is less. The stream of payments for future pain and suffering shall be calculated by dividing the remaining amount of damages for future pain and suffering by the number of years over which such payments shall be made to determine the first year's payment and the payment due in each succeeding year shall be computed by adding four percent to the previous year's payment. The court shall determine the present value of the stream of payments by applying a discount rate to the stream of payments.

(d) The findings of future economic and pecuniary damages except in wrongful death actions, shall be used to determine a stream of payments for each such item of damages by applying (i) the growth rate, to the (ii) annual amount in current dollars, for the (iii) period of years, all of such items as determined by the finder of fact for each such item of damages. The court shall determine the present value of the stream of payments for each such item of damages by applying a discount rate to the stream of payments. After determining the present value of the stream of payments for future economic and pecuniary damages, thirty-five percent of that present value shall be paid in a lump sum, and the stream of payments for future economic and pecuniary damages shall be adjusted accordingly by proportionately reducing each item of the remaining stream of payments for future economic and pecuniary damages and paying those amounts over time in the form of an annuity in accordance with the provisions set forth in subdivision (g) of this section, subject to the adjustments and deductions specified in subdivision (f) of this section.

(e) The discount rate to be used in determining the present value of all streams of payments for periods of up to twenty years shall be the rate in effect for the ten-year United States Treasury Bond on the date of the verdict. As to any streams of payments for which the period of years exceeds twenty years, the discount rate to be used in determining the present value shall be calculated by averaging, on an annual basis, the rate in effect for the ten-year United States Treasury Bond on the date of the verdict for the first twenty years and two percentage points above the rate in effect for the ten-year United States Treasury Bond on the date of the verdict for the years after twenty years.

(f) After making the applicable calculations set forth above:

(1) The court shall apply any set-offs for comparative negligence and settlements by deducting them proportionately from each item of the damages awards, including the lump sum payments specified in subdivisions (b), (c), and (d) of this section, and the present value of the streams of payments specified in such subdivisions (c) and (d). After such deductions, the streams of payments specified in such subdivisions (c) and (d) and their present value shall be adjusted accordingly.

(2) The court shall then deduct the litigation expenses of the plaintiff's attorney proportionately from each remaining item of the damages awards, including the remaining lump sum payments specified in such subdivisions (b), (c), and (d), and the present value of the remaining streams of payments specified in such subdivisions (c) and (d), and such expenses shall be paid in a lump sum. After said deductions, the streams of payments specified in such subdivisions (c) and (d) and their present value shall be adjusted accordingly.

(3) The court shall then determine the attorney's fees based upon the remaining damages awards, including the remaining lump sum payments specified in such subdivisions (b), (c), and (d), and the present value of the remaining streams of payments specified in such subdivisions (c) and (d). The attorney's fees shall be deducted proportionately from each item of the remaining damages awards, including the remaining lump sum payments specified in such subdivisions (b), (c), and (d), and the present value of the remaining streams of payments specified in such subdivisions (c) and (d), and such fees shall be paid in a lump sum. After said deductions, the stream of payments specified in such subdivisions (c) and (d) and their present value shall be adjusted accordingly.

(4) Any liens which are not the subject of a separate award by the finder of fact shall then be deducted proportionately from each

CPLR

item of the remaining damages awards, including the remaining lump sum payments specified in such subdivisions (b), (c), and (d), and the present value of the remaining streams of payments specified in such subdivisions (c) and (d), and such liens shall be paid in a lump sum. After said deductions, the stream of payments specified in such subdivisions (c) and (d) and their present value shall be adjusted accordingly.

(g) The defendants and their insurance carriers shall be required to offer and to guarantee the purchase and payment of an annuity contract to make annual payments in equal monthly installments of the remaining streams of payments specified in such subdivisions (c) and (d), after making the deductions and adjustments prescribed in subdivision (f) of this section. The annuity contract shall provide that the payments shall run from the date of the verdict (unless some other date is specified in the verdict) for the period of years determined by the finder of fact (except the stream of payments for future pain and suffering, which shall not exceed eight years) or the life of the plaintiff, whichever is shorter, except that:

(1) awards for lost earnings shall be paid for the full term of the award determined by the finder of fact; and

(2) awards for any item of economic or pecuniary damages as to which the finder of fact found that the loss or item of damage is permanent, the payments for that item shall continue to run for the entire life of the plaintiff, increasing each year beyond the period of years determined by the finder of fact at the same growth rate as determined by the finder of fact.

(h) The judgment shall be entered on the lump sum payments and the present value of the streams of payments required to be made by the defendants under this section.

2003 AMENDMENTS

L. 2003, ch. 86, §§ 2, 4, eff. July 26, 2003, repealing and replacing the entire section.

1986 AMENDMENTS

L. 1986, ch. 485, eff. July 21, 1986, and applicable to acts, omissions or failures occurring on or after such date, amended CPLR 5031 to apply to podiatric malpractice actions.

1985 AMENDMENTS

L. 1985, ch. 294, eff. July 1, 1985, added Article 50-A, comprising CPLR 5031–5039. Article 50-A is applicable to any action for dental or medical malpractice commenced on or after July 1, 1985.

§ 5032. Form of security.

Security authorized or required for payment of a judgment for periodic installments entered in accordance with this article must be in the form of an annuity contract, executed by a qualified insurer and approved by the superintendent of insurance pursuant to section five thousand thirty-nine of this article, and approved by the court.

1985 AMENDMENTS

L. 1985, ch. 294, eff. July 1, 1985, added Article 50-A, comprising CPLR 5031–5039. Article 50-A is applicable to any action for dental or medical malpractice commenced on or after July 1, 1985.

§ 5033. Posting and maintaining security.

(a) If the court enters a judgment for periodic installments, each party liable for all or a portion of such judgment shall separately or jointly with one or more others post security in an amount necessary to secure payment for the amount of the judgment for future periodic installments within thirty days after the date the judgment is entered. A liability insurer having a contractual obligation and any other person adjudged to have an obligation to pay all or part of a judgment for periodic installments on behalf of a judgment debtor is obligated to post security to the extent of its contractual or adjudged obligation if the judgment debtor has not done so.

(b) A judgment creditor or successor in interest and any party having rights may move that the court find that security has not been posted and maintained with regard to a judgment obligation owing to the moving party. Upon so finding, the court shall order that security complying with this article be posted within thirty days. If security is not posted within that time and subdivision (c) of this section does not apply, the court shall enter a judgment for the lump sum as such sum is determinable under the law without regard to this article.

(c) If a judgment debtor who is the only person liable for a portion of a judgment for periodic installments fails to post and maintain security, the right to lump sum payment described in subdivision (b) of

CPLR

this section applies only against that judgment debtor and the portion of the judgment so owed.

(d) If more than one party is liable for all or a portion of a judgment requiring security under this article and the required security is posted by one or more but fewer than all of the parties liable, the security requirements are satisfied and those posting security may proceed under subdivision (b) of this section to enforce rights for security or lump sum payment to satisfy or protect rights of reimbursement from a party not posting security.

1985 AMENDMENTS

L. 1985, ch. 294, eff. July 1, 1985, added Article 50-A, comprising CPLR 5031–5039. Article 50-A is applicable to any action for dental or medical malpractice commenced on or after July 1, 1985.

§ 5034. Failure to make payment.

If at any time following entry of judgment, a judgment debtor fails for any reason to make a payment in a timely fashion according to the terms of this article, the judgment creditor may petition the court which rendered the original judgment for an order requiring payment by the judgment debtor of the outstanding payments in a lump sum. In calculating the amount of the lump sum judgment, the court shall total the remaining periodic payments due and owing to the judgment creditor, as calculated pursuant to subdivision (e) of section five thousand thirty-one of this article, and shall not convert these amounts to their present value. The court may also require the payment of interest on the outstanding judgment.

1999 AMENDMENTS

L. 1999, ch. 446, eff. July 27, 1999, amended CPLR § 5034 by changing the reference to the section providing for the calculation of the amount of lump sum judgments from CPLR § 5031(b) to CPLR § 5031(e).

1985 AMENDMENTS

L. 1985, ch. 294, eff. July 1, 1985, added Article 50-A, comprising CPLR 5031–5039. Article 50-A is applicable to any action for dental or medical malpractice commenced on or after July 1, 1985.

§ 5035. [Repealed]

§ 5036. Adjustment of payments.

(a) If, at the time after entry of judgment, a judgment creditor or successor in interest can establish that the continued payment of the judgment in periodic installments will impose a hardship, the court may, in its discretion, order that the remaining payments or a portion thereof shall be made to the judgment creditor in a lump sum. The court shall, before entering such an order, find that: (i) unanticipated and substantial medical, dental or other needs have arisen that warrant the payment of the remaining payments, or a portion thereof, in a lump sum; (ii) ordering such a lump sum payment would not impose an unreasonable financial burden on the judgment debtor or debtors; (iii) ordering such a lump sum payment will accommodate the future medical and other needs of the judgment creditor; and (iv) ordering such a lump sum payment would further the interests of justice.

(b) If a lump sum payment is ordered by the court, such payment shall be made by the medical malpractice insurance association created pursuant to article fifty-five of the insurance law and shall not be the obligation of the insurer providing the initial annuity contract. Such insurer shall thereafter make all future payments due under its annuity contract to the association, except that, if the lump sum payment ordered by the court is a portion of the remaining periodic payments, such insurer shall appropriately apportion future payments due under its annuity contract between the association and the judgment creditor or successor in interest. Such lump sum payment to be paid to the judgment creditor or successor in interest by the association shall be calculated on the basis of the present value of the annuity contract, which shall be based on its cost at such time, for remaining periodic payments, or portions thereof, that are converted into a lump sum payment. In no event shall such lump sum payment be greater than the present value of the annuity contract for the remaining periodic payments.

CROSS REFERENCES

Insurance Law Article 55, referred to in subdivision (b), governs the operations and management of the Medical Malpractice Insurance Association.

1988 AMENDMENTS

L. 1988, ch. 184, eff. July 1, 1988, repealed subdivision (b) and replaced it with a new (b) requiring lump-sum payments to be made by the medical malpractice insurance association (See Insurance Law § 55).

CPLR

1985 AMENDMENTS

L. 1985, ch. 294, eff. July 1, 1985, added Article 50-A, comprising CPLR 5031–5039. Article 50-A is applicable to any action for dental or medical malpractice commenced on or after July 1, 1985.

§ 5037. Settlements.

Nothing in this article shall be construed to limit the right of a plaintiff, defendant and any insurer to settle dental, medical or podiatric malpractice claims as they consider appropriate and in their complete discretion.

1986 AMENDMENTS

L. 1986, ch. 485, eff. July 21, 1986, and applicable to acts, omissions or failures occurring on or after such date, amended CPLR 5037 to apply to podiatric malpractice actions.

1985 AMENDMENTS

L. 1985, ch. 294, eff. July 1, 1985, added Article 50-A, comprising CPLR 5031–5039. Article 50-A is applicable to any action for dental or medical malpractice commenced on or after July 1, 1985.

§ 5038. Assignment of periodic installments.

An assignment of or an agreement to assign any right to periodic installments for future damages contained in a judgment entered under this article is enforceable only as to amounts: (a) to secure payment of alimony, maintenance, or child support; (b) for the cost of products, services, or accommodations provided or to be provided by the assignee for medical, dental or other health care; or (c) for attorney's fees and other expenses of litigation incurred in securing the judgment.

1985 AMENDMENTS

L. 1985, ch. 294, eff. July 1, 1985, added Article 50-A, comprising CPLR 5031–5039. Article 50-A is applicable to any action for dental or medical malpractice commenced on or after July 1, 1985.

§ 5039. Duties of superintendent of insurance.

The superintendent of insurance shall establish rules and procedures for determining which insurers, self-insurers, plans or arrangements are financially qualified to provide the security required under this article and to be designated as qualified insurers.

1985 AMENDMENTS

L. 1985, ch. 294, eff. July 1, 1985, added Article 50-A, comprising CPLR
5031–5039. Article 50-A is applicable to any action for dental or medical
malpractice commenced on or after July 1, 1985.

CPLR

Article 50-B

PERIODIC PAYMENT OF JUDGMENTS IN PERSONAL INJURY, INJURY TO PROPERTY AND WRONGFUL DEATH ACTIONS

SUMMARY OF ARTICLE

CPLR

§ 5041. Basis for determining judgment to be entered.

In order to determine what judgment is to be entered on a verdict in an action to recover damages for personal injury, injury to property or wrongful death under this article, and not subject to article fifty-A of this chapter, the court shall proceed as follows:

(a) The court shall apply to the findings of past and future damages any applicable rules of law, including set-offs, credits, comparative negligence pursuant to section fourteen hundred eleven of this chapter, additurs, and remittiturs, in calculating the respective amounts of past and future damages claimants are entitled to recover and defendants are obligated to pay.

(b) The court shall enter judgment in lump sum for past damages, for future damages not in excess of two hundred fifty thousand dollars, and for any damages, fees or costs payable in lump sum or otherwise under subdivisions (c) and (d) of this section. For the purposes of this section, any lump sum payment of a portion of future damages shall be deemed to include the elements of future damages in the same proportion as such elements comprise of the total award for future damages as determined by the trier of fact.

(c) Payment of litigation expenses and that portion of the attorney's fees related to past damages shall be payable in a lump sum. Payment of that portion of the attorney's fees related to future damages for which, pursuant to this article, the claimant is entitled to a lump sum payment shall also be payable in a lump sum. Payment of that portion of the attorney's fees related to the future periodically paid damages shall also be payable in a lump sum, based on the present value of the annuity contract purchased to provide payment of such future periodically paid damages pursuant to subdivision (e) of this section.

(d) Upon election of a subrogee or a lien holder, including an employer or insurer who provides workers' compensation, filed within the time permitted by rule of court, any part of future damages allocable to reimbursement of payments previously made by the subrogee or the lien holder shall be paid in lump sum to the subrogee or the lien holder in such amount as is calculable and determinable under the law in effect at the time of such payment.

(e) With respect to awards of future damages in excess of two hundred fifty thousand dollars in an action to recover damages for personal injury, injury to property or wrongful death, the court shall enter judgment as follows:

After making any adjustment prescribed by subdivision (b), (c) and (d) of this section, the court shall enter a judgment for the amount of the present value of an annuity contract that will provide for the payment of the remaining amounts of future damages in periodic installments. The present value of such contract shall be determined in accordance with generally accepted actuarial practices by applying the discount rate in effect at the time of the award to the full amount of the remaining future damages, as calculated pursuant to this subdivision. The period of time over which such periodic payments shall be made and the period of time used to calculate the present value of the annuity contract shall be the period of years determined by the trier of fact in arriving at the itemized verdict; provided, however, that the period of time over which such periodic payments shall be made and the period of time used to calculate the present value for damages attributable to pain and suffering shall be ten years or the period of time determined by the trier of fact, whichever is less. The court, as part of its judgment, shall direct that the defendants and their insurance carriers shall be required to offer and to guarantee the purchase and payment of such an annuity contract. Such annuity contract shall provide for the payment of the annual payments of such remaining future damages over the period of time determined pursuant to this subdivision. The annual payment for the first year shall be calculated by dividing the remaining amount of future damages by the number of years over which such payments shall be made and the payment due in each succeeding year shall be computed by adding four percent to the previous year's payment. Where payment of a portion of the future damages terminates in accordance with the provisions of this article, the four percent added payment shall be based only upon that portion of the damages that remains subject to continued payment. Unless otherwise agreed, the annual sum so arrived at shall be paid in equal monthly installments and in advance.

(f) With the consent of the claimant and any party liable, in whole or in part, for the judgment, the court shall enter judgment for the amount found for future damages attributable to said party as such are determinable without regard to the provisions of this article.

1986 AMENDMENTS

L. 1986, ch. 682, eff. July 30, 1986, and applicable to actions commenced or claims filed on or after such date, added new Article 50–B, comprising CPLR 5041 through 5049.

§ 5042.   Form of security.

Security authorized or required for payment of a judgment for periodic installments entered in accordance with this article must be in the form of an annuity contract, executed by a qualified insurer and approved by the superintendent of insurance pursuant to section five thousand forty-nine of this article, and approved by the court.

1986 AMENDMENTS

L. 1986, ch. 682, eff. July 30, 1986, and applicable to actions commenced or claims filed on or after such date, added new Article 50–B, comprising CPLR 5041 through 5049.

§ 5043.   Posting and maintaining security.

(a) If the court enters a judgment for periodic installments, each party liable for all or a portion of such judgment shall separately or jointly with one or more others post security in an amount necessary to secure payment for the amount of the judgment for future periodic installments within thirty days after the date the judgment is entered. A liability insurer having a contractual obligation and any other person adjudged to have an obligation to pay all or part of a judgment for periodic installments on behalf of a judgment debtor is obligated to post security to the extent of its contractual or adjudged obligation if the judgment debtor has not done so.

(b) A judgment creditor or successor in interest and any party having rights may move that the court find that security has not been posted and maintained with regard to a judgment obligation owing to the moving party. Upon so finding, the court shall order that security complying with this article be posted within thirty days. If security is not posted within that time and subdivision (c) of this section does not apply, the court shall enter a judgment for the lump sum as such sum is determinable under the law without regard to this article.

(c) If a judgment debtor who is the only person liable for a portion of a judgment for periodic installments fails to post and maintain security, the right to lump sum payment described in subdivision (b) of this section applies only against that judgment debtor and the portion of judgment so owed.

(d) If more than one party is liable for all or a portion of a judgment requiring security under this article and the required security is posted by one or more but fewer than all of the parties liable, the security requirements are satisfied and those posting security may proceed under subdivision (b) of this section to enforce rights for security or lump sum payment to satisfy or protect rights of reimbursement from a party not posting security.

1986 AMENDMENTS

L. 1986, ch. 682, eff. July 30, 1986, and applicable to actions commenced or claims filed on or after such date, added new Article 50–B, comprising CPLR 5041 through 5049.

§ 5044.   Failure to make payment.

If at any time following entry of judgment, a judgment debtor fails for any reason to make a payment in a timely fashion according to the terms of this article, the judgment creditor may petition the court which rendered the original judgment for an order requiring payment by the judgment debtor of the outstanding payments in a lump sum. In calculating the amount of the lump sum judgment, the court shall total the remaining periodic payments due and owing to the judgment creditor, as calculated pursuant to subdivision (e) of section five thousand forty-one of this article, and shall not convert these amounts to their present value. The court may also require the payment of interest on the outstanding judgment.

1999 AMENDMENTS

L. 1999, ch. 446, eff. July 27, 1999, amended by changing the reference to the section providing for the calculation of the amount of lump sum judgments from CPLR § 5041(b) to CPLR § 5041(e).

1986 AMENDMENTS

L. 1986, ch. 682, eff. July 30, 1986, and applicable to actions commenced or claims filed on or after such date, added new Article 50–B, comprising CPLR 5041 through 5049.

§ 5045. Effect of death of judgment creditor.

(a) Unless otherwise agreed between the parties at the time security is posted pursuant to section five thousand forty-three of this article, in all cases covered by this article in which future damages are payable in periodic installments, the liability for payment of any installments for medical, dental or other costs of health care or non-economic loss not yet due at the death of the judgment creditor terminates upon the death of the judgment creditor.

(b) The portion of any periodic payment allocable to loss of future earnings shall not be reduced or terminated by reason of the death of the judgment creditor, but shall be paid to persons to whom the judgment creditor owed a duty of support immediately prior to his death to the extent that such duty of support exists under applicable law at the time of the death of the judgment creditor. Such payments to such persons shall continue for the remainder of the period as originally found by the jury or until such duty of support ceases to exist, whichever occurs first. In such cases, the court which rendered the original judgment may, upon petition of any party in interest, modify the judgment to award and apportion the future payments of such unpaid future damages in accordance with this subdivision which apportioned amounts shall be payable in the future as provided for in this article. In the event that the judgment credit does not owe a duty of support to any person at the time of the death of the judgment creditor or such duty ceases to exist, the remaining payments shall be considered part of the estate of the judgment creditor. In such cases, the court which rendered the original judgment may, upon petition of any party in interest, convert those portions of such periodic payments allocable to the loss of future earnings to a lump sum by calculating the present value of such payments in order to assist in the settlement of the estate of the judgment creditor.

1986 AMENDMENTS

L. 1986, ch. 682, eff. July 30, 1986, and applicable to actions commenced or claims filed on or after such date, added new Article 50–B, comprising CPLR 5041 through 5049.

§ 5046. Adjustment of payments.

(a) If, at any time after entry of judgment, a judgment creditor or successor in interest can establish that the continued payment of the judgment in periodic installments will impose a hardship, the court may, in its discretion, order that the remaining payments or a portion thereof shall be made to the judgment creditor in a lump sum. The court shall, before entering such an order, find that: (i) unanticipated and substantial medical, dental or other health needs have arisen that warrant the payment of the remaining payments, or a portion thereof, in a lump sum; (ii) ordering such a lump sum payment would not impose an unreasonable financial burden on the judgment debtor or debtors; (iii) ordering such a lump sum payment will accommodate the future medical, dental and other health needs of the judgment creditor; and (iv) ordering such a lump sum payment would further the interests of justice.

(b) If a lump sum payment is ordered by the court, such lump sum shall be calculated on the basis of the present value of remaining periodic payments, or portions thereof, that are converted into a lump sum payment. Unless specifically waived by all parties, the annuity contract executed pursuant to section five thousand forty-two of this article shall contain a provision authorizing such a lump sum payment if such payment is approved pursuant to this section. The remaining future periodic payments, if any, shall be reduced accordingly. For the purposes of this section, present value shall be calculated based on the interest rate and mortality assumptions at the time such a lump sum payment is made as determined by the insurer who has provided the annuity contract, in accordance with regulations issued by the superintendent of insurance.

1986 AMENDMENTS

L. 1986, ch. 682, eff. July 30, 1986, and applicable to actions commenced or claims filed on or after such date, added new Article 50–B, comprising CPLR 5041 through 5049.

§ 5047. Settlements.

Nothing in this article shall be construed to limit the right of a plaintiff, defendant or defendants and any insurer to settle property damage, personal injury or wrongful death claims as they consider appropriate and in their complete discretion.

1986 AMENDMENTS

L. 1986, ch. 682, eff. July 30, 1986, and applicable to actions commenced or claims filed on or after such date, added new Article 50–B, comprising CPLR 5041 through 5049.

§ 5048. Assignment of periodic installments.

An assignment of or an agreement to assign any right to periodic installments for future damages contained in a judgment entered under this article is enforceable only as to amounts: (a) to secure payment of alimony, maintenance, or child support; (b) for the cost of products, services, or accommodations provided or to be provided by the assignee for medical, dental or other health care; or (c) for attorney's fees and other expenses of litigation incurred in securing the judgment.

1986 AMENDMENTS

L. 1986, ch. 682, eff. July 30, 1986, and applicable to actions commenced or claims filed on or after such date, added new Article 50–B, comprising CPLR 5041 through 5049.

§ 5049. Duties of superintendent of insurance.

The superintendent of insurance shall establish rules and procedures for determining which insurers, self-insurers, plans or arrangements are financially qualified to provide the security required under this article

CPLR

and to be designated as qualified insurers.

1986 AMENDMENTS

L. 1986, ch. 682, eff. July 30, 1986, and applicable to actions commenced or claims filed on or after such date, added new Article 50–B, comprising CPLR 5041 through 5049.

Article 51

ENFORCEMENT OF JUDGMENTS AND ORDERS GENERALLY

---

§ 5101. Enforcement of money judgment or order.

A money judgment and an order directing the payment of money, including motion costs, may be enforced as prescribed in article fifty-two. An order of support, alimony or maintenance of any court of competent jurisdiction where arrears/past-due support have not been reduced to judgment, including motion costs, may be enforced as prescribed in article fifty-two upon the default of a debtor as such term is defined in paragraph seven of subdivision (a) of section fifty-two hundred forty-one of this article, except that for the purposes of this section only, a default shall not be founded upon retroactive child support obligations as defined in paragraph (a) of subdivision one of section four hundred forty of the family court act and subdivision one of section two hundred forty, and paragraph b of subdivision nine of section two hundred thirty-six of the domestic relations law. The establishment of a default shall be subject to the procedures established for the determination of a mistake of fact for income executions pursuant to subdivision (e) of section fifty-two hundred forty-one of this article.

1993 AMENDMENTS

L. 1993, ch. 59, eff. July 1, 1993, to address the enforceability of support, alimony or maintenance orders upon the debtor's default.

§ 5102. Enforcement of judgment or order awarding possession of real property or a chattel.

A judgment or order, or a part thereof, awarding possession of real property or a chattel may be enforced by an execution, which shall particularly describe the property and designate the party to whom the judgment or order awards its possession. The execution shall comply with the provisions of section 5230, except that it shall direct the sheriff to deliver possession of the property to the party designated. In an action to recover a chattel, where the judgment awards possession of the chattel and in the alternative its value, the execution shall also direct the sheriff, if the chattel cannot be found within his county, to levy upon real and personal property as upon an execution to enforce a money judgment. After the death of a party against whom a judgment or order awarding possession of real property has been obtained, an order granting leave to issue such execution may be granted upon twenty days' notice, to be served in the same manner as a summons, to the occupants of the real property and to the heirs or devisees of the deceased party.

§ 5103. Enforcement of judgment or order directing sale of real property.

(a) Entry in county where real property situated. Where real property directed by a judgment or order to be sold is not situated in the county in which the judgment or order is entered, the judgment or order shall also be entered by the clerk of the county in which the property is situated upon filing with him a certified copy of the judgment or order. A purchaser of the property is not required to pay the purchase money or accept a deed until the judgment or order is so entered.

(b) Place and mode of sale; security. Where a judgment or order directs that real property shall be sold, it shall be sold in such manner as the judgment or order may direct in the county where it is situated by the sheriff of that county or by a referee appointed by the court for the purpose. If the property is situated in more than one county, it may be sold in a county in which any part is situated unless the judgment or order directs otherwise. If a referee is appointed to sell the property, the court may require him to give an undertaking in an amount fixed by it for the proper application of the proceeds of the sale. The conveyance shall specify in the granting clause the party whose right, title or interest is directed to be sold by the judgment or order and is being conveyed.

§ 5104. Enforcement of judgment or order by contempt.

Any interlocutory or final judgment or order, or any part thereof, not enforceable under either article fifty-two or section 5102 may be enforced by serving a certified copy of the judgment or order upon the party or other person required thereby or by law to obey it and, if he refuses or wilfully neglects to obey it, by punishing him for a contempt of the court.

CROSS REFERENCES

See selected provisions governing procedures to punish for contempt under **Judiciary Law, Article 19,** in Appendix, *below.*

§ 5105. Alternative enforcement of judgment or order.

An interlocutory or final judgment or order, or any part thereof, may be enforced either by the method prescribed in article fifty-two or that prescribed in section 5104, or both, where such judgment or part:

1. requires the payment of money into court or to an officer of, or receiver appointed by, the court, except where the money is due upon an express or implied contract or as damages for non-performance of a contract; or

2. requires a trustee or person acting in a fiduciary relationship to pay a sum of money for a willful default or dereliction of his duty.

§ 5106. Appointment of receiver.

A court, by or after judgment, may appoint a receiver of property which is the subject of an action, to carry the judgment into effect or to dispose of the property according to its directions. Unless the court otherwise orders, such a receivership shall be subject to the provisions of article sixty-four.

§ 5107. Conveyance by sheriff.

The court may require the sheriff to convey real property in conformity with its directions.

1964 AMENDMENTS

L. 1964, ch. 262, eff. Sept. 1, 1964, deleted the last sentence of CPLR 2703 and reenacted the same as CPLR 5107.

Article 52

ENFORCEMENT OF MONEY JUDGMENTS

SUMMARY OF ARTICLE

CPLR

* [**Editor's note:** No official heading.]

CPLR

CPLR

§ 5201. Debt or property subject to enforcement; proper garnishee.

(a) Debt against which a money judgment may be enforced. A money judgment may be enforced against any debt, which is past due or which is yet to become due, certainly or upon demand of the judgment debtor, whether it was incurred within or without the state, to or from a resident or non-resident, unless it is exempt from application to the satisfaction of the judgment. A debt may consist of a cause of action which could be assigned or transferred accruing within or without the state.

(b) Property against which a money judgment may be enforced. A money judgment may be enforced against any property which could be assigned or transferred, whether it consists of a present or future right or interest and whether or not it is vested, unless it is exempt from application to the satisfaction of the judgment. A money judgment entered upon a joint liability of two or more persons may be enforced against individual property of those persons summoned and joint property of such persons with any other persons against whom the judgment is entered.

(c) Proper garnishee for particular property or debt.

1. Where property consists of a right or share in the stock of an association or corporation, or interests or profits therein, for which a certificate of stock or other negotiable instrument is not outstanding, the corporation, or the president or treasurer of the association on behalf of the association, shall be the garnishee.

2. Where property consists of a right or interest to or in a decedent's estate or any other property or fund held or controlled by a fiduciary, the executor or trustee under the will, administrator or other fiduciary shall be the garnishee.

3. Where property consists of an interest in a partnership, any partner other than the judgment debtor, on behalf of the partnership, shall be the garnishee.

4. Where property or a debt is evidenced by a negotiable instrument for the payment of money, a negotiable document of title or a certificate of stock of an association or corporation, the instrument, document or certificate shall be treated as property capable of delivery and the person holding it shall be the garnishee; except that section 8—112 of the uniform commercial code shall govern the extent to which and the means by which any interest in a certificated security, uncertificated security or security entitlement (as defined in article eight of the uniform commercial code) may be reached by garnishment, attachment or other legal process.

CROSS REFERENCES

See **U.C.C. § 8-112,** referred to in paragraph (4) of subdivision (c), *above.*

1997 AMENDMENTS

L. 1997, ch. 566, § 20, eff. Oct. 10, 1997, amended subdivision (c)(4) to replace the Uniform Commercial Code reference.

1964 AMENDMENTS

L. 1964, ch. 298, eff. Sept. 1, 1964, amended paragraph 4 of Subd. (c) to add the provision following the semi-colon in respect to a security transferable in the manner set forth in the Uniform Commercial Code § 8-320.

§ 5202. Judgment creditor's rights in personal property.

(a) Execution creditor's rights. Where a judgment creditor has delivered an execution to a sheriff, the judgment creditor's rights in a debt owed to the judgment debtor or in an interest of the judgment

CPLR

debtor in personal property, against which debt or property the judgment may be enforced, are superior to the extent of the amount of the execution to the rights of any transferee of the debt or property, except:

1. a transferee who acquired the debt or property for fair consideration before it was levied upon; or

2. a transferee who acquired a debt or personal property not capable of delivery for fair consideration after it was levied upon without knowledge of the levy.

(b) Other judgment creditor's rights. Where a judgment creditor has secured an order for delivery of, payment of, or appointment of a receiver of, a debt owed to the judgment debtor or an interest of the judgment debtor in personal property, the judgment creditor's rights in the debt or property are superior to the rights of any transferee of the debt or property, except a transferee who acquired the debt or property for fair consideration and without notice of such order.

CROSS REFERENCES

As to definition of fair consideration, see **Debtor and Creditor Law § 272**, in Appendix, *below.*

§ 5203. Priorities and liens upon real property.

(a) Priority and lien on docketing judgment. No transfer of an interest of the judgment debtor in real property, against which property a money judgment may be enforced, is effective against the judgment creditor either from the time of the docketing of the judgment with the clerk of the county in which the property is located until ten years after filing of the judgment-roll, or from the time of the filing with such clerk of a notice of levy pursuant to an execution until the execution is returned, except:

1. a transfer or the payment of the proceeds of a judicial sale, which shall include an execution sale, in satisfaction either of a judgment previously so docketed or of a judgment where a notice of levy pursuant to an execution thereon was previously so filed; or

2. a transfer in satisfaction of a mortgage given to secure the payment of the purchase price of the judgment debtor's interest in the property; or

3. a transfer to a purchaser for value at a judicial sale, which shall include an execution sale; or

4. when the judgment was entered after the death of the judgment debtor; or

5. when the judgment debtor is the state, an officer, department, board or commission of the state, or a municipal corporation; or

6. when the judgment debtor is the personal representative of a decedent and the judgment was awarded in an action against him in his representative capacity.

(b) Extension of lien. Upon motion of the judgment creditor, upon notice to the judgment debtor, served personally or by registered or certified mail, return receipt requested, to the last known address of the judgment debtor, the court may order that the lien of a money judgment upon real property be effective after the expiration of ten years from the filing of the judgment-roll, for a period no longer than the time during which the judgment creditor was stayed from enforcing the judgment, or the time necessary to complete advertisement and sale of real property in accordance with section 5236, pursuant to an execution delivered to a sheriff prior to the expiration of ten years from the filing of the judgment roll. The order shall be effective from the time it is filed with the clerk of the county in which the property is located and an appropriate entry is made upon the docket of the judgment.

1972 AMENDMENTS

L. 1972, ch. 968, eff. Sept. 1, 1972, added new subparagraph (a)(6).

1965 AMENDMENTS

L. 1965, ch. 974, eff. Sept. 1, 1965, inserted the words "which shall include an execution sale" in Subd. (a), paragraphs 1 and 3.

1964 AMENDMENTS

L. 1964, ch. 388, eff. Sept. 1, 1964, corrected the cross-reference in Subd. (b) to "5235" to read "5236".

§ 5204. Release of lien or levy upon appeal.

Upon motion of the judgment debtor, upon notice to the judgment creditor, the sheriff and the sureties upon the undertaking, the court may order, upon such terms as justice requires, that the lien of a money judgment, or that a levy made pursuant to an execution issued upon a money judgment, be released as to all or specified real or personal property upon the ground that the judgment debtor has given an undertaking upon appeal sufficient to secure the judgment creditor.

1970 AMENDMENTS

L. 1970, ch. 600, eff. July 1, 1970, amended the section by requiring that the sheriff receive notice of a motion to release a lien of a money judgment or a levy made pursuant to an execution issued upon a money judgment.

§ 5205. Personal property exempt from application to the satisfaction of money judgments.

(a) Exemption for personal property. The following personal property when owned by any person is exempt from application to the satisfaction of a money judgment except where the judgment is for the purchase price of the exempt property or was recovered by a domestic, laboring person or mechanic for work performed by that person in such capacity:

     1. all stoves kept for use in the judgment debtor's dwelling house and necessary fuel therefor for sixty days; one sewing machine with its appurtenances;

     2. the family bible, family pictures, and school books used by the judgment debtor or in the family; and other books, not exceeding fifty dollars in value, kept and used as part of the family or judgment debtor's library;

     3. a seat or pew occupied by the judgment debtor or the family in a place of public worship;

     4. domestic animals with the necessary food for those animals for sixty days, provided that the total value of such animals and food does not exceed four hundred fifty dollars; all necessary food actually provided for the use of the judgment debtor or his family for sixty days;

     5. all wearing apparel, household furniture, one mechanical, gas or electric refrigerator, one radio receiver, one television set, crockery, tableware and cooking utensils necessary for the judgment debtor and the family;

     6. a wedding ring; a watch not exceeding thirty-five dollars in value; and

7. necessary working tools and implements, including those of a mechanic, farm machinery, team, professional instruments, furniture and library, not exceeding six hundred dollars in value, together with the necessary food for the team for sixty days, provided, however, that the articles specified in this paragraph are necessary to the carrying on of the judgment debtor's profession or calling.

(b) Exemption of cause of action and damages for taking or injuring exempt personal property. A cause of action, to recover damages for taking or injuring personal property exempt from application to the satisfaction of a money judgment, is exempt from application to the satisfaction of a money judgment. A money judgment and its proceeds arising out of such a cause of action is exempt, for one year after the collection thereof, from application to the satisfaction of a money judgment.

(c) Trust exemption.

1. Except as provided in paragraphs four and five of this subdivision, all property while held in trust for a judgment debtor, where the trust has been created by, or the fund so held in trust has proceeded from, a person other than the judgment debtor, is exempt from application to the satisfaction of a money judgment.

2. For purposes of this subdivision, all trusts, custodial accounts, annuities, insurance contracts, monies, assets or interests established as part of, and all payments from, either any trust or plan, which is qualified as an individual retirement account under section four hundred eight or section four hundred eight A of the United States Internal Revenue Code of 1986, as amended, a Keogh (HR-10), retirement or other plan established by a corporation, which is qualified under section 401 of the United States Internal Revenue Code of 1986, as amended, or created as a result of rollovers from such plans pursuant to sections 402 (a) (5), 403 (a) (4), 408 (d) (3) or 408A of the Internal Revenue Code of 1986, as amended, or a plan that satisfies the requirements of section 457 of the Internal Revenue Code of 1986, as amended, shall be considered a trust which has been created by or which has proceeded from a person other than the judgment debtor, even though such judgment debtor is (i) in the case of an individual retirement account plan, an

individual who is the settlor of and depositor to such account plan, or (ii) a self-employed individual, or (iii) a partner of the entity sponsoring the Keogh (HR-10) plan, or (iv) a shareholder of the corporation sponsoring the retirement or other plan or (v) a participant in a section 457 plan.

3. All trusts, custodial accounts, annuities, insurance contracts, monies, assets, or interests described in paragraph two of this subdivision shall be conclusively presumed to be spendthrift trusts under this section and the common law of the state of New York for all purposes, including, but not limited to, all cases arising under or related to a case arising under sections one hundred one to thirteen hundred thirty of title eleven of the United States Bankruptcy Code, as amended.

4. This subdivision shall not impair any rights an individual has under a qualified domestic relations order as that term is defined in section 414(p) of the United States Internal Revenue Code of 1986, as amended or under any order of support, alimony or maintenance of any court of competent jurisdiction to enforce arrears/past due support whether or not such arrears/past due support have been reduced to a money judgment.

5. Additions to an asset described in paragraph two of this subdivision shall not be exempt from application to the satisfaction of a money judgment if (i) made after the date that is ninety days before the interposition of the claim on which such judgment was entered, or (ii) deemed to be fraudulent conveyances under article ten of the debtor and creditor law.

(d) Income exemptions. The following personal property is exempt from application to the satisfaction of a money judgment, except such part as a court determines to be unnecessary for the reasonable requirements of the judgment debtor and his dependents:

1. ninety per cent of the income or other payments from a trust the principal of which is exempt under subdivision (c); provided, however, that with respect to any income or payments made from trusts, custodial accounts, annuities, insurance contracts, monies, assets or interest established as part of an individual retirement account plan or as part of a Keogh (HR-10), retirement or other plan

described in paragraph two of subdivision (c) of this section, the exception in this subdivision for such part as a court determines to be unnecessary for the reasonable requirements of the judgment debtor and his dependents shall not apply, and the ninety percent exclusion of this paragraph shall become a one hundred percent exclusion;

2. ninety per cent of the earnings of the judgment debtor for his personal services rendered within sixty days before, and at any time after, an income execution is delivered to the sheriff or a motion is made to secure the application of the judgment debtor's earnings to the satisfaction of the judgment; and

3. payments pursuant to an award in a matrimonial action, for the support of a wife, where the wife is the judgment debtor, or for the support of a child, where the child is the judgment debtor; where the award was made by a court of the state, determination of the extent to which it is unnecessary shall be made by that court.

(e) Exemptions to members of armed forces. The pay and bounty of a non-commissioned officer, musician or private in the armed forces of the United States or the state of New York; a land warrant, pension or other reward granted by the United States, or by a state, for services in the armed forces; a sword, horse, medal, emblem or device of any kind presented as a testimonial for services rendered in the armed forces of the United States or a state; and the uniform, arms and equipments which were used by a person in the service, are exempt from application to the satisfaction of a money judgment; provided, however, that the provisions of this subdivision shall not apply to the satisfaction of any order or money judgment for the support of a person's child, spouse, or former spouse.

(f) Exemption for unpaid milk proceeds. Ninety per cent of any money or debt due or to become due to the judgment debtor for the sale of milk produced on a farm operated by him and delivered for his account to a milk dealer licensed pursuant to article twenty-one of the agriculture and markets law is exempt from application to the satisfaction of a money judgment.

(g) Security deposit exemption. Money deposited as security for the rental of real property to be used as the residence of the judgment

CPLR

debtor or the judgment debtor's family; and money deposited as security with a gas, electric, water, steam, telegraph or telephone corporation, or a municipality rendering equivalent utility services, for services to judgment debtor's residence or the residence of judgment debtor's family, are exempt from application to the satisfaction of a money judgment.

(h) The following personal property is exempt from application to the satisfaction of money judgment, except such part as a court determines to be unnecessary for the reasonable requirements of the judgment debtor and his dependents:

1. any and all medical and dental accessions to the human body and all personal property or equipment that is necessary or proper to maintain or assist in sustaining or maintaining one or more major life activities or is utilized to provide mobility for a person with a permanent disability; and

2. any guide dog, service dog or hearing dog, as those terms are defined in section one hundred eight of the agriculture and markets law, or any animal trained to aid or assist a person with a permanent disability and actually being so used by such person, together with any and all food or feed for any such dog or other animal.

(i) Exemption for life insurance policies. The right of a judgment debtor to accelerate payment of part or all of the death benefit or special surrender value under a life insurance policy, as authorized by paragraph one of subsection (a) of section one thousand one hundred thirteen of the insurance law, or enter into a viatical settlement pursuant to the provisions of article seventy-eight of the insurance law, is exempt from application to the satisfaction of a money judgment.

(j) Exemption for New York state college choice tuition savings program trust fund payment monies. Monies in an account created pursuant to article fourteen-A of the education law are exempt from application to the satisfaction of a money judgment as follows:

1. one hundred percent of monies in an account established in connection with a scholarship program established pursuant to such article is exempt;

2. one hundred percent of monies in an account is exempt where the judgment debtor is the account owner and designated beneficiary

of such account and is a minor; and

3. an amount not exceeding ten thousand dollars in an account, or in the aggregate for more than one account, is exempt where the judgment debtor is the account owner of such account or accounts.

For purposes of this subdivision, the terms "account owner" and "designated beneficiary" shall have the meanings ascribed to them in article fourteen-A of the education law.

(k) Notwithstanding any other provision of law to the contrary, where the judgment involves funds of a convicted person as defined in paragraph (c) of subdivision one of section six hundred thirty-two-a of the executive law, and all or a portion of such funds represent compensatory damages awarded by judgment to a convicted person in a separate action, a judgment obtained pursuant to such section six hundred thirty-two-a shall not be subject to execution or enforcement against the first ten percent of the portion of such funds that represents compensatory damages in the convicted person's action; provided, however, that this exemption from execution or enforcement shall not apply to judgments obtained by a convicted person prior to the effective date of the chapter of the laws of two thousand one which added this sentence or to any amendment to such judgment where such amendment was obtained on or after the effective date of this subdivision. For the purpose of determining the amount of a judgment which is not subject to execution or enforcement pursuant to this subdivision: (i) the court shall deduct attorney's fees from that portion of the judgment that represents compensatory damages and multiply the remainder of compensatory damages by ten percent; and (ii) when the judgment includes compensatory and punitive damages, attorney's fees shall be pro rated among compensatory and punitive damages in the same proportion that all attorney's fees bear to all damages recovered.

(l) Exemption of banking institution accounts into which statutorily exempt payments are made electronically or by direct deposit.

1. If direct deposit or electronic payments reasonably identifiable as statutorily exempt payments were made to the judgment debtor's account in any banking institution during the forty-five day period preceding the date a restraining notice was served on the banking

CPLR

institution or an execution was served upon the banking institution by a marshal or sheriff, then two thousand five hundred dollars in the judgment debtor's account is exempt from application to the satisfaction of a money judgment. Nothing in this subdivision shall be construed to limit a creditor's rights under 42 U.S.C. § 659 or 38 U.S.C. § 5301 or to enforce a child support, spousal support, alimony or maintenance obligation. Nothing in this subdivision shall alter the exempt status of funds that are protected from execution, levy, attachment, garnishment or other legal process, pursuant to this section or under any other provision of state or federal law, or shall affect the right of a judgment debtor to claim such exemption.

2. For purposes of this article, "statutorily exempt payments" means any personal property exempt from application to the satisfaction of a money judgment under any provision of state or federal law. Such term shall include, but not be limited to, payments from any of the following sources: social security, including retirement, survivors' and disability benefits, supplemental security income or child support payments; veterans administration benefits; public assistance; workers' compensation; unemployment insurance; public or private pensions; railroad retirement; and black lung benefits.

3. (i) Beginning on April first, two thousand twelve, and at each three-year interval ending on April first thereafter, the dollar amount of the exemption provided in this section, subdivisions (e) and (h) of section fifty-two hundred twenty-two, subdivision (a) of section fifty-two hundred thirty and subdivision (e) of section fifty-two hundred thirty-two of this article in effect immediately before that date shall be adjusted as provided in subparagraph (ii) of this paragraph.

(ii) The superintendent of banks shall determine the amount of the adjustment based on the change in the Consumer Price Index for All Urban Consumers, New York-Northern New Jersey-Long Island, NY-NJ-CT-PA, published by the U.S. Department of Labor, Bureau of Labor Statistics, for the most recent three-year period ending on December thirty-first preceding the adjustment, with each adjusted amount rounded to the nearest twenty-five dollars.

(iii) Beginning on April first, two thousand twelve, and at each three-year interval ending on April first thereafter, the superintendent of banks shall publish the current dollar amount of the exemption provided in this section, subdivisions (e) and (h) of section fifty-two hundred twenty-two, subdivision (a) of section fifty-two hundred thirty and subdivision (e) of section fifty-two hundred thirty-two of this chapter, together with the date of the next scheduled adjustment. The publication shall be substantially in the form set below:

CURRENT DOLLAR AMOUNT OF EXEMPTION FROM EN-FORCEMENT OF JUDGMENT UNDER NEW YORK CIVIL PRACTICE LAW AND RULES Sections 5205(l), 5222(e), 5222(h), 5230(a), and 5232(e)

The following is the current dollar amount of exemption from enforcement of money judgments under CPLR sections 5205(l), 5222(e), 5222(h), 5230(a), and 5232(e), as required by CPLR section 5205(l)(3):

(Amount)

This amount is effective on April 1, (year) and shall not apply to cases commenced before April 1, (year). The next adjustment is scheduled for April 1, (year).

(iv) Adjustments made under subparagraph (i) of this paragraph shall not apply with respect to restraining notices served or executions effected before the date of the adjustment.

(m) Nothing in subdivision (l) of this section limits the judgment debtor's exemption rights in this section or under any other law.

(n) Notwithstanding any other provision of law to the contrary, the term "banking institution" when used in this article shall mean and include all banks, trust companies, savings banks, savings and loan associations, credit unions, foreign banking corporations incorporated, chartered, organized or licensed under the laws of this state, foreign banking corporations maintaining a branch in this state, and nationally chartered banks.

(o) The provisions of subdivisions (l), (m) and (n) of this section do not apply when the state of New York, or any of its agencies or municipal corporations is the judgment creditor, or if the debt enforced is for child support, spousal support, maintenance or alimony, provided that the restraining notice or execution contains a legend at the top thereof, above the caption, in sixteen point bold type with the following language: "The judgment creditor is the state of New York, or any of its agencies or municipal corporations, AND/OR the debt enforced is for child support, spousal support, maintenance or alimony."

CROSS REFERENCES

See **Debtor and Creditor Law, Article 10-A,** in Appendix, *below,* regarding exemptions for debtors in federal bankruptcy proceedings.

2009 AMENDMENTS

L. 2009, ch. 24, eff. May 4, 2009, amending subdivision (l) and adding subdivision (o) to provide that personal property that is otherwise exempt from application for satisfaction of a debt, may be applied to a debt to the state or its political subdivisions, or if the debt is for child support, spousal support, alimony or maintenance.

2008 AMENDMENTS

L. 2008, ch. 575, § 1, eff. Jan. 1, 2009, adding new subdivisions (l), (m), and (n) to establish a procedure for claiming exemption of certain income from levy of execution by judgment debtors; provides that certain accounts shall be exempt from execution.

2001 AMENDMENTS

L. 2001, ch. 62, § 11, eff. June 25, 2001, adding new subdivision (k). Notwithstanding the expiration of any other statute of limitations, this amendment shall apply to: (i) all judgments originally entered prior to such effective date, regardless whether such judgment is subsequently amended or satisfied on or after such effective date; and (ii) all judgments, obligations, or agreements to pay profits from a crime or funds of a convicted person entered, incurred, or entered into on or after the effective date of this act.

L. 2001, ch. 141, § 1, eff. Aug. 6, 2001, amending subdivision (c)(2) to include a plan that satisfies the requirements of I.R.C. § 457.

1998 AMENDMENTS

L. 1998, ch. 206, § 1, eff. July 7, 1998 and deemed to have been in full force and effect on and after January 1, 1998, amended CPLR 5205(c)(2) by adding the references to Internal Revenue Code § 408A.

1997 AMENDMENTS

L. 1997, ch. 398, § 61, eff. Jan. 1, 1998, amended CPLR 5205(c)(4) to provide for reaching such funds to enforce a qualified domestic relations order or other orders of support, alimony or maintenance.

L. 1997, ch. 546, § 5, eff. Sept. 10, 1997, and applicable to taxable years beginning after December 31, 1997, added new subdivision (j).

1995 AMENDMENTS

L. 1995, ch. 93, section 1, eff. Sept. 1, 1995, amended CPLR 5205(c)(2) by deleting the words "the corpus of" from the first sentence [following the word "either"], by replacing the word "qualifying" with the words "or plan, which is qualified," by adding the words "in the case of an individual retirement account plan, an individual who is the settlor of and depositor to such account plan," and by renumbering the remaining categories.

L. 1995, ch. 93, § 2, eff. Sept. 1, 1995, amended CPLR 5205(d)(1) by adding to subparagraph (1) the words "an individual retirement account plan or as part of."

1994 AMENDMENTS

L. 1994, ch. 127, eff. Sept. 1, 1994, amended CPLR 5205(c)(2), to add to the trust exemption provisions the corpus of a federally qualified Individual Retirement Account trust.

1993 AMENDMENTS

L. 1993, ch. 638, eff. Aug. 4, 1993, added subdivision (i) to exempt from application to the satisfaction of a money judgment the right of a judgment debtor to accelerate payment of part or all of the death benefit or special surrender value provided in a life insurance policy, or to enter into a viatical settlement as the owner of a life insurance policy covering catastrophic or life-threatening illness and providing that the insured may agree to accept compensation in return for assigning the right to receive a death benefit.

1989 AMENDMENTS

L. 1989, ch. 84, eff. May 11, 1989; ch. 84 superseded by L. 1989, ch. 280, eff. July 7, 1989.

1987 AMENDMENTS

L. 1987, ch. 108, eff. June 8, 1987, amended subd. (c) by designating language following words "Trust exemption," as par. 1, adding references therein to pars. 3 and 4, and adding pars. 2, 3 and 4.

1986 AMENDMENTS

L. 1986, ch. 404, eff. July 21, 1986, amended CPLR 5205(h)(2) to exempt "service dogs" (dogs that assist persons with disabilities) from property applicable to the satisfaction of a money judgment.

1980 AMENDMENTS

L. 1980, ch. 116, eff. May 13, 1980, amended CPLR 5205 by adding new subdivision (h).

1979 AMENDMENTS

L. 1979, ch. 148, eff. June 28, 1979, amended subd. (d) par. 1 by making a technical correction.

1978 AMENDMENTS

L. 1978, ch. 17, eff. March 14, 1978, added subdivision (g).

1977 AMENDMENTS

L. 1977, ch. 516, eff. July 1, 1977, amended subd. (e) to provide that exemptions to members of the armed forces shall not apply to the satisfaction of any order or money judgment for support of a child, spouse or former spouse.

1976 AMENDMENTS

L. 1976, ch. 129, eff. Sept. 1, 1976, amended Subd. (a), deleted former Subd. (b), and relettered the remaining subdivisions accordingly, in order to eliminate an improper sex distinction in the designation of items constituting exempt personal property.

L. 1976, ch. 697, eff. Aug. 23, 1976, amended paragraph 5 of Subd. (a) by adding one television set to the list of personal property exempt from application to the satisfaction of a money judgment.

1965 AMENDMENTS

L. 1965, ch. 623, eff. June 28, 1965, amended subsection (f), by raising the exemption from 60% to 90%.

§ 5206. Real property exempt from application to the satisfaction of money judgments.

(a) Exemption of homestead. Property of one of the following types, not exceeding fifty thousand dollars in value above liens and encumbrances, owned and occupied as a principal residence, is exempt from application to the satisfaction of a money judgment, unless the judgment was recovered wholly for the purchase price thereof:

1. a lot of land with a dwelling thereon,

2. shares of stock in a cooperative apartment corporation,

3. units of a condominium apartment, or

4. a mobile home.

But no exempt homestead shall be exempt from taxation or from sale for nonpayment of taxes or assessments.

(b) Homestead exemption after owner's death. The homestead exemption continues after the death of the person in whose favor the property was exempted for the benefit of the surviving spouse and surviving children until the majority of the youngest surviving child and until the death of the surviving spouse.

(c) Suspension of occupation as affecting homestead. The homestead exemption ceases if the property ceases to be occupied as a residence by a person for whose benefit it may so continue, except where the suspension of occupation is for a period not exceeding one year, and occurs in consequence of injury to, or destruction of, the dwelling house upon the premises.

(d) Exemption of homestead exceeding fifty thousand dollars in value. The exemption of a homestead is not void because the value of the property exceeds fifty thousand dollars but the lien of a judgment attaches to the surplus.

(e) Sale of homestead exceeding fifty thousand dollars in value. A judgment creditor may commence a special proceeding in the county in which the homestead is located against the judgment debtor for the sale, by a sheriff or receiver, of a homestead exceeding fifty thousand dollars in value. The court may direct that the notice of petition be served upon any other person. The court, if it directs such a sale, shall so marshal the proceeds of the sale that the right and interest of each person in the proceeds shall correspond as nearly as may be to his right and interest in the property sold. Money, not exceeding fifty thousand dollars, paid to a judgment debtor, as representing his interest in the proceeds, is exempt for one year after the payment, unless, before the expiration of the year, he acquires an exempt homestead, in which case, the exemption ceases with respect to so much of the money as was not expended for the purchase of that property; and the exemption of the property so acquired extends to every debt against which the property sold was exempt. Where the exemption of property sold as prescribed in this subdivision has been continued after the judgment debtor's death, or where he dies after the sale and before payment to him of his portion of the proceeds of the sale, the court may direct that portion of the proceeds which represents his interest be invested for the benefit of the person or persons entitled to the benefit of the exemption, or be otherwise disposed of as justice requires.

(f) Exemption of burying ground. Land, set apart as a family or private burying ground, is exempt from application to the satisfaction of a money judgment, upon the following conditions only:

CPLR

1. a portion of it must have been actually used for that purpose;

2. it must not exceed in extent one-fourth of an acre; and

3. it must not contain any building or structure, except one or more vaults or other places of deposit for the dead, or mortuary monuments.

CROSS REFERENCES

See **Debtor and Creditor Law, Article 10-A,** in Appendix, *below,* regarding exemptions for debtors in federal bankruptcy proceedings.

2005 AMENDMENTS

L. 2005, ch. 623, eff. Aug. 30, 2005, amended CPLR 5206(a)(d) and (e) by increasing the homestead exemption amount from civil judgments from $10,000 to $50,000.

1980 AMENDMENTS

L. 1980, ch. 717, eff. June 26, 1980, amended CPLR 5206(a) by adding mobile homes to the list of properties qualifying for the homestead exemption.

1977 AMENDMENTS

L. 1977, ch. 181, § 1, eff. Aug. 22, 1977, amended subd. (a) by making the homestead exemption applicable to shares in a cooperative apartment corporation and units of a condominium, and by increasing the value of the exemption from "two thousand dollars" to "ten thousand dollars . . . above liens and encumbrances;" deleted former subd. (b), which had required that property intended to be held as an exempt homestead be designated as such, and which had provided for the recording of such designation; relettered the remaining subdivisions accordingly, and deleted references therein to designation of exempt property; amended subds. (d) and (e) by increasing the value of the exemption from two thousand to ten thousand dollars; eliminated requirements from subd. (f) that land intended for use as burying ground must be so designated in order to attain exempt status, and that such designation be recorded as provided; and deleted former subd. (h) which had provided for cancellation of exemption of real property.

L. 1977, ch. 181, section 2 provided that the act shall not affect the application of property to the satisfaction of a money judgment for a debt contracted before the effective date. The section, as it appeared prior to the 1977 amendment is set forth below:

"§ 5206.   Real property exempt from application to the satisfaction of money judgments.

"(a) Exemption of homestead. A lot of land, with one or more buildings thereon, not exceeding two thousand dollars in value, owned and occupied as a principal residence by any person, and designated for that purpose, is exempt from application to the satisfaction of a money judgment, unless the judgment was recovered wholly for a debt contracted before the designation of the property, or for the purchase price thereof. But no property designated as an exempt homestead shall be exempt from taxation or from sale for non-payment of taxes or assessments.

"(b) Designation of exempt homestead. In order to be exempted as a homestead, a conveyance thereof, stating in substance that it is designed to be held as a homestead, exempt from application to the satisfaction of a money judgment, must be recorded, as prescribed by law; or a notice containing a full description of the property and stating that it is designed to be so held shall be subscribed by the owner, acknowledged or proved, and certified, in like manner as a deed to be recorded in the county where the property is situated, and must be recorded in the office of the recording officer of that county, in a book kept for that purpose, and styled the "homestead exemption book." In those counties where the clerk of the county is not the recording officer, designations heretofore recorded in the office of the clerk of the county shall be transferred to the office of the recording officer of that county.

"(c) Homestead exemption after owner's death. The homestead exemption continues after the death of the person in whose favor the property was exempted for the benefit of the youngest surviving child and until the death of the surviving spouse.

"(d) Suspension of occupation as affecting homestead. The homestead exemption ceases if the property ceases to be occupied as a residence by a person for whose benefit it may so continue, except where the suspension of occupation is for a period not exceeding one year, and occurs in consequence of injury to, or destruction of, the dwelling house upon the premises.

"(e) Exemption of homestead exceeding two thousand dollars in value. The exemption of a homestead is not void because the value of the property designated as exempt exceeds two thousand dollars but the lien of a judgment attaches to the surplus.

"(f) Sale of homestead exceeding two thousand dollars in value. A judgment creditor may commence a special proceeding in the county in which the homestead is located against the judgment debtor for the sale, by a sheriff or receiver, of a homestead exceeding two thousand dollars in value. The court may direct that the notice of petition be served upon any other person. The court, if it directs such a sale, shall so marshall the proceeds of the sale that the right and interest of each person in the proceeds shall correspond as nearly as may be to his right and interest in the property sold. Money, not exceeding two thousand dollars, paid to a judgment debtor, as representing his interest in the proceeds, is exempt for one year after the payment, unless, before the expiration of the year, he causes real property to be designated as an exempt homestead, in which case, the exemption ceases with respect to so

CPLR

much of the money as was not expended for the purchase of that property; and the exemption of the property so designated extends to every debt against which the property sold was exempt. Where the exemption of property sold as prescribed in this subdivision has been continued after the judgment debtor's death, or where he dies after the sale and before payment to him of his proportion of the proceeds of the sale, the court may direct that portion of the proceeds which represents his interest be invested for the benefit of the person or persons entitled to the benefit of the exemption, or be otherwise disposed of as justice requires.

"(g) Exemption of burying ground. Land, set apart as a family or private burying ground and heretofore designated as prescribed by law in order to exempt the same, or hereafter designated as prescribed in this subdivision for that purpose, is exempt from application to the satisfaction of a money judgment, upon the following conditions only:

"1. a portion of it must have been actually used for that purpose;

"2. it must not exceed in extent one-fourth of an acre; and

"3. it must not contain at the time of its designation, or at any time afterwards, any building or structure, except one or more vaults or other places of deposit for the dead, or mortuary monuments.

"In order to designate land to be exempted as prescribed in this subdivision, a notice containing a full description of the land to be exempted and stating that it has been set apart for a family or private burying ground must be subscribed by the owner; acknowledged or proved, and certified, in like manner as a deed to be recorded in the county where the land is situated; and recorded in the office of the clerk or register of that county, in the proper book for recording deeds, at least three days before the sale of the land by virtue of a procedure to secure its application to the satisfaction of a judgment.

"(h) Cancellation of exemption of real property. The owner of real property exempt as prescribed in this section may subscribe a notice, at any time, and personally acknowledge the execution thereof before an officer authorized by law to take the acknowledgment of a deed, to the effect that he cancels all exemptions from application of the property, or a particular part thereof, fully described in the notice, to the satisfaction of a money judgment. The cancellation takes effect when such a notice is recorded as prescribed in this section for recording a notice to effect the exemption so canceled. Nothing herein contained shall be so construed as to prevent a husband and wife from jointly conveying or mortgaging property so exempt."

1976 AMENDMENTS

L. 1976, ch. 129, eff. Sept. 1, 1976, amended Subd. (a) by deleting a provision which made the section applicable to the principal residence of a "woman or householder" and providing that the exemption apply instead to "any person."

1969 AMENDMENTS

L. 1969, ch. 961, eff. Jan. 1, 1970, amended subds. (a), (d) and (e).

§ 5207. Enforcement involving the state.

None of the procedures for the enforcement of money judgments are applicable to a judgment against the state. All procedures for the enforcement of money judgments against other judgment debtors are applicable to the state, its officers, agencies and subdivisions, as a garnishee, except where otherwise prescribed by law, and except that an order in such a procedure shall only provide for the payment of moneys not claimed by the state, and no judgment shall be entered against the state, or any officer, department, board or commission thereof, in such a procedure. This section shall not be deemed to grant any court jurisdiction to hear and determine claims or actions against the state not otherwise given by law to such court.

§ 5208. Enforcement after death of judgment debtor; leave of court; extension of lien.

Except where otherwise prescribed by law, after the death of a judgment debtor, an execution upon a money judgment shall not be levied upon any debt owed to him or any property in which he has an interest, nor shall any other enforcement procedure be undertaken with respect to such debt or property, except upon leave of the surrogate's court which granted letters testamentary or letters of administration upon the estate. If such letters have not been granted within eighteen months after the death, leave to issue such an execution or undertake such enforcement procedure may thereafter be granted, upon motion of the judgment creditor upon such notice as the court may require, by any court from which the execution could issue or in which the enforcement procedure could be commenced. A judgment lien existing against real property at the time of a judgment debtor's death shall expire two years thereafter or ten years after filing of the judgment-roll, whichever is later.

CROSS REFERENCES

As to obtaining leave from the Surrogate's Court to issue execution against decedent's estate, see **Surrogate's Court Procedures Act § 1812,** in Appendix, *below.*

§ 5209.   Discharge of garnishee's obligation.

A person who, pursuant to an execution or order, pays or delivers, to the judgment creditor or a sheriff or receiver, money or other personal property in which a judgment debtor has or will have an interest, or so pays a debt he owes the judgment debtor, is discharged from his obligation to the judgment debtor to the extent of the payment or delivery.

§ 5210.   Power of court to punish for contempt.

Every court in which a special proceeding to enforce a money judgment may be commenced, shall have power to punish a contempt of court committed with respect to an enforcement procedure.

CROSS REFERENCES

See selected provisions governing procedures to punish for contempt under **Judiciary Law, Article 19**, in Appendix, *below.*

§ 5211.   Privilege on examination; immunity.

The court may confer immunity upon any witness in accordance with the provisions of section 50.20 of the criminal procedure law for testimony or evidence in an enforcement procedure relating to disposition of property in which the judgment debtor has an interest, or relating to his or another person's claim to be entitled, as against the judgment creditor or a receiver, to hold property derived from or through the judgment debtor, or to be discharged from the payment of a debt which was due to the judgment debtor; provided, however, that no immunity shall be conferred except upon twenty-four hours' prior written notice to the appropriate district attorney having an official interest therein.

CROSS REFERENCES

CPL §§ 50.10 and 50.20, providing for compulsion of evidence by offer of immunity, appear in the Appendix, *below.*

1971 AMENDMENTS

L. 1971, ch. 1097, eff. Sept. 1, 1971, amended CPLR 5211 by deleting the reference to the Code of Criminal Procedure and substituting reference to the Criminal Procedure Law § 50.20.

1967 AMENDMENTS

L. 1967, ch. 680, eff. Sept. 1, 1967, inserted reference to Code of Criminal Procedure in place of reference to Penal Law.

§§ 5212–5220. [Not used.]

§ 5221. Where enforcement proceeding commenced.

(a) Court and county in which proceeding commenced.

1. If the judgment sought to be enforced was entered in the city court of any city outside the city of New York, and the respondent resides or is regularly employed or has a place for the regular transaction of business in person within the county in which the court is or was located, a special proceeding authorized by this article shall be commenced in that court or in the county court of that county.

2. If the judgment sought to be enforced was entered in a district court, or by a justice of the peace whose office has been or is by law to be abolished and whose jurisdiction has been or is by law to be superseded by a district court, and the respondent resides or is regularly employed or has a place for the regular transaction of business in person within the county in which such district court is established, a special proceeding authorized by this article shall be commenced in such district court.

3. If the judgment sought to be enforced was entered in the municipal court of the city of New York, the city court of the city of New York or the civil court of the city of New York, and the respondent resides or is regularly employed or has a place for the regular transaction of business in person within that city, a special proceeding authorized by this article shall be commenced in the civil court of the city of New York.

4. In any other case, if the judgment sought to be enforced was entered in any court of this state, a special proceeding authorized by this article shall be commenced, either in the supreme court or a county court, in a county in which the respondent resides or is regularly employed or has a place for the regular transaction of business in person or, if there is no such county, in any county in which he may be served or the county in which the judgment was

CPLR

entered.

5. If no court in which a special proceeding authorized by this article could be commenced is in session, the special proceeding may be commenced in the supreme court or a county court in any county within the judicial district in which the proceeding could otherwise be commenced or in any county adjoining the county in which the proceeding could otherwise be commenced.

(b) Notices, subpoenas and motions. A notice or subpoena authorized by this article may be issued from, and a motion authorized by this article may be made before, any court in which a special proceeding authorized by this article could be commenced if the person served with the notice, subpoena or notice of motion were respondent.

1989 AMENDMENTS

L.1989, ch. 124, eff. June 2, 1989, amended paragraph 1 of subdivision (a) to eliminate the list of cities and substitute the phrase "any city outside the city of New York."

1983 AMENDMENTS

L. 1983, ch. 341, eff. Sept. 1, 1983, amended CPLR 5221(a)(1) by adding Binghamton and Jamestown to the list of city courts to which the statute applies.

1980 AMENDMENTS

L. 1980, ch. 289, eff. Sept. 1, 1980, amended CPLR 5221(a)(1) by adding a reference to the courts of the city of White Plains.

1979 AMENDMENTS

L. 1979, ch. 92, eff. Sept. 1, 1979, amended par. 1 of subd. (a) of CPLR 5221 by adding the cities of Lockport, Niagara Falls and North Tonawanda to the list of cities to which the statute applies.

1976 AMENDMENTS

L. 1976, ch. 164, eff. May 18, 1976, amended CPLR 5221(a)(1) by adding thereto the City Court of New Rochelle.

1971 AMENDMENTS

L. 1971, ch. 1069, eff. Sept. 1, 1971, amended CPLR 5221(a)(1) by adding thereto the City Court of Long Beach.

1970 AMENDMENTS

L. 1970, ch. 554, eff. Sept. 1, 1970, amended Subd. (a)(1) by adding thereto the City Court of Rome.

1965 AMENDMENTS

L. 1965, ch. 518, eff. Sept. 1, 1965, renumbered paragraphs 2, 3 and 4 of Subd. (a), to 3, 4 and 5 respectively, and added a new paragraph 2 which begins "If the judgment sought to be enforced was entered in a district court . . ."

§ 5222.   Restraining notice.

(a) Issuance; on whom served; form; service.   A restraining notice may be issued by the clerk of the court or the attorney for the judgment creditor as officer of the court, or by the support collection unit designated by the appropriate social services district. It may be served upon any person, except the employer of a judgment debtor or obligor where the property sought to be restrained consists of wages or salary due or to become due to the judgment debtor or obligor. It shall be served personally in the same manner as a summons or by registered or certified mail, return receipt requested or if issued by the support collection unit, by regular mail, or by electronic means as set forth in subdivision (g) of this section. It shall specify all of the parties to the action, the date that the judgment or order was entered, the court in which it was entered, the amount of the judgment or order and the amount then due thereon, the names of all parties in whose favor and against whom the judgment or order was entered, it shall set forth subdivision (b) and shall state that disobedience is punishable as a contempt of court, and it shall contain an original signature or copy of the original signature of the clerk of the court or attorney or the name of the support collection unit which issued it. Service of a restraining notice upon a department or agency of the state or upon an institution under its direction shall be made by serving a copy upon the head of the department, or the person designated by him or her and upon the state department of audit and control at its office in Albany; a restraining notice served upon a state board, commission, body or agency which is not within any department of the state shall be made by serving the restraining notice upon the state department of audit and control at its office in Albany. Service at the office of a department of the state in Albany may be made by the sheriff of any county by registered or certified mail, return receipt requested, or if issued by the support collection unit, by regular mail.

(b) Effect of restraint; prohibition of transfer; duration.   A judgment debtor or obligor served with a restraining notice is forbidden to make or suffer any sale, assignment, transfer or interference with any property in which he or she has an interest, except upon direction of the sheriff or pursuant to an order of the court, until the judgment or order is satisfied or vacated. A restraining notice served upon a person other than the judgment debtor or obligor is effective only if, at the time of service, he or she owes a debt to the judgment debtor or obligor or he or she is in the possession or custody of property in which he or she knows or has reason to believe the judgment debtor or obligor has an interest, or if the judgment creditor or support collection unit has stated in the notice that a specified debt is owed by the person served to the judgment debtor or obligor or that the judgment debtor or obligor has an interest in specified property in the possession or custody of the person served. All property in which the judgment debtor or obligor is known or believed to have an interest then in and thereafter coming into the possession or custody of such a person, including any specified in the notice, and all debts of such a person, including any specified in the notice, then due and thereafter coming due to the judgment debtor or obligor, shall be subject to the notice. Such a person is forbidden to make or suffer any sale, assignment or transfer of, or any interference with, any such property, or pay over or otherwise dispose of any such debt, to any person other than the sheriff or the support collection unit, except upon direction of the sheriff or pursuant to an order of the court, until the expiration of one year after the notice is served upon him or her, or until the judgment or order is satisfied or vacated, whichever event first occurs. A judgment creditor or support collection unit which has specified personal property or debt in a restraining notice shall be liable to the owner of the property or the person to whom the debt is owed, if other than the judgment debtor or obligor, for any damages sustained by reason of the restraint. If a garnishee served with a restraining notice withholds the payment of money belonging or owed to the judgment debtor or obligor in an amount equal to twice the amount due on the judgment or order, the restraining notice is not effective as to other property or money.

(c) Subsequent notice. Leave of court is required to serve more than one restraining notice upon the same person with respect to the same judgment or order.

(d) Notice to judgment debtor or obligor. If a notice in the form prescribed in subdivision (e) has not been given to the judgment debtor or obligor within a year before service of a restraining notice, a copy of the restraining notice together with the notice to judgment debtor or obligor shall be mailed by first class mail or personally delivered to each judgment debtor or obligor who is a natural person within four days of the service of the restraining notice. Such notice shall be mailed to the defendant at his or her residence address; or in the event such mailing is returned as undeliverable by the post office, or if the residence address of the defendant is unknown, then to the defendant in care of the place of employment of the defendant if known, in an envelope bearing the legend "personal and confidential" and not indicating on the outside thereof, by the return address or otherwise, that the communication is from an attorney or concerns a judgment or order; or if neither the residence address nor the place of employment of the defendant is known then to the defendant at any other known address.

(e) Content of notice. The notice required by subdivision (d) of this section shall be in substantially the following form and may be included in the restraining notice:

NOTICE TO JUDGMENT DEBTOR OR OBLIGOR

Money or property belonging to you may have been taken or held in order to satisfy a judgment or order which has been entered against you. Read this carefully.

YOU MAY BE ABLE TO GET YOUR MONEY BACK

State and federal laws prevent certain money or property from being taken to satisfy judgments or orders. Such money or property is said to be "exempt". The following is a partial list of money which may be exempt:

1. Supplemental security income, (SSI);

2. Social security;

3. Public assistance (welfare);

4. Spousal support, maintenance (alimony) or child support;

5. Unemployment benefits;

6. Disability benefits;

7. Workers' compensation benefits;

CPLR

8. Public or private pensions;

9. Veterans benefits;

10. Ninety percent of your wages or salary earned in the last sixty days;

11. Twenty-five hundred dollars of any bank account containing statutorily exempt payments that were deposited electronically or by direct deposit within the last forty-five days, including, but not limited to, your social security, supplemental security income, veterans benefits, public assistance, workers' compensation, unemployment insurance, public or private pensions, railroad retirement benefits, black lung benefits, or child support payments;

12. Railroad retirement; and

13. Black lung benefits.

If you think that any of your money that has been taken or held is exempt, you must act promptly because the money may be applied to the judgment or order. If you claim that any of your money that has been taken or held is exempt, you may contact the person sending this notice.

Also, YOU MAY CONSULT AN ATTORNEY, INCLUDING ANY FREE LEGAL SERVICES ORGANIZATION IF YOU QUALIFY. You can also go to court without an attorney to get your money back. Bring this notice with you when you go. You are allowed to try to prove to a judge that your money is exempt from collection under New York civil practice law and rules, sections fifty-two hundred twenty-two-a, fifty-two hundred thirty-nine and fifty-two hundred forty. If you do not have a lawyer, the clerk of the court may give you forms to help you prove your account contains exempt money that the creditor cannot collect. The law (New York civil practice law and rules, article four and sections fifty-two hundred thirty-nine and fifty-two hundred forty) provides a procedure for determination of a claim to an exemption.

(f) For the purposes of this section "order" shall mean an order issued by a court of competent jurisdiction directing the payment of support, alimony or maintenance upon which a "default" as defined in paragraph seven of subdivision (a) of section fifty-two hundred forty-one of this article has been established subject to the procedures established for the determination of a "mistake of fact" for income executions pursuant to subdivision (e) of section fifty-two hundred forty-one of this article except that for the purposes of this section only a default shall not be founded upon retroactive child support obligations as defined in paragraph (a) of subdivision one of section four hundred forty of the family court act and subdivision one of section two hundred forty and paragraph b of subdivision nine of section two hundred thirty-six of the domestic relations law.

(g) Restraining notice in the form of magnetic tape or other electronic means. Where such person consents thereto in writing, a restraining notice in the form of magnetic tape or other electronic means, as defined in subdivision (f) of rule twenty-one hundred three of this chapter, may be served upon a person other than the judgment debtor or obligor. A restraining notice in such form shall contain all of the information required to be specified in a restraining notice under subdivision (a), except for the original signature or copy of the original signature of the clerk or attorney who issued the restraining notice. The provisions of this subdivision notwithstanding, the notice required by subdivisions (d) and (e) shall be given to the judgment debtor or obligor in the written form set forth therein.

(h) Effect of restraint on judgment debtor's banking institution account into which statutorily exempt payments are made electronically or by direct deposit. Notwithstanding the provisions of subdivision (b) of this section, if direct deposit or electronic payments reasonably identifiable as statutorily exempt payments as defined in paragraph two of subdivision (l) of section fifty-two hundred five of this article were made to the judgment debtor's account during the forty-five day period preceding the date that the restraining notice was served on the banking institution, then the banking institution shall not restrain two thousand five hundred dollars in the judgment debtor's account. If the account contains an amount equal to or less than two thousand five hundred dollars, the account shall not be restrained and the restraining notice shall be deemed void. Nothing in this subdivision shall be construed to limit a banking institution's right or obligation to restrain or remove such funds from the judgment debtor's account if required by 42 U.S.C. § 659 or 38 U.S.C. § 5301 or by a court order. Nothing in this subdivision shall alter the exempt status of funds that are protected from execution, levy, attachment, garnishment or other legal process, under section fifty-two hundred five of this article or under any other provision of state or federal law, or affect the right of a judgment debtor to claim such exemption.

(i) Effect of restraint on judgment debtor's banking institution account. A restraining notice issued pursuant to this section shall not apply to an amount equal to or less than the greater of two hundred forty times the federal minimum hourly wage prescribed in the Fair Labor Standards Act of 1938 or two hundred forty times the state minimum hourly wage prescribed in section six hundred fifty-two of the labor law as in effect at the time the earnings are payable (as published on the websites of the United States department of labor and the state department of labor) except such part thereof as a court determines to be unnecessary for the reasonable requirements of the judgment debtor and his or her dependents. This amount shall be equal to seventeen hundred sixteen dollars on the effective date of this subdivision, and shall rise to seventeen hundred forty dollars on July twenty-fourth, two thousand nine, and shall rise thereafter in tandem with the minimum wage. Nothing in this subdivision shall be construed to limit a banking institution's right or obligation to restrain or remove such funds from the judgment debtor's account if required by 42 U.S.C. § 659 or 38 U.S.C. § 5301 or by a court order. Where a judgment debtor's account contains an amount equal to or less than ninety percent of the greater of two hundred forty times the federal minimum hourly wage prescribed in the Fair Labor Standards Act of 1938 or two hundred forty times the state minimum hourly wage prescribed in section six hundred fifty-two of the labor law as in effect at the time the earnings are payable (as published on the websites of the United States department of labor and the state department of labor), the account shall not be restrained and the restraining notice shall be deemed void, except as to those funds that a court determines to be unnecessary for the reasonable requirements of the judgment debtor and his or her dependents. Nothing in this subdivision shall alter the exempt status of funds which are exempt from execution, levy, attachment or garnishment, under section fifty-two hundred five of this article or under any other provision of state or federal law, or the right of a judgment debtor to claim such exemption.

(j) Fee for banking institution's costs in processing a restraining notice for an account. In the event that a banking institution served with a restraining notice cannot lawfully restrain a judgment debtor's banking institution account, or a restraint is placed on the judgment debtor's account in violation of any section of this chapter, the banking institution shall charge no fee to the judgment debtor regardless of any terms of agreement, or schedule of fees, or other contract between the judgment debtor and the banking institution.

(k) The provisions of subdivisions (h), (i) and (j) of this section do not apply when the state of New York, or any of its agencies or municipal corporations is the judgment creditor, or if the debt enforced is for child support, spousal support, maintenance or alimony, provided that the restraining notice contains a legend at the top thereof, above the caption, in sixteen point bold type with the following language: "The judgment creditor is the state of New York, or any of its agencies or municipal corporations, AND/OR the debt enforced is for child support, spousal support, maintenance or alimony."

2009 AMENDMENTS

L. 2009, ch. 24, eff. May 4, 2009, adding subdivision (k) to provide that personal property that is otherwise exempt from application for satisfaction of a debt, may be applied to a debt to the state or its political subdivisions, or if the debt is for child support, spousal support, alimony or maintenance.

2008 AMENDMENTS

L. 2008, ch. 575, eff. Jan. 1, 2009, amending subdivisions (b), (c), (d), and (e), and adding subdivisions (h), (i), and (j) to establish a procedure for claiming exemption of certain income from levy of execution by judgment debtors; provides that certain accounts shall be exempt from execution.

2000 AMENDMENTS

L. 2000, ch. 409, eff. Sept. 29, 2000, amending subdivisions (a) and (g) pertaining to use of other electronic means.

1994 AMENDMENTS

L. 1994, ch. 35, eff. April 4, 1994, added a new subdivision (g) pertaining to restraining notices in the form of magnetic tape.

1993 AMENDMENTS

L. 1993, ch. 59, eff. July 1, 1993, amended subdivision (a) by adding the words "or by the support collection unit designated by the appropriate social services district"; by adding the words "support collection unit" throughout the section; by adding the words "or obligor" following the words "judgment debtor" throughout the section; by adding the words "or if issued by the support collection unit, by regular mail" to the third sentence and the final sentence of subdivision (a); to add the words "or order" following the word "judgment" throughout the section; to add the words "or the name of the support collection unit which" to the fifth sentence of subdivision (a); to add the words "or her" following the words "to him" throughout the section; and to add a new subdivision (f).

1991 AMENDMENTS

L. 1991, ch. 314, eff. July 15, 1991, amended subdivision (a) by requiring that a restraining notice contain the original signature or copy of the original signature of the clerk of the court or attorney who issued it.

1982 AMENDMENTS

L. 1982, ch. 882, eff. Sept. 1, 1982, amended CPLR 5222 by adding two new subdivisions (d) and (e).

1969 AMENDMENTS

L. 1969, ch. 1137, eff. May 26, 1969, amended Subd. (a) by adding to the second sentence thereof, "except the employer of a judgment debtor where the property sought to be restrained consists of wages or salary due or to become due to the judgment debtor."

1968 AMENDMENTS

L. 1968, ch. 743, eff. Sept. 1, 1968, inserted last two sentences in Subd. (a) pertaining to service of a restraining notice upon the state of New York.

§ 5222-a. Service of notices and forms and procedure for claim of exemption.

(a) Applicability. Any person authorized under subdivision (a) of section fifty-two hundred twenty-two of this article issuing a restraining notice affecting a natural person's account at a banking institution pursuant to such subdivision must comply with this section, in addition to the general provisions set forth in such section. Any sheriff levying against a natural person's account at a banking institution pursuant to section fifty-two hundred thirty-two of this article must comply with this section, in addition to the general provisions set forth in section fifty-two hundred thirty-two of this article. The procedures set forth in subdivisions (b), (c), (d), (e), (f) and (g) of this section shall not apply where pursuant to subdivision (h) and/or (i) of section fifty-two hundred twenty-two or subdivision (e) of section fifty-two hundred thirty-two of this article, no funds in the account are restrained or levied upon.

(b) Service of exemption notice and exemption claim form.

1. Service with restraining notice upon banking institution. The person issuing the restraining notice pursuant to subdivision (a) of section fifty-two hundred twenty-two of this article shall provide the banking institution with the restraining notice, a copy of the restraining notice, an exemption notice and two exemption claim forms with sections titled "ADDRESS A" and "ADDRESS B" completed. The exemption notice and exemption claim forms shall be in the forms set forth in paragraph four of this subdivision. The notice and the forms shall be served on the banking institution together with the restraining notice and copy of the restraining notice. Service must be accomplished in accordance with subdivision (a) or (g) of section fifty-two hundred twenty-two of this article. Failure to serve the notice and forms together with the restraining notice renders the restraining notice void, and the banking institution shall not restrain the account.

2. Service of execution by levy upon a garnishee banking institution. When serving an execution pursuant to subdivision (a) of section fifty-two hundred thirty-two of this article, the sheriff shall provide the banking institution with an exemption notice and two exemption claim forms, which shall be in the forms set forth in paragraph four of this subdivision. The sheriff shall serve both the exemption notice and the exemption claim forms on the banking institution together with the execution notice. Service must be accomplished in accordance with subdivision (a) of section fifty-two hundred thirty-two of this article. Failure to serve the notice and forms renders the execution void, and the banking institution shall not levy upon the account.

3. Service upon judgment debtor. Within two business days after receipt of the restraining notice or execution, exemption notice and exemption claim forms, the banking institution shall serve upon the judgment debtor the copy of the restraining notice, the exemption notice and two exemption claim forms. The banking institution shall serve the notice and forms by first class mail to the last known address of the judgment debtor. The inadvertent failure by a depository

institution to provide the notice required by this subdivision shall not give rise to liability on the part of the depository institution.

4. Content of exemption notice and exemption claim form.

a. The exemption notice shall be in the following form:

"EXEMPTION NOTICE

as required by New York Law

YOUR BANK ACCOUNT IS RESTRAINED OR "FROZEN"

The attached Restraining Notice or notice of Levy by Execution has been issued against your bank account. You are receiving this notice because a creditor has obtained a money judgment against you, and one or more of your bank accounts has been restrained to pay the judgment. A money judgment is a court's decision that you owe money to a creditor.

You should be aware that FUTURE DEPOSITS into your account(s) might also be restrained if you do not respond to this notice. You may be able to "vacate" (remove) the judgment. If the judgment is vacated, your bank account will be released. Consult an attorney (including free legal services) or visit the court clerk for more information about how to do this.

Under state and federal law, certain types of funds cannot be taken from your bank account to pay a judgment. Such money is said to be "exempt."

DOES YOUR BANK ACCOUNT CONTAIN ANY OF THE FOL-LOWING TYPES OF FUNDS?

1. Social security;

2. Social security disability (SSD);

3. Supplemental security income (SSI);

4. Public assistance (welfare);

5. Income earned while receiving SSI or public assistance;

6. Veterans benefits;

7. Unemployment insurance;

8. Payments from pensions and retirement accounts;

9. Disability benefits;

10. Income earned in the last 60 days (90% of which is exempt);

11. Workers' compensation benefits;

12. Child support;

13. Spousal support or maintenance (alimony);

14. Railroad retirement; and/or

15. Black lung benefits.

If YES, you can claim that your money is exempt and cannot be taken.

To make the claim, you must

(a) complete the EXEMPTION CLAIM FORM attached;

(b) deliver or mail the form to the bank with the restrained or "frozen" account; and

(c) deliver or mail the form to the creditor or its attorney at the address listed on the form.

You must send the forms within 20 DAYS of the postmarked date on the envelope holding this notice. You may be able to get your account released faster if you send to the creditor or its attorney written proof that your money is exempt. Proof can include an award letter from the government, an annual statement from your pension, pay stubs, copies of checks, bank records showing the last two months of account activity, or other papers showing that the money in your bank account is exempt. If you send the creditor's attorney proof that the money in your account is exempt, the attorney must release that money within seven days. You do not need an attorney to make an exemption claim using the form."

b. The exemption claim form shall be in the following form:

CPLR

NAME OF COURT, NAME
OF COUNTY

_____

PLAINTIFF/PETITIONER/
CLAIMANT   INDEX NO.

                        V.   EXEMPTION CLAIM FORM

DEFENDANT/
RESPONDENT

_____

NAME AND ADDRESS OF JUDG-   NAME AND ADDRESS OF FI-
MENT CREDITOR OR   NANCIAL INSTITUTION
ATTORNEY   (To be completed by judgment
(To be completed by judgment creditor or attorney)
creditor or attorney)   ADDRESS
ADDRESS
A _____   B _____

Directions: To claim that some or all of the funds in your account are exempt, complete both copies of this form, and make one copy for yourself. Mail or deliver one form to ADDRESS A and one form to ADDRESS B within twenty days of the date on the envelope holding this notice.

** If you have any documents, such as an award letter, an annual statement from your pension, paystubs, copies of checks or bank records showing the last two months of account activity, include copies of the documents with this form. Your account may be released more quickly.

_____

I state that my account contains the following type(s) of funds (check all that apply):

—   Social security

—   Social security disability (SSD)

—   Supplemental security income (SSI)

—   Public assistance

—   Wages while receiving SSI or public assistance

— Veterans benefits

— Unemployment insurance

— Payments from pensions and retirement accounts

— Income earned in the last 60 days (90% of which is exempt)

— Child support

— Spousal support or maintenance (alimony)

— Workers' compensation

— Railroad retirement or black lung benefits

— Other (describe exemption)_____

CPLR

I request that any correspondence to me regarding my claim be sent to the following address:

_____

(FILL IN YOUR COMPLETE ADDRESS)

I certify under penalty of perjury that the statement above is true to the best of my knowledge and belief.

_____

DATE   SIGNATURE OF JUDGMENT DEBTOR

_____

(c) Claim of exemption. 1. To claim an exemption pursuant to the procedures in this section, the judgment debtor shall complete the exemption claim forms, sign them under penalty of perjury, and serve them within twenty days of the date postmarked on the correspondence containing the notice and forms. The judgment debtor shall serve one completed exemption claim form on the banking institution and the other on the attorney for the judgment creditor. In the event that there is no attorney for the judgment creditor, then the exemption claim form must be served directly on the judgment creditor. The judgment debtor may serve the exemption claim forms in person or by first-class mail.

2. Where the banking institution receives an exemption claim form, it shall notify the judgment creditor forthwith of the date on which the funds will be released pursuant to paragraph three of this subdivision.

3. The banking institution shall release all funds in the judgment debtor's account eight days after the date postmarked on the envelope containing the executed exemption claim form mailed to the banking institution or the date of personal delivery of the executed exemption claim form to the banking institution, and the restraint shall be deemed void, except where the judgment creditor interposes an objection to the exemption within that time.

4. Where the executed exemption claim form sent to the judgment creditor is accompanied by information demonstrating that all funds in the account are exempt, the judgment creditor shall, within seven days of the postmark on the envelope containing the exemption claim form and accompanying information, instruct the banking institution to release the account, and the restraint shall be deemed void. Where the account contains some funds from exempt sources, and other funds from unknown sources, the judgment creditor shall apply the lowest intermediate balance principle of accounting and, within seven days of the postmark on the envelope containing the exemption claim form and accompanying information, shall instruct the banking institution to release the exempt money in the account. The provisions of paragraph two of subdivision (b) of rule twenty-one hundred three of this chapter shall not enlarge the judgment creditor's time to move pursuant to this section. Information demonstrating that funds are exempt includes, but is not limited to, originals or copies of benefit award letters, checks, check stubs or any other document that discloses the source of the judgment debtor's income, and bank records showing the last two months of account activity. If the judgment creditor fails to act in accordance with this subdivision, the judgment creditor shall be deemed to have acted in bad faith and the judgment debtor may seek a court award of the damages, costs, fees and penalties provided for in subdivision (g) of this section.

5. If no claim of exemption is received by the banking institution within twenty-five days after the notice and forms are mailed to the judgment debtor, the funds remain subject to the restraining notice or execution. Failure of the judgment debtor to deliver the executed exemption claim form does not constitute a waiver of any right to an exemption.

(d) Objection to exemption claim and request for hearing. A judgment creditor may object to the claim of exemption by moving for an order pursuant to section fifty-two hundred forty of this article. The judgment creditor must serve the banking institution and the judgment debtor with its motion papers within eight days after the date postmarked on the envelope containing the executed exemption claim form or the date of personal delivery of the executed exemption claim form to the banking institution, and the provisions of paragraph one of subdivision (b) of rule twenty-one hundred three of this chapter shall not enlarge the judgment creditor's time to move pursuant to this section. The judgment debtor shall be served at the address provided on the exemption claim form. The affirmation or affidavit in support of the motion shall demonstrate a reasonable belief that such judgment debtor's account contains funds that are not exempt from execution and the amount of such nonexempt funds. The executed exemption claim form shall be attached to the affirmation or affidavit. The affirmation or affidavit shall not be conclusory, but is required to show the factual basis upon which the reasonable belief is based. The hearing to decide the motion shall be noticed for seven days after service of the moving papers. The executed exemption claim form shall be prima facie evidence at such hearing that the funds in the account are exempt funds. The burden of proof shall be upon the judgment creditor to establish the amount of funds that are not exempt. The court shall, within five days of the hearing, issue an order stating whether or not funds in the account are exempt and ordering the appropriate relief. The judgment creditor or its attorney must serve the order on the banking institution and the judgment debtor no later than two business days after the court issues the order.

(e) Duties of banking institution if objection is made to exemption claim. Upon receipt of a written objection pursuant to subdivision (d) of this section from the judgment creditor or its attorney within the specified eight-day period, the banking institution shall retain the funds claimed to be exempt for twenty-one days unless otherwise ordered by the court. If the period of twenty-one days expires and the banking institution has not been otherwise ordered by the court, the banking institution shall release the funds to the judgment debtor.

(f) Release of funds. At any time during the procedure specified in this section, the judgment debtor or the judgment creditor may, by a writing dated after the service of the restraining notice, direct the banking institution to release the funds in question to the other party. Upon receipt of a release, the banking institution shall release the funds as directed.

(g) Proceedings; bad faith claims. Where the judgment creditor objects to a claim of exemption pursuant to subdivision (d) of this section and the court finds that the judgment creditor disputed the claim of exemption in bad faith, as provided in paragraph four of subdivision (c) of this section, the judgment debtor shall be awarded costs, reasonable attorney fees, actual damages and an amount not to exceed one thousand dollars.

(h) Rights of judgment debtor. Nothing in this section shall in any way restrict the rights and remedies otherwise available to a judgment debtor, including but not limited to, rights to property exemptions under federal and state law.

(i) The provisions of this section do not apply when the state of New York, or any of its agencies or municipal corporations is the judgment creditor, or if the debt enforced is for child support, spousal support, maintenance or alimony, provided that the restraining notice contains a legend at the top thereof, above the caption, in sixteen point bold type with the following language: "The judgment creditor is the state of New York, or any of its agencies or municipal corporations, AND/OR the debt enforced is for child support, spousal support, maintenance or alimony."

2009 AMENDMENTS

L. 2009 ch. 24, eff. May 4, 2009, amended subds. (a), (b) and (c) of CPLR 5222-a and added subd. (i) to provide that personal property that is otherwise exempt from application for satisfaction of a debt, may be applied to a debt to the state or its political subdivisions, or if the debt is for child support, spousal support, alimony or maintenance.

2008 AMENDMENTS

L. 2008, ch. 575, § 4, eff. Jan. 1, 2009, added CPLR 5222-a to establish a procedure for claiming exemption of certain income from levy of execution by judgment debtors; provides that certain accounts shall be exempt from execution.

§ 5223. Disclosure.

At any time before a judgment is satisfied or vacated, the judgment creditor may compel disclosure of all matter relevant to the satisfaction of the judgment, by serving upon any person a subpoena, which shall specify all of the parties to the action, the date of the judgment, the court in which it was entered, the amount of the judgment and the amount then due thereon, and shall state that false swearing or failure to comply with the subpoena is punishable as a contempt of court.

R 5224.   Subpoena; procedure.

(a) Kinds and service of subpoena. Any or all of the following kinds of subpoenas may be served:

1. a subpoena requiring attendance for the taking of a deposition upon oral or written questions at a time and place named therein; or

2. a subpoena duces tecum requiring the production of books and papers for examination at a time and place named therein; or

3. an information subpoena, accompanied by a copy and original of written questions and a prepaid, addressed return envelope. Service of an information subpoena may be made by registered or certified mail, return receipt requested. Answers shall be made in writing under oath by the person upon whom served, if an individual, or by an officer, director, agent or employee having the information, if a corporation, partnership or sole proprietorship. Each question shall be answered separately and fully and each answer shall refer to the question to which it responds. Answers shall be returned together with the original of the questions within seven days after receipt. Where the person serving the subpoena is a judgment creditor, other than where the state, a municipality or an agency or officer of the state or a municipality is the judgment creditor, the following additional rules shall apply:

(i) information subpoenas, served on an individual or entity other than the judgment debtor, may be served on an individual, corporation, partnership or sole proprietorship only if the judgment creditor or the judgment creditor's attorney has a reasonable belief that the party receiving the subpoena has in their possession information about the debtor that will assist the creditor in collecting his or her judgment. Any information subpoena served pursuant to this subparagraph shall contain a certification signed by the judgment creditor or his or her attorney stating the following: I HEREBY CERTIFY THAT THIS INFORMATION SUBPOENA COMPLIES WITH RULE 5224 OF THE CIVIL PRACTICE LAW AND RULES AND THAT I HAVE A REASONABLE BELIEF THAT THE PARTY RECEIVING THIS SUBPOENA HAS IN THEIR POSSESSION INFORMATION ABOUT THE DEBTOR THAT WILL ASSIST THE CREDITOR IN COLLECTING THE JUDGMENT. By signing the certification, the judgment creditor or attorney certifies that, to the best of that person's knowledge, information and belief, formed after an inquiry reasonable under the circumstances, that the individual or entity receiving the subpoena has relevant information about the debtor.

(ii) if an information subpoena, served on an individual or entity other than the judgment debtor, does not contain the certification provided for in subparagraph (i) of this paragraph, such subpoena shall be deemed null and void.

(iii) if an information subpoena, served on an individual or entity other than the judgment debtor, does contain the certification provided for in subparagraph (i) of this paragraph, the individual, corporation, partnership or sole proprietorship receiving the subpoena, may move to quash the subpoena pursuant to section twenty-three hundred four of this chapter, except that such motion shall be made in the court that issued the underlying judgment.

(iv) failure to comply with an information subpoena shall be governed by subdivision (b) of section twenty-three hundred eight of this chapter, except that such motion shall be made in the court that issued the underlying judgment.

4. an information subpoena in the form of magnetic tape or other electronic means. Where the person to be served consents thereto in writing, an information subpoena in the form of magnetic tape or electronic means, as defined in subdivision (f) of rule twenty-one hundred three of this chapter, may be served upon the individual, or if a corporation, partnership, limited liability company, or sole proprietorship, upon the officer, director, agent or employee having the information. Answers shall be provided within seven days.

(a-1) Scope of subpoena duces tecum. A subpoena duces tecum authorized by this rule and served on a judgment debtor, or on any individual while in the state, or on a corporation, partnership, limited liability company or sole proprietorship doing business, licensed, qualified, or otherwise entitled to do business in the state, shall subject the person or other entity or business served to the full disclosure prescribed by section fifty-two hundred twenty-three of this article whether the materials sought are in the possession, custody or control of the subpoenaed person, business or other entity within or without the state. Section fifty-two hundred twenty-nine of this article shall also apply to disclosure under this rule.

(b) Fees. A judgment debtor served with a subpoena under this section and any other person served with an information subpoena shall not be entitled to any fee. Any other person served with a subpoena requiring attendance or the production of books and papers shall be paid or tendered in advance authorized traveling expenses and one day's witness fee.

(c) Time and place of examination. A deposition on oral or written questions or an examination of books and papers may proceed upon not less than ten days' notice to the person subpoenaed, unless the court orders shorter notice, before any person authorized by subdivision (a) of rule 3113. An examination shall be held during business hours and, if taken within the state, at a place specified in rule 3110. Upon consent of the witness, an examination may be held at any other place within the state and before any officer authorized to administer an oath.

(d) Conduct of examination. The officer before whom the deposition is to be taken shall put the witness on oath. If requested by the person conducting the examination, the officer shall personally, or by some one acting under his direction, record and transcribe the testimony and shall list all appearances by the parties and attorneys. Examination and cross-examination of the witness shall proceed as permitted in the trial of actions in open court. Cross-examination need not be limited to the subject matter of the examination in chief. All objections made at the time of the examination to the qualifications of the officer taking the deposition, or of a person recording it, or to the manner of taking it, or to the testimony presented, or to the conduct of any person, and any other objection to the proceedings, shall be noted by the officer upon

CPLR

the deposition and the deposition shall proceed subject to the right of a person to apply for a protective order. The deposition shall be taken continuously and without unreasonable adjournment, unless the court orders or the witness agrees otherwise. If the witness does not understand the English language, the judgment creditor shall, at his own expense, provide a translation of all questions and answers. Unless the court orders otherwise, a person other than the judgment debtor served with a subpoena duces tecum requiring the production of books of account may produce in place of the original books of account a sworn transcript of such accounts as are relevant.

(e) Signing deposition; physical preparation. At the request of the person conducting the examination, a deposition on written questions or a deposition on oral questions which has been transcribed shall be submitted to the witness and shall be read to or by him, and any changes in form or substance which the witness desires to make shall be entered upon the deposition with a statement of the reasons given by the witness for making them; and the deposition shall then be signed by the witness before any officer authorized to administer an oath. If the witness fails to sign the deposition, the officer before whom the deposition was taken shall sign it and state on the record the fact of the witness's failure or refusal to sign together with any reason given. The deposition may then be used as fully as though signed. Where testimony is transcribed, the officer before whom the deposition was taken shall certify on the deposition that the witness was duly sworn by him and that the deposition is a true record of the testimony given by the witness.

(f) Subsequent examination. Leave of court is required to compel a judgment debtor to appear for the taking of his deposition or to compel the production by him of books and papers within one year after the conclusion of a previous examination of him with respect to the same judgment.

2006 AMENDMENTS

L. 2006, ch. 452 and ch. 552, both eff. on and after Jan. 1, 2007, amended CPLR R 5224(a)(3) to require that information subpoenas contain a certification declaring that the individual signing the subpoena has a reasonable belief that the party receiving the information subpoena has information about the debtor that will assist in the collection of the underlying judgment. This provision does not apply where the state, municipality or an agency or officer of the state or municipality is a judgment creditor.

L. 2006, ch. 257, § 1, eff. Aug. 25, 2006, added CPLR R 5224(a-1) to provide that a subpoena duces tecum shall subject a person or other entity or business served to full disclosure whether the materials sought are in the possession, custody or control of the subpoenaed person, business or other entity within or without the state.

2000 AMENDMENTS

L. 2000, ch. 409, eff. Sept. 29, 2000, added subparagraph (4) to subdivision (a) pertaining to service of subpoena by magnetic tape or other electronic means.

1994 AMENDMENTS

L. 1994, ch. 302, eff. July 20, 1994, amended CPLR 5224(b) by adding the words "and any other person served with an information subpoena" and by deleting the final sentence relating to fees.

§ 5225. Payment or delivery of property of judgment debtor.

(a) Property in the possession of judgment debtor. Upon motion of the judgment creditor, upon notice to the judgment debtor, where it is shown that the judgment debtor is in possession or custody of money or other personal property in which he has an interest, the court shall order that the judgment debtor pay the money, or so much of it as is sufficient to satisfy the judgment, to the judgment creditor and, if the amount to be so paid is insufficient to satisfy the judgment, to deliver any other personal property, or so much of it as is of sufficient value to satisfy the judgment, to a designated sheriff. Notice of the motion shall be served on the judgment debtor in the same manner as a summons or by registered or certified mail, return receipt requested.

(b) Property not in the possession of judgment debtor. Upon a special proceeding commenced by the judgment creditor, against a person in possession or custody of money or other personal property in which the judgment debtor has an interest, or against a person who is a transferee of money or other personal property from the judgment debtor, where it is shown that the judgment debtor is entitled to the possession of such property or that the judgment creditor's rights to the property are superior to those of the transferee, the court shall require such person to pay the money, or so much of it as is sufficient to satisfy the judgment to the judgment creditor and, if the amount to be so paid is insufficient to satisfy the judgment, to deliver any other personal property, or so much of it as is of sufficient value to satisfy the judgment, to a designated sheriff. Costs of the proceedings shall not be awarded against a person who did not dispute the judgment debtor's interest or right to possession. Notice of the proceeding shall also be served upon the judgment debtor in the same manner as a summons or by registered or certified mail, return receipt requested. The court may permit the judgment debtor to intervene in the proceeding. The court may permit any adverse claimant to intervene in the proceeding and may determine his rights in accordance with section 5239.

(c) Documents to effect payment or delivery. The court may order any person to execute and deliver any document necessary to effect payment or delivery.

1964 AMENDMENTS

L. 1964, ch. 388, eff. Sept. 1, 1964, corrected the cross-reference to "5238" in Subd. (b) to read "5239."

§ 5226.   Installment payment order.

Upon motion of the judgment creditor, upon notice to the judgment debtor, where it is shown that the judgment debtor is receiving or will receive money from any source, or is attempting to impede the judgment creditor by rendering services without adequate compensation, the court shall order that the judgment debtor make specified installment payments to the judgment creditor. Notice of the motion shall be served on the judgment debtor in the same manner as a summons or by registered or certified mail, return receipt requested. In fixing the amount of the payments, the court shall take into consideration the reasonable requirements of the judgment debtor and his dependents, any payments required to be made by him or deducted from the money he would otherwise receive in satisfaction of other judgments and wage assignments, the amount due on the judgment, and the amount being or to be received, or, if the judgment debtor is attempting to impede the judgment creditor by rendering services without adequate compensation, the reasonable value of the services rendered.

§ 5227.   Payment of debts owed to judgment debtor.

Upon a special proceeding commenced by the judgment creditor, against any person who it is shown is or will become indebted to the judgment debtor, the court may require such person to pay to the judgment creditor the debt upon maturity, or so much of it as is sufficient to satisfy the judgment, and to execute and deliver any document necessary to effect payment; or it may direct that a judgment be entered against such person in favor of the judgment creditor. Costs of the proceeding shall not be awarded against a person who did not dispute the indebtedness. Notice of the proceeding shall also be served upon the judgment debtor in the same manner as a summons or by registered or certified mail, return receipt requested. The court may permit the judgment debtor to intervene in the proceeding. The court may permit any adverse claimant to intervene in the proceeding and may determine his rights in accordance with section 5239.

§ 5228. Receivers.

(a) Appointment of receiver. Upon motion of a judgment creditor, upon such notice as the court may require, the court may appoint a receiver who may be authorized to administer, collect, improve, lease, repair or sell any real or personal property in which the judgment debtor has an interest or to do any other acts designed to satisfy the judgment. As far as practicable, the court shall require that notice be given to the judgment debtor and to any other judgment creditors of the judgment debtor. The order of appointment shall specify the property to be received, the duties of the receiver and the manner in which they are to be performed. A receiver shall have no power to employ counsel unless expressly so authorized by order of the court. A receiver shall be entitled to necessary expenses and to such commissions, not exceeding five percent of the sums received and disbursed by him, as the court which appointed him allows, but if a judgment creditor is appointed receiver, he shall not be entitled to compensation. If a receiver has been appointed, a court making an order directing payment, or delivery, of property shall direct that payment, or delivery, be made to the receiver rather than to a sheriff. Sections 6402, 6403, 6404 and 6405 are applicable to receivers appointed under this subdivision.

(b) Extension of receivership. Where a receiver has been appointed, the court, upon motion of a judgment creditor, upon such notice as it may require, shall extend the receivership to his judgment.

§ 5229. Enforcement before judgment entered.

In any court, before a judgment is entered, upon motion of the party in whose favor a verdict or decision has been rendered, the trial judge may order examination of the adverse party and order him restrained with the same effect as if a restraining notice had been served upon him after judgment.

1964 AMENDMENTS

L. 1964, ch. 279, eff. Sept. 1, 1964, added the words "In any court" at the beginning of the sentence.

§ 5230. Executions.

(a) Form. An execution shall specify the date that the judgment or order was entered, the court in which it was entered, the amount of the judgment or order and the amount due thereon and it shall specify the names of the parties in whose favor and against whom the judgment or order was entered. An execution shall direct that only the property in which a named judgment debtor or obligor who is not deceased has an interest, or the debts owed to the named judgment debtor or obligor, be levied upon or sold thereunder and shall specify the last known address of that judgment debtor or obligor. Except in cases when the state of New York, or any of its agencies or municipal corporations is the judgment creditor, or if the debt enforced is for child support, spousal support, maintenance or alimony, provided that in those instances the execution contains a legend at the top thereof, above the caption, in sixteen point bold type with the following language: "The judgment creditor is the state of New York, or any of its agencies or municipal corporations, AND/OR the debt enforced is for child support, spousal support, maintenance or alimony.", an execution notice shall state that, pursuant to subdivision (l) of section fifty-two hundred five of this article, two thousand five hundred dollars of an account containing direct deposit or electronic payments reasonably identifiable as statutorily exempt payments, as defined in paragraph two of subdivision (l) of section fifty-two hundred five of this article, is exempt from execution and that the garnishee cannot levy upon or restrain two thousand five hundred dollars in such an account. Except in cases when the state of New York, or any of its agencies or municipal corporations is the judgment creditor, or if the debt enforced is for child support, spousal support, maintenance or alimony, provided that in those instances the execution contains a legend at the top thereof, above the caption, in sixteen point bold type with the following language: "The judgment creditor is the state of New York, or any of its agencies or municipal corporations, AND/OR the debt enforced is for child support, spousal support, maintenance or alimony.", an execution notice shall likewise state that pursuant to subdivision (i) of section fifty-two hundred twenty-two of this article, an execution shall not apply to an amount equal to or less than ninety percent of the greater of two hundred forty times the federal minimum hourly wage prescribed in the Fair Labor Standards Act of 1938 or two hundred forty times the state minimum hourly wage prescribed in section six hundred fifty-two of the labor law as in effect at the time the earnings are payable, except such part as a court determines to be unnecessary for the reasonable requirements of the judgment debtor and his or her dependents. Where the judgment or order was entered in a court other than the supreme, county or a family court, the execution shall also specify the date on which a transcript of the judgment or order was filed with the clerk of the county in which the judgment was entered. Where jurisdiction in the action was based upon a levy upon property or debt pursuant to an order of attachment, the execution shall also state that fact, describe all property and debts levied upon, and direct that only such property and debts be sold thereunder. Where the judgment or order was recovered for all or part of a mortgage debt, the execution shall also describe the mortgaged property, specify the book and page where the mortgage is recorded, and direct that no part of the mortgaged property be levied upon or sold thereunder.

CPLR

(b) Issuance. At any time before a judgment or order is satisfied or vacated, an execution may be issued from the supreme court, county court or a family court, in the county in which the judgment was first docketed, by the clerk of the court or the attorney for the judgment creditor as officer of the court, to the sheriffs of one or more counties of the state, directing each of them to satisfy the judgment or order out of the real and personal property of the judgment debtor or obligor and the debts due to him or her. Where the judgment or order is for support and is payable to the support collection unit designated by the appropriate social services district, such unit shall be authorized to issue the execution and to satisfy the judgment or order out of the real and personal property of the judgment debtor or obligor and the debts due to him or her.

(c) Return. An execution shall be returned to the clerk of the court from which it was issued or to the support collection unit within sixty days after issuance unless the execution has been served in accordance with section 5231 or subdivision (a) of section 5232. The time may be extended in writing for a period of not more than sixty additional days by the attorney for the judgment creditor or by the support collection unit. Further like extensions may be given by the attorney for the judgment creditor or by the support collection unit unless another execution against the same judgment debtor or obligor has been delivered to the same enforcement officer and has not been returned.

(d) Records of sheriff or support collection unit. Each sheriff or support collection unit shall keep a record of executions delivered showing the names of the parties and the judgment debtor or obligor; the dates of issue and return; the date and time of delivery, which shall be endorsed upon the execution; the amount due at the time the execution was delivered; and the amount of the judgment or order and of the sheriff's fees unpaid, if any, at the time of the return.

(e) For the purposes of this section "order" shall mean an order issued by a court of competent jurisdiction directing the payment of support, alimony or maintenance upon which a "default" as defined in paragraph seven of subdivision (a) of section fifty-two hundred forty-one of this article has been established subject to the procedures established for the determination of a "mistake of fact" for income executions pursuant to subdivision (e) of section fifty-two hundred forty-one of this article, except that for the purposes of this section only, a default shall not be founded upon retroactive child support obligations as defined in paragraph (a) of subdivision one of section four hundred forty of the family court act and subdivision one of section two hundred forty, and paragraph b of subdivision nine of section two hundred thirty-six of the domestic relations law.

2009 AMENDMENTS

L. 2009 ch. 24, eff. May 4, 2009, amended subd. (a) of CPLR 5230 to provide that personal property that is otherwise exempt from application for satisfaction of a debt, may be applied to a debt to the state or its political subdivisions, or if the debt is for child support, spousal support, alimony or maintenance.

2008 AMENDMENTS

L. 2008, ch. 575, eff. Jan. 1, 2009, amended subdivision (a) to establish a procedure for claiming exemption of certain income from levy of execution by judgment debtors; provides that certain accounts shall be exempt from execution.

1993 AMENDMENTS

L.1993, ch. 59, eff. July 1, 1993, added a new final sentence to subdivision (b); added a new subdivision (e); added the word "orders" following the word "judgments" throughout the section; added the word "obligor" following the word "judgment debtor" throughout the section; and added references to "support collection unit" throughout the section.

§ 5231. Income execution.

(a) Form. An income execution shall specify, in addition to the requirements of subdivision (a) of section 5230, the name and address of the person from whom the judgment debtor is receiving or will receive money; the amount of money, the frequency of its payment and the amount of the installments to be collected therefrom; and shall contain a notice to the judgment debtor that he shall commence payment of the installments specified to the sheriff forthwith and that, upon his default, the execution will be served upon the person from whom he is receiving or will receive money.

(b) Issuance. Where a judgment debtor is receiving or will receive money from any source, an income execution for installments therefrom of not more than ten percent thereof may be issued and delivered to the sheriff of the county in which the judgment debtor resides or, where the judgment debtor is a non-resident, the county in which he is employed; provided, however, that (i) no amount shall be withheld from the judgment debtor's earnings pursuant to an income execution for any week unless the disposable earnings of the judgment debtor for that week exceed the greater of thirty times the federal minimum hourly wage prescribed in the Fair Labor Standards Act of 1938 or thirty times the state minimum hourly wage prescribed in section six hundred fifty-two of the labor law as in effect at the time the earnings are payable; (ii) the amount withheld from the judgment debtor's earnings pursuant to an income execution for any week shall not exceed twenty-five percent of the disposable earnings of the judgment debtor for that week, or, the amount by which the disposable earnings of the judgment debtor for that week exceed the greater of thirty times the federal minimum hourly wage prescribed by the Fair Labor Standards Act of 1938 or thirty times the state minimum hourly wage

CPLR

prescribed in section six hundred fifty-two of the labor law as in effect at the time the earnings are payable, whichever is less; (iii) if the earnings of the judgment debtor are also subject to deductions for alimony, support or maintenance for family members or former spouses pursuant to section five thousand two hundred forty-one or section five thousand two hundred forty-two of this article, the amount withheld from the judgment debtor's earnings pursuant to this section shall not exceed the amount by which twenty-five percent of the disposable earnings of the judgment debtor for that week exceeds the amount deducted from the judgment debtor's earnings in accordance with section five thousand two hundred forty-one or section five thousand two hundred forty-two of this article. Nothing in this section shall be construed to modify, abrogate, impair, or affect any exemption from the satisfaction of a money judgment otherwise granted by law.

(c) Definition of earnings and disposable earnings.

(i) As used herein earnings means compensation paid or payable for personal services, whether denominated as wages, salary, commission, bonus, or otherwise, and includes periodic payments pursuant to a pension or retirement program.

(ii) As used herein disposable earnings means that part of the earnings of any individual remaining after the deduction from those earnings of any amounts required by law to be withheld.

(d) Service upon debtor. Within twenty days after an income execution is delivered to the sheriff, the sheriff shall serve a copy of it upon the judgment debtor, in the same manner as a summons or, in lieu thereof, by certified mail return receipt requested provided an additional copy is sent by regular mail to the debtor. If service is by mail as herein provided, the person effecting service shall retain the receipt together with a post office certificate of mailing as proof of such service.

(e) Levy upon default or failure to serve debtor. If a judgment debtor fails to pay installments pursuant to an income execution served upon him for a period of twenty days, or if the sheriff is unable to serve an income execution upon the judgment debtor within twenty days after the execution is delivered to the sheriff, the sheriff shall levy upon the money that the judgment debtor is receiving or will receive by serving a copy of the income execution, indorsed to indicate the extent to which paid installments have satisfied the judgment, upon the person from whom the judgment debtor is receiving or will receive money personally within the county in the same manner as a summons or by certified mail return receipt requested, except that such service shall not be made by delivery to a person authorized to receive service of summons solely by a designation filed pursuant to a provision of law other than rule 318.

(f) Withholding of installments. A person served with an income execution shall withhold from money then or thereafter due to the judgment debtor installments as provided therein and pay them over to the sheriff. If such person shall fail to so pay the sheriff, the judgment creditor may commence a proceeding against him for accrued installments. If the money due to the judgment debtor consists of salary or wages and his employment is terminated by resignation or dismissal at any time after service of the execution, the levy shall thereafter be ineffective, and the execution shall be returned, unless the debtor is reinstated or re-employed within ninety days after such termination.

(g) Statement on income execution. Any income execution delivered to the sheriff on or after the effective date of this act shall contain the following statement:

THIS INCOME EXECUTION DIRECTS THE WITHHOLDING OF UP TO TEN PERCENT OF THE JUDGMENT DEBTOR'S GROSS INCOME. IN CERTAIN CASES, HOWEVER, STATE OR FEDERAL LAW DOES NOT PERMIT THE WITHHOLDING OF THAT MUCH OF THE JUDGMENT DEBTOR'S GROSS INCOME. THE JUDGMENT DEBTOR IS REFERRED TO NEW YORK CIVIL PRACTICE LAW AND RULES § 5231 AND 15 UNITED STATES CODE § 1671 ET SEQ.

I. LIMITATIONS ON THE AMOUNT THAT CAN BE WITHHELD.

A. AN INCOME EXECUTION FOR INSTALLMENTS FROM A JUDGMENT DEBTOR'S GROSS INCOME CANNOT EXCEED TEN PERCENT (10%) OF THE JUDGMENT DEBTOR'S GROSS INCOME.

B. IF A JUDGMENT DEBTOR'S WEEKLY DISPOSABLE EARNINGS ARE LESS THAN THIRTY (30) TIMES THE CUR-

CPLR

RENT FEDERAL MINIMUM WAGE (, PER HOUR), OR
(   ), NO DEDUCTION CAN BE MADE FROM THE JUDG-
MENT DEBTOR'S EARNINGS UNDER THIS INCOME EXECU-
TION.

C. A JUDGMENT DEBTOR'S WEEKLY DISPOSABLE EARN-
INGS CANNOT BE REDUCED BELOW THE AMOUNT ARRIVED
AT BY MULTIPLYING THIRTY (30) TIMES THE CURRENT
FEDERAL MINIMUM WAGE (, PER HOUR), OR (   ),
UNDER THIS INCOME EXECUTION.

D. IF DEDUCTIONS ARE BEING MADE FROM A JUDGMENT
DEBTOR'S EARNINGS UNDER ANY ORDERS FOR ALIMONY,
SUPPORT OR MAINTENANCE FOR FAMILY MEMBERS OR
FORMER SPOUSES, AND THOSE DEDUCTIONS EQUAL OR
EXCEED TWENTY-FIVE PERCENT (25%) OF THE JUDGMENT
DEBTOR'S DISPOSABLE EARNINGS, NO DEDUCTION CAN BE
MADE UNDER THIS INCOME EXECUTION.

E. IF DEDUCTIONS ARE BEING MADE FROM A JUDGMENT
DEBTOR'S EARNINGS UNDER ANY ORDERS FOR ALIMONY,
SUPPORT OR MAINTENANCE FOR FAMILY MEMBERS OR
FORMER SPOUSES, AND THOSE DEDUCTIONS ARE LESS
THAN TWENTY-FIVE PERCENT (25%) OF THE JUDGMENT
DEBTOR'S DISPOSABLE EARNINGS, DEDUCTIONS MAY BE
MADE FROM THE JUDGMENT DEBTOR'S EARNINGS UNDER
THIS INCOME EXECUTION. HOWEVER, THE AMOUNT AR-
RIVED AT BY ADDING THE DEDUCTIONS FROM EARNINGS
MADE UNDER THE EXECUTION TO THE DEDUCTIONS MADE
FROM EARNINGS UNDER ANY ORDERS FOR ALIMONY, SUP-
PORT OR MAINTENANCE FOR FAMILY MEMBERS OR
FORMER SPOUSES CANNOT EXCEED TWENTY-FIVE PER-
CENT (25%) OF THE JUDGMENT DEBTOR'S DISPOSABLE
EARNINGS.

NOTE: NOTHING IN THIS NOTICE LIMITS THE PROPOR-
TION OR AMOUNT WHICH MAY BE DEDUCTED UNDER
ANY ORDER FOR ALIMONY, SUPPORT OR MAINTE-
NANCE FOR FAMILY MEMBERS OR FORMER SPOUSES.

II.   EXPLANATION OF LIMITATIONS.

DEFINITIONS:

DISPOSABLE EARNINGS

   DISPOSABLE EARNINGS ARE THAT PART OF AN INDIVIDU-AL'S EARNINGS LEFT AFTER DEDUCTING THOSE AMOUNTS THAT ARE REQUIRED BY LAW TO BE WITHHELD (FOR EXAMPLE, TAXES, SOCIAL SECURITY, AND UNEMPLOY-MENT INSURANCE, BUT NOT DEDUCTIONS FOR UNION DUES, INSURANCE PLANS, ETC.).

GROSS INCOME

   GROSS INCOME IS SALARY, WAGES OR OTHER INCOME, INCLUDING ANY AND ALL OVERTIME EARNINGS, COMMIS-SIONS, AND INCOME FROM TRUSTS, BEFORE ANY DEDUC-TIONS ARE MADE FROM SUCH INCOME.

ILLUSTRATIONS REGARDING EARNINGS:

IF DISPOSABLE EARNINGS IS:	AMOUNT TO PAY OR DEDUCT FROM EARNINGS UNDER THIS INCOME EXECUTION IS:
(A) 30 TIMES FEDERAL MINI-MUM WAGE ( ) OR LESS	NO PAYMENT OR DEDUCTION ALLOWED
(B) MORE THAN 30 TIMES FEDERAL MINIMUM WAGE ( ) AND LESS THAN 40 TIMES FEDERAL MINIMUM WAGE ( )	THE LESSER OF: THE EXCESS OVER 30 TIMES THE FEDERAL MINIMUM WAGE ( ) IN DIS-POSABLE EARNINGS, OR 10% OF GROSS EARNINGS
(C) 40 TIMES THE FEDERAL MINIMUM WAGE ( ) OR MORE	THE LESSER OF: 25% OF DIS-POSABLE EARNINGS OR 10% OF GROSS EARNINGS.

III.   NOTICE: YOU MAY BE ABLE TO CHALLENGE THIS IN-COME EXECUTION THROUGH THE PROCEDURES PRO-VIDED IN CPLR § 5231(g)* AND CPLR § 5240

   IF YOU THINK THAT THE AMOUNT OF YOUR INCOME BEING DEDUCTED UNDER THIS INCOME EXECUTION EX-CEEDS THE AMOUNT PERMITTED BY STATE OR FEDERAL LAW, YOU SHOULD ACT PROMPTLY BECAUSE THE MONEY WILL BE APPLIED TO THE JUDGMENT. IF YOU CLAIM THAT THE AMOUNT OF YOUR INCOME BEING DEDUCTED UNDER

CPLR

THIS INCOME EXECUTION EXCEEDS THE AMOUNT PERMIT-
TED BY STATE OR FEDERAL LAW, YOU SHOULD CONTACT
YOUR EMPLOYER OR OTHER PERSON PAYING YOUR IN-
COME. FURTHER, YOU MAY CONSULT AN ATTORNEY, IN-
CLUDING LEGAL AID IF YOU QUALIFY. NEW YORK STATE
LAW PROVIDES TWO PROCEDURES THROUGH WHICH AN
INCOME EXECUTION CAN BE CHALLENGED:

CPLR § 5231(i) MODIFICATION. AT ANY TIME, THE JUDG-
MENT DEBTOR MAY MAKE A MOTION TO A COURT FOR AN
ORDER MODIFYING AN INCOME EXECUTION.

CPLR § 5240 MODIFICATION OR PROTECTIVE ORDER: SU-
PERVISION OF ENFORCEMENT. AT ANY TIME, THE JUDG-
MENT DEBTOR MAY MAKE A MOTION TO A COURT FOR AN
ORDER DENYING, LIMITING, CONDITIONING, REGULATING,
EXTENDING OR MODIFYING THE USE OF ANY POST-
JUDGMENT ENFORCEMENT PROCEDURE, INCLUDING THE
USE OF INCOME EXECUTIONS.

(h) Levy upon money payable by municipal corporation or the state.
The levy of an income execution served upon a municipal or public
benefit corporation, or board of education, shall be effective fifteen
days after such service. Such an execution shall specify the title or
position of the judgment debtor and the bureau, office, department or
subdivision in which he is employed and the municipal or public
benefit corporation, or board of education, shall be entitled to a fee of
two dollars upon being served. A levy upon money payable directly by
a department of the state, or by an institution under its jurisdiction,
shall be made by serving the income execution upon the head of the
department, or upon a person designated by him, at the office of the
department in Albany; a levy upon money payable directly upon the
state comptroller's warrant, or directly by a state board, commission,
body or agency which is not within any department of the state, shall
be made by serving the income execution upon the state department of
audit and control at its office in Albany. Service at the office of a
department of the state in Albany may be made by the sheriff of any
county by registered or certified mail, return receipt requested.

(i) Modification. At any time, the judgment creditor or the judgment debtor may move, upon such notice as the court may direct, for an order modifying an income execution.

(j) Priority; delivery to another sheriff. Two or more income executions issued against the same judgment debtor, specifying the same person from whom the money is received and delivered to the same or different enforcement officers shall be satisfied out of that money in the order in which the executions are delivered to an officer authorized to levy in the county, town or city in which the debtor resides or, where the judgment debtor is a non-resident, the county, town or city in which he is employed. If an income execution delivered to a sheriff is returned unsatisfied in whole or in part because the sheriff to whom it was delivered is unable to find within the county the person from whom the judgment debtor is receiving or will receive money, the execution may be delivered to the sheriff of any county in which such person may be found. The priority of an income execution delivered to a sheriff within twenty days after its return by each previous sheriff shall be determined by the time of delivery to the first sheriff.

(k) Accounting by sheriff. It shall be the duty of the sheriff to whom such income execution shall be delivered, from time to time and at least once every ninety days from the time a levy shall be made thereunder, to account for and pay over to the person entitled thereto all monies collected thereon, less his lawful fees and expenses for collecting the same.

* **[Editor's note:** So in original. Probably should read "5231(i)."]

CPLR

CROSS REFERENCES

Personal Property Law § 48-a deals with the manner of collection of income executions, the percentage of earnings deductible and restrictions against multiple deductions.

2008 AMENDMENTS

L. 2008, ch. 575, eff. Jan. 1, 2009, amended subdivision (b) to establish a procedure for claiming exemption of certain income from levy of execution by judgment debtors; provides that certain accounts shall be exempt from execution.

1990 AMENDMENTS

L. 1990, ch. 178, eff. May 24, 1990, amended CPLR 5231 subdivision (b) by deleting "earnings from any person" and adding "money from any source;" adding to subparagraphs (i), (ii) and (iii) the words "from the judgment debtor's earnings;" and adding a new final sentence: "Nothing in this section shall be construed to modify, abrogate, impair or affect any exemption from the satisfaction of a money judgment otherwise granted by law." The same enactment amended subdivision (g) by changing the first sentence from "state and federal law" to "state or federal law;" replacing the references in I(D) and I(E) to "gross income" with "earnings," and adding to phrases "from the judgment debtor's earnings" and "from earnings;" changing the phrase in I(E) from "the income execution" to "this income execution;" modifying the Illustrations portion of the prescribed form by adding the phrase "regarding earnings" after "Illustrations;" adding "from earnings" after "Amount to Pay or Deduct;" replacing "Gross Income" with "Gross Earnings;" modifying Part III, the Notice portion of the prescribed form by changing the reference from CPLR 5231(g) to CPLR 5231(i); changing "earnings" to "income;" and changing "state and federal law" to "state or federal law."

L. 1990, ch. 183, eff. May 24, 1990, amended CPLR 5231 subdivision (d) by providing that one additional copy of the income execution by sent to the debtor by regular mail, and by repealing that part of the subdivision that provided that a copy of the income execution be sent by regular mail to the debtor in care of his last known employer.

1987 AMENDMENTS

L. 1987, ch. 829, eff. Aug. 7, 1987, added new subdivisions (c) and (g), amended subdivision (b), amended and relettered subdivision (f) and relettered the remaining subdivisions accordingly.

1986 AMENDMENTS

L. 1986, ch. 241, eff. July 31, 1986, amended former Subd.(i) [relettered subd. (k) in 1987] by reducing the amount of time for an accounting of monies collected by a sheriff from at least once every six months to ninety days.

1975 AMENDMENTS

L. 1975, ch. 88, eff. May 13, 1975, amended subds. (c) and (d).

1970 AMENDMENTS

L. 1970, ch. 298, eff. Sept. 1, 1970, amended Subd. (b) by increasing the amount which a judgment debtor receives for which an income execution may be issued from more than thirty dollars to more than eighty-five dollars per week.

§ 5232. Levy upon personal property.

(a) Levy by service of execution. The sheriff or support collection unit designated by the appropriate social services district shall levy upon any interest of the judgment debtor or obligor in personal property not capable of delivery, or upon any debt owed to the judgment debtor or obligor, by serving a copy of the execution upon the garnishee, in the same manner as a summons, except that such service shall not be made by delivery to a person authorized to receive service of summons solely by a designation filed pursuant to a provision of law other than rule 318. In the event the garnishee is the state of New York, such levy shall be made in the same manner as an income execution pursuant to section 5231 of this article. A levy by service of the execution is effective only if, at the time of service, the person served owes a debt to the judgment debtor or obligor or he or she is in the possession or custody of property not capable of delivery in which he or she knows or has reason to believe the judgment debtor or obligor has an interest, or if the judgment creditor or support collection unit has stated in a notice which shall be served with the execution that a specified debt is owed by the person served to the judgment debtor or obligor or that the judgment debtor or obligor has an interest in specified property not capable of delivery in the possession or custody of the person served. All property not capable of delivery in which the judgment debtor or obligor is known or believed to have an interest then in or thereafter coming into the possession or custody of such a person, including any specified in the notice, and all debts of such a person, including any specified in the notice, then due or thereafter coming due to the judgment debtor or obligor, shall be subject to the levy. The person served with the execution shall forthwith transfer all such property, and pay all such debts upon maturity, to the sheriff or to the support collection unit and execute any document necessary to effect the transfer or payment. After such transfer or payment, property coming into the possession or custody of the garnishee, or debt incurred by him, or her shall not be subject to the levy. Until such transfer or payment is made, or until the expiration of ninety days after the service of the execution upon him or her, or of such further time as is provided by any order of the court served upon him or her, whichever event first occurs, the garnishee is forbidden to make or suffer any sale, assignment or transfer of, or any interference with, any such property, or pay over or otherwise dispose of any such debt, to any person other than the sheriff or the support collection unit, except upon direction of the sheriff or the support collection unit or pursuant to an order of the court. At the expiration of ninety days after a levy is made by service of the execution, or of such further time as the court, upon motion of the judgment creditor or support collection unit has provided, the levy shall be void except as to property or debts which have been transferred or paid to the sheriff or to the support collection unit or as to which a proceeding under sections 5225 or 5227 has been brought. A judgment creditor who, or support collection unit which, has specified personal property or debt to be levied upon in a notice served with an execution shall be liable to the owner of the property or the person to whom the debt is owed, if other than the judgment debtor or obligor, for any damages sustained by reason of the levy.

(b) Levy by seizure. The sheriff or support collection unit of the appropriate social services district shall levy upon any interest of the judgment debtor in personal property capable of delivery by taking the property into custody without interfering with the lawful possession of pledgees and lessees. The sheriff or support collection unit shall forthwith serve a copy of the execution in the manner prescribed by subdivision (a) upon the person from whose possession or custody the property was taken.

(c) Notice to judgment debtor or obligor. Where an execution does not state that a notice in the form presented by subdivision (e) of section fifty-two hundred twenty-two of this chapter has been duly served upon the judgment debtor or obligor within a year, the sheriff or support collection unit shall, not later than four days after service of the execution upon any garnishee, mail by first class mail, or personally deliver, to each judgment debtor or obligor who is a natural person, a copy of the execution together with such notice. The sheriff or support collection unit shall specify on the notice to judgment debtor or obligor the name and address of the judgment creditor or the judgment creditor's attorney or the support collection unit. The notice shall be mailed to the judgment debtor or obligor at his or her residence address; and in the event such mailing is returned as undeliverable by the post office, or if the residence address of the judgment debtor or obligor is unknown, then to the judgment debtor or obligor in care of the place of employment of the judgment debtor or obligor if known, in an envelope bearing the legend "personal and confidential" and not indicating on the outside thereof, by the return address or otherwise, that the communication is from a sheriff or support collection unit or concerns a debt; or if neither the residence nor the place of employment of the judgment debtor or obligor is known, then to the judgment debtor or obligor at any other known address.

(d) For the purposes of this section "obligor" shall mean an individual other than a judgment debtor obligated to pay support, alimony or maintenance pursuant to an order of a court of competent jurisdiction who has been found to be in "default" of such order as such term is defined in paragraph seven of subdivision (a) of section fifty-two hundred forty-one of this article and the establishment of such default has been subject to the procedures established for the determination of a "mistake of fact" for income executions pursuant to subdivision (e) of section fifty-two hundred forty-one of this article, except that for the purposes of this section only, a default shall not be founded upon retroactive child support obligations as defined in paragraph (c) of subdivision one of section four hundred forty and subdivision one of section two hundred forty, and paragraph b of subdivision nine of section two hundred thirty-six of the domestic relations law.

(e) Notwithstanding the provisions of subdivision (a) of this section, if direct deposit or electronic payments reasonably identifiable as statutorily exempt payments as defined in paragraph two of subdivision (l) of section fifty-two hundred five of this article were made to the judgment debtor's account during the forty-five day period preceding the date that the execution notice was served on the garnishee banking institution, then a garnishee banking institution shall not execute, levy, attach, garnish or otherwise restrain or encumber two thousand five hundred dollars in the judgment debtor's account. Notwithstanding the provisions of subdivision (a) of this section, an execution shall not apply to an amount equal to or less than the greater of two hundred forty times the federal minimum hourly wage prescribed in the Fair Labor Standards Act of 1938 or two hundred forty times the state minimum hourly wage prescribed in section six hundred fifty-two of the labor law as in effect at the time the earnings are payable (as published on the websites of the United States department of labor and the state department of labor) except such part thereof as a court determines to be unnecessary for the reasonable requirements of the judgment debtor and his or her dependents. This amount shall be equal to seventeen hundred sixteen dollars on the effective date of this subdivision, and shall rise to seventeen hundred forty dollars on July twenty-fourth, two thousand nine, and shall rise thereafter in tandem with the minimum wage. Nothing in this subsection shall be construed to limit a banking institution's right or obligation to restrain, remove or execute upon such funds from the judgment debtor's account if required by 42 U.S.C. § 659 or 38 U.S.C. § 5301 or to enforce a child support, spousal support, alimony or maintenance obligation or by a court order. Nothing in this subdivision shall alter the exempt status of funds that are protected from execution, levy, attachment, garnishment, or other legal process, under section fifty-two hundred five of this article or under any other provision of state or federal law, or affect the right of a judgment debtor to claim such exemption.

(f) Fee for banking institution's costs in processing a levy by service of execution when account contains only exempt, direct deposit or electronic payments. In the event that a banking institution cannot lawfully garnish or execute upon on a judgment debtor's banking institution account or funds are garnished or executed upon in violation of any section of this chapter, the banking institution shall charge no fee to the judgment debtor regardless of any terms of agreement, or schedule of fees, or other contract between the judgment debtor and the banking institution.

(g) Where a levy by execution pursuant to this section is made against a natural person's account at a banking institution, the sheriff or support collection unit shall serve the banking institution with the exemption notice and two exemption claim forms prescribed in subdivision (b) of section fifty-two hundred twenty-two-a of this article. The notice and forms must be served upon the banking institution simultaneously with the execution and section fifty-two hundred twenty-two-a of this article shall apply, and all procedures stated therein must be followed. The banking institution shall not transfer the funds in the account to the sheriff or support collection unit for at least twenty-seven days. If, after thirty days, the banking institution has not received an exemption claim form from the judgment debtor, or a court order directing otherwise, it may thereafter transfer the funds to the sheriff or support collection unit.

(h) The provisions of subdivisions (e), (f) and (g) of this section do not apply when the state of New York, or any of its agencies or municipal corporations is the judgment creditor, or if the debt enforced is for child support, spousal support, maintenance or alimony provided that in those instances the execution contains a legend at the top thereof, above the caption, in sixteen point bold type with the following language: "The judgment creditor is the state of New York, or any of its agencies or municipal corporations, AND/OR the debt enforced is for child support, spousal support, maintenance or alimony."

2009 AMENDMENTS

L. 2009 ch. 24, eff. May 4, 2009, amended subd. (e) of CPLR 5230 and added subd. (h) to provide that personal property that is otherwise exempt from application for satisfaction of a debt, may be applied to a debt to the state or its political subdivisions, or if the debt is for child support, spousal support, alimony or maintenance.

2008 AMENDMENTS

L. 2008, ch. 575, eff. Jan. 1, 2009, added subdivisions (e), (f), and (g) to establish a procedure for claiming exemption of certain income from levy of execution by judgment debtors; provides that certain accounts shall be exempt from execution.

1993 AMENDMENTS

L. 1993, ch. 59, eff. July 1, 1993, added references to "support collection unit" throughout the section; added the words "or her" after the word "him" throughout the section; added the words "or obligor" following the words "judgment debtor" throughout the section; substituted the words "this article" in place of the words "civil practice law and rules" in subdivision (a); and added a new subdivision (d).

1982 AMENDMENTS

L. 1982, ch. 882, eff. Sept. 1, 1982, amended CPLR 5232 by adding a new subdivision (c).

1968 AMENDMENTS

L. 1968, ch. 743, eff. Sept. 1, 1968, inserted second sentence in Subd. (a) pertaining to a levy when the state of New York is the garnishee.

§ 5233. Sale of personal property.

(a) Public auction. The interest of the judgment debtor in personal property obtained by a sheriff pursuant to execution or order, other than legal tender of the United States, shall be sold by the sheriff at public auction at such time and place and as a unit or in such lots, or combination thereof, as in his judgment will bring the highest price, but no sale may be made to that sheriff or to his deputy or undersheriff. The property shall be present and within the view of those attending the sale unless otherwise ordered by the court.

(b) Public notice. A printed notice of the time and place of the sale shall be posted at least six days before the sale in three public places in the town or city in which the sale is to be held, provided however, in the city of New York, in lieu of posting such notice may be advertised in the auction columns of any morning newspaper published daily and Sunday in such city an edition of which appears on the newsstands the previous night and has a circulation of not less than three hundred thousand. An omission to so post or advertise notice, or the defacing or removal of a posted notice, does not affect the title of a purchaser without notice of the omission or offense.

(c) Order for immediate sale or disposition. The court may direct immediate sale or other disposition of property with or without notice if the urgency of the case requires.

(d) Unsaleable material. If property seized by the sheriff is considered by him to be material which, by law, may not be sold, he shall apply to the court for a determination whether the property can legally be sold. Reasonable notice of such application shall also be given to the owner of such property. If the court decides the property may not be legally sold, it shall order appropriate disposition of the property which may include its destruction.

1979 AMENDMENTS

L. 1979, ch. 457, eff. July 5, 1979, amended CPLR 5233 by adding a new subdivision (d).

1976 AMENDMENTS

L. 1976, ch. 795, eff. July 24, 1976, amended Subd. (b) to provide that in New York City the notice may be published in a qualifying newspaper in lieu of posting.

§ 5234. Distribution of proceeds of personal property; priorities.

(a) Distribution of proceeds of personal property. After deduction for and payment of fees, expenses and any taxes levied upon sale, delivery, transfer or payment, the proceeds of personal property or debt acquired by a receiver or a sheriff or other officer authorized to enforce the judgment shall be distributed to the judgment creditor and any excess shall be paid over to the judgment debtor. No distribution of proceeds shall be made until fifteen days after service of the execution except upon order of the court.

(b) Priority among execution creditors. Where two or more executions or orders of attachment are issued against the same judgment debtor or obligor and delivered to the same enforcement officer or issued by the support collection unit designated by the appropriate social services district, they shall be satisfied out of the proceeds of personal property or debt levied upon by the officer or by the support collection unit in the order in which they were delivered, such executions for child support shall have priority over any other assignment, levy or process. Where two or more executions or orders of attachment are issued against the same judgment debtor or obligor and delivered to different enforcement officers, and personal property or debt is levied upon within the jurisdiction of all of the officers, the proceeds shall be first applied in satisfaction of the execution or order of attachment delivered to the officer who levied, and thereafter shall be applied in satisfaction of the executions or orders of attachment delivered to those of the other officers who, before the proceeds are distributed, make a demand upon the officer who levied, in the order of such demands, except that such executions for child support shall have priority over any other assignment, levy or process. Where there is more than one past-due child support order, the proceeds shall be applied to the orders in proportion to the amount each order's claim bears to the combined total. Nothing herein shall be deemed to defeat or impair the rights of any secured party as such term is defined in paragraph seventy-two of subsection (a) of section 9–102 of the uniform commercial code. An execution or order of attachment returned by an officer before a levy or delivered to him after the proceeds of the levy have been distributed shall not be satisfied out of those proceeds.

(c) Priority of other judgment creditors. Where personal property or debt has been ordered delivered, transferred or paid, or a receiver thereof has been appointed by order, or a receivership has been extended thereto by order, and the order is filed before the property or debt is levied upon, the rights of the judgment creditor who secured the order are superior to those of the judgment creditor entitled to the proceeds of the levy. Where two or more such orders affecting the same interest in personal property or debt are filed, the proceeds of the property or debt shall be applied in the order of filing. Where delivery,

CPLR

transfer, or payment to the judgment creditor, a receiver, or a sheriff or other officer is not completed within sixty days after an order is filed, the judgment creditor who secured the order is divested of priority, unless otherwise specified in the order or in an extension order filed within the sixty days.

2001 AMENDMENTS

L. 2001, ch. 84, § 40, eff. July 1, 2001, amending subdivision (b).

1993 AMENDMENTS

L. 1993, ch. 59, eff. July 1, 1993, added the words "or obligor" following the words "judgment debtor"; added the words "or issued by the support collection unit designated by the appropriate social services district" after the words "same enforcement officer"; added the words "or by the support collection unit" following the words "by the officer"; added the words "such executions for child support shall have priority over any other assignment, levy or process" following the words "in which they were delivered"; added the words "except that such executions for child support shall have priority over any other assignment, levy or process" following the words "in the order of such demands"; and added the two sentences immediately preceding the last sentence in subdivision (b).

1982 AMENDMENTS

L. 1982, ch. 882, eff. Sept. 1, 1982, amended CPLR 5234 by adding a new sentence at the end of subdivision (a).

§ 5235. Levy upon real property.

After the expiration of ten years after the filing of the judgment-roll, the sheriff shall levy upon any interest of the judgment debtor in real property, pursuant to an execution other than one issued upon a judgment for any part of a mortgage debt upon the property, by filing with the clerk of the county in which the property is located a notice of levy describing the judgment, the execution and the property. The clerk shall record and index the notice against the name of the judgment debtor, or against the property, in the same books, and in the same manner as a notice of the pendency of an action.

§ 5236. Sale of real property.

(a) Time of sale; public auction. Between the fifty-sixth and the sixty-third day after the first publication of a copy of the notice of sale, unless the time is extended by order or the sale postponed by the sheriff, the interest of the judgment debtor in real property which has been levied upon under an execution delivered to the sheriff or which was subject to the lien of the judgment at the time of such delivery shall be sold by the sheriff pursuant to the execution at public auction at such time and place within the county where the real property is situated and as a unit or in such parcels, or combination thereof, as in his judgment will bring the highest price, but no sale may be made to that sheriff or to his deputy or undersheriff. If the property is situated in more than one county, it may be sold in a county in which any part is situated, unless the court orders otherwise.

(b) Sale of mortgaged property. Real property mortgaged shall not be sold pursuant to an execution issued upon a judgment recovered for all or part of the mortgage debt.

(c) Notice of sale. A printed notice of the time and place of the sale containing a description of the property to be sold shall be posted at least fifty-six days before the sale in three public places in the town or city in which the property is located, and, if the sale is to be held in another town or city, in three public places therein. Service by the sheriff of a copy of said notice on the judgment debtor shall be made as provided in section 308. A list containing the name and address of the judgment debtor and of every judgment creditor whose judgment was a lien on the real property to be sold and of every person who had of record any interest in or lien on such property forty-five days prior to the day fixed for the sale shall be furnished the sheriff by the judgment creditor, and each person on the list shall be served by the sheriff with a copy of the notice by personal delivery or by registered or certified mail, return receipt requested, at least thirty days prior to the day fixed for the sale. A copy of the notice shall be published at least once in each of four periods of fourteen successive days, the first of which periods may be measured from any day between the fifty-sixth and sixty-third days, preceding the time fixed for the sale in a newspaper published in the county in which the property is located or, if there is none, in a newspaper published in an adjoining county. An omission to give any notice required by this or the following subdivision, or the defacing or removal of a notice posted pursuant to either, does not affect the title of a purchaser without notice of the omission or offense.

(d) Notice of postponement of sale. Any person may, in a writing served on the sheriff either by personal delivery or by registered or certified mail, return receipt requested, request that the sheriff notify him in the event that a scheduled sale is postponed. Such writing shall contain the person's name and mailing address. If the sale is for any reason postponed, notice of the postponed date need be given only to:

1. those whose requests, made as above provided, have been received by the sheriff at least five days prior to the postponed date,

2. those who appeared at the time and place previously appointed for the sale, and

3. the judgment debtor at his last known address.

The notice may be served either by personal delivery or by registered or certified mail, return receipt requested. Unless the court shall otherwise direct, it need not be posted or published.

(e) Effect of notice as against judgment creditors. A judgment creditor duly notified pursuant to subdivisions (c) or (d) who fails to deliver an execution to the sheriff prior to the sale shall have no further lien on the property and, except as against the judgment debtor, no further interest in the proceeds of the sale.

(f) Conveyance; proof of notice. Within ten days after the sale, the sheriff shall execute and deliver to the purchaser proofs of publication, service and posting of the notice of sale, and a deed which shall convey the right, title and interest sold. Such proofs may be filed and recorded in the office of the clerk of the county where the property is located.

(g) Disposition of proceeds of sale. After deduction for and payment of fees, expenses and any taxes levied on the sale, transfer or delivery, the sheriff making a sale of real property pursuant to an execution shall, unless the court otherwise directs,

1. distribute the proceeds to the judgment creditors who have delivered executions against the judgment debtor to the sheriff before the sale, which executions have not been returned, in the order in which their judgments have priority, and

2. pay over any excess to the judgment debtor.

1975 AMENDMENTS

L. 1975, ch. 570, eff. Sept. 1, 1975, amended Subd. (c) by rewording it so as to resolve the conflict between the section and CPLR 308, as amended in 1970.

1969 AMENDMENTS

L. 1969, ch. 1089, eff. Jan. 1, 1970, amended subds. (c) and (d).

1968 AMENDMENTS

L. 1968, ch. 498, eff. Sept. 1, 1968, amended the second sentence of Subd. (c) to expand the class of those persons who are to be given notice of the sale of realty pursuant to an execution to include anyone whose interest was of record thirty days prior to the sale.

1967 AMENDMENTS

L. 1967, ch. 57, eff. Sept. 1, 1967, amended Subd. (c) to require that notice of sale be given to owner of fee title if owner, at time of execution, is other than the judgment debtor.

1965 AMENDMENTS

L. 1965, ch. 974, eff. Sept. 1, 1965, amended subds. (a) and (c), added new subds. (d) and (e), and relettered subds. (d) and (e) to be subds. (f) and (g), respectively. In relation to the amendment of subd. (c) the Judicial Conference noted:

"The net effect of the time changes proposed would be that only creditors with liens at least 30 days old prior to the sale, instead of 20 days old, would be notified. The levying judgment creditor could complete his list of the judgment creditors and mortgagees on or after the 30th day before the sale instead of the 20th day. . . . The sheriff would have a possible 15 days in which to effect service on the listed judgment creditors and mortgagees instead of 10 days. . . . The notified judgment creditors would have 15 days prior to the sale in which to issue and deliver their own executions to the sheriff. . . .

"The sheriffs have expressed some apprehension that the present provision as it relates to the time of sale might be construed as permitting the sale only on the 63rd day following the first publication. The purpose of the present provision, however, is to permit the sale to take place on any day between the 56th and the 63rd day after first publication. The proposed amendment, requested by the sheriffs, is designed to clarify this point."

1964 AMENDMENTS

L. 1964, ch. 347, eff. Sept. 1, 1964, amended the third sentence of Subd. (c) to change the time periods for publication.

§ 5237. Failure of title to property sold.

The purchaser of property sold by a sheriff pursuant to execution or order may recover the purchase money from the judgment creditors who received the proceeds if the property is recovered from such purchaser in consequence of an irregularity in the sale or a vacatur, reversal or setting aside of the judgment upon which the execution or order was based. If a judgment for the purchase money is so recovered against a judgment creditor in consequence of an irregularity in the sale, such judgment creditor may enforce his judgment as if no levy or sale had been made, and, for that purpose, he may move without notice for an order restoring any lien or priority or amending any docket entry affected by the sale.

§ 5238.   Directions to the sheriff.

Upon motion of any party, on notice to the sheriff and all other parties, the court may direct the sheriff to dispose of, account for, assign, return or release all or any part of any property or debt, or the proceeds thereof, or to file additional returns, subject to the payment of the sheriff's fees and expenses. As far as practicable, the court shall direct that notice of the motion be given to any other judgment creditors, at the addresses shown on the judgment docket and to any persons who have secured orders of attachment affecting any property or debt, or the proceeds thereof, sought to be returned or released.

§ 5239.   Proceeding to determine adverse claims.

Prior to the application of property or debt by a sheriff or receiver to the satisfaction of a judgment, any interested person may commence a special proceeding against the judgment creditor or other person with whom a dispute exists to determine rights in the property or debt. Service of process in such a proceeding shall be made by service of a notice of petition upon the respondent, the sheriff or receiver, and such other person as the court directs, in the same manner as a notice of motion. The proceeding may be commenced in the county where the property was levied upon, or in a court or county specified in subdivision (a) of section 5221. The court may vacate the execution or order, void the levy, direct the disposition of the property or debt, or direct that damages be awarded. Where there appear to be disputed questions of fact, the court shall order a separate trial, indicating the person who shall have possession of the property pending a decision and the undertaking, if any, which such person shall give. If the court determines that any claim asserted was fraudulent, it may require the claimant to pay to any party adversely affected thereby the reasonable expenses incurred by such party in the proceeding, including reasonable attorneys' fees, and any other damages suffered by reason of the claim. The court may permit any interested person to intervene in the proceeding.

1994 AMENDMENTS

L. 1994, ch. 563, eff. July 26, 1994, amended CPLR 5239 by deleting the words "by serving" in the first sentence and inserting in their place the words "Service of process in such a proceeding shall be made by service of."

1965 AMENDMENTS

L. 1965, ch. 974, eff. Sept. 1, 1965, amended the section.

§ 5240. Modification or protective order; supervision of enforcement.

The court may at any time, on its own initiative or the motion of any interested person, and upon such notice as it may require, make an order denying, limiting, conditioning, regulating, extending or modifying the use of any enforcement procedure. Section 3104 is applicable to procedures under this article.

§ 5241. Income execution for support enforcement.

(a) Definitions. As used in this section and in section fifty-two hundred forty-two of this chapter, the following terms shall have the following meanings:

1. "Order of support" means any temporary or final order, judgment, agreement or stipulation incorporated by reference in such judgment or decree in a matrimonial action or family court proceeding, or any foreign support order, judgment or decree, registered pursuant to article five-B of the family court act which directs the payment of alimony, maintenance, support or child support.

2. "Debtor" means any person directed to make payments by an order of support.

3. "Creditor" means any person entitled to enforce an order of

support, including a support collection unit.

4. "Employer" means any employer, future employer, former employer, union or employees' organization.

5. "Income payor" includes:

(i) the auditor, comptroller, trustee or disbursing officer of any pension fund, benefit program, policy of insurance or annuity;

(ii) the state of New York or any political subdivision thereof, or the United States; and

(iii) any person, corporation, trustee, unincorporated business or association, partnership, financial institution, bank, savings and loan association, credit union, stock purchase plan, stock option plan, profit sharing plan, stock broker, commodities broker, bond broker, real estate broker, insurance company, entity or institution.

6. "Income" includes any earned, unearned, taxable or non-taxable income, benefits, or periodic or lump sum payment due to an individual, regardless of source, including wages, salaries, commissions, bonuses, workers' compensation, disability benefits, unemployment insurance benefits, payments pursuant to a public or private pension or retirement program, federal social security benefits as defined in 42 U.S.C. section 662(f) (2), and interest, but excluding public assistance benefits paid pursuant to the social services law and federal supplemental security income.

7. "Default" means the failure of a debtor to remit to a creditor three payments on the date due in the full amount directed by the order of support, or the accumulation of arrears equal to or greater than the amount directed to be paid for one month, whichever first occurs.

8. "Mistake of fact" means any error in the amount of current support or arrears or in the identity of the debtor or that the order of support does not exist or has been vacated.

9. "Support collection unit" means any support collection unit established by a social services district pursuant to the provisions of section one hundred eleven-h of the social services law.

10. "Date of withholding" means the date on which the income

would otherwise have been paid or made available to the debtor were it not withheld by the employer or income payor.

11. "Health insurance benefits" means any medical, dental, optical and prescription drugs and health care services or other health care benefits which may be provided for dependents through an employer or organization, including such employers or organizations which are self-insured.

12. "Business day" means a day on which state offices are open for regular business.

(b) Issuance.

(1) When a debtor is in default, an execution for support enforcement may be issued by the support collection unit, or by the sheriff, the clerk of court or the attorney for the creditor as an officer of the court. Where a debtor is receiving or will receive income, an execution for deductions therefrom in amounts not to exceed the limits set forth in subdivision (g) of this section may be served upon an employer or income payor after notice to the debtor. The amount of the deductions to be withheld shall be sufficient to ensure compliance with the direction in the order of support, and shall include an additional amount to be applied to the reduction of arrears. The creditor may amend the execution before or after service upon the employer or income payor to reflect additional arrears or payments made by the debtor after notice pursuant to subdivision (d) of this section, or to conform the execution to the facts found upon a determination made pursuant to subdivision (e) of this section.

(2) (i) Where the court orders the debtor to provide health insurance benefits for specified dependents, an execution for medical support enforcement may, except as provided for herein, be issued by the support collection unit, or by the sheriff, the clerk of court or the attorney for the creditor as an officer of the court; provided, however, that when the court issues an order of child support or combined child and spousal support on behalf of persons other than those in receipt of public assistance or in receipt of services pursuant to section one hundred eleven-g of the social services law, such medical execution shall be in the form of a separate qualified medical child support order as provided by

subdivision (j) of section four hundred sixteen of the family court act and paragraph (h) of subdivision one of section two hundred forty of the domestic relations law. Such execution for medical support enforcement may require the debtor's employer, organization or group health plan administrator to purchase on behalf of the debtor and the debtor's dependents such available health insurance benefits. Such execution shall direct the employer, organization or group health plan administrator to provide to the dependents for whom such benefits are required to be provided or such dependents' custodial parent or legal guardian or social services district on behalf of persons applying for or in receipt of public assistance any identification cards and benefit claim forms and to withhold from the debtor's income the employee's share of the cost of such health insurance benefits, and to provide written confirmation of such enrollment indicating the date such benefits were or become available or that such benefits are not available and the reasons therefor to the issuer of the execution. An execution for medical support enforcement shall not require a debtor's employer, organization or group health plan administrator to purchase or otherwise acquire health insurance or health insurance benefits that would not otherwise be available to the debtor by reason of his or her employment or membership. Nothing herein shall be deemed to obligate or otherwise hold any employer, organization or group health plan administrator responsible for an option exercised by the debtor in selecting medical insurance coverage by an employee or member.

(ii) Where the child support order requires the debtor to provide health insurance benefits for specified dependents, and where the debtor provides such coverage and then changes employment, and the new employer provides health care coverage, an amended execution for medical support enforcement may be issued by the support collection unit, or by the sheriff, the clerk of the court or the attorney for the creditor as an officer of the court without any return to court. The issuance of the amended execution shall transfer notice of the requirements of the order and the execution to the new employer, organization or group health plan administrator, and shall have the same effect as the original execution for medical support issued pursuant to this section unless the debtor contests the execution.

(3) Any inconsistent provisions of this title or other law notwithstanding, in any case in which a parent is required by a court order to provide health coverage for a child and the parent is eligible for health insurance benefits as defined in this section through an employer or organization, including those which are self-insured, doing business in the state, such employer or organization must, in addition to implementing the provisions of a medical support execution:

(i) permit such parent to immediately enroll under such health insurance benefit coverage any such dependent who is otherwise eligible for such coverage without regard to any seasonal enrollment restrictions;

(ii) if such a parent is enrolled but fails to make application to obtain coverage of such dependent child, immediately enroll such dependent child under such health benefit coverage upon application by such child's other parent or by the office of temporary and disability assistance or social services district furnishing medical assistance to such child, and

(iii) not disenroll, or eliminate coverage of, such a child unless:

(A) the employer or organization is provided with satisfactory written evidence that such court order is no longer in effect, or the child is or will be enrolled in comparable health coverage through another insurer which will take effect not later than the effective date of such disenrollment, or

(B) such employer or organization has eliminated health insurance coverage for all similarly situated employees.

(c) Execution for support enforcement; form.

(1) The income execution shall contain the caption of the order of support, and specify the date that the order of support was entered, the court in which it was entered, the amount of the periodic payments directed, the amount of arrears, the nature of the default and the names of the debtor and creditor. In addition, the income execution shall include:

(i) The name and address of the employer or income payor from whom the debtor is receiving or will receive income;

(ii) the amount of the deductions to be made therefrom on account of current support, and the amount to be applied to the reduction of arrears;

(iii) a notice that deductions will apply to current and subsequent income;

(iv) a notice that the income execution will be served upon any current or subsequent employer or income payor unless a mistake of fact is shown within fifteen days, a notice of the manner in which a mistake of fact may be asserted, and a notice that, if the debtor claims a mistake of fact, a determination will be made within forty-five days after notice to the debtor as provided in subdivision (d) of this section, and that the debtor will receive written notice whether the income execution will be served and of the time that deductions will begin;

(v) a notice that the employer or income payor must commence deductions no later than the first pay period that occurs after fourteen days following the service of the income execution and that payment must be remitted within seven business days of the date that the debtor paid;

(vi) a notice that the income execution is binding until further notice;

(vii) a notice of the substance of the provisions of section fifty-two hundred fifty-two of this chapter and that a violation thereof is punishable as a contempt of court by fine or imprisonment or both;

(viii) a notice of the limitations upon deductions from wages set forth in subdivision (g) of this section;

(ix) a notice that an employer must notify the issuer promptly when the debtor terminates employment and provide the debtor's last address and the name and address of the new employer, if known;

(x) a notice that when an employer receives an income withholding instrument issued by another state, the employer shall apply the income withholding law of the state of the debtor's principal place of employment in determining:

(A) the employer's fee for processing income withholding;

(B) the maximum amount permitted to be withheld from the debtor's income;

(C) the time periods within which the employer must implement the income withholding and forward the child support payment;

(D) the priorities for withholding and allocating income withheld for multiple child support creditors; and

(E) any withholding terms or conditions not specified in the withholding instrument; and

(xi) a notice that an employer who complies with an income withholding notice that is regular on its face shall not be subject to civil liability to any individual or agency for conduct in compliance with the notice.

(2) The medical support execution shall contain the caption of the order of support and specify the date that the order of support was entered and the court in which it was entered. Such execution shall include the name and address of the employer or organization and shall include:

(i) a notice that the debtor has been ordered by the court to enroll the dependents in any available health insurance benefits and to maintain such coverage for such dependents as long as such benefits remain available;

(ii) a notice inquiring of the employer or organization as to whether such health insurance benefits are presently in effect for the eligible dependents named in the execution, the date such benefits were or become available, or that such benefits are not available and the reasons therefor and directing that the response to such inquiry immediately be forwarded to the issuer of such execution;

(iii) a statement directing the employer or organization to purchase on behalf of the debtor any available health insurance benefits to be made available to the debtor's dependents as

CPLR

directed by the execution, including the enrollment of such eligible dependents in such benefit plans and the provision to the dependents or such dependents' custodial parent or legal guardian or social services district on behalf of persons applying for or in receipt of public assistance of any identification cards and benefit claim forms;

(iv) a statement directing the employer or organization to deduct from the debtor's income such amount which is the debtor's share of the premium, if any, for such health insurance benefits for such dependents who are otherwise eligible for such coverage without regard to any seasonal enrollment restrictions;

(v) a notice that the debtor's employer must notify the issuer promptly at any time the debtor terminates or changes such health insurance benefits;

(vi) a statement that the debtor's employer or organization shall not be required to purchase or otherwise acquire health insurance or health insurance benefits for such dependents that would not otherwise be available to the debtor by reason of his employment or membership;

(vii) a statement that failure to enroll the eligible dependents in such health insurance plan or benefits or failure to deduct from the debtor's income the debtor's share of the premium for such plan or benefits shall make such employer or organization jointly and severally liable for all medical expenses incurred on the behalf of the debtor's dependents named in the execution while such dependents are not so enrolled to the extent of the health insurance benefits that should have been provided under the execution;

(viii) the name and last known mailing address of the debtor and the name and mailing address of the dependents; provided however, that the name and mailing address of a social services official may be substituted on behalf of such dependents;

(ix) a reasonable description of the type of coverage to be provided to each dependent, or the manner in which such type of coverage is to be determined;

(x) the period to which such execution applies; and

(xi) a statement that the debtor's employer or organization shall not be required to provide any type or form of benefit or option not otherwise provided under the group health plan except to the extent necessary to meet the requirements of a law relating to medical child support described in section one thousand three hundred ninety-six-g-1 of title forty-two of the United States Code.

(d) Notice to debtor. The creditor shall serve a copy of the execution upon the debtor by regular mail to the debtor at his last known residence or such other place where he is likely to receive notice, or in the same manner as a summons may be served.

(e) Determination of mistake of fact. Where the execution has been issued by the support collection unit, the debtor may assert a mistake of fact and shall have an opportunity to make a submission in support of the objection within fifteen days from service of a copy thereof. Thereafter, the agency shall determine the merits of the objection, and shall notify the debtor of its determination within forty-five days after notice to the debtor as provided in subdivision (d) of this section. If the objection is disallowed, the debtor shall be notified that the income execution will be served on the employer or income payor, and of the time that deductions will begin. Where the income execution has been issued by an attorney as officer of the court, or by the sheriff, or by the clerk of the court, the debtor may assert a mistake of fact within fifteen days from service of a copy thereof by application to the supreme court or to the family court having jurisdiction in accordance with section four hundred sixty-one of the family court act. If application is made to the family court, such application shall be by petition on notice to the creditor and it shall be heard and determined in accordance with the provisions of section four hundred thirty-nine of the family court act, and a determination thereof shall be made, and the debtor notified thereof within forty-five days of the application. If application is made to the supreme court such application shall be by order to show cause or motion on notice to the creditor in the action in which the order or judgement sought to be enforced was entered and a determination thereof shall be made, and the debtor notified thereof within forty-five days of the application.

(f) Levy. If a debtor fails to show mistake of fact within fifteen days,

CPLR

or after a determination pursuant to subdivision (e) of this section has been made, or if the creditor is unable to serve the execution upon the debtor, the creditor may levy upon the income that the debtor is receiving or will receive by serving the execution upon the employer or income payor personally in the same manner as a summons or by regular mail, except that such service shall not be made by delivery to a person authorized to receive service of summons solely by a designation filed pursuant to a provision of law other than rule 318.

(g) Deduction from income.

(1) An employer or income payor served with an income execution shall commence deductions from income due or thereafter due to the debtor no later than the first pay period that occurs fourteen days after service of the execution, and shall remit payments to the creditor within seven business days of the date that the debtor is paid. Each payment remitted by an employer or income payor shall include, in addition to the identity and social security number of the debtor, the date and amount of each withholding of the debtor's income included in the payment. If the money due to the debtor consists of salary or wages and his or her employment is terminated by resignation or dismissal at any time after service of the execution, the levy shall thereafter be ineffective, and the execution shall be returned, unless the debtor is reinstated or re-employed within ninety days after such termination. An employer must notify the issuer promptly when the debtor terminates employment and provide the debtor's last address and name and address of the new employer, if known. Where the income is compensation paid or payable to the debtor for personal services, the amount of the deductions to be withheld shall not exceed the following:

(i) Where a debtor is currently supporting a spouse or dependent child other than the creditor, the amount of the deductions to be withheld shall not exceed fifty percent of the earnings of the debtor remaining after the deduction therefrom of any amounts required by law to be withheld ("disposable earnings"), except that if any part of such deduction is to be applied to the reduction of arrears which shall have accrued more than twelve weeks prior to the beginning of the week for which such earnings are payable, the amount of such deduction shall not exceed fifty-five percent of disposable earnings.

(ii) Where a debtor is not currently supporting a spouse or dependent child other than the creditor, the amount of the deductions to be withheld shall not exceed sixty percent of the earnings of the debtor remaining after the deduction therefrom of any amounts required by law to be withheld ("disposable earnings"), except that if any part of such deduction is to be applied to the reduction of arrears which shall have accrued more than twelve weeks prior to the beginning of the week for which such earnings are payable, the amount of such deduction shall not exceed sixty-five percent of disposable earnings.

(2)   (A) An employer or income payor served with an income execution in accordance with paragraph one of this subdivision shall be liable to the creditor for failure to deduct the amounts specified. The creditor may commence a proceeding against the employer or income payor for accrued deductions, together with interest and reasonable attorney's fees.

(B) An employer or income payor served with an income execution in accordance with paragraph one of this subdivision shall be liable to the creditor and the debtor for failure to remit any amounts which have been deducted as directed by the income execution. Either party may commence a proceeding against the employer or income payor for accrued deductions, together with interest and reasonable attorney's fees.

(C) The actions of the employer or income payor in deducting or failing to deduct amounts specified by an income execution shall not relieve the debtor of the underlying obligation of support.

(D) In addition to the remedies herein provided and as may be otherwise authorized by law, upon a finding by the family court that the employer or income payor failed to deduct or remit deductions as directed in the income execution, the court shall issue to the employer or income payor an order directing compliance and may direct the payment of a civil penalty not to exceed five hundred dollars for the first instance and one thousand dollars per instance for the second and subsequent instances of employer or income payor noncompliance. The penalty shall be paid to the creditor and may be enforced in the same manner as a civil judgment or in any other manner permitted by law.

(3) If an employer, organization or group health plan administrator is served with an execution for medical support enforcement, such employer, organization or group health plan administrator shall: (i) purchase on behalf of the debtor any health insurance benefits which may be made available to the debtor's dependents as ordered by the execution, including the immediate enrollment of such eligible dependents in such benefit plans; (ii) provide the dependents for whom such benefits are required, or a social services official substituted for such dependents, identification cards and benefit claim forms; (iii) commence deductions from income due or thereafter due to the debtor of such amount which is the debtor's share of the premium, if any, for such health insurance benefits, provided, however, that such deduction when combined with deductions for support does not exceed the limitations set forth in paragraph one of this subdivision and is consistent with the priority provisions set forth in subdivision (h) of this section; and (iv) provide a confirmation of such enrollment indicating the date such benefits were or become available or that such benefits are not available and the reasons therefor to the issuer of the execution. Except as otherwise provided by law, nothing herein shall be deemed to obligate an employer or organization to maintain or continue an employee's or member's health insurance benefits.

(4) If such employer, organization or group health plan administrator shall fail to so enroll such eligible dependents or to deduct from the debtor's income the debtor's share of the premium, such employer, organization or group health plan administrator shall be jointly and severally liable for all medical expenses incurred on behalf of the debtor's dependents named in the execution while such dependents are not so enrolled to the extent of the insurance benefits that should have been provided under such execution. Except as otherwise provided by law, nothing herein shall be deemed to obligate an employer, organization or group health plan administrator to maintain or continue an employee's or member's health insurance benefits.

(h) Priority. A levy pursuant to this section or an income deduction order pursuant to section 5242 of this chapter shall take priority over any other assignment, levy or process. If an employer or income payor is served with more than one execution pursuant to this section, or with an execution pursuant to this section and also an order pursuant to section 5242 of this chapter, and if the combined total amount of the deductions to be withheld exceeds the limits set forth in subdivision (g) of this section, the employer or income payor shall withhold the maximum amount permitted thereby and pay to each creditor that proportion thereof which such creditor's claim bears to the combined total. Any additional deduction authorized by subdivision (g) of this section to be applied to the reduction of arrears shall be applied to such arrears in proportion to the amount of arrears due to each creditor. Deductions to satisfy current support obligations shall have priority over deductions for the debtor's share of health insurance premiums which shall have priority over any additional deduction authorized by subdivision (g) of this section.

(i) Levy upon money payable by the state. A levy upon money payable directly by a department of the state, or by an institution under its jurisdiction, shall be made by serving the income execution upon the head of the department, or upon a person designated by him, at the office of the department in Albany; a levy upon money payable directly upon the state comptroller's warrant, or directly by a state board, commission, body or agency which is not within any department of the state, shall be made by serving the execution upon the state department of audit and control at its office in Albany. Service at the office of a department or any agency or institution of the state in Albany may be made by registered or certified mail, return receipt requested.

2009 AMENDMENTS

L. 2009, ch. 215, eff. Oct. 9, 2009, amended CPLR 5241, subds. (b) and (h), to amend the priority for deductions via an income execution.

2008 AMENDMENTS

L. 2008, ch. 94 § 1, eff. May 27, 2008, amended CPLR 5241(e) to require that, where an income execution is issued, applications to assert a mistake of fact in Supreme Court be made by order to show cause or motion on notice to the creditor in the same action in which the order or judgment sought to be enforced was entered.

CPLR

2007 AMENDMENTS

L. 2007, ch. 5241, eff. Aug. 15, 2007, amended CPLR 5241(b)(3)(ii) by replacing "department" with "office of temporary and disability assistance".

2006 AMENDMENTS

L. 2006, ch. 335, § 1, eff. Oct. 24, 2006, amended CPLR 5241(g)(2)(D) to provide that the penalties assessed against employers and income payors for the failure to comply with income execution for child support and for discrimination against an employee involved in a child support proceeding shall be paid to the creditor and may be enforced in the same manner as a civil judgment or in any other manner permitted by law.

1999 AMENDMENTS

L. 1999, ch. 533, § 8, eff. Sept. 28, 1999, amended CPLR 5241 by adding the language providing that when a court issues a child support order or combined child and spousal support order for persons other than those receiving public assistance, the medical execution shall be in the form of a separate qualified medical support order pursuant to F.C.A. § 416(f) and D.R.L. § 240(1)(f).

1998 AMENDMENTS

L. 1998, ch. 214, §§ 51–55-a, eff. Nov. 4, 1998, amended CPLR 5241 subdivisions (b)(2) and (3), (c)(1) and (2), added four new subparagraphs (c)(2)(viii)–(xi), and amended (g)(3). The amendments to 5241(b), (c) and (g) delete references to qualified medical child support orders and replace them with references to medical support executions; change the recipient of information from employers, organizations and health plan administrators; add to the informational requirements for such parties; and add the references to income executions. L. 1998, ch. 214, § 79, eff. July 7, 1998, deemed in full force and effect on and after Nov. 11, 1997, amended CPLR 5241 (g)(2)(D), by adding the phrase "and as may be otherwise authorized by law" and by substituting "civil penalty" for "fine."

1997 AMENDMENTS

L. 1997, ch. 398, §§ 20–28, eff. Nov. 11, 1997, amended CPLR 5241 as follows: amended subd. (a) para. (1) by replacing the reference to D.R.L. § 37-a with F.C.A. Article 5-B; amended subd. (a) para. (6) by expanding the definition of "income" to include benefits, periodic or lump sum payments including wages, salaries, commissions and bonuses, payments pursuant to a public or private pension or retirement program and interest; amended subd. (a) para. (9) by deleting the reference to a local public agency responsible for the functions of the support collection unit pursuant to S.S.L. § 111-h; amended subd. (a) by adding a new para. (12) defining a "business day"; amended subd. (c) para. (1) subpara. (v) by changing the notice of the time that the payment under an execution for support enforcement must be remitted from ten to seven business days of the date the debtor paid;

amended subd. (c) para. (1) by adding two new subparas. (x) and (xi) providing that the execution shall also include a notice that the employer shall apply the income withholding law of the state of the debtor's principal place of employment in determining listed factors and that an employer complying with an income withholding notice that is regular on its face shall not be subject to civil liability; amended subd. (g) para. (1) by changing the date to remit payments to the creditor from ten to seven business days and deleting the third and fourth sentences; amended subd. (g) by adding a new para. (2) providing that the employer or income payor served with an income execution order shall be liable to the creditor for failing to deduct and remit the specified amounts; §§ 137–140, eff. Jan. 1, 1998, amended CPLR 5241 as follows: amended subd. (b) para. (2) by replacing "order of support orders" with "qualified medical child support orders," by extending the scope of executions for medical support enforcement to include the administrator of a group health plan and by adding new (b)(2)(ii), authorizing a support collection unit to amend an execution for medical support to reflect a change in employment by the support debtor; amended subd. (g) para. (2) by renumbering to para. (3), by adding group health plan administrators to those subject to the provision, changing the party to be notified to an alternate recipient named on the execution and providing limits for the maximum deduction allowed under this subpara.; amended subd. (g) by adding a new para. (4), providing that any administrator who fails to comply with a medical support execution may be liable for all of the medical expenses incurred by the support debtor's dependents; amended subd. (h) by giving priority to deductions that satisfy support obligations.

CPLR

1994 AMENDMENTS

L. 1994, ch. 170, eff. June 9, 1994, amended CPLR 5241(b)(2) by deleting the final sentence pertaining to executions for medical support enforcement, and by adding a new subparagraph (3); amended CPLR 5241(c)(2)(iv) by deleting the words "no later than the first enrollment period allowable under the applicable provider's terms of enrollment subsequent to the service of the execution," and inserting in their place the words "who are otherwise eligible for such coverage without regard to any seasonal enrollment restrictions"; amended CPLR 5241(g)(1)(ii) by deleting the final sentence, which read "The provisions of this paragraph shall not apply to executions for medical support enforcement as described in paragraph two of subdivision (b) of this section"; amended CPLR 5241(g)(2) by adding the word "immediate" and by deleting the words "no later than the first enrollment subsequent to the service of the execution" and inserting in their place the words "who are otherwise eligible for such coverage without regard to any seasonal enrollment restrictions."

1993 AMENDMENTS

L. 1993, ch. 59, eff. July 1, 1993, amended subdivision (a) by adding a new paragraph (11), defining "health insurance benefits," and amended subdivisions (b), (c) and (g).

1990 AMENDMENTS

L. 1990, ch. 818, eff. Sept. 30, 1990, amended CPLR 5241 by adding a new paragraph (a)(10), and by adding a provision to subdivision (g) mandating that each payment remitted by an employer or income payor include the identity and social security number of the debtor, as well as the date and amount of each withholding of the debtor's income included in the payment.

1988 AMENDMENTS

L. 1988, ch. 327, eff. July 25, 1988, and applying to all judgments, orders or agreements or stipulations incorporated by reference in a judgment, relating to actions for divorce, separation or annulment of a marriage or of support, entered or issued both before and after such date. The amendment added "agreements or stipulations incorporated by reference in a judgment" to the definition of "order of support".

1987 AMENDMENTS

L. 1987, ch. 815, eff. Aug. 7, 1987, and applicable to any action or proceeding commenced on or after such date, amended Subd. (e) to add the provision that determinations of mistake of fact applications on income executions issued by the sheriff or the clerk of the court, shall be made by the court; and deleting the provision that such determinations be made by the issuer; to add reference to Family Court Act § 461; to provide that applications to the Family Court be brought by petition on notice to the creditor; to add the last sentence specifying the procedure for application to the supreme court on a mistake of fact.

1985 AMENDMENTS

L. 1985, ch. 809, eff. Nov. 1, 1985, added CPLR 5241.

§ 5242. Income deduction order for support enforcement.

(a) Upon application of a creditor, for good cause shown, and upon such terms as justice may require, the court may correct any defect, irregularity, error or omission in an income execution for support enforcement issued pursuant to section 5241 of this article.

(b) Upon application of a creditor, for good cause shown, the court may enter an income deduction order for support enforcement. In determining good cause, the court may take into consideration evidence of the degree of such debtor's past financial responsibility, credit references, credit history, and any other matter the court considers relevant in determining the likelihood of payment in accordance with the order of support. Proof of default establishes a prima facie case against the debtor, which can be overcome only by proof of the debtor's inability to make the payments. Unless the prima facie case is overcome, the court shall enter an income deduction order for support enforcement pursuant to this section.

(c) (1) When the court enters an order of support on behalf of persons other than those in receipt of public assistance or in receipt of services pursuant to section one hundred eleven-g of the social services law, or registers pursuant to article five-B of the family court act an order of support which has been issued by a foreign jurisdiction and which is not to be enforced pursuant to title six-A of article three of the social services law, where the court determines that the respondent earns wages that could be subject to an income deduction order, the court shall issue an income deduction order to obtain payment of the order at the same time it issues or registers the order. The court shall enter the income deduction order unless the court finds and sets forth in writing (i) the reasons that there is good cause not to require immediate income withholding; or (ii) that an agreement providing for an alternative arrangement has been reached between the parties. Such agreement may include a written agreement or an oral stipulation, made on the record, that results in a written order. For purposes of this subdivision, good cause shall mean substantial harm to the debtor. The absence of an arrearage or the mere issuance of an income deduction order shall not constitute good cause. When the court determines that there is good cause not to issue an income deduction order immediately or when the parties agree to an alternative arrangement as provided in this paragraph, the court shall state expressly in the order of support the basis for its decision. In entering the income deduction order, the court shall specify an amount to be withheld by the debtor's employer, which shall be sufficient to ensure compliance with the order of support and also shall include an additional amount to be applied to the reduction of arrears, if any, and shall specify the names, addresses, and social security numbers of the parties to the support proceeding and the mailing address of the unit within the state office of temporary and disability assistance designated to receive such deductions. The court shall transmit copies of such order to the parties and to such unit.

(2) An employer served with an income deduction order entered

pursuant to this subdivision shall commence deductions from the income due or thereafter due to the debtor no later than the first pay period that occurs fourteen days after service of the income deduction order, and shall remit payments to the state office of temporary and disability assistance pursuant to subdivision fourteen of section one hundred eleven-b of the social services law within ten days of the date that the debtor is paid. Each payment remitted by the employer shall be made payable to the creditor named in the order, and shall include the names, addresses, and social security numbers of the debtor and the creditor, and the date and the amount of each withholding of the debtor's income included in the payment. An employer shall be liable to the creditor for failure to deduct the amounts specified in the income deduction order, provided however that deduction by the employer of the amounts specified shall not relieve the debtor of the underlying obligation of support. If an employer shall fail to so pay the creditor, the creditor may commence a proceeding against the employer for accrued deductions, together with interest and reasonable attorney's fees. If the debtor's employment is terminated by resignation or dismissal at any time after service of the income deduction order, the order shall cease to have force and effect unless the debtor is reinstated or re-employed by the same employer. An employer must notify the creditor promptly when the debtor terminates employment and must provide the debtor's last address and the name and address of the debtor's new employer, if known. Where the income is compensation paid or payable to the debtor for personal services, the amount withheld by the employer shall not exceed the following:

(i) Where the debtor currently is supporting a spouse or dependent child other than the creditor's dependent child, the amount withheld shall not exceed fifty percent of the earnings of the debtor remaining after the deduction therefrom of any amounts required by law to be withheld ("disposable earnings"), except that if any part of the deduction is to be applied to the reduction of arrears which shall have accrued more than twelve weeks prior to the beginning of the week for which such earnings are payable, the amount withheld shall not exceed fifty-five percent of disposable earnings.

(ii) Where the debtor currently is not supporting a spouse or dependent child other than the creditor's dependent child, the amount withheld shall not exceed sixty percent of the earnings of the debtor remaining after the deduction therefrom of any amounts required by law to be withheld ("disposable earnings"), except that if any part of the deduction is to be applied to the reduction of arrears which shall have accrued more than twelve weeks prior to the beginning of the week for which such earnings are payable, the amount withheld shall not exceed sixty-five percent of disposable earnings.

(d) An order pursuant to this section shall take priority over any other assignment, levy or process. If an employer or income payor is served with more than one income deduction order pertaining to a single employee pursuant to this section, or with an order issued pursuant to this section and also an execution pursuant to section 5241 of this chapter, and if the combined total amount of the income to be withheld exceeds the limits set forth in subdivision (c) of this section, the employer or income payor shall withhold the maximum amount permitted thereby and pay to each creditor that proportion thereof which such creditor's claim bears to the combined total.

(e) An employer or income payor shall be liable to the creditor for failure to deduct the amounts specified, provided however that deduction of the amounts specified by the employer or income payor shall not relieve the debtor of the underlying obligation of support.

(f) A creditor shall not be required to issue process under section 5241 of this article prior to obtaining relief pursuant to this section.

(g) Where the court issues an income deduction order for support enforcement payable to the support collection unit, as defined in paragraph nine of subdivision (a) of section 5241 of this article, each payment remitted by an employer or income payor shall include, in addition to the identity and social security number of the debtor, the date and amount of each withholding of the debtor's income included in the payment.

2007 AMENDMENTS

L. 2007, ch. 601, eff. Jan. 1, 2008, amended CPLR 5242(c)(1) and (2) by replacing "department of social services" with "office of temporary and disability assistance."

CPLR

1997 AMENDMENTS

L. 1997, ch. 398, eff. Jan. 1, 1998, amended CPLR 5242(c)(1) by replacing the reference to D.R.L. § 37-a with F.C.A. Article 5-B.

1994 AMENDMENTS

L. 1994, ch. 170, eff. June 15, 1994, amended CPLR 5242 by adding a new subdivision (c) authorizing the court to issue an income deduction order in certain cases, based upon a determination that the respondent earns wages in New York and that enforcement may not otherwise be available; by renumbering former subdivisions (c) through (f) to become subdivisions (d) through (g); and by adding to subdivision (d) all of the language after the initial sentence, providing that if multiple support enforcement orders are served, whether pursuant to CPLR 5241, CPLR 5242 or both, the employer shall deduct the maximum amount authorized and distribute the deduction to each creditor in proportion to the amount of that creditor's claim.

1990 AMENDMENTS

L. 1990, ch. 818, eff. Sept. 30, 1990, amended CPLR 5242 by adding subdivision (f).

1987 AMENDMENTS

L. 1987, ch. 815, eff. Aug. 7, 1987, and applicable to any action or proceeding commenced on or after such date, added new subd. (e), which provides that a creditor is not required to issue process under CPLR 5241 before obtaining relief under CPLR 5242.

1985 AMENDMENTS

L. 1985, ch. 809, eff. Nov. 1, 1985, added CPLR 5242.

§§ 5243–5249. [Not used.]

§ 5250. Arrest of judgment debtor.

Upon motion of the judgment creditor without notice, where it is shown that the judgment debtor is about to depart from the state, or keeps himself concealed therein, and that there is reason to believe that he has in his possession or custody property in which he has an interest, the court may issue a warrant directed to the sheriff of any county in which the judgment debtor may be located. The warrant shall command the sheriff to arrest the judgment debtor forthwith and bring him before the court. The sheriff shall serve a copy of the warrant and the papers upon which it was based upon the judgment debtor at the time he makes the arrest. When the judgment debtor is brought before the court, the court may order that he give an undertaking, in a sum to be fixed by the court, that he will attend before the court for examination and that he will obey the terms of any restraining notice contained in the order.

CROSS REFERENCES

See selected provisions governing procedures to punish for contempt under **Judiciary Law, Article 19,** in Appendix, *below.*

§ 5251. Disobedience of subpoena, restraining notice or order; false swearing; destroying notice of sale.

Refusal or willful neglect of any person to obey a subpoena or restraining notice issued, or order granted, pursuant to this title; false swearing upon an examination or in answering written questions; and willful defacing or removal of a posted notice of sale before the time fixed for the sale, shall each be punishable as a contempt of court.

CROSS REFERENCES

See selected provisions governing procedures to punish for contempt under **Judiciary Law, Article 19,** in Appendix, *below.*

1965 AMENDMENTS

L. 1965, ch. 773, eff. Sept. 1, 1965, amended the section.

§ 5252. Discrimination against employees and prospective employees based upon wage assignment or income execution.

1. No employer shall discharge, lay off, refuse to promote, or discipline an employee, or refuse to hire a prospective employee, because one or more wage assignments or income executions have been served upon such employer or a former employer against the employee's or prospective employee's wages or because of the pendency of any action or judgment against such employee or prospective employee for nonpayment of any alleged contractual obligation. In addition to being subject to the civil action authorized in subdivision two of this section, where any employer discharges, lays off, refuses to promote or disciplines an employee or refuses to hire a prospective employee because of the existence of one or more income executions and/or income deduction orders issued pursuant to section fifty-two hundred forty-one or fifty-two hundred forty-two of this article, the court may direct the payment of a civil penalty not to exceed five hundred dollars for the first instance and one thousand dollars per instance for the second and subsequent instances of

employer or income payor discrimination. The penalty shall be paid to the creditor and may be enforced in the same manner as a civil judgment or in any other manner permitted by law.

2. An employee or prospective employee may institute a civil action for damages for wages lost as a result of a violation of this section within ninety days after such violation. Damages recoverable shall not exceed lost wages for six weeks and in such action the court also may order the reinstatement of such discharged employee or the hiring of such prospective employee. Except as provided for in subdivision (g) of section fifty-two hundred forty-one, not more than ten per centum of the damages recovered in such action shall be subject to any claims, attachments or executions by any creditors, judgment creditors or assignees of such employee or prospective employee. A violation of this section may also be punished as a contempt of court pursuant to the provisions of section seven hundred fifty-three of the judiciary law.

2006 AMENDMENTS

L. 2006, ch. 335, § 2, eff. Oct. 24, 2006, amended CPLR 5252(1) to provide that the penalties assessed against employers and income payors for the failure to comply with income execution for child support and for discrimination against an employee involved in a child support proceeding shall be paid to the creditor and may be enforced in the same manner as a civil judgment or in any other manner permitted by law.

1998 AMENDMENTS

L. 1998, ch. 214, § 80, eff. July 7, 1998, deemed in full force and effect on and after Nov. 11, 1997, amended CPLR 5252(1) by substituting "civil penalty" for "fine."

1997 AMENDMENTS

L. 1997, ch. 398, eff. Nov. 11, 1997, amended CPLR 5252(1) by adding the last sentence providing for monetary fines for discrimination based upon wage assignment or income execution.

1985 AMENDMENTS

L. 1985, ch. 809, eff. Nov. 1, 1985, amended CPLR 5252 to apply to prospective employees, to cross refer to CPLR 5241(g) governing the maximum amount deductible for support enforcement, and to make violation of the section punishable as a contempt of court.

1977 AMENDMENTS

L. 1977, ch. 344, eff. Jan. 1, 1978, amended CPLR 5252 by adding the provision to subd. (1) prohibiting discharge of an employee because of pendency of action or judgment against such employee for nonpayment of a contractual obligation.

1974 AMENDMENTS

L. 1974, ch. 981, eff. Sept. 1, 1974, amended subd. (1) of section 5252 by inserting the reference to "one or more wage assignments" and by prohibiting an employer from discharging or laying off an employee because income "executions" have been served upon the employer against the employee's wages. Previously the section referred to "an income execution" in the singular. In addition the word "employees'" was amended to read "employee's."

Prior to the enactment of chapter 981 of the L. of 1974, ch. 753 of the L. of 1974, eff. Sept. 1, 1974, provided for a more limited amendment of CPLR 5252 by inserting a reference to a "wage assignment" and by changing the word "employees'" to read "employee's." The provisions of chapter 753 of the Laws of 1974 pertaining to CPLR 5252 have been superseded by the provisions of chapter 981 of the Laws of 1974.

1969 AMENDMENTS

L. 1969, ch. 1138, eff. May 26, 1969, amended paragraph (1) by deleting "provided, however, that this provision shall not apply if more than one income execution against such employee is served upon the employer within any period of twelve consecutive months after January first, nineteen hundred sixty-seven."

1966 AMENDMENTS

L. 1966, ch. 613, eff. Jan. 1, 1967, added new section 5252.

CPLR

Article 53

RECOGNITION OF FOREIGN COUNTRY MONEY JUDGMENTS

SUMMARY OF ARTICLE

§ 5301. Definitions.

As used in this article the following definitions shall be applicable.

(a) Foreign state. "Foreign state" in this article means any governmental unit other than the United States, or any state, district, commonwealth, territory, insular possession thereof, or the Panama Canal Zone or the Trust Territory of the Pacific Islands.

(b) Foreign country judgment. "Foreign country judgment" in this article means any judgment of a foreign state granting or denying recovery of a sum of money, other than a judgment for taxes, a fine or other penalty, or a judgment for support in matrimonial or family matters.

1979 AMENDMENTS

L. 1979, ch. 119. eff. Jan. 1, 1980, amended CPLR 5301 subd. (a) by eliminating the Ryukyu Islands from the list of exceptions to the term "foreign state". The exception was once appropriate, when the Ryukyu Islands were under the treaty control of the United States. However, they were returned to Japan in 1972.

1970 AMENDMENTS

L. 1970, ch. 981, eff. Sept. 1, 1970, added new Article 53 (CPLR 5301-5309) concerning the recognition of foreign country money judgments.

The new Article 53 was recommended by the Judicial Conference Jan. 2, 1970 Report to the Legislature wherein it was stated:

"This bill would insert into the CPLR a new Article 53 entitled 'Recognition of Foreign Country Money Judgments'. This would in effect, incorporate in New York law the 'Uniform Foreign Money-Judgments Recognition Act' which has already been adopted by seven states, among them California and Illinois. . . .

"*The basic purpose of this proposal is to procure for New York judgments in foreign countries much better reciprocal treatment at the hands of foreign courts than they now receive.* The lack of recognition of New York judgments in foreign countries stems frequently from the fact that many foreign countries of civil law background do not accept *decisional* law as proof that New York treats foreign judgments liberally, but they rather require *statutory* proof of this fact. It is the opinion of experts in the field of international litigation that this codifying legislation would answer the reciprocity requirements of many foreign countries and would therefore result in obtaining better treatment for New York citizens engaged in litigation abroad.

"The Uniform Act codifies, rather than reforms, existing decisional law in New York and other states respecting the recognition of foreign country judgments. Indeed, New York's standards of recognition are even more liberal than those prescribed by the Uniform Act. The liberal tendency of New York courts in respect to the recognition of foreign country judgments is reflected in a long line of cases. Two such examples are *Coudenhove-Kalergi v. Dieterle* (36 N.Y.S.2d 313; Sup. Ct. 1942) wherein the New York court recognized an award of an arbitration tribunal in Germany over the objection that this was not a final judgment of a court of record and *Regierungspraesident Land Nordrheim Westfolen v. Rosenthal* (17 A.D.2d 145, 232 N.Y.S.2d 963; 1962) wherein the New York court enforced a revocation award of a German administrative tribunal. Neither of these decisions would be authorized by the provisions of Article 53 but neither would be overruled by this Article since they represent an aspect of decisional law more liberal than Article 53 and the New York courts would be free to exceed Article 53 in liberality if they should so choose under a saving clause contained in the draft statute.

"Article 53 as proposed would be applicable only to judgments of foreign countries and not to judgments of United States courts or sister-state courts. Only money judgments would be recognizable under the proposed article and only those which are final, conclusive and enforceable where rendered. Qualifying foreign country judgments would be enforceable by the procedures presently provided in the CPLR for the enforcement of judgments (action on the judgment or motion for summary judgment in lieu of complaint).

"A foreign country judgment under this bill, *would be refused* recognition in New York if the judgment was rendered under a system which does not provide impartial tribunals or procedures compatible with the requirements of due process, or if the foreign court did not have personal jurisdiction over the defendants. In addition, the New York court, in its discretion, *could refuse* recognition in a wide variety of instances specified in the bill and conforming to present case law.

"Provision is also made for a stay of the New York proceedings if an appeal is pending in the foreign country."

§ 5302. Applicability.

This article applies to any foreign country judgment which is final, conclusive and enforceable where rendered even though an appeal therefrom is pending or it is subject to appeal.

§ 5303. Recognition and enforcement.

Except as provided in section 5304, a foreign country judgment meeting the requirements of section 5302 is conclusive between the parties to the extent that it grants or denies recovery of a sum of money. Such a foreign judgment is enforceable by an action on the judgment, a motion for summary judgment in lieu of complaint, or in a pending action by counterclaim, cross-claim or affirmative defense.

§ 5304. Grounds for non-recognition.

(a) No recognition. A foreign country judgment is not conclusive if:

1. the judgment was rendered under a system which does not provide impartial tribunals or procedures compatible with the requirements of due process of law;

2. the foreign court did not have personal jurisdiction over the defendant.

(b) Other grounds for non-recognition. A foreign country judgment need not be recognized if:

1. the foreign court did not have jurisdiction over the subject matter;

2. the defendant in the proceedings in the foreign court did not receive notice of the proceedings in sufficient time to enable him to defend;

3. the judgment was obtained by fraud;

4. the cause of action on which the judgment is based is repugnant to the public policy of this state;

5. the judgment conflicts with another final and conclusive judgment;

6. the proceeding in the foreign court was contrary to an agreement between the parties under which the dispute in question was to be settled otherwise than by proceedings in that court;

7. in the case of jurisdiction based only on personal service, the foreign court was a seriously inconvenient forum for the trial of the action; or

8. the cause of action resulted in a defamation judgment obtained in a jurisdiction outside the United States, unless the court before which the matter is brought sitting in this state first determines that the defamation law applied in the foreign court's adjudication provided at least as much protection for freedom of speech and press in that case as would be provided by both the United States and New York constitutions.

2008 AMENDMENTS

L. 2008, ch. 66 § 2, eff. April 28, 2008, amended CPLR 5304(b) by adding par (8) to prohibit enforcement in New York of a foreign defamation judgment unless a New York court determines that the foreign court's defamation law provides at least as much free speech protections (including freedom of the press) guaranteed by the New York and United States constitutions.

§ 5305. Personal jurisdiction.

(a) Bases of jurisdiction. The foreign country judgment shall not be refused recognition for lack of personal jurisdiction if:

1. the defendant was served personally in the foreign state;

2. the defendant voluntarily appeared in the proceedings, other than for the purpose of protecting property seized or threatened with seizure in the proceedings or of contesting the jurisdiction of the court over him;

3. the defendant prior to the commencement of the proceedings had agreed to submit to the jurisdiction of the foreign court with respect to the subject matter involved;

4. the defendant was domiciled in the foreign state when the proceedings were instituted, or, being a body corporate had its principal place of business, was incorporated, or had otherwise acquired corporate status, in the foreign state;

5. the defendant had a business office in the foreign state and the proceedings in the foreign court involved a cause of action arising out of business done by the defendant through that office in the foreign state; or

6. the defendant operated a motor vehicle or airplane in the foreign state and the proceedings involved a cause of action arising out of such operation.

(b) Other bases of jurisdiction.   The courts of this state may recognize other bases of jurisdiction.

§ 5306.   Stay in case of appeal.

If the defendant satisfies the court either that an appeal is pending or that he is entitled and intends to appeal from the foreign country judgment, the court may stay the proceedings until the appeal has been determined or until the expiration of a period of time sufficient to enable the defendant to prosecute the appeal.

§ 5307.   Recognition in other situations.

This article does not prevent the recognition of a foreign country judgment in situations not covered by this article.

§ 5308.   Uniformity of interpretation.

This article shall be so construed as to effectuate its general purpose to make uniform the law of those states which enact these provisions.

§ 5309.   Citation.

This article may be cited as the "Uniform Foreign Country Money-Judgments Recognition Act."

Article 54

ENFORCEMENT OF JUDGMENTS ENTITLED TO FULL FAITH AND CREDIT

SUMMARY OF ARTICLE

§ 5401. Definition.

In this article "foreign judgment" means any judgment, decree, or order of a court of the United States or of any other court which is entitled to full faith and credit in this state, except one obtained by default in appearance, or by confession of judgment.

1970 AMENDMENTS

L. 1970, ch. 982, eff. Sept. 1, 1970, added new Article 54 (CPLR 5401-5408) concerning the enforcement of judgments entitled to full faith and credit.

The new Article 54 was recommended by the Judicial Conference Jan. 2, 1970, Report to the Legislature wherein it was stated in part: "This proposal would insert into the CPLR a new Article 54, captioned 'Enforcement of Judgments Entitled to Full Faith and Credit'. It would thereby incorporate into the law of New York the major features of the 1964 Uniform Enforcement of Foreign Judgments Act, recommended for adoption in New York in a study prepared for the Judicial Conference by Professor Barbara

CPLR

Kulzer of the State University of New York at Buffalo (now of Rutgers University School of Law), published in the *Thirteenth Annual Report of the Judicial Conference* (1968). The terms 'foreign judgment' and 'American judgment' as used in this discussion to describe the scope of this bill are identical in meaning; they include judgments of courts of states of the United States and courts in the Federal jurisdiction; they *do not* include judgments of courts of foreign countries. . . .

"Article 54 would provide a registration procedure for the enforcement of American judgments. This procedure is similar to that used in the Federal District Courts for the registration of federal judgments for money or property (28 U.S.C. § 1963) and is based upon the 1964 Uniform Enforcement of Foreign Judgments Act. *However, it is more conservative in its approach than the Uniform Act. The Uniform Act would apply to default and consent judgments. Article 54 would expressly exclude default and consent judgments from its scope.*

"The purpose of this bill is to cure a procedural defect in our law in respect to the modes of enforcement of American judgments which has been criticized by legal writers for upwards of 40 years and which has led to the enactment of 28 U.S.C. § 1963 for federal courts, and to the drafting of the 1948 Uniform Enforcement of Foreign Judgments Act as well as the revised 1964 Uniform Enforcement of Foreign Judgments Act for state courts. Proposed Article 54 is designed to provide for American judgments, *aside from default and consent judgments*, which are sought to be enforced in New York, the simpler, speedier and less expensive method of enforcement which is now available in the Federal system for the enforcement of judgments of United States district courts. It is comparable to registration systems now in successful operation in Canada and Australia. The Uniform Act has been adopted by seven sister states.

"Proposed Article 54 would establish a procedure whereby a copy of any foreign judgment entitled to full faith and credit and not rendered by default or by consent, if properly authenticated, could be filed within 90 days of authentication in the office of any county clerk. The clerk, under the proposed Article, would treat the foreign judgment in the same manner as a judgment of the Supreme Court of this state. A judgment so filed would have the same effect and be subject to the same procedures, defenses and proceedings for reopening, vacating, or staying as a judgment of the Supreme Court of this state and could be enforced or satisfied in like manner. The Article would permit the court to stay enforcement for good cause shown.

"The right of a judgment creditor to proceed by an action on the judgment or a motion for summary judgment in lieu of complaint instead of proceeding under this Article remains unimpaired.

"The success of the Federal courts in working with a registration enforcement procedure very similar to that here proposed indicates the practicality and desirability of this proposal. It should be necessary as a matter of equity only to ensure that a defendant has his full day in court. If he has his full day in court in one state, it should be unnecessary, in a federal system such as ours, especially in view of our full faith and credit concepts, that he be given another full day in court in every state where the winning plaintiff attempts to enforce his judgment. Indeed, the present procedures are most inequitable to the plaintiff who has fairly won his case against a defendant whose properties happen to be located in other states. This proposal is more extensively discussed in the CPLR Report of the Judicial Conference to the 1969 Legislature.

. . . .

"The bill . . . contains a provision for notice of registration to the judgment debtor. More specifically, the notice provision would require that within 30 days after the filing of the judgment and the affidavit, the judgment creditor shall mail notice of filing of the foreign judgment to the judgment debtor at his last known address and, while execution may issue immediately, the proceeds of the execution shall not be distributed to the judgment creditor earlier than 30 days after filing of proof of service. . . . [The] notice by mail . . . is timed so that normally it will not interfere with the judgment creditor's collection efforts; yet it will alert the judgment debtor to the filing of the judgment and enable him to raise objections before distribution of the proceeds of an execution. Notice will also enable the judgment debtor to ensure the discharge of a registered judgment if he satisfies the judgment without being aware of the registration."

§ 5402. Filing and status of foreign judgments.

(a) Filing.   A copy of any foreign judgment authenticated in accordance with an act of congress or the statutes of this state may be filed within ninety days of the date of authentication in the office of any county clerk of the state. The judgment creditor shall file with the judgment an affidavit stating that the judgment was not obtained by default in appearance or by confession of judgment, that it is unsatisfied in whole or in part, the amount remaining unpaid, and that its enforcement has not been stayed, and setting forth the name and last known address of the judgment debtor.

(b) Status of foreign judgments.   The clerk shall treat the foreign judgment in the same manner as a judgment of the supreme court of this state. A judgment so filed has the same effect and is subject to the same procedures, defenses and proceedings for reopening, vacating, or staying as a judgment of the supreme court of this state and may be enforced or satisfied in like manner.

§ 5403.   Notice of filing.

Within thirty days after filing of the judgment and the affidavit, the judgment creditor shall mail notice of filing of the foreign judgment to the judgment debtor at his last known address. The proceeds of an execution shall not be distributed to the judgment creditor earlier than thirty days after filing of proof of service.

§ 5404.   Stay.

(a) Based upon security in foreign jurisdiction.   If the judgment debtor shows the supreme court that an appeal from the foreign judgment is pending or will be taken, or that a stay of execution has been granted, the court shall stay enforcement of the foreign judgment until the appeal is concluded, the time for appeal expires, or the stay of execution expires or is vacated, upon proof that the judgment debtor has furnished the security for the satisfaction of the judgment required by the state in which it was rendered.

(b) Based upon other grounds.   If the judgment debtor shows the supreme court any ground upon which enforcement of a judgment of the supreme court of this state would be stayed, the court shall stay enforcement of the foreign judgment for an appropriate period, upon requiring the same security for satisfaction of the judgment which is required in this state.

§ 5405.   Fees.

When a foreign judgment is filed pursuant to this article, an index number shall be assigned in accordance with the provisions of subdivision (a) of section 8018 and the fee shall be as prescribed therein.

§ 5406.   Optional procedure.

The right of a judgment creditor to proceed by an action on the judgment or a motion for summary judgment in lieu of complaint, instead of proceeding under this article, remains unimpaired.

§ 5407.   Uniformity of interpretation.

This article shall be so construed as to effectuate its general purpose to make uniform the law of those states which enact these provisions.

§ 5408. Citation.

This article may be cited as the "Uniform Enforcement of Foreign Judgments Act."

Article 55

APPEALS GENERALLY

CPLR

§ 5501. Scope of review.

(a) Generally, from final judgment. An appeal from a final judgment brings up for review:

1. any non-final judgment or order which necessarily affects the final judgment, including any which was adverse to the respondent on the appeal from the final judgment and which, if reversed, would entitle the respondent to prevail in whole or in part on that appeal, provided that such non-final judgment or order has not previously been reviewed by the court to which the appeal is taken;

2. any order denying a new trial or hearing which has not previously been reviewed by the court to which the appeal is taken;

3. any ruling to which the appellant objected or had no opportunity to object or which was a refusal or failure to act as requested by the appellant, and any charge to the jury, or failure or refusal to charge as requested by the appellant, to which he objected;

CPLR

4. any remark made by the judge to which the appellant objected; and

5. a verdict after a trial by jury as of right, when the final judgment was entered in a different amount pursuant to the respondent's stipulation on a motion to set aside the verdict as excessive or inadequate; the appellate court may increase such judgment to a sum not exceeding the verdict or reduce it to a sum not less than the verdict.

(b) Court of appeals. The court of appeals shall review questions of law only, except that it shall also review questions of fact where the appellate division, on reversing or modifying a final or interlocutory judgment, has expressly or impliedly found new facts and a final judgment pursuant thereto is entered. On an appeal pursuant to subdivision (d) of section fifty-six hundred one, or subparagraph (ii) of paragraph one of subdivision (a) of section fifty-six hundred two, or subparagraph (ii) of paragraph two of subdivision (b) of section fifty-six hundred two, only the non-final determination of the appellate division shall be reviewed.

(c) Appellate division. The appellate division shall review questions of law and questions of fact on an appeal from a judgment or order of a court of original instance and on an appeal from an order of the supreme court, a county court or an appellate term determining an appeal. The notice of appeal from an order directing summary judgment, or directing judgment on a motion addressed to the pleadings, shall be deemed to specify a judgment upon said order entered after service of the notice of appeal and before entry of the order of the appellate court upon such appeal, without however affecting the taxation of costs upon the appeal. In reviewing a money judgment in an action in which an itemized verdict is required by rule forty-one hundred eleven of this chapter in which it is contended that the award is excessive or inadequate and that a new trial should have been granted unless a stipulation is entered to a different award, the appellate division shall determine that an award is excessive or inadequate if it deviates materially from what would be reasonable compensation.

(d) Appellate term. The appellate term shall review questions of law and questions of fact.

CROSS REFERENCES

See **N.Y. Const., Art. VI, §§ 3** (Court of appeals), **5** (Appellate courts generally), **8** (Appellate term) and **11** (Appellate jurisdiction of county courts), in Appendix, *below.*

1997 AMENDMENTS

L. 1997, ch. 474, eff. Nov. 24, 1997, amended subdivision (c) to provide that a notice of appeal from an order directing judgment upon a motion addressed to the pleadings or for summary judgment shall be deemed to specify a judgment on that order entered after service of the notice of appeal and before entry of the order of the appellate court without affecting the taxation of costs on the appeal.

1988 AMENDMENTS

L. 1988, ch. 184, eff. July 1, 1988, amending L. 1986, ch. 682, to make subdivision (c) applicable to all actions in which trial has not begun as of August 1, 1988.

1986 AMENDMENTS

L. 1986, ch. 682, eff. July 30, 1986 and applicable to actions commenced or claims filed on or after such date, amended CPLR 5501(c) by adding provisions relating to review of money judgments in actions in which an itemized verdict is required and it is contended that the award is excessive or inadequate.

§§ 5502–5510. [Not used.]

§ 5511. Permissible appellant and respondent.

An aggrieved party or a person substituted for him may appeal from any appealable judgment or order except one entered upon the default of the aggrieved party. He shall be designated as the appellant and the adverse party as the respondent.

§ 5512. Appealable paper; entry of order made out of court.

(a) Appealable paper. An initial appeal shall be taken from the judgment or order of the court of original instance and an appeal seeking review of an appellate determination shall be taken from the order entered in the office of the clerk of the court whose order is sought to be reviewed. If a timely appeal is taken from a judgment or order other than that specified in the last sentence and no prejudice results therefrom and the proper paper is furnished to the court to which the appeal is taken, the appeal shall be deemed taken from the proper judgment or order.

CPLR

(b) Entry of order made out of court. Entry of an order made out of court and filing of the papers on which the order was granted may be compelled by order of the court from or to which an appeal from the order might be taken.

§ 5513. Time to take appeal, cross-appeal or move for permission to appeal.

(a) Time to take appeal as of right. An appeal as of right must be taken within thirty days after service by a party upon the appellant of a copy of the judgment or order appealed from and written notice of its entry, except that when the appellant has served a copy of the judgment or order and written notice of its entry, the appeal must be taken within thirty days thereof.

(b) Time to move for permission to appeal. The time within which a motion for permission to appeal must be made shall be computed from the date of service by a party upon the party seeking permission of a copy of the judgment or order to be appealed from and written notice of its entry, or, where permission has already been denied by order of the court whose determination is sought to be reviewed, of a copy of such order and written notice of its entry, except that when such party seeking permission to appeal has served a copy of such judgment or order and written notice of its entry, the time shall be computed from the date of such service. A motion for permission to appeal must be made within thirty days.

(c) Additional time where adverse party takes appeal or moves for permission to appeal. A party upon whom the adverse party has served a notice of appeal or motion papers on a motion for permission to appeal may take an appeal or make a motion for permission to appeal within ten days after such service or within the time limited by subdivision (a) or (b) of this section, whichever is longer, if such appeal or motion is otherwise available to such party.

(d) Additional time where service of judgment or order and notice of entry is served by mail or overnight delivery service. Where service of the judgment or order to be appealed from and written notice of its entry is made by mail pursuant to paragraph two of subdivision (b) of rule twenty-one hundred three or by overnight delivery service pursuant to paragraph six of subdivision (b) of rule twenty-one hundred three of this chapter, the additional days provided by such paragraphs shall apply to this action, regardless of which party serves the judgment or order with notice of entry.

1999 AMENDMENTS

L. 1999, ch. 94, eff. June 22, 1999, and shall apply to judgments and orders with notices of entry served on or after June 22, 1999, amended CPLR § 5513 by adding new subdivision (d) relating to additional time to appeal where service of the notice of entry upon an attorney is made by mail or overnight delivery service.

1996 AMENDMENTS

L. 1996, ch. 214, eff. Jan. 1, 1997, amended subdivisions (a) and (b) by adding the phrase "by a party"; further amended subdivision (b) by adding the phrase "seeking permission to appeal"; and made the section gender neutral.

1977 AMENDMENTS

L. 1977, ch. 30, eff. Sept. 1, 1977, repealed former subdivision (b) governing the time to take a cross-appeal and relettered former subdivision (c), governing time to move for permission to appeal, to be subdivision (b). The matter repealed in former subdivision (b) is now covered in new subdivision (c) enacted by L. 1977, ch. 30, eff. Sept. 1, 1977.

The effect of the amendment is to specifically provide that the ten-day minimal period for cross-appeal be applicable in those instances where either the appeal or the cross-appeal, or both, are made by motion for permission to appeal, and that such ten-day period not be limited to instances where the appeal or cross-appeal is taken as of right.

1970 AMENDMENTS

L. 1970, ch. 108, eff. Sept. 1, 1970, amended Subd. (a) to provide that when an appellant has served a copy of the judgment or order and written notice of its entry, his appeal must be taken within thirty days thereof; amended Subd. (c) [now (b)] to provide that when a party seeking permission to appeal has served a copy of the judgment or order and written notice of its entry, the time to appeal shall be computed from the date of such service.

§ 5514. Extension of time to take appeal or to move for permission to appeal.

(a) Alternate method of appeal. If an appeal is taken or a motion for permission to appeal is made and such appeal is dismissed or motion is denied and, except for time limitations in section 5513, some other method of taking an appeal or of seeking permission to appeal is available, the time limited for such other method shall be computed from the dismissal or denial unless the court to which the appeal is sought to be taken orders otherwise.

(b) Disability of attorney. If the attorney for an aggrieved party dies, is removed or suspended, or becomes physically or mentally incapacitated or otherwise disabled before the expiration of the time limited for taking an appeal or moving for permission to appeal without having done so, such appeal may be taken or such motion for permission to appeal may be served within sixty days from the date of death, removal or suspension, or commencement of such incapacity or disability.

(c) Other extensions of time; substitutions or omission. No extension of time shall be granted for taking an appeal or for moving for permission to appeal except as provided in this section, section 1022, or section 5520.

§ 5515. Taking an appeal; notice of appeal.

1. An appeal shall be taken by serving on the adverse party a notice of appeal and filing it in the office where the judgment or order of the court of original instance is entered except that where an order granting permission to appeal is made, the appeal is taken when such order is entered. A notice shall designate the party taking the appeal, the judgment or order or specific part of the judgment or order appealed from and the court to which the appeal is taken.

2. Whenever an appeal is taken to the court of appeals, a copy of the notice of appeal shall be sent forthwith to the clerk of the court of appeals by the clerk of the office where the notice of appeal is required to be filed pursuant to this section.

3. Where leave to appeal to the court of appeals is granted by permission of the appellate division, a copy of the order granting such permission to appeal shall be sent forthwith to the clerk of the court of appeals by the clerk of the appellate division.

1975 AMENDMENTS

L. 1975, ch. 491, eff. Aug. 28, 1975, amended the first paragraph by designating it Subd. (1), and adding new Subds. (2) and (3), requiring the clerk of the court of original instance, or the Appellate Division Clerk, to forward to the Court of Appeals Clerk a copy of the notice of appeal, or the order granting permission to appeal.

R 5516. Motion for permission to appeal.

A motion for permission to appeal shall be noticed to be heard at a motion day at least eight days and not more than fifteen days after notice of the motion is served, unless there is no motion day during that period, in which case at the first motion day thereafter.

1978 AMENDMENTS

L. 1978, ch. 209, eff. June 2, 1978, amended CPLR 5516 by adoption of proposals made by the Judicial Conference in its Report to the 1978 Legislature, in which it stated:

"CPLR 5516, which governs motions for permission to appeal, and which now provides that such motion shall be noticed to be heard 'at the next motion day more than seven days' after the notice is served, would be amended to provide instead that such motions shall be noticed to be heard 'at least eight days and not more than fifteen days' after the notice is served. The proposed amendment would clarify the rule so as to assure avoidance of potential problems.

"The phrase 'more than seven days' means the same as 'at least eight days' and therefore a motion under CPLR 5516 served by mail must be made on 11 days' notice, pursuant to CPLR 2103(b)(2) which provides, *inter alia*, that 'where a period of time prescribed by law is measured from the service of a paper and service is by mail, three days shall be added to the prescribed period.'

"The wording of CPLR 5516, however, could easily be misread by the practitioner to result in the addition of 3 days to 7 days in the instance of service by mail. This would result in a jurisdictionally defective motion (*see* 7 Weinstein, Korn & Miller, New York Civil Practice-CPLR ¶ 5516.01 (Matthew Bender)).

"The difficulty is complicated by the fact that CPLR 5516 requires a motion for permission to appeal to be noticed to be heard 'at the next motion day.' This phrase could be literally construed to mean that there is only one day on which such motion can be made returnable, rather than on any of the days specified in the rules of the appellate courts.

"The proposed change would allow the clerk to move the return date further ahead if necessary to prevent a jurisdictional defect, thus conforming the language to the intent of the draftsmen (*see* 7 Weinstein, Korn &Miller, New York Civil Practice - CPLR ¶ 5516.01(Matthew Bender))."

1968 AMENDMENTS

Proposal No. 3, eff. Sept. 1, 1968, made by the Judicial Conference Feb. 1, 1968, Report to the Legislature, inserted word "seven" in place of word "four."

§ 5517. Subsequent orders.

(a) Appeal not affected by certain subsequent order. An appeal shall not be affected by:

CPLR

1. the granting of a motion for reargument or the granting of an order upon reargument making the same or substantially the same determination as is made in the order appealed from; or

2. the granting of a motion for resettlement of the order appealed from; or

3. the denial of a motion, based on new or additional facts, for the same or substantially the same relief applied for in the motion on which the order appealed from was made.

(b) Review of subsequent orders. A court reviewing an order may also review any subsequent order made upon a motion specified in subdivision (a), if the subsequent order is appealable as of right.

§ 5518. Preliminary injunction or temporary restraining order by appellate division.

The appellate division may grant, modify or limit a preliminary injunction or temporary restraining order pending an appeal or determination of a motion for permission to appeal in any case specified in section 6301.

§ 5519. Stay of enforcement.

(a) Stay without court order. Service upon the adverse party of a notice of appeal or an affidavit of intention to move for permission to appeal stays all proceedings to enforce the judgment or order appealed from pending the appeal or determination on the motion for permission to appeal where:

1. the appellant or moving party is the state or any political subdivision of the state or any officer or agency of the state or of any political subdivision of the state; provided that where a court, after considering an issue specified in question four of section seventy-eight hundred three of this chapter, issues a judgment or order directing reinstatement of a license held by a corporation with no more than five stockholders and which employs no more than ten employees, a partnership with no more than five partners and which employs no more than ten employees, a proprietorship or a natural person, the stay provided for by this paragraph shall be for a period of fifteen days; or

2. the judgment or order directs the payment of a sum of money, and an undertaking in that sum is given that if the judgment or order appealed from, or any part of it, is affirmed, or the appeal is dismissed, the appellant or moving party shall pay the amount directed to be paid by the judgment or order, or the part of it as to which the judgment or order is affirmed; or

3. the judgment or order directs the payment of a sum of money, to be paid in fixed installments, and an undertaking in a sum fixed by the court of original instance is given that the appellant or moving party shall pay each installment which becomes due pending the appeal and that if the judgment or order appealed from, or any part of it, is affirmed, or the appeal is dismissed, the appellant or moving party shall pay any installments or part of installments then due or the part of them as to which the judgment or order is affirmed; or

4. the judgment or order directs the assignment or delivery of personal property, and the property is placed in the custody of an officer designated by the court of original instance to abide the direction of the court to which the appeal is taken, or an undertaking in a sum fixed by the court of original instance is given that the appellant or moving party will obey the direction of the court to which the appeal is taken; or

5. the judgment or order directs the execution of any instrument, and the instrument is executed and deposited in the office where the original judgment or order is entered to abide the direction of the court to which the appeal is taken; or

6. the appellant or moving party is in possession or control of real property which the judgment or order directs be conveyed or delivered, and an undertaking in a sum fixed by the court of original instance is given that the appellant or moving party will not commit or suffer to be committed any waste and that if the judgment or order appealed from, or any part of it, is affirmed, or the appeal is dismissed, the appellant or moving party shall pay the value of the use and occupancy of such property, or the part of it as to which the judgment or order is affirmed, from the taking of the appeal until the delivery of possession of the property; if the judgment or order directs the sale of mortgaged property and the payment of any deficiency, the undertaking shall also provide that the appellant or

moving party shall pay any such deficiency; or

7. the judgment or order directs the performance of two or more of the acts specified in subparagraphs two through six and the appellant or moving party complies with each applicable subparagraph.

(b) Stay in action defended by insurer. If an appeal is taken from a judgment or order entered against an insured in an action which is defended by an insurance corporation, or other insurer, on behalf of the insured under a policy of insurance the limit of liability of which is less than the amount of said judgment or order, all proceedings to enforce the judgment or order to the extent of the policy coverage shall be stayed pending the appeal, and no action shall be commenced or maintained against the insurer for payment under the policy pending the appeal, where the insurer:

1. files with the clerk of the court in which the judgment or order was entered a sworn statement of one of its officers, describing the nature of the policy and the amount of coverage together with a written undertaking that if the judgment or order appealed from, or any part of it, is affirmed, or the appeal is dismissed, the insurer shall pay the amount directed to be paid by the judgment or order, or the part of it as to which the judgment or order is affirmed, to the extent of the limit of liability in the policy, plus interest and costs;

2. serves a copy of such sworn statement and undertaking upon the judgment creditor or his attorney; and

3. delivers or mails to the insured at the latest address of the insured appearing upon the records of the insurer, written notice that the enforcement of such judgment or order, to the extent that the amount it directs to be paid exceeds the limit of liability in the policy, is not stayed in respect to the insured. A stay of enforcement of the balance of the amount of the judgment or order may be imposed by giving an undertaking, as provided in paragraph two of subdivision (a), in an amount equal to that balance.

(c) Stay and limitation of stay by court order. The court from or to which an appeal is taken or the court of original instance may stay all proceedings to enforce the judgment or order appealed from pending an appeal or determination on a motion for permission to appeal in a case not provided for in subdivision (a) or subdivision (b), or may grant a limited stay or may vacate, limit or modify any stay imposed by subdivision (a), subdivision (b) or this subdivision, except that only the court to which an appeal is taken may vacate, limit or modify a stay imposed by paragraph one of subdivision (a).

(d) Undertaking. On an appeal from an order affirming a judgment or order, the undertaking shall secure both the order and the judgment or order which is affirmed.

(e) Continuation of stay. If the judgment or order appealed from is affirmed or modified, the stay shall continue for five days after service upon the appellant of the order of affirmance or modification with notice of its entry in the court to which the appeal was taken. If an appeal is taken or a motion is made for permission to appeal from such an order, before the expiration of the five days, the stay shall continue until five days after service of notice of the entry of the order determining such appeal or motion. When a motion for permission to appeal is involved, the stay, or any other stay granted pending determination of the motion for permission to appeal, shall:

    (i) if the motion is granted, continue until five days after the appeal is determined; or

    (ii) if the motion is denied, continue until five days after the movant is served with the order of denial with notice of its entry.

(f) Proceedings after stay. A stay of enforcement shall not prevent the court of original instance from proceeding in any matter not affected by the judgment or order appealed from or from directing the sale of perishable property.

(g) Appeals in medical, dental or podiatric malpractice judgments. In an action for medical, dental or podiatric malpractice, if an appeal is taken from a judgment in excess of one million dollars and an undertaking in the amount of one million dollars or the limit of insurance coverage available to the appellant for the occurrence, whichever is greater, is given together with a joint undertaking by the appellant and any insurer of the appellant's professional liability that, during the period of such stay, the appellant will make no fraudulent conveyance without fair consideration as described in section two hundred seventy-three-a of the debtor and creditor law, the court to which such an appeal is taken shall stay all proceedings to enforce the judgment pending such appeal if it finds that there is a reasonable probability that the judgment may be reversed or determined excessive. In making a determination under this subdivision, the court shall not consider the availability of a stay pursuant to subdivision (a) or (b) of this section. Liability under such joint undertaking shall be limited to fraudulent conveyances made by the appellant subsequent to the execution of such undertaking and during the period of such stay, but nothing herein shall limit the liability of the appellant for fraudulent conveyances pursuant to article ten of the debtor and creditor law or any other law. An insurer that pays money to a beneficiary of such a joint undertaking shall thereupon be subrogated, to the extent of the amount to be paid, to the rights and interests of such beneficiary, as a judgment creditor, against the appellant on whose behalf the joint undertaking was executed.

1988 AMENDMENTS

L. 1988, ch. 184, eff. July 1, 1988, added new subdivision (g) governing stays in large-verdict (*i.e.*, one million dollars and above) medical, dental, and podiatric malpractice actions. L. 1988, ch. 493, eff. Sept. 1, 1988, amended 5519(a) paragraph 1 to set at 15 days an automatic stay pending appeal by the state or a political subdivision or agency of the state, of an adverse decision in specified Article 78 proceedings.

1979 AMENDMENTS

L. 1979, ch. 239, eff. Jan. 1, 1980, amended CPLR 5519 subd. (e) by making certain stylistic changes and by clarifying the meaning of the statute with respect to procedures for continuation of a stay of proceedings where an appeal as of right is timely taken, or a timely motion is made for permission to take an appeal from an affirmance or modification of an order determining a prior appeal.

The Judicial Conference report on the CPLR to the 1979 Legislature stated that the statute, ". . . has been troublesome for lack of precision and because reference to motions for permission to appeal was not included . . .

"CPLR 5519(e) now provides for continuance of the stay after the determination of the first appeal, for five days from service upon the appellant of the notice of entry, in the court to which the first appeal was taken, of the order determining that appeal. Where an appeal is taken from such an order, the stay continues until determination of the appeal. *DFI Communications Inc. v. Greenberg,* 394 N.Y.S.2d 586, 41 N.Y.2d 1017, 363 N.E. 2d 312 (1977) held that a motion to continue the stay is unnecessary since the filing of the notice of appeal automatically continues the stay. CPLR 5519(e) would be clarified to reflect the decision by providing for such automatic continuation if the second appeal is taken within the designated 5-day period after the determination of the first appeal, except that the 5-day period would now be measured from service on appellant of the order of affirmation or modification as well as the notice of entry. It would also be provided that the stay continue until 5 days after determination of the appeal.

"CPLR 5519(e) would be further clarified by providing a similar mechanism to govern the continuation of a stay where a motion for permission to appeal is made. Absence of such specific provision has generated unnecessary applications in such cases for continuation of the stay until determination of the appeal (*Created Gemstones, Inc. v. Union Carbide Corporation,* 408 N.Y.S.2d 507, 45 N.Y.2d 772, 380 N.E.2d 333 (1978)). Thus, where a motion for permission to appeal is made within the designated 5-day period, any stay would continue until the motion is granted or denied. If the motion is granted, whether or not the designated 5-day period has elapsed, the stay would continue until 5 days after the determination of the appeal. If the motion is denied, the stay would continue for 5 days after the movant is served with the order of denial with notice of its entry.

"The last sentence of CPLR 5519(e), which relates to the duration of any stay granted pending a motion for permission to appeal, would be stricken as unnecessary because of the proposed amendments."

1975 AMENDMENTS

L. 1975, ch. 70, eff. Sept. 1, 1975, upon the recommendation of the Judicial Conference, amended Subd. (e).

1965 AMENDMENTS

L. 1965, ch. 744, eff. Sept. 1, 1965, deleted the words "and the judgment or order directs either the payment of a sum of money, the assignment or delivery of personal property, or the conveyance of real property" in paragraph 1 of subdivision (a).

§ 5520. Omissions; appeal by improper method.

(a) Omissions. If an appellant either serves or files a timely notice of appeal or notice of motion for permission to appeal, but neglects through mistake or excusable neglect to do another required act within the time limited, the court from or to which the appeal is taken or the court of original instance may grant an extension of time for curing the omission.

(b) Appeal by permission instead of as of right. An appeal taken by permission shall not be dismissed upon the ground that the appeal would lie as of right and was not taken within the time limited for an appeal as of right, provided the motion for permission was made within the time limited for taking the appeal.

(c) Defects in form. Where a notice of appeal is premature or contains an inaccurate description of the judgment or order appealed from, the appellate court, in its discretion, when the interests of justice so demand, may treat such a notice as valid.

1979 AMENDMENTS

L. 1979, ch. 120, eff. Jan. 1, 1980, amended CPLR 5520 subd. (a) by ". . . supplying a missing reference therein to a notice of motion for permission to appeal . . .", the Judicial Conference Report on the CPLR to the 1979 Legislature stated. The report continued:

"CPLR 5520(a) provides that the court of original instance or the court from or to which an appeal is taken may grant an extension of time to cure an omission by mistake or excusable neglect on the part of an appellant who has either served or filed a timely notice of appeal, but has omitted some other act necessary to perfect the appeal.

"No good reason exists for the failure to extend the benefit of this provision to a notice of motion for leave to appeal . . . This obviously unintended deficiency would be corrected by this bill, which specifically includes a notice of motion for permission to appeal within the scope of the provision."

1966 AMENDMENTS

L. 1966, ch. 594, eff. Sept. 1, 1966, added new Subd. (c).

R 5521. Preferences.

(a) Preferences in the hearing of an appeal may be granted in the discretion of the court to which the appeal is taken.

(b) Consistent with the provisions of section one thousand one hundred twelve of the family court act, appeals from orders, judgments or decrees in proceedings brought pursuant to articles three, seven, ten and ten-A and parts one and two of article six of the family court act, and pursuant to sections three hundred fifty-eight-a, three hundred eighty-three-c, three hundred eighty-four, and three hundred eighty-four-b of the social services law, shall be given preference and may be brought on for argument on such terms and conditions as the court may direct without the necessity of a motion.

2005 AMENDMENTS

L. 2005, ch. 65 (PartA), eff. Dec. 21, 2005, was amended to create a preference for appeals under the new Article 10-A of the Family Court Act and SSL §§ 383-c and 384 without the necessity for a motion.

1991 AMENDMENTS

L. 1991, ch. 582, eff. Jan. 1, 1992, relettered the previously undesignated first paragraph as subdivision (a) and added new subdivision (b).

R 5522. Disposition of appeal.

(a) A court to which an appeal is taken may reverse, affirm, or modify, wholly or in part, any judgment or order before it, as to any party. The court shall render a final determination or, where necessary or proper, remit to another court for further proceedings. A court reversing or modifying a judgment or order without opinion shall briefly state the grounds of its decision.

(b) In an appeal from a money judgment in an action in which an itemized verdict is required by rule forty-one hundred eleven of this chapter in which it is contended that the award is excessive or inadequate, the appellate division shall set forth in its decision the reasons therefor, including the factors it considered in complying with subdivision (c) of section fifty-five hundred one of this chapter.

CPLR

1988 AMENDMENTS

L. 1988, ch. 184, eff. July 1, 1988, amended L. 1986, ch. 682, to make subdivision (b) applicable to all actions in which trial has not begun as of August 1, 1988.

1986 AMENDMENTS

L. 1986, ch. 682, eff. July 30, 1986, and applicable to actions commenced or claims filed on or after such date, amended CPLR 5522 by restructuring the rule and adding new paragraph (b), requiring the Appellate Division, in appeals from money judgments in actions where an itemized verdict is required by CPLR 4111, to set forth in its decision the reasons it found such award to be excessive or inadequate.

1977 AMENDMENTS

CPLR 5522 was amended by proposal No. 3 of the Judicial Conference in its Report to the 1977 Legislature, effective September 1, 1977, by eliminating the requirement that a court affirming a judgment or order without opinion briefly state the grounds of its decision. The 1977 amendment reverts to the text as it read before the amendment effected by ch. 407 of the Laws of 1975.

1975 AMENDMENTS

L. 1975, ch. 407, eff. Sept. 1, 1975, amended CPLR 5522.

§ 5523. Restitution.

A court reversing or modifying a final judgment or order or affirming such a reversal or modification may order restitution of property or rights lost by the judgment or order, except that where the title of a purchaser in good faith and for value would be affected, the court may order the value or the purchase price restored or deposited in court.

R 5524.   Entry of order; remittitur and further proceedings.

(a) Entry of order in appellate court. An order of a court to which an appeal is taken shall be entered in the office of the clerk of that court.

(b) Remittitur and further proceedings. A copy of the order of the court to which an appeal is taken determining the appeal, together with the record on appeal, shall be remitted to the clerk of the court of original instance except that where further proceedings are ordered in another court, they shall be remitted to the clerk of such court. The entry of such copy shall be authority for any further proceedings. Any judgment directed by the order shall be entered by the clerk of the court to which remission is made.

R 5525.   Preparation and settlement of transcript; statement in lieu of transcript.

(a) Preparation of transcript. Where a stenographic record of the proceedings is made, the appellant, within the time for taking the appeal, shall serve upon the stenographic reporter a request for a transcript of the proceedings and, unless the appellant is the state or any political subdivision of the state or an officer or agency of the state or of any political subdivision of the state, shall deposit a sum sufficient to pay the fee. As soon as possible after receiving such notice the reporter shall serve upon the appellant the ribbon copy and a carbon copy of the typewritten transcript, or two copies of the transcript if it is reproduced by any other means. The appellate division in each department may by rule applicable in the department to all appeals taken from judgments or orders entered in the department, provide that only a ribbon copy of the typewritten transcript be prepared and provide for the use of such copy by the parties and the court.

(b) Omission of part of transcript. The parties may stipulate that only a portion of the record be transcribed. No transcript is necessary where a party appeals from a judgment entered upon a referee's report, or a decision of the court upon a trial without a jury, and he relies only upon exceptions to rulings on questions of law made after the case is finally submitted.

(c) Settlement of transcript. 1. Within fifteen days after receiving the transcript from the court reporter or from any other source, the appellant shall make any proposed amendments and serve them and a copy of the transcript upon the respondent. Within fifteen days after such service the respondent shall make any proposed amendments or objections to the proposed amendments of the appellant and serve them upon the appellant. At any time thereafter and on at least four days' notice to the adverse party, the transcript and the proposed amendments and objections thereto shall be submitted for settlement to the judge or referee before whom the proceedings were had if the parties cannot agree on the amendments to the transcript. The original of the transcript shall be corrected by the appellant in accordance with the agreement of the parties or the direction of the court and its correctness shall be certified to thereon by the parties or the judge or referee before whom the proceedings were had. When he serves his brief upon the respondent the appellant shall also serve a conformed copy of the transcript or deposit it in the office of the clerk of the court of original instance who shall make it available to respondent.

2. If the appellant has timely proposed amendments and served them with a copy of the transcript on respondent, and no amendments or objections are proposed by the respondent within the time limited by paragraph 1, the transcript, certified as correct by the court reporter, together with appellant's proposed amendments, shall be deemed correct without the necessity of a stipulation by the parties certifying to its correctness or the settlement of the transcript by the judge or referee. The appellant shall affix to such transcript an affirmation, certifying to his compliance with the time limitation, the service of the notice provided by paragraph 3 and the respondent's failure to propose amendments or objections within the time prescribed.

3. Appellant shall serve on respondent together with a copy of the transcript and the proposed amendments, a notice of settlement containing a specific reference to subdivision (c) of this rule, and stating that if respondent fails to propose amendments or objections within the time limited by paragraph 1, the provisions of paragraph

CPLR

2 shall apply.

(d) *Statement in lieu of stenographic transcript.* Where no stenographic record of the proceedings is made, the appellant, within ten days after taking his appeal, shall prepare and serve upon the respondent a statement of the proceedings from the best available sources, including his recollection, for use instead of a transcript. The respondent may serve upon the appellant objections or proposed amendments to the statement within ten days after such service. The statement, with objections or proposed amendments, shall be submitted for settlement to the judge or referee before whom the proceedings were had.

(e) *Special rules prescribing time limitations in settlement of transcript or statement in lieu thereof authorized.* The appellate division in each department may by rule applicable in the department prescribe other limitations of time different from those prescribed in subdivisions (c) and (d) for serving transcripts, or statements in lieu of transcripts, and proposed amendments or objections, and for submission thereof for settlement.

1975 AMENDMENTS

CPLR 5525(c) was amended by Proposal No. 1 of the Judicial Conference Report to the 1975 Legislature, effective September 1, 1975, by designating the text of the first paragraph of Subd. (c) as Paragraph "1."; by changing the ten day time limits in the first and second sentences to fifteen day time limits; by inserting in the first sentence, following the phrase "after receiving the transcript," the clause "from the court reporter or from any other source"; and by adding thereto two new paragraphs, numbered Paragraphs "2." and "3."

R 5526.   Content and form of record on appeal.

The record on appeal from a final judgment shall consist of the notice of appeal, the judgment-roll, the corrected transcript of the proceedings or a statement pursuant to subdivision (d) of rule 5525 if a trial or hearing was held, any relevant exhibits, or copies of them, in the court of original instance, any other reviewable order, and any opinions in the case. The record on appeal from an interlocutory judgment or any order shall consist of the notice of appeal, the judgment or order appealed from, the transcript, if any, the papers and other exhibits upon which the judgment or order was founded and any opinions in the case. All printed or reproduced papers comprising the record on appeal shall be eleven inches by eight and one-half inches. The subject matter of each page of the record shall be stated at the top thereof, except that in the case of papers other than testimony, the subject matter of the paper may be stated at the top of the first page of each paper, together with the page numbers of the first and last pages thereof. In the case of testimony, the name of the witness, by whom he was called and whether the testimony is direct, cross, redirect or recross examination shall be stated at the top of each page.

1976 AMENDMENTS

Proposal No. 1, effective September 1, 1976, made by the Judicial Conference 1976 Report to the Legislature, amended CPLR 5526 by adding the last two sentences specifying the form of page headings.

1968 AMENDMENTS

Proposal No. 4, effective Sept. 1, 1968, made by the Judicial Conference Feb. 1, 1968 Report to the Legislature, amended caption and text of rule 5526 to read as above. (See 1975 Amendments.)

R 5527.   Statement in lieu of record on appeal.

When the questions presented by an appeal can be determined without an examination of all the pleadings and proceedings, the parties may prepare and sign a statement showing how the questions arose and were decided in the court from which the appeal is taken and setting forth only so much of the facts averred and proved or sought to be proved as are necessary to a decision of the questions. The statement may also include portions of the transcript of the proceedings and other relevant matter. It shall include a copy of the judgment or order appealed from, the notice of appeal and a statement of the issues to be determined. Within twenty days after the appellant has taken his appeal, the statement shall be presented to the court from which the appeal is taken for approval as the record on appeal. The court may make corrections or additions necessary to present fully the questions raised by the appeal. The approved statement shall be printed as a joint appendix.

R 5528.   Content of briefs and appendices.

(a) Appellant's brief and appendix. The brief of the appellant shall contain in the following order:

1. a table of contents, which shall include the contents of the appendix, if it is not bound separately, with references to the initial page of each paper printed and of the direct, cross, and redirect examination of each witness;

2. a concise statement, not exceeding two pages, of the questions involved without names, dates, amounts or particulars, with each question numbered, set forth separately and followed immediately by the answer, if any, of the court from which the appeal is taken;

3. a concise statement of the nature of the case and of the facts which should be known to determine the questions involved, with supporting references to pages in the appendix;

4. the argument for the appellant which shall be divided into points by appropriate headings distinctively printed; and

5. an appendix, which may be bound separately, containing only such parts of the record on appeal as are necessary to consider the questions involved, including those parts the appellant reasonably assumes will be relied upon by the respondent; provided, however, that the appellate division in each department may by rule applicable in the department authorize an appellant at his election to proceed upon a record on appeal printed or reproduced in like manner as an appendix, and in the event of such election an appendix shall not be required.

(b) Respondent's brief and appendix. The brief of the respondent shall conform to the requirements of subdivision (a), except that a counterstatement of the questions involved or a counterstatement of the nature and facts of the case shall be included only if the respondent disagrees with the statement of the appellant and the appendix shall contain only such additional parts of the record as are necessary to consider the questions involved.

(c) Appellant's reply brief and appendix. Any reply brief of the appellant shall conform to the requirements of subdivision (a) without repetition.

(d) Joint appendix. A joint appendix bound separately may be used. It shall be filed with the appellant's brief.

(e) Sanction. For any failure to comply with subdivision (a), (b) or

(c) the court to which the appeal is taken may withhold or impose costs.

R 5529. Form of briefs and appendices.

(a) Form of reproduction; size; paper; binding.

1. Briefs and appendices shall be reproduced by any method that produces a permanent, legible, black image on white paper. Paper shall be of a quality approved by the chief administrator of the courts.

2. Briefs and appendices shall be on white paper eleven inches along the bound edge by eight and one-half inches.

3. An appellate court may by rule applicable to practice therein prescribe the size of margins and type of briefs and appendices and the line spacing and the length of briefs.

(b) Numbering. Pages of briefs shall be numbered consecutively. Pages of appendices shall be separately numbered consecutively, each number preceded by the letter A.

(c) Page headings. The subject matter of each page of the appendix shall be stated at the top thereof, except that in the case of papers other than testimony, the subject matter of the paper may be stated at the top of the first page of each paper, together with the page numbers of the first and last pages thereof. In the case of testimony, the name of the witness, by whom he was called and whether the testimony is direct, cross, redirect, or recross examination shall be stated at the top of each page.

(d) Quotations. Asterisks or other appropriate means shall be used to indicate omissions in quoted excerpts. Reference shall be made to the source of the excerpts quoted. Where an excerpt in the appendix is testimony of a witness quoted from the record the beginning of each page of the transcript shall be indicated by parenthetical insertion of the transcript page number.

(e) Citations of decisions. New York decisions shall be cited from the official reports, if any. All other decisions shall be cited from the official reports, if any, and also from the National Reporter System if they are there reported. Decisions not reported officially or in the National Reporter System shall be cited from the most available

CPLR

source.

(f) Questions and answers. The answer to a question in the appendix shall not begin a new paragraph.

2002 AMENDMENTS

L. 2002, ch. 595, § 1, eff. Jan.1, 2003, amended subparagraphs (1)–(3) in subdivision (a).

1976 AMENDMENTS

Proposal No. 1, effective September 1, 1976, made by the Judicial Conference 1976 Report to the Legislature, amended Subd. (c) to permit subject matter of the paper to be stated at the top of the first page only, instead of requiring such statement at the top of every page.

1975 AMENDMENTS

Proposal No. 2 of the 1975 Judicial Conference, effective September 1, 1975, amended CPLR 5529(a)(3).

1968 AMENDMENTS

Proposal No. 5, effective Sept. 1, 1968, made by the Judicial Conference Feb. 1, 1968 Report to the Legislature amended paragraphs (2) and (3) of subdivision (a).

R 5530. Filing record and briefs; service of briefs.

(a) Generally. Within twenty days after settlement of the transcript or after settlement of the statement in lieu of stenographic transcript or after approval of the statement in lieu of record, the appellant shall file with the clerk of the court to which the appeal is taken the record on appeal or statement in lieu of record, and the required number of copies of his brief, and shall also serve upon the adverse party three copies of his brief. The respondent shall file and serve a like number of copies of his brief within fifteen days after service of the appellant's brief. The appellant may file and serve a like number of copies of a reply brief within ten days after service of the respondent's brief.

(b) Upon cross-appeal. Unless the court to which the appeals are taken otherwise orders, where both parties take an appeal from the same judgment or order, the plaintiff, or appellant in the court from which the appeal is taken, shall file and serve his brief first. The answering brief shall be filed and served within fifteen days after service of the first brief and shall include the points and arguments on the cross-appeal. A reply brief shall be filed and served within fifteen days after service of the answering brief, and shall include answering points and arguments on the cross-appeal. A reply brief to the cross-appeal may thereafter be served and filed within ten days after the service of the reply to the first brief.

(c) Special rules prescribing times for filing and serving authorized.

The appellate division in each department may by rule applicable in the department prescribe other limitations of time different from those prescribed in subdivisions (a) and (b) for filing and serving records on appeal, or statements in lieu of records, and briefs in appeals taken therein.

R 5531. Description of action.

The appellant shall file together with the record on appeal, in both criminal and civil actions, a statement containing the following information listed and numbered in the following order:

1. the index number of the case in the court below,

2. the full names of the original parties and any change in the parties,

3. the court and county in which the action was commenced,

4. the date the action was commenced and the dates on which each pleading was served,

5. a brief description of the nature and object of the action,

6. a statement as to whether the appeal is from a judgment or an order or both, the dates of entry of each judgment or order appealed from, and the name of the judge or justice who directed the entry of the judgment or made the order being appealed, and

7. a statement as to the method of appeal being used:

(a) whether the appeal is on full record, printed or reproduced, or

(b) on the original record, in which event, state whether the appendix method is being used, or leave to prosecute the appeal on the original record was granted by the court or by statute.

The statement shall be prefixed to the papers constituting the record on appeal. A copy of this statement shall be filed with the clerk at the time the record on appeal is filed.

CPLR

1974 AMENDMENTS

L. 1974, ch. 433, eff. Sept. 1, 1974, amended paragraphs 6 and 7.

1966 AMENDMENTS

Amendment No. 3, effective Sept. 1, 1966, made by the Judicial Conference Feb. 1, 1966, Report to the Legislature. The reason stated was that the requirement of "CPLR 5531 that the statement referred to therein be filed with the appellant's brief if a brief is filed has caused some confusion among the bar because of the change from Rule 234 of the Rules of Civil Practice, under which the statement was required to be prefixed to the papers on appeal. The former practice, which resulted in earlier filing of the statement than at present and its inclusion in the record on appeal, is preferable for administrative purposes. For these reasons it seems desirable to revert to the former practice.

"Since the statement required by CPLR 5531 is also used for statistical purposes by the Judicial Conference, the proposed change would require that an additional copy be filed. This will facilitate transmission of the information contained in the statement by the clerk of the appellate court to the Judicial Conference."

1964 AMENDMENTS

Amendment No. 10 made by the Judicial Conference Feb. 1, 1964, Report to the Legislature, pursuant to Judiciary Law § 229, effective Sept. 1, 1964, revised the requirements of the statement to be filed with the record on appeal.

R 5532.   Stipulation in lieu of certification.

The parties or their attorneys may stipulate as to the correctness of the entire record on appeal or any portion thereof in lieu of certification.

1964 AMENDMENTS

Amendment No. 9 made by the Judicial Conference Feb. 1, 1964, Report to the Legislature, effective Sept. 1, 1964, added this new Rule 5532.

Article 56
APPEALS TO THE COURT OF APPEALS

§ 5601. Appeals to the court of appeals as of right.

(a) Dissent. An appeal may be taken to the court of appeals as of right in an action originating in the supreme court, a county court, a surrogate's court, the family court, the court of claims or an administrative agency, from an order of the appellate division which finally determines the action, where there is a dissent by at least two justices on a question of law in favor of the party taking such appeal.

(b) Constitutional grounds. An appeal may be taken to the court of appeals as of right:

CPLR

1. from an order of the appellate division which finally determines an action where there is directly involved the construction of the constitution of the state or of the United States; and

2. from a judgment of a court of record of original instance which finally determines an action where the only question involved on the appeal is the validity of a statutory provision of the state or of the United States under the constitution of the state or of the United States.

(c) From order granting new trial or hearing, upon stipulation for judgment absolute. An appeal may be taken to the court of appeals as of right in an action originating in the supreme court, a county court, a surrogate's court, the family court, the court of claims or an administrative agency, from an order of the appellate division granting or affirming the granting of a new trial or hearing where the appellant stipulates that, upon affirmance, judgment absolute shall be entered against him.

(d) Based upon nonfinal determination of appellate division. An appeal may be taken to the court of appeals as of right from a final judgment entered in a court of original instance, from a final determination of an administrative agency or from a final arbitration award, or from an order of the appellate division which finally determines an appeal from such a judgment or determination, where the appellate division has made an order on a prior appeal in the action which necessarily affects the judgment, determination or award and which satisfies the requirements of subdivision (a) or of paragraph one of subdivision (b) except that of finality.

CROSS REFERENCES

See **N.Y. Const., Art. VI, §§ 3** (Court of appeals), **5** (Appellate courts generally), **8** (Appellate term) and **11** (Appellate jurisdiction of county courts), in Appendix, *below.*

1986 AMENDMENTS

L. 1986, ch. 316, eff. Jan. 1, 1987, and applicable to every notice of appeal filed or motion for leave to appeal to the court of appeals made on or after such date, amended Subd. (d) of CPLR 5601 by providing for appeal as of right to the Court of Appeals from a final arbitration award.

1985 AMENDMENTS

L. 1985, ch. 300, eff. Jan. 1, 1986, and applicable to every notice of appeal taken or motion for leave to appeal to the Court of Appeals made on or after that date, amended CPLR 5601(a) to limit appeals as of right to the Court of Appeals to cases where there is a dissent by at least two justices of the Appellate Division on a question of law in favor of the party taking the appeal.

1973 AMENDMENTS

L. 1973, ch. 95, § 1, eff. immediately and retroactive to and deemed to be in full force and effect from and after March 1, 1973, amended L. 1969, ch. 999 by eliminating the time limit on the effectiveness of ch. 999. This makes the 1969 amendment of CPLR 5601(a) (L. 1969, ch. 999, as amended by L. 1971, ch. 44) permanent. See "1971" and "1969 Amendments," *below.*

L. 1973, ch. 95, § 2, amended CPLR 5601 (a) by deleting "stated" before "question of law," and by making grammatical changes.

1971 AMENDMENTS

L. 1971, ch. 44, eff. March 1, 1971 until March 1, 1973, amended L. 1969, ch. 999, § 2, entitled "An Act to Amend the Civil Practice Law and Rules, in Relation to Appeals as of Right to the Court of Appeals" (CPLR 5601(a)), by extending the effective date of ch. 999 until March 1, 1973.

1969 AMENDMENTS

L. 1969, ch. 999, eff. Sept. 2, 1969 until March 1, 1971, amended Subd. (a) by deleting "of such judgment or order"; by dividing the material following "an order of the appellate division which finally determines the action," into subparagraphs (i), (ii) and (iii); by adding to new subparagraph (i), "on a stated question of law in favor of the party taking such appeal"; and by adding to new subparagraph (iii), "thereof in a substantial respect, which is within the power of the court of appeals to review on such appeal, and the party taking the appeal is aggrieved by the modification."

1967 AMENDMENTS

L. 1967, ch. 342, eff. Sept. 1, 1967, added reference to family court in Subd. (a) and Subd. (c).

§ 5602. Appeals to the court of appeals by permission.

(a) Permission of appellate division or court of appeals. An appeal may be taken to the court of appeals by permission of the appellate division granted before application to the court of appeals, or by permission of the court of appeals upon refusal by the appellate division or upon direct application. Permission by an appellate division for leave to appeal shall be pursuant to rules authorized by that appellate division. Permission by the court of appeals for leave to appeal shall be pursuant to rules authorized by the court which shall provide that leave to appeal be granted upon the approval of two judges of the court of appeals. Such appeal may be taken:

1. in an action originating in the supreme court, a county court, a surrogate's court, the family court, the court of claims, an administrative agency or an arbitration,

(i) from an order of the appellate division which finally determines the action and which is not appealable as of right, or

(ii) from a final judgment of such court, final determination of such agency or final arbitration award where the appellate division has made an order on a prior appeal in the action which necessarily affects the final judgment, determination or award and the final judgment, determination or award is not appealable as of right pursuant to subdivision (d) of section 5601 of this article; and

2. in a proceeding instituted by or against one or more public officers or a board, commission or other body of public officers or a court or tribunal, from an order of the appellate division which does not finally determine such proceeding, except that the appellate division shall not grant permission to appeal from an order granting or affirming the granting of a new trial or hearing.

(b) Permission of appellate division. An appeal may be taken to the court of appeals by permission of the appellate division:

1. from an order of the appellate division which does not finally determine an action, except an order described in paragraph two of subdivision (a) or subparagraph (iii) of paragraph two of subdivision (b) of this section or in subdivision (c) of section 5601;

2. in an action originating in a court other than the supreme court, a county court, a surrogate's court, the family court, the court of claims or an administrative agency,

(i) from an order of the appellate division which finally determines the action, and which is not appealable as of right pursuant to paragraph one of subdivision (b) of section 5601, or

(ii) from a final judgment of such court or a final determination of such agency where the appellate division has made an order on a prior appeal in the action which necessarily affects the final judgment or determination and the final judgment or determination is not appealable as of right pursuant to subdivision (d) of section 5601, or

(iii) from an order of the appellate division granting or affirming the granting of a new trial or hearing where the appellant stipulates that, upon affirmance, judgment absolute shall be entered against him.

1986 AMENDMENTS

L. 1986, ch. 316, eff. Jan. 1, 1987, and applicable to every notice of appeal filed or motion for leave to appeal to the court of appeals made on or after such date, amended Subd. (1)(a) of CPLR 5602 by providing for appeal by permission in an action originating in an arbitration from a final arbitration award.

1985 AMENDMENTS

L. 1985, ch. 300, eff. Jan. 1, 1986, and applicable to every notice of appeal taken or motion for leave to appeal to the court of appeals made on or after that date, amended CPLR 5602(a) to provide that permission for leave to appeal to the Court of Appeals shall be pursuant to rules authorized by the Appellate Division and the Court of Appeals.

1967 AMENDMENTS

L. 1967, ch. 342, eff. Sept. 1, 1967, added reference to family court in Subd. (a)(1) and Subd. (b)(2).

§§ 5603–5610.   [Not used.]

§ 5611.   When appellate division order deemed final.

If the appellate division disposes of all the issues in the action its order shall be considered a final one, and a subsequent appeal may be taken only from that order and not from any judgment or order entered pursuant to it. If the aggrieved party is granted leave to replead or to perform some other act which would defeat the finality of the order, it shall not take effect as a final order until the expiration of the time limited for such act without his having performed it.

§ 5612.   Presumptions as to determinations of questions of fact.

(a) Appeal from reversal or modification. On an appeal from an order of the appellate division reversing, modifying or setting aside a determination and rendering a final or interlocutory determination, except when it reinstates a verdict, the court of appeals shall presume that questions of fact as to which no findings are made in the order or

CPLR

opinion of the appellate division were not considered by it, where such findings are required to be made by paragraph two of subdivision (b)* of rule 5712.

(b) Appeal on certified questions of law. On an appeal on certified questions of law, the court of appeals shall presume that questions of fact as to which no findings are made in the order granting permission to appeal or in the order appealed from or in the opinion of the appellate division were determined in favor of the party who is respondent in the court of appeals.

   * **[Editor's note:** So in original. Reference probably should be to subdivision (c) of rule 5712.]

§ 5613.   Disposition upon reversal or modification.

The court of appeals, upon reversing or modifying a determination of the appellate division, when it appears or must be presumed that questions of fact were not considered by the appellate division, shall remit the case to that court for determination of questions of fact raised in the appellate division.

§ 5614.   Disposition upon certified questions.

The order of the court of appeals determining an appeal upon certified questions shall certify its answers to the questions certified and direct entry of the appropriate judgment or order.

§ 5615.   Disposition upon appeal from order granting new trial or hearing.

When an appeal to the appellate division presented questions of fact and a further appeal is taken pursuant to subdivision (c) of section 5601, or subparagraph (iii) of paragraph two of subdivision (b) of section 5602, the court of appeals shall affirm the order appealed from and shall render judgment or order absolute against the appellant unless the order or opinion of the appellate division recites either that the questions of fact have not been considered or that the court has considered the questions of fact and has determined that it would not grant a new trial or hearing upon those questions.

Article 57

APPEALS TO THE APPELLATE DIVISION

§ 5701. Appeals to appellate division from supreme and county courts.

(a) Appeals as of right. An appeal may be taken to the appellate division as of right in an action, originating in the supreme court or a county court:

   1. from any final or interlocutory judgment except one entered subsequent to an order of the appellate division which disposes of all

CPLR

the issues in the action; or

2. from an order not specified in subdivision (b), where the motion it decided was made upon notice and it:

(i) grants, refuses, continues or modifies a provisional remedy; or

(ii) settles, grants or refuses an application to resettle a transcript or statement on appeal; or

(iii) grants or refuses a new trial; except where specific questions of fact arising upon the issues in an action triable by the court have been tried by a jury, pursuant to an order for that purpose, and the order grants or refuses a new trial upon the merits; or

(iv) involves some part of the merits; or

(v) affects a substantial right; or

(vi) in effect determines the action and prevents a judgment from which an appeal might be taken; or

(vii) determines a statutory provision of the state to be unconstitutional, and the determination appears from the reasons given for the decision or is necessarily implied in the decision; or

(viii) grants a motion for leave to reargue made pursuant to subdivision (d) of rule 2221 or determines a motion for leave to renew made pursuant to subdivision (e) of rule 2221; or

3. from an order, where the motion it decided was made upon notice, refusing to vacate or modify a prior order, if the prior order would have been appealable as of right under paragraph two had it decided a motion made upon notice.

(b) Orders not appealable as of right. An order is not appealable to the appellate division as of right where it:

1. is made in a proceeding against a body or officer pursuant to article 78; or

2. requires or refuses to require a more definite statement in a pleading; or

3. orders or refuses to order that scandalous or prejudicial matter be stricken from a pleading.

(c) Appeals by permission. An appeal may be taken to the appellate division from any order which is not appealable as of right in an action originating in the supreme court or a county court by permission of the judge who made the order granted before application to a justice of the appellate division; or by permission of a justice of the appellate division in the department to which the appeal could be taken, upon refusal by the judge who made the order or upon direct application.

CROSS REFERENCES

See **N.Y. Const., Art. VI, §§ 3** (Court of appeals), **5** (Appellate courts generally), **8** (Appellate term) and **11** (Appellate jurisdiction of county courts), in Appendix, *below.*

1999 AMENDMENTS

L. 1999, ch. 281, eff. July 20, 1999, added new subparagraph (viii) to provide that an appeal as of right may be taken to the appellate division in an action originating in supreme or county court from an order granting a motion for leave to reargue (CPLR § 2221(d)) or determining a motion for leave to renew (CPLR § 2221(e)).

§ 5702. Appeals to appellate division from other courts of original instance.

An appeal may be taken to the appellate division from any judgment or order of a court of original instance other than the supreme court or a county court in accordance with the statute governing practice in such court.

§ 5703. Appeals to appellate division from appellate courts.

(a) From appellate terms. An appeal may be taken to the appellate division, from an order of the appellate term which determines an appeal from a judgment or order of a lower court, by permission of the appellate term or, in case of refusal, of the appellate division. When permission to appeal is sought from an order granting or affirming the granting of a new trial or hearing, the appellant shall stipulate that, upon affirmance, judgment absolute may be entered against him.

(b) From other appellate courts. An appeal may be taken to the appellate division as of right from an order of a county court or a special term of the supreme court which determines an appeal from a judgment of a lower court.

§ 5704. Review of ex parte orders.

(a) By appellate division. The appellate division or a justice thereof may vacate or modify any order granted without notice to the adverse party by any court or a judge thereof from which an appeal would lie to such appellate division; and the appellate division may grant any order or provisional remedy applied for without notice to the adverse party and refused by any court or a judge thereof from which an appeal would lie to such appellate division.

(b) By appellate term. The appellate term in the first or second judicial department or a justice thereof may vacate or modify any order granted without notice to the adverse party by any court or a judge thereof from which an appeal would lie to such appellate term; and such appellate term may grant any order or provisional remedy applied for without notice to the adverse party and refused by any court or a judge thereof from which an appeal would lie to such appellate term.

1972 AMENDMENTS

L. 1972, ch. 435, eff. Sept. 1, 1972 amended CPLR 5704(a).

The 1972 Judicial Conference Report stated:

"At present, section 5704 (a) specifies, substantially, that the Appellate Division or a Justice thereof may vacate or modify an ex parte order of the Supreme Court (or a Justice thereof) only; and that the Appellate Division may grant an ex-parte order or provisional remedy refused by the Supreme Court (or a Justice thereof) only. The proposed amendment would remove the foregoing arbitrary limitation to the Supreme Court by providing that the specified power to the review extends to similar orders or decisions of any court, or a Judge thereof, from which an appeal would lie to the Appellate Division.

1966 AMENDMENTS

L. 1966, ch. 577, eff. Sept. 1, 1966, amended Subd. (b) by deleting references to the Civil Court of the City of New York and the Justices thereof, and substituting therefore references to "any court or a judge thereof from which an appeal would lie to such appellate term."

§§ 5705–5710. [Not used.]

§ 5711. Where appeal heard.

Except as provided in subdivision (d) of rule 511, an appeal to the appellate division shall be brought in the department embracing the county in which the judgment or order appealed from is entered and there heard and determined unless, in furtherance of justice, the appeal is sent to another department.

1965 AMENDMENTS

L. 1965, ch. 338, eff. Sept. 1, 1965, added the words "Except as provided in subdivision (d) of rule 511" at the beginning of the section.

§ 5712. Content of order determining appeal.

(a) Dissents. Every order of the appellate division determining an appeal shall state whether one or more justices dissent from the determination.

(b) Order of affirmance. Whenever the appellate division, although affirming a final or interlocutory judgment or order, reverses or modifies any findings of fact, or makes new findings of fact, its order shall comply with the requirement of subdivision (c).

(c) Order of reversal or modification. Whenever the appellate division reverses or modifies or sets aside a determination and thereupon makes a determination, except when it reinstates a verdict, its order shall state whether its determination is upon the law, or upon the facts, or upon the law and the facts:

1. if the determination is stated to be upon the law alone, the order shall also state whether or not the findings of fact below have been affirmed; and

2. if the determination is stated to be upon the facts, or upon the law and the facts, the order shall also specify the findings of fact which are reversed or modified, and set forth any new findings of fact made by the appellate division with such particularity as was employed for the statement of the findings of fact in the court of original instance; except that the order need not specify the findings of fact which are reversed or modified nor set forth any new findings of fact if the appeal is either from a determination by the court without any statement of the findings of fact or from a judgment entered upon a general verdict without answers to interrogatories.

1964 AMENDMENTS

L. 1964, ch. 388, eff. Sept. 1, 1964, corrected "court or original instance" in

CPLR

Subd. (c)(2) to read "court of original instance."

§ 5713. Content of order granting permission to appeal to court of appeals.

When the appellate division grants permission to appeal to the court of appeals, its order granting such permission shall state that questions of law have arisen which in its opinion ought to be reviewed. When the appeal is from a non-final order, the order granting such permission shall also state that the findings of fact have been affirmed, or reversed or modified and new findings of fact made, or have not been considered, shall specify the findings of fact which have been reversed or modified and set forth new findings of fact with at least the same particularity as was employed for the findings of fact below and shall certify the questions of law decisive of the correctness of its determination or of any separable portion of it.

Article 60

PROVISIONAL REMEDIES GENERALLY

SUMMARY OF ARTICLE

§ 6001.   **Kinds of provisional remedies; when remedy available to defendant.**

§ 6001. Kinds of provisional remedies; when remedy available to defendant.

The provisional remedies are attachment, injunction, receivership and notice of pendency. On a motion for a provisional remedy, the plaintiff shall state whether any other provisional remedy has been secured or sought in the same action against the same defendant, and the court may require the plaintiff to elect between those remedies to which he would otherwise be entitled; for this purpose, seizure of a chattel in an action to recover a chattel is a provisional remedy. A cause of action contained in a counterclaim or a cross-claim, and a judgment demanded thereon, shall entitle the defendant to the same provisional remedies to which he would be entitled if he were the plaintiff, the party against whom the judgment is demanded were the defendant and the cause of action were contained in a complaint.

1984 AMENDMENTS

L. 1984, ch. 313, eff. July 3, 1984, amended CPLR 6001 by deleting the reference to the provisional remedy of arrest.

Article 61

ARREST [Repealed.]

[**Editor's note:** *L. 1979, ch. 409, eff. June 29, 1979, repealed CPLR Article 61.*]

Article 62
ATTACHMENT

SUMMARY OF ARTICLE

§ 6201.   Grounds for attachment.

An order of attachment may be granted in any action, except a matrimonial action, where the plaintiff has demanded and would be entitled, in whole or in part, or in the alternative, to a money judgment against one or more defendants, when:

    1. the defendant is a nondomiciliary residing without the state, or is a foreign corporation not qualified to do business in the state; or

    2. the defendant resides or is domiciled in the state and cannot be personally served despite diligent efforts to do so; or

    3. the defendant, with intent to defraud his creditors or frustrate the enforcement of a judgment that might be rendered in plaintiff's favor, has assigned, disposed of, encumbered or secreted property, or removed it from the state or is about to do any of these acts; or

    4. the action is brought by the victim or the representative of the victim of a crime, as defined in subdivision six of section six hundred twenty-one of the executive law, against the person or the legal representative or assignee of the person convicted of committing such crime and seeks to recover damages sustained as a result of such crime pursuant to section six hundred thirty-two-a of the executive law; or

    5. the cause of action is based on a judgment, decree or order of a court of the United States or of any other court which is entitled to full faith and credit in this state, or on a judgment which qualifies for

recognition under the provisions of article 53.

1992 AMENDMENTS

L. 1992, ch. 618, eff. July 24, 1992 and applying only to actions commenced on or after the effective date, renumbered prior Subdivision (4) as (5) and added a new Subdivision (4), expanding the list of situations in which an order of attachment may be granted to include a civil action for damages brought by a crime victim or his or her representative against the person convicted of committing the crime or that person's representative or assignee.

1977 AMENDMENTS

L. 1977, ch. 860, eff. Sept. 1, 1977, amended CPLR 6201 by adoption of proposals made by the Judicial Conference in its Report to the 1977 Legislature, in which it stated:

"The proposed amendment of subparagraph 1 of this section would subject foreign corporations to attachment only where such corporations are not qualified to do business in the state. There is never a need for a jurisdictional attachment when a foreign corporation has obtained a certificate of authority to do business in New York.

"Present subparagraph 3 is eliminated as archaic and unnecessary. While at one time such a provision was needed to secure jurisdiction in certain cases, the provision has been outmoded by the availability of new jurisdictional tools (CPLR 308(5)). Moreover, the provision largely overlaps with present subparagraphs 1 and 2. The Weinstein, Korn and Miller Treatise (§ 6201.11) [12 Weinstein, Korn & Miller, New York Civil Practice, CPLR ¶ 6201] properly points out that 'it is difficult to imagine an instance in which attachment could be granted under subparagraph 3 against a defendant trying to avoid service that would not fall within subparagraphs 1 and 2.' If the defendant is a resident or domiciliary, or a corporation qualified to do business in the state, the plaintiff should be able to effect personal service without resorting to attachment. If the defendant is a nondomiciliary residing without the state or a foreign corporation not qualified to do business in the state, attachment is available under subparagraph 1 as proposed to be amended.

"Paragraphs 5, 6 and 8 are repealed because each of the provisions grounds attachment solely on the nature of the action (fraud in inducing contract (paragraph 5)); (peculation (paragraph 6)); conversion, fraud or deceit (paragraph 8)). The present statute, in authorizing attachment in these cases, apparently indulges in the unproved presumption that defendants charged with the stated wrongs are more likely to indulge in conduct frustrating the enforcement of a future judgment in plaintiff's favor than defendants in other cases. The provisions are of dubious constitutional validity. There is no reason why a defendant charged, for example, with conversion is more likely to tamper with his property than one sued for assault, wrongful death or negligence. In the absence of compelling reasons, drastic interference with the free use and enjoyment of defendant's property should not be authorized on the basis of limited judicial cognition, long before defendant has his full day in court and his liability has been established.

"Paragraph 7 would be renumbered paragraph 4, but would otherwise remain as it presently reads, because attachment should be available to secure judgments entitled to full faith and credit or qualifying for registration under Article 53. These are situations sui generis where the defendant had his day in court, or at least an opportunity for a day in court, although the court was foreign rather than domestic."

CROSS REFERENCES

Domestic Relations Law § 233 deals with the sequestration of defendant's property for the purpose of securing quasi in rem jurisdiction in matrimonial actions.

1970 AMENDMENTS

L. 1970, ch. 980, eff. Sept. 1, 1970, amended the section by adding a new Subd. (7), renumbered as Subd. (4) by L. 1977, ch. 860, eff. Sept. 1, 1977, and by renumbering former Subd. (7) as Subd. (8).

§ 6202. Debt or property subject to attachment; proper garnishee.

Any debt or property against which a money judgment may be enforced as provided in section 5201 is subject to attachment. The proper garnishee of any such property or debt is the person designated in section 5201; for the purpose of applying the provisions to attachment, references to a "judgment debtor" in section 5201 and in subdivision (i) of section 105 shall be construed to mean "defendant."

1977 AMENDMENTS

L. 1977, ch. 860, eff. Sept. 1, 1977, amended CPLR 6202 by correcting the former cross-reference to subd. (h) of section 105 to refer to subd. (i) of section 105, as relettered by L. 1973, ch. 238.

§ 6203. Attaching creditor's rights in personal property.

Where a plaintiff has delivered an order of attachment to a sheriff, the plaintiff's rights in a debt owed to the defendant or in an interest of the defendant in personal property against which debt or property a judgment may be enforced, are superior to the extent of the amount of the attachment to the rights of any transferee of the debt or property, except:

1. a transferee who acquired the debt or property before it was levied upon for fair consideration or without knowledge of the order of attachment; or

2. a transferee who acquired the debt or property for fair consideration after it was levied upon without knowledge of the levy while it was not in the possession of the sheriff.

§ 6204. Discharge of garnishee's obligation.

A person who, pursuant to an order of attachment, pays or delivers to the sheriff money or other personal property in which a defendant has or will have an interest, or so pays a debt he owes the defendant, is discharged from his obligation to the defendant to the extent of the payment or delivery.

§ 6210. Order of attachment on notice; temporary restraining order; contents.

Upon a motion on notice for an order of attachment, the court may, without notice to the defendant, grant a temporary restraining order prohibiting the transfer of assets by a garnishee as provided in subdivision (b) of section 6214. The contents of the order of attachment granted pursuant to this section shall be as provided in subdivision (a) of section 6211.

1977 AMENDMENTS

L. 1977, ch. 860, eff. Sept. 1, 1977, added section 6210, as proposed by the Judicial Conference in its Report to the 1977 Legislature, in which it stated:

"Proposed new CPLR 6210 would effect two basic changes. It would expressly provide in statutory form that the plaintiff may apply for an order of attachment on notice. It would further provide that the court may prohibit the transfer of assets by a garnishee or the defendant, as provided in CPLR 6214 (b), through a temporary restraining order, issued ex parte.

"At present the only explicit provision governing the granting of an order of attachment to the plaintiff sets forth an ex parte procedure (CPLR 6211). Thus, proposed CPLR 6210 would codify plaintiff's option of proceeding on notice which was always available in practice, although not spelled out in a separate provision in the CPLR. However, the plaintiff's option was rarely used because the motion-on-notice method offered no protection to plaintiff in restraining the transfer of assets by the garnishee before the hearing.

"Spelling out the proposed procedure, with the restraining order component, would codify a practice employed by some courts as a result of constitutional concerns about the ex parte procedure. The utility of obtaining an order of attachment on notice is enhanced by permitting the use of an ex parte temporary restraining order pending the hearing on the motion. This both encourages pre-attachment hearings (protecting defendants) and permits use of a temporary restraining order (protecting plaintiffs).

"Ordinarily the most practicable method of moving on notice for an order of attachment, while simultaneously seeking a temporary restraining order without notice, would be to proceed by order to show cause on a single set of motion papers. However, nothing would preclude a plaintiff from proceeding on separate motion papers, by ordinary motion on notice, for an order of attachment and for a temporary restraining order. The temporary restraining order is designed to protect the plaintiff during the period which will elapse from the time the plaintiff moves for an order of attachment to the time the sheriff is able to levy upon each garnishee under the order, after it has been granted.

"By making reference to CPLR 6211(a), this provision also makes it clear that the contents of an order of attachment obtained on notice are the same as the contents of an order of attachment obtained ex parte."

§ 6211. Order of attachment without notice.

(a) When granted; contents. An order of attachment may be granted without notice, before or after service of summons and at any time prior to judgment. It shall specify the amount to be secured by the order of attachment including any interest, costs and sheriff's fees and expenses, be indorsed with the name and address of the plaintiff's attorney and shall be directed to the sheriff of any county or of the city of New York where any property in which the defendant has an interest is located or where a garnishee may be served. The order shall direct the sheriff to levy within his jurisdiction, at any time before final judgment, upon such property in which the defendant has an interest and upon such debts owing to the defendant as will satisfy the amount specified in the order of attachment.

(b) Confirmation of order. Except where an order of attachment is granted on the ground specified in subdivision one of section 6201, an order of attachment granted without notice shall provide that within a period not to exceed five days after levy, the plaintiff shall move, on such notice as the court shall direct to the defendant, the garnishee, if any, and the sheriff, for an order confirming the order of attachment. Where an order of attachment without notice is granted on the ground specified in subdivision one of section 6201, the court shall direct that the statement required by section 6219 be served within five days, that a copy thereof be served upon the plaintiff, and the plaintiff shall move within ten days after levy for an order confirming the order of attachment. If the plaintiff upon motion shall show that the statement has not been served and that the plaintiff will be unable to satisfy the requirement of subdivision (b) of section 6223 until the statement has been served, the court may grant one extension of the time to move for confirmation for a period not to exceed ten days. If plaintiff fails to make such motion within the required period, the order of attachment and any levy thereunder shall have no further effect and shall be vacated upon motion. Upon the motion to confirm, the provisions of subdivision (b) of section 6223 shall apply. An order of attachment granted without notice may provide that the sheriff refrain from taking any property levied upon into his actual custody, pending further order of the court.

CPLR

1985 AMENDMENTS

L. 1985, ch. 566, eff. Sept. 1, 1985, amended CPLR 6211(b) in relation to confirmation of an order of attachment without notice granted on the ground specified in CPLR 6201(1) (defendant is a nondomiciliary or a corporation not qualified to do business within the state).

1977 AMENDMENTS

L. 1977, ch. 860, eff. Sept. 1, 1977, amended CPLR 6211 by adoption of proposals made by the Judicial Conference in its Report to the 1977 Legislature, in which it stated in part:

"The present section, now headed 'order of attachment,' would be amended to make it clear that it applies to an order granted ex parte. The section would be divided into two subdivisions, (a) and (b), the text of subdivision (b) being new.

"Subdivision (a) would be clarified to indicate that the amount specified in the order of attachment is the amount to be secured by that order, including any interest, costs and sheriff's fees and expenses.

"New subdivision (b) would provide that where the ex parte motion for attachment is used, the defendant is protected by the requirement that within a period not to exceed five days after the levy, the plaintiff shall move, on such notice as the court shall direct to the defendant, the garnishee, if any, and the sheriff, for an order confirming the order of attachment. If plaintiff fails to make such motion, the order of attachment and any levy thereunder shall have no further effect. Thus, where an ex parte motion for attachment is used, the defendant is protected by the requirement that the levy be swiftly followed by a motion by the plaintiff to confirm the attachment. This procedure largely codifies the minimum guidelines for attachment contained in the directive of October 28, 1974 of Honorable Edward Thompson, Administrative Judge of the Civil Court of the City of New York, and a similar rule promulgated by the Appellate Division, Fourth Judicial Department (22 N.Y.C.R.R. § 1039.13).

"Under the procedure established by the proposed amendment, a garnishee would no longer be bound by the levy or the attachment if the motion to confirm was not made within five days of the levy, or within a shorter period set by the court. Although a motion of vacatur is not required to void an attachment and levy under this provision, it is permitted. A defendant, for example, may desire to make a motion to secure an order formally vacating the attachment in order to lay a procedural foundation for recovering damages suffered on account of an improper attachment."

R 6212.   Motion papers; undertaking; filing; demand; damages.

(a) Affidavit; other papers. On a motion for an order of attachment or for an order to confirm an order of attachment, the plaintiff shall show, by affidavit and such other written evidence as may be submitted, that there is a cause of action, that it is probable that the plaintiff will succeed on the merits, that one or more grounds for attachment provided in section 6201 exist, and that the amount demanded from the defendant exceeds all counterclaims known to the plaintiff.

(b) Undertaking. On a motion for an order of attachment, the plaintiff shall give an undertaking, in a total amount fixed by the court, but not less than five hundred dollars, a specified part thereof conditioned that the plaintiff shall pay to the defendant all costs and damages, including reasonable attorney's fees, which may be sustained by reason of the attachment if the defendant recovers judgment or if it is finally decided that the plaintiff was not entitled to an attachment of the defendant's property, and the balance conditioned that the plaintiff shall pay to the sheriff all of his allowable fees. The attorney for the plaintiff shall not be liable to the sheriff for such fees. The surety on the undertaking shall not be discharged except upon notice to the sheriff.

(c) Filing. Within ten days after the granting of an order of attachment, the plaintiff shall file it and the affidavit and other papers upon which it was based and the summons and complaint in the action. Unless the time for filing has been extended, the order shall be invalid if not so filed, except that a person upon whom it is served shall not be liable for acting upon it as if it were valid without knowledge of the invalidity.

(d) Demand for papers. At any time after property has been levied upon, the defendant may serve upon the plaintiff a written demand that the papers upon which the order of attachment was granted and the levy made be served upon him. Not more than one day after service of the demand, the plaintiff shall cause the papers demanded to be served at the address specified in the demand. A demand under this subdivision shall not of itself constitute an appearance in the action.

(e) Damages. The plaintiff shall be liable to the defendant for all costs and damages, including reasonable attorney's fees, which may be sustained by reason of the attachment if the defendant recovers judgment, or if it is finally decided that the plaintiff was not entitled to an attachment of the defendant's property. Plaintiff's liability shall not be limited by the amount of the undertaking.

CPLR

1978 AMENDMENTS

L. 1977, ch. 15, eff. Sept. 1, 1977, amended subd. (b) by adding the final sentence thereof, requiring notice to the sheriff of discharge of the surety. Section 2 of L. 1977, ch. 15 provided that the act shall take effect on Sept. 1, 1977 and shall expire one year from that date. L. 1978, ch. 530, eff. July 24, 1978, repealed the expiration date of September 1, 1978, thus ending the provisional status of the notice requirement. L. 1977, ch. 860, eff. Sept. 1, 1977, amended CPLR 6212 by adoption of proposals made by the Judicial Conference in its Report to the 1977 Legislature, in which it stated:

"Subdivision (a) would be amended to contain a new requirement that the plaintiff's affidavit, on the motion for an order of attachment or for a confirming order, show that it is probable that the plaintiff will succeed on the merits and that one or more grounds for attachment exist. This would conform the statutory requirement to dicta in the United States Supreme Court cases cited previously . . . . An erroneous cross-reference would also be corrected.

"Subdivision (b) would be amended to increase the $250 minimum amount of an undertaking to $500 to reflect inflation since 1963 when the CPLR became effective and to make it clear that reasonable attorney's fees are recoverable costs under the undertaking.

"Subdivision (e) is new."

§ 6213. Service of summons.

An order of attachment granted before service is made on the defendant against whom the attachment is granted is valid only if, within sixty days after the order is granted, a summons is served upon the defendant or first publication of the summons against the defendant is made pursuant to an order and publication is subsequently completed, except that a person upon whom the order of attachment is served shall not be liable for acting upon it as if it were valid without knowledge of the invalidity. If the defendant dies within sixty days after the order is granted and before the summons is served upon him or publication is completed, the order is valid only if the summons is served upon his executor or administrator within sixty days after letters are issued. Upon such terms as may be just and upon good cause shown the court may extend the time, not exceeding sixty days, within which the summons must be served or publication commenced pursuant to this section, provided that the application for extension is made before the expiration of the time fixed.

1992 AMENDMENTS

L. 1992, ch. 216, eff. July 1, 1992, amended the first sentence of CPLR 6213 by deleting the words "an action is commenced" after the words "attachment granted before" and inserting in their place "service is made on the defendant against whom the attachment is granted."

1969 AMENDMENTS

L. 1969, ch. 208, eff. Sept. 1, 1969; thirty day limitation for service of summons increased to sixty days and last sentence added permitting the court to extend the time, not exceeding sixty days, within which the summons must be served or publication commenced.

§ 6214.   Levy upon personal property by service of order.

(a) Method of levy.   The sheriff shall levy upon any interest of the defendant in personal property, or upon any debt owed to the defendant, by serving a copy of the order of attachment upon the garnishee, or upon the defendant if property to be levied upon is in the defendant's possession or custody, in the same manner as a summons except that such service shall not be made by delivery of a copy to a person authorized to receive service of summons solely by a designation filed pursuant to a provision of law other than rule 318.

(b) Effect of levy; prohibition of transfer.   A levy by service of an order of attachment upon a person other than the defendant is effective only if, at the time of service, such person owes a debt to the defendant or such person is in the possession or custody of property in which such person knows or has reason to believe the defendant has an interest, or if the plaintiff has stated in a notice which shall be served with the order that a specified debt is owed by the person served to the defendant or that the defendant has an interest in specified property in the possession or custody of the person served. All property in which the defendant is known or believed to have an interest then in and thereafter coming into the possession or custody of such a person, including any specified in the notice, and all debts of such a person, including any specified in the notice, then due and thereafter coming due to the defendant, shall be subject to the levy. Unless the court orders otherwise, the person served with the order shall forthwith transfer or deliver all such property, and pay all such debts upon maturity, up to the amount specified in the order of attachment, to the sheriff and execute any document necessary to effect the payment, transfer or delivery. After such payment, transfer or delivery, property coming into the possession or custody of the garnishee, or debt incurred by him, shall not be subject to the levy. Until such payment, transfer or delivery is made, or until the expiration of ninety days after the service of the order of attachment upon him, or of such further time as is provided by any subsequent order of the court served upon him, whichever event first occurs, the garnishee is forbidden to make or suffer any sale, assignment or transfer of, or any interference with any such property, or pay over or otherwise dispose of any such debt, to any person other than the sheriff, except upon direction of the sheriff or pursuant to an order of the court. A garnishee, however, may collect or redeem an instrument received by him for such purpose and he may sell or transfer in good faith property held as collateral or otherwise pursuant to pledge thereof or at the direction of any person other than the defendant authorized to direct sale or transfer, provided that the proceeds in which the defendant has an interest be retained subject to the levy. A plaintiff who has specified personal property or debt to be levied upon in a notice served with an order of attachment shall be liable to the owner of the property or the person to whom the debt is owed, if other than the defendant, for any damages sustained by reason of the levy.

(c) Seizure by sheriff; notice of satisfaction. Where property or debts have been levied upon by service of an order of attachment, the sheriff shall take into his actual custody all such property capable of delivery and shall collect and receive all such debts. When the sheriff has taken into his actual custody property or debts having value

CPLR

sufficient to satisfy the amount specified in the order of attachment, the sheriff shall notify the defendant and each person upon whom the order of attachment was served that the order of attachment has been fully executed.

(d) Proceeding to compel payment or delivery. Where property or debts have been levied upon by service of an order of attachment, the plaintiff may commence a special proceeding against the garnishee served with the order to compel the payment, delivery or transfer to the sheriff of such property or debts, or to secure a judgment against the garnishee. Notice of petition shall also be served upon the parties to the action and the sheriff. A garnishee may interpose any defense or counterclaim which he might have interposed against the defendant if sued by him. The court may permit any adverse claimant to intervene in the proceeding and may determine his rights in accordance with section 6221.

(e) Failure to proceed. At the expiration of ninety days after a levy is made by service of the order of attachment, or of such further time as the court, upon motion of the plaintiff on notice to the parties to the action, has provided, the levy shall be void except as to property or debts which the sheriff has taken into his actual custody, collected or received or as to which a proceeding under subdivision (d) has been commenced.

1977 AMENDMENTS

L. 1977, ch. 860, eff. Sept. 1, 1977, amended CPLR 6214 by adoption of proposals made by the Judicial Conference in its Report to the 1977 Legislature, in which it stated:

"The amendments to the several subdivisions of this section, relating to levy by the sheriff upon personal property pursuant to an order of attachment, are designed to clarify the language and to require that parties and other interested persons receive appropriate notice of proceedings authorized under the statute. The addition of the phrase 'unless the court orders otherwise' in § 6214(b) in respect to the transfer of assets to the sheriff is required to conform to new § 6211(b) which permits the court in its discretion in an ex parte order of attachment to provide that the sheriff refrain from taking the property levied upon into his actual custody."

1965 AMENDMENTS

L. 1965, ch. 773, eff. Sept. 1, 1965, deleted the word "manual" in the phrase "capable of manual delivery" in Subd. (c).

§ 6215. Levy upon personal property by seizure.

If the plaintiff shall so direct and shall furnish the sheriff indemnity satisfactory to him or fixed by the court, the sheriff, as an alternative to the method prescribed by section 6214, shall levy upon property capable of delivery by taking the property into his actual custody. The sheriff shall forthwith serve a copy of the order of attachment in the manner prescribed by subdivision (a) of section 6214 upon the person from whose possession or custody the property was taken.

1963 AMENDMENTS

L. 1963, ch. 532, deleted the word "rule" from the cross-reference to "section 6214" in the first sentence of CPLR 6215.

§ 6216. Levy upon real property.

The sheriff shall levy upon any interest of the defendant in real property by filing with the clerk of the county in which the property is located a notice of attachment indorsed with the name and address of the plaintiff's attorney and stating the names of the parties to the action, the amount specified in the order of attachment and a description of the property levied upon. The clerk shall record and index the notice in the same books, in the same manner and with the same effect, as a notice of the pendency of an action.

1977 AMENDMENTS

L. 1977, ch. 860, eff. Sept. 1, 1977, amended CPLR 6216 by adoption of proposals made by the Judicial Conference in its Report to the 1977 Legislature, in which it stated:

"The phrase 'the amount of plaintiff's claim' would be superseded by the phrase 'the amount specified in the order of attachment,' which is more precise. It applies to all items to be secured by the order of attachment, including interest, costs and the sheriff's fees and expenses."

§ 6217. Additional undertaking to carrier garnishee.

A garnishee who is a common carrier may transport or deliver property actually loaded on a conveyance, notwithstanding the service upon him of an order of attachment, if it was loaded without reason to believe that an order of attachment affecting the property had been granted, unless the plaintiff gives an undertaking in an amount fixed by the court, that the plaintiff shall pay any such carrier all expenses and damages which may be incurred for unloading the property and for

CPLR

detention of the conveyance necessary for that purpose.

§ 6218. Sheriff's duties after levy.

(a) Retention of property. The sheriff shall hold and safely keep all property or debts paid, delivered, transferred or assigned to him or taken into his custody to answer any judgment that may be obtained against the defendant in the action, unless otherwise directed by the court or the plaintiff, subject to the payment of the sheriff's fees and expenses. Any money shall be held for the benefit of the parties to the action in an interest-bearing trust account at a national or state bank or trust company. If the urgency of the case requires, the court may direct sale or other disposition of property, specifying the manner and terms thereof, with notice to the parties to the action and the garnishee who had possession of such property.

(b) Inventory. Within fifteen days after service of an order of attachment or forthwith after such order has been vacated or annulled, the sheriff shall file an inventory of property seized, a description of real property levied upon, the names and addresses of all persons served with the order of attachment, and an estimate of the value of all property levied upon.

1977 AMENDMENTS

L. 1977, ch. 860, eff. Sept. 1, 1977, amended CPLR 6218 by adoption of proposals made by the Judicial Conference in its Report to the 1977 Legislature, in which it stated:

"This provision would be amended to assure that any attached monies shall be held for the benefit of the parties to the action in an interest-bearing trust account at a national or state bank or trust company . . .

"The provision would also be amended to require notice to parties and garnishees when the court directs the sale or other disposition of attached property."

1964 AMENDMENTS

L. 1964, ch. 342, eff. Sept. 1, 1964, amended Subd. (b), to change period for filing of inventory from 10 to 15 days.

§ 6219. Garnishee's statement.

Within ten days after service upon a garnishee of an order of attachment, or within such shorter time as the court may direct, the garnishee shall serve upon the sheriff a statement specifying all debts of the garnishee to the defendant, when the debts are due, all property in the possession or custody of the garnishee in which the defendant has an interest, and the amounts and value of the debts and property specified. If the garnishee has money belonging to, or is indebted to, the defendant in at least the amount of the attachment, he may limit his statement to that fact.

§ 6220. Disclosure.

Upon motion of any interested person, at any time after the granting of an order of attachment and prior to final judgment in the action, upon such notice as the court may direct, the court may order disclosure by any person of information regarding any property in which the defendant has an interest, or any debts owing to the defendant.

CPLR

§ 6221. Proceedings to determine adverse claims.

Prior to the application of property or debt to the satisfaction of a judgment, any interested person may commence a special proceeding against the plaintiff to determine the rights of adverse claimants to the property or debt. Service of process in such a proceeding shall be made by serving a notice of petition upon the sheriff and upon each party in the same manner as a notice of motion. The proceeding may be commenced in the county where the property was levied upon, or in the county where the order of attachment is filed. The court may vacate or discharge the attachment, void the levy, direct the disposition of the property or debt, direct that undertakings be provided or released, or direct that damages be awarded. Where there appear to be disputed questions of fact, the court shall order a separate trial, indicating the person who shall have possession of the property pending a decision and the undertaking, if any, which such person shall give. If the court determines that the adverse claim was fraudulent, it may require the claimant to pay the plaintiff the reasonable expenses incurred in the proceeding, including reasonable attorney's fees, and any other damages suffered by reason of the claim. The commencement of the proceeding shall not of itself subject the adverse claimant to personal jurisdiction with respect to any matter other than the claim asserted in the proceeding.

1994 AMENDMENTS

L. 1994, ch. 563, eff. July 26, 1994, amended CPLR 6221 by adding to the phrase "Service of process in such a proceeding shall be made."

1977 AMENDMENTS

L. 1977, ch. 860, eff. Sept. 1, 1977, amended CPLR 6221 by adoption of proposals made by the Judicial Conference in its Report to the 1977 Legislature, in which it stated:

"This section, governing proceedings to determine adverse claims, would be clarified by providing that the commencement of the proceeding shall not of itself subject the adverse claimant to personal jurisdiction with respect to any matter other than the claim asserted in the proceeding."

§ 6222. Discharge of attachment.

A defendant whose property or debt has been levied upon may move, upon notice to the plaintiff and the sheriff, for an order discharging the attachment as to all or a part of the property or debt upon payment of the sheriff's fees and expenses. On such a motion, the defendant shall give an undertaking, in an amount equal to the value of the property or debt sought to be discharged, that the defendant will pay to the plaintiff the amount of any judgment which may be recovered in the action against him, not exceeding the amount of the undertaking. Making a motion or giving an undertaking under this section shall not of itself constitute an appearance in the action.

§ 6223. Vacating or modifying attachment.

(a) Motion to vacate or modify. Prior to the application of property or debt to the satisfaction of a judgment, the defendant, the garnishee or any person having an interest in the property or debt may move, on notice to each party and the sheriff, for an order vacating or modifying the order of attachment. Upon the motion, the court may give the plaintiff a reasonable opportunity to correct any defect. If, after the defendant has appeared in the action, the court determines that the attachment is unnecessary to the security of the plaintiff, it shall vacate the order of attachment. Such a motion shall not of itself constitute an appearance in the action.

(b) Burden of proof. Upon a motion to vacate or modify an order of attachment the plaintiff shall have the burden of establishing the grounds for the attachment, the need for continuing the levy and the probability that he will succeed on the merits.

1977 AMENDMENTS

L. 1977, ch. 860, eff. Sept. 1, 1977, amended CPLR 6223 by adoption of proposals made by the Judicial Conference in its Report to the 1977 Legislature, in which it stated:

"At present this section, which is headed 'Vacating or modifying attachment,' has no subdivisions. It would be divided into two subdivisions under the amendment. Subdivision (a) would be entitled 'Motion to vacate or modify.'

"At present, §6223 provides that on this motion the court shall give the plaintiff a reasonable opportunity to correct any defect. The proposed amendment would give the court discretion to provide the plaintiff with a reasonable opportunity to correct any defect, since the court may feel that correction may or may not be wise under the circumstances.

"A new subdivision (b), entitled 'burden of proof,' would be added to provide that upon a motion to vacate or modify an order of attachment the plaintiff shall have the burden of establishing the grounds for the attachment, the need for continuing the levy and the probability that he will succeed on the merits.

"The recent line of cases of the Supreme Court of the United States on provisional remedies, referred to previously [*Carey v. Sugar*, 425 U.S. 73, 96 S. Ct. 1208, 47 L. Ed. 2d 587 (1976); *North Georgia Finishing, Inc. v. Di-Chem Inc.*, 419 U.S. 601, 95 S. Ct. 719, 42 L. Ed. 2d 751 (1975); *Mitchell v. W. T. Grant Company*, 416 U.S. 600, 94 S. Ct. 1895, 40 L. Ed. 2d 406 (1974); *Fuentes v. Shevin*, 407 U. S. 67, 92 S. Ct. 1983, 32 L. Ed. 2d 556 (1972); *Sniadach v. Family Finance Corp. of Bay View*, 395 US 337, 89 SCt 1820, 23 L. Ed. 2d 349 (1969)], indicates the desirability of the proposed amendment.

"When the court has granted an order of attachment without a prior hearing the court must determine at a post-taking hearing brought on by the plaintiff on motion whether to confirm the order. The standards of confirming or granting an order are the same. Where the court grants an order of attachment before a hearing, or where the defendant has defaulted, the court must apply these standards on the basis of the papers and proof presented by the plaintiff. In other instances there will usually be opposing papers and proof presented by the defendant. The burden of proof will be upon the plaintiff in all cases.

"The Supreme Court in *North Georgia Finishing, Inc. v. Di-Chem*, 419 U.S. 601 (1975), required 'an early hearing at which the creditor would be required to demonstrate at least probable cause' for the taking. The concurring opinion of Justice Powell which represents the minimal position of the Court states: 'Due process further requires that the State afford an opportunity for a prompt post-garnishment judicial hearing in which the garnishor has the burden of showing probable cause to continue the garnishment for a sufficient period of time to allow proof and satisfaction of the alleged debt.' 419 U.S. at 611.

"The court must in addition find that the plaintiff has presented a prima facie case and with reasonable probability will be entitled to final judgment. This provision resembles a provision found in the revised claim and delivery procedures in California. California Code of Civil Procedure § 510(e) Supp. 1973. As in *Long Island Trust Co. v. Porta Aluminum Corp.* 44 A.D. 2d 118 (2nd Dept. 1974), if the court cannot find probable cause to believe that plaintiff will succeed, the court should refuse to grant or confirm an order of attachment. By a cross-reference contained in proposed new CPLR 6211 (b), this provision on the burden of proof is made applicable to the motion to confirm.

"Any determination made by the court on a motion to confirm, modify, or vacate an order of attachment, in respect to the probability that the plaintiff will ultimately prevail on the merits, is, of course, inadmissible on the merits of the action in the case-in-chief."

§ 6224. Annulment of attachment.

An order of attachment is annulled when the action in which it was granted abates or is discontinued, or a judgment entered therein in favor of the plaintiff is fully satisfied, or a judgment is entered therein in favor of the defendant. In the last specified case a stay of proceedings suspends the effect of the annulment, and a reversal or vacating of the judgment revives the order of attachment.

§ 6225. Return of property; directions to clerk and sheriff.

Upon motion of any interested person, on notice to the sheriff and each party, the court may direct the clerk of any county to cancel a notice of attachment and may direct the sheriff to dispose of, account for, assign, return or release any property or debt, or the proceeds thereof, or any undertakings, or to file additional inventories or returns, subject to the payment of the sheriff's fees and expenses. The court shall direct that notice of the motion be given to the plaintiffs in other orders of attachment, if any, and to the judgment creditors of executions, if any, affecting any property or debt, or the proceeds thereof, sought to be returned or released.

§ 6226. Disposition of attached property after execution issued; priority of orders of attachment.

Where an execution is issued upon a judgment entered against the defendant, the sheriff's duty with respect to custody and disposition of property or debt levied upon pursuant to an order of attachment is the same as if he had levied upon it pursuant to the execution. The priority among two or more orders of attachment against the same defendant shall be in the order in which they were delivered to the officer who levied upon the property or debt. The priority between an order of attachment and an execution, or a payment, delivery or receivership order, is set forth in section 5234.

Article 63
INJUNCTION

---

§ 6301.   Grounds for preliminary injunction and temporary restraining order.

A preliminary injunction may be granted in any action where it appears that the defendant threatens or is about to do, or is doing or procuring or suffering to be done, an act in violation of the plaintiff's rights respecting the subject of the action, and tending to render the judgment ineffectual, or in any action where the plaintiff has demanded and would be entitled to a judgment restraining the defendant from the commission or continuance of an act, which, if committed or continued during the pendency of the action, would produce injury to the plaintiff. A temporary restraining order may be granted pending a hearing for a preliminary injunction where it appears that immediate and irreparable injury, loss or damage will result unless the defendant is restrained

CPLR

before the hearing can be had.

§ 6311. Preliminary injunction.

1. A preliminary injunction may be granted only upon notice to the defendant. Notice of the motion may be served with the summons or at any time thereafter and prior to judgment. A preliminary injunction to restrain a public officer, board or municipal corporation of the state from performing a statutory duty may be granted only by the supreme court at a term in the department in which the officer or board is located or in which the duty is required to be performed.

2. Notice of motion for a preliminary injunction to restrain state officers or boards of state officers under the provisions of this section must be upon notice served upon the defendant or respondent, state officers or board of state officers and must be served upon the attorney general by delivery of such notice to an assistant attorney general at an office of the attorney general in the county in which venue of the action is designated or if there is no office of the attorney general in such county, at the office of the attorney general nearest such county.

1972 AMENDMENTS

L. 1972, ch. 455, eff. May 24, 1972 and ch. 752, eff. May 30, 1972, amended CPLR 6311 by adding subparagraph 2 and numbering the prior matter as subparagraph 1.

R 6312. Motion papers; undertaking; issues of fact.

(a) Affidavit; other evidence. On a motion for a preliminary injunction the plaintiff shall show, by affidavit and such other evidence as may be submitted, that there is a cause of action, and either that the defendant threatens or is about to do, or is doing or procuring or suffering to be done, an act in violation of the plaintiff's rights respecting the subject of the action and tending to render the judgment ineffectual; or that the plaintiff has demanded and would be entitled to a judgment restraining the defendant from the commission or continuance of an act, which, if committed or continued during the pendency of the action, would produce injury to the plaintiff.

(b) Undertaking. Except as provided in section 2512, prior to the granting of a preliminary injunction, the plaintiff shall give an undertaking in an amount to be fixed by the court, that the plaintiff, if it is finally determined that he or she was not entitled to an injunction, will pay to the defendant all damages and costs which may be sustained by reason of the injunction, including:

1. if the injunction is to stay proceedings in another action, on any ground other than that a report, verdict or decision was obtained by actual fraud, all damages and costs which may be, or which have been, awarded in the other action to the defendant as well as all damages and costs which may be awarded him or her in the action in which the injunction was granted; or,

2. if the injunction is to stay proceedings in an action to recover real property, or for dower, on any ground other than that a verdict, report or decision was obtained by actual fraud, all damages and costs which may be, or which have been, awarded to the defendant in the action in which the injunction was granted, including the reasonable rents and profits of, and any wastes committed upon, the real property which is sought to be recovered or which is the subject of the action for dower, after the granting of the injunction; or,

3. if the injunction is to stay proceedings upon a judgment for a sum of money on any ground other than that the judgment was obtained by actual fraud, the full amount of the judgment as well as all damages and costs which may be awarded to the defendant in the action in which the injunction was granted.

(c) Issues of fact. Provided that the elements required for the issuance of a preliminary injunction are demonstrated in the plaintiff's papers, the presentation by the defendant of evidence sufficient to raise an issue of fact as to any of such elements shall not in itself be grounds for denial of the motion. In such event the court shall make a determination by hearing or otherwise whether each of the elements required for issuance of a preliminary injunction exists.

1996 AMENDMENTS

L. 1996, ch. 24, eff. Jan. 1, 1997, amended the heading by adding the words, "issues of fact"; amended subdivision (a) by replacing the word "paper" with "evidence"; amended subdivision (b) by deleting the comma at the end and replacing with a colon; added a new subdivision (c) entitled "Issues of fact"; and made the section gender neutral.

§ 6313. Temporary restraining order.

(a) Generally. If, on a motion for a preliminary injunction, the plaintiff shall show that immediate and irreparable injury, loss or damages will result unless the defendant is restrained before a hearing can be had, a temporary restraining order may be granted without notice. Upon granting a temporary restraining order, the court shall set the hearing for the preliminary injunction at the earliest possible time. No temporary restraining order may be granted in an action arising out of a labor dispute as defined in section eight hundred seven of the labor law, nor against a public officer, board or municipal corporation of the state to restrain the performance of statutory duties.

(b) Service. Unless the court orders otherwise, a temporary restraining order together with the papers upon which it was based, and a notice of hearing for the preliminary injunction, shall be personally served in the same manner as a summons.

(c) Undertaking. Prior to the granting of a temporary restraining order the court may, in its discretion, require the plaintiff to give an undertaking in an amount to be fixed by the court, containing terms similar to those set forth in subdivision (b) of rule 6312, and subject to the exception set forth therein.

CROSS REFERENCES

See **Article 7-A of the State Finance Law §§ 123-123j**, authorizing temporary restraining orders against public servants, notwithstanding the provisions of CPLR 6313, in citizen taxpayer suits for improper disbursement of state funds or property.

1982 AMENDMENTS

L. 1982, ch. 235, eff. June 15, 1982, amended CPLR 6313(a) by deleting the last sentence which had made this section inapplicable to the attorney-general in a proceeding under Article 23-A of the **General Business Law.**

1964 AMENDMENTS

L. 1964, ch. 263, eff. Sept. 1, 1964, added new Subd. (c).

§ 6314. Vacating or modifying preliminary injunction or temporary restraining order.

A defendant enjoined by a preliminary injunction may move at any time, on notice to the plaintiff, to vacate or modify it. On motion, without notice, made by a defendant enjoined by a temporary restraining order, the judge who granted it, or in his absence or disability, another judge, may vacate or modify the order. An order granted without notice and vacating or modifying a temporary restraining order shall be effective when, together with the papers upon which it is based, it is filed with the clerk and served upon the plaintiff. As a condition to granting an order vacating or modifying a preliminary injunction or a temporary restraining order, a court may require the defendant, except where the defendant is a public body or officer, to give an undertaking, in an amount to be fixed by the court, that the defendant shall pay to the plaintiff any loss sustained by reason of the vacating or modifying order.

§ 6315. Ascertaining damages sustained by reason of preliminary injunction or temporary restraining order.

The damages sustained by reason of a preliminary injunction or temporary restraining order may be ascertained upon motion on such notice to all interested persons as the court shall direct. Where the defendant enjoined was an officer of a corporation or joint-stock association or a representative of another person, and the amount of the undertaking exceeds the damages sustained by the defendant by reason of the preliminary injunction or temporary restraining order, the damages sustained by such corporation, association or person represented, to the amount of such excess, may also be ascertained. The amount of damages so ascertained is conclusive upon all persons who were served with notice of the motion and such amount may be recovered by the person entitled thereto in a separate action.

§ 6330. Obscene prints and articles; jurisdiction.

The supreme court has jurisdiction to enjoin the sale or distribution of obscene prints and articles, as hereinafter specified:

1. The district attorney of any county, the chief executive officer of any city, town or village or the corporation counsel, or if there be none, the chief legal officer of any city, town, or village, in which a person, firm or corporation publishes, sells or distributes or displays or is about to sell or distribute or display or has in his possession with intent to sell or display or distribute or is about to acquire possession with intent to sell, display or distribute any book, magazine, pamphlet, comic book, story paper, writing, paper, picture, motion picture, drawing, photograph, figure, image or any

written or printed matter of an indecent character, which is obscene, lewd, lascivious, filthy, indecent or disgusting, or which contains an article or instrument of indecent or immoral use or purports to be for indecent or immoral use or purpose; or in any other respect defined in section 235.00 of the penal law, may maintain an action for an injunction against such person, firm or corporation in the supreme court to prevent the sale or further sale or the distribution or further distribution or the acquisition, publication or possession within the state of any book, magazine, pamphlet, comic book, story paper, writing, paper, picture, motion picture, drawing, photograph, figure or image or any written or printed matter of an indecent character, herein described or described in section 235.00 of the penal law.

2. The person, firm or corporation sought to be enjoined shall be entitled to a trial of the issues within one day after joinder of issue and a decision shall be rendered by the court within two days of the conclusion of the trial.

3. In the event that a final order or judgment of injunction be entered in favor of such officer of the city, town or village and against the person, firm or corporation sought to be enjoined, such final order of* judgment shall contain a provision directing the person, firm or corporation to surrender to such peace officer, acting pursuant to his special duties, or police officer, as the court may direct or to the sheriff of the county in which the action was brought any of the matter described in paragraph one hereof and such officer or sheriff shall be directed to seize and destroy the same.

4. In any action brought as herein provided such officer of the city, town or village shall not be required to file any undertaking before the issuance of an injunction order provided for in paragraph two hereof, shall not be liable for costs and shall not be liable for damages sustained by reason of the injunction order in cases where judgment is rendered in favor of the person, firm or corporation sought to be enjoined.

5. Every person, firm or corporation who sells, distributes, or acquires possession with intent to sell or distribute any of the matter described in paragraph one hereof, after the service upon him of a summons and complaint in an action brought by such officer of any county, city, town or village pursuant to this section is chargeable

with knowledge of the contents thereof.

6. The court, in its adjudication, may (1) grant the relief sought (2) deny the relief sought or (3) enjoin the sale, further sale, display, distribution, further distribution, acquisition, publication, or possession of the material, to persons under the age of seventeen, upon a finding that the material is of the kind described in paragraph a or b of subdivision one of section 235.21 of the penal law.

* **[Editor's note:** So in original. Probably should read "or."]

1980 AMENDMENTS

L. 1980, ch. 843, eff. Sept. 1, 1980, amended subdivision three of CPLR 6330 by inserting a reference to police officers, as well as qualifying the term peace officer by adding the words ". . . acting pursuant to his special duties."

1972 AMENDMENTS

L. 1972, ch. 826, eff. Aug. 31, 1972, amended CPLR 6330(1) by including "displays" of indecent matter, adding "motion picture," making a technical amendment, and by adding a new paragraph (6).

1971 AMENDMENTS

L. 1971, ch. 545, § 8, eff. Sept. 1, 1971, added new CPLR 6330. It is derived from former section 22-a of the Code of Criminal Procedure.

CPLR

Article 64

RECEIVERSHIP

SUMMARY OF ARTICLE

§ 6401. Appointment and powers of temporary receiver.

(a) Appointment of temporary receiver; joinder of moving party. Upon motion of a person having an apparent interest in property which is the subject of an action in the supreme or a county court, a temporary receiver of the property may be appointed, before or after service of summons and at any time prior to judgment, or during the pendency of an appeal, where there is danger that the property will be removed from the state, or lost, materially injured or destroyed. A motion made by a person not already a party to the action constitutes an appearance in the action and the person shall be joined as a party.

(b) Powers of temporary receiver. The court appointing a receiver may authorize him to take and hold real and personal property, and sue for, collect and sell debts or claims, upon such conditions and for such purposes as the court shall direct. A receiver shall have no power to employ counsel unless expressly so authorized by order of the court. Upon motion of the receiver or a party, powers granted to a temporary receiver may be extended or limited or the receivership may be extended to another action involving the property.

(c) Duration of temporary receivership. A temporary receivership

CPLR

shall not continue after final judgment unless otherwise directed by the court.

§ 6402. Oath.

A temporary receiver, before entering upon his duties, shall be sworn faithfully and fairly to discharge the trust committed to him. The oath may be administered by any person authorized to take acknowledgments of deeds by the real property law. The oath may be waived upon consent of all parties.

CROSS REFERENCES

See **Real Prop. L. § 298,** *et seq.,* in Appendix, *below*, for provisions authorizing the taking of acknowledgments of deeds.

§ 6403. Undertaking.

A temporary receiver shall give an undertaking in an amount to be fixed by the court making the appointment, that he will faithfully discharge his duties.

§ 6404. Accounts.

A temporary receiver shall keep written accounts itemizing receipts and expenditures, and describing the property and naming the depository of receivership funds, which shall be open to inspection by any person having an apparent interest in the property. Upon motion of the receiver or of any person having an apparent interest in the property, the court may require the keeping of particular records or direct or limit inspection or require presentation of a temporary receiver's accounts. Notice of a motion for the presentation of a temporary receiver's accounts shall be served upon the sureties on his undertaking as well as upon each party.

§ 6405. Removal.

Upon motion of any party or upon its own initiative, the court which appointed a receiver may remove him at any time.

Article 65
NOTICE OF PENDENCY

---

§ 6501. Notice of pendency; constructive notice.

A notice of pendency may be filed in any action in a court of the state or of the United States in which the judgment demanded would affect the title to, or the possession, use or enjoyment of, real property, except in a summary proceeding brought to recover the possession of real property. The pendency of such an action is constructive notice, from the time of filing of the notice only, to a purchaser from, or incumbrancer against, any defendant named in a notice of pendency indexed in a block index against a block in which property affected is situated or any defendant against whose name a notice of pendency is indexed. A person whose conveyance or incumbrance is recorded after the filing of the notice is bound by all proceedings taken in the action after such filing to the same extent as a party.

1993 AMENDMENTS

L. 1993, ch. 657, eff. Jan. 1, 1994, amended to specifically exclude summary proceedings brought to recover possession of real property.

§§ 6502–6510. [Not used.]

R 6511. Filing, content and indexing of notice of pendency.

(a) Filing. In a case specified in section 6501, the notice of pendency shall be filed in the office of the clerk of any county where property affected is situated, before or after service of summons and at any time prior to judgment. Unless it has already been filed in that county, the complaint shall be filed with the notice of pendency.

(b) Content; designation of index. A notice of pendency shall state the names of the parties to the action, the object of the action and a description of the property affected. A notice of pendency filed with a clerk who maintains a block index shall contain a designation of the number of each block on the land map of the county which is affected by the notice. Except in an action for partition a notice of pendency filed with a clerk who does not maintain a block index shall contain a designation of the names of each defendant against whom the notice is directed to be indexed.

(c) Indexing. Each county clerk with whom a notice of pendency is filed shall immediately record it and index it against the blocks or names designated. A county clerk who does not maintain a block index shall index a notice of pendency of an action for partition against the names of each plaintiff and each defendant not designated as wholly fictitious.

(d) Electronic indexing. A county clerk may adopt a new indexing system utilizing electro-mechanical, electronic or any other method he deems suitable for maintaining the indexes.

1991 AMENDMENTS

L. 1991, ch. 648, eff. July 26, 1991, added subdivision (d).

§ 6512. Service of summons.

A notice of pendency is effective only if, within thirty days after filing, a summons is served upon the defendant or first publication of the summons against the defendant is made pursuant to an order and publication is subsequently completed. If the defendant dies within thirty days after filing and before the summons is served upon him or publication is completed, the notice is effective only if the summons is served upon his executor or administrator within sixty days after letters are issued.

1994 AMENDMENTS

L. 1994, ch. 563, eff. July 26, 1994, amended CPLR 6512 by deleting the words "filed before an action is commenced" after the words "notice of pendency."

§ 6513. Duration of notice of pendency.

A notice of pendency shall be effective for a period of three years from the date of filing. Before expiration of a period or extended period, the court, upon motion of the plaintiff and upon such notice as it may require, for good cause shown, may grant an extension for a like additional period. An extension order shall be filed, recorded and indexed before expiration of the prior period.

§ 6514. Motion for cancellation of notice of pendency.

(a) Mandatory cancellation. The court, upon motion of any person aggrieved and upon such notice as it may require, shall direct any county clerk to cancel a notice of pendency, if service of a summons has not been completed within the time limited by section 6512; or if the action has been settled, discontinued or abated; or if the time to appeal from a final judgment against the plaintiff has expired; or if enforcement of a final judgment against the plaintiff has not been stayed pursuant to section 5519.

(b) Discretionary cancellation. The court, upon motion of any person aggrieved and upon such notice as it may require, may direct any county clerk to cancel a notice of pendency, if the plaintiff has not commenced or prosecuted the action in good faith.

(c) Costs and expenses. The court, in an order canceling a notice of pendency under this section, may direct the plaintiff to pay any costs

CPLR

and expenses occasioned by the filing and cancellation, in addition to any costs of the action.

(d) Cancellation by stipulation. At any time prior to entry of judgment, a notice of pendency shall be canceled by the county clerk without an order, on the filing with him of

1. an affidavit by the attorney for the plaintiff showing which defendants have been served with process, which defendants are in default in appearing or answering, and which defendants have appeared or answered and by whom, and

2. a stipulation consenting to the cancellation, signed by the attorney for the plaintiff and by the attorneys for all the defendants who have appeared or answered including those who have waived all notices, and executed and acknowledged, in the form required to entitle a deed to be recorded, by the defendants who have been served with process and have not appeared but whose time to do so has not expired, and by any defendants who have appeared in person.

(e) Cancellation by plaintiff. At any time prior to the entry of judgment a notice of pendency of action shall be canceled by the county clerk without an order, on the filing with him of an affidavit by the attorney for the plaintiff showing that there have been no appearances and that the time to appear has expired for all parties.

1971 AMENDMENTS

L. 1971, ch. 668, eff. June 22, 1971, added new CPLR 6514(e) providing for cancellation of notice of pendency of action by plaintiff.

1967 AMENDMENTS

L. 1967, ch. 440, eff. Sept. 1, 1967, added Subd. (d) permitting cancellation of notice of pendency by stipulation.

§ 6515. Undertaking for cancellation of notice of pendency; security by plaintiff.

In any action other than a foreclosure action as defined in subdivision (b) of section 6516 of this article or for partition or dower, the court, upon motion of any person aggrieved and upon such notice as it may require, may direct any county clerk to cancel a notice of pendency, upon such terms as are just, whether or not the judgment demanded would affect specific real property, if the moving party shall give an undertaking in an amount to be fixed by the court, and if:

1. the court finds that adequate relief can be secured to the plaintiff by the giving of such an undertaking; or

2. in such action, the plaintiff fails to give an undertaking, in an amount to be fixed by the court, that the plaintiff will indemnify the moving party for the damages that he or she may incur if the notice is not cancelled.

2005 AMENDMENTS

L. 2005, ch. 347, eff. Aug. 2, 2005 amended CPLR 6515 to clarify the definition of foreclosure action.

1973 AMENDMENTS

L. 1973, ch. 1029, eff. Sept. 1, 1973 amended paragraph (2) of CPLR 6515 by eliminating the restriction of paragraph 2 to actions for specific performance only.

§ 6516. Successive notices of pendency.

(a) In a foreclosure action, a successive notice of pendency may be filed to comply with section thirteen hundred thirty-one of the real property actions and proceedings law, notwithstanding that a previously filed notice of pendency in such action or in a previous foreclosure action has expired pursuant to section 6513 of this article or has become ineffective because service of a summons had not been completed within the time limited by section 6512 of this article, whether or not such expiration or such ineffectiveness has been determined by the court. This subdivision is inapplicable to an action to foreclose a mechanic's lien, notwithstanding section forty-three of the lien law.

(b) For the purposes of this article, the term "foreclosure action" shall mean any action or proceeding in which the provisions of section thirteen hundred thirty-one of the real property actions and proceedings law are applicable or in which a similar requirement is imposed by law.

(c) Except as provided in subdivision (a) of this section, a notice of pendency may not be filed in any action in which a previously filed notice of pendency affecting the same property had been cancelled or vacated or had expired or become ineffective.

(d) Nothing contained in this section shall be construed as making the requirements of section thirteen hundred thirty-one of the real

CPLR

property actions and proceedings law applicable to a proceeding to foreclose a tax lien in which a list of delinquent taxes has been filed pursuant to subdivision seven of section eleven hundred twenty-two of the real property tax law or any comparable law, or as precluding the filing of a successive list of delinquent taxes in such a proceeding.

2005 AMENDMENTS

L. 2005, ch. 347, eff. Aug. 2, 2005 added CPLR 6516.

Article 70

HABEAS CORPUS

SUMMARY OF ARTICLE

§ 7001. Application of article; special proceeding.

Except as otherwise prescribed by statute, the provisions of this article are applicable to common law or statutory writs of habeas corpus and common law writs of certiorari to inquire into detention. A proceeding under this article is a special proceeding.

§ 7002. Petition.

(a) By whom made. A person illegally imprisoned or otherwise restrained in his liberty within the state, or one acting on his behalf or a party in a child abuse proceeding subsequent to an order of the family court, may petition without notice for a writ of habeas corpus to inquire into the cause of such detention and for deliverance. A judge authorized to issue writs of habeas corpus having evidence, in a judicial proceeding before him, that any person is so detained shall, on his own initiative, issue a writ of habeas corpus for the relief of that person.

(b) To whom made. Except as provided in paragraph five of this subdivision, a petition for the writ shall be made to:

1. the supreme court in the judicial district in which the person is detained; or

2. the appellate division in the department in which the person is detained; or

3. any justice of the supreme court; or

4. a county judge being or residing within the county in which the person is detained; where there is no judge within the county capable

of issuing the writ, or if all within the county capable of doing so have refused, the petition may be made to a county judge being or residing within an adjoining county.

5. in a city having a population of one million or more inhabitants, a person held as a trial inmate in a city detention institution shall petition for a writ to the supreme court in the county in which the charge for which the inmate is being detained is pending. Such inmate may also petition for a writ to the appellate division in the department in which he is detained or to any justice of the supreme court provided that the writ shall be made returnable before a justice of the supreme court held in the county in which the charge for which the inmate is being detained is pending.

(c) Content. The petition shall be verified and shall state, or shall be accompanied by an affidavit which shall state,

1. that the person in whose behalf the petition is made is detained, naming the person by whom he is detained and the place of detention if they are known, or describing them if they are not known; where the detention is by virtue of a mandate, a copy of it shall be annexed to the petition, or sufficient reason why a copy could not be obtained shall be stated;

2. the cause or pretense of the detention, according to the best knowledge and belief of the petitioner;

3. that a court or judge of the United States does not have exclusive jurisdiction to order him released;

4. if the writ is sought because of an illegal detention, the nature of the illegality;

5. whether any appeal has been taken from any order by virtue of which the person is detained, and, if so, the result;

6. the date, and the court or judge to whom made, of every previous application for the writ, the disposition of each such application and of any appeal taken, and the new facts, if any, presented in the petition that were not presented in any previous application; and

7. if the petition is made to a county judge outside the county in which the person is detained, the facts which authorize such judge to

CPLR

act.

1986 AMENDMENTS

L. 1986, ch. 355, eff. July 17, 1986, amended CPLR 7002(b)(1) and (5) by deleting references to special term.

1971 AMENDMENTS

L. 1971, ch. 803, eff. July 1, 1971 amended CPLR 7002 (b) the addition of new paragraph 5.

1969 AMENDMENTS

L. 1969, ch. 264, eff. June 1, 1969, amended Subd. (a) by adding that ". . . party in a child abuse proceeding subsequent to an order of the family court" may petition for a writ of habeas corpus.

§ 7003.   When the writ shall be issued.

(a) Generally. The court to whom the petition is made shall issue the writ without delay on any day, or, where the petitioner does not demand production of the person detained or it is clear that there is no disputable issue of fact, order the respondent to show cause why the person detained should not be released. If it appears from the petition or the documents annexed thereto that the person is not illegally detained or that a court or judge of the United States has exclusive jurisdiction to order him released, the petition shall be denied.

(b) Successive petitions for writ. A court is not required to issue a writ of habeas corpus if the legality of the detention has been determined by a court of the state on a prior proceeding for a writ of habeas corpus and the petition presents no ground not theretofore presented and determined and the court is satisfied that the ends of justice will not be served by granting it.

(c) Penalty for violation. For a violation of this section in refusing to issue the writ, a judge, or, if the petition was made to a court, each member of the court who assents to the violation, forfeits to the person detained one thousand dollars to be recovered by an action in his name or in the name of the petitioner to his use.

§ 7004.   Content of writ.

(a) For whom issued. The writ shall be issued on behalf of the state, and where issued upon the petition of a private person, it shall show that it was issued upon his relation.

(b) To whom directed. The writ shall be directed to, and the respondent shall be, the person having custody of the person detained.

(c) Before whom returnable. A writ to secure the discharge of a person from a state institution shall be made returnable before a justice of the supreme court or a county judge being or residing within the county in which the person is detained; if there is no such judge it shall be made returnable before the nearest accessible supreme court justice or county judge. In all other cases, the writ shall be made returnable in the county where it was issued, except that where the petition was made to the supreme court or to a supreme court justice outside the county in which the person is detained, such court or justice may make the writ returnable before any judge authorized to issue it in the county of detention.

(d) When returnable. The writ may be made returnable forthwith or on any day or time certain, as the case requires.

(e) Expenses; undertaking. A court issuing a writ directed to any person other than a public officer may require the petitioner to pay the charges of bringing up the person detained and to deliver an undertaking to the person having him in custody in an amount fixed by the court, to pay the charges for taking back the person detained if he should be remanded. Service of the writ shall not be complete until such charge is paid or tendered and such undertaking is delivered.

1964 AMENDMENTS

L. 1964, ch. 388, eff. Sept. 1, 1964, made a mechanical correction.

§ 7005. Service of the writ.

A writ of habeas corpus may be served on any day. Service shall be made by delivering the writ and a copy of the petition to the person to whom it is directed. If he cannot with due diligence be found, the writ may be served by leaving it and a copy of the petition with any person who has custody of the person detained at the time. Where the person to whom the writ is directed conceals himself or refuses admittance, the writ may be served by affixing it and a copy of the petition in a conspicuous place on the outside either of his dwelling or of the place where the person is detained and mailing a copy of the writ and the petition to him at such dwelling or place, unless the court which issues the writ determines, for good cause shown, that such mailing shall be dispensed with, or directs service in some other manner which it finds

CPLR

reasonably calculated to give notice to such person of the proceeding. If the person detained is in the custody of a person other than the one to whom the writ is directed, a copy of the writ may be served upon the person having such custody with the same effect as if the writ had been directed to him.

1970 AMENDMENTS

L. 1970, ch. 395, eff. Sept. 1, 1970, amended the section by adding new material to the penultimate sentence, after the word "detained."

The amendment was recommended by the Judicial Conference Jan. 2, 1970 Report to the Legislature which stated, in part:

"This bill would amend CPLR 7005, which prescribes methods of service of the writ of habeas corpus, to provide a more desirable method for service where the person to whom the writ is directed conceals himself or refuses admittance. Presently, under such circumstances, the statute prescribes service by affixing the writ and a copy of the petition in a conspicuous place on the outside either of his dwelling place or of the place where the person is detained. No adequate reason appears for the existence of a difference between the method of substituted service of the writ of habeas corpus, which requires only the 'nailing' of the writ, and the method of substituted service of process, which requires 'nailing and mailing'.

"Although there is need for haste in some habeas corpus matters, emotions frequently run high in such situations, and the evidence of concealment or refusal is often circumstantial. Where the need for haste is paramount, the proposed bill would allow the court, upon good cause shown, to dispense with mailing or to direct service in some other manner which it finds reasonably calculated to give notice. The latter clause of the proposed amendment would introduce desirable flexibility into service of the writ, allowing even greater haste when warranted, than is presently possible. For example, the court could direct that service be made orally by use of the telephone or of an electric bullhorn, if the circumstances of the case were sufficiently urgent to warrant doing so."

§ 7006. Obedience to the writ.

(a) Generally; defects in form. A person upon whom the writ or a copy thereof is served, whether it is directed to him or not, shall make a return to it and, if required by it, produce the body of the person detained at the time and place specified, unless the person detained is too sick or infirm to make the required trip. A writ of habeas corpus shall not be disobeyed for defect of form so long as the identity of the person detained may be derived from its contents.

(b) Compelling obedience. If the person upon whom the writ or a copy thereof is served refuses or neglects fully to obey it, without showing sufficient cause, the court before whom the writ is returnable, upon proof of its service, shall forthwith issue a warrant of attachment against him directed to the sheriff in any county in which such person may be found requiring him to be brought before the court issuing the warrant; he may be ordered committed in close custody to the county jail until he complies with the order of the court. Where such person is a sheriff, the warrant shall be directed to a person specifically designated to execute it. Such person shall have power to call to his aid the same assistance as the sheriff in executing the warrant; a sheriff shall be committed to a jail in a county other than his own.

(c) Precept to bring up person detained. A court issuing a warrant of attachment as prescribed in subdivision (b) may at the same time, or thereafter, issue a precept to the person to whom the warrant is directed ordering him immediately to bring before the court the person detained.

§ 7007. Warrant preceding or accompanying writ.

A court authorized to issue a writ of habeas corpus, upon satisfactory proof that a person is wrongfully detained and will be removed from the state or suffer irreparable injury before he can be relieved by habeas corpus, shall issue a warrant of attachment directed to an appropriate officer requiring him immediately to bring the person detained before the court. A writ of habeas corpus directed to the person having custody of the person detained shall also be issued. Where it appears that the detention constitutes a criminal offense, the warrant may order the apprehension of the person responsible for the detention, who shall then be brought before the court issuing the warrant and examined as in a criminal case.

§ 7008. Return.

(a) When filed and served. The return shall consist of an affidavit to be served in the same manner as an answer in a special proceeding and filed at the time and place specified in the writ, or, where the writ is returnable forthwith, within twenty-four hours after its service.

(b) Content. The affidavit shall fully and explicitly state whether the

CPLR

person detained is or has been in the custody of the person to whom the writ is directed, the authority and cause of the detention, whether custody has been transferred to another, and the facts of and authority for any such transfer. A copy of any mandate by virtue of which the person is detained shall be annexed to the affidavit, and the original mandate shall be produced at the hearing; where the mandate has been delivered to the person to whom the person detained was transferred, or a copy of it cannot be obtained, the reason for failure to produce it and the substance of the mandate shall be stated in the affidavit.

§ 7009.   Hearing.

(a) Notice before hearing. Where the detention is by virtue of a mandate, the court shall not adjudicate the issues in the proceeding until written notice of the time and place of the hearing has been served either personally eight days prior to the hearing, or in any other manner or time as the court may order,

1. where the mandate was issued in a civil cause, upon the person interested in continuing the detention or upon his attorney; or,

2. where a person is detained by order of the family court, or by order of any court while a proceeding affecting him or her is pending in the family court, upon the judge who made the order. In all such proceedings, the court shall be represented by the attorney-general; or,

3. in any other case, upon the district attorney of the county in which the person was detained when the writ was served and upon the district attorney of the county from which he was committed.

(b) Reply to return. The petitioner or the person detained may deny under oath, orally or in writing, any material allegation of the answering affidavits or allege any fact showing that the person detained is entitled to be discharged.

(c) Hearing to be summary. The court shall proceed in a summary manner to hear the evidence produced in support of and against the detention and to dispose of the proceeding as justice requires.

(d) Sickness or infirmity of person detained. Where it is proved to the satisfaction of the court that the person detained is too sick or infirm to be brought to the appointed place, the hearing may be held without his presence, may be adjourned, or may be held at the place where the prisoner is detained.

(e) Custody during proceeding. Pending final disposition, the court may place the person detained in custody or parole him or admit him to bail as justice requires.

2007 AMENDMENTS

L. 2007, ch. 40, eff. May 29, 2007, amended CPLR 7009(a)(2) by replacing "corporation counsel of the city of New York, or outside the city of New York, by the county attorney" with "attorney-general".

§ 7010. Determination of proceeding.

(a) Discharge. If the person is illegally detained a final judgment shall be directed discharging him forthwith. No person detained shall be discharged for a defect in the form of the commitment, or because the person detaining him is not entitled to do so if another person is so entitled. A final judgment to discharge a person may be enforced by the court issuing the order by attachment in the manner prescribed in subdivision (b) of section 7006.

(b) Bail. If the person detained has been admitted to bail but the amount fixed is so excessive as to constitute an abuse of discretion, and he is not ordered discharged, the court shall direct a final judgment reducing bail to a proper amount. If the person detained has been denied bail, and he is not ordered discharged, the court shall direct a final judgment admitting him to bail forthwith, if he is entitled to be admitted to bail as a matter of right, or if it appears that the denial of bail constituted an abuse of discretion. Such judgment must fix the amount of bail, specify the time and place at which the person detained is required to appear, and order his release upon bail being given in accordance with the criminal procedure law.

(c) Remand. If the person detained is not ordered discharged and not admitted to bail, a final judgment shall be directed dismissing the proceeding, and, if he was actually produced in court, remanding him to the detention from which he was taken, unless the person then detaining him was not entitled to do so, in which case he shall be remanded to proper detention.

CROSS REFERENCES

Criminal Procedure Law bail provisions referred to in Subd. (b), *above*,

CPLR

appear in **Crim. Pro. L. §§ 500-550.10.**

1971 AMENDMENTS

L. 1971, ch. 1097, eff. Sept. 1, 1971, amended CPLR 7010(b) by deleting the reference to the Code of Criminal Procedure and substituting reference to the Criminal Procedure Law.

§ 7011.   Appeal.

An appeal may be taken from a judgment refusing to grant a writ of habeas corpus or refusing an order to show cause issued under subdivision (a) of section 7003, or from a judgment made upon the return of such writ or order to show cause. A person to whom notice is given pursuant to subdivision (a) of section 7009 is a party for purposes of appeal. The attorney-general may appeal in the name of the state in any case where a district attorney might do so. Where an appeal from a judgment admitting a person to bail is taken by the state, his release shall not be stayed thereby.

§ 7012.   Redetention after discharge.

A person discharged upon the return of a writ of habeas corpus shall not be detained for the same cause, except by virtue of a subsequent lawful mandate.

Article 71
RECOVERY OF CHATTEL

SUMMARY OF ARTICLE

CPLR

§ 7101.   When action may be brought.

An action under this article may be brought to try the right to possession of a chattel.

§ 7102.   Seizure of chattel on behalf of plaintiff.

(a) Seizure of chattel. When the plaintiff delivers to a sheriff an order of seizure, the papers on which the order was granted, the undertaking and a summons and complaint bearing the index number and the date of filing with the clerk of the court, in the action to recover the chattel, he shall seize the chattel in accordance with the provisions of the order and without delay.

(b) Service. The sheriff shall serve upon the person from whose possession the chattel is seized a copy of the order of seizure, the papers on which the order was granted, and the undertaking delivered to him by the plaintiff. Unless the order of seizure provides otherwise, the papers delivered to him by the plaintiff, shall be personally served by the sheriff on each defendant not in default in the same manner as a summons or as provided in section 314; if a defendant has appeared he shall be served in the manner provided for service of papers generally.

(c) Affidavit. The application for an order of seizure shall be supported by an affidavit which shall clearly identify the chattel to be seized and shall state:

    1. that the plaintiff is entitled to possession by virtue of facts set forth;

    2. that the chattel is wrongfully held by the defendant named;

    3. whether an action to recover the chattel has been commenced, the defendants served, whether they are in default, and, if they have appeared, where papers may be served upon them;

    4. the value of each chattel or class of chattels claimed, or the aggregate value of all chattels claimed;

5. if the plaintiff seeks the inclusion in the order of seizure of a provision authorizing the sheriff to break open, enter and search for the chattel, the place where the chattel is located and facts sufficient to establish probable cause to believe that the chattel is located at the place;

6. that no defense to the claim is known to the plaintiff; and

7. if the plaintiff seeks an order of seizure without notice, facts sufficient to establish that unless such order is granted without notice, it is probable the chattel will become unavailable for seizure by reason of being transferred, concealed, disposed of, or removed from the state, or will become substantially impaired in value.

(d) Order of seizure.

1. Upon presentation of the affidavit and undertaking and upon finding that it is probable the plaintiff will succeed on the merits and the facts are as stated in the affidavit, the court may grant an order directing the sheriff of any county where the chattel is found to seize the chattel described in the affidavit and including, if the court so directs, a provision that, if the chattel is not delivered to the sheriff, he may break open, enter and search for the chattel in the place specified in the affidavit. The plaintiff shall have the burden of establishing the grounds for the order.

2. Upon a motion for an order of seizure, the court, without notice to the defendant, may grant a temporary restraining order that the chattel shall not be removed from the state if it is a vehicle, aircraft or vessel or, otherwise, from its location, transferred, sold, pledged, assigned or otherwise disposed of or permitted to become subject to a security interest or lien until further order of the court. Unless the court otherwise directs, the restraining order does not prohibit a disposition of the chattel to the plaintiff. Disobedience of the order may be punished as contempt of court.

3. An order as provided in paragraph one of this subdivision may be granted without notice only if, in addition to the other prerequisites for the granting of the order, the court finds that unless such order is granted without notice it is probable the chattel will become unavailable for seizure by reason of being transferred, concealed, disposed of, or removed from the state, or will become substantially

CPLR

impaired in value.

4. An order of seizure granted without notice shall provide that the plaintiff shall move for an order confirming the order of seizure on such notice to the defendant and sheriff and within such period, not to exceed five days after seizure, as the court shall direct. Unless the motion is made within such period, the order of seizure shall have no further effect and shall be vacated on motion and any chattel seized thereunder shall be returned forthwith to the defendant. Upon the motion to confirm, the plaintiff shall have the burden of establishing the grounds for confirmation.

(e) Undertaking. The undertaking shall be executed by sufficient surety, acceptable to the court. The condition of the undertaking shall be that the surety is bound in a specified amount, not less than twice the value of the chattel stated in the plaintiff's affidavit, for the return of the chattel to any person to whom possession is awarded by the judgment, and for payment of any sum awarded by the judgment against the person giving the undertaking. A person claiming only a lien on or security interest in the chattel may except to the plaintiff's surety.

(f) Disposition of chattel by sheriff. Unless the court orders otherwise, the sheriff shall retain custody of a chattel for a period of ten days after seizure where seizure is pursuant to an order granted on notice, and until served with an order of confirmation where seizure is pursuant to an order granted without notice. At the expiration of such period, the sheriff shall deliver the chattel to the plaintiff if there has not been served upon him a notice of exception to plaintiff's surety, a notice of motion for an impounding or returning order, or the necessary papers to reclaim the chattel. Upon failure of the surety on plaintiff's undertaking to justify, the sheriff shall deliver possession of the chattel to the person from whom it was seized.

1994 AMENDMENTS

L. 1994, ch. 563, eff. July 26, 1994, amended CPLR 7102(a) by deleting the word "and" following "order was granted"; deleting the clause "if an action to recover a chattel has not been commenced" following "the undertaking and"; and by adding the phrase "in the action to recover the chattel."

1992 AMENDMENTS

L. 1992, ch. 216, eff. July 1, 1992, amended subdivision (a) by adding the words "bearing the index number and the date of filing with the clerk of the court."

1978 AMENDMENTS

L. 1978, ch. 81, eff. Jan. 1, 1979, amended CPLR 7102. The amendments were recommended by the Judicial Conference in its Report to the 1978 Legislature, wherein it stated:

"The purpose of this proposal to amend CPLR Article 71 is twofold: (1) to assure that New York's statutory replevin procedure is constitutional and (2) to replace the vague reference to due process in the present statute with specific statements of the requirements of due process, thus affording clear guidance to the bench and bar.

"In 1970, a three-judge federal court held that the provision of Article 71 'permitting the prejudgment seizure of chattels by the plaintiff in a replevin action without an order of a judge or of a court of competent jurisdiction . . .' violated the Fourth Amendment of the United States Constitution as applied to the states by the Fourteenth Amendment and the procedural due process requirements of the Fourteenth Amendment (*LaPrease v. Raymours Furniture Company,* (D.C.N.Y.) 315 F.Supp. 716, 725 (N.D.N.Y. 1970)).

"Article 71 was amended in 1971 (L. 1971, ch. 1051) to comply with the requirements of constitutional due process suggested by the *LaPrease* decision. However, as amended, Article 71 simply authorizes the courts to grant the order of seizure and to direct the sheriff to break into the place where the chattel is located when it is constitutional to do so (see CPLR 7102(d) (1)).

"In 1972, when the United States Supreme Court decided *Fuentes v. Shevin,* 92 S.Ct. 1983, 407 U.S. 67, 32 L.Ed. 556 (1972), it appeared that constitutional due process required notice and a hearing aimed at establishing the probable validity of the underlying claim before the chattel may be seized, except in unusual circumstances (see *Fuentes,* 407 U.S. at 93, 97). In *Fuentes* the Court held unconstitutional the Florida and Pennsylvania replevin statutes that allowed seizure of goods by a sheriff without notice, hearing, and judicial order.

"Shortly after *Fuentes* was decided, the judges and clerks of the Civil Court of the City of New York were directed to deny all applications for the prejudgment seizure of chattels unless the defendant had been given notice and an opportunity to be heard (Edward Thompson, J.S.C., Administrative Judge, Notice to Clerks of Special Term (July 11, 1972)).

"However, in 1974, the United States Supreme Court held constitutional the Louisiana replevin statute allowing ex parte pre-judgment seizure of property (*Mitchell v. W. T. Grant Company,* 94 S.Ct. 1895, 416 U.S. 600, 40 L.Ed.2d 406 (1974)). Furthermore, in *Mitchell* and in a 1975 opinion, *North Georgia Finishing Co., Inc. v. Di-Chem, Inc.,* 95 S.Ct. 719, 419 U.S. 601, 42 L.Ed.2d 751 (1975), the Court clarified due process requirements and

CPLR

established a balancing test to determine the constitutionality of a replevin procedure.

"Due process requires 'notice and . . . opportunity for a hearing or other safeguard against mistaken repossession . . . .' (*North Georgia Finishing Co., Inc. v. Di-Chem, Inc.,* 95 S.Ct. 719, 419 U.S. at 606, 42 L.Ed.2d 751 (1975), holding unconstitutional the impounding, in a commercial litigation, of respondent's bank account pursuant to a Georgia garnishment statute because of the absence of a prompt hearing at which the creditor would be required to demonstrate at least 'probable cause' to justify the garnishment). The replevin procedure must accommodate the conflicting interests of the plaintiff and defendant and minimize the risk of mistaken repossession (*Mitchell v. W. T. Grant Co.,* 94 S.Ct. 1895, 416 U.S. at 607, 618, 40 L.Ed.2d 406 (1974)). Plaintiffs are concerned that property they they [sic] are entitled to possess will deteriorate in the hands of the defendant or will become unavailable. Defendants are interested in enjoying the use and possession of property they are entitled to and in being compensated for all damages if the order of seizure is mistakenly granted.

"The ex parte procedure in *Mitchell* constitutionally accommodated the interests of both parties and minimized the risk of mistaken repossession. The main features of that procedure are: 1) the plaintiff must establish the probability of success; 2) the plaintiff must present the factual basis of his claim instead of conclusory allegations; 3) there is judicial supervision throughout; 4) the defendant is entitled to an early post-seizure hearing in which the plaintiff must prove his claim; 5) the plaintiff must put up a bond to guarantee the defendant against damages and expenses resulting from mistaken repossession.

"Whether the Fourth Amendment applies to replevin procedures was not decided by the United States Supreme Court in *Fuentes, Mitchell,* or *North Georgia Finishing Co., Inc.* However, lower federal courts have held that the Fourth Amendment applies to orders of seizure authorizing the sheriff to forcibly enter and search the place where the chattel is located (*LaPrease,* 315 F.Supp. at 721-22; *Hamrick v. Ashland Finance Co. of W. Va.,* (D.C.W.Va) 423 F.Supp. 1033, 1036-37 (S.D.W.Va. 1976)).

"Using the guidance provided by the United States Supreme Court in *Mitchell* and *North Georgia Finishing Co., Inc.* on the procedural due process problem and by lower federal courts on the Fourth Amendment problem, it is now possible to amend Article 71 to assure that it is constitutional and to rectify 'the failure of the 1971 amendment to Art. 71 to establish clear and easily usable standards to guide attorneys and the courts in taking action under the statute.' Edward Thompson, J.S.C., Administrative Judge, *Notice to Judges and Clerks, No. 176* (March 17, 1972 (quoting Governor Rockefeller's statement on signing the measure amending Article 71 in 1971)).

"This proposal to amend Article 71 establishes procedures for granting the order of seizure on notice (revised section 7102(d)(1)) and the order of seizure without notice (new section 7102(d)(3)). A temporary restraining order is available in both proceedings (see revised section 7102(d)(2)). If a seizure is made pursuant to an order of seizure without notice, new section 7102(d)(4) provides for an early hearing to minimize the risk and harm of mistaken repossession, and a new provision of section 7108(a) makes the plaintiff liable to the defendant for all damages if the order of seizure without notice is not confirmed under new section 7102(d)(4).

"Because of Fourth Amendment concerns, the revised section governing the order of seizure requires probable cause to believe that the chattel is located as specified before the court may authorize the sheriff to break in and search (see revised section 7102(d)(1)). In addition, if the order of seizure is without notice, the court must find exigent circumstances under new section 7102(d)(3).

"The Committee has considered the replevin provisions in light of *Shaffer v. Heitner,* (U.S.Del.), 97 S.Ct. 2569, 45 U.S.L.W. 4849 (U.S. Supreme Court, June 24, 1977) which held that when the property serving as the basis for the exercise of jurisdiction by a state court in a quasi-in-rem action is completely unrelated to the plaintiff's cause of action, the presence of the property alone is not sufficient to support the state's jurisdiction under due process. The Committee has concluded that no revision of the replevin article is necessary in light of *Shaffer* because in replevin the property to be seized is the very subject matter of the underlying claim.

"The Advisory Committee wishes to highlight a major change made by the bill that could otherwise be overlooked. The substitution of 'may' for 'shall' in section 7102(d)(1) and (2) makes replevin a discretionary remedy. This is justified because, although not formally a provisional remedy, replevin is functionally a provisional remedy since it involves a prejudgment seizure of property. All the provisional remedies save lis pendens are discretionary and in view of the drastic nature of the remedy and the infinite variety of possible fact patterns, replevin should also be discretionary.

Subdivision (a). "The amendment to section 7102(a) provides that the documents to be delivered by the plaintiff to the sheriff shall include, among other things, the papers on which the order was granted. This amendment is not intended to change the meaning of section 7102(a). Rather, the amendment simply makes it clear that the court examines the papers, and grants the order before the order, and the papers on which the order was granted are given to the sheriff and that the sheriff then acts pursuant to court order."

Subdivision (b). "The amendment to section 7102(b) provides that the documents that the sheriff shall serve upon the person from whose possession the chattel is seized include, in addition to a copy of the order of seizure, copies of the papers on which the order was granted, and the undertaking delivered to the sheriff by the plaintiff. The purpose of this amendment is to conform section 7102(b) to section 7102 (a) as amended."

Subdivision (c). "The purpose of the proposed amendments to section 7102(c) is to coordinate the affidavit requirements with the factual issues that the court must focus on in deciding whether to issue an order of seizure under revised section 7102(d)(1) or new section 7102(d)(3).

"The general reference in section 7102(c)(5) to due process has been deleted and replaced by a specific statement of the due process standard. Under revised paragraph (5) of section 7102(c), if the plaintiff seeks the inclusion in the order of seizure of a provision authorizing the sheriff to break open, enter and search for the chattel, the affidavit shall state where the chattel is located and facts sufficient to establish probable cause to believe that such chattel is located there.

"The statement in revised paragraph (5) is necessary to enable the court to determine under revised section 7102(d)(1) whether the order of seizure should authorize the sheriff to break in and search for the chattel. The plaintiff's factual statement must show that the information and the informant are reliable and credible (*see Aguilar v. State of Texas,* 84 S.Ct. 1509, 378 U.S. 108, 12 L.Ed.2d 723 (1964)).

"Under new paragraph (6), the plaintiff must state that he knows of no defense to his claim. The statement focuses attention on the possibility that defenses to the claim exist that would defeat plaintiff's right to possession of the chattel. If an order of seizure without notice is granted and, at the hearing on the plaintiff's motion for an order of confirmation under new paragraph (4) of section 7102(d), the defendant establishes that he has a defense to the claim and that the plaintiff knew about the defense at the time of plaintiff's motion for an order of seizure without notice, the court, in ruling on the motion for an order of confirmation and in assessing damages, may consider the fact that the plaintiff stated in his affidavit that he knew of no defense.

"New paragraph (6) of section 7102(c) also is in aid of section 601 of the General Business Law which prohibits a principal creditor (as defined in section 600 of the General Business Law) or his agent from claiming or attempting or threatening to enforce a right with knowledge or reason to know that the right does not exist. N.Y. General Business Law § 601.

"Under new paragraph (7) of section 7102(c), if the plaintiff seeks an order of seizure without notice, he shall state facts sufficient to establish that unless such order is granted without notice it is probable the chattel will become unavailable for seizure by reason of being transferred, concealed, disposed of, or removed from the state, or will become substantially impaired in value.

"The statement in new paragraph (7) of section 7102(c) is necessary to enable the court to decide under new paragraph (3) of section 7102(d) whether to grant an order of seizure without notice."

Subdivision (d). "Section 7102(d) has been divided into four paragraphs: (1), (2), (3), and (4). As amended, section 7102(d) spells out the due process requirements for an order of seizure and for authorizing the sheriff to break in and search, permits the court to grant a temporary restraining order, and establishes the procedure for the new requirement that an order of seizure without notice must be confirmed.

"Revised paragraph (1) of section 7102(d) is the core provision governing orders of seizure. It governs the order of seizure on notice and, in conjunction with new paragraphs (3) and (4) of section 7102(d), the order of seizure without notice.

"Paragraph (1), as revised, permits the court to grant an order of seizure upon presentation of the affidavit and undertaking and upon finding that it is probable that the plaintiff will succeed on the merits and the facts are as stated in the affidavit. This proposed provision states that the court 'may' grant an order of seizure, rather than 'shall' grant an order of seizure as at present, to make it clear that the court has discretion 'to prevent unfair and mistaken deprivations of property . . .' (*Fuentes,* 407 U.S. at 97), and to conform the replevin procedure, which is functionally a provisional remedy, to other provisional remedies which are discretionary. The court must find it 'probable' that the plaintiff will succeed on the merits because due process requires that the plaintiff establish 'the probability that his case will succeed' (*Mitchell*, 94 S.Ct. 1895, 416 U.S. at 609, 40 L.Ed.2d 406. Accord, *Fuentes,* 407 U.S. at 97; *Long Is. Trust Co. v. Porta Aluminum*, 354 N.Y.S.2d 134, 44 A.D.2d 118, 124 (2nd Dept. 1974)).

"Revised paragraph (1) of section 7102(d) also provides that if the facts are as stated in the affidavit, the court may include in the order of seizure a provision that, if the chattel is not delivered to the sheriff, the sheriff may break open, enter and search for the chattel in the place specified in the affidavit. Thus, if the court finds probable cause to believe that the chattel is located at the place specified in the affidavit, the court may authorize the sheriff to break into and search that place if the chattel is not delivered to the sheriff. Under the Fourth Amendment, the location of the chattel must be specified and there must be probable cause to believe that the chattel is located at that place (*LaPrease v. Raymours Furniture Company*, (D.C.N.Y.) 315 F.Supp. 716, 721 (N.D.N.Y. 1970); *Hamrick v. Ashland Finance Co. of W. Va.*, (D.C.W.Va.) 423 F.Supp. 1033, 1036-37 (S.D.W.Va. 1976)). The court is given discretion to permit the sheriff to break in and search because the Fourth Amendment requires that breaking and entering be allowed only in the court's sound discretion. (*Hamrick*, (D.C.W.Va.) 432 F.Supp. at 1036).

"Finally, revised paragraph (1) of section 7102(d) provides that the plaintiff shall have the burden of establishing the grounds for the order. The purpose of this provision is to clarify that the plaintiff has the burden to establish all the grounds for the granting of the order of seizure.

"Revised paragraph (2) of section 7102(d) provides that the court, without notice to the defendant, may grant a temporary restraining order upon any motion for an order of seizure, not, as at present, only when the order of seizure does not include a provision authorizing the sheriff to break in and search. As with the granting of an order of seizure and the inclusion of the breaking and search provision, the authority to grant a temporary restraining order is discretionary, not, as at present, mandatory.

"The temporary restraining order in new paragraph (2) of section 7102(d) provides the plaintiff with the immediate protection of having the status quo preserved without significantly interfering with the defendant's use and possession of the chattel. The temporary restraining order is available even if the court decides that the order of seizure without notice is inappropriate.

"By providing for the granting of a temporary restraining order upon a motion for an order of seizure, revised paragraph (2) of section 7102(d) encourages plaintiffs to proceed on notice. When a plaintiff weighs the need to proceed without notice against the cost of proceeding without notice (*e.g.,* the greater proof requirements under new paragraph (3) of section 7102(d) and the greater potential damages liability under revised section 7108(a)), the fact that a temporary restraining order is available to protect his interest in the property if he moves for an order of seizure on notice may lead him to proceed on notice.

"New paragraph (3) of section 7102(d) has been added to govern the order of seizure without notice. Under new paragraph (3), an order as provided in section 7102(d)(1) may be granted without notice only if, in addition to the other prerequisites for the granting of the order, the court finds that unless such order is granted without notice it is probable that the chattel will become unavailable for seizure by reason of being transferred, concealed, disposed of, or removed from the state, or will become substantially impaired in value.

"After the decisions in *LaPrease and Fuentes,* which raised doubts about the constitutionality of the ex parte order of seizure, the Civil Court of the City of New York, since 1972, has granted orders of seizure only on notice to the defendant and has protected plaintiffs in special situations by granting 'stays' enjoining defendants from disposing of or destroying the chattels in dispute (see Edward Thompson, J.S.C., Administrative Judge, *Notice to Clerks of Special Term* (July 11, 1972) and *Directive to Judges, Clerks and Special Term II Clerks No. 219* (December 5, 1972)).

"It is now clear that an ex parte replevin procedure is constitutional if it accommodates the interests of the plaintiff and the defendant and minimizes the risk and harm of mistaken repossession (see *Mitchell,* 94 S.Ct. 1895, 416 U.S. 600, 40 L.Ed. 2d 406). Under new paragraph (3) of section 7102(d), the court has discretion to grant an order of seizure without notice if the court finds it probable that the plaintiff will succeed on the merits and that the facts are as stated in the affidavit and the court finds that, unless such order of seizure is granted without notice, it is probable that the chattel will become unavailable for seizure by reason of being transferred, concealed, disposed of, or removed from the state or will become substantially impaired in value.

"The harm to the defendant that would flow from mistaken repossession is minimized by the early post-seizure hearing provided for in new paragraph (4) of section 7102(d).

"New paragraph (3) of section 7102(d) also takes into account the concern that a number of judges have expressed about the constitutionality of including in an ex parte order of seizure permission for the sheriff to break in and search (see, *e.g., LaPrease,* (D.C.N.Y.) 315 F.Supp. at 721-22; Edward Thompson J.S.C., Administrative Judge, *Notice to Judges and Clerks, No. 176* (March 17, 1972)). Because the danger of mistaken repossession is greater when the order is granted ex parte and because the interference with the defendant's expectation of privacy is greater when the sheriff is permitted to break in and search, new paragraph (3) requires not only probable cause to believe that the chattel is located as specified in the affidavit (as is required by revised section 7102(d)(1)), but also that the court be satisfied that, unless the order is granted without notice, the chattel will become unavailable for seizure by reason of being transferred, concealed, disposed of, or removed from the state, or will become substantially impaired in value. This exigency requirement comports with Judge Thompson's *Notice to Judges and Clerks, No. 176* (March 17, 1972).

"New paragraph (4) of section 7102(d) provides that an order of seizure granted without notice shall provide that the plaintiff shall move for an order confirming the order of seizure on such notice to the defendant and sheriff and within such period, not to exceed five days after seizure, as the court shall direct. Unless the motion is made within such period, the order of seizure shall have no further effect and shall be vacated on motion and any chattel seized thereunder shall be returned forthwith to the defendant. Upon the motion to confirm, the plaintiff shall have the burden of establishing the grounds for confirmation.

"Thus, where the order of seizure without notice is used, the defendant is protected by the requirement that the seizure be swiftly followed by a hearing and order of confirmation or else the order of seizure will be void and the chattel will be returned to the defendant. At the hearing on the motion for the order of confirmation, the court has discretion to confirm the order of seizure if the plaintiff establishes all the grounds for the granting of the order of seizure without notice under section 7102(d)(3). Where the order of seizure is granted without notice, due process requires an early noticed hearing with the plaintiff having the burden of establishing the probability of success in establishing his claim.

"Although a motion to vacate is not required to void the seizure, it is permitted. A defendant may, for example, wish to secure an order vacating the seizure in order to lay a procedural foundation for recovering damages on account of improper seizure."

Subdivision (f). "This amendment provides that, where seizure is pursuant to an order granted on notice, unless the court orders otherwise, the sheriff shall retain custody of the chattel for a period of ten days after seizure, and, where seizure is pursuant to an order granted without notice, unless the court orders otherwise, the sheriff shall retain custody of the chattel for a period of ten days after seizure and until served with an order of confirmation.

"The purpose of this revision is to coordinate section 7102(f) with new paragraph (4) of section 7102(d), which governs the confirmation of the order of seizure without notice.

"The word 'either' that appears in the second sentence of section 7102(f) has been deleted for grammatical reasons."

1971 AMENDMENTS

L. 1971, ch. 1051, eff. July 2, 1971, amended CPLR 7102.

§ 7103.   Reclaiming, impounding or returning chattel.

(a) Reclaiming chattel. A chattel may be reclaimed by any person claiming the right to its possession, except a defendant claiming only a lien thereon or security interest therein, by service upon the sheriff, and upon all parties to the action, of a notice that the reclaiming party requires a return of all or part of the chattels replevied; an undertaking executed as required by subdivision (e) of section 7102 and an affidavit stating that the reclaiming party is entitled to possession by virtue of facts set forth. The sheriff shall retain custody of the chattel for ten days after such papers have been served upon him. At the expiration of such period he shall deliver the chattel to the person serving the notice if there has not been served upon him a notice of exception to sureties or a notice of motion for an impounding order. Upon failure by the surety to justify, the sheriff shall deliver possession of the chattel to the plaintiff. If more than one person serves a reclaiming notice on the sheriff, the sheriff shall move, on notice to all parties, to have the court determine to whom the chattel shall be delivered.

(b) Impounding chattel. A chattel which is in the custody of the sheriff may be impounded pending judgment or further order of the court, upon motion of any person claiming the right to its possession, upon notice to the sheriff and to all parties to the action. The motion shall be granted if the chattel is of such a nature, or the circumstances are such, that the moving party, if found to be entitled to possession, would not be adequately compensated for its loss by the payment of its pecuniary value. An undertaking shall accompany the motion, in an amount not less than two hundred and fifty dollars, that the moving party will indemnify the sheriff for all expenses incurred by him in transporting, handling and safekeeping the chattel pending determination of the motion, and, if the motion is granted, pending judgment or further order of the court. All expenses resulting from impounding shall be taxed as disbursements in the action as the court may direct.

(c) Returning chattel.

1. If a chattel which is in the custody of the sheriff is personal property which if owned by a defendant would be exempt from application to the satisfaction of a money judgment, if the value of the possession of the chattel to the defendant is greater than the value of its possession to the plaintiff, if the interest of the plaintiff would not thereby be prejudiced and if the interests of justice so require, upon motion of the defendant, upon notice to the sheriff and to all parties to the action, and on such terms and on such security and conditions as to the court may seem proper, the court may order its return to the defendant.

2. If the court orders the return of the chattel to the defendant, it shall grant a restraining order that the chattel shall not be removed from the state if it is a vehicle, aircraft or vessel or, otherwise, from its location, transferred, sold, pledged, assigned or otherwise disposed of or permitted to become subject to a security interest or lien until further order of the court. Unless the court otherwise directs, the restraining order does not prohibit a disposition of the chattel to the plaintiff. Disobedience of the order may be punished as a contempt of court.

(d) Additional parties. A motion under this section, or service upon plaintiff of a notice of reclamation or exception to surety by a person not a party to the action, makes such a person a party to the action. Plaintiff shall serve a copy of the complaint upon such person within twenty days after he becomes a party.

1971 AMENDMENTS

L. 1971, ch. 1051, eff. July 2, 1971, amended subd. (a), added new subd. (c) and relettered former subd. (c) to be subd. (d).

§ 7104. Seizing, reclaiming or returning less than all chattels.

Where the seizure of two or more chattels is required by the order of seizure, the sheriff shall seize those chattels which can be found. Less than all of the seized chattels may be impounded, reclaimed, or returned. The value of the chattels seized, as stated in the affidavit of the plaintiff, or as determined by the court upon application of the defendant, shall be the value for the purposes of subsequent undertakings in the action. Unless the court orders otherwise, the sheriff may, at any time before entry of judgment, seize those chattels not yet seized; the proceedings for reclaiming, impounding or returning a chattel subsequently seized are the same as on a former seizure.

1978 AMENDMENTS

L. 1978, ch. 81, eff. Jan. 1, 1979, amended CPLR 7104 by adoption of proposals made by the Judicial Conference in its Report to the 1978 Legislature, in which it stated:

"Section 7104 has been amended to provide that the value of the chattels seized for the purposes of subsequent undertakings in the action shall be as stated in the affidavit or as determined by the court upon application of the defendant.

"The purpose of this amendment is to make it clear that in determining the value of the chattel, the court may take into consideration the value that the defendant asserts is the value of the chattel as well as the value that the plaintiff has alleged in his affidavit. This amendment is intended to obviate the danger that the plaintiff may have overvalued or undervalued the chattel because of mistake or for other reasons. For example, the plaintiff may have undervalued the chattel in order to be able to put up a smaller bond under section 7102(e); the plaintiff may have overvalued the chattel in order to show that it is urgent that an order of seizure be granted."

See notes under the 1978 amendment to CPLR 7102 for the extensive commentary by the Judicial Conference recommending the 1978 amendment of Article 71.

1971 AMENDMENTS

L. 1971, ch. 1051, eff. July 2, 1971, amended CPLR 7104.

§ 7105. Sale of perishable property.

Upon motion with such notice as the court may require, the court may order the sheriff to sell perishable property which has been seized. The court shall prescribe the time and place of the sale, and the manner and time in which notice thereof shall be given. Unless the court orders otherwise, the sheriff, after deducting his fees and necessary expenses, shall pay the proceeds into court to be held pending determination of the action.

§ 7106. Payment of sheriff's fees and expenses; liability of sheriff.

(a) Payment of sheriff's fees and expenses. The sheriff shall not deliver a chattel to the person entitled to possession unless such person shall, upon request, pay to the sheriff his lawful fees and the expenses necessarily incurred in taking and keeping the chattel. Such fees and expenses shall be taxed as costs in the action or may be taxed immediately upon motion and the sheriff may be required to refund any amount not found to be necessarily incurred.

(b) Liability of sheriff. A sheriff is liable for damages caused by his delivery of a chattel in violation of this article only to the extent that such damages can not be collected from the party to whom the chattel was delivered, or his surety. When a chattel is delivered by the sheriff to any party, as prescribed in this article, the sheriff ceases to be responsible for the sufficiency of the sureties of any party; until then, he is responsible for the sufficiency of the sureties of any party.

§ 7107. Sheriff's return.

The sheriff shall file with the clerk a return within twenty days after he has delivered a chattel; it shall include all papers delivered to or served on him and a statement of all action taken by him. Where the sheriff has not filed a return before the hearing of a motion made by any party to punish him for contempt for such failure, he may be punished for contempt. At least ten days' notice of such motion shall be given to the sheriff.

§ 7108. Judgment; execution in certain cases; enforcement by contempt.

(a) Generally. Damages for wrongful taking or detention or for injury to or depreciation of a chattel may be awarded to a party. If an order of seizure granted without notice is not confirmed as required pursuant to paragraph four of subdivision (d) of section 7102, the plaintiff, unless the court orders otherwise upon good cause shown, shall be liable to the defendant for all costs and damages, including reasonable attorney's fees, which may be sustained by reason of the granting of the order of seizure without notice, and the plaintiff's liability shall not be limited to the amount of the undertaking. Except as provided in subdivision (b), judgment shall award possession of

CPLR

each chattel to the prevailing party or, if the action is discontinued or dismissed, to the person from whom it was seized; and where the person awarded possession is not in possession when judgment is entered, it shall in the alternative, award the value of each chattel at the time of trial or the sum for which it was sold under section 7105, decreased by the value of the interest of an unsuccessful party.

(b) Where value of chattel should not be awarded; execution. A verdict, report or decision in favor of the defendant where the chattel is in possession of the plaintiff at the time it is rendered shall not fix the value of the chattel where:

1. the plaintiff is the owner of the chattel but it was rightfully distrained doing damage, and the value of the chattel is greater than the damages sustained by the defendant; or

2. the plaintiff is the owner of the chattel, but the defendant has a special property therein, the value of which is less than the value of the chattel.

The verdict, report or decision shall state why the value of the chattel is not fixed, and the final judgment shall award to the defendant the amount of damages or value of his special property and, if such sum is not collected, possession of the chattel. An execution shall direct the sheriff to deliver possession of the chattel to the defendant unless the party in possession pays the sum awarded to the defendant with interest and sheriff's fees and in case the chattel cannot be found within his county, then to satisfy that sum from the property of the party against whom the judgment is entered. If the chattel is in possession of the defendant, it may remain in his possession until the amount awarded is paid.

(c) Failure of jury to fix sum. If the jury shall fail to fix any sum required to be fixed by this section, such sum shall be fixed by a jury empanelled for the purpose upon motion made before the judge who presided at the trial within fifteen days after verdict.

1978 AMENDMENTS

L. 1978, ch. 81, eff. Jan. 1, 1979, amended CPLR 7108 by adoption of proposals made by the Judicial Conference in its Report to the 1978 Legislature, in which it stated:

"A new sentence has been added to section 7108(a) to provide that if an order of seizure granted without notice is not confirmed as required pursuant to section 7102(d)(4), the plaintiff, unless the court orders otherwise upon good cause shown, shall be liable to the defendant for all costs and damages, including reasonable attorney's fees, which may be sustained by reason of the granting of the order of seizure without notice, and the plaintiff's liability shall not be limited to the amount of the undertaking.

"This provision protects defendants and, by not limiting damages to the amount of the undertaking, provides an incentive to plaintiffs to move on notice for an order of seizure."

See notes under the 1978 amendment to CPLR 7102 for the extensive commentary by the Judicial Conference recommending the 1978 amendment of Article 71.

§ 7109. Unique chattel.

(a) Injunction, temporary restraining order. Where the chattel is unique, the court may grant a preliminary injunction or temporary restraining order that the chattel shall not be removed from the state, transferred, sold, pledged, assigned or otherwise disposed of until the further order of the court.

(b) Judgment enforceable by contempt. Where the chattel is unique, the court, in addition to granting a judgment under section 7108, may direct that a party in possession deliver the chattel to the party entitled to possession. Disobedience of a judgment or order so directing may be punished as a contempt of court. If a party accepts the value of the chattel awarded to him by the judgment, he shall have no claim to the chattel.

§ 7110. Sheriff's powers.

If the order of seizure so provides, the sheriff in accordance with the order of seizure, may break open, enter and search for the chattel in the place where the chattel may be and take the chattel into his possession.

1971 AMENDMENTS

L. 1971, ch. 1051, eff. July 2, 1971, amended CPLR 7110 by deleting all the language after the word "powers" in the catchline; by deleting and adding language to reflect the charges made in Article 71 by the repeal of the use of a requisition and the substitution of an order of seizure in its stead.

§ 7111. Action on undertaking.

An action on an undertaking cannot be maintained after final judgment until the return, wholly or partly unsatisfied, of an execution on the judgment for delivery of possession of the chattel or for payment of a sum of money in lieu of the chattel.

§ 7112. Testimony by deposition to ascertain location of chattel.

A party to an action to recover a chattel may move, upon such notice as the court may direct, upon a showing that he lacks knowledge of the location of the chattel or a part thereof, for an order to examine any person for the purpose of obtaining information with reference to such location. The order may be granted before or after service of summons and complaint, or anytime before or after final judgment, and may also restrain the adverse party from acting in violation of whatever rights the moving party may have in the chattel, upon the execution of a reasonable undertaking, with sufficient sureties, to reimburse the adverse party for all damages wrongfully caused by such restraint.

1978 AMENDMENTS

L. 1978, ch. 81, eff. Jan. 1, 1979, amended CPLR 7112 by adoption of proposals made by the Judicial Conference in its Report to the 1978 Legislature, in which it stated:

"A new phrase has been added to provide that a motion to examine any person for the purpose of obtaining information with reference to the location of a chattel shall be 'upon such notice as the court may direct.' "

See notes under the 1978 amendment to CPLR 7102 for the extensive commentary by the Judicial Conference recommending the 1978 amendment of Article 71.

1968 AMENDMENTS

L. 1968, ch. 355, eff. Sept. 1, 1968, added CPLR 7112.

Article 72

RECOVERY OF PENALTY OR FORFEITURE

§ 7201. Action by state.

(a) Statutory penalty or forfeiture. Where property has been forfeited or a penalty incurred to the state or to an officer, for its use, pursuant to statute, the attorney-general, or the district attorney of the county in which the action is triable, if such an action has not already been brought by the attorney-general, shall commence an action to recover the property or penalty. A recovery in such an action bars the recovery in any other action brought for the same cause.

(b) Forfeiture on conviction for treason. Where personal property is forfeited to the state upon a conviction of outlawry for treason, the attorney-general shall commence an action to recover the property or its value.

(c) Forfeiture of recognizance. Where the condition of a recognizance is broken, the recognizance is wholly forfeited by an order of the court directing its prosecution. Where a recognizance to the state is forfeited, it is not necessary to allege or prove any damages.

§ 7202. Action by person aggrieved.

Where a penalty or forfeiture is given by a statute to a person aggrieved by the act or omission of another, the person aggrieved may commence an action to recover it.

§ 7203. Action by common informer.

(a) When maintainable. Where a penalty or forfeiture is given by a statute to any person, an action to recover it may be maintained by any person in his own name; but the action cannot be compromised or settled without the leave of the court.

(b) Service. The summons can be served only by an officer authorized by law to collect upon an execution issued out of the same court. The summons cannot be countermanded by the plaintiff before service. Immediately after it has been served, the officer shall file it with his certificate of service with the judge who issued it or with the clerk of the court.

(c) Action not barred by collusive recovery. The plaintiff may recover, notwithstanding the recovery of a judgment, for or against the defendant, in an action brought by another person, if the former judgment was recovered collusively and fraudulently.

§ 7204. Recovery of part of penalty or forfeiture.

Where a statute gives a pecuniary penalty or forfeiture not exceeding a specified sum, the whole sum or a part proportionate to the offense may be awarded.

§ 7205. Defense of good faith reliance on judicial decision.

No action for a penalty or forfeiture may be brought for an act done in good faith and pursuant to a construction given to a statute by a decision of an appellate court and adjudged lawful thereby, where such act was done prior to a reversal or the overruling of such decision.

Article 75

ARBITRATION

SUMMARY OF ARTICLE

CPLR

§ 7501. Effect of arbitration agreement.

A written agreement to submit any controversy thereafter arising or any existing controversy to arbitration is enforceable without regard to the justiciable character of the controversy and confers jurisdiction on the courts of the state to enforce it and to enter judgment on an award. In determining any matter arising under this article, the court shall not consider whether the claim with respect to which arbitration is sought is tenable, or otherwise pass upon the merits of the dispute.

§ 7502. Applications to the court; venue; statutes of limitation; provisional remedies.

(a) Applications to the court; venue. A special proceeding shall be used to bring before a court the first application arising out of an arbitrable controversy which is not made by motion in a pending action.

(i) The proceeding shall be brought in the court and county specified in the agreement. If the name of the county is not specified, proceedings to stay or bar arbitration shall be brought in the county where the party seeking arbitration resides or is doing business, and other proceedings affecting arbitration are to be brought in the county where at least one of the parties resides or is doing business or where the arbitration was held or is pending.

(ii) If there is no county in which the proceeding may be brought under paragraph (i) of this subdivision, the proceeding may be brought in any county.

(iii) Notwithstanding the entry of judgment, all subsequent applications shall be made by motion in the special proceeding or action in which the first application was made.

(iv) If an application to confirm an arbitration award made within the one year as provided by section seventy-five hundred ten of this article, or an application to vacate or modify an award made within the ninety days as provided by subdivision (a) of section seventy-five hundred eleven of this article, was denied or dismissed solely on the ground that it was made in the form of a motion captioned in an earlier special proceeding having reference to the arbitration instead of as a distinct special proceeding, the time in which to apply to confirm the award and the time in which to apply to vacate or modify the award may, notwithstanding that the applicable period of time has expired, be made at any time within ninety days after the effective date of this paragraph, and may be made in whatever form is appropriate (motion or special proceeding) pursuant to this subdivision.

(b) Limitation of time. If, at the time that a demand for arbitration was made or a notice of intention to arbitrate was served, the claim sought to be arbitrated would have been barred by limitation of time had it been asserted in a court of the state, a party may assert the limitation as a bar to the arbitration on an application to the court as provided in section 7503 or subdivision (b) of section 7511. The failure to assert such bar by such application shall not preclude its assertion before the arbitrators, who may, in their sole discretion, apply or not apply the bar. Except as provided in subdivision (b) of section 7511, such exercise of discretion by the arbitrators shall not be subject to review by a court on an application to confirm, vacate or modify the award.

(c) Provisional remedies. The supreme court in the county in which an arbitration is pending or in a county specified in subdivision (a) of this section, may entertain an application for an order of attachment or for a preliminary injunction in connection with an arbitration that is pending or that is to be commenced inside or outside this state, whether or not it is subject to the United Nations convention on the recognition and enforcement of foreign arbitral awards, but only upon the ground

CPLR

that the award to which the applicant may be entitled may be rendered ineffectual without such provisional relief. The provisions of articles 62 and 63 of this chapter shall apply to the application, including those relating to undertakings and to the time for commencement of an action (arbitration shall be deemed an action for this purpose), except that the sole ground for the granting of the remedy shall be as stated above. It an arbitration is not commenced within thirty days of the granting of the provisional relief, the order granting such relief shall expire and be null and void and costs, including reasonable attorney's fees, awarded to the respondent. The court may reduce or expand this period of time for good cause shown. The form of the application shall be as provided in subdivision (a) of this section.

2005 AMENDMENTS

L. 2005, ch. 703, eff. Oct. 4, 2005, amended subdivision (c) to permit attachment orders or preliminary injunctions in connection with arbitrations that are pending or will be commenced inside or outside New York whether or not they are subject to the United Nations convention on the recognition and enforcement of foreign arbitral awards.

2001 AMENDMENTS

L. 2001, ch. 567, eff. Dec. 19, 2001, added new paragraph (iv) to subdivision (a).

2000 AMENDMENTS

L. 2000, ch. 226, eff. Aug. 16, 2000, repealed and added subdivision (a) to CPLR 7502

1985 AMENDMENTS

L. 1985, ch. 253, eff. Jan. 1, 1986, added subdivision (c) to CPLR 7502.

§ 7503. Application to compel or stay arbitration; stay of action; notice of intention to arbitrate.

(a) Application to compel arbitration; stay of action. A party aggrieved by the failure of another to arbitrate may apply for an order compelling arbitration. Where there is no substantial question whether a valid agreement was made or complied with, and the claim sought to be arbitrated is not barred by limitation under subdivision (b) of section 7502, the court shall direct the parties to arbitrate. Where any such question is raised, it shall be tried forthwith in said court. If an issue claimed to be arbitrable is involved in an action pending in a court having jurisdiction to hear a motion to compel arbitration, the application shall be made by motion in that action. If the application is granted, the order shall operate to stay a pending or subsequent action, or so much of it as is referable to arbitration.

(b) Application to stay arbitration. Subject to the provisions of subdivision (c), a party who has not participated in the arbitration and who has not made or been served with an application to compel arbitration, may apply to stay arbitration on the ground that a valid agreement was not made or has not been complied with or that the claim sought to be arbitrated is barred by limitation under subdivision (b) of section 7502.

(c) Notice of intention to arbitrate. A party may serve upon another party a demand for arbitration or a notice of intention to arbitrate, specifying the agreement pursuant to which arbitration is sought and the name and address of the party serving the notice, or of an officer or agent thereof if such party is an association or corporation, and stating that unless the party served applies to stay the arbitration within twenty days after such service he shall thereafter be precluded from objecting that a valid agreement was not made or has not been complied with and from asserting in court the bar of a limitation of time. Such notice or demand shall be served in the same manner as a summons or by registered or certified mail, return receipt requested. An application to stay arbitration must be made by the party served within twenty days after service upon him of the notice or demand, or he shall be so precluded. Notice of such application shall be served in the same manner as a summons or by registered or certified mail, return receipt requested. Service of the application may be made upon the adverse party, or upon his attorney if the attorney's name appears on the demand for arbitration or the notice of intention to arbitrate. Service of the application by mail shall be timely if such application is posted within the prescribed period. Any provision in an arbitration agreement or arbitration rules which waives the right to apply for a stay of arbitration is hereby declared null and void.

1973 AMENDMENTS

L. 1973, ch. 1028, eff. Sept. 1, 1973, amended CPLR 7503(c) by changing the ten day period for applying to stay arbitration to twenty days; by providing that service of the application to stay arbitration may be made upon the adverse party's attorney if his name appears on the notice of intention to arbitrate or on the demand; by providing that service of the application by mail shall be timely if made within the prescribed period; by adding to the first, second and third sentence references to demands for arbitration to conform to CPLR 7502(b); and by adding a requirement that any provision in an arbitration agreement which waives the right to apply for a stay be deemed void.

1964 AMENDMENTS

L. 1964, ch. 388, eff. Sept. 1, 1964, deleted comma formerly appearing between "be" and "arbitrated" in Subd. (b).

§ 7504.   Court appointment of arbitrator.

If the arbitration agreement does not provide for a method of appointment of an arbitrator, or if the agreed method fails or for any reason is not followed, or if an arbitrator fails to act and his successor has not been appointed, the court, on application of a party, shall appoint an arbitrator.

§ 7505.   Powers of arbitrator.

An arbitrator and any attorney of record in the arbitration proceeding has the power to issue subpoenas. An arbitrator has the power to administer oaths.

§ 7506.   Hearing.

(a) Oath of arbitrator.   Before hearing any testimony, an arbitrator shall be sworn to hear and decide the controversy faithfully and fairly by an officer authorized to administer an oath.

(b) Time and place.   The arbitrator shall appoint a time and place for the hearing and notify the parties in writing personally or by registered or certified mail not less than eight days before the hearing. The arbitrator may adjourn or postpone the hearing. The court, upon application of any party, may direct the arbitrator to proceed promptly with the hearing and determination of the controversy.

(c) Evidence.   The parties are entitled to be heard, to present evidence and to cross-examine witnesses. Notwithstanding the failure of a party duly notified to appear, the arbitrator may hear and determine the controversy upon the evidence produced.

(d) Representation by attorney.   A party has the right to be represented by an attorney and may claim such right at any time as to any part of the arbitration or hearings which have not taken place. This right may not be waived. If a party is represented by an attorney, papers to be served on the party shall be served upon his attorney.

(e) Determination by majority. The hearing shall be conducted by all the arbitrators, but a majority may determine any question and render an award.

(f) Waiver. Except as provided in subdivision (d), a requirement of this section may be waived by written consent of the parties and it is waived if the parties continue with the arbitration without objection.

§ 7507. Award; form; time; delivery.

Except as provided in section 7508, the award shall be in writing, signed and affirmed by the arbitrator making it within the time fixed by the agreement, or, if the time is not fixed, within such time as the court orders. The parties may in writing extend the time either before or after its expiration. A party waives the objection that an award was not made within the time required unless he notifies the arbitrator in writing of his objection prior to the delivery of the award to him. The arbitrator shall deliver a copy of the award to each party in the manner provided in the agreement, or, if no provision is so made, personally or by registered or certified mail, return receipt requested.

1981 AMENDMENTS

L. 1981, ch. 952, eff. July 31, 1981, amended CPLR 7507 by requiring that an arbitrator now affirm a written arbitration award instead of acknowledging it.

§ 7508. Award by confession.

(a) When available. An award by confession may be made for money due or to become due at any time before an award is otherwise made. The award shall be based upon a statement, verified by each party, containing an authorization to make the award, the sum of the award or the method of ascertaining it, and the facts constituting the liability.

(b) Time of award. The award may be made at any time within three months after the statement is verified.

(c) Person or agency making award. The award may be made by an arbitrator or by the agency or person named by the parties to designate the arbitrator.

§ 7509. Modification of award by arbitrator.

On written application of a party to the arbitrators within twenty days after delivery of the award to the applicant, the arbitrators may modify the award upon the grounds stated in subdivision (c) of section 7511. Written notice of the application shall be given to other parties to the arbitration. Written objection to modification must be served on the arbitrators and other parties to the arbitration within ten days of receipt of the notice. The arbitrators shall dispose of any application made under this section in writing, signed and acknowledged by them, within thirty days after either written objection to modification has been served on them or the time for serving said objection has expired, whichever is earlier. The parties may in writing extend the time for such disposition either before or after its expiration.

§ 7510. Confirmation of award.

The court shall confirm an award upon application of a party made within one year after its delivery to him, unless the award is vacated or modified upon a ground specified in section 7511.

§ 7511. Vacating or modifying award.

(a) When application made. An application to vacate or modify an award may be made by a party within ninety days after its delivery to him.

(b) Grounds for vacating.

1. The award shall be vacated on the application of a party who either participated in the arbitration or was served with a notice of intention to arbitrate if the court finds the rights of that party were prejudiced by:

(i) corruption, fraud or misconduct in procuring the award; or

(ii) partiality of an arbitrator appointed as a neutral; except where the award was by confession; or

(iii) an arbitrator, or agency or person making the award exceeded his power or so imperfectly executed it that a final and definite award upon the subject matter submitted was not made; or

(iv) failure to follow the procedure of this article, unless the party applying to vacate the award continued with the arbitration with notice of the defect and without objection.

2. The award shall be vacated on the application of a party who neither participated in the arbitration nor was served with a notice of intention to arbitrate if the court finds that:

(i) the rights of that party were prejudiced by one of the grounds specified in paragraph one; or

(ii) a valid agreement to arbitrate was not made; or

(iii) the agreement to arbitrate had not been complied with; or

(iv) the arbitrated claim was barred by limitation under subdivision (b) of section 7502.

(c) Grounds for modifying. The court shall modify the award if:

1. there was a miscalculation of figures or a mistake in the description of any person, thing or property referred to in the award; or

2. the arbitrators have awarded upon a matter not submitted to them and the award may be corrected without affecting the merits of the decision upon the issues submitted; or

3. the award is imperfect in a matter of form, not affecting the merits of the controversy.

(d) Rehearing. Upon vacating an award, the court may order a rehearing and determination of all or any of the issues either before the same arbitrator or before a new arbitrator appointed in accordance with this article. Time in any provision limiting the time for a hearing or award shall be measured from the date of such order or rehearing, whichever is appropriate, or a time may be specified by the court.

(e) Confirmation. Upon the granting of a motion to modify, the court shall confirm the award as modified; upon the denial of a motion to vacate or modify, it shall confirm the award.

CROSS REFERENCES

See **Insurance Law § 675** as to arbitration of "no-fault" claims against insurers. Special provisions for review of arbitrators' awards are contained therein.

§ 7512. Death or incompetency of a party.

Where a party dies after making a written agreement to submit a controversy to arbitration, the proceedings may be begun or continued upon the application of, or upon notice to, his executor or administrator or, where it relates to real property, his distributee or devisee who has succeeded to his interest in the real property. Where a committee of the property or of the person of a party to such an agreement is appointed, the proceedings may be continued upon the application of, or notice to, the committee. Upon the death or incompetency of a party, the court may extend the time within which an application to confirm, vacate or modify the award or to stay arbitration must be made. Where a party has died since an award was delivered, the proceedings thereupon are the same as where a party dies after a verdict.

§ 7513. Fees and expenses.

Unless otherwise provided in the agreement to arbitrate, the arbitrators' expenses and fees, together with other expenses, not including attorney's fees, incurred in the conduct of the arbitration, shall be paid as provided in the award. The court, on application, may reduce or disallow any fee or expense it finds excessive or allocate it as justice requires.

§ 7514. Judgment on an award.

(a) Entry. A judgment shall be entered upon the confirmation of an award.

(b) Judgment-roll. The judgment-roll consists of the original or a copy of the agreement and each written extension of time within which to make an award; the statement required by section 7508 where the award was by confession; the award; each paper submitted to the court and each order of the court upon an application under sections 7510 and 7511; and a copy of the judgment.

1964 AMENDMENTS

L. 1964, ch. 388, eff. Sept. 1, 1964, changed reference in Subd. (b) to section "seventy-five hundred eight" to the figures "7508."

Article 75-A
HEALTH CARE ARBITRATION

SUMMARY OF ARTICLE

§ 7550. Definitions.

As used in this article:

(a) "Arbitration administrator" means an entity designated by the superintendent of insurance to administer the arbitration of disputes pursuant to this article.

(b) "Hospital" has the same meaning as is set forth in subdivision ten of section twenty-eight hundred one of the public health law.

(c) "Health maintenance organization" has the same meaning as is set forth in subdivision one of section forty-four hundred one of the public health law and shall include health maintenance organizations authorized pursuant to article forty-three of the insurance law.

(d) "Health care provider" includes any person or entity employed or otherwise involved in the provision of health care or treatment.

1986 AMENDMENTS

L. 1986, ch. 266, eff. July 8, 1986, added new Article 75-a, comprising CPLR 7550 through 7565.

§ 7551. Applicability.

The provisions of this article shall apply to all claims for damages because of injury or death resulting from health care or treatment rendered or failed to be rendered to enrollees and other covered family members of health maintenance organizations and all other claims, cross-claims, counter-claims, and claims for contribution and indemnity arising from claims subject to agreements to arbitrate made pursuant to section forty-four hundred six-a of the public health law and to arbitrations authorized pursuant to section thirty hundred forty-five of this chapter.

1986 AMENDMENTS

L. 1986, ch. 266, eff. July 8, 1986, added new Article 75-a, comprising CPLR 7550 through 7565.

§ 7552. Health care arbitration proceedings.

(a) Proceedings pursuant to this article shall be commenced and conducted in accordance with article seventy-five of this chapter, except as otherwise provided by this article, and in accordance with rules promulgated by the arbitration administrator and approved by the superintendent of insurance.

(b) The standards of duty, practice, or care to be applied to a physician, dentist, hospital, health maintenance organization or other health care provider in the arbitration shall be the same standards as would be applied in a comparable medical or dental malpractice action.

(c) Damages shall be determined in accordance with provisions of law applicable to medical and dental malpractice actions. Attorney contingency fee agreements shall be valid and subject to provisions of law applicable to medical and dental malpractice actions.

1986 AMENDMENTS

L. 1986, ch. 266, eff. July 8, 1986, added new Article 75-a, comprising CPLR 7550 through 7565.

§ 7553. Costs of the proceeding.

The administrative expense of arbitrations shall be paid from the arbitration fund established pursuant to section five thousand six hundred three of the insurance law.

1986 AMENDMENTS

L. 1986, ch. 266, eff. July 8, 1986, added new Article 75-a, comprising CPLR 7550 through 7565.

§ 7554. Selection of arbitrators.

(a) An arbitration under this article shall be heard by a panel of three arbitrators. The chairperson of the panel shall be an attorney who shall be appointed to serve in such capacity on a full-time basis for a fixed term. The chairperson shall have jurisdiction over prehearing procedures. Qualifications for the selection of such chairpersons shall be established by the arbitration administrator, subject to the approval of the superintendent of insurance.

(b) Except as otherwise provided in subdivision (e) of this section, the remaining two arbitrators, hereinafter referred to as associate arbitrators, shall be selected from a pool of candidates established pursuant to the rules and procedures promulgated by the arbitration administrator and approved by the superintendent of insurance. Attorneys whose practice substantially involves representation in personal injury matters, physicians, dentists, hospital and health maintenance organization personnel and other health care providers shall not be eligible to serve as associate arbitrators. The rules and procedures pertaining to selection of associate arbitrators under this article shall provide that the arbitration administrator send simultaneously to each party an identical list of associate arbitrator candidates, together with a brief biographical statement on each candidate. A party may strike from the list any names which is unacceptable and shall number the remaining names in order of preference. When the lists are returned to the arbitration administrator they shall be compared and the first two mutually agreeable associate arbitrator candidates shall be invited to serve.

CPLR

(c) When two mutually agreed upon associate arbitrators have not been selected from the first list, a second list of such candidates shall be sent in the manner provided for in subdivision (b) of this section.

(d) If a complete panel is not selected by mutual agreement of the parties pursuant to subdivisions (b) and (c) of this section, then, under applicable rules and procedures of the arbitration administrator, which are approved by the superintendent of insurance, the arbitration administrator shall appoint the remaining associate arbitrators. Any appointment of an associate arbitrator by the arbitration administrator shall be subject to challenge by any party for cause. To be sufficient, a challenge must allege facts which establish that community, professional or other pressures are likely to influence the objectivity of the appointed associate arbitrator. A decision on a request to strike an arbitrator for cause shall be made by the arbitration administrator.

(e) The parties shall not be restricted to the associate arbitrator candidates submitted for consideration. If all parties mutually agree upon one or more associate arbitrators, such arbitrators shall be invited to serve.

1986 AMENDMENTS

L. 1986, ch. 266, eff. July 8, 1986, added new Article 75-a, comprising CPLR 7550 through 7565.

§ 7555. Screening for bias; communication with arbitrator candidates.

(a) Prior to inclusion on a list of proposed associate arbitrators, the arbitration administrator shall make an appropriate initial screening for bias and shall require associate arbitrator candidates for a particular case to complete a current personal disclosure statement under oath. In addition to other relevant information, the statement shall disclose any personal acquaintance with any of the parties or their counsel and the nature of such acquaintance. If the statement reveals facts which suggest the possibility of partiality, the arbitration administrator shall communicate those facts to the parties.

(b) No party shall communicate with an associate arbitrator candidate, directly or indirectly, except through the arbitration administrator, at any time after the filing of the demand for arbitration. Any candidate who is aware of such communication shall immediately notify the arbitration administrator.

1986 AMENDMENTS

L. 1986, ch. 266, eff. July 8, 1986, added new Article 75-a, comprising CPLR 7550 through 7565.

§ 7556. Demand for arbitration; minors; consolidation of proceedings.

(a) Any person subject to an arbitration agreement may seek to compel arbitration, pursuant to section seventy-five hundred three or section thirty-hundred forty-five of this chapter.

(b) Notwithstanding the provisions of section twelve hundred nine of this chapter, a minor child and a person judicially determined to be incompetent shall be bound to arbitrate disputes, controversies, or issues upon the execution of an arbitration election on the person's behalf by a parent, legal guardian, committee, conservator or other person legally authorized to enroll such minor or incompetent person in a health maintenance organization, in accordance with the provisions of section forty-five hundred six-a of the public health law.

(c) Separate arbitration proceedings brought pursuant to this article, which involve common question of law and fact, shall be consolidated into a single arbitration proceeding.

(d) Except for arbitrations commenced pursuant to section thirty hundred forty-five of this chapter, any case involving a person who is not bound to participate in the arbitration proceeding pursuant to subdivision (e) of section forty-four hundred six-a of the public health law shall not be subject to the arbitration proceeding, unless such person and all parties who are subject to the arbitration consent to the arbitration of the claim. Absent such consent, any party may seek to stay such arbitrations, pursuant to section seventy-five hundred three of this chapter, notwithstanding any time limits that may otherwise apply to such a stay, and require the matter to proceed as a civil action. In the event that such an arbitration is stayed, the arbitration administrator shall forthwith transfer the case to the clerk of the court in the venue designated by the plaintiff, where the case shall be expeditiously reviewed and assigned in accordance with rules promulgated by the chief administrator of the courts. If the demand for arbitration was made or a notice of intention to arbitrate was served within the limitations of time specified by article two of this chapter, and the arbitration was subsequently stayed and transferred to a court, the

CPLR

action shall be deemed to have been timely commenced, in accordance with the provisions of subdivision (a) of section two hundred five of this chapter.

1986 AMENDMENTS

L. 1986, ch. 266, eff. July 8, 1986, added new Article 75-a, comprising CPLR 7550 through 7565.

§ 7557. Reparation offers; denials of liability.

All communications incidental to settlement made orally or in writing by any party shall not be disclosed to the arbitration panel, unless all parties consent to such disclosure.

1986 AMENDMENTS

L. 1986, ch. 266, eff. July 8, 1986, added new Article 75-a, comprising CPLR 7550 through 7565.

§ 7558. Depositions and discovery; rules of the arbitration administrator; adjournments.

(a) After the appointment of the panel of arbitrators and notwithstanding inconsistent provisions of sections four hundred eight and three thousand one hundred two of this chapter, the parties to the arbitration may take depositions and obtain discovery regarding the subject matter of the arbitration and, to that end, use and exercise the same rights, remedies, and obligations in the arbitration as if the subject matter of the arbitration were pending in a civil action.

(b) The arbitration administrator shall promulgate rules, subject to the approval of the superintendent of insurance, to ensure the expeditious completion of discovery and the prompt commencement and conclusion of the hearing, consistent with applicable provisions of rule thirty-four hundred six of this chapter.

(c) An adjournment at the request of counsel for any of the parties may be granted only by the chairperson of the panel for good cause shown. A proceeding under this article shall be treated in the same manner as an action or proceeding in supreme court for the purpose of any claim by counsel of actual engagement.

1986 AMENDMENTS

L. 1986, ch. 266, eff. July 8, 1986, added new Article 75-a, comprising CPLR 7550 through 7565.

§ 7559. Hearing; evidence; record; neutral experts.

(a) An arbitration hearing shall be informal and the rules of evidence shall be those applicable to arbitrations conducted pursuant to article seventy-five of this chapter.

(b) Testimony at the hearing shall be taken under oath and a record of the proceedings shall be made by a recording device. Any party may obtain a copy of the recording of the proceeding, which shall be provided without charge. A party, at that party's expense, may also utilize the services of a stenographic reporter. The cost of any transcription ordered by the panel of arbitrators for its own use shall be deemed part of the cost of the proceedings.

(c) The panel on its own motion may call a neutral expert witness who shall be subject to cross-examination by the parties. The cost of the expert will be deemed a cost of the proceeding.

1986 AMENDMENTS

L. 1986, ch. 266, eff. July 8, 1986, added new Article 75-a, comprising CPLR 7550 through 7565.

§ 7560. Subpoenas.

The chairperson of the panel and any attorney of record in the proceeding has the power to issue subpoenas, in accordance with section seventy-five hundred five of this chapter.

1986 AMENDMENTS

L. 1986, ch. 266, eff. July 8, 1986, added new Article 75-a, comprising CPLR 7550 through 7565.

§ 7561. Use of depositions; enforcement of discovery procedures.

(a) On application of a party to the arbitration, the chairperson may permit the deposition of a witness to be used as evidence, in accordance with the provisions of rule three thousand one hundred seventeen of this chapter.

(b) Depositions shall be taken in the manner prescribed by law for the taking of depositions in civil actions.

(c) The chairperson may enforce the failure of parties to comply with applicable discovery obligations in the same manner as a court,

CPLR

pursuant to section three thousand one hundred twenty-six of this chapter, including through the imposition of costs, payable to the arbitration fund, provided, however, that the chairperson shall not have the power to find a party in contempt.

1986 AMENDMENTS

L. 1986, ch. 266, eff. July 8, 1986, added new Article 75-a, comprising CPLR 7550 through 7565.

§ 7562.   Witnesses' fees and mileage; arbitrator's fees and expenses.

(a) Except for the parties to the arbitration and their agents, officers, and employees, all witnesses appearing pursuant to subpoena are entitled to receive fees and mileage in the same amount and under the same circumstances as prescribed by law for witnesses in civil actions. The fee and mileage of a witness subpoenaed upon the application of a party to the arbitration shall be paid by that party. The fee and mileage of a witness subpoenaed solely at the request of an arbitrator shall be deemed to be a cost of the proceeding.

(b) Each arbitrator's salary or fees and expenses, together with any other costs of the proceeding shall be paid from the arbitration administration fund established pursuant to section five thousand six hundred three of the insurance law. The range of such salary or fees and expenses and the manner of their payment shall be established by regulation of the superintendent of insurance.

1986 AMENDMENTS

L. 1986, ch. 266, eff. July 8, 1986, added new Article 75-a, comprising CPLR 7550 through 7565.

§ 7563.   Briefs; award; decision.

(a) The panel may order that written briefs be submitted within thirty days after the close of hearings. In written briefs each party may summarize the evidence and testimony and may propose a comprehensive award of compensatory elements.

(b) The panel of arbitrators shall render its decision by majority vote and the decision shall be rendered within thirty days after the close of the hearing or the receipt of briefs, if briefs are requested.

1986 AMENDMENTS

L. 1986, ch. 266, eff. July 8, 1986, added new Article 75-a, comprising CPLR 7550 through 7565.

§ 7564. Form of decision; costs upon frivolous claims and counterclaims.

(a) The decision in the arbitration proceeding shall be in the form required by sections seven thousand five hundred seven and four thousand two hundred thirteen of this chapter and shall be filed with the arbitration administrator.

(b) The panel of arbitrators shall be empowered to award costs and reasonable attorney's fees to a successful party in an arbitration, if the panel finds that the action, claim, counterclaim, defense or cross claim of an unsuccessful party is frivolous, in accordance with the provisions and subject to the limitations of section eight thousand three hundred three-a of this chapter. The arbitration fee paid by the claimant shall be recoverable by the claimant in the event an award is made to the claimant.

CPLR

1986 AMENDMENTS

L. 1986, ch. 266, eff. July 8, 1986, added new Article 75-a, comprising CPLR 7550 through 7565.

§ 7565. Modification and judicial review of decision.

A decision of a panel of arbitrators shall be binding on all parties, unless modified or vacated pursuant to section seven thousand five hundred nine or seven thousand five hundred eleven of this chapter.

1986 AMENDMENTS

L. 1986, ch. 266, eff. July 8, 1986, added new Article 75-A, comprising CPLR 7550 through 7565.

Article 76

PROCEEDING TO ENFORCE AGREEMENT FOR DETERMINATION OF ISSUE

SUMMARY OF ARTICLE

§ 7601.   Special proceeding to enforce agreement that issue or controversy be determined by a person named or to be selected.

§ 7601. Special proceeding to enforce agreement that issue or controversy be determined by a person named or to be selected.

A special proceeding may be commenced to specifically enforce an agreement, other than one contained in the standard fire insurance policy of the state, that a question of valuation, appraisal or other issue or controversy be determined by a person named or to be selected. The court may enforce such an agreement as if it were an arbitration agreement, in which case the proceedings shall be conducted as if brought under article seventy-five. Where there is a defense which would require dismissal of an action for breach of the agreement, the proceeding shall be dismissed.

CPLR

Article 77

PROCEEDING RELATING TO EXPRESS TRUST

SUMMARY OF ARTICLE

§ 7701. Special proceeding relating to express trust.

A special proceeding may be brought to determine a matter relating to any express trust except a voting trust, a mortgage, a trust for the benefit of creditors, a trust to carry out any plan of reorganization of real property acquired on foreclosure or otherwise of a mortgage or mortgages against which participation certificates have been issued and guaranteed by a corporation and for which the superintendent of insurance or the superintendent of banks has been or may hereafter be appointed rehabilitator or liquidator or conservator, a trust to carry out any plan of reorganization pursuant to sections one hundred nineteen through one hundred twenty-three of the real property law or pursuant to section seventy-seven B of the national bankruptcy act, and trusts for cemetery purposes, as provided for by sections 8-1.5 and 8-1.6 of the estates, powers and trusts law.

Any party to the proceeding shall have the right to examine the trustees, under oath, either before or after filing an answer or objections, as to any matter relating to their administration of the trust, in accordance with the provisions of article thirty-one.

1976 AMENDMENTS

L. 1976, ch. 193, eff. Sept. 1, 1976, amended the section by updating the cross-references contained therein, without changing substance, and by adding the final paragraph providing for examination of trustees.

CPLR

CPLR 408, which requires leave of court for disclosure in special proceedings, was also amended by Chapter 193, so as to exclude Article 77 proceedings from the provisions of § 408, and to provide that disclosure in such proceedings be governed by the general provisions of Article 31.

Amendment of CPLR 408 and CPLR 7701 was recommended by the Judicial Conference Report to the 1976 Legislature, wherein it stated:

"This bill would conform the practice under the CPLR relating to *inter vivos* trust proceedings to that in Surrogate's Court, thus rectifying a previous legislative oversight.

"At present, by virtue of the general provisions of CPLR 408, a court order is required for disclosure in *inter vivos* trust proceedings, whereas in testamentary trust proceedings, under SCPA 2211, no such order is necessary. SCPA 2211 also provides that in testamentary trust accountings the fiduciary may be examined under oath by any party to the proceeding, either before or after filing objections. There is no comparable provision in Article 77 of the CPLR with respect to *inter vivos* trusts.

"There is no good reason why the procedure in *inter vivos* trust accountings should be different in this respect from testamentary trust accountings."

1964 AMENDMENTS

L. 1964, ch. 322, eff. Sept. 1, 1964, amended the section to clarify its meaning and scope.

§ 7702.　Verified account accompanying petition.

A petition by a trustee praying that his intermediate or final account be judicially settled shall be accompanied by an account verified in the form required by section twenty-two hundred nine of the surrogate's court procedure act.

CROSS REFERENCES

See **SCPA § 2209** in Appendix, *below.*

1970 AMENDMENTS

L. 1970, ch. 348, eff. Sept. 1, 1970, amended the section to provide that a trustee seeking to have his account judicially settled shall submit, with his petition, an account verified in the form required by section 2209 of the Surrogate's Court Procedure Act.

§ 7703.　Joinder and representation of persons interested in trust property.

The provisions as to joinder and representation of persons interested in estates as provided in the surrogate's court procedure act shall govern joinder and representation of persons interested in express trusts. For these purposes, the term "will" used in the surrogate's court procedure act shall be construed to mean the instrument creating the trust.

CROSS REFERENCES

See **SCPA § 315** ("Joinder and representation of persons interested in estates.") in appendix, *below.*

1981 AMENDMENTS

L. 1981, ch. 178, eff. June 2, 1981, which applies to estates of deceased persons and trusts in existence after such date, repealed CPLR 7703 ("Representation in case of remainder to class") and substituted a new section 7703.

§ 7704. Reference.

No referee shall be appointed to examine and audit a trustee's account, or to hear and report on or to determine any questions arising upon the settlement of such account, where:

1. a question of law exclusively is involved; or

2. no objections have been filed to the transactions set forth in the account by any of the persons interested in the trust or by any representative authorized under section 1201 to appear for an infant or incompetent interested in the trust or by a guardian ad litem of a person not in being interested in the trust.

1964 AMENDMENTS

L. 1964, ch. 388, eff. Sept. 1, 1964, inserted "a" before "question" in Subd. (1).

§ 7705. Recording or filing instrument settling account.

There may be recorded or filed in the office of the clerk or register of the county where any trustee under an express trust not created by will, if an individual, resides, or, if a corporation, has its principal office, any instrument settling an account, in whole or in part, executed by one or more such trustees and by one or more of the persons interested in the subject-matter of the trust, none of whom is under the disability of infancy or incompetency. Every such instrument to be recorded or filed shall be acknowledged; and if recorded the record thereof, or a certified copy of the record or instrument shall be prima facie evidence of the contents of such instrument and its due execution.

CPLR

1981 AMENDMENTS

L. 1981, ch. 199, eff. June 9, 1981, amended CPLR 7705.

§ 7706. Order on filing instrument settling account.

Where an instrument described in section seven thousand seven hundred five of this article has been executed by all of the persons who would be necessary parties in a proceeding under section seven thousand seven hundred one of this article, none of whom is under the disability of infancy or incompetency, one or more of the trustees may present to the court a petition showing the names and post office addresses of all persons interested in the trust, whether or not the trust has been fully executed, that the petitioner has fully accounted and made full disclosure in writing of his administration of the trust to all persons interested, and praying that his intermediate or final account be judicially settled. There shall be filed with the petition the instrument described in section seven thousand seven hundred five of this article. The court may thereupon make an order settling the petitioner's account and discharging the petitioner and sureties on his bond, if any, from any further liability to all persons interested therein.

1981 AMENDMENTS

L. 1981, ch. 199, eff. June 9, 1981, added a new section 7706 to the CPLR.

Article 78

PROCEEDING AGAINST BODY OR OFFICER

SUMMARY OF ARTICLE

CPLR

§ 7801. Nature of proceeding.

Relief previously obtained by writs of certiorari to review, mandamus or prohibition shall be obtained in a proceeding under this article. Wherever in any statute reference is made to a writ or order of certiorari, mandamus or prohibition, such reference shall, so far as applicable, be deemed to refer to the proceeding authorized by this article. Except where otherwise provided by law, a proceeding under this article shall not be used to challenge a determination:

1. which is not final or can be adequately reviewed by appeal to a court or to some other body or officer or where the body or officer making the determination is expressly authorized by statute to rehear the matter upon the petitioner's application unless the determination to be reviewed was made upon a rehearing, or a rehearing has been denied, or the time within which the petitioner can procure a rehearing has elapsed; or

2. which was made in a civil action or criminal matter unless it is an order summarily punishing a contempt committed in the presence of the court.

§ 7802. Parties.

(a) Definition of "body or officer." The expression "body or officer" includes every court, tribunal, board, corporation, officer, or other person, or aggregation of persons, whose action may be affected by a proceeding under this article.

(b) Persons whose terms of office have expired; successors. Whenever necessary to accomplish substantial justice, a proceeding under this article may be maintained against an officer exercising judicial or quasi-judicial functions, or member of a body whose term of office has expired. Any party may join the successor of such officer or member of a body or other person having custody of the record of proceedings under review.

(c) Prohibition in favor of another. Where the proceeding is brought to restrain a body or officer from proceeding without or in excess of jurisdiction in favor of another, the latter shall be joined as a party.

(d) Other interested persons. The court may direct that notice of the proceeding be given to any person. It may allow other interested persons to intervene.

1981 AMENDMENTS

L. 1981, ch. 502, eff. July 15, 1981, amended CPLR 7802(b) by deleting the requirement of serving a notice of a proceeding under Article 78 upon the attorney-general when it is brought against an officer exercising judicial or quasi-judicial functions or a member of a body whose term of office has expired. That service requirement is now found at CPLR 7804(c).

§ 7803. Questions raised.

The only questions that may be raised in a proceeding under this article are:

1. whether the body or officer failed to perform a duty enjoined upon it by law; or

2. whether the body or officer proceeded, is proceeding or is about to proceed without or in excess of jurisdiction; or

3. whether a determination was made in violation of lawful procedure, was affected by an error of law or was arbitrary and capricious or an abuse of discretion, including abuse of discretion as to the measure or mode of penalty or discipline imposed; or

4. whether a determination made as a result of a hearing held, and at which evidence was taken, pursuant to direction by law is, on the entire record, supported by substantial evidence.

5. A proceeding to review the final determination or order of the state review officer pursuant to subdivision three of section forty-four hundred four of the education law shall be brought pursuant to article four of this chapter and such subdivision; provided, however, that the provisions of this article shall not apply to any proceeding commenced on or after the effective date of this subdivision.

2003 AMENDMENTS

L. 2003, ch. 492, eff. Sept.1, 2003, added 7803 (5).

§ 7804. Procedure.

(a) Special proceeding. A proceeding under this article is a special proceeding.

(b) Where proceeding brought. A proceeding under this article shall be brought in the supreme court in the county specified in subdivision (b) of section 506 except as that subdivision otherwise provides.

(c) Time for service of notice of petition and answer. Unless the court grants an order to show cause to be served in lieu of a notice of petition at a time and in a manner specified therein, a notice of petition, together with the petition and affidavits specified in the notice, shall be served on any adverse party at least twenty days before the time at which the petition is noticed to be heard. An answer and supporting affidavits, if any, shall be served at least five days before such time. A

CPLR

reply, together with supporting affidavits, if any, shall be served at least one day before such time. In the case of a proceeding pursuant to this article against a state body or officers, or against members of a state body or officers whose terms have expired as authorized by subdivision (b) of section 7802 of this chapter, commenced either by order to show cause or notice of petition, in addition to the service thereof provided in this section, the order to show cause or notice of petition must be served upon the attorney general by delivery of such order or notice to an assistant attorney general at an office of the attorney general in the county in which venue of the proceeding is designated, or if there is no office of the attorney general within such county, at the office of the attorney general nearest such county. In the case of a proceeding pursuant to this article against members of bodies of governmental subdivisions whose terms have expired as authorized by subdivision (b) of section 7802 of this chapter, the order to show cause or notice of petition must be served upon such governmental subdivision in accordance with section 311 of this chapter.

(d) Pleadings. There shall be a verified petition, which may be accompanied by affidavits or other written proof. Where there is an adverse party there shall be a verified answer, which must state pertinent and material facts showing the grounds of the respondent's action complained of. There shall be a reply to a counterclaim denominated as such and there shall be a reply to new matter in the answer or where the accuracy of proceedings annexed to the answer is disputed. The court may permit such other pleadings as are authorized in an action upon such terms as it may specify.

(e) Answering affidavits; record to be filed; default. The body or officer shall file with the answer a certified transcript of the record of the proceedings under consideration, unless such a transcript has already been filed with the clerk of the court. The respondent shall also serve and submit with the answer affidavits or other written proof showing such evidentiary facts as shall entitle him to a trial of any issue of fact. The court may order the body or officer to supply any defect or omission in the answer, transcript or an answering affidavit. Statements made in the answer, transcript or an answering affidavit are not conclusive upon the petitioner. Should the body or officer fail either to file and serve an answer or to move to dismiss, the court may either issue a judgment in favor of the petitioner or order that an answer be submitted.

(f) Objections in point of law. The respondent may raise an objection in point of law by setting it forth in his answer or by a motion to dismiss the petition, made upon notice within the time allowed for answer. If the motion is denied, the court shall permit the respondent to answer, upon such terms as may be just; and unless the order specifies otherwise, such answer shall be served and filed within five days after service of the order with notice of entry; and the petitioner may re-notice the matter for hearing upon two days' notice, or the respondent may re-notice the matter for hearing upon service of the answer upon seven days' notice. The petitioner may raise an objection in point of law to new matter contained in the answer by setting it forth in his reply or by moving to strike such matter on the day the petition is noticed or re-noticed to be heard.

(g) Hearing and determination; transfer to appellate division. Where the substantial evidence issue specified in question four of section 7803 is not raised, the court in which the proceeding is commenced shall itself dispose of the issues in the proceeding. Where such an issue is raised, the court shall first dispose of such other objections as could terminate the proceeding, including but not limited to lack of jurisdiction, statute of limitations and res judicata, without reaching the substantial evidence issue. If the determination of the other objections does not terminate the proceeding, the court shall make an order directing that it be transferred for disposition to a term of the appellate division held within the judicial department embracing the county in which the proceeding was commenced. When the proceeding comes before it, whether by appeal or transfer, the appellate division shall dispose of all issues in the proceeding, or, if the papers are insufficient, it may remit the proceeding.

(h) Trial. If a triable issue of fact is raised in a proceeding under this article, it shall be tried forthwith. Where the proceeding was transferred to the appellate division, the issue of fact shall be tried by a referee or by a justice of the supreme court and the verdict, report or decision rendered after the trial shall be returned to, and the order thereon made by, the appellate division.

(i) Appearance by judicial officer. Notwithstanding any other provision of law, where a proceeding is brought under this article

CPLR

against a justice, judge, referee or judicial hearing officer appointed by a court and (1) it is brought by a party to a pending action or proceeding, and (2) it is based upon an act or acts performed by the respondent in that pending action or proceeding either granting or denying relief sought by a party thereto, and (3) the respondent is not a named party to the pending action or proceeding, in addition to service on the respondent, the petitioner shall serve a copy of the petition together with copies of all moving papers upon all other parties to the pending action or proceeding. All such parties shall be designated as respondents. Unless ordered by the court upon application of a party the respondent justice, judge, referee or judicial hearing officer need not appear in the proceeding in which case the allegations of the petition shall not be deemed admitted or denied by him. Upon election of the justice, judge, referee, or judicial hearing officer not to appear, any ruling, order or judgment of the court in such proceeding shall bind said respondent. If such respondent does appear he shall respond to the petition and shall be entitled to be represented by the attorney general. If such respondent does not elect to appear all other parties shall be given notice thereof.

5. A proceeding to review the final determination or order of the state review officer pursuant to subdivision three of section forty-four hundred four of the education law shall be brought pursuant to article four of this chapter and such subdivision; provided, however, that the provisions of this article shall not apply to any proceeding commenced on or after the effective date of this subdivision.

2003 AMENDMENTS

L. 2003, ch. 492, eff. Sept. 1, 2003, and shall apply to proceedings commenced on or after such effective date. Amended CPLR 7803 by adding Subd. (5).

1993 AMENDMENTS

L. 1993, ch. 202, eff. July 6, 1993, amended subdivision (f) by allowing respondents to "re-notice the matter for hearing upon service of the answer upon seven days' notice."

1990 AMENDMENTS

L. 1990, ch. 575, eff. Jan. 1, 1991, amended CPLR 7804(g) to require the court, when the substantial evidence issue specified in CPLR 7803(4) is raised, to first dispose of those objections that could terminate the proceeding, such as lack of jurisdiction, statute of limitations and res judicata, before reaching the substantial evidence issue; and deleting the words "the court may, however, itself pass on objections in point of law."

1987 AMENDMENTS

L. 1987, ch. 384, eff. July 23, 1987, amended CPLR 7804(i), making provisions applicable to proceedings brought by a party to a pending action or proceeding, and eliminating the requirement that the proceeding be brought by a party to a "pending criminal action" or proceeding "involving the custody of a child."

1986 AMENDMENTS

L. 1986, ch. 355, eff. July 17, 1986, amended CPLR 7804 (b) and (h) by deleting references to special term and trial term.

1983 AMENDMENTS

L. 1983, ch. 840, eff. April 1, 1983, amended CPLR 7804(i).

1981 AMENDMENTS

L. 1981, ch. 502, eff. July 15, 1981, amended subdivision (c) of CPLR 7804 by expanding the kinds of Article 78 proceedings wherein service of initiatory papers must be made upon the attorney-general to include proceedings against members of a state body or officers whose terms have expired as authorized by CPLR 7802(b) and by requiring that in any proceeding pursuant to Article 78 which is brought against a member of a governmental subdivision whose term has expired as authorized by CPLR 7802(b), the order to show cause or notice of petition must be served upon such governmental subdivision in accordance with CPLR 311.

L. 1981, ch. 580, eff. Aug. 14, 1981, amended CPLR 7804 by adding a new subdivision (i).

1972 AMENDMENTS

L. 1972, ch. 455, eff. May 24, 1972, and ch. 752, eff. May 30, 1972, amended CPLR 7804(c) by providing that in an Article 78 proceeding against a state body of officers, the order to show cause or notice of petition must be served on the attorney general.

1965 AMENDMENTS

L. 1965, ch. 814, eff. Sept. 1, 1965, amended subds. (d) and (e).

Amendments recommended by the Judicial Conference Feb. 1, 1965, Report to the Legislature: "Article 78 proceedings under the C.P.A. were summary in nature. The recommended change restores language inadvertently omitted in the CPLR, and permits the disposition of these proceedings on the return day expeditiously as an application for summary judgment, in accordance with practice under the C.P.A. See the 1937 *Report of the Judicial Council* (page 129 et seq.)"

§ 7805.   Stay.

On the motion of any party or on its own initiative, the court may stay further proceedings, or the enforcement of any determination under review, upon terms including notice, security and payment of costs, except that the enforcement of an order or judgment granted by the appellate division in a proceeding under this article may be stayed only by order of the appellate division or the court of appeals. Unless otherwise ordered, security given on a stay is effective in favor of a person subsequently joined as a party under section 7802.

§ 7806.   Judgment.

The judgment may grant the petitioner the relief to which he is entitled, or may dismiss the proceeding either on the merits or with leave to renew. If the proceeding was brought to review a determination, the judgment may annul or confirm the determination in whole or in part, or modify it, and may direct or prohibit specified action by the respondent. Any restitution or damages granted to the petitioner must be incidental to the primary relief sought by the petitioner, and must be such as he might otherwise recover on the same set of facts in a separate action or proceeding suable in the supreme court against the same body or officer in its or his official capacity.

Article 80
FEES

SUMMARY OF ARTICLE

CPLR

(b)   Legible copies.

(c)   Notice to county clerk.

(d)   Exemptions for state or city of New York.

(e)   Size of page and type.

(f)   Copies of records.

§ 8020.   County clerks as clerks of court.

(a)   Placing cause on calendar.

(b)   Calendar fee for transferred cause, joint trial, retrial, or separate trial.

(c)   Filing demand for jury trial.

(d)   Filing a stipulation of settlement or a voluntary discontinuance.

(e)   Jury fee for transferred cause, joint trial, retrial, or separate trial.

(f)   Certification, exemplification, and copies of papers.

(g)   Searches.

(h)   Production of court records.

§ 8021.   County clerks other than as clerks of court.

(a)   Services in connection with papers or instruments relating to real property and not filed under the uniform commercial code.

(b)   Filing, other than in connection with papers or instruments relating to real property or filed under the uniform commercial code.

(c)   Certification, issuing certificates, other papers and copies of papers, records, and related services, other than in connection with papers or instruments relating to real property or filed under the uniform commercial code.

(d)   Searches of records not filed under the uniform commercial code.

(e)   Production of records.

(f)   Services rendered pursuant to part four of article nine of the uniform commercial code.

(g)   Services rendered in relation to federal tax liens filed pursuant to the lien law.

§ 8001. Persons subpoenaed; examination before trial; transcripts of records.

(a) Persons subpoenaed. Any person whose attendance is compelled by a subpoena, whether or not actual testimony is taken, shall receive for each day's attendance fifteen dollars for attendance fees and twenty-three cents as travel expenses for each mile to the place of attendance from the place where he or she was served, and return. There shall be no mileage fee for travel wholly within a city.

(b) Persons subpoenaed upon an examination before trial. If a witness who is not a party, or agent or employee of a party, is subpoenaed to give testimony, or produce books, papers and other things at an examination before trial, he shall receive an additional three dollars for each day's attendance.

(c) Transcripts of records. Wherever the preparation of a transcript of records is required in order to comply with a subpoena, the person subpoenaed shall receive an additional fee of ten cents per folio upon demand.

1988 AMENDMENTS

L. 1988, ch. 23, eff. Jan. 1, 1989, amended subdivision (a) to increase subpoenaed-witness fees from two to fifteen dollars for attendance, and from eight to twenty-three cents per mile for travel expenses; and to make statute gender neutral.

§ 8002. Stenographers.

Unless otherwise provided by law, a stenographer is entitled, for a copy fully written out from his or her stenographic notes of testimony or other proceedings taken in a court, and furnished upon request to a party or his or her attorney, to the fee set forth in the rules promulgated by the chief administrator of the courts.

2000 AMENDMENTS

L. 2000, ch. 279, eff. Aug. 16, 2000.

1984 AMENDMENTS

L. 1984, ch. 846, eff. Aug. 5, 1984, amended CPLR 8002 by providing that the fee shall be that set forth in the rules promulgated by the chief administrator. The new fee is applicable only to transcripts ordered on or after the date of the formal promulgation of the rules and regulations by the chief administrator of the courts. The former fee was 30 cents per folio.

1973 AMENDMENTS

L. 1973, ch. 458, eff. Sept. 1, 1973, amended CPLR 8002 by increasing the fee to thirty cents for each folio.

1965 AMENDMENTS

L. 1965, ch. 980, eff. Sept. 1, 1965, increased the fee to twenty cents per folio.

§ 8003. Referees.

(a) Generally. A referee is entitled, for each day spent in the business of the reference, to fifty dollars unless a different compensation is fixed by the court or by the consent in writing of all parties not in default for failure to appear or plead.

(b) Upon sale of real property. A referee appointed to sell real property pursuant to a judgment is entitled to the same fees and disbursements as those allowed to a sheriff. Where a referee is required to take security upon a sale, or to distribute, apply, or ascertain and report upon the distribution or application of any of the proceeds of the sale, he or she is also entitled to one-half of the commissions upon the amount secured, distributed or applied as are allowed by law to an executor or administrator for receiving and paying out money. Commissions in excess of fifty dollars shall not be allowed upon a sum bid by a party, and applied upon that party's judgment, without being paid to the referee. A referee's compensation, including commissions, upon a sale pursuant to a judgment in any action cannot exceed five hundred dollars, unless the property sold for fifty thousand dollars or more, in which event the referee may receive such additional compensation as to the court may seem proper.

(c) This section shall not apply to judicial hearing officers who have been designated referees.

1996 AMENDMENTS

L. 1996, ch. 225, eff. June 26, 1996, amended the final sentence of subdivision (b) to change the phrase "an action to foreclose a mortgage" to"any action"; to delete the phrase "two hundred dollars, or pursuant to any other judgment," prior to the phrase "five hundred dollars"; to increase the sum of ten thousand dollars to fifty thousand dollars; and to make the section gender neutral.

1983 AMENDMENTS

L. 1983, ch. 840, eff. April 1, 1983, added CPLR 8003(c).

1976 AMENDMENTS

L. 1976, ch. 700, eff. Aug. 23, 1976, amended CPLR 8003 by increasing fees for referees.

§ 8004. Commissions of receivers.

(a) Generally. A receiver, except where otherwise prescribed by statute, is entitled to such commissions, not exceeding five percent upon the sums received and disbursed by him, as the court by which he is appointed allows, but if in any case the commissions, so computed, do not amount to one hundred dollars, the court, may allow the receiver such a sum, not exceeding one hundred dollars, as shall be commensurate with the services he rendered.

(b) Allowance where funds depleted. If, at the termination of a receivership, there are no funds in the hands of the receiver, the court, upon application of the receiver, may fix the compensation of the receiver and the fees of his attorney, in accordance with the respective services rendered, and may direct the party who moved for the appointment of the receiver to pay such sums, in addition to the necessary expenditures incurred by the receiver. This subdivision shall not apply to a receiver or his attorney appointed pursuant to article twenty-three-a of the general business law.

CROSS REFERENCES

Article 23-A of the General Business Law, referred to in Subd. (b), *above,* deals with fraudulent practices with respect to stocks, bonds and other securities.

§ 8005. Commissions of trustees; advance payment of fees of an attorney-trustee.

A trustee of an express trust shall be entitled to commissions and the allowance of his expenses and compensation and, if he be an attorney admitted to practice in this state, to the allowance of a sum on account of his compensation for legal services theretofore rendered to the trust, in the same manner and amount as that provided by sections twenty-one hundred eleven, twenty-three hundred eight and twenty-three hundred eleven of the surrogate's court procedure act for testamentary trustees, if the trust was established on or before August thirty-first, nineteen hundred fifty-six, or as that provided by sections twenty-one hundred eleven, twenty-three hundred nine and twenty-three hundred eleven of the surrogate's court procedure act for testamentary trustees, if the trust was established after August thirty-first, nineteen hundred fifty-six or as that provided for by sections twenty-one hundred eleven and twenty-three hundred eleven for testamentary trustees and twenty-three hundred twelve of the surrogate's court procedure act except that the statements required thereunder to be furnished annually in order to retain certain annual commissions need be furnished during the settlor's lifetime only to beneficiaries currently receiving income. The court shall make such determinations and allowances as the named sections require or authorize the surrogate to make, and the term "will" used in those sections shall be construed to mean the instrument creating the trust and the phrase "the court from which his letters were issued" shall be construed to mean the court having jurisdiction of the trust.

1984 AMENDMENTS

L. 1984, ch. 936, eff. Aug. 6, 1984, amended CPLR 8005 by adding references to SCPA §§ 2211, 2311 and 2312. L. 1984, ch. 936, § 12, reads as follows:

§ 12. This act shall take effect immediately, and shall apply to any trust whether in existence on or after the effective date of this act provided, however, nothing contained in this act shall be deemed to change, alter, reduce, eliminate or otherwise affect the right of any trustee to any receiving or paying commission or annual commission which such trustee has earned or is entitled to claim or be paid immediately prior to the effective date of this act and further provided however that an individual trustee shall continue to receive commissions in the manner provided for an individual trustee under sections twenty-three hundred eight and twenty-three hundred nine of the surrogate's court procedure act, as the case may be, in effect immediately before the effective date of this act until the end of the then current trust year, and thereafter, at the rates then in effect under such sections.

1980 AMENDMENTS

L. 1980, ch. 185, eff. June 2, 1980, amended CPLR 8005 to provide for the advance payment of fees to an attorney who is also a trustee of an express trust.

1972 AMENDMENTS

L. 1972, ch. 172, eff. April 25, 1972, amended CPLR 8005 be deleting references to Surrogate's Court Act §§ 285-a, 285-b, and 285-d and substituting references to Surrogate's Court Procedure Act §§ 2308, 2309, and 2311.

1965 AMENDMENTS

L. 1965, ch. 542, eff. June 1, 1965, amended section.

Amendment recommended jointly by the Temporary State Commission on the Law of Estates and the Judicial Conference. The phrase "on the settlement of the account" was eliminated to make it clear that the trustees are entitled to commissions not only on the settlement of the account but also annually in the same manner and amount as under the Surrogate's Court Act. Reference to § 285-d was inserted to enable inter vivos trustees to make an ex parte application for advance payment of commissions in the same manner as testamentary trustees under the Surrogate's Court Act. Reference to annual statements was inserted to make it clear that an inter vivos trustee must make the same broad disclosures to beneficiaries as testamentary trustees except that while the settlor of the trust is alive the statements need only be furnished to the beneficiaries currently receiving income. See Report No. 7.11B [Leg. Doc. (1964) No. 19, p. 691] and 1964 Supplement to same.

§ 8006. Premiums on undertakings by fiduciaries.

A receiver, assignee, guardian, trustee, committee, conservator or person appointed under section one hundred eleven of the real property law or under section twenty of the personal property law, required by law to give an undertaking as such, may include as a part of his necessary expenses such reasonable sum, not exceeding one percent per annum upon the amount of such undertaking paid his surety thereon, as the court appointing him shall allow.

CROSS REFERENCES

Real Prop. L. § 111 and Pers. Prop. L. § 20 were repealed by EPTL § 14-1.1 (L. 1966, ch. 952, eff. Sept. 1, 1967) and their provisions were reenacted, with minor revisions, as **EPTL §7-2.3.**

1981 AMENDMENTS

L. 1981, ch. 115, eff. May 18, 1981, amended CPLR 8006 by adding a reference to a conservator.

§ 8007. Printers.

Except where otherwise prescribed by law, the proprietor of a newspaper is entitled for publishing a summons, notice, order or other advertisement, required to be published by law or by the order of any court, or of the clerk of a court, to twenty-nine cents per line of a column width not less than ten pica ems, provided that in computing such charge per line the line shall average at least five words for each insertion in newspapers having a circulation of less than two thousand five hundred; twenty-nine and one-half cents per line for newspapers having two thousand five hundred or more circulation and less than five thousand; thirty and one-half cents per line for newspapers having five thousand or more circulation and less than seven thousand five hundred; thirty-one and one-half cents per line for newspapers having seven thousand five hundred or more circulation and less than ten thousand; thirty-two and one-half cents per line for newspapers having ten thousand or more circulation and less than fifteen thousand; and three and one-half cents per line, in addition to the thirty-two and one-half cents for the initial fifteen thousand circulation, for each additional five thousand circulation up to thirty-five thousand circulation and one and one-half cents per line for each additional five thousand possessed by a newspaper. To all of the above rates nine cents per line shall be added to the initial insertion charge of each separate advertisement. To all of the above rates for the initial insertion eight cents per line shall also be added for tabular matter or intricate composition. In reckoning line charges allowance shall be made for date lines, paragraph endings, titles, signatures and similar short lines as full lines where the same are set to conform to the usual rules of composition. Display advertising shall be charged agate measurement (fourteen lines to each inch), ten to thirteen pica ems wide, depending on the makeup of the newspaper publishing such copy. This rate shall not apply to any newspaper printed, principally circulated or having its principal office in the counties of New York or Bronx within the first judicial district or in the county of Kings within the second judicial district or in the county of Richmond within the thirteenth judicial district or in the county of Nassau within the tenth judicial district or in the county of Queens within the eleventh judicial district or in the county of Westchester within the ninth judicial district or in any city having a population of over one hundred seventy-five thousand inhabitants within the eighth judicial district, where the rate for such publication may be equal to but shall not exceed the regularly established classified advertising rate of such newspapers. Every newspaper making claim for compensation under the provisions of this section must be established at least one year and entered in the post office as second class matter.

CPLR

2009 AMENDMENTS

L. 2009, ch. 450, eff. Sept. 16, 2009.

1991 AMENDMENTS

L. 1991, ch. 449, eff. Sept. 1, 1991.

1990 AMENDMENTS

L. 1990, ch. 776, eff. Sept. 1, 1990.

1988 AMENDMENTS

L. 1988, ch. 354, eff. Aug. 28, 1988, amended 8007 to exempt Westchester County from the fee structure for display advertising of legal notices.

1984 AMENDMENTS

L. 1984, ch. 679, eff. Sept. 1, 1984.

1980 AMENDMENTS

L. 1980, ch. 500, eff. Sept. 1, 1980.

1979 AMENDMENTS

L. 1979, ch. 719, eff. Sept. 1, 1979.

1974 AMENDMENTS

L. 1974, ch. 691, sec. 2, eff. Jan. 1, 1975.

1971 AMENDMENTS

L. 1971, ch. 1198, eff. Jan. 1, 1972.

1966 AMENDMENTS

L. 1966, ch. 885 and ch. 458, eff. Jan. 1, 1967.

§ 8008. Fees and expenses of officer to be paid before transmission of paper.

Each provision of law requiring a judge, clerk or other officer to transmit a paper to another officer, for the benefit of a party, is to be construed as requiring the transmission only at the request of the person so to be benefited, and upon payment by him of the fees allowed by law for the paper transmitted, or any copy or certificate connected therewith, and the expenses specified in section sixty-eight of the public officers law.

CROSS REFERENCES

See **Public Officers Law § 68** in Appendix, *below.*

§ 8009. Oaths; acknowledgments; certification or exemplification.

Any authorized officer is entitled, for the services specified to the following fees:

1. for administering an oath or affirmation, and certifying it when required, except where another fee is specially prescribed by statute, two dollars;

2. for taking and certifying the acknowledgment or proof of the execution of a written instrument, two dollars for one person and two dollars for each additional person, and two dollars for swearing each witness thereto; and

3. for certifying or exemplifying a typewritten or printed copy of any document, paper, book or record in his custody, twenty-five cents for each folio with a minimum of one dollar.

1991 AMENDMENTS

L. 1991, ch. 143, eff. July 23, 1991.

1972 AMENDMENTS

L. 1972, ch. 734 and ch. 735, eff. July 1, 1972.

§ 8010. County treasurers.

The treasurer of a county or the commissioner of finance of the city of New York is entitled for the services specified to the following fees:

1. two per cent upon a sum of money paid out of court by him;

2. one-half of one per cent upon a sum of money invested by him;

3. two per cent of the par value of investments transferred or assigned out of court by him, when the investments have been made by him;

4. two per cent of the par value of securities deposited into court and received by him, to be paid at the time of the deposit by the parties making it; and

5. one dollar for each certificate issued by him certifying as to the amount of deposit to the credit of court funds.

2004 AMENDMENTS

L. 2004, ch. 520, § 1, eff. Sept. 28, 2004, amended CPLR 8010.

CPLR

1978 AMENDMENTS

L. 1978, ch. 655, eff. July 24, 1978, amended CPLR 8010.

1970 AMENDMENTS

L. 1970, ch. 547, eff. July 1, 1970, amended subparagraph (5).

1969 AMENDMENTS

L. 1969, ch. 407, eff. May 9, 1969.

1964 AMENDMENTS

L. 1964, ch. 576, eff. April 16, 1964.

§ 8011. Fixed fees of sheriffs.

For the services specified, a sheriff is entitled to the following fees and, where indicated, these shall be paid in advance.

(a) Order of attachment.

1. For receiving an order of attachment, entering it in the appropriate books, and return when required, fifteen dollars, in advance.

2. For levying upon real or personal property, forty dollars, in advance.

3. For each additional levy upon real or personal property by virtue of an order of attachment, forty dollars, in advance.

4. For serving a copy of an order of attachment on a defendant, and for serving a copy on each additional defendant, fifteen dollars, in advance.

5. For serving a summons with or without a complaint, fifteen dollars, in advance.

6. For making and filing a description of real property, or an inventory of personal property, levied upon by virtue of an order of attachment, or an estimate of the value thereof, fifteen dollars.

7. Mileage for services covered in paragraphs two, three and four of this subdivision, in advance, provided, however, that where the services covered in such paragraphs are performed at the same time and place, there shall be only one mileage fee.

(b) Property execution.

1. For receiving an execution against property, entering it in the

appropriate books, and return when required, fifteen dollars, in advance, except that in an execution which arises out of an action brought pursuant to article eighteen of the uniform district court act, article eighteen of the uniform city court act, article eighteen of the New York city civil court act or article eighteen of the uniform justice court act, the fees provided in this subdivision shall not be collected in advance.

2. For levying upon property by virtue of an execution, fifteen dollars.

3. For making an inventory of property levied upon by virtue of an execution, fifteen dollars.

4. Mileage for services covered in paragraphs two and three of this subdivision, in advance, provided however, that where the services covered in such paragraphs are performed at the same time, there shall be only one mileage fee.

(c) Income execution; service upon judgment debtor.

1. For receiving an income execution, entering it in appropriate books, and return when required, fifteen dollars, in advance.

2. For serving the income execution upon the judgment debtor, fifteen dollars, in advance.

3. Mileage for service covered in paragraph two of this subdivision, unless such execution is served by mail.

(d) Income execution; levy upon default or failure to serve judgment debtor.

1. For serving an income execution, entering it in the appropriate books, and return when required, fifteen dollars, in advance.

2. For levying upon the money that the judgment debtor is receiving or will receive, fifteen dollars, in advance.

3. Mileage for services covered in paragraph two of this subdivision unless such levy is made by mail.

(e) Recovery of chattel.

1. For receiving an order to recover chattel, entering it in the appropriate books, and return when required, fifteen dollars, in

advance.

2. For executing the order of seizure against the defendant's chattel or chattels, seventy-five dollars, in advance.

3. For executing the order of seizure against the chattel or chattels of an additional defendant or any other person in whose possession said chattel or chattels may be found, forty dollars, in advance.

4. For serving an additional copy of the required papers, fifteen dollars, in advance.

5. For serving the summons with or without a complaint, fifteen dollars, in advance.

6. Mileage for services covered in paragraphs two, three, four and five of this subdivision, in advance, provided however, that where the services covered in such paragraphs are performed at the same time and place, there shall be only one mileage fee.

(f) Summary proceeding.

1. Notice of petition and petition.

(i) For receiving a notice of petition and petition, obtaining an index number when required, entering it in the appropriate books, and return, fifteen dollars, in advance.

(ii) For serving the notice of petition on a tenant or other person in possession, fifteen dollars, in advance.

(iii) For serving the notice of petition on each additional tenant, undertenant, subtenant, person or persons in possession, or person or persons not in possession to be served, fifteen dollars, in advance.

(iv) For making an affidavit of military or nonmilitary service, fifteen dollars for each affidavit, in advance.

(v) Mileage for services covered in subparagraph (ii) of this paragraph, and where person or persons named in the petition are to be served at an address or addresses other than the premises described in the petition, additional mileage shall be paid, in advance, except where two or more notices of petition are to be served at the same time, within the same site or location, there shall be only one mileage fee.

2. Warrant of eviction or any mandate requiring delivery of possession of real property and removal of person or persons in possession.

(i) For requisitioning, receiving, entering in the appropriate books, and for the return of a warrant of eviction or any other mandate, fifteen dollars, in advance.

(ii) For service of notice of eviction on a person or persons to be served, fifteen dollars for each person to be served, in advance.

(iii) Mileage of services covered in subparagraph (ii) of this paragraph, in advance, except where two or more notices of eviction are to be served at the same time, within the same site or location, there shall be only one mileage fee.ge shall be paid, in advance, except where two or more notices of petition are to be served at the

(iv) For executing a warrant of eviction or any mandate requiring him or her to put a person in possession of real property and removing person or persons in possession, seventy-five dollars, in advance.

(v) Mileage for services covered in subparagraph (iv) of this paragraph, in advance.

(g) Sales.

1. For posting of notice, including advertising real or personal property for sale by virtue of an execution, order of attachment, or other mandate, or in pursuance of a direction contained in a judgment, or for a notice of postponement of a sale, fifteen dollars.

2. For drawing and executing a conveyance upon a sale of real property, twenty dollars, to be paid by the grantee, in advance.

3. For attending a sale of real or personal property, fifteen dollars.

4. For conducting a sale of real or personal property, fifteen

dollars.

5. Mileage for services covered in paragraphs three and four of this subdivision provided, however, that where the services covered in such paragraphs are performed at the same time and place, there shall be only one mileage fee.

(h) Summons, subpoenas and other mandates.

1. For serving a summons, with or without a complaint or notice, for serving a subpoena, or for serving civil process, fifteen dollars, in advance.

2. For serving or executing an order of arrest, or any other mandate for the service or execution of which no other fee is specifically prescribed by law, forty-five dollars, in advance, except that when a court has directed the service of an order of protection, there shall be no fee for service of such order and of any related orders or papers to be served simultaneously.

3. Mileage for services subject to fees under paragraphs one and two of this subdivision, in advance.

4. For receiving a precept issued by commissioners appointed to inquire concerning the incompetency of a person, the fee allowed the clerk by subdivision (a) of section eight thousand twenty of this article for placing a cause on the calendar, and for notifying a county clerk or commissioner of jurors pursuant to such a precept, the fee, if any, allowed the clerk by subdivision (c) of section eight thousand twenty of this article for filing a demand for jury trial.

(j) Prisoners.

1. For each person committed to or discharged from prison, ten dollars, in advance, to be paid by the person at whose instance he or she is imprisoned.

2. For attending before an officer for the purpose of surrendering a prisoner, or receiving into custody a prisoner surrendered, in exoneration of his or her bail, ten dollars, for all his or her services upon such a surrender or receipt.

(k) Jurors; view; constables' services.

1. For notifying jurors to attend upon a writ of inquiry, two dollars and fifty cents for each juror notified, including the making and return of the inquisition, when required; and for attending a jury when required in such a case, twenty-eight dollars.

2. For attending a view, ten dollars for each day.

3. For any services which may be rendered by a constable, other than those specifically provided for in this section, section eight thousand twelve or eight thousand thirteen of this article, to the same fees as are allowed by law to a constable for those services.

2007 AMENDMENTS

L. 2007, ch. 36, eff. Aug. 19, 2007, amended CPLR 8011 (h) by providing that where the court directs the service of an order of protection there is to be no fee for service of the order and any related papers served simultaneaously.

2003 AMENDMENTS

L. 2003, ch. 11, §§ 1, 2, eff. February 24, 2003, amending subds. (h)(1) and (h)(2)

2002 AMENDMENTS

L. 2002, ch. 655, eff. Feb. 24, 2003, amended CPLR 8011.

1996 AMENDMENTS

L. 1996, ch. 190, eff. January 1, 1997, amended subparagraph (b)(1) by adding a reference to Article 18 of the Uniform Justice Court Act.

1992 AMENDMENTS

L. 1992, ch. 55, eff. April 10, 1992, added this section, replacing former CPLR 8011, 8011-a and 8011-b.

§ 8011-a. [Repealed.]

§ 8011-b. [Repealed.]

§ 8012. Mileage fees, poundage fees, additional compensation, and limitation on compensation of sheriffs.

(a) Mileage fees. A sheriff is entitled to the current federal internal revenue service mileage reimbursement rate for each mile necessarily travelled in performing the following services, payable in advance:

1. in serving or executing a mandate upon or against one person, or upon or against two or more persons in the course of one journey, computed from the nearest office of the sheriff in the county to the

place of service or execution, and return;

2. in serving or executing two or more mandates in one action upon or against one person at one time, computed from the nearest office of the sheriff in the county to the place of service or execution, and return; and

3. in attending a view, computed from the nearest office of the sheriff in the county to the place of attendance, and return.

(b) Poundage fees.

1. A sheriff is entitled, for collecting money by virtue of an execution, an order of attachment, or an attachment for the payment of money in an action, or a warrant for the collection of money issued by the comptroller or by a county treasurer or by any agency of the state or a political subdivision thereof, or for collecting a fine by virtue of a commitment for civil contempt, to poundage of, in the counties within the city of New York, five per cent of the sum collected and in all other counties, five percent upon the first two hundred fifty thousand dollars collected, and three percent upon the residue of the sum collected.

2. Where a settlement is made after a levy by virtue of service of an execution, the sheriff is entitled to poundage upon the judgment or settlement amount, whichever is less. Where an execution is vacated or set aside after levy, the sheriff is entitled to poundage upon the value of the property levied upon, not exceeding the amount specified in the execution, and the court may order the party liable therefore to pay the same to the sheriff.

3. Where a settlement is made, either before or after judgment, after a levy by virtue of service of an order of attachment, the sheriff is entitled to poundage upon the judgment or settlement amount, whichever is less. Where an order of attachment is vacated or set aside after levy, the sheriff is entitled to poundage upon the value of the property levied upon, not exceeding the amount specified in the order of attachment, and the court may order the party at whose instance the order of attachment was granted to pay the same to the sheriff. Where an order of attachment is otherwise discharged by order of the court, the sheriff is entitled to the same poundage, to be paid by the party at whose instance the order of attachment is

discharged, and the sheriff is entitled to retain the property levied upon until the poundage is paid. The maximum amount upon which poundage shall be computed, if such a settlement is made or the order of attachment is vacated or set aside, is one million dollars.

4. Where a settlement is made (i) after service of an income execution upon the debtor pursuant to subdivision (d) of section fifty-two hundred thirty-one of this chapter or upon the garnishee pursuant to subdivision (e) of section fifty-two hundred thirty-one of this chapter, or (ii) after issuance of a property execution pursuant to section fifty-two hundred thirty of this chapter and levy against personal or real property pursuant to section fifty-two hundred thirty- two or fifty-two hundred thirty-five of this chapter, the sheriff is entitled to poundage upon the judgment amount or settlement amount, whichever is less. Where an income or property execution is vacated or set aside after levy, the sheriff is entitled to poundage upon the value of the property levied upon, not exceeding the amount specified in the execution, and the court may order the party liable therefor to pay the same to the sheriff.

5. A sheriff who brings an action in a court of competent jurisdiction to collect such amount provided for in this subdivision may also be awarded reasonable attorney's fees and court costs.

(c) Additional compensation. A sheriff is entitled in any case, including an instance in which a mandate has been stayed, vacated or set aside, or a settlement has been made after a levy, to such additional compensation for his trouble and expenses in taking possession of and preserving property under any mandate or in removing a person in possession of real property and the said person's property, as the court allows, and the court may make an order requiring the party liable therefor to pay the same to the sheriff.

(d) Mileage fees in the city of New York. For mileage travelled wholly within the city of New York the sheriff of the city of New York shall be entitled to twenty-five dollars payable in advance, as provided in section eight thousand eleven of this chapter.

2009 AMENDMENTS

L. 2009, ch. 381, § 1, deemed to be eff. Aug. 5, 2008, amended paragraph 4 of CPLR 8012(b) to grant poundage to the sheriff upon a settlement when a property execution has been issued and the property has been levied against.

2008 AMENDMENTS

L. 2008, ch. 441, § 1, eff. Aug. 5, 2008, amended paragraphs 2 and 3 of CPLR 8012(b) to provide that where a settlement is made (1) after a levy by service of an execution (CPLR 8012(b)(2)) or (2) either before or after judgment, after levy by service of an order of attachment (CPLR 8012(b)(3)), the Sheriff is entitled to poundage fees on the judgment or settlement amount, whichever is less.and added new paragraphs 4 and 5 to provide that: (a) where a settlement occurs after service of an income or property execution on the debtor (as per CPLR 5231(d)) or upon a garnishee under CPLR 5231(e), the Sheriff is entitled to receive poundage fees on the judgment or settlement amount, whichever is less; (b) if after levy, an income or property execution is set aside or vacated, the Sheriff is entitled to poundage fees upon the value of the levied property, not to exceed the amount set forth in the execution, and the court can order the liable party to pay the Sheriff; (c) if the Sheriff brings an action to collect the poundage fees, the court can also award attorneys' fees and costs.

2006 AMENDMENTS

L. 2006, ch. 31, § 1, eff. May 2, 2006, amended CPLR 8012(a) to establish that a sheriff is entitled to the current Internal Revenue Service mileage reimbursement rate for each mile necessarily traveled in performing certain services.

2000 AMENDMENTS

L. 2000, ch. 337, eff. Oct. 1, 2000, amended subd. (d) to increase the mileage fees of the sheriff in the city of New York, from fifteen dollars to twenty-five dollars.

1987 AMENDMENTS

L. 1987, ch. 218, eff. Sept. 1, 1987, amended subd. (d) to increase the mileage fees of the sheriff in the city of New York, from ten dollars to fifteen dollars.

1985 AMENDMENTS

L. 1985, ch. 565, eff. July 26, 1985, amended CPLR 8012(a) to increase the sheriff's mileage fee to twenty-three cents per mile.

1976 AMENDMENTS

L. 1976, ch. 695, eff. July 24, 1976, amended CPLR 8012(d) by increasing the sheriff's mileage fee in the city of New York and adding a reference to the general provisions governing sheriff's fees in New York city in the newly enacted CPLR 8011-a.

1972 AMENDMENTS

L. 1972, ch. 734 and ch. 735, eff. July 1, 1972, amended CPLR 8012(b)(1).

L. 1972, ch. 734, eff. July 1, 1972, repealed CPLR 8012(d), relettered subdivision (e) as (d), and amended new subdivision (d).

1970 AMENDMENTS

L. 1970, ch. 859, § 4, eff. July 1, 1970, amended CPLR 8012(b)(1).

1969 AMENDMENTS

L. 1969, ch. 441, eff. July 1, 1969, added new subdivision (e), now (d).

§ 8013. Expenses of sheriffs.

(a) Publication of notice of sale. A sheriff, where real property is to be sold by virtue of an execution or in pursuance of a direction contained in a judgment, is entitled to reimbursement for printer's fees, paid by him for the publication of a notice of the sale. Where the notice is published more than four times, or the sale is postponed, the expense of continuing the publication, or of publishing the notice of postponement, shall be paid by the person requesting it. Where two or more executions against the property of one judgment debtor are in the hands of the sheriff at the time when the proceeds are distributed, the sheriff is entitled to reimbursement for printer's fees upon only the execution issued upon the judgment first docketed in the county.

(b) Appraisal of attached property. A sheriff, where an estimate of the value of property levied upon by virtue of an order of attachment is made, shall be entitled to reimbursement for such compensation to appraisers actually employed thereupon as the court which granted the order of attachment may allow.

(c) Other expenses. A sheriff is entitled to reimbursement of all expenses necessarily incurred in the execution of any mandate and in the protection, presentation, transportation or sale of property.

(d) Payment in advance. A sheriff, whenever he deems it necessary, may require payment to him in advance to cover any or all expenses for which he is entitled to reimbursement; advance payments made in connection with a mandate or direction affecting property shall be repaid by the sheriff out of the proceeds of the sale of the property, if any.

§ 8014. Collection of sheriff's fees on execution.

The fees of a sheriff, upon an execution against property, which are not required by statute to be paid by a particular person and which are not included in the bill of costs of the party in whose favor the execution is issued, shall be collected by virtue of the execution in the

CPLR

same manner as the sum therein directed to be collected.

§ 8015. County clerk where sheriff is a party or otherwise disqualified.

A county clerk is entitled for the services specified to the following fees:

1. for performing any duty of a sheriff in an action in which the sheriff, for any cause, is disqualified, the same compensation to which a sheriff is entitled for the same services; and

2. for confining a sheriff in a house by virtue of a mandate, and maintaining him while there, two dollars for each day, to be paid by the sheriff, before he is entitled to be discharged.

§ 8016. Clerks of courts of record generally.

(a) Fees of clerks in actions. Except where a greater fee is allowed by another statute for the same service, each clerk of a court of record, except the clerk of the civil court of the city of New York, except a county clerk, except clerks of the family courts, and except the clerks of the district courts, is entitled for the services specified to the following fees, payable in advance:

1. upon the trial of an action, or the hearing, upon the merits, of a special proceeding, from the party bringing it on, one dollar;

2. for entering final judgment, including the filing of the judgment-roll and a copy of the judgment to insert therein, fifty cents, and fifteen cents in addition for each folio, exceeding five, contained in the judgment;

3. for entering any order or an interlocutory judgment, fifty cents, and fifteen cents in addition for each folio, exceeding five;

4. for a certified or other copy of an order, record or other paper in an action brought or transferred to the court of which he is clerk and entered or filed in his office, ten cents for each folio;

5. for a certified transcript of the docket of a judgment, fifty cents; and

6. for filing a transcript or docketing or redocketing a judgment thereupon, fifty cents, and fifty cents in addition for each defendant,

exceeding two.

(b) Certifying judgment-roll on appeal. Where, on an appeal from a judgment or order, a party shall present to the clerk of a court of record, except the clerk of the civil court of the city of New York, except a county clerk, except clerks of the family courts, and except the clerks of the district courts, a printed copy of the judgment-roll or order appealed from, it shall be the duty of the clerk to compare and certify the same, for which service he shall be entitled to be paid at the rate of fifty cents per page or portion thereof, unless a greater fee is allowed by another statute.

1969 AMENDMENTS

L. 1969, ch. 219, eff. Sept. 1, 1969, amended Subd. (a) and Subd. (b) by excepting clerks of the district courts from the provisions respecting fees of clerks in civil actions. Fees payable to clerks of the district courts provided for in Uniform District Court Act § 1911.

1965 AMENDMENTS

L. 1965, ch. 437, eff. Sept. 1, 1965, added words "and except clerks of the family courts" to Subds. (a) and (b).

§ 8017. Exemption of the state and counties, and agencies and officers thereof, from fees of clerks.

(a) Notwithstanding any other provision of this article or any other general, special or local law relating to fees of clerks, no clerk shall charge or collect a fee from the state, or an agency or officer thereof, for any service rendered in an action in which any of them is involved, nor shall any clerk charge or collect a fee for filing, recording or indexing any paper, document, map or proceeding filed, recorded or indexed for the county, or an agency or officer thereof acting in an official capacity, nor for furnishing a transcript, certification or copy of any paper, document, map or proceeding to be used for official purposes.

(b) Notwithstanding any other provision of law the exemption of subdivision (a) of this section shall not apply to the fees of clerks where the action is on behalf of the New York State Higher Education Services Corporation to recover money due as a result of default of a student loan.

1988 AMENDMENTS

L. 1988, ch. 192, eff. July 31, 1988, relocated the previously-misplaced "(a)" after the section heading.

1984 AMENDMENTS

L. 1984, ch. 858, eff. Aug. 5, 1984, added CPLR 8017(b).

1965 AMENDMENTS

L. 1965, ch. 147, eff. Sept. 1, 1965, repealed former § 8017 entitled "Exemption of actions by the state or state agencies from fees of clerks." Former 8017-a, entitled "Exemption of counties from fees of county clerks" was revised and enacted as a new § 8017.

§ 8018.   Index number fees of county clerks.

(a) Amount of fee.

1. A county clerk is entitled, for the assignment of an index number to an action pending in a court of which he or she is clerk, to a fee of one hundred ninety dollars, payable in advance.

2. The filing of a transcript of judgment in the county clerk's office is not to be deemed an action pending in the supreme or county court of the county in which it is filed, nor does it constitute the commencement of an action in such courts.

3. In addition, a county clerk is entitled, for the assignment of an index number to an action pending in a court of which he or she is clerk, to the following fee: an additional five dollars, to be paid monthly by the county clerk to the commissioner of education, after deducting twenty five cents, for deposit into the New York state local government records management improvement fund and an additional fifteen dollars, after deducting seventy five cents, for deposit to the cultural education account.

(b) Exemptions from index number fee. No fee shall be charged for the assignment of an index number:

1. upon the filing of an order of the appellate term of the supreme court or of an order or certificate of commitment under the mental hygiene law; or

2. upon the transfer of papers from the clerk of any other court, pursuant to an order for change of venue; or

3. to a criminal case or to any action at the request of a public

agency, officer or poor person entitled by law to exemption from payment of fees to a county clerk; or

4. to any case in a county court on appeal from a judgment or order of the district court or a town, village or city court; or

5. to a civil cause of action in which a city, town, village, fire district, district corporation, school district or board of cooperative educational services is the plaintiff.

(c) Endorsement of index number on papers. No paper in an action in the supreme or a county court, other than an order submitted for signature to a judge out of court, shall be submitted for any purpose to the supreme or county court or to a clerk thereof unless there is endorsed on such paper the index number of the action assigned by the clerk of the county.

(d) Additional services without fee where index number assigned. A county clerk who has assigned an index number shall charge no further fee in the action to which the index number is assigned:

1. for the filing, entering, indexing, or docketing, and in the counties within the city of New York, for recording, as required by statute, of any and all papers in the action, or preliminary thereto or supplementary to judgment;

2. for furnishing an extract of minutes for filing with the clerk of the court, for affixing a certificate to a filed paper, for taxing costs, for sealing writs, for issuing commissions, for certifying a copy of the clerk's minutes to accompany papers transmitted upon entry of an order for change of venue, or for entering a judgment in the action;

3. for docketing of a satisfaction, a partial satisfaction, an assignment, a reversal, a modification, an amendment, a cancellation or a continuance of a previous entry or docket of a previously filed paper in the action;

4. for certifying a copy of an order of an appellate term of the supreme court for transmittal to the civil court of the city of New York or a city, municipal or district court, or for certifying a copy of an order for use in a division of the clerk's office or for transmittal to a city or county treasurer;

CPLR

5. for docketing of a return of execution, satisfied, unsatisfied or partially satisfied;

6. for filing a notice or order continuing or canceling a notice of pendency of action or a notice of attachment against real property; and

7. for discharging a judgment of record by deposit with the clerk.

2004 AMENDMENTS

L. 2004, ch. 520, eff. Sept. 28, 2004, amending to make permanent portions of subd. (a)(3) relating to the Local Government Records Management Improvement Act.

2003 AMENDMENTS

L. 2003, ch. 62, Part J, § 23, eff. July 14, 2003, amending subd. (a)(1).

2002 AMENDMENTS

L. 2002, ch. 83, amended subd. (a), eff. July 1, 2002, effectively raising the filing fees in Supreme Court and County Court to $185.

2000 AMENDMENTS

L. 2000, ch. 314, eff. July 1, 2001, added new paragraph (5) to subdivision (b) pertaining to exemptions from index number fee.

1999 AMENDMENTS

L. 1999, ch. 483, eff. Sept. 7, 1999, extended expiration date of the third undesignated paragraph of subdivision (a) to Dec. 21, 2005.

1990 AMENDMENTS

L. 1990, ch. 190, eff. May 25, 1990, amended CPLR 8018(a) to increase the fee for an index number from one hundred dollars to one hundred sixty-five dollars.

1989 AMENDMENTS

Unnumbered paragraph three of subdivision (a), relating to additional fees, was added by L. 1989, ch. 78, eff. Aug. 1, 1989, but to be deemed repealed on Dec. 31, 1995; paragraph 4 of subdivision (b) was added by L. 1989, ch. 488, eff. July 16, 1989.

1988 AMENDMENTS

L. 1988, ch. 192, eff. July 31, 1988, repealed subdivision (e), and included its provisions in the amended subdivision (d) as paragraphs (5), (6) and (7).

1987 AMENDMENTS

L. 1987, ch. 825, eff. Nov. 5, 1987, amended subd. (a) to increase the fee to a county clerk for the assignment of an index number from thirty-five dollars to one-hundred dollars.

1983 AMENDMENTS

L. 1983, ch. 15, eff. April 1, 1983, amended CPLR 8018(a).

1981 AMENDMENTS

L. 1981, ch. 997, eff. July 31, 1981, amended CPLR 8018(a).

1980 AMENDMENTS

L. 1980, ch. 39, eff. April 1, 1980, amended CPLR 8018(a).

1977 AMENDMENTS

L. 1977, ch. 33, section 1, eff. April 1, 1977, amended subd. (a).

L. 1977, ch. 688, eff. Sept. 1, 1977, amended subd. (e)(2).

1972 AMENDMENTS

L. 1972, ch. 734, eff. July 1, 1972, amended subdivisions (a)(1) and (e)(3) by increasing fees.

L. 1972, ch. 709, eff. Sept. 1, 1972, renumbered subdivision (a)(2) as (a)(3) and added new subdivision (a)(2).

1971 AMENDMENTS

L. 1971, ch. 404, eff. July 1, 1971 amended CPLR 8018(a)(1) and (e)(3).

1970 AMENDMENTS

L. 1970, ch. 105, eff. March 24, 1970, amended Subd. (a)(1).

1966 AMENDMENTS

L. 1966, ch. 752, eff. Sept. 1, 1966, amended Subd. (e).

1964 AMENDMENTS

L. 1964, ch. 286, eff. Sept. 1, 1964, added new unnumbered paragraph at end of Subd. (a).

§ 8019. County clerks generally.

(a) Application. The fees of a county clerk specified in this article shall supersede the fees allowed by any other statute for the same services, except in so far as the administrative code of the city of New York sets forth different fees for the city register of the city of New York and the county clerk of Richmond, and except that such fees do not include the block fees as set out in the Nassau county administrative code, which are to be charged in addition to the fees specified in this article. This subdivision does not apply to the fees specified in subdivision (f) of section 8021.

(b) Legible copies. Whenever a paper or document, presented to a county clerk for filing or recording, is not legible or otherwise suitable for copying or recording by the photocopying process, the county clerk may require a legible or suitable copy thereof along with such paper or document, and the same fees shall be payable for the copy as are payable for the paper or document.

(c) Notice to county clerk. A county clerk need not make an entry which is required by a court order unless proper notice is given to the clerk by a party to the action or a person legally interested therein.

(d) Exemptions for state or city of New York. A clerk of a county within the city of New York shall not charge or receive any fee from the city of New York or the state of New York or from any agency or officer of either acting in official capacity.

(e) Size of page and type. For purposes of this article, the size of each page accepted by a county clerk for recording and indexing shall not exceed nine inches by fourteen inches, except that in the counties of Cattaraugus, Columbia, Delaware, Herkimer, Monroe and Otsego, the size of the page shall not exceed eight and a half inches by fourteen inches, and every printed portion thereof shall be plainly printed in not smaller than eight point type. The county clerk acting as recording officer may in special circumstances accept a page exceeding the size or with smaller print than that prescribed herein, on such terms and at such fee, subject to review by the supreme court, as he may deem appropriate, but the fee for such recording and indexing shall not be less than double the fees otherwise chargeable by law therefor.

(f) Copies of records. The following fees, up to a maximum of forty dollars per record shall be payable to a county clerk or register for copies of the records of the office except records filed under the uniform commercial code:

1. to prepare a copy of any paper or record on file in the office, except as otherwise provided, sixty-five cents per page with a minimum fee of one dollar thirty cents;

2. to certify a prepared copy of any record or paper on file, sixty-five cents per page with a minimum fee of five dollars twenty cents;

3. to prepare and certify a copy of any record or paper on file, one dollar twenty-five cents per page with a minimum fee of five dollars;

4. to prepare and certify a copy of a certificate of honorable discharge, except as provided for in the military law, two dollars fifty cents; and

5. to prepare a copy of any paper or record on file in the office in a medium other than paper, the actual cost of reproducing the record in accordance with paragraph (c) of subdivision one of section eighty-seven of the public officers law.

2008 AMENDMENTS

L. 2008, ch. 223, Part 7, § 24, eff. Aug. 6, 2008, amending subd. (f), par (3) and (4) and adding par (5).

2003 AMENDMENTS

L. 2003, ch. 62, Part J, § 24, eff. July 14, 2003, amending subd. (f).

1988 AMENDMENTS

L. 1988, ch. 192, eff. July 31, 1988, added new subdivision (f) setting fees for copying and certification of county clerk or county register records.

1965 AMENDMENTS

L. 1965, ch. 773, eff. Sept. 1, 1965, made mechanical changes.

1964 AMENDMENTS

L. 1964, ch. 476, eff. Sept. 27, 1964, added to Subd. (a): "This subdivision does not apply to the fees specified in subdivision (f) of section eight thousand twenty-one of this chapter." This amendment is part of law amending the Uniform Commercial Code and relates thereto. See CPLR 8021.

§ 8020. County clerks as clerks of court.

Whenever a county clerk renders a service in his capacity as clerk of the supreme or a county court, in an action pending in such court, he is entitled to the fees specified in this section, payable in advance.

(a) Placing cause on calendar. For placing a cause on a calendar for trial or inquest, one hundred twenty-five dollars in the supreme court and county court; except that where rules of the chief administrator of the courts require that a request for judicial intervention be made in an action pending in supreme court or county court, the county clerk shall be entitled to a fee of ninety-five

CPLR

dollars, payable before a judge may be assigned pursuant to such request, and thereafter, for placing such a cause on a calendar for trial or inquest, the county clerk shall be entitled to an additional fee of thirty dollars, and no other fee may be charged thereafter pursuant to this subdivision; except that the county clerk shall be entitled to a fee of forty-five dollars upon the filing of each motion or cross motion in such action. However, no fee shall be imposed for a motion which seeks leave to proceed as a poor person pursuant to subdivision (a) of section eleven hundred one of this chapter.

(b) Calendar fee for transferred cause, joint trial, retrial, or separate trial. Where a cause which has been placed upon a calendar is transferred before trial to a court for which a larger calendar fee is prescribed, the difference in calendar fee shall be paid at the time the cause is placed upon the calendar of the latter court, except that no additional fee shall be required when the action is transferred for the purpose of consolidation or trial jointly with another action. No separate calendar fee shall be imposed for a retrial of a cause or for the trial of a separate issue in a cause.

(c) Filing demand for jury trial. For filing a demand for a jury trial in the following counties, where the right to a jury trial is duly demanded:

    1. in the counties within the city of New York, sixty-five dollars in the supreme court;

    2. in all other counties, sixty-five dollars in the supreme court and county court.

(d) Filing a stipulation of settlement or a voluntary discontinuance. For filing a stipulation of settlement pursuant to rule twenty-one hundred four of this chapter or a notice, stipulation, or certificate pursuant to subdivision (d) of rule thirty-two hundred seventeen of this chapter, the defendant shall file and pay:

    1. in the counties within the city of New York, thirty-five dollars in the supreme court.

    2. in all other counties, thirty-five dollars in the supreme court and county court.

Provided, however, that only one such fee shall be charged for each notice, stipulation or certificate filed pursuant to this subdivision.

(e) Jury fee for transferred cause, joint trial, retrial or separate trial. Where a cause in which a jury has been demanded is transferred before trial to a court for which a larger jury fee is prescribed, the difference in the jury fee shall be paid at the time the cause is placed upon the calendar of the latter court, except that no additional fee shall be required when the action is transferred for the purpose of consolidation or trial jointly with another action in which a jury fee has previously been paid. No separate jury fee shall be imposed for a retrial of a cause or for the trial of a separate issue in a cause.

(f) Certification, exemplification, and copies of papers.

1. For issuing any certificate, in counties within the city of New York, eight dollars, and in all other counties, four dollars, except as otherwise expressly provided in this article.

2. For a certificate of exemplification, exclusive of certification, in counties within the city of New York, twenty-five dollars, and in all other counties, ten dollars.

(g) Searches. For certifying to a search of any court records for a consecutive two-year period or fraction thereof, for each name so searched, five dollars.

(h) Production of court records. For each day or part thereof in attendance in any action pursuant to a subpoena duces tecum, twenty dollars, and in addition thereto, mileage fees of twelve cents per mile each way and the necessary expenses of the messenger, except that if the subpoena duces tecum be served within the city of New York and the place of attendance is within the city of New York, then actual transportation costs shall be charged instead of the mileage fees.

2003 AMENDMENTS

L. 2003, ch. 62, Part J, § 25, eff. July 14, 2003, amending subds. (a) and (c) and adding subd. (d).

CPLR

1996 AMENDMENTS

L. 1996, ch. 309, eff. July 23, 1996, amended subdivision (a) by adding an additional fee to be paid to the clerk for placing a cause on a calendar for trial or inquest after a request for judicial intervention.

1992 AMENDMENTS

L. 1992, ch. 55, eff. April 15, 1992, amended CPLR 8020(f) to set forth the amounts payable to a county clerk acting in the capacity of court clerk for issuing any certificate or a certificate of exemplification in a county within New York City.

1990 AMENDMENTS

L. 1990, ch. 190, eff. May 25, 1990, amended CPLR 8020(a) to increase the fee for placing a case on the calendar for trial or inquest from seventy dollars to one hundred dollars, and to increase the fee for assigning a judge pursuant to a request for judicial intervention from fifty dollars to seventy-five dollars.

1988 AMENDMENTS

L. 1988, ch. 192, eff. July 31, 1988, deleted paragraphs 2, 3, and 4 from subdivision (f), and renumbered paragraph 5 as paragraph 2.

1987 AMENDMENTS

L. 1987, ch. 825, eff. Nov. 5, 1987, amended Subd. (a), clarifying language by deleting subsections (1) and (2) which had distinguished between the Supreme Court in counties within the city of New York, and the Supreme Court and County Court in all other counties, and adding the exception for the payment of the fee of fifty dollars where the rules of the chief administrator of the courts require that a request for judicial intervention be made in a pending action.

1983 AMENDMENTS

L. 1983, ch. 15, eff. April 1, 1983, amended CPLR 8020(a) and (c).

L. 1983, ch. 784, eff. Aug. 29, 1983, amended CPLR 8020(f), (g) and (h).

1980 AMENDMENTS

L. 1980, ch. 39, eff. April 1, 1980, amended CPLR 8020(a) and (c).

1977 AMENDMENTS

L. 1977, ch. 33, sections 2 and 3, eff. April 1, 1977, amended subdivisions (a) and (c).

1972 AMENDMENTS

L. 1972, ch. 185, § 4, eff. May 28, 1972, repealed Subdivisions (c) and (d) and inserted a new Subdivision (c). Subdivision (d) was not replaced nor were subsequent subdivisions relettered.

L. 1972, ch. 709, eff. Sept. 1, 1972, added new Subd. (a)(3).

L. 1972, ch. 734, eff. July 1, 1972, amended CPLR 8020 (a)(1), (c)(1), (f), (g) and (h) by increasing the fees payable.

1971 AMENDMENTS

L. 1971, ch. 404, eff. July 1, 1971, and ch. 829, eff. Sept. 1, 1971, amended Subds. (a), (c), (f) and (g).

1970 AMENDMENTS

L. 1970, ch. 440, eff. May 1, 1970, amended paragraph (a).

L. 1970, ch. 104, eff. March 24, 1970, amended Subd. (h).

1969 AMENDMENTS

L. 1969, ch. 801, eff. Sept. 1, 1969, amended subd. (a)(2).

1968 AMENDMENTS

L. 1968, ch. 14, eff. Sept. 1, 1968, added paragraph 4-a to Subd. (a), since repealed.

§ 8021. County clerks other than as clerks of court.

Whenever a county clerk renders a service other than in his capacity as clerk of the supreme or a county court, or other than in an action pending in a court of which he is clerk, he is entitled to the fees specified in this section, payable in advance.

(a) Services in connection with papers or instruments relating to real property and not filed under the uniform commercial code.

1. For filing any paper, document or other instrument of any nature or description which is required or permitted by law to be filed in his office, five dollars, except as otherwise expressly provided in this article and in article twelve of the real property law.

2. For filing and indexing any map, ten dollars.

3. For affixing and indexing a notice of foreclosure of a mortgage, as prescribed in section fourteen hundred four of the real property actions and proceedings law, ten dollars.

4. a.(1) For recording, entering, indexing and endorsing a certificate on any instrument, five dollars, and, in addition thereto, three dollars for each page or portion of a page, and fifty cents for each additional town, city, block or other indices in which such instrument is to be indexed as directed by the

endorsement thereon. On the assignment of a mortgage which assigns more than one mortgage or on a release of lease which releases more than one lease, then there shall be an additional fee of three dollars for every mortgage assigned or lease released in excess of one.

(2) Notwithstanding clause one of this subparagraph, any county may opt by county law to increase the fee for recording, entering, indexing and endorsing a certificate on any instrument from five dollars to twenty dollars and, in addition thereto, increase from three dollars to five dollars for each page or portion of a page. Such increase shall take effect thirty days after the county enacts such fees. For the purpose of determining the appropriate recording fee, the fee for any cover page shall be deemed an additional page of the instrument. A cover page shall not include any social security account number or date of birth. To the extent a county clerk has placed an image of such cover page online, such county clerk shall make a good faith effort to redact such information.

b. For recording, entering, indexing and endorsing a certificate on any instrument, an additional fee of five dollars to be paid monthly by county clerks to the commissioner of education, after deducting twentyfive cents, for deposit into the New York state local government records management improvement fund and an additional fifteen dollars, after deducting seventy five cents, for deposit to the cultural education account.

5. For re-indexing a recorded instrument, two dollars for each town, city, block or other indices so re-indexed upon presentation of the instrument with such additional endorsement thereon or, if the original instrument is not obtainable, by request in writing sworn to by an interested party, setting forth the facts.

6. For copying and mailing any map, such fees as may be fixed by the county clerk subject to review by the supreme court.

7. For entering a cross reference of the record of any instrument on the margin of the record of any other instrument referred to therein by liber and page, fifty cents for each cross reference.

8. For examining the record of each assignment of mortgage or

other instrument recited in a certificate of discharge of mortgage, fifty cents.

9. For searching for any filed or recorded instrument, upon a written request specifying the kind of instrument, the location by town, city or block if a real property instrument, and the names and period to be searched, such fee as may be fixed by the county clerk subject to review by the supreme court.

10. For filing or recording a notice of pendency of action or a notice of attachment against real property, or an amended notice of pendency of action or an amended notice of action against real property, in counties within the city of New York, thirty-five dollars, and in all other counties, fifteen dollars, but no fee shall be charged for filing or recording a notice or order continuing or canceling same.

11. For filing federal tax liens payment shall be made in the manner provided by section two hundred forty-three of the lien law.

(b) Filing, other than in connection with papers or instruments relating to real property or filed under the uniform commercial code.

1. For filing any paper, document or other instrument of any nature or description which is required or permitted by law to be filed in his office, five dollars, except as otherwise expressly provided in this article, and except that no fee shall be charged for filing a commission of appointment to public office or an oath of office of a public officer or employee, other than a notary public or commissioner of deeds.

2. For filing any certificate, instrument or document in relation to a corporation, or any certificate pursuant to section forty-nine-a of the personal property law, or any certificate, instrument or document in relation to a joint stock association, limited partnership, continued use of firm name or registration of hotel name, in counties within the city of New York, one hundred dollars, and in all other counties, twenty-five dollars. For filing any certificate pursuant to section one hundred thirty of the general business law, in counties within the city of New York, one hundred dollars, and

CPLR

in all other counties, twenty-five dollars. No fee shall be charged for filing proof of publication or a cancellation, discontinuance or dissolution certificate.

3. For filing an assignment of or order for the payment of salary or wages, in counties within the city of New York, ten dollars, and in all other counties, five dollars. No fee shall be charged for filing of a satisfaction, assignment, cancellation or vacation thereof.

4. For filing a notice of mechanics lien, or a notice of lending, in counties within the city of New York, thirty dollars, and in all other counties, fifteen dollars. No fee shall be charged for filing a notice or order continuing, amending or canceling same, but when a mechanics lien is discharged by deposit with a clerk of the court, there shall be a fee of three dollars in all counties other than those within the city of New York.

5. For filing, examining and entering an absolute bill of sale of chattels, or any instrument affecting chattels, or a copy of the foregoing, or an assignment of any such instrument, or a satisfaction of a chattel mortgage or conditional bill of sale, in all counties except those within the city of New York, one dollar and fifty cents. For filing, examining and entering a notice of lien on merchandise, one dollar and fifty cents. Every instrument affecting chattels must be endorsed on the outside thereof with the character of the instrument, the names of all the parties thereto and the location of the property affected thereby, which must be distinguished from the address of the parties by the words "property located at," or similar words.

6. For filing a notice of hospital lien, five dollars. No fee shall be charged for filing a satisfaction, partial satisfaction, modification, assignment, cancellation, discharge of amendment thereof.

7. For filing a transcript of judgment, in counties within the city of New York, twenty-five dollars, and in all other counties, ten dollars. No fee shall be charged for filing a certificate or order of satisfaction, partial satisfaction, modification, assignment, reversal, cancellation or amendment, of judgment or lien.

8. For filing and indexing a certificate of appointment or official character of a notary public, or for filing and indexing a certificate

of appointment as commissioner of deeds, ten dollars.

9. For filing an assignment of money due on a contract, or an order on owner, twenty-five dollars. No fee shall be charged for filing a notice or order continuing, amending or canceling same.

10. For filing a building loan contract, in counties within the city of New York, fifty dollars, and in all other counties, twenty-five dollars.

11. (a) For recording any instrument required by statute to be recorded, in counties within the city of New York, ten dollars, and in all other counties, five dollars, and, in addition thereto, three dollars for each page or portion of a page recorded, except that the charge for instruments of surrender and orders of commitment required to be filed and recorded pursuant to section three hundred eighty-four of the social services law shall be ten dollars per instrument or order in counties within the city of New York, and in all other counties, five dollars per instrument or order.

(b) For recording any instrument required by statute to be recorded, an additional fee of five dollars to be paid monthly by county clerks to the commissioner of education, after deducting twenty-five cents, for deposit into the New York state local government records management improvement fund and an additional fifteen dollars, after deducting seventy-five cents, for deposit to the cultural education account.

(c) Certification, issuing certificates, other papers and copies of papers, records, and related services, other than in connection with papers or instruments relating to real property or filed under the uniform commercial code.

1. For issuing any certificate, except as otherwise expressly provided for in this article, in counties within the city of New York, ten dollars, and in all other counties, five dollars.

2. For an execution of a judgment, five dollars.

3. For issuing a transcript of the docket of a judgment or other lien, in counties within the city of New York, fifteen dollars, and in all other counties, five dollars.

4. For issuing a certificate of appointment of a notary public, five dollars.

5. For issuing a certificate authenticating an official act by a notary public, commissioner of deeds or other public officer, three dollars, except that no fee shall be charged for a certificate on a paper required by the United States veterans' administration.

6. For issuing an official receipt for any instrument affecting personal property, two dollars.

7. For a certificate of exemplification, exclusive of certification, ten dollars.

8. For preparing and certifying a copy of a marriage record, five dollars.

9. No fee shall be charged to any county officer, employee or institution required to file or record any instrument in connection with the official duties thereof, or to any public official in connection with the filing of his undertaking.

(d) Searches of records not filed under the uniform commercial code. For certifying to a search of any records, other than those in an action or relating to real property, for a consecutive two-year period or fraction thereof, for each name so searched, five dollars; except that in the counties within the city of New York, when the records so searched are the census records of the state of New York, the charge shall be one dollar for a consecutive two-year period or fraction thereof.

(e) Production of records. The production in any action of any filed or recorded paper, document, map or other instrument which is part of the public records and papers of a county clerk's office, except the papers in an action which have been filed with the county clerk in his capacity as clerk of the court, is hereby prohibited in the interest of the safety and preservation thereof, unless the county clerk consents to such production, or the judge presiding in the court in which such production is sought so orders. Instead of the original, a certified copy of such filed or recorded paper, document, map or other instrument shall be produced in evidence as provided in section 4540 without an order. In the event that the original is to be produced on order of such judge, there shall be a fee for each day or part thereof in attendance pursuant to a subpoena duces tecum of twenty dollars and, in addition thereto, mileage fees of twelve cents per mile each way and the necessary expenses of the messenger, except that if the subpoena duces tecum be served within the city of New York and the place of attendance is within the city of New York, then actual transportation cost shall be charged instead of the mileage fees. In the event that a certified photo copy of the records subpoenaed is produced, there shall be the same fee as if the original was produced on the order of a judge.

(f) Services rendered pursuant to part four of article nine of the uniform commercial code.

1. For filing, indexing and furnishing filing data for a financing statement or a continuation statement on a form conforming to standards prescribed by the secretary of state, three dollars, or if the statement otherwise conforms to the requirements of part four of such article, four dollars and fifty cents, plus, in either case,

(a) if the statement covers collateral which is crops or goods which are or are to become fixtures, fifty cents and, in addition;

(b) if the real estate is in the city of New York or the county of Nassau, any block fees allowed by the administrative code of the city of New York or the Nassau county administrative code;

(c) for each additional person, firm or organization, beyond the first, named as a debtor in the statement, seventy-five cents.

2. For filing and indexing an assignment or statement of assignment on a form conforming to standards prescribed by the secretary of state, of a security interest included in or accompanying a termination statement, three dollars, or if the assignment or statement of assignment otherwise conforms to the requirements of part four of such article, four dollars and fifty cents, plus, in either case, for each additional person, firm or organization, beyond the first, named as a debtor in the assignment or statement, seventy-five cents.

3. For filing and indexing a termination statement, including sending or delivering the financing statement and any continua-

CPLR

tion statement, statement of assignment or statement of release pertaining thereto, or an acknowledgment of the filing of the termination statement, one dollar and fifty cents and, otherwise, shall be three dollars, plus, in each case an additional fee of seventy-five cents for each name more than one against which the termination statement is required to be indexed.

4. For filing, indexing and furnishing filing data for a financing statement indicating an assignment of a security interest in the collateral on a form conforming to standards prescribed by the secretary of state, three dollars, or if the financing statement otherwise conforms to the requirements of part four of such article, four dollars and fifty cents, and seventy-five cents for each additional person, firm or organization, beyond the first, named as a debtor in the statement.

5. For filing, indexing and furnishing filing data about a statement of assignment on a form conforming to standards prescribed by the secretary of state, separate from a financing statement, three dollars, or if the statement of assignment otherwise conforms to the requirements of part four of such article, four dollars and fifty cents plus, in either case, for each additional person, firm or organization, beyond the first, named as a debtor in the statement, seventy-five cents.

6. For filing and noting a statement of release of collateral on a form conforming to standards prescribed by the secretary of state, three dollars, or if the statement of release otherwise conforms to the requirements of part four of such article, four dollars and fifty cents plus, in either case, for each additional person, firm or organization, beyond the first, named as a debtor in the statement, seventy-five cents.

7. For noting the file number and date and hour of the filing of the original upon a copy thereof furnished by the person filing any financing statement, termination statement, statement of assignment, or statement of release, and delivering or sending the copy to such person, when the filed statement contains more than one page or the statements and copy are not on forms conforming to standards prescribed by the secretary of state, an amount equal to the product of one dollar and fifty cents multiplied by the number

of pages the filed statement contains.

8. For issuing a certificate showing whether there is on file a presently effective financing statement naming a particular debtor and any statement of assignment thereof or statement of release of collateral pertaining thereto, and if there is, giving the date and hour of filing of each such statement and the names and addresses of each secured party therein, four dollars and fifty cents if the request for the certificate is on a form conforming to standards prescribed by the secretary of state or, otherwise, seven dollars and fifty cents.

9. For furnishing a copy of any filed financing statement, continuation statement, termination statement, statement of assignment or statement of release, one dollar and fifty cents per page; provided, however, that the county clerk may furnish duplicate copies of microfilm records of all financing statements, continuation statements, termination statements, statements of assignment and statements of release filed during any month to any person requesting the same at a fee, to be determined by the county clerk, of less than one dollar and fifty cents per page.

(g) Services rendered in relation to federal tax liens filed pursuant to the lien law.

1. For filing and indexing a notice of lien for taxes payable to the United States of America and certificates and notices affecting such liens, four dollars and fifty cents.

2. For issuing a certificate showing whether there is on file on the date and hour stated therein, any notice of federal tax lien or certificate or notice affecting such lien, filed on or after July third, nineteen hundred sixty-six, and if there is, giving the date and hour of filing each such notice or certificate, four dollars and fifty cents.

CROSS REFERENCES

Reference in Subd. (a)(1), *above,* to provisions of Article 12 of the Real Property Law refers to **Real Prop. L. § 432**, which sets forth fees to be charged for registering title to real property.

2008 AMENDMENTS

L. 2008, ch. 288, § 1, eff. July 7, 2008, amended subparagraph (a) and added subparagraph (a)(2) to allow county governments, at local option, to increase the fee for recording, entering, indexing and endorsing a certificate on any instrument from $5 to $20 and to increase the per-page fee from $3 per page to $5 per page. The amendments also prohibit a cover page from including social security numbers and/or dates of birth.

2004 AMENDMENTS

L. 2004, ch. 520, § 1, eff. Sept. 28, 2004, amended subparagraphs (a)(4)(b) and (b)(11)(b) to make the Local Government Improvement Fund permanent.

2002 AMENDMENTS

L. 2002, ch. 83, Part B, § 2, 3, eff. July 1, 2002, amended subparagraphs (a)(4)(b) and (b)(11)(b) raising certain fees.

1999 AMENDMENTS

L. 1999, ch. 483, eff. Sept. 7, 1999, extending the expiration dates of subds. (a)(4) and (b)(11) to Dec. 31, 2005.

1992 AMENDMENTS

L. 1992, ch. 55, eff. April 15, 1992, amended CPLR 8021(a)(10); (b)(2), (3), (4), (7), (10), and (11)(a); and (c)(1) and (3), by setting forth the amount payable to a clerk of a county within New York City, who is not acting as a court clerk, for performing the services described in these subsections.

1989 AMENDMENTS

L. 1989, ch. 78, eff. July 30, 1989, amended paragraph 4 of subdivision (a) and paragraph 11 of subdivision (b) regarding additional fees; however, these provisions will be deemed repealed on Dec. 31, 1995.

1988 AMENDMENTS

L. 1988, ch. 192, eff. July 31, 1988, deleted paragraphs 6 and 7 from subdivision (a), renumbered paragraphs 8 through 13 as 6 through 11, and amended renumbered paragraph 10 to include recording a notice or amended notice of pendency; amended paragraph 10 of subdivision (b) to eliminate restriction to the counties within New York City; deleted paragraphs 6, 8 and 9 from subdivision (c), renumbered paragraph 7 as 6 and 10 through 12 as 7 through 9.

1983 AMENDMENTS

L. 1983, ch. 783, eff. Aug. 29, 1983, amended CPLR 8021(a)–(g).

1982 AMENDMENTS

L. 1982, ch. 692, eff. Aug. 21, 1982, amended subds. (f) and (g).

1977 AMENDMENTS

L. 1977, ch. 688, eff. Sept. 1, 1977, amended subds. (a)(4), (b)(7), (b)(8), (c)(3) and (c)(4).

1972 AMENDMENTS

L. 1972, chs. 324, 734 and 735, eff. July 1, 1975, amended Subd. (a)(4).

L. 1972, chs. 734 and 735, eff. July 1, 1975, also amended Subd. (b), (c), (d) and (e) by increasing fees.

1971 AMENDMENTS

L. 1971, ch. 404, eff. July 1, 1971, amended CPLR 8021(a), (b), (c), (d) and (e).

1969 AMENDMENTS

L. 1969, ch. 680, eff. May 21, 1969, amended Subd. (f)(4).

1968 AMENDMENTS

L. 1968, ch. 133, eff. July 1, 1968, amended Subd. (a) by adding paragraph (13).

L. 1968, ch. 721, eff. Sept. 1, 1968, amended Subd. (b)(11).

1967 AMENDMENTS

L. 1967, ch. 338, eff. April 18, 1967, added Subd. (g).

L. 1967, ch. 680, eff. Sept. 1, 1967, amended subd. (b)(2).

L. 1967, ch. 689, eff. April 27, 1967, amended Subd. (f).

1965 AMENDMENTS

L. 1965, ch. 128, eff. Sept. 1, 1965, amended Subd. (b).

L. 1965, ch. 773, eff. Sept. 1, 1965, amended subd. (a)(3).

1964 AMENDMENTS

L. 1964, ch. 476, eff. Sept. 27, 1964, amending the Uniform Commercial Code, made related amendments to CPLR 8021.

§ 8022.   Fee on civil appeals and proceedings before appellate courts.

(a) A county clerk, upon filing a notice of appeal, is entitled to a fee of sixty-five dollars, payable in advance.

(b) The clerks of the appellate divisions of the supreme court and the clerk of the court of appeals are entitled, upon the filing of a record on a civil appeal or a statement in lieu of record on a civil appeal, as required by rule 5530 of this chapter, to a fee of three hundred fifteen dollars, payable in advance. The clerks of the appellate divisions also shall be entitled to such fee upon the filing of a notice of petition or order to show cause commencing a special proceeding in their respective courts. In addition, the clerks of the appellate divisions of the supreme court and the clerk of the court of appeals are entitled, upon the filing of each motion or cross motion with respect to a civil appeal or special proceeding, to a fee of forty-five dollars, payable in advance. However, no fee shall be imposed for a motion or cross motion which seeks leave to prosecute or defend a civil appeal or special proceeding as a poor person pursuant to subdivision (a) of section eleven hundred one of this chapter.

2003 AMENDMENTS

L. 2003, ch. 62, Part J, § 27, eff. July 14, 2003, amending subds. (a) and (b).

L. 2003, ch. 686, Part B, § 6, eff. July 14, 2003, amending subd. (b).

1996 AMENDMENTS

L. 1996 ch. 390, eff. July 23, 1996, amended the heading by replacing the word "appeal" with the words, "appeals and proceedings before appellate courts"; amended paragraph (b) by adding the last sentence.

1990 AMENDMENTS

L. 1990 ch. 190, eff. May 25, 1990, amended CPLR 8022 by adding a new subdivision (a) authorizing a county clerk to receive a fee of fifty dollars before filing a notice of appeal; and by renumbering the former provision to become subdivision (b), and increasing the fee on appeal to the Appellate Division and Court of Appeals from two hundred dollars to two hundred fifty dollars.

1987 AMENDMENTS

L. 1987, ch. 825, eff. Nov. 5, 1987, added section 8022.

§ 8023. Payment of fee by credit card.

Notwithstanding any provision of law to the contrary, a party may pay any of the fees specified in subdivision (a) of section 8018, subdivisions (a) and (c) of section 8020 and section 8022 of this article by means of a credit card or similar device; provided, however, notwithstanding any other provision of law, any party paying a fee hereunder in such manner also may be required to pay a reasonable administrative fee. The amount of such fee and the time and manner of its payment shall be in accordance with the system established pursuant to paragraph (j) of subdivision two of section two hundred twelve of the judiciary law.

2009 AMENDMENTS

L. 2009, ch. 416, eff. Sept. 1, 2009, eliminated the expiration date.

2005 AMENDMENTS

L. 2005, ch. 504, eff. Aug. 16, 2005, extended the expiration date until Sept. 1, 2009.

2003 AMENDMENTS

L. 2003, ch. 261, § 1, eff. July 29, 2003, extended the expiration date until Sept. 1, 2005.

2002 AMENDMENTS

L. 2002, ch. 110, § 1, eff. June 28, 2002, extended the effective date of the statute until July 1, 2003.

1999 AMENDMENTS

L. 1999, ch. 367, eff. July 27, 1999, and shall expire July 1, 2002 when upon such date the amendments made by such sections of this act shall be deemed repealed.

CPLR

Article 81

COSTS GENERALLY

---

§ 8101. Costs in an action.

The party in whose favor a judgment is entered is entitled to costs in the action, unless otherwise provided by statute or unless the court determines that to so allow costs would not be equitable, under all of the circumstances.

§ 8102. Limitation of costs where action brought in higher court.

A plaintiff is not entitled to costs:

1. in an action brought in the supreme court in a county within the city of New York which could have been brought, except for the amount claimed, in the civil court of the city of New York, unless he shall recover six thousand dollars or more; or,

2. in an action brought in the supreme court in a county not within the city of New York which could have been brought, except for the amount claimed, in any court of limited monetary jurisdiction in the

county, unless he shall recover five hundred dollars or more; or,

3. in an action brought in the county court which could have been brought, except for the amount claimed, in any court of lesser monetary jurisdiction in the county, unless he shall recover two hundred fifty dollars or more.

§ 8103.   Costs where parties prevail upon separate issues.

Upon the recovery of a judgment in favor of the plaintiff, the court may award costs in the action to a defendant without denying costs to the plaintiff, if it determines that a cause of action upon which the defendant prevailed is not substantially the same as any cause of action upon which the plaintiff recovered the judgment.

§ 8104.   Costs in consolidated, severed or removed action.

Where two or more actions are consolidated, costs shall be awarded in the consolidated action as if it had been instituted as a single action, unless the order of consolidation otherwise provides. Where an action is severed into two or more actions, costs shall be awarded in each such action as if it had been instituted as a separate action, unless the order of severance otherwise provides. Where an action is removed, except pursuant to subdivision (d) of section three hundred twenty-five of this chapter, costs in the action shall be awarded as if it had been instituted in the court to which it is removed, unless the order of removal otherwise provides and as limited by section eighty-one hundred two of this chapter. Where an action is removed pursuant to subdivision (d) of section three hundred twenty-five of this chapter, costs in the action shall be awarded as if it had remained in the court from which it was removed, as limited by section eighty-one hundred two of this chapter.

1990 AMENDMENTS

L. 1990, ch. 64, eff. Jan. 1, 1991, amended § 8104 by providing that costs in an action removed pursuant to § 325(d) shall be awarded as if the action had remained in the court from which it was removed, as limited by § 8102.

§ 8105.   Costs where more than one plaintiff or defendant.

Where a judgment is entered in favor of two or more parties, they shall be entitled, in all, to the same costs in the action as a single party, unless the court otherwise orders.

§ 8106. Costs upon motion.

Costs upon a motion may be awarded to any party, in the discretion of the court, and absolutely or to abide the event of the action.

§ 8107. Costs upon appeal.

The party in whose favor an appeal is decided in whole or in part is entitled to costs upon the appeal, whether or not he is entitled to costs in the action, unless otherwise provided by statute, rule or order of the appellate court. Where a new trial is directed upon appeal, costs upon the appeal may be awarded absolutely or to abide the event.

§ 8108. Specification of denial or award of costs.

A denial of costs in an action to a party in whose favor the judgment is entered, an award of costs in an action to a party against whom the judgment is entered, an award of separate costs in an action to one or more parties, or an apportionment of costs among several parties, shall be made in the direction of the court for judgment, or in the report or decision upon which judgment is entered, or, upon motion of the party to be benefited thereby, by an order of the judge or referee who presided at the trial. The decision on a motion shall specify the amount of costs awarded upon the motion, if any, and each party to whom they are awarded. The decision on appeal shall specify the disposition made in regard to costs.

§ 8109. Defendant's costs against the state.

(a) Action brought for benefit of municipal corporation. Costs awarded to the defendant in an action brought by the state for the benefit of a municipal corporation shall be awarded against the municipal corporation and not against the state.

(b) Payment of defendant's costs against the state. Where costs are awarded to the defendant and against the state in an action brought by a public officer, and the proceedings have not been stayed, the comptroller shall draw his warrant upon the treasurer for the payment of the costs out of any money in the treasury appropriated for that

CPLR

purpose, upon the production to him of an exemplified copy of the judgment or order awarding the costs, a copy of a taxed bill of costs and a certificate of the attorney-general to the effect that the action was brought pursuant to law. The fees of the clerk for the exemplified copy shall be certified thereupon by him and included in the warrant.

§ 8110. Costs against a fiduciary.

Where costs are awarded against a fiduciary, they shall be chargeable only upon the estate, fund or person he represents, unless the court directs them to be paid personally for mismanagement or bad faith in the prosecution or defense of the action.

Article 82

AMOUNT OF COSTS

SUMMARY OF ARTICLE

§ 8201.   **Amount of costs in an action.**

§ 8202.   **Amount of costs on motion.**

§ 8203.   **Amount of costs on appeal to appellate division and appellate term.**

§ 8204.   **Amount of costs on appeal to court of appeals.**

§ 8201. Amount of costs in an action.

Costs awarded in an action shall be in the amount of:

1. two hundred dollars for all proceedings before a note of issue is filed; plus

2. two hundred dollars for all proceedings after a note of issue is filed and before trial; plus

3. three hundred dollars for each trial, inquest or assessment of damages.

1988 AMENDMENTS

L. 1988, ch. 101, eff. Jan. 1, 1989, applicable to all bills of costs entered on or after effective date, regardless of when claim accrued or action was commenced, amended 8201 to increase costs awarded in proceedings before note of issue is filed from fifty dollars (or twenty-five dollars outside New York City) to two hundred dollars in all counties; to increase costs awarded after note of issue is filed but before trial from one hundred dollars (or fifty dollars outside New York City) to two hundred dollars in all counties; and to increase costs awarded for each trial, inquest or assessment of damages from one hundred fifty dollars (or seventy-five dollars outside New York City) to three hundred dollars in all counties.

1972 AMENDMENTS

L. 1972, ch. 734 and ch. 735, eff. July 1, 1972, amended CPLR 8201 by increasing the costs in an action in New York City.

§ 8202. Amount of costs on motion.

Costs awarded on a motion shall be in an amount fixed by the court, not exceeding one hundred dollars.

1988 AMENDMENTS

L. 1988, ch. 101, eff. Jan. 1, 1989, applicable to all bills of costs entered on or after effective date, regardless of when claim accrued or action was commenced, amended to increase costs awarded on a motion from forty dollars (or twenty dollars outside New York City) to one hundred dollars for all counties.

1972 AMENDMENTS

L. 1972, ch. 734 and ch. 735, eff. July 1, 1972, amended CPLR 8202 by increasing the costs on a motion in New York City.

§ 8203. Amount of costs on appeal to appellate division and appellate term.

(a) Unless the court awards a lesser amount, costs awarded on an appeal to the appellate division shall be in the amount of two hundred fifty dollars.

(b) Costs on an appeal from a county court to an appellate term may be awarded by the appellate term in its discretion, and if awarded shall be as follows:

1. to the appellant upon reversal, not more than thirty dollars;

2. to the respondent upon affirmance, not more than twenty-five dollars;

3. to either party on modification, not more than twenty-five dollars.

On appeal from any other court to an appellate term costs shall be governed by the provisions of the applicable court act.

1988 AMENDMENTS

L. 1988, ch. 101, eff. Jan. 1, 1989, applicable to all bills of costs entered on or after effective date, regardless of when claim accrued or action was commenced, amended subdivision (a) to eliminate the differential between pre-argument and argument costs, setting costs at two hundred fifty dollars.

1972 AMENDMENTS

L. 1972, ch. 391, eff. Sept. 1, 1972, amended CPLR 8203 by adding to the title, "appellate term," by lettering the prior material as subdivision (a), and by adding new subdivision (b).

L. 1972, ch. 734 eff. July 1, 1972, amended CPLR 8203. Effect of amendment canceled by L. 1972, ch. 735, eff. July 1, 1972.

§ 8204. Amount of costs on appeal to court of appeals.

Unless the court awards a lesser amount, costs awarded on an appeal to the court of appeals shall be in the amount of five hundred dollars.

1988 AMENDMENTS

L. 1988, ch. 101, eff. Jan. 1, 1989, applicable to all bills of costs entered on or after effective date, regardless of when claim accrued or action was commenced, amended 8204 to eliminate the pre-argument/argument costs differential, and to set costs at five hundred dollars.

1972 AMENDMENTS

L. 1972, ch. 734, eff. July 1, 1972, amended CPLR 8204. Effect of amendment cancelled by L. 1972, ch. 735, eff. July 1, 1972.

CPLR

Article 83

DISBURSEMENTS AND ADDITIONAL ALLOWANCES

CPLR

SUMMARY OF ARTICLE

§ 8301. Taxable disbursements.

(a) Disbursements in action or on appeal. A party to whom costs are awarded in an action or on appeal is entitled to tax his necessary disbursements for:

    1. the legal fees of witnesses and of referees and other officers;

    2. the reasonable compensation of commissioners taking depositions;

    3. the legal fees for publication, where publication is directed pursuant to law;

4. the legal fees paid for a certified copy of a paper necessarily obtained for use on the trial;

5. the expense of securing copies of opinions and charges of judges;

6. the reasonable expenses of printing the papers for a hearing, when required;

7. the prospective charges for entering and docketing the judgment;

8. the sheriff's fees for receiving and returning one execution;

9. the reasonable expense of taking, and making two transcripts of testimony on an examination before trial, not exceeding two hundred fifty dollars in any one action;

10. the expenses of searches made by title insurance, abstract or searching companies, or by any public officer authorized to make official searches and certify to the same, or by the attorney for the party to whom costs are awarded, taxable at rates not exceeding the cost of similar official searches;

11. the reasonable expenses actually incurred in securing an undertaking to stay enforcement of a judgment subsequently reversed; and

12. such other reasonable and necessary expenses as are taxable according to the course and practice of the court, by express provision of law or by order of the court.

(b) Disbursements on motion. Upon motion of any party made after the determination of a motion, or upon its own initiative, the court may allow any party thereto to tax as disbursements his reasonable and necessary expenses of the motion.

(c) Disbursements to party not awarded costs. The court may allow taxation of disbursements by a party not awarded costs in an action or on appeal; and shall allow taxation of disbursements by a party not awarded costs in an action for a sum of money only where he recovers the sum of fifty dollars or more.

(d) Reasonable fees taxable. Where an expense for a service performed, other than a search, is a taxable disbursement, the court may allow its taxation in an amount equal to the reasonable sum actually and necessarily expended therefor, if it is the usual charge made by private persons for the service, although it is in excess of the fee allowed a public officer.

§ 8302. Additional allowance to plaintiff as of right in real property actions.

(a) Actions in which allowance made. A plaintiff, if a judgment is entered in his favor and he recovers costs, is entitled to an additional allowance, in an action:

> 1. to foreclose a mortgage upon real property; or
>
> 2. for the partition of real property; or
>
> 3. to compel the determination of a claim to real property.

(b) Amount of allowance. An additional allowance under this rule shall be computed upon the amount found to be due upon the mortgage, or the value of the property which is partitioned or the claim to which is determined, at the rate of:

> 1. ten per cent of a sum not exceeding two hundred dollars; plus
>
> 2. five per cent of any additional sum not exceeding eight hundred dollars; plus
>
> 3. two per cent of any additional sum not exceeding two thousand dollars; plus
>
> 4. one per cent of any additional sum not exceeding five thousand dollars.

(c) Additional allowance where action settled. Where an action specified in subdivision (a) is settled before judgment, the plaintiff is entitled to an additional allowance upon the amount paid upon the settlement, computed at one-half of the rates set forth in subdivision (b).

(d) Additional allowance in foreclosure action. In an action to foreclose a mortgage upon real property, a plaintiff entitled to an additional allowance pursuant to subdivision (a) or (c) shall also be entitled to the sum of fifty dollars. Where a part of the mortgage debt is not due, if the judgment directs the sale of the whole property, the additional allowance specified in subdivision (a) shall be computed as provided in subdivision (b) upon the whole sum unpaid upon the mortgage. If the judgment directs the sale of a part only, it shall be computed upon the sum actually due, and if the court thereafter grants an order directing the sale of the remainder or a part thereof, it shall be computed upon the amount then due. The aggregate of additional allowances so computed shall not exceed the sum which would have been allowed if the entire sum secured by the mortgage had been due when the judgment was entered.

§ 8303. Additional allowance in the discretion of the court.

(a) Discretionary allowance in action. Whether or not costs have been awarded, the court before which the trial was had, or in which judgment was entered, on motion, may award:

1. to any party to an action to foreclose a mortgage upon real property, a sum not exceeding two and one half per cent of the sum due or claimed to be due upon such mortgage, and not exceeding the sum of three hundred dollars; or

2. to any party to a difficult or extraordinary case, where a defense has been interposed, a sum not exceeding five per cent of the sum recovered or claimed, or of the value of the subject matter involved, and not exceeding the sum of three thousand dollars; or

3. to any party to an action for the partition of real property, a sum not exceeding five per cent of the value of the subject matter involved and not exceeding the sum of three thousand dollars; or

4. to the fiduciary or to any party to an action which involves the construction of a will or an inter vivos trust instrument, such sums as it deems reasonable for counsel fees and other expenses necessarily incurred with respect to such construction in the action; and the court may direct that the whole or any part of such allowance shall be paid to the attorney rendering the services in the action, and may provide that the determination of the amount of any allowance in connection therewith be reserved for a supplemental order to be entered after the time to appeal has expired, or if an appeal be taken, then after final determination of the appeal; and a court on appeal may make a like award and direction on appeal; or

5. to the attorney for the petitioner in a proceeding to dispose of

an infant's property, such sum as to the court may seem just and proper; or

6. to the plaintiffs in an action or proceeding brought by the attorney-general under articles twenty-two, twenty-two-A, twenty-three-A or thirty-three or section three hundred ninety-one-b or five hundred twenty-a of the general business law, or under subdivision twelve of section sixty-three of the executive law, or under article twenty-three of the arts and cultural affairs law, or in an action or proceeding brought by the attorney-general under applicable statutes to dissolve a corporation or for usurpation of public office, or unlawful exercise of franchise or of corporate right, a sum not exceeding two thousand dollars against each defendant.

(b) Discretionary allowance on enforcement motion. The court, on a motion relating to the enforcement of a judgment, may award to the judgment creditor a sum not exceeding five per cent of the judgment or fifty dollars, whichever is more.

CPLR

2002 AMENDMENTS

L. 2002, ch. 530, § 2, eff. March 16, 2003, amended subparagraph (a)(6). 6.

1988 AMENDMENTS

L. 1988, ch. 500, eff. Aug. 1, 1988, amended paragraph 6 of subdivision (a) to permit discretionary award of costs to plaintiff in an action brought under General Business Law § 520-a (requirements for credit card transaction forms); L. 1988, ch. 547, eff. Nov. 1, 1988, amended paragraph 6 of subdivision (a) to delete reference to former General Business Law Article 26-A (regulation of theatrical syndication financing) and to add reference to Arts and Cultural Affairs Law Article 23, paralleling the legislature's relocation of this section by L. 1983, ch. 876, § 1.

1982 AMENDMENTS

L. 1982, ch. 846, eff. Sept. 1, 1982, amended CPLR 8303(a)(6) by adding a reference to General Business Law § 33.

1971 AMENDMENTS

L. 1971, ch. 430, eff. Sept. 1, 1971, amended CPLR 8303(a) (6) by adding a reference to General Business Law Article 22-a.

1966 AMENDMENTS

L. 1966, ch. 224, eff. Sept. 1, 1966, amended Subd. (a).

The amendments were recommended by the Judicial Conference Feb. 1, 1966, Report to the Legislature: "Both CPLR 8301 and CPLR 8302 are applicable only to a party to whom costs are awarded. The silence of CPLR 8303(a) on this point has occasioned some confusion. The provision should be clarified to reflect the revisers' intention that a party may be eligible for an additional allowance even though he is not the party who taxes costs (See 1960 N.Y.Leg.Doc.No. 20, p. 331)." The change to § 8303(a)(1) is one of form merely.

"§ 1513 of the Civil Practice Act, the counterpart of CPLR 8303(a)(1), provided explicitly that it applied only to mortgages on real property. Since no change in substance was intended by the revisers, CPLR 8303(a)(1) should be clarified accordingly in order to prevent any misconstruction. The proposed clarification would also remove an inconsistency with CPLR 8302(a)(1), which expressly applies to mortgages on real property only."

1965 AMENDMENTS

L. 1965, ch. 577, eff. June 28, 1965, amended paragraph 6 of subd. (a).

§ 8303-a. Costs upon frivolous claims and counterclaims in actions to recover damages for personal injury, injury to property or wrongful death.

(a) If in an action to recover damages for personal injury, injury to property or wrongful death, or an action brought by the individual who committed a crime against the victim of the crime, and such action or claim is commenced or continued by a plaintiff or a counterclaim, defense or cross claim is commenced or continued by a defendant and is found, at any time during the proceedings or upon judgment, to be frivolous by the court, the court shall award to the successful party costs and reasonable attorney's fees not exceeding ten thousand dollars.

(b) The costs and fees awarded under subdivision (a) of this section shall be assessed either against the party bringing the action, claim, cross claim, defense or counterclaim or against the attorney for such party, or against both, as may be determined by the court, based upon the circumstances of the case. Such costs and fees shall be in addition to any other judgment awarded to the successful party.

(c) In order to find the action, claim, counterclaim, defense or cross claim to be frivolous under subdivision (a) of this section, the court must find one or more of the following:

(i) the action, claim, counterclaim, defense or cross claim was commenced, used or continued in bad faith, solely to delay or prolong the resolution of the litigation or to harass or maliciously injure another;

(ii) the action, claim, counterclaim, defense or cross claim was commenced or continued in bad faith without any reasonable basis in law or fact and could not be supported by a good faith argument for an extension, modification or reversal of existing law. If the action, claim, counterclaim, defense or cross claim was promptly discontinued when the party or the attorney learned or should have learned that the action, claim, counterclaim, defense or cross claim lacked such a reasonable basis, the court may find that the party or the attorney did not act in bad faith.

1997 AMENDMENTS

L. 1997, ch. 620, eff. Nov. 1, 1997, and applicable to cases in which a final judgment has been ordered on or after such date, amended paragraph (a) by adding in reference to an action brought by the individual who committed a crime against the crime victim.

1986 AMENDMENTS

L. 1986, ch. 220, eff. June 28, 1986, and applicable to actions or proceedings commenced on or after such date, amended paragraph (a) by providing for costs upon frivolous claims and counterclaims in actions for personal injury, injury to property or wrongful death, and deleting references to dental and medical malpractice actions.

L. 1986, ch. 485, eff. July 21, 1986, amended CPLR 8303-a to apply to podiatric malpractice actions. Such amendment is applicable to acts, omissions or failures occurring on or after such date.

1985 AMENDMENTS

L. 1985, ch. 294, eff. July 1, 1985, and applicable to any action for dental or medical malpractice commenced on or after such date, added CPLR 8303-a.

CPLR

Article 84

TAXATION OF COSTS

§ 8401. Computation by clerk.

Costs, disbursements and additional allowances shall be taxed by the clerk upon the application of the party entitled thereto. A valuation of property necessary for fixing an additional allowance shall be ascertained by the court, unless it has been fixed by the decision of the court, verdict of the jury, or report of the referee or commissioners, upon which the judgment is entered. The clerk, whether or not objection is made, shall examine the bills presented to him for taxation; shall satisfy himself that all the items allowed by him are correct and allowable; and shall strike out all items of disbursements, other than the prospective charges expressly allowed by law, not supported by affidavit showing that they have been necessarily incurred and are reasonable in amount. The clerk shall insert in the judgment the total of the amount taxed as costs, disbursements and additional allowances.

§ 8402. Taxation with notice.

Costs may be taxed upon at least five days' notice to each adverse party interested in reducing the amount thereof except one against whom judgment was entered on default in appearance. A copy of the bill of costs, specifying the items in detail, and a copy of any supporting affidavits shall be served with the notice.

§ 8403. Taxation without notice.

Costs may also be taxed without notice. A party who has taxed costs without notice shall immediately serve a copy of the bill of costs upon each party who is entitled to notice under section 8402. Within five days after such service, any such party may serve notice of retaxation of costs upon five days' notice to the party who has taxed the costs, specifying the item as to which retaxation is sought.

§ 8404. Judicial review of taxation or retaxation.

Upon motion of any interested party, on notice, the court may allow or disallow any item objected to before the clerk; or it may order a retaxation before the clerk and it may specify the grounds or the proof upon which an item may be allowed or disallowed.

Article 85
SECURITY FOR COSTS

SUMMARY OF ARTICLE

§ 8501.   Security for costs.

   (a) As of right.

   (b) In court's discretion.

§ 8502.   Stay and dismissal on failure to give security.

§ 8503.   Undertaking.

§ 8501. Security for costs.

(a) As of right. Except where the plaintiff has been granted permission to proceed as a poor person or is the petitioner in a habeas corpus proceeding, upon motion by the defendant without notice, the court or a judge thereof shall order security for costs to be given by the plaintiffs where none of them is a domestic corporation, a foreign corporation licensed to do business in the state or a resident of the state when the motion is made.

(b) In court's discretion. Upon motion by the defendant with notice, or upon its own initiative, the court may order the plaintiff to give security for costs in an action by or against an assignee or trustee for the benefit of creditors, a trustee, a receiver or debtor in possession in bankruptcy, an official trustee or a committee of a person imprisoned in this state, an executor or administrator, the committee of a person judicially declared to be incompetent, the conservator of a conservatee, a guardian ad litem, or a receiver.

1981 AMENDMENTS

L. 1981, ch. 115, eff. May 18, 1981, amended CPLR 8501(b) by adding actions by or against a conservator of a conservatee to those actions in which a court may, in its discretion, require the plaintiff to give security for costs.

§ 8502. Stay and dismissal on failure to give security.

Until security for costs is given pursuant to the order of the court, all proceedings other than to review or vacate such order shall be stayed.

If the plaintiff shall not have given security for costs at the expiration of thirty days from the date of the order, the court may dismiss the complaint upon motion by the defendant, and award costs in his favor.

§ 8503. Undertaking.

Security for costs shall be given by an undertaking in an amount of five hundred dollars in counties within the city of New York, and two hundred fifty dollars in all other counties, or such greater amount as shall be fixed by the court that the plaintiff shall pay all legal costs awarded to the defendant.

1972 AMENDMENTS

L. 1972, ch. 734 and ch. 735, eff. July 1, 1972, increased the amount of the undertaking for security for costs in New York City to five hundred dollars.

Article 86

COUNSEL FEES AND EXPENSES IN CERTAIN ACTIONS AGAINST THE STATE

§ 8600.   Intent and short title.

It is the intent of this article, which may hereafter be known and cited as the "New York State Equal Access to Justice Act," to create a mechanism authorizing the recovery of counsel fees and other reasonable expenses in certain actions against the state of New York, similar to the provisions of federal law contained in 28 U.S.C. § 2412(d) and the significant body of case law that has evolved thereunder.

1990 AMENDMENTS

L. 1990, ch. 73, eff. April 1, 1990 to March 31, 1992, amended CPLR 8600 to replace the erroneous reference to 5 U.S.C. § 504 with the correct reference, 28 U.S.C. § 2412(d).

§ 8601. Fees and other expenses in certain actions against the state.

(a) When awarded. In addition to costs, disbursements and additional allowances awarded pursuant to sections eight thousand two hundred one through eight thousand two hundred four and eight thousand three hundred one through eight thousand three hundred three of this chapter, and except as otherwise specifically provided by statute, a court shall award to a prevailing party, other than the state, fees and other expenses incurred by such party in any civil action brought against the state, unless the court finds that the position of the state was substantially justified or that special circumstances make an award unjust. Whether the position of the state was substantially justified shall be determined solely on the basis of the record before the agency or official whose act, acts, or failure to act gave rise to the civil action. Fees shall be determined pursuant to prevailing market rates for the kind and quality of the services furnished, except that fees and expenses may not be awarded to a party for any portion of the litigation in which the party has unreasonably protracted the proceedings.

(b) Application for fees. A party seeking an award of fees and other expenses shall, within thirty days of final judgment in the action, submit to the court an application which sets forth (1) the facts supporting the claim that the party is a prevailing party and is eligible to receive an award under this section, (2) the amount sought, and (3) an itemized statement from every attorney or expert witness for whom fees or expenses are sought stating the actual time expended and the rate at which such fees and other expenses are claimed.

1990 AMENDMENTS

L. 1990, ch. 73, eff. April 1, 1990 to March 31, 1992, amended CPLR 8601 to provide discussion of fees and other expenses in certain actions against the state; and amended to replace the original references to "plaintiff or petitioner" with "party;" the original references to "defendant" with "state;" and the reference to "action" in the final sentence of subdivision (a) with "act, acts."

§ 8602. Definitions.

For the purpose of this article:

(a) "Action" means any civil action or proceeding brought to seek judicial review of an action of the state as defined in subdivision (g) of this section, including an appellate proceeding, but does not include an action brought in the court of claims.

(b) "Fees and other expenses" means the reasonable expenses of expert witnesses, the reasonable cost of any study, analysis, consultation with experts, and like expenses, and reasonable attorney fees, including fees for work performed by law students or paralegals under the supervision of an attorney incurred in connection with an administrative proceeding and judicial action.

(c) "Final judgment" means a judgment that is final and not appealable, and settlement.

(d) "Party" means (i) an individual whose net worth, not including the value of a homestead used and occupied as a principal residence, did not exceed fifty thousand dollars at the time the civil action was filed; (ii) any owner of an unincorporated business or any partnership, corporation, association, real estate developer or organization which had no more than one hundred employees at the time the civil action was filed, (iii) any organization described in section 501(c)(3) of the Internal Revenue Code of 1954 (26 U.S.C. 501(c)(3)) exempt from taxation under section 501(a) of such Code regardless of the number of employees.

(e) "Position of the state" means the act, acts or failure to act from which judicial review is sought.

(f) "Prevailing party" means a plaintiff or petitioner in the civil action against the state who prevails in whole or in substantial part where such party and the state prevail upon separate issues.

(g) "State" means the state or any of its agencies or any of its officials acting in his or her official capacity.

§ 8603. Interest.

If the state appeals an award made pursuant to this section and the award is affirmed in whole or in part, interest shall be paid on the amount of the award. Such interest shall run from the date of the award

CPLR

through the day before the date of the affirmance.

§ 8604. Annual report.

The department of audit and control shall file with the governor, the speaker of the assembly and the majority leader of the senate an annual report describing the number, nature and amount of each award in the previous fiscal year including the agency involved in each action, and other relevant information which might aid the legislature and the governor in evaluating the scope and impact of such awards.

§ 8605. Applicability.

(a) Nothing contained in this article shall be construed to alter or modify the other provisions of this chapter where applicable to actions other than actions against the state.

(b) Nothing contained in this article shall be deemed to authorize the institution of a civil action for the sole purpose of obtaining fees incurred by a party to an administrative proceeding.

(c) Nothing contained in this article shall affect or preclude the right of any party to recover fees or other expenses authorized by common law or by any other statute, law or rule.

1992 AMENDMENTS

L. 1992, ch. 36, § 1, amended L. 1989, ch. 770, by omitting "except that the provisions of article 86 of the civil practice law and rules, as added by section one of this act, shall expire and be deemed repealed on March 31, 1992."

1989 AMENDMENTS

L. 1989, ch. 770, eff. April 1, 1990, created this new Article 86; Section 2 of that chapter provided that the new Article 86 "shall apply to all actions commenced on or after such date, except that the provisions of article 86 of the civil practice law and rules, as added by section one of this act, shall expire and be deemed repealed on March 31, 1992."

Article 87
PUNITIVE DAMAGE AWARDS; PUBLIC SHARE

[**Editor's note:** *L. 1992, ch. 55, eff. April 10, 1992 and deemed repealed on April 1, 1994, pursuant to L. 1992, ch. 55, § 427(dd).*]

Article 90

FAILURE OR ADJOURNMENT OF TERM OF COURT

SUMMARY OF ARTICLE

R 9001.   No abatement by failure, adjournment, or change of time or place of term of court.

R 9002.   Death, disability or incapacity of judge following verdict, report, decision, or determination of motion or special proceeding.

R 9003.   Running of time when county judge disqualified from acting in a case.

R 9001. No abatement by failure, adjournment, or change of time or place of term of court.

When a term of a court fails or is adjourned or the time or place of holding it is changed, all persons are bound to appear and all proceedings shall continue at the time and place to which the term is adjourned or changed, or, if it has failed, at the next term, with like effect as if the term had been held as originally appointed.

R 9002. Death, disability or incapacity of judge following verdict, report, decision, or determination of motion or special proceeding.

The death, sickness, resignation, removal from or expiration of office or other disability or legal incapacity of a judge following his verdict, report, decision or determination of a motion or special proceeding in any matter in a civil judicial proceeding shall not affect its validity. Unless otherwise provided by rule of the chief administrator of the courts, any other judge of the same court may, on the application of a party, give effect to such verdict, report, decision or determination and make and sign an appropriate order or judgment based thereon, which shall have the same effect as if it had been made by the judge upon whose verdict, report, decision or determination it is based.

CPLR

CROSS REFERENCES

See **Judiciary Law § 7-c** in Appendix, *below*, as to continuance of special proceeding before another officer.

1986 AMENDMENTS

L. 1986, ch. 355, eff. July 17, 1986, amended CPLR 9002 by adding "Unless otherwise provided by rule of the chief administrator of the courts" at the beginning of the second sentence.

1974 AMENDMENTS

Amended by proposal No. 4 of the Judicial Conference Report to the 1974 Legislature by adding the reference to a "determination of a motion or special proceeding." As stated by the 1974 Judicial Conference Report: "[A]t present there is no statute or rule providing that in case of death, sickness, resignation, removal from or expiration of office or other disability or legal incapacity of a judge after determining a motion or special proceeding, any judge of the same court may sign an order determining such motion or special proceeding. Thus, the proposed amendment would remove the present necessity in such case for duplicative proceedings."

1969 AMENDMENTS

Amendment promulgated by Judicial Conference Feb. 1, 1969 Report to the Legislature, effective Sept. 1, 1969, so as to permit any judge of the same court to sign the concluding order or judgment where the judge who rendered the verdict, report or decision cannot sign the concluding order or judgment because of "sickness, resignation, removal from or expiration of office or other disability or legal incapacity."

R 9003. Running of time when county judge disqualified from acting in a case.

If a county judge is disqualified from acting in any case pending in his court and files a certificate pursuant to judiciary law section one hundred ninety-two, the time within which any proceeding may be taken, as fixed by statute or rule, does not begin to run until the certificate is filed.

CROSS REFERENCES

Judiciary Law § 192 was repealed by L. 1964, ch. 53, eff. Sept. 1, 1964.

Article 94

ADMISSION TO PRACTICE

***

SUMMARY OF ARTICLE

R 9401.   Committee.

The appellate division in each judicial department shall appoint a committee of not less than three practicing lawyers for each judicial district within the department, for the purpose of investigating the character and fitness of every applicant for admission to practice as an attorney and counselor at law in the courts of this state. Each member of such committee shall serve until his death, resignation or the appointment of his successor. A lawyer who has been or who shall be appointed a member of the committee for one district may be appointed a member of the committee for another district within the same department.

R 9402.   Application for admission.

Every application for admission to practice pursuant to the provisions of paragraph a of subdivision one of section ninety of the judiciary law by a person who has been certified by the state board of law examiners, in accordance with the provisions of section four hundred sixty-four of said law, shall be referred by the appellate division to the committee for a district in its judicial department. Every application for admission to practice which is made on motion without the taking of the bar examination, pursuant to rules of the court of appeals and the provisions of paragraph b of subdivision one of section ninety of the judiciary law, by a person already admitted to practice in another jurisdiction, shall be referred by the appellate division to the committee for a district in its judicial department.

1985 AMENDMENTS

L. 1985, ch. 226, eff. June 15, 1985, amended CPLR 9402 to provide that the appellate division shall refer applications for admission to the committee in a district in its judicial department.

R 9403. Referral to another judicial district.

Notwithstanding rule 9402, any application for admission to practice pending before a committee, may be referred to the committee for another judicial district in the same or another department by order or direction of the presiding justice of the appellate division of the department embracing the district in which the application is pending. Such order or direction may be made only upon the written request of the chairman or acting chairman of the committee before which the application is pending and only upon his written certification either:

1. that the applicant, since he applied to take the bar examination or to dispense with such examination or since he applied on motion to be admitted to practice, has changed his actual residence to such other judicial district in the same or other department, or, if not a resident of the state, has acquired full-time employment in or changed his place of full-time employment to such other judicial district in the same or other department; or

2. that the majority of the members of such committee are not qualified to vote on the application or have disqualified themselves from voting or have refrained from voting thereon; or

3. that the members of such committee are equally divided in their opinion as* the application; or

4. that strict compliance with rule 9402 will cause undue hardship to the applicant.

* **[Editor's note:** So in original. Probably should read "as to."]

1985 AMENDMENTS

L. 1985, ch. 226, eff. June 18, 1985, amended CPLR 9403 to provide for transfer of an application for admission in the case of a non-resident acquiring full-time employment in a judicial district or where strict compliance with CPLR 9402 will cause undue hardship.

1973 AMENDMENTS

CPLR 9403 was amended by proposal No. 6 of the Judicial Conference Report to the 1973 Legislature, effective Sept. 1, 1973, to provide for the transfer of an application for admission to the bar from one judicial department to another.

R 9404. Certificate of character and fitness.

Unless otherwise ordered by the appellate division, no person shall be admitted to practice without a certificate from the proper committee that it has carefully investigated the character and fitness of the applicant and that, in such respects, he is entitled to admission. To enable the committee to make such investigation, the justices of the appellate division are authorized to prescribe and from time to time to amend a form of statement or questionnaire to be submitted by the applicant, including specifically his present and such past places of actual residence as may be required therein, listing the street and number, if any, and the period of time he resided at each place.

CPLR

1973 AMENDMENTS

CPLR 9404 was amended by proposal No. 7 of the Judicial Conference Report to the 1973 Legislature, effective Sept. 1, 1973.

1965 AMENDMENTS

L. 1965, ch. 675, eff. Sept. 1, 1965.

R 9405. Prior application.

In the event that any applicant has made a prior application for admission to practice in this state or in any other jurisdiction, then upon said statement or questionnaire or in an accompanying signed statement, he shall set forth in detail all the facts with respect to such prior application and its disposition. If such prior application had been filed in any appellate division of this state and if the applicant failed to obtain a certificate of good character and fitness from the appropriate character committee or if for any reason such prior application was disapproved or rejected either by said committee or said appellate division, he shall obtain and submit the written consent of said appellate division to the renewal of his application in that appellate division or in any other appellate division.

R 9406.   Proof.

No person shall receive said certificate from any committee and no person shall be admitted to practice as an attorney and counselor at law in the courts of this state, unless he shall furnish satisfactory proof to the effect:

    1. that he supports the constitutions of the United States and of the state of New York; and

    2. that he has complied with all the requirements of the applicable statutes of this state, the applicable rules of the court of appeals and the applicable rules of the appellate division in which his application is pending, relating to the admission to practice as an attorney and counselor at law.

CROSS REFERENCES

See **Judiciary Law** § 464 as to certification of non-residents employed within the state.

1985 AMENDMENTS

L. 1985, ch. 226, eff. June 18, 1985, amended CPLR 9406 by deleting subd. (2), mandating a six-month residency requirement for admission to practice, and amending subd. (1) to require applicants to prove they support the United States and New York constitutions.

1978 AMENDMENTS

L. 1978, ch. 294, eff. June 19, 1978, and applicable to applications for admission to practice made after June 1, 1975, eliminated from subd. (2) the former requirement that an applicant furnish proof that his residence in New York State has continued until the final disposition of his application.

1974 AMENDMENTS

Amended by proposal No. 5 of the Judicial Conference Report to the 1974 Legislature by deleting the second subdivision which provided that no person may be admitted to the bar in New York State unless he is a citizen of the United States. The remaining subdivisions were renumbered accordingly.

1965 AMENDMENTS

L. 1965, ch. 675, eff. Sept. 1, 1965, amended Subd. 3, now Subd. 2.

R 9407.   Filing.

Every application for admission to practice, together with all the papers submitted thereon, upon its final disposition by the appellate division shall be filed in the office of the clerk of such appellate division.

Article 97

RECORDS OF CLERKS OF THE COURTS

SUMMARY OF ARTICLE

R 9701.   Records to be kept by the clerk of appellate division.

R 9702.   Books to be kept by the clerks of other courts.

R 9703.   Form of records.

R 9701. Records to be kept by the clerk of appellate division.

The clerk of the appellate division in each department shall keep:

1. a book, properly indexed, or an index, in which shall be entered the title of all proceedings in that court, with entries under each, showing the proceedings taken therein and the final disposition thereof; and

2. a book in which shall be indexed all undertakings filed in the clerk's office, with a statement of the proceedings in which they are given, and a statement of any disposition or order made of or concerning them; and

3. a book, properly indexed, or an index, which shall contain (a) the name of each attorney admitted to practice, in the department, with the date of the attorney's admission, and (b) the name of each person who has been refused admission or who has been disbarred, disciplined or censured by the court. The clerk of each department shall transmit to the clerk of the court of appeals and to the clerks of the other departments the names of all applicants who have been refused admission, and the names of all attorneys who have resigned or who have been disbarred, disciplined, censured or reinstated by the court.

1990 AMENDMENTS

L. 1990, ch. 623, eff. July 18, 1990, redesignated former subdivisions (3) and (4) as (2) and (3), respectively, and deleted subdivision (2); L. 1990, ch. 184, eff. May 24, 1990, deleted the reference in subdivision (3), clause (b), prior to its redesignation as subdivision (3) by L. 1990, ch. 623, eff. May 24, 1990, to "the names of all attorneys who have been admitted to practice."

CPLR

1975 AMENDMENTS

CPLR 9701 was amended by Proposal No. 3 of the Judicial Conference Report to the 1975 Legislature, effective Sept. 1, 1975, to conform the language to the recordkeeping practices actually employed by the clerks of the Appellate Divisions.

R 9702.   Books to be kept by the clerks of other courts.

The clerks of the other courts shall keep:

1. a "judgment-book," in which shall be recorded all judgments entered in their offices;

2. a book, properly indexed, in which shall be entered the title of all civil judicial proceedings, with proper entries under each denoting the papers filed and the orders made and the steps taken therein, with the dates of the filing of the several papers in the proceeding;

3. a book, properly indexed, in which shall be entered the name and address of each conservator, committee or guardian who is appointed pursuant to the provisions of the mental hygiene law, the title of the proceeding, the name and address of any surety, the papers filed, and any orders made or steps taken therein;

4. a book in which shall be recorded at length each undertaking of a public officer or any officer appointed by the court, filed in their offices, except the undertakings of receivers appointed under section 5228, with a statement showing when the undertaking was filed and a notation on the margin of the record showing any disposition, or order, made of or concerning it;

5. such other books, properly indexed, as may be necessary, or convenient, to contain the docket of judgments, the entry of orders, and all other necessary matters and proceedings; and

6. such other books as the chief administrator of the courts may direct to be kept.

1990 AMENDMENTS

L. 1990, ch. 184, eff. May 24, 1990, amended CPLR 9702 by deleting the phrase "the minutes of the court" in subdivision (5); L. 1990, Ch. 623, eff. July 18, 1990, amended CPLR 9702 by substituting the reference to the appellate divisions in subdivision (6) with "chief administrator of the courts."

1977 AMENDMENTS

L. 1977, ch. 28, eff. Sept. 1, 1977, amended CPLR 9702 by adding a new subdivision (3), and by renumbering the remaining subdivisions accordingly.

R 9703. Form of records.

A clerk shall keep books and records in such form and style as may be prescribed by the chief administrator of the courts.

1990 AMENDMENTS

L. 1990, ch. 623, eff. July 18, 1990, amended CPLR 9703 by designating that the form of books and records will now be as prescribed by the chief administrator of the courts.

CPLR

Article 98
ACTIONS AGAINST VILLAGES

SUMMARY OF ARTICLE

§ 9801.	Actions against the village.
§ 9802.	Liability of villages in certain actions.
§ 9803.	Place of trial of actions and proceedings against villages.
§ 9804.	Notice of defects in certain actions.

§ 9801. Actions against the village.

1. No action shall be maintained against the village for a personal injury or injury to property alleged to have been sustained by reason of the negligence or wrongful act of the village or of any officer, agent or employee thereof, unless a notice of claim shall have been made and served in compliance with section fifty-e of the general municipal law.

2. Every such action shall be commenced pursuant to the provisions of section fifty-i of the general municipal law.

CROSS REFERENCES

General Municipal Law § 50-e, referred to in paragraph (1), *above*, appears in Appendix, *below*. General Municipal Law § 50-i, referred to in paragraph (2), *above*, appears in Appendix, *below*.

1972 AMENDMENTS

L. 1972, ch. 890, § 3, eff. Sept. 1, 1973, added new CPLR Article 98 (CPLR 9801-9803) concerning actions against villages.

§ 9802. Liability of villages in certain actions.

Except as provided otherwise in this chapter no action shall be maintained against the village upon or arising out of a contract of the village unless the same shall be commenced within eighteen months after the cause of action therefor shall have accrued, nor unless a written verified claim shall have been filed with the village clerk within one year after the cause of action shall have accrued, and no other action shall be maintained against the village unless the same shall be commenced within one year after the cause of action therefor shall have accrued, nor unless a notice of claim shall have been made and served in compliance with section fifty-e of the general municipal law. The omission to present a claim or to commence an action thereon within the respective periods of time above stated applicable to such claim, shall be a bar to any claim or action therefor against said village; but no action shall be brought upon any such claim until forty days have elapsed after the filing of the claim in the office of the village clerk.

CROSS REFERENCES

See **General Municipal Law §§ 50-e, 50-h and 50-i** in Appendix, *below.*

§ 9803. Place of trial of actions and proceedings against villages.

The place of trial of all actions and proceedings against a village or any of its officers or boards shall be the county in which the village is situated.

§ 9804. Notice of defects in certain actions.

No civil action shall be maintained against the village for damages or injuries to person or property sustained in consequence of any street, highway, bridge, culvert, sidewalk or crosswalk being defective, out of repair, unsafe, dangerous or obstructed or for damages or injuries to persons or property sustained solely in consequence of the existence of snow or ice upon any sidewalk, crosswalk, street, highway, bridge or culvert unless written notice of the defective, unsafe, dangerous or obstructive condition, or of the existence of the snow or ice, relating to the particular place, was actually given to the village clerk and there was a failure or neglect within a reasonable time after the receipt of such notice to repair or remove the defect, danger or obstruction complained of or to cause the snow or ice to be removed, or the place otherwise made reasonably safe.

CROSS REFERENCES

The provisions of this section are also found in **Village Law § 6-628**. See also **Town Law §65-a**, as to liability of towns and town superintendents of highways, and notice requirements applicable thereto.

1973 AMENDMENTS

L. 1973, ch. 739, eff. Sept. 1, 1973, added new CPLR 9804.

Article 100

REPEAL; SAVING CLAUSES; EFFECTIVE DATE

SUMMARY OF ARTICLE

§ 10001.	Repeal of the civil practice act.
§ 10002.	Abrogation of rules of civil practice.
§ 10003.	Pending and subsequent proceedings.
§ 10004.	Effect of unconstitutionality in part.
§ 10005.	Effective date.

§ 10001. Repeal of the civil practice act.

Chapter nine hundred twenty-five of the laws of nineteen hundred twenty, entitled "An act in relation to the civil practice in the courts of the state of New York," and all acts amendatory thereof and supplemental thereto, constituting the civil practice act, as heretofore in effect, are hereby repealed.

§ 10002. Abrogation of rules of civil practice.

The rules of practice adopted by the convention provided for by chapter nine hundred two of the laws of nineteen hundred twenty, as amended or supplemented by appropriate action of the justices of the appellate division in the several departments pursuant to section eighty-three of the judiciary law, comprising the rules of civil practice, as heretofore in effect, are hereby abrogated and shall no longer be in effect.

§ 10003. Pending and subsequent proceedings.

This act shall apply to all actions hereafter commenced. This act shall also apply to all further proceedings in pending actions, except to the extent that the court determines that application in a particular pending action would not be feasible or would work injustice, in which event the former procedure applies. Proceedings pursuant to law in an action taken prior to the time this act takes effect shall not be rendered ineffectual or impaired by this act.

§ 10004.   Effect of unconstitutionality in part.

If any clause, sentence, paragraph, subdivision, section, rule or part of this chapter shall be adjudged by any court of competent jurisdiction to be invalid, such judgment shall not affect, impair or invalidate the remainder thereof, but shall be confined in its operation to the clause, sentence, paragraph, subdivision, section, rule or part thereof directly involved in the controversy in which such judgment shall have been rendered.

§ 10005.   Effective date.

This act shall take effect September first, nineteen hundred sixty-three.

UNIFORM RULES FOR THE NEW YORK STATE TRIAL COURTS (Part 202)

(Parts relating to Civil Practice)

CT RULES

CT RULES

§ 202.1   Application of Part; waiver; additional rules; application of CPLR; definitions.

(a) *Application.* This Part shall be applicable to civil actions and proceedings in the Supreme Court and the County Court.

(b) *Waiver.* For good cause shown, and in the interests of justice, the court in an action or proceeding may waive compliance with any of the rules in this Part, other than sections 202.2 and , unless prohibited from doing so by statute or by a rule of the Chief Judge.

(c) *Additional rules.* Local court rules, not inconsistent with law or with these rules, shall comply with Part 9 of the Rules of the Chief Judge (22 NYCRR Part 9).

(d) *Application of CPLR.* The provisions of this Part shall be construed consistent with the Civil Practice Law and Rules (CPLR), and matters not covered by these provisions shall be governed by the CPLR.

(e) *Definitions.*

(1) *Chief Administrator of the Courts* in this Part also includes a designee of the Chief Administrator.

(2) The term *clerk* shall mean the chief clerk or other appropriate

clerk of the trial court unless the context otherwise requires.

(3) Unless otherwise defined in this Part, or the context otherwise requires, all terms used in this Part shall have the same meaning as they have in the CPLR.

§ 202.2   Terms and parts of court.

(a) *Terms of court.* A term of court is a four-week session of court, and there shall be 13 terms of court in a year, unless otherwise provided in the annual schedule of terms established by the Chief Administrator of the Courts, which also shall specify the dates of such terms.

(b) *Parts of court.* A part of court is a designated unit of the court in which specified business of the court is to be conducted by a judge or quasi-judicial officer. There shall be such parts of court as may be authorized from time to time by the Chief Administrator of the Courts.

§ 202.3   Individual assignment system; structure.

(a) *General.* There shall be established for all civil actions and proceedings heard in the Supreme Court and County Court an individual assignment system which provides for the continuous supervision of each action and proceeding by a single judge. Except as otherwise may be authorized by the Chief Administrator or by these rules, every action and proceeding shall be assigned and heard pursuant to the individual assignment system.

(b) *Assignments.* Actions and proceedings shall be assigned to the judges of the court upon the filing with the court of a request for judicial intervention pursuant to section 202.6 of this Part. Assignments shall be made by the clerk of the court pursuant to a method of random selection authorized by the Chief Administrator. The judge thereby assigned shall be known as the "assigned judge" with respect to that matter and, except as otherwise provided in subdivision (c) of this section, shall conduct all further proceedings therein.

(c) *Exceptions.*

(1) Where the requirements of matters already assigned to a judge are such as to limit the ability of that judge to handle additional cases, the Chief Administrator may authorize that new assignments to that judge be suspended until the judge is able to handle additional cases.

CT RULES

(2) The Chief Administrator may authorize the establishment in any court of special categories of actions and proceedings, including but not limited to matrimonial actions, medical malpractice actions, tax assessment review proceedings, condemnation actions and actions requiring protracted consideration, for assignment to judges specially assigned to hear such actions or proceedings. Where more than one judge is specially assigned to hear a particular category of action or proceeding, the assignment of such actions or proceedings to the judges so assigned shall be at random.

(3) The Chief Administrator may authorize the assignment of one or more special reserve trial judges. Such judges may be assigned matters for trial in exceptional circumstances where the needs of the courts require such assignment.

(4) Matters requiring immediate disposition may be assigned to a judge designated to hear such matters when the assigned judge is not available.

(5) The Chief Administrator may authorize the transfer of any action or proceeding and any matter relating to an action or proceeding from one judge to another in accordance with the needs of the court.

(6) The Chief Administrator may authorize the establishment in any court or county or judicial district of a dual track system of assignment. Under such system each action and proceeding shall be supervised continuously by the individually assigned judge until the note of issue and certificate of readiness have been filed and the pretrial conference, if one is ordered, has been held. The action or proceeding then may be assigned to another judge for trial in a manner prescribed by the Chief Administrator.

§ 202.4   County Court judge; *ex parte* applications in Supreme Court actions; applications for settlement of Supreme Court actions.

Ex parte applications in actions or proceedings in the Supreme Court, and applications for the settlement of actions or proceedings pending in the Supreme Court, where judicial approval is necessary, may be heard and determined by a judge of the County Court in the county where venue is laid, during periods when no Supreme Court term is in session in the county.

§ 202.5   Papers filed in court.

(a) *Index number; form; label.* The party filing the first paper in an action, upon payment of the proper fee, shall obtain from the county clerk an index number, which shall be affixed to the paper. The party causing the first paper to be filed shall communicate in writing the county clerk's index number forthwith to all other parties to the action. Thereafter such number shall appear on the outside cover and first page to the right of the caption of every paper tendered for filing in the action. Each such cover and first page also shall contain an indication of the county of venue and a brief description of the nature of the paper and, where the case has been assigned to an individual judge, shall contain the name of the assigned judge to the right of the caption. In addition to complying with the provisions of CPLR 2101, every paper filed in court shall have annexed thereto appropriate proof of service on all parties where required, and if typewritten, shall have at least double space between each line, except for quotations and the names and addresses of attorneys appearing in the action, and shall have at least one-inch margins. In addition, every paper filed in court, other than an exhibit or printed form, shall contain writing on one side only, except that papers that are fastened on the side may contain writing on both sides. Papers that are stapled or bound securely shall not be rejected for filing simply because they are not bound with a backer of any kind.

(b) *Submission of papers to judge.* All papers for signature or consideration of the court shall be presented to the clerk of the trial court in the appropriate courtroom or clerk's office, except that where the clerk is unavailable or the judge so directs, papers may be submitted to the judge and a copy filed with the clerk at the first available opportunity. All papers for any judge that are filed in the clerk's office shall be promptly delivered to the judge by the clerk. The papers shall be clearly addressed to the judge for whom they are intended and prominently show the nature of the papers, the title and index number of the action in which they are filed, the judge's name and the name of the attorney or party submitting them.

(c) *Papers filed to commence an action or special proceeding.* For purposes of CPLR 304, governing the method of commencing actions and special proceedings, the term "clerk of the court" shall mean the county clerk. Each county clerk, and each chief clerk of the Supreme Court, shall post prominently in the public areas of his or her office notice that filing of papers in order to commence an action or special proceeding must be with the county clerk. Should the county clerk, as provided by CPLR 304, designate a person or persons other than himself or herself to accept delivery of the papers required to be filed in order to commence an action or special proceeding, the posted notice shall so specify.

§ 202.5-a   Filing by facsimile transmission.

(a) *Application.* (1) There is hereby established a pilot program in which papers may be filed by facsimile transmission with the Supreme Court and, as is provided in section 206.5-a of these rules, with the Court of Claims. In the Supreme Court, the program shall be limited to commercial claims and tax certiorari, conservatorship, and mental hygiene proceedings in Monore, Westchester, New York and Suffolk Counties.

(2) "Facsimile transmission" for purposes of these rules shall mean any method of transmission of documents to a facsimile machine at a remote location which can automatically produce a tangible copy of such document.

(b) *Procedure.*

(1) Papers in any civil actions or proceedings designated pursuant to this section, including those commencing an action or proceeding, may be filed with the appropriate court clerk by facsimile transmission at a facsimile telephone number provided by the court for that purpose. The cover page of each facsimile transmission shall be in a form prescribed by the Chief Administrator and shall state the nature of the paper being filed; the name, address and telephone number of the filing party or party's attorney; the facsimile telephone number that may receive a return facsimile transmission, and the number of total pages, including the cover page, being filed. The papers, including exhibits, shall comply with the requirements of CPLR 2101(a) and section 202.5 of these rules and shall be signed as required by law. Whenever a paper is filed that requires the payment of a filing fee, a separate credit card or debit card

authorization sheet shall be included and shall contain the credit or debit card number or other information of the party or attorney permitting such card to be debited by the clerk for payment of the filing fee. The card authorization sheet shall be kept separately by the clerk and shall not be a part of the public record. The clerk shall not be required to accept papers more than 50 pages in length, including exhibits but excluding the cover page and the card authorization sheet.

(2) Papers may be transmitted at any time of the day or night to the appropriate facsimile telephone number and will be deemed filed upon receipt of the facsimile transmission, provided, however, that where payment of a fee is required, the papers will not be deemed filed unless accompanied by a completed credit card or debit card authorization sheet. The clerk shall date-stamp the papers with the date that they were received. Where the papers initiate an action, the clerk also shall mark the papers with the index number. No later than the following business day, the clerk shall transmit a copy of the first page of each paper, containing the date of filing and, where appropriate, the index number, to the filing party or attorney, either by facsimile or first class mail. If any page of the papers filed with the clerk was missing or illegible, a telephonic, facsimile, or postal notification transmitted by the clerk to the party or attorney shall so state, and the party or attorney shall forward the new or corrected page to the clerk for inclusion in the papers.

(c) *Technical Failures.* The appropriate clerk shall deem the UCS fax server to be subject to a technical failure on a given day if the server is unable to accept filings continuously or intermittently over the course of any period of time greater than one hour after 12:00 noon of that day The clerk shall provide notice of all such technical failures by means of the UCS fax server which persons may telephone in order to learn the current status of the Service which appears to be down. When filing by fax is hindered by a technical failure of the UCS fax server, with the exception of deadlines that by law cannot be extended, the time for filing of any paper that is delayed due to technical failure shall be extended for one day for each day in which such technical failure occurs, unless otherwise ordered by the court.

§ 202.5-b   Electronic Filing in Supreme Court.

(a) *Application.* (1) There is hereby established a pilot program in which documents may be filed and served by electronic means in civil actions in Supreme Court. Documents may be filed or served by such means only to the extent and in the manner authorized in this section and only in the following actions: (i) tax certiorari actions (including small claims actions under Title 1-A of Article 7 of the Real Property Tax Law) and tort and commercial actions in the Supreme Court in Albany, Bronx, Essex, Kings, Livingston, Monroe, Nassau, New York, Niagara, Onondaga, Queens, Richmond, Suffolk, Sullivan and Westchester Counties; and (ii) actions in Supreme Court in Broome County and Erie County of any type designated by the appropriate Administrative Judge.

(2) For purposes of these rules:

(i) *electronic means* shall mean any method of transmission of information between computers or other machines, other than facsimile machines, designed for the purpose of sending and receiving such transmissions, and which allows the recipient to reproduce the information transmitted in a tangible medium of expression

(ii) the *e-filing Internet site* shall mean the website located at www.nycourts.gov/efile;

(iii) *e-filing, electronic filing and electronically filing* shall mean the filing and service of documents in a civil action by electronic means through the e-filing Internet site;

(iv) an *authorized e-filing user* shall mean a person who has registered to use e-filing pursuant to subdivision (c) of this section;

(v) an *action* shall include a special proceeding.

(vi) *hard copy* shall mean information set forth in paper form; and

(vii) *party or parties* shall mean the party or parties to an action or counsel thereto.

(b) *E–Filing in Actions in Supreme Court.* (1) *Commencing an action by electronic means.* A party may commence any action specified in paragraph (1) of subdivision (a) of this section by electronically filing the initiating documents with the County Clerk.

(2) *E-filing in an action after commencement.*

(i) *Consent of the parties required.* After commencement of an action specified in paragraph (1) of subdivision (a) of this section, documents may be electronically filed and served, but only if and when all parties have consented thereto or, if fewer than all parties have so consented, only by and between consenting parties with the permission of the court.

(ii) *Consent to e-filing; how obtained.* A consent to e-filing in an action shall state that the party providing it agrees to the use of e-filing in the action and to be bound by the filing and service provisions in this section. Consent may be obtained by stipulation or a party who seeks to use e-filing in a pending action may serve upon all other parties to the action a notice regarding use of e-filing in a form approved by the Chief Administrator of the Courts. Service of such a notice shall constitute consent to e-filing in the action by the party causing such service to be made. A party served with such a notice may consent to e-filing in the action not later than ten days after receipt of such service, either by filing with the court and serving on all parties of record a consent to e-filing or if such party or the attorney of record therefor is an authorized e-filing user, by filing the consent electronically in the manner provided at the e-filing Internet site; provided, however, the court, in its discretion, may permit a consent to e-filing at any time thereafter. The filing of a consent to e-filing hereunder shall not constitute an appearance in the action.

(iii) *Filing and service after consent to e-filing in an action.* Once an action is made subject to e-filing, all documents filed and served by consenting parties shall be served and filed in accordance with this section.

(iv) *Documents previously filed with the court; termination or modification of e-filing procedures.* When an action becomes subject to e-filing, the court may direct that documents previously filed in the action in hard copy be filed electronically by the parties. The court may at any time order discontinuation of e-filing in such action or modification of e-filing procedures therein in order to prevent prejudice and promote substantial justice. Where a court orders discontinuation of e-filing in an action, the court may direct the clerk

CT RULES

to convert into hard copy those documents comprising the case file which had been received electronically.

(c) *Authorized E-Filing Users, Passwords and Other Information.*

(1) *Registration required.* Documents may be filed or served electronically only by a person who has registered as an authorized e-filing user or as otherwise provided in this subdivision.

(2) *Registering as an authorized e-filing user.* Documents may be filed or served electronically only by a person who has registered as an authorized e-filing user or as otherwise provided in this subdivision.

(i) *Who may register.* An attorney admitted to practice in the State of New York, or a person seeking to use e-filing as an authorized agent on behalf of attorneys of record in action or actions (hereinafter "filing agent") may register as an authorized e-filing user of the e-filing Internet site. An attorney admitted *pro hac vice* in an action, a party to an action subject to e-filing who is not represented by an attorney, or a person who has been authorized in writing by an owner or owners of real property to submit a petition as provided in section 730 of the Real Property Tax Law and who has been licensed to engage in such business by the jurisdiction in which the business is operated (hereinafter "small claims assessment review filing agent") may also register as an authorized e-filing user, but solely for purposes of such action or, in the case of a small claims assessment review filing agent, solely for those proceedings under section 730 of the Real Property Tax Law in which he or she has been authorized to submit a petition.

(ii) *How to register.* Registration shall be on a form prescribed by the Chief Administrator, which shall require such information as he or shall shall specify. If so provided by the Chief Administrator, registration shall not be complete until the registering person has been approved as an e-filing user. An authorized e-filing user shall notify the appropriate clerk immediately of any change in the information provided on his or her registration form.

(3) *Identification and password.* Upon registration, an authorized e-filing user shall be issued a confidential User Identification Designation ("User ID") and a password by the Unified Court System ("UCS"). An authorized e-filing user shall maintain his or her User ID and password as confidential, except as provided in paragraph (4) of

this subdivision. Upon learning of the compromise of the confidentiality of either the User ID or the password, an authorized e-filing user shall immediately notify the appropriate clerk. At its initiative or upon request, the UCS may at any time issue a new User ID or password to any authorized e-filing user.

(4) An authorized e-filing user may authorize a another person to file a document electronically on his or her behalf in a particular action using the User ID and Password of the user, but in such event, the authorized e-filing user shall retain full responsibility for any document filed.

(d) *Electronic Filing of Documents.* (1) In any action subject to e-filing, all documents required to be filed with the court by a party that has consented to such e-filing shall be filed electronically , except as expressly provided herein. Each document to be filed electronically by a filing agent (other than one employed by a governmental entity) shall be accompanied by a statement of authorization from counsel of record in a form approved by the Chief Administrator.

(2) *Payment of fees.* Whenever documents are filed electronically that require the payment of a filing fee, the person who files the documents shall provide, in payment of the fee: (i) such credit or debit card information as shall be required at the e-filing Internet site to permit a card to be charged or debited by the County Clerk; or (ii) the form or information required by the County Clerk to permit him or her to debit an account maintained with the County Clerk by an attorney or law firm appearing for a party to the case; or (iii) any other form of payment authorized by the Chief Administrator. Notwithstanding the foregoing, an authorized e-filing user who electronically files documents that require the payment of a filing fee may cause such fee to be paid thereafter in person at the office of the County Clerk.

(3) *Filing and receipt of documents; confirmation; secure information.* (i) *When documents are filed.* Documents may be transmitted at any time of the day or night to the e-filing Internet site. Documents are deemed filed on the date on which their electronic transmission is recorded at that site, provided, however,

CT RULES

that where payment of a fee is required upon the filing of a document, the document will not be deemed filed until transmission of the information or form or information as required in (i) or (ii), respectively, of paragraph (2) of this subdivision is recorded at the e-filing Internet site; or, if no such transmission is recorded, until payment is physically presented to the County Clerk.

(ii) *Confirmation.* No later than the close of business on the business day following the electronic filing of a document, a confirmation notice shall be transmitted electronically by the e-filing Internet site to person filing such document. When documents initiating an action are filed electronically, the County Clerk shall assign an index number or filing number to the action and shall cause that number to be transmitted to the person filing such documents as part of the confirmation notice. If payment is submitted in person after the initiating documents have been transmitted electronically, the County Clerk shall assign the number upon presentation of that payment.

(iii) *Secure information.* When electronically filing a document, the person filing such document shall indicate whether it contains any of the following: individually identifiable health information, a social security number, a credit card number, a bank account number, an individual's date of birth, an individual's home address, a minor child's name, or trade secrets. If such person indicates that any of this information is contained in the document, access to it on the e-fling Internet site may be restricted to consenting parties to the action, the County Clerk and the court. The document will, however, be available for the public inspection at the office of the County Clerk unless sealed by the court.

(4) *Official record;courtesy copies* When a document has been filed electronically pursuant to this section, the official record shall be the electronic recording of the document stored by the clerk. The court may require the parties to provide courtesy hard copies of the documents filed electronically. Unless the court directs otherwise, each such copy shall bear a conspicuous notice on the first page that the document has been electronically filed.

(5) *Orders and judgments.* Unless the courts direct otherwise, any document that requires a judge's signature shall also be transmitted

electronically and in hard copy to the court. Orders Unless the Chief Administrator authorizes use of electronic signatures, orders and judgments signed by a judge shall be signed in hard copy, and shall be converted into electronic form by the appropriate clerk. The County Clerk may sign judgments in hard copy, or may affix a digital image of his or her signature to judgments in electronic form.,

(6) *Exhibits in hard copy.* Notwithstanding any other provision of this section, the clerk may permit a party to file in hard copy an exhibit which it is impractical or inconvenient to file electronically.

(e) *Signatures.*

(1) *Signing of a document.* An electronically filed document shall be considered to have been signed by, and shall be binding upon, the person identified as a signatory if:

(i) it bears the physical signature of such person and is scanned into an electronic format that reproduces such signature; or

(ii) the signatory has electronically affixed the digital image of his or her signature to the document; or

(iii) it is electronically filed under the User ID and password of that person; or

(iv) in a tax certiorari action in which the parties have stipulated to this procedure, it is an initiating document that is electronically filed without the signature of the signatory in a form provided above in this subparagraph, provided that, prior to filing, the document is signed in hard copy form (which hard copy must be preserved until the conclusion of all proceedings, including appeals, in the case in which it is filed) and the electronic record of the document bears the word "Signed" typed on the signature line; or

(v) it otherwise bears the electronic signature of the signatory in a format conforming to such standards and requirements as may hereafter be established by the Chief Administrator.

(2) *Compliance with Part 130.* A document shall be considered to have been signed by an attorney or party in compliance with section 130-1.1-a of the Rules of the Chief Administrator (22 NYCRR § 130-1.1-a) if it has been signed by such attorney or party as provided in paragraph (1) of this subdivision and it bears the

signatory's name, address and telephone number.

(3) *Certification of Signature.* A party or attorney may add his or her signature to a stipulation or other filed document by signing and filing a Certification of Signature for such document in a form prescribed by the Chief Administrator.

(f) *Service of Documents.* (1) *Service of initiating documents in an action.* Initiating documents may be served in hard copy pursuant to Article 3 of the CPLR, or in tax certiorari cases, pursuant to the Real Property Tax Law, or by electronic means if the party served agrees to accept such service. A party served by electronic means shall, within 24 hours of service, provide the serving party or attorney with an electronic confirmation that the service has been effected.

(2) *Service of interlocutory documents.*

(i) *E-mail address for service.* Each party in an action subject to electronic filing that has consented thereto shall identify on an appropriate form an e-mail address at which service of interlocutory documents on that party may be made through notification transmitted by the e-filing Internet site (hereinafter the "e-mail service address"). Each attorney of record and each self-represented party shall promptly notify the appropriate clerk in the event he or she changes his or her e-mail service address.

(ii) *How service is made.* Where parties have consented to e-filing, upon the receipt of an interlocutory document by the e-filing Internet site, the site shall automatically transmit electronic notification to all mail service addresses. Such notification shall provide the title of the document received, and the names of those appearing on the list of e-mail service addresses to whom that notification is being sent. Each party receiving the notification shall be responsible for accessing the e-filing Internet site to obtain a copy of the document received. The electronic transmission of the notification shall constitute service of the document on the mail service addresses identified therein, except that such service will not be effective if the filing party learns that it did not reach the address of the person to be served. Proof of such service will be recorded on the e-filing Internet site. A party may, however, utilize other service methods permitted by the CPLR provided that, if one of such other methods is used, proof of service shall be filed electronically.

(g) *Addition of Parties or Proposed Intervenors in a Pending E-Filed Action.* A party to be added in an action subject to e-filing shall be served with initiating documents in hard copy together with the notice regarding use of e-filing specified in paragraph (2)(ii) of subdivision (b) of this section, to which response shall be made as set forth in that paragraph. A proposed intervenor or other person seeking non-party who seeks relief from the court in an action subject to e-filing, if consenting to e-filing, shall promptly file and serve a consent to e-filing. If an added party or intervenor does not so consent, subsequent documents shall be served by and on that party or intervenor in hard copy but the action shall continue as an e-filed one as to all consenting parties.

(h) *Entry of Orders and Judgments and Notice of Entry.* In an action subject to e-filing, the County Clerk or his or her designee shall file orders and judgments of the court electronically, which shall constitute entry of the order or judgment. The date of entry shall be the date on which transmission of the order or judgment is recorded at the e-filing Internet site. The County Clerk may require that a party seeking entry of judgment electronically serve upon the County Clerk a request for entry of judgment. Upon entry of an order or judgment, the County Clerk, his or her designee, or the e-filing Internet site shall transmit to e-mail service addresses a notification of such entry, which shall not constitute service of notice of entry by any party. A party shall serve notice of entry of an order or judgment on another party by serving a copy of the notification received from the County Clerk, his or her designee or the e-filing Internet site, a copy of the order or judgment, and an express statement that the transmittal constitutes notice of entry. Service may be made through the e-filing Internet site, or by any other service methods permitted by the CPLR provided that, if one of such other methods is used, proof of service shall be filed electronically.

(i) Technical Failures. The appropriate clerk shall deem the e-filing Internet site to be subject to a technical failure on a given day if the site is unable to accept filings or provide access to filed documents continuously or intermittently over the course of any period of time greater than one hour after 12:00 noon of that day. The clerk shall provide notice of all such technical failures on site. When filing by electronic means is hindered by a technical failure, a party may file with the appropriate clerk in hard copy. With the exception of deadlines that by law cannot be extended, the time for filing of any paper that is delayed due to technical failure of the site shall be extended for one day for each day on which such failure occurs, unless otherwise ordered by the court.

(j) *Electronic Filing of Discovery Materials.* In any action subject to e-filing, parties and non-parties producing materials in response to discovery demands may enter into a stipulation authorizing the electronic filing of discovery responses and discovery materials to the degree and upon terms and conditions set forth in the stipulation. In the absence of such a stipulation , no party shall file electronically any such materials except in the form of excerpts, quotations, or selected exhibits from such materials as part of motion papers, pleadings or other filings with the court.

(k) *Copyright, Confidentiality, and Other Proprietary Rights.* (1) Submissions pursuant to e-filing procedures shall have the same copyright, confidentiality and proprietary rights as paper documents.

(2) In an action subject to e-filing , any person may apply for an order prohibiting or restricting the electronic filing in the action of specifically identified materials on the grounds that such materials are subject to copyright or other proprietary rights, or trade secret or other privacy interests, and that electronic filing in the action is likely to result in substantial prejudice to those rights or interests. Unless otherwise permitted by the court, a motion for such an order shall be filed not less than ten days before the materials to which the motion pertains are due to be produced or filed with the court.

§ 202.6   Request for judicial intervention.

(a) At any time after service of process, a party may file a request for judicial intervention. Except as provided in subdivision (b), in an action not yet assigned to a judge, the court shall not accept for filing a notice of motion, order to show cause, application for an ex parte order, notice of petition, note of issue, notice of medical, dental or podiatric malpractice action, statement of net worth pursuant to section 236 of the Domestic Relations Law or request for a preliminary conference pursuant to section 202.12(a) of this Part, unless such notice or application is accompanied by a request for judicial intervention. Where an application for poor person relief is made, payment of the fee for filing the request for judicial intervention accompanying the application shall be required only upon denial of the application. A request for judicial intervention must be submitted, in duplicate, on a form authorized by the Chief Administrator of the Courts, with proof of service on the other parties to the action (but proof of service is not required where the application is *ex parte*).

(b) The filing of a request for judicial intervention and payment of the fee required by CPLR 8020(a) for said filing shall not be required with respect to an application not filed in an action or proceeding, nor with respect to a petition for the sale of church property, an application for change of name, a habeas corpus proceeding where the movant is institutionalized, an application for default judgment to the clerk pursuant to CPLR 3215(a), an application under 3102(e) for court assistance in obtaining disclosure in an action pending in another state, a retention proceeding authorized by Article 9 of the Mental Hygiene Law, an appeal to a county court of a civil case brought in a court of limited jurisdiction, an application to vacate a judgment on account of bankruptcy, a motion for an order authorizing emergency surgery, or within the City of New York, an uncontested action for a judgment for annulment, divorce or separation commenced pursuant to Articles 9, 10 or 11 of the Domestic Relations Law.

(c) In the counties within the City of New York, when a request for judicial intervention is filed, the clerk shall require submission of a copy of the receipt of purchase of the index number provided by the county clerk, or a written statement of the county clerk that an index number was purchased in the action. Unless otherwise authorized by the Chief Administrator, the filing of a request for judicial intervention pursuant to this section shall cause the assignment of the action to a judge pursuant to section 202.3 of this Part. The clerk may require that a self-addressed and stamped envelope accompany the request for judicial intervention.

§ 202.7   Calendaring of motions; uniform notice of motion form; affirmation of good faith.

(a) There shall be compliance with the procedures prescribed in the CPLR for the bringing of motions. In addition, except as provided in

CT RULES

subdivision (d), no motion shall be filed with the court unless there have been served and filed with the motion papers (1) a notice of motion and (2) with respect to a motion relating to disclosure or to a bill of particulars, an affirmation that counsel has conferred with counsel for the opposing party in a good faith effort to resolve the issues raised by the motion.

(b) The notice of motion shall read substantially as follows:

COURT OF THE STATE OF NEW YORK COUNTY OF

A.B., Plaintiff,

-against-

C.D., Defendant.

Notice of Motion

Index No.

_ _ _ _ _ _ _ _

Name of Assigned Judge

_ _ _ _ _ _ _ _

Oral argument is requested
☑
(check box if applicable)

Upon the affidavit of _ _ _ _ _ _ _ _ _ , sworn to on _ _ _ _ _ _ _ _ 20,
and upon (list supporting papers if any), the _ _ _ _ _ _ _ _ will move
this court (in Room _ _ _ _ _ _ _ _) at the _ _ _ _ _ _ _ _ Courthouse _ _ _ _ _ _ _ _ _ , _ _ _ _ _ _ _ _ , New York, on the
_ _ _ _ _ _ _ _ day of _ _ _ _ _ _ _ _ , 20 _ _ _ _ _ ,
at _ _ _ _ _ _ _ _ (a.m.) (p.m.) for an order (briefly indicate relief
requested).

The above-entitled action is for (briefly state nature of action, e.g.
personal injury, medical malpractice, divorce, etc.).

This is a motion for or related to interim maintenance or child support
☑
(check box if applicable)

An affirmation that a good faith effort has been made to resolve the
issues raised in this motion is annexed hereto. (required only where the
motion related to disclosure or to a bill of particulars)

Pursuant to CPLR 2214(b), answering affidavits, if any, are required to
be served upon the undersigned at least seven days before the return
date of this motion. ☑

(check box if applicable)

Date:

(Printed Name) _____

Attorney * (for Attorney
in charge of case if law
firm for moving party
Address:
Telephone number:

CT RULES

TO: (Print Name)

_____

Attorney[*] for (other party)
Address:
Telephone number:
(Print Name)

_____c

Attorney[*] for (other party)
Address:
Telephone number

_____

  [*] If any party is appearing pro se, the name, address and telephone number
  of such party shall be stated.

(c) The affirmation of the good faith effort to resolve the issues raised by the motion shall indicate the time, place and nature of the consultation and the issues discussed and any resolutions, or shall indicate good cause why no such conferral with counsel for opposing parties was held.

(d) An order to show cause or an application for _ex parte_ relief need not contain the notice of motion set forth in this section, but shall contain the affirmation of good faith set forth in this section if such affirmation otherwise is required by this section.

(e) _Ex parte_ motions submitted to a judge outside of the county where the underlying action is venued or will be venued shall be referred to the appropriate court in the county of venue unless the judge determines that the urgency of the motion requires immediate determination.

(f) Any application for temporary injunctive relief, including but not limited to a motion for a stay or a temporary restraining order, shall contain, in addition to the other information required by this section, an affirmation demonstrating there will be significant prejudice to the party seeking the restraining order by the giving of notice. In the absence of a showing of significant prejudice, the affirmation must demonstrate that a good faith effort has been made to notify the party against whom the temporary restraining order is sought of the time, date and place that the application will be made in a manner sufficient to permit the party an opportunity to appear in response to the application. This subdivision shall not be applicable to orders to show cause or motions in special proceedings brought under Article 7 of the Real Property Actions and Proceedings Law, nor to orders to show cause or motions requesting an order of protection under section 240 of the Domestic Relations Law, unless otherwise ordered by the court.

§ 202.8   Motion procedure.

(a) All motions shall be returnable before the assigned judge, and all papers shall be filed with the court on or before the return date.

(b) *Special procedure for unassigned cases.* If a case has not been assigned to a judge, the motion shall be made returnable before the court, and a copy of the moving papers, together with a request for judicial intervention, shall be filed with the court, with proof of service upon all other parties, where required by section 202.6, within five days of service upon the other parties. The moving party shall give written notice of the index number to all other parties immediately after filing of the papers. Copies of all responding papers shall be submitted to the court, with proof of service and with the index number set forth in the papers, on or before the return date. The case shall be assigned to a judge as soon as practicable after the filing of the request for judicial intervention pursuant to section 202.6 of this Part, but in no event later than the return date. After assignment to the judge, the court shall provide for appropriate notice to the parties of the name of the assigned judge. Motion papers noticed to be heard in a county other than the county where the venue of the action has been placed by the plaintiff shall be assigned to a judge in accordance with procedures established by the Chief Administrator.

(c) The moving party shall serve copies of all affidavits and briefs upon all other parties at the time of service of the notice of motion. The answering party shall serve copies of all affidavits and briefs as required by CPLR 2214. Affidavits shall be for a statement of the relevant facts, and briefs shall be for a statement of the relevant law.

(d) Motion papers received by the clerk of the court on or before the return date shall be deemed submitted as of the return date. The assigned judge, in his or her discretion or at the request of a party, thereafter may determine that any motion be orally argued and may fix a time for oral argument. A party requesting oral argument shall set

CT RULES

forth such request in its notice of motion or in its order to show cause or on the first page of the answering papers, as the case may be. Where all parties to a motion request oral argument, oral argument shall be granted unless the court shall determine it to be unnecessary. Where a motion is brought on by order to show cause, the court may set forth in the order that oral argument is required on the return date of the motion.

(e) (1) Stipulations of adjournment of the return date made by the parties shall be in writing and shall be submitted to the assigned judge. Such stipulation shall be effective unless the court otherwise directs. No more than three stipulated adjournments for an aggregate period of 60 days shall be submitted without prior permission of the court. (2) Absent agreement by the parties, a request by any party for an adjournment shall be submitted in writing, upon notice to the other party, to the assigned judge on or before the return date. The court will notify the requesting party whether the adjournment has been granted.

(f) Where the motion relates to disclosure or to a bill of particulars, and a preliminary conference has not been held, the court shall notify all parties of a scheduled date to appear for a preliminary conference, which shall be not more than 45 days from the return date of the motion unless the court orders otherwise, and a form of a stipulation and order, prescribed by the Chief Administrator of the Courts, shall be made available which the parties may sign, agreeing to a timetable which shall provide for completion of disclosure within 12 months, and for a resolution of any other issues raised by the motion. If all parties sign the form and return it to the court before the return date of the motion, such form shall be "so ordered" by the court, and the motion shall be deemed withdrawn. If such stipulation is not returned by all parties, the conference shall be held on the assigned date. Issues raised by the motion and not resolved at the conference shall be determined by the court.

(g) Unless the circumstances require settlement of an order, a judge shall incorporate into the decision an order effecting the relief specified in the decision.

(h) *Reports of pending motions in the Supreme Court.* (1) To assist in preparing the quarterly report of pending civil matters required by section 4.1 of the Rules of the Chief Judge, the Chief Administrator of the Court or his or her designee shall provide to a justice of the Supreme Court, upon request, an automated open motion report of all motions pending before the justice which appear undecided 60 days after final submission. This open motion report may be used by the justice to assist in the preparation of his or her official quarterly report.

(2) Since motions are decided on a daily basis and further submissions may be received on a pending motion, the only report that shall be considered current is the official quarterly report submitted by the particular justice.

§ 202.9   Special proceedings.

Special proceedings shall be commenced and heard in the same manner as motions that have not yet been assigned to a judge as set forth in section 202.8 of this Part, except that they shall be governed by the time requirements of the CPLR relating to special proceedings.

§ 202.10   [Reserved]

§ 202.11   [Reserved]

§ 202.12   Preliminary conference.

(a) A party may request a preliminary conference at any time after service of process. The request shall state the title of the action; index number, names, addresses and telephone numbers of all attorneys appearing in the action; and the nature of the action. If the action has not been assigned to a judge, the party shall file a request for judicial intervention together with the request for a preliminary conference. The request shall be served on all other parties and filed with the clerk for transmittal to the assigned judge. The court shall order a preliminary conference in any action upon compliance with the requirements of this subdivision.

(b) The court shall notify all parties of the scheduled conference date, which shall be not more than 45 days from the date the request for judicial intervention is filed unless the court orders otherwise, and a form of a stipulation and order, prescribed by the Chief Administrator of the Courts, shall be made available which the parties may sign, agreeing to a timetable which shall provide for completion of disclosure within 12 months of the filing of the request for judicial intervention for a standard case, or within 15 months of such filing for a complex case. If all parties sign the form and return it to the court before the scheduled preliminary conference, such form shall be "so ordered" by the court, and, unless the court orders otherwise, the scheduled preliminary conference shall be canceled. If such stipulation is not returned signed by all parties, the parties shall appear at the conference. Except where a party appears in the action pro se, an attorney thoroughly familiar with the action and authorized to act on behalf of the party shall appear at such conference.

(c) The matters to be considered at the preliminary conference shall include:

(1) simplification and limitation of factual and legal issues, where appropriate;

(2) establishment of a timetable for the completion of all disclosure, proceedings, provided that all such procedures must be completed within the timeframes set forth in subdivision (b), unless otherwise shortened or extended by the court depending upon the circumstances of the case;

(3) Where the court deems appropriate, establishment of the method and scope of any electronic discovery, included but not limited to (a) retention of electronic data and implementation of a data preservation plan, (b) scope of electronic data review, (c) identification of relevant data (d) identification and redaction of privileged electronic data, (e) the scope, extent and form of production, (f) anticipated cost of data recovery and proposed initial allocation of such cost, (g) disclosure of the programs and manner in which the data is maintained, (h) identification of computer system(s) utilized, and (i) identification of the individual(s) responsible for data preservation;

(4) addition of other necessary parties;

(5) settlement of the action;

(6) removal to a lower court pursuant to CPLR 325, where appropriate; and

(7) any other matters that the court may deem relevant.

(d) At the conclusion of the conference the court shall make a written order including its directions to the parties as well as stipulations of counsel. Alternatively, in the court's discretion, all directions of the court and stipulations of counsel may be recorded by a reporter. Where the latter procedure is followed, the parties shall procure and share equally the cost of a transcript thereof unless the court in its discretion otherwise provides. The transcript, corrected if necessary on motion or by stipulation of the parties approved by the court, shall have the force and effect of an order of the court. The transcript shall be filed by the plaintiff with the clerk of the court.

(e) The granting or continuation of a special preference shall be conditional upon full compliance by the party who has requested any such preference with the foregoing order or transcript. When a note of issue and certificate of readiness are filed pursuant to section 202.21 of this Part, in an action to which this section is applicable, the filing party, in addition to complying with all other applicable rules of the court, shall file with the note of issue and certificate of readiness an affirmation or affidavit, with proof of service on all parties who have appeared, showing specific compliance with the preliminary conference order or transcript.

(f) In the discretion of the court, failure by a party to comply with the order or transcript resulting from the preliminary conference, or with the so-ordered stipulation provided for in subdivision (b) of this section, or the making of unnecessary or frivolous motions by a party, shall result in the imposition upon such party of costs or such other sanctions as are authorized by law.

(g) A party may move to advance the date of a preliminary conference upon a showing of special circumstances.

(h) Motions in actions to which this section is applicable made after the preliminary conference has been scheduled may be denied unless there is shown good cause why such relief is warranted before the preliminary conference is held.

(i) No action or proceeding to which this section is applicable shall be deemed ready for trial unless there is compliance with the provisions of this section and any order issued pursuant thereto.

(j) The court, in its discretion, at any time may order such

CT RULES

conferences as the court may deem helpful or necessary in any matter before the court.

(k) The provisions of this section shall apply to preliminary conferences required in matrimonial actions and actions based upon a separation agreement, in medical malpractice actions, and in real property tax assessment review proceedings within the City of New York, only to the extent that these provisions are not inconsistent with the provisions of sections 202.16, 202.56 and 202.60 of this Part, respectively.

(l) The provisions of this section shall apply where a request is filed for a preliminary conference in an action involving a terminally ill party governed by CPLR 3407 only to the extent that the provisions of this section are not inconsistent with the provisions of CPLR 3407. In an action governed by CPLR 3407 the request for a preliminary conference may be filed at any time after commencement of the action, and shall be accompanied by the physician's affidavit required by that provision.

§ 202.12-a   Residential Mortgage Foreclosure Actions; Settlement Conference.

(a) Applicability. This section shall be applicable to residential mortgage foreclosure actions brought on or after September 1, 2008, involving one- to four-family dwellings owned and occupied by the defendant where the underlying loan is high-cost, subprime or non-traditional, as defined in section 6-1 of the Banking Law and section 1304.5(c) and (e) of the Real Property Actions and Proceedings Law, and was entered into between January 1, 2003, and September 1, 2008.

(b) Request for judicial intervention. At the time that proof of service of the summons and complaint is filed with the county clerk, plaintiff shall file with the county clerk a specialized request for judicial intervention (RJI), on a form prescribed by the Chief Administrator of the Courts, applicable to residential mortgage foreclosure actions covered by this section. The RJI shall contain the name, address, telephone number and e-mail address, if available, of the defendant in the action and shall request that a settlement conference be scheduled.

(c) Settlement conference.

(1) The court shall promptly send to the parties a Notice scheduling a settlement conference to be held within 60 days after the date of the filing of the RJI. The Notice shall be mailed to all parties or their attorneys, which must include mailing to the address of the property subject to the mortgage. The Notice shall be on a form prescribed by the Chief Administrator, and it shall set forth the purpose of the conference, instructions to the parties on how to prepare for the conference, and what information and documents to bring to the conference. The Notice shall further provide that the defendant contact the court by telephone, no later than seven days before the conference is scheduled, to advise whether the defendant will be able to attend the scheduled conference.

(2) The conference shall include settlement discussions pertaining to the relative rights and obligations of the parties under the mortgage loan documents, including determining whether the parties can reach a unilaterally agreeable resolution to help the defendant avoid losing his or her home, and evaluating the potential for a resolution in which payment schedules or amounts may be modified or other workout options may be agreed to. The court may also use the conference for whatever other purposes the court deems appropriate. Where appropriate, the court may permit a representative of the plaintiff to attend the conference telephonically or by video-conference.

(3) If the parties appear by counsel, such counsel must be fully authorized to dispose of the case. If the defendant appears at the conference without counsel, the court shall treat the defendant as having made a motion to proceed as a poor person and shall determine whether permission to so appear shall be granted pursuant to the standards set forth in CPLR 1101.

(4) The court may schedule such other conferences as may be necessary to help resolve the action.

§ 202.13   Removal of actions without consent to courts of limited jurisdiction.

Actions may be removed to courts of limited jurisdiction without consent pursuant to the provisions of CPLR 325(d) as follows:

(a) from the Supreme Court in counties within the First, Second,

Eleventh and Twelfth Judicial Districts to the Civil Court of the City of New York;

(b) from the Supreme Court in counties within the Ninth Judicial District to county and city courts within such counties;

(c) from the Supreme Court in counties within the Tenth Judicial District to county courts within such counties;

(d) from the Supreme Court in counties within the Third Judicial Department to county and city courts within such counties;

(e) from the Supreme Court in counties within the Fourth Judicial Department to county and city courts within such counties;

(f) from the County Court of Broome County to the City Court of Binghamton;

(g) from the County Court of Albany County to the City Court of Albany;

(h) from the Supreme Court and County Court of Nassau County to the District Court of Nassau County and to the city courts within such county; and

(i) from the Supreme Court and County Court of Suffolk County to the District Court of Suffolk County.

§ 202.14   Special masters.

The Chief Administrator of the Courts may authorize the creation of a program for the appointment of attorneys as special masters in designated courts to preside over conferences and hear and report on applications to the court. Special masters shall serve without compensation.

§ 202.15   Videotape recording of civil depositions.

(a) *When permitted.* Depositions authorized under the provisions of the Civil Practice Law and Rules or other law may be taken, as permitted by section 3113(b) of the Civil Practice Law and Rules, by means of simultaneous audio and visual electronic recording, provided such recording is made in conformity with this section.

(b) *Other rules applicable.* Except as otherwise provided in this section, or where the nature of videotaped recording makes compliance impossible or unnecessary, all rules generally applicable to examinations before trial shall apply to videotaped recording of depositions.

(c) *Notice of taking deposition.* Every notice or subpoena for the taking of a videotaped deposition shall state that it is to be videotaped and the name and address of the videotape operator and of the operator's employer, if any. The operator may be an employee of the attorney taking the deposition. Where an application for an order to take a videotaped deposition is made, the application and order shall contain the same information.

(d) *Conduct of the examination.* (1) The deposition shall begin by one of the attorneys or the operator stating on camera:

(i) the operator's name and address;

(ii) the name and address of the operator's employer;

(iii) the date, the time and place of the deposition; and

(iv) the party on whose behalf the deposition is being taken.

The officer before whom the deposition is taken shall be a person authorized by statute and shall identify himself or herself and swear the witness on camera. If the deposition requires the use of more than one tape, the end of each tape and the beginning of each succeeding tape shall be announced by the operator.

(2) Every videotaped deposition shall be timed by means of a time-date generator which shall permanently record hours, minutes and seconds. Each time the videotape is stopped and resumed, such times shall be orally announced on the tape.

(3) More than one camera may be used, either in sequence or simultaneously.

(4) At the conclusion of the deposition, a statement shall be made on camera that the recording is completed. As soon as practicable thereafter, the videotape shall be shown to the witness for examination, unless such showing and examination are waived by the witness and the parties.

(5) Technical data, such as recording speeds and other information

CT RULES

needed to replay or copy the tape, shall be included on copies of the videotaped deposition.

(e) Copies and transcription. The parties may make audio copies of the deposition and thereafter may purchase additional audio and audio-visual copies. A party may arrange to have a stenographic transcription made of the deposition at his or her own expense.

(f) *Certification.* The officer before whom the videotape deposition is taken shall cause to be attached to the original videotape recording a certification that the witness was fully sworn or affirmed by the officer and that the videotape recording is a true record of the testimony given by the witness. If the witness has not waived the right to a showing and examination of the videotape deposition, the witness shall also sign the certification in accordance with the provisions of section 3116 of the Civil Practice Law and Rules.

(g) *Filing and objections.* (1) If no objections have been made by any of the parties during the course of the deposition, the videotape deposition may be filed by the proponent with the clerk of the trial court and shall be filed upon the request of any party.

(2) If objections have been made by any of the parties during the course of the deposition, the videotape deposition, with the certification, shall be submitted to the court upon the request of any of the parties within 10 days after its recording, or within such other period as the parties may stipulate, or as soon thereafter as the objections may be heard by the court, for the purpose of obtaining rulings on the objections. An audio copy of the sound track may be submitted in lieu of the videotape for this purpose, as the court may prefer. The court may view such portions of the videotape recording as it deems pertinent to the objections made, or may listen to an audiotape recording. The court, in its discretion, may also require submission of a stenographic transcript of the portion of the deposition to which objection is made, and may read such transcript in lieu of reviewing the videotape or audio copy.

(3) (i) The court shall rule on the objections prior to the date set for trial and shall return the recording to the proponent of the videotape with notice to the parties of its rulings and of its instructions as to editing. The editing shall reflect the rulings of

the court and shall remove all references to the objections. The proponent, after causing the videotape to be edited in accordance with the court's instructions, may cause both the original video-tape recording and the deleted version of the recording, clearly identified, to be filed with the clerk of the trial court, and shall do so at the request of any party. Before such filing, the proponent shall permit the other party to view the edited videotape.

(ii) The court may, in respect to objectionable material, instead of ordering its deletion, permit such material to be clearly marked so that the audio recording may be suppressed by the operator during the objectionable portion when the videotape is presented at the trial. In such case the proponent may cause both the original videotape recording and a marked version of that recording, each clearly identified, to be filed with the clerk of the trial court, and shall do so at the request of any party.

(h) *Custody of tape.* When the tape is filed with the clerk of the court, the clerk shall give an appropriate receipt for the tape and shall provide secure and adequate facilities for the storage of videotape recordings.

(i) *Use at trial.* The use of videotape recordings of depositions at the trial shall be governed by the provisions of the Civil Practice Law and Rules and all other relevant statutes, court rules and decisional law relating to depositions and relating to the admissibility of evidence. The proponent of the videotaped deposition shall have the responsi-bility of providing whatever equipment and personnel may be neces-sary for presenting such videotape deposition.

(j) *Applicability to audio taping of depositions.* Except where clearly inapplicable because of the lack of a video portion, these rules are equally applicable to the taking of depositions by audio recording alone. However, in the case of the taking of a deposition upon notice by audio recording alone, any party, at least five days before the date noticed for taking the deposition, may apply to the court for an order establishing additional or alternate procedures for the taking of such audio deposition, and upon the making of the application, the deposi-tion may be taken only in accordance with the court order.

(k) *Cost.* The cost of videotaping or audio recording shall be borne

CT RULES

by the the party who served the notice for the videotaped or audio recording of the deposition, and such cost shall be a taxable disbursement in the action unless the court in its discretion orders otherwise in the interest of justice.

(l) *Transcription for appeal.* On appeal, visual and audio depositions shall be transcribed in the same manner as other testimony and transcripts filed in the appellate court. The visual and audio depositions shall remain part of the original record in the case and shall be transmitted therewith. In lieu of the transcribed deposition and, on leave of the appellate court, a party may request a viewing of portions of the visual deposition by the appellate court but, in such case, a transcript of pertinent portions of the deposition shall be filed as required by the court.

§ 202.16   **Matrimonial actions; calendar control of financial disclosure in actions and proceedings involving alimony, maintenance, child support and equitable distribution; motions for alimony, counsel fees** *pendente lite,* **and child support; special rules.**

(a) *Applicability:* This section shall be applicable to all contested actions and proceedings in the Supreme Court in which statements of net worth are required by section 236 of the Domestic Relations Law to be filed and in which a judicial determination may be made with respect to alimony, counsel fees *pendente lite,* maintenance, custody and visitation, child support, or the equitable distribution of property, including those referred to Family Court by the Supreme Court pursuant to section 464 of the Family Court Act.

(b) *Form of Statements of Net Worth.* Sworn statements of net worth, except as provided in subdivision (k) hereof, exchanged and filed with the court pursuant to section 236 of the Domestic Relations Law, shall be in substantial compliance with the Statement of Net Worth form contained in appendix A of this Part.

(c) *Retainer agreements.* (1) A signed copy of the attorney's retainer agreement with the client shall accompany the statement of net worth filed with the court, and the court shall examine the agreement to assure that it conforms to Appellate Division attorney conduct and disciplinary rules. Where substitution of counsel occurs after the filing with the court of the net worth statement, a signed copy of the attorney's retainer agreement shall be filed with the court within 10 days of its execution.

(2) An attorney seeking to obtain an interest in any property of his or her client to secure payment of the attorney's fee shall make application to the court for approval of said interest on notice to the client and to his or her adversary. The application may be granted only after the court reviews the finances of the parties and an application for attorney's fees.

(d) *Request for judicial intervention.* A request for judicial intervention shall be filed with the court by the plaintiff no later than 45 days from the date of service of the summons and complaint or summons with notice upon the defendant, unless both parties file a notice of no necessity with the court, in which event the request for judicial intervention may be filed no later than 120 days from the date of service of the summons and complaint or summons with notice upon the defendant. Notwithstanding section 202.6(a) of this Part, the court shall accept a request for judicial intervention that is not accompanied by other papers to be filed in court.

(e) *Certification.* Every paper served on another party or filed or submitted to the court in a matrimonial action shall be signed as provided in section 130-1.1-a of the Rules of the Chief Administrator.

(f) *Preliminary conference.* (1) In all actions or proceedings to which this section of the rules is applicable, a preliminary conference shall be ordered by the court to be held within 45 days after the action has been assigned. Such order shall set the time and date for the conference and shall specify the papers that shall be exchanged between the parties. These papers must be exchanged no later than 10 days prior to the preliminary conference, unless the court directs otherwise. These papers shall include:

(i) statements of net worth, which also shall be filed with the court no later than 10 days prior to the premliminary conference;

(ii) all paycheck stubs for the current calendar year and the last paycheck stub for the immediately preceding calendar year;

(iii) all filed state and federal income tax returns for the previous three years, including both personal returns filed on

CT RULES

behalf of any partnership or closely held corporation of which the party is a partner or shareholder;

(iv) all W-2 wage and tax statements, 1099 forms and K-1 forms for any year in the past three years in which the party did not file state and federal income tax returns;

(v) all statements of accounts received during the past three years from each financial institution in which the party has maintained any account in which cash or securities are held;

(vi) the statements immediately preceding and following the date of commencement of the matrimonial action pertaining to: (A) any policy of life insurance having a cash or dividend surrender value; and (B) any deferred compensation plan of any type or nature in which the party has an interest including, but not limited to, Individual Retirement Accounts, pensions, profit-sharing plans Keogh plans, 401K plans and other retirement plans.

Both parties personally must be present in court at the time of the conference, and the judge personally shall address the parties at some time during the conference.

(2) The matters to be considered at the conference may include, among other things:

(i) applications for pendente lite relief, including interim counsel fees;

(ii) compliance with the requirement of compulsory financial disclosure, including the exchange and filing of a supplemental statement of net worth indicating material changes in any previously exchanged and filed statement of net worth;

(iii) simplification and limitation of issues;

(iv) the establishment of a timetable for the completion of all disclosure proceedings, provided that all such procedures must be completed within six months from the commencement of the conference, unless otherwise shortened or extended by the court depending upon the circumstances of the case;

(v) and any other matters which the court shall deem appropriate.

(3) At the close of the conference, the court shall direct the parties to stipulate, in writing or on the record, as to all resolved issues, which the court then shall "so order," and as to all issues with respect to fault, custody and finance that remain unresolved. Any issues with respect to fault, custody and finance that are not specifically described in writing or on the record at that time may not be raised in the action unless good cause is shown. The court shall fix a schedule for discovery as to all unresolved issues and, in a noncomplex case, shall schedule a date for trial not later than six months from the date of the conference. The court may appoint a law guardian for the infant children, or may direct the parties to file with the court, within 30 days of the conference, a list of suitable law guardians for selection by the court. The court also may direct that a list of expert witnesses be filed with the court within 30 days of the conference from which the court may select a neutral expert to assist the court. The court shall schedule a compliance conference unless the court dispenses with the conference based upon a stipulation of compliance filed by the parties. Unless the court excuses their presence, the parties personally must be present in court at the time of the compliance conference. If the parties are present in court, the judge personally shall address them at some time during the conference.

(g) *Expert witnesses.* (1) Responses to demands for expert information pursuant to CPLR § 3101(d) shall be served within 20 days following service of such demands.

(2) Each expert witness whom a party expects to call at the trial shall file with the court a written report, which shall be exchanged and filed with the court no later than 60 days before the date set for trial, and reply reports, if any, shall be exchanged and filed no later than 30 days before such date. Failure to file with the court a report in conformance with these requirements may, in the court's discretion, preclude the use of the expert. Except for good cause shown, the reports exchanged between the parties shall be the only reports admissible at trial. Late retention of experts and consequent late submission of reports shall be permitted only upon a showing of good cause as authorized by CPLR § 3101(d)(1)(i). In the discretion

of the court, written reports may be used to substitute for direct testimony at the trial, but the reports shall be submitted by the expert under oath, and the expert shall be present and available for cross-examination. In the discretion of the court, in a proper case, parties may be bound by the expert's report in their direct case.

(h) *Statement of Proposed Disposition.*

(1) Each party shall exchange a statement setting forth the following:

(i) the assets claimed to be marital property;

(ii) the assets claimed to be separate property;

(iii) an allocation of debts or liabilities to specific marital or separate assets, where appropriate;

(iv) the amount requested for maintenance, indicating and elaborating upon the statutory factors forming the basis for the maintenance requests;

(v) the proposal for equitable distribution, where appropriate, indicating and elaborating upon the statutory factors forming the basis for the proposed distribution;

(vi) the proposal for a distributive award, if requested, including a showing of the need for a distributive award;

(vii) the proposed plan for child support, indicating and elaborating upon the statutory factors upon which the proposal is based; and

(viii) the proposed plan for custody and visitation of any children involved in the proceeding, setting forth the reasons therefor.

(2) A copy of any written agreement entered into by the parties relating to financial arrangements or custody or visitation shall be annexed to the statement referred to in paragraph (1) of this subdivision.

(3) The statement referred to in paragraph (1) of this subdivision, with proof of service upon the other party, shall, with the note of issue, be filed with the court. The other party, if he or she has not

already done so, shall file with the court a statement with paragraph (1) within 20 days of such service.

(i) *Filing of Note of Issue.* No action or proceeding to which this section is applicable shall be deemed ready for trial unless there is compliance with this section by the party filing the note of issue and certificate of readiness.

(j) *Referral to Family Court.* In all actions or proceedings to which this section is applicable referred to the Family Court by the Supreme Court pursuant to section 464 of the Family Court Act, all statements, including supplemental statements, exchanged and filed by the parties pursuant to this section shall be transmitted to the Family Court with the order of referral.

(k) Motions for Alimony, Maintenance, Counsel Fees Pendente Lite and Child Support (Other Than Under Section 237(c) or Section 238 of the Domestic Relations Law). Unless, on application made to the court, the requirements of this subdivision be waived for good cause shown, or unless otherwise expressly provided by any provision of the CPLR or other statute, the following requirements shall govern motions for alimony, maintenance, counsel fees (other than a motion made pursuant to section 237(c) or section 238 of the Domestic Relations Law for counsel fees for services rendered by an attorney to secure the enforcement of a previously granted order or decree) or child support or any modification of an award thereof:

(1) Such motion shall be made before or at the preliminary conference, if practicable.

(2) No motion shall be heard unless the moving papers include a statement of net worth in the official form prescribed by subdivision (b) of this section.

(3) No motion for counsel fees shall be heard unless the moving papers also include the affidavit of the movant's attorney stating the moneys, if any, received on account of such attorney's fee from the movant or any other person on behalf of the movant, and the moneys such attorney has been promised by, or the agreement made with, the movant or other persons on behalf of the movant, concerning or in payment of the fee.

(4) The party opposing any motion shall be deemed to have

CT RULES

admitted, for the purpose of the motion but not otherwise, such facts set forth in the moving party's statement of net worth as are not contraverted in:

(i) a statement of net worth, in the official form prescribed by this section, completed and sworn to by the opposing party, and made a part of the answering papers, or

(ii) other sworn statements or affidavits with respect to any fact which is not feasible to controvert in the opposing party's statement of net worth.

(5) The failure to comply with the provisions of this subdivision shall be good cause, in the discretion of the judge presiding, either:

(i) to draw an inference favorable to the adverse party with respect to any disputed fact or issue affected by such failure; or

(ii) to deny the motion without prejudice to renewal upon compliance with the provisions of this section.

(6) The notice of motion submitted with any motion for or related to interim maintenance or child support shall contain a notation indicating the nature of the motion. Any such motion shall be determined within 30 days after the motion is submitted for decision.

(7) Upon any application for an award of counsel fees or appraisal/accounting fees made prior to the conclusion of the trial of the action, the court shall set forth in specific detail, in writing or on the record, the factors it considered and the reasons for its decision.

(l) Hearings or trials pertaining to temporary or permanent custody or visitation shall proceed from day to day conclusion. With respect to other issues before the court, to the extent feasible, trial should proceed from day to day to conclusion.

§ 202.16a   Matrimonial actions; automatic orders.

(a) *Applicability.* This section shall be applicable to all matrimonial actions and proceedings in the Supreme Court authorized by section 236(2) of the Domestic Relations Law.

(b) *Service.* The plaintiff in a matrimonial action shall cause to be served upon the defendant, simultaneous with the service of the summons, a copy of the automatic orders set forth in this section in a notice that substantially conforms to the notice contained in Appendix F. The automatic orders shall be binding upon the plaintiff immediately upon filing of the summons, or summons and complaint, and upon the defendant immediately upon service of the automatic orders with the summons..

(c) *Automatic orders.* The automatic orders served with the

summons shall provide as follows: (1) Neither part shall sell, transfer, encumber, conceal, assign, remove or in any way dispose of, without the consent of the other party in writing, or by order of the court, any property (including, but not limited to, real estate, personal property, cash accounts, stocks, mutual funds, bank accounts, cars and boats) individually or jointly held by the parties, except in the usual course of business, for customary and usual household expenses or for reasonable attorney's fees in connection with this action.

(2) Neither party shall transfer, encumber, assign, remove, withdraw or in any way dispose of any tax deferred funds, stocks or other assets held in any individual retirement accounts, 401K accounts, profit sharing plans, Keogh accounts, or any other pension or retirement account, and the parties shall further refrain from applying for or requesting the payment of retirement benefits or annuity payments of any kind, without the consent of the other party in writing, or upon further order of the court.

(3) Neither party shall incur unreasonable debts hereafter, including but not limited to further borrowing against any credit line secured by the family residence, further encumbrancing any assets, or unreasonably using credit cards or cash advances against credit cards, except in the usual course of business or for customary or usual household expenses, or for reasonable attorney's fees in connection with this action.

(4) Neither party shall cause the other party or the children of the marriage to be removed from any existing medical, hospital and dental insurance coverage, and each party shall maintain the existing medical, hospital and dental insurance coverage in full force and effect.

(5) Neither party shall change the beneficiaries of any existing life insurance policies, and each party shall maintain the existing life insurance, automobile insurance, homeowners and renters insurance

policies in full force and effect.

§ 202.17   Exchange of medical reports in personal injury and wrongful death actions.

Except where the court otherwise directs, in all actions in which recovery is sought for personal injuries, disability or death, physical examinations and the exchange of medical information shall be governed by the provisions hereinafter set forth:

(a) At any time after joinder of issue and service of a bill of particulars the party to be examined or any other party may serve on all other parties a notice fixing the time and place of examination. Unless otherwise stipulated the examination shall be held not less than 30 nor more than 60 days after service of the notice. If served by any party to be examined, the notice shall name the examining medical provider or providers. If the notice is served by the party to be examined, the examining parties shall, within five days of receipt thereof, submit to the party to be examined the name of the medical providers who will conduct the examination. Any party may move to modify or vacate the notice fixing the time and place of examination or the notice naming the examining medical providers within ten days of the receipt thereof, on the grounds that the time or place fixed or the medical provider named is objectionable, or that the nature of the action is such that the interests of justice will not be served by an examination, exchange of medical reports or delivery of authorization.

(b) At least 20 days before the date of such examination, or on such other date as the court may direct, the party to be examined shall server upon and deliver to all other parties the following, which may be used by the examining medical provider:

(1) copies of the medical reports of those medical providers who have previously treated or examined the party seeking recovery. These shall include a recital of the injuries and conditions as to which testimony will be offered at the trial, referring to and identifying those x-ray and technicians' reports which will be offered at the trial, including a description of the injuries, a diagnosis and a prognosis. Medical reports may consist of completed medical provider, workers' compensation, or insurance forms that provide the information required by this paragraph.

(2) duly executed and acknowledged written authorizations permitting all parties to obtain and make copies of all hospital records and such other records, including x-ray and technicians reports, as may be referred to and identified in the reports of those medical providers who have treated or examined the party seeking recovery.

(c) Copies of the reports of the medical providers making examinations pursuant to this section shall be served on all other parties 45 days after completion of the examination. These shall comply with the requirements of paragraph (1) of subdivision (b).

(d) In actions where the cause of death is in issue, each party shall serve upon all other parties copies of the reports of all treating and examining medical providers whose testimony will be offered at the trial, complying with the requirements of paragraph (1) of subdivision (b) and the party seeking to recover shall deliver to all other parties authorizations to examine and obtain copies of all hospital records, autopsy or post-mortem reports, and such other records as provided in paragraph (2) of subdivision (b). Copies of these reports and the required authorizations shall be served and delivered with the bill of particulars by the party seeking to recover. All other parties shall serve copies of the reports of their medical providers within 45 days thereafter. In any case where the interests of justice will not be promoted by service of such reports and delivery of such authorizations, an order dispensing with either or both may be obtained.

(e) Parties relying solely on hospital records may so certify in lieu of serving medical providers' reports.

(f) No case otherwise eligible to be noticed for trial may be noticed unless there has been compliance with this rule, or an order dispensing with compliance or extending the time therefor has been obtained; or, where the party to be examined was served a notice as provided in subdivision (a) of this section, and the party so served has not responded thereto.

(g) In the event that the party examined intends at the trial to offer evidence of further or additional injuries or conditions, nonexistent or not known to exist at the time of service of the original medical

CT RULES

reports, such party shall, within 30 days after the discovery thereof, and not later than 30 days before trial, serve upon all parties a supplemental medical report complying with the requirements of paragraph (1) of subdivision (b) and shall specify a time not more than 10 days thereafter and a place at which a further examination may be had. Further authorization to examine and make copies of additional hospital records, other records, x-ray or other technicians reports as provided in paragraph (2) of subdivision (b) must also be delivered with the medical reports. Copies of the reports of the examining medical providers, complying with the requirements of subdivision (c), shall be served within 10 days after completion of such further examination. If any party desires at the trial to offer the testimony of additional treating or examining medical providers other than whose medical reports have been previously exchanged, the medical reports of such medical providers, complying with the requirements of paragraph (1) of subdivision (b) shall be served upon all parties at least 30 days before trial.

(h) Unless an order to the contrary is made or unless the judge presiding at the trial in the interests of justice and upon a showing of good cause shall hold otherwise, the party seeking to recover damages shall be precluded at the trial from offering in evidence any part of the hospital records and all other records, including autopsy or post-mortem records, x-ray reports or reports of other technicians, not made available pursuant to this rule, and no party shall be permitted to offer any evidence of injuries or conditions not set forth or put in issue in the respective medical reports previously exchanged, nor will the court hear the testimony of any treating or examining medical providers whose medical reports have not been served as provided by this rule.

(i) Orders transferring cases pending in other courts which are subject to the provisions of this section, whether or not such cases are consolidated with cases pending in the court to which transferred, shall contain such provisions as are required to bring the transferred cases into compliance with this rule.

(j) Any party may move to compel compliance or to be relieved from compliance with this rule or any provision thereof, but motions directed to the sufficiency of medical reports must be made within

20 days of receipt of such reports. All motions under this rule may be made on affidavits of attorneys, shall be made on notice, and shall be granted or denied on such terms as to costs, calendar position and dates of compliance with any provision of this rule as the court in its discretion shall direct.

(k) Where an examination is conducted on consent prior to the institution of an action, the party to be examined shall deliver the documents specified in paragraphs (1) and (2) of subdivision (b) hereof, and the report of the examining medical provider shall be delivered as provided in subdivision (c) hereof. In that event, examination after institution of the action may be waived. The waiver, which shall recite that medical reports have been exchanged and that all parties waive further physical examination, shall be filed with the note of issue. This shall not be a bar, however, to proceeding under subdivision (g) in a proper case.

§ 202.18   Testimony of court-appointed expert witness in matrimonial action or proceeding.

In any action or proceeding tried without a jury to which section 237 of the Domestic Relations Law applies, the court may appoint a psychiatrist, psychologist, social worker or other appropriate expert to give testimony with respect to custody or visitation, and may appoint an accountant, appraiser, actuary or other appropriate expert to give testimony with respect to equitable distribution or a distributive award. In the First and Second Judicial Departments, appointments shall be made as appropriate from a panel of mental health professionals pursuant to 22 NYCRR Parts 623 and 680. The cost of such expert witness shall be paid by a party or parties as the court shall direct.

§ 202.19   Differentiated case management.

(a) *Applicability.* This section shall apply to such categories of cases designated by the Chief Administrator of the Courts as being subject to differentiated case management, and shall be implemented in such counties, courts or parts of courts as designated by the Chief Administrator. The provisions of section 202.12 of these rules, relating to the preliminary conference, and section 202.26 of these rules, relating to the pretrial conference, shall apply to the extent not inconsistent with this section.

CT RULES

(b) *Preliminary conference.* (1) In all actions and proceedings to which this section of the rules is applicable, a preliminary conference shall be ordered by the court to be held within 45 days after the request for judicial intervention is filed.

(2) At the preliminary conference, the court shall designate the track to which the case shall be assigned in accordance with the following:

    (i) Expedited—discovery to be completed within eight months

    (ii) Standard—discovery to be completed within 12 months

    (iii) Complex—discovery to be completed within 15 months

    The timeframes must be complied with unless otherwise shortened or extended by the court depending upon the circumstances of the case.

(3) No later than 60 days before the date fixed for completion of discovery, a compliance conference shall be held to monitor the progress of discovery, explore potential settlement, and set a deadline for the filing of the Note of Issue.

(c) *Pretrial conference.* (1) A pretrial conference shall be held within 180 days of the filing of the Note of Issue.

(2) At the pretrial conference, the court shall fix a date for the commencement of trial, which shall be no later than eight weeks after the date of the conference.

§ 202.20   [Reserved]

§ 202.21   Note of Issue and Certificate of Readiness.

(a) *General.* No action or special proceeding shall be deemed ready for trial or inquest unless there is first filed a note of issue accompanied by a certificate of readiness, with proof of service on all parties entitled to notice, in the form prescribed by this section. Filing of a note of issue and certificate of readiness is not required for an application for court approval of the settlement of the claim of an infant, incompetent or conservatee. The note of issue shall include the county clerk's index number; the name of the judge to whom the action is assigned; the name, office address and telephone number of each attorney who has appeared; the name, address and telephone number of any party who has appeared pro se; and the name of any insurance carrier acting on behalf of any party. Within 10 days after service, the original note of issue, and the certificate of readiness where required, with proof of service where service is required, shall be filed in duplicate with the county clerk together with payment of the calendar fee prescribed by CPLR 8020 or a copy of an order permitting the party filing the note of issue to proceed as a poor person, and a duplicate original with proof of service shall be filed with the clerk of the trial court. The county clerk shall forward one of the duplicate originals of the note of issue to the clerk of the trial court stamped "Fee Paid" or "Poor Person Order."

(b) *Forms.* The note of issue and certificate of readiness shall read substantially as follows:

NOTE OF ISSUE

Calendar No. (if any) _____   For use of clerk

Index No. _____

_____ Court _____

County

Name of assigned judge _____

Notice for trial

Trial by jury demanded _____

_____ of all issues

_____ of issues specified below

or attached hereto

Trial without jury _____

Filed by attorney for _____

Date summons served _____

Date service completed _____

Date issue joined _____

Nature of action or special proceeding

Tort:

Motor vehicle
negligence   _____

Medical malpractice   _____

Other tort   _____

Contract   _____

Contested matrimonial   _____

Uncontested
matrimonial _____
Special preference claimed
under _____
on the ground that _____
Tax certiorari _____
_____
Condemnation _____
Other (not itemized
above) _____
_____
(specify_____
Indicate if this action is brought as a class
action _____

> Attorney(s) for
> Plaintiff(s)
> Office and P.O. Ad-
> dress:
> Phone No.

Amount demanded $ _____.
Other relief _____
Insurance carrier(s), if known:
NOTE: The clerk will not accept this note
of issue unless accompanied by a certifi-
cate of readiness.

CERTIFICATE OF READINESS FOR TRIAL
(Items 1-7 must be checked)

		Complete	Waived	Not required
1.	All pleadings served	_____	_____	_____
2.	Bill of particulars served	_____	_____	_____
3.	Physical examinations com-pleted	_____	_____	_____
4.	Medical reports exchanged	_____	_____	_____
5.	Appraisal reports exchanged	_____	_____	_____
6.	Compliance with section 202.16 of the Rules of the Chief Ad-ministrator (22 NYCRR 202.16) in matrimonial actions	_____	_____	_____

		Complete	Waived	Not required
7.	Discovery proceedings now known to be necessary completed	_____	_____	_____
8.	There are no out-standing requests for discovery			
9.	There has been a reasonable opportunity to complete the foregoing proceedings			
10.	There has been compliance with any order issued pursuant to section 202.12 of the Rules of the Chief Administrator (22 NY-CRR 202.12)			
11.	If a medical malpractice action, there has been compliance with any order issued pursuant to section 202.56 of the Rules of the Chief Administrator (22 NY-CRR 202.56)			
12.	The case is ready for trial			

Dated:_____

(Signature)_____

Attorney(s) for:_____

Office and P.O. address:_____

(c) *Jury trials.* A trial by jury may be demanded as provided by CPLR 4102. Where a jury trial has been demanded, the action or special proceeding shall be scheduled for jury trial upon payment of the fee prescribed by CPLR 8020 by the party first filing the demand. If no demand for a jury trial is made, it shall constitute a waiver by all parties and the action or special proceeding shall be scheduled for nonjury trial.

(d) *Pretrial proceedings.* Where a party is prevented from filing a note of issue and certificate of readiness because a pretrial proceeding has not been completed for any reason beyond the control of the party, the court, upon motion supported by affidavit, may permit the party to file a note of issue upon such conditions as the court deems appropriate. Where unusual or unanticipated circumstances develop subsequent to the filing of a note of issue and certificate of readiness which require additional pretrial proceedings to prevent substantial prejudice, the court, upon motion supported by affidavit, may grant permission to conduct such necessary proceedings.

(e) *Vacating note of issue.* Within 20 days after service of a note of issue and certificate of readiness, any party to the action or special proceeding may move to vacate the note of issue, upon affidavit showing in what respects the case is not ready for trial, and the court may vacate the note of issue if it appears that a material fact in the certificate of readiness is incorrect, or that the certificate of readiness fails to comply with the requirements of this section in some material respect. However, the 20-day time limitation to make such motion shall not apply to tax assessment review proceedings. After such period, except in a tax assesssment review proceeding, no such motion shall be allowed except for good cause shown. At any time, the court on its own motion may vacate a note of issue if it appears that a material fact in the certificate of readiness is incorrect, or that the certificate of readiness fails to comply with the requirements of this section in some material respect. If the motion to vacate a note of issue is granted, a copy of the order vacating the note of issue shall be served upon the clerk of the trial court.

(f) *Reinstatement of note of issue.* Motions to reinstate notes of issue vacated pursuant to this section shall be supported by a proper and sufficient certificate of readiness and by affidavit by a person having first-hand knowledge showing that there is merit to the action, satisfactorily showing the reasons for the acts or omissions which led to the note of issue being vacated, stating meritorious reasons for its reinstatement and showing that the case is presently ready for trial.

(g) *Limited specification of damages demanded in certain actions.* This subdivision shall apply only in counties where the Chief Administrator of the Courts has established arbitration programs pursuant to Part 28 of the Rules of the Chief Judge of the State of New York pertaining to the arbitration of certain actions (22 NYCRR Part 28). In a medical malpractice action or an action against a municipality seeking a sum of money only, where the party filing the note of issue is prohibited by the provisions of CPLR 3017(c) from stating in the pleadings the amount of damages sought in the action, the party shall indicate on the note of issue whether the amount of damages exceeds $ 6,000, exclusive of costs and interest. If it does not, the party shall also indicate if it exceeds $ 2,000, exclusive of costs and interest.

(h) *Change in title of action.* In the event of a change in title of an action by reason of a substitution of any party, no new note of issue will be required. Notice of such substitution and change in title shall be given to the assigned judge and to the clerk within 10 days of the date of an order or stipulation effecting the party substitution or title change.

(i) *Additional requirements with respect to uncontested matrimonial actions.*

(1) Uncontested matrimonial actions, proceedings for dissolution of marriages and applications of declaratory judgments shall be assigned to judges or special parts of court as the Chief Administrator shall authorize.

(2) There shall be a Unified Court System Uncontested Divorce Packet which shall contain the official forms for use in uncontested matrimonial actions. The Packet shall be available in the Office of the Clerk of the Supreme Court in each county, and the forms shall be filed with the appropriate clerk in accordance with the instructions in the Packet. These forms shall be accepted by the Court for obtaining an uncontested divorce, and no other forms shall be necessary. The Court, in its discretion, may accept other forms that comply with the requirements of law.

(3) The proposed judgments shall be numbered in the order in which they are received and submitted in sequence to the judge or referee.

(4) Unless the court otherwise directs, the proof required by statute must be in writing, by affidavits, which shall include a sufficient factual statement to establish jurisdiction, as well as all elements of the cause of action warranting the relief sought.

(5) If the judge or referee believes that the papers are insufficient, the complaint shall either be dismissed for failure of proof or a hearing shall be directed to determine whether sufficient evidence exists to support the cause of action.

(6) Whether upon written proof or at the conclusion of a hearing,

CT RULES

the judge or referee shall render a decision and sign the findings of fact, conclusions of law and the judgment, unless for reasons stated on the record decisions is reserved.

(7) Where a hearing has been held, no transcript of testimony shall be required as a condition precedent to the signing of the judgment, unless the judge or referee presiding shall so direct.

§ 202.22   Calendars.

(a) A judge to whom cases are assigned under the individual assignment system may establish such calendars of cases as the judge shall deem necessary or desirable for proper case management. These calendars may include:

(1) Preliminary conference calendar. A preliminary conference calendar is for the calendaring for conference of cases in which a note of issue and certificate of readiness have not yet been filed.

(2) Motion calendar. A motion calendar is for the hearing of motions.

(3) General calendar. A general calendar is for actions in which a note of issue and a certificate of readiness have been filed but which have not as yet been transferred to a pretrial conference calendar or a calendar containing cases that are ready for trial.

(4) Pretrial conference calendar. A pretrial conference calendar is for actions awaiting conference after the note of issue and certificate of readiness have been filed.

(5) Reserve calendar. A reserve calendar is for actions that have had a pretrial conference or where such conference was dispensed with by the court, but where the actions have not yet been transferred to a ready calendar.

(6) Ready calendar. A ready calendar is for actions in which a trial is imminent.

(7) Military calendar. A military calendar is for cases where a party to an action or a witness necessary upon the trial is in military service and is not presently available for trial, and a deposition cannot be taken, or, if taken, would not provide adequate evidence.

(8) Continuous calendars. In any court not continuously in

session, the calendars at the close of one term shall be used to open the following term and actions on the calendars shall retain their positions.

(b) *Calendar progression.* With due regard to the requirements of statutory preferences and of section 202.24 of this Part, when actions are advanced from one calendar to another they shall progress from the head of one calendar to the foot of the next calendar and otherwise progress in order insofar as practicable unless otherwise determined by the court.

(c) *Call of calendars.* Judges to whom actions and proceedings are assigned pursuant to the individual assignment system may schedule calls of any calendars they have established at such times as they deem appropriate.

(d) *Readiness for trial.* When an action has been announced "ready" but a trial is not immediately available, counsel may arrange with the judge to be summoned by telephone, provided they agree to hold themselves available and to appear on one hour's notice, or at such other time as the court may order, at the time assigned for trial.

§ 202.23   [Reserved]

§ 202.24   **Special preferences.**

(a) *Applications.* Any party claiming a preference under CPLR 3403 may apply to the court in the manner prescribed by that rule.

(b) *Special requirements in personal injury and wrongful death action.* A party seeking a preference pursuant to CPLR 3403(a)(3) in an action for damages for personal injuries or for causing death shall serve and file in support of the demand or application, whether in the note of issue or subsequent thereto, a copy of:

(1) the summons;

(2) the complaint, answer and bill of particulars, conforming to CPLR 3043 and 3044;

(3) each report required by this Part to be served by the parties relating to medical information;

(4) a statement that the venue of the action was properly laid; and

(5) all other papers material to the application.

(c) *Counterclaims and cross-claims.* A counterclaim or cross-claim which is not entitled to a preference shall not itself defeat the plaintiff's right to a preference under this section.

(d) Result of preference being granted. If a preference is granted, the case shall be placed ahead of all non-preferred cases pending as of that date, unless the court otherwise orders.

§ 202.25   Objections to applications for special preference.

(a) Within 20 days of the filing of the note of issue, if the notice of motion for a special preference is filed therewith, or within 10 days of the service of a notice of motion to obtain a preference, if served and filed subsequent to service and filing of the note of issue, any other party may serve upon all other parties and file with the court affidavits and other relevant papers, with proof of service, in opposition to granting the preference. In the event opposing papers are filed, the party applying for the preference may, within five days thereafter, serve and file in like manner papers in rebuttal.

(b) In any action which has been accorded a preference in trial upon a motion, the court shall not be precluded, on its own motion at any time thereafter, from ordering that the action is not entitled to a preference under these rules.

(c) Notwithstanding the failure of any party to oppose the application, no preference shall be granted by default unless the court finds that the action is entitled to a preference.

§ 202.26   Pretrial conference.

(a) After the filing of a note of issue and certificate of readiness in any action, the judge shall order a pretrial conference, unless the judge dispenses with such a conference in any particular case.

(b) To the extent practicable, pretrial conferences shall be held not less than 15 nor more than 45 days before trial is anticipated.

(c) The judge shall consider at the conference with the parties or their counsel the following:

(1) simplification and limitation of the issues;

(2) obtaining admission of fact and of documents to avoid unnecessary proof;

(3) disposition of the action including scheduling the action for trial;

(4) amendment of pleadings or bill of particulars;

(5) limitation of number of expert witnesses; and

(6) insurance coverage where relevant.

The judge also may consider with the parties any other matters deemed relevant.

(d) In actions brought under the simplified procedure sections of the CPLR, the court shall address those matters referred to in CPLR 3036(5).

(e) Where parties are represented by counsel, only attorneys fully familiar with the action and authorized to make binding stipulations, or accompanied by a person empowered to act on behalf of the party represented, will be permitted to appear at a pre-trial conference. Where appropriate, the court may order parties, representatives of parties, representatives of insurance carriers or persons having an interest in any settlement, including those holding liens on any settlement or verdict, to also attend in person or telephonically at the settlement conference. Plaintiff shall submit marked copies of the pleadings. A verified bill of particulars and a doctors report or hospital record, or both, as to the nature and extent of injuries claimed, if any, shall be submitted by the plaintiff and by any defendant who counterclaims. The judge may require additional data, or may waive any requirement for submission of documents on suitable alternate proof of damages. Failure to comply with this paragraph may be deemed a default under CPLR 3404. Absence of an attorneys file shall not be acceptable excuse for failing to comply with this paragraph.

(f) If any action is settled or discontinued by stipulation at a pretrial conference, complete minutes of such stipulation shall be made at the direction of the court. Such transcribed stipulation shall be enforceable as though made in open court.

(g) (1) At the pretrial conference, if it appears that the action falls within the monetary jurisdiction of a court of limited jurisdiction, there is nothing to justify its being retained in the court in which it is then pending, and it would be reached for trial more quickly in a lower court, the judge shall order the case transferred to the appropriate lower court, specifying the paragraph of CPLR 325 under which the action is taken. (2) With respect to transfers to the New York City Civil Court pursuant to CPLR 325, if, at the pretrial conference, the conditions in paragraph (1) are met except that the case will not be reached for trial more quickly in the lower court, the judge, in his or her discretion, may order the case so transferred if it will be reached for trial in the lower court within 30 days of the conference. In determining whether the action will be reached for trial in the lower court within 30 days, the judge shall consult with the administrative judge of his or her court, who shall advise, after due inquiry, whether calendar conditions and clerical considerations will permit the trial of actions in the lower court within the 30-day timeframe. If the action is not transferred to a lower court, it shall be tried in the superior court in its proper calendar progression.

§ 202.27　Defaults.

At any scheduled call of a calendar or at any conference, if all parties do not appear and proceed or announce their readiness to proceed immediately or subject to the engagement of counsel, the judge may note the default on the record and enter an order as follows:

　(a) if the plaintiff appears but the defendant does not, the judge may grant judgment by default or order an inquest.

　(b) if the defendant appears but the plaintiff does not, the judge may dismiss the action and may order a severance of counterclaims or cross-claims.

　(c) if no party appears, the judge may make such order as appears just.

§ 202.28　Discontinuance of civil actions.

In any discontinued action, the attorney for the defendant shall file a stipulation or statement of discontinuance with the county clerk within 20 days of such discontinuance. If the action has been noticed for judicial activity within 20 days of such discontinuance, the stipulation or statement shall be filed before the date scheduled for such activity.

§ 202.29   [Reserved]

§ 202.30   [Reserved]

§ 202.31   Identification of trial counsel.

Unless the court otherwise provides, where the attorney of record for any party arranges for another attorney to conduct the trial, the trial counsel must be identified in writing to the court and all parties no later than 15 days after the pretrial conference or, if there is no pretrial conference, at least ten days before trial. The notice must be signed by both the attorney of record and the trial counsel.

§ 202.32   Engagement of counsel.

No adjournment shall be granted on the ground of engagement of counsel except in accordance with Part 125 of the Rules of the Chief Administrator of the Courts (22 NYCRR Part 125).

§ 202.33   Conduct of the voir dire.

(a) *Trial judge.* All references to the trial judge in this section shall include any judge designated by the administrative judge in those instances where the case processing system or other logistical considerations do not permit the trial judge to perform the acts set forth in this section.

(b) *Pre-voir dire settlement conference.* Where the court has directed that jury selection begin, the trial judge shall meet prior to the actual commencement of jury selection with counsel who will be conducting the voir dire and shall attempt to bring about a disposition of the action.

(c) *Method of jury selection.* The trial judge shall direct the method of jury selection that shall be used for the voir dire from among the methods specified in subdivision (f) below.

(d) *Time limitations.* The trial judge shall establish time limitations for the questioning of prospective jurors during the voir dire. At the discretion of the judge, the limits established may consist of a general period for the completion of the questioning, a period after which attorneys shall report back to the judge on the progress of the voir dire, and/or specific time periods for the questioning of panels of jurors or individual jurors.

(e) *Presence of judge at the voir dire.* In order to ensure an efficient and dignified selection process, the trial judge shall preside at the commencement of the voir dire and open the voir dire proceeding. The trial judge shall determine whether supervision of the voir dire should continue after the voir dire has commenced and, in his or her discretion, preside over part of or all of the remainder of the *voir dire.*

(f) *Methods of jury selection.* Counsel shall select prospective jurors in accordance with the general principles applicable to jury selection set forth in Appendix "E" * and using the method designated by the judge pursuant to subdivision (c). The methods that may be selected are:

   * See Appendix E following § 202.70.

   (1) "White's method," as set forth in Appendix "E"* of this Part;
   * See Appendix E following § 202.70.

   (2) "Struck method," as set forth in Appendix "E"* of this Part;
   * See Appendix E following § 202.70.

   (3) "Strike and replace method," in districts where the specifics of that method have been submitted to the Chief Administrator by the Administrative Judge and approved by the Chief Administrator for that district. The strike and replace method shall be approved only in those districts where the Chief Administrator, in his or her discretion, has determined that experience with the method in the district has resulted in an efficient and orderly selection process; or

   (4) Other methods that may be submitted to the Chief Administrator for use on an experimental basis by the appropriate Administrative Judge and approved by the Chief Administrator.

§ 202.34   [Reserved]

§ 202.35   Submission of papers for trial.

(a) Upon the trial of an action, the following papers, if not yet submitted, shall be submitted to the court by the party who has filed the note of issue:

(1) copies of all pleadings marked as required by CPLR 4012; and

(2) a copy of the bill of particulars, if any.

(b) Upon the trial of an action, a copy of any statutory provision in effect at the time the cause of action arose shall be submitted to the court by the party who intends to rely upon such statute.

(c) If so ordered, the parties shall submit to the court, before the commencement of trial, trial memoranda which shall be exchanged among counsel.

§ 202.36   Absence of attorney during trial.

All trial counsel shall remain in attendance at all stages of the trial until the jury retires to deliberate, unless excused by the judge presiding. The court may permit counsel to leave, provided that counsel remain in telephone contact with the court. Any counsel not present during the jury deliberation, further requests to charge, or report of the jury verdict shall be deemed to stipulate that the court may proceed in his or her absence and to waive any irregularity in proceedings taken in his or her absence.

§§ 202.37-202.39   [Reserved]

§ 202.40   Jury trial of less than all issues; procedure.

Unless otherwise ordered by the court, whenever a trial by jury is demanded on less than all issues of fact in an action, and such issues as to which a trial by jury is demanded have been specified in the note of issue or in the jury demand, as the case may be, served and filed pursuant to section 202.21 of this Part, the court without a jury first shall try all issues of fact as to which a trial by jury is not demanded. If the determination of these issues by the court does not dispose of the action, a jury shall be empanelled to try the issues as to which a trial by jury is demanded.

§ 202.41   [Reserved]

§ 202.42   Bifurcated trials.

(a) Judges are encouraged to order a bifurcated trial of the issues of liability and damages in any action for personal injury where it appears

CT RULES

that bifurcation may assist in a clarification or simplification of issues and a fair and more expeditious resolution of the action.

(b) Where a bifurcated trial is ordered, the issues of liability and damages shall be severed and the issue of liability shall be tried first, unless the court orders otherwise.

(c) During the *voir dire* conducted prior to the liability phase of the trial, if the damage phase of the trial is to be conducted before the same jury, counsel may question the prospective jurors with respect to the issue of damages in the same manner as if the trial were not bifurcated.

(d) In opening to the jury on the liability phase of the trial, counsel may not discuss the question of damages. However, if the verdict of the jury shall be in favor of the plaintiff on the liability issue or in favor of the defendant on any counterclaim on the liability issue, all parties shall then be afforded an opportunity to address the jury on the question of damages before proof in that regard is presented to the jury.

(e) In the event of a plaintiff's verdict on the issue of liability or a defendant's verdict on the issue of liability on a counterclaim, the damage phase of the trial shall be conducted immediately thereafter before the same judge and jury, unless the judge presiding over the trial, for reasons stated in the record, finds such procedures to be impracticable.

§ 202.43   References of triable issues and proceedings to judicial hearing officers or referees.

(a) No application to refer an action or special proceeding to a judicial hearing officer or referee will be entertained unless a note of issue, where required, has been filed and the index number is set forth in the moving papers and the proposed order.

(b) The proposed order of reference shall be presented in duplicate, and a signed original order shall be delivered to the referee. If such order is not presented for signature within 20 days after the court directs a reference, the application shall be deemed abandoned.

(c) The proposed order of reference, and the actual order of reference, shall indicate whether the reference is one to hear and determine or to hear and report.

(d) Every order of reference which does not set forth a date certain for commencement of the trial or hearing shall contain the following provision:

and it is further ORDERED that if trial of the issue or action hereby referred is not begun within 60 days from the date of this order, or before such later date as the referee or judicial hearing officer may fix upon good cause shown, this order shall be cancelled and revoked, shall be remitted by the referee or judicial hearing officer to the court from which it was issued, and the matter hereby referred shall immediately be returned to the court for trial.

(e) The term "referee" in this section shall include, but not be limited to, commissioners of appraisal, and shall not include receivers or referees in incompetency proceedings or mortgage foreclosure proceedings.

§ 202.44   Motion to confirm or reject judicial hearing officer's or referee's report.

(a) When a judicial hearing officer or a referee appointed to hear and report has duly filed his or her report, together with the transcript of testimony taken and all papers and exhibits before him or her in the proceedings, if any, and has duly given notice to each party of the filing of the report, the plaintiff shall move on notice to confirm or reject all or part of the report within 15 days after notice of such filing was given. If plaintiff fails to make the motion, the defendant shall so move within 30 days after notice of such filing was given.

(b) If no party moves as specified above, the court, on its own motion, shall issue its determination. Costs of such motion, including reasonable attorneys' fees, shall be borne by the parties pro rata, except a party who did not request any relief. However, the Attorney General of New York, or State, Federal or local governmental agencies or officers thereof, shall not be liable for costs. This subdivision shall not apply to a reference to a special referee or a judicial hearing officer or to a reference to a referee in an uncontested matrimonial action.

(c) The term *referee* in this section shall be used as defined in of section 202.43(e) of this Part.

§ 202.45   Rescheduling after jury disagreement, mistrial or order for new trial.

An action in which there has been an inability by a jury to reach a verdict, a mistrial or a new trial granted by the trial justice or an appellate court shall be rescheduled for trial. Where a new trial is granted by an appellate court, a notice to reschedule shall be filed with the appropriate clerk.

§ 202.46   Damages, inquest after default; proof.

(a) In an inquest to ascertain damages upon a default, pursuant to CPLR 3215, if the defaulting party fails to appear in person or by representative, the party entitled to judgment, whether a plaintiff, third-party plaintiff, or a party who has pleaded a cross-claim or counterclaim, may be permitted to submit, in addition to the proof required by CPLR 3215(e), properly executed affidavits as proof of damages.

(b) In any action where it is necessary to take an inquest before the court, the party seeking damages may submit the proof required by oral testimony of witnesses in open court or by written statements of the witnesses, in narrative or question and answer form, signed and sworn to.

§ 202.47   Transcript of judgment; receipt stub.

Whenever a county clerk issues a transcript of judgment, which shall be in the form prescribed by law, such clerk shall at the same time issue a stub. Such stub shall be 3⅝ × 8½ inches and shall have imprinted thereon the name and address of the issuing county clerk. The stub shall also contain such other information as shall be required to identify it with the transcript with which it was issued, so that it may be readily identified upon its return to the issuing county clerk, with the name of, and the date of receipt by, the receiving clerk endorsed thereon.

§ 202.48   Submission of orders, judgments and decrees for signature.

(a) Proposed orders or judgments, with proof of service on all parties where the order is directed to be settled or submitted on notice, must be submitted for signature, unless otherwise directed by the court, within 60 days after the signing and filing of the decision directing that the order be settled or submitted.

(b) Failure to submit the order or judgment timely shall be deemed an abandonment of the motion or action, unless for good cause shown.

(c) (1) When settlement of an order or judgment is directed by the court, a copy of the proposed order or judgment with notice of settlement, returnable at the office of the clerk of the court in which the order or judgment was granted, or before the judge if the court has so directed or if the clerk is unavailable, shall be served on all parties either:

(i) by personal service not less than five days before the date of settlement; or

(ii) by mail not less than 10 days before the date of settlement.

(2) Proposed counter-orders or judgments shall be made returnable on the same date and at the same place, and shall be served on all parties by personal service, not less than two days, or by mail, not less than seven days, before the date of settlement. Any proposed counter-order or judgment shall be submitted with a copy clearly marked to delineate each proposed change to the order or judgment to which objection is made.

§ 202.49   [Reserved]

§ 202.50   Proposed judgments in matrimonial actions; forms.

(a) Form of Judgments. Findings and conclusions shall be in a separate paper from the judgment, which papers shall be labelled "FINDINGS OF FACT AND CONCLUSIONS OF LAW" and "JUDGMENT", respectively.

(b) Approved Forms.

(1) Contested Actions. The paragraphs contained in Appendix B of this Part, modified or deleted as may be necessary to conform to the law and facts in a particular action, shall be used in the preparation of "FINDINGS OF FACT AND CONCLUSIONS OF LAW," "JUDGMENT," or "REFEREE'S REPORT OF FINDINGS OF FACT AND CONCLUSIONS OF LAW." Parenthesized portions indicate alternate provisions.

(2) Uncontested Actions. Parties in uncontested matrimonial actions shall use the forms in the Unified Court System Uncontested

Divorce Packet as set forth in Section 202.21(i)(2) of this Part, unless the court permits otherwise pursuant to that Section.

(c) Judgments submitted to the court shall be accompanied by a completed form UCS 111 (Child Support Summary Form).

§ 202.51   Proof required in dissolution proceedings.

In all actions in which the accounts of a receiver appointed in an action for the dissolution of a corporation are presented for settlement or to be passed upon by the court, a notice or a copy of an advertisement requiring the creditors to present their claims to a referee must be mailed, with the postage thereon prepaid, to each creditor whose name appears on the books of the corporation, at least 20 days before the date specified in such notice or advertisement. Proof of such mailing shall be required on the application for a final decree passing the accounts of the receiver unless proof is furnished that personal service of such notice or copy of advertisement has been made upon the creditors.

§ 202.52   Deposit of funds by receivers and assignees.

(a) Every receiver or assignee who, as such, receives any funds shall promptly deposit them in a checking account or in an interest-bearing account, as determined by the court, in a bank or trust company designated by the court. Such account shall be in his or her name as receiver or assignee and shall show the name of the case. The depository shall furnish monthly statements to the receiver or assignee and to the attorney for the receiver or the assignee.

(b) No funds shall be withdrawn from a receiver's or assignee's account, and no check thereon shall be honored, unless directed by court order or the check is countersigned by the receiver's or assignee's surety.

(c) The order appointing a receiver or assignee shall incorporate subdivisions (a) and (b) of this section.

(d) All checks by a receiver or assignee for the withdrawal of moneys shall be numbered consecutively. On the stub of each check shall be noted the number, the date, the payee's name and the purpose for which the check is drawn. Checkbooks, stubs, cancelled checks and bank statements of such bank accounts shall be maintained at the office of the receiver or assignee or his or her attorney and shall be available for inspection by creditors or parties during business hours.

(e) Receivers shall file with the court an accounting at least once each year. An application by a receiver for final settlement of his or her account or by an assignee for leave to sell assets shall include a county clerk's certificate stating the date that the bond of the applicant was filed, that it is still on file and that no order has been entered cancelling the bond or discharging the surety thereon.

§ 202.53   Trust accountings; procedure.

(a) Applications by trustees for interlocutory or final judgments or final orders in trust accountings or to terminate trusts shall be by notice of petition or order to show cause after the account has been filed in the county clerk's office.

(b) In all actions involving an accounting of a testamentary trustee or a trustee under a deed, notice must be given to the State Tax Commission before the accounts of such trustees may be approved.

(c) Where all parties file a written consent to the entry of a judgment or order, it may be presented at a motion part for consideration by the court.

§ 202.54   Proceedings relating to appointments of guardians with respect to patients in facilities defined in the Mental Hygiene Law.

Where a patient in a facility defined in the Mental Health Law is the subject of a proceeding for the appointment of a guardian, pursuant to the Mental Hygiene Law or to article 17-A of the Surrogate's Court Procedure Act, or for any substitute for or successor to such person:

(a) A copy of the notice of application for the appointment shall be served on the director of the Mental Hygiene Legal Service in the department in which the facility is located. The director shall submit to the court for its consideration such papers as the director may deem appropriate.

(b) Within 10 days after the order determining the application is signed, a copy shall be served on the director.

CT RULES

(c) Within 10 days after qualification of the guardian, proof of qualification shall be served on the director.

(d) A notice of an application for a judicial accounting by the guardian shall be served on the director.

(e) With respect to a patient in a facility located in a judicial department other than the department where the proceeding is initiated, copies of the application, order or proof of qualification shall be served upon the directors in both departments.

(f) Whenever the patient, or a person on behalf of the patient, or the director requests a court hearing, at least five days notice, if notice is given personally or by delivery at the home of the person receiving notice, or eight days notice, if notice is given by mail, excluding Sundays and holidays, of the date and place of the hearing, shall be given to the patient and any person requesting the hearing.

§ 202.55   Procedure for perfection of civil appeals to the county court.

(a) Within 20 days after the papers described in section 1704 of the Uniform Justice Court Act or section 1704 of the Uniform City Court Act have been filed with the County Court, appellants shall notice the appeal for the next term or special term of County Court by filing with the clerk of the county court, not less than 14 days prior to the date for which the appeal has been noticed, a notice of argument and a brief or statement of contentions with proof of service of a copy of each upon respondent. Respondent's papers shall be filed with the judge of the County Court within 12 days after service of appellant's brief or statement of contentions, with proof of service of a copy upon appellant.

(b) If appellant does not comply herewith, the County Court may, upon respondent's motion or upon its own motion, dismiss the appeal.

(c) Upon motion, the County Court judge hearing the appeal may for good cause shown extend the time to a subsequent term or special term, in which case the appellant must notice the appeal for such subsequent term. Unless otherwise ordered by the court, appeals may be submitted without oral argument. Motions for reargument may be made after decision is rendered, and must be made within 30 days after service upon the moving party of a copy of the order entered on the decision, with written notice of its entry.

§ 202.56   Medical, dental and podiatric malpractice actions; special rules.

(a) *Notice of medical, dental or podiatric malpractice action.* (1) Within 60 days after joinder of issue by all defendants named in the complaint in an action for medical, dental or podiatric malpractice, or after the time for a defaulting party to appear, answer or move with respect to a pleading has expired, the plaintiff shall obtain an index number and file a notice of such medical, dental or podiatric malpractice action with the appropriate clerk of the county of venue, together with

(i) proof of service of the notice upon all other parties to the action,

(ii) proof that, if demanded, authorizations to obtain medical, dental and hospital records have been served upon the defendants in the action,

(iii) copies of the summons, notice of appearance and all pleadings, including the certificate of merit if required by CPLR 3012-a,

(iv) a copy of the bill of particulars, if one has been served,

(v) a copy of any arbitration demand, election of arbitration or concession of liability served pursuant to CPLR 3045, and

(vi) if requested and available, all information required by CPLR 3101(d)(1)(i).

The notice shall be served simultaneously upon all such parties. If the bill of particulars, papers served pursuant to CPLR 3045, and information required by CPLR 3101(d)(1)(i) are not available, but later become available, they shall be filed with the court simultaneously when served on other parties. The notice shall be in substantially the following form:

CT RULES

NOTICE OF
MEDICAL, DENTAL OR PODIATRIC MALPRACTICE ACTION

Malpractice

Calendar No.
(if any)_____

_____

Reserved for Clerk's use

Index No._____

Name of Assigned Judge_____

SUPREME COURT
_____ County

_____

Plaintiff(s)

       vs.

_____

Defendants(s)

   Please take notice that the above action for medical, dental or podiatric malpractice was commenced by service of summons on _____, that issue was joined therein on _____, and that the action has not been dismissed, settled or otherwise terminated.

1. State full name, address and age of each plaintiff.

2. State full name and address of each defendant.

3. State alleged medical specialty of each individual defendant, if known.

4. Indicate where claim is for

_____ medical malpractice

_____ dental malpractice

_____ podiatric malpractice

5. State date and place claim arose

6. State substance of claim

7. (Following items must be checked)

(a) Proof is attached that authorization to obtain medical, dental, podiatric and hospital records have been served upon the defendants in the action _____

   or

demand has not been made for such authorizations. _____

(b) Copies of the summons, notice of appearance, all pleadings, certificate of merit, if required, and the bill of particulars if one has been served, are attached. _____

(c) A copy of any demand for arbitration, election of arbitration or concession of liability is attached _____

   or

demand has not been made for arbitration. _____

(d) All information required by CPLR 3101(d)(1)(i) is attached _____

   or

a request for such information has not been made _____

   or

such information is not available. _____

8. State names, addresses and telephone numbers of counsel for all parties

_____ (PRINT NAME)   Telephone number
Attorney for Plaintiff   Dated:
Address   Instructions:

1. Attach additional 8½ × 11 rider sheets if necessary.

2. Attach proof of service of this notice upon all other parties to the action.

   (2) The filing of the notice of medical, dental or podiatric malpractice action in an action to which a judge has not been assigned shall be accompanied by a request for judicial intervention, pursuant to section 202.6 of this Part, and shall cause the assignment of the action to a judge.

(3) Such notice shall be filed after the expiration of 60 days only by leave of the court on motion and for good cause shown. The court shall impose such conditions as may be just, including the assessment of costs.

(b) Medical, dental and podiatric malpractice preliminary conference.

(1) The judge, assigned to the medical, dental or podiatric malpractice action, as soon as practicable after the filing of the notice of medical, dental or podiatric malpractice action, shall order and conduct a preliminary conference and shall take whatever action is warranted to expedite the final disposition of the case, including but not limited to:

(i) directing any party to utilize or comply forthwith with any pretrial disclosure procedure authorized by the Civil Practice Law and Rules;

(ii) fixing the date and time for such procedure provided that all such procedures must be completed within 12 months of the filing of the notice of medical, dental or podiatric malpractice action unless otherwise ordered by the court;

(iii) establishing a timetable for offers and depositions pursuant to CPLR 3101(d)(1)(ii);

(iv) directing the filing of a note of issue and a certificate of readiness when the action otherwise is ready for trial, provided that the filing of the note of issue and certificate of readiness, to the extent feasible, be no later than 18 months after the notice of medical, dental or podiatric malpractice action is filed;

(v) fixing a date for trial;

(vi) signing any order required;

(vii) discussing and encouraging settlement, including use of the arbitration procedures set forth in CPLR 3045;

(viii) limiting issues and recording stipulations of counsel; and

(ix) scheduling and conducting any additional conferences as may be appropriate.

(2) A party failing to comply with a directive of the court authorized by the provisions of this subdivision shall be subject to appropriate sanctions, including costs, imposition of appropriate attorney's fees, dismissal of an action, claim, cross-claim, counter-claim or defense, or rendering a judgment by default. A certificate of readiness and a note of issue may not be filed until a precalendar conference has been held pursuant to this subdivision.

(3) Where parties are represented by counsel, only attorneys fully familiar with the action and authorized to make binding stipulations or commitments, or accompanied by a person empowered to act on behalf of the party represented, shall appear at the conference.

§ 202.57   Judicial review of orders of the State Division of Human Rights; procedure.

(a) Any complainant, respondent or other person aggrieved by any order of the State Commissioner of Human Rights or the State Division of Human Rights may obtain judicial review of such order by commencing a special proceeding, within 60 days after service of the order, in the Supreme Court in the county where the alleged discrimi-natory practice which is the subject of the order occurred or where any person required by the order to cease and desist from an unlawful discriminatory practice or to take other affirmative action resides or transacts business. Such proceeding shall be commenced by the filing of a notice of petition and petition naming as respondents the State Division of Human Rights and all other parties appearing in the proceeding before the State Division of Human Rights.

(b) Except as set forth in subdivision (c) of this section, and unless otherwise ordered by the court, the State Division of Human Rights shall have 20 days after service of the notice of petition and petition to file with the court the written transcript of the record of all prior proceedings upon which its order was made.

(c) Where the petition seeks review of an order issued after a public hearing held pursuant to section 297(4)(a) of the Executive Law:

(1) the petition shall have annexed to it a copy of such order;

(2) the Supreme Court, upon the filing of the petition, shall make an order directing that the proceeding be transferred for disposition to the Appellate Division in the judicial department embracing the

CT RULES

county in which the proceeding was commenced; and

(3) the time and manner of the filing of the written transcript of the record of all prior proceedings shall be determined by the Appellate Division to which the proceeding is transferred.

§ 202.58   Small claims tax assessment review proceedings; small claims sidewalk assessment review proceedings; special rules.

(a) *Establishment.*

(1) There is hereby established in the Supreme Court of the State of New York in each county a program to hear special proceedings for small claims tax assessment review pursuant to title 1-A of Article 7 of the Real Property Tax Law; provided, however, that insofar as Hamilton County may lack required personnel and facilities, Fulton and Hamilton Counties shall be deemed one county for the purposes of this rule.

(2) There also is established in the Supreme Court in each county within the City of New York a program to hear special proceedings for small claims sidewalk assessment review pursuant to section 19-152.3 of the Administrative Code of the City of New York.

(b) *Commencement of small claims tax assessment review proceeding.*

(1) A special proceeding pursuant to title 1-A of article 7 of the Real Property Tax Law shall be commenced by a petition in a form in substantial compliance with the forms prescribed by the Chief Administrator of the Courts. Forms shall be available at no cost at each county clerk's office.

(2) Three copies of the petition shall be filed with the county clerk in the county in which the property is located within 30 days after the final completion and filing of the assessment roll containing the assessment at issue, except that in the City of New York, the petition shall be filed before the 25th day of October following the time when the determination sought to be reviewed was made. The petition may be filed with the county clerk by ordinary mail if mailed within the 30-day time period, or in the City of New York, if mailed prior to the 25th day of October, as evidenced by the postmark. A filing fee of

$ 25 shall be paid at the time of filing, which may be in the form of a check payable to the county clerk.

(3) Within 10 days of filing the petition with the county clerk, the petitioner shall send by mail, a copy of the petition to:

(i) the clerk of the assessing unit named in the petition or, if there is no such clerk, to the officer who performs the customary duties of the clerk, except that in the City of New York the petition shall be mailed to the president of the New York City Tax Commission or to a designee of the president;

(ii) except in the cities of Buffalo, New York, Rochester, Syracuse and Yonkers, to the clerk of any school district within which any part of the real property on which the assessment to be reviewed is located or, if there is no clerk of the school district or such name and address cannot be obtained, to a trustee of the school district;

(iii) the treasurer of any county in which any part of the real property is located; and

(iv) the clerk of a village which has enacted a local law, in accordance with the provisions of subdivision 3 of section 1402 of the Real Property Tax Law, providing that the village shall cease to be an assessing unit and that village taxes shall be levied on a copy of the part of the town or county assessment roll.

(4) The county clerk shall assign a small claims assessment review filing number to each petition, shall retain one copy and shall forward two copies within two days of filing to the clerk designated by the appropriate administrative judge to process assessment review petitions.

(c) *Commencement of small claims sidewalk assessment review proceeding.*

(1) A special proceeding pursuant to section 19-152.3 of the Administrative Code of the City of New York shall be commenced by a petition in a form prescribed by the Department of Transportation of the City of New York in consultation with the Office of Court Administration. Forms shall be available at no cost at each county clerk's office within the City of New York.

CT RULES

(2) Three copies of the petition shall be filed with the county clerk in the county in which the property is located, provided that at least 30 days have elapsed from the presentation of the notice of claim to the Office of the Comptroller pursuant to section 19-152.2 of the Administrative Code. The petition may be filed with the county clerk by ordinary mail. A filing fee of $25 shall be paid at the time of filing, which may be in the form of a check payable to the county clerk.

(3) Within seven days of filing the petition with the county clerk, the petitioner personally shall deliver or send by certified mail, return receipt requested, a copy of the petition to the Commissioner of Transportation of the City of New York or the Commissioner's designee.

(4) The county clerk shall assign a sidewalk assessment review filing number to each petition, shall retain one copy and shall forward two copies within two days of filing to the clerk designated by the appropriate administrative judge to process sidewalk assessment review petitions.

(d) *Selection of hearing officer panels.*

(1) The Chief Administrator of the Courts shall establish panels of small claims hearing officers found qualified to hear small claims tax assessment review proceedings pursuant to title 1-A of article 7 of the Real Property Tax Law and panels of small claims hearing officers found qualified to hear small claims sidewalk assessment review proceedings pursuant to section 19-152.3 of the Administrative Code of the City of New York.

(2) The administrative judge of the county in which the panel will serve, or the deputy chief administrative judge for the courts within the City of New York, if the panel is to serve in New York City, shall invite applicants to apply by publishing an announcement in the appropriate law journals, papers of general circulation or trade journals, and by communicating directly with such groups as may produce qualified candidates.

(3) The announcements and communications shall set forth the nature of the position, the qualifications for selection as contained in section 731 of the Real Property Tax Law, or section 19-152.3(d) of

the Administrative Code of the City of New York, and the compensation.

(4) The administrative judge shall screen each applicant in conformance with the requirements set forth in section 731 of the Real Property Tax Law or section 19-152.3(d) of the Administrative Code of the City of New York, for qualifications, character and ability to handle the hearing officer responsibilities, and shall forward the names of recommended nominees, with a summary of their qualifications, to the Chief Administrator for appointment.

(5) Hearing officers shall serve at the pleasure of the chief administrator, and their appointments may be rescinded by the chief administrator at any time.

(6) The chief administrator may provide for such orientation courses, training courses and continuing education courses for persons applying to be hearing officers and for persons serving on hearing officer panels as the chief administrator may deem necessary and desirable.

(e) *Assignment of hearing officers.*

(1) The assessment review clerk of the county in which the panel will serve shall draw names of hearing officers at random from the panel and shall assign to each hearing officer at least the first three, but no more than six, petitions filed with the county clerk pursuant to these rules; provided, however, where necessary to ensure the fair and expeditious administration of justice, the Chief Administrator may authorize the assignment of related petitions and the assignment of more than six petitions to a single hearing officer.

(2) No person who has served as a hearing officer shall be eligible to serve again until all other hearing officers on the panel have had an opportunity to serve.

(3) A hearing officer shall disqualify himself or herself from hearing a matter where a conflict exists as defined by the Public Officers Law or, with respect to small claims tax assessment review hearing officers, by subdivision 2 of section 731 of the Real Property Tax Law. Where a hearing officer disqualifies himself or herself, such hearing officer shall notify the chief administrator or designee and the matter shall be reassigned to another hearing officer.

CT RULES

(4) The hearing officer shall determine, after contacting the parties, the date, time and place for the hearing, which shall be held within 45 days with respect to a small claims tax assessment review proceeding, and within 30 days with respect to a small claims sidewalk assessment review proceeding, after the filing of the petition, or as soon thereafter as is practicable, and which shall be held, where practicable, at a location within the county where the real property is located. The hearing officer shall schedule hearings in the evening at the request of any party, unless special circumstances require otherwise. Written notice of the date, time and place of the hearing shall be sent by mail by the hearing officer to the parties or their attorneys, if represented, at least 10 working days prior to the date of the hearing, provided however, failure to receive such notice in such period shall not bar the holding of a hearing.

(5) Adjournments shall not be granted by the hearing officer except upon good cause shown.

(6) All parties are required to appear at the hearing. Failure to appear shall result in the petition being dismissed or in the petition being determined upon inquest by the hearing officer based upon the available evidence submitted.

(f) *Decision and order.*

(1) The decision and order of the hearing officer shall be rendered expeditiously, and, in a small claims tax assessment review proceeding, the notice required by section 733(4) of the Real Property Tax Law shall be attached to the petition form.

(2) Costs. (i) In a small claims tax assessment review proceeding, if the assessment is reduced by an amount equal to or greater than half the reduction sought, the hearing officer shall award the petitioner costs against the respondent assessing unit in the amount of $25. If the assessment is reduced by an amount less than half of the reduction sought, the hearing officer may award the petitioner costs against the respondent assessing unit in an amount not to exceed $25. (ii) In a small claims sidewalk assessment review proceeding, if the hearing officer grants the petition in full or in part, the hearing officer shall award the petitioner costs against the respondent in the amount of $25. In

any other case, the hearing officer, in his or her discretion, may award the petitioner costs in the amount of $25, if he or she deems it appropriate.

(3) The hearing officer in a small claims tax assessment review proceeding shall transmit one copy of the decision and order, by ordinary mail, to the petitioner, the clerk of the assessing unit and the assessment review clerk of the court. The hearing officer in a small claims sidewalk assessment review proceeding shall transmit one copy of the decision and order, by ordinary mail, to the petitioner, the Commissioner of Transportation of the City of New York or the Commissioner's designee, and the assessment review clerk of the court.

(4) The assessment review clerk shall file the petition and the attached decision and order with the county clerk.

(5) The assessment review clerk shall make additional copies of the decision and order, as necessary, and, in the case of the small claims tax assessment review proceeding, shall transmit a copy to the clerk of each tax district relying on the assessment that is named in the petition and to the treasurer of any county in which any part of the real property is located. In the case of a small claims sidewalk assessment review proceeding, where the order grants the petition in full or in part, the assessment review clerk shall mail a copy of the decision and order to the Collector of the City of New York.

(g) *Advertising by hearing officers.* No person who is appointed a hearing officer shall, in any public advertisement published or distributed to advance such person's business or professional interests, refer to his or her status as a hearing officer. No hearing officer shall use letterhead or business cards bearing the title of hearing officer except in direct connection with such person's official duties as hearing officer.

(h) (1) Proceedings pursuant to title 1-A of article 7 of Real Property Tax Law may be heard and determined by a judicial hearing officer. The judicial hearing officer shall be designated and assigned by the appropriate administrative judge to hear such proceedings as determined by that judge or by the assessment review clerk, and the hearing shall be conducted in accordance with this section.

(2) Judicial hearing officers appointed to hear proceedings pursuant to this section shall receive compensation as provided in section 122.8 of the rules of this Title. A location in which a hearing is held pursuant to this section shall be deemed a "facility designated for court appearances" within the meaning of section 122.8 of this Title.

(i) *Collateral proceedings.* All applications for judicial relief shall be made in the Supreme Court in the county where the real property subject to review is located. If a judicial hearing officer has heard and determined a proceeding under this section, any application for judicial relief may not be heard by a judicial hearing officer, except upon consent of the parties.

§ 202.59   Tax assessment review proceedings in counties outside the City of New York; special rules

(a) *Applicability.* This section shall apply to every tax assessment review proceeding brought pursuant to title 1 of article 7 of the Real Property Tax Law in counties outside the City of New York.

(b) *Statement of income and expenses.* Before the note of issue and certificate of readiness may be filed, the petitioner shall have served on the respondent, in triplicate, a statement that the property is not income-producing or a copy of a verified or certified statement of the income and expenses on the property for each tax year under review. For the purposes of this section, a cooperative or condominium apartment building shall be considered income-producing property; an owner-occupied business property shall be considered income-producing as determined by the amount reasonably allocable for rent, but the petitioner is not required to make an estimate of rental income.

(c) *Audit.* Within 60 days after the service of the statement of income and expenses, the respondent, for the purpose of substantiating petitioner's statement of income and expenses, may request in writing an audit of the petitioner's books and records for the tax years under review. If requested, the audit must be completed within 120 days after the request has been made unless the court, upon good cause shown, extends the time for the audit. Failure of the respondent to request or complete the audit within the time limits shall be deemed a waiver of such privilege. If an audit is requested and the petitioner fails to furnish its books and records within a reasonable time after receipt of the request, or otherwise unreasonably impedes or delays the audit, the court, on motion of the respondent, may dismiss the petition or petitions or make such other order as the interest of justice requires.

(d) *Filing note of issue and certificate of readiness; additional requirements.* (1) A note of issue and certificate of readiness shall not be filed unless all disclosure proceedings have been completed and the statement of income and expenses has been served and filed.

(2) A separate note of issue shall be filed for each property for each tax year.

(e) *Pretrial conference.* (1) At any time after filing of the note of issue and certificate of readiness, any party to a tax assessment review proceeding may demand, by application served on all other parties and filed with the court, together with proof of such service, a pretrial conference, or the court on its own motion may direct a pretrial conference at a time and date to be fixed by the court. At the pretrial conference, the judge shall take whatever action is warranted to expedite final disposition of the proceedings, including, but not limited to:

(i) directing the parties to obtain appraisals and sales reports, and to exchange and file appraisal reports and sales reports by dates certain before the trial, provided that if the court dispenses with a pretrial conference, such exchange and filings shall be accomplished at least ten days before trial;

(ii) fixing a date for trial, or by which the parties must be ready for trial;

(iii) signing any order required;

(iv) conducting conferences for the purpose of facilitating settlement; and

(v) limiting issues and recording stipulations of counsel.

(2) Failure to comply with any order or directive of the court authorized by this subdivision shall be subject to the appropriate sanctions.

(f) *Consolidation or joint trial.* Consolidation or joint trial of real property tax assessment review proceedings in the discretion of the

CT RULES

court shall be conditioned upon service having been made of the verified or certified income and expense statement, or a statement that the property is not income-producing, for each of the tax years under review.

(g) *Exchange and filing of appraisal reports.* (1) The exchange and filing of appraisal reports shall be accomplished by the following procedure:

(i) The respective parties shall file with the clerk of the trial court one copy, or in the event that there are two or more adversaries, a copy for each adversary, of all appraisal reports intended to be used at the trial.

(ii) When the clerk shall have received all such reports, the clerk forthwith shall distribute simultaneously to each of the other parties a copy of the reports filed.

(iii) Where multiple parties or more than one parcel is involved, each appraisal report need be served only upon the taxing authority and the party or parties contesting the value of the property which is the subject of the report. Each party shall provide an appraisal report copy for the court.

(2) The appraisal reports shall contain a statement of the method of appraisal relied on and the conclusions as to value reached by the expert, together with the facts, figures and calculations by which the conclusions were reached. If sales, leases or other transactions involving comparable properties are to be relied on, they shall be set forth with sufficient particularity as to permit the transaction to be readily identified, and the report shall contain a clear and concise statement of every fact that a party will seek to prove in relation to those comparable properties. The appraisal reports also may contain photographs of the property under review and of any comparable property that specifically is relied upon by the appraiser, unless the court otherwise directs.

(3) Where an appraiser appraises more than one parcel in any proceeding, those parts of the separate appraisal reports for each parcel that would be repetitious may be included in one general appraisal report to which reference may be made in the separate appraisal reports. Such general appraisal reports shall be served and

filed as provided in paragraph (1) of this subdivision.

(4) Appraisal reports shall comply with any official form for appraisal reports that may be prescribed by the Chief Administrator of the Courts.

(h) *Use of appraisal reports at trial.* Upon the trial, expert witnesses shall be limited in their proof of appraised value to details set forth in their respective appraisal reports. Any party who fails to serve an appraisal report as required by this section shall be precluded from offering any expert testimony on value, provided, however, upon the application of any party on such notice as the court shall direct, the court may, upon good cause shown, relieve a party of a default in the service of a report, extend the time for exchanging reports, or allow an amended or supplemental report to be served upon such conditions as the court may direct. After the trial of the issues has begun, any such application must be made to the trial judge and shall be entertained only in unusual and extraordinary circumstances.

§ 202.60   Tax assessment review proceedings in counties within the City of New York; special rules.

(a) *Applicability.* This section shall apply to every tax assessment review proceeding brought pursuant to title 1 of article 7 of the Real Property Tax Law in a county within the City of New York.

(b) *Preliminary conference.*

(1) Any party to a tax assessment review proceeding may demand, by application served on all other parties and filed with the court, together with proof of such service, a preliminary conference, or the court on its own motion may direct a preliminary conference. The court, in its notice to the parties setting the date for the conference, shall direct the petitioner to serve upon the respondent by a date certain before the date of the conference, the completed statement of income and expenses required by this section, together with any ancillary papers or documents that may be necessary. No note of issue may be filed until a preliminary conference has been held.

(2) The judge presiding at the preliminary conference shall take whatever action is warranted to expedite final disposition of the case, including, but not limited to:

(i) directing any party to utilize or comply by a date certain with any pretrial disclosure or bill of particulars procedure authorized by the Civil Practice Law and Rules;

(ii) directing the parties to obtain appraisals and sales reports, and to exchange and file appraisal reports and sales reports by dates certain before the trial;

(iii) directing the filing of a note of issue and certificate of readiness;

(iv) fixing a date for trial, or by which the parties must be ready for trial;

(v) signing any order required;

(vi) conducting conferences for the purpose of facilitating settlement; and

(vii) limiting issues and recording stipulations of counsel.

(3) Failure to comply with any order or directive of the court authorized by this subdivision shall be subject to appropriate sanctions.

(4) Where parties are represented by counsel, only attorneys fully familiar with the action and authorized to make binding stipulations or commitments, or accompanied by a person empowered to act on behalf of the party represented, shall appear at the conference.

(c) *Statement of income and expenses.* Before the note of issue and certificate of readiness may be filed, the petitioner shall have served on the respondent, in triplicate, a statement that the property is not income-producing or a copy of a verified or certified statement of the income and expenses of the property for each tax year under review. If the property is income-producing, the petitioner must serve the statement of income and expenses on forms provided by the Tax Certiorari Division of the Office of the Corporation Counsel of the City of New York. The petitioner shall complete all items listed on such such form. A copy of such completed form shall also be filed with the note of issue and certificate of readiness. For the purposes of this section, a cooperative or condominium apartment building shall be considered income-producing property; an owner-occupied business property shall be considered income-producing as determined by the amount reasonably allocable for rent, but the petitioner is not required to make an estimate of rental income.

(d) *Audit.* Within 60 days after the first preliminary conference, the respondent, for the purpose of substantiating petitioner's completed statement of income and expenses, as required by subdivision (c) of this section, may request in writing an audit of the petitioner's books and records for the tax years under review. If requested, the audit must be completed within 120 days after the request has been made unless the court, upon good cause shown, extends the time for the audit. Failure of the respondent to request or complete the audit within the time limits shall be deemed a waiver of such privilege. If an audit is requested and the petitioner fails to furnish its books and records within a reasonable time after receipt of the request, or otherwise unreasonably impedes or delays the audit, the court, on motion of the respondent, may dismiss the petition or petitions or make such other order as the interest of justice requires.

(e) *Filing note of issue and certificate of readiness; additional requirements.*

(1) A note of issue and certificate of readiness shall not be filed unless all disclosure proceedings have been completed and the statement of income and expenses has been served and filed. A note of issue and certificate of readiness may not be filed in any action where a preliminary conference was requested or was directed by the court until the conference has been held and there has been compliance with any orders or directives of the court or stipulations of counsel made at such conference.

(2) A separate note of issue shall be filed for each property for each tax year.

(f) *Consolidation or joint trial.* Consolidation or joint trial of real property tax assessment review proceedings in the discretion of the court shall be conditioned upon service having been made of the verified or certified income and expense statement, or a statement that the property is not income-producing, for each of the tax years under review.

(g) *Exchange and filing of appraisal reports.*

(1) Upon the filing of the note of issue and certificate of readiness,

the court, if it has not previously so directed, shall direct that appraisal reports and sales reports be obtained and that appraisal reports and sales reports be exchanged and filed by a date certain a specified time before the date scheduled for trial.

(2) The exchange and filing of appraisal reports shall be accomplished by the following procedure:

(i) The respective parties shall file with the clerk of the trial court one copy, or in the event that there are two or more adversaries, a copy for each adversary, of all appraisal reports intended to be used at the trial.

(ii) When the clerk shall have received all such reports, the clerk forthwith shall distribute simultaneously to each of the other parties a copy of the reports filed.

(iii) Where multiple parties or more than one parcel is involved, each appraisal report need be served only upon the taxing authority and the party or parties contesting the value of the property which is the subject of the report. Each party shall provide an appraisal report copy for the court.

(3) The appraisal reports shall contain a statement of the method of appraisal relied on and the conclusions as to value reached by the expert, together with the facts, figures and calculations by which the conclusions were reached. If sales, leases or other transactions involving comparable properties are to be relied on, they shall be set forth with sufficient particularity as to permit the transaction to be readily identified, and the report shall contain a clear and concise statement of every fact that a party will seek to prove in relation to those comparable properties. The appraisal reports also shall contain photographs of the property under review and of any comparable property that specifically is relied upon by the appraiser, unless the court otherwise directs.

(4) Where an appraiser appraises more than one parcel in any proceeding, those parts of the separate appraisal reports for each parcel that would be repetitious may be included in one general appraisal report to which reference may be made in the separate appraisal reports. Such general appraisal reports shall be served and filed as provided in paragraph (1) of this subdivision.

(5) Appraisal reports shall comply with any official form for appraisal reports that may be prescribed by the Chief Administrator of the Courts.

(h) Use of appraisal reports at trial. Upon the trial, expert witnesses shall be limited in their proof of appraised value to details set forth in their respective appraisal reports. Any party who fails to serve an appraisal report as required by this section shall be precluded from offering any expert testimony on value provided, however, upon the application of any party on such notice as the court shall direct, the court may, upon good cause shown, relieve a party of a default in the service of a report, extend the time for exchanging reports, or allow an amended or supplemental report to be served upon such conditions as the court may direct. After the trial of the issues has begun, any such application must be made to the trial judge and shall be entertained only in unusual and extraordinary circumstances.

§ 202.61 Exchange of appraisal reports in eminent domain proceedings.

(a) (1) In all proceedings for the determination of the value of property taken pursuant to eminent domain, the exchange of appraisal reports shall be accomplished in the same manner as provided for the exchange of such reports by subdivision (g) of section 202.59 and subdivision (g) of section 202.60 of this Part, except that such reports shall be filed no later than nine months after service of the claim, demand or notice of appearance required by section 503 of the Eminent Domain Procedure Law, unless otherwise extended by the court. A note of issue may not be filed until such reports have been filed.

(2) If a party intends to offer at trial expert evidence in rebuttal to any report, an expert's report shall be filed within 60 days after receipt of the document sought to be rebutted.

(3) Upon application of any party upon such notice as the court in which the proceeding is pending shall direct, the court may, upon good cause shown, relieve a party of a default in filing a report, extend the time for filing reports, or allow an amended or supplemental report to be filed upon such conditions as the court may direct.

CT RULES

(b) In proceedings where more than one parcel is involved, the appraisal reports shall be distributed only to the taking authority and to the claimant or claimants who are owners of parcels which are the subject of the appraisal report. In the event that a party defaults in filing an appraisal report within the time limitation prescribed, the clerk shall return the filed copies of each party's appraisal report, with notice to the party in default.

(c) The contents and form of each appraisal report, including any rebuttal, amended or supplementary report, shall conform to the requirements of subdivision (g) of section 202.59 and subdivision (g) of section 202.60 of this Part.

(d) All appraisals of fixtures submitted on behalf of the claimants and the condemnor for which claim is made shall be filed and distributed as provided by these rules with respect to appraisal reports and shall set forth the appraisal value of each item in the same numerical order as in the inventory annexed to the claim.

(1) Where the condemnor puts in issue the existence of any item in the inventory, the appraisal submitted on its behalf shall so state.

(2) Where the condemnor puts in issue the description of any item in the inventory, the appraisal submitted on behalf of the condemnor shall state its appraiser's description of such item and his or her estimate of value.

(3) Where the condemnor puts in issue the compensability of any item in the inventory, the appraisal report submitted by the condemnor shall so state and shall state the ground therefor, as well as its appraiser's estimate of the value of such item for consideration in the event that the court should determine that it is compensable.

(e) Upon trial, all parties shall be limited in their affirmative proof of value to matters set forth in their respective appraisal reports. Any party who fails to file an appraisal report as required by this section shall be precluded from offering any appraisal testimony on value.

§ 202.62   Payment of eminent domain award to other than the named awardee.

On all applications for payment of awards in eminent domain proceedings by parties other than the party named in the decree, the applicant shall give notice of its motion to all parties with an interest in the award.

§ 202.63   Assignment for benefit of creditors.

(a) *Records and papers.*

(1) In assignments for the benefit of creditors, the clerk shall keep a register and docket. The clerk shall enter in the register in full every final order according to date; the docket shall contain a brief note of each day's proceedings under the respective title.

(2) Every petition, order, decree or other paper shall have endorsed on the outside the nature of such paper, the date of filing, and the name, number and page of the book in which the proceedings are entered by the clerk.

(3) The papers in each proceeding shall be kept in a separate file, as required by section 18 of the Debtor and Creditor Law. No paper shall be removed from the files of the court except by order of the court.

(4) Except as otherwise provided by law, every notice or citation, subpoena, and all process shall issue out of the court under seal and be attested by the clerk.

(b) *Appearances.*

(1) Any person interested in an assignment for the benefit of creditors may appear either in person or by attorney. If in person, his or her address and telephone number, and if by attorney, the name, address and telephone number, shall be endorsed on every appearance filed by such attorney. The name of such person or attorney shall be entered in the docket.

(2) The assignee's attorney shall file a written notice of appearance as soon as possible, but not later than 10 days after being retained.

(3) When an assignee is removed, voluntarily or involuntarily, and another person has been appointed as assignee, a certified copy of the order shall be filed with the clerk of the county where the original assignment was recorded. The clerk shall make an entry on the

CT RULES

record of the original assignment to show the appointment of the substituted assignee, and the copy of the order of substitution shall be attached to the original assignment.

(c) *Duties of the assignor and assignee.*

(1) The assignor shall deliver all books, records and documents to the assignee immediately upon filing the assignment, but the assignee shall make them available to the assignor to prepare the schedules.

(2) The assignee's attorney shall require the person in charge of the assignor's business to submit to examination under oath and shall complete such examinations within 30 days, unless extended by the court for good cause.

(3) The assignee shall promptly require the assignor, if an individual, or its officers and persons in charge of its finances, if a corporation, to pay to the assignee all trust funds withheld for accounting to any governmental authorities, together with any preferential payments paid to them or to others by the assignor.

(4) (i) Upon the filing of an assignment, the court, upon application, may stay any prospective sale or transfer to enforce a lien against property in the custody of the court whether by a secured creditor, a judgment creditor, a lienor or otherwise.

(ii) With respect to property not in the custody of the court, possession having been acquired by the secured creditor, judgment creditor or lienor, the assignee may, upon notice to the adverse party, apply to the court where such assignment proceedings are pending to enjoin any prospective sale and to permit the assignee to conduct the sale, whether private or a public auction, upon such terms and conditions as in its discretion will not prejudice the interest of the secured party and yet preserve the interest of the assigned estate by affording the assignee an opportunity to liquidate the assets under the most favorable terms and conditions.

(5) Every assignee shall keep full, exact and regular books of account of all receipts, payments and expenditures of monies.

(6) In making sales at auction of personal property, the assignee

shall give at least 10 days' notice of the time and place of sale and of the articles to be sold, by advertisement in one or more newspapers. Such sale shall be held within 15 days after the entry of the order authorizing the same, unless in the meantime an order of the court has been obtained granting an extension of the time for such sale; and he or she shall give notice of the sale at auction of any real estate at least 20 days before such sale. Upon such sale, the assignee shall sell by printed catalogue, in parcels, and shall file a copy of such catalogue with the prices obtained for the goods sold, within 20 days after the date of such sale.

(7) (i) Notwithstanding subdivision (f) of this section, upon receipt of an offer for all or a substantial part of the assets, an assignee may for good cause shown make application to the court for leave to sell at a private sale in lieu of a public auction sale. A hearing thereon shall be scheduled for the purpose of considering that offer or any higher or better offers that may be submitted upon such notice and advertising as the court may deem appropriate.

(ii) Upon application by an assignee or a creditor, setting forth that a part or the whole of the estate is perishable, the nature and location of such perishable property, and that there will be a loss if the same is not sold immediately, the judge presiding, if satisfied of the facts stated and that the sale is required in the interest of the estate, may order the same to be sold with or without notice to creditors.

(8) Upon an application made for a notice of filing of his or her account and for a hearing thereon, the assignee shall file with his or her petition his or her account with the vouchers.

(d) *Accounting and schedules.*

(1) The assignee must file and account in all cases.

(2) Failure to file an interim accounting in a pending proceeding within six months after the filing of an assignment may cause a forfeiture of commissions and fees of the assignee and his or her attorney and shall constitute grounds for their removal.

(3) Where more than one sheet of paper is necessary to contain the schedule of liabilities and inventory of assets required to be filed by

CT RULES

the assignor or assignee, each page shall be signed by the person or persons verifying the same. Contingent liabilities shall appear on a separate sheet of paper. The sheets on which such schedule and inventory are written shall be securely fastened before the filing thereof and shall be endorsed with the full name of the assignor and assignee; and when filed by an attorney, the name and address of such attorney shall also be endorsed thereon. Such schedule and inventory shall fully and fairly state the nominal and actual value of the assets and the cause of differences between such values. A separate affidavit will be required explaining such stated cause of difference. If it is deemed necessary, affidavits of disinterested experts as to the claimed values must be furnished; and if such schedule and inventory are filed by the assignee, they must be accompanied by affidavits made by such assignee and by some disinterested expert showing, in detail, the nature and value of the property assigned. The name, residence, occupation and place of business of the assignor, and the name and place of residence of the assignee must be annexed to the schedule and inventory or incorporated in the affidavit verifying the same. There shall be a recapitulation at the end of such schedule and inventory, as follows:

Debts and liabilities amount to _____ $_____

Fair value of assets _____ $_____

Assets realized on liquidation _____ $_____

(4) Application to amend the schedule shall be made by verified petition in which the amendment sought to be made shall appear in full, and such amendment shall be verified in the same manner as the original schedule.

(5) The account of the assignee shall be in the nature of a debit and credit statement; he or she shall debit himself or herself with the assets as shown in the schedule, as filed, and credit himself or herself with any decrease and expenses.

(6) The statement of expenditures shall be full and complete and the vouchers for all payments shall be attached to the account.

(7) The affirmative on the accounting shall be with the assignee; the objections to the account may be presented to the court or

designated referee in writing or be brought out on a cross-examination. In the latter case, they must be specifically taken and entered in the minutes.

(8) The testimony taken and all exhibits marked in evidence shall be filed with the report of the referee.

(9) It shall be the duty of the assignee to close up the estate as expeditiously as possible; and, unless good cause for greater delay can be shown and authorized by an order of the court obtained prior to the expiration of the permissible time, the assignee's account shall be filed within 15 months from the date of the execution of the assignment deed.

(10) The court may order notice to creditors by publication to present their claims as provided in section 5 of the Debtor and Creditor Law.

(e) *Court-appointed referee.*

(1) The court may appoint a referee to take and state any contested account or to hear and report on any issue of fact raised in an application to the court by any interested party.

(2) Notice of the time and place of the hearing before a referee appointed to take and state an assignee's account or to hear and report on a referred issue of fact shall be given by mail, with the postage thereon prepaid, at least 20 days before the date specified in said notice, to the assignor, the assignee's surety and to each creditor whose name appears on the books of the assignor or on the schedule, or who has presented her or her claim or address to the assignee, and to each attorney who has appeared for any person interested in the assigned estate.

(3) A notice or a copy of an advertisement, requiring the creditors to present their claims, with the vouchers therefor duly verified to the referee, must be mailed to each creditor whose name appears on the books of the assignor or on the schedule, with the postage thereon prepaid, at least 10 days before the date specified in such notice or advertisement. Proof of such mailing shall be required on the application for a final decree approving the account of the assignee unless proof is furnished that personal service of such notice or a copy of such advertisement has been made upon the

creditor.

(4) The report of the referee shall show all the jurisdictional facts necessary to confer power on the court, such as the proper execution and acknowledgement of the assignment, its recording, the filing of the schedule and bond, the publication and mailing of notice to creditors to present claims, the filing of the assignee's account, the issuance and service of notice of application for settlement of the account, and, where any items in the account of the assignee are disallowed, the same shall be fully set out in the report, together with the reason therefor.

(5) The report of the referee after a hearing of a disputed claim under the statute shall be filed with the clerk of the court and a copy served on each party to the proceeding. The court shall, on application of any party, or on its own motion, confirm or disaffirm the referee's report; such report shall then be reviewed only by appeal to the Appellate Division.

(f) *Discharge of assignee.*

(1) No discharge shall be granted an assignee who has not advertised for claims pursuant to section 5 of the Debtor and Creditor Law and the applicable provisions of this section.

(2) No discharge shall be granted an assignee and his or her sureties in any case, whether or not the creditors have been paid, or have released, or have entered into composition, except in a regular proceeding for an accounting under the applicable provisions of the Debtor and Creditor Law, commenced by petition, and after due and timely notice thereof to all persons interested in the estate.

(3) Provisional and final bond. The affidavit upon which application is made for leave to file a provisional bond must show fully and fairly the nature and extent of the property assigned, and good and sufficient reason must be shown why the schedule and inventory cannot be filed. It must appear satisfactorily to the court that a necessity exists for filing of such provisional bond; and the affidavits filed shall be deemed a schedule and inventory of the assigned property until such time as the regular schedule and inventory of the assigned property shall be filed. Upon the filing of the schedule and inventory, the amount of the bond shall be determined finally.

Should the provisional bond already filed by deemed sufficient, an order may be granted making such bond, as approved, the final bond.

(4) Upon all applications made to the court by assignees under general assignments for the benefit of creditors for the filing of a provisional bond, or for permission to sell the property of the assignor, the applicant shall present proof by affidavit whether any petition in bankruptcy has been filed by or against the assignor.

(5) The final bond shall be joint and several in form and must be accompanied by the affidavit prescribed by CPLR 2502, and also by the affidavit of each surety, setting forth his business, where it is carried on, and the amount in which he or she is required to justify over and above his debts and liabilities.

(g) *Justification of sureties.* The court may in its discretion require any surety to appear and justify. If the penalty of the bond be $ 20,000 or over, it may be executed by two sureties each justifying in that sum, or by more than two sureties, the amount of whose justification, united, is double the penalty of the bond.

(h) *Application to continue business of assignor.* An application for authority to continue the business of an assignor must be made upon duly verified petition and upon notice given to, or order to show cause served upon, the assignor, the assignee's surety and all creditors, secured, general or otherwise, of the assigned estate. If more than one application for such authority is subsequently made, the petition must set forth, by a statement of receipts, disbursements and expenses, the result of the continuance of such business for or during the period for which the same was previously authorized.

(i) *Involuntary petition in bankruptcy of the assigned estate.* Where an order for relief pursuant to section 503 of Title 11 of the United States Code has been entered, the assignee shall file with the clerk a certified copy of such petition in bankruptcy, together with proof by affidavit on the part of the assignee showing that he has turned over all assets of the assigned estate to the trustee or receiver in bankruptcy.

(j) *Assignee's commissions and attorneys fees.* Assignee's allowances and attorney fees are to be fixed by the court upon a motion to settle and approve the assignee's account or upon the confirmation of the referee's report regarding the account. No allowances, fees or commissions shall be paid out until so fixed and directed by the court.

(k) *Service of notice by mail.* When any notice is served by mail on the creditors of the insolvent debtor pursuant to the provisions of the applicable statute or this section, every envelope containing such notice shall have upon it a direction to the postmaster at the place to which it is sent, to return the same to the sender whose name and address shall appear thereon, unless called for or delivered.

§ 202.64   Election law proceedings.

(a) All applications to the Supreme Court, or to a judge thereof, pursuant to the Election Law, shall be made at the special part designated for such proceedings, and where there is no special part, before the judge to whom the proceeding is assigned. As far as practicable, the application shall be brought in the county in which it arose.

(b) The judge may hear and determine the proceeding or assign it to a referee for hearing or decision, and such proceedings shall have preference over all other business of the part to which it is assigned or before the judge to whom it is assigned.

(c) The final order in an election proceeding shall state the determination and the facts upon which it was made.

§ 202.65   Registration of title to real property; sales of real estate under court direction.

(a) *Petitions for registration.* Petitions for the registration of titles to land made pursuant to article 12 of the Real Property Law shall be made to the Supreme Court in the county where the land or portion thereof affected by the petition is situated. Where a particular part has been designated for this purpose as a title part under the provisions of section 371 of the such law, all petitions to register titles to land under the law must be returnable at the said title part. If there is no such part, petitions shall be returnable before the judge is assigned. Such title part or assigned judge is hereinafter denominated as the appropriate part or judge in this section.

(b) *Application for final order and judgment of registration.* After the time provided in the notice of hearing shall have expired, or within such further time as may have been allowed by the court, if there have been no appearances or answers to the petition, the petitioner may apply to the appropriate part or judge for a final order and judgment of registration, as provided for in the law. In all applications for such final order and judgment of registration, the applicant or petitioner must present to the court proof by affidavit that all the provisions of the law entitling the petitioner to such final order and judgment of registration have been complied with.

(c) *Application for jury trial.* Where an answer is interposed which raises an issue of fact which in an action relating to the title to real property would be triable by a jury, either or any party to the registration proceeding who is entitled to have such issue determined may apply to the appropriate part or judge within 20 days after the issue has been joined to have the issues framed to be tried by a jury, as provided by CPLR 4102(b). The trial of such issues shall be had and the subsequent proceedings in relation thereto shall be such as are prescribed by the CPLR. After such issues are disposed of, either or any party to the registration proceeding may apply to the appropriate part or judge, upon eight days' notice to all who have appeared in the registration proceeding, for a final order and judgment of registration, and on such application the court shall try all other issues in the proceeding not disposed of by the jury, or may refer any such issues undisposed of to be tried by an official examiner of title as referee. Where all issues have been disposed of, any party, upon eight days' notice to all who have appeared in the proceeding, may apply for the final order and judgment of registration at the appropriate part or before the appropriate assigned judge.

(d) *Applications; notice requirements.* All applications to the court after a certificate of registration of title has been issued under the provisions of the law must be made at the appropriate part or before the appropriate assigned judge hereinbefore designated upon 20 days' notice to all persons interested in the said application. All applications to the court under sections 404-a and 422 of the Real Property Law shall be made to the appropriate part or judge upon eight days' notice to all persons in interest, as provided by that section. All applications made to the court under section 428 of the Real Property Law shall also be made to the appropriate part or judge, upon eight days' notice to the city or county treasurer and all other parties who have appeared in the proceeding to recover for loss or damage or deprivation of real property out of the assurance fund provided for by law.

(e) Sales of real estate. All sales of real estate or an interest therein, made pursuant to a judgment, decree or order, or by an officer of the court under its direction, shall be made pursuant to section 231 of the Real Property Actions and Proceedings Law, after notice as prescribed in that section. An auctioneer selected for this purpose must be an attorney, or a licensed real estate broker, or a salesman licensed for at least five years. The auctioneer's fee for conducting the sale shall be as prescribed by law.

§ 202.66   Workers' compensation settlements.

(a) Applications for approval of compromises of third-party actions pursuant to subdivision 5 of section 29 of the Workers' Compensation Law must include all papers described therein, and a proposed order providing that the appropriate insuring body file an affidavit within a specified time consenting to or opposing the application. A copy of all such application papers shall be served on the insurance carrier that is liable for the payment of claims under the Workers' Compensation Law.

(b) If prior to the return of the application the court directs that the parties place their stipulation on the record, the transcript shall be filed as part of the papers. In such cases the matter shall be marked settled subject to written consent of the insuring body, or the entry of an order pursuant to subdivision 5 of section 29 of the Workers' Compensation Law.

(c) On the return of the application, the court may hear the matter forthwith or schedule the matter for later hearing if affidavits in opposition to the compromise show that the amount is grossly inadequate in view of the injuries involved, the potential monetary recovery against the third party and the possible exposure of the insuring body to future claims by the plaintiff-petitioner arising out of the same accident.

(d) Nothing in this section shall preclude the insuring body from consenting to a reduction of its lien.

§ 202.67   Infants' and incapacitated persons' claims and proceedings.

(a) The settlement of an action or claim by an infant or judicially declared incapacitated person (including an incompetent or conservatee) shall comply with CPLR 1207 and 1208 and, in the case of an infant, with section 474 of the Judiciary Law. The proposed order in such cases may provide for deduction of the following disbursements from the settlement:

(1) motor vehicle reports;

(2) police reports;

(3) photographs;

(4) deposition stenographic expenses;

(5) service of summons and complaint and of subpoenas;

(6) expert's fees, including analysis of materials; and

(7) other items approved by court order.

The order shall not provide for attorney's fees in excess of one-third of the amount remaining after deduction of the above disbursements unless otherwise specifically authorized by the court.

(b) The petition or affidavit in support of the application also shall set forth the total amount of the charge incurred for each doctor and hospital in the treatment and care of the infant or incapacitated person, and the amount remaining unpaid to each doctor and hospital for such treatment and care. If an order be made approving the application, the order shall provide that all such charges for doctors and hospitals shall be paid from the proceeds, if any, received by the parent, guardian or other person, in settlement of any action or claim for the loss of the infant's or incapacitated person's services; provided, however, that if there be any bona fide dispute as to such charges, the judge presiding, in the order, may make such provision with respect to them as justice requires. With respect to an incapacitated person, the judge presiding may provide for the posting of a bond as required by the Mental Hygiene Law.

(c) If the net amount obtained for the infant or incapacitated person in any approved settlement does not exceed the amount set forth in CPLR 1206(b), the court may permit it to be paid pursuant to CPLR

1206(b). The court may order in any case that the money be deposited or invested pursuant to CPLR 1206(c) or held for the use and benefit of the infant or incapacitated person as provided in CPLR 1206(d) and CPLR 1210(d).

(d) The affidavit of the attorney for a plaintiff, in addition to complying with CPLR 1208, must show compliance with the requirements for filing a retainer statement and recite the number assigned by the Office of Court Administration, or show that such requirements do not apply.

(e) Applications for approval of an infant's or incapacitated person's compromise shall be made returnable before the judge who presided over the compromise or, where the agreement was reached out-of-court, before the appropriate assigned judge.

(f) A petition for the expenditure of the funds of an infant shall comply with CPLR Article 12, and also shall set forth:

(1) a full explanation of the purpose of the withdrawal;

(2) a sworn statement of the reasonable cost of the proposed expenditure;

(3) the infant's age;

(4) the date and amounts of the infant's and parents' recovery;

(5) the balance from such recovery;

(6) the nature of the infant's injuries and present condition;

(7) a statement that the family of the infant is financially unable to afford the proposed expenditures;

(8) a statement as to previous orders authorizing such expenditures; and

(9) any other facts material to the application.

(g) No authorization will be granted to withdraw such funds, except for unusual circumstances, where the parents are financially able to support the infant and to provide for the infant's necessaries, treatment and education.

(h) Expenditures of the funds of an incapacitated person shall comply with the provisions of the Mental Hygiene Law.

(i) The required notice of the filing of a final account by an incapacitated person's guardian and of a petition for settlement thereof shall show the amounts requested for additional services of the guardian and for legal services. Prior to approving such allowances, the court shall require written proof of the nature and extent of such services. Where notice is given to the attorney for the Veterans Administration, if the attorney for the Veterans Administration does not appear after notice, the court shall be advised whether the Veterans' Administration attorney has examined the account and whether he objects to it or to any proposed commission or fee.

§ 202.68   Proceedings involving custody of an Indian child.

In any proceeding in which the custody of a child is to be determined, the court, when it has reason to believe that the child is an Indian child within the meaning of the Indian Child Welfare Act of 1948 (92 Stat. 3069), shall require the verification of the child's status in accordance with that act and, proceed further, as appropriate, in accordance with the provisions of that act.

§ 202.69.   Coordination of related actions pending in more than one judicial district.

(a) *Application.*   This section shall apply when related actions are pending in the courts of the Unified Court System in more than one judicial district and it may be appropriate for these actions to be coordinated pursuant to the criteria and procedures set forth in this section. Coordination pursuant to this section shall apply to pretrial proceedings, including dispositive motions.

(b) Litigation Coordinating Panel.   (1) Composition.   The Chief Administrator of the Courts, in consultation with the Presiding Justice of each Appellate Division, shall create a Litigation Coordinating Panel composed of one justice of the Supreme Court from each judicial department of the state.

(2) Procedure.   The Panel shall determine, *sua sponte* or upon application of a party to an action, a justice before whom such an action is pending, or an administrative judge, whether the related actions should be coordinated before one or more individual justices.

CT RULES

The Panel shall provide notice and an opportunity to be heard to all parties to the actions sought to be coordinated and shall inform the justices before whom such actions are pending of the initiation of proceedings before the Panel.

(3) Standards for Coordination. In determining whether to issue an administrative order of coordination, the Panel shall consider, among other things, the complexity of the actions; whether common questions of fact or law exist, and the importance of such questions to the determination of the issues; the risk that coordination may unreasonably delay the progress, increase the expense, or complicate the processing of any action or otherwise prejudice a party; the risk of duplicative or inconsistent rulings, orders or judgments; the convenience of the parties, witnesses and counsel; whether coordinated discovery would be advantageous; efficient utilization of judicial resources and the facilities and personnel of the court; the manageability of a coordinated litigation; whether issues of insurance, limits on assets and potential bankruptcy can be best addressed in coordinated proceedings; and the pendency of related matters in the federal courts and in the courts of other states. The Panel may exclude particular actions from an otherwise applicable order of coordination when necessary to protect the rights of parties.

(4) Determination.

(i) The Panel shall issue a written decision on each application. If the Panel determines to direct coordination, it shall issue an administrative order identifying the actions that shall be coordinated. The order may address actions subsequently filed or not otherwise then before the Panel.

(ii) The order of the Panel shall specify the number of Coordinating Justices and the county or counties in which the coordinated proceedings shall take place. In making this decision, the Panel shall consider, among other things, the venues of origin of the cases to be coordinated; whether the actions arise out of an accident or events in a particular county; judicial caseloads in prospective venues; fairness to parties; the convenience of the parties and witnesses; the convenience of counsel; and whether the purposes of this section can best be advanced by coordination before more than one Coordinating Justice.

(c) *Coordinating Justice.* (1) Designation. The Administrative Judge charged with supervision of the local jurisdiction within which coordinated proceedings are to take place shall select the Coordinating Justice or Justices, in consultation with the appropriate Deputy Chief Administrative Judge. In deciding whom to designate, the Administrative Judge shall consider, among other things, the existing caseload of each prospective appointee and the overall needs of the court in which that justice serves; the familiarity of that justice with the litigation at issue; the justice's managerial ability; and the previous experience of the justice with the field of law involved and with coordinated litigation. The Administrative Judge may designate a justice from another local jurisdiction as a Coordinating Justice with the approval of the Administrative Judge thereof.

(2) Authority. The Coordinating Justice shall have authority to make any order consistent with this section and its purposes, including to remand to the court of origin any portion of a case not properly subject to coordination under the administrative order of the Panel; assign a master caption; create a central case file and docket; establish a service list; periodically issue case management orders after consultation with counsel; appoint and define the roles of steering committees and counsel of parties and liaison counsel, provided that the committees and counsel shall not deprive any party of substantive rights; issue protective orders pursuant to Article 31 of the Civil Practice Law and Rules; establish a document depository; direct the parties to prepare coordinated pleadings and deem service upon liaison counsel or steering committee service upon the respective parties; require service of uniform requests for disclosure and establish a uniform method for the conduct of physical and mental examinations; rule upon all motions; require the parties to participate in settlement discussions and court-annexed alternative dispute resolution; and try any part of any coordinated case on consent of the parties to that action.

(3) Coordination with Federal or Other States' Actions. If actions related to those pending before a Coordinating Justice are proceeding in federal courts or in the courts of other states, the Coordinating Justice shall consult with the presiding judge(s) in an effort to advance the purposes of this section. Where appropriate, the Coordinating Justice, while respecting the rights of parties under the

CT RULES

Civil Practice Law and Rules, may require that discovery in the cases coordinated pursuant to this section proceed jointly or in coordination with discovery in the federal or other states' actions.

(d) *Termination of Coordination.* The Coordinating Justice, *sua sponte*, or upon motion by any party, may terminate coordination, in whole or in part, if the Justice determines that coordination has been completed or that the purposes of this section can be best advanced by termination of the coordination. Upon termination, the actions shall be remanded to their counties of origin for trial unless the parties to an action consent to trial of that action before the Coordinating Justice.

§ 202.70   Rules of the Commercial Division of the Supreme Court.

(a) *Monetary thresholds.* Except as set forth in subdivision (b), the monetary thresholds of the Commercial Division, exclusive of punitive damages, interests, costs, disbursements and counsel fees claimed, is established as follows:

Albany County: $25,000

Eighth Judicial District: $50,000

Kings County: $75,000

Nassau County: $100,000

New York County: $150,000

Onondaga County $25,000

Queens County: $50,000

Seventh Judicial District: $25,000

Suffolk County: $50,000

Westchester County: $75,000

(b) *Commercial cases.* Actions in which the principal claims involve or consist of the following will be heard in the Commercial Division provided that the monetary threshold is met or equitable or declaratory relief is sought:

(1) Breach of contract or fiduciary duty, fraud, misrepresentation, business tort (e.g., unfair competition), or statutory and/or common

law violation where the breach or violation is alleged to arise out of business dealings (e.g., sales of assets or securities; corporate restructuring; partnership, shareholder, joint venture, and other business agreements; trade secrets; restrictive covenants; and employment agreements not including claims that principally involve alleged discriminatory practices);

(2) Transactions governed by the Uniform Commercial Code (exclusive of those concerning individual cooperative or condominium units);

(3) Transactions involving commercial real property, including Yellowstone injunctions and excluding actions for the payment of rent only;

(4) Shareholder derivative actions—without consideration of the monetary threshold;

(5) Commercial class actions—without consideration of the monetary threshold;

(6) Business transactions involving or arising out of dealings with commercial banks and other financial institutions;

(7) Internal affairs of business organizations;

(8) Malpractice by accountants or actuaries, and legal malpractice arising out of representation in commercial matters;

(9) Environmental insurance coverage;

(10) Commercial insurance coverage (e.g. directors and officers, errors and omissions, and business interruption coverage);

(11) Dissolution of corporations, partnerships, limited liability companies, limited liability partnerships and joint ventures—without consideration of the monetary threshold; and

(12) Applications to stay or compel arbitration and affirm or disaffirm arbitration awards and related injunctive relief pursuant to CPLR Article 75 involving any of the foregoing enumerated commercial issues–without consideration of the monetary threshold.

(c) *Non-commercial cases.* The following will not be heard in the Commercial Division even if the monetary threshold is met:

CT RULES

(1) Suits to collect professional fees;

(2) Cases seeking a declaratory judgment as to insurance coverage for personal injury or property damage;

(3) Residential real estate disputes, including landlord-tenant matters, and commercial real estate disputes involving the payment of rent only;

(4) Proceedings to enforce a judgment regardless of the nature of the underlying case;

(5) First-party insurance claims and actions by insurers to collect premiums or rescind non-commercial policies; and

(6) Attorney malpractice actions except as otherwise provided in paragraph (b)(8).

(d) *Assignment to the Commercial Division.* (1) A party seeking assignment of a case to the Commercial Division shall indicate on the Request for Judicial Intervention (RJJ) that the case is "commercial."A party seeking a designation of a special proceeding as a commercial case shall check the "other commercial" box on the RJI, not the "special proceedings" box.

(2) The party shall submit with the RJI a brief signed statement justifying the Commercial Division designation, together with a copy of the proceedings.

(e) *Transfer into the Commercial Division.* If a case is assigned to a non-commercial part because the filing party did not designate the case as "commercial" on the RJI, any other party may apply by letter application (with a copy to all parties) to the Administrative Judge, within ten days after receipt of a copy of the RJI, for a transfer of the case into the Commercial Division. The determination of the Administrative Judge shall be final and subject to no further administrative review or appeal.

(f) *Transfer from the Commercial Division.* (1) In the discretion of the Commercial Division justice assigned, if a case does not fall within the jurisdiction of the Commercial Division as set forth in this section, it shall be transferred to a noncommercial part of the court.

(2) Any party aggrieved by a transfer of a case to a non-

commercial part may seek review by letter application (with a copy to all parties) to the Administrative Judge within ten days of receipt of the designation of the case to a non-commercial part. The determination of the Administrative Judge shall be final and subject to no further administrative review or appeal.

(g) *Rules of practice for the Commercial Division.* Unless these rules of practice for the Commercial Division provide specifically to the contrary, the rules of Part 202 also shall apply to the Commercial Division, except that Rules 7 through 15 shall supersede section 202.12 (Preliminary Conference) and Rules 16 through 24 shall supersede section 202.8 (Motion Procedure).

Rule 1. *Appearance by Counsel with Knowledge and Authority.* Counsel who appear in the Commercial Division must be fully familiar with the case in regard to which they appear and fully authorized to enter into agreements, both substantive and procedural, on behalf of their clients. Counsel should also be prepared to discuss any motions that have been submitted and are outstanding. Failure to comply with this rule may be regarded as a default and dealt with appropriately. See Rule 12. It is important tat counsel be on time for all scheduled appearances.

Rule 2. *Settlements and Discontinuances.* If an action is settled, discontinued, or otherwise disposed of, counsel shall immediately inform the court by submission of a copy of the stipulation or a letter directed to the clerk of the part along with notice to chambers via telephone or e-mail. This notification shall be made in addition to the filing of a stipulation with the County Clerk.

Rule 3. *Alternative Dispute Resolution (ADR).* At any stage of the matter, the court may direct or counsel may seek the appointment of an uncompensated mediator for the purpose of mediating a resolution of all or some of the issues presented in the litigation.

Rule 4. *Electronic Submission of Papers.*

(a) *Papers and correspondence by fax.* Papers and correspondence filed by fax should comply with the requirements of section 202.5-a except that papers shall not be submitted to the court by fax without advance approval of the justice assigned. Correspondence sent by fax should not be followed by hard copy unless

CT RULES

requested.

(b) *Papers submitted in digital format.* In cases not pending in the court's Filing by Electronic Means System, the court may permit counsel to communicate with the court and each other by e-mail. In the court' s discretion, counsel may be requested to submit memoranda of law by e-mail or on a computer disk along with an original and courtesy copy.

Rule 5. *Information on Cases.* (This rule shall apply only in the First and Second Judicial Departments)

Information on future court appearances can be found at the court system's future appearance site (www.nycourts.gov/ecourts). Decisions can be found on the Commercial Division home page of the Unified Court System's internet website: www.courts.state.ny.us/ comdiv or in the New York Law Journal. The clerk of the part can also provide information about scheduling in the part (trials, conferences, and arguments on motions). Where circumstances require exceptional notice, it will be furnished directly by chambers.

Rule 6. *Form of Papers.* All papers submitted to the Commercial Division shall comply with CPLR 2101 and section 202.5(a). Papers shall be double-spaced and contain print no smaller than twelve-point, or 8 1/2x 11 inch paper, bearing margins no smaller than one inch. The print size of footnotes shall be no smaller than ten-point. Papers also shall comply with Part 130 of the Rules of the Chief Administrator.

Rule 7. *Preliminary Conference; Request.* A preliminary conference shall be held within 45 days of assignment of the case to a Commercial Division justice, or as soon thereafter as is practicable. Except for good cause shown, no preliminary conference shall be adjourned more than once or for more than 30 days. If a Request for Judicial Intervention is accompanied by a dispositive motion, the preliminary conference shall take place within 30 days following the decision of such motion (if not rendered moot) or at such earlier date as scheduled by the justice presiding. Notice of the preliminary conference date will be sent by the court at least five days prior thereto.

Rule 8. *Consultation prior to Preliminary and Compliance Conferences.*

(a) Counsel for all parties shall consult prior to a preliminary or compliance conference about (i) resolution of the case, in whole or in part; (ii) discovery and any other issues to be discussed at the conference; and (iii) the use of alternate dispute resolution to resolve all or some issues in the litigation. Counsel shall make a good faith effort to reach agreement on these matters in advance of the conference.

(b) Prior to the preliminary conference, counsel shall confer with regard to anticipated electronic discovery issues. Such issues shall be addressed with the court at the preliminary conference and shall include but not be limited to (i) implementation of a data preservation plan; (ii) identification of relevant data; (iii) the scope, extent and form of production; (iv) anticipated cost of data recovery and proposed initial allocation of such cost; (v) disclosure of the programs and manner in which the data is maintained; (vi) identification of computer system(s) utilized; (vii) identification of the individual(s) responsible for data preservation; (viii) confidentiality and privilege issues; and (ix) designation of experts.

Rule 9. (Reserved)

Rule 10. *Submission of Information.* At the preliminary conference, counsel shall be prepared to furnish the court with the following: (i) a complete caption, including the index number; (ii) the name, address, telephone number, e~mail address and fax number of all counsel; (iii) the dates the action was commenced and issue joined; (iv) a statement as to what motions, if any, are anticipated; and (v) copies of any decisions previously rendered in the case.

Rule 11. *Discovery.*

(a) The preliminary conference will result in the issuance by the court of a preliminary conference order. Where appropriate, the order will contain specific provisions for means of early disposition of the case, such as (i) directions for submission to the alternative dispute resolution program; (ii) a schedule of limited-

CT RULES

issue discovery in aid of early dispositive motions or settlement; and/or (iii) a schedule for dispositive motions before disclosure or after limited-issue disclosure.

(b) The order will also contain a comprehensive disclosure schedule, including dates for the service of third-party pleadings, discovery, motion practice, a compliance conference, if needed, a date for filing the note of issue, a date for a pre-trial conference and a trial date.

(c) The preliminary conference order may provide for such limitations of interrogatories and other discovery as may be necessary to the circumstances of the case.

(d) The court will determine, upon application of counsel, whether discovery will be stayed, pursuant to CPLR 3214(b), pending the determination of any dispositive motion.

Rule 12. *Non-Appearance at Conference.* The failure of counsel to appear for a conference may result in a sanction authorized by section 130.2.1 of the Rules of the Chief Administrator or section 202.27, including dismissal, the striking of an answer, an inquest or direction for judgment, or other appropriate sanction.

Rule 13. *Adherence to Discovery Schedule.*

(a) Parties shall strictly comply with discovery obligations by the dates set forth in all case scheduling orders. Such deadlines, however, may be modified upon the consent of all parties, provided that all discovery shall be completed by the discovery cutoff date set forth in the preliminary conference order. Applications for extension of a discovery deadline shall be made as soon as practicable and prior to the expiration of such deadline. Non-compliance with such an order may result in the imposition of an appropriate sanction against that party pursuant to CPLR 3126.

(b) If a party seeks documents as a condition precedent to a deposition and the documents are not produced by the date fixed, the party seeking disclosure may ask the court to preclude the non-producing party from introducing such demanded documents at trial.

Rule 14. *Disclosure Disputes.* Counsel must consult with one another in a good faith effort to resolve all disputes about disclosure. See section 202.7. Except as provided in Rule 24 hereof, if counsel are unable to resolve any disclosure dispute in this fashion, the aggrieved party shall contact the court to arrange a conference as soon as practicable to avoid exceeding the discovery cutoff date. Counsel should request a conference by telephone if that would be more convenient and efficient than an appearance in court.

Rule 15. *Adjournments of Conferences.* Adjournments on consent are permitted with the approval of the court for good cause where notice of the request is given to all parties. Adjournment of a conference will not change any subsequent date in the preliminary conference order, unless otherwise directed by the court.

Rule 16. *Motions in General.*

(a) *Form of Motion Papers.* The movant shall specify in the notice of motion, order to show cause, and in a concluding section of a memorandum of law, the exact relief sought. Counsel must attach copies of all pleadings and other documents as required by the CPLR and as necessary for an informed decision on the motion (especially on motions pursuant to CPLR 3211 and 3212). Counsel should use tabs when submitting papers containing exhibits. Copies must be legible. If a document to be annexed to an affidavit or affirmation is voluminous and only discrete portions are relevant to the motion, counsel shall attach excerpts and submit the full exhibit separately. Documents in a foreign language shall be properly translated. CPLR 2101(b). Whenever reliance is placed upon a decision or other authority not readily available to the court, a copy of the case or of pertinent portions of the authority shall be submitted with the motion papers.

(b) *Proposed Orders.* When appropriate, proposed orders should be submitted with motions, e.g., motions to be relieved, *pro hac vice* admissions, open commissions, etc. No proposed order should be submitted with motion papers on a dispositive motion.

(c) *Adjournment of Motions.* Dispositive motions (made pursuant to CPLR 3211, 3212 or 3213) may be adjourned only

CT RULES

with the court's consent. Non-dispositive motions may be adjourned on consent no more than three times for a total of no more than 60 days unless otherwise directed by the court.

Rule 17. *Length of Papers.* Unless otherwise permitted by the court: (i) briefs or memoranda of law shall be limited to 25 pages each; (ii) reply memoranda shall be no more than 15 pages and shall not contain any arguments that do not respond or relate to those made in the memoranda in chief; (iii) affidavits and affirmations shall be limited to 25 pages each.

Rule 18. *Sur-Reply and Post-Submission Papers.* Absent express permission in advance, sur-reply papers, including correspondence, addressing the merits of a motion are not permitted, except that counsel may inform the court by letter of the citation of any post-submission court decision that is relevant to the pending issues, but there shall be no additional argument. Materials submitted in violation hereof will not be read or considered. Opposing counsel who receives a copy of materials submitted in violation of this Rule shall not respond in kind.

Rule 19. *Orders to Show Cause.* Motions shall be brought on by order to show cause only when there is genuine urgency (e.g., applications for provisional relief), a stay is required or a statute mandates so proceeding. See Rule 20. Absent advance permission, reply papers shall not be submitted on orders to show cause.

Rule 19-a. *Motions for Summary Judgment; Statements of Material Facts..*

(a) Upon any motion for summary judgment, other than a motion made pursuant to CPLR 3213, the court may direct that there shall be annexed to the notice of motion a separate, short and concise statement, in numbered paragraphs, of the material facts as to which the moving party contends there is no genuine issue to be tried.

(b) In such a case, the papers opposing a motion for summary judgment shall include a correspondingly numbered paragraph responding to each numbered paragraph in the statement of the moving party and, if necessary, additional paragraphs containing a separate short and concise statement of the material facts as to which it is contended that there exists a genuine issue to be tried.

(c) Each numbered paragraph in the statement of material facts required to be served by the moving party will be deemed to be admitted for purposes of the motion unless specifically controverted by a correspondingly numbered paragraph in the statement required to be served by the opposing party.

(d) Each statement of material fact by the movant or opponent pursuant to subdivision (a) or (b), including each statement controverting any statement of material fact, must be followed by citation to evidence submitted in support of or in opposition to the motion.

Rule 20. *Temporary Restraining Orders.* Unless the moving party can demonstrate that there will be significant prejudice by reason of giving notice, a temporary restraining order will not be issued. The applicant must give notice to the opposing parties sufficient to permit them an opportunity to appear and contest the application.

Rule 21. *Courtesy Copies.* Courtesy copies should not be submitted unless requested or as herein provided. However, courtesy copies of all motion papers and proposed orders shall be submitted in cases in the court's Filing by Electronic Means System.

Rule 22. *Oral Argument.* Any party may request oral argument on the face of its papers or in an accompanying letter. Except in cases before justices who require oral argument on all motions, the court will determine, on a case-by-case basis, whether oral argument will be heard and, if so, when counsel shall appear. Notice of the date selected by the court shall be given, if practicable, at least 14 days before the scheduled oral argument. At that time, counsel shall be prepared to argue the motion, discuss resolution of the issue(s) presented and/or schedule a trial or hearing.

Rule 23. *60-Day Rule.* If 60 days have elapsed after a motion has been finally submitted or oral argument held, whichever was later, and no decision has been issued by the court, counsel for the movant shall send the court a letter alerting it to this fact with copies to all parties to the motion.

Rule 24. *Advance Notice of Motions.*

CT RULES

(a) Nothing in this rule shall be construed to prevent or limit counsel from making any motion deemed appropriate to best represent a party's interests. However, in order to permit the court the opportunity to resolve issues before motion practice ensues, and to control its calendar in the context of the discovery and trial schedule, pre-motion conferences in accordance herewith must be held. The failure of counsel to comply with this rule may result in the motion being held in abeyance until the court has an opportunity to conference the matter.

(b) This rule shall not apply to disclosure disputes covered by Rule 14 nor to dispositive motions pursuant to CPLR 3211, 3212 or 3213 made at the time of the filing of the Request for Judicial Intervention or after discovery is complete. Nor shall the rule apply to motions to be relieved as counsel, for *pro hac vice* admission, for reargument or *in limine*.

(c) Prior to the making or filing of a motion, counsel for the moving party shall advise the Court in writing (no more than two pages) on notice to opposing counsel outlining the issue(s) in dispute and requesting a telephone conference. If a cross-motion is contemplated, a similar motion notice letter shall be forwarded to the court and counsel. Such correspondence shall not be considered by the court in reaching its decision on the merits of the motion.

(d) Upon review of the motion notice letter, the court will schedule a telephone or in-court conference with counsel. Counsel fully familiar with the matter and with authority to bind their client must be available to participate in the conference. The unavailability of counsel for the scheduled conference, except for good cause shown, may result in granting of the application without opposition and/or the imposition of sanctions.

(e) If the matter can be resolved during the conference, an order consistent with such resolution may be issued or counsel will be directed to forward a letter confirming the resolution to be "so ordered." At the discretion of the court, the conference may be held on the record.

(f) If the matter cannot be resolved, the parties shall set a briefing schedule for the motion which shall be approved by the court. Except for good cause shown, the failure to comply with the briefing schedule may result in the submission of the motion unopposed or the dismissal of the motion, as may be appropriate.

(g) On the face of all notices of motion and orders to show cause, there shall be a statement that there has been compliance with this rule.

(h) Where a motion must be made within a certain time pursuant to the CPLR, the submission of a motion notice letter, as provided in subdivision (a), within the prescribed time shall be deemed the timely making of the motion. This subdivision shall not be construed to extend any jurisdictional limitations period.

Rule 25. *Trial Schedule.* Counsel are expected to be ready to proceed either to select a jury or to begin presentation of proof on the scheduled trial date. Once a trial date is set, counsel shall immediately determine the availability of witnesses. If, for any reason, counsel are not prepared to proceed on the scheduled date, the court is to be notified within ten days of the date on which counsel are given the trial date or, in extraordinary circumstances, as soon as reasonably practicable. Failure of counsel to provide such notification will be deemed a waiver of any application to adjourn the trial because of the unavailability of a witness. Witnesses are to be scheduled so that trials proceed without interruption. Trials shall commence each court day promptly at such times as the court directs. Failure of counsel to attend the trial at the time scheduled without good cause shall constitute a waiver of the right of that attorney and his or her client to participate in the trial for the period of counsel's absence. There shall be no adjournment of a trial except for good cause shown. With respect to trials scheduled more than 60 days in advance, section 125.1(g) of the Rules of the Chief Administrator shall apply and the actual engagement of trial counsel in another matter will not be recognized as an acceptable basis for an adjournment of the trial.

Rule 26. *Estimated Length of Trial.* At least ten days prior to trial or such other time as the court may set, the parties, after considering the expected testimony of and, if necessary, consulting with their witnesses, shall furnish the court with a realistic estimate of the

CT RULES

length of the trial.

Rule 27. *Motions in Limine.* The parties shall make all motions in limine no later than ten days prior to the scheduled pre-trial conference date, and the motions shall be returnable on the date of the pre-trial conference, unless otherwise directed by the court.

Rule 28. *Pre-Marking of Exhibits.* Counsel for the parties shall consult prior to the pre-trial conference and shall in good faith attempt to agree upon the exhibits that will be offered into evidence without objection. At the pre-trial conference date, each side shall then mark its exhibits into evidence as to those to which no objection has been made. All exhibits not consented to shall be marked for identification only. If the trial exhibits are voluminous, counsel shall consult the clerk of the part for guidance. The court will rule upon the objections to the contested exhibits at the earliest possible time. Exhibits not previously demanded which are to be used solely for credibility or rebuttal need not be pre-marked.

Rule 29. *Identification of Deposition Testimony.* Counsel for the parties shall consult prior to trial and shall in good faith attempt to agree upon the portions of deposition testimony to be offered into evidence without objection. The parties shall delete from the testimony to be read questions and answers that are irrelevant to the point for which the deposition testimony is offered. Each party shall prepare a list of deposition testimony to be offered by it as to which objection has not been made and, identified separately, a list of deposition testimony as to which objection has been made. At least ten days prior to trial or such other time as the court may set, each party shall submit its list to the court and other counsel, together with a copy of the portions of the deposition testimony as to which objection has been made. The court will rule upon the objections at the earliest possible time after consultation with counsel.

Rule 30. *Settlement and Pre-Trial Conferences.* (a) *Settlement Conference.* At the time of certification of the matter as ready for trial or at any time after the discovery cut-off date, the court may schedule a settlement conference which shall be attended by counsel and the parties, who are expected to be fully prepared to discuss the settlement of the matter.

(b) *Pre-trial Conference.* Prior to the pre-trial conference, counsel shall confer in a good faith effort to identify matters not in contention, resolve disputed questions without need for court intervention and further discuss settlement of the case. At the pre-trial conference, counsel shall be prepared to discuss all matters as to which there is disagreement between the parties, including those identified in Rules 27-29, and settlement of the matter. At or before the pre-trial conference, the court may require the parties to prepare a written stipulation of undisputed facts.

Rule 31. *Pre-Trial Memoranda, Exhibit Book and Requests for Jury Instructions.* (a) Counsel shall submit pre-trial memoranda at the pre-trial conference, or such other time as the court may set. Counsel shall comply with CPLR 2103(e). A single memorandum no longer than 25 pages shall be submitted by each side. No memoranda in response shall be submitted.

(b) At the pre-trial conference or at such other time as the court may set, counsel shall submit an indexed binder or notebook of trial exhibits for the court's use. A copy for each attorney on trial and the originals in a similar binder or notebook for the witnesses shall be prepared and submitted. Plaintiff's exhibits shall be numericaily tabbed and defendant's exhibits shall be tabbed alphabetically.

(c) Where the trial is by jury, counsel shall, on the pre-trial conference date or such other time as the court may set, provide the court with case-specific requests to charge and proposed jury interrogatories. Where the requested charge is from the New York Pattern Jury Instructions—Civil, a reference to the PJ1 number will suffice. Submissions should be by hard copy and disk or e-mail attachment in WordPerfect 12 format, as directed by the court.

Rule 32. *Scheduling of witnesses.* At the pre-trial conference or at such time as the court may direct, each party shall identify in writing for the court the witnesses it intends to call, the order in which they shall testify and the estimated length of their testimony, and shall provide a copy of such witness list to opposing counsel. Counsel shall separately identify for the court only a list of the

CT RULES

witnesses who may be called solely for rebuttal or with regard to credibility.

Rule 33. *Preclusion.* Failure to comply with Rules 28, 29, 31 and 32 may result in preclusion pursuant to CPLR 3126.

APPENDIX

APPENDIX

Chapter III.   Supreme and County Court Forms

Subchapter A. Forms Authorized by Section 202.16(b)
APPENDIX A

Statement of Net Worth ("Official" Form)[1]

_____ COURT OF THE STATE OF NEW YORK

COUNTY OF _____

_____,
                    Plaintiff,

        –against–

_____,
                    Defendant.

STATEMENT OF
NET WORTH
(D.R.L. § 236)

Index No. _____

Date of commencement of action _____

Complete all items, marking "NONE," "INAPPLICABLE" and "UNKNOWN," if appropriate)

STATE OF _____

COUNTY OF_____

} ss.:

_____, the (Petitioner) (Respondent) (Plaintiff) (Defendant) herein, being duly sworn, deposes and says that the following is an accurate statement as of _____, of my net worth (assets of whatsoever kind and nature and wherever situated minus liabilities), statement of income from all sources and statement of assets transferred of whatsoever kind and nature and wherever situated:

I. FAMILY DATA:

[1]**Form**—Revised 12/7/98

(a)	Husband's age	_____
(b)	Wife's age	_____
(c)	Date married	_____
(d)	Date (separated) (divorced)	_____
(e)	Number of dependent children under 21 years	_____
(f)	Names and ages of children	

_____

_____

_____

(g)   Custody of Children _____Husband _____Wife

(h)   Minor   children   of   prior   marriage:
        _____Husband _____Wife

(i)   (Husband) (Wife) (paying) (receiving) $_____ as alimony
        (maintenance) and/or $_____ child support in connection
        with prior marriage:

(j)   Custody of children of prior marriage:
        Name _____

        Address _____

(k)   Is marital residence occupied by Husband _____
        Wife_____Both _____

(l)   Husband's present address
        _____

        Wife's present address
        _____

(m)   Occupation of Husband _____ Occupation of Wife
        _____

(n)   Husband's employer
        _____

(o)   Wife's employer
        _____

(p)   Education, training and skills [Include dates of attainment of de-
        grees, etc.]
            Husband _____
            Wife _____

(q)   Husband's health _____

(r)   Wife's health _____

(s)   Children's health _____

II.   EXPENSES: (You may elect to list all expenses on a weekly basis or all expenses on a monthly basis, however, you must be consistent. If any items are paid on a monthly basis, divide by 4.3 to obtain weekly payments; if any items are paid on a weekly basis, multiply by 4.3 to obtain monthly payment. Attach additional sheet, if needed. Items included under "Other" should be listed separately with separate dollar amounts.)

        Expenses listed [ ] weekly   [ ] monthly

(a)   Housing

1.	Rent	_____	4.	Condominium charges	_____
2.	Mortgage and amortization	_____	5.	Cooperative apartment maintenance	_____
3.	Real estate taxes	_____			

Total: Housing
$_____

(b) Utilities

1.	Fuel oil	_____	4.	Telephone	_____
2.	Gas	_____	5.	Water	_____
3.	Electricity	_____			

Total: Utilities
$_____

(c) Food

1.	Groceries	_____	5.	Liquor/alcohol	_____
2.	School lunches	_____	6.	Home entertainment	_____
3.	Lunches at work	_____	7.	Other _____	_____
4.	Dining Out	_____			

Total: Food
$_____

(d) Clothing

| 1. | Husband | _____ | 3. | Children | _____ |
| 2. | Wife | _____ | 4. | Other _____ | _____ |

Total: Clothing
$_____

(e) Laundry

| 1. | Laundry at home | _____ | 3. | Other _____ | _____ |
| 2. | Dry cleaning | _____ | | | |

Total: Laundry
$_____

(f) Insurance

1.	Life	_____	6.	Medical plan	_____
2.	Homeowner's /tenant's	_____	7.	Dental plan	_____
3.	Fire, theft and liability	_____	8.	Optical plan	_____
4.	Automotive	_____	9.	Disability	_____
5.	Umbrella policy	_____	10.	Worker's compensation	_____
			11.	Other _____	_____

Total: Insurance
$_____

(g) Unreimbursed medical

| 1. | Medical | _____ | 5. | Surgical, nursing, | |

2. Dental _____   hospital _____
3. Optical _____   6. Other _____
4. Pharma- _____
   ceutical

Total:
Unreimbursed medical
$_____

(h) Household
    maintenance
   1. Repairs _____   5. Painting _____
   2. Furniture, fur-   6. Sanitation/carting _____
      nishings,
      housewares _____   7. Gardening/ _____
                                      landscaping
   3. Cleaning Sup- _____   8. Snow removal _____
      plies
   4. Appliances, _____   9. Extermination _____
      including
      maintenance _____   10. Other _____ _____
                                         Total:
                                         Household maintenance
                                         $_____

(i) Household
    help
   1. Babysitter _____   3. Other _____ _____
   2. Domestic _____
      (housekeeper,
      maid, etc.)

Total: Household help
$_____

(j) Automotive
Year: _____ Make: _____ Personal: _____ Business: _____
Year: _____ Make: _____ Personal: _____ Business: _____
Year: _____ Make: _____ Personal: _____ Business: _____
   1. Payments _____   4. Car wash _____
   2. Gas and oil _____   5. Registration and _____
                                      license
   3. Repairs _____   6. Parking and tolls _____
                                7. Other _____ _____
                                   Total: Automotive
                                   $_____

(k) Educational
   1. Nursery and _____   6. School transporta- _____
      pre-school   tion
   2. Primary and _____   7. School supplies/ _____
      secondary   books
   3. College _____   8. Tutoring _____
   4. Post-graduate _____   9. School events _____

5. Religious in- _____ 10. Other _____ _____
struction

Total: Educational
$_____

(l) Recreational

1. Summer camp _____ 9. Country club/pool _____
club

2. Vacations _____ 10. Health club _____
3. Movies _____ 11. Sporting goods _____
4. Theatre, ballet, _____ 12. Hobbies _____
etc.
5. Video rentals _____ 13. Music/dance les- _____
sons
6. Tapes, CD's, _____ 14. Sports lessons _____
etc.
7. Cable televi- _____ 15. Birthday parties _____
sion
8. Team sports _____ 16. Other _____ _____

Total: Recreational
$_____

(m) Income taxes

1. Federal _____ 3. City _____
2. State _____ 4. Social Security _____
and Medicare

Total: Income taxes
$_____

(n) Miscellaneous

1. Beauty parlor/ _____ 9. Union and organi-
barber zation dues

2. Beauty aids/
cosmetics,
drug items _____ 10. Commutation and _____
3. Cigarettes/ _____ transportation _____
tobacco
4. Books, maga- 11. Veterinarian/pet
zines,
newspapers _____ expenses _____
5. Children's _____ 12. Child support pay-
allowances ments
6. Gifts _____ (prior marriage) _____
7. Charitable _____ 13. Alimony and
contributions maintenance payments
8. Religious or- (prior marriage) _____
ganization
dues _____ 14. Loan payments _____
15. Unreimbursed
business

expenses _____

Total: Miscellaneous
$_____

(o)   Other

    1. _____ _____   3. _____ _____

    3. _____ _____   4. _____ _____

Total: Other
$_____

TOTAL EXPENSES: $_____

III. GROSS INCOME: (State source of income and annual amount. Attach additional sheet, if needed).

(a)   Salary or wages: (State whether income has changed during the year preceding date of this affidavit _____. If so, set forth name and address of all employers during preceding year and average weekly wage paid by each. Indicate overtime earnings separately. Attach previous year's W-2 or income tax return.)

    _____   _____

    _____   _____

(b)   Weekly deductions:

    1.   Federal tax   _____

    2.   New York State tax   _____

    3.   Local tax   _____

    4.   Social security   _____

    5.   Medicare   _____

    6.   Other payroll deductions (specify)   _____

(c)   Social Security number _____

(d)   Number and names of dependents claimed: _____

(e)   Bonus, commissions, fringe benefits (use of auto, memberships, etc.) _____

(f)   Partnership, royalties, sale of assets (income and installment payments) _____   _____

(g)   Dividends and interest (state whether taxable or not)_____   _____

(h)   Real estate (income only) _____   _____

(i)   Trust, profit sharing and annuities (principal distribution and income) _____   _____

(j)   Pension (income only) _____   _____

(k)	Awards, prizes, grants (state whether taxable)		_____
(l)	Bequests, legacies and gifts ____		_____
(m)	Income from all other sources __ (including alimony, mainte- nance or child support from prior marriage)		_____
(n)	Tax preference items:		
	1.	Long term capital gain de- duction _____	_____
	2.	Depreciation, amortization or depletion _____	_____
	3.	Stock options—excess of fair market value over amount paid _____	_____
(o)	If any child or other member of your household is employed, set forth name and that person's an- nual income		_____
(p)	Social Security _____		_____
(q)	Disability benefits _____		_____
(r)	Public assistance _____		_____
(s)	Other_____		_____

TOTAL INCOME: _____

IV. ASSETS: (If any asset is held jointly with spouse or another, so state, and set forth your respective shares. Attach additional sheets, if needed.)

A. Cash Accounts
   Cash
   1.1   a.   Location_____
         b.   Source of funds_____
         c.   Amount _____ $_____
                  Total: Cash
                  $_____

   Checking Accounts
   2.1   a.   Financial institution ____
         b.   Account number _____
         c.   Title holder. _____
         d.   Date opened _____

        e.   Source of Funds _____

        f.   Balance _____ $_____

2.2   a.   Financial institution _____

        b.   Account number _____

        c.   Title Holder _____

        d.   Date opened_____

        e.   Source of Funds_____

        f.   Balance_____ $_____

                            Total: Checking
                            $_____

Savings accounts (including individual, joint, totten trust, certificates of deposit, treasury notes)

3.1   a.   Financial institution _____

        b.   Account number _____

        c.   Title holder _____

        d.   Type of account_____

        e.   Date opened_____

        f.   Source of funds_____

        g.   Balance_____ $_____

3.2   a.   Financial institution _____

        b.   Account number _____

        c.   Title holder _____

        d.   Type of account_____

        e.   Date opened_____

        f.   Source of funds_____

        g.   Balance_____ $_____

                            Total: Savings
                            $_____

Security deposits, earnest money, etc.

4.1   a.   Location _____

        b.   Title owner _____

        c.   Type of deposit _____

        e.   Source of funds_____

        f.   Date of deposit _____

        g.   Amount_____ $_____

                            Total: Security Deposits, etc.
                            $_____

Other

5.1   a.   Location _____

CT RULES

      b.   Title owner _____

      c.   Type of account _____

      d.   Source of funds_____

      e.   Date of deposit _____

      f.   Amount_____ $_____

                          Total: Other
                          $_____

                          Total: Cash Accounts
                          $_____

B. Securities

    Bonds, notes, mortgages

      1.1   a.   Description of security ____

            b.   Title holder _____

            c.   Location _____

            d.   Date of acquisition _____

            e.   Original price
                 or value _____

            f.   Source of funds to acquire

                 _____

            g.   Current value_____ $_____

                          Total: Bonds,
                          notes, etc.
                          $_____

    Stocks, options and commodity con-
    tracts

      2.1   a.   Description
                 of security _____

            b.   Title holder _____

            c.   Location _____

            d.   Date of acquisition _____

            e.   Original price
                 or value _____

            f.   Source of funds to acquire

                 _____

            g.   Current value_____ $_____

      2.2   a.   Description
                 of security _____

            b.   Title holder _____

            c.   Location _____

            d.   Date of acquisition _____

            e.   Original price or value ____

      f.   Source of funds to acquire

      _____

      g.   Current value_____ $_____

2.3   a.   Description of security ___

      b.   Title holder _____

      c.   Location _____

      d.   Date of acquisition _____

      e.   Original price
          or value _____

      f.   Source of funds to acquire

      _____

      g.   Current value_____ $_____

                                         $ Total: Stocks, options, etc.
                                         $_____

Broker margin accounts

   3.1   a.   Name and address of
              broker_____

      b.   Title holder_____

      c.   Date account opened _____

      d.   Original value of account_

      e.   Source of funds_____

      f.   Current value_____ $_____

                                       Total:
                                       Margin accounts
                                       $_____

                                       Total value of securities:
                                       $_____

C.   Loans to others and accounts receivable

   1.1   a.   Debtor's name and address

      _____

      b.   Original amount of loan or
           debt _____

      c.   Source of funds from
           which loan made or origin
           of debt _____

      d.   Date
           payment(s) due _____

      e.   Current amount due _____ $_____

   1.2   a.   Debtor's name and
              address_____

    b. Original amount of loan or debt _____

    c. Source of funds from which loan made or origin of debt _____

    d. Date payment(s) due_____

    e. Current amount due_____ $_____

        Total: Loans and accounts receivable $_____

D. Value of interest in any business

    1.1 a. Name and address of business_____

        b. Type of business (corporate, partnership, sole proprietorship or other) _____

        c. Your capital contribution _

        d. Your percentage of interest _____

        e. Date of acquisition _____

        f. Original price or value _____

        g. Source of funds to acquire _____

        h. Method of valuation _____

        i. Other relevant information_____

        j. Current net worth of business _____ $_____

        Total: Value of business interest $_____

E. Cash surrender value of life insurance

    1.1 a. Insurer's name and address _____

        b. Name of insured _____

        c. Policy number _____

        d. Face amount of policy _____

    e.   Policy owner _____

    f.   Date of acquisition _____

    g.   Source of funding to
        acquire_____

    h.   Current cash surrender $_____
        value _____

                  Total: Value of life insurance
                  $_____

F.   Vehicles (automobile, boat, plane, truck, camper, etc.)

     1.1   a.   Description _____

          b.   Title owner _____

          c.   Date of acquisition _____

          d.   Original price _____

          e.   Source of funds to
              acquire_____

          f.   Amount of current lien
              unpaid _____

          g.   Current fair market value $_____

              _____

     1.2   a.   Description _____

          b.   Title owner _____

          c.   Date of acquisition _____

          d.   Original price _____

          e.   Source of funds to acquire

              _____

          f.   Amount of current lien
              unpaid _____

          g.   Current fair market value $_____

              _____

                  Total: Value of Vehicles
                $_____

G.   Real estate (including real property, leaseholds, life estates, etc. at market value—do not deduct any mortgage)

     1.1   a.   Description _____

          b.   Title owner _____

          c.   Date of acquisition _____

          d.   Original price _____

          e.   Source of funds to acquire

              _____

          f.   Amount of mortgage or
              lien unpaid _____

       g. Estimated current market $_____
          value _____

1.2 a. Description _____

       b. Title owner _____

       c. Date of acquisition _____

       d. Original price _____

       e. Source of funds to acquire

          _____

       f.   Amount of mortgage or
          lien unpaid _____

       g. Estimated current market $_____
          value _____

1.3 a. Description _____

       b. Title owner _____

       c. Date of acquisition _____

       d. Original price _____

       e. Source of funds to acquire

          _____

       f.   Amount of mortgage or
          lien unpaid _____

       g. Estimated current market $_____
          value _____

                     Total: Value of real estate
                     $_____

H. Vested interests in trusts (pension, profit sharing, legacies, deferred compensation and others)

    1.1 a. Description of trust _____

         b. Location of assets_____

         c. Title owner _____

         d. Date of acquisition _____

         e. Original investment _____

         f.   Source of funds_____

         g. Amount of unpaid liens __

         h. Current value _____ $_____

    1.2 a. Description of trust _____

         b. Location of assets _____

         c. Title owner _____

         d. Date of acquisition _____

         e. Original investment _____

         f.   Source of funds _____

     g.   Amount of unpaid liens __

     h.   Current value _____ $_____

             Total: Vested interest in trusts
             $_____

I.   Contingent interests (stock options, interests subject to life estates, prospective inheritances, etc.)

     1.1 a.   Description _____

          b.   Location _____

          c.   Date of vesting _____

          d.   Title owner _____

          e.   Date of acquisition _____

          f.   Original price
             or value _____

          g.   Source of funds to acquire

             _____

          h.   Method of valuation _____

          i.   Current value _____ $_____

             Total: Contingent interests
             $_____

J.   Household furnishings

     1.1 a.   Description _____

          b.   Location _____

          c.   Title owner _____

          d.   Original price _____

          e.   Source of funds to acquire

             _____

          f.   Amount of lien unpaid ___

          g.   Current value _____ $_____

             Total: Household furnishings
             $_____

K.   Jewelry, art, antiques, precious objects, gold and precious metals (only if valued at more than $500)

     1.1 a.   Description _____

          b.   Title owner _____

          c.   Location _____

          d.   Original price
             or value _____

          e.   Source of funds to acquire

             _____

          f.   Amount of
             lien unpaid _____

          g. Current value _____ $_____

1.2 a. Description _____

      b. Title owner _____

      c. Location _____

      d. Original price or value ____

      e. Source of funds to acquire

         _____

      f. Amount of lien unpaid ____

      g. Current value _____ $_____

                       Total: Jewelry, art, etc.:

                       $_____

L. Other (e.g., tax shelter investments, collections, judgments, causes of action, patents, trademarks, copyrights, and any other asset not hereinabove itemized)

          1.1 a. Description _____

              b. Title owner _____

              c. Location _____

              d. Original price or value _____

              e. Source of funds to acquire

                   _____

              f. Amount of lien unpaid _____

              g. Current value _____ $_____

          1.2 a. Description _____

              b. Title owner _____

              c. Location _____

              d. Original price or value _____

              e. Source of funds to acquire

                   _____

              f. Amount of lien unpaid _____

              g. Current value _____ $_____

                       Total: Other

                       $_____

                       TOTAL: ASSETS

                       $_____

V.   LIABILITIES

A.   Accounts payable

    1.1   a.   Name   and   address   of creditor_____

          b.   Debtor_____

          c.   Amount of original debt _____

          d.   Date of incurring debt _____

          e.   Purpose _____

          f.   Monthly or other periodic payment ____

          g.   Amount of current debt_____ $_____

    1.2   a.   Name   and   address   of creditor_____

          b.   Debtor_____

          c.   Amount of original debt _____

          d.   Date of incurring debt _____

          e.   Purpose _____

          f.   Monthly or other periodic payment ____

          g.   Amount of current debt_____ $_____

    1.3   a.   Name   and   address   of creditor_____

          b.   Debtor_____

          c.   Amount of original debt _____

          d.   Date of incurring debt _____

          e.   Purpose _____

          f.   Monthly or other periodic payment ____

          g.   Amount of current debt_____ $_____

    1.4   a.   Name   and   address   of creditor_____

          b.   Debtor_____

          c.   Amount of original debt _____

          d.   Date of incurring debt _____

          e.   Purpose _____

          f.   Monthly or other periodic payment ____

          g.   Amount of current debt_____ $_____

    1.5   a.   Name   and   address   of creditor_____

          b.   Debtor_____

          c.   Amount of original debt _____

          d.   Date of incurring debt _____

          e.   Purpose _____

          f.   Monthly or other periodic payment ____

          g.   Amount of current debt_____ $_____

CT RULES

Total: Accounts payable
$_____

B.   Notes payable
    1.1   a.   Name and address of note holder_____
            b.   Debtor_____
            c.   Amount of original debt _____
            d.   Date of incurring debt _____
            e.   Purpose _____
            f.   Monthly or other periodic payment_____
            g.   Amount of current debt_____ $_____
    1.2   a.   Name and address of note holder_____
            b.   Debtor_____
            c.   Amount of original debt _____
            d.   Date of incurring debt _____
            e.   Purpose _____
            f.   Monthly or other periodic payment ____
            g.   Amount of current debt_____ $_____

Total: Notes payable
$_____

C.   Installment accounts payable (security agreements, chattel mortgages)
    1.1   a.   Name and address of creditor _____
            b.   Debtor_____
            c.   Amount of original debt _____
            d.   Date of incurring debt _____
            e.   Purpose _____
            f.   Monthly or other periodic payment_____
            g.   Amount of current debt_____ $_____
    1.2   a.   Name and address of creditor _____
            b.   Debtor_____
            c.   Amount of original debt _____
            d.   Date of incurring debt _____
            e.   Purpose _____
            f.   Monthly or other periodic payment ____
            g.   Amount of current debt_____ $_____

Total: Installment accounts
$_____

D.   Brokers' margin accounts
    1.1   a.   Name and address of broker
                _____
            b.   Amount of original debt _____
            c.   Date of incurring debt _____
            d.   Purpose _____
            e.   Monthly or other periodic payment_____
            f.   Amount of current debt_____ $_____

Total: Brokers' margin
accounts
$_____

E. Mortgages payable on real estate
  1.1 a. Name and address of mortgagee _____
      b. Address of property mortgaged _____
      c. Mortgagor(s) _____
      d. Original debt _____
      e. Date of incurring debt _____
      f. Monthly or other periodic payment ____
      g. Maturity Date _____
      h. Amount of current debt_____ $_____
  1.2 a. Name and address of mortgagee _____
      b. Address of property mortgaged _____
      c. Mortgagor(s)_____
      d. Original debt _____
      e. Date of incurring debt _____
      f. Monthly or other periodic payment_____
      g. Maturity date _____
      h. Amount of current debt_____ $_____

Total: Mortgages payable
$_____

F. Taxes payable
  1.1 a. Description of tax _____
      b. Amount of tax _____
      c. Date due _____

Total: Taxes payable
$_____

G. Loans on life insurance policies
  1.1 a. Name and address of insurer _____
      b. Amount of loan _____
      c. Date incurred _____
      d. Purpose _____
      e. Name of borrower _____
      f. Monthly or other periodic payment ____
      g. Amount of current debt _____ $_____

Total: Life insurance loans
$_____

H. Other liabilities
  1.1 a. Description _____
      b. Name and address of creditor _____
      c. Debtor _____
      d. Original amount of debt _____
      e. Date incurred _____
      f. Purpose _____

    g.   Monthly or other periodic payment ____

    h.   Amount of current debt _____ $_____

1.2   a.   Description _____

    b.   Name and address of creditor _____

    c.   Debtor _____

    d.   Original amount of debt _____

    e.   Date incurred _____

    f.   Purpose _____

    g.   Monthly or other periodic payment ____

    h.   Amount of current debt _____ $_____

Total: Other liabilities
$_____

TOTAL LIABILITIES:
$_____

NET WORTH

TOTAL ASSETS: $_____

TOTAL LIABILITIES: (minus)   ($_____)

NET WORTH: $_____

VI.   **ASSETS TRANSFERRED:** (List all assets transferred in any manner during the preceding three years, or length of the marriage, whichever is shorter [transfers in the routine course of business which resulted in an exchange of assets of substantially equivalent value need not be specifically disclosed where such assets are otherwise identified in the statement of net worth]).

Description of Property	To Whom Transferred and Relationship to Transferee	Date of Transfer	Value
_____	_____	_____	_____
_____	_____	_____	_____
_____	_____	_____	_____
_____	_____	_____	_____

VII.   **SUPPORT REQUIREMENTS:**

(a)   Deponent is at present (paying) (receiving) $_____ per (week) (month), and prior to separation (paid) (received) $_____ per (week) (month) to cover expenses for _____

These payments are being made (voluntarily) (pursuant to court order or judgment) (pursuant to separation agreement), and there are (no) arrears outstanding (in the sum of $_____ to date).

(b)   Deponent requests for support of each child $_____ per (week) (month). Total for children $_____.

(c)   Deponent requests for support of self $_____ per (week) (month).

(d)   The day of the (week) (month) on which payment should be made is _____

VIII.   COUNSEL FEE REQUIREMENTS:

(a)   Deponent requests for counsel fee and disbursements the sum of $_____ .

(b)   Deponent has paid counsel the sum of $_____ and has agreed with counsel concerning fees as follows:

_____
_____
_____

(c)   There is (not) a retainer agreement or written agreement relating to payment of legal fees. (A copy of any such agreement must be annexed.)

IX.   ACCOUNTANT AND APPRAISAL FEES REQUIREMENTS:

(a)   Deponent requests for accountants' fees and disbursements the sum of $_____ . (Include basis for fee, e.g., hourly rate, flat rate)

(b)   Deponent requests for appraisal fees and disbursements the sum of $_____. (Include basis for fee, e.g., hourly rate, flat rate)

(c)   Deponent requires the services of an accountant for the following reasons:

_____
_____

(d)   Deponent requires the services of an appraiser for the following reasons:

_____
_____

CT RULES

X. Other data concerning the financial circumstances of the parties that should be brought to the attention of the Court are:

_____
_____
_____
_____
_____
_____

The foregoing statements and a rider consisting of _____ page(s) annexed hereto and made part hereof, have been carefully read by the undersigned who states that they are true and correct.

_____

                       (Petitioner)

                                 (Respondent)

                       (Plaintiff)

                                 (Defendant)

Sworn to before me this
_____ day of
_____, 19_____

Signature of Attorneys

_____
Attorney's Name (Print or Type)

_____
_____
_____
Attorney's Address & Telephone Number

Subchapter B. Forms Authorized by Section 202.50(b).

APPENDIX B   FINDINGS OF FACT AND CONCLUSIONS OF LAW

Title

The issues of this action having duly come on for _____ hearing before me as one of the Justices of this Court at _____ Part _____ hereof, held in and for the County of _____, on the _____ day(s) of _____, 20_____, and having heard the allegations and proofs of the respective parties, and due deliberation having been held thereon NOW, after hearing _____, Esq., attorney for the plaintiff, and _____, Esq., attorney for the defendant, I do hereby make the following findings of essential facts which I deem established by the evidence and reach the following conclusions of law.

Age of Parties—No Guardian Needed

FIRST: That plaintiff and defendant were both over the age of 18 when this action was commenced.

Age of Parties—Under Age Party

FIRST: That (plaintiff) (defendant) was over the age of 18 years when this action commenced and (defendant) (plaintiff) was then and now is under 18, to wit:

_____ years of age and appears herein by _____ (parent and natural guardian) (duly appointed as _____ guardian by order dated _____ 20_____).

Residence—One Year

SECOND: That at the time of the commencement of this action and for a continuous period of at least one year immediately preceding such commencement (plaintiff) (defendant) resided in this State and (the parties were married in the State) (the parties have resided in this State as husband and wife) (the cause occurred in this State).

Residence—Two Years

SECOND: That for a continuous period of at least two years immediately preceding commencement of this action (plaintiff) (defendant) resided in this State.

Residence—No Required Time

SECOND: That at the time of the commencement of this action both plaintiff and defendant resided in this State and the cause occurred in this State.

Marriage

THIRD: That plaintiff and defendant were married on _____, 20_____ in _____

No Children

FOURTH: That there is no issue of this marriage.

Children

FOURTH: That there are _____ children (born of) _____ (adopted by) the parties to this marriage, whose names and dates of birth are as follows:

Cruelty

FIFTH: That at the following times, none of which is earlier than five years before the date of commencement of this action, defendant committed the following acts which endangered the plaintiff's (physical) (mental) (physical and mental well-being) and rendered it (unsafe) (improper) (unsafe and improper) for plaintiff to continue to reside with defendant.

(Spell out in letter subparagraphs, the acts or omissions to act for which there is proof in the minutes).

Abandonment

FIFTH: That the defendant without cause or justification and without plaintiff's consent on the _____ day of _____ 20_____ abandoned plaintiff with intent not to return and has been wilfully and continuously absent from the home of the parties since

(in divorce actions add: for a period of one year prior to the commencement of this action)

Confinement to Prison

FIFTH: (a) That after the marriage of plaintiff and defendant, defendant was confined in prison for a period of three or more consecutive years, to wit:

that defendant was confined in _____prison on the _____ day of _____ 20_____ and remained confined until the _____ day of _____ 20_____; and

    (b) not more than five years elapsed between the date the cause of action arose and the date of commencement of this action.

Adultery

FIFTH: (a) That on the _____ day of _____ 20_____ at premises _____the defendant committed adultery with _____; and

    (b) not more than five years elapsed between the date of said adultery and the date of commencement of this action.

Neglect to Support

FIFTH: (a) That defendant has (neglected) (refused) to provide for the support of plaintiff since the _____ day of _____ 20_____; and

    (b) not more than five years elapsed between the date the cause of action arose and the date of commencement of this action.

Living Apart under Separation Decree

FIFTH: (a) That a judgment separating the parties was entered on the _____ day of _____ 20_____ by the _____Court of the State of _____; and

    (b) that the parties have lived apart pursuant to said judgment for a period of one year after the granting of such judgment; and

    (c) that the plaintiff has substantially performed all the terms and conditions of such judgment.

Living Apart Under Separation Agreement

FIFTH: (a) That the plaintiff and defendant entered into a written agreement of separation, which they subscribed and acknowledged on the _____ day of _____ 20_____ in the form required to entitle a deed to be recorded; and

    (b) that the (agreement) (a memorandum of said agreement) was filed in the office of the Clerk of the County of _____, wherein (plaintiff) (defendant) resided on the _____ day of _____ 20_____; and

(c) that the parties have lived separate and apart for a period of one year after the execution of said agreement; and

(d) that the plaintiff has substantially performed all the terms and conditions of such agreement.

Annulment for Fraud

FIFTH: (a) That prior to the marriage of the parties the defendant represented to plaintiff that_____ *(state representation)*; and

(b) that said representation was false; and

(c) that said representation was made to induce plaintiff to enter into the marriage; and

(d) that plaintiff believed and relied upon said representation, and would not have entered into the marriage had the representation not been made or had plaintiff known that defendant did not intend to _____ *(refer to representation)*; and

(e) that defendant after the marriage refused to *(refer to representation)*; and

(f) that plaintiff has not cohabited with defendant since discovery of the falsity of the representation; and

(g) that three years have not elapsed since discovery of the facts constituting the fraud.

(for other grounds see 140 D.R.L.).

Declaration of Nullity of Void Marriage

FIFTH: (a) That prior to his marriage to plaintiff and on the _____ day of _____ 20_____, defendant married _____ (name) in _____ (place); and

(b) that on the date of the marriage of plaintiff and defendant the marriage between defendant and _____ (name) had not been terminated by the judgment of any court; and

(c) on the date of the marriage of plaintiff and defendant, defendant's prior spouse was alive and the prior marriage of defendant was valid and subsisting.

Arrears Due Under Temporary Order

SIXTH: (a) That by order of this court (or by order of the Family Court, _____County) dated the _____ day of _____ 20_____, defendant was required to pay to plaintiff as and for maintenance and child support, the sum of $ _____ per week and as counsel fee, the sum of $ _____; and

(b) that there became due under said order through the week of _____ 20_____, the total sum of $ _____, no part of which has been paid except $ _____; and

(c) that defendant is in arrears under said order in the total sum of $ _____ for said period.

Separate and Marital Property

SEVENTH: (a) That the following is separate property owned by plaintiff:_____ _____; and

(b) that the following is separate property owned by defendant: _____; and

(c) that the following is marital property to be disposed of equitablly pursuant to D.R.L. 236B(5):

(List findings required under D.R.L. 236(5)(d) (1-10)).

Custody

EIGHTH: That the children of the marriage now reside with (plaintiff) (defendant).

Visitation

NINTH: That the (plaintiff) (defendant) is entitled to visitation with the infant child(ren) away from the custodial residence.

Exclusive Occupancy

TENTH: That the parties hereto are the owners of premises known as _____

_____ (P.O. address)

Maintenance (pursuant to D.R.L. 236B(6))

ELEVENTH: (a) That plaintiff is (not) employed and is earning $ _____ (net) _____per week; and

(b) that defendant is (not) employed and is earning $ _____ (net) _____per week; and

(c) that (plaintiff) (defendant) now receives $ _____ per _____pursuant to an outstanding Court order.

(d) that (plaintiff) (defendant) now requires $ _____ per week for maintenance; and

(List findings required under D.R.L. 236B(6)(a)(1-10)); and

(e) that the parties have entered into (a stipulation) (or/and agreement) dated _____wherein (plaintiff) (defendant) agrees to accept and (plaintiff) (defendant) agrees to pay $ _____ per week child as and for child support, which (stipulation) (agreement) includes a provision stating that the parties have been advised of the provisions of D.R.L. 240(1-b)(h).) That the terms of the agreement were fair and reasonable at the time of the making of the agreement and are not unconscionable at the time of the entry of judgment herein.

(f) Neither of the parties seeks equitable distribution of the marital property.

Child Support

TWELFTH: (a) The award of child support in accordance with D.R.L. 240(1-b) is based on the following findings:

(i) the children of the marriage entitled to receive parental support are: [state names and dates of birth];

(ii) the income of the plaintiff, who is the (custodial) (non-custodial) parent, is $ _____ per year;

(iii) the income of the defendant, who is the (custodial) (non-custodial) parent, is $ _____ year;

(iv) the applicable child support percentage is _____%;

(v) the basic child support obligation is $ _____ per (week) (month) [plus, if applicable, expenses for child care, health care not covered by insurance, and educational or other extraordinary expenses]

(vi) the non-custodial parent's pro rata share of the basic child support obligation is calculated as follows:

A. $ _____ per (week) (month) representing _____% of the combined parental income under $ 80,000 per year; plus

B. $ _____ per (week) (month), representing _____% of the combined parental income, if any, over $ 80,000 per year;

C. _____% of future reasonable health care expenses not covered by insurance; [delete if inapplicable]

D. _____% of the reasonable child care expenses; [delete if inapplicable]

E. _____% of educational or other extraordinary expenses; [delete if inapplicable]

* (b) The non-custodial parent's pro rate share of the basic child support obligation is neither unjust nor inappropriate.

OR

* (b) Upon consideration of the following factors specified in Section 140(1-b)(f) of the Domestic Relations Law:
the non-custodial parent's pro rata share of the basic child support obligation is unjust or inappropriate in that:

OR

* (b) The parties have entered into a (stipulation) (agreement) dated _____wherein (plaintiff) (defendant) agrees to pay $ _____ per (week) (month) for child support, such (stipulation) (agreement) reciting, in compliance with D.R.L. 240(1-b)(h), that:

The parties have been advised of the provisions of Section

240(1-b) of the Domestic Relations Law;

The unrepresented party, if any, has received a copy of the child support standards chart promulgated by the commissioner of Social Services pursuant to Social Services Law 111-i;

The basic child support obligation as defined in DRL Section 240(1-b) presumptively results in the correct amount of child support to be awarded;

The basic child support obligation in this case is $ _____ per _____; [plus, if applicable, expenses for child care, health care not covered by insurance, and educational or other extraordinary expenses]; and [*]

[**] Only one of the three alternative subparagraphs (b) will be appropriate; delete the inapplicable provisions.

[**] (c) The amount of child support agreed to therein conforms to the basic child support obligation.

OR

[**] (c) The amount of child support agreed to therein deviates from the basic child support obligation, and the parties' reasons for not providing that amount are And the court having found the parties' agreement to deviate from the basic child support obligation is approved for the following reasons: [See DRL 240(1-b)(f)]

Counsel Fees

THIRTEENTH: That the attorney for the (plaintiff) (defendant) is entitled to counsel fees.

Jurisdiction Obtained

FOURTEENTH: _____That jurisdiction as required by Section 230 of the Domestic Relations Law has been obtained.

Removal of Barriers to Remarriage

FIFTEENTH: That plaintiff has filed a verified statement that (he) (she) has taken all steps solely within (his) (her) power to remove all barriers to defendant's remarriage following the (annulment) (divorce).

Plaintiff Entitled to Judgment

SIXTEENTH: That plaintiff is entitled to _____ judgment (of divorce) (of separation) (of annulment)
(declaring the nullity of the marriage) and granting the incidental relief awarded (herein) (in the JUDGMENT signed this
date) **

** Only one of the two alternative subparagraphs (c) will be appropriate;
delete the inapplicable provisions.

Dated:

_____

Justice Supreme Court

MATRIMONIAL JUDGMENTS

Title

Nature of Action—Divorce

The plaintiff having brought this action for a judgment of
absolute divorce by reason of_____

(Insert one or more of the following grounds:)

* the cruel and inhuman treatment of the plaintiff by the
defendant

* the abandonment of the plaintiff by the defendant for a period
for one or more years

* the confinement of defendant in prison for a period of three
or more consecutive years after the marriage of plaintiff and
defendant

* the commission by the defendant of adultery

* the plaintiff and defendant having lived apart after the
granting of a judgment of separation for a period of one or more
years

* the plaintiff and defendant having lived separate and apart
pursuant to a written agreement for a period of one or more
years

Nature of Action—Separation

The plaintiff having brought this action for a judgment of
separation by reason of_____

(Insert one or more of the following grounds:)

* the cruel and inhuman treatment of the plaintiff by the defendant

* the abandonment of the plaintiff by the defendant the neglect or refusal of defendant to provide for plaintiff

* the commission by defendant of adultery

* the confinement of defendant in prison for a period of three or more consecutive years after the marriage of plaintiff and defendant

Nature of Action—Annulment

The plaintiff having brought this action for a judgment of annulment by reason of the fraud of the defendant in inducing the marriage_____ (or other grounds, see 140 DRL)

Nature of Action—Declaration of the Nullity of a Void Marriage

The plaintiff having brought this action for a judgment declaring the nullity of (his) (her) marriage to the defendant by reason of the prior subsisting marriage of the defendant

Service of Process

and the summons bearing the notation ("Action for a Divorce") ("Action for a Separation") ("Action to Annul a Marriage") ("Action to Declare the Nullity of a Void Marriage") and a statement of any ancillary relief demanded having been duly served upon the defendant (personally within this State) (personally without this State by publication)

Defendant's Non-Appearance

and the defendant not having appeared within the time prescribed therefor by statute, and it appearing from (non-military affidavit) (testimony given in open court) that the defendant is not in the military service of the United States

Defendant's Appearance and Non-Answer

and the defendant having appeared _____ by _____ Esq. and plaintiff's verified complaint having been duly served upon the attorney for defendant and the defendant not having answered although the time to do so has fully expired

Defendant's Appearance, Answer and Withdrawal of Answer

and the defendant having appeared by _____, Esq. and plaintiff's verified complaint having been duly served upon the attorney for defendant and the defendant having answered the complaint and having thereafter (by written stipulation) (in open court) withdrawn (his) (her) answer

Defendant's Appearance and Answer-Contested Action

and the defendant having appeared by _____, Esq. and plaintiff's verified complaint having been duly served upon the attorney for defendant and defendant having answered the complaint

Inquest held

and the plaintiff having applied (if defendant has appeared insert: on due notice to defendant's attorney) to the court for judgment for the relief demanded in the complaint and the matter having been set down for trial on the _____ day of _____ 20_____, and the plaintiff having on that day appeared before me and presented written and oral proof of service and in support of the essential allegations of the complaint, and such proof having been heard and considered by me, I decide and find as stated in the separate FINDINGS OF FACT AND CONCLUSIONS OF LAW of even date herewith

Contested Trial—Non-Jury

and the matter having come on for trial before me on the following days _____ and the parties having appeared before me and presented their written and oral proof, and the court having made and filed its _____ memorandum decision dated _____

Contested Trial—Jury

and the matter having come on before the undersigned and a jury on the following days _____ and the parties having presented their written and oral proof before the court and jury, and the jury having been instructed to answer each of the following questions "Yes" or "No"

1.

CT RULES

2.

and having after due deliberation, made written answers to said questions as follows:

Question 1 _____; Question 2 _____

NOW, on motion of _____, Esq. attorney for the (plaintiff) (defendant) it is _____ Adjudged that the marriage between _____, plaintiff, and _____, defendant, is dissolved by reason of _____ (State ground or grounds in the language set forth above); and it is further _____

Separation

Adjudged that _____, plaintiff be and (s)he hereby is separated from the bed and board of _____, defendant by reason of _____ (State ground or grounds in the language set forth above); and it is further_____

Annulment

Adjudged that the marriage contract heretofore existing between _____, plaintiff, and _____, defendant, is annulled because of the fraud of the defendant; and it is further

Declaration of Nullity of Void Marriage

Adjudged that the marriage entered into between _____, plaintiff, and _____, defendant, on the _____ day of _____ 20_____ is declared null and void because of the prior subsisting marriage of the defendant; and it is further

Custody of Children

Adjudged that (plaintiff) (defendant) is awarded custody of the infant issue of the marriage to wit:
born [year]
born [year]
born [year]
and it is further

Visitation

Ordered and Adjudged that (plaintiff) (defendant) may have visitation with the _____ (*number*) _____ infant children away from the custodial residence during the following periods: (a) on Saturday or Sunday of each week between the hours of _____ a.m. and _____p.m., provided (defendant) (plaintiff) shall notify (defendant) (plaintiff) not later than Wednesday of each week of the day selected; (b) on the following holiday days, between the hours of _____ a.m. and _____p.m., in odd numbered years (specify holidays); (c) on the following holiday days between the hours of _____ a.m. and _____ p.m. in even numbered years (specify holidays); and (d) for a period of _____consecutive calendar weeks during the summer recess from school beginning on Sunday of the first week selected, provided (defendant) (plaintiff) shall notify (plaintiff) (defendant) not later than June 10th in each year of the particular weeks selected; and it is further

Family Court Order Continued

Ordered and Adjudged that the order made the _____ day of _____ 20_____ by the Family Court of the State of New York, County of _____ in the proceeding bearing Docket number _____ is continued, and a copy of this judgment shall be served by plaintiff's attorney upon the Clerk of said Court within 10 days after the date hereof; and it is further

Findings as to Pro Rata Share

and it is further Adjudged that:

(a) The basic child support obligation in this case is $ _____ per _____; [plus, if applicable, expenses for child care, health care not covered by insurance, and educational or other extraordinary expenses]; and

* (b) The non-custodial parent's pro rata share of the basic child support obligation is neither unjust nor inappropriate.

OR

* (b) Upon consideration of the following factors specified in 240(1-b)(f): the non-custodial parent's pro rata share of the basic child support obligation is unjust or inappropriate in that:

OR

* (b) The parties have voluntarily agreed to child support for the child(ren) [names] _____ payable by _____ to _____ in the amount of $ _____ per _____, such stipulation reciting, in compliance with D.R.L. 240(1-b):

The parties have been advised of the provisions of D.R.L. 240(1-b);

The unrepresented party, if any, has received a copy of the child support standards chart promulgated by the commissioner of Social Services pursuant to Social Services Law 111-i;

The basic child support obligation as defined in D.R.L. 240(1-b) presumptively results in the correct amount of child support to be awarded; The basic child support obligation in this case is $ _____ per _____[plus, if applicable, expenses for child care, health care not covered by insurance, and educational or other extraordinary expenses]; and

** (c) The amount of child support agreed to therein conforms to the basic child support obligation.

OR

** (c) The amount of child support agreed to therein deviates from the basic child support obligation, for the following reasons:

  * Only one of the three alternative sub-paragraphs (b) will be appropriate in each case; delete the inapplicable paragraphs.

  ** Only one of the two sub-paragraphs (c) will be appropriate to the agreement or stipulation; delete the inapplicable provisions.

And the Court having found the parties' agreement to deviate from the basic child support obligation is approved for the following reasons: [See D.R.L. 240(1-b)(f)] and it is further

Maintenance Payable to (Plaintiff) (Defendant)

Ordered and Adjudged that the (defendant) (plaintiff) shall pay to the (plaintiff) (defendant) (third party _____) by check or money order drawn to (his) (her) order and forwarded on _____ (*day*) of _____ each week commencing with _____ (*date*) 20_____, the first _____ (*day*) after the date of this judgment, to the (defendant) (plaintiff) (third party _____) at (his) (her) residence or at such other place as (he) (she) may designate in writing, the sum of $ _____

per week as maintenance, which sum is inclusive of all obligations of (defendant) (plaintiff) for the maintenance of (plaintiff) (defendant) except extraordinary medical or dental expense

(if exclusive possession of marital premises is awarded, add: and extraordinary repairs of marital premises; consider requirement for purchase of insurance policy); and it is further

Child Support Payable to (Plaintiff) (Defendant)

Ordered and Adjudged that (defendant) (plaintiff) shall pay to (defendant) (plaintiff) (third party _____) by check or money order drawn to (his) (her) order and forwarded on _____ (day) of each week commencing with _____ (*date*) 19_____, the first _____ (*day*) after the date of this judgment, to (defendant) (plaintiff) (third party _____) at (his) (her) residence or at such other place as (he) (she) may designate in writing, the sum of $ _____ per week per child for the support of the child(ren), making a total sum of $ _____ per week; and it is further

Ordered and Adjudged that (defendant) (plaintiff) shall pay to (defendant) (plaintiff) (third party _____) as and for child care expenses the sum of $ _____ by check or money order drawn to (his) (her) order as follows: ; and it is further

Ordered and Adjudged that (defendant) (plaintiff) shall pay to (defendant) (plaintiff) (third party _____) the sum of $ _____, as and for future reasonable health care expenses not covered by insurance as follows: ; and it is further

Ordered and Adjudged that (defendant) (plaintiff) shall pay to (defendant) (plaintiff) (third party _____) the sum of $ _____, as and for (present) (future) (post-secondary) (private) (special) (enriched) education for the child(ren) as follows:

Exclusive Possession of Real Property

Ordered and Adjudged that (plaintiff) (defendant) is awarded exclusive possession of the marital premises to wit:

(*set forth either street address, or if there is no street number, the metes and bounds description*) until the youngest child is 21, or

CT RULES

sooner emancipated and (plaintiff) (defendant) shall within
_____ days after service upon (him) (her) of a copy of this
judgment with notice of entry remove (himself) (herself) therefrom
and upon proof by affidavit of (plaintiff) (defendant) and (his) (her)
attorney of (defendant's) (plaintiff's) failure to remove from said
premises within the time therein provided, a writ of assistance shall
issue without further notice to (defendant) (plaintiff); and it is further

Equitable Distribution

Ordered and Adjudged that the marital property shall be distributed
as follows:

(*include disposition of property upon termination of exclusive
possession of real property, if any.*); and it is further

Counsel Fee

Ordered and Adjudged that the defendant shall pay to the plaintiff,
by check or money order, forwarded to (him) (her) at (his) (her)
(residence) (the office of (his) (her) attorney) within _____
days after service upon him of a copy of this judgment with notice
of entry, as and for counsel fee and expenses, the sum of
$ _____; and it is further

Separation Agreement or Stipulation

Ordered and Adjudged that the (separation agreement) (stipulation)
entered into between the parties on the _____ day of
_____ 19_____, a copy of which is attached to and
incorporated in this judgment by reference, shall (not survive and
shall be merged) (survive and shall not be merged) in this judgment,
and the parties hereby are directed to comply with every legally
enforceable term and provision of such (separation agreement)
(stipulation) including any provision to submit an appropriate issue
to arbitration before a single arbitrator, as if such term or provision
were set forth in its entirety herein, and the court retains jurisdiction
of the matter concurrently with the Family Court for the purpose of
specifically enforcing such of the provisions of that (separation
agreement) (stipulation) as are capable of specific enforcement, to
the extent permitted by law, and of making such further judgment
with respect to maintenance, support, custody or visitation as it finds
appropriate under the circumstances existing at the time application
for that purpose is made to it, or both; and it is further

Permission to Resume Prior Surname

Ordered and Adjudged that (plaintiff) (defendant) is authorized to resume the use of her maiden name or other former surname, to wit_____ _____; and it is further

Money Judgment for Arrears

Ordered and Adjudged that plaintiff, _____, residing at _____recover   from   _____   residing   at _____the sum of $ _____, as arrears due under the order of this court, (Family Court, _____County) dated _____ 19_____ and that plaintiff have execution therefor.

Signature
ENTER (IN _____COUNTY
Justice Supreme Court

REFEREE'S REPORT—FINDINGS OF FACT
AND CONCLUSIONS OF LAW

SUPREME COURT OF THE
STATE OF NEW YORK
COUNTY OF
TITLE OF ACTION
Cal. No.
Index No.

Nature of Action—Divorce

The plaintiff having brought this action for a judgment of absolute divorce by reason of

(*Insert one or more of the following grounds:*)

* the cruel and inhuman treatment of the plaintiff by the defendant

* the abandonment of the plaintiff by the defendant for a period of one or more years

* the confinement of defendant in prison for a period of three or more consecutive years after the marriage of plaintiff and defendant

* the commission by the defendant of adultery

* the plaintiff and defendant having lived apart after the granting of a judgment of separation for a period of one or more years

* the plaintiff and defendant having lived separate and apart pursuant

to a written agreement for a period of one or more years

Nature of Action—Separation

The plaintiff having brought this action for a judgment of separation by reason of

(*Insert one or more of the following grounds:*)

☐ the cruel and inhuman treatment of the plaintiff by the defendant

☐ the abandonment of the plaintiff by the defendant

☐ the neglect or refusal of defendant to provide for plaintiff

☐ the commission by defendant of adultery

☐ the confinement of defendant in prison for a period of three or more consecutive years after the marriage of plaintiff and defendant

Nature of Action—Annulment

The plaintiff having brought this action for a judgment of annulment by reason of the fraud of the defendant in inducing the marriage (or other grounds, see 140 DRL)

Nature of Action—Declaration of the Nullity of a Void Marriage

The plaintiff having brought this action for a judgment declaring the nullity of (his) (her) marriage to the defendant by reason of the prior subsisting marriage of the defendant

Service of Process

and the summons bearing the notation ("Action for a Divorce") ("Action for a Separation") ("Action to Annul a Marriage") ("Action to Declare the Nullity of a Void Marriage") and a statement of any ancillary relief demanded having been duly served upon the defendant (personally within this State) (personally without this State by publication)

Defendant's Non-Appearance

and the defendant not having appeared within the time prescribed therefor by statute, and it appearing from (non-military affidavit) (testimony given in open court) that the defendant is not in the military service of the United States

Defendant's Appearance and Non-Answer

and the defendant having appeared by _____, Esq. and

plaintiff's verified complaint having been duly served upon the attorney for defendant and defendant having answered the complaint

Inquest held

and the plaintiff having applied

(*if defendant has appeared insert:* on due notice to defendant's attorney)

to the court for judgment for the relief demanded in the complaint and the matter having been set down for trial on the _____ day of _____ 20_____, and the plaintiff having on that day appeared before me and presented written and oral proof of service and in support of the essential allegations of the complaint, and such proof having been heard and considered by me, I decide and find as follows:

Contested Trial—Non-Jury

and the matter having come on for trial before me on the following days _____ and the parties having appeared before me and presented their written and oral proof, and the court having made and filed its memorandum decision dated

Contested Trial—Jury

and the matter having come on before the undersigned and a jury on the following days _____ and the parties having presented their written and oral proof before the court and jury, and the jury having been instructed to answer each of the following questions "Yes" or "No"

1.
2.

and having after due deliberation, made written answers to said questions as follows: Question 1 _____; Question 2

_____

Age of Parties—No Guardian Needed

FIRST: That plaintiff and defendant were both over the age of 18 when this action was commenced.

Age of Parties—Under Age Party

FIRST: That (plaintiff) (defendant) was over the age of 18 years when this action commenced and (defendant) (plaintiff) was then and now is under 18, to wit: _____ years of age and appears herein by _____, (parent and natural guardian) (duly appointed as guardian by order dated _____ 19_____).

Residence—One Year

SECOND: That at the time of the commencement of this action and for a continuous period of at least one year immediately preceding such commencement (plaintiff) (defendant) resided in this State and (the parties were married in the State) (the parties have resided in this State as husband and wife) (the cause occurred in this State).

Residence—Two Years

SECOND: That for a continuous period of at least two years immediately preceding commencement of this action (plaintiff) (defendant) resided in this State.

Residence—No Required Time

SECOND: That at the time of the commencement of this action both plaintiff and defendant resided in this State and the cause occurred in this State.

Marriage

THIRD: That plaintiff and defendant were married on _____, 20_____ in

No Children

FOURTH: That there is no issue of this marriage.

Children

FOURTH: That there are _____children (born of) (adopted by) the parties to this marriage, whose names and dates of birth are as follows:

Cruelty

FIFTH: That at the following times, none of which is earlier than five years before the date of commencement of this action, defendant committed the following acts which endangered the plaintiff's (physical) (mental) (physical and mental well-being) and rendered it (unsafe) (improper) (unsafe and improper) for plaintiff to continue to reside with defendant. (*Spell out in letter subparagraphs, the acts or omissions to act for which there is proof in the minutes*).

Abandonment

FIFTH: That the defendant without cause or justification and without plaintiff's consent on the _____ day of _____ 19_____ abandoned plaintiff with intent not to return and has been wilfully and continuously absent from the home of the parties since in divorce actions add: for a period of one year prior to the commencement of this action

Confinement to Prison

FIFTH: (a) That after the marriage of plaintiff and defendant, defendant was confined in prison for a period of three or more consecutive years, to wit:

that defendant was confined in _____prison on the _____ day of _____20_____ and remained confined until the _____ day of _____ 20_____; and (b) not more than five years elapsed between the date the cause of action arose and the date of commencement of this action.

Adultery

FIFTH: (a) That on the _____ day of _____ _____20_____ at premises _____ the defendant committed adultery with _____; and (b) not more than five years elapsed between the date of said adultery and the date of commencement of this action.

Neglect to Support

FIFTH: (a) That defendant has (neglected) (refused) to provide for the support of plaintiff since the _____ day of _____ 20_____, and has not done so; and (b) not more than five years elapsed between the date the cause of action arose and the date of commencement of this action.

Living Apart under Separation Decree

FIFTH: (a) That a judgment separating the parties was entered on the _____ day of _____ 20_____ by the _____ Court of the State of _____; and (b) that the parties have lived apart pursuant to said judgment for a period of one year after the granting of such judgment; and (c) that the plaintiff has substantially performed all the terms and conditions of such judgment.

Living Apart Under Separation Agreement

CT RULES

FIFTH: (a) That the plaintiff and defendant entered into a written agreement of separation, which they subscribed and acknowledged on the _____ day of _____ 20_____ in the form required to entitle a deed to be recorded; and

(b) that the (agreement) (a memorandum of said agreement) was filed in the office of the Clerk of the County of _____, wherein (plaintiff) (defendant) resides on the _____ day of _____ 20_____; and (c) that the parties have lived separate and apart for a period of one year after the execution of said agreement; and (d) that the plaintiff has substantially performed all the terms and conditions of such agreement.

Annulment for Fraud

FIFTH: (a) That prior to the marriage of the parties the defendant represented to plaintiff that (*state representation*); and (b) that said representation was false; and (c) that said representation was made to induce plaintiff to enter into the marriage; and (d) that plaintiff believed and relied upon said representation, and would not have entered into the marriage had the representation not been made or had plaintiff known that defendant did not intend to (*refer to representation*); and (e) that defendant after the marriage refused to (*refer to representation*); and (f) that plaintiff has not cohabited with defendant since discovery of the falsity of the representation; and (g) that three years have not elapsed since discovery of the facts constituting the fraud. (*for other grounds see 140 D.R.L.*).

Declaration of Nullity of Void Marriage

FIFTH: (a) That prior to the marriage to plaintiff and on the _____ day of _____ 20_____, defendant married _____ (*name*) in _____ (*place*); and (b) that on the date of the marriage of plaintiff and defendant the marriage between defendant and _____ (*name*) had not been terminated by the judgment of any court; and (c) on the date of the marriage of plaintiff and defendant, defendant's prior spouse was alive and the prior marriage of defendant was valid and subsisting.

Arrears Due Under Temporary Order

SIXTH: (a) That by order of this court (or by order of the Family

Court, _____County) dated the _____ day of
_____ 20_____, defendant was required to pay to
plaintiff as and for maintenance and child support, the sum of
$ _____ per week and as counsel fee, the sum of
$ _____; and (b) that there became due under said order
through the week of _____ 20_____, the total sum of $
_____, no part of which has been paid except
$ _____; and (c) that defendant is in arrears under said
order in the total sum of $ _____ for said period.

Separate and Marital Property

SEVENTH: (a) That the following is separate property owned by
plaintiff:_____ _____ _____; and

(b) that the following is separate property owned by
defendant:_____ _____; and

(c) that the following is marital property to be disposed of
equitably pursuant to D.R.L. 236B(5):

(*List findings required under D.R.L. 236(5)(d)(1–10)*)

Custody

EIGHTH: That the children of the marriage now reside with
(plaintiff) (defendant).

Visitation

NINTH: That the (plaintiff) (defendant) is entitled to visitation
with the infant child(ren) away from the custodial residence.

Exclusive Occupancy

TENTH: That the parties hereto are the owners of premises
known as_____
_____ (*P.O. address*).

Maintenance (*pursuant to D.R.L. 236B(6)*)

ELEVENTH: (a) That plaintiff is (not) employed and is earning $
_____ (net) _____per week; and

(b) that defendant is (not) employed and is earning
$ _____ (net) _____per week; and

CT RULES

(c) that (plaintiff) (defendant) now receives $ _____ per _____ pursuant to an out-standing Court order.

(d) that (plaintiff) (defendant) now required $ _____ per week for maintenance; and

(*List findings required under D.R.L. 236B(6)(a)(1–10)*; and

(e) that the parties have entered into (a stipulation) (or/and agreement) dated _____ wherein (plaintiff) (defendant) agrees to accept and (plaintiff) (defendant) agrees to pay $ _____ per week as maintenance (and $ _____ per week per child as and for child support, which (stipulation) (agreement) includes a provision stating that the parties have been advised of the provisions of D.R.L. 240(1-b)(h).) That the terms of the agreement were fair and reasonable at the time of the making of the agreement and are not unconscionable at the time of the entry of judgment herein.

(f) Neither of the parties seeks equitable distribution of the marital property.

Child Support

TWELFTH: (a) The award of child support in accordance with D.R.L. 240(1-b) is based on the follows findings:

(i) the children of the marriage entitled to receive parental support are: [*state names and dates of birth*];

(ii) the income of the plaintiff, who is the (custodial) (non-custodial) parent, is $ _____ per year;

(iii) the income of the defendant, who is the (custodial) (non-custodial) parent, is $ _____ year;

(iv) the applicable child support percentage is _____ %;

(v) the basic child support obligation is $ _____ per (week) (month) [*plus, if applicable, expenses for child care, health care not covered by insurance, and educational or other extraordinary expenses*]

(vi) the non-custodial parent's pro rata share of the basic

child support obligation is calculated as follows:

    A. $ _____ per (week) (month) representing _____% of the combined parental income under $ d80,000 per year; plus

    B. $ _____ per (week) (month), representing _____% of the combined parental income, if any, over $ 80,000 per year;

    C. _____% of future reasonable health care expenses not covered by insurance; [*delete if inapplicable*]

    D. _____% of the reasonable child care expenses; [*delete if inapplicable*]

    E. _____% of educational or other extraordinary expenses; [*delete if inapplicable*]

* (b) The non-custodial parent's pro rata share of the basic child support obligation is neither unjust nor inappropriate.

OR

* (b) Upon consideration of the following factors specified in Section 140(1-b)(f) of the Domestic Relations Law: the non-custodial parent's pro rata share of the basic child support obligation is unjust or inappropriate in that

OR

* (b) The parties have entered into a (stipulation) (agreement) dated _____wherein (plaintiff) (defendant) agrees to pay $ _____ per (week) (month) for child support, such (stipulation) (agreement) reciting, in compliance with D.R.L. 240(1-b)(h), that: The parties have been advised of the provisions of Section 240(1-b) of the Domestic Relations Law; The unrepresented party, if any, has received a copy of the child support standards chart promulgated by the commissioner of Social Services pursuant to Social Services Law 111-i;

The basic child support obligation as defined in DRL Section 240(1-b) presumptively results in the correct amount of child support to be awarded; The basic child support obligation in this case is $ _____ per _____; [plus, if applicable, expenses for child care, health care not covered by insurance, and educational or other extraordinary expenses]; and

** (c) The amount of child support agreed to therein conforms to the basic child support obligation.

OR

** (c) The amount of child support agreed to therein deviates from the basic child support obligation, and the parties' reasons for not providing that amount are;

And the court having found the parties' agreement to deviate from the basic child support obligation is approved for the following reasons: [See DRL 240(1-b)(f)]

Counsel Fees

THIRTEENTH: That the attorney for the (plaintiff) (defendant) is entitled to counsel fees.

Jurisdiction Obtained

FOURTEENTH: That jurisdiction as required by Section 230 of the Domestic Relations Law has been obtained.

FIFTEENTH: That plaintiff has filed a verified statement that (he) (she) has taken all steps solely within (his) (her) power to remove all barriers to defendant's remarriage following the (annulment) (divorce).

Plaintiff Entitled to Judgment

SIXTEENTH: That plaintiff is entitled to judgment (of divorce) (of separation) (of annulment) (declaring the nullity of the marriage) and granting the incidental relief awarded (herein) (in the JUDGMENT signed this date)

Dated: New York, New York
_____ day of _____, 20 _____.

Referee

* Only one of the three alternative subparagraphs (b) will be appropriate; delete the inapplicable provisions.

** Only one of the two alternative subparagraphs (c) will be appropriate; delete the inapplicable provisions.

MATRIMONIAL JUDGMENT ENTERED UPON
REFEREE'S REPORT

**At the Supreme Court, _____
County, held at the courthouse
at _____, New York, on the
_____ day of _____, 20_____.**

PRESENT:

HON. (Justice Supreme Court)

TITLE OF ACTION

The issues in this action having been referred to a referee to hear and report, and the referee having submitted his report,

NOW, on motion of _____, Esq., attorney for the (plaintiff) (defndant), it is

ORDERED, that the Referee's Report is confirmed; and it is further

Adjudged that the marriage between _____, plaintiff, and _____, defendant, is dissolved by reason of

(*State ground or grounds in the language set forth above*); and it is further

Separation

Adjudged that _____, plaintiff be and (s)he hereby is separated from the bed and board of _____, defendant by reason of _____ (*State ground or grounds in the language set forth above*); and it is further

Annulment

Adjudged that the marriage contract heretofore existing between _____, plaintiff, and _____, defendant, is annulled because of the fraud of the defendant; and it is further

Declaration of Nullity of Void Marriage

Adjudged that the marriage entered into between _____, plaintiff, and _____, defendant, on the _____ day of _____ 20_____ is declared null and void because of the prior subsisting marriage of the defendant; and it is further

Custody of Children

Adjudged that (plaintiff) (defendant) is awarded custody of the infant issue of the marriage to wit:

born 19_____

born 19_____

born 19_____

and it is further

Visitation

Ordered and Adjudged that (plaintiff) (defendant) may have visitation with the _____ (number) _____ infant children away from the custodial residence during the following periods:

(a) on Saturday or Sunday of each week between the hours of _____ a.m. and _____p.m., provided (defendant) (plaintiff) shall notify (defendant) (plaintiff) not later than Wednesday of each week of the day selected;

(b) on the following holiday days, between the hours of _____ a.m. and _____p.m., in odd numbered years (specify holidays);

(c) on the following holiday days between the hours of _____ a.m. and _____p.m. in even numbered years (specify holidays); and

(d) for a period of _____consecutive calendar weeks during the summer recess from school beginning on Sunday of the first week selected, provided (defendant) (plaintiff) shall notify (plaintiff) (defendant) not later than June 10th in each year of the particular weeks selected; and it is further

Family Court Order Continued

Ordered and Adjudged that the order made the _____ day of _____ 19_____ by the Family Court of the State of New York, County of _____ in the proceeding bearing Docket number _____ is continued, and a copy of this judgment shall be served by plaintiff's attorney upon the Clerk of said Court within 10 days after the date hereof; and it is further

Findings as to Pro Rata Share

and it is further Adjudged that:

(a) The basic child support obligation in this case is $ _____ per _____; [*plus, if applicable, expenses for child care, health care not covered by insurance, and educational or other extraordinary expenses*]; and

(b) The non-custodial parent's pro rata share of the basic child support obligation is neither unjust nor inappropriate.

OR

* (b) Upon consideration of the following factors specified In Section 140(1-b)(f) of the Domestic Relations Law:

the non-custodial parent's pro rata share of the basic child support obligation is unjust or inappropriate in that:

OR

* (b) The parties have voluntarily agreed to child support for the child(ren) [*names*] _____ payable by _____ to _____ in the amount of $ _____ per _____, such stipulation reciting, in compliance with D.R.L. 240(1-b):

The parties have been advised of the provisions of D.R.L. 240(1-b);

The unrepresented party, if any, has receive a copy of the child support standards chart promulated by the Commissioner of Social Services pursuant to Social Services Law 111-i;

The basic child support obligation in this case is $ _____ per _____; and

The basic child support obligation as defined in D.R.L. 240(1-b) presumptively results in the correct amount of child support to be awarded;

The basic child support obligation in this case is $ _____ per _____[plus, if applicable, expenses for child care, health care not covered by insurance, and educational or other extraordinary expenses]; and

** (c) The amount of child support agreed to therein conforms to the basic child support obligation.

OR

** (c) The amount of child support agreed to therein deviates from the basic child support obligation, for the following reasons:

And the Court having found the parties' agreement to deviate from the basic child support obligation is approved for the following reasons: [*See D.R.L. 240(1(b)(f)*] and it is further

Maintenance Payable to (Plaintiff) (Defendant)

Ordered and Adjudged that the (defendant) (plaintiff) shall pay to the (plaintiff) (defendant) (third party _____) by check or money order drawn to (his) (her) order and forwarded on _____ (day) of each week commencing with _____ (date) 19_____, the first _____ (day) after the date of this judgment, to the (defendant) (plaintiff) (third party _____) at (his) (her) residence or at such other place as (he) (she) may designate in writing, the sum of $ _____ per week as maintenance, which sum is inclusive of all obligations of (defendant) (plaintiff) for the maintenance of (plaintiff) (defendant) except extraordinary medical or dental expense (if exclusive possession of marital premises, is awarded add: and extraordinary repairs of marital premises; consider requirement for purchase of insurance policy); and it is further

Child Support Payable to (Plaintiff) (Defendant)

Ordered and Adjudged that (defendant) (plaintiff) shall pay to (defendant) (plaintiff) (third party _____) by check or money order drawn to (his) (her) order and forwarded on _____ (day) of each week commencing with _____ (date) 20_____, the first _____ (day) after the date of this judgment, to (defendant) (plaintiff) (third party _____) at (his) (her) residence or at such other palce as (he) (she) may designate in writing, the sum of $ _____ per week per child for the support of the child(ren) making a total sum of $ _____ per week; and it is further

Ordered and Adjudged that (defendant) (plaintiff) shall pay to (defendant) (plaintiff) (third party _____) as and for child care expenses the sum of $ _____ by check or money order drawn to (his) (her) order as follows: ; and it is further

Ordered and Adjudged that (defendant) (plaintiff) shall pay to (defendant) (plaintiff) (third party _____) the sum of $ _____, as and for future reasonable health care expenses not covered by insurance as follows: _____ ; and it is further

Ordered and Adjudged that (defendant) (plainitff) shall pay to (defendant) (plaintiff) (third party _____) the sum of $ _____, as and for (present) (future) (post-secondary) (private) (special) (enriched) education for the child(ren) as follows:

Maintenance and Child Support Payable to (Plaintiff) (Defendant) Only

Ordered and Adjudged that the defendant shall pay to the plaintiff (third party _____) by check or money order drawn to (his) (her) order and forwarded on _____ (*day*) of each week commencing with _____ (*date*) 20_____, the first _____ (*date*) after the date of this judgment, to (the plaintiff) (third party _____) at (his) (her) residence or at such other place as (he) (she) may designate in writing, the sum of $ _____ per week as maintenance, plus the sum of $ _____ per week per child for the support of the children making a total sum of $ _____ per week, which total sum is inclusive of all obligations of defendant for the support and maintenance of plaintiff and the children except extraordinary medical or dental expense (if plaintiff is awarded exclusive possession of marital premises, add: and extraordinary repairs of marital premises; consider requirement for purchase of insurance policy); and it is further

Exclusive Possession of Real Property

Ordered and Adjudged that (plaintiff) (defendant) is awarded exclusive possession of the marital premises to wit:

(*set forth either street address, or if there is no street number, the metes and bounds description*)

until the youngest child is 21, or sooner emancipated and (plaintiff) (defendant) shall within _____ days after service upon (him) (her) of a copy of this judgment with notice of entry remove (himself) (herself) therefrom and upon proof by affidavit of (plaintiff) (defendant) and (his) (her) attorney of (defendant's) (plaintiff's) failure to remove from said premises within the time herein provided, a writ of assistance shall issue without further notice to (defendant) (plaintiff); and it is further

CT RULES

Equitable Distribution

Ordered and Adjudged that the marital property shall be distributed as follows:

(include disposition of property upon termination of exclusive possession of real property, if any);

and it is further

Counsel Fee

Ordered and Adjudged that the defendant shall pay to the plaintiff, by check or money order, forwarded to (him) (her) at (his) (her) (residence) (the office of (his) (her) attorney) within _____ days after service upon him of a copy of this judgment with notice of entry, as and for counsel fee and expenses, the sum of $ _____; and it is further

Separation Agreement or Stipulation

Ordered and Adjudged that the (separation agreement) (stipulation) entered into between the parties on the _____ day of _____ 20_____, a copy of which is attached to and incorporated in this judgment by reference, shall (not survive and shall be merged) (survive and shall not be merged) in this judgment, and the parties hereby are directed to comply with every legally enforceable term and provision of such (separation agreement) (stipulation) including any provision to submit an appropriate issue to arbitration before a single arbitrator, as if such term or provision were set forth in its entirety herein, and the court retains jurisdiction of the matter concurrently with the Family Court for the purpose of specifically enforcing such of the provisions of that (separation agreement) (stipulation) as are capable of specific enforcement, to the extent permitted by law, and of making such further judgment with respect to maintenance, support, custody or visitation as it finds appropriate under the circumstances existing at the time application for that purpose is made to it, or both; and it is further

Permission to Resume Prior Surname

Ordered and Adjudged that (plaintiff) (defendant) is authorized to resume the use of her maiden name or other former surname, to wit _____; and it is further

Money Judgment for Arrears

Ordered and Adjudged that plaintiff, _____, residing at _____recover from _____ residing at _____, the sum of $ _____, as arrears due under the order of this court, (Family Court, _____County) dated _____ 20_____ and that plaintiff have execution therefor.

Signature
ENTER (IN _____COUNTY
Justice Supreme Court

REQUEST FOR JUDICIAL INTERVENTION

SUPREME (COUNTY) COURT, _____ COUNTY

INDEX #: _____ DATE PURCHASED _____

NOTICE: Court rules and related materials supplied by the courts are included. Since all rules and amendments may not have been supplied, the clerk of the appropriate court should be consulted to determine the current rules.

PLAINTIFF(S):   **IAS ENTRY DATE**

DEFENDANT(S):   **JUDGE ASSIGNED**

R J I DATE

Date issue joined: _____ Bill of particulars served (Y/N): _____

NATURE OF JUDICIAL INTERVENTION
(check ONE box only and enter information)
[ ] Request for preliminary conference
[ ] Note of issue and/or certificate of readiness
[ ] Notice of motion (return date _____)   Relief sought _____
[ ] Order to show cause (clerk enter return date _____)   Relief sought _____
[ ] Other ex parte application (specify __)
[ ] Notice of petition (return date _____)   Relief sought _____
[ ] Notice of medical or dental malpractice action (specify _____)
[ ] Statement of net worth
[ ] Writ of habeas corpus
[ ] Other (specify _____)

NATURE OF ACTION OR PROCEEDING (check ONE box only)

MATRIMONIAL
[ ] Contested	— CM	
[ ] Uncontested	— UM	

TORTS
Malpractice
[ ] Medical/Podiatric	— MM
[ ] Dental	— DM
[ ] * Other Professional	— OPM

COMMERCIAL
[ ] Contract	— CONT
[ ] Corporate	— CORP
[ ] Insurance (where insurer is a party, except arbitration)	— INS
[ ] UCC (including sales, negotiable instruments	— UCC
[ ] * Other Commercial _____	— OC

[ ] Motor Vehicle	— MV
[ ] * Products Liability	— PL

[ ] Environmental	— EN
[ ] Asbestos	— ASB
[ ] Breast Implant	— BI
[ ] * Other Negligence	— OTN

[ ] * Other Tort (including intentional)	— OT

REAL PROPERTY
[ ] Tax Certiorari   — TAX
[ ] Foreclosure   — FOR
[ ] Condemnation   — COND
[ ] Landlord/Tenant   — LT
[ ] * Other Real Property   — ORP

_____

SPECIAL PROCEEDINGS
[ ] Art. 75 (Arbitration)   — ART 75
[ ] Art. 77 (Trusts)   — ART 77
[ ] Article 78   — ART 78
[ ] Election Law   — ELEC
[ ] Guardianship (MHL Art.   — GUARD 81
     81)
[ ] * Other Mental Hygiene   — MHYG
[ ] * Other Special Proceeding   — OSP

OTHER MATTERS
[ ] * _____ — OTH
   * If asterisk used, please specify further.

Check "YES" or "NO" for each of the following questions.

Is this action/proceeding against a

YES	NO		YES	NO	
[ ]	[ ]	Municipality:	[ ]	[ ]	Public Authority:
		(specify _____)			(specify _____)

YES   NO
[ ]   [ ]   Does this action/proceeding seek equitable relief?
[ ]   [ ]   Does this action/proceeding seek recovery for personal injury?
[ ]   [ ]   Does this action/proceeding seek recovery for property damage?

ATTORNEY(S) FOR PLAINTIFF(S): (NAME(S), ADDRESS(ES), PHONE NO.)

ATTORNEY(S) FOR DEFENDANT(S): (NAME(S), ADDRESS(ES), PHONE NO.)

Parties appearing *pro se* (without attorney) should enter information in space provided above for attorneys.

INSURANCE CARRIERS:

RELATED CASES: (IF NONE, write "NONE" below)
Title   Index #   Court   Nature of Relationship

    I AFFIRM UNDER PENALTY OF PERJURY THAT, TO MY KNOWLEDGE, OTHER THAN AS NOTED ABOVE, THERE ARE AND HAVE BEEN NO RELATED ACTIONS OR PROCEEDINGS, NOR HAS A REQUEST FOR JUDICIAL INTERVENTION PREVIOUSLY BEEN FILED IN THIS ACTION OR PROCEEDING.

Dated: _____

_____
(SIGNATURE)

_____
(PRINT OR TYPE NAME)

_____
ATTORNEY FOR

Attach rider sheets if necessary to provide required information.

CT RULES

APPENDIX C   **[Reserved]**

APPENDIX D   **[Reserved]**

APPENDIX E

Procedures for questioning, challenging and selecting jurors authorized by section 202.33 of the Rules of the Chief Administrator of the Courts.

A. General principles applicable to Jury selection. Selection of jurors pursuant to any of the methods authorized by section 202.33(e) of the Rules of the Chief Administrator shall be governed by the following:

(1) If for any reason jury selection cannot proceed immediately, counsel shall return promptly to the courtroom of the assigned trial judge or the Trial Assignment Part or any other designated location for further instructions.

(2) Generally, a total of eight jurors, including two alternates, shall be selected. The court may permit a greater number of alternates if a lengthy trial is expected or for any appropriate reason. Counsel may consent to the use of "nondesignated" alternate jurors, in which even no distinction shall be made during jury selection between jurors and alternates, but the number of peremptory challenges, in such cases shall consist of the sum of the peremptory challenges that would have been available to challenge both jurors and designated alternates.

(3) All prospective jurors shall complete a background questionnaire supplied by the court in a form approved by the Chief Administrator. Prior to the commencement of jury selection, completed questionnaires shall be made available to counsel. Upon completion of jury selection, or upon removal of a prospective juror, the questionnaires shall be either returned to the respective jurors or collected and discarded by court staff in a manner that ensures juror privacy. With Court approval, which shall take into consideration concern for juror privacy, the parties may supplement the questionnaire to address concerns unique to a specific case.

(4) During the voir dire each attorney may state generally the

contentions of his or her client, and identify the parties, attorneys and the witnesses likely to be called. However, counsel may not read from any of the pleadings in the action or inform potential jurors of the amount of money at issue.

(5) Counsel shall exercise peremptory challenges outside of the presence of the panel of prospective jurors.

(6) Counsel shall avoid discussing legal concepts such as burden of proof, which are the province of the court.

(7) If an unusual delay or a lengthy trial is anticipated, counsel may so advise prospective jurors.

(8) If counsel objects to anything said or done by any other counsel during the selection process, the objecting counsel shall unobtrusively request that all counsel step outside the juror's presence, and counsel shall make a determined effort to resolve the problem. Should that effort fail, counsel shall immediately bring the problem to the attention of the assigned trial judge, the Trial Assignment Part judge or any other designated judge.

(9) After jury selection is completed, counsel shall advise the clerk of the assigned Trial Part or of the Trial Assignment Part or other designated part. If counsel anticipates the need during trial of special equipment (if available) or special assistance, such as an interpreter, counsel shall so inform the clerk at that time.

B. "White's Method."

(1) Prior to the identification of the prospective jurors to be seated in the jury box, counsel shall ask questions generally to all of the jurors in the room to determine whether any prospective juror in the room has knowledge of the subject matter, the parties, their attorneys or the prospective witnesses. A response from a juror that requires elaboration may be the subject of further questioning of that juror by counsel on an individual basis. Counsel may exercise challenges for cause at this time.

(2) After general questions have been asked to the group of prospective jurors, jury selection shall continue in rounds, with each round to consist of the following: (1) seating prospective jurors in

CT RULES

the jury box; (2) questioning of seated prospective jurors; and (3) removal of seated prospective jurors upon exercise of challenges. Jurors removed for cause shall immediately be replaced during each round. The first round shall begin initially with the seating of six prospective jurors (where undesignated alternates are used, additional prospective jurors equal to the number of alternate jurors shall be seated as well).

(3) In each round, the questioning of the seated prospective jurors shall be conducted first by counsel for the plaintiff, followed by counsel for the remaining parties in the order in which their names appear in the caption. Counsel may be permitted to ask follow-up questions. Within each round, challenges for cause shall be exercised by any party prior to the exercise of peremptory challenges and as soon as the reason therefor becomes apparent. Upon replacement of a prospective juror removed for cause, questioning shall revert to the plaintiff.

(4) Following questioning and the exercise of challenges for cause, peremptory challenges shall be exercised one at a time and alternately as follows: In the first round, in caption order, each attorney shall exercise one peremptory challenge by removing a prospective juror's name from a "board" passed back and forth between or among counsel. An attorney alternatively may waive the making of a peremptory challenge. An attorney may exercise a second, single peremptory challenge within the round only after all other attorneys have either exercised or waived their first peremptory challenges. The board shall continue to circulate among the attorneys until no other peremptory challenges are exercised. An attorney who waives a challenge may not thereafter exercise a peremptory challenge within the round, but may exercise remaining peremptory challenges in subsequent rounds. The counsel last able to exercise a peremptory challenge in the round is not confined to the exercise of a single challenge but may then exercise one or more peremptory challenges.

(5) In subsequent rounds, the first exercise of peremptory challenges shall alternate from side to side. Where a side consists of multiple parties, commencement of the exercise of peremptory challenges in subsequent rounds shall rotate among the parties

within the side. In each such round, before the board is to be passed to the other side, the board must be passed to all remaining parties within the side, in caption order, starting from the first party in the rotation for that round.

(6) At the end of each round, those seated jurors who remain unchallenged shall be sworn and removed from the room. The challenged jurors shall be replaced, and a new round shall commenced.

(7) The selection of designated alternate jurors shall take place after the selection of the six jurors. Designated alternate jurors shall be selected in the same manner as described above, with the order of exercise of peremptory challenges continuing as the next round following the last completed round of challenges to regular jurors. The total number of peremptory challenges to alternates may be exercised against any alternate, regardless of seat.

C. "Struck Method."

(1) Unless otherwise ordered by the Court, selection of jurors shall be made from an initial panel of 25 prospective jurors, who shall be seated randomly and who shall maintain the order of seating throughout the voir dire. If fewer prospective jurors are needed due to the use of designated alternate jurors or for any other reason, the size of the panel may be decreased.

(2) Counsel first shall ask questions generally to the prospective jurors as a group to determine whether any prospective juror has knowledge of the subject matter, the parties, their attorneys or the prospective witnesses. A response from a juror that requires further elaboration may be the subject of further questioning of that juror by counsel on an individual basis. Counsel may exercise challenges for cause at this time.

(3) After the general questioning has been completed, in an action with one plaintiff and one defendant, counsel for the plaintiff initially shall question the prospective jurors, followed by questioning by defendant's counsel. Counsel may be permitted to ask follow-up questions. In cases with multiple parties, questioning shall be undertaken by counsel in the order in which the parties' names

appear in the caption. A challenge for cause may be made by counsel to any party as soon as the reason therefor becomes apparent. At the end of the period, all challenges for cause to any prospective juror on the panel must have been exercised by respective counsel.

(4) After challenges for cause are exercised, the number of prospective jurors remaining shall be counted. If that number is less than the total number of jurors to be selected (including alternates where non-designated alternates are being used) plus the maximum number of peremptory challenges allowed by the court or by statute that may be exercised by the parties (such sum shall be referred to as the "jury panel number"), additional prospective jurors shall be added until the number of prospective jurors not subject to challenge for cause equals or exceeds the jury panel number. Counsel for each party then shall question each replacement juror pursuant to the procedure set forth in paragraph 3.

(5) After all prospective jurors in the panel have been questioned, and all challenges for cause have been made, counsel for each party, one at a time beginning with counsel for the plaintiff, shall then exercise allowable peremptory challenges by alternately striking a single juror's name from a list or ballot passed back and forth between or among counsel until all challenges are exhausted or waived. In cases with multiple plaintiffs and/or defendants, peremptory challenges shall be exercised by counsel in the order in which the parties' names appear in the caption, unless following that order would, in the opinion of the court, unduly favor a side. In that event, the court, after consulting with the parties, shall specify the order in which the peremptory challenges shall be exercised in a manner that shall balance the interests of the parties.

An attorney who waives a challenge may not thereafter exercise a peremptory challenge. Any Batson or other objections shall be resolved by the court before any of the struck jurors are dismissed.

(6) After all peremptory challenges have been made, the trial jurors (including alternates when non-designated alternates are used) then shall be selected in the order in which they have been seated from those prospective jurors remaining on the panel.

(7) The selection of designated alternate jurors shall take place

after the selection of the six jurors. Counsel shall select designated alternates in the same manner as set forth in these rules, but with an initial panel of not more than 10 prospective alternates unless otherwise directed by the court. The jury panel number for designated alternate jurors shall be equal to the number of alternates plus the maximum number of peremptory challenges allowed by the court or by statute that may be executed by the parties. The total number of peremptory challenges to alternates may be exercised against any alternate, regardless of seat.

A-1

APPENDIX
SELECTED PRACTICE
PROVISIONS

CONTENTS

App Pract Provs

CONSTITUTION OF THE STATE OF NEW YORK

SYNOPSIS OF SELECTED PROVISIONS

Article III LEGISLATURE

App Pract Provs

§ 19. [Private claims not to be audited by legislature; claims barred by lapse of time.]

The legislature shall neither audit nor allow any private claim or account against the state, but may appropriate money to pay such claims as shall have been audited and allowed according to law.

No claim against the state shall be audited, allowed or paid which, as between citizens of the state, would be barred by lapse of time. But if the claimant shall be under legal disability the claim may be presented within two years after such disability is removed.

Article VI JUDICIARY

§ 1. [Unified court system; courts of record; statewide service and execution.]

a. There shall be a unified court system for the state. The state-wide courts shall consist of the court of appeals, the supreme court including the appellate divisions thereof, the court of claims, the county court, the surrogate's court and the family court, as hereinafter provided. The legislature shall establish in and for the city of New York, as part of the unified court system for the state, a single, city-wide court of civil jurisdiction and a single, city-wide court of criminal jurisdiction, as hereinafter provided, and may upon the request of the mayor and the local legislative body of the city of New York, merge the two courts into one city-wide court of both civil and criminal jurisdiction. The unified court system for the state shall also include the district, town, city and village courts outside the city of New York, as hereinafter provided.

b. The court of appeals, the supreme court including the appellate divisions thereof, the court of claims, the county court, the surrogate's court, the family court, the courts or court of civil and criminal jurisdiction of the city of New York, and such other courts as the legislature may determine shall be courts of record.

c. All processes, warrants and other mandates of the court of appeals, the supreme court including the appellate divisions thereof, the court of claims, the county court, the surrogate's court and the family court may be served and executed in any part of the state. All processes, warrants and other mandates of the courts or court of civil and criminal jurisdiction of the city of New York may, subject to such limitation as may be prescribed by the legislature, be served and executed in any part of the state. The legislature may provide that processes, warrants and other mandates of the district court may be served and executed in any part of the state and that processes, warrants and other mandates of town, village and city courts outside the city of New York may be served and executed in any part of the county in which such courts are located or in any part of any adjoining county.

    See also Judiciary Law §§ 2, 2-b, *below,* as to courts of record.

§ 3.   [Court of appeals; subject matter jurisdiction.]

a. The jurisdiction of the court of appeals shall be limited to the review of questions of law except where the judgment is of death, or where the appellate division, on reversing or modifying a final or interlocutory judgment in an action or a final or interlocutory order in a special proceeding, finds new facts and a final judgment or a final order pursuant thereto is entered; but the right to appeal shall not depend upon the amount involved.

b. Appeals to the court of appeals may be taken in the classes of cases hereafter enumerated in this section;

In criminal cases, directly from a court of original jurisdiction where the judgment is of death, and in other criminal cases from an appellate division or otherwise as the legislature may from time to time provide.

In civil cases and proceedings as follows:

    (1) As of right, from a judgment or order entered upon the decision of an appellate division of the supreme court which finally determines an action or special proceeding wherein is directly involved the construction of the constitution of the state or of the United States, or where one or more of the justices of the appellate division dissents from the decision of the court, or where the judgment or order is one of reversal or modification.

    (2) As of right, from a judgment or order of a court of record of original jurisdiction which finally determines an action or special proceeding where the only question involved on the appeal is the validity of a statutory provision of the state or of the United States under the constitution of the state or of the United States; and on any

such appeal only the constitutional question shall be considered and determined by the court.

(3) As of right, from an order of the appellate division granting a new trial in an action or a new hearing in a special proceeding where the appellant stipulates that, upon affirmance, judgment absolute or final order shall be rendered against him.

(4) From a determination of the appellate division of the supreme court in any department, other than a judgment or order which finally determines an action or special proceeding, where the appellate division allows the same and certifies that one or more questions of law have arisen which, in its opinion, ought to be reviewed by the court of appeals, but in such case the appeal shall bring up for review only the question or questions so certified; and the court of appeals shall certify to the appellate division its determination upon such question or questions.

(5) From an order of the appellate division of the supreme court in any department, in a proceeding instituted by or against one or more public officers or a board, commission or other body of public officers or a court or tribunal, other than an order which finally determines such proceeding, where the court of appeals shall allow the same upon the ground that, in its opinion, a question of law is involved which ought to be reviewed by it, and without regard to the availability of appeal by stipulation for final order absolute.

(6) From a judgment or order entered upon the decision of an appellate division of the supreme court which finally determines an action or special proceeding but which is not appealable under paragraph (1) of this subdivision where the appellate division or the court of appeals shall certify that in its opinion a question of law is involved which ought to be reviewed by the court of appeals. Such an appeal may be allowed upon application (a) to the appellate division, and in case of refusal, to the court of appeals, or (b) directly to the court of appeals. Such an appeal shall be allowed when required in the interest of substantial justice.

(7) No appeal shall be taken to the court of appeals from a judgment or order entered upon the decision of an appellate division of the supreme court in any civil case or proceeding where the

appeal to the appellate division was from a judgment or order entered in an appeal from another court, including an appellate or special term of the supreme court, unless the construction of the constitution of the state or of the United States is directly involved therein, or unless the appellate division of the supreme court shall certify that in its opinion a question of law is involved which ought to be reviewed by the court of appeals.

(8) The legislature may abolish an appeal to the court of appeals as of right in any or all of the cases or classes of cases specified in paragraph (1) of this subdivision wherein no question involving the construction of the constitution of the state or of the United States is directly involved, provided, however, that appeals in any such case or class of cases shall thereupon be governed by paragraph (6) of this subdivision.

§ 5.   [Appellate courts; power to determine appeal; transfer of appeal by court not authorized to review.]

a. Upon an appeal from a judgment or an order, any appellate court to which the appeal is taken which is authorized to review such judgment or order may reverse or affirm, wholly or in part, or may modify the judgment or order appealed from, and each interlocutory judgment or intermediate or other order which it is authorized to review, and as to any or all of the parties. It shall thereupon render judgment of affirmance, judgment of reversal and final judgment upon the right of any or all of the parties, or judgment of modification thereon according to law, except where it may be necessary or proper to grant a new trial or hearing, when it may grant a new trial or hearing.

b. If any appeal is taken to an appellate court which is not authorized to review such judgment or order, the court shall transfer the appeal to an appellate court which is authorized to review such judgment or order.

§ 7.   [Supreme court; subject matter jurisdiction; new classes of actions.]

a. The supreme court shall have general original jurisdiction in law and equity and the appellate jurisdiction herein provided. In the city of New York, it shall have exclusive jurisdiction over crimes prosecuted by indictment, provided, however, that the legislature may grant to the city-wide court of criminal jurisdiction of the city of New York jurisdiction over misdemeanors prosecuted by indictment and to the family court in the city of New York jurisdiction over crimes and offenses by or against minors or between spouses or between parent and child or between members of the same family or household.

b. If the legislature shall create new classes of actions and proceedings, the supreme court shall have jurisdiction over such classes of actions and proceedings, but the legislature may provide that another court or other courts shall also have jurisdiction and that actions and proceedings of such classes may be originated in such other court or courts.

§ 8.   [Appellate terms authorized; composition; jurisdiction.]

a. The appellate division of the supreme court in each judicial department may establish an appellate term in and for such department or in and for a judicial district or districts or in and for a county or counties within such department. Such an appellate term shall be composed of not less than three nor more than five justices of the supreme court who shall be designated from time to time by the chief administrator of the courts with the approval of the presiding justice of the appropriate appellate division, and who shall be residents of the department or of the judicial district or districts as the case may be and the chief administrator of the courts shall designate the place or places where such appellate terms shall be held.

b. Any such appellate term may be discontinued and re-established as the appellate division of the supreme court in each department shall determine from time to time and any designation to service therein may be revoked by the chief administrator of the courts with the approval of the presiding justice of the appropriate appellate division.

c. In each appellate term no more than three justices assigned thereto shall sit in any action or proceeding. Two of such justices shall constitute a quorum and the concurrence of two shall be necessary to decision.

d. If so directed by the appellate division of the supreme court establishing an appellate term, an appellate term shall have jurisdiction to hear and determine appeals now or hereafter authorized by law to be taken to the supreme court or to the appellate division other than appeals from the supreme court, a surrogate's court, the family court or appeals in criminal cases prosecuted by indictment or by information as provided in section six of Article one.

e. As may be provided by law, an appellate term shall have jurisdiction to hear and determine appeals from the district court or a town, village or city court outside the city of New York.

§ 9.   [Court of claims continued; composition; jurisdiction.]

The court of claims is continued. It shall consist of the eight judges now authorized by law, but the legislature may increase such number and may reduce such number to six or seven. The judges shall be appointed by the governor by and with the advice and consent of the senate and their terms of office shall be nine years. The court shall have jurisdiction to hear and determine claims against the state or by the state against the claimant or between conflicting claimants as the legislature may provide.

§ 11.   [County court; subject matter jurisdiction; appellate jurisdiction.]

a. The county court shall have jurisdiction over the following classes of actions and proceedings which shall be originated in such county court in the manner provided by law, except that actions and proceedings within the jurisdiction of the district court or a town, village or city court outside the city of New York may, as provided by law, be originated therein: actions and proceedings for the recovery of money, actions and proceedings for the recovery of chattels and actions and proceedings for the foreclosure of mechanics liens and liens on personal property where the amount sought to be recovered or the value of the property does not exceed twenty-five thousand dollars exclusive of interest and costs; over all crimes and other violations of law; over summary proceedings to recover possession of real property and to remove tenants therefrom; and over such other actions and proceedings, not within the exclusive jurisdiction of the supreme court, as may be provided by law.

b. The county court shall exercise such equity jurisdiction as may be provided by law and its jurisdiction to enter judgment upon a counterclaim for the recovery of money only shall be unlimited.

c. The county court shall have jurisdiction to hear and determine all appeals arising in the county in the following actions and proceedings: as of right, from a judgment or order of the district court or a town, village or city court which finally determines an action or proceeding and, as may be provided by law, from a judgment or order of any such court which does not finally determine an action or proceeding. The legislature may provide, in accordance with the provisions of section eight of this article, that any or all of such appeals be taken to an appellate term of the supreme court instead of the county court.

d. The provisions of this section shall in no way limit or impair the jurisdiction of the supreme court as set forth in section seven of this article.

See also Judiciary Law § 190, below.

§ 12. [Surrogate's court continued; composition; subject matter jurisdiction.]

a. The surrogate's court is continued in each county in the state. There shall be at least one judge of the surrogate's court in each county and such number of additional judges of the surrogate's court as may be provided by law.

b. The judges of the surrogate's court shall be residents of the county and shall be chosen by the electors of the county.

c. The terms of the judges of the surrogate's court in the city of New York shall be fourteen years, and in other counties ten years, from and including the first day of January next after their election.

d. The surrogate's court shall have jurisdiction over all actions and proceedings relating to the affairs of decedents, probate of wills, administration of estates and actions and proceedings arising thereunder or pertaining thereto, guardianship of the property of minors, and such other actions and proceedings, not within the exclusive jurisdiction of the supreme court, as may be provided by law.

e. The surrogate's court shall exercise such equity jurisdiction as may be provided by law.

f. The provisions of this section shall in no way limit or impair the jurisdiction of the supreme court as set forth in section seven of this article.

§ 13.   [Family court established; composition; subject matter jurisdiction.]

a. The family court of the state of New York is hereby established. It shall consist of at least one judge in each county outside the city of New York and such number of additional judges for such counties as may be provided by law. Within the city of New York it shall consist of such number of judges as may be provided by law. The judges of the family court within the city of New York shall be residents of such city and shall be appointed by the mayor of the city of New York for terms of ten years. The judges of the family court outside the city of New York, shall be chosen by the electors of the counties wherein they reside for terms of ten years.

b. The family court shall have jurisdiction over the following classes of actions and proceedings which shall be originated in such family court in the manner provided by law: (1) the protection, treatment, correction and commitment of those minors who are in need of the exercise of the authority of the court because of circumstances of neglect, delinquency or dependency, as the legislature may determine; (2) the custody of minors except for custody incidental to actions and proceedings for marital separation, divorce, annulment of marriage and dissolution of marriage; (3) the adoption of persons; (4) the support of dependents except for support incidental to actions and proceedings in this state for marital separation, divorce, annulment of marriage or dissolution of marriage; (5) the establishment of paternity; (6) proceedings for conciliation of spouses; and (7) as may be provided by law: the guardianship of the person of minors and, in conformity with the provisions of section seven of this article, crimes and offenses by or against minors or between spouses or between parent and child or between members of the same family or household. Nothing in this section shall be construed to abridge the authority or jurisdiction of courts to appoint guardians in cases originating in those courts.

c. The family court shall also have jurisdiction to determine, with the same powers possessed by the supreme court, the following matters when referred to the family court from the supreme court: habeas corpus proceedings for the determination of the custody of minors; and in actions and proceedings for marital separation, divorce, annulment of marriage and dissolution of marriage, applications to fix temporary

App Pract Provs

or permanent support and custody, or applications to enforce judgments and orders of support and of custody, or applications to modify judgments and orders of support and of custody which may be granted only upon the showing to the family court that there has been a subsequent change of circumstances and that modification is required.

d. The provisions of this section shall in no way limit or impair the jurisdiction of the supreme court as set forth in section seven of this article.

§ 15.   [New York City civil and criminal courts; merger authorized; subject matter jurisdiction.]

a. The legislature shall by law establish a single court of city-wide civil jurisdiction and a single court of city-wide criminal jurisdiction in and for the city of New York and the legislature may, upon the request of the mayor and the local legislative body of the city of New York, merge the two courts into one city-wide court of both civil and criminal jurisdiction. The said city-wide courts shall consist of such number of judges as may be provided by law. The judges of the court of city-wide civil jurisdiction shall be residents of such city and shall be chosen for terms of ten years by the electors of the counties included within the city of New York from districts within such counties established by law. The judges of the court of city-wide criminal jurisdiction shall be residents of such city and shall be appointed for terms of ten years by the mayor of the city of New York.

b. The court of city-wide civil jurisdiction of the city of New York shall have jurisdiction over the following classes of actions and proceedings which shall be originated in such court in the manner provided by law: actions and proceedings for the recovery of money, actions and proceedings for the recovery of chattels and actions and proceedings for the foreclosure of mechanics liens and liens on personal property where the amount sought to be recovered or the value of the property does not exceed twenty-five thousand dollars exclusive of interest and costs, or such smaller amount as may be fixed by law; over summary proceedings to recover possession of real property and to remove tenants therefrom and over such other actions and proceedings, not within the exclusive jurisdiction of the supreme court, as may be provided by law. The court of city-wide civil jurisdiction shall further exercise such equity jurisdiction as may be provided by law and its jurisdiction to enter judgment upon a counterclaim for the recovery of money only shall be unlimited.

c. The court of city-wide criminal jurisdiction of the city of New York shall have jurisdiction over crimes and other violations of law, other than those prosecuted by indictment, provided, however, that the legislature may grant to said court jurisdiction over misdemeanors prosecuted by indictment; and over such other actions and proceedings, not within the exclusive jurisdiction of the supreme court, as may be provided by law.

d. The provisions of this section shall in no way limit or impair the jurisdiction of the supreme court as set forth in section seven of this article.

§ 16.   [District courts authorized; subject matter jurisdiction.]

a. The district court of Nassau county may be continued under existing law and the legislature may, at the request of the board of supervisors or other elective governing body of any county outside the city of New York, establish the district court for the entire area of such county or for a portion of such county consisting of one or more cities, or one or more towns which are contiguous, or of a combination of such cities and such towns provided at least one of such cities is contiguous to one of such towns.

b. No law establishing the district court for an entire county shall become effective unless approved at a general election on the question of the approval of such law by a majority of the votes cast thereon by the electors within the area of any cities in the county considered as one unit and by a majority of the votes cast thereon by the electors within the area outside of cities in the county considered as one unit.

c. No law establishing the district court for a portion of a county shall become effective unless approved at a general election on the question of the approval of such law by a majority of the votes cast thereon by the electors within the area of any cities included in such portion of the county considered as one unit and by a majority of the votes cast thereon by the electors within the area outside of cities included in such portion of the county considered as one unit.

d. The district court shall have such jurisdiction as may be provided by law, but not in any respect greater than the jurisdiction of the courts

App Pract Provs

for the city of New York as provided in section fifteen of this article, provided, however, that in actions and proceedings for the recovery of money, actions and proceedings for the recovery of chattels and actions and proceedings for the foreclosure of mechanics liens and liens on personal property, the amount sought to be recovered or the value of the property shall not exceed fifteen thousand dollars exclusive of interest and costs.

e. The legislature may create districts of the district court which shall consist of an entire county or of an area less than a county.

f. There shall be at least one judge of the district court for each district and such number of additional judges in each district as may be provided by law.

g. The judges of the district court shall be apportioned among the districts as may be provided by law, and to the extent practicable, in accordance with the population and the volume of judicial business.

h. The judges shall be residents of the district and shall be chosen by the electors of the district. Their terms shall be six years from and including the first day of January next after their election.

i. The legislature may regulate and discontinue the district court in any county or portion thereof.

§ 17.   [Town, village and city courts continued; subject matter jurisdiction.]

a. Courts for towns, villages and cities outside the city of New York are continued and shall have the jurisdiction prescribed by the legislature but not in any respect greater than the jurisdiction of the district court as provided in section sixteen of this article.

b. The legislature may regulate such courts, establish uniform jurisdiction, practice and procedure for city courts outside the city of New York and may discontinue any village or city court outside the city of New York existing on the effective date of this article. The legislature may discontinue any town court existing on the effective date of this Article only with the approval of a majority of the total votes cast at a general election on the question of a proposed discontinuance of the court in each such town affected thereby.

c. The legislature may abolish the legislative functions on town boards of justices of the peace and provide that town councilmen be elected in their stead.

d. The number of the judges of each of such town, village and city courts and the classification and duties of the judges shall be prescribed by the legislature. The terms, method of selection and method of filling vacancies for the judges of such courts shall be prescribed by the legislature, provided, however, that the justices of town courts shall be chosen by the electors of the town for terms of four years from and including the first day of January next after their election.

§ 18.   [Trial by jury.]

a. Trial by jury is guaranteed as provided in Article one of this constitution. The legislature may provide that in any court of original jurisdiction a jury shall be composed of six or of twelve persons and may authorize any court which shall have jurisdiction over crimes and other violations of law, other than crimes prosecuted by indictment, to try such matters without a jury, provided, however, that crimes prosecuted by indictment shall be tried by a jury composed of twelve persons, unless a jury trial has been waived as provided in section two of Article one of this constitution.

b. The legislature may provide for the manner of trial of actions and proceedings involving claims against the state.

§ 19.   [Transfer of actions and proceedings.]

a. The supreme court may transfer any action or proceeding, except one over which it shall have exclusive jurisdiction which does not depend upon the monetary amount sought, to any other court having jurisdiction of the subject matter within the judicial department provided that such other court has jurisdiction over the classes of persons named as parties. As may be provided by law, the supreme court may transfer to itself any action or proceeding originated or pending in another court within the judicial department other than the court of claims upon a finding that such a transfer will promote the administration of justice.

b. The county court shall transfer to the supreme court or surrogate's court or family court any action or proceeding which has not been transferred to it from the supreme court or surrogate's court or family court and over which the county court has no jurisdiction. The county

App Pract
Provs

court may transfer any action or proceeding, except a criminal action or proceeding involving a felony prosecuted by indictment or an action or proceeding required by this Article to be dealt with in the surrogate's court or family court, to any court, other than the supreme court, having jurisdiction of the subject matter within the county provided that such other court has jurisdiction over the classes of persons named as parties.

c. As may be provided by law, the supreme court or the county court may transfer to the county court any action or proceeding originated or pending in the district court or a town, village or city court outside the city of New York upon a finding that such a transfer will promote the administration of justice.

d. The surrogate's court shall transfer to the supreme court or the county court or the family court or the courts for the city of New York established pursuant to section fifteen of this Article any action or proceeding which has not been transferred to it from any of said courts and over which the surrogate's court has no jurisdiction.

e. The family court shall transfer to the supreme court or the surrogate's court or the county court or the courts for the city of New York established pursuant to section fifteen of this Article any action or proceeding which has not been transferred to it from any of said courts and over which the family court has no jurisdiction.

f. The courts for the city of New York established pursuant to section fifteen of this Article shall transfer to the supreme court or the surrogate's court or the family court any action or proceeding which has not been transferred to them from any of said courts and over which the said courts for the city of New York have no jurisdiction.

g. As may be provided by law, the supreme court shall transfer any action or proceeding to any other court having jurisdiction of the subject matter in any other judicial district or county provided that such other court has jurisdiction over the classes of persons named as parties.

h. As may be provided by law, the county court, the surrogate's court, the family court and the courts for the city of New York established pursuant to section fifteen of this Article may transfer any action or proceeding, other than one which has previously been transferred to it, to any other court, except the supreme court, having jurisdiction of the subject matter in any other judicial district or county provided that such other court has jurisdiction over the classes of persons named as parties.

i. As may be provided by law, the district court or a town, village or city court outside the city of New York may transfer any action or proceeding, other than one which has previously been transferred to it, to any court, other than the county court or the surrogate's court or the family court or the supreme court, having jurisdiction of the subject matter in the same or an adjoining county provided that such other court has jurisdiction over the classes of persons named as parties.

j. Each court shall exercise jurisdiction over any action or proceeding transferred to it pursuant to this section.

k. The legislature may provide that the verdict or judgment in actions and proceedings so transferred shall not be subject to the limitation or monetary jurisdiction of the court to which the actions and proceedings are transferred if that limitation be lower than that of the court in which the actions and proceedings were originated.

§ 28.   [Administrative supervision of the courts.]

a. The chief judge of the court of appeals shall be the chief judge of the state of New York and shall be the chief judicial officer of the unified court system. There shall be an administrative board of the courts which shall consist of the chief judge of the court of appeals as chairman and the presiding justice of the appellate division of the supreme court of each judicial department. The chief judge shall, with the advice and consent of the administrative board of the courts, appoint a chief administrator of the courts who shall serve at his pleasure.

b. The chief administrator, on behalf of the chief judge, shall supervise the administration and operation of the unified court system. In the exercise of such responsibility, the chief administrator of the courts shall have such powers and duties as may be delegated to him by the chief judge and such additional powers and duties as may be provided by law.

c. The chief judge, after consultation with the administrative board, shall establish standards and administrative policies for general appli-

App Pract Provs

cation throughout the state, which shall be submitted by the chief judge to the court of appeals, together with the recommendations, if any, of the administrative board. Such standards and administrative policies shall be promulgated after approval by the court of appeals.

§ 35.   [Abolition of certain courts; abolition of referee's office.] [Selections]

a. The children's courts, the court of general sessions of the county of New York, the county courts of the counties of Bronx, Kings, Queens and Richmond, the city court of the city of New York, the domestic relations court of the city of New York, the municipal court of the city of New York, the court of special sessions of the city of New York and the city magistrates' courts of the city of New York are abolished from and after the effective date of this Article and thereupon the seals, records, papers and documents of or belonging to such courts shall, unless otherwise provided by law, be deposited in the offices of the clerks of the several counties in which these courts now exist.

*   *   *

k. The office of official referee is abolished, provided, however, that official referees in office on the effective date of this Article shall, for the remainder of the terms for which they were appointed or certified, be official referees of the court in which appointed or certified or the successor court, as the case may be. At the expiration of the term of any official referee, his office shall be abolished and thereupon such former official referee shall be subject to the relevant provisions of section twenty-five of this article.

BUSINESS CORPORATION LAW

Article 3.   Corporate name and service of process.

§ 304.   Statutory designation of secretary of state as agent for service of process.

(a) The secretary of state shall be the agent of every domestic corporation and every authorized foreign corporation upon whom process against the corporation may be served.

(b) No domestic or foreign corporation may be formed or authorized to do business in this state under this chapter unless in its certificate of incorporation or application for authority it designates the secretary of state as such agent.

(c) Any designation by a domestic or a foreign corporation of the secretary of state as such agent, which designation is in effect on the effective date of this chapter, shall continue. Every domestic or foreign corporation, existing or authorized on the effective date of this chapter, which has not designated the secretary of state as such agent, shall be deemed to have done so. Any designation prior to the effective date of this chapter by a foreign corporation of any agent other than the secretary of state shall terminate on the effective date of this chapter.

(d) Any designated post office address to which the secretary of state shall mail a copy of process served upon him as agent of a domestic corporation or a foreign corporation, shall continue until the filing of a certificate under this chapter directing the mailing to a different post

App Pract Provs

office address.

§ 306. Service of process.

(a) Service of process on a registered agent may be made in the manner provided by law for service of a summons, as if the registered agent was a defendant.

(b) (1) Service of process on the secretary of state as agent of a domestic or authorized foreign corporation shall be made by personally delivering to and leaving with the secretary of state or a deputy, or with any person authorized by the secretary of state to receive such service, at the office of the department of state in the city of Albany, duplicate copies of such process together with the statutory fee, which fee shall be a taxable disbursement. Service of process on such corporation shall be complete when the secretary of state is so served. The secretary of state shall promptly send one of such copies by certified mail, return receipt requested, to such corporation, at the post office address, on file in the department of state, specified for the purpose. If a domestic or authorized foreign corporation has no such address on file in the department of state, the secretary of state shall so mail such copy, in the case of a domestic corporation, in care of any director named in its certificate of incorporation at the director's address stated therein or, in the case of an authorized foreign corporation, to such corporation at the address of its office within this state on file in the department.

(c) If an action or special proceeding is instituted in a court of limited jurisdiction, service of process may be made in the manner provided in this section if the office of the domestic or foreign corporation is within the territorial jurisdiction of the court.

(d) Nothing in this section shall affect the right to serve process in any other manner permitted by law.

§ 306-A. Resignation for receipt of process.

(a) The party (or his/her legal representative) whose post office address has been supplied by a domestic corporation or authorized foreign corporation as its address for process may resign. A certificate entitled "Certificate of Resignation for Receipt of Process under Section 306-A of the Business Corporation Law" shall be signed by such party and delivered to the department of state. It shall set forth:

(1) The name of the corporation and the date that its certificate of incorporation or application of authority was filed by the department of state.

(2) That the address of the party has been designated by the corporation as the post office address to which the secretary of state shall mail a copy of any process served on the secretary of state as agent for such corporation, and that such party wishes to resign.

(3) That sixty days prior to the filing of the certificate of resignation with the department of state the party has sent a copy of the certificate of resignation for receipt of process by registered or certified mail to the address of the registered agent of the designating corporation, if other than the party filing the certificate of resignation, for receipt of process, or if the resigning corporation has no registered agent, then to the last address of the designating corporation known to the party, specifying the address to which the copy was sent. If there is no registered agent and no known address of the designating corporation, the party shall attach an affidavit to the certificate stating that a diligent but unsuccessful search was made by the party to locate the corporation, specifying what efforts were made.

(4) That the designating corporation is required to deliver to the department of state a certificate of amendment or change providing for the designation by the corporation of a new address and that upon its failure to file such certificate, its authority to do business in this state shall be suspended, unless the corporation has previously filed a biennial statement under section four hundred eight of this chapter, in which case the address of the principal executive office stated in the last filed biennial statement shall constitute the new address for process of the corporation, and no such certificate of amendment or change need be filed.

(b) Upon the failure of the designating corporation to file a certificate of amendment or change providing for the designation by the corporation of the new address after the filing of a certificate of resignation for receipt of process with the secretary of state, its authority to do business in this state shall be suspended unless the corporation has previously filed a statement of addresses and directors under section four hundred eight of this chapter, the address of the principal

App Pract
Provs

executive office stated in the last filed statement of addresses and directors shall constitute the new address for process of the corporation, and the corporation shall not be deemed suspended.

(c) The filing by the department of state of a certificate of amendment or change providing for a new address by a designating corporation shall annul the suspension and its authority to do business in this state shall be restored and continue as if no suspension had occurred.

(d) The resignation for receipt of process shall become effective upon the filing by the department of state of a certificate of resignation for receipt of process.

(e) (1) In any case in which a corporation suspended pursuant to this section would be subject to the personal or other jurisdiction of the courts of this state under article three of the civil practice law and rules, process against such corporation may be served upon the secretary of state as its agent pursuant to this section. Such process may issue in any court in this state having jurisdiction of the subject matter.

(2) Service of such process upon the secretary of state shall be made by personally delivering to and leaving with him or his deputy, or with any person authorized by the secretary of state to receive such service, at the office of the department of state in the city of Albany, a copy of such process together with the statutory fee, which fee shall be a taxable disbursement. Such service shall be sufficient if notice thereof and a copy of the process are:

(i) delivered personally within or without this state to such corporation by a person and in manner authorized to serve process by law of the jurisdiction in which service is made, or

(ii) sent by or on behalf of the plaintiff to such corporation by registered or certified mail with return receipt requested to the last address of such corporation known to the plaintiff.

(3) (i) Where service of a copy of process was effected by personal service, proof of service shall be by affidavit of compliance with this section filed, together with the process, within thirty days after such service, with the clerk of the court in which the action or special proceeding is pending. Service of process shall

complete ten days after such papers are filed with the clerk of the court.

(ii) Where service of a copy of process was effected by mailing in accordance with this section, proof of service shall be by affidavit of compliance with this section filed, together with the process, within thirty days after receipt of the return receipt signed by the corporation, or other official proof of delivery or of the original envelope mailed. If a copy of the process is mailed in accordance with this section, there shall be filed with the affidavit of compliance either the return receipt signed by such corporation or other official proof of delivery, if acceptance was refused by it, the original envelope with a notation by the postal authorities that acceptance was refused. If acceptance was refused, a copy of the notice and process together with notice of the mailing by registered or certified mail and refusal to accept shall be promptly sent to such corporation at the same address by ordinary mail and the affidavit of compliance shall so state. Service of process shall be complete ten days after such papers are filed with the clerk of the court. The refusal to accept delivery of the registered or certified mail or to sign the return receipt shall not affect the validity of the service and such corporation refusing to accept such registered or certified mail shall be charged with knowledge of the contents thereof.

(4) Service made as provided in this section without the state shall have the same force as personal service made within this state.

(5) Nothing in this section shall affect the right to serve process in any other manner permitted by law.

§ 307. Service of process on unauthorized foreign corporation.

(a) In any case in which a non-domiciliary would be subject to the personal or other jurisdiction of the courts of this state under Article three of the civil practice law and rules, a foreign corporation not authorized to do business in this state is subject to a like jurisdiction. In any such case, process against such foreign corporation may be served upon the secretary of state as its agent. Such process may issue in any court in this state having jurisdiction of the subject matter.

App Pract Provs

(b) Service of such process upon the secretary of state shall be made by personally delivering to and leaving with him or his deputy, or with any person authorized by the secretary of state to receive such service, at the office of the department of state in the city of Albany, a copy of such process together with the statutory fee, which fee shall be a taxable disbursement. Such service shall be sufficient if notice thereof and a copy of the process are:

(1) Delivered personally without this state to such foreign corporation by a person and in the manner authorized to serve process by law of the jurisdiction in which service is made, or

(2) Sent by or on behalf of the plaintiff to such foreign corporation by registered mail with return receipt requested, at the post office address specified for the purpose of mailing process, on file in the department of state, or with any official or body performing the equivalent function, in the jurisdiction of its incorporation, or if no such address is there specified, to its registered or other office there specified, or if no such office is there specified, to the last address of such foreign corporation known to the plaintiff.

(c) (1) Where service of a copy of process was effected by personal service, proof of service shall be by affidavit of compliance with this section filed, together with the process, within thirty days after such service, with the clerk of the court in which the action or special proceeding is pending. Service of process shall be complete ten days after such papers are filed with the clerk of the court.

(2) Where service of a copy of process was effected by mailing in accordance with this section, proof of service shall be by affidavit of compliance with this section filed, together with the process, within thirty days after receipt of the return receipt signed by the foreign corporation, or other official proof of delivery or of the original envelope mailed. If a copy of the process is mailed in accordance with this section, there shall be filed with the affidavit of compliance either the return receipt signed by such foreign corporation or other official proof of delivery or, if acceptance was refused by it, the original envelope with a notation by the postal authorities that acceptance was refused. If acceptance was refused, a copy of the notice and process together with notice of the mailing by registered mail and refusal to accept shall be promptly sent to such foreign

corporation at the same address by ordinary mail and the affidavit of compliance shall so state. Service of process shall be complete ten days after such papers are filed with the clerk of the court. The refusal to accept delivery of the registered mail or to sign the return receipt shall not affect the validity of the service and such foreign corporation refusing to accept such registered mail shall be charged with knowledge of the contents thereof.

(d) Service made as provided in this section shall have the same force as personal service made within this state.

(e) Nothing in this section shall affect the right to serve process in any other manner permitted by law.

App Pract Provs

COURT OF CLAIMS ACT

Article II.   Jurisdiction.

§ 10.   Time of filing claims and notice of intention to file claims. [Selection]

No judgment shall be granted in favor of any claimant unless such claimant shall have complied with the provisions of this section applicable to his claim.

*   *   *

5. If the claimant shall be under legal disability, the claim may be presented within two years after such disability is removed.

*   *   *

App Pract Provs

CRIMINAL PROCEDURE LAW

SYNOPSIS OF SELECTED PROVISIONS

Article 50. Compulsion of evidence by offer of immunity.

§ 50.10. Compulsion of evidence by offer of immunity; definitions of terms.

The following definitions are applicable to this article:

1. "Immunity." A person who has been a witness in a legal proceeding, and who cannot, except as otherwise provided in this subdivision, be convicted of any offense or subjected to any penalty or forfeiture for or on account of any transaction, matter or thing concerning which he gave evidence therein, possesses "immunity" from any such conviction, penalty or forfeiture. A person who possesses such immunity may nevertheless be convicted of perjury as a result of having given false testimony in such legal proceeding, and may be convicted of or adjudged in contempt as a result of having contumaciously refused to give evidence therein.

2. "Legal proceeding" means a proceeding in or before any court or grand jury, or before any body, agency or person authorized by law to conduct the same and to administer the oath or to cause it to be administered.

3. "Give evidence" means to testify or produce physical evidence.

§ 50.20. Compulsion of evidence by offer of immunity.

1. Any witness in a legal proceeding, other than a grand jury proceeding, may refuse to give evidence requested of him on the ground that it may tend to incriminate him and he may not, except as provided in subdivision two, be compelled to give such evidence.

2. Such a witness may be compelled to give evidence in such a proceeding notwithstanding an assertion of his privilege against self-incrimination if:

(a) The proceeding is one in which, by express provision of statute, a person conducting or connected therewith is declared a competent authority to confer immunity upon witnesses therein; and

(b) Such competent authority

(i) orders such witness to give the requested evidence notwithstanding his assertion of his privilege against self-incrimination, and

(ii) advises him that upon so doing he will receive immunity.

3. A witness who is ordered to give evidence pursuant to subdivision two and who complies with such order receives immunity. Such witness is not deprived of such immunity because such competent authority did not comply with statutory provisions requiring notice to a specified public servant of intention to confer immunity.

4. A witness who, without asserting his privilege against self-incrimination, gives evidence in a legal proceeding other than a grand jury proceeding does not receive immunity.

5. The rules governing the circumstances in which witnesses may be compelled to give evidence and in which they receive immunity therefor in a grand jury proceeding are prescribed in section 190.40.

DEBTOR AND CREDITOR LAW

SYNOPSIS OF SELECTED PROVISIONS

Article 10.   Fraudulent conveyances.

§ 272.   Fair consideration.

Fair consideration is given for property, or obligation,

   a. When in exchange for such property, or obligation, as a fair equivalent therefor, and in good faith, property is conveyed or an antecedant debt is satisfied, or

   b. When such property, or obligation is received in good faith to secure a present advance or antecedent debt in amount not disproportionately small as compared with the value of the property, or obligation obtained.

Article 10-A.   Personal bankruptcy exemptions.

§ 282.   Permissible exemptions in bankruptcy.

Under section five hundred twenty-two of title eleven of the United States Code, entitled "Bankruptcy", an individual debtor domiciled in this state may exempt from the property of the estate, to the extent permitted by subsection (b) thereof, only (i) personal and real property exempt from application to the satisfaction of money judgments under sections fifty-two hundred five and fifty-two hundred six of the civil practice law and rules, (ii) insurance policies and annuity contracts and the proceeds and avails thereof as provided in section three thousand two hundred twelve of the insurance law and (iii) the following property:

1. Bankruptcy exemption of a motor vehicle. One motor vehicle not exceeding twenty-four hundred dollars in value above liens and encumbrances of the debtor.

2. Bankruptcy exemption for right to receive benefits. The debtor's right to receive or the debtor's interest in: (a) a social security benefit, unemployment compensation or a local public assistance benefit; (b) a veterans' benefit; (c) a disability, illness, or unemployment benefit; (d) alimony, support, or separate maintenance, to the extent reasonably necessary for the support of the debtor and any dependent of the debtor; and (e) all payments under a stock bonus, pension, profit sharing, or similar plan or contract on account of illness, disability, death, age, or length of service unless (i) such plan or contract, except those qualified under section 401, 408 or 408A of the United States Internal Revenue Code of 1986, as amended, was established by the debtor or under the auspices of an insider that employed the debtor at the time the debtor's rights under such plan or contract arose, (ii) such plan is on account of age or length of service, and (iii) such plan or contract does not qualify under section four hundred one (a), four hundred three (a), four hundred three (b), four hundred eight, four hundred eight A, four hundred nine or four hundred fifty-seven of the Internal Revenue Code of nineteen hundred eighty-six, as amended.

3. Bankruptcy exemption for right to receive certain property. The debtor's right to receive, or property that is traceable to: (i) an award under a crime victim's reparation law; (ii) a payment on account of the wrongful death of an individual of whom the debtor was a dependent to the extent reasonably necessary for the support of the debtor and any dependent of the debtor; (iii) a payment, not to exceed seventy-five hundred dollars on account of personal bodily injury, not including pain and suffering or compensation for actual pecuniary loss, of the debtor or an individual of whom the debtor is a dependent; and (iv) a payment in compensation of loss of future earnings of the debtor or an individual of whom the debtor is or was a dependent, to the extent reasonably necessary for the support of the debtor and any dependent of the debtor.

§ 283.   Aggregate individual bankruptcy exemption for certain

annuities and personal property.

1. General application. The aggregate amount the debtor may exempt from the property of the estate for personal property exempt from application to the satisfaction of a money judgment under subdivision (a) of section fifty-two hundred five of the civil practice law and rules and for benefits, rights, privileges, and options of annuity contracts described in the following sentence shall not exceed five thousand dollars. Annuity contracts subject to the foregoing limitation are those that are: (a) initially purchased by the debtor within six months of the debtor's filing a petition in bankruptcy, (b) not described in any paragraph of section eight hundred five (d) of the Internal Revenue Code of nineteen hundred fifty-four, and (c) not purchased by application of proceeds under settlement options of annuity contracts purchased more than six months before the debtor's filing a petition in bankruptcy or under settlement options of life insurance policies.

2. Contingent alternative bankruptcy exemption. Notwithstanding section two hundred eighty-two of this article, a debtor, who (a) does not elect, claim, or otherwise avail himself of an exemption described in section fifty-two hundred six of the civil practice law and rules; (b) utilizes to the fullest extent permitted by law as applied to said debtor's property, the exemptions referred to in subdivision one of this section which are subject to the five thousand dollar aggregate limit; and (c) does not reach such aggregate limit, may exempt cash in the amount by which five thousand dollars exceeds the aggregate of his exemptions referred to in subdivision one of this section or in the amount of two thousand five hundred dollars, whichever amount is less. For purposes of this subdivision, cash means currency of the United States at face value, savings bonds of the United States at face value, the right to receive a refund of federal, state and local income taxes, and deposit accounts in any state or federally chartered depository institution.

§ 284. **Exclusivity of exemptions.**

In accordance with the provisions of section five hundred twenty-two (b) of title eleven of the United States Code, debtors domiciled in this state are not authorized to exempt from the estate property that is specified under subsection (d) of such section.

DOMESTIC RELATIONS LAW

SYNOPSIS OF SELECTED PROVISIONS

Article 11-A.   Special provisions relating to divorce and separation.

§ 211.   Pleadings, proof and motions.

A matrimonial action shall be commenced by the filing of a summons with the notice designated in section two hundred thirty-two of this chapter, or a summons and verified complaint as provided in section three hundred four of the civil practice law and rules. A final judgment shall be entered by default for want of appearance or pleading, or by consent, only upon competent oral proof or upon written proof that may be considered on a motion for summary judgment. Where a complaint or counterclaim in an action for divorce or separation charges adultery, the answer or reply thereto may be made without verifying it, except that an answer containing a counterclaim must be verified as to that counterclaim. All other pleadings in a matrimonial action shall be verified.

Article 13.   Provisions applicable to more than one type of matrimonial action.

§ 232.   Notice of nature of matrimonial action; proof of service.

a. In an action to annul a marriage or for divorce or separation, if the complaint is not personally served with the summons, the summons shall have legibly written or printed upon the face thereof: "Action to annul a marriage", "Action to declare the nullity of a void marriage",

"Action for a divorce", or "Action for a separation", as the case may be, and shall specify the nature of any ancillary relief demanded. A judgment shall not be rendered in favor of the plaintiff upon the defendant's default in appearing or pleading, unless either (1) the summons and a copy of the complaint were personally delivered to the defendant; or (2) the copy of the summons (a) personally delivered to the defendant, or (b) served on the defendant pursuant to an order directing the method of service of the summons in accordance with the provisions of section three hundred eight or three hundred fifteen of the civil practice law and rules, shall contain such notice.

b. An affidavit or certificate proving service shall state affirmatively in the body thereof that the required notice was written or printed on the face of the copy of the summons delivered to the defendant and what knowledge the affiant or officer who executed the certificate had that he was the defendant named and how he acquired such knowledge. The court may require the affiant or officer who executed the affidavit or certificate to appear in court and be examined in respect thereto.

§ 236 Part B(4).   Compulsory financial disclosure.*

a. In all matrimonial actions and proceedings in which alimony, maintenance or support is in issue, there shall be compulsory disclosure by both parties of their respective financial states. No showing of special circumstances shall be required before such disclosure is ordered. A sworn statement of net worth shall be provided upon receipt of a notice in writing demanding the same, within twenty days after the receipt thereof. In the event said statement is not demanded, it shall be filed with the clerk of the court by each party, within ten days after joinder of issue, in the court in which the proceeding is pending. As used in this part, the term "net worth" shall mean the amount by which total assets including income exceed total liabilities including fixed financial obligations. It shall include all income and assets of whatsoever kind and nature and wherever situated and shall include a list of all assets transferred in any manner during the preceding three years, or the length of the marriage, whichever is shorter; provided, however that transfers in the routine course of business which resulted in an exchange of assets of substantially equivalent value need not be specifically disclosed where such assets are otherwise identified in the statement of net worth. All such sworn statements of net worth shall be accompanied by a current and representative paycheck stub and the most recently filed state and federal income tax returns including a copy of the W-2(s) wage and tax statement(s) submitted with the returns. In addition, both parties shall provide information relating to any and all group health plans available to them for the provision of care or other medical benefits by insurance or otherwise for the benefit of the child or children for whom support is sought, including all such information as may be required to be included in a qualified medical child support order as defined in section six hundred nine of the employee retirement income security act of 1974 (29 USC 1169) including, but not limited to: (i) the name and last known mailing address of each party and of each dependent to be covered by the order; (ii) the identification and a description of each group health plan available for the benefit or coverage of the disclosing party and the child or children for whom support is sought; (iii) a detailed description of the type of coverage available from each group health plan for the potential benefit of each such dependent; (iv) the identification of the plan administrator for each such group health plan and the address of such administrator; (v) the identification numbers for each such group health plan; and (vi) such other information as may be required by the court. Noncompliance shall be punishable by any or all of the penalties prescribed in section thirty-one hundred twenty-six of the civil practice law and rules, in examination before or during trial.

b. As soon as practicable after a matrimonial action has been commenced, the court shall set the date or dates the parties shall use for the valuation of each asset. The valuation date or dates may be anytime from the date of commencement of the action to the date of trial.

* **[Editor's note:** DRL Part B(4) applies to actions commenced on or after July 19, 1980. Identical provisions, contained in DRL 236 Part A(2), apply to actions commenced on or after September 1, 1975, but before July 19, 1980.]

App Pract Provs

EDUCATION LAW

SYNOPSIS OF SELECTED PROVISIONS

Article 1.   Short title and definitions.

§ 2.   Definitions.

Whenever used in this chapter, the following terms shall have the respective meanings hereinafter set forth or indicated:

*   *   *

13. School officer. The term "school officer" means a clerk, collector, or treasurer of any school district; a trustee; a member of a board of education or other body in control of the schools by whatever name known in a union free school district, central school district, central high school district, or in a city school district; a superintendent of schools; a district superintendent; a supervisor of attendance or attendance officer; or other elective or appointive officer in a school district whose duties generally relate to the administration of affairs connected with the public school system.

App Pract
Provs

ESTATES, POWERS AND TRUSTS LAW

SYNOPSIS OF SELECTED PROVISIONS

Article 7.   Trusts.

Part 2.   Rules governing trustees.

Article 7.   Trusts.

Part 2.   Rules governing trustees.

§ 7-2.3.   Trust estate not to descend on death of trustee; appointment, duties and rights of successor trustee.

(a) On the death of the sole surviving trustee of an express trust, the trust estate does not vest in his personal representative or pass to his distributees or devisees, but, in the absence of a contrary direction by the creator, if the trust has not been executed, the trust estate vests in the supreme court or the surrogate's court, as the case may be, and the trust shall be executed by a person appointed by the court.

(b) Upon such notice to the beneficiaries of the trust as the court may direct of an application for the appointment of a successor trustee, unless the creator has directed otherwise, the court may appoint a successor trustee, even though the trust has terminated, whenever in the opinion of the court such appointment is necessary for the effective administration and distribution of the trust estate, subject to the following:

(1) A successor trustee shall give security in such amount as the court may direct.

(2) A successor trustee shall be subject to the same duties, as to accounting and trust administration, as are imposed by law on trustees and, in addition to the reasonable expenses incurred in the course of trust administration, shall be entitled to such commissions

as may be fixed by any court having jurisdiction to pass upon such trustee's final account, which shall in no case exceed the commissions allowable by law to trustees.

GENERAL ASSOCIATIONS LAW

SYNOPSIS OF SELECTED PROVISIONS

Article 3.   Action or proceeding by or against unincorporated associations.

§ 12.   Action or proceeding by unincorporated association.

An action or special proceeding may be maintained, by the president or treasurer of an unincorporated association to recover any property, or upon any cause of action, for or upon which all the associates may maintain such an action or special proceeding, by reason of their interest or ownership therein, either jointly or in common. An action may likewise be maintained by such president or treasurer to recover from one or more members of such association his or their proportionate share of any moneys lawfully expended by such association for the benefit of such associates, or to enforce any lawful claim of such association against such member or members.

§ 13.   Action or proceeding against unincorporated association.

An action or special proceeding may be maintained, against the president or treasurer of such an association, to recover any property, or upon any cause of action, for or upon which the plaintiff may maintain such an action or special proceeding, against all the associates, by reason of their interest or ownership, or claim of ownership therein, either jointly or in common, or their liability therefor, either jointly or severally. Any partnership, or other company of persons, which has a president or treasurer, is deemed an association within the meaning of this section.

The service of summons, subpoena or other legal process of any court upon the president, vice president, treasurer, assistant treasurer, secretary, assistant secretary, or business agent, in his capacity as such, shall constitute service upon a labor organization. Such service shall be made on such individuals in the manner provided by law for the service of a summons on a natural person.

GENERAL CONSTRUCTION LAW

SYNOPSIS OF SELECTED PROVISIONS

Article 2.   Meaning of terms.

§ 20.   Day, computation.

A number of days specified as a period from a certain day within which or after or before which an act is authorized or required to be done means such number of calendar days exclusive of the calendar day from which the reckoning is made. If such period is a period of two days, Saturday, Sunday or a public holiday must be excluded from the reckoning if it is an intervening day between the day from which the reckoning is made and the last day of the period. In computing any specified period of time from a specified event, the day upon which the event happens is deemed the day from which the reckoning is made. The day from which any specified period of time is reckoned shall be excluded in making the reckoning.

§ 25.   Public holiday, Saturday or Sunday in contractual obligations; extension of time where performance of act authorized or required by contract is due on Saturday, Sunday or public holiday.

1. Where a contract by its terms authorizes or requires the payment of money or the performance of a condition on a Saturday, Sunday or a public holiday, or authorizes or requires the payment of money or the performance of a condition within or before or after a period of time computed from a certain day, and such period of time ends on a Saturday, Sunday or a public holiday, unless the contract expressly or impliedly indicates a different intent, such payment may be made or condition performed on the next succeeding business day, and if the period ends at a specified hour, such payment may be made or condition performed, at or before the same hour of such next succeeding business day, with the same force and effect as if made or performed in accordance with the terms of the contract.

2. Where time is extended by virtue of the provisions of this section, such extended time shall not be included in the computation of interest unless the contract so provides, except that when the period is specified as a number of months, such extended time shall be included in the computation of interest unless the contract otherwise provides.

3. Notwithstanding any other provision of law, all time deposits and certificates of deposit of banking organizations that mature on a Saturday, Sunday or bank holiday shall continue to accrue interest at the same rate fixed for the term of the deposit or certificate until the first banking day next succeeding the date of maturity, at which the principal and all accrued interest may be withdrawn, unless sooner withdrawn by the depositor.

§ 25-a.   Public holiday, Saturday or Sunday in statutes; extension of time where performance of act is due on Saturday, Sunday or public holiday.

1. When any period of time, computed from a certain day, within which or after which or before which an act is authorized or required to be done, ends on a Saturday, Sunday or a public holiday, such act may be done on the next succeeding business day and if the period ends at a specified hour, such act may be done at or before the same hour of

such next succeeding business day, except that where a period of time specified by contract ends on a Saturday, Sunday or a public holiday, the extension of such period is governed by section twenty-five of this chapter.

2. Where time is extended by virtue of the provisions of this section, such extended time shall not be included in the computation of interest, except that when the period is specified as a number of months, such extended time shall be included in the computation of interest.

§ 25-b.   Injury to property.

"Injury to property" is an actionable act, whereby the estate of another is lessened, other than a personal injury, or the breach of a contract.

§ 30.   Month, computation.

A number of months after or before a certain day shall be computed by counting such number of calendar months from such day, exclusive of the calendar month in which such day occurs, and shall include the day of the month in the last month so counted having the same numerical order in days of the month as the day from which the computation is made, unless there be not so many days in the last month so counted, in which case the period computed shall expire with the last day of the month so counted.

§ 31.   Month in statute, contract and public or private instrument.

In a statute, contract or public or private instrument, unless otherwise provided in such contract or instrument or by law, the term month means a calendar month and not a lunar month.

§ 37-a.   Personal injury.

"Personal injury" includes libel, slander and malicious prosecution; also an assault, battery, false imprisonment, or other actionable injury to the person either of the plaintiff, or of another.

§ 58.   Year in statute, contract and public or private instrument.

App Pract Provs

The term year in a statute, contract, or any public or private instrument, means three hundred and sixty-five days, but the added day of a leap year and the day immediately preceding shall for the purpose of such computation be counted as one day. In a statute, contract or public or private instrument, the term year means twelve months, the term half year, six months, and the term a quarter of a year, three months.

§ 60.   Newspapers.

a In any case in which notice of any fact is required by law to be published or advertised in a newspaper, the term "newspaper" shall mean a paper of general circulation which is printed and distributed ordinarily not less frequently than once a week, and has been so for at least one year immediately preceding such publication or advertisement, and which contains news, articles of opinion (as editorials), features, advertising, or other matter regarded as of current interest, has a paid circulation and (except for such a paper which has been printed and distributed not less frequently than once a week for a period of ten years prior to January one, nineteen hundred seventy-five) has been entered at United States post-office as second-class matter. A publication which is distributed or made available primarily for advertising purposes to the public generally without consideration being paid therefor shall not be deemed to be a "newspaper" for the purpose of publication or advertisement of such notice required by law. Notwithstanding any provision of this subdivision to the contrary, a publication which was designated and publishing notice as an official newspaper prior to the year nineteen hundred forty and continued to be so designated and publishing for at least thirty years after such year shall be deemed to be a newspaper within the meaning of this subdivision.

b The terms "daily newspaper" and "newspaper published each business day" in a statute, contract, or any public or private instrument, mean respectively, a newspaper customarily published on each business day of the year, whether or not such newspaper is published on any other day. The term "business day" when used herein does not include Saturdays, Sundays or legal holidays.

c The term "newspaper of a county, city, town or village" when used in a statute shall mean a newspaper published, circulated, printed or distributed in the county, city, town or village.

GENERAL MUNICIPAL LAW

SYNOPSIS OF SELECTED PROVISIONS

Article 4. Negligence and malfeasance of public officers; taxpayers' remedies.

§ 50-e. Notice of claim.

1. When service required; time for service; upon whom service required. (a) In any case founded upon tort where a notice of claim is required by law as a condition precedent to the commencement of an action or special proceeding against a public corporation, as defined in the general construction law, or any officer, appointee or employee thereof, the notice of claim shall comply with and be served in accordance with the provisions of this section within ninety days after the claim arises except that in wrongful death actions, the ninety days shall run from the appointment of a representative of the decedent's estate.

(b) Service of the notice of claim upon an officer, appointee or employee of a public corporation shall not be a condition precedent to the commencement of an action or special proceeding against such person. If an action or special proceeding is commenced against such person, but not against the public corporation, service of the notice of claim upon the public corporation shall be required only if the corporation has a statutory obligation to indemnify such person under this chapter or any other provision of law.

2. Form of notice; contents. The notice shall be in writing, sworn to by or on behalf of the claimant, and shall set forth: (1) the name and post-office address of each claimant, and of his attorney, if any; (2) the

App Pract
Provs

nature of the claim; (3) the time when, the place where and the manner in which the claim arose; and (4) the items of damage or injuries claimed to have been sustained so far as then practicable but a notice with respect to a claim against a municipal corporation other than a city with a population of one million or more persons shall not state the amount of damages to which the claimant deems himself entitled, provided, however, that the municipal corporation, other than a city with a population of one million or more persons, may at any time request a supplemental claim setting forth the total damages to which the claimant deems himself entitled. A supplemental claim shall be provided by the claimant within fifteen days of the request. In the event the supplemental demand is not served within fifteen days, the court, on motion, may order that it be provided by the claimant.

3. How served; when service by mail complete; defect in manner of service; return of notice improperly served. (a) The notice shall be served on the public corporation against which the claim is made by delivering a copy thereof personally, or by registered or certified mail, to the person designated by law as one to whom a summons in an action in the supreme court issued against such corporation may be delivered or to an attorney regularly engaged in representing such public corporation.

(b) Service by registered or certified mail shall be complete upon deposit of the notice of claim, enclosed in a postpaid properly addressed wrapper, in a post office or official depository under the exclusive care and custody of the United States post office department within the state.

(c) If the notice is served within the period specified by this section, but in a manner not in compliance with the provisions of this subdivision, the service shall be valid if the public corporation against which the claim is made demands that the claimant or any other person interested in the claim be examined in regard to it, or if the notice is actually received by a proper person within the time specified by this section, and the public corporation fail to return the notice, specifying the defect in the manner of service, within thirty days after the notice is received.

(d) If the notice is served within the period specified by this section and is returned for the reason and within the time provided in this subdivision, the claimant may serve a new notice in a manner complying with the provisions of this subdivision within ten days after the returned notice is received. If a new notice is so served within that period, it shall be deemed timely served.

4. Requirements of section exclusive except as to conditions precedent to liability for certain defects or snow or ice. No other or further notice, no other or further service, filing or delivery of the notice of claim, and no notice of intention to commence an action or special proceeding, shall be required as a condition to the commencement of an action or special proceeding for the enforcement of the claim; provided, however, that nothing herein contained shall be deemed to dispense with the requirement of notice of the defective, unsafe, dangerous or obstructed condition of any street, highway, bridge, culvert, sidewalk or crosswalk, or of the existence of snow or ice thereon, where such notice now is, or hereafter may be, required by law, as a condition precedent to liability for damages or injuries to person or property alleged to have been caused by such condition, and the failure or negligence to repair or remove the same after the receipt of such notice.

5. Application for leave to serve a late notice.

Upon application, the court, in its discretion, may extend the time to serve a notice of claim specified in paragraph (a) of subdivision one. The extension shall not exceed the time limited for the commencement of an action by the claimant against the public corporation. In determining whether to grant the extension, the court shall consider, in particular, whether the public corporation or its attorney or its insurance carrier acquired actual knowledge of the essential facts constituting the claim within the time specified in subdivision one or within a reasonable time thereafter. The court shall also consider all other relevant facts and circumstances, including: whether the claimant was an infant, or mentally or physically incapacitated, or died before the time limited for service of the notice of claim; whether the claimant failed to serve a timely notice of claim by reason of his justifiable reliance upon settlement representations made by an authorized representative of the public corporation or its insurance carrier; whether the claimant in serving a notice of claim made an excusable error concerning the identity of the public corporation against which the claim should be asserted; and whether the delay in serving the notice of claim substantially prejudiced the public corporation in maintaining its defense on the merits.

An application for leave to serve a late notice shall not be denied on the ground that it was made after commencement of an action against the public corporation.

6. Mistake, omission, irregularity or defect. At any time after the service of a notice of claim and at any stage of an action or special proceeding to which the provisions of this section are applicable, a mistake, omission, irregularity or defect made in good faith in the notice of claim required to be served by this section, not pertaining to the manner or time of service thereof, may be corrected, supplied or disregarded, as the case may be, in the discretion of the court, provided it shall appear that the other party was not prejudiced thereby.

7. Applications under this section. All applications under this section shall be made to the supreme court or to the county court: (a)in a county where the action may properly be brought for trial, (b)if an action to enforce the claim has been commenced, where the action is pending, or (c) in the event that there is no motion term available in any of the counties specified in clause (a) or (b) hereof, in any adjoining county.Where the application is for leave to serve a late notice of claim, it shall be accompanied by a copy of the proposed notice of claim.

8. Inapplicability of section. This section shall not apply to claims arising under the provisions of the workers' compensation law, the volunteer firefighters' benefit law, or the volunteer ambulance workers' benefit law or to claims against public corporations by their own infant wards.

§ 50-h. Examination of claims.

1. Wherever a notice of claim is filed against a city, county, town, village, fire district, ambulance district or school district the city, county, town, village, fire district, ambulance district or school district shall have the right to demand an examination of the claimant relative to the occurrence and extent of the injuries or damages for which claim is made, which examination shall be upon oral questions unless the parties otherwise stipulate and may include

a physical examination of the claimant by a duly qualified physician. If the party to be examined desires, he or she is entitled to have such examination in the presence of his or her own personal physician and such relative or other person as he or she may elect. Exercise of the right to demand a physical examination of the claimant as provided in this section shall in no way affect the right of a city, county, town, village, fire district, ambulance district or school district in a subsequent action brought upon the claim to demand a physical examination of the plaintiff pursuant to statute or court rule.

2. The demand for examination as provided in subdivision one of this section shall be made by the chief executive officer or, where there is no such officer, by the chairman of the governing body of the city, county, town, village, fire district or school district or by such officer, agent or employee as may be designated by him for that purpose. The demand shall be in writing and shall be served personally or by registered or certified mail upon the claimant unless the claimant is represented by an attorney, when it shall be served personally or by mail upon his attorney. The demand shall give reasonable notice of the examination. It shall state the person before whom the examination is to be held, the time, place and subject matter thereof and, if a physical examination is to be required, it shall so state. If the place of examination is located outside the municipality against which the claim is made, the claimant may demand, within ten days of such service, that the examination be held at a location within such municipality. Such location shall be determined by the municipality. If a physical examination is to be required and there is no appropriate place for such an examination within the municipality, such examination shall be given at a location as close to such municipality as practicable. No demand for examination shall be effective against the claimant for any purpose unless it shall be served as provided in this subdivision within ninety days from the date of filing of the notice of claim.

3. In any examination required pursuant to the provisions of this section the claimant shall have the right to be represented by counsel. The examination shall be conducted upon oath or affirmation. The officer or person before whom the examination is had shall take down or cause to be taken down every question and answer unless the parties consent that only the substance of the testimony be

inserted. The testimony so taken, together with the report of the examining physician where a physical examination is required, shall constitute the record of the examination. The transcript of the record of an examination shall not be subject to or available for public inspection, except upon court order upon good cause shown, but shall be furnished to the claimant or his attorney upon request.

4. A transcript of the testimony taken at an examination pursuant to the provisions of this section may be read in evidence by either party, in an action founded upon the claim in connection with which it was taken, at the trial thereof or upon assessment of damages or upon motion. In an action by an executor or administrator to recover damages for a wrongful act, neglect or default by which a decedent's death was caused, the testimony of such decedent taken pursuant to the provisions of this section in respect of such wrongful act, neglect or default may be read in evidence.

5. Where a demand for examination has been served as provided in subdivision two of this section no action shall be commenced against the city, county, town, village, fire district or school district against which the claim is made unless the claimant has duly complied with such demand for examination, which compliance shall be in addition to the requirements of section fifty-e of this chapter. If such examination is not conducted within ninety days of service of the demand, the claimant may commence the action. The action, however, may not be commenced until compliance with the demand for examination if the claimant fails to appear at the hearing or requests an adjournment or postponement beyond the ninety day period. If the claimant requests an adjournment or postponement beyond the ninety day period, the city, county, town, village, fire district or school district shall reschedule the hearing for the earliest possible date available.

§ 50-i.   Presentation of tort claims; commencement of actions.

1. No action or special proceeding shall be prosecuted or maintained against a city, county, town, village, fire district or school district for personal injury, wrongful death or damage to real or personal property alleged to have been sustained by reason of the negligence or wrongful act of such city, county, town, village, fire district or school district or of any officer, agent or employee thereof,

including volunteer firemen of any such city, county, town, village, fire district or school district or any volunteer fireman whose services have been accepted pursuant to the provisions of section two hundred nine-i of this chapter, unless, (a) a notice of claim shall have been made and served upon the city, county, town, village, fire district or school district in compliance with section fifty-e of this chapter, (b) it shall appear by and as an allegation in the complaint or moving papers that at least thirty days have elapsed since the service of such notice and that adjustment or payment thereof has been neglected or refused, and (c) the action or special proceeding shall be commenced within one year and ninety days after the happening of the event upon which the claim is based; except that wrongful death actions shall be commenced within two years after the happening of the death.

2. This section shall be applicable notwithstanding any inconsistent provisions of law, general, special or local, or any limitation contained in the provisions of any city charter.

3. Nothing contained herein or in section fifty-h of this chapter shall operate to extend the period limited by subdivision one of this section for the commencement of an action or special proceeding.

4. (a) Notwithstanding any other provision of law to the contrary, including any other subdivision of this section, section fifty-e of this article, section thirty-eight hundred thirteen of the education law, and the provisions of any general, special or local law or charter requiring as a condition precedent to commencement of an action or special proceeding that a notice of claim be filed or presented, any cause of action against a public corporation for personal injuries suffered by a participant in World Trade Center rescue, recovery or cleanup operations as a result of such participation which is barred as of the effective date of this subdivision because the applicable period of limitation has expired is hereby revived, and a claim thereon may be filed and served and prosecuted provided such claim is filed and served within one year of the effective date of this subdivision.

(b) For the purposes of this subdivision:

(1) "participant in World Trade Center rescue, recovery or

cleanup operations" means any employee or volunteer that:

(i) participated in the rescue, recovery or cleanup operations at the World Trade Center site; or

(ii) worked at the Fresh Kills Land Fill in the city of New York after September eleventh, two thousand one; or

(iii) worked at the New York city morgue or the temporary morgue on pier locations on the west side of Manhattan after September eleventh, two thousand one; or

(iv) worked on the barges between the west side of Manhattan and the Fresh Kills Land Fill in the city of New York after September eleventh, two thousand one.

(2) "World Trade Center site" means anywhere below a line starting from the Hudson River and Canal Street; east on Canal Street to Pike Street; south on Pike Street to the East River; and extending to the lower tip of Manhattan.

GENERAL OBLIGATIONS LAW

Article 5.   Creation, definition and enforcement of contractual obligations.

Title 14.   Enforceability of clauses respecting choice of law and choice of forum in certain transactions.

§ 5-1401.   Choice of law.

1. The parties to any contract, agreement or undertaking, contingent or otherwise, in consideration of, or relating to any obligation arising out of a transaction covering in the aggregate not less than two hundred fifty thousand dollars, including a transaction otherwise covered by subsection one of section 1-105 of the uniform commercial code, may agree that the law of this state shall govern their rights and duties in

whole or in part, whether or not such contract, agreement or undertaking bears a reasonable relation to this state. This section shall not apply to any contract, agreement or undertaking (a) for labor or personal services, (b) relating to any transaction for personal, family or household services, or (c) to the extent provided to the contrary in subsection two of section 1-105 of the uniform commercial code.

2. Nothing contained in this section shall be construed to limit or deny the enforcement of any provision respecting choice of law in any other contract, agreement or undertaking.

§ 5-1402. Choice of forum.

1. Notwithstanding any act which limits or affects the right of a person to maintain an action or proceeding, including, but not limited to, paragraph (b) of section thirteen hundred fourteen of the business corporation law and subdivision two of section two hundred-b of the banking law, any person may maintain an action or proceeding against a foreign corporation, non-resident, or foreign state where the action or proceeding arises out of or relates to any contract, agreement or undertaking for which a choice of New York law has been made in whole or in part pursuant to section 5-1401 and which (a) is a contract, agreement or undertaking, contingent or otherwise, in consideration of, or relating to any obligation arising out of a transaction covering in the aggregate, not less than one million dollars, and (b) which contains a provision or provisions whereby such foreign corporation or non-resident agrees to submit to the jurisdiction of the courts of this state.

2. Nothing contained in this section shall be construed to affect the enforcement of any provision respecting choice of forum in any other contract, agreement or undertaking.

Article 7. Obligations relating to property received as security.

Title 3. Bonds and undertakings.

§ 7-301. Liability of surety on an undertaking.

When any undertaking executed within or without the state specifies that it is to be void upon payment of an amount or performance of an act, the undertaking shall be deemed to contain a covenant either to pay the amount or to perform the act specified. In the event of payment, the amount recoverable from a surety shall not exceed the amount specified in the undertaking except that interest in addition to this amount shall be awarded from the time of default by the surety.

Article 15.   Modification and discharge of obligations.
Title 1.   Discharge of joint obligors.
§ 15-102.   Co-obligor not a party.

A judgment against one or more of several obligors, or against one or more of joint, or of joint and several obligors shall not discharge a co-obligor who was not a party to the proceeding wherein the judgment was rendered.

§ 15-108.   Release or covenant not to sue.

(a) Effect of release of or covenant not to sue tortfeasors. When a release or a covenant not to sue or not to enforce a judgment is given to one of two or more persons liable or claimed to be liable in tort for the same injury, or for the same wrongful death, it does not discharge any of the other tortfeasors from liability for the injury or wrongful death unless its terms expressly so provide, but it reduces the claim of the releasor against the other tortfeasors to the extent of any amount stipulated by the release or the covenant, or in the amount of the consideration paid for it or in the amount of the released tortfeasor's equitable share of the damages under Article fourteen of the civil practice law and rules, whichever is the greatest.

(b) Release of tortfeasor. A release given in good faith by the injured person to one tortfeasor as provided in subdivision (a) relieves him from liability to any other person for contribution as provided in Article fourteen of the civil practice law and rules.

(c) Waiver of contribution. A tortfeasor who has obtained his own release from liability shall not be entitled to contribution from any other person.

(d) Releases and covenants within the scope of this section. A release or a covenant not to sue between a plaintiff or claimant and a person who is liable or claimed to be liable in tort shall be deemed a release or covenant for the purposes of this section only if:

(1) the plaintiff or claimant receives, as part of the agreement, monetary consideration greater than one dollar;

(2) the release or covenant completely or substantially terminates the dispute between the plaintiff or claimant and the person who was claimed to be liable; and

(3) such release or covenant is provided prior to entry of judgment.

Article 17. Revival or extension; waiver of defense or bar.

Title 1. Obligations barred by statutes of limitation.

§ 17-101. Acknowledgment or new promise must be in writing.

An acknowledgment or promise contained in a writing signed by the party to be charged thereby is the only competent evidence of a new or continuing contract whereby to take an action out of the operation of the provisions of limitations of time for commencing actions under the civil practice law and rules other than an action for the recovery of real property. This section does not alter the effect of a payment of principal or interest.

§ 17-103. Agreements waiving the statute of limitation.

1. A promise to waive, to extend, or not to plead the statute of limitation applicable to an action arising out of a contract express or implied in fact or in law, if made after the accrual of the cause of action and made, either with or without consideration, in a writing signed by the promisor or his agent is effective, according to its terms, to prevent interposition of the defense of the statute of limitation in an action or proceeding commenced within the time that would be applicable if the cause of action had arisen at the date of the promise, or within such shorter time as may be provided in the promise.

2. A promise to waive, to extend, or not to plead the statute of limitation may be enforced as provided in this section by the person to whom the promise is made or for whose benefit it is expressed to be made or by any person who, after the making of the promise, succeeds or is subrogated to the interest of either of them.

3. A promise to waive, to extend, or not to plead the statute of limitation has no effect to extend the time limited by statute for commencement of an action or proceeding for any greater time or in any other manner than that provided in this section, or unless made as

provided in this section.

4. This section

a. does not change the requirements of the effect with respect to the statute of limitation, of an acknowledgment or promise to pay, or a payment or part payment of principal or interest, or a stipulation made in an action or proceeding;

b. does not affect the power of the court to find that by reason of conduct of the party to be charged it is inequitable to permit him to interpose the defense of the statute of limitation; and

c. does not apply in any respect to a cause of action to foreclose a mortgage of real property or a mortgage of a lease of real property, or to a cause of action to recover a judgment affecting the title to or the possession, use or enjoyment of real property, or a promise or waiver with respect to any statute of limitation applicable thereto.

App Pract
Provs

INSURANCE LAW

SYNOPSIS OF SELECTED PROVISIONS

Article 34. Insurance contracts—property/casualty.

§ 3420. Liability insurance; standard provisions; right of injured person [Selections].

*   *   *

(g) No policy or contract shall be deemed to insure against any liability of an insured because of death of or injuries to his or her spouse or because of injury to, or destruction of property of his or her spouse unless express provision relating specifically thereto is included in the policy as provided in paragraphs one and two of this subsection. This exclusion shall apply only where the injured spouse, to be entitled to recover, must prove the culpable conduct of the insured spouse.

(1) Upon written request of an insured, and upon payment of a reasonable premium established in accordance with article twenty-three of this chapter, an insurer issuing or delivering any policy that satisfies the requirements of article six of the vehicle and traffic law shall provide coverage against liability of an insured because of death of or injuries to his or her spouse up to the liability insurance limits provided under such policy even where the injured spouse, to be entitled to recover, must prove the culpable conduct of the insured

App Pract
Provs

spouse. Such insurance coverage shall be known as "supplemental spousal liability insurance".

(2) Upon issuance of a motor vehicle liability policy that satisfies the requirements of article six of the vehicle and traffic law and that becomes effective on or after January first, two thousand three, pursuant to regulations promulgated by the superintendent, the insurer shall notify the insured, in writing, of the availability of supplemental spousal liability insurance. Such notification shall be contained on the front of the premium notice in boldface type and include a concise statement that supplementary spousal coverage is available, an explanation of such coverage, and the insurer's premium for such coverage. Subsequently, a notification of the availability of supplementary spousal liability coverage shall be provided at least once a year in motor vehicle liability policies issued pursuant to article six of the vehicle and traffic law, including those originally issued prior to January first, two thousand three. Such notice must include a concise statement that supplementary spousal coverage is available, an explanation of such coverage, and the insurer's premium for such coverage.

Article 51. Comprehensive motor vehicle insurance reparations [No-fault] [Selections].

§ 5102. Definitions.

In this chapter:

(a) "Basic economic loss" means, up to fifty thousand dollars per person of the following combined items, subject to the limitations of section five thousand one hundred eight of this article:

(1) All necessary expenses incurred for: (i) medical, hospital (including services rendered in compliance with article forty-one of the public health law, whether or not such services are rendered directly by a hospital), surgical, nursing, dental, ambulance, x-ray, prescription drug and prosthetic services; (ii) psychiatric, physical therapy (provided that treatment is rendered pursuant to a referral) and occupational therapy and rehabilitation; (iii) any non-medical remedial care and treatment rendered in accordance with a religious method of healing recognized by the laws of this state; and (iv) any other professional health services; all without

limitation as to time, provided that within one year after the date of the accident causing the injury it is ascertainable that further expenses may be incurred as a result of the injury. For the purpose of determining basic economic loss, the expenses incurred under this paragraph shall be in accordance with the limitations of section five thousand one hundred eight of this article.

(2) Loss of earnings from work which the person would have performed had he not been injured, and reasonable and necessary expenses incurred by such person in obtaining services in lieu of those that he would have performed for income, up to two thousand dollars per month for not more than three years from the date of the accident causing the injury. An employee who is entitled to receive monetary payments, pursuant to statute or contract with the employer, or who receives voluntary monetary benefits paid for by the employer, by reason of the employee's inability to work because of personal injury arising out of the use or operation of a motor vehicle, is not entitled to receive first party benefits for "loss of earnings from work" to the extent that such monetary payments or benefits from the employer do not result in the employee suffering a reduction in income or a reduction in the employee's level of future benefits arising from a subsequent illness or injury.

(3) All other reasonable and necessary expenses incurred, up to twenty-five dollars per day for not more than one year from the date of the accident causing the injury.

(4) "Basic economic loss" shall not include any loss incurred on account of death; subject, however, to the provisions of paragraph four of subsection (a) of section five thousand one hundred three of this article.

(5) "Basic economic loss" shall also include an additional option to purchase, for an additional premium, an additional twenty-five thousand dollars of coverage which the insured or his legal representative may specify will be applied to loss of earnings from work and/or psychiatric, physical or occupational therapy and rehabilitation after the initial fifty thousand dollars of basic economic loss has been exhausted. This optional additional coverage shall be made available and notice with explanation of

App Pract
Provs

such coverage shall be provided by an insurer at the first policy renewal after the effective date of this paragraph, or at the time of application.

(b) "First party benefits" means payments to reimburse a person for basic economic loss on account of personal injury arising out of the use or operation of a motor vehicle, less:

(1) Twenty percent of lost earnings computed pursuant to paragraph two of subsection (a) of this section.

(2) Amounts recovered or recoverable on account of such injury under state or federal laws providing social security disability benefits, or workers' compensation benefits, or disability benefits under Article nine of the workers' compensation law, or medicare benefits, other than lifetime reserve days and provided further that the medicare benefits utilized herein do not result in a reduction of such person's medicare benefits for a subsequent illness or injury.

(3) Amounts deductible under the applicable insurance policy.

(c) "Non-economic loss" means pain and suffering and similar nonmonetary detriment.

(d) "Serious injury" means a personal injury which results in death; dismemberment; significant disfigurement; a fracture; loss of a fetus; permanent loss of use of a body organ, member, function or system; permanent consequential limitation of use of a body organ or member; significant limitation of use of a body function or system; or a medically determined injury or impairment of a non-permanent nature which prevents the injured person from performing substantially all of the material acts which constitute such person's usual and customary daily activities for not less than ninety days during the one hundred eighty days immediately following the occurrence of the injury or impairment.

(e) "Owner" means an owner as defined in section one hundred twenty-eight of the vehicle and traffic law.

(f) "Motor vehicle" means a motor vehicle as defined in section three hundred eleven of the vehicle and traffic law and also includes fire and police vehicles. It shall not include any motor vehicle not required to carry financial security pursuant to Article six, eight or forty-eight-A of the vehicle and traffic law or a motorcycle, as defined in subsection (m) hereof.

(g) "Insurer" means the insurance company or self-insurer, as the case may be, which provides the financial security required by Article six or eight of the vehicle and traffic law.

(h) "Member of his household" means a spouse, child or relative of the named insured who regularly resides in his household.

(i) "Uninsured motor vehicle" means a motor vehicle, the owner of which is (i) a financially irresponsible motorist as defined in subsection (j) of section five thousand two hundred two of this chapter or (ii) unknown and whose identity is unascertainable.

(j) "Covered person" means any pedestrian injured through the use or operation of, or any owner, operator or occupant of, a motor vehicle which has in effect the financial security required by Article six or eight of the vehicle and traffic law or which is referred to in subdivision two of section three hundred twenty-one of such law; or any other person entitled to first party benefits.

(k) "Bus" means both a bus and a school bus as defined in sections one hundred four and one hundred forty-two of the vehicle and traffic law.

(l) "Compensation provider" means the state insurance fund, or the person, association, corporation or insurance carrier or statutory fund liable under state or federal laws for the payment of workers' compensation benefits or disability benefits under Article nine of the workers' compensation law.

(m) "Motorcycle" means any motorcycle, as defined in section one hundred twenty-three of the vehicle and traffic law, and which is required to carry financial security pursuant to Article six, eight or forty-eight-A of the vehicle and traffic law.

*   *   *

§ 5103.   Entitlement to first party benefits; additional financial security required.

(a) Every owner's policy of liability insurance issued on a motor vehicle in satisfaction of the requirements of Article six or eight of the vehicle and traffic law shall also provide for; every owner who maintains another form of financial security on a motor vehicle in satisfaction of the requirements of such articles shall be liable for; and every owner of a motor vehicle required to be subject to the provisions of this Article by subdivision two of section three hundred twenty-one of the vehicle and traffic law shall be liable for; the payment of first party benefits to:

(1) Persons, other than occupants of another motor vehicle or a motorcycle, for loss arising out of the use or operation in this state of such motor vehicle. In the case of occupants of a bus other than operators, owners, and employees of the owner or operator of the bus, the coverage for first party benefits shall be afforded under the policy or policies, if any, providing first party benefits to the injured person and members of his household for loss arising out of the use or operation of any motor vehicle of such household. In the event there is no such policy, first party benefits shall be provided by the insurer of such bus.

(2) The named insured and members of his household, other than occupants of a motorcycle, for loss arising out of the use or operation of (i) an uninsured motor vehicle or motorcycle, within the United States, its territories or possessions, or Canada; and (ii) an insured motor vehicle or motorcycle outside of this state and within the United States, its territories or possessions, or Canada.

(3) Any New York resident who is neither the owner of a motor vehicle with respect to which coverage for first party benefits is required by this Article nor, as a member of a household, is entitled to first party benefits under paragraph two of this subsection, for loss arising out of the use or operation of the insured or self-insured motor vehicle outside of this state and within the United States, its territories or possessions, or Canada.

(4) The estate of any covered person, other than an occupant of another motor vehicle or a motorcycle, a death benefit in the amount of two thousand dollars for the death of such person arising out of the use or operation of such motor vehicle which is in addition to any first party benefits for basic economic loss.

(b) An insurer may exclude from coverage required by subsection (a) hereof a person who:

(1) Intentionally causes his own injury.

(2) Is injured as a result of operating a motor vehicle while in an intoxicated condition or while his ability to operate such vehicle is impaired by the use of a drug within the meaning of section eleven hundred ninety-two of the vehicle and traffic law.

(3) Is injured while he is: (i) committing an act which would constitute a felony, or seeking to avoid lawful apprehension or arrest by a law enforcement officer, or (ii) operating a motor vehicle in a race or speed test, or (iii) operating or occupying a motor vehicle known to him to be stolen, or (iv) operating or occupying any motor vehicle owned by such injured person with respect to which the coverage required by subsection (a) hereof is not in effect, or (v) a pedestrian, through being struck by any motor vehicle owned by such injured pedestrian with respect to which the coverage required by subsection (a) hereof is not in effect, or (vi) repairing, servicing or otherwise maintaining a motor vehicle if such conduct is within the course of a business of repairing, servicing or otherwise maintaining a motor vehicle and the injury occurs on the business premises.

(c) Insurance offered by any insurer to satisfy the requirements of subsection (a) of this section shall be offered: (1) without a deductible; and (2) with a family deductible of up to two hundred dollars (which deductible shall apply only to the loss of the named insured and members of that household). The superintendent may approve a higher deductible in the case of insurance policies providing additional benefits or pursuant to a plan designed and implemented to coordinate first party benefits with other benefits. The superintendent may approve appropriate deductible or co-insurance provisions for medical and other health care services provided through approved managed care programs.

(d) Insurance policy forms for insurance to satisfy the requirements of subsection (a) hereof shall be subject to approval pursuant to Article twenty-three of this chapter. Minimum benefit standards for such policies and for self-insurers, and rights of subrogation, exami-

App Pract Provs

nation and other such matters, shall be established by regulation pursuant to section three hundred one of this chapter.

(e) Every owner's policy of liability insurance issued in satisfaction of Article six or eight of the vehicle and traffic law shall also provide, when a motor vehicle covered by such policy is used or operated in any other state or in any Canadian province, insurance coverage for such motor vehicle at least in the minimum amount required by the laws of that state or province.

(f) Every owner's policy of liability insurance issued on a motor-cycle or an all terrain vehicle in satisfaction of the requirements of Article six or eight of the vehicle and traffic law or section twenty-four hundred seven of such law shall also provide for; every owner who maintains another form of financial security on a motorcycle or an all terrain vehicle in satisfaction of the requirements of such articles or section shall be liable for; and every owner of a motorcycle or an all terrain vehicle required to be subject to the provisions of this Article by subdivision two of section three hundred twenty-one of such law shall be liable for; the payment of first party benefits to persons, other than the occupants of such motorcycle or all terrain vehicle, another motorcycle or all terrain vehicle, or any motor vehicle, for loss arising out of the use or operation of the motorcycle or all terrain vehicle within this state. Every insurer and self-insurer may exclude from the coverage required by this subsection a person who intentionally causes his own injury or is injured while committing an act which would constitute a felony or while seeking to avoid lawful apprehension or arrest by a law enforcement officer.

(g) A company authorized to provide the insurance specified in paragraph three of subsection (a) of section one thousand one hundred thirteen of this chapter or a corporation organized pursuant to Article forty-three of this chapter may, individually or jointly, with the approval of the superintendent upon a showing that the company or corporation is qualified to provide for all of the items of basic economic loss specified in paragraph one of subsection (a) of section five thousand one hundred two of this article, provide coverage for such items of basic economic loss to the extent that an insurer would be required to provide under this article. Where a policyholder elects to be covered under such an arrangement the insurer providing coverage for the automobile shall be furnished with the names of all persons covered by the company or corporation under the arrangement and such persons shall not be entitled to benefits for any of the items of basic economic loss specified in such paragraph. The premium for the automobile insurance policy shall be appropriately reduced to reflect the elimination of coverage for such items of basic economic loss. Coverage by the automobile insurer of such eliminated items shall be effected or restored upon request by the insured and payment of the premium for such coverage. All companies and corporations providing coverage for items of basic economic loss pursuant to the authorization of this subsection shall have only those rights and obligations which are applicable to an insurer subject to this article.

(h) Any policy of insurance obtained to satisfy the financial security requirements of Article six or eight of the vehicle and traffic law which does not contain provisions complying with the requirements of this article, shall be construed as if such provisions were embodied therein.

*   *   *

§ 5104.   Causes of action for personal injury.

(a) Notwithstanding any other law, in any action by or on behalf of a covered person against another covered person for personal injuries arising out of negligence in the use or operation of a motor vehicle in this state, there shall be no right of recovery for non-economic loss, except in the case of a serious injury, or for basic economic loss. The owner, operator or occupant of a motorcycle which has in effect the financial security required by Article six or eight of the vehicle and traffic law, or which is referred to in subdivision two of section three hundred twenty-one of such law, shall not be subject to an action by or on behalf of a covered person for recovery for non-economic loss, except in the case of a serious injury, or for basic economic loss.

(b) In any action by or on behalf of a covered person, against a non-covered person, where damages for personal injuries arising out of the use or operation of a motor vehicle or a motorcycle may be recovered, an insurer which paid or is liable for first party benefits on account of such injuries has a lien against any recovery to the extent of benefits paid or payable by it to the covered person. No such action may be compromised by the covered person except with the written consent of the insurer, or with the approval of the court, or where the amount of such settlement exceeds fifty thousand dollars. The failure of such person to commence such action within two years after accrual gives the insurer a cause of action for the amount of first party benefits paid or payable against any person who may be liable to the covered person for his personal injuries. The insurer's cause of action shall be in addition to the cause of action of the covered person except that in any action subsequently commenced by the covered person for such injuries, the amount of his basic economic loss shall not be recoverable.

(c) Where there is no right of recovery for basic economic loss, such loss may nevertheless be pleaded and proved to the extent that it is relevant to the proof of non-economic loss.

§ 5108.   Limit on charges by providers of health services.

(a) The charges for services specified in paragraph one of subsection (a) of section five thousand one hundred two of this Article and any further health service charges which are incurred as a result of the injury and which are in excess of basic economic loss, shall not exceed the charges permissible under the schedules prepared and established by the chairman of the workers' compensation board for industrial accidents, except where the insurer or arbitrator determines that unusual procedures or unique circumstances justify the excess charge.

(b) The superintendent, after consulting with the chairman of the workers' compensation board and the commissioner of health, shall promulgate rules and regulations implementing and coordinating the provisions of this Article and the workers' compensation law with respect to charges for the professional health services specified in paragraph one of subsection (a) of section five thousand one hundred two of this article, including the establishment of schedules for all such services for which schedules have not been prepared and established by the chairman of the workers' compensation board. Payments for medical and other health care services provided by managed care organizations pursuant to managed care programs approved pursuant to paragraph one of subsection (i) of section five thousand one hundred three of this Article shall not exceed amounts otherwise payable by application of the fee schedules established by the superintendent or the chair of the workers' compensation board.

(c) No provider of health services specified in paragraph one of subsection (a) of section five thousand one hundred two of this Article may demand or request any payment in addition to the charges authorized pursuant to this section. Every insurer shall report to the commissioner of health any patterns of overcharging, excessive treatment or other improper actions by a health provider within thirty days after such insurer has knowledge of such pattern.

App Pract Provs

JUDICIARY LAW

SYNOPSIS OF SELECTED PROVISIONS

App Pract
Provs

Article 2.   General provisions relating to courts and judges.

§ 2.   Courts of record.

Each of the following courts of the state is a court of record:

1. The court for the trial of impeachments.

2. A court of the judiciary.

3. The court of appeals.

4. The appellate division of the supreme court in each department.

5. The supreme court.

6. The court of claims.

7. A county court in each county, except the counties of New York, Bronx, Kings, Queens, and Richmond.

8. The family court.

9. A surrogate's court in each county.

10. Each city court outside the city of New York.

11. The district court in each county or portion thereof in which such court shall be established.

12. The civil court of the city of New York and the criminal court of the city of New York.

All courts other than those specified in this section are courts not of record.

§ 2-b.   General powers of courts of record.

A court of record has power

1. to issue a subpoena requiring the attendance of a person found in the state to testify in a cause pending in that court, subject, however, to the limitations prescribed by law with respect to the portion of the state in which the process of the local court of record may be served;

2. to administer an oath to a witness in the exercise of the powers and duties of the court and;

3. to devise and make new process and forms of proceedings, necessary to carry into effect the powers and jurisdiction possessed by it.

§ 7-c.   Continuance of special proceeding before another officer.

In case of the death, sickness, resignation, removal from office, absence from the county, or other disabililty of an officer before whom or in whose court a special proceeding has been instituted, where no express provision is made by law for the continuance thereof, it may be continued before or in the court of

1. the officer's successor, or

2. if there is no successor capable of acting, any other officer residing in the same county before whom it might have been originally instituted, or

3. if there is neither a successor nor an officer specified in paragraph two capable of acting, an officer in an adjoining county who would originally have had jurisdiction of the subject matter had it occurred or existed in the latter county. An officer substituted, as prescribed by law, to continue a special proceeding instituted before another, may exercise all powers in the special proceeding, as if it had been originally instituted before him.

§ 35-a.   Statements to be filed by judges or justices fixing or approving fees, commissions or other compensation for persons appointed by courts to perform services in actions and proceedings.

1. (a) On the first business day of each week any judge or justice who has during the preceding week fixed or approved one or more fees or allowances of more than five hundred dollars for services performed by any person appointed by the court in any capacity, including but not limited to appraiser, special guardian, guardian ad litem, general guardian, referee, counsel, special referee, auctioneer, special examiner, conservator, committee of incompetent or receiver, shall file a statement with the office of court administration on a form to be prescribed by the state administrator. The statement shall show the name and address of the appointee, the county and the title of the court in which the services of the appointee were performed, the court docket index or file number assigned to the

action or proceeding, if any, the title of the action or proceeding, the nature of the action or proceeding, the name of the judge or justice who appointed the person, the person or interest which the appointee represented, whether or not the proceeding was contested, the fee fixed or approved by the judge or justice, the gross value of the subject matter of the proceeding, the number of hours spent by the appointee in performing the service, the nature of the services performed and such other information relating to the appointment as the state administrator shall require. The judge or justice shall certify that the fee, commission, allowance or other compensation fixed or approved is a reasonable award for the services rendered by the appointee, or is fixed by statute. If the fee, commission, allowance or other compensation for services performed pursuant to an appointment described in this section is either specified as to amount by statute or fixed by statute as a percentage of the value of the subject matter of the action or proceeding, the judge or justice shall specify the statutory fee, commission or allowance and shall specify the section of the statute authorizing the payment of the fee, commission, allowance or other compensation.

(b) Paragraph (a) shall not apply to any compensation awarded to appointees assigned to represent indigent persons pursuant to Article 18-B of the county law, counsel assigned pursuant to section thirty-five of the judiciary law, law guardians or counsel appointed pursuant to the family court act, or referees appointed pursuant to section 78.25 of the mental hygiene law.

(c) Any judge or justice who fixes or approves compensation for services performed by persons appointed as referees to examine accounts of incompetents pursuant to section 78.25 of the mental hygiene law shall file, annually, with the office of court administration a statement containing such information regarding such appointments as the state administrator shall require.

2. The office of court administration shall annually submit to the appellate division of the supreme court in each of the judicial departments of the state a report containing a summary of the information contained in the statements filed with it pursuant to this section by the judges and justices sitting in courts in that department during the preceding year. Each appellate division of the supreme court

shall keep and file such reports and shall have power to make such rules respecting the supervision of all such court appointees within its judicial department as it may deem necessary.

3. The statements and reports required by this section shall be matters of public record and available for public inspection. Each court may permit the information contained therein to be made available for publication at such times and in such manner as it may deem proper.

Article 5. Supreme court.

§ 140-b. General jurisdiction of supreme court.

The general jurisdiction in law and equity which the supreme court possesses under the provisions of the constitution includes all the jurisdiction which was possessed and exercised by the supreme court of the colony of New York at any time, and by the court of chancery in England on the fourth day of July, seventeen hundred seventy-six, with the exceptions, additions and limitations created and imposed by the constitution and laws of the state. Subject to those exceptions and limitations the supreme court of the state has all the powers and authority of each of those courts and may exercise them in like manner.

§ 148-a. [Repealed].

Article 7. County court.

§ 190. Jurisdiction of county court.

The jurisdiction of each county court, except the county courts of counties within the city of New York, extends to the following actions and special proceedings, in addition to the jurisdiction, power and authority conferred upon a county court in a particular case by special statutory provision:

1. An action for the partition of real property, for dower, for the foreclosure, redemption or satisfaction of a mortgage upon real property, for the foreclosure of a lien arising out of a contract for the sale of real property, for specific performance of a contract relating to real property, for the enforcement or foreclosure of a mechanic's lien on real property, for reformation or rescission of a deed, contract or mortgage affecting real property, or to compel the determination of a claim to real property under Article fifteen of the real property

App Pract Provs

actions and proceedings law, where the real property to which the action relates is situated within the county; or to foreclose a lien upon a chattel in a case specified in section two hundred six of the lien law where the lien does not exceed twenty-five thousand dollars in amount and the chattel is found within the county.

2. An action in favor of the executor, administrator or assignee of a judgment creditor, or in a proper case in favor of the judgment creditor, to recover a judgment for money remaining due upon a judgment rendered in the same court.

3. An action for any other cause, where the defendant, or if there are two or more defendants, where all of them, at the time of the commencement of the action, reside in the county, or where a defendant has an office for the transaction of business within the county and the cause of action arose therein, or where the defendant is a foreign corporation that is doing business within the county and the cause of action arose therein and where the complaint in such action demands judgment for a sum of money only not exceeding twenty-five thousand dollars; or to recover one or more chattels the aggregate value of which does not exceed twenty-five thousand dollars with or without damages for the taking or detention thereof.

4. The custody of the person and the care of the property, concurrently with the supreme court, of a resident of the county who is adjudicated incompetent to manage his affairs by reason of age, drunkenness, mental illness or other cause or for whom a conservator has been appointed; and any special proceeding which the supreme court has jurisdiction to entertain for the appointment of a committee of the person or of the property of such an incompetent person or conservatee or for the sale or other disposition of the real property situated within the county of a person wherever resident who is incompetent, who is a conservatee, or who is an infant, or for the sale or other disposition of the real property, situated within the county, of a domestic religious corporation.

5. Notwithstanding any other provision of law to the contrary, any proceeding which the supreme court has jurisdiction to entertain to review the actions or determinations of the state board of parole.

6. An action for any claim against a restitution fund established by

such court resulting from its criminal jurisdiction.

§ 190-a. When domestic or foreign corporation or joint-stock association deemed resident.

For the purpose of determining jurisdiction under section one hundred ninety, a domestic corporation or joint-stock association is deemed a resident of a county in which its principal place of business is established by or pursuant to a statute or by its articles of association, or in which its principal place of business or any part of its plant, shops, factories or offices is actually located, or in the case of a railroad corporation, in which any portion of the road operated by it is located, and a foreign corporation is to be deemed a resident of a county if it maintains any plant, store, office, warehouse or other facility for doing business within such county; and personal service of a paper by which an action or special proceeding is commenced, made within the county, as prescribed in the civil practice law and rules, is sufficient service thereof upon a domestic corporation wherever it is located.

§ 190-b. Power of county court and county judge co-extensive with that of supreme court and supreme court justice.

1. Where a county court has jurisdiction of an action or a special proceeding, it possesses the same jurisdiction, power and authority in and over the same, and in the course of the proceedings therein, that the supreme court possesses in a like case; and it may render any judgment or grant either party any relief that the supreme court may render or grant in a like case, and may send its process and other mandates into any county of the state for service or execution and enforce obedience thereto in the same manner as the supreme court.

2. The county judge possesses the same power and authority in such action or special proceeding that a justice of the supreme court possesses in a like action or special proceeding brought in the supreme court.

3. The county judge possesses the same power and authority in a special proceeding which can be lawfully instituted before him out of court that a justice of the supreme court possesses in a like special proceeding instituted before him out of court.

Article 19.   Contempts (selections).

§ 756.   Application to punish for contempt; procedure.

An application to punish for a contempt punishable civilly may be commenced by notice of motion returnable before the court or judge authorized to punish for the offense, or by an order of such court or judge requiring the accused to show cause before it, or him, at a time and place therein specified, why the accused should not be punished for the alleged offense. The application shall be noticed, heard and determined in accordance with the procedure for a motion on notice in an action in such court, provided, however, that, except as provided in section fifty-two hundred fifty of the civil practice law and rules or unless otherwise ordered by the court, the moving papers shall be served no less than ten and no more than thirty days before the time at which the application is noticed to be heard. The application shall contain on its face a notice that the purpose of the hearing is to punish the accused for a contempt of court, and that such punishment may consist of fine or imprisonment, or both, according to law together with the following legend printed or type written in a size equal to at least eight point bold type:

WARNING: YOUR FAILURE TO APPEAR IN COURT MAY RESULT IN YOUR IMMEDIATE ARREST AND IMPRISONMENT FOR CONTEMPT OF COURT.

§ 757.   Application to punish for contempt committed before referee.

Where the offense is committed upon the trial of an issue referred to a referee appointed by the court, or consists of a witness's non-attendance, or refusal to be sworn or testify, before him, the application prescribed in this section may be made returnable before him or before the court. The application shall contain on its face a notice that the purpose of the hearing is to punish the accused for a contempt of court, and that such punishment may consist of fine or imprisonment, or both, according to law.

§ 760.   When application may be made.

An application may be made, either before or after the final judgment in the action, or the final order in the special proceeding.

§ 761.   Notice to accused; service.

An application to punish for contempt in a civil contempt proceeding shall be served upon the accused, unless service upon the attorney for the accused be ordered by the court or judge.

§ 767.   When habeas corpus may issue.

If the accused is in the custody of a sheriff, or other officer, by virtue of an execution against his person, or by virtue of a mandate for any other contempt or misconduct, or a commitment on a criminal charge, the court, upon proof of the facts, may issue a writ of habeas corpus, directed to the officer, requiring him to bring the accused before it, to answer for the offense charged. The officer to whom the writ is directed, or upon whom it is served, must bring him before the court, and detain him at the place where the court is sitting, until the further order of the court.

§ 770.   Final order directing punishment; exception.

Upon the return of an application to punish for contempt, or upon a hearing held upon a warrant of commitment issued pursuant to section seven hundred seventy-two or seven hundred seventy-three of this article, the court shall inform the offender that he has the right to the assistance of counsel, and when it appears that the offender is financially unable to obtain counsel, the court may in its discretion assign counsel to represent him. If it is determined that the accused has committed the offense charged; and that it was calculated to, or actually did, defeat, impair, impede, or prejudice the rights or remedies of a party to an action or special proceeding, brought in the court, or before the judge or referee; the court, judge, or referee must make a final order directing that he be punished by fine or imprisonment, or both, as the nature of the case requires. A warrant of commitment must issue accordingly, except as hereinafter provided. Where an application is made under this Article and in pursuance of section two hundred forty-five of the domestic relations law or any other section of law for a final order directing punishment for failure to pay alimony and/or

App Pract Provs

counsel fees pursuant to an order of the court or judge in an action for divorce or separation and the husband appear and satisfy the court or a judge before whom the application may be pending that he has no means or property or income to comply with the terms of the order at the time, the court or judge may, in its or his discretion, deny the application to punish the husband, without prejudice to the wife's rights and without prejudice to a renewal of the application by the wife upon notice and after proof that the financial condition of the husband is changed.

Where an application is made to punish an offender for an offense committed with respect to an enforcement procedure under the civil practice law and rules, if the offender appear and comply and satisfy the court or a judge before whom the application shall be pending that he has at the time no means or property or income which could be levied upon pursuant to an execution issued in such an enforcement procedure, the court or judge shall deny the application to punish the offender without prejudice to the applicant's rights and without prejudice to a renewal of the application upon notice and after proof that the financial condition of the offender has changed.

§ 772. Punishment upon return of application.

Upon the return of an application to punish for contempt, the questions which arise must be determined, as upon any other motion; and, if the determination is to the effect specified in section seven hundred and seventy, the order thereupon must be to the same effect as the final order therein prescribed.

Except as hereinafter provided, the offender may be committed upon a certified copy of the order so made, without further process. Where the commitment is ordered to punish an offense committed with respect to an enforcement procedure under the civil practice law and rules or pursuant to section two hundred forty-five of the domestic relations law, and the defendant has not appeared upon the return of the application, the final order directing punishment and commitment of the offender shall include a provision granting him leave to purge himself of the contempt within ten days after personal service of the order by performance of the act or duty the omission of which constitutes the misconduct for which he is to be punished, and the act or duty to be performed shall be specified in the order. Upon a certified copy of the order, together with proof by affidavit that more than ten days have elapsed since personal service thereof upon the offender, and that the act or duty specified has not been performed, the court may issue without notice a warrant directed to the sheriff or other enforcement officer of any jurisdiction in which the offender may be found. The warrant shall command such officer to arrest the offender forthwith and bring him before the court, or a judge thereof, to be committed or for such further disposition as the court in its discretion shall direct.

§ 773.　　Amount of fine.

If an actual loss or injury has been caused to a party to an action or special proceeding, by reason of the misconduct proved against the offender, and the case is not one where it is specially prescribed by law, that an action may be maintained to recover damages for the loss or injury, a fine, sufficient to indemnify the aggrieved party, must be imposed upon the offender, and collected, and paid over to the aggrieved party, under the direction of the court. The payment and acceptance of such a fine constitute a bar to an action by the aggrieved party, to recover damages for the loss or injury.

Where it is not shown that such an actual loss or injury has been caused, a fine may be imposed, not exceeding the amount of the complainant's costs and expenses, and two hundred and fifty dollars in addition thereto, and must be collected and paid, in like manner. A corporation may be fined as prescribed in this section.

If a fine is imposed to punish an offense committed with respect to an enforcement procedure under the civil practice law and rules or pursuant to section two hundred forty-five of the domestic relations law, and it has not been shown that such an actual loss or injury has been caused and the defendant has not appeared upon the return of the application, the order imposing fine, if any, shall include a provision granting the offender leave to purge himself of the contempt within ten days after personal service of the order by appearing and satisfying the court that he is unable to pay the fine or, in the discretion of the court, by giving an undertaking in a sum to be fixed by the court conditioned upon payment of the fine plus costs and expenses and his appearance and performance of the act or duty, the omission of which constitutes

App Pract Provs

the misconduct for which he is to be punished. The order may also include a provision committing the offender to prison until the fine plus costs and expenses are paid, or until he is discharged according to law. Upon a certified copy of the order imposing fine, together with proof by affidavit that more than ten days have elapsed since personal service thereof upon the offender, and that the fine plus costs and expenses has not been paid, the court may issue without notice a warrant directed to the sheriff or other enforcement officer of any jurisdiction in which the offender may be found. The warrant shall command such officer to arrest the offender forthwith and bring him before the court, or a judge thereof, to be committed or for such other disposition as the court in its discretion shall direct.

§ 774. Length of imprisonment and periodic review of proceedings.

1. Where the misconduct proved consists of an omission to perform an act or duty, which is yet in the power of the offender to perform, he shall be imprisoned only until he has performed it, and paid the fine imposed, but if he shall perform the act or duty required to be performed, he shall not be imprisoned for the fine imposed more than three months if the fine is less than five hundred dollars, or more than six months if the fine is five hundred dollars or more. In such case, the order, and the warrant of commitment, if one is issued, must specify the act or duty to be performed, and the sum to be paid. In every other case, where special provision is not otherwise made by law, the offender may be imprisoned for a reasonable time, not exceeding six months, and until the fine, if any, is paid; and the order, and the warrant of commitment, if any, must specify the amount of the fine, and the duration of the imprisonment. If the term of imprisonment is not specified in the order, the offender shall be imprisoned for the fine imposed three months if the fine is less than five hundred dollars, and six months if the fine imposed is five hundred dollars or more. If the offender is required to serve a specified term of imprisonment, and in addition to pay a fine, he shall not be imprisoned for the nonpayment of such fine for more than three months if such fine is less than five hundred dollars or more than six months if the fine imposed is five hundred dollars or more in addition to the specified time of imprisonment.

2. In all instances where any offender shall have been imprisoned pursuant to Article nineteen of the judiciary law and where the term of such imprisonment is specified to be an indeterminate period of time or for a term of more than three months, such offender, if not then discharged by law from imprisonment, shall within ninety days after the commencement of such imprisonment be brought, by the sheriff, or other officer, as a matter of course personally before the court imposing such imprisonment and a review of the proceedings shall then be held to determine whether such offender shall be discharged from imprisonment. At periodic intervals of not more than ninety days following such review, the offender, if not then discharged by law from imprisonment, shall be brought, by the sheriff, or other officer, as a matter of course personally before the court imposing such imprisonment and further reviews of the proceedings shall then be held to determine whether such offender shall be discharged from imprisonment. Where such imprisonment shall have arisen out of or during the course of any action or proceeding, the clerk of the court before which such review of the proceedings shall be held, or the judge or justice of such court in case there be no clerk, shall give reasonable notice in writing of the date, time and place of each such review to each party or his attorney who shall have appeared of record in such action or proceeding, at their last known address.

§ 775.   When court may release offender.

Where an offender, imprisoned as prescribed in this article, is unable to endure the imprisonment, or to pay the sum, or perform the act or duty, required to be paid or performed, in order to entitle him to be released, the court, judge, or referee may, in its or his discretion, and upon such terms as justice requires, make an order, directing him to be discharged from the imprisonment.

Where the commitment was made to punish a contempt of court committed with respect to an enforcement procedure under the civil practice law and rules, and the offender has purged himself of contempt as provided in section seven hundred seventy-two or seven hundred seventy-three of this article, the court out of which the execution was issued shall make an order directing him to be discharged from the imprisonment.

App Pract
Provs

§ 777.   Proceedings when accused does not appear.

Where a person has given an undertaking for his appearance, as prescribed in this Article and fails to appear, on the return day of the application, the court may either issue a warrant of commitment, or make an order, directing the undertaking to be prosecuted; or both.

LIEN LAW

Article 10-A.   Liens for taxes payable to the United States of America and other federal liens.

§ 243.   Fees.

The fee to be paid to the secretary of state or a clerk or register for filing and indexing each notice of lien or certificate or notice affecting any such lien shall be determined in accordance with the provisions of section ninety-six-a of the executive law. Such officers shall bill the district directors of internal revenue or other appropriate federal officers on a monthly basis for fees for documents filed by them.

NEW YORK CITY CIVIL COURT ACT

SYNOPSIS

SYNOPSIS

Article 1. Organization.

§ 101. Short title.

This act shall be known as the New York city civil court act, and may be cited as "CCA."

§ 102. Court established.

The civil court of the city of New York is hereby established as a single city-wide court, as provided by sections one and fifteen of article six of the constitution; it shall be a part of the unified court system for the state, and a court of record with such power and jurisdiction as are herein or elsewhere provided by law. The court in each county of the city shall have an official seal on which shall be engraved the arms of the state, the name of the court, and the county.

§ 102-a. Vacancies and composition of court.

1. The civil court of the city of New York shall consist of one hundred thirty-one judges, all of whom shall be residents of the city of New York. No person may serve in the office of judge of this court after the effective date of this section unless he or she has been admitted to practice law in this state for at least ten years as of the date he or she commences the duties of office.

2. The twenty-five additional judges of the civil court of the city of new york authorized on June first, nineteen hundred sixty-eight by chapter nine hundred eighty-seven of the laws of nineteen hundred sixty-eight shall be elected in and from the residents of the following

counties in the indicated numbers: from the county of New York, seven; from the county of Kings, seven; from the county of Queens, six; from the county of Bronx, four; and from the county of Richmond, one. Such additional judges shall receive the same compensation as the existing judges of the civil court of the city of New York. The eleven additional judges of the civil court of the city of New York authorized by this section shall be chosen by the electors of the counties included within the city of New York from districts within such counties as shall be established by law.

3. A vacancy occurring otherwise than by the expiration of term in the office of judge of the civil court of the city of New York shall be filled by the mayor of the city of New York by an appointment which shall continue until and including the last day of December next after the election at which the vacancy shall be filled.

4. Vacancies in the office of judge of the civil court of the city of new york occurring by the expiration of the term on the last day of december, nineteen hundred seventy-eight of a justice elected or appointed to the city court of the city of New York or the municipal court of the city of New York, who was continued as a judge of the civil court pursuant to the provisions of subdivision c of section thirty-five of article six of the constitution, or of their successors, shall be filled for a full term at the general election to be held in November, nineteen hundred seventy-eight. Judges to fill such vacancies shall be chosen by the electors of the county or district from which the judge whose term expires on December thirty-first, nineteen hundred seventy-eight or his predecessor, was elected or appointed.

§ 103.   Powers of appellate division.

In addition to the powers conferred upon them in this act and in any other provision of law, all the powers heretofore conferred by law upon the chief justice of the city court of the city of New York and upon the president justice and board of justices of the municipal court of the city of New York are vested in the appellate divisions of the supreme court in the first and second judicial departments. As provided by section twenty-eight of article six of the constitution and article seven-a of the judiciary law, the appellate divisions of the supreme court in the first and second judicial departments shall supervise the administration and operation of the court in their respective departments, either separately

App Pract Provs

or jointly; provided, however, that if the administrative board shall so direct, a single administrative judge shall be designated by the appellate divisions or the administrative board as provided by law to administer and regulate the operations of the court.

§ 104. Expenses of court.

All salaries of both judicial and nonjudicial personnel of the court and all other expenses of the court whatsoever shall be a charge upon the city of New York. As provided in subdivision d of section twenty-nine of article six of the constitution, the governing body of the city shall annually include in its final estimate such sums as may be necessary to pay such salaries and expenses.

§ 109. Clerk of the court.

There shall be a chief clerk of the court. The chief clerk and such other non-judicial personnel as shall be authorized by rule or order of court shall each have the power to administer oaths, take acknowledgments and sign the process or mandate of the court.

§ 110. Housing part.

(a) A part of the court shall be devoted to actions and proceedings involving the enforcement of state and local laws for the establishment and maintenance of housing standards, including, but not limited to, the multiple dwelling law and the housing maintenance code, building code and health code of the administrative code of the city of New York, as follows:

(1) Actions for the imposition and collection of civil penalties for the violation of such laws.

(2) Actions for the collection of costs, expenses and disbursements incurred by the city of New York in the elimination or correction of a nuisance or other violation of such laws, or in the removal or demolition of any dwelling pursuant to such laws.

(3) Actions and proceedings for the establishment, enforcement or foreclosure of liens upon real property and upon the rents therefrom for civil penalties, or for costs, expenses and disbursements incurred

by the city of New York in the elimination or correction of a nuisance or other violation of such laws.

(4) Proceedings for the issuance of injunctions and restraining orders or other orders for the enforcement of housing standards under such laws.

(5) Actions and proceedings under article seven-A of the real property actions and proceedings law, and all summary proceedings to recover possession of residential premises to remove tenants therefrom, and to render judgment for rent due, including without limitation those cases in which a tenant alleges a defense under section seven hundred fifty-five of the real property actions and proceedings law, relating to stay or proceedings or action for rent upon failure to make repairs, section three hundred two-a of the multiple dwelling law, relating to the abatement of rent in case of certain violations of section D26–41.21 of such housing mainte-nance code.

(6) Proceedings for the appointment of a receiver of rents, issues and profits of buildings in order to remove or remedy a nuisance or to make repairs required to be made under such laws.

(7) Actions and proceedings for the removal of housing violations recorded pursuant to such laws, or for the imposition of such violation or for the stay of any penalty thereunder.

(8) Special proceedings to vest title in the city of New York to abandoned multiple dwellings.

(9) The city department charged with enforcing the multiple dwelling law, housing maintenance code, and other state and local laws applicable to the enforcement of proper housing standards may commence any action or proceeding described in paragraphs one, two, three, four, six and seven of this subdivision by an order to show cause, returnable within five days, or within any other time period in the discretion of the court. Upon the signing of such order, the clerk of the housing part shall issue an index number.

(b) On the application of any city department, any party, or on its own motion, the housing part of the civil court shall, unless good cause is shown to the contrary, consolidate all actions and proceedings pending in such part as to any building.

App Pract
Provs

(c) Regardless of the relief originally sought by a party the court may recommend or employ any remedy, program, procedure or sanction authorized by law for the enforcement of housing standards, if it believes they will be more effective to accomplish compliance or to protect and promote the public interest; provided in the event any such proposed remedy, program or procedure entails the expenditure of monies appropriated by the city, other than for the utilization and deployment of personnel and services incidental thereto, the court shall give notice of such proposed remedy, program or procedure to the city department charged with the enforcement of local laws relating to housing maintenance and shall not employ such proposed remedy, program or procedure, as the case may be, if such department shall advise the court in writing within the time fixed by the court, which shall not be less than fifteen days after such notice has been given, of the reasons such order should not be issued, which advice shall become part of the record. The court may retain continuing jurisdiction of any action or proceeding relating to a building until all violations of law have been removed.

(d) In any of the actions or proceedings specified in subdivision (a) and on the application of any party, any city department or the court, on its own motion, may join any other person or city department as a party in order to effectuate proper housing maintenance standards and to promote the public interest.

(e) Actions and proceedings before the housing part shall be tried before civil court judges, acting civil court judges, or housing judges. Housing judges shall be appointed pursuant to subdivision (f) of this section and shall be duly constituted judicial officers empowered to hear, determine and grant any relief within the powers of the housing part in any action or proceeding except those to be tried by jury. Such housing judges shall have the power of judges of the court to punish for contempts. Rules of evidence shall be applicable in actions and proceedings before the housing part. The determination of a housing judge shall be final and shall be entered and may be appealed in the same manner as a judgment of the court; provided that the assignment of actions and proceedings to housing judges, the conduct of the trial and the contents and filing of a housing judge's decision, and all matters incidental to the operation of the housing part, shall be in accordance with rules jointly promulgated by the first and second departments of the appellate division for such part.

(f) The housing judges shall be appointed by the administrative judge from a list of persons selected annually as qualified by training, interest, experience, judicial temperament and knowledge of federal, state and local housing laws and programs by the advisory council for the housing part. The list of persons who have been approved by such advisory council, whether or not appointed to such judicial position, shall be deemed public information and be published in the city record immediately after such list is submitted to the administrative judge. The annual salary of a housing judge shall be one hundred fifteen thousand four hundred dollars.

(g) The advisory council for the housing part shall be composed of two members representative of each of the following: the real estate industry, tenants' organizations, civic groups and bar associations and four members from the public at large. Such members shall be appointed by the administrative judge, with the approval of the presiding justices of the first and second departments of the appellate division. The members of the advisory council shall be appointed for non-renewable terms of three years. In addition the mayor of the city of New York shall appoint one member to serve at his pleasure and the commissioner of housing and community renewal shall be a member.

(h) The advisory council shall meet at least four times a year, and on such additional occasions as they may require or as may be required by the administrative judge. Members shall receive no compensation. Members shall visit the housing part from time to time to review the manner in which the part is functioning, and make recommendations to the administrative judge and to the advisory council. A report on the work of the part shall be prepared annually and submitted to the administrative judge, the administrative board of the judicial conference, the majority and minority leaders of the senate and assembly, the governor, the chairpersons of the judiciary committee in the senate and assembly and the mayor of the city of New York by the thirty-first day of January of each year.

(i) Housing judges have been admitted to the bar of the state for at least five years, two years of which shall have been in active practice. Each housing judge shall serve full-time for five years. Reappointment shall be at the discretion of the administrative judge and on the basis

App Pract Provs

of the performance, competency and results achieved during the preceding term.

(j) [Repealed].

(k) Unless a party requests a manual stenographic record by filing a notice with the clerk two working days prior to the date set for an appearance before the court, hearings shall be recorded mechanically. A party may request a transcript from a mechanical recording. Any party making a request for a copy of either a mechanically or manually recorded transcript shall bear the cost thereof and shall furnish a copy of the transcript to the court, and to the other parties.

(l) Any city department charged with enforcing any state or local law applicable to the enforcement of proper housing standards may be represented in the housing part by its department counsel in any action or proceeding in which it is a party. A corporation which is a party may be represented by an officer, director or a principal stockholder.

(m) The service of process in any of the actions or proceedings specified in subdivision (a) which are brought under the housing maintenance code of the administrative code of the city of New York shall be made as herein provided:

(1) Service of process shall be made in the manner prescribed for actions or proceedings in this court, except where the manner of such service is provided for in the housing maintenance code of the administrative code of the city of New York, such service may, as an alternative, be made as therein provided.

(2) Where the manner of service prescribed for actions or proceedings in this court includes delivery of the summons to a person at the actual place of business of the person to be served, such delivery may be made alternatively to a person of suitable age and discretion at the address registered with the department charged with the enforcement of local laws relating to housing maintenance pursuant to article forty-one of such code, hereinafter referred to as the "registered address".

(3) Where the manner of service prescribed for actions or

proceedings in this court includes affixing the summons to the door of the actual place of business of the person to be served, the summons may, as an alternative, be posted in a conspicuous place on either the premises specified in the summons or the registered address.

(4) Where the manner of service for actions or proceedings in this court includes mailing the summons to the person to be served at his last known residence, the summons may, as an alternative, be mailed to the registered address; however, if the person to be served has not registered as required by article forty-one of such housing maintenance code, such summons may, as an alternative, be mailed to an address registered in the last registration statement filed with such department other than the address of the managing agent of the premises and to the last known address of the person to be served.

(5) Where the manner of service for actions or proceedings in this court includes mailing the summons to the person to be served at his last known residence, if the person to be served is a corporation and if either: (i) an officer of such corporation, (ii) the managing agent of such corporation for the premises involved in the suit or (iii) a person designated by such corporation to receive notices in its behalf, other than the secretary of state, has been named a party to the suit, the summons may, as an alternative, be mailed to the registered address of such corporation or, if such corporation has not registered as required by such code, to the address of such corporation set forth in a document filed or recorded with a governmental agency.

(6) A copy of the summons with proof of service shall be filed in the manner provided in section four hundred nine, except that such filing shall be made with the clerk of the housing part in the county in which the action is brought.

(n) Nothing contained in the section one hundred ten shall in any way affect the right of any party to trial by jury as heretofore provided by law.

(o) There shall be a sufficient number of pro se clerks of the housing part to assist persons without counsel. Such assistance shall include, but need not be limited to providing information concerning court

App Pract
Provs

procedure, helping to file court papers, and, where appropriate, advising persons to seek administrative relief.

(p) The court shall review the performance and records of administrators appointed pursuant to article seven-a of the real property actions and proceedings law or receivers appointed pursuant to paragraph six of subdivision (a) of this section. Such review shall include but not be limited to an examination of the accountings submitted by such administrators or receivers and an examination of the plan submitted to the court pursuant to subdivision nine of section seven hundred seventy eight of the real property actions and proceedings law. The court may compel the production of any records it deems necessary to perform such review.

SYNOPSIS

Article 2.   Jurisdiction.

§ 201.   Jurisdiction; in general.

The court shall have jurisdiction as set forth in this article and as elsewhere provided by law. The phrase "$25,000" whenever it appears herein, shall be taken to mean "$25,000 exclusive of interest and costs."

§ 202.   Money actions and actions involving chattels.

The court shall have jurisdiction of actions and proceedings for the recovery of money, actions and proceedings for the recovery of chattels and actions and proceedings for the foreclosure of liens on personal property where the amount sought to be recovered on the value of the property does not exceed $25,000.

§ 203.   Actions involving real property.

The court shall have jurisdiction of the following actions provided that the real property involved or part of it is situate within the county in the city of New York in which the action is brought:

(a) An action for the partition of real property where the assessed valuation of the property at the time the action is commenced does not exceed $25,000.

(b) An action for the foreclosure, redemption or satisfaction of a mortgage on real property where the amount of the mortgage lien at the time the action is commenced does not exceed $25,000.

(c) An action for the foreclosure of a lien arising out of a contract for the sale of real property where the amount of the lien sought to be foreclosed does not, at the time the action is commenced, exceed $25,000.

(d) An action for the specific performance of a contract for the sale of real property where the contract price of the property does not exceed $25,000.

(e) An action for the establishment, enforcement or foreclosure of a mechanic's lien on real property where the lien asserted does not, at the time the action is commenced, exceed $25,000.

(f) An action to reform or rescind a deed to real property where

App Pract
Provs

the assessed valuation of property does not exceed the $25,000 at the time the action is commenced.

(g) An action to reform or rescind a contract for the sale of real property where the agreed price of the property as stated in the contract does not exceed $25,000; or, if the controversy shall be with regard to the price of the property, where the agreed price as claimed by plaintiff does not exceed $25,000.

(h) An action to reform or rescind a mortgage on real property where the unpaid balance of the debt secured by the mortgage does not exceed $25,000 at the time the action is commenced.

(i) An action to compel the determination of a claim to real property under article fifteen of the real property actions and proceedings law where the assessed valuation of the property does not exceed $25,000 at the time the action is commenced.

(j) An action of ejectment where the assessed valuation of the real property does not exceed $25,000 at the time the action is commenced.

(k) An action brought to impose and collect a civil penalty for a violation of state or local laws for the establishment and maintenance of housing standards, including, but not limited to, the multiple dwelling law and the housing maintenance code, building code and health code of the administrative code of the city of New York.

(l) An action to recover costs, expenses and disbursements incurred by the city of New York in the elimination or correction of a nuisance or other violation of any law described in subdivision (k) of this section, or in the removal or demolition of any building pursuant to such law or laws.

(m) An action or proceeding to establish, enforce or foreclose a lien upon real property and the rents therefrom, for civil penalties, or for costs, expenses and disbursements incurred by the city of New York in the elimination of a nuisance or other violation of any law described in subdivision (k) of this section, or in the removal or demolition of any building pursuant to such law or laws.

(n) Actions and proceedings for the removal of housing violations recorded pursuant to any law described in subdivision (k) of this section, or for the imposition of such violation or for the stay of any penalty thereunder.

(o) An action or proceeding for the issuance of an injunction, restraining orders or other orders for the enforcement of housing standards under any law described in subdivision (k) of this section.

(p) Special proceedings to vest title in the city of New York to abandoned multiple dwellings.

§ 204. Summary proceedings.

The court shall have jurisdiction over summary proceedings to recover possession of real property located within the city of New York, to remove tenants therefrom, and to render judgment for rent due without regard to amount, and in such a proceeding after the court has determined that a warrant of eviction be issued, it shall not be necessary for the court to sign the warrant, but it may be signed by the clerk of said court. The court shall also have jurisdiction over special proceedings by tenants of multiple dwellings in the city of New York for judgment directing deposit of rents and the use thereof for the purpose of remedying conditions dangerous to life, health or safety, as authorized by article seven-a of the real property actions and proceedings law.

§ 205. Interpleader.

The court shall have jurisdiction of an action of interpleader and defensive interpleader as defined and governed by the CPLR, provided that the amount in controversy or the value of the property involved does not exceed $25,000.

§ 206. Arbitration.

(a) Threshold questions under CPLR article 75. If an action of which the court has jurisdiction has been duly commenced therein, and there arise in such action any questions relating to the arbitrability of the controversy, the court shall have jurisdiction completely to dispose of such questions and CPLR article 75 shall be applicable thereto. But the court shall not have jurisdiction of the special proceeding, as set forth

App Pract Provs

in CPLR § 7502(a), used to bring before a court the first application arising out of an arbitrable controversy, except as provided in subdivision (b).

(b) Proceedings on award under CPLR article 75. Where a controversy has been duly arbitrated and an award made therein is for relief which is within the court's jurisdiction, the court shall have jurisdiction of proceedings under CPLR §§ 7510 through 7514, relating to judicial recognition of such awards, which provisions shall be applicable thereto.

(c) Arbitration distinct from CPLR article 75. The rules may provide systems of arbitration and conciliation of claims within the court's jurisdiction without reference to CPLR article 75. Where the chief administrator of the courts has provided by rule for an alternative method of dispute resolution by arbitration and has established by order this arbitration program in any county in this court, applicable in each such county to civil actions for a sum of money only, except those commenced in small claims parts and not subsequently transferred to a regular part of court, that on or after the effective date of such order are noticed for trial or commenced in this court, all such actions shall be heard and decided by a panel of arbitrators where the recovery sought for each cause of action is ten thousand dollars or less, exclusive of costs and interest.

§ 207.   Small claims.

The court shall have jurisdiction of small claims as defined in article 18 of this act.

§ 208.   Counterclaims.

The court shall have jurisdiction of counterclaims as follows:

(a) Of any counterclaim the subject matter of which would be within the jurisdiction of the court if sued upon separately.

(b) Of any counterclaim for money only, without regard to amount.

(c) Of any counterclaim for:

    1. the rescission or reformation of the transaction upon which

the plaintiff's cause of action is founded, if the amount in controversy on such counterclaim does not exceed $25,000; or

2. an accounting between partners after the dissolution of the partnership, where the book value of the partnership assets does not exceed $25,000 and the plaintiff's cause of action arises out of the partnership.

(d) In an action commenced in the housing part by the city department charged with enforcing the multiple dwelling law, housing maintenance code, or other state or local laws applicable to the enforcement of proper housing standards, no counterclaim may be interposed or maintained except if it relates to an action or proceeding specified in subdivision (a) of § 110 of this act.

§ 209. Provisional remedies.

(a) Attachment, arrest, seizure of chattel. An order of attachment or of arrest, a warrant to seize a chattel as provided in §207 of the lien law, and an order of seizure of a chattel may issue out of this court if such remedy might issue out of supreme court in a like case.

(b) Injunction or restraining order. No injunction or restraining order or notice shall issue out of or by this court unless:

(1) pursuant to §§ 7102(d), 7103(c) and 7109 of the CPLR, in conjunction with the recovery of a chattel; or

(2) pursuant to §211 of the Real Property Actions and Proceedings Law, in conjunction with the prevention of waste; or

(3) pursuant to §1508 of this act, in conjunction with an enforcement proceeding; or

(4) pursuant to section three hundred six of the multiple dwelling law, or article fifty-three of the housing maintenance code of the administrative code of the city of New York in conjunction with enforcement of housing standards.

(c) Receivers. No receiver shall be appointed by this court except pursuant to §1508 of this act, relative to an enforcement proceeding, or in an action for the foreclosure of a mortgage on real property, brought pursuant to the provisions of §203(b) of this act, or in an action brought pursuant to subdivision five of section three hundred nine of the

App Pract Provs

multiple dwelling law, relative to the appointment of a receiver for the recovery of costs, expenses and disbursements incurred by the city of New York in the elimination or correction of a nuisance or in the removal or demolition of a building pursuant thereto.

(d) Notice of pendency. A notice of pendency may be filed with the county clerk, as provided in article 65 of the CPLR, in any action within the court's jurisdiction in which the same might be filed in a like action in the supreme court. The city department charged with the enforcement of the multiple dwelling law, housing maintenance code, and other state and local laws applicable to the enforcement of proper housing standards may file a notice of pendency as authorized by section 308 of the multiple dwelling law or section D26–50.07 of the housing maintenance code of the administrative code of the city of New York.

§ 210. Contempt.

All of the provisions of law governing civil and criminal contempts in like instances in supreme court shall apply in this court, except that this court shall have no power to punish for contempt a judge or justice of any court.

§ 211. Joinder of causes of action in complaint; effect on jurisdiction.

Where several causes of action are asserted in the complaint and each of them would be within the jurisdiction of the court if sued upon separately, the court shall have jurisdiction of the action. In such case judgment may be rendered by the court in excess of $25,000 if such excess result solely because of such joinder. Nothing herein shall be construed to prevent the court from granting judgment in an unlimited amount on a counterclaim.

§ 212. Additional jurisdiction and powers.

In the exercise of its jurisdiction the court shall have all of the powers that the supreme court would have in like actions and proceedings.

§ 212-a. Declaratory judgments involving obligations of

insurers.

The court shall have the jurisdiction defined in section 3001 of the CPLR to make a declaratory judgment with respect to any controversy involving the obligation of an insurer to indemnify or defend a defendant in an action in which the amount sought to be recovered does not exceed $25,000.

§ 213. Jurisdiction for rescission or reformation of certain transactions.

The court shall have jurisdiction of actions for rescission or reformation of a transaction if the amount in controversy does not exceed $25,000.

SYNOPSIS

Article 3. Venue.

Article 3. Venue.

§ 301. Transitory actions; venue.

An action, other than a real property action, shall be brought:

(a) in an action arising out of a consumer credit transaction where a purchaser, borrower, or a debtor is a defendant, if a defendant resides in the city of New York, or if such transaction took place therein, in the county in which a defendant resides at the commencement thereof or in the county in which such transaction took place, and in all other cases, in the county in which one of the parties resides at the commencement thereof; or

(b) if no party resides in the city of New York, in the county in which one of the parties has regular employment or a place for the regular transaction of business; or

(c) if no party has such employment or place of business within the city of New York, in the county in which the cause of action arose; or

(d) if none of the foregoing are applicable in any county.

§ 302. Real property actions; venue.

A real property action, as defined in § 203 of this act, whether asserted by a plaintiff or by any party by way of counterclaim, cross-claim or third-party claim, shall be brought and adjudicated only in the county in which such real property or a part thereof is situated. If by virtue of the venue applicable to the cause of action asserted by plaintiff the main action is triable in a county other than that in which the real property is situated, the court must either:

(a) transfer the entire action to the county wherein the real property is situated, if the transfer may be effected without prejudice to the rights of any party; or

(b) strike the real property cause of action, no matter by whom asserted, without prejudice to the party asserting it to commence it in the proper county.

If more than one real property cause of action appear, the court may make such disposition as is just under the circumstances, and a real property action, no matter by whom asserted, may be tried in a county other than that in which the real property or a part thereof is situated only if there is reason to believe that an impartial trial cannot be had in the latter county.

§ 303. Summary proceedings; venue.

A summary proceeding to recover possession of real property or to remove tenants therefrom shall be brought in the county in which the real property or a part thereof is situated.

§ 304.   Actions by or against the city of New York; or against the New York city transit authority; venue.

(a) An action shall by or on behalf of the city of New York or any department thereof shall be brought in the county of New York or in the county within said city where the cause of action arose.

(b) An action against the city of New York or the New York city transit authority shall be brought in the county within said city where the cause of action arose. If the cause of action arose outside the city of New York, the action shall be brought in the county of New York.

§ 305.   Assignees; corporations and associations.

(a) If the plaintiff is an assignee of the cause of action, the original owner of the cause of action shall be deemed the plaintiff for the purpose of determining proper venue.

(b) A corporation, joint-stock association or other unincorporated association shall be deemed a resident of any county wherein it transacts business, keeps an office, has an agency or is established by law.

§ 306.   Change of venue; procedure.

The bringing of an action or proceeding in the wrong county shall not be deemed a jurisdictional defect, but the court may of its own motion and must on the motion of a party defendant transfer the action or proceeding to a proper county. The motion by the defendant for such relief must be made in writing and on notice and must be filed with the clerk before or at joinder of issue. It must specify the county to which the defendant desires the action or proceeding to be transferred and must state under oath facts showing the ground exists for such transfer. In the absence of timely motion by the defendant, he shall be deemed to have waived any objection relating to proper venue, except in the case of a real property action.

The transfer of a real property action from an improper to the proper county may be had at any time by motion or otherwise.

App Pract
Provs

§ 307.   Venue; rules.

Notwithstanding the provisions of this article, the rules may establish a part or parts of the court where designated classes of cases shall be brought or tried.

————

SYNOPSIS

Article 4.   Summons.

§ 400.   Method of commencing action or special proceeding.

1. An action is commenced in this court by filing a summons and complaint. A special proceeding is commenced by filing a notice of petition and petition or order to show cause and petition. For purposes of this section, and for purposes of section two hundred three of the

civil practice law and rules, filing shall mean the delivery of the summons and complaint, the notice of petition and petition or order to show cause and petition to the clerk of the court in the county in which the action or special proceeding is brought together with any fee required by section nineteen hundred eleven of this act. At the time of filing, the original and a copy of the papers shall be date stamped by the court clerk who shall file the original and maintain a record of the filing and shall return the copy to the party who brought the filing. The clerk shall accept the fee and file the papers as soon as reasonably practicable.

2. Jurisdiction is acquired over a party to an action or special proceeding by service upon such party of a copy of the summons and complaint, the notice of petition and petition or the order to show cause and petition.

3. The actual index number shall be on the summons, notice of petition or order to show cause as served. Failure to include the index number on the papers as served shall be cured by stipulation between the parties or by leave of court, which shall not be unreasonably withheld.

§ 401.   Summons; issuance; form; issuance of notice of petition.

(a) The summons may be issued by the plaintiff's attorney or, if the plaintiff appears without attorney, by the clerk.

(b) The summons shall direct the defendant to file his answer with the clerk and shall otherwise be in such form as may be provided by rule. It shall contain the residence address of the plaintiff and, if it is issued by the plaintiff's attorney, the latter's office address.

(c) Notwithstanding the provisions of section 731 of the real property actions and proceedings law, regarding issuance by an attorney, the notice of petition in a summary proceeding to recover possession of real property shall be issued only by a judge or the clerk of the court. The original petition shall be filed with the clerk at the time the notice of petition is issued.

(d) The summons served in an action arising from a consumer credit transaction must be printed legibly in both Spanish and English.

§ 402.   Summons; time to appear and answer.

App Pract
Provs

(a) If the summons is personally delivered to the defendant within the city of New York, it shall require him to appear and answer within twenty days after its service.

(b) If the summons is served by any means other than personal delivery to the defendant within the city of New York, it shall provide that the defendant must appear and answer within thirty days after proof of service is filed with the clerk.

§ 403. Summons; method and place of service.

Service of summons shall be made in the manner prescribed in supreme court practice, including the optional method of service by mail authorized by CPLR 312–a, but it shall be made only within the city of New York unless service beyond the city be authorized by this act or by such other provision of law, other than the CPLR, as expressly applies to courts of limited jurisdiction or to all courts of the state.

§ 404. Summons; personal jurisdiction by acts of non-residents.

(a) Acts which are the basis of jurisdiction. The court may exercise personal jurisdiction over any non-resident of the city of New York, or his executor or administrator, as to a cause of action arising from any of the acts enumerated in this section, in the same manner as if he were a domiciliary of the state and a resident of the city of New York if, in person or through an agent, he:

1. transacts any business within the city of New York or contracts anywhere to supply goods or services in the city of New York; or

2. commits a tortious act within the city of New York, except as to a cause of action for defamation of character arising from the act; or

3. owns, uses or possesses any real property situated within the city of New York.

(b) Service of summons. Service of summons under this section may be made in such manner and at such place, regardless of city or state lines, as would confer jurisdiction on supreme court in a like case.

(c) Effect of appearance. Where personal jurisdiction is based solely upon this section, an appearance does not confer such jurisdiction with respect to causes of action not arising from an act enumerated in this section.

(d) Corporation or association. If service of the summons cannot be effected by personal delivery thereof within the city of New York so as to acquire in personam jurisdiction of a corporation or unincorporated association, such corporation or association shall be deemed a non-resident of the city of New York for purposes of this section.

§ 405.   Summons; service without the city of New York permissible but not giving personal jurisdiction in certain actions.

Service may be made without the city of New York or the state by any person authorized to make service in a like instance in supreme court and in the same manner as service in such court may be made:

(a) in a real property action as defined in § 203 of this act; or

(b) in an action to foreclose a lien on, or to recover, a chattel seized within the city of New York; or

(c) where a levy upon property of the person to be served has been made within the city of New York pursuant to an order of attachment; or

(d) where the case is within CPLR § 1006(g) and a sum of money has been paid or deposited as provided for therein.

§ 406.   Summons; service by publication authorized.

The court, upon motion without notice, shall order service of a summons by publication in an action described in § 405 if service cannot be made by another method with due diligence. Practice and procedure on service by publication shall be governed by the CPLR, except insofar as this act otherwise provides.

§ 407.   Summons; action commenced pursuant to CPLR § 303.

In any action in this court to be commenced by service of summons upon an attorney or a clerk as agent, as authorized by CPLR § 303, such service may be made in such manner and at such place regardless of city lines, as would confer jurisdiction on the supreme court in a like

App Pract
Provs

case.

§ 408.   Summons; service outside city to bring in certain additional parties or on domiciliary-resident.

A summons may be served in such manner and at such place, regardless of city or state lines, as would confer jurisdiction on supreme court in a like instance, upon:

(a) a third-party defendant as set forth in CPLR §1007;

(b) a person not a party against whom a counterclaim is asserted pursuant to CPLR § 3019(a);

(c) a person not a party against whom a cross-claim is asserted pursuant to CPLR § 3019(b);

(d) a claimant whom a defendant stakeholder seeks to bring into the action pursuant to CPLR § 1006(b);

(e) a person whom the court has ordered joined as a party pursuant to CPLR § 1001; and

(f) a defendant who is a domiciliary of the state and a resident of the city.

§ 409.   Summons and complaint, notice of petition and petition or order to show cause and petition; filing proof of service.

(a) Proof of service of the summons and complaint, notice of petition and petition or order to show cause and petition shall be filed with the clerk of the court in the county in which the action is brought.

(b) Proof of service shall be made by the certificate of the sheriff or marshal or by the affidavit of the person by whom the service was made.

§ 410.   Summons; when service complete.

The service of summons is complete:

(a) immediately upon personal delivery to the defendant, where § 402(a) is applicable; or

(b) upon the filing of proof of service, where § 402(b) is

applicable.

§ 411.   Service of summons and complaint, third-party summons and complaint, petition with a notice of petition or order to show cause and petition upon defendant.

Service of the summons and complaint, third-party summons and complaint, petition with a notice of petition or order to show cause and petition shall be made within one hundred twenty days after the filing of the summons and complaint, third-party summons and complaint, or petition with notice of petition or order to show cause and petition, provided that if service is not made upon a defendant within the time provided in this section, the court, upon motion, shall dismiss the action without prejudice as to that defendant, or upon good cause shown or in the interest of justice, extend the time for service.

§ 412.   Accrual of interest.

In any action, petition, order to show cause or other proceeding wherein interest accrues from the date of the inception of the action, petition, order or proceeding, said entitlement to interest shall not begin to accrue until service is completed by the actual index number being properly depicted on the summons and provided to the party to be charged with the payment of interest.

App Pract Provs

SYNOPSIS

Article 7.   Mandates.

§ 701.   Direction and execution of mandates.

(a) In an action or proceeding brought in the court, all processes and mandates may be served or executed only within the city of New York unless this act otherwise provides. They shall be served or executed by the sheriff of the city of New York or by a city marshal. Where this act empowers the court's process or mandate to be served or executed without the city of New York, it shall be served or executed by such officer as could serve or execute the process or mandate of the supreme court of the county in a like instance.

(b) The provisions of law applicable in supreme court practice, relating to the execution of mandates by a sheriff and the power and control of the court over the sheriff executing the same, shall apply in this court; and they shall apply equally to both sheriffs and marshals.

(c) In any instance where a return by the enforcement officer is required by law to be made to the court or the clerk thereof, such provision shall be deemed to refer to this court in that county out of which the process or mandate issued, or the clerk of this court in such county, as the case may be.

(d) In a case wherein a marshal serves or executes the process or mandate of the court, the return or certificate of a marshall and the service of a paper by him shall have the same force and effect as the like return, certificate or service of or by a sheriff.

(e) Nothing herein contained shall be construed to prevent the service of a summons, petition, notice of petition, subpoena or other paper by any person who might serve the same in a like instance in the supreme court.

§ 702.   Execution of mandates by marshals.

The authority of a marshall shall extend throughtout the city of New York. But where a transcript of a money judgment has been filed with the county clerk, an execution shall thereafter issue only to a sheriff, as if the judgement on which execution is sought were rendered by the supreme court.

SYNOPSIS

Article 8.   Provisional remedies.

§ 801.   Provisional remedies; procedure.

Whenever the remedies set forth in § 209 of this act may issue out of this court under the terms of said section, practice and procedure thereon shall be governed, insofar as consistent with this act, by the CPLR and such other provisions of law governing practice and procedure thereon in the supreme court, subject to the following:

(a) The remedy may be executed only within the city of New York, against persons or property within the city of New York.

(b) When a return is required, the return shall be made to the clerk of this court in the county out of which the remedy issued.

(c) 1. Where a notice of pendency may be filed with the county clerk, pursuant to § 209(d) of this act, the original complaint shall be filed simultaneously with such county clerk; service of summons shall thereafter be made within the time provided in CPLR § 6512. A copy of the complaint shall be sufficient for the purpose of filing the same, after service thereof, with the clerk of this court.

2. Where a notice of pendency is filed with the county clerk after the action has been commenced in this court, a copy of the complaint may be filed therewith in lieu of the original complaint.

§ 802.   Tender and offer.

The provisions of Rules 3219, 3220 and 3221 of the CPLR, treating respectively of tender, offer to liquidate damages conditionally and offer to compromise, shall be applicable in this court, with the additional requirement that at the time of service upon the other party of the "written tender," "written offer" or "written notice," as referred to in said rules, a copy of such tender, offer or notice shall be filed with the clerk.

SYNOPSIS

Article 9. Pleadings.

§ 901. Pleadings; in general.

Pleadings between plaintiff and defendant shall consist of complaint and anwer and, when ordered, a reply. Such order may be made by motion on notice or by the court of its own motion.

§ 902. Pleadings; form.

(a) All pleadings shall be formal pleadings, as in supreme court practice, except that:

(1) If the plaintiff's cause of action is for money only, the cause of action may be set forth by indorsement upon the summons. The indorsement shall consist of a statement of the nature and substance of the cause of action, and the summons in such instance shall set forth the amount in which the plaintiff will take judgment in the event of default. If the plaintiff shall appear without attorney, such indorsement shall be made by the clerk.

(2) Where the plaintiff's cause of action is for money only and the defendant appears without attorney, he may describe his answer to

the clerk, who shall indorse the nature and substance of the answer on, or annex it to, the summons.

(b) If a formal complaint must be or is used, it shall be served with the summons, except that if service is made by publication the CPLR shall govern.

(c) The address of the defendant, and that of his attorney if he shall appear by attorney, shall be stated with or in the answer.

(d) The rules may provide, in actions for money only in designated categories in which a party might otherwise proceed by indorsement as above provided, that a formal complaint, or a formal answer, or both, shall be required.

(e) The court in any case may, at any time before judgment, on its own motion or on the motion on notice of a party, direct the service and filing of a formal pleading.

§ 903. Pleadings; requirements of formal pleading inapplicable to indorsement pleading.

The requirements of this act or of the CPLR applicable to a formal pleading shall not be applicable to an indorsement pleading.

§ 905. Pleadings; defenses.

The court may consider any defense to a cause of action or claim asserted by any party, whether such defense be denominated or deemed legal or equitable in nature.

App Pract
Provs

§ 907. Pleadings; subsequent pleading containing cause of action.

(a) Counterclaim. The plaintiff may reply to a counterclaim but shall not be required to do so except by court order. If the plaintiff elects voluntarily to reply, he shall do so within ten days after service of the answer containing the counterclaim. In the absence of a reply the allegations of the counterclaim shall be deemed denied by the plaintiff. An answer containing a counterclaim against the plaintiff and another person shall be replied to by such other person, as required by CPLR § 3019(d), within the time provided in § 402 of this act, based upon the time and method of service.

(b) Cross-claim. A cross-claim shall be answered within ten days after the answer containing it is served.

(c) Third-party claim and claim by defendant stakeholder. A third-party complaint, and an interpleader complaint served by a defendant stakeholder under CPLR § 1006(b), shall be answered within the time provided in § 402 of this act, based upon the time and method of service.

§ 908.   Pleadings; verification.

Verification of pleadings shall be governed by the CPLR, except that if a pleading be not formal it need not be verified. The court in such instance may require a formal pleading as provided in subdivision (e) of § 902 and order its verification.

§ 909.   Pleadings; amended and supplemental.

(a) A party may amend his pleading once without leave of court at any time before the period for responding to it expires, or within ten days after its service or the service of a pleading responding to it. An amended pleading which requires a responsive pleading shall be responded to within ten days after it is served, or within ten days after the expiration of the period during which the original pleading could have been responded to, whichever is later.

(b) Except as provided in subdivision (a), the CPLR shall govern amended and supplemental pleadings in this court.

§ 910.   Simplified procedure for court determination of disputes; action without pleadings.

The simplified procedure for court determination of disputes set forth in CPLR §§ 3031, 3035 and 3037, and rules 3032 and 3036, shall apply in this court insofar as they may be applicable and the relief demanded is within the jurisdiction of this court.

Article 10.   Motions.

§ 1001.   Motion practice.

Motion practice in the court, including time provisions for the making and decision of motions, practice relating to show cause orders, and practice relating to motions before, during and after trial, shall be governed by the CPLR, except as this act otherwise provides.

§ 1002.   Motion to dismiss.

CPLR rule 3211, relating to a motion to dismiss, shall apply in this court, except that, with reference to subdivision (e) of said rule, a party's time to move to dismiss a cause of action contained in a pleading to which no response is required shall be within ten days after the service of such pleading. A motion based on paragraphs two, seven or ten of subdivision (a) of said rule may, as provided in its subdivision (e), be made at any time.

§ 1003.   Motion to correct pleadings.

Rule 3024 of the CPLR shall apply to motions to correct formal pleadings in this court, except that the notice of motion shall be served within the time allowed for responding to the challenged pleading or, in the case of a pleading requiring no response, within ten days after the service of such pleading.

§ 1004.   CPLR § 3213 applicable; return time varied.

CPLR § 3213, relating to a motion for summary judgment in lieu of complaint, shall be applicable in this court, except that the minimum period for return of the motion shall be as provided by § 402 of this act for answering a summons, based upon the time and method of service. The summons served with such motion papers shall instruct the defendant to answer as provided in the accompanying notice of motion. If the plaintiff adds days to the period for return provided herein, he may require the defendant to serve a copy of his answering papers upon plaintiff an equal number of days prior to such return day.

SYNOPSIS

Article 11.   Disclosure.

§ 1101.   Disclosure.

(a) CPLR applicable. The procedures set forth in the CPLR relative to disclosure, bill of particulars and the procuring of a copy of the items of an account, shall govern in this court, subject to subdivision (b). In an action to impose or collect a civil penalty for violation of the multiple dwelling law or the housing maintenance code of the New York city administrative code, leave of court, obtained by motion to the housing part thereof, shall be required for disclosure or for a bill of particulars except for a notice under CPLR 3123, which leave shall be granted only upon a showing that such disclosure or bill of particulars is necessary to the prosecution or defense of the action. If it is so noted on the summons, any motion for disclosure or a bill of particulars must be made in writing and on notice and must be filed with the clerk with proof of service not later than thirty days after joinder of issue.

(b) Parties and non-parties. All notices, orders, subpoenas and other papers relating to disclosure:

  1. by a party, may be served by such means and at such place, regardless of city or state lines, as would be permissible in the supreme court in a like instance;

  2. by a person not a party, may be served and executed only within the city, unless the court shall find that the interest of justice require that service not be so limited, in which case the court may permit

service as in paragraph one. Such permission may be granted only after motion on notice to all adverse parties.

(c) Protective order. The protective order provided for in CPLR § 3103 shall be available in this court with regard to all of the foregoing, and shall not be limited to the disclosure devices provided in article 31 of the CPLR.

§ 1102. Implied admissions.

The following provisions governing matters deemed admitted and the imposition of additional costs for unreasonable denials shall be applicable in this court.

(a) Ownership, operation or control of: 1. Vehicle. In an action for negligence arising from the ownership, operation or control of a vehicle required to be registered or licensed, where the pleading containing the cause of action states the registration or license number of such vehicle, the pleader need not prove upon the trial the ownership, operation or control of such vehicle by the other party and the same shall be deemed admitted, unless specifically denied in the responsive pleading.

2. Streetcar or bus. In an action for negligence arising from the ownership, operation or control of any streetcar or omnibus in the state of New York, where the pleading containing the cause of action states the avenue or street upon which the said streetcar or omnibus was operated, the place where the accident occurred, and the number of the streetcar or omnibus or the name or number of any of the employees operating the said streetcar or omnibus at the time in question, the pleader need not prove upon the trial the ownership, operation or control of the particular streetcar or omnibus by the other party and the same shall be deemed admitted, unless specifically denied in the responsive pleading.

3. Building. In an action for negligence arising from the ownership, operation or control of any building, dwelling or tenement house, where the pleading containing the cause of action states the full address of the building, dwelling or tenement house and the date when the acts complained of took place, the pleader need not prove upon the trial the ownership, operation or control of such building, dwelling or tenement house by the other party

and the same shall be deemed admitted, unless specifically denied in the responsive pleading.

(b) Signature. A signature to a written instrument which is pleaded shall be deemed genuine unless the other party, in his responsive pleading, specifically denies its genuineness and makes demand that it be proved.

(c) Corporate existence. In an action by or against a corporation organized or authorized to do business pursuant to the laws of the state of New York, the existence of such corporation shall be deemed admitted unless specifically denied in the responsive pleading.

(d) In the event of the unreasonable or unjustifiable denial of any of the matters contained in subdivisions (a), (b) or (c), and the satisfactory proof thereof, upon trial, by the party who pleaded them, the court may allow such party, if he prevails in the action, additional costs not to exceed twenty-five dollars for each such denial.

SYNOPSIS

Article 12   Subpoenas.

§ 1201.   Subpoenas.

A subpoena and subpoena duces tecum, and the powers of the court with reference to them, shall elsewhere outside governed by the CPLR, except that they shall be served only within the city of New York or in a county adjoining such city. But the court, upon motion of a party which need not be on notice, may issue either kind of subpoena and permit its service elsewhere outside the city of New York if satisfied that the interests of justice would be served thereby.

Article 13. Trial.

§ 1301. How cause brought on for trial; notice of trial.

Upon joinder of issue the clerk shall place the case upon a general calendar. Where any party appears in person, the clerk shall fix a date for trial not less than five nor more than fifteen days after joinder of issue, and shall immediately notify all the parties by mail of such date. If any of the parties has appeared by attorney, the clerk shall notify the attorney. Where all parties appear by attorney any party may serve a notice on the others fixing a date for trial not less than five nor more than eight days after the service of such notice, and shall file such notice, with proof of service thereof, with the clerk, who shall thereupon place the case on the calendar for trial. The case shall be set down for trial as provided for by the rules.

§ 1302. Adjournment of trial.

The trial of an action may be adjourned:

(a) By the court for good cause shown and upon such terms and conditions as the court may deem just.

(b) By stipulation of the parties with the approval of the court, such stipulation to be filed with the clerk; or upon request of the plaintiff where the defendant has made default; or, if the court approve, upon consent of the parties in open court.

§ 1303. Jury trial; how obtained; jury fee.

(a) Either party after joinder of issue may demand a trial by jury. The demand must be made in writing and must be filed with the clerk with the notice of trial set forth in § 1301. Any other party to the action

App Pract
Provs

within ten days after the service of a copy of the notice of trial upon him unaccompanied by a written notice demanding a trial by jury, may serve upon the attorneys for all the other parties to the action a written notice demanding a jury trial and file a copy of such notice with the clerk within three days after service thereof. In a summary proceeding to recover possession of real property, the demand may be made by the tenant at the time of answering or by the landlord at any time before the day of trial.

(b) Unless a demand is made and the jury fee paid as provided in section nineteen hundred eleven of this act, a jury trial is waived.

(c) The Court may relieve a party from the effect of failing to comply with this section if no undue prejudice to the rights of another party would result.

§ 1305. Number of jurymen.

A jury shall be composed of six persons.

§ 1306. Jury terms.

Jury terms shall be held as may from time to time be directed by rule or order. All provisions of law applicable to trial jurors in supreme court, insofar as such provisions are not inconsistent with this act, shall apply as nearly as may be in this court.

§ 1307. Jurors; challenges.

Challenges to jurors shall be as provided in the CPLR.

SYNOPSIS

Article 14. Judgment.

§ 1401. Judgments; in general.

Within the limits of its jurisdiction as defined in this act or as elsewhere provided by law, the court shall have power to render any judgment that the supreme court might render in a like case. The judgment in an action shall be prepared by the attorney for the successful party, except that if such party does not appear by attorney the judgment shall be prepared by the clerk. If the judgment is not prepared within thirty days after it is rendered, the attorney for the unsuccessful party may prepare the judgment, except that if such party does not appear by attorney, the judgment shall be prepared by the clerk upon request of such party. In a summary proceeding to recover possession of real property, the judgment shall be prepared by the clerk.

§ 1402. Default judgment.

A judgment by default may be entered as provided in CPLR § 3215.

A summons stating the amount for which the plaintiff will take judgment if the defendant fails to appear and answer, and containing a statement of the nature and substance of the cause of action, or a summons accompanied by a formal complaint, shall be deemed "the summons and the complaints" referred to in subdivision (e) of said section.

§ 1403. Confession of judgment.

The provisions of CPLR § 3218, relating to judgment by confession, shall be applicable in this court where the relief for which the judgment is confessed is within the jurisdiction of this court. For such purpose the words "clerk of the county" as used in CPLR § 3218(b) shall be deemed a reference to the clerk of this court in such county, and such judgment shall be entered in this court and shall be enforcible in the same manner and with the same effect as a judgment in an action in this court.

App Pract Provs

SYNOPSIS

Article 15.   Execution.

§ 1501.   Execution; when and how issued.

An execution, including an income execution, upon a judgment may be issued by the judgment-creditor's attorney or, if he does not appear by attorney, by the clerk of the court in the county where the judgment was entered. It shall be issued within the time prescribed by law applicable in the supreme court.

A "judgment," as used in this article, shall be deemed to include an order directing the payment of money.

§ 1502.   Transcript of judgment.

(a) Upon application of a judgment-creditor the clerk must deliver to him a transcript of the judgment. If the judgment is for other than money only, the clerk shall insert in the transcript a brief statement of the nature of the action and the relief awarded by the judgment; such statement may be inserted under "remarks" as contained in the form set forth in § 255–c of the judiciary law.

(b) The docketing of the judgment with the clerk of the county, and thereafter with other county clerks, shall be governed by the CPLR.

§ 1503.   Executions against marshals or sheriffs.

(a) Execution on a judgment against a marshal or his sureties shall issue only to the sheriff after transcript filed with the county clerk and must be made returnable to said clerk.

(b) Execution on a judgment against a sheriff shall issue to such person as the same would issue to in supreme court practice on a like judgment, and it shall issue only after transcript filed with the county clerk and must be made returnable to said clerk.

§ 1504.   Executions issued out of this court; requisites.

An execution issued out of this court may be levied only against personal property of the judgment-debtor. It shall be directed either to a marshal or the sheriff of the city of New York, and if directed to the sheriff it must be delivered to the office of the sheriff in the county in which it is to be levied. It must be subscribed by either the clerk of the court in the county in which the judgment was entered, or the attorney for the judgment-creditor, and must bear, in addition to such other matter as is required by the CPLR, the date of its delivery. It may be levied in any part of the city of New York, and for such purpose it is not necessary that the judgment have been docketed with any county clerk.

§ 1505.   Execution to be levied against real property.

An execution out of this court may not be levied against real property. In order for an execution on a judgment of this court to be levied against real property, a transcript of such judgment must be filed with the county clerk of the county wherein judgment was entered, pursuant to § 1502 of this act. After such transcripting, CPLR § 5018(a) shall be applicable and the judgment enforceable accordingly. This shall not be construed to prevent the issuance of an execution out of this court, pursuant and subject to § 1504 of this act, after such transcripting.

§ 1506.   Execution where order of attachment issued.

Where the real property of the judgment-debtor has been duly attached under an order of attachment that has not been vacated, the execution may not issue out of this court. In such a case, a transcript of the judgment must be filed and docketed with the county clerk and the execution issued out of supreme court.

§ 1507.   Limitation on execution against property of tenant.

No levy shall be made on the property of a tenant dispossessed for nonpayment of rent under any execution within twenty-four hours of the time of dispossess, if the property of which the tenant is being dispossessed was his residence.

§ 1508. Enforcement proceeding; injunction, receivership.

(a) An injunction or restraining order or notice may issue out of or by, and a receiver may be appointed by, the court if:

1. the court has been granted jurisdiction of an enforcement proceeding by CPLR § 5221; and

2. such remedy is utilized in furtherance of the enforcement of a money judgment.

(b) In any enforcement proceeding of which the court has jurisdiction, all processes, mandates, subpoenas, orders, notices and other papers therein may be served or executed by such means and at such place, regardless of city or state lines, as would be authorized in the supreme court in a like instance; and the powers of a receiver appointed in such proceeding, pursuant to subdivision (a), shall extend throughout the state.

§ 1509. Contempt; extension of court's process.

In an instance where a contempt of the court has been committed, the court's process or mandate relating to the punishment of the contemptuous person may beserved and executed in any part of the state, and proceedings thereon shall follow supreme court practice.

SYNOPSIS

Article 16.   Marshals.

§ 1601.   Marshals to continue in office; appointment of marshals; vacancies.

1. No more than eighty-three city marshals shall be appointed by the mayor. Upon the expiration of the terms of office of the duly appointed incumbents the mayor shall appoint their successors for terms of five years. Every marshal shall be, at the time of his or her appointment and during his or her term of office, a domiciliary of the city of New York, and his or her removal from the city shall vacate his or her office, provided that no marshal holding office on the effective date of this section as hereby amended shall be required to establish a domicile in the city of New York as a condition to remaining in office for the remainder of the term for which he or she was appointed. If a vacancy in the office of a marshal shall occur otherwise than by the expiration of a term the person appointed by the mayor to fill such vacancy shall hold office for the unexpired term of the marshal whom he or she succeeds.

2. An independent committee on city-marshals is hereby created. The committee shall consist of fifteen members, of whom six shall be selected by the mayor, three each shall be selected by the presiding justices of the first and second judicial departments and three shall be selected by the deans of law schools located within the city of New York. Performance of this function shall be rotated annually among such eligible deans. The members chosen by the mayor and the presiding justices shall serve for a term concurrent with the mayor's

term of office. The members chosen by the law school deans shall serve one year. Vacancies in the committee shall be filled in the same manner as initial appointments.

3. The committee shall establish and publish criteria for the appointment of marshals and shall recommend up to three qualified persons meeting such criteria for each appointment to the office of city marshal to be made by the mayor. In addition to any criteria established by the committee, all persons to be recommended to the mayor shall be required to provide to the department of investigation of the city of New York or any successor agency thereto, information relating to their background and financial resources in a form prescribed by such department. All communications to the committee, and its proceedings and all applications, correspondence, interviews, transcripts, reports and all other papers, files and records of the committee shall be confidential and shall be exempt from public disclosure.

4. No person shall be appointed to the office of city marshal except upon the recommendation of the committee on city marshals. No person shall be recommended to the mayor for appointment or reappointment as a marshal unless (i) a report on such person's background has been received by the committee from the department of investigation, and (ii) in the case of a reappointment, the committee has reviewed his or her record of performance in office and has determined it to be satisfactory.

5. The mayor shall, by executive order, establish or authorize the committee to establish such procedures to be followed by the committee in its review and recommendation of candidates for the office of city marshal as are consistent with the provisions of this article and as may be necessary to effectuate its purposes.

§ 1601–a.   City marshals; qualifications, prohibitions.

1. a. No person shall assume the office of city marshal on or after the effective date of this section unless he or she: (i) shall have earned a high school diploma or its equivalent: (ii) shall have satisfactorily completed, as of the date of his or her appointment, a training program: and (iii) shall have demonstrated that he or she has obtained or will be able to obtain a bond in the amount prescribed by this article. Prior service as a marshal for a period of two years or

more shall be deemed to satisfy the requirement that a marshal has obtained a high school diploma or its equivalent as a condition to qualifying for appointment.

b. The appellate division shall promulgate rules and regulations which specify what constitutes an acceptable training program and shall either establish such a program or provide for its establishment. Such rules and regulations shall set forth with particularity standards for performance which must be met by participants in the program in order that they may satisfactorily complete such program. The appellate division shall provide for the proper issuance of a certificate of satisfactory completion of training, which shall be submitted to the committee on marshals established pursuant to this article.

2. a. Except as provided by paragraph b of this subdivision, no marshal shall actively engage or participate in any other occupation or employment, nor shall any marshall engage or participate in any trade or business which creates or might tend to create an actual or potential conflict of interest. No marshal or member of his or her immediate family shall maintain any financial interest, direct or indirect, in a process serving agency, a towing company or a furniture moving and storage company. A violation of any of the provisions of this subdivision shall be cause for discipline, including removal pursuant to the procedures specified in section sixteen hundred ten of this article. For purposes of this subdivision, "immediate family" means spouse, parent, child, stepchild or sibling.

b. During any period of suspension pending a hearing on charges provided for by section sixteen hundred ten of this article, a marshal may actively engage in another occupation or employment, provided that such occupation or employment does not create or does not tend to creat an actual or potential conflict of interest.

§ 1602.   City marshals; badges.

The mayor is hereby authorized to prescribe the style, form and size of a badge to be known and designated as the official badge of the city marshals, a description of which he shall file in the office of the city clerk. Each city marshal shall provide himself at his own expense, with one such badge, and shall wear the same at all times while engaged in

App Pract Provs

the discharge of his official duties. Every city marshal shall display his badge upon demand. Every city marshal shall forthwith surrender his official badge to the city clerk upon the expiration of his term or upon the vacation of his office for any reason and the city clerk is hereby authorized to refund the sum originally charged therefor. Any person violating the provisions of this section shall be punished by imprisonment for a term not exceeding thirty days or a fine not exceeding two hundred dollars for each offense.

§ 1603. Persons pretending to be city marshals.

It shall be unlawful for any person, other than a marshal of the city of New York, to hold himself out to the public as being a marshal or as being in any way authorized to act as a marshal or to perform the duties of a marshal; and it shall be unlawful for any person, other than a marshal, to exhibit any sign with the words "marshal's bureau" thereon or any other words or terms whereby the public may be led to believe that he is a city marshal or authorized to act as such, or that his office is the office of a city marshal. It shall be unlawful for any city marshal to permit any person, other than a city marshal, to perform any act in his name, or to sign or to use his name in the performance of any act which must be performed personally by a city marshal. Any person violating any of the provisions of this section shall be guilty of a misdemeanor and shall be punished by imprisonment for a term not exceeding one month or a fine not exceeding two hundred dollars for each offense.

§ 1604. Bond of marshal.

(a) No marshal shall be permitted to enter upon the duties of his office until he shall have given a bond as herein prescribed. The bond shall be executed by the marshal with two sufficient sureties, who shall be residents of the city of New York and each of whom shall be the owner of real estate therein of the value of double the penalty of the bond. The penalty of the bond shall be the sum of sixty thousand dollars. Except as hereinafter provided, beginning July first, nineteen hundred ninety-nine, the penalty of the bond shall increase to the sum of eighty thousand dollars and beginning July first, two thousand, the penalty of the bond shall increase to the sum of one hundred thousand dollars. If on June thirtieth, nineteen hundred ninety-nine the provisions of subdivision (s-1) of section one hundred five of the civil practice law and rules and paragraph b of subdivision one of section sixteen hundred nine of the New York city civil court act are repealed pursuant to section three of chapter four hundred fifty-five of the laws of nineteen hundred ninety-seven, the penalty of the bond shall remain sixty thousand dollars and shall not increase to the sum of eighty thousand dollars on July first, nineteen hundred ninety-nine or to the sum of one hundred thousand dollars on July first, two thousand. The bond shall provide that the marshal and the sureties shall jointly and severally answer to the city of New York and any persons that may complain, for the true and faithful execution by such marshal of the duties of his office. The bond shall be submitted for approval to a judge of the court and such judge shall have power to require that the sureties justify before him within five days after the bond shall have been submitted, and shall approve or reject the bond within five days thereafter. When so approved, the bond shall be filed with the city clerk of the city of New York. A marshal already qualified for and in office on any date upon which the penalty of the bond shall increase pursuant to this subdivision shall within thirty days after such date file with the city clerk an additional bond, otherwise executed as provided for herein and approved by a judge of the court, in an amount sufficient to bring the total amount of such bond to the penalty amount provided in this subdivision. If on June thirtieth, nineteen hundred ninety-nine the provisions of subdivision (s-1) of section one hundred five of the civil practice law and rules and paragraph b of subdivision one of section sixteen hundred nine of the New York city civil court act are repealed pursuant to section three of chapter four hundred fifty-five of the laws of nineteen hundred ninety-seven, the penalty of the bond shall remain sixty thousand dollars and shall not increase to the sum of eighty thousand dollars on July first, nineteen hundred ninety-nine or to the sum of one hundred thousand dollars on July first, two thousand. The bond shall provide that the marshal and the sureties shall jointly and severally answer to the city of New York and any persons that may complain, for the true and faithful execution by such marshal of the duties of his office. The bond shall be submitted for approval to a judge of the court and such judge shall have power to require that the sureties justify before him within five days after the bond shall have been submitted, and shall approve or reject the bond within five days

App Pract Provs

thereafter. When so approved, the bond shall be filed with the city clerk of the city of New York. A marshal already qualified for and in office on any date upon which the penalty of the bond shall increase pursuant to this subdivision shall within thirty days after such date file with the city clerk an additional bond, otherwise executed as provided for herein and approved by a judge of the court, in an amount sufficient to bring the total amount of such bond to the penalty amount provided in this subdivision.

(b) The bond must be executed, approved and filed within thirty days after the appointment of the marshal or he shall be deemed to have declined his appointment and another person shall be appointed in his place.

§ 1605.   Action on marshal's bond.

An action upon the bond of a marshal may be brought and prosecuted to judgment in this court, upon leave obtained from a judge of this court, according to the provisions relating to an action in the supreme court by a private person upon an official bond.

§ 1606.   Filing of transcript of judgment with city clerk; reducing bond.

Upon the filing with the city clerk of a transcript of a judgment on the bond of a marshal, the city clerk shall make a memorandum on the bond of the time when and the court by which such judgment was rendered and the amount thereof, and he shall be entitled to a fee of fifty cents therefor, which the court rendering the judgment shall have power to include therein; and the bond shall be reduced by the amount of the judgment.

§ 1607.   Reducing bond on payment.

Whenever the sureties of the marshal shall pay the amount for which the action on the marshal's bond is brought, and the costs and disbursements incurred therein, or any part thereof, they shall be entitled to have such sum credited upon the bond upon presenting to the city clerk the affidavit of the plaintiff or his attorney in such action, acknowledging the payment; whereupon such clerk shall endorse the payment on the bond and the bond shall be reduced by the amount so paid.

§ 1608.   Appellate division to compel renewal of marshal's bond; removal of marshal.

Whenever judgement shall be rendered on the bond of a marshal, or the bond shall be reduced as provided in the last preceding section, the city clerk shall report the fact to the appellate division. If the amount of the judgment is equal to or greater than the amount of the bond the appellate division shall direct the marshal to furnish a new bond; or, if the amount of the judgment is less than the amount of the bond, or in case of a reduction thereof, the appellate division shall direct the marshal to furnish an additional bond in the penal sum of double the amount of the judgment or the reduction. If the marshal fails to comply with such direction within ten days after notice thereof, his failure shall constitute ground for his removal from office.

§ 1609.   General powers, duties and liabilities of marshals; small claims judgments.

App Pract
Provs

[*Effective until June 30, 2014, pursuant to L. 2009, Ch. 103*]

1. a. The authority of a marshal extends throughout the city of New York and all provisions of law relating to the powers, duties and liabilities of sheriffs in like cases and in respect to the taking and restitution of property, shall apply to marshals. Every marshal shall keep a record of his or her official acts in such manner as shall be prescribed by the appellate division. Such records shall show, in addition to the official acts of the marshal, all fees and sums received by the marshal therefor, the expenses of the marshal in connection with the performance of his or her official duties and his gross and net income as such marshal. The records of every marshal shall be open to inspection by the appellate division and such officers or employees of the court, or other persons, agencies or officials, as may be designated by the appellate division.

b. Notwithstanding any inconsistent provision of this act or of any other general, special or local law, code, charter, or ordinance, all provisions of law relating to the powers, duties and liabilities of the city sheriff in like cases in respect to the enforcement within the city of money judgments rendered by any family court or money judgments entered in any supreme court or docketed with the clerk of any county, shall apply to marshals, except that city marshals shall have no power to levy upon or sell real property and city marshals shall have no power of arrest.

2. The appellate division shall promulgate rules and regulations concerning performance of official duties of marshals.

3. a. The appellate division shall promulgate rules and regulations providing for the assignment of specified marshals on a rotating basis during fixed time periods, to the task of executing and enforcing small claims judgments within the city of New York whenever executions of such judgments are delivered to such marshals in accordance with law. Such rules and regulations shall include provisions requiring such marshals to submit quarterly reports to an agency designated by the appellate division, reporting each such judgment collected and each unsuccessful attempt at collection and the reason or reasons for any lack of success at collection.

b. The clerk of the small claims part in each county shall freely distribute to litigants copies of a list of the names, office addresses and phone numbers and dates and counties of assignment of all marshals currently assigned within the city of New York pursuant to this subdivision. He shall also provide to litigants a list, in a form approved by the appellate division, containing information which a judgment creditor should provide to a marshal to assist him or her in the execution or enforcement of a judgment.

§ 1610.   Discipline, suspension and removal on charges.

The appellate division may discipline by reprimand or censure, or may temporarily suspend or permanently remove any marshal for cause, provided that written charges are first filed with said court, and that the marshal be given due notice thereof and be afforded an opportunity to be heard at a full and complete hearing. The appellate division may, in its discretion, suspend a marshal from the performance of his or her official duties pending a hearing upon the charges. Upon charges being preferred against a marshal by a judge of the appellate division, such court shall forthwith cause notice of suspension of the marshal to be served upon him or her, and the marshal shall thereupon remain suspended until the hearing and determination of the charges. Such hearing shall be held within sixty days from the date of service of notice of suspension upon a marshal, except that the period of time prescribed herein may be extended for good cause shown upon application. In lieu of discipline by temporary suspension or removal, the appellate division may assess a fine, not to exceed five hundred dollars, against any marshal who has been found, after a hearing, to be in violation of the provisions of this article or of the rules and regulations promulgated pursuant thereto.

§ 1611.   Fees to the city of New York.

1. Every city marshal who serves in office for any portion of the calendar year shall pay an annual fee to the city of New York of fifteen hundred dollars.

2. Every city marshal shall, in addition to the fee required by subdivision one, pay annually to the city of New York 4.50 percent of the gross fees, including poundage, received by the marshal during the preceding calendar year.

App Pract
Provs

3. The fees paid to the city of New York pursuant to this section shall be disbursed for the purposes of this article.

§ 1612.   Appellate division to continue authority.

The appellate division may continue to delegate its authority under this article, except that its authority permanently to remove a marshall shall not be delegated.

———

SYNOPSIS

Article 17.   Appeals.

§ 1701.   Appeals; to what court.

Appeals shall be taken from the court to the appellate division of the supreme court in the department in which the action or proceeding is pending, unless an appellate term of the supreme court has been established by said appellate division and it has directed that such appeals be taken to such term, in which case the appeal shall be taken to the appellate term.

§ 1702.   Appeals; judgments and orders appealable.

(a) Appeals as of right. An appeal may be taken as of right:

1. from any final or interlocutory judgment except one entered subsequent to an order of an appellate court which disposes of all the issues in the action; or

2. from an order not specified in subdivision (b), where the motion it decided was made upon notice and it:

(i) grants, refuses, continues or modifies a provisional remedy; or

(ii) settles, grants or refuses an application to resettle a transcript or statement on appeal; or

(iii) grants or refuses a new trial; except where specific questions of fact arising upon the issues in an action triable by the court have been tried by a jury, pursuant to an order for that purpose, and the order grants or refuses a new trial upon the merits; or

(iv) involves some part of the merits; or

(v) affects a substantial right; or

(vi) in effect determines the action and prevents a judgment from which an appeal might be taken; or

(vii) determines a statutory provision of the state to be unconstitutional, and the determination appears from the reasons given for the decision or is necessarily implied in the decision; or

3. from an order, where the motion it decided was made upon notice, refusing to vacate or modify a prior order, if the prior order would have been appealable as of right under paragraph two had it decided a motion made upon notice.

(b) Orders not appealable as of right. An order is not appealable as of right where it:

1. requires or refuses to require a more definite statement in a pleading; or

2. orders or refuses to order that scandalous or prejudicial matter be stricken from a pleading.

(c) Appeals by permission. An appeal may be taken from any order which is not appealable as of right by permission of the judge who made the order granted before application to a justice of the appellate court; or by permission of a justice of the appellate court upon refusal by the judge who made the order or upon direct application.

(d) On any appeal taken hereunder the appellate court shall have full power to review any exercise of discretion by the court or judge below.

§ 1703.   Appeals; practice and procedure in general.

(a) Practice and procedure on appeals shall be as provided in article 55 of the CPLR except insofar as this act or the rules of this court consistent with this act otherwise provide.

(b) An appeal as of right from a judgment entered in a small claim or a commercial claim must be taken within thirty days of the following, whichever first occurs:

1. service by the court of a copy of the judgment appealed from upon the appellant.

2. service by a party of a copy of the judgment appealed from upon the appellant.

3. service by the appellant of a copy of the judgment appealed from upon a party.

Where service as provided in paragraphs one through three of this subdivision is by mail, five days shall be added to the thirty day period prescribed in this section.

§ 1704.   Settlement of case and return on appeal.

(a) When an appeal has been taken as herein prescribed, the stenographer's original transcript of minutes must be furnished to the clerk within ten days after the fees therefor have been paid. Immediately upon receiving such minutes the clerk shall cause notice of that fact to be sent to the attorney for the appellant, or to the appellant if he or she has not appeared by attorney. Within fifteen days after receiving the transcript from the clerk, or from any other source, the appellant or the appellant's attorney shall make any proposed amendments and cause them to be served, together with a copy of the transcript, on the attorney for the respondent, or on the respondent if he or she has not appeared by attorney. Within fifteen days after such service, the respondent or the respondent's attorney shall make any proposed amendments to the transcript or objections to the proposed amendments of the appellant and cause them to be served on the appellant's attorney or on the appellant if he or she has not appeared by attorney.

The appellant or his or her attorney shall then procure the case to be settled on a written notice of at least four days to the clerk and to the attorney for the respondent or to the respondent if he or she has not appeared by attorney, returnable before the judge who tried the case. The clerk must thereupon make a return to the appellate court, which must contain the summons or notice of petition, pleadings, evidence, judgment and all other necessary papers and proceedings, and have annexed thereto the opinion of the court, if any, and the notice of appeal. The judge before whom the case was tried shall within five days from the date of the submission to the court of the case on appeal, settle the case and indorse his or her settlement on the return. In lieu of the judge settling the case and indorsing his or her settlement on the return, the parties may stipulate that the transcript together with the proposed amendments, if any, and all other elements of the return are correct. The clerk must thereupon cause the return to be filed with the clerk of the appellate court. After a judge is out of office he or she may settle the case in any action or proceeding tried before him or her and may be compelled by the appellate court so to do.

(b) When no testimony was taken and a settlement of a case is not required, the return shall be made by the clerk forthwith upon filing the notice of appeal. Such return shall contain the judgment or order appealed from and all the original papers upon which the judgment or order was rendered or made, duly authenticated by the certificate of the clerk having the custody thereof, or copies thereof duly certified by such clerk, and shall have annexed thereto the opinion of the court, if any, and the notice of appeal.

(c) Upon an appeal from an order granting or denying a motion for a new trial, upon the ground of fraud or newly discovered evidence, the stenographer's minutes of the trial shall be included in the return of the clerk and the provisions of subdivision (a) of this section shall apply to such an appeal.

§ 1705. Printing; record and briefs.

The printing of neither the record nor the briefs shall be required except as the rules of the court to which the appeal is taken shall provide in designated classes of appeals.

§ 1706. Appeals from appellate court.

App Pract Provs

Appeals from the judgment or order of an appellate court, or appeal from this court, shall be governed by the CPLR.

§ 1707. Appeal to the court of appeals.

An appeal may be taken direct to the court of appeals from a judgment or order which finally determines an action or special proceeding where the only question involved on the appeal is the validity of a statutory provision of the state or of the United States under the constitution of the state or of the United States. On any such appeal only the constitutional question shall be considered and determined by the court.

SYNOPSIS

Article 18.   Small claims.

§ 1801.   Small claims defined.

The term "small claim" or "small claims" as used in this act shall mean and include any cause of action for money only not in excess of five thousand dollars exclusive of interest and costs, provided that the defendant either resides, or has an office for the transaction of business or a regular employment, within the city of New York.

§ 1802.   Parts for the determination of small claims established.

The chief administrator shall assign the times and places for holding, and the judges who shall hold one or more parts of the court in each county for the hearing of small claims as herein defined, and the rules may regulate the practice and procedure controlling the determination of such claims and prescribe and furnish the forms for instituting the same. There shall be at least one evening session of each part every month for the hearing of small claims, provided however, that the chief administrator may provide for exemption from this requirement where there exists no demonstrated need for evening sessions. Such practice, procedure and forms shall differ from the practice, procedure and forms used in the court for other than small claims, notwithstanding any provision of law to the contrary. They shall constitute a simple, informal and inexpensive procedure for the prompt determination of such claims in accordance with the rules and principles of substantive law. The procedure established pursuant to this article shall not be exclusive of but shall be alternative to the procedure now or hereafter established with respect to actions commenced in the court by the service of a summons. No rule to be enacted pursuant to this article shall dispense with or interfere with the taking of stenographic minutes of any hearing of any small claim hereunder.

§ 1803.   Commencement of action upon small claims.

(a) Small claims shall be commenced upon the payment by the claimant of a filing fee of fifteen dollars for claims in the amount of one thousand dollars or less and twenty dollars for claims in the amount of more than one thousand dollars, without the service of a summons and, except by special order of the court, without the service of any pleading other than a statement of his cause of action by the claimant or someone in his behalf to the clerk, who shall reduce the same to a concise, written form and record it in a docket kept especially for such purpose. Such procedure shall provide for the sending of notice of such claim by ordinary first class mail and certified mail with return receipt requested to the party complained against at his residence, if he resides within the city of New York, and his residence is known to the claimant, or at his office or place of regular employment within the city of New York if he does not reside therein or his residence within the city of New York is not known to the claimant. If, after the expiration of twenty-one days, such ordinary first class mailing has not been returned as undeliverable, the party complained against shall be presumed to have received notice of such claim. Such notice shall include a clear description of the procedure for filing a counterclaim, pursuant to subdivision (c) of this section.

Such procedure shall further provide for an early hearing upon and determination of such claim. No filing fee, however, shall be demanded or received on small claims of employees who shall comply with § 1912 (a) of this act which is hereby made applicable, except that necessary mailing costs shall be paid.

(b) The clerk shall furnish every claimant, upon commencement of the action, with information written in clear and coherent language which shall be prescribed and furnished by the office of court administration, concerning the small claims court. Such information shall include, but not be limited to, an explanation of the following terms and procedures; adjournments, counterclaims, jury trial requests, subpoenas, arbitration, collection methods and fees, the responsibility of the judgment creditor to collect data on the judgment debtor's assets, the ability of the court prior to entering judgment to order examination of or disclosure by, the defendant and restrain him, the utilization of section eighteen hundred twelve of this article concerning treble damage awards and information subpoenas including, but not limited to, specific questions to be used on information subpoenas, and the claimant's right to notify the appropriate state or local licensing or certifying authority of an unsatisfied judgment if it arises out of the carrying on, conducting or transaction of a licensed or certified business or if such business appears to be engaged in fraudulent or illegal acts or otherwise demonstrates fraud or illegality in the carrying on, conducting or transaction of its business and a list of at least the most prominent state or local licensing or certifying authorities and a description of the business categories such licensing or certifying authorities oversee. The information shall be available in English. Large signs in English shall be posted in conspicuous locations in each small claims court clerk's office, advising the public of its availability.

(c) A defendant who wishes to file a counterclaim shall do so by filing with the clerk a statement containing such counterclaim within five days of receiving the notice of claim. At the time of such filing the defendant shall pay to the clerk a filing fee of five dollars plus the cost of mailings which are required pursuant to this subdivision. The clerk shall forthwith send notice of the counterclaim by ordinary first class mail to the claimant. If the defendant fails to file the counterclaim in accordance with the provisions of this subdivision, the defendant retains the right to file the counterclaim, however the claimant may, but shall not be required to, request and obtain adjournment of the hearing to a later date. The claimant may reply to the counterclaim but shall not be required to do so.

§ 1804.   Informal and simplified procedure on small claims.

The court shall conduct hearings upon small claims in such manner as to do substantial justice between the parties according to the rules of substantive law and shall not be bound by statutory provisions or rules of practice, procedure, pleading or evidence, except statutory provisions relating to privileged communications and personal transactions or communications with a decedent or mentally ill person. An itemized bill or invoice, receipted or marked paid, or two itemized estimates for services or repairs, are admissible in evidence and are prima facie evidence of the reasonable value and necessity of such services and repairs. Disclosure shall be unavailable in small claims procedure except upon order of the court on showing of proper circumstances. In every small claims action, where the claim arises out of the conduct of the defendant's business at the hearing on the matter, the judge or arbitrator shall determine the appropriate state or local licensing or certifying authority and any business or professional association of which the defendant is a member. The provisions of this act and the rules of this court, together with the statutes and rules governing supreme court practice, shall apply to claims brought under this article

App Pract
Provs

so far as the same can be made applicable and are not in conflict with the provisions of this article; in case of conflict, the provisions of this article shall control.

§ 1805.   Remedies available; transfer of small claims.

(a) Upon determination of a small claim, the court shall direct judgment in accordance with its findings, and, when necessary to do substantial justice between the parties, may condition the entry of judgment upon such terms as the court shall deem proper. Pursuant to section fifty-two hundred twenty-nine of the civil practice law and rules, prior to entering judgment, the court may order the examination of or disclosure by, the defendant and restrain him to the same extent as if a restraining notice had been served upon him after judgment was entered.

(b) The court shall have power to transfer any small claim or claims to any other part of the court upon such terms as the rules may provide, and proceed to hear the same according to the usual practice and procedure applicable to other parts of the court.

(c) No counterclaim shall be permitted in a small claims action, unless the court would have had monetary jurisdiction over the counterclaim if it had been filed as a small claim. Any other claim sought to be maintained against the claimant may be filed in any court of competent jurisdiction.

(d) If the defendant appears to be engaged in repeated fraudulent or illegal acts or otherwise demonstrates persistent fraud or illegality in the carrying on, conducting or transaction of business, the court shall either advise the attorney general in relation to his authority under subdivision twelve of section sixty-three of the executive law, or shall advise the claimant to do same, but shall retain jurisdiction over the small claim.

(e) If the defendant appears to be engaged in fraudulent or illegal acts or otherwise demonstrates fraud or illegality in the carrying on, conducting or transaction of a licensed or certified business, the court shall either advise the appropriate state or local licensing or certifying authority or shall advise the claimant to do same, but shall retain jurisdiction over the small claim.

§ 1806.   Trial by jury; how obtained; discretionary costs.

A person commencing an action upon a small claim under this article shall be deemed to have waived a trial by jury, but if said action shall be removed to a regular part of the court, the plaintiff shall have the same right to demand a trial by jury as if such action had originally been begun in such part. Any party to such action, other than the plaintiff, prior to the day upon which he is notified to appear or answer, may file with the court a demand for a trial by jury and his affidavit that there are issues of fact in the action requiring such a trial, specifying the same and stating that such trial is desired and intended in good faith. Such demand and affidavit shall be accompanied with the jury fee required by law and an undertaking in the sum of fifty dollars in such form as may be approved by the rules, payable to the other party or parties, conditioned upon the payment of any costs which may be entered against him in the said action or any appeal within thirty days after the entry thereof; or, in lieu of said undertaking, the sum of fifty dollars may be deposited with the clerk of the court and thereupon the clerk shall forthwith transmit such original papers or duly attested copies there of as may be provided by the rules to the part of the court to which the action shall have been transferred and assigned and such part may require pleadings in such action as though it had been begun by the service of a summons. Such action may be considered a preferred cause of action. In any small claim which may have been transferred to another part of the court, the court may award costs up to twenty-five dollars to the plaintiff if he prevails.

§ 1807.   Review.

A person commencing an action upon a small claim under this article shall be deemed to have waived all right to appeal, except that either party may appeal on the sole grounds that substantial justice has not been done between the parties according to the rules and principles of substantive law.

§ 1808.   Judgment obtained to be res judicata in certain cases.

A judgment obtained under this article shall not be deemed an adjudication of any fact at issue or found therein in any other action or court; except that a subsequent judgment obtained in another action or court involving the same facts, issues and parties shall be reduced by the amount of a judgment awarded under this article.

§ 1809.   Procedures relating to corporations, associations, insurers and assignees.

1. No corporation, except a municipal corporation, public benefit corporation, school district or school district public library wholly or partially within the municipal corporate limit, no partnership, or association and no assignee of any small claim shall institute an action or proceeding under this article, nor shall this article apply to any claim or cause of action brought by an insurer in its own name or in the name of its insured whether before or after payment to the insured on the policy.

2. A corporation may appear in the defense of any small claim action brought pursuant to this article by an attorney as well as by any authorized officer, director or employee of the corporation provided that the appearance by a non-lawyer on behalf of a corporation shall be deemed to constitute the requisite authority to bind the corporation in a settlement or trial. The court or arbitrator may make reasonable inquiry to determine the authority of any person who appears for the corporation in defense of a small claims court case.

§ 1810.   Limitation on right to resort to small claims procedures.

If the clerk shall find that the procedures of the small claims part are sought to be utilized by a claimant for purposes of oppression or harassment, as where a claimant has previously resorted to such procedures on the same claim and has been unsuccessful after the hearing thereon, the clerk may in his discretion compel the claimant to make application to the court for leave to prosecute the claim in the small claims part. The court upon such application may inquire into the circumstances and, if it shall find that the claim has already been adjudicated, or that the claim is sought to be brought on solely for purposes of oppression or harassment and not under color of right, it may make an order denying the claimant the use of the small claims part to prosecute the claim.

§ 1811.   Notice of small claims judgments and indexing of

unpaid claims.

(a) Notice of judgment sent to judgment debtor shall specify that a failure to satisfy a judgment may subject the debtor to any one or combination of the following actions:

1. garnishment of wage;

2. garnishment of bank account;

3. a lien on personal property;

4. seizure and sale of real property;

5. seizure and sale of personal property, including automobiles;

6. suspension of motor vehicle license and registration, if claim is based on defendant's ownership or operation of a motor vehicle;

7. revocation, suspension, or denial of renewal of any applicable business license or permit;

8. investigation and prosecution by the attorney general for fraudulent or illegal business practices; and

9. a penalty equal to three times the amount of the unsatisfied judgment plus attorney's fees, if there are other unpaid claims.

(b) Notice of judgment sent to judgment creditor shall contain but not be limited to the following information:

1. the claimant's right to payment within thirty days following the debtor's receipt of the judgment notice;

2. the procedures for use of section eighteen hundred twelve of this article concerning the identification of assets of the judgment debtor, including the use of information subpoenas, access to consumer credit reports and the role of sheriffs and marshals, and actions to collect three times the judgment award and attorney's fees if there are two other unsatisfied claims against the debtor;

3. the claimant's right to initiate actions to recover the unpaid judgment through the sale of the debtor's real property, or personal property;

4. the claimant's right to initiate actions to recover the unpaid judgment through suspension of debtor's motor vehicle license and

App Pract Provs

registration, if claim is based on defendant's ownership or operation of a motor vehicle;

5. the claimant's right to notify the appropriate state or local licensing or certifying authority of an unsatisfied judgment as a basis for possible revocation, suspension, or denial of renewal of business license; and

6. a statement that upon satisfying the judgment, the judgment debtor shall present appropriate proof thereof to the court; and

7. the claimant's right to notify the attorney general if the debtor is a business and appears to be engaged in fraudulent or illegal business practices.

(c) Notice of judgment sent to each party shall include the following statement: "An appeal from this judgment must be taken no later than the earliest of the following dates: (i) thirty days after receipt in court of a copy of the judgment by the appealing party, (ii) thirty days after personal delivery of a copy of the judgment by another party to the action to the appealing party (or by the appealing party to another party), or (iii) thirty-five days after the mailing of a copy of the judgment to the appealing party by the clerk of the court or by another party to the action."

(d) All wholly or partially unsatisfied small claims court judgments shall be indexed alphabetically and chronologically under the name of the judgment debtor. Upon satisfying the judgment, the judgment debtor shall present appropriate proof to the court and the court shall indicate such in the records.

§ 1812.   Enforcement of small claims judgments.

(a) The special procedures set forth in subdivision (b) hereof shall be available only where:

1. there is a recorded judgment of a small claims court; and

2. (i) the aforesaid judgment resulted from a transaction in the course of the trade or business of the judgment debtor, or arose out of a repeated course of dealing or conduct of the judgment debtor, and

(ii) there are at least two other unsatisfied recorded judgments of a small claims court arising out of such trade or business or repeated course of dealing or conduct, against that judgment debtor; and

3. the judgment debtor failed to satisfy such judgment within a period of thirty days after receipt of notice of such judgment. Such notice shall be given in the same manner as provided for the service of a summons or by certified mail, return receipt requested, and shall contain a statement that such judgment exists, that at least two other unsatisfied recorded judgments exist, and that failure to pay such judgment may be the basis for an action, for treble the amount of such unsatisfied judgment, pursuant to this section.

(b) Where each of the elements of subdivision (a) of this section are present the judgment creditor shall be entitled to commence an action against said judgment debtor for treble the amount of such unsatisfied judgment, together with reasonable counsel fees, and the costs and disbursements of such action, provided, however, that in any such action it shall be a defense that the judgment debtor did not have resources to satisfy such judgment within a period of thirty days after receipt of notice of such judgment. The failure to pay a judgment obtained in an action pursuant to this section shall not be the basis for another such action pursuant to this section.

(c) Where the judgment is obtained in an action pursuant to subdivision (b), and arises from a business of the defendant, the court shall, in addition to its responsibilities under this article, advise the attorney general in relation to his authority under subdivision twelve of section sixty-three of the executive law, and if such judgment arises from a certified or licensed business of the defendant, advise the state or local licensing or certifying authority.

(d) Where a judgment has been entered in a small claims court and remains unsatisfied, the small claims clerk shall, upon request, issue information subpoenas, at nominal cost, for the judgment creditor and provide the creditor with assistance on their preparation and use. The court shall have the same power as the supreme court to punish a contempt of court committed with respect to an information subpoena.

§ 1813. Duty to pay judgments.

(a) Any person, partnership, firm or corporation which is sued in a

App Pract
Provs

small claims court for any cause of action arising out of its business activities, shall pay any judgment rendered against it in its true name or in any name in which it conducts business. "True name" includes the legal name of a natural person and the name under which a partnership, firm or corporation is licensed, registered, incorporated or otherwise authorized to do business. "Conducting business" as used in this section shall include, but not be limited to, maintaining signs at business premises or on business vehicles; advertising; entering into contracts; and printing or using sales slips, checks, invoices or receipts. Whenever a judgment has been rendered against a person, partnership, firm or corporation in other than its true name and the judgment has remained unpaid for thirty-five days after receipt by the judgment debtor of notice of its entry, the aggrieved judgment creditor shall be entitled to commence an action in small claims court or in any other court of otherwise competent jurisdiction against such judgment debtor, notwithstanding the jurisdictional limit of the court, for the sum of the original judgment, costs, reasonable attorney's fees, and one hundred dollars.

(b) Whenever a judgment which relates to activities for which a license is required has been rendered against a business which is licensed by a state or local licensing authority and which remains unpaid for thirty-five days after receipt by the judgment debtor of notice of its entry and the judgment has not been stayed or appealed, the state or local licensing authority shall consider such failure to pay if deliberate or part of a pattern of similar conduct indicating recklessness, as a basis for the revocation, suspension, conditioning or refusal to grant or renew such license. Nothing herein shall be construed to preempt an authority's existing policy if it is more restrictive.

(c) The clerk shall attach to the notice of suit required under this article a notice of the duty imposed by this section.

§ 1814. Designation of defendant; amendment procedure.

(a) A party who is ignorant, in whole or in part, of the true name of a person, partnership, firm or corporation which may properly be made a party defendant, may proceed against such defendant in any name used by the person, partnership, firm or corporation in conducting business, as defined in subdivision (a) of section eighteen hundred thirteen of this article.

(b) If the true name of the defendant becomes known at any time prior to the hearing on the merits, such information shall be brought to the attention of the clerk, who shall immediately amend all prior proceedings and papers. The clerk shall send an amended notice to the defendant, without payment of additional fees by the plaintiff, and all subsequent proceedings and papers shall be amended accordingly.

(c) In every action in the small claims part, at the hearing on the merits, the judge or arbitrator shall determine the defendant's true name. The clerk shall amend all prior proceedings and papers to conform to such determination, and all subsequent proceedings and papers shall be amended accordingly.

(d) A party against whom a judgment has been entered pursuant to this article, in any proceeding under section five thousand fifteen of the civil practice law and rules for relief from such judgment, shall, disclose its true name; any and all names in which it is conducting business; and any and all names in which it was conducting business at the time of the transaction or occurrence on which such judgment is based. All subsequent proceedings and papers shall be amended to conform to such disclosure.

§ 1815.   [*VERSION ONE*] Appearance by non-attorney representatives.

The court may permit, upon the request of a party, that a non-attorney representative, who is related by consanguinity or affinity to such party, be allowed to appear on behalf of such party when the court finds that due to the age, mental or physical capacity or other disability of such party that it is in the interests of justice to permit such representation. No person acting as a non-attorney representative shall be permitted to charge a fee or be allowed to accept any form of remuneration for such services.

§ 1815.   [*VERSION TWO*] Access to daytime pro se part.

1. Senior citizens, disabled persons and members of the work force whose normal work schedule requires them to work during evening hours may institute a small claims action or proceeding returnable to the daytime pro se part of the court.

App Pract
Provs

2. The clerk of the court shall verbally inform all claimants who appear to qualify or who submit adequate documentation, upon commencement of the small claims action, of the right to have any small claims heard in the daytime pro se part upon such terms as provided herein. Notwithstanding any inconsistent provision of law, a claimant shall have the right upon presenting proof to the clerk that he is sixty-five years of age or older, that he is disabled as defined in subdivision twenty-one of section two hundred ninety-two of the executive law or that he is employed in a capacity which requires him to work during evening hours and the court shall proceed to hear the case according to the practice and procedure applicable to the small claims part.

3. The clerk of the court shall publicize the availability of such forum. Such publicity shall include but not be limited to prerecorded taped messages and large signs in English and Spanish to be posted in conspicuous locations in each small claims court clerk's office, advising the public of the availability.

SYNOPSIS

Article 18-A.   Commercial claims.

§ 1801-A.   Commercial claims defined.

(a) The term "commercial claim" or "commercial claims" as used in this article shall mean and include any cause of action for money only not in excess of the maximum amount permitted for a small claim in the small claims part of the court, exclusive of interest and costs, provided that subject to the limitations contained in section eighteen hundred nine-A of this article, the claimant is a corporation, partnership or association, which has its principal office in the state of New York and provided that the defendant either resides, or has an office for the transaction of business or a regular employment, within the city of New York.

(b) Consumer transaction defined. The term "consumer transaction" means a transaction between a claimant and a natural person, wherein the money, property or service which is the subject of the transaction is primarily for personal, family or household purposes.

§ 1802-A.   Parts for the determination of commercial claims established.

The chief administrator shall assign the times and places for holding, and the judges who shall hold, one or more parts of the court in each county for the hearing of commercial claims as herein defined, and the rules may regulate the practice and procedure controlling the determination of such claims and prescribe and furnish the forms for instituting the same. There shall be at least one evening session of each part every month for the hearing of commercial claims, provided however, that the chief administrator may provide for exemption from this requirement where there exists no demonstrated need for evening sessions. The chief administrator shall not combine commercial claims part actions with small claims part actions for purposes of convenience unless a preference is given to small claims and to commercial claims arising out of consumer transactions. Such practice, procedure and forms shall differ from the practice, procedure and forms used in the court for other than small claims and commercial claims, notwithstanding any provision of law to the contrary. They shall constitute a simple, informal and inexpensive procedure for the prompt determination of commercial claims in accordance with the rules and principles of substantive law. The procedure established pursuant to this article shall not be exclusive of but shall be alternative to the procedure now or hereafter established with respect to actions commenced in the court by the service of a summons. No rule to be enacted pursuant to this article shall dispense with or interfere with the taking of stenographic minutes of any hearing of any commercial claim hereunder.

§ 1803-A.   Commencement of action upon commercial claim.

(a) Commercial claims other than claims arising out of consumer transactions shall be commenced upon the payment by the claimant of a filing fee of twenty-five dollars and the cost of mailings as herein provided, without the service of a summons and, except by special order of the court, without the service of any pleading other than a required certification verified as to its truthfulness by the claimant on a form prescribed by the state office of court administration and filed with the clerk, that no more than five such actions or proceedings (including the instant action or proceeding) have been instituted during that calendar month, and a required statement of its cause of action by the claimant or someone in its behalf to the clerk, who shall reduce the same to a concise, written form and record it in a docket kept especially for such purpose. Such procedure shall provide that the commercial claims part of the court shall have no jurisdiction over, and shall dismiss, any case with respect to which the required certification is not made upon the attempted institution of the action or proceeding. Such procedure shall provide for the sending of notice of such claim by ordinary first class mail and certified mail with return receipt requested to the party complained against at his residence, if he resides within the city of New York, and his residence is known to the claimant, or at his office or place of regular employment within the city of New York if he does not reside therein or his residence within the city of New York is not known to the claimant. If, after the expiration of twenty-one days, such ordinary first class mailing has not been returned as undeliverable, the party complained against shall be presumed to have received notice of such claim. Such notice shall include a clear description of the procedure for filing a counterclaim, pursuant to subdivision (d) of this section.

Such procedure shall further provide for an early hearing upon and determination of such claim. The hearing shall be scheduled in a manner which, to the extent possible, minimizes the time the party complained against must be absent from employment.

Either party may request that the hearing be scheduled during evening hours, provided that the hearing shall not be scheduled during evening hours if it would cause unreasonable hardship to either party. The court shall not unreasonably deny requests for evening hearings if such requests are made by the claimant upon commencement of the action or by the party complained against within fourteen days of receipt of the notice of claim.

(b) Commercial claims in actions arising out of consumer transactions shall be commenced upon the payment by the claimant of a filing fee of twenty-five dollars and the cost of mailings as herein provided, without the service of a summons and, except by special order of the court, without the service of any pleading other than a required statement of the cause of action by the claimant or someone on its behalf of the clerk, who shall reduce the same to a concise written form including the information required by subdivision (c) of this section, denominate it conspicuously as a consumer transaction, and record it in the docket marked as a consumer transaction, and by filing with the clerk a required certificate verified as to its truthfulness by the claimant on forms prescribed by the state office of court administration.

Such verified certificate shall certify (i) that the claimant has mailed by ordinary first class mail to the party complained against a demand letter, no less than ten days and no more than one hundred eighty days prior to the commencement of the claim, and (ii) that, based upon information and belief, the claimant has not instituted more than five actions or proceedings (including the instant action or proceeding) during the calendar month.

A form for the demand letter shall be prescribed and furnished by the state office of court administration and shall require the following information: the date of the consumer transaction; the amount that remains unpaid; a copy of the original debt instrument or other document underlying the debt and an accounting of all payments, and, if the claimant was not a party to the original transaction, the names and addresses of the parties to the original transaction; and a statement that the claimant intends to use this part of the court to obtain a judgment, that further notice of a hearing date will be sent, unless payment is received by a specified date, and that the party complained against will be entitled to appear at said hearing and present any defenses to the claim.

In the event that the verified certificate is not properly completed by the claimant, the court shall not allow the action to proceed until the verified certificate is corrected. Notice of such claim shall be sent by the clerk by both ordinary first class mail and certified mail with return receipt requested to the party complained against at his residence, if he resides within the city of New York, and his residence is known to the claimant, or at his office or place of regular employment within the city of New York if he does not reside therein or his residence within the city of New York is not known to the claimant. If, after the expiration of thirty days, such ordinary first class mailing has not been returned as undeliverable, the party complained against shall be presumed to have received notice of such claim.

Such procedure shall further provide for an early hearing upon and determination of such claim. The hearing shall be scheduled in a manner which, to the extent possible, minimizes the time the party complained against must be absent from employment. Either party may request that the hearing be scheduled during evening hours, provided that the hearing shall not be scheduled during evening hours if it would cause unreasonable hardship to either party. The court shall not unreasonably deny requests for evening hearings if such requests are made by the claimant upon commencement of the action or by the party complained against within fourteen days of receipt of the notice of claim.

(c) The clerk shall furnish every claimant, upon commencement of the action, and every party complained against, with the notice of claim, and with information written in clear and coherent language which shall be prescribed and furnished by the state office of court administration, concerning the commercial claims part. Such information shall include, but not be limited to, the form for certification and filing by the claimant that no more than five such actions or proceedings have been instituted during that calendar month, and an explanation of the following terms and procedures: adjournments, counterclaims, jury trial requests, evening hour requests, demand letters in cases concerning consumer transactions, default judgments, subpoenas, arbitration and collection methods, the responsibility of the judgment creditor to collect data on the judgment debtor's assets, the ability of the court prior to entering judgment to order examination of or disclosure by, the defendant and restrain him, and a statement in Spanish that such information is available in Spanish upon request. The information shall be available in English and Spanish. Large signs in English and Spanish shall be posted in conspicuous locations in each commercial claims part clerk's office, advising the public of its availability.

(d) A defendant who wishes to file a counterclaim shall do so by filing with the clerk a statement containing such counterclaim within five days of receiving the notice of claim. At the time of such filing the defendant shall pay to the clerk a filing fee of five dollars plus the cost of mailings which are required pursuant to this subdivision. The clerk shall forthwith send notice of the counterclaim by ordinary first class mail to the claimant. If the defendant fails to file the counterclaim in accordance with the provisions of this subdivision, the defendant retains the right to file the counterclaim, however the claimant may, but shall not be required to, request and obtain adjournment of the hearing to a later date. The claimant may reply to the counterclaim but shall not be required to do so.

§ 1804-A.   Informal and simplified procedure on commercial claims.

The court shall conduct hearings upon commercial claims in such manner as to do substantial justice between the parties according to the rules of substantive law and shall not be bound by statutory provisions or rules of practice, procedure, pleading or evidence, except statutory provisions relating to privileged communications and personal transactions or communications with a decedent or mentally ill person. An itemized bill or invoice, receipted or marked paid, or two itemized estimates for services or repairs, are admissible in evidence and are prima facie evidence of the reasonable value and necessity of such services and repairs. Disclosure shall be unavailable in commercial claims procedure except upon order of the court on showing of proper circumstances. The provisions of this act and the rules of this court, together with the statutes and rules governing supreme court practice, shall apply to claims brought under this article so far as the same can be made applicable and are not in conflict with the provisions of this article; in case of conflict, the provisions of this article shall control.

§ 1805-A.   Remedies available; transfer of commercial claims.

(a) Upon determination of a commercial claim, the court shall direct judgment in accordance with its findings, and, when necessary to do substantial justice between the parties, may condition the entry of judgment upon such terms as the court shall deem proper. Pursuant to section fifty-two hundred twenty-nine of the civil practice law and rules, prior to entering a judgment, the court may order the examination of or disclosure by, the defendant and restrain him to the same extent as if a restraining notice had been served upon him after judgment was entered.

(b) The court shall have power to transfer any commercial claim or claims to any other part of the court upon such terms as the rules may provide, and proceed to hear the same according to the usual practice and procedure applicable to other parts of the court.

(c) No counterclaim shall be permitted in a commercial claims action, unless the court would have had monetary jurisdiction over the counterclaim if it had been filed as a commercial claim. Any other claim sought to be maintained against the claimant may be filed in any court of competent jurisdiction.

(d) If the defendant appears to be engaged in repeated fraudulent or illegal acts or otherwise demonstrates persistent fraud or illegality in the carrying on, conducting or transaction of business, the court shall either advise the attorney general in relation to his authority under subdivision twelve of section sixty-three of the executive law, or shall advise the claimant to do same, but shall retain jurisdiction over the commercial claim.

(e) If the defendant appears to be engaged in fraudulent or illegal acts or otherwise demonstrates fraud or illegality in the carrying on, conducting or transaction of a licensed or certified business, the court shall either advise the appropriate state or local licensing or certifying authority or shall advise the claimant to do same, but shall retain jurisdiction over the commercial claim.

§ 1806-A.   Trial by jury; how obtained; discretionary costs.

A claimant commencing an action upon a commercial claim under this article shall be deemed to have waived a trial by jury, but if said action shall be removed to a regular part of the court, the claimant shall have the same right to demand a trial by jury as if such action had originally been begun in such part. Any party to such action, other than the claimant, prior to the day upon which he is notified to appear or answer, may file with the court a demand for a trial by jury and his affidavit that there are issues of fact in the action requiring such a trial, specifying the same and stating that such trial is desired and intended in good faith. Such demand and affidavit shall be accompanied with the jury fee required by law and an undertaking in the sum of fifty dollars in such form as may be approved by the rules, payable to the other party or parties, conditioned upon the payment of any costs which may be entered against him in the said action or any appeal within thirty days after the entry thereof; or, in lieu of said undertaking, the sum of fifty dollars may be deposited with the clerk of the court and thereupon the clerk shall forthwith transmit such original papers or duly attested copies thereof as may be provided by the rules to the part of the court to which the action shall have been transferred and assigned and such part may require pleadings in such action as though it had been begun by the service of a summons. Such action may be considered a preferred cause of action. In any commercial claim which may have been transferred to another part of the court, the court may award costs up to twenty-five dollars to the claimant if the claimant prevails.

§ 1807-A.   Proceedings on default and review of judgments.

(a) A claimant commencing an action upon a commercial claim under this article shall be deemed to have waived all right to appeal, except that either party may appeal on the sole grounds that substantial justice has not been done between the parties according to the rules and principles of substantive law.

(b) The clerk shall mail notice of the default judgment by first class mail, both to the claimant and to the party complained against. Such notice shall inform the defaulting party, in language promulgated by the state office of court administration, of such party's legal obligation to pay; that failure to pay may result in garnishments, repossessions, seizures and similar actions; and that if there was a reasonable excuse for the default, the defaulting party may apply to have the default vacated by submitting a written request to the court.

(c) Proceedings on default under this article are to be governed by, but are not limited to, section five thousand fifteen of the civil practice law and rules.

§ 1808-A.   Judgment obtained to be res judicata in certain cases.

A judgment obtained under this article shall not be deemed an adjudication of any fact at issue or found therein in any other action or court; except that a subsequent judgment obtained in another action or court involving the same facts, issues and parties shall be reduced by the amount of a judgment awarded under this article.

§ 1809-A.   Procedures relating to corporations, associations, insurers and assignees.

(a) Any corporation, including a municipal corporation or public benefit corporation, partnership, or association, which has its principal office in the city of New York and an assignee of any commercial claim may institute an action or proceeding under this article.

(b) No person or co-partnership, engaged directly or indirectly in the business of collection and adjustment of claims, and no corporation or association, directly or indirectly, itself or by or through its officers, agents or employees, shall solicit, buy or take an assignment of, or be in any manner interested in buying or taking an assignment of a bond, promissory note, bill of exchange, book debt, or other thing in action, or any claim or demand, with the intent and for the purpose of bringing an action or proceeding thereon under this article.

(c) A corporation, partnership or association, which institutes an action or proceeding under this article shall be limited to five such actions or proceedings per calendar month. Such corporation, partnership or association shall complete and file with the clerk the required certification, provided it is true and verified as to its truthfulness, as a prerequisite to the institution of an action or proceeding in this part of the court.

(d) A corporation may appear as a party in any action brought pursuant to this article by an attorney as well as by any authorized officer, director or employee of the corporation provided that the appearance by a non-lawyer on behalf of a corporation shall be deemed to constitute the requisite authority to bind the corporation in a settlement or trial. The court or arbitrator may make reasonable inquiry to determine the authority of any person who appears for the corporation in a commercial claims part case.

§ 1810-A.   Limitation on right to resort to commercial claims procedures.

If the clerk shall find that the procedures of the commercial claims part are sought to be utilized by a claimant for purposes of oppression or harassment, as where a claimant has previously resorted to such procedures on the same claim and has been unsuccessful after the hearing thereon, the clerk may in his discretion compel the claimant to make application to the court for leave to prosecute the claim in the commercial claims part. The court upon such application may inquire into the circumstances and, if it shall find that the claim has already been adjudicated, or that the claim is sought to be brought on solely for purposes of oppression or harassment and not under color of right, it may make an order denying the claimant the use of the commercial claims part to prosecute the claim.

§ 1811-A.   Indexing commercial claims part judgments.

All wholly or partially unsatisfied commercial claims part judgments shall be indexed alphabetically and chronologically under the name of the judgment debtor. Upon satisfying the judgment, the judgment debtor shall present appropriate proof to the court and the court shall indicate such in the records.

§ 1812-A.   Enforcement of commercial claims judgments.

Where a judgment has been entered in a commercial claims part and remains unsatisfied, the commercial claims clerk shall, upon request, issue information subpoenas, at nominal cost, for the judgment creditor and provide the creditor with assistance on their preparation and use.

App Pract
Provs

§ 1813-A.   Duty to pay judgments.

(a) Any person, partnership, firm or corporation which is sued in a commercial claims part for any cause of action arising out of its business activities, shall pay any judgment rendered against it in its true name or in any name in which it conducts business. "True name" includes the legal name of a natural person and the name under which a partnership, firm or corporation is licensed, registered, incorporated or otherwise authorized to do business. "Conducting business" as used in this section shall include, but not be limited to, maintaining signs at business premises or on business vehicles; advertising; entering into contracts; and printing or using sales slips, checks, invoices or receipts. Whenever a judgment has been rendered against a person, partnership, firm or corporation in other than its true name and the judgment has remained unpaid for thirty-five days after receipt by the judgment debtor of notice of its entry, the aggrieved judgment creditor shall be entitled to commence an action in commercial claims part or in any other court of otherwise competent jurisdiction against such judgment debtor, notwithstanding the jurisdictional limit of the court, for the sum of the original judgment, costs, reasonable attorney's fees, and one hundred dollars.

(b) Whenever a judgment which relates to activities for which a license is required has been rendered against a business which is licensed by a state or local licensing authority and which remains unpaid for thirty-five days after receipt by the judgment debtor of notice of its entry and the judgment has not been stayed or appealed, the state or local licensing authority shall consider such failure to pay if deliberate or part of a pattern of similar conduct indicating recklessness, as a basis for the revocation, suspension, conditioning or refusal to grant or renew such license. Nothing herein shall be construed to preempt an authority's existing policy if it is more restrictive.

(c) The clerk shall attach to the notice of suit required under this article a notice of the duty imposed by this section.

§ 1814-A.   Designation of defendant; amendment procedure.

(a) A party who is ignorant, in whole or in part, of the true name of a person, partnership, firm or corporation which may properly be made a party defendant, may proceed against such defendant in any name used by the person, partnership, firm or corporation in conducting business, as defined in subdivision (a) of section eighteen hundred thirteen-A of this article.

(b) If the true name of the defendant becomes known at any time prior to the hearing on the merits, such information shall be brought to the attention of the clerk, who shall immediately amend all prior proceedings and papers. The clerk shall send an amended notice to the defendant, without payment of additional fees by the plaintiff, and all subsequent proceedings and papers shall be amended accordingly.

(c) In every action in the commercial claims part, at the hearing on the merits, the judge or arbitrator shall determine the defendant's true name. The clerk shall amend all prior proceedings and papers to conform to such determination, and all subsequent proceedings and papers shall be amended accordingly.

(d) A party against whom a judgment has been entered pursuant to this article, in any proceeding under section five thousand fifteen of the civil practice law and rules for relief from such judgment, shall disclose its true name; any and all names in which it is conducting business; and any and all names in which it was conducting business at the time of the transaction or occurrence on which such judgment is based. All subsequent proceedings and papers shall be amended to conform to such disclosure.

App Pract
Provs

SYNOPSIS

Article 19.   Costs and fees.

§ 1900.   Security for costs.

Article 85 of the CPLR, entitled "security for costs," shall apply in this court, except that the minimum undertaking of CPLR 8503 shall be $200 rather than the amount therein provided.

§ 1901.   Amount of costs in an action.

(a) Ordinary costs. Except as provided in subdivisions (b) and (c) of this section, costs awarded in an action shall be in the amount of:

1. fifty dollars for all proceedings before a notice of trial is filed; plus

2. one hundred dollars for all proceedings after a notice of trial is filed and before trial; plus

3. one hundred fifty dollars for each trial, inquest or assessment of damages.

(b) Limited costs in certain actions. Costs awarded in an action for a sum of money only where the amount of the judgment is not more than six thousand dollars, shall be in the amount of:

1. twenty dollars for all proceedings before a notice of trial is filed; plus

2. thirty-five dollars for all proceedings after a notice of trial is filed and before trial; plus

3. sixty dollars for each trial, inquest or assessment of damages.

(c) This section shall not apply to costs in a summary proceeding or in a small claims actions.

§ 1902.   [Repealed]

§ 1903.   Costs; additional provisions.

The provisions of CPLR §§ 8101, 8103, 8104, 8105 and 8106 shall apply in actions and proceedings in this court.

§ 1904.   Certain costs added; additional allowance.

(a) Certain costs added. Costs on appeal, and those awarded under § 1102 of this act, may be added to the amount of costs otherwise applicable in the action.

(b) Additional allowance. 1. Section 8302 of the CPLR, relating to an additional allowance as of right in certain real property actions in which plaintiff has recovered judgment, shall apply in this court. The allowance so calculated shall be added to the amount of costs first calculated under other provisions of this article without reference to CPLR § 8302.

2. Section 8303 (a) of the CPLR, relating to an additional allowance in the court's discretion in certain actions, shall apply in this court to an action within its jurisdiction which falls within CPLR § 8303 (a). The allowance so calculated shall be added to the amount of costs first calculated under other provisions of this article without reference to CPLR § 8303 (a).

(c) Discretionary allowance on enforcement motion.   Section 8303(b) of the CPLR, relating to costs on a motion relating to the enforcement of a judgment, shall apply in this court without reference to the foregoing subdivisions of this section.

§ 1905.   No costs on plea of bankruptcy.

Where the defendant recovers judgment upon the defense of bankruptcy, he shall not be entitled to costs.

§ 1906.   Costs allowed by court.

App Pract
Provs

The court may in its discretion impose costs not exceeding fifty dollars in the following cases:

(a) Upon granting or denying a motion.

(b) Upon allowing an amendment of a pleading.

(c) Upon adjournment of a trial.

§ 1906–a.   Costs in a summary proceeding.

In a summary proceeding to recover possession of real property, petitioner shall be allowed as costs for each necessary respondent served with the notice of petition by a person other than a sheriff or marshal, five dollars, and if there is a default in appearance by the respondent, the sum of five dollars for securing the affidavit that the respondent is not in military service, required by the statutes of the United States; plus as a disbursement, the fee paid pursuant to § 1911 (k) of this act. Such costs shall be exclusive in such proceeding and shall constitute the sum to be awarded as cost by the judgment pursuant to § 747 of the real property actions and proceedings law, except insofar as additional costs may be imposed pursuant to subdivision three of said section.

§ 1907.   Taxation of costs and disbursements.

Costs together with fees paid to the clerk and the fee for issuing execution to the sheriff or marshal, must be taxed by the clerk forthwith upon rendition of judgment and inserted therein. Upon issuing a transcript the clerk shall include therein the prospective fees of the county clerk and sheriff. Other taxable disbursements shall be taxed by the clerk on two days' notice to be given by the party entitled thereto to the adverse party. The clerk shall also tax costs allowed by an appellate court and shall enter all items of costs and disbursements in the docket book. All disbursements taxable on notice must be verified by affidavit. The clerk must examine all items presented to him for taxation and, before allowing any disbursements, must be satisfied that the items were necessarily incurred or that the services for which they are charged were necessarily performed.

§ 1908.   Disbursements allowable.

Except where the contrary is specifically provided by law, a party to whom costs are awarded, or a prevailing party who has appeared in person, shall be allowed his necessary disbursements as follows:

(a) All fees paid to the clerk, the sheriff or a marshal, including jury fees, and the reasonable expense of serving process where service is made by other than the sheriff or a marshal.

(b) The legal fees of witnesses.

(c) The legal fees paid for a certified copy of a deposition or other paper recorded or filed in any public office, necessarily used or obtained for use on the trial.

(d) The reasonable compensation of commissioners for taking depositions.

(e) Prospective charges for filing a transcript with the county clerk and the sheriff's fees for receiving and returning an execution.

(f) Such other reasonable and necessary expenses as are taxable pursuant to the provisions of CPLR § 8301.

App Pract
Provs

§ 1908–a.   Disbursement where service of process by mail is not acknowledged.

In any action where service of process is made by mail pursuant to CPLR 312–a, and where the signed acknowledgement of receipt is not returned within thirty (30) days after receipt of the documents mailed pursuant to that section, the reasonable expense of serving process by an alternative method shall be taxed by the court as a disbursement, payable to the party serving process, if that party is awarded costs in the action or proceeding.

§ 1909.   Review of taxation.

Within ten days the clerk's taxation may be reviewed by the court upon two days' notice. The order must disallow any items wrongfully included in the judgment or add any items wrongfully omitted therefrom, and direct that any sum so disallowed be credited upon any execution or other mandate issued to enforce the judgment. Unless a motion for review of the taxation is made, the clerk's taxation cannot be questioned on appeal.

§ 1910.   Costs upon appeal.

(a) Costs upon an appeal may be awarded by the appellate court in its discretion, and if awarded shall be as follows:

1. To the appellant upon reversal, not more than thirty dollars.

2. To the respondent upon affirmance, not more than twenty-five dollars.

3. To either party upon modification, not more than twenty-five dollars.

(b) Costs upon appeal from the judgment or order of the appellate court shall be as provided in the CPLR.

§ 1911.   Fees payable to the clerk.

There shall be paid to the clerk the following sums as court fees in an action:

(a) Upon issuance of a summons, order of arrest or attachment, or requisition or warrant of seizure by the clerk, together with copies thereof, forty-five dollars.

(b) Upon filing summons with proof of service thereof, or upon filing of the first paper in that county in any action or proceeding, forty-five dollars, unless there has been paid in that county a fee of forty-five dollars pursuant to subdivision (a) hereof.

(c) Upon filing an infant's compromise, where no summons was filed, forty dollars.

(d) On filing a notice of trial, forty dollars.

(e) For entry of judgment upon confession, forty-five dollars, unless there has been paid a fee pursuant to subdivision (a) or subdivision (b) hereof.

(f) On filing notice of appeal, thirty dollars.

(g) For issuing a satisfaction of judgment, or a certificate regarding the judgment, six dollars.

(h) Upon demand for a trial by jury, seventy dollars; to be paid by the party demanding the jury, at the time of demand.

(i) For exemplification of any paper filed, fifteen dollars.

(j) For certifying a copy of a paper on file in the clerk's office, six dollars.

(k) For issuing a notice of petition, or an order to show cause in lieu thereof, in a summary proceeding to recover possession of real property, forty-five dollars.

(l) For issuing a petition for change of name, sixty-five dollars.

(m) For any other matter, not provided for above, for which there would be a fee payable in the supreme court of a county within the city of New York, the same fee; except that this subdivision shall not apply to the fees required to be paid in supreme court (i) upon the filing of a motion or cross-motion pursuant to subdivision (a) of section 8020 of the civil practice law and rules, and (ii) upon the filing of a stipulation of settlement or a voluntary discontinuance pursuant to subdivision (d) of such section.

All fees shall be prepaid before the service shall be performed.

§ 1912. Actions in which no fees to be charged; employees; state or city actions.

(a) Employee's action. When the action is brought by an employee against an employer for services performed by such employee, the clerk shall not demand or receive any fees whatsoever from the plaintiff or his attorney, if the plaintiff shall present proof by his own affidavit that his demand does not exceed three hundred dollars exclusive of interest and costs; that he is a resident of or an employee in the city of New York; that he has a good and meritorious cause of action against the defendant and the nature thereof; and that he has made either a written or a personal demand upon the defendant or his agent for payment thereof and payment was refused; provided that if the plaintiff shall demand a trial by jury, he must pay to the clerk the fees therefor.

(b) State or city actions. In an action brought in the name of the people of the state of New York by the attorney-general, or in the name of the city of New York or of any department, board or officer thereof, by the corporation counsel or any municipal department, board or officer of the city of New York, for the recovery of a penalty, no fees shall be required to be paid by the plaintiff to the clerk and no costs shall be taxed against the plaintiff; but in case such plaintiff recovers judgment, the costs and taxable disbursements shall be included therein, and if collected shall be accounted for.

§ 1913. Witnesses' fees.

Witnesses in an action or a special proceeding or before a commissioner or judge of this court taking a deposition, are entitled to the same fees, including mileage, as a witness in an action in the supreme court.

§ 1914. Stenographer's fees.

In all cases of appeal from an order or judgment, where a transcript of the stenographer's minutes or mechanical record of the testimony given on trial or hearing becomes a necessary part of the return on appeal, the stenographer's fees for making up such transcript shall be thirty cents for each folio and shall be paid in the first instance by the appellant and be taxable by him as a disbursement on the appeal; provided, however, that in any case in which an appeal has been taken by the city of New York or by any department, board or officer thereof, the stenographer, upon demand of the corporation counsel or the department, board or officer of the city shall, within ten days, make up the transcript as herein provided and furnish a copy of such transcript to the corporation counsel or the department, board or officer, the stenographer's fees in such case to be audited and paid by the comptroller of the city of New York out of the fund or appropriations applicable thereto.

§ 1915.   Fees of sheriff and marshal.

In performing a function within their respective jurisdiction and powers elsewhere provided in this act, the sheriff of the City of New York and the city marshals shall be allowed and paid the same fees to which a sheriff would be entitled for like services in supreme court.

SYNOPSIS

Article 20.   Criminal Jurisdiction and procedure

§ 2001.   Criminal jurisdiction; procedures.

(1) The court shall have such jurisdiction of criminal matters as is prescribed by the criminal procedure law.

(2) Unless otherwise specifically prescribed, the practice and procedure of the court shall be governed by the criminal procedure law.

§ 2005.   Further powers of judges; process and mandates.

The judges of the court shall have the power and jurisdiction to send processes and other mandates in any matter of which they have jurisdiction into any part of the county or any adjoining county, for service or execution, as provided by the criminal procedure law; and particularly to compel the attendance of witnesses, to order the conditional examination of witnesses, to issue commissions for the examination of witnesses within or without the state, to inquire into the sanity of a defendant and to dismiss the prosecution of an action conformably to the provisions of the criminal procedure law, and to punish for criminal contempt a person guilty thereof in the manner and subject to the limitations prescribed for courts of record by the judiciary law.

§ 2009.   Judge before whom defendant arraigned or tried.

An accused person need not be arraigned or tried before the judge signing or issuing the summons or warrant, but may be arraigned or tried before any judge of the court; provided, however, that whenever trial has been commenced, it shall be continued and concluded by and before the same judge before whom it was commenced, except as hereinbefore provided.

§ 2012.   Drawing of jurors.

Jurors may be drawn and summoned in the manner provided by rules of the appellate division of the department in which the court is located. Jurors drawn for civil actions pursuant to this act may also be used in the trial of criminal cases.

§ 2013.   Jury trial; submission to jury.

Whenever a case is submitted to the jury, the jury shall be placed in charge of any peace officer, acting pursuant to his special duties, or police officer designated by the court.

§ 2014.   Impanelment and fees of jurors.

The system for impaneling, and the fees of, trial jurors shall be as provided by law for the particular court or, in the absence of such governing provisions, as provided for the supreme court of the county in which the court sits. No fee shall be paid to a juror who has been excused from service as a juror, for the day or days so excused.

§ 2015. Correction of technical errors.

Technical errors in the commitment of any accused person may be corrected by the judge at any time after the committment is signed. The judge may alter or modify a sentence or correct any technical error in the record not affecting the substantial rights of the defendant at any time before the execution of the sentence has been commenced.

§ 2019. Records.

All judges of the court shall keep or cause to be kept legible and suitable records and dockets of all criminal actions and proceedings separate and apart from the records and dockets of civil actions and proceedings kept by them or by clerks of their respective courts.

§ 2020. Disposition of fines and penalties.

All fines and penalties collected by the court shall be paid over to the persons or agencies entitled to the same pursuant to law.

App Pract
Provs

SYNOPSIS

Article 21. General.

§ 2101. Definitions; construction of act.

The following words used in this act shall have the meaning defined in this section, unless otherwise apparent from the context:

(a) "Administrative board" means the administrative board of the judicial conference of the state.

(b) "Administrative judge" means the officer designated by the appellate divisions of the department in which the court is located.

(c) "Appellate division" means the appellate division of the supreme court in and for the department in which the court is located, or its designated administrative judge.

(d) "City" means the city in which the court is located.

(e) "City clerk" means the clerk of the city in which the court is located, or the person, by whatever other title, performing equivalent duties.

(f) "Clerk" means the chief clerk or any other clerk or non-judicial person, regardless of title, employed by the court and designated to perform the function referred to in the particular section.

(g) "Common council" means the local governing body of the city in which the court is located.

(h) "County" means the county in which the court is located.

(i) "Court" means the court to which this act applies pursuant to § 2300, whether called "city court" or otherwise titled, or one of the judges thereof, unless the context clearly indicates reference to some other court.

(j) "Enforcement officer" means such officer or officers, whether sheriffs or marshals or otherwise titled, designated pursuant to law to execute the civil mandates of the court.

(k) "Judge" means any judicial officer of the court, unless the context clearly indicates reference to some other judge.

(l) "Rules" means the rules adopted pursuant to § 2103 of this act.

§ 2102. Civil practice; general provisions; CPLR applicable.

The CPLR and other provisions of law relating to practice and procedure in the supreme court, notwithstanding reference by name or classification therein to any other court, shall apply in this court as far as the same can be made applicable and are not in conflict with this act.

§ 2103.   Rules of court.

The appellate division may adopt, amend and rescind rules for the court not inconsistent with this act, with the CPLR or with the standards and policies adopted by the administrative board. A copy of the rules shall be available at all times in the office of the clerk of the court, and shall be published as directed by the administrative board or, absent the board's direction, by the appellate division. Three copies of the rules shall be filed with the administrative board.

§ 2104.   Organization of city courts.

(a) The number of judges for each city court outside the city of New York, their jurisdiction and terms of office, and the methods of their selection and of filling vacancies in their offices shall be as provided in this section.

(b) Each judge of a city court, including acting city court judges, shall:

(1) be an attorney admitted to practice law in this state for at least five years as of the date he or she commences the duties of office, and be a resident of the city in which he or she is elected or appointed, except that the judges of the Sherrill city court may reside anywhere in either Oneida or Madison counties, the acting judge of the Port Jervis city court may reside anywhere in either Sullivan or Orange counties, the acting judge of the Port Jervis city court may reside anywhere in either Sullivan or Orange Counties and the judges of the Hudson city court may reside anywhere in Columbia county.

(2) exercise all jurisdiction possessed by the court on which he or she serves.

(3) serve a term of six years, except that full-time judges each shall serve a term of ten years.

(c) An acting city court judge shall serve during the absence or disability of a judge of the court on which he or she serves, or when requested to serve by a judge of the court or an administrative judge.

App Pract Provs

City courts in each of the following cities shall each have one acting city court judge: Auburn, Beacon, Canandaigua, Corning, Dunkirk, Fulton, Geneva, Glens Falls, Gloversville, Hudson, Ithaca, Jamestown, Johnstown, Little Falls, Mechanicville, Norwich, Olean, Oneida, Oneonta, Oswego, Plattsburgh, Port Jervis, Rensselaer, Rye, Salamanca, Saratoga Springs, Tonawanda, and Watervliet. The city court of White Plains shall have two acting city court judges.

(d) A full-time judge of a city court shall not engage in the practice of law, act as an arbitrator, referee, or compensated mediator in any action or proceeding, or engage in the conduct of any other professional business that interferes with the performance of his or her judicial duties.

(e) The number of judges of the city court in each city, exclusive of acting city court judges, shall be as provided herein. Full-time judgeships are specifically so designated, all others are part-time:

Par.	Name of city
1	Albany, three full-time and one part-time;
2	Amsterdam, two;
3	Auburn, one full-time;
4	Batavia, two;
5	Beacon, one;
6	Binghamton, two full-time;
7	Buffalo, twelve full-time;
8	Canandaigua, one;
9	Cohoes, two;
10	Corning, one;
11	Cortland, one full-time and one part-time;
12	Dunkirk, one;
13	Elmira, one full-time and one part-time;
14	Fulton, one;
15	Geneva, two;
16	Glen Cove, two;
17	Glens Falls, one full-time;
18	Gloversville, one;
19	Hornell, two;
20	Hudson, one;
21	Ithaca, one full-time;

Par.	Name of city
22	Jamestown, one full-time;
23	Johnstown, one;
24	Kingston, one full-time and one part-time;
25	Lackawanna, two;
26	Little Falls, one;
27	Lockport, two;
28	Long Beach, one full-time and one part-time;
29	Mechanicville, one;
30	Middletown, one full-time and one part-time;
31	Mount Vernon, three full-time and one part-time;
32	Newburgh, one full-time and one part-time;
33	New Rochelle, one full-time and one part-time;
34	Niagra Falls, two full-time and one part-time;
35	North Tonawanda, two;
36	Norwich, one;
37	Ogdensburg, two;
38	Olean, one;
39	Oneida, one;
40	Oneonta, one;
41	Oswego, one;
42	Peekskill, two;
43	Plattsburgh, one;
44	Port Jervis, one;
45	Poughkeepsie, one full-time and one part-time;
46	Rensselaer, one;
47	Rochester, eight full-time;
48	Rome, one full-time and one part-time;
49	Rye, one;
50	Salamanca, one;
51	Saratoga Springs, one full-time;
52	Schenectady, one full-time and one part-time;
53	Sherrill, one;
54	Syracuse, six full-time and one part-time;
55	Tonawanda, one;
56	Troy, one full-time and one part-time;
57	Utica, three full-time;
58	Watertown, one full-time and one part-time;
59	Watervliet, one;

App Pract
Provs

Par.	Name of city
60	White Plains, two full-time;
61	Yonkers, six full-time.

(f) Method of selection; vacancies.

(1) Each judge of a city court, including acting city court judges, shall be elected for the term provided in this section, except that each of the following judges shall be appointed:

(i) by the mayor of the city for which the court on which he or she will serve has been established, with the advice and consent of the city council: acting city court judge of Beacon, acting city court judge of Corning, part-time city court judge of Cortland, acting city court judge of Gloversville, one city court judge of Glen Cove, acting city court judge of Ithaca, acting city court judge of Jamestown, acting city court judge of Olean, city court judge and acting city court judge of Plattsburgh, acting city court judge of Port Jervis, city court judge and acting city court judge of Rye, acting city court judge of Salamanca and the part-time city court judge of Watertown.

(ii) by the city council of the city for which the court on which he or she will serve has been established: acting city court judge of Auburn, city court judge of Batavia who serves in the office that formerly was that of acting city court judge of Batavia, acting city court judge of Canandaigua, acting city court judge of Johnstown, part-time city court judge of Newburgh, acting city court judge of Norwich, city court judges of Peekskill, and city court judges and acting city court judges of White Plains.

(iii) by the mayor of the city for which the court on which he or she will serve has been established: city court judges of Cohoes, acting city court judge of Dunkirk, acting city court judge of Fulton, acting city court judge of Geneva, city court judge of Hornell who serves in the office that formerly was that of acting city court judge of Hornell, acting city court judge of Hudson, part-time city court judge of Kingston, city court judge of Lackawanna who serves in the office that on June thirtieth, nineteen hundred eighty-eight was that of the acting city court judge of Lackawanna, acting city court judge of Little Falls, city court judge of Lockport who serves in the office that formerly was that of acting city court judge of Lockport, acting city court judge of Mechanicville, part-time city court judge of Middletown, the part-time city court judge of Mount Vernon, the part-time city court judges of New Rochelle, city court judge of North Tonawanda who serves in the office that on the day immediately preceding the effective date of this section was that of the acting city court judge of North Tonawanda, city court judge of Ogdensburg who serves in the office that formerly was that of acting City court judge of Ogdensburg, acting city court judge of Oneida, acting city court judge of Oneonta, acting city court judge of Oswego, city court judges of Poughkeepsie, acting city court judge of Rensselaer, acting city court judge of Saratoga Springs, acting city court judge of Tonawanda and acting city court judge of Watervliet.

(iv) by the city commission of the city in which the court on which he or she will serve has been established: city court judge of Sherrill.

(2) Whenever a vacancy in the office of city court judge occurs other than by expiration of term, it shall be filled as herein provided:

(i) If the office is elective, the acting city court judge of the court on which the vacancy has occurred or, if there be more than one acting city court judge of such court, the acting city court judge senior in service, shall fill the vacancy temporarily until the thirty-first day of December following the next general city election at which the vacancy can be filled. At such election, a successor shall be elected to fill the vacancy for a full term of office, to commence on January first next thereafter. If there is no acting city court judge of the court on which the vacancy has occurred or if the incumbent acting city court judge declines to serve as provided herein or if the vacancy is in the office of acting city court judge, the mayor of the city in which the court on which the vacancy has occurred is located shall appoint a qualified person to fill it temporarily as provided in this subparagraph. Where an acting city court judge fills a vacancy in the office of city court judge pursuant to this subparagraph:

App Pract Provs

(a) he or she shall not be deemed to have vacated the office of acting city court judge, his or her term in such office shall not be deemed to have been interrupted and, upon expiration of service as city court judge hereunder, he or she shall resume service as acting city court judge for the remainder of such term;

(b) for the duration of such service, he or she shall be paid the compensation provided by law for the office of city court judge thereby filled; and

(c) the mayor may appoint a qualified person to serve as acting city court judge in his or her stead for a period not to exceed the period during which he or she serves as city court judge hereunder.

(ii) If the office is appointive, a successor shall be selected for a full term in the manner provided in paragraph one of this subdivision.

(g) Notwithstanding the designation hereunder of a judge of a city court as part-time or as an acting city court judge, such judge shall, for purposes of determining his or her entitlement to credit under the retirement and social security law for service rendered prior to April first, nineteen hundred ninety-four, be deemed to work full time.

SYNOPSIS

Article 22.   Transition.

§ 2203.   Cases carried over.

All actions and proceedings pending in any court to which this act applies, at the time this act takes effect, shall remain in the court and shall be governed by the following subdivisions of this section.

(a) No such action or proceeding, or appeal taken therein, shall abate by virtue of the application of this act to the court.

(b) For the purpose of the disposition of such pending action or proceeding only, the jurisdiction of the court shall be deemed expanded to that of the court under provisions applicable prior to the effective date of this act whenever necessary to sustain the jurisdiction of the court over such action or proceeding if the court had jurisdiction of the same under such provisions.

(c) Except as provided for in the foregoing, practice and procedure in such actions and proceedings shall be as if the same were instituted after the effective date of this act. But if the court shall find that a practice or procedure available prior to the effective date of this act, but unavailable after such effective date, is necessary to the disposition of such action or proceedings, the court may permit recourse to or completion of the same.

§ 2204.   Appeal involving pending action or proceeding; judgment or order of court.

(a) If on the effective date of this act there existed a right of appeal from a judgment or order entered before the effective date of this act in any court to which this act applies, and the time in which to appeal as provided for in the practice obtaining in such court prior to the effective date hereof has not expired, such time shall continue ro run as if this act did not take effect and an appeal may be taken within such time by the service of a notice of appeal upon the respondent or respondents and by the filing of the same with the clerk of this court.

(b) Such appeal shall be taken to the county court or, if an appellate term has been established in the department and the appellate division has directed that such appeal be taken to such term, it shall be so taken. Further appeal from either of such courts shall be governed by the same provisions as would govern judgments or orders entered in this court after the effective date of this act.

(c) If the judgment or order is entered by this court after the effective date of this act, it shall be treated, for purposes of appeal, as if the action or proceeding were commenced in this court after such effective date, except as provided in subdivision (d).

(d) If in any action or proceeding decided prior to the effective date of this act, a party had a right of direct appeal from the court to the court of appeals, such appeal may be taken directly to the court of appeals during the time such party would have had under the practice obtaining in the court prior to the effective date hereof; and if the judgment or order in such case is entered after the effective date of this act, the time in which to take such direct appeal shall be governed by the practice obtaining in the court as if such court entered the judgment or order prior to the effective date hereof. The notice of appeal, if not filed as of the effective date of this act, shall be served on the respondent or respondents and shall be filed with the clerk of this court.

(e) For all purposes except appeal, a judgment or order entered by the court before the effective date hereof shall be treated as if the action or proceeding in which the same was entered was commenced in this court and the judgment or order entered herein after such effective date.

SYNOPSIS

Article 23.   Application

§ 2300.   Application of this act.

(a) All references to the "uniform city court act" or to the "UCCA" in any law of the state shall be deemed a reference to this act or to the appropriate portions thereof.

(b) This act shall apply to each city court of the state outside the city of New York; provided, however, the following, with regard to each court to which this act is applicable as herein provided, shall not be governed by this act but shall be governed by such other provisions of law as may be applicable to each such court:

1. All matters regarding the compensation of judges.

2. Matters regarding expenses of the court and matters regarding the duties of judges and employees of the court to account for and

pay over fines, penalties, fees and any other monies received by them.

(c) Notwithstanding any other provision of law, where, on the day immediately preceding the effective date of this subdivision a city court exercised greater jurisdiction or powers than are provided under this act, such city court shall continue to exercise such greater jurisdiction or powers.

§ 2301.   Effective date.

This act shall take effect April first, nineteen hundred sixty-five, except that subdivision (f) of section twenty-three hundred shall take effect immediately.

App Pract
Provs

PROFESSIONAL DISCIPLINARY RULES

Part 1200.   Rules of Professional Conduct

Sec.

App Pract
Provs

Part 1200.   Rules of Professional Conduct

RULE 1.0   Terminology.

(a) "Advertisement" means any public or private communication made by or on behalf of a lawyer or law firm about that lawyer or law firm's services, the primary purpose of which is for the retention of the lawyer or law firm. It does not include communications to existing clients or other lawyers.

(b) "Belief" or "believes" denotes that the person involved actually believes the fact in question to be true. A person's belief may be inferred from circumstances.

(c) "Computer-accessed communication" means any communication made by or on behalf of a lawyer or law firm that is disseminated through the use of a computer or related electronic device, including, but not limited to, web sites, weblogs, search engines, electronic mail, banner advertisements, pop-up and pop-under advertisements, chat rooms, list servers, instant messaging, or other internet presences, and any attachments or links related thereto.

(d) "Confidential information" is defined in Rule 1.6.

(e) "Confirmed in writing," denotes (i) a writing from the person to the lawyer confirming that the person has given consent, (ii) a writing that the lawyer promptly transmits to the person confirming the person's oral consent, or (iii) a statement by the person made on the record of any proceeding before a tribunal. If it is not feasible to obtain or transmit the writing at the time the person gives oral consent, then the lawyer must obtain or transmit it within a reasonable time thereafter.

(f) "Differing interests" include every interest that will adversely affect either the judgment or the loyalty of a lawyer to a client, whether it be a conflicting, inconsistent, diverse, or other interest.

(g) "Domestic relations matter" denotes representation of a client in a claim, action or proceeding, or preliminary to the filing of a claim, action or proceeding, in either Supreme Court or Family Court, or in any court of appellate jurisdiction, for divorce, separation, annulment, custody, visitation, maintenance, child support, alimony, or to enforce or modify a judgment or order in connection with any such claim, action or proceeding.

(h) "Firm" or "law firm" includes, but is not limited to, a lawyer or lawyers in a law partnership, professional corporation, sole proprietorship or other association authorized to practice law; or lawyers employed in a qualified legal assistance organization, a government law office, or the legal department of a corporation or other organization.

(i) "Fraud" or "fraudulent" denotes conduct that is fraudulent under the substantive or procedural law of the applicable jurisdiction or has a purpose to deceive, provided that it does not include conduct that, although characterized as fraudulent by statute or administrative rule, lacks an element of scienter, deceit, intent to mislead, or knowing failure to correct misrepresentations that can be reasonably expected to induce detrimental reliance by another.

(j) "Informed consent" denotes the agreement by a person to a proposed course of conduct after the lawyer has communicated information adequate for the person to make an informed decision, and after the lawyer has adequately explained to the person the material risks of the proposed course of conduct and reasonably available alternatives.

(k) "Knowingly," "known," "know," or "knows" denotes actual knowledge of the fact in question. A person's knowledge may be inferred from circumstances.

(l) "Matter" includes any litigation, judicial or administrative proceeding, case, claim, application, request for a ruling or other determination, contract, controversy, investigation, charge, accusation, arrest, negotiation, arbitration, mediation or any other representation involving a specific party or parties.

(m) "Partner" denotes a member of a partnership, a shareholder in a law firm organized as a professional legal corporation or a member of an association authorized to practice law.

(n) "Person" includes an individual, a corporation, an association, a trust, a partnership, and any other organization or entity.

(o) "Professional legal corporation" means a corporation, or an association treated as a corporation, authorized by law to practice law for profit.

(p) "Qualified legal assistance organization" means an office or organization of one of the four types listed in Rule 7.2(b)(1)-(4) that meets all of the requirements thereof.

(q) "Reasonable" or "reasonably," when used in relation to

conduct by a lawyer, denotes the conduct of a reasonably prudent and competent lawyer. When used in the context of conflict of interest determinations, "reasonable lawyer" denotes a lawyer acting from the perspective of a reasonably prudent and competent lawyer who is personally disinterested in commencing or continuing the representation.

(r) "Reasonable belief" or "reasonably believes," when used in reference to a lawyer, denotes that the lawyer believes the matter in question and that the circumstances are such that the belief is reasonable.

(s) "Reasonably should know," when used in reference to a lawyer, denotes that a lawyer of reasonable prudence and competence would ascertain the matter in question.

(t) "Screened" or "screening" denotes the isolation of a lawyer from any participation in a matter through the timely imposition of procedures within a firm that are reasonably adequate under the circumstances to protect information that the isolated lawyer or the firm is obligated to protect under these Rules or other law.

(u) "Sexual relations" denotes sexual intercourse or the touching of an intimate part of the lawyer or another person for the purpose of sexual arousal, sexual gratification or sexual abuse.

(v) "State" includes the District of Columbia, Puerto Rico, and other federal territories and possessions.

(w) "Tribunal" denotes a court, an arbitrator in an arbitration proceeding or a legislative body, administrative agency or other body acting in an adjudicative capacity. A legislative body, administrative agency or other body acts in an adjudicative capacity when a neutral official, after the presentation of evidence or legal argument by a party or parties, will render a legal judgment directly affecting a party's interests in a particular matter.

(x) "Writing" or "written" denotes a tangible or electronic record of a communication or representation, including handwriting, typewriting, printing, photocopying, photography, audio or video recording and email. A "signed" writing includes an electronic sound, symbol or process attached to or logically associated with a writing

App Pract
Provs

and executed or adopted by a person with the intent to sign the writing.

RULE 1.1 COMPETENCE.

(a) A lawyer should provide competent representation to a client. Competent representation requires the legal knowledge, skill, thoroughness and preparation reasonably necessary for the representation.

(b) A lawyer shall not handle a legal matter that the lawyer knows or should know that the lawyer is not competent to handle, without associating with a lawyer who is competent to handle it.

(c) A lawyer shall not intentionally:

(1) fail to seek the objectives of the client through reasonably available means permitted by law and these Rules; or

(2) prejudice or damage the client during the course of the representation except as permitted or required by these Rules.

RULE 1.2 SCOPE OF REPRESENTATION AND ALLOCATION OF AUTHORITY BETWEEN CLIENT AND LAWYER.

(a) Subject to the provisions herein, a lawyer shall abide by a client's decisions concerning the objectives of representation and, as required by Rule 1.4, shall consult with the client as to the means by which they are to be pursued. A lawyer shall abide by a client's decision whether to settle a matter. In a criminal case, the lawyer shall abide by the client's decision, after consultation with the lawyer, as to a plea to be entered, whether to waive jury trial and whether the client will testify.

(b) A lawyer's representation of a client, including representation by appointment, does not constitute an endorsement of the client's political, economic, social or moral views or activities.

(c) A lawyer may limit the scope of the representation if the limitation is reasonable under the circumstances, the client gives informed consent and where necessary notice is provided to the tribunal and/or opposing counsel.

(d) A lawyer shall not counsel a client to engage, or assist a client, in conduct that the lawyer knows is illegal or fraudulent, except that the lawyer may discuss the legal consequences of any proposed course of conduct with a client.

(e) A lawyer may exercise professional judgment to waive or fail to assert a right or position of the client, or accede to reasonable requests of opposing counsel, when doing so does not prejudice the rights of the client.

(f) A lawyer may refuse to aid or participate in conduct that the lawyer believes to be unlawful, even though there is some support for an argument that the conduct is legal.

(g) A lawyer does not violate this Rule by being punctual in fulfilling all professional commitments, by avoiding offensive tactics, and by treating with courtesy and consideration all persons involved in the legal process.

RULE 1.3   DILIGENCE.

(a) A lawyer shall act with reasonable diligence and promptness in representing a client.

(b) A lawyer shall not neglect a legal matter entrusted to the lawyer.

(c) A lawyer shall not intentionally fail to carry out a contract of employment entered into with a client for professional services, but the lawyer may withdraw as permitted under these Rules.

RULE 1.4   COMMUNICATION.

(a) A lawyer shall:

(1) promptly inform the client of:

(i) any decision or circumstance with respect to which the client's informed consent, as defined in Rule 1.0(j), is required by these Rules;

(ii) any information required by court rule or other law to be communicated to a client; and

(iii) material developments in the matter including settlement or plea offers.

(2) reasonably consult with the client about the means by which the client's objectives are to be accomplished;

(3) keep the client reasonably informed about the status of the matter;

App Pract Provs

(4) promptly comply with a client's reasonable requests for information; and

(5) consult with the client about any relevant limitation on the lawyer's conduct when the lawyer knows that the client expects assistance not permitted by these Rules or other law.

(b) A lawyer shall explain a matter to the extent reasonably necessary to permit the client to make informed decisions regarding the representation.

RULE 1.5   FEES AND DIVISION OF FEES.

(a) A lawyer shall not make an agreement for, charge, or collect an excessive or illegal fee or expense. A fee is excessive when, after a review of the facts, a reasonable lawyer would be left with a definite and firm conviction that the fee is excessive. The factors to be considered in determining whether a fee is excessive may include the following:

(1) the time and labor required, the novelty and difficulty of the questions involved, and the skill requisite to perform the legal service properly;

(2) the likelihood, if apparent or made known to the client, that the acceptance of the particular employment will preclude other employment by the lawyer;

(3) the fee customarily charged in the locality for similar legal services;

(4) the amount involved and the results obtained;

(5) the time limitations imposed by the client or by circumstances;

(6) the nature and length of the professional relationship with the client;

(7) the experience, reputation and ability of the lawyer or lawyers performing the services; and

(8) whether the fee is fixed or contingent.

(b) A lawyer shall communicate to a client the scope of the representation and the basis or rate of the fee and expenses for which the client will be responsible. This information shall be communicated to the client before or within a reasonable time after commencement of the representation and shall be in writing where required by statute or court rule. This provision shall not apply when the lawyer will charge a regularly represented client on the same basis or rate and perform services that are of the same general kind as previously rendered to and paid for by the client. Any changes in the scope of the representation or the basis or rate of the fee or expenses shall also be communicated to the client.

(c) A fee may be contingent on the outcome of the matter for which the service is rendered, except in a matter in which a contingent fee is prohibited by paragraph (d) or other law. Promptly after a lawyer has been employed in a contingent fee matter, the lawyer shall provide the client with a writing stating the method by which the fee is to be determined, including the percentage or percentages that shall accrue to the lawyer in the event of settlement, trial or appeal; litigation and other expenses to be deducted from the recovery; and whether such expenses are to be deducted before or, if not prohibited by statute or court rule, after the contingent fee is calculated. The writing must clearly notify the client of any expenses for which the client will be liable regardless of whether the client is the prevailing party. Upon conclusion of a contingent fee matter, the lawyer shall provide the client with a writing stating the outcome of the matter and, if there is a recovery, showing the remittance to the client and the method of its determination.

(d) A lawyer shall not enter into an arrangement for, charge or collect:

(1) a contingent fee for representing a defendant in a criminal matter;

(2) a fee prohibited by law or rule of court;

(3) a fee based on fraudulent billing;

(4) a nonrefundable retainer fee. A lawyer may enter into a retainer agreement with a client containing a reasonable minimum fee clause, if it defines in plain language and sets forth the circumstances under which such fee may be incurred and how it will be calculated; or

(5) any fee in a domestic relations matter if:

(i) the payment or amount of the fee is contingent upon the securing

App Pract Provs

of a divorce or of obtaining child custody or visitation or is in any way determined by reference to the amount of maintenance, support, equitable distribution, or property settlement;

(ii) a written retainer agreement has not been signed by the lawyer and client setting forth in plain language the nature of the relationship and the details of the fee arrangement; or

(iii) the written retainer agreement includes a security interest, confession of judgment or other lien without prior notice being provided to the client in a signed retainer agreement and approval from a tribunal after notice to the adversary. A lawyer shall not foreclose on a mortgage placed on the marital residence while the spouse who consents to the mortgage remains the titleholder and the residence remains the spouse's primary residence.

(e) In domestic relations matters, a lawyer shall provide a prospective client with a statement of client's rights and responsibilities at the initial conference and prior to the signing of a written retainer agreement.

(f) Where applicable, a lawyer shall resolve fee disputes by arbitration at the election of the client pursuant to a fee arbitration program established by the Chief Administrator of the Courts and approved by the Administrative Board of the Courts.

(g) A lawyer shall not divide a fee for legal services with another lawyer who is not associated in the same law firm unless:

(1) the division is in proportion to the services performed by each lawyer or, by a writing given to the client, each lawyer assumes joint responsibility for the representation;

(2) the client agrees to employment of the other lawyer after a full disclosure that a division of fees will be made, including the share each lawyer will receive, and the client's agreement is confirmed in writing; and

(3) the total fee is not excessive.

(h) Rule 1.5(g) does not prohibit payment to a lawyer formerly associated in a law firm pursuant to a separation or retirement agreement.

RULE 1.6   CONFIDENTIALITY OF INFORMATION.

(a) A lawyer shall not knowingly reveal confidential information, as defined in this Rule, or use such information to the disadvantage of a client or for the advantage of the lawyer or a third person, unless:

(1) the client gives informed consent, as defined in Rule 1.0(j);

(2) the disclosure is impliedly authorized to advance the best interests of the client and is either reasonable under the circumstances or customary in the professional community; or

(3) the disclosure is permitted by paragraph (b).

"Confidential information" consists of information gained during or relating to the representation of a client, whatever its source, that is (a) protected by the attorney-client privilege, (b) likely to be embarrassing or detrimental to the client if disclosed, or (c) information that the client has requested be kept confidential. "Confidential information" does not ordinarily include (i) a lawyer's legal knowledge or legal research or (ii) information that is generally known in the local community or in the trade, field or profession to which the information relates.

(b) A lawyer may reveal or use confidential information to the extent that the lawyer reasonably believes necessary:

(1) to prevent reasonably certain death or substantial bodily harm;

(2) to prevent the client from committing a crime;

(3) to withdraw a written or oral opinion or representation previously given by the lawyer and reasonably believed by the lawyer still to be relied upon by a third person, where the lawyer has discovered that the opinion or representation was based on materially inaccurate information or is being used to further a crime or fraud;

(4) to secure legal advice about compliance with these Rules or other law by the lawyer, another lawyer associated with the lawyer's firm or the law firm;

(5)(i) to defend the lawyer or the lawyer's employees and associates against an accusation of wrongful conduct; or

App Pract
Provs

(ii) to establish or collect a fee; or

(6) when permitted or required under these Rules or to comply with other law or court order.

(c) A lawyer shall exercise reasonable care to prevent the lawyer's employees, associates, and others whose services are utilized by the lawyer from disclosing or using confidential information of a client, except that a lawyer may reveal the information permitted to be disclosed by paragraph (b) through an employee.

RULE 1.7   CONFLICT OF INTEREST: CURRENT CLIENTS.

(a) Except as provided in paragraph (b), a lawyer shall not represent a client if a reasonable lawyer would conclude that either:

(1) the representation will involve the lawyer in representing differing interests; or

(2) there is a significant risk that the lawyer's professional judgment on behalf of a client will be adversely affected by the lawyer's own financial, business, property or other personal interests.

(b) Notwithstanding the existence of a concurrent conflict of interest under paragraph (a), a lawyer may represent a client if:

(1) the lawyer reasonably believes that the lawyer will be able to provide competent and diligent representation to each affected client;

(2) the representation is not prohibited by law;

(3) the representation does not involve the assertion of a claim by one client against another client represented by the lawyer in the same litigation or other proceeding before a tribunal; and

(4) each affected client gives informed consent, confirmed in writing.

RULE 1.8   CURRENT CLIENTS: SPECIFIC CONFLICT OF INTEREST RULES.

(a) A lawyer shall not enter into a business transaction with a client if they have differing interests therein and if the client expects the lawyer to exercise professional judgment therein for the protection of the client, unless:

(1) the transaction is fair and reasonable to the client and the terms of the transaction are fully disclosed and transmitted in writing in a manner that can be reasonably understood by the client;

(2) the client is advised in writing of the desirability of seeking, and is given a reasonable opportunity to seek, the advice of independent legal counsel on the transaction; and

(3) the client gives informed consent, in a writing signed by the client, to the essential terms of the transaction and the lawyer's role in the transaction, including whether the lawyer is representing the client in the transaction.

(b) A lawyer shall not use information relating to representation of a client to the disadvantage of the client unless the client gives informed consent, except as permitted or required by these Rules.

(c) A lawyer shall not:

(1) solicit any gift from a client, including a testamentary gift, for the benefit of the lawyer or a person related to the lawyer; or

(2) prepare on behalf of a client an instrument giving the lawyer or a person related to the lawyer any gift, unless the lawyer or other recipient of the gift is related to the client and a reasonable lawyer would conclude that the transaction is fair and reasonable.

For purposes of this paragraph, related persons include a spouse, child, grandchild, parent, grandparent or other relative or individual with whom the lawyer or the client maintains a close, familial relationship.

(d) Prior to conclusion of all aspects of the matter giving rise to the representation or proposed representation of the client or prospective client, a lawyer shall not negotiate or enter into any arrangement or understanding with:

(1) a client or a prospective client by which the lawyer acquires an interest in literary or media rights with respect to the subject matter of the representation or proposed representation; or

(2) any person by which the lawyer transfers or assigns any interest in literary or media rights with respect to the subject matter of the representation of a client or prospective client.

App Pract
Provs

(e) While representing a client in connection with contemplated or pending litigation, a lawyer shall not advance or guarantee financial assistance to the client, except that:

(1) a lawyer may advance court costs and expenses of litigation, the repayment of which may be contingent on the outcome of the matter;

(2) a lawyer representing an indigent or pro bono client may pay court costs and expenses of litigation on behalf of the client; and

(3) a lawyer, in an action in which an attorney's fee is payable in whole or in part as a percentage of the recovery in the action, may pay on the lawyer's own account court costs and expenses of litigation. In such case, the fee paid to the lawyer from the proceeds of the action may include an amount equal to such costs and expenses incurred.

(f) A lawyer shall not accept compensation for representing a client, or anything of value related to the lawyer's representation of the client, from one other than the client unless:

(1) the client gives informed consent;

(2) there is no interference with the lawyer's independent professional judgment or with the client-lawyer relationship; and

(3) the client's confidential information is protected as required by Rule 1.6.

(g) A lawyer who represents two or more clients shall not participate in making an aggregate settlement of the claims of or against the clients, absent court approval, unless each client gives informed consent in a writing signed by the client. The lawyer's disclosure shall include the existence and nature of all the claims involved and of the participation of each person in the settlement.

(h) A lawyer shall not:

(1) make an agreement prospectively limiting the lawyer's liability to a client for malpractice; or

(2) settle a claim or potential claim for such liability with an unrepresented client or former client unless that person is advised in writing of the desirability of seeking, and is given a reasonable opportunity to seek, the advice of independent legal counsel in connection therewith.

(i) A lawyer shall not acquire a proprietary interest in the cause of action or subject matter of litigation the lawyer is conducting for a client, except that the lawyer may:

(1) acquire a lien authorized by law to secure the lawyer's fee or expenses; and

(2) contract with a client for a reasonable contingent fee in a civil matter subject to Rule 1.5(d) or other law or court rule.

(j)(1) A lawyer shall not:

(i) as a condition of entering into or continuing any professional representation by the lawyer or the lawyer's firm, require or demand sexual relations with any person;

(ii) employ coercion, intimidation or undue influence in entering into sexual relations incident to any professional representation by the lawyer or the lawyer's firm; or

(iii) in domestic relations matters, enter into sexual relations with a client during the course of the lawyer's representation of the client.

(2) Rule 1.8(j)(1) shall not apply to sexual relations between lawyers and their spouses or to ongoing consensual sexual relationships that predate the initiation of the client-lawyer relationship.

(k) Where a lawyer in a firm has sexual relations with a client but does not participate in the representation of that client, the lawyers in the firm shall not be subject to discipline under this Rule solely because of the occurrence of such sexual relations.

RULE 1.9   DUTIES TO FORMER CLIENTS.

(a) A lawyer who has formerly represented a client in a matter shall not thereafter represent another person in the same or a substantially related matter in which that person's interests are materially adverse to the interests of the former client unless the former client gives informed consent, confirmed in writing.

(b) Unless the former client gives informed consent, confirmed in writing, a lawyer shall not knowingly represent a person in the same or a substantially related matter in which a firm with which the lawyer formerly was associated had previously represented a client:

App Pract
Provs

(1) whose interests are materially adverse to that person; and

(2) about whom the lawyer had acquired information protected by Rules 1.6 and paragraph (c) that is material to the matter.

(c) A lawyer who has formerly represented a client in a matter or whose present or former firm has formerly represented a client in a matter shall not thereafter:

(1) use confidential information of the former client protected by Rule 1.6 to the disadvantage of the former client, except as these Rules would permit or require with respect to a current client or when the information has become generally known; or

(2) reveal confidential information of the former client protected by Rule 1.6 except as these Rules would permit or require with respect to a current client.

RULE 1.10   IMPUTATION OF CONFLICTS OF INTEREST.

(a) While lawyers are associated in a firm, none of them shall knowingly represent a client when any one of them practicing alone would be prohibited from doing so by Rule 1.7, 1.8 or 1.9, except as otherwise provided therein.

(b) When a lawyer has terminated an association with a firm, the firm is prohibited from thereafter representing a person with interests that the firm knows or reasonably should know are materially adverse to those of a client represented by the formerly associated lawyer and not currently represented by the firm if the firm or any lawyer remaining in the firm has information protected by Rule 1.6 or Rule 1.9(c) that is material to the matter.

(c) When a lawyer becomes associated with a firm, the firm may not knowingly represent a client in a matter that is the same as or substantially related to a matter in which the newly associated lawyer, or a firm with which that lawyer was associated, formerly represented a client whose interests are materially adverse to the prospective or current client unless the newly associated lawyer did not acquire any information protected by Rule 1.6 or Rule 1.9(c) that is material to the current matter.

(d) A disqualification prescribed by this Rule may be waived by the affected client or former client under the conditions stated in Rule 1.7.

(e) A law firm shall make a written record of its engagements, at or near the time of each new engagement, and shall implement and maintain a system by which proposed engagements are checked against current and previous engagements when:

(1) the firm agrees to represent a new client;

(2) the firm agrees to represent an existing client in a new matter;.

(3) the firm hires or associates with another lawyer; or

(4) an additional party is named or appears in a pending matter.

(f) Substantial failure to keep records or to implement or maintain a conflict-checking system that complies with paragraph (e) shall be a violation thereof regardless of whether there is another violation of these Rules.

(g) Where a violation of paragraph (e) by a law firm is a substantial factor in causing a violation of paragraph (a) by a lawyer, the law firm, as well as the individual lawyer, shall be responsible for the violation of paragraph (a).

(h) A lawyer related to another lawyer as parent, child, sibling or spouse shall not represent in any matter a client whose interests differ from those of another party to the matter who the lawyer knows is represented by the other lawyer unless the client consents to the representation after full disclosure and the lawyer concludes that the lawyer can adequately represent the interests of the client.

RULE 1.11   SPECIAL CONFLICTS OF INTEREST FOR FORMER AND CURRENT GOVERNMENT OFFICERS AND EMPLOYEES.

(a) Except as law may otherwise expressly provide, a lawyer who has formerly served as a public officer or employee of the government:

(1) shall comply with Rule 1.9(c); and

(2) shall not represent a client in connection with a matter in which the lawyer participated personally and substantially as a public officer or employee, unless the appropriate government agency gives its informed consent, confirmed in writing, to the representation. This provision shall not apply to matters governed by Rule 1.12(a).

App Pract
Provs

(b) When a lawyer is disqualified from representation under paragraph (a), no lawyer in a firm with which that lawyer is associated may knowingly undertake or continue representation in such a matter unless:

(1) the firm acts promptly and reasonably to:

(i) notify, as appropriate, lawyers and nonlawyer personnel within the firm that the personally disqualified lawyer is prohibited from participating in the representation of the current client;

(ii) implement effective screening procedures to prevent the flow of information about the matter between the personally disqualified lawyer and the others in the firm;

(iii) ensure that the disqualified lawyer is apportioned no part of the fee therefrom; and

(iv) give written notice to the appropriate government agency to enable it to ascertain compliance with the provisions of this Rule; and

(2) there are no other circumstances in the particular representation that create an appearance of impropriety.

(c) Except as law may otherwise expressly provide, a lawyer having information that the lawyer knows is confidential government information about a person, acquired when the lawyer was a public officer or employee, may not represent a private client whose interests are adverse to that person in a matter in which the information could be used to the material disadvantage of that person. As used in this Rule, the term "confidential government information" means information that has been obtained under governmental authority and that, at the time this Rule is applied, the government is prohibited by law from disclosing to the public or has a legal privilege not to disclose, and that is not otherwise available to the public. A firm with which that lawyer is associated may undertake or continue representation in the matter only if the disqualified lawyer is timely and effectively screened from any participation in the matter in accordance with the provisions of paragraph (b).

(d) Except as law may otherwise expressly provide, a lawyer currently serving as a public officer or employee shall not:

(1) participate in a matter in which the lawyer participated person-

ally and substantially while in private practice or nongovernmental employment, unless under applicable law no one is, or by lawful delegation may be, authorized to act in thelawyer's stead in the matter; or

(2) negotiate for private employment with any person who is involved as a party or as lawyer for a party in a matter in which the lawyer is participating personally and substantially.

(e) As used in this Rule, the term "matter" as defined in Rule 1.0(l) does not include or apply to agency rule making functions.

(f) A lawyer who holds public office shall not:

(1) use the public position to obtain, or attempt to obtain, a special advantage in legislative matters for the lawyer or for a client under circumstances where the lawyer knows or it is obvious that such action is not in the public interest;

(2) use the public position to influence, or attempt to influence, a tribunal to act in favor of the lawyer or of a client; or

(3) accept anything of value from any person when the lawyer knows or it is obvious that the offer is for the purpose of influencing the lawyer's action as a public official

RULE 1.12   SPECIFIC CONFLICTS OF INTEREST FOR FORMER JUDGES, ARBITRATORS, MEDIATORS OR OTHER THIRD-PARTY NEUTRALS.

(a) A lawyer shall not accept private employment in a matter upon the merits of which the lawyer has acted in a judicial capacity.

(b) Except as stated in paragraph (e), and unless all parties to the proceeding give informed consent, confirmed in writing, a lawyer shall not represent anyone in connection with a matter in which the lawyer participated personally and substantially as:

(1) an arbitrator, mediator or other third-party neutral; or

(2) a law clerk to a judge or other adjudicative officer or an arbitrator, mediator or other third-party neutral.

(c) A lawyer shall not negotiate for employment with any person

App Pract
Provs

who is involved as a party or as lawyer for a party in a matter in which the lawyer is participating personally and substantially as a judge or other adjudicative officer or as an arbitrator, mediator or other third-party neutral.

(d) When a lawyer is disqualified from representation under this Rule, no lawyer in a firm with which that lawyer is associated may knowingly undertake or continue representation in such a matter unless:

(1) the firm acts promptly and reasonably to:

(i) notify, as appropriate, lawyers and nonlawyer personnel within the firm that the personally disqualified lawyer is prohibited from participating in the representation of the current client;

(ii) implement effective screening procedures to prevent the flow of information about the matter between the personally disqualified lawyer and the others in the firm;

(iii) ensure that the disqualified lawyer is apportioned no part of the fee therefrom; and

(iv) give written notice to the parties and any appropriate tribunal to enable it to ascertain compliance with the provisions of this Rule; and

(2) there are no other circumstances in the particular representation that create an appearance of impropriety.

(e) An arbitrator selected as a partisan of a party in a multimember arbitration panel is not prohibited from subsequently representing that party.

RULE 1.13   ORGANIZATION AS CLIENT.

(a) When a lawyer employed or retained by an organization is dealing with the organization's directors, officers, employees, members, shareholders or other constituents, and it appears that the organization's interests may differ from those of the constituents with whom the lawyer is dealing, the lawyer shall explain that the lawyer is the lawyer for the organization and not for any of the constituents.

(b) If a lawyer for an organization knows that an officer, employee or other person associated with the organization is engaged in action or intends to act or refuses to act in a matter related to the representation that (i) is a violation of a legal obligation to the organization or a violation of law that reasonably might be imputed to the organization, and (ii) is likely to result in substantial injury to the organization, the lawyer shall proceed as is reasonably necessary in the best interest of the organization. In determining how to proceed, the lawyer shall give due consideration to the seriousness of the violation and its consequences, the scope and nature of the lawyer's representation, the responsibility in the organization and the apparent motivation of the person involved, the policies of the organization concerning such matters and any other relevant considerations. Any measures taken shall be designed to minimize disruption of the organization and the risk of revealing information relating to the representation to persons outside the organization. Such measures may include, among others:

(1) asking reconsideration of the matter;

(2) advising that a separate legal opinion on the matter be sought for presentation to an appropriate authority in the organization; and

(3) referring the matter to higher authority in the organization, including, if warranted by the seriousness of the matter, referral to the highest authority that can act in behalf of the organization as determined by applicable law.

(c) If, despite the lawyer's efforts in accordance with paragraph (b), the highest authority that can act on behalf of the organization insists upon action, or a refusal to act, that is clearly in violation of law and is likely to result in a substantial injury to the organization, the lawyer may reveal confidential information only if permitted by Rule 1.6, and may resign in accordance with Rule 1.16.

(d) A lawyer representing an organization may also represent any of its directors, officers, employees, members, shareholders or other constituents, subject to the provisions of Rule 1.7. If the organization's consent to the concurrent representation is required by Rule 1.7, the consent shall be given by an appropriate official of the organization other than the individual who is to be represented, or by the shareholders.

RULE 1.14   CLIENT WITH DIMINISHED CAPACITY.

(a) When a client's capacity to make adequately considered decisions in connection with a representation is diminished, whether because of minority, mental impairment or for some other reason, the lawyer shall, as far as reasonably possible, maintain a conventional relationship with the client.

(b) When the lawyer reasonably believes that the client has diminished capacity, is at risk of substantial physical, financial or other harm unless action is taken and cannot adequately act in the client's own interest, the lawyer may take reasonably necessary protective action, including consulting with individuals or entities that have the ability to take action to protect the client and, in appropriate cases, seeking the appointment of a guardian ad litem, conservator or guardian.

(c) Information relating to the representation of a client with diminished capacity is protected by Rule 1.6. When taking protective action pursuant to paragraph (b), the lawyer is impliedly authorized under Rule 1.6(a) to reveal information about the client, but only to the extent reasonably necessary to protect the client's interests.

RULE 1.15 PRESERVING IDENTITY OF FUNDS AND PROPERTY OF OTHERS; FIDUCIARY RESPONSIBILITY; COMMINGLING AND MISAPPROPRIATION OF CLIENT FUNDS OR PROPERTY; MAINTENANCE OF BANK ACCOUNTS; RECORD KEEPING; EXAMINATION OF RECORDS.

(a) Prohibition Against Commingling and Misappropriation of Client Funds or Property. A lawyer in possession of any funds or other property belonging to another person, where such possession is incident to his or her practice of law, is a fiduciary, and must not misappropriate such funds or property or commingle such funds or property with his or her own.

(b) Separate Accounts. (1) A lawyer who is in possession of funds belonging to another person incident to the lawyer's practice of law shall maintain such funds in a banking institution within New York State that agrees to provide dishonored check reports in accordance with the provisions of 22 N.Y.C.R.R. Part 1300. "Banking institution" means a state or national bank, trust company, savings bank, savings and loan association or credit union. Such funds shall be maintained, in the lawyer's own name, or in the name of a firm of lawyers of which the lawyer is a member, or in the name of the lawyer or firm of lawyers by whom the lawyer is employed, in a special account or accounts, separate from any business or personal accounts of the lawyer or lawyer's firm, and separate from any accounts that the lawyer may maintain as executor, guardian, trustee or receiver, or in any other fiduciary capacity; into such special account or accounts all funds held in escrow or otherwise entrusted to the lawyer or firm shall be deposited; provided, however, that such funds may be maintained in a banking institution located outside New York State if such banking institution complies with 22 N.Y.C.R.R. Part 1300 and the lawyer has obtained the prior written approval of the person to whom such funds belong specifying the name and address of the office or branch of the banking institution where such funds are to be maintained.

(2) A lawyer or the lawyer's firm shall identify the special bank account or accounts required by Rule 1.15(b)(1) as an "Attorney Special Account," or "Attorney Trust Account," or "Attorney Escrow Account," and shall obtain checks and deposit slips that bear such title. Such title may be accompanied by such other descriptive language as the lawyer may deem appropriate, provided that such additional language distinguishes such special account or accounts from other bank accounts that are maintained by the lawyer or the lawyer's firm.

(3) Funds reasonably sufficient to maintain the account or to pay account charges may be deposited therein.

(4) Funds belonging in part to a client or third person and in part currently or potentially to the lawyer or law firm shall be kept in such special account or accounts, but the portion belonging to the lawyer or law firm may be withdrawn when due unless the right of the lawyer or law firm to receive it is disputed by the client or third person, in which event the disputed portion shall not be withdrawn until the dispute is finally resolved.

(c) Notification of Receipt of Property; Safekeeping; Rendering Accounts; Payment or Delivery of Property.

A lawyer shall:

(1) promptly notify a client or third person of the receipt of funds, securities, or other properties in which the client or third person has an

interest;

(2) identify and label securities and properties of a client or third person promptly upon receipt and place them in a safe deposit box or other place of safekeeping as soon as practicable;

(3) maintain complete records of all funds, securities, and other properties of a client or third person coming into the possession of the lawyer and render appropriate accounts to the client or third person regarding them; and

(4) promptly pay or deliver to the client or third person as requested by the client or third person the funds, securities, or other properties in the possession of the lawyer that the client or third person is entitled to receive.

(d) Required Bookkeeping Records.

(1) A lawyer shall maintain for seven years after the events that they record:

(i) the records of all deposits in and withdrawals from the accounts specified in Rule 1.15(b) and of any other bank account that concerns or affects the lawyer's practice of law; these records shall specifically identify the date, source and description of each item deposited, as well as the date, payee and purpose of each withdrawal or disbursement;

(ii) a record for special accounts, showing the source of all funds deposited in such accounts, the names of all persons for whom the funds are or were held, the amount of such funds, the description and amounts, and the names of all persons to whom such funds were disbursed;

(iii) copies of all retainer and compensation agreements with clients;

(iv) copies of all statements to clients or other persons showing the disbursement of funds to them or on their behalf;

(v) copies of all bills rendered to clients;

(vi) copies of all records showing payments to lawyers, investigators or other persons, not in the lawyer's regular employ, for services rendered or performed;

(vii) copies of all retainer and closing statements filed with the Office of Court Administration; and

(viii) all checkbooks and check stubs, bank statements, prenumbered canceled checks and duplicate deposit slips.

(2) Lawyers shall make accurate entries of all financial transactions in their records of receipts and disbursements, in their special accounts, in their ledger books or similar records, and in any other books of account kept by them in the regular course of their practice, which entries shall be made at or near the time of the act, condition or event recorded.

(3) For purposes of Rule 1.15(d), a lawyer may satisfy the requirements of maintaining "copies" by maintaining any of the following items: original records, photocopies, microfilm, optical imaging, and any other medium that preserves an image of the document that cannot be altered without detection.

(e) Authorized Signatories. All special account withdrawals shall be made only to a named payee and not to cash. Such withdrawals shall be made by check or, with the prior written approval of the party entitled to the proceeds, by bank transfer. Only a lawyer admitted to practice law in New York State shall be an authorized signatory of a special account.

(f) Missing Clients. Whenever any sum of money is payable to a client and the lawyer is unable to locate the client, the lawyer shall apply to the court in which the action was brought if in the unified court system, or, if no action was commenced in the unified court system, to the Supreme Court in the county in which the lawyer maintains an office for the practice of law, for an order directing payment to the lawyer of any fees and disbursements that are owed by the client and the balance, if any, to the Lawyers' Fund for Client Protection for safeguarding and disbursement to persons who are entitled thereto.

(g) Designation of Successor Signatories.

(1) Upon the death of a lawyer who was the sole signatory on an attorney trust, escrow or special account, an application may be made to the Supreme Court for an order designating a successor signatory for such trust, escrow or special account, who shall be a member of the bar in good standing and admitted to the practice of law in New York State.

App Pract Provs

(2) An application to designate a successor signatory shall be made to the Supreme Court in the judicial district in which the deceased lawyer maintained an office for the practice of law. The application may be made by the legal representative of the deceased lawyer's estate; a lawyer who was affiliated with the deceased lawyer in the practice of law; any person who has a beneficial interest in such trust, escrow or special account; an officer of a city or county bar association; or counsel for an attorney disciplinary committee. No lawyer may charge a legal fee for assisting with an application to designate a successor signatory pursuant to this Rule.

(3) The Supreme Court may designate a successor signatory and may direct the safeguarding of funds from such trust, escrow or special account, and the disbursement of such funds to persons who are entitled thereto, and may order that funds in such account be deposited with the Lawyers' Fund for Client Protection for safeguarding and disbursement to persons who are entitled thereto.

(h) Dissolution of a Firm. Upon the dissolution of any firm of lawyers, the former partners or members shall make appropriate arrangements for the maintenance, by one of them or by a successor firm, of the records specified in Rule 1.15(d).

(i) Availability of Bookkeeping Records: Records Subject to Production in Disciplinary Investigations and Proceedings. The financial records required by this Rule shall be located, or made available, at the principal New York State office of the lawyers subject hereto, and any such records shall be produced in response to a notice or subpoena duces tecum issued in connection with a complaint before or any investigation by the appropriate grievance or departmental disciplinary committee, or shall be produced at the direction of the appropriate Appellate Division before any person designated by it. All books and records produced pursuant to this Rule shall be kept confidential, except for the purpose of the particular proceeding, and their contents shall not be disclosed by anyone in violation of the attorney-client privilege.

(j) Disciplinary Action. A lawyer who does not maintain and keep the accounts and records as specified and required by this Rule, or who does not produce any such records pursuant to this Rule, shall be deemed in violation of these Rules and shall be subject to disciplinary proceedings.

RULE 1.16   DECLINING OR TERMINATING REPRESENTATION.

(a) A lawyer shall not accept employment on behalf of a person if the lawyer knows or reasonably should know that such person wishes to:

(1) bring a legal action, conduct a defense, or assert a position in a matter, or otherwise have steps taken for such person, merely for the purpose of harassing or maliciously injuring any person; or

(2) present a claim or defense in a matter that is not warranted under existing law, unless it can be supported by a good faith argument for an extension, modification, or reversal of existing law.

(b) Except as stated in paragraph (d), a lawyer shall withdraw from the representation of a client when:

(1) the lawyer knows or reasonably should know that the representation will result in a violation of these Rules or of law;

(2) the lawyer's physical or mental condition materially impairs the lawyer's ability to represent the client;

(3) the lawyer is discharged; or

(4) the lawyer knows or reasonably should know that the client is bringing the legal action, conducting the defense, or asserting a position in the matter, or is otherwise having steps taken, merely for the purpose of harassing or maliciously injuring any person.

(c) Except as stated in paragraph (d), a lawyer may withdraw from representing a client when:

(1) withdrawal can be accomplished without material adverse effect on the interests of the client;

(2) the client persists in a course of action involving the lawyer's services that the lawyer reasonably believes is criminal or fraudulent;

(3) the client has used the lawyer's services to perpetrate a crime or fraud;

(4) the client insists upon taking action with which the lawyer has a

App Pract
Provs

fundamental disagreement;

(5) the client deliberately disregards an agreement or obligation to the lawyer as to expenses or fees;

(6) the client insists upon presenting a claim or defense that is not warranted under existing law and cannot be supported by good faith argument for an extension, modification, or reversal of existing law;

(7) the client fails to cooperate in the representation or otherwise renders the representation unreasonably difficult for the lawyer to carry out employment effectively;

(8) the lawyer's inability to work with co-counsel indicates that the best interest of the client likely will be served by withdrawal;

(9) the lawyer's mental or physical condition renders it difficult for the lawyer to carry out the representation effectively;

(10) the client knowingly and freely assents to termination of the employment;

(11) withdrawal is permitted under Rule 1.13(c) or other law;

(12) the lawyer believes in good faith, in a matter pending before a tribunal, that the tribunal will find the existence of other good cause for withdrawal; or

(13) the client insists that the lawyer pursue a course of conduct which is illegal or prohibited under these Rules.

(d) If permission for withdrawal from employment is required by the rules of a tribunal, a lawyer shall not withdraw from employment in a matter before that tribunal without its permission. When ordered to do so by a tribunal, a lawyer shall continue representation notwithstanding good cause for terminating the representation.

(e) Even when withdrawal is otherwise permitted or required, upon termination of representation, a lawyer shall take steps, to the extent reasonably practicable, to avoid foreseeable prejudice to the rights of the client, including giving reasonable notice to the client, allowing time for employment of other counsel, delivering to the client all papers and property to which the client is entitled, promptly refunding any part of a fee paid in advance that has not been earned and complying with applicable laws and rules.

RULE 1.17   SALE OF LAW PRACTICE.

(a) A lawyer retiring from a private practice of law; a law firm, one or more members of which are retiring from the private practice of law with the firm; or the personal representative of a deceased, disabled or missing lawyer, may sell a law practice, including goodwill, to one or more lawyers or law firms, who may purchase the practice. The seller and the buyer may agree on reasonable restrictions on the seller's private practice of law, notwithstanding any other provision of these Rules. Retirement shall include the cessation of the private practice of law in the geographic area, that is, the county and city and any county or city contiguous thereto, in which the practice to be sold has been conducted.

(b) Confidential information.

(1) With respect to each matter subject to the contemplated sale, the seller may provide prospective buyers with any information not protected as confidential information under Rule 1.6.

(2) Notwithstanding Rule 1.6, the seller may provide the prospective buyer with information as to individual clients:

(i) concerning the identity of the client, except as provided in paragraph (b)(6);

(ii) concerning the status and general nature of the matter;

(iii) available in public court files; and

(iv) concerning the financial terms of the client-lawyer relationship and the payment status of the client's account.

(3) Prior to making any disclosure of confidential information that may be permitted under paragraph (b)(2), the seller shall provide the prospective buyer with information regarding the matters involved in the proposed sale sufficient to enable the prospective buyer to determine whether any conflicts of interest exist. Where sufficient information cannot be disclosed without revealing client confidential information, the seller may make the disclosures necessary for the prospective buyer to determine whether any conflict of interest exists, subject to paragraph (b)(6). If the prospective buyer determines that conflicts of interest exist prior to reviewing the information, or determines during the course of review that a conflict of interest exists,

App Pract
Provs

the prospective buyer shall not review or continue to review the information unless the seller shall have obtained the consent of the client in accordance with Rule 1.6(a)(1).

(4) Prospective buyers shall maintain the confidentiality of and shall not use any client information received in connection with the proposed sale in the same manner and to the same extent as if the prospective buyers represented the client.

(5) Absent the consent of the client after full disclosure, a seller shall not provide a prospective buyer with information if doing so would cause a violation of the attorney-client privilege.

(6) If the seller has reason to believe that the identity of the client or the fact of the representation itself constitutes confidential information in the circumstances, the seller may not provide such information to a prospective buyer without first advising the client of the identity of the prospective buyer and obtaining the client's consent to the proposed disclosure.

(c) Written notice of the sale shall be given jointly by the seller and the buyer to each of the seller's clients and shall include information regarding:

(1) the client's right to retain other counsel or to take possession of the file;

(2) the fact that the client's consent to the transfer of the client's file or matter to the buyer will be presumed if the client does not take any action or otherwise object within 90 days of the sending of the notice, subject to any court rule or statute requiring express approval by the client or a court;

(3) the fact that agreements between the seller and the seller's clients as to fees will be honored by the buyer;

(4) proposed fee increases, if any, permitted under paragraph (e); and

(5) the identity and background of the buyer or buyers, including principal office address, bar admissions, number of years in practice in New York State, whether the buyer has ever been disciplined for professional misconduct or convicted of a crime, and whether the buyer currently intends to resell the practice.

(d) When the buyer's representation of a client of the seller would give rise to a waivable conflict of interest, the buyer shall not undertake such representation unless the necessary waiver or waivers have been obtained in writing.

(e) The fee charged a client by the buyer shall not be increased by reason of the sale, unless permitted by a retainer agreement with the client or otherwise specifically agreed to by the client.

RULE 1.18   DUTIES TO PROSPECTIVE CLIENTS.

(a) A person who discusses with a lawyer the possibility of forming a client-lawyer relationship with respect to a matter is a "prospective client."

(b) Even when no client-lawyer relationship ensues, a lawyer who has had discussions with a prospective client shall not use or reveal information learned in the consultation, except as Rule 1.9 would permit with respect to information of a former client.

(c) A lawyer subject to paragraph (b) shall not represent a client with interests materially adverse to those of a prospective client in the same or a substantially related matter if the lawyer received information from the prospective client that could be significantly harmful to that person in the matter, except as provided in paragraph (d). If a lawyer is disqualified from representation under this paragraph, no lawyer in a firm with which that lawyer is associated may knowingly undertake or continue representation in such a matter, except as provided in paragraph (d).

(d) When the lawyer has received disqualifying information as defined in paragraph (c), representation is permissible if:

(1) both the affected client and the prospective client have given informed consent, confirmed in writing; or

(2) the lawyer who received the information took reasonable measures to avoid exposure to more disqualifying information than was reasonably necessary to determine whether to represent the prospective client; and

(i) the firm acts promptly and reasonably to notify, as appropriate, lawyers and nonlawyer personnel within the firm that the personally

App Pract Provs

disqualified lawyer is prohibited from participating in the representation of the current client;

(ii) the firm implements effective screening procedures to prevent the flow of information about the matter between the disqualified lawyer and the others in the firm;

(iii) the disqualified lawyer is apportioned no part of the fee therefrom; and

(iv) written notice is promptly given to the prospective client; and

(3) a reasonable lawyer would conclude that the law firm will be able to provide competent and diligent representation in the matter.

(e) A person who:

(1) communicates information unilaterally to a lawyer, without any reasonable expectation that the lawyer is willing to discuss the possibility of forming a client lawyer relationship; or

(2) communicates with a lawyer for the purpose of disqualifying the lawyer from handling a materially adverse representation on the same or a substantially related matter, is not a prospective client with the meaning of paragraph (a).

RULE 2.1   ADVISOR.

In representing a client, a lawyer shall exercise independent professional judgment and render candid advice. In rendering advice, a lawyer may refer not only to law but to other considerations such as moral, economic, social, psychological, and political factors that may be relevant to the client's situation.

RULE 2.2   [RESERVED].

RULE 2.3   EVALUATION FOR USE BY THIRD PERSONS.

(a) A lawyer may provide an evaluation of a matter affecting a client for the use of someone other than the client if the lawyer reasonably believes that making the evaluation is compatible with other aspects of the lawyer's relationship with the client.

(b) When the lawyer knows or reasonably should know that the evaluation is likely to affect the client's interests materially and adversely, the lawyer shall not provide the evaluation unless the client gives informed consent.

(c) Unless disclosure is authorized in connection with a report of an evaluation, information relating to the evaluation is protected by Rule 1.6.

RULE 2.4 LAWYER SERVING AS THIRD-PARTY NEUTRAL.

(a) A lawyer serves as a "third-party neutral" when the lawyer assists two or more persons who are not clients of the lawyer to reach a resolution of a dispute or other matter that has arisen between them. Service as a third-party neutral may include service as an arbitrator, a mediator or in such other capacity as will enable the lawyer to assist the parties to resolve the matter.

(b) A lawyer serving as a third-party neutral shall inform unrepresented parties that the lawyer is not representing them. When the lawyer knows or reasonably should know that a party does not understand the lawyer's role in the matter, the lawyer shall explain the difference between the lawyer's role as a third-party neutral and a lawyer's role as one who represents a client.

RULE 3.1 NON-MERITORIOUS CLAIMS AND CONTENTIONS.

(a) A lawyer shall not bring or defend a proceeding, or assert or controvert an issue therein, unless there is a basis in law and fact for doing so that is not frivolous. A lawyer for the defendant in a criminal proceeding or for the respondent in a proceeding that could result in incarceration may nevertheless so defend the proceeding as to require that every element of the case be established.

(b) A lawyer's conduct is "frivolous" for purposes of this Rule if:

(1) the lawyer knowingly advances a claim or defense that is unwarranted under existing law, except that the lawyer may advance such claim or defense if it can be supported by good faith argument for an extension, modification, or reversal of existing law;

(2) the conduct has no reasonable purpose other than to delay or prolong the resolution of litigation, in violation of Rule 3.2, or serves merely to harass or maliciously injure another; or

App Pract Provs

(3) the lawyer knowingly asserts material factual statements that are false.

RULE 3.2   DELAY OF LITIGATION.

In representing a client, a lawyer shall not use means that have no substantial purpose other than to delay or prolong the proceeding or to cause needless expense.

RULE 3.3   CONDUCT BEFORE A TRIBUNAL.

(a) A lawyer shall not knowingly:

(1) make a false statement of fact or law to a tribunal or fail to correct a false statement of material fact or law previously made to the tribunal by the lawyer;

(2) fail to disclose to the tribunal controlling legal authority known to the lawyer to be directly adverse to the position of the client and not disclosed by opposing counsel; or

(3) offer or use evidence that the lawyer knows to be false. If a lawyer, the lawyer's client, or a witness called by the lawyer has offered material evidence and the lawyer comes to know of its falsity, the lawyer shall take reasonable remedial measures, including, if necessary, disclosure to the tribunal. A lawyer may refuse to offer evidence, other than the testimony of a defendant in a criminal matter, that the lawyer reasonably believes is false.

(b) A lawyer who represents a client before a tribunal and who knows that a person intends to engage, is engaging or has engaged in criminal or fraudulent conduct related to the proceeding shall take reasonable remedial measures, including, if necessary, disclosure to the tribunal.

(c) The duties stated in paragraphs (a) and (b) apply even if compliance requires disclosure of information otherwise protected by Rule 1.6.

(d) In an ex parte proceeding, a lawyer shall inform the tribunal of all material facts known to the lawyer that will enable the tribunal to make an informed decision, whether or not the facts are adverse.

(e) In presenting a matter to a tribunal, a lawyer shall disclose, unless privileged or irrelevant, the identities of the clients the lawyer represents and of the persons who employed the lawyer.

(f) In appearing as a lawyer before a tribunal, a lawyer shall not:

(1) fail to comply with known local customs of courtesy or practice of the bar or a particular tribunal without giving to opposing counsel timely notice of the intent not to comply;

(2) engage in undignified or discourteous conduct;

(3) intentionally or habitually violate any established rule of procedure or of evidence; or

(4) engage in conduct intended to disrupt the tribunal.

RULE 3.4   FAIRNESS TO OPPOSING PARTY AND COUNSEL.

A lawyer shall not:

(a)(1) suppress any evidence that the lawyer or the client has a legal obligation to reveal or produce;

(2) advise or cause a person to hide or leave the jurisdiction of a tribunal for the purpose of making the person unavailable as a witness therein;

(3) conceal or knowingly fail to disclose that which the lawyer is required by law to reveal;

(4) knowingly use perjured testimony or false evidence;

(5) participate in the creation or preservation of evidence when the lawyer knows or it is obvious that the evidence is false; or

(6) knowingly engage in other illegal conduct or conduct contrary to these Rules;

(b) offer an inducement to a witness that is prohibited by law or pay, offer to pay or acquiesce in the payment of compensation to a witness contingent upon the content of the witness's testimony or the outcome of the matter. A lawyer may advance, guarantee or acquiesce in the payment of:

(1) reasonable compensation to a witness for the loss of time in attending, testifying, preparing to testify or otherwise assisting counsel, and reasonable related expenses; or

App Pract
Provs

(2) a reasonable fee for the professional services of an expert witness and reasonable related expenses;

(c) disregard or advise the client to disregard a standing rule of a tribunal or a ruling of a tribunal made in the course of a proceeding, but the lawyer may take appropriate steps in good faith to test the validity of such rule or ruling;

(d) in appearing before a tribunal on behalf of a client:

(1) state or allude to any matter that the lawyer does not reasonably believe is relevant or that will not be supported by admissible evidence;

(2) assert personal knowledge of facts in issue except when testifying as a witness;

(3) assert a personal opinion as to the justness of a cause, the credibility of a witness, the culpability of a civil litigant or the guilt or innocence of an accused but the lawyer may argue, upon analysis of the evidence, for any position or conclusion with respect to the matters stated herein;

(4) ask any question that the lawyer has no reasonable basis to believe is relevant to the case and that is intended to degrade a witness or other person; or

(e) present, participate in presenting, or threaten to present criminal charges solely to obtain an advantage in a civil matter.

RULE 3.5   MAINTAINING AND PRESERVING THE IMPARTIALITY OF TRIBUNALS AND JURORS.

(a) A lawyer shall not:

(1) seek to or cause another person to influence a judge, official or employee of a tribunal by means prohibited by law or give or lend anything of value to such judge, official, or employee of a tribunal when the recipient is prohibited from accepting the gift or loan but a lawyer may make a contribution to the campaign fund of a candidate for judicial office in conformity with Part 100 of the Rules of the Chief Administrator of the Courts;

(2) in an adversary proceeding communicate or cause another person

to do so on the lawyer's behalf, as to the merits of the matter with a judge or official of a tribunal or an employee thereof before whom the matter is pending, except:

(i) in the course of official proceedings in the matter;

(ii) in writing, if the lawyer promptly delivers a copy of the writing to counsel for other parties and to a party who is not represented by a lawyer;

(iii) orally, upon adequate notice to counsel for the other parties and to any party who is not represented by a lawyer; or

(iv) as otherwise authorized by law, or by Part 100 of the Rules of the Chief Administrator of the Courts;

(3) seek to or cause another to influence a juror or prospective juror by means prohibited by law;

(4) communicate or cause another to communicate with a member of the jury venire from which the jury will be selected for the trial of a case or, during the trial of a case, with any member of the jury unless authorized to do so by law or court order;

(5) communicate with a juror or prospective juror after discharge of the jury if:

(i) the communication is prohibited by law or court order;

(ii) the juror has made known to the lawyer a desire not to communicate;

(iii) the communication involves misrepresentation, coercion, duress or harassment; or

(iv) the communication is an attempt to influence the juror's actions in future jury service; or

(6) conduct a vexatious or harassing investigation of either a member of the venire or a juror or, by financial support or otherwise, cause another to do so.

(b) During the trial of a case a lawyer who is not connected therewith shall not communicate with or cause another to communicate with a juror concerning the case.

(c) All restrictions imposed by this Rule also apply to communications with or investigations of members of a family of a member of the venire or a juror.

(d) A lawyer shall reveal promptly to the court improper conduct by a member of the venire or a juror, or by another toward a member of the venire or a juror or a member of his or her family of which the lawyer has knowledge.

RULE 3.6 TRIAL PUBLICITY.

(a) A lawyer who is participating in or has participated in a criminal or civil matter shall not make an extrajudicial statement that the lawyer knows or reasonably should know will be disseminated by means of public communication and will have a substantial likelihood of materially prejudicing an adjudicative proceeding in the matter.

(b) A statement ordinarily is likely to prejudice materially an adjudicative proceeding when it refers to a civil matter triable to a jury, a criminal matter or any other proceeding that could result in incarceration, and the statement relates to:

(1) the character, credibility, reputation or criminal record of a party, suspect in a criminal investigation or witness, or the identity of a witness or the expected testimony of a party or witness;

(2) in a criminal matter that could result in incarceration, the possibility of a plea of guilty to the offense or the existence or contents of any confession, admission or statement given by a defendant or suspect, or that person's refusal or failure to make a statement;

(3) the performance or results of any examination or test, or the refusal or failure of a person to submit to an examination or test, or the identity or nature of physical evidence expected to be presented;

(4) any opinion as to the guilt or innocence of a defendant or suspect in a criminal matter that could result in incarceration;

(5) information the lawyer knows or reasonably should know is likely to be inadmissible as evidence in a trial and would, if disclosed, create a substantial risk of prejudicing an impartial trial; or

(6) the fact that a defendant has been charged with a crime, unless there is included therein a statement explaining that the charge is

merely an accusation and that the defendant is presumed innocent until and unless proven guilty.

(c) Provided that the statement complies with paragraph (a), a lawyer may state the following without elaboration:

(1) the claim, offense or defense and, except when prohibited by law, the identity of the persons involved;

(2) information contained in a public record;

(3) that an investigation of a matter is in progress;

(4) the scheduling or result of any step in litigation;

(5) a request for assistance in obtaining evidence and information necessary thereto;

(6) a warning of danger concerning the behavior of a person involved, when there is reason to believe that there exists the likelihood of substantial harm to an individual or to the public interest; and

(7) in a criminal matter:

(i) the identity, age, residence, occupation and family status of the accused;

(ii) if the accused has not been apprehended, information necessary to aid in apprehension of that person;

(iii) the identity of investigating and arresting officers or agencies and the length of the investigation; and

(iv) the fact, time and place of arrest, resistance, pursuit and use of weapons, and a description of physical evidence seized, other than as contained only in a confession, admission or statement.

(d) Notwithstanding paragraph (a), a lawyer may make a statement that a reasonable lawyer would believe is required to protect a client from the substantial prejudicial effect of recent publicity not initiated by the lawyer or the lawyer's client. A statement made pursuant to this paragraph shall be limited to such information as is necessary to mitigate the recent adverse publicity.

(e) No lawyer associated in a firm or government agency with a lawyer subject to paragraph (a) shall make a statement prohibited by paragraph (a).

RULE 3.7   LAWYER AS WITNESS.

(a) A lawyer shall not act as advocate before a tribunal in a matter in which the lawyer is likely to be a witness on a significant issue of fact unless:

(1) the testimony relates solely to an uncontested issue;

(2) the testimony relates solely to the nature and value of legal services rendered in the matter;

(3) disqualification of the lawyer would work substantial hardship on the client;

(4) the testimony will relate solely to a matter of formality, and there is no reason to believe that substantial evidence will be offered in opposition to the testimony; or

(5) the testimony is authorized by the tribunal.

(b) A lawyer may not act as advocate before a tribunal in a matter if:

(1) another lawyer in the lawyer's firm is likely to be called as a witness on a significant issue other than on behalf of the client, and it is apparent that the testimony may be prejudicial to the client; or

(2) the lawyer is precluded from doing so by Rule 1.7 or Rule 1.9.

RULE 3.8   SPECIAL RESPONSIBILITIES OF PROSECUTORS AND OTHER GOVERNMENT LAWYERS.

(a) A prosecutor or other government lawyer shall not institute, cause to be instituted or maintain a criminal charge when the prosecutor or other government lawyer knows or it is obvious that the charge is not supported by probable cause.

(b) A prosecutor or other government lawyer in criminal litigation shall make timely disclosure to counsel for the defendant or to a defendant who has no counsel of the existence of evidence or information known to the prosecutor or other government lawyer that tends to negate the guilt of the accused, mitigate the degree of the offense, or reduce the sentence, except when relieved of this responsibility by a protective order of a tribunal.

RULE 3.9   ADVOCATE IN NON-ADJUDICATIVE MATTERS.

A lawyer communicating in a representative capacity with a legislative body or administrative agency in connection with a pending non-adjudicative matter or proceeding shall disclose that the appearance is in a representative capacity, except when the lawyer seeks information from an agency that is available to the public.

RULE 4.1   TRUTHFULNESS IN STATEMENTS TO OTHERS.

In the course of representing a client, a lawyer shall not knowingly make a false statement of fact or law to a third person.

RULE 4.2   COMMUNICATION WITH PERSON REPRESENTED BY COUNSEL.

(a) In representing a client, a lawyer shall not communicate or cause another to communicate about the subject of the representation with a party the lawyer knows to be represented by another lawyer in the matter, unless the lawyer has the prior consent of the other lawyer or is authorized to do so by law.

(b) Notwithstanding the prohibitions of paragraph (a), and unless otherwise prohibited by law, a lawyer may cause a client to communicate with a represented person unless the represented person is not legally competent, and may counsel the client with respect to those communications, provided the lawyer gives reasonable advance notice to the represented person's counsel that such communications will be taking place.

RULE 4.3   COMMUNICATING WITH UNREPRESENTED PERSONS.

In communicating on behalf of a client with a person who is not represented by counsel, a lawyer shall not state or imply that the lawyer is disinterested. When the lawyer knows or reasonably should know that the unrepresented person misunderstands the lawyer's role in the matter, the lawyer shall make reasonable efforts to correct the misunderstanding. The lawyer shall not give legal advice to an unrepresented person other than the advice to secure counsel if the lawyer knows or reasonably should know that the interests of such person are or have a reasonable possibility of being in conflict with the interests of the client.

RULE 4.4   RESPECT FOR RIGHTS OF THIRD PERSONS.

(a) In representing a client, a lawyer shall not use means that have no substantial purpose other than to embarrass or harm a third person or use methods of obtaining evidence that violate the legal rights of such a person.

(b) A lawyer who receives a document relating to the representation of the lawyer's client and knows or reasonably should know that the document was inadvertently sent shall promptly notify the sender.

RULE 4.5   COMMUNICATION AFTER INCIDENTS INVOLVING PERSONAL INJURY OR WRONGFUL DEATH.

(a) In the event of a specific incident involving potential claims for personal injury or wrongful death, no unsolicited communication shall be made to an individual injured in the incident or to a family member or legal representative of such an individual, by a lawyer or law firm, or by any associate, agent, employee or other representative of a lawyer or law firm representing actual or potential defendants or entities that may defend and/or indemnify said defendants, before the 30th day after the date of the incident, unless a filing must be made within 30 days of the incident as a legal prerequisite to the particular claim, in which case no unsolicited communication shall be made before the 15th day after the date of the incident.

(b) An unsolicited communication by a lawyer or law firm, seeking to represent an injured individual or the legal representative thereof under the circumstance described in paragraph (a) shall comply with Rule 7.3(e).

RULE 5.1   RESPONSIBILITIES OF LAW FIRMS, PARTNERS, MANAGERS AND SUPERVISORY LAWYERS.

(a) A law firm shall make reasonable efforts to ensure that all lawyers in the firm conform to these Rules.

(b)(1) A lawyer with management responsibility in a law firm shall make reasonable efforts to ensure that other lawyers in the law firm conform to these Rules.

(2) A lawyer with direct supervisory authority over another lawyer shall make reasonable efforts to ensure that the supervised lawyer conforms to these Rules.

(c) A law firm shall ensure that the work of partners and associates is adequately supervised, as appropriate. A lawyer with direct supervisory authority over another lawyer shall adequately supervise the work of the other lawyer, as appropriate. In either case, the degree of supervision required is that which is reasonable under the circumstances, taking into account factors such as the experience of the person whose work is being supervised, the amount of work involved in a particular matter and the likelihood that ethical problems might arise in the course of working on the matter.

(d) A lawyer shall be responsible for a violation of these Rules by another lawyer if:

(1) the lawyer orders or directs the specific conduct or, with knowledge of the specific conduct, ratifies it; or

(2) the lawyer is a partner in a law firm or is a lawyer who individually or together with other lawyers possesses comparable managerial responsibility in a law firm in which the other lawyer practices or is a lawyer who has supervisory authority over the other lawyer; and

(i) knows of such conduct at a time when it could be prevented or its consequences avoided or mitigated but fails to take reasonable remedial action; or

(ii) in the exercise of reasonable management or supervisory authority should have known of the conduct so that reasonable remedial action could have been taken at a time when the consequences of the conduct could have been avoided or mitigated.

RULE 5.2   RESPONSIBILITIES OF A SUBORDINATE LAWYER.

(a) A lawyer is bound by these Rules notwithstanding that the lawyer acted at the direction of another person.

App Pract
Provs

(b) A subordinate lawyer does not violate these Rules if that lawyer acts in accordance with a supervisory lawyer's reasonable resolution of an arguable question of professional duty.

RULE 5.3 LAWYER'S RESPONSIBILITY FOR CONDUCT OF NONLAWYERS.

(a) A law firm shall ensure that the work of nonlawyers who work for the firm is adequately supervised, as appropriate. A lawyer with direct supervisory authority over a nonlawyer shall adequately supervise the work of the nonlawyer, as appropriate. In either case, the degree of supervision required is that which is reasonable under the circumstances, taking into account factors such as the experience of the person whose work is being supervised, the amount of work involved in a particular matter and the likelihood that ethical problems might arise in the course of working on the matter.

(b) A lawyer shall be responsible for conduct of a nonlawyer employed or retained by or associated with the lawyer that would be a violation of these Rules if engaged in by a lawyer, if:

(1) the lawyer orders or directs the specific conduct or, with knowledge of the specific conduct, ratifies it; or

(2) the lawyer is a partner in a law firm or is a lawyer who individually or together with other lawyers possesses comparable managerial responsibility in a law firm in which the nonlawyer is employed or is a lawyer who has supervisory authority over the nonlawyer; and

(i) knows of such conduct at a time when it could be prevented or its consequences avoided or mitigated but fails to take reasonable remedial action; or

(ii) in the exercise of reasonable management or supervisory authority should have known of the conduct so that reasonable remedial action could have been taken at a time when the consequences of the conduct could have been avoided or mitigated.

RULE 5.4 PROFESSIONAL INDEPENDENCE OF A LAWYER.

(a) A lawyer or law firm shall not share legal fees with a nonlawyer, except that:

(1) an agreement by a lawyer with the lawyer's firm or another lawyer associated in the firm may provide for the payment of money, over a reasonable period of time after the lawyer's death, to the lawyer's estate or to one or more specified persons;

(2) a lawyer who undertakes to complete unfinished legal business of a deceased lawyer may pay to the estate of the deceased lawyer that portion of the total compensation that fairly represents the services rendered by the deceased lawyer; and

(3) a lawyer or law firm may compensate a nonlawyer employee or include a nonlawyer employee in a retirement plan based in whole or in part on a profit-sharing arrangement.

(b) A lawyer shall not form a partnership with a nonlawyer if any of the activities of the partnership consist of the practice of law.

(c) Unless authorized by law, a lawyer shall not permit a person who recommends, employs or pays the lawyer to render legal service for another to direct or regulate the lawyer's professional judgment in rendering such legal services or to cause the lawyer to compromise the lawyer's duty to maintain the confidential information of the client under Rule 1.6.

(d) A lawyer shall not practice with or in the form of an entity authorized to practice law for profit, if:

(1) a nonlawyer owns any interest therein, except that a fiduciary representative of the estate of a lawyer may hold the stock or interest of the lawyer for a reasonable time during administration;

(2) a nonlawyer is a member, corporate director or officer thereof or occupies a position of similar responsibility in any form of association other than a corporation; or

(3) a nonlawyer has the right to direct or control the professional judgment of a lawyer.

RULE 5.5   UNAUTHORIZED PRACTICE OF LAW.

(a) A lawyer shall not practice law in a jurisdiction in violation of the regulation of the legal profession in that jurisdiction.

(b) A lawyer shall not aid a non-lawyer in the unauthorized practice of law.

App Pract
Provs

RULE 5.6 RESTRICTIONS ON RIGHT TO PRACTICE.

(a) A lawyer shall not participate in offering or making:

(1) a partnership, shareholder, operating, employment, or other similar type of agreement that restricts the right of a lawyer to practice after termination of the relationship, except an agreement concerning benefits upon retirement; or

(2) an agreement in which a restriction on a lawyer's right to practice is part of the settlement of a client controversy.

(b) This Rule does not prohibit restrictions that may be included in the terms of the sale of a law practice pursuant to Rule 1.17.

RULE 5.7 RESPONSIBILITIES REGARDING NONLEGAL SERVICES.

(a) With respect to lawyers or law firms providing nonlegal services to clients or other persons:

(1) A lawyer or law firm that provides nonlegal services to a person that are not distinct from legal services being provided to that person by the lawyer or law firm is subject to these Rules with respect to the provision of both legal and nonlegal services.

(2) A lawyer or law firm that provides nonlegal services to a person that are distinct from legal services being provided to that person by the lawyer or law firm is subject to these Rules with respect to the nonlegal services if the person receiving the services could reasonably believe that the nonlegal services are the subject of a client-lawyer relationship.

(3) A lawyer or law firm that is an owner, controlling party or agent of, or that is otherwise affiliated with, an entity that the lawyer or law firm knows to be providing nonlegal services to a person is subject to these Rules with respect to the nonlegal services if the person receiving the services could reasonably believe that the nonlegal services are the subject of a client-lawyer relationship.

(4) For purposes of paragraphs (a)(2) and (a)(3), it will be presumed that the person receiving nonlegal services believes the services to be the subject of a client-lawyer relationship unless the lawyer or law firm has advised the person receiving the services in writing that the

services are not legal services and that the protection of a client-lawyer relationship does not exist with respect to the nonlegal services, or if the interest of the lawyer or law firm in the entity providing nonlegal services is *de minimis.*

(b) Notwithstanding the provisions of paragraph (a), a lawyer or law firm that is an owner, controlling party, agent, or is otherwise affiliated with an entity that the lawyer or law firm knows is providing nonlegal services to a person shall not permit any nonlawyer providing such services or affiliated with that entity to direct or regulate the professional judgment of the lawyer or law firm in rendering legal services to any person, or to cause the lawyer or law firm to compromise its duty under Rule 1.6(a) and (c) with respect to the confidential information of a client receiving legal services.

(c) For purposes of this Rule, "nonlegal services" shall mean those services that lawyers may lawfully provide and that are not prohibited as an unauthorized practice of law when provided by a nonlawyer.

RULE 5.8   CONTRACTUAL RELATIONSHIP BETWEEN LAWYERS AND NONLEGAL PROFESSIONALS.

(a) The practice of law has an essential tradition of complete independence and uncompromised loyalty to those it serves. Recognizing this tradition, clients of lawyers practicing in New York State are guaranteed "independent professional judgment and undivided loyalty uncompromised by conflicts of interest". Indeed, these guarantees represent the very foundation of the profession and allow and foster its continued role as a protector of the system of law. Therefore, a lawyer must remain completely responsible for his or her own independent professional judgment, maintain the confidences and secrets of clients, preserve funds of clients and third parties in his or her control, and otherwise comply with the legal and ethical principles governing lawyers in New York State.

Multi-disciplinary practice between lawyers and nonlawyers is incompatible with the core values of the legal profession and therefore, a strict division between services provided by lawyers and those provided by nonlawyers is essential to protect those values. However, a lawyer or law firm may enter into and maintain a contractual relationship with a nonlegal professional or nonlegal professional service firm for the purpose of offering to the public, on a systematic and continuing basis, legal services performed by the lawyer or law firm as well as other nonlegal professional services, notwithstanding the provisions of Rule 1.7(a), provided that:

(1) the profession of the nonlegal professional or nonlegal professional service firm is included in a list jointly established and maintained by the Appellate Divisions pursuant to Section 1205.3 of the Joint Appellate Division Rules;

(2) the lawyer or law firm neither grants to the nonlegal professional or nonlegal professional service firm, nor permits such person or firm to obtain, hold or exercise, directly or indirectly, any ownership or investment interest in, or managerial or supervisory right, power or position in connection with the practice of law by the lawyer or law firm, nor, as provided in Rule 7.2(a)(1), shares legal fees with a nonlawyer or receives or gives any monetary or other tangible benefit for giving or receiving a referral; and

(3) the fact that the contractual relationship exists is disclosed by the lawyer or law firm to any client of the lawyer or law firm before the client is referred to the nonlegal professional service firm, or to any client of the nonlegal professional service firm before that client receives legal services from the lawyer or law firm; and the client has given informed written consent and has been provided with a copy of the "Statement of Client's Rights In Cooperative Business Arrangements" pursuant to section 1205.4 of the Joint Appellate Divisions Rules.

(b) For purposes of paragraph (a):

(1) each profession on the list maintained pursuant to a joint rule of the Appellate Divisions shall have been designated sua sponte, or approved by the Appellate Divisions upon application of a member of a nonlegal profession or nonlegal professional service firm, upon a determination that the profession is composed of individuals who, with respect to their profession:

(i) have been awarded a bachelor's degree or its equivalent from an accredited college or university, or have attained an equivalent combination of educational credit from such a college or university and work experience;

(ii) are licensed to practice the profession by an agency of the State of New York or the United States Government; and

(iii) are required under penalty of suspension or revocation of license to adhere to a code of ethical conduct that is reasonably comparable to that of the legal profession;

(2) the term "ownership or investment interest" shall mean any such interest in any form of debt or equity, and shall include any interest commonly considered to be an interest accruing to or enjoyed by an owner or investor.

(c) This Rule shall not apply to relationships consisting solely of non-exclusive reciprocal referral agreements or understandings between a lawyer or law firm and a nonlegal professional or nonlegal professional service firm.

RULE 6.1   VOLUNTARY PRO BONO SERVICE.

Lawyers are strongly encouraged to provide pro bono legal services to benefit poor persons.

(a) Every lawyer should aspire to:

(1) provide at least 20 hours of pro bono legal services each year to poor persons; and

(2) contribute financially to organizations that provide legal services to poor persons.

(b) Pro bono legal services that meet this goal are:

(1) professional services rendered in civil matters, and in those criminal matters for which the government is not obliged to provide funds for legal representation, to persons who are financially unable to compensate counsel;

(2) activities related to improving the administration of justice by simplifying the legal process for, or increasing the availability and quality of legal services to, poor persons; and

(3) professional services to charitable, religious, civic and educational organizations in matters designed predominantly to address the needs of poor persons.

(c) Appropriate organizations for financial contributions are:

App Pract
Provs

(1) organizations primarily engaged in the provision of legal services to the poor; and

(2) organizations substantially engaged in the provision of legal services to the poor, provided that the donated funds are to be used for the provision of such legal services.

(d) This Rule is not intended to be enforced through the disciplinary process, and the failure to fulfill the aspirational goals contained herein should be without legal consequence.

RULE 6.2   [RESERVED].

RULE 6.3   MEMBERSHIP IN A LEGAL SERVICES ORGANIZATION.

A lawyer may serve as a director, officer or member of a not-for-profit legal services organization, apart from the law firm in which the lawyer practices, notwithstanding that the organization serves persons having interests that differ from those of a client of the lawyer or the lawyer's firm. The lawyer shall not knowingly participate in a decision or action of the organization:

(a) if participating in the decision or action would be incompatible with the lawyer's obligations to a client under Rules 1.7 through 1.13; or

(b) where the decision or action could have a material adverse effect on the representation of a client of the organization whose interests differ from those of a client of the lawyer or the lawyer's firm.

RULE 6.4   LAW REFORM ACTIVITIES AFFECTING CLIENT INTERESTS.

A lawyer may serve as a director, officer or member of an organization involved in reform of the law or its administration, notwithstanding that the reform may affect the interests of a client of the lawyer. When the lawyer knows that the interests of a client may be materially benefitted by a decision in which the lawyer actively participates, the lawyer shall disclose that fact to the organization, but need not identify the client. When the lawyer knows that the interests of a client may be adversely affected by a decision in which the lawyer actively participates, the lawyer shall disclose that fact to the client.

RULE 6.5   PARTICIPATION IN LIMITED PRO BONO

LEGAL SERVICE PROGRAMS.

(a) A lawyer who, under the auspices of a program sponsored by a court, government agency, bar association or not-for-profit legal services organization, provides short-term limited legal services to a client without expectation by either the lawyer or the client that the lawyer will provide continuing representation in the matter:

(1) shall comply with Rules 1.7, 1.8 and 1.9, concerning restrictions on representations where there are or may be conflicts of interest as that term is defined in these Rules, only if the lawyer has actual knowledge at the time of commencement of representation that the representation of the client involves a conflict of interest; and

(2) shall comply with Rule 1.10 only if the lawyer has actual knowledge at the time of commencement of representation that another lawyer associated with the lawyer in a law firm is affected by Rules 1.7, 1.8 and 1.9.

(b) Except as provided in paragraph (a)(2), Rule 1.7 and Rule 1.9 are inapplicable to a representation governed by this Rule.

(c) Short-term limited legal services are services providing legal advice or representation free of charge as part of a program described in paragraph (a) with no expectation that the assistance will continue beyond what is necessary to complete an initial consultation, representation or court appearance.

(d) The lawyer providing short-term limited legal services must secure the client's informed consent to the limited scope of the representation, and such representation shall be subject to the provisions of Rule 1.6.

(e) This Rule shall not apply where the court before which the matter is pending determines that a conflict of interest exists or, if during the course of the representation, the lawyer providing the services becomes aware of the existence of a conflict of interest precluding continued representation.

RULE 7.1   ADVERTISING.

(a) A lawyer or law firm shall not use or disseminate or participate in the use or dissemination of any advertisement that:

(1) contains statements or claims that are false, deceptive or misleading; or

(2) violates a Rule.

(b) Subject to the provisions of paragraph (a), an advertisement may include information as to:

(1) legal and nonlegal education, degrees and other scholastic distinctions, dates of admission to any bar; areas of the law in which the lawyer or law firm practices, as authorized by these Rules; public offices and teaching positions held; publications of law related matters authored by the lawyer; memberships in bar associations or other professional societies or organizations, including offices and committee assignments therein; foreign language fluency; and bona fide professional ratings;

(2) names of clients regularly represented, provided that the client has given prior written consent;

(3) bank references; credit arrangements accepted; prepaid or group legal services programs in which the lawyer or law firm participates; nonlegal services provided by the lawyer or law firm or by an entity owned and controlled by the lawyer or law firm; the existence of contractual relationships between the lawyer or law firm and a nonlegal professional or nonlegal professional service firm, to the extent permitted by Rule 5.8, and the nature and extent of services available through those contractual relationships; and

(4) legal fees for initial consultation; contingent fee rates in civil matters when accompanied by a statement disclosing the information required by paragraph (p); range of fees for legal and nonlegal services, provided that there be available to the public free of charge a written statement clearly describing the scope of each advertised service; hourly rates; and fixed fees for specified legal and nonlegal services.

(c) An advertisement shall not:

(1) include an endorsement of, or testimonial about, a lawyer or law firm from a client with respect to a matter still pending;

(2) include a paid endorsement of, or testimonial about, a lawyer or law firm without disclosing that the person is being compensated therefor;

(3) include the portrayal of a judge, the portrayal of a fictitious law firm, the use of a fictitious name to refer to lawyers not associated together in a law firm, or otherwise imply that lawyers are associated in a law firm if that is not the case;

(4) use actors to portray the lawyer, members of the law firm, or clients, or utilize depictions of fictionalized events or scenes, without disclosure of same;

(5) rely on techniques to obtain attention that demonstrate a clear and intentional lack of relevance to the selection of counsel, including the portrayal of lawyers exhibiting characteristics clearly unrelated to legal competence;

(6) be made to resemble legal documents; or

(7) utilize a nickname, moniker, motto or trade name that implies an ability to obtain results in a matter.

(d) An advertisement that complies with paragraph (e) may contain the following:

(1) statements that are reasonably likely to create an expectation about results the lawyer can achieve;

(2) statements that compare the lawyer's services with the services of other lawyers;

(3) testimonials or endorsements of clients, where not prohibited by paragraph (c)(1), and of former clients; or

(4) statements describing or characterizing the quality of the lawyer's or law firm's services.

(e) It is permissible to provide the information set forth in paragraph (d) provided:

(1) its dissemination does not violate paragraph (a);

(2) it can be factually supported by the lawyer or law firm as of the date on which the advertisement is published or disseminated; and

(3) it is accompanied by the following disclaimer: "Prior results do not guarantee a similar outcome."

(f) Every advertisement other than those appearing in a radio, television or billboard advertisement, in a directory, newspaper, magazine or other periodical (and any web sites related thereto), or made in person pursuant to Rule 7.3(a)(1), shall be labeled "Attorney Advertising" on the first page, or on the home page in the case of a web site. If the communication is in the form of a self-mailing brochure or postcard, the words "Attorney Advertising" shall appear therein. In the case of electronic mail, the subject line shall contain the notation "ATTORNEY ADVERTISING."

(g) A lawyer or law firm shall not utilize:

(1) a pop-up or pop-under advertisement in connection with computer-accessed communications, other than on the lawyer or law firm's own web site or other internet presence; or

(2) meta tags or other hidden computer codes that, if displayed, would violate these Rules.

(h) All advertisements shall include the name, principal law office address and telephone number of the lawyer or law firm whose services are being offered.

(i) Any words or statements required by this Rule to appear in an advertisement must be clearly legible and capable of being read by the average person, if written, and intelligible if spoken aloud. In the case of a web site, the required words or statements shall appear on the home page.

(j) A lawyer or law firm advertising any fixed fee for specified legal services shall, at the time of fee publication, have available to the public a written statement clearly describing the scope of each advertised service, which statement shall be available to the client at the time of retainer for any such service. Such legal services shall include all those services that are recognized as reasonable and necessary under local custom in the area of practice in the community where the services are performed.

(k) All advertisements shall be pre-approved by the lawyer or law firm, and a copy shall be retained for a period of not less than three years following its initial dissemination. Any advertisement contained in a computer-accessed communication shall be retained for a period of not less than one year. A copy of the contents of any web site covered by this Rule shall be preserved upon the initial publication of the web site, any major web site redesign, or a meaningful and extensive content change, but in no event less frequently than once every 90 days.

(l) If a lawyer or law firm advertises a range of fees or an hourly rate for services, the lawyer or law firm shall not charge more than the fee advertised for such services. If a lawyer or law firm advertises a fixed fee for specified legal services, or performs services described in a fee schedule, the lawyer or law firm shall not charge more than the fixed fee for such stated legal service as set forth in the advertisement or fee schedule, unless the client agrees in writing that the services performed or to be performed were not legal services referred to or implied in the advertisement or in the fee schedule and, further, that a different fee arrangement shall apply to the transaction.

(m) Unless otherwise specified in the advertisement, if a lawyer publishes any fee information authorized under this Rule in a publication that is published more frequently than once per month, the lawyer shall be bound by any representation made therein for a period of not less than 30 days after such publication. If a lawyer publishes any fee information authorized under this Rule in a publication that is published once per month or less frequently, the lawyer shall be bound by any representation made therein until the publication of the succeeding issue. If a lawyer publishes any fee information authorized under this Rule in a publication that has no fixed date for publication of a succeeding issue, the lawyer shall be bound by any representation made therein for a reasonable period of time after publication, but in no event less than 90 days.

(n) Unless otherwise specified, if a lawyer broadcasts any fee information authorized under this Rule, the lawyer shall be bound by any representation made therein for a period of not less than 30 days after such broadcast.

(o) A lawyer shall not compensate or give any thing of value to representatives of the press, radio, television or other communication medium in anticipation of or in return for professional publicity in a news item.

(p) All advertisements that contain information about the fees charged by the lawyer or law firm, including those indicating that in the

App Pract
Provs

absence of a recovery no fee will be charged, shall comply with the provisions of Judiciary Law § 488(3).

(q) A lawyer may accept employment that results from participation in activities designed to educate the public to recognize legal problems, to make intelligent selection of counsel or to utilize available legal services.

(r) Without affecting the right to accept employment, a lawyer may speak publicly or write for publication on legal topics so long as the lawyer does not undertake to give individual advice.

RULE 7.2   PAYMENT FOR REFERRALS.

(a) A lawyer shall not compensate or give anything of value to a person or organization to recommend or obtain employment by a client, or as a reward for having made a recommendation resulting in employment by a client, except that:

(1) a lawyer or law firm may refer clients to a nonlegal professional or nonlegal professional service firm pursuant to a contractual relationship with such nonlegal professional or nonlegal professional service firm to provide legal and other professional services on a systematic and continuing basis as permitted by Rule 5.8, provided however that such referral shall not otherwise include any monetary or other tangible consideration or reward for such, or the sharing of legal fees; and

(2) a lawyer may pay the usual and reasonable fees or dues charged by a qualified legal assistance organization or referral fees to another lawyer as permitted by Rule 1.5(g).

(b) A lawyer or the lawyer's partner or associate or any other affiliated lawyer may be recommended, employed or paid by, or may cooperate with one of the following offices or organizations that promote the use of the lawyer's services or those of a partner or associate or any other affiliated lawyer, or request one of the following offices or organizations to recommend or promote the use of the lawyer's services or those of the lawyer's partner or associate, or any other affiliated lawyer as a private practitioner, if there is no interference with the exercise of independent professional judgment on behalf of the client:

(1) a legal aid office or public defender office:

(i) operated or sponsored by a duly accredited law school;

(ii) operated or sponsored by a bona fide, non-profit community organization;

(iii) operated or sponsored by a governmental agency; or

(iv) operated, sponsored, or approved by a bar association;

(2) a military legal assistance office;

(3) a lawyer referral service operated, sponsored or approved by a bar association or authorized by law or court rule; or

(4) any bona fide organization that recommends, furnishes or pays for legal services to its members or beneficiaries provided the following conditions are satisfied:

(i) Neither the lawyer, nor the lawyer's partner, nor associate, nor any other affiliated lawyer nor any nonlawyer, shall have initiated or promoted such organization for the primary purpose of providing financial or other benefit to such lawyer, partner, associate or affiliated lawyer;

(ii) Such organization is not operated for the purpose of procuring legal work or financial benefit for any lawyer as a private practitioner outside of the legal services program of the organization;

(iii) The member or beneficiary to whom the legal services are furnished, and not such organization, is recognized as the client of the lawyer in the matter;

(iv) The legal service plan of such organization provides appropriate relief for any member or beneficiary who asserts a claim that representation by counsel furnished, selected or approved by the organization for the particular matter involved would be unethical, improper or inadequate under the circumstances of the matter involved; and the plan provides an appropriate procedure for seeking such relief;

(v) The lawyer does not know or have cause to know that such organization is in violation of applicable laws, rules of court or other legal requirements that govern its legal service operations; and

(vi) Such organization has filed with the appropriate disciplinary

App Pract
Provs

authority, to the extent required by such authority, at least annually a report with respect to its legal service plan, if any, showing its terms, its schedule of benefits, its subscription charges, agreements with counsel and financial results of its legal service activities or, if it has failed to do so, the lawyer does not know or have cause to know of such failure.

RULE 7.3   SOLICITATION AND RECOMMENDATION OF PROFESSIONAL EMPLOYMENT.

(a) A lawyer shall not engage in solicitation:

(1) by in-person or telephone contact, or by real-time or interactive computer-accessed communication unless the recipient is a close friend, relative, former client or existing client; or

(2) by any form of communication if:

(i) the communication or contact violates Rule 4.5, Rule 7.1(a), or paragraph (e) of this Rule;

(ii) the recipient has made known to the lawyer a desire not to be solicited by the lawyer;

(iii) the solicitation involves coercion, duress or harassment;

(iv) the lawyer knows or reasonably should know that the age or the physical, emotional or mental state of the recipient makes it unlikely that the recipient will be able to exercise reasonable judgment in retaining a lawyer; or

(v) the lawyer intends or expects, but does not disclose, that the legal services necessary to handle the matter competently will be performed primarily by another lawyer who is not affiliated with the soliciting lawyer as a partner, associate or of counsel.

(b) For purposes of this Rule, "solicitation" means any advertisement initiated by or on behalf of a lawyer or law firm that is directed to, or targeted at, a specific recipient or group of recipients, or their family members or legal representatives, the primary purpose of which is the retention of the lawyer or law firm, and a significant motive for which is pecuniary gain. It does not include a proposal or other writing prepared and delivered in response to a specific request of a prospective client.

(c) A solicitation directed to a recipient in this State, shall be subject to the following provisions:

(1) A copy of the solicitation shall at the time of its dissemination be filed with the attorney disciplinary committee of the judicial district or judicial department wherein the lawyer or law firm maintains its principal office. Where no such office is maintained, the filing shall be made in the judicial department where the solicitation is targeted. A filing shall consist of:

(i) a copy of the solicitation;

(ii) a transcript of the audio portion of any radio or television solicitation; and

(iii) if the solicitation is in a language other than English, an accurate English-language translation.

(2) Such solicitation shall contain no reference to the fact of filing.

(3) If a solicitation is directed to a predetermined recipient, a list containing the names and addresses of all recipients shall be retained by the lawyer or law firm for a period of not less than three years following the last date of its dissemination.

(4) Solicitations filed pursuant to this subdivision shall be open to public inspection.

(5) The provisions of this paragraph shall not apply to:

(i) a solicitation directed or disseminated to a close friend, relative, or former or existing client;

(ii) a web site maintained by the lawyer or law firm, unless the web site is designed for and directed to or targeted at a prospective client affected by an identifiable actual event or occurrence or by an identifiable prospective defendant; or

(iii) professional cards or other announcements the distribution of which is authorized by Rule 7.5(a).

(d) A written solicitation shall not be sent by a method that requires the recipient to travel to a location other than that at which the recipient ordinarily receives business or personal mail or that requires a signature on the part of the recipient.

App Pract
Provs

(e) No solicitation relating to a specific incident involving potential claims for personal injury or wrongful death shall be disseminated before the 30th day after the date of the incident, unless a filing must be made within 30 days of the incident as a legal prerequisite to the particular claim, in which case no unsolicited communication shall be made before the 15th day after the date of the incident.

(f) Any solicitation made in writing or by computer-accessed communication and directed to a pre-determined recipient, if prompted by a specific occurrence involving or affecting a recipient, shall disclose how the lawyer obtained the identity of the recipient and learned of the recipient's potential legal need.

(g) If a retainer agreement is provided with any solicitation, the top of each page shall be marked "SAMPLE" in red ink in a type size equal to the largest type size used in the agreement and the words "DO NOT SIGN" shall appear on the client signature line.

(h) Any solicitation covered by this section shall include the name, principal law office address and telephone number of the lawyer or law firm whose services are being offered.

(i) The provisions of this Rule shall apply to a lawyer or members of a law firm not admitted to practice in this State who solicit retention by residents of this State.

RULE 7.4   IDENTIFICATION OF PRACTICE AND SPECIALTY.

(a) A lawyer or law firm may publicly identify one or more areas of law in which the lawyer or the law firm practices, or may state that the practice of the lawyer or law firm is limited to one or more areas of law, provided that the lawyer or law firm shall not state that the lawyer or law firm is a specialist or specializes in a particular field of law, except as provided in Rule 7.4(c).

(b) A lawyer admitted to engage in patent practice before the United States Patent and Trademark Office may use the designation "Patent Attorney" or a substantially similar designation.

(c) A lawyer may state that the lawyer has been recognized or certified as a specialist only as follows:

(1) A lawyer who is certified as a specialist in a particular area of law

or law practice by a private organization approved for that purpose by the American Bar Association may state the fact of certification if, in conjunction therewith, the certifying organization is identified and the following statement is prominently made: "The [name of the private certifying organization] is not affiliated with any governmental authority. Certification is not a requirement for the practice of law in the State of New York and does not necessarily indicate greater competence than other attorneys experienced in this field of law;"

(2) A lawyer who is certified as a specialist in a particular area of law or law practice by the authority having jurisdiction over specialization under the laws of another state or territory may state the fact of certification if, in conjunction therewith, the certifying state or territory is identified and the following statement is prominently made "Certification granted by the [identify state or territory] is not recognized by any governmental authority within the State of New York. Certification is not a requirement for the practice of law in the State of New York and does not necessarily indicate greater competence than other attorneys experienced in this field of law;"

RULE 7.5   PROFESSIONAL NOTICES, LETTERHEADS, AND SIGNS.

(a) A lawyer or law firm may use internet web sites, professional cards, professional announcement cards, office signs, letterheads or similar professional notices or devices, provided the same do not violate any statute or court rule and are in accordance with Rule 7.1, including the following:

(1) a professional card of a lawyer identifying the lawyer by name and as a lawyer, and giving addresses, telephone numbers, the name of the law firm, and any information permitted under Rule 7.1(b) or Rule 7.4. A professional card of a law firm may also give the names of members and associates;

(2) a professional announcement card stating new or changed associations or addresses, change of firm name, or similar matters pertaining to the professional offices of a lawyer or law firm or any nonlegal business conducted by the lawyer or law firm pursuant to Rule 5.7. It may state biographical data, the names of members of the firm and associates, and the names and dates of predecessor firms in a

App Pract
Provs

continuing line of succession. It may state the nature of the legal practice if permitted under Rule 7.4;

(3) a sign in or near the office and in the building directory identifying the law office and any nonlegal business conducted by the lawyer or law firm pursuant to Rule 5.7. The sign may state the nature of the legal practice if permitted under Rule 7.4; or

(4) a letterhead identifying the lawyer by name and as a lawyer, and giving addresses, telephone numbers, the name of the law firm, associates and any information permitted under Rule 7.1(b) or Rule 7.4. A letterhead of a law firm may also give the names of members and associates, and names and dates relating to deceased and retired members. A lawyer or law firm may be designated "Of Counsel" on a letterhead if there is a continuing relationship with a lawyer or law firm, other than as a partner or associate. A lawyer or law firm may be designated as "General Counsel" or by similar professional reference on stationery of a client if the lawyer or the firm devotes a substantial amount of professional time in the representation of that client. The letterhead of a law firm may give the names and dates of predecessor firms in a continuing line of succession.

(b) A lawyer in private practice shall not practice under a trade name, a name that is misleading as to the identity of the lawyer or lawyers practicing under such name, or a firm name containing names other than those of one or more of the lawyers in the firm, except that the name of a professional corporation shall contain "PC" or such symbols permitted by law, the name of a limited liability company or partnership shall contain "LLC," "LLP" or such symbols permitted by law and, if otherwise lawful, a firm may use as, or continue to include in its name the name or names of one or more deceased or retired members of the firm or of a predecessor firm in a continuing line of succession. Such terms as "legal clinic," "legal aid," "legal service office," "legal assistance office," "defender office" and the like may be used only by qualified legal assistance organizations, except that the term "legal clinic" may be used by any lawyer or law firm provided the name of a participating lawyer or firm is incorporated therein. A lawyer or law firm may not include the name of a nonlawyer in its firm name, nor may a lawyer or law firm that has a contractual relationship with a nonlegal professional or nonlegal professional service firm pursuant to Rule 5.8 to provide legal and other professional services on a systematic and continuing basis include in its firm name the name of the nonlegal professional service firm or any individual nonlegal professional affiliated therewith. A lawyer who assumes a judicial, legislative or public executive or administrative post or office shall not permit the lawyer's name to remain in the name of a law firm or to be used in professional notices of the firm during any significant period in which the lawyer is not actively and regularly practicing law as a member of the firm and, during such period, other members of the firm shall not use the lawyer's name in the firm name or in professional notices of the firm.

(c) Lawyers shall not hold themselves out as having a partnership with one or more other lawyers unless they are in fact partners.

(d) A partnership shall not be formed or continued between or among lawyers licensed in different jurisdictions unless all enumerations of the members and associates of the firm on its letterhead and in other permissible listings make clear the jurisdictional limitations on those members and associates of the firm not licensed to practice in all listed jurisdictions; however, the same firm name may be used in each jurisdiction.

(e) A lawyer or law firm may utilize a domain name for an internet web site that does not include the name of the lawyer or law firm provided:

(1) all pages of the web site clearly and conspicuously include the actual name of the lawyer or law firm;

(2) the lawyer or law firm in no way attempts to engage in the practice of law using the domain name;

(3) the domain name does not imply an ability to obtain results in a matter; and

(4) the domain name does not otherwise violate these Rules.

(f) A lawyer or law firm may utilize a telephone number which contains a domain name, nickname, moniker or motto that does not otherwise violate these Rules.

RULE 8.1   CANDOR IN THE BAR ADMISSION PROCESS.

App Pract Provs

(a) A lawyer shall be subject to discipline if, in connection with the lawyer's own application for admission to the bar previously filed in this state or in any other jurisdiction, or in connection with the application of another person for admission to the bar, the lawyer knowingly:

(1) has made or failed to correct a false statement of material fact; or

(2) has failed to disclose a material fact requested in connection with a lawful demand for information from an admissions authority.

RULE 8.2   JUDICIAL OFFICERS AND CANDIDATES.

(a) A lawyer shall not knowingly make a false statement of fact concerning the qualifications, conduct or integrity of a judge or other adjudicatory officer or of a candidate for election or appointment to judicial office.

(b) A lawyer who is a candidate for judicial office shall comply with the applicable provisions of Part 100 of the Rules of the Chief Administrator of the Courts.

RULE 8.3   REPORTING PROFESSIONAL MISCONDUCT.

(a) A lawyer who knows that another lawyer has committed a violation of the Rules of Professional Conduct that raises a substantial question as to that lawyer's honesty, trustworthiness or fitness as a lawyer shall report such knowledge to a tribunal or other authority empowered to investigate or act upon such violation.

(b) A lawyer who possesses knowledge or evidence concerning another lawyer or a judge shall not fail to respond to a lawful demand for information from a tribunal or other authority empowered to investigate or act upon such conduct.

(c) This Rule does not require disclosure of:

(1) information otherwise protected by Rule 1.6; or

(2) information gained by a lawyer or judge while participating in a bona fide lawyer assistance program.

RULE 8.4   MISCONDUCT.

A lawyer or law firm shall not:

(a) violate or attempt to violate the Rules of Professional Conduct, knowingly assist or induce another to do so, or do so through the acts of another;

(b) engage in illegal conduct that adversely reflects on the lawyer's honesty, trustworthiness or fitness as a lawyer;

(c) engage in conduct involving dishonesty, fraud, deceit or misrepresentation;

(d) engage in conduct that is prejudicial to the administration of justice;

(e) state or imply an ability:

(1) to influence improperly or upon irrelevant grounds any tribunal, legislative body or public official; or

(2) to achieve results using means that violate these Rules or other law;

(f) knowingly assist a judge or judicial officer in conduct that is a violation of applicable rules of judicial conduct or other law;

(g) unlawfully discriminate in the practice of law, including in hiring, promoting or otherwise determining conditions of employment on the basis of age, race, creed, color, national origin, sex, disability, marital status or sexual orientation. Where there is a tribunal with jurisdiction to hear a complaint, if timely brought, other than a Departmental Disciplinary Committee, a complaint based on unlawful discrimination shall be brought before such tribunal in the first instance. A certified copy of a determination by such a tribunal, which has become final and enforceable and as to which the right to judicial or appellate review has been exhausted, finding that the lawyer has engaged in an unlawful discriminatory practice shall constitute prima facie evidence of professional misconduct in a disciplinary proceeding; or

(h) engage in any other conduct that adversely reflects on the lawyer's fitness as a lawyer.

RULE 8.5   DISCIPLINARY AUTHORITY AND CHOICE OF LAW.

(a) A lawyer admitted to practice in this state is subject to the disciplinary authority of this state, regardless of where the lawyer's conduct occurs. A lawyer may be subject to the disciplinary authority of both this state and another jurisdiction where the lawyer is admitted for the same conduct.

(b) In any exercise of the disciplinary authority of this state, the rules of professional conduct to be applied shall be as follows:

(1) For conduct in connection with a proceeding in a court before which a lawyer has been admitted to practice (either generally or for purposes of that proceeding), the rules to be applied shall be the rules of the jurisdiction in which the court sits, unless the rules of the court provide otherwise; and

(2) For any other conduct:

(i) If the lawyer is licensed to practice only in this state, the rules to be applied shall be the rules of this state, and

(ii) If the lawyer is licensed to practice in this state and another jurisdiction, the rules to be applied shall be the rules of the admitting jurisdiction in which the lawyer principally practices; provided, however, that if particular conduct clearly has its predominant effect in another jurisdiction in which the lawyer is licensed to practice, the rules of that jurisdiction shall be applied to that conduct.

Part 1205. Cooperative Business Arrangements Between Lawyers and Non-legal Professionals

§ 1205.1. Application

This Part shall apply to all lawyers who, pursuant to a cooperative business arrangement:

(a) undertake to provide legal services to a client referred by a nonlegal service provider; or

(b) refer an existing client to a nonlegal service provider.

§ 1205.2. Definition.

A "cooperative business arrangement" is a contractual relationship between a lawyer or law firm and a nonlegal professional or nonlegal professional service firm for the purpose of offering to the public, on a systematic and continuing basis, legal services performed by the lawyer or law firm, as well as other nonlegal professional services, as authorized by section 1200.5-c of this Title.

§ 1205.3.   List of Professions

(a) The Appellate Divisions jointly shall establish and maintain a list of professions,set forth in section 1205.5 of this Part designated by the Appellate Divisions *sua sponte* or approved by them upon application of a member of a nonlegal profession or nonlegal professional service firm, with whose members a lawyer may enter into a cooperative business arrangement to perform legal and nonlegal services as authorized by section 1200.5-c of this Title.

(b) A member of a nonlegal profession may apply to the Appellate Division to have that profession included in the list by submitting to the Appellate Division Clerk's Office in any Judicial Department a petition to establish that the profession is composed of individuals who, with respect to their profession, meet the requirements set forth in section 1200.5-c(b)(1)of this Title.

§ 1205.4.   Statement of Client's Rights in Cooperative Business Arrangements

In the furtherance of a cooperative business arrangement:

(a) prior to the commencement of legal representation of a client referred by a nonlegal service provider; or

(b) prior to the referral of an existing client to a nonlegal service provider; a lawyer shall provide the client with a statement of the client's right. That statement shall include a consent to the referral to be signed by the client and shall contain the following:

STATEMENT OF CLIENT'S RIGHT IN COOPERATIVE BUSINESS ARRANGEMENTS

Your lawyer is providing you with this document to explain how your rights may be affected by the referral of your particular matter by your lawyer to a nonlegal service provider, or by the referral of your particular matter by a nonlegal service provider to your lawyer.

To help avoid any misunderstanding between you and your lawyer please read this document carefully. If you have any questions about these rights, do not hesitate to ask your lawyer.

Your lawyer has entered into a contractual relationship with a nonlegal professional or professional service firm, in the form of a cooperative business arrangement which may include sharing of costs and expenses, to provide legal and nonlegal services. Such an arrangement may substantially affect your rights in a number of respects. Specifically, you are advised:

1. A lawyer's clients are guaranteed the independent professional judgment and undivided loyalty of the lawyer, uncompromised by conflicts of interest. The lawyer's business arrangement with a provider of nonlegal services may not diminish these rights.

2. Confidences and secrets imparted by a client to a lawyer are protected by the attorney/client privilege and may not be disclosed by the lawyer as part of a referral to a nonlegal service provider without the separate written consent of the client.

3. The protections afforded to a client by the attorney/client privilege may not carry over to dealings between the client and a nonlegal service provider. Information that would be protected as a confidence or secret, if imparted by the client to a lawyer, may not be so protected when disclosed by the client to a nonlegal service provider. Under some circumstances, the nonlegal service provider may be required by statute or a code of ethics to make disclosure to a government agency.

4. Even where a lawyer refers a client to a nonlegal service provider for assistance in financial matters, the lawyer's obligation to preserve and safeguard client funds in his or her possession continues.

You have the right to consult with an independent lawyer or other third party before signing this agreement.

Client's Consent:

I have read the above Statement of Client's Rights in Cooperative Business Arrangements and I consent to the referral of my particular matter in accordance with that Statement.

_____

Client's signature

_____

Date

§ 1205.5. Nonlegal professions eligible to form cooperative business arrangements with lawyers.

Members of the following nonlegal professions are eligible to form contractual business relationships with lawyers:

Architecture

Certified Public Accountancy

Professional Engineering

Land Surveying

Certified Social Work

Part 1210. Statement of Client's Rights.

§ 1210.1. Posting.

Every attorney with an office located in the State of New York shall insure that there is posted in that office, in a manner visible to clients of the attorney, a statement of client's rights in the form set forth below. Attorneys in offices that provide legal services without fee may delete from the statement those provisions dealing with fees. The statement shall contain the following:

STATEMENT OF CLIENT'S RIGHTS

1. You are entitled to be treated with courtesy and consideration at all times by your lawyer and the other lawyers and personnel in your lawyer's office.

2. You are entitled to an attorney capable of handling your legal matter competently and diligently, in accordance with the highest standards of the profession. If you are not satisfied with how your matter is being handled, you have the right to withdraw from the attorney-client relationship at any time (court approval may be required in some matters and your attorney may have a claim against you for the value of services rendered to you up to the point of discharge).

App Pract Provs

3. You are entitled to your lawyer's independent professional judgment and undivided loyalty uncompromised by conflicts of interest.

4. You are entitled to be charged a reasonable fee and to have your lawyer explain at the outset how the fee will be computed and the manner and frequency of billing. You are entitled to request and receive a written itemized bill from your attorney at reasonable intervals. You may refuse to enter into any fee arrangement that you find unsatisfactory. In the event of a fee dispute, you may have the right to seek arbitration: your attorney will provide you with the necessary information regarding arbitration in the event of a fee dispute, or upon your request.

5. You are entitled to have your questions and concerns addressed in a prompt manner and to have your telephone calls returned promptly.

6. You are entitled to be kept informed as to the status of your matter and to request and receive copies of papers. You are entitled to sufficient information to allow you to participate meaningfully in the development of your matter.

7. You are entitled to have your legitimate objectives respected by your attorney, including whether or not to settle your matter (court approval of a settlement is required in some matters).

8. You have the right to privacy in your dealings with your lawyer and to have your secrets and confidences preserved to the extent permitted by law.

9. You are entitled to have your attorney conduct himself or herself ethically in accordance with the Code of Professional Responsibility.

10. You may not be refused representation on the basis of race, creed, color, religion, sex, sexual orientation, age, national origin or disability.

Part 1215.   WRITTEN LETTER OF ENGAGEMENT

§ 1215.1.   Requirements.

(a) Effective March 4, 2002, an attorney who undertakes to represent a client and enters into an arrangement for, charges or collects any fee from a client shall provide to the client a written letter of engagement before commencing the representation, or within a reasonable time thereafter:

(1) if otherwise impracticable; or

(2) if the scope of services to be provided cannot be determined at the time of the commencement of representation.

"Client" shall include any person or entity that is responsible for the payment of the attorney's fees. Where there is a significant change in the scope of services or the fee to be charged, an updated letter of engagement shall be provided to the client.

(b) The letter of engagement shall address the following matters:

(1) explanation of the scope of the legal services to be provided;

(2) explanation of attorney's fees to be charged, expenses and billing practices; and

(3) where applicable, shall provide that the client may have a right to arbitrate fee disputes under Part 137 of this Title.

(c) Instead of providing the client with a written letter of engagement, an attorney may comply with the provisions of subdivision (a) of this section by entering into a signed written retainer agreement with the client, before or within a reasonable time after commencing the representation, provided that the agreement addresses the matters set forth in subdivision (b) of this section.

§ 1215.2.   Exceptions.

This section shall not apply to:

(a) representation of a client where the fee to be charged is expected to be less than $3000;

(b) representation where the attorney's services are of the same general kind as previously rendered to and paid for by the client; or

(c) representation in domestic relations matters subject to Part 1400 of this Title.

Part 1230.   FEE ARBITRATION

§ 1230.1. Establishment of fee arbitration program.

(a) The Chief Administrator of the Courts shall establish a fee arbitration program, which shall be approved by the justices of the Appellate Divisions and which shall provide for the resolution by arbitrators of fee disputes between an attorney and client based upon representation in civil matters.

(b) The fee arbitration program established by the Chief Administrator pursuant to this Part shall provide for arbitration that shall be binding upon both attorney and client unless *de novo* review is sought in the courts.

Part 1300. Dishonored Check Reporting Rules for Attorney Special, Trust and Escrow Accounts

§ 1300.1. Dishonored check reports.

(a) Special bank accounts required by Disciplinary Rule 9–102 (22 NYCRR 1200.46) shall be maintained only in banking institutions which have agreed to provide dishonored check reports in accordance with the provisions of this section.

(b) An agreement to provide dishonored check reports shall be filed with the Lawyers' Fund for Client Protection, which shall maintain a central registry of all banking institutions which have been approved in accordance with this section, and the current status of each such agreement. The agreement shall apply to all branches of each banking institution that provides special bank accounts for attorneys engaged in the practice of law in this State, and shall not be cancelled by a banking institution except on 30 days' prior written notice to the Lawyers' Fund for Client Protection.

(c) A dishonored check report by a banking institution shall be required whenever a properly payable instrument is presented against an attorney special, trust or escrow account which contains insufficient available funds, and the banking institution dishonors the instrument for that reason. A *properly payable instrument* means an instrument which, if presented in the normal course of business, is in a form requiring payment under the laws of the State of New York.

(d) A dishonored check report shall be substantially in the form of the notice of dishonor which the banking institution customarily forwards to its customer, and may include a photocopy or a computer-generated duplicate of such notice.

(e) Dishonored check reports shall be mailed to the Lawyers' Fund for Client Protection, 119 Washington Avenue, Albany, NY 12210, within five banking days after the date of presentment against insufficient available funds.

(f) The Lawyers' Fund for Client Protection shall hold each dishonored check report for 10 business days to enable the banking institution to withdraw a report provided by inadvertence or mistake; except that the curing of an insufficiency of available funds by a lawyer or law firm by the deposit of additional funds shall not constitute reason for withdrawing a dishonored check report.

(g) After holding the dishonored check report for 10 business days, the Lawyers' Fund for Client Protection shall forward it to the attorney disciplinary committee for the judicial department or district having jurisdiction over the account holder, as indicated by the law office or other address on the report, for such inquiry and action that attorney disciplinary committee deems appropriate.

(h) Every lawyer admitted to the Bar of the State of New York shall be deemed to have consented to the dishonored check reporting requirements of this section. Lawyers and law firms shall promptly notify their banking institutions of existing or new attorney special, trust, or escrow accounts for the purpose of facilitating the implementation and administration of the provisions of this section.

Part 1400. Procedure for Attorneys in Domestic Relations Matters

§ 1400.1. Application.

This Part shall apply to all attorneys who, on or after November 30, 1993, undertake to represent a client in a claim, action or proceeding, or preliminary to the filing of a claim, action or proceeding, in either Supreme Court or Family Court, or in any court of appellate jurisdiction, for divorce, separation, annulment, custody, visitation, maintenance, child support, or alimony, or to enforce or modify a judgment or order in connection with any such claims, actions or proceedings. This Part shall not apply to attorneys representing clients without compensation paid by the client, except that where the client is other than a

App Pract
Provs

minor, the provisions of section 1400.2 shall apply to the extent they are not applicable to compensation.

§ 1400.2. Statement of Client's Rights and Responsibilities.

An attorney shall provide a prospective client with a statement of client's rights and responsibilities, in a form prescribed by the Appellate Divisions, at the initial conference and prior to the signing of a written retainer agreement. If the attorney is not being paid a fee from the client for the work to be performed on the particular case, the attorney may delete from the statement those provisions dealing with fees. The attorney shall obtain a signed acknowledgment of receipt from the client. The statement shall contain the following:

Your attorney is providing you with this document to inform you of what you, as a client, are entitled to by law or by custom. To help prevent any misunderstanding between you and your attorney please read this document carefully.

If you ever have any questions about these rights, or about the way your case is being handled, do not hesitate to ask your attorney. He or she should be readily available to represent your best interests and keep you informed about your case.

An attorney may not refuse to represent you on the basis of race, creed, color, sex, sexual orientation, age, national origin or disability.

You are entitled to an attorney who will be capable of handling your case; show you courtesy and consideration at all times; represent you zealously; and preserve your confidences and secrets that are revealed in the course of the relationship.

You are entitled to a written retainer agreement which must set forth, in plain language, the nature of the relationship and the details of the fee arrangement. At your request, and before you sign the agreement, you are entitled to have your attorney clarify in writing any of its terms, or include additional provisions.

You are entitled to fully understand the proposed rates and retainer fee before you sign a retainer agreement, as in any other contract.

You may refuse to enter into any fee arrangement that you find unsatisfactory.

Your attorney may not request a fee that is contingent on the securing of a divorce or on the amount of money or property that may be obtained.

Your attorney may not request a retainer fee that is nonrefundable. That is, should you discharge your attorney, or should your attorney withdraw from the case, before the retainer is used up, he or she is entitled to be paid commensurate with the work performed on your case and any expenses, but must return the balance of the retainer to you. However, your attorney may enter into a minimum fee arrangement with you that provides for the payment of a specific amount below which the fee will not fall based upon the handling of the case to its conclusion.

You are entitled to know the approximate number of attorneys and other legal staff members who will be working on your case at any given time and what you will be charged for the services of each.

You are entitled to know in advance how you will be asked to pay legal fees and expenses, and how the retainer,if any, will be spent.

At your request, and after your attorney has had a reasonable opportunity to investigate your case, you are entitled to be given an estimate of approximate future costs of your case, which estimate shall be made in good faith but may be subject to change due to facts and circumstances affecting the case.

You are entitled to receive a written, itemized bill on a regular basis, at least every 60 days.

You are expected to review the itemized bills sent by counsel, and to raise any objections or errors in a timely manner. Time spent in discussion or explanation of bills will not be charged to you.

You are expected to be truthful in all discussions with your attorney, and to provide all relevant information and documentation to enable him or her to competently prepare your case.

You are entitled to be kept informed of the status of your case, and to be provided with copies of correspondence and documents prepared on your behalf or received from the court or your adversary.

You are entitled to make the ultimate decision on the objectives to be pursued in your case,and to make the final decision regarding the settlement of your case.

App Pract Provs

Your attorney's written retainer agreement must specify under what circumstances he or she might seek to withdraw as your attorney for nonpayment of legal fees. If an action or proceeding is pending, the court may give your attorney a "charging lien," which entitles your attorney to payment for services already rendered at the end of the case out of the proceeds of the final order or judgment.

You are under no legal obligation to sign a confession of judgment or promissory note, or to agree to a lien or mortgage on your home to cover legal fees. Your attorney's written retainer agreement must specify whether, and under what circumstances, such security may be requested. In no event may such security interest be obtained by your attorney without prior court approval and notice to your adversary. An attorney's security interest in the marital residence cannot be foreclosed against you.

You are entitled to have your attorney's best efforts exerted on your behalf, but no particular results can be guaranteed.

If you entrust money with an attorney for an escrow deposit in your case, the attorney must safeguard the escrow in a special bank account. You are entitled to a written escrow agreement, a written receipt, and a complete record concerning the escrow. When the terms of the escrow agreement have been performed, the attorney must promptly make payment of the escrow to all persons who are entitled to it.

In the event of a fee dispute, you may have the right to seek arbitration. Your attorney will provide you with the necessary information regarding arbitration in the event of a fee dispute, or upon your request.

Receipt Acknowledged:

. . . .
Attorney's signature

. . . .
Client's signature

. . . .
Date

Form 1400.2-1(1/95)

Your attorney is providing you with this document to inform you of what you, as a client, are entitled to by law or by custom. To help prevent any misunderstanding between you and your attorney please read this document carefully.

If you ever have any questions about these rights, or about the way your case is being handled, do not hesitate to ask your attorney. He or she should be readily available to represent your best interests and keep you informed about your case.

An attorney may not refuse to represent you on the basis of race, creed, color, sex, sexual orientation, age, national origin or disability.

You are entitled to an attorney who will be capable of handling your case; show you courtesy and consideration at all times; represent you zealously; and preserve your confidences and secrets that are revealed in the course of the relationship.

You are expected to be truthful in all discussions with your attorney, and to provide all relevant information and documentation to enable him or her to competently prepare your case.

You are entitled to be kept informed of the status of your case, and to be provided with copies of correspondence and documents prepared on your behalf or received from the court or your adversary.

You have the right to be present in court at the time that conferences are held.

You are entitled to make the ultimate decision on the objectives to be pursued in your case,and to make the final decision regarding the settlement of your case.

You are entitled to have your attorney's best efforts exerted on your behalf, but no particular results can be guaranteed.

App Pract
Provs

If you entrust money with an attorney for an escrow deposit in your case, the attorney must safeguard the escrow in a special bank account. You are entitled to a written escrow agreement, a written receipt, and a complete record concerning the escrow. When the terms of the escrow agreement have been performed, the attorney must promptly make payment of the escrow to all persons who are entitled to it.

Receipt Acknowledged:

. . . .
Attorney's signature
. . . .
Client's signature
. . . .
Date

Form 1400.2-2 (12/94)

§ 1400.3.   Written Retainer Agreement.

An attorney who undertakes to represent a party and enters into an arrangement for, charges or collects any fee from a client shall execute a written agreement with the client setting forth in plain language the terms of compensation and the nature of services to be rendered. The agreement, and any amendment thereto, shall be signed by both client and attorney, and, in actions in Supreme Court, a copy of the signed agreement shall be filed with the court with the statement of net worth. Where substitution of counsel occurs after the filing of the net worth statement, a signed copy of the attorney's retainer agreement shall be filed with the court within 10 days of its execution. A copy of a signed amendment shall be filed within 15 days of signing. A duplicate copy of the filed agreement and any amendment shall be provided to the client. The agreement shall be subject to the provisions governing confidentiality contained in Domestic Relations Law, section 235(1). The agreement shall contain the following information:

RETAINER AGREEMENT

1.   Names and addresses of the parties entering into the agreement;

2.   Nature of the services to be rendered;

3.   Amount of the advance retainer, if any, and what it is intended to cover;

4.   Circumstances under which any portion of the advance retainer may be refunded. Should the attorney withdraw from the case or be discharged prior to the depletion of the advance retainer, the written retainer agreement shall provide how the attorney's fees and expenses are to be determined, and the remainder of the advance retainer shall be refunded to the client;

5.   Client's right to cancel the agreement at any time; how the attorney's fee will be determined and paid should the client discharge the attorney at any time during the course of the representation;

6.   How the attorney will be paid through the conclusion of the case after the retainer is depleted; whether the client may be asked to pay another lump sum;

7.   Hourly rate of each person whose time may be charged to the client; any out-of-pocket disbursements for which the client will be required to reimburse the attorney. Any changes in such rates or fees shall be incorporated into a written agreement constituting an amendment to the original agreement, which must be signed by the client before it may take effect;

8.   Any clause providing for a fee in addition to the agreed-upon rate, such as a reasonable minimum fee clause, must be defined in plain language and set forth the circumstances under which such fee may be incurred and how it will be calculated.

9.   Frequency of itemized billing, which shall be at least every 60 days; the client may not be charged for time spent in discussion of the bills received;

10.   Client's right to be provided with copies of correspondence and documents relating to the case, and to be kept apprised of the status of the case;

11.   Whether and under what circumstances the attorney might seek a security interest from the client, which can be obtained only upon court approval and on notice to the adversary;

12.   Under what circumstances the attorney might seek to withdraw from the case for nonpayment of fees, and the attorney's right to seek a charging lien from the court.

13.   Should a dispute arise concerning the attorney's fee, the client may seek arbitration; the attorney shall provide information concerning

App Pract Provs

fee arbitration in the event of such dispute or upon the client's request.

§ 1400.4.   Nonrefundable Retainer Fee.

An attorney shall not enter into an arrangement for, charge or collect a nonrefundable retainer fee from a client. An attorney may enter into a "minimum fee" arrangement with a client that provides for the payment of a specific amount below which the fee will not fall based upon the handling of the case to its conclusion.

§ 1400.5.   Security Interests.

(a) An attorney may obtain a confession of judgment or promissory note, take a lien on real property, or otherwise obtain a security interest to secure his or her fee only where:

(1) the retainer agreement provides that a security interest may be sought;

(2) notice of an application for a security interest has been given to the other spouse; and,

(3) the court grants approval for the security interest after submission of an application for counsel fees.

(b) Notwithstanding the provisions of subdivision (a) of this section, an attorney shall not foreclose on a mortgage placed on the marital residence while the spouse who consents to the mortgage remains the titleholder and the residence remains the spouse's primary residence.

§ 1400.6.   [Repealed.]

§ 1400.7.   Fee Arbitration.

In the event of a fee dispute between attorney and client, the client may seek to resolve the dispute by arbitration pursuant to a fee arbitration program established by the Chief Administrator of the Courts and subject to the approval of the justices of the Appellate Divisions.

Part 1500.   Mandatory Continuing Legal Education Program for Attorneys in the State of New York
Subpart A.   STRUCTURE OF PROGRAM

§ 1500.1.   Scope.

There shall be a mandatory continuing legal education program in the State of New York (hereinafter Program) which shall include a transitional legal education program for newly admitted attorneys, as set forth in Subpart B, and a legal education program for all other admitted attorneys, as set forth in Subpart C. A Continuing Legal Education Board shall accredit and oversee, as set forth in this Subpart, the courses, programs and other educational activities that will satisfy the requirements of the Program.

§ 1500.2.   Definitions.

(a) *Accredited Course or Program* is a continuing legal education course or program that has met the standards set forth in § 1500.4(b) and has received advance accreditation approval by the Continuing Legal Education Board.

(b) *Accredited Provider* is a person or entity whose continuing legal education program has been accredited by the Continuing Legal Education Board, and who has been certified by the Continuing Legal Education Board as an accredited provider of continuing legal education courses and programs in accordance with § 1500.4(c).

(c) *Ethics and Professionalism* may include, among other things, the following: the norms relating to lawyers' professional obligations to clients (including the obligation to provide legal assistance to those in need, confidentiality, competence, conflicts of interest, the allocation of decision making, and zealous advocacy and its limits); the norms relating to lawyers' professional relations with prospective clients, courts and other legal institutions, and third parties (including the lawyers' fiduciary, accounting and record-keeping obligations when entrusted with law client and escrow monies, as well as the norms relating to civility); the sources of lawyers' professional obligations (including disciplinary rules, judicial decisions, and relevant constitutional and statutory provisions); recognition and resolution of ethical dilemmas; the mechanisms for enforcing professional norms; substance abuse control; and professional values (including professional development, improving the profession, and the promotion of fairness, justice and morality).

(d) *Skills* must relate to the practice of law and may include, among other things, problem solving, legal analysis and reasoning, legal research and writing, drafting documents, factual investigation (as taught in courses on areas of professional practice), communication, counseling, negotiation, mediation, arbitration, organization and trial advocacy.

(e) *Law Practice Management* must relate to the practice of law and may encompass, among other things, law office management, state, applications of technology, state and federal court procedures, stress management, management of legal work and avoiding malpractice and litigation.

(f) *Areas of Professional Practice* may include, among other things, corporations, wills/trusts, elder law, estate planning/administration, real estate, commercial law, civil litigation, criminal litigation, family law, labor and employment law, administrative law, securities, tort/insurance practice, bankruptcy, taxation, compensation, intellectual property, municipal law, landlord/tenant, environmental law, entertainment law, international law, social security and other government benefits, and alternative dispute resolution procedures.

(g) *Regulations and Guidelines* refers to the regulations and guidelines of the Continuing Legal Education Board set forth in Part 7500 of this title.

§ 1500.3.   The Continuing Legal Education Board.

(a) *The Continuing Legal Education Board.* The Continuing Legal Education Board (CLE Board) is hereby established.

(b) *Board Composition.* The CLE board shall consist of 16 resident members of the bench and bar. Three members shall be chosen by each of the presiding justices of the Appellate Divisions, and four members shall be chosen by the Chief Judge of the State of New York. The Chief Judge shall designate the chair. Board members shall serve at the pleasure of the Administrative Board of the Courts.

(c) *Quorum.* Nine members shall constitute a quorum of the entire CLE board.

(d) *Term of Service.* The term of board members shall be three years. Board members shall be appointed for no more than one three-year term.

(e) *Duties and Responsibilities.* The CLE board is authorized to: accredit providers of courses, programs, and other educational activities that will satisfy the requirements of the program; determine the number of hours for which continuing legal education credit will be given for particular courses or programs; adopt or repeal regulations and forms consistent with these rules; examine course materials and the qualifications of continuing legal education instructors; consult and appoint committees in furtherance of its official duties as necessary; foster and encourage the offering of accredited courses and programs, particularly in geographically isolated regions; and report annually on its activities to the Chief Judge, the presiding justices of the Appellate Divisions and the Chief Administrator of the Courts.

(f) *Expenses.* Members of the CLE board shall serve without compensation but shall be reimbursed for their reasonable, actual and direct expenses incurred in furtherance of their official duties.

(g) *Confidentiality.* The files, records and proceedings of the CLE board, as they relate to an attorney's satisfying the requirements of this Part, shall be confidential and shall not be disclosed except in furtherance of the duties of the board or upon the request of the attorney affected, or as they may be introduced in evidence or otherwise produced in proceedings implementing this Part.

(h) *Appeal of Determinations.* Any person or organization aggrieved by a determination pursuant to this Part may seek administrative review of that determination pursuant to the regulations and guidelines adopted by the CLE board.

§ 1500.4. Accreditation.

(a) *Procedure.* Unless a provider has been granted accredited provider status pursuant to subdivision (c), accreditation of continuing legal education courses or programs must be sought and granted at least 60 days prior to the occurrence of the course or program except in extenuating circumstances and with prior permission of the CLE board.

(b) *Standards.* Continuing legal education courses or programs to be accredited shall comply with the following guidelines:

App Pract
Provs

(1) One hour of continuing legal education credit shall consist of at least 50 minutes of instruction, exclusive of introductory remarks, meals, breaks, or other noneducational activities.

(2) The course or program must have significant intellectual or practical content and its primary objective must be to increase the professional legal competency of the attorney in ethics and professionalism, skills, practice management and/or areas of professional practice.

(3) The course or program shall be taught by instructors with expertise in the subject matter being taught and shall be specifically tailored to attorneys.

(4) The faculty of the course or program shall include at least one attorney in good standing who shall actively participate in the course or program.

(5) The course or program shall not be taught by a disbarred attorney, whether the disbarred attorney is the sole presenter or one of several instructors.

(6) The cost of continuing legal education courses or programs to the participating attorney shall be reasonable.

(7) Providers must have a financial hardship policy as provided in the regulations and guidelines.

(8) The course or program must be conducted in a physical setting that is comfortable and conducive to learning.

(9) At the conclusion of the course or program, each participant must be given the opportunity to complete an evaluation questionnaire addressing the quality, effectiveness and usefulness of the particular course or program. A summary of the results of the survey(s) must be submitted to the CLE board at the end of the calendar year in which the course or program was given. Providers must maintain the questionnaires for a period of four (4) years following the course or program.

(10) Providers of continuing legal education courses or programs shall provide a certificate of attendance to all persons completing the continuing legal education course or program.

(11) Providers of continuing legal education courses or programs must maintain an official attendance list of participants in the program, and the time, date, location, title, speaker(s) and amount of approved CLE credit for each course or program, for at least four (4) years after the completion date.

(12) Programs that satisfy these standards and that cross academic lines, such as accounting-tax seminars, may be considered for approval by the CLE board.

(c) *Accredited provider status.*

(1) Procedure. Application may be made for accredited provider status by submitting the appropriate forms and materials to the CLE board pursuant to CLE board regulations and guidelines.

(2) Requirements. Accredited provider status may be granted at the discretion of the CLE board to applicants satisfying the requirements of this section and, as well, the following requirements:

(i) The provider has presented, within the prior three years, separate programs of continuing legal education that meet the standards set forth in subdivision (b) and the regulations and guidelines of the CLE board; or

(ii) The provider has demonstrated to the board that its CLE activities have consistently met the standards set forth in subdivision (b) and the regulations and guidelines of the CLE board.

Providers that meet the foregoing requirements may include bar associations, law schools, law firms and legal departments (including corporate, nonprofit and municipal and state law departments).

(3) Duration of accredited provider status. Once a provider has been granted accredited provider status, the continuing legal education courses or programs sponsored by that provider are presumptively approved for credit for a period of three years from the date of the grant of such status.

(4) Accredited provider reports. Providers granted accredited provider status shall file a written report with the CLE board each year at a time fixed by the board. The report shall describe the

continuing legal education activities conducted during the prior 12 months and shall be in such detail and form as required by the board and by the regulations and guidelines. The accredited status of a provider may be continued by filing an application for renewal with the board before the end of the provider's accreditation period.

(5) Renewal of accredited provider status. Renewal of accredited provider status shall be for periods of three years. The CLE board shall determine if there are pending or past breaches of these rules or regulations and guidelines, and the board, in its discretion, may condition renewal upon the provider meeting additional requirements specified by the board.

(i) If an application for renewal is timely filed, the accredited status shall continue until the board acts on the application.

(ii) If an application for renewal is not filed before the end of the provider's accreditation period, the provider's accredited status will terminate at the end of the period. Any application received thereafter shall be considered by the board as an initial application for accredited provider status.

(6) Revocation. Accredited provider status may be revoked by the board if the reporting requirements of these rules and regulations and guidelines are not met or, if upon review of the provider's performance, the CLE board determines that the content of the course or program materials, the quality of the CLE activities, or the provider's performance does not meet the standards set forth in these rules and regulations and guidelines. In such event, the CLE board shall send the provider a 30-day notice of revocation by first class mail. The provider may request a review of such revocation, and the CLE board shall determine the request within 90 days of receipt of such request. The decision of the CLE board shall be final after such review.

(d) *Provider List.* A list of accredited providers whose continuing legal education courses or activities have been presumptively approved for credit shall be compiled and published periodically by the CLE board. Lists shall be made available at each of the appellate divisions and at such other offices and electronic sites as the Chief Administrator of the Courts shall determine.

(e) *Announcement.* Providers who have received approval for continuing legal education courses and programs may indicate that their course or program has received CLE Board approval as follows:

"This (transitional) continuing legal education course (or program) has been approved in accordance with the requirements of the Continuing Legal Education Board for a maximum of . . . . . . credit hours, of which . . . . . . credit hours can be applied toward the . . . . . . requirement, and . . . . . . credit hours can be applied toward the requirement."

Where a program or segment of a program might reasonably be used to satisfy more than one category of instruction, *e.g.,* either skills or areas of professional practice, the approved provider may so indicate, but must state that duplicate credit for the same hour of instruction is not permitted; an election must be made by the attendee, and each hour may be counted as satisfying only one category of instruction. The following language may be used:

and an aggregate of . . . . . . credit hours can be applied toward the . . . . . . requirement or the . . . . . . requirement.

§ 1500.5.   Waivers, Modifications and Exemptions.

(a) *Waivers and Modifications.* The continuing legal education board may, in individual cases involving undue hardship or extenuating circumstances, grant waivers and modifications of program requirements to attorneys, upon written request, in accordance with the regulations and guidelines established by the CLE board and this Part.

(b) *Exemptions.* The following persons shall be exempt from the requirements of New York's continuing legal education program:

(1) subject to the requirements in §§ 1500.12(f) and 1500.22(n), attorneys who do not practice law in New York. Attorneys practice law pursuant to this section if, during the reporting period, they give legal advice or counsel to, or provide legal representation for, a particular body or individual in a particular situation in either the public or private sector. The practice of law does not include the performance of judicial or quasi-judicial (e.g., administrative law judge, hearing officer) functions;

(2) full-time active members of the United States Armed Forces

and members of the military service of the State serving on active duty;

(3) Attorneys with offices outside of New York who are temporarily admitted to practice in a court within New York for a case or proceeding;and

(4) Attorneys who certify that they are retired from the practice of law pursuant to § 468-a of the Judiciary Law.

Subpart B.   MANDATORY CONTINUING LEGAL EDUCATION FOR NEWLY ADMITTED ATTORNEYS

§ 1500.10.   Application.

(a) The requirements of this subpart shall apply to all newly admitted attorneys, who are not exempt from these requirements pursuant to § 1500.5(b), during the first two years after their admission to the Bar of the State of New York.

(b) A newly admitted attorney is an attorney who has successfully passed the New York State Bar examination administered by the State Board of Law Examiners and who becomes duly admitted to the practice of law in New York after October 1, 1997.

(c) Attorneys who have been engaged in the practice of law in another state, the District of Columbia, any territory of the United States or any foreign jurisdiction, for at least five of the seven years immediately preceding admission to the New York Bar, shall not be deemed newly admitted attorneys for the purposes of this subpart, and shall be required to comply with the requirements of Subpart C to the extent they are applicable.

§ 1500.11.   Statement of Purpose.

Mandatory continuing legal education for newly admitted attorneys in the State of New York is a transitional continuing legal education program designed to help recent graduates and newly admitted attorneys become competent to deliver legal services at an acceptable level of quality as they enter practice and assume primary client service responsibilities. The program seeks to help the newly admitted attorney establish a foundation in certain practical skills, techniques and procedures, which are and can be essential to the practice of law, but may not have been adequately addressed in law school. It includes courses targeting ethics and professionalism, skills, practice management and areas of professional practice.

§ 1500.12.   Minimum Requirements.

(a) *Credit Hours.* Each newly admitted attorney shall complete a minimum of 32 hours of accredited transitional education within the first two years of the date of admission to the Bar. Sixteen accredited hours shall be completed in each of the first two years of admission to the Bar as follows:

(1) three hours of ethics and professionalism;

(2) six hours of skills; and

(3) seven hours of law practice management and areas of professional practice.

Ethics and professionalism, skills, law practice management and areas of professional practice are defined in § 1500.2. The ethics and professionalism and skills components may be intertwined with other courses.

(b) *Carry-over credit.* Except as provided in section 1500.13(b)(2), a newly admitted attorney who accumulates more than the 16 hours of credit required in the first year of admission to the Bar may carry over to the second year of admission to the Bar a maximum of eight credits. Six credits in excess of the 16-hour requirement in the second year of admission to the Bar may be carried over to the following biennial reporting cycle to fulfill the requirements of Subpart C. Ethics and professionalism credit may not be carried over.

(c) *Accredited courses or programs only.* Transitional continuing legal education credit will be granted only for courses and programs approved as such by the CLE board, except as provided in subdivision (d) of this section. No transitional continuing legal education course or program consisting of nontraditional formats, such as self-study, correspondence work, videotapes, audiotapes, motion picture presentations or on-line programs may be accepted for credit without prior permission from the CLE board, except as provided in the regulations and guidelines.

(d) *Other Jurisdictions.* Transitional continuing legal education courses approved by another state, the District of Columbia, any territory of the United States or any foreign jurisdiction with requirements meeting the standards adopted by the CLE board shall count toward the newly admitted attorney's compliance with New York's transitional CLE program requirements in writing in accordance with the regulations and guidelines established by the CLE board and this Part.

(e) *Post-Graduation/Pre-Admission.* A maximum of 16 hours of approved transitional CLE courses taken from the date of graduation from law school up through the date of admission to the New York Bar may be applied toward a newly admitted attorney's first-year CLE program requirements. Credit hours in excess of 16 may not be carried over and applied toward the second-year CLE requirement.

(f) *Obligations of attorneys exempt from the program requirements.*

(1) An attorney who is exempt from the requirements of this program and who is required to comply with the continuing legal education requirements of another jurisdiction shall comply with those requirements and shall certify to this compliance on the attorney's biennial attorney registration statement.

(2) An attorney who is exempt from the requirements of this program and who is not required to comply with the continuing legal education requirements of another jurisdiction shall so certify on the attorney's biennial attorney registration statement.

(3) An attorney who is exempt from the requirements of this program and who thereafter ceases to be exempt and commences the practice of law in New York during the first two years after admission to the Bar shall be required to complete by the end of those two years 1.5 credit hours of accredited continuing legal education as set forth in section 1500.12(a), in any combination of categories set forth in said section, for each full month of the two-year period during which the attorney practices law in New York.

(4) An attorney who permanently ceases to practice law in New York while commencing or continuing the practice of law in another jurisdiction shall be exempt from the requirements of this program

for the year in which the permanent cessation from New York practice occurred, and shall comply with the requirements of any jurisdiction in which the attorney practices law during that year.

§ 1500.13.   Reporting Requirements.

(a) *Attorney Obligations.* Each newly admitted attorney subject to New York's transitional continuing legal education requirements shall retain the certificate of attendance for each approved transitional education course or program for at least four years from the date of the course or program.

(b) *Certification.* (1) Except as otherwise authorized by this Part, each newly admitted attorney subject to New York's transitional continuing legal education requirements is required to certify along with the submission of his or her biennial attorney registration statement that the attorney has satisfactorily completed 32 credit hours of transitional continuing legal education (16 credit hours in the first year of admission to the Bar, 16 credit hours in the second year of admission to the Bar) and that the attorney has retained the certificates of attendance or other documentation required by the CLE board for the accredited courses or programs.

(2) A newly admitted attorney who is required to file his or her biennial attorney registration statement prior to completing the second year of admission to the Bar shall certify the actual number of credit hours of transitional continuing legal education completed at the time the statement is filed. The attorney shall remain responsible for completing the 16 second-year credit hours of transitional continuing legal education by the end of that second year after admission, but may apply 12 of the 16 credit hours to fulfilling the requirements of Subpart C as set forth in § 1500.22(b)(3).

§ 1500.14.   Waivers or Modifications

(a) A newly admitted attorney may apply in writing to the CLE board for a waiver or modification of program requirements based upon extenuating circumstances preventing the newly admitted attorney from complying with the requirements, in accordance with the regulations and guidelines established by the CLE board and this Part.

(b) Requests for extensions of time in which to complete program requirements based upon extenuating circumstances shall be made pursuant to the procedures contained in the regulations and guidelines and shall not be granted for a period of greater than 90 days absent special circumstances. If an extension is granted, the period of time by which a newly admitted attorney must complete the mandatory continuing legal education requirements applicable to all attorneys as set forth in subpart C remains the same.

§ 1500.15.   Noncompliance.

The names of newly admitted attorneys who fail to comply with transitional continuing legal education requirements will be submitted to the Appellate Division for appropriate action.

§ 1500.16.   Effective date.

Mandatory continuing legal education for newly admitted attorneys in the State of New York shall become effective on October 1, 1997.

Subpart C.   MANDATORY CONTINUING LEGAL EDUCATION FOR ATTORNEYS OTHER THAN NEWLY ADMITTED ATTORNEYS

§ 1500.20.   Application.

The requirements of this subpart shall apply to all attorneys who have been duly admitted to the practice of law in New York, are not exempt from these requirements pursuant to § 1500.5(b), and are not newly admitted attorneys subject to the requirements of subpart B of this Part.

§ 1500.21.   Statement of purpose.

It is of utmost importance to members of the Bar and to the public that attorneys maintain their professional competence by continuing their legal education throughout the period of their active practice of law. This program establishes the minimum requirements for continuing legal education for attorneys other than newly admitted attorneys in New York State.

§ 1500.22.   Minimum requirements.

(a) *Credit hours.* Each attorney shall complete a minimum of 24 credit hours of accredited continuing legal education each biennial reporting cycle in ethics and professionalism, skills, law practice management or areas of professional practice, at least four credit hours of which shall be in ethics and professionalism. Ethics and professionalism, skills, law practice management and areas of professional practice are defined in § 1500.2. The ethics and professionalism components may be intertwined with other courses.

(b) *Biennial reporting cycle.*

(1) The biennial reporting cycle shall be the two-year period between the dates of submission of the attorney's biennial registration statement.

(2) An attorney shall comply with the requirements of this subpart commencing from the time of the filing of the attorney's biennial attorney registration statement in the second calendar year following admission to the Bar.

(3) A newly admitted attorney whose transitional two-year post-Bar admission period has not been completed as of the last day the attorney registration statement in paragraph (2) is required to be filed may apply 12 hours of the second-year accredited transitional education credits required in section 1500.12(a) to fulfilling the requirements of this subpart.

(c) *Carry-over credit.* An attorney who accumulates more than the 24 hours of credit in any one biennial reporting cycle may carry over a maximum of six credits to the next biennial reporting cycle.

(d) *Course or program formats.* Continuing legal education courses or programs may include traditional live classroom or audience settings; teleconferences; video conferences; satellite transmissions; videotapes; audiotapes; motion picture presentations; interactive video instruction; activities electronically transmitted from another location; self-study; correspondence work; and on-line computer courses.

(e) *Credit for speaking and teaching activities.* Credit may be earned through speaking, teaching or participating in a panel in an accredited CLE program. Where teaching is done in tandem or by panel, teaching credit shall be given to all participants.

(f) *Credit for teaching law school classes.* Credit may be earned

App Pract
Provs

through teaching in an ABA-accredited law school as may be permitted pursuant to the regulations and guidelines of the CLE board.

(g) *Credit for attending law school courses.* Credit may be earned for attending courses at an ABA-accredited law school after admission to practice in New York provided:

(1) the attorney is officially registered for the course; and

(2) the attorney completed the course as required by the terms of registration.

(h) *Credit for judging law competitions.* Credit may be earned for preparing students for and judging law competitions, mock trials and moot court arguments, including those in high school, pursuant to the regulations and guidelines of the CLE board.

(i) *Credit for publications.* Credit may be earned, as may be permitted pursuant to the regulations and guidelines of the CLE board, for legal research-based writing upon application to the CLE board, provided the activity:

(1) produced material published or to be published, in print or electronically, in the form of an article, chapter or book written, in whole or in substantial part, by the applicant; and

(2) contributed substantially to the continuing legal education of the applicant and other attorneys.

(j) *Credit for performing pro bono legal services.* Credit may be earned for performing uncompensated legal services for clients unable to afford counsel pursuant to:

(1) assignment by a court; or

(2) a program, accredited by the CLE board, of a bar association, legal services provider or other entity.

Credit shall be awarded pursuant to the regulations and guidelines of the CLE board, provided that no more than six hours of CLE credit may be awarded in a two-year reporting period for performing *pro bono* legal services, and no more than one credit hour of CLE credit may be awarded for every six hours of legal work performed.

(k) *Accredited courses, programs and activities only.* Continuing legal education credit will be granted only for courses, programs and activities approved by the CLE board, except where credit is extended as provided in subdivision (m).

(l) *Individual course approval.* An attorney seeking approval of a course or program that has not otherwise been approved shall apply to the CLE board for approval in accordance with board procedures. Such approval must be sought at least 60 days prior to the occurrence of the course or program, except in extenuating circumstances and only with prior permission of the board.

(m) *Other jurisdictions.* Continuing legal education courses approved by another state, the District of Columbia, any territory of the United States or any foreign jurisdiction with requirements meeting the standards adopted by the CLE board shall count toward the attorney's compliance with New York's CLE program requirements.

(n) *Obligations of attorneys exempt from the program requirements.*

(1) An attorney who is exempt from the requirements of this program and who is required to comply with the continuing legal education requirements of another jurisdiction shall comply with those requirements and shall certify this compliance on the attorney's biennial attorney registration statement.

(2) An attorney who is exempt from the requirements of this program and who is not required to comply with the continuing legal education requirements of another jurisdiction shall so certify on the attorney's biennial attorney registration statement.

(3) An attorney who is exempt from the requirements of this program and who thereafter ceases to be exempt and commences the practice of law in New York during a biennial reporting cycle shall be required to complete by the end of the reporting cycle one credit hour of accredited continuing legal education as set forth in section 1500.22(a), in any combination of categories set forth in said section, for each full calendar month of the biennial reporting cycle during which the attorney practices law in New York.

(4) An attorney who permanently ceases to practice law in New York while commencing or continuing the practice of law in another jurisdiction shall be exempt from the requirements of this program

for the reporting cycle in which the permanent cessation from New York practice occurred, and shall comply with the requirements of the jurisdiction in which the attorney practices law during that cycle.

§ 1500.23.   Reporting Requirements.

(a) *Attorney obligations.* Each attorney subject to New York's continuing legal education requirements shall retain the certificate of attendance or other documentation required by the board for each approved education course, program or activity for at least four years from the date of the course, program or activity.

(b) *Certification.* Except as otherwise authorized by this Part, each attorney subject to New York's continuing legal education requirements is required to certify along with the submission of his or her biennial attorney registration statement that the attorney has satisfactorily completed 24 credit hours of continuing legal education for the current biennial reporting cycle and that the attorney has retained the certificates of attendance or other documentation required by the CLE board for the accredited courses, programs or activities.

§ 1500.24.   Waivers or Modifications

(a) An attorney may apply in writing to the CLE board for a waiver or modification of program requirements based upon extenuating circumstances preventing the attorney from complying with the requirements, in accordance with the regulations and guidelines established by the CLE board and this Part.

(b) Requests for extensions of time in which to complete program requirements based upon extenuating circumstances shall be made pursuant to the procedures contained in the regulations and guidelines and shall not be granted for a period of greater than 90 days absent special circumstances. If an extension is granted, the period of time by which the attorney must complete the mandatory continuing legal education requirements of the next biennial reporting cycle remains the same.

§ 1500.25.   Noncompliance.

The names of attorneys who fail to comply with continuing legal education requirements will be submitted to the Appellate Division for appropriate action.

§ 1500.26.   Effective Date and Transition.

The requirements of this subpart shall become effective on December 31, 1998. Compliance with the certification requirement shall commence with biennial attorney registration statements filed on or after January 1, 2000, as follows:

(a) Attorneys who file their biennial registration statement in calendar year 2000 shall complete 12 credit hours of accredited continuing legal education as of the date of the filing in any combination of the categories set forth in § 1500.22(a). Attorneys who accumulate more than 12 credit hours at the time of this filing may carry over a maximum of six (6) credit hours to the next biennial cycle;

(b) Attorneys who file their biennial registration statement in calendar year 2001 must complete the full 24 credit hours of accredited continuing legal education as set forth in § 1500.22(a). Approved CLE credits earned from January 1, 1998, may be applied toward fulfilling the requirements for the initial biennial reporting cycle.

App Pract
Provs

PUBLIC HEALTH LAW

SYNOPSIS OF SELECTED PROVISIONS

Article 28.   Hospitals.

§ 2805-d.   Limitation of medical, dental or podiatric malpractice action based upon lack of informed consent.

1. Lack of informed consent means the failure of the person providing the professional treatment or diagnosis to disclose to the patient such alternatives thereto and the reasonably foreseeable risks and benefits involved as a reasonable medical, dental or podiatric practitioner under similar circumstances would have disclosed, in a manner permitting the patient to make a knowledgeable evaluation.

2. The right of action to recover for medical, dental or podiatric malpractice based on a lack of informed consent is limited to those cases involving either (a) non emergency treatment, procedure or surgery, or (b) a diagnostic procedure which involved invasion or disruption of the integrity of the body.

3. For a cause of action therefore it must also be established that a reasonably prudent person in the patient's position would not have undergone the treatment or diagnosis if he had been fully informed and that the lack of informed consent is a proximate cause of the injury or condition for which recovery is sought.

4. It shall be a defense to any action for medical, dental or podiatric malpractice based upon an alleged failure to obtain such an informed consent that:

(a) the risk not disclosed is too commonly known to warrant disclosure; or

App Pract
Provs

(b) the patient assured the medical, dental or podiatric practitioner he would undergo the treatment, procedure or diagnosis regardless of the risk involved, or the patient assured the medical, dental or podiatric practitioner that he did not want to be informed of the matters to which he would be entitled to be informed; or

(c) consent by or on behalf of the patient was not reasonably possible; or

(d) the medical, dental or podiatric practitioner, after considering all of the attendant facts and circumstances, used reasonable discretion as to the manner and extent to which such alternatives or risks were disclosed to the patient because he reasonably believed that the manner and extent of such disclosure could reasonably be expected to adversely and substantially affect the patient's condition.

PUBLIC OFFICERS LAW

SYNOPSIS OF SELECTED PROVISIONS

Article 4.   Powers and duties of public officers.

§ 68.   Allowance of additional fees and expenses.

Where an officer or other person is required, in the course of a duty imposed upon him by law, to take an oath, to acknowledge an instrument, to cause an instrument to be filed or recorded, or to transmit a paper to another officer, he is entitled, in addition to the fees, or other compensation for the service, prescribed by law, to the fees necessarily paid by him, to the officer who administered the oath, or took the acknowledgment, or filed or recorded the instrument; and to the expense of transmitting the paper, including postage, where the transmission is lawfully made through the post-office.

Article 6.   Freedom of information law.

§ 84.   Legislative declaration.

The legislature hereby finds that a free society is maintained when government is responsive and responsible to the public, and when the public is aware of governmental actions. The more open a government

App Pract Provs

is with its citizenry, the greater the understanding and participation of the public in government.

As state and local government services increase and public problems become more sophisticated and complex and therefore harder to solve, and with the resultant increase in revenues and expenditures, it is incumbent upon the state and its localities to extend public accountability wherever and whenever feasible.

The people's right to know the process of governmental decision-making and to review the documents and statistics leading to determinations is basic to our society. Access to such information should not be thwarted by shrouding it with the cloak of secrecy or confidentiality.

The legislature therefore declares that government is the public's business and that the public, individually and collectively and represented by a free press, should have access to the records of government in accordance with the provisions of this article.

§ 85.   Short title.

This Article shall be known and may be cited as the "Freedom of Information Law."

§ 86.   Definitions.

As used in this article, unless the context requires otherwise:

1. "Judiciary" means the courts of the state, including any municipal or district court, whether or not of record.

2. "State Legislature" means the legislature of the state of New York, including any committee, subcommittee, joint committee, select committee, or commission thereof.

3. "Agency" means any state or municipal department, board, bureau, division, commission, committee, public authority, public corporation, council, office or other governmental entity performing a governmental or proprietary function for the state or any one or more municipalities thereof, except the judiciary or the state legislature.

4. "Record" means any information kept, held, filed, produced or

reproduced by, with or for an agency or the state legislature, in any physical form whatsoever including, but not limited to, reports, statements, examinations, memoranda, opinions, folders, files, books, manuals, pamphlets, forms, papers, designs, drawings, maps, photos, letters, microfilms, computer tapes or discs, rules, regulations or codes.

5. "Critical infrastructure" means systems, assets, places or things, whether physical or virtual, so vital to the state that the disruption, incapacitation or destruction of such systems, assets, places or things could jeopardize the health, safety, welfare or security of the state, its residents or its economy.

§ 87.   Access to agency records.

1. (a) Within sixty days after the effective date of this article, the governing body of each public corporation shall promulgate uniform rules and regulations for all agencies in such public corporation pursuant to such general rules and regulations as may be promulgated by the committee on open government in conformity with the provisions of this article, pertaining to the administration of this article.

(b) Each agency shall promulgate rules and regulations, in conformity with this Article and applicable rules and regulations promulgated pursuant to the provisions of paragraph (a) of this subdivision, and pursuant to such general rules and regulations as may be promulgated by the committee on open government in conformity with the provisions of this article, pertaining to the availability of records and procedures to be followed, including, but not limited to:

     i. the times and places such records are available;

     ii. the persons from whom such records may be obtained, and

     iii. the fees for copies of records which shall not exceed twenty-five cents per photocopy not in excess of nine inches by fourteen inches, or the actual cost of reproducing any other record in accordance with the provisions of paragraph (c) of this subdivision, except when a different fee is otherwise prescribed

by statute. (c) In determining the actual cost of reproducing a

App Pract Provs

record, an agency may include only:

i. an amount equal to the hourly salary attributed to the lowest paid agency employee who has the necessary skill required to prepare a copy of the requested record;

ii. the actual cost of the storage devices or media provided to the person making the request in complying with such request;

iii. the actual cost to the agency of engaging an outside professional service to prepare a copy of a record, but only when an agency's information technology equipment is inadequate to prepare a copy, if such service is used to prepare the copy; and

iv. preparing a copy shall not include search time or administrative costs, and no fee shall be charged unless at least two hours of agency employee time is needed to prepare a copy of the record requested. A person requesting a record shall be informed of the estimated cost of preparing a copy of the record if more than two hours of an agency employee's time is needed, or if an outside professional service would be retained to prepare a copy of the record.

2. Each agency shall, in accordance with its published rules, make available for public inspection and copying all records, except that such agency may deny access to records or portions thereof that:

(a) are specifically exempted from disclosure by state or federal statute;

(b) if disclosed would constitute an unwarranted invasion of personal privacy under the provisions of subdivision two of section eighty-nine of this article;

(c) if disclosed would impair present or imminent contract awards or collective bargaining negotiations;

(d) are trade secrets or submitted to an agency by a commercial enterprise or derived from information obtained from a commercial enterprise and which if disclosed would cause substantial injury to the competitive position of the subject enterprise;

(e) are compiled for law enforcement purposes and which, if disclosed, would:

i. interfere with law enforcement investigations or judicial proceedings;

ii. deprive a person of a right to a fair trial or impartial adjudication;

iii. identify a confidential source or disclose confidential information relating to a criminal investigation; or

iv. reveal criminal investigative techniques or procedures, except routine techniques and procedures.

(f) if disclosed could endanger the life or safety of any person;

(g) are inter-agency or intra-agency materials which are not:

i. statistical or factual tabulations or data;

ii. instructions to staff that affect the public;

iii. final agency policy or determinations;

iv. external audits, including but not limited to audits performed by the comptroller and the federal government; or

(h) are examination questions or answers which are requested prior to the final administration of such questions.

(i) if disclosed, would jeopardize an agency's capacity to guarantee the security of its information technology assets, such assets encompassing both electronic information systems and infrastructures; or

(j) are photographs, microphotographs, videotape or other recorded images prepared under authority of section eleven hundred eleven-a of the vehicle and traffic law. [*Effective until December 1, 2014, pursuant to L. 2009, Ch. 18, eff. Apr. 28, 2009.*]

(k) are photographs, microphotographs, videotape or other recorded images prepared under authority of section eleven hundred eleven-b of the vehicle and traffic law. [*Effective until December 1, 2014, pursuant to L. 2009, Ch.19, eff. Apr. 28, 2009.*

3. Each agency shall maintain:

(a) a record of the final vote of each member in every agency proceeding in which the member votes;

App Pract Provs

(b) a record setting forth the name, public office address, title and salary of every officer or employee of the agency; and

(c) a reasonably detailed current list by subject matter of all records in the possession of the agency, whether or not available under this article. Each agency shall update its subject matter list annually, and the date of the most recent update shall be conspicuously indicated on the list. Each state agency as defined in subdivision four of this section that maintains a website shall post its current list on its website and such posting shall be linked to the website of the committee on open government. Any such agency that does not maintain a website shall arrange to have its list posted on the website of the committee on open government.

4. (a) Each state agency which maintains records containing trade secrets, to which access may be denied pursuant to paragraph (d) of subdivision two of this section, shall promulgate regulations in conformity with the provisions of subdivision five of section eighty-nine of this Article pertaining to such records, including, but not limited to the following:

(1) the manner of identifying the records or parts;

(2) the manner of identifying persons within the agency to whose custody the records or parts will be charged and for whose inspection and study the records will be made available;

(3) the manner of safeguarding against any unauthorized access to the records.

(b) As used in this subdivision the term "agency" or "state agency" means only a state department, board, bureau, division, council or office and any public corporation the majority of whose members are appointed by the governor.

(c) Each state agency that maintains a website shall post information related to this article and article six-A of this chapter on its website. Such information shall include, at a minimum, contact information for the persons from whom records of the agency may be obtained, the times and places such records are available for inspection and copying, and information on how to request records in person, by mail, and, if the agency accepts requests for records electronically, by e-mail. This posting shall be linked to the website of the committee on open government.

5. (a) An agency shall provide records on the medium requested by a person, if the agency can reasonably make such copy or have such copy made by engaging an outside professional service. Records provided in a computer format shall not be encrypted.

(b) No agency shall enter into or renew a contract for the creation or maintenance of records if such contract impairs the right of the public to inspect or copy the agency's records.

§ 88.   Access to state legislative records.

1. The temporary president of the senate and the speaker of the assembly shall promulgate rules and regulations for their respective houses in conformity with the provisions of this article, pertaining to the availability, location and nature of records, including, not limited to:

(a) the times and places such records are available;

(b) the persons from whom such records may be obtained;

(c) the fees for copies of such records, which shall not exceed twenty-five cents per photocopy not in excess of nine inches by fourteen inches, or the actual cost of reproducing any other record, except when a different fee is otherwise prescribed by law.

2. The state legislature shall, in accordance with its published rules, make available for public inspection and copying:

(a) bills and amendments thereto, fiscal notes, introducers' bill memoranda, resolutions and amendments thereto, and index records;

(b) messages received from the governor or the other house of the legislature, and home rule messages;

(c) legislative notification of the proposed adoption of rules by an agency;

(d) transcripts or minutes, if prepared, and journal records of public sessions including meetings of committees and subcommittees and public hearings, with the records of attendance of members thereat and records of any votes taken;

(e) internal or external audits and statistical or factual tabulations

App Pract Provs

of, or with respect to, material otherwise available for public inspection and copying pursuant to this section or any other applicable provision of law;

(f) administrative staff manuals and instructions to staff that affect members of the public;

(g) final reports and formal opinions submitted to the legislature;

(h) final reports or recommendations and minority or dissenting reports and opinions of members of committees, subcommittees, or commissions of the legislature;

(i) any other files, records, papers or documents required by law to be made available for public inspection and copying.

(j) external audits conducted pursuant to section ninety-two of the legislative law and schedules issued pursuant to subdivision two of section ninety of the legislative law.

3. Each house shall maintain and make available for public inspection and copying:

(a) a record of votes of each member in every session and every committee and subcommittee meeting in which the member votes;

(b) a record setting forth the name, public office address, title, and salary of every officer or employee; and

(c) a current list, reasonably detailed, by subject matter of any records required to be made available for public inspection and copying pursuant to this section.

§ 89 General provisions relating to access to records; certain cases

The provisions of this section apply to access to all records, except as hereinafter specified:

1. (a) The committee on open government is continued and shall consist of the lieutenant governor or the delegate of such officer, the secretary of state or the delegate of such officer, whose office shall act as secretariat for the committee, the commissioner of the office of general services or the delegate of such officer, the director of the budget or the delegate of such officer, and seven

other persons, none of whom shall hold any other state or local public office except the representative of local governments as set forth herein, to be appointed as follows: five by the governor, at least two of whom are or have been representatives of the news media, one of whom shall be a representative of local government who, at the time of appointment, is serving as a duly elected officer of a local government, one by the temporary president of the senate, and one by the speaker of the assembly. The persons appointed by the temporary president of the senate and the speaker of the assembly shall be appointed to serve, respectively, until the expiration of the terms of office of the temporary president and the speaker to which the temporary president and speaker were elected. The four persons presently serving by appointment of the governor for fixed terms shall continue to serve until the expiration of their respective terms. Thereafter, their respective successors shall be appointed for terms of four years. The member representing local government shall be appointed for a term of four years, so long as such member shall remain a duly elected officer of a local government. The committee shall hold no less than two meetings annually, but may meet at any time. The members of the committee shall be entitled to reimbursement for actual expenses incurred in the discharge of their duties.

(b) The committee shall:

i. furnish to any agency advisory guidelines, opinions or other appropriate information regarding this article;

ii. furnish to any person advisory opinions or other appropriate information regarding this article;

iii. promulgate rules and regulations with respect to the implementation of subdivision one and paragraph (c) of subdivision three of section eighty-seven of this article;

iv. request from any agency such assistance, services and information as will enable the committee to effectively carry out its powers and duties;

v. develop a form, which shall be made available on the internet, that may be used by the public to request a record; and

App Pract Provs

vi. report on its activities and findings regarding this article and article seven of this chapter, including recommendations for changes in the law, to the governor and the legislature annually, on or before December fifteenth.

2. (a) The committee on public access to records may promulgate guidelines regarding deletion of identifying details or withholding of records otherwise available under this article to prevent unwarranted invasions of personal privacy. In the absence of such guidelines, an agency may delete identifying details when it makes records available.

(b) An unwarranted invasion of personal privacy includes, but shall not be limited to:

i. disclosure of employment, medical or credit histories or personal references of applicants for employment;

ii. disclosure of items involving the medical or personal records of a client or patient in a medical facility;

iii. sale or release of lists of names and addresses if such lists would be used for solicitation or fund-raising purposes;

iv. disclosure of information of a personal nature when disclosure would result in economic or personal hardship to the subject party and such information is not relevant to the work of the agency requesting or maintaining it; or

v. disclosure of information of a personal nature reported in confidence to an agency and notrelevant to the ordinary work of such agency; or

vi. information of a personal nature contained in a workers' compensation record, except as provided by section one hundred ten-a of the workers' compensation law.

(c) Unless otherwise provided by this article, disclosure shall not be construed to constitute an unwarranted invasion of personal privacy pursuant to paragraphs (a) and (b) of this subdivision:

i. when identifying details are deleted;

ii. when the person to whom a record pertains consents in writing to disclosure;

iii. when upon presenting reasonable proof of identity, a person seeks access to records pertaining to him or her; or

iv. when a record or group of records relates to the right, title or interest in real property, or relates to the inventory, status or characteristics of real property, in which case disclosure and providing copies of such record or group of records shall not be deemed an unwarranted invasion of personal privacy.

2-a. Nothing in this article shall permit disclosure which constitutes an unwarranted invasion of personal privacy as defined in subdivision two of this section if such disclosure is prohibited under section ninety-six of this chapter.

3. (a) Each entity subject to the provisions of this article, within five business days of the receipt of a written request for a record reasonably described, shall make such record available to the person requesting it, deny such request in writing or furnish a written acknowledgement of the receipt of such request and a statement of the approximate date, which shall be reasonable under the circumstances of the request, when such request will be granted or denied, including, where appropriate, a statement that access to the record will be determined in accordance with subdivision five of this section. An agency shall not deny a request on the basis that the request is voluminous or that locating or reviewing the requested records or providing the requested copies is burdensome because the agency lacks sufficient staffing or on any other basis if the agency may engage an outside professional service to provide copying, programming or other services required to provide the copy, the costs of which the agency may recover pursuant to paragraph (c) of subdivision one of section eighty-seven of this article. An agency may require a person requesting lists of names and addresses to provide a written certification that such person will not use such lists of names and addresses for solicitation or fund-raising purposes and will not sell, give or otherwise make available such lists of names and addresses to any other person for the purpose of allowing that person to use such lists of names and addresses for solicitation or fund-raising purposes. If an agency determines to grant a request in whole or in part, and if circumstances prevent disclosure to the

App Pract
Provs

person requesting the record or records within twenty business days from the date of the acknowledgement of the receipt of the request, the agency shall state, in writing, both the reason for the inability to grant the request within twenty business days and a date certain within a reasonable period, depending on the circumstances, when the request will be granted in whole or in part. Upon payment of, or offer to pay, the fee prescribed therefor, the entity shall provide a copy of such record and certify to the correctness of such copy if so requested, or as the case may be, shall certify that it does not have possession of such record or that such record cannot be found after diligent search. Nothing in this article shall be construed to require any entity to prepare any record not possessed or maintained by such entity except the records specified in subdivision three of section eighty-seven and subdivision three of section eighty-eight of this article. When an agency has the ability to retrieve or extract a record or data maintained in a computer storage system with reasonable effort, it shall be required to do so. When doing so requires less employee time than engaging in manual retrieval or redactions from non-electronic records, the agency shall be required to retrieve or extract such record or data electronically. Any programming necessary to retrieve a record maintained in a computer storage system and to transfer that record to the medium requested by a person or to allow the transferred record to be read or printed shall not be deemed to be the preparation or creation of a new record.

(b) All entities shall, provided such entity has reasonable means available, accept requests for records submitted in the form of electronic mail and shall respond to such requests by electronic mail, using forms, to the extent practicable, consistent with the form or forms developed by the committee on open government pursuant to subdivision one of this section and provided that the written requests do not seek a response in some other form.

4. (a) Except as provided in subdivision five of this section, any person denied access to a record may within thirty days appeal in writing such denial to the head, chief executive or governing body of the entity, or the person therefor designated by such head, chief executive, or governing body, who shall within ten business days of the receipt of such appeal fully explain in writing to the person

requesting the record the reasons for further denial, or provide access to the record sought. In addition, each agency shall immediately forward to the committee on open government a copy of such appeal when received by the agency and the ensuing determination thereon. Failure by an agency to conform to the provisions of subdivision three of this section shall constitute a denial.

(b) Except as provided in subdivision five of this section, a person denied access to a record in an appeal determination under the provisions of paragraph (a) of this subdivision may bring a proceeding for review of such denial pursuant to article seventy-eight of the civil practice law and rules. In the event that access to any record is denied pursuant to the provisions of subdivision two of section eighty-seven of this article, the agency involved shall have the burden of proving that such record falls within the provisions of such subdivision two. Failure by an agency to conform to the provisions of paragraph (a) of this subdivision shall constitute a denial.

(c) The court in such a proceeding may assess, against such agency involved, reasonable attorney's fees and other litigation costs reasonably incurred by such person in any case under the provisions of this section in which such person has substantially prevailed, when:

i. the agency had no reasonable basis for denying access; or

ii. the agency failed to respond to a request or appeal within the statutory time.

5. (a) (1) A person acting pursuant to law or regulation who, subsequent to the effective date of this subdivision, submits any information to any state agency may, at the time of submission, request that the agency except such information from disclosure under paragraph (d) of subdivision two of section eighty-seven of this article. Where the request itself contains information which if disclosed would defeat the purpose for which the exception is sought, such information shall also be excepted from disclosure.

(1-a) A person or entity who submits or otherwise makes

App Pract
Provs

available any records to any agency, may, at any time, identify those records or portions thereof that may contain critical infrastructure information, and request that the agency that maintains such records except such information from disclosure under subdivision two of section eighty-seven of this article. Where the request itself contains information which if disclosed would defeat the purpose for which the exception is sought, such information shall also be excepted from disclosure.

(2) The request for an exception shall be in writing and state the reasons why the information should be excepted from disclosure.

(3) Information submitted as provided in subparagraphs one and one-a of this paragraph shall be excepted from disclosure and be maintained apart by the agency from all other records until fifteen days after the entitlement to such exception has been finally determined or such further time as ordered by a court of competent jurisdiction.

(b) On the initiative of the agency at any time, or upon the request of any person for a record excepted from disclosure pursuant to this subdivision, the agency shall:

(1) inform the person who requested the exception of the agency's intention to determine whether such exception should be granted or continued;

(2) permit the person who requested the exception, within ten business days of receipt of notification from the agency, to submit a written statement of the necessity for the granting or continuation of such exception;

(3) within seven business days of receipt of such written statement, or within seven business days of the expiration of the period prescribed for submission of such statement, issue a written determination granting, continuing or terminating such exception and stating the reasons therefor; copies of such determination shall be served upon the person, if any, requesting the record, the person who requested the exception, and the committee on public access to records.

(c) A denial of an exception from disclosure under paragraph

(b) of this subdivision may be appealed by the person submitting the information and a denial of access to the record may be appealed by the person requesting the record in accordance with this subdivision:

(1) Within seven business days of receipt of written notice denying the request, the person may file a written appeal from the determination of the agency with the head of the agency, the chief executive officer or governing body or their designated representatives.

(2) The appeal shall be determined within ten business days of the receipt of the appeal. Written notice of the determination shall be served upon the person, if any, requesting the record, the person who requested the exception and the committee on public access to records. The notice shall contain a statement of the reasons for the determination.

(d) A proceeding to review an adverse determination pursuant to paragraph (c) of this subdivision may be commenced pursuant to article seventy-eight of the civil practice law and rules. Such proceeding, when brought by a person seeking an exception from disclosure pursuant to this subdivision, must be commenced within fifteen days of the service of the written notice containing the adverse determination provided for in subparagraph two of paragraph (c) of this subdivision.

(e) The person requesting an exception from disclosure pursuant to this subdivision shall in all proceedings have the burden of proving entitlement to the exception.

(f) Where the agency denies access to a record pursuant to paragraph (d) of subdivision two of section eighty-seven of this article, the agency shall have the burden of proving that the record falls within the provisions of such exception.

(g) Nothing in this subdivision shall be construed to deny any person access, pursuant to the remaining provisions of this article, to any record or part excepted from disclosure upon the express written consent of the person who had requested the exception.

(h) As used in this subdivision the term "agency" or "state agency" means only a state department, board, bureau, division, council or office and any public corporation the majority of whose members are appointed by the governor.

6. Nothing in this article shall be construed to limit or abridge any otherwise available right of access at law or in equity of any party to records.

7. Nothing in this article shall require the disclosure of the home address of an officer or employee, former officer or employee, or of a retiree of a public employees' retirement system; nor shall anything in this article require the disclosure of the name or home address of a beneficiary of a public employees' retirement system or of an applicant for appointment to public employment; provided however, that nothing in this subdivision shall limit or abridge the right of an employee organization, certified or recognized for any collective negotiating unit of an employer pursuant to article fourteen of the civil service law, to obtain the name or home address of any officer, employee or retiree of such employer, if such name or home address is otherwise available under this article.

8. Any person who, with intent to prevent the public inspection of a record pursuant to this article, willfully conceals or destroys any such record shall be guilty of a violation.

9. When records maintained electronically include items of information that would be available under this article, as well as items of information that may be withheld, an agency in designing its information retrieval methods, whenever practicable and reasonable, shall do so in a manner that permits the segregation and retrieval of available items in order to provide maximum public access.

* [Editor's Note:
Subdivision two-a of section eighty-nine takes effect Sept. 1, 1984, provided that agency actions necessary to the functioning of new Article Six-A of the Public Officers Law on such date shall be taken prior thereto.
Subdivision five of section eighty-nine applies only to records submitted on or after January 1, 1982.
Subdivision seven of section eighty-nine applies to any request pursuant to the Public Officers Law for which there is no final determination, including judicial review.]

§ 90. Severability.

If any provision of this Article or the application thereof to any person or circumstances is adjudged invalid by a court of competent jurisdiction, such judgment shall not affect or impair the validity of the other provisions of the Article or the application thereof to other persons and circumstances.

App Pract
Provs

REAL PROPERTY LAW

Article 9.   Recording instruments affecting real property.

§ 298.   Acknowledgments and proofs within the state.

The acknowledgment or proof, within this state, of a conveyance of real property situate in this state may be made:

1. At any place within the state, before (a) a justice of the supreme court; (b) an official examiner of title; (c) an official referee; or (d) a notary public.

2. Within the district wherein such officer is authorized to perform official duties, before (a) a judge or clerk of any court of record; (b) a commissioner of deeds outside of the city of New York, or a commissioner of deeds of the city of New York within the five counties comprising the city of New York; (c) the mayor or recorder of a city; (d) a surrogate, special surrogate, or special county judge; or (e) the county clerk or other recording officer of a county.

3. Before a justice of the peace, town councilman, village police justice or a judge of any court of inferior local jurisdiction, anywhere within the county containing the town, village or city in which he is

App Pract
Provs

authorized to perform official duties.

§ 299. Acknowledgments and proofs without the state, but within the United States or any territory, possession, or dependency thereof.

The acknowledgment or proof of a conveyance of real property situate in this state, if made (a) without the state but within the United States, (b) within any territory, possession, or dependency of the United States, or (c) within any place over which the United States, at the time when such acknowledgment or proof is taken, has or exercises jurisdiction, sovereignty, control, or a protectorate, may be made before any of the following officers acting within his territorial jurisdiction or within that of the court of which he is an officer:

1. A judge or other presiding officer of any court having a seal, or the clerk or other certifying officer thereof.

2. A mayor or other chief civil officer of any city or other political subdivision.

3. A notary public.

4. A commissioner of deeds appointed pursuant to the laws of this state to take acknowledgments or proofs without this state.

5. Any person authorized, by the laws of the state, District of Columbia, territory, possession, dependency, or other place where the acknowledgment or proof is made, to take the acknowledgment or proof of deeds to be recorded therein.

§ 299-a. Acknowledgment to conform to law of New York or of place where taken; certificate of conformity.

1. An acknowledgment or proof made pursuant to the provisions of section two hundred ninety-nine of this chapter may be taken in the manner prescribed either by the laws of the state of New York or by the laws of the state, District of Columbia, territory, possession, dependency, or other place where the acknowledgment or proof is taken. The acknowledgment or proof, if taken in the manner prescribed by such state, District of Columbia, territory, possession, dependency, or other place, must be accompanied by a certificate to the effect that it conforms with such laws. Such certificate may be made by

(a) An attorney-at-law admitted to practice in the state of New York, resident in the place where the acknowledgment or proof is taken, or by

(b) An attorney-at-law admitted to practice in the state, District of Columbia, territory, possession, dependency, or other place where the acknowledgment or proof is taken, or by

(c) Any other person deemed qualified by any court of the state of New York, if, in any action, proceeding, or other matter pending before such court, it be necessary to determine that such acknowledgment or proof conforms with the laws of such state, District of Columbia, territory, possession, dependency, or other place; or by the supreme court of the state of New York, on application for such determination. The justice, judge, surrogate, or other presiding judicial officer shall append to the instrument so acknowledged or proved his signed statement that he deemed such person qualified to make such certificate.

2. (a) The signature to such a certificate of conformity shall be presumptively genuine, and the qualification of the person whose name is so signed as a person authorized to make such certificate shall be presumptively established by the recital thereof in the certificate.

(b) The statement of a judicial officer appended to the instrument that he deemed the person making such certificate qualified shall establish the qualification of the person designated therein to make such certificate; and the recording, filing, registering or use as evidence of the instrument shall not depend on the power of the court to make the statement and proof shall not be required of any action, proceeding, matter or application in which or in connection with which the statement is made.

(c) When an instrument so acknowledged or proved is accompanied by the certificate of conformity and the statement of a judicial officer, if any be required, the acknowledgment or proof of the instrument, for the purpose of recording, filing or registering in any recording or filing office in this state or for use as evidence, shall be equivalent to one taken or made in the form prescribed by law for use in this state; and if the acknowledgment or proof is properly authenticated, where authentication is required by law, and if the instrument be otherwise entitled to record, filing or registering, such instrument, together with the acknowledgment or proof, the certificate of conformity and any certificate of authentication or statement of a judicial officer, may be recorded, filed or registered in any recording or filing office in this state, and shall be so recorded, filed or registered upon payment or tender of lawful fees therefor. In fixing the fees of a recording, filing or registering officer, the certificate of conformity and the statement of a judicial officer appended, if any, shall be treated as certificates of authentication required by other provisions of this chapter.

§ 300.   Acknowledgments and proofs by persons in or with the armed forces of the United States.

The acknowledgment or proof of a conveyance of real property situate in this state, if made by a person enlisted or commissioned in or serving in or with the armed forces of the United States or by a dependent of any such person, wherever located, or by a person attached to or accompanying the armed forces of the United States, whether made within or without the United States, may be made before any commissioned officer in active service of the armed forces of the United States with the rank of second lieutenant or higher in the Army, Air Force or Marine Corps, or ensign or higher in the Navy or Coast Guard, or with equivalent rank in any other component part of the armed forces of the United States.

In addition to the requirements of sections three hundred and three, three hundred and four, and three hundred and six of this chapter, the certificate of an acknowledgment or proof taken under this section shall state (a) the rank and serial number of the officer taking the same, and the command to which he is attached, (b) that the person making such acknowledgment or proof was, at the time of making the same, enlisted or commissioned in or serving in or with the armed forces of the United States or the dependent of such a person, or a person attached to or accompanying the armed forces of the United States, and (c) the serial number of the person who makes, or whose dependent makes the acknowledgment or proof if such person is enlisted or commissioned in the armed forces of the Unites States. The place where such acknowledgment or proof is taken need not be disclosed.

No authentication of the officer's certificate of acknowledgment or proof shall be required.

Notwithstanding any of the provisions of this section, the acknowledgment or proof of a conveyance of real property situate in this state may also be made as provided in sections two hundred ninety-eight, two hundred ninety-nine, two hundred ninety-nine-a, three hundred one, and three hundred one-a, of this chapter.

§ 301.　　Acknowledgments and proofs in foreign countries.

The acknowledgment or proof of a conveyance of real property situate in this state may be made in foreign countries before any of the following officers acting within his territorial jurisdiction or within that of the court of which he is an officer:

1. An ambassador, envoy, minister, charge d'affaires, secretary of legation, consul-general, consul, vice-consul, consular agent, vice-consular agent, or any other diplomatic or consular agent or representative of the United States, appointed or accredited to, and residing within, the country where the acknowledgment or proof is taken.

2. A judge or other presiding officer of any court having a seal, or the clerk or other certifying officer thereof.

3. A mayor or other chief civil officer of any city or other political subdivision.

4. A notary public.

5. A commissioner of deeds appointed pursuant to the laws of this state to take acknowledgments or proofs without this state.

6. A person residing in, or going to, the country where the acknowledgment or proof is to be taken, and specially authorized for that purpose by a commission issued to him under the seal of the supreme court of the state of New York.

7. Any person authorized, by the laws of the country where the acknowledgment or proof is made, to take acknowledgments of conveyances of real estate or to administer oaths in proof of the execution thereof.

App Pract
Provs

§ 301-a.   Acknowledgment to conform to law of New York or of foreign country; certificate of conformity.

1. An acknowledgment or proof made pursuant to the provisions of section three hundred one of this chapter may be taken in the manner prescribed either by the laws of the state of New York or by the laws of the country where the acknowledgment or proof is taken. The acknowledgment or proof, if taken in the manner prescribed by the laws of such foreign country, must be accompanied by a certificate to the effect that it conforms with such laws. Such certificate may be made by

(a) An attorney-at-law admitted to practice in the state of New York, resident in such foreign country, or by

(b) A consular officer of the United States, resident in such foreign country, under the seal of his office, or by

(c) A consular officer of such foreign country, resident in the state of New York, under the seal of his office, or by

(d) Any other person deemed qualified by any court of the state of New York, if, in any action, proceeding, or other matter pending before such court, it be necessary to determine that such acknowledgment or proof conforms with the laws of such foreign country; or by the supreme court of the state of New York, on application for such determination.

The justice, judge, surrogate, or other presiding judicial officer shall append to the instrument so acknowledged or proved his signed statement that he deemed such person qualified to make such certificate.

2. (a) The signature to such a certificate of conformity shall be presumptively genuine, and the qualification of the person whose name is so signed as a person authorized to make such certificate shall be presumptively established by the recital thereof in the certificate.

(b) The statement of a judicial officer appended to the instrument that he deemed the person making such certificate qualified shall establish the qualification of the person designated therein to make such certificate; and the recording, filing, registering or use as evidence of the instrument shall not depend on the power of the court to make the statement and proof shall not be required of any action, proceeding, matter or application in which or in connection with which the statement is made.

(c) When an instrument so acknowledged or proved is accompanied by the certificate of conformity and the statement of a judicial officer, if any be required, the acknowledgment or proof of the instrument, for the purpose of recording, filing or registering in any recording or filing office in this state or for use as evidence, shall be equivalent to one taken or made in the form prescribed by law for use in this state; and if the acknowledgment or proof is properly authenticated, where authentication is required by law, and if the instrument be otherwise entitled to record, filing or registering, such instrument, together with the acknowledgment of proof, the certificate of conformity and any certificate of authentication or statement of a judicial officer, may be recorded, filed or registered in any recording or filing office in this state, or shall be so recorded, filed or registered upon payment or tender of lawful fees therefor. In fixing the fees of a recording, filing or registering officer, the certificate of conformity and the statement of a judicial officer appended, if any, shall be treated as certificates of authentication required by other provisions of this chapter.

App Pract
Provs

SURROGATE'S COURT PROCEDURE ACT

SYNOPSIS OF SELECTED PROVISIONS

Article 3.   Proceedings, pleadings and process.

§ 315.   Joinder and representation of persons interested in estates.

1. The provisions of this section shall apply in any proceeding in which all persons interested in the estate are required to be served with process. For the purposes of this section, the term "an interest in the estate" includes both interests in income and interests in principal.

2. Representation of class interests.

(a) Where an interest in the estate has been limited as follows, it shall not be necessary to serve process on any other person than as herein provided:

(i) In any contingency to the persons who shall compose a certain class upon the happening of a future event, the persons in being who would constitute the class if such event had happened immediately before the commencement of the proceeding.

(ii) To a person who is a party to the proceeding and the same interest has been further limited upon the happening of a future event to a class of persons described in terms of their relationship to such party, the party to the proceeding.

(iii) to unborn or unascertained persons, none of such persons, but if it appears that there is no person in being or ascertained, having the same interest, the court shall appoint a guardian ad litem to represent or protect the persons who eventually may become entitled to the interest.

(b) Where a party to the proceeding has a power of appointment it shall not be necessary to serve the potential appointees and if it is a general power of appointment it shall not be necessary to serve the takers in default of the exercise thereof.

3. Representation of contingent interests.

Where an interest in the estate has been limited to a person who is a party to the proceeding and the same interest has been further limited upon the happening of a future event to any other person it shall not be necessary to serve such other person.

4. Representation in probate proceeding. In a proceeding for probate of a testamentary instrument, the interests of the respective persons specified in subdivisions 2(a)(ii) and 3 of this section shall be deemed to be the same interest, whether or not their respective interests are in income or in principal or in both, provided that they are beneficiaries of the same trust or fund, that they have a common interest in proving or disproving the instrument offered for probate and that the person who is a party under subdivision 2(a)(ii) or the person to whom the interest has been limited under subdivision 3 would not receive greater financial benefit if such instrument were denied probate (in the case where such beneficiaries have a common interest in proving such instrument) or admitted to probate, (in the case where such beneficiaries have a common interest in disproving such instrument).

5. Representation of persons under a disability. If the instrument expressly so provides, where a party to the proceeding has the same interest as a person under a disability, it shall not be necessary to serve the person under a disability.

6. The decree or order entered in any such proceeding shall be

binding and conclusive on all persons upon whom service of process is not required.

7. In any proceeding in which service of process upon persons interested in the estate may be dispensed with pursuant to the provisions of this section or section twenty-two hundred ten, in addition to such other requirements as may be applicable to the petition in the particular proceeding, the petition shall (i) set forth in a form satisfactory to the court the information required by subdivision three of section three hundred four with respect to the persons interested in the estate upon whom service of process may be dispensed with, the nature of the interests of such persons and the basis upon which service of process may be dispensed with, and (ii) state whether the fiduciary or any other person has discretion to affect the present or future beneficial enjoyment of the estate and, if so, set forth the discretion possessed and, if exercised, the manner in which it has been exercised. Notwithstanding the foregoing provisions of this section and any provisions of the instrument to the contrary, if the court finds that the representation of a person's interest is or may be inadequate it may require that he be served. The basis for such finding shall be set forth specifically in the order.

8. Nonjudicial settlements of accounts of fiduciaries. Unless the instrument expressly provides otherwise, an instrument settling an account, executed by all the persons upon whom service of process would be required in a proceeding for the judicial settlement of the account, shall be binding and conclusive on all persons upon whom service of process would not be required to the same extent as that instrument binds the persons who executed it.

Article 8.   General provisions relating to bonds.

§ 801.   Amount; condition; number of sureties; obligees.

1. Amount. Whenever a fiduciary or legal life tenant shall be required to file a bond, the amount thereof, except where the court has reduced it or dispensed therewith, shall be fixed as follows:

(a) Executor, administrator, administrator c.t.a., administrator d.b.n. and temporary administrator.   (a) Not Less Than:

i. Value of all personal property receivable by the fiduciary.

ii. Estimated gross rents of real property receivable by the fiduciary for 18 months.

iii. Probable recovery in any cause of action prosecuted by the fiduciary.

In fixing the amount of a bond under this paragraph the court must also take into consideration in the case of a successor executor, administrator, administrator c. t. a., or administrator d. b. n., how much of the estate, if any, has already been administered.

No bond shall be required of any of the above mentioned fiduciaries if the value of the assets to be administered does not exceed the monetary amount defined as a small estate pursuant to subdivision one of section 1301 of this act.

(b) Guardian of the property of an infant

(b) Not less than:

i. Value of all personal property receivable by the guardian.

ii. Estimated gross rents of real property receivable by the guardian for three years.

iii. Estimated gross income for three years from sources other than moneys or other assets committed to the guardian for administration.

(c) i. Testamentary trustee, or executor required to hold, manage or invest property for the benefit of another,

ii. ancillary fiduciaries,

iii. guardian of the person of an infant,

iv. legal life tenant, or

v. any case not provided for in this article where the filing of a bond is required.

(c) In such amount as the court directs.

(d) In granting limited and restrictive letters pursuant to the provisions of 702 the court may dispense with a bond altogether or fix the amount at such sum as it may deem sufficient.

(e) In addition to such powers as are conferred by CPLR 2508, the court may at any time increase or decrease the bond of a fiduciary or legal life tenant when good reason therefore appears.

(f) In fixing the amount of a bond, the court may require evidence as to the character and value of the assets to be committed to the fiduciary and may examine the applicant or any other person under oath or take such other steps as it deems necessary.

2. Condition. Unless the court directs otherwise the condition of the bond shall be that the fiduciary will faithfully discharge his trust, obey all lawful decrees and orders touching the administration of the assets committed to him including but not limited to decrees or orders directing repayment of amounts allowed as advances on commissions and render a verified account of his administration whenever required to do so by the court. In the case of a legal life tenant the condition shall be that the principal account for and deliver to his successors in interest the property held as life tenant.

3. Sureties. The court may authorize or direct the execution and filing of a bond with a sole surety or with two or more sureties or it may dispense with sureties altogether when good reason therefor appears.

4. Obligees of bond. The bond of a fiduciary shall run to the people of the state for the security and benefit of the persons then or thereafter interested in the estate.

Article 17.   Guardians and custodians.

§ 1708.   Bonding Requirements; Investment of Guardianship Funds.

1. Except as provided in this section, all property of the infant shall be secured by bond as provided in this act.

2. (a) The court may dispense with a bond wholly or partly and direct that the guardian jointly with a person or depositary designated collect and receive the moneys and other property of the infant as directed by order and that such moneys and property as it directs be deposited in the name of the guardian, subject to the order of the court, with a bank, savings bank, trust company, safe deposit

App Pract Provs

company, or state or federal credit union designated in the order or invested in the name of the guardian, subject to the order of the court, in the shares of a savings and loan association or the savings account of a federal savings and loan association designated in the order, provided that no deposit or investment of the funds of any one infant in any single bank, savings bank, trust company, savings and loan association, federal savings and loan association, or state or federal credit union shall exceed the maximum amount insured by the federal deposit insurance corporation or the national credit union share insurance fund.

(b) The court may also dispense with a bond wholly or partly when it authorizes the guardian to purchase and invest in United States savings bonds, treasury bills, treasury notes, treasury bonds, or bonds of the state of New York or bonds or other obligations of any county, city, town, village or school district of the state of New York for the benefit of the infant and directs the guardian to deposit such bonds, bills, notes or other municipal obligations in joint custody with a bank, savings bank, trust company, safe deposit company, or state or federal credit union invested in the name of the guardian, subject to the order of the court. The guardian shall collect and receive all interest and income from such United States savings bonds, treasury notes, treasury bonds or bonds of the state of New York or bonds or other obligations of any county, city, town, village or school district of the state of New York and deposit such interest and income in an account in the name of the guardian, subject to the order of the court, as authorized pursuant to this section with the bank, savings bank, trust company, safe deposit company, or state or federal credit union having joint custody with the guardian of such United States savings bonds, treasury bills, treasury notes, treasury bonds, or bonds of the state of New York or bonds or other obligations of any county, city, town, village or school district of the state of New York.

(c) The court may also dispense with a bond wholly or partly when it authorizes the guardian to invest the guardianship funds pursuant to an investment advisory agreement with a bank, trust company, brokerage house, or other financial services entity acceptable to the court. The investment advisory agreement shall provide that the guardianship funds will be invested in accordance with the provisions of section 11-2.3 of the estates, powers[,]* and trusts law and that the funds so invested shall not be released from the custody of the custodian identified therein except on order of the court. The petition to invest the guardianship funds pursuant to this subdivision shall be accompanied by a copy of the proposed investment advisory agreement. If the custodian of the funds is not the same person or entity providing the investment advice, a separate custodial agreement shall also accompany the petition to invest the guardianship** pursuant to this subdivision. Such custodial agreement shall be with an institution acceptable to the court for the purpose of retaining control of the guardianship funds and shall also provide that the funds under the control of the custodian shall not be released from custody except on order of the court.

(d) Such deposit or investment shall be withdrawn or removed only on the order of the court, except that no court order shall be required to pay over to the infant who has attained the age of eighteen years all the moneys so held unless the depository is in receipt of an order from a court of competent jurisdiction directing it to withhold such payment beyond the infant's eighteenth birthday.

3. Where an infant is a beneficiary of a contract of life insurance under which moneys are payable to the infant or under which rights may accrue to the infant pursuant to election made by his guardian under the terms of the contract, the court may by order dispense wholly or partly with a bond and direct that the insurance company and the guardian shall make no withdrawal of the funds due to the infant under the contract except by joint check to the order of the guardian and a person designated by the court to receive such moneys.

4. The letters issued shall contain the substance of the order.

Article 18.   Claims; debts and expenses.

§ 1812.   Leave to issue execution against decedent's real property.

For the purpose of procuring a decree granting leave to issue execution against a decedent's real property a judgment creditor shall

----

*   So in original.

**   **Ed. Note:** Probably should read "guardianship funds".

present to the court a verified petition showing the facts and praying for such decree and that the person whose interest in the property will be affected by a sale by virtue of the execution and the fiduciary of the judgment debtor may be required to show cause why it should not be granted. Upon the presentation of the petition the court must issue process accordingly. The process must be served either personally or in such manner as directed by the court and upon the return thereof the court may make such decree as justice shall require.

Article 22.   Accounting.

§ 2209.   Affidavit to account.

To each account filed in the court, as prescribed in this article, must be appended the affidavit of the accounting party to the effect that the account contains according to the best of his knowledge and belief a true statement of all his receipts and disbursements on account of the estate and of all money or other property belonging to the estate which have come into his hands or been received by any other person by his order or authority for his use and that he does not know of any error or omission in the account to the prejudice of any creditor of, or person interested in, the estate.

UNIFORM COMMERCIAL CODE

SYNOPSIS OF SELECTED PROVISIONS

Article 2.   Sales.

§ 2-725.   Statute of limitations in contracts for sale.

(1) An action for breach of any contract for sale must be commenced within four years after the cause of action has accrued. By the original agreement the parties may reduce the period of limitation to not less than one year but may not extend it.

(2) A cause of action accrues when the breach occurs, regardless of the aggrieved party's lack of knowledge of the breach. A breach of warranty occurs when tender of delivery is made, except that where a warranty explicitly extends to future performance of the goods and discovery of the breach must await the time of such performance the cause of action accrues when the breach is or should have been discovered.

(3) Where an action commenced within the time limited by subsection (1) is so terminated as to leave available a remedy by another action for the same breach such other action may be commenced after the expiration of the time limited and within six months after the termination of the first action unless the termination resulted from voluntary discontinuance or from dismissal for failure or neglect to prosecute.

(4) This section does not alter the law on tolling of the statute of limitations nor does it apply to causes of action which have accrued before this Act becomes effective.

App Pract
Provs

Article 3.　Commercial paper.

§ 3-122.　Accrual of cause of action.

* * *

(3) A cause of action against a drawer of a draft or an indorser of any instrument accrues upon demand following dishonor of the instrument. Notice of dishonor is a demand.

VEHICLE AND TRAFFIC LAW

SYNOPSIS OF SELECTED PROVISIONS

Article 3.   Exemption of non-resident owners and operators.

§ 253.   Service of summons on non-residents.

1. The use or operation by a non-resident of a vehicle in this state, or the use or operation in this state of a vehicle in the business of a non-resident, or the use or operation in this state of a vehicle owned by a non-resident if so used or operated with his permission, express or implied, shall be deemed equivalent to an appointment by such nonresident of the secretary of state to be his true and lawful attorney upon whom may be served the summons in any action against him, growing out of any accident or collision in which such non-resident may be involved while using or operating such vehicle in this state or in which such vehicle may be involved while being used or operated in this state in the business of such non-resident or with the permission, express or implied, of such non-resident owner; and such use or operation shall be deemed a signification of his agreement that any such summons against him which is so served shall be of the same legal force and validity as if served on him personally within the state and within the territorial jurisdiction of the court from which the summons issues, and that such appointment of the secretary of state shall be irrevocable and binding upon his executor or administrator. Where such non-resident has died prior to the commencement of an action brought pursuant to this section, service of process shall be made on the executor or administrator of such non-resident in the same manner and on the same notice as is provided in the case of the non-resident himself. Where an action has been duly commenced

App Pract Provs

under the provisions of this section against a non-resident who dies thereafter, the court must allow the action to be continued against his executor or administrator upon motion with such notice as the court deems proper.

2. A summons in an action described in this section may issue in any court in the state having jurisdiction of the subject matter and be served as hereinafter provided. Service of such summons shall be made by mailing a copy thereof to the secretary of state at his office in the city of Albany, or by personally delivering a copy thereof to one of his regularly established offices, with a fee of ten dollars, and such service shall be sufficient service upon such non-resident provided that notice of such service and a copy of the summons and complaint are forthwith sent by or on behalf of the plaintiff to the defendant by certified mail or registered mail with return receipt requested. The plaintiff shall file with the clerk of the court in which the action is pending, or with the judge or justice of such court in case there be no clerk, an affidavit of compliance herewith, a copy of the summons and complaint, and either a return receipt purporting to be signed by the defendant or a person qualified to receive his certified mail or registered mail, in accordance with the rules and customs of the post-office department; or, if acceptance was refused by the defendant or his agent, the original envelope bearing a notation by the postal authorities that receipt was refused, and an affidavit by or on behalf of the plaintiff that notice of such mailing and refusal was forthwith sent to the defendant by ordinary mail; or, if the registered or certified letter was returned to the post office unclaimed, the original envelope bearing a notation by the postal authorities of such mailing and return, an affidavit by or on behalf of the plaintiff that the summons was posted again by ordinary mail and proof of mailing certificate of ordinary mail. Where the summons is mailed to a foreign country, other official proof of the delivery of the mail may be filed in case the post-office department is unable to obtain such a return receipt. The foregoing papers shall be filed within thirty days after the return receipt or other official proof of delivery or the original envelope bearing a notation of refusal, as the case may be, is received by the plaintiff. Service of process shall be complete when such papers are filed. The return receipt or other official proof of delivery shall constitute presumptive evidence that the summons mailed was received by the defendant or a person qualified

to receive his certified mail or registered mail; and the notation of refusal shall constitute presumptive evidence that the refusal was by the defendant or his agent. Service of such summons also may be made by mailing a copy thereof to the secretary of state at his office in the city of Albany, or by personally delivering a copy thereof to one of his regularly established offices, with a fee of ten dollars, and by delivering a duplicate copy thereof with the complaint annexed thereto, to the defendant personally without the state by a resident or citizen of the state of New York or a sheriff, under-sheriff, deputy-sheriff or constable of the county or other political sub-division in which the personal service is made, or an officer authorized by the laws of this state, to take acknowledgments of deeds to be recorded in this state, or an attorney and/or counselor at law, solicitor, advocate or barrister duly qualified to practice in the state or country where such service is made, or by a United States marshall or deputy United States marshall. Proof of personal service without the state shall be filed with the clerk of the court in which the action is pending within thirty days after such service. Personal service without the state is complete when proof thereof is filed. The court in which the action is pending may order such extensions as may be necessary to afford the defendant reasonable opportunity to defend the action.

3. As used in this section, the term "vehicle" means a "motor vehicle," "motorcycle," "semitrailer," and "trailer" as defined in sections one hundred twenty-five, one hundred twenty-three, one hundred forty-three and one hundred fifty-six, respectively, of this chapter, whether or not such vehicles are used or operated upon a public highway.

§ 254. **Service of summons on residents who depart from state and on residents' executors or administrators who are non-residents or who depart from state.**

The provisions of section two hundred fifty-three of this chapter shall also apply (a) to a resident who departs from the state subsequent to the accident or collision and remains absent therefrom for thirty days continuously, whether such absence is intended to be temporary or permanent, and to any executor or administrator of such resident, and (b) to an executor or administrator of a resident if such executor or administrator is a non-resident or if, being a resident, he departs from the state and remains absent therefrom for thirty days continuously,

App Pract
Provs

whether such absence is intended to be temporary or permanent.

COURT DIRECTORY

STATE-WIDE COURT ADMINISTRATIVE OFFICES

Office of Court Administration

25 Beaver Street–11th Floor
New York, New York 10004
Honorable Jonathan Lippman, Chief Administrative Judge
(212) 428-2150 (New York City Office)
Fax: (212) 428-2188
Internet: http://www.courts.state.ny.us

Commission on Judicial Conduct

61 Broadway, 12th Floor
New York, New York 10006
(646) 386–4800
Fax: (646) 458–0037
www.scjc.state.ny.us (for all offices)

Corning Tower Suite
2301 Empire State Plaza
Albany, New York 12223 (518) 453-4600
Fax: (518) 486-1850
www.scjc.state.ny.us

400 Andrews Street, Suite 700
Rochester, New York 14604
(585) 232-5756
Fax: (585) 232-7834
www.scjc.state.ny.us

Lawyers' Fund for Client Protection

119 Washington Avenue
Albany, New York 12210
(518) 434-1935
(800) 442-3863
Fax: (518) 434-5641
E-mail: raywood@nylawfund.org or info@nylawfund.org
Internet: http://www.nylawfund.org

Department of State

One Commerce Plaza

99 Washington Avenue
Albany, New York 12231-1001
(518) 474-4752; (518) 474-6740
Fax: (518) 474-4597
E-mail: info@dos.state.ny.us; counsel@dos.state.ny.us
Internet: http://www.dos.state.ny.us

New York City Regional Office

123 William Street
19th Floor
New York, New York 10038
(212) 417-5800
Fax: (212) 417-2383
www.dos.state.ny.us

Division of Corporations and State Records

One Commerce Plaza
99 Washington Avenue
Albany, New York 12231-1001
(518) 473-2492
Fax: (518) 474-1418
State Records: (518) 478-4770
Uniform Commercial Codes: (518) 474-4763
Fax: (518) 474-4478
Email: corporations@dos.state.ny.us
Internet: http://www.dos.state.ny.us

NEW YORK STATE COURTS
www.nycourts.gov (Information for all NYS courts)

Court of Appeals

Court of Appeals Hall
20 Eagle Street
Albany, New York 12207-1095
(518) 455-7700
Internet: http://www.courts.state.ny.us/ctapps

Appellate Division

First Department

27 Madison Avenue
New York, New York 10010
(212) 340-0400

Fax: (212) 889-4412

Second Department

45 Monroe Place
Brooklyn, New York 11201
(718) 875-1300
www.nycourts.gov/court/ad2/

Third Department

Justice Building
Empire State Plaza, Fifth Floor, Room 511
Albany, New York 12223
(518) 471-4777
Fax: (518) 471-4750
www.courts.state.ny.us

mailing address:
Capitol Station
P.O. Box 7288
Albany, New York 12224–0288

Fourth Department

50 East Avenue
Suite 200
Rochester, New York 14604
(585) 530-3100
www.courts.state.ny.us

Court of Claims

Justice Building
P.O. Box 7344
Capitol Station
Albany, New York 12224-0902
(518) 432-3411
Clerk: Robert T. DeCataldo
(518) 432-3463
Fax for filing: (866) 413-1069
www.nyscourtofclaims.state.ny.us

26 Broadway, 10th Floor
New York, New York 10004
(212) 361-8100
Receptionist: (212) 361-8150

Court Directory

Fax: (212) 361-8163

COUNTY DIRECTORY

Albany County

(Third Department, Third Judicial District)
www.nycourts.gov

Supreme Court

Albany County Courthouse
16 Eagle Street Albany, New York 12207
(518) 285–8989
Fax: (518) 487-5020
County Clerk: (518)487–5100

Criminal Court

One Morton Avenue
Albany, New York 12202
(518)462–6714
Fax: (518)477–8778

Surrogate's Court

30 Clinton Avenue
Albany, New York 12207
(518) 462–0194
Chief Clerk: Stacy L. Pettit
Fax: (518) 487-5087

County Court

Albany County Courthouse
16 Eagle Street
Albany, New York 12207
Chief Clerk: Charles E. Diamond
(518) 285–8989
Fax: (518) 487-5020

Family Court

30 Clinton Avenue
Albany, New York 12207
(518) 285-8600
Fax: (518) 462-4248

City Court

Civil Court

City Hall
Albany, New York 12207
Chief Clerk: Linda File
(518) 453–4640
Fax: (518) 434-5034
www.nycourts.gov

97 Mohawk Street
P.O. Box 678
Cohoes, New York 12047-0678
Chief Clerk: Janet LeBeau
(518) 233-2133
Fax: (518) 233-8202

#2
15th Street
Watervliet, New York 12189
Chief Clerk: Robin Robillard
(518) 270-3803
Fax: (518) 270-3812

Sheriff

16 Eagle Street
Albany, New York 12207
(518) 487-5400
Civil Unit Fax: (518) 487-5352

Allegany County

(Fourth Department, Eighth Judicial District)

Supreme Court

Courthouse
7 Court Street
Belmont, New York 14813–1084
Chief Clerk: Kathleen Johnson
Deputy Chief Clerk: Laura Gabler
(585) 268-5800
Fax: (585) 268-7090

Surrogate's Court

Courthouse

7 Court Street
Belmont, New York 14813
Chief Clerk: Karen R. Harkenrider
(585) 268-5815
Fax: (585) 268-7090

County Court

Courthouse
7 Court Street
Belmont, New York 14813–1084
(585) 268-5813;
Fax: (585) 268-7090
Clerk: (585) 268–9270

Family Court

Courthouse
7 Court Street
Belmont, New York 14813
(585) 268-5816
Fax: (585) 268-7090

Sheriff

7 Court Street
Belmont, New York 14813
(716) 268-9200, 08
Fax: (716) 268-9475

Bronx County

(First Department, Twelfth Judicial District)

Supreme Court

Civil Term
851 Grand Concourse, Rm 217
Bronx, New York 10451
County Clerk: (866)797–7214
General Information (646) 386–5700
Civil Division: (718) 618-1400
Chief Clerk: Tracy Pardo
(718) 590–3985
Fax: (718)618–3545
Criminal Term
215 East 161st Street

Bronx, New York 10451
(718) 618–3100
Fax: (718)618–3545
Internet: www.nycourts.gov

Surrogate's Court

851 Grand Concourse,
Bronx, New York 10451
(718) 618–2300
General Information (646) 386–5700
Records: (718) 590–3618
Chief Clerk: Tracy Pardo
(718) 590–3985
Fax: (718)618–3545

Family Court

900 Sheridan Avenue
Bronx, New York 10451
Judge's Chambers: (718) 618–2098
Clerk of Court: (718) 590–3318
Fax: (718) 590-2681

Civil Court

851 Grand Concourse
Bronx, New York 10451
Chief Clerk: Tracy Pardo
General Information
(646) 386–5700
(718)618–2561
Fax: (718)590–7294

Broome County

(Third Department, Sixth Judicial District)

Supreme Court

92 Court Street
Courthouse
Binghamton, New York 13901
(607) 778-2448
Fax: (607) 778-6426
County Clerk: (607) 778–2451

Surrogate's Court

92 Court Street

Binghamton, New York 13901
Chief Clerk: Rebecca Malmquist
(607) 778-2111
Fax: (607) 778-2308

County Court

65 Hawley Street
Binghamton, New York 13901
(607) 778-2448
Fax: (607) 778-6426

Family Court

65 Hawley Street
Binghamton, New York 13901
(607) 778-2156
Fax:
(607) 778–2439
District Office: (607) 721–8541

City Court

City Hall Governmental Plaza
38 Hawley Street 5th Floor
Binghamton, New York 13901
(607) 772-7006
Fax: (607) 772-7041
District Office: (607) 721–8541

Sheriff

155 Lt. Van Winkle Drive
Binghamton, New York 13905
(607) 778-2492
Fax: (607) 778-2100

Cattaraugus County

(Fourth Department, Eighth Judicial District)

Supreme Court

County Center
303 Court Street
Little Valley, New York 14755
Deputy Chief Clerk: Kim Reed
(716) 938-9111, Ext. 2388

Fax: (716) 938-6413
Email: ydry@courts.state.ny.us

Surrogate's Court

303 Court Street
Little Valley, New York 14755
(716) 938-2327
Fax: (716) 938-6983
Chief Clerk: Christine Wrona
E-mail: cwrona@courts.state.ny.us

County Court

County Center
303 Court Street
Little Valley, New York 14755
(716) 938-9111, Ext. 388
Fax: (716) 938-6413
County Clerk: (716) 938-9111, ext. 2297

Family Court

1 Leo Moss Drive
Olean, New York 14760
(716) 373-8035
Fax: (716) 373-0449
Chief Clerk: Ruth Dickerson
E-mail: rdickers@courts.state.ny.us

City Court

101 East State Street
P.O. Box 631
Olean, New York 14760
(716) 376-5621
Fax: (716) 376-5623
Deputy Chief Clerk: Stella S. Johnston
Email: ssjohnst@courts.state.ny.us.

225 Wildwood Avenue
Salamanca, New York 14779
(716) 945–4135
Fax: (716) 9452362
Deputy Chief Clerk: Stella S. Johnston

Sheriff

County Center

301 Court Street
Little Valley, New York 14755
(716) 938-9111 Ext. 2204

Cayuga County

(Fourth Department, Seventh Judicial District)

Supreme Court

152 Genesee Street
Auburn, New York 13021
(315) 255-4320
Fax: (315) 255-4322
E-mail: kwejko@courts.state.ny.us
Internet: www.courts.state.ny.us
County Clerk: (315) 253-1271

Surrogate's Court

152 Genesee Street
Auburn, New York 13021
(315) 255-4316
Fax: (315) 255-4324
E-mail: mmarr@courts.state.ny.us

County Court

152 Genesee Street
Auburn, New York 13021
(315) 255-4320
Fax: (315) 255-4322
E-mail: kwejko@courts.state.ny.us

Family Court

Old Historic Post Office Building
157 Genesee Street, 2nd Floor
Auburn, New York 13021
(315) 255-4306
Fax: (315) 255-4312

City Court

157 Genesee Street
Auburn, New York 13021
(315) 253-1570
Fax: (315) 253-1085

Sheriff

Public Safety Building
7445 County House Road
Auburn, New York 13021
(315) 253-1222
Fax: (315) 253-1192

Chautauqua County

(Fourth Department, Eighth Judicial District)

Supreme Court

P.O. Box 292
Mayville, New York 14757-0292
(716) 753-4266
Fax: (716) 753-4993
County Clerk: (716) 753-4331

Surrogate's Court

2 Academy Street Suite 5
Mayville, New York 14757
(716) 753-4339
Fax: (716) 753-4600

County Court

Courthouse
1 North Erie Street
P.O. Box 292
Mayville, New York 14757-0292
(716) 753-4266
Fax: (716) 753-4162; (716) 753-4993

Family Court

2 Academy Street Suite 5
Mayville, New York 14757
(716) 753-4351
Fax: (716) 753-4350

City Court

Dunkirk City Court—City Hall
342 Central Avenue
Dunkirk, New York 14048-2122
(716) 366-2055

Fax: (716) 366-3622

City Hall
Municipal Building
200 East 3rd Street
Jamestown, New York 14701
(716) 483-7561, (716) 483–7562
Fax: (716) 483-7519

Sheriff

Sheriff's Office
15 East Chautauqua Street
P.O.Box 128
Mayville, New York 14757
(716) 753-2131
(716) 753-4276

Chemung County

(Third Department, Sixth Judicial District)

Supreme Court

Hazlett Building
203–205 Lake Street,
Elmira, New York 14901
(607) 737–2084
Fax: (607) 732-8879

Surrogate's Court

224 Lake Street
Elmira, New York 14901
(607) 737-2873
Fax: (607) 737-2874

County Court

Hazlett Building
203–205 Lake Street,
Elmira, New York 14901
(607) 737–2084
Fax: (607) 732-8879

Family Court

Justice Building
203-209 William Street

Elmira, New York 14901
(607) 737-2902
Fax: (607) 737-2898

City Court
City Hall
317 East Church Street
Elmira, New York 14901
(607) 737-5681
Fax: (607) 737-5820

Sheriff

Justice Building
203 William Street
Elmira, New York 14902-0588
(607) 737-2987
Fax: (607) 737-2931

Chenango County

(Third Department, Sixth Judicial District)

Supreme Court

County Office Building
5 Court Street
Norwich, New York 13815
Catherine A. Schell, Chief Clerk
Irene R. Williams, Deputy Chief Clerk
(607) 337-1457
Fax: (607) 337-1835

Surrogate's Court

County Office Building
5 Court Street
Norwich, New York 13815
Linda J. Wiley, Chief Clerk
(607) 337-1827
Fax: (607) 337-1834

County Court

County Office Building
5 Court Street
Norwich, New York 13815
(607) 337-1457

Fax: (607) 337-1835
Judge's Chambers: (607) 337–1825
Catherine A. Schell, Chief Clerk
Irene R. Williams, Deputy Chief Clerk
County Clerk: (607) 337-1450

Family Court

County Office Building 5 Court St. Norwich, NY 13815
Carole S. Dunham, Chief Clerk
Sharon B. Mason, Deputy Chief Clerk
(607) 337-1820
Fax: (607) 337-1835

City Court

1 Court Plaza
Norwich, New York 13815
Linda Roys-Jones, Chief Clerk
(607) 334-1224
Fax: (607) 334-8494

Sheriff

14 West Park Place
Norwich, New York 13815
(607) 334-2000
Fax: (607) 336-1568

Clinton County

(Third Department, Fourth Judicial District)

Supreme Court
Clerk's Office

County Government Center
137 Margaret Street
Plattsburgh, New York 12901
(518) 565-4715
Fax: (607) 565-4708

Surrogate's Court

County Government Center
137 Margaret Street, Suite 315
Plattsburgh, New York 12901
(518) 565-4630

Fax: (518) 565-4769

County Court

County Government Center
137 Margaret Street
Plattsburgh, New York 12901
(518) 565-4715
Fax: (607) 565-4708
County Clerk: (518) 565-4700

Family Court

County Government Center
137 Margaret Street
Plattsburgh, New York 12901
(518) 565-4658
Fax: (518) 565-4688

City Court

24 U.S. Oval
Plattsburgh, New York 12903
(518) 563-7870
Fax: (518) 563-3124

Sheriff

25 McCarthy Drive
Plattsburgh, New York 12901
(518) 561-4338
Fax: (518) 565-4333

Columbia County

(Third Department, Third Judicial District)

Supreme Court

401 Union Street
Hudson, New York 12534
(518) 828-7858
Fax: (518) 828-1603

Surrogate's Court

401 Union Street
Hudson, New York 12534
(518) 828-0414

Fax: (518) 828-1603

County Court

401 Union Street
Hudson, New York 12534
(518) 828-7858
Fax: (518) 828-1603

Family Court

401 Union Street
Hudson, New York 12534
Dorothy Prestigiacomo, Chief Clerk
(518) 828-7858
Fax: (518) 828-1603

City Court

427–429 Warren Street
Hudson, New York 12534
(518) 828-3100
Fax: (518) 828-3628

Sheriff

85 Industrial Tract
Hudson, New York 12534
Emergency: (518) 828-3344
Business: (518) 828-0601
Fax: (518) 828-9088

Cortland County

(Third Department, Sixth Judicial District)

Supreme Court

46 Greenbush Street, Suite 301
Cortland, New York 13045
Christina DeMass, Chief Clerk
(607) 753-5013
Fax: (607) 756-3409

Surrogate's Court

46 Greenbush Street, Suite 301
Cortland, New York 13045
Maxine B. Ripley, Chief Clerk

(607) 753-5355
Fax: (607) 756-3409

County Court

46 Greenbush Street, Suite 301
Cortland, New York 13045
Christina DeMass, Chief Clerk
(607) 753-5013
Fax: (607) 756-3409

Family Court

46 Greenbush Street, Suite 301
Cortland, New York 13045
Laurie L. Case, Chief Clerk
Deborah A. Elliott, Deputy Chief Clerk
(607) 753-5353
Fax: (607) 756-3409

City Court

City Hall
25 Court Street
Cortland, New York 13045
Kelly Preston, Chief Clerk
E-mail: kpreston@courts.state.ny.us
(607) 428-5420
Fax: (607) 428-5435

Sheriff

Courthouse
54 Greenbush Street
Cortland, New York 13045-5590
Lee A. Price, Sheriff
(607) 753-3311
Fax: (607) 753-7815

Delaware County

(Third Department, Sixth Judicial District)

Supreme Court

Delaware County Courthouse
3 Court Street
Delhi, New York 13753

Alison P. Barnes, Chief Clerk
(607) 746-2131
Fax: (607) 746-3253

Surrogate's Court

Delaware County Courthouse
3 Court Street
Delhi, New York 13753
Lisa Loucks, Chief Clerk
(607) 746-2126
Fax: (607) 746-3253

County Court

Delaware County Courthouse
3 Court Street
Delhi, New York 13753
Alison P. Barnes, Chief Clerk
(607) 746-2131
Fax: (607) 746-3253

Family Court

Delaware County Courthouse
3 Court Street
Delhi, New York 13753
Lori L. Metzko, Chief Clerk
(607) 746-2298
Fax: (607) 746-2288

Sheriff

280 Phoebe Lane
Suite 1
Delhi, New York 13753
(607) 746-2336
(607) 746-2632

Dutchess County

(Second Department, Ninth Judicial District)

Supreme Court

10 Market Street
Poughkeepsie, New York 12601
Ronald P. Varricchio, Chief Clerk

Fern G. Kaelber, Deputy Chief Clerk
(845) 486-2260
Fax: (845) 473-5403

Surrogate's Court

10 Market Street
Poughkeepsie, New York 12601
John Atherton, Chief Clerk
Michael Thompson, Deputy Chief Clerk
(845) 486-2235
Fax: (845) 486-2234

County Court

10 Market Street
Poughkeepsie, New York 12601
(845) 486-2260
Ronald P. Varricchio, Chief Clerk
Michael Thompson, Deputy Chief Clerk
Fax: (845) 473-5403

Family Court

50 Market Street
Poughkeepsie, New York 12601
Peter Palladino, Chief Clerk
(845) 486-2500
Fax: (845) 486-2510

City Court

1 Municipal Plaza
Suite 2
Beacon, New York 12508
Debra Antonelli, Chief Clerk
(845) 838-5030
Fax: (845) 838-5041

62 Civic Center Plaza
P.O. Box 300
Poughkeepsie, New York 12602
Jean Jicha, Chief Clerk
Cheryl Jolie, Deputy Chief Clerk
(845) 451-4091
Fax: (845) 451-4094

Court Directory

Sheriff

150 North Hamilton Street
Poughkeepsie, New York 12601
(845) 486-3800
Fax: (845) 452-2987

Erie County

(Fourth Department, Eighth Judicial District)

Supreme Court

25 Delaware Avenue
Buffalo, New York 14202
(716) 845-9300
Fax: (716) 851-3293

Surrogate's Court

92 Franklin Street
Buffalo, New York 14202
(716) 845-2560
Fax: (716) 853-3741
E-mail: mmartoch@courts.state. ny.us

County Court

25 Delaware Avenue
Buffalo, New York 14202
(716) 845-9300
Fax: (716) 851-3293

Family Court

1 Niagara Plaza
Buffalo, New York 14202
Frank J. Boccio, Chief Clerk
E-mail: fboccio@courts.state.ny.us
Daniel S. Johnston, Deputy Clerk Clerk
E-mail: djohnston@courts.state.ny.us
(716) 845-7400
Fax: (716) 845-8432

City Court

50 Delaware Avenue
Buffalo, New York 14202
(716) 845-2600

Fax: (716) 847-8257
E-mail: sthomas@courts.state. ny.us

City Hall

714 Ridge Road
Lackawanna, New York 14218
(716) 827-6486
Fax: (716) 825-1874

City Hall

200 Niagara Street
Tonawanda, New York 14150
(716) 845-2160
Fax: (716) 693-1612

Sheriff

10 Delaware Avenue
Buffalo, New York 14202
(716) 858-7608
Fax: (716) 858-7680

Essex County

(Third Department, Fourth Judicial District)

Supreme Court

7559 Court Street
P.O. Box 217
Elizabethtown, New York 12932
(518) 873-3371
Fax: (518) 873-3376

Surrogate's Court

7559 Court Street
P.O. Box 505
Elizabethtown, New York 12932
(518) 873-3385
Fax: 518-873-3731

County Court

7559 Court Street
P.O. Box 217
Elizabethtown, New York 12932

(518) 873-3371
Fax: (518) 873-3376

Family Court

7559 Court Street
P.O. Box 217
Elizabethtown, New York 12932
(518) 873-3320
Fax: (518) 873-3626

Sheriff

7551 Court Street
P.O. Box 278
Elizabethtown, New York 12932
(518) 873-6321
Fax: (518) 873-3340

Franklin County

(Third Department, Fourth Judicial District)

Supreme Court

355 West Main Street
Malone, New York 12953
Kimberly A. Crow, Chief Clerk
Lisa Johnston, Deputy Chief Clerk
(518) 481-1817
Fax: (518) 481-5456

Surrogate's Court

355 West Main Street Suite 3223
Malone, New York 12953
(518) 481-1736
Fax: (518) 481-7583

County Court

355 West Main Street
Malone, New York 12953
Kimberly A. Crow, Chief Clerk
Lisa Johnston, Deputy Chief Clerk
(518) 481-1817
Fax: (518) 481-5456

Family Court

355 West Main Street Suite 3223

Malone, New York 12953
Janice F. Mock, Chief Clerk
(518) 481-1742
Fax: (518) 481-5453

Commissioner of Jurors

Courthouse
63 West 355 Main Street
Malone, New York 12953
Kathleen M. Monette, Commissioner of Jurors
(518) 481-1756
Fax: (518) 481-6204

Sheriff

Courthouse
45 Bare Hill Road
Malone, New York 12953
(518) 483-3304
Fax: (518) 483-3139

Fulton County

(Third Department, Fourth Judicial District)

Supreme Court

223 West Main Street
Johnstown, New York 12095
(518) 736-5539
Fax: (518) 762-5078

Surrogate's Court

223 West Main Street
Johnstown, New York 12095
(518) 736-5695
Fax: (518) 762-6372

County Court

223 West Main Street
Johnstown, New York 12095
(518) 736-5539
Fax: (518) 762-5078

Family Court

11 North William Street

Johnstown, New York 12095
(518) 762-3840
Fax: (518) 762-9540

City Court

City Hall
3 Frontage Road
Gloversville, New York 12078
(518) 773-4527
Fax: (518) 773-4599

City Hall
33-41 East Main Street Suite 105
Johnstown, New York 12095
(518) 762-0007
(518) 762-2720

Sheriff

2712 State Highway 29
P.O. Box 20
Johnstown, New York 12095
(518) 736-2100
Fax: (518) 736-2126

Genesee County

(Fourth Department, Eighth Judicial District)

Supreme Court

Courts Facility Building
1 West Main Street
Batavia, New York 14020
Nelson Green, Chief Clerk
(585) 344-2310
Fax: (585) 344-8517
E-mail: ngreen@courts.state.ny.us

Surrogate's Court

Courts Facility Building
1 West Main Street
Batavia, New York 14020
Michele Westfall-Owens, Chief Clerk
(585) 344-2237
Fax: (585) 344-8517

E-mail: ckelly@courts.state.ny.us

County Court

Courts Facility Building
1 West Main Street
Batavia, New York 14020
Nelson Green, Chief Clerk
(585) 344-2310
Fax: (585) 344-8517
E-mail: ngreen@courts.state.ny.us

Family Court

Courts Facility Building
1 West Main Street
Batavia, New York 14020
Kathleen Blake, Chief Clerk
(585) 344-2228
Fax: (585) 344-8520
E-mail: kblake@courts.state.ny.us
Elaine Pommerening, Deputy Chief Clerk
E-mail: epommere@courts.state.ny.us

City Court

Courts Facility Building
1 West Main Street
Batavia, New York 14020
(585) 344-2417
Fax: (585) 344-8556
E-mail: lgiambro@courts.state.ny.us

Sheriff

14 West Main Street
P.O. Box 151
Batavia, New York 14020-0151
(585) 343-0911
Fax: (585) 343-9129

Greene County

(Third Department, Third Judicial District)

Supreme Court

80 Woodland Avenue

Catskill, New York 12414
Kathleen Barry Gorczyca, Chief Clerk
(518) 943-2230
Fax: (518) 943-0247

Surrogate's Court

80 Woodland Avenue Catskill, New York 12414
Eric Maurer, Chief Clerk
(518)943–2484
Fax (518) 943–1864

County Court

80 Woodland Avenue
Catskill, New York 12414
Kathleen Barry Gorczyca, Chief Clerk
(518) 943-2230
Fax: (518) 943-0247

Family Court

80 Woodland Avenue
Catskill, New York 12414
Brenda VanDermark, Chief Clerk
Carol Peters, Deputy Chief Clerk
(518) 943-5711
Fax: (518) 943-1864
E-mail: bvanderm@courts.state.ny.us

Sheriff

80 Bridge Street
P.O. Box 231
Catskill, New York 12414
(518) 943-3300
Fax: (518) 943-6832

Hamilton County

(Third Department, Fourth Judicial District)

Supreme Court

No sessions held *(See Fulton County for information)*
Hamilton County Court Law Library
Hamilton County Court House
Route 8

Lake Pleasant, New York 12108
(518) 648–5411
Fax: (518) 648-6286

Surrogate's Court
mailing address:
P.O. Box 780
Indian Lake, New York 12842-0780

Court sessions held at: Route 8
Lake Pleasant, New York 12142
(518) 648-5411
Fax: (518) 648-6286

County Court *mailing address*:
P.O. Box 780
Indian Lake, New York 12842-0780

Court sessions held at:
Courthouse
Route 8
Lake Pleasant, New York 12108
(518) 548-3211

Chambers
White Birch Lane
Indian Lake, New York 12842-0780
(518) 648-5411
Fax: (518) 648-6286

Family Court *mailing address*:
White Birch Lane
P.O. Box 780
Indian Lake, New York 12842-0780

Court sessions held at:
Courthouse
Route 8
Lake Pleasant, New York 12108
(518) 648-5411
Fax: (518) 648-6286

Sheriff

P.O. Box 210
South Shore Road
Lake Pleasant, New York 12108

(518) 548-3113
(518) 548-3113 (call to fax)

Herkimer County

(Fourth Department, Fifth Judicial District)

Supreme Court

Herkimer County Office and Courts Facility
301 North Washington Street
5th Floor Suite 5550
Herkimer, New York 13350
Constance A. Vertucci, Chief Clerk IV
Shirley D. French, Deputy Chief Clerk II
Civil Phone: (315) 867-1209
Criminal Phone: (315) 867-1282
Fax: (315) 866-1802

Surrogate's Court

Herkimer County Office and Courts Facility
Fifth Floor, Suite 5550
301 North Washington Street
Herkimer, NY 13350
Constance A. Vertucci, Chief Clerk IV
Shirley D. French, Deputy Chief Clerk II
(315) 867-1367
Fax: (315) 866-1722

County Court

Herkimer County Office and Courts Facility
301 North Washington Street
5th Floor Suite 5550
Herkimer, New York 13350
Constance A. Vertucci, Chief Clerk IV
Shirley D. French, Deputy Chief Clerk II
Civil Phone: (315) 867-1209
Criminal Phone: (315) 867-1282
Fax: (315) 866-1802

Family Court

Herkimer County Office and Court Facility
301 North Washington Street
4th Floor P.O. Box 749

Herkimer, New York 13350
Lynn M. Kohl, Chief Clerk IV
Mary Leahy, Deputy Chief Clerk II
(315) 867-1139
Fax: (315) 867-1369

City Court

City Hall
659 East Main Street
Little Falls, New York 13365
Jane B. Fortuna, Chief Clerk I
(315) 823-1690
Fax: (315) 823-1623

Sheriff

320 North Main Street, Suite 2900
Herkimer, New York 13350-1949
(315) 867-1167
Fax: (315) 867-1354

Jefferson County

Fourth Department, Fifth Judicial District)

Supreme Court

Dulles State Office Building
317 Washington Street, 10th Floor
Watertown, New York 13601
Bonnie S. Johnson, Chief Clerk III
(315) 785-7906
Fax: (315) 785-7909

Surrogate's Court

Jefferson County Court Complex
163 Arsenal Street
Watertown, New York 13601
(315) 785-3019
Benjamin Cobb, Chief Clerk I
Fax: (315) 785-5194

County Court

Jefferson County Court Complex
163 Arsenal Street

Watertown, New York 13601
Bonnie S. Johnson, Chief Clerk III
(315) 785-3044
Fax: (315) 785-7409

Family Court

Jefferson County Court Complex
163 Arsenal Street
Watertown, New York 13601
Tanice Gebo, Chief Clerk IV
(315) 785-3001
Fax: (315) 785-3198

City Court

245 Washington Street
Watertown, New York 13601
Julie M. Call, Chief Clerk II
Agnes J. Zaremba, Chief Clerk III
(315) 785-7785
Fax: (315) 785-7856

Sheriff

753 Waterman Drive
Watertown, New York 13601
(315) 786-2600, 2700
Fax: (315) 786-2684

Kings County

(Second Department, Second Judicial District)

Supreme Court

Civil Term
360 Adams Street
Brooklyn, New York 11201
Nancy T. Sunshine, Chief Clerk
Louis D. Fiorillo, Deputy Chief Clerk
(718) 675–7699

Criminal Term

320 Jay Street
Brooklyn, New York 11201
(347) 296–1076

Fax:
(347) 296-71977

Surrogate's Court

2 Johnson Street
Brooklyn, New York 11201
Public access may be had through Supreme Court, Kings County
main entrance at 360 Adams Street
(347) 404-9700
Fax:
(718) 643-6237

Family Court

330 Jay Street
Brooklyn, New York 11201
(347) 401-9610
Fax: (347) 401-9609

Civil Court

141 Livingston Street
Brooklyn, New York 11201
General Information: (212) 791-6000
Civil: (347) 404–9123
Housing General Information: (646) 386–5750
Housing: (347) 404–9201
Small Claims: (347) 404–9021

Criminal Court

120 Schermerhorn Street
Brooklyn New York 11201
(347) 404–9400
Fax: (718) 643–7733

Under Sheriff

Municipal Building
210 Joralemon Street
Brooklyn, New York 11201
(718) 802-3543
Fax: (718) 802-3715

Lewis County

(Fourth Department, Fifth Judicial District)

Supreme Court

7660 North State Street
Lowville, New York 13367
Bart R, Pleskach, Chief Clerk I
(315) 376-5380
Fax: (315) 376-1656

Surrogate's Court

7660 North State Street
Lowville, New York 13367
(315) 376-5344
Fax: (315) 376-4145

County Court

7660 North State Street
Lowville, New York 13367
Bart R, Pleskach, Chief Clerk I
(315) 376-5380
Fax: (315) 376-1656

Family Court

7660 North State Street
Lowville, New York 13367
Judy C. Meekins, Chief Clerk I
(315) 376-5345
Fax: (315) 376-5189

Sheriff

Public Safety Building
5252 Outer Stowe Street
P.O. Box 233
Lowville, New York 13367
(315) 376-3511
Fax: (315) 376-5232

Livingston County

(Fourth Department, Seventh Judicial District)

Supreme Court

2 Court Street

Geneseo, New York 14454
(585) 243-7060
Diane C. Murphy, Court Clerk
Fax: (585) 243-7067
E-mail: livingstonsandc@courts.state.ny.us

Surrogate's Court

2 Court Street
Geneseo, New York 14454
(585) 243-7095
Fax: (585) 243-7080
E-mail: tmoore@courts.state.ny.us

County Court

2 Court Street
Geneseo, New York 14454
(585) 243-7060
Fax: (585) 243-7067
E-mail: livingstonsandc@courts.state.ny.us

Family Court

2 Court Street
Geneseo, New York 14454
(585) 243-7070
Fax: (585) 243-7076

Sheriff

4 Court Street
Geneseo, New York 14454
(585) 243-7120
(585) 243-7926

Madison County

(Third Department, Sixth Judicial District)

Supreme Court

North Court Street
Wampsville, New York 13163
Marianne Kincaid, Chief Clerk
(315) 366-2267
Fax: (315) 366-2539

Surrogate's Court

138 North Court Street

Andrea L. Slivinski, Chief Clerk
Wampsville, New York 13163
(315) 366-2392
Fax: (315) 366-2539

County Court

North Court Street
Wampsville, New York 13163
Marianne Kincaid, Chief Clerk
(315) 366-2267
Fax: (315) 366-2539

Family Court

North Court Street
Wampsville, New York 13163
Cheryl Collins, Chief Clerk
(315) 366-2291
Fax: (315) 366-2828

City Court

Oneida Municipal Building
109 North Main Street
Oneida, New York 13421
Lynne Mondrick, Chief Clerk
(315) 363-1310
Fax: (315) 363-3230

Sheriff

County Correctional Facility
North Court Street
Wampsville, New York 13163
(315) 366-2289
Fax: (315) 366-2286

Monroe County

(Fourth Department, Seventh Judicial District)

Supreme Court

Hall of Justice
Room 545
99 Exchange Boulevard
Rochester, New York 14614

(585) 428-2020, 2331
Chief Clerk: (585) 428–5001
Fax: (585) 428-2190

Surrogate's Court

Hall of Justice
Room 541
99 Exchange Boulevard
Rochester, New York 14614
James L. Hendricks, Esq., Chief Clerk
(585) 428-5200
Fax: (585) 428-2650
E-Filing Specialist: esimpson@courts.state.ny.us
Email Inquiries: mannunzi@courts.state.ny.us

County Court

Hall of Justice
Room 545
99 Exchange Boulevard
Rochester, New York 14614
James L. Hendricks, Esq., Chief Clerk
(585) 428-2020, 2331
Chief Clerk: (585) 428–5001
Fax: (585) 428-2190

Family Court

Hall of Justice
Room 361
99 Exchange Boulevard
Rochester, New York 14614
(585) 428-5429
Fax: (585) 428-2597

City Court

Civil Branch
Hall of Justice
99 Exchange Boulevard Room 6
Rochester, New York 14614
Civil: (585) 428-2444
Fax: (585) 428-2588; Criminal: (585) 428-2447
Fax: (585) 428–2732

Sheriff

130 South Plymouth Avenue
Rochester, New York 14614
(585) 428-5780, 1
Fax: (585) 428-5851

Montgomery County

(Third Department, Fourth Judicial District)

Supreme Court

58 Broadway
P.O. Box 1500
Fonda, New York 12068
(518) 853-4516
Fax: (518)853-3596

Surrogate's Court

58 Broadway
P.O. Box 1500
Fonda, New York 12068
(518) 853-8108
Fax: (518)853-8230

County Court

58 Broadway
P.O. Box 1500
Fonda, New York 12068
(518) 853-4516
Fax: (518)853-3596

Family Court

58 Broadway
P.O. Box 1500
Fonda, New York 12068
(518) 853-8134
Fax: (518)853-8148

City Court

1 Guy Park Avenue Ext.
Public Safety Building, Room 208
Amsterdam, New York 12010
(518) 842-9510

Fax: (518) 843-8474

Sheriff

Sheriff's Office
200 Clark Drive
Fultonville, New York 12072
Civil: (518) 853-5515
Sheriff Fax: (518) 853-4969

Nassau County

(Second Department, Tenth Judicial District)

Supreme Court

100 Supreme Court Drive
Mineola, New York 11501
(516) 571-2904
Fax: (516) 571-1575

Surrogate's Court

262 Old Country Road
Mineola, New York 11501
(516) 571-2082
Fax: (516) 571-3803

County Court

262 Old Country Road
Mineola, New York 11501
(516) 571-2720
Fax: (516) 571-2160

Family Court

1200 Old Country Road
Westbury, New York 11590
(516) 571-9033
Fax: (516) 571-9335

First District Court

99 Main Street
Hempstead, New York 11550
Civil (516) 572-2256
Criminal (516) 572-2355
Fax: (516) 572-2507

Court Directory

Second District Court

99 Main Street
Hempstead, New York 11550
Civil (516) 572-2256
Criminal (516) 572-2355
Fax: (516) 572-2507

Third District Court

435 Middleneck Road
Great Neck, New York 11023
(516) 571-8400
Fax: (516) 571-8403, 02

Fourth District Court

99 Main Street
Hempstead, New York 11550
(516) 572-2261

City Court

13 Glen Street
Glen Cove, New York 11542
Heddy Amstel, Chief Clerk
(516) 676-0109
Fax: (516) 676-1570

1 West Chester Street
Long Beach, New York 11561
Joann Spiritis, Chief Clerk
(516) 431-1000
Fax: (516) 889-3511

Sheriff

Civil Bureau
Nassau County Office Building
240 Old Country Road
Mineola, New York 11501
(516) 571-2113
Fax: (516) 571-5086

New York County
(First Department, First Judicial District)

Supreme Court

Civil Term:

60 Centre Street
New York, New York 10007
80 Centre Street
New York, New York 10013
111 Centre Street
New York, New York 10013
71 Thomas Street
New York, New York 10013
(646) 386–3600
Fax: (212)374–3326
Criminal Term:
100 Centre Street
New York, New York 10013
Courtrooms also located at 111 Centre Street, 100 Centre Street
(646) 386-4000
Fax: (212) 374-3177
111 Centre Street
(646) 386-4300
Fax: (212) 374-2637

Surrogate's Court

31 Chambers Street
New York, New York 10007
Jane Passenaut, Chief Clerk
Jana Cohn, Deputy Chief Clerk
(646) 386-5000
Fax: (212) 374-3250

Family Court

60 Lafayette Street
New York, New York 10013
(646) 386-5200
Fax: (212) 748-5272

Civil Court

111 Centre Street
New York, New York 10013
Civil Gen'l Info. (646) 386-5700
Civil (646) 386-5600
Housing Gen'l Info. (646) 386-5750
Housing (646) 386-5500
Small Claims (646) 386-5480
Fax: (212) 374-8053

Criminal Court

100 Centre St., New York, New York 10013
(212) 374-5880
Fax: (212) 374-5293

Sheriff

31 Chambers Street Room 608
New York, New York 10007
(212) 788-8731
Fax: (212) 766-9666

Niagara County

(Fourth Department, Eighth Judicial District)

Supreme Court

775 3rd Street
Niagara Falls, New York 14302-1710
(716) 278-1800
Fax: (716) 278-1809

Surrogate's Court

175 Hawley Street
Lockport, New York 14094
(716) 439-7130
Fax: (716) 439-7319

County Court

175 Hawley Street
Lockport, New York 14094
(716) 439-7148
Fax: (716) 439-7157

Family Court

Two Locations:
175 Hawley Street, Lockport, New York 14094
Phone/fax: (716) 439-7172
Fax: (716) 439-7170
775 3rd Street, Niagara Falls, NY 14302
Phone/fax: (716) 278-1880
Fax: (716) 278-1877

City Court

One Locks Plaza

Lockport, New York 14094
Criminal: (716) 439-6671
Civil (716) 439-6660
Traffic (716) 439-6680
Fax: (716) 439-6684

Niagara Falls Municipal Complex
1925 Main Street
Niagara Falls, New York 14305
(716) 278-9800
Fax: (716) 278-9809

City Hall
216 Payne Avenue
North Tonawanda, New York 14120
(716) 693-1010
Fax: (716) 743-1754

Sheriff

P.O. Box 496
5526 Niagara Street
Lockport, New York 14094-1898
(716) 438-3393
Fax: (716) 438-3302

Oneida County

(Fourth Department, Fifth Judicial District)

Supreme Court

200 Elizabeth Street
Utica, New York 13501
Joseph P. Panella, Chief Clerk IV
Kathleen Aiello, Deputy Chief Clerk IV
(315) 798-5890
Fax: (315) 798-6436

Surrogate's Court

Oneida County Office Building
800 Park Avenue, 8th Floor
Utica, New York 13501
Martha R. Hoffman, Chief Clerk V
Kristine K. Pecheone, Chief Clerk II
Carra L. Applebee, Deputy Chief Clerk II

Court Directory

(315) 797-9230
Fax: (315) 797-9237

County Court

200 Elizabeth Street
Utica, New York 13501 (315)798-5890
Fax: (315)798-6438

Family Court

200 Elizabeth Street, Utica, New York 13501
Barbara A. Porta, Chief Clerk
Sherre Jackson, Chief Clerk III
Phone/fax: (315) 798-5925
Fax: (315) 798-6404
Special services:
Children's Center: (315) 793-6035
301 West Dominick Street, Rome, New York 13440
Barbara L. Tokarsky, Deputy Chief Clerk
Phone/fax: (315) 337-7492
Fax: (315) 336-3828
Hours: 8:30 a.m. - 4:30 p.m.
Summer: 8:30 a.m. - 4:00 p.m.

City Court

100 West Court Street
Rome, New York 13440
Eleanor T. Coniglio, Chief Clerk II
Susan G. Exner, Deputy Chief Clerk II
(315) 337-6440
Fax: (315) 338-0343

373 Sherrill Road
Sherrill, New York 13461
Carol A. Shea, Chief Clerk I
(315) 363-0996
Fax: (315) 363-1176

411 Oriskany Street West
Utica, New York 13502
Steven R. Pecheone, Chief Clerk IV
Lori O'Brien, Deputy Chief Clerk II
Civil: (315) 724-8157
Criminal: (315) 724-8227
Traffic (315) 724-8158

Fax::
Civil: (315) 792-8038
Criminal: (315) 724-0762
Traffic: (315) 724-0762

Sheriff

Law Enforcement Building
6065 Judd Road
Oriskany, New York 13424
(315) 765-2222
Fax: (315) 765-2205

Onondaga County

(Fourth Department, Fifth Judicial District)

Supreme Court

401 Montgomery Street
Syracuse, New York 13202
Patricia J. Noll, Chief Clerk VI
James E. Makowiec, Deputy Chief Clerk IV
Criminal: (315) 671-1020
Civil: (315) 671-1030
Fax: (315) 671-1176

Surrogate's Court

401 Montgomery Street
Syracuse, New York 13202
Ava S. Raphael, Chief Clerk VI
(315) 671-2100
Fax: (315) 671-1162

County Court

505 South State Street
Syracuse, New York 13202
(315) 671-1020
Fax: (315) 671-1191

Family Court

401 Montgomery Street
Syracuse, New York 13202
Bobette J. Morin, Chief Clerk VI
Sherree Jackson, Chief Clerk IV

Florence Walsh, Deputy Chief Clerk IV
(315) 671-2000
Fax: (315) 671-1163

City Court

505 South State Street
Suite 130
Syracuse, New York 13202
Criminal: (315) 671-2760
Civil: (315) 671-2782
Traffic: (315) 671-2770
Fax:
Criminal: (315) 671-2744
Civil: (315) 671-2741
Traffic: (315) 671-2743

Sheriff

407 South State Street
Syracuse, New York 13202
(315) 435-3044
Fax: (315) 435-2942

Ontario County

(Fourth Department, Seventh Judicial District)

Supreme Court

27 North Main Street
Canandaigua, New York 14424
Kathleen D. Sweeney, Chief Clerk
(585) 396-4239
Fax: (585) 396-4576
E-mail: ksweeney@courts.state.ny.us

Surrogate's Court

27 North Main Street
Canandaigua, New York 14424
(585) 396-4812
Fax: (585) 396-4576
E-mail: esimpson@courts.state.ny.us

County Court

27 North Main Street

Canandaigua, New York 14424
Kathleen D. Sweeney, Chief Clerk
(585) 396-4239
Fax: (585) 396-4576
E-mail: ksweeney@courts.state.ny.us

Family Court

27 North Main Street
Canandaigua, New York 14424
(585) 396-4272
Fax: (585) 396-4576 e-mail:
ontariofamilycourt@ courts.state.ny.us

City Court

2 North Main Street
Canandaigua, New York 14424
Lisa Schutz, Chief Clerk
(585) 396-5011
Fax: (585) 396-5012
E-mail: lschutz@courts.state.ny.us

Public Safety Building
255 Exchange Street
Geneva, New York 14456
(315) 789-6560
Fax: (315) 781-2802
E-mail: jguard@courts.state.ny.us

Sheriff

Sheriff's Office
74 Ontario Street
Canandaigua, New York 14424
(585) 394-4560
Fax: (585) 394-3245

Orange County

(Second Department, Ninth Judicial District)

Supreme Court

Government Center
255-285 Main Street
Goshen, New York 10924
(845) 291-3111

Fax: (845) 291-2595

Surrogate's Court

30 Park Place
Goshen, New York 10924
Joy V. Morse, Chief Clerk
Jeanne Smith, Deputy Chief Clerk
(845) 291-2193
Fax: (845) 291-2196

County Court

Government Center
255-285 Main Street
Goshen, New York 10924
(845) 291-3100
Fax: (845) 291-2525

Family Court

Government Center
255-285 Main Street
Goshen, New York 10924
(845) 291-3030
Fax: (845) 291-3054

City Court

2 James Street
Middletown, New York 10940
Linda Padden, Chief Clerk
Robin Siegel, Deputy Chief Clerk
(845) 346-4050
Fax: (845) 343-5737

300 Broadway
Newburgh, New York 12550
Sharon Reed, Chief Clerk
Irene Grant, Deputy Chief Clerk
(845) 483-8100
Fax: Civil/Traffic/Housing - (845) 565-0230
Criminal: (845) 565-0241

20 Hammond Street
Port Jervis, New York 12771
Catherine Quinn, Chief Clerk
(845) 858-4034

Fax: (845) 856-2767, 858-9883

Sheriff

110 Wells Farm Road
Goshen, New York 10924
(845) 294-4033
Fax: (845) 294-1590; (845) 291-7603 (Civil Unit)

Orleans County

(Fourth Department, Eighth Judicial District)

Supreme Court

1 South Main Street, Suite 3
Albion, New York 14411
Barbara Hale
(585) 589-5458
Fax: (585) 589-0632
E-mail: bhale@courts.state.ny.us

Surrogate's Court

1 South Main Street, Suite 3
Albion, New York 14411
Deborah Berry, Chief Clerk
(585) 589-4457
Fax: (585) 589-0632
E-mail: dberry@courts.state.ny.us

County Court

1 South Main Street, Suite 3
Albion, New York 14411
Barbara Hale
(585) 589-5458
Fax: (585) 589-0632
E-mail: bhale@courts.state.ny.us

Family Court

1 South Main Street, Suite 3
Albion, New York 14411
Laurie A.Bower, Chief Clerk
(585) 589-4457
Fax: (585) 589-0632
E-mail: lbower@courts.state.ny.us

Sheriff

13925 Route 31
Albion, New York 14411
(585) 589-5528
Fax: (585) 589-6761

Oswego County

(Fourth Department, Fifth Judicial District)

Supreme Court

25 E. Oneida Street
Oswego, New York 13126
Theresa M. Stephens, Chief Clerk II
(315) 349-3286
Fax: (315) 349-8525
County Clerk: (315) 349-8385

Surrogate's Court

25 E. Oneida Street
Oswego, New York 13126
Judy L. Cooper, Chief Clerk III
(315) 349-3295
Fax: (315) 349-8514

County Court

39 Churchill Road
Oswego, New York 13126
Theresa M. Stephens, Chief Clerk II
(315) 349-3280
Fax: (315) 349-8513
County Clerk: (315) 349-8385

Family Court

39 Churchill Road
Oswego, New York 13126
Sherryl A. Waldron, Chief Clerk IV
Kathleen Halstead, Deputy Chief Clerk II
(315) 349-3350
Fax: (315) 349-3457

City Court

Conway Municipal Building

20 West Oneida Street
Oswego, New York 13126
Cassie Kinney, Chief Clerk II
(315) 343-0415
Fax: (315) 343-0531

141 South First Street
Fulton, New York 13069
(315) 593-8400
Fax: (315) 592-3415

Sheriff

39 Churchill Road
Oswego, New York 13126-6613
(315) 349-3309
Civil Division Fax: (315) 349-3303
Sheriff Direct Fax: (315) 349-3483
Corrections Fax: (315) 349-3349

Otsego County

(Third Department, Sixth Judicial District)

Supreme Court

193 Main Street
Cooperstown, New York 13326
Gloria Chandler, Chief Clerk
(607) 547-4364
Fax: (607) 547-7567
County Clerk: (607) 547-4276
E-mail: gchandle@courts.state.ny.us

Surrogate's Court

County Office Building
197 Main Street
Cooperstown, New York 13326
Judy M. McBrearty, Chief Clerk
(607) 547-4213
Fax: (607) 547-7566

County Court

193 Main Street
Cooperstown, New York 13326
Gloria Chandler, Chief Clerk

(607) 547-4364
Fax: (607) 547-7567
County Clerk: (607) 547-4276
E-mail: gchandle@courts.state.ny.us

Family Court

Otsego County Annex Building
32 Chestnut Street
Cooperstown, New York 13326
Karen A. Nichols, Chief Clerk
Deborah J. Honohan, Deputy Chief Clerk
(607) 547-4264
Fax: (607) 547-6412

City Court

Public Safety Building
81 Main Street
Oneonta, New York 13820
(607) 432-4480
Fax: (607) 432-2328

Sheriff

Sheriff's Office

172 County Highway 33 West
Cooperstown, New York 13326
(607) 547-4271
Fax: (607) 547-6413

Putnam County

(Second Department, Ninth Judicial District)

Supreme Court
County Office Building
20 County Center
Carmel, New York 10512
Leonard A. Pace, Chief Clerk
Phone: (845) 208-7830
Fax: (845) 228-9611
County Clerk: (845) 225-3641
Judge John W. Sweeny, Jr.
44 Gleneida Avenue
Carmel, New York 10512

(845) 225-3641, Ext. 222
Fax: (845) 228-0837

Surrogate's Court

Historic Courthouse
44 Gleneida Avenue
Carmel, New York 10512
Phone: (845) 208-7860
Fax: (845) 228-9620
Linda Schwark, Chief Clerk

County Court

County Office Building
20 County Center
Carmel, New York 10512
Leonard A. Pace, Chief Clerk
Phone: (845) 208-7830
Fax: (845) 228-9611
County Clerk: (845) 225-3641

Family Court

County Office Building
20 County Center
Carmel, New York 10512
Karen O'Connor, Chief Clerk
(845) 208–7805
Fax: (845) 228-5761

Sheriff

3 County Center
Carmel, New York 10512
(845) 225-4300
Fax: (845) 228-5227

Queens County

(Second Department, Eleventh Judicial District)

Supreme Court

Civil Term:

88-11 Sutphin Boulevard
Jamaica, New York 11435
(718) 298-1000

Fax: (718) 298-1176

Criminal Term:

125-01 Queens Boulevard
Kew Gardens, New York 11415
(718) 298–1000
Fax: (718) 520-2494

Surrogate's Court

88-11 Sutphin Boulevard 7th Floor
Jamaica, New York 11435
(718) 298-0500

Family Court

151-20 Jamaica Avenue
Jamaica, New York 11432
(718) 298-0197
Fax: (718) 297-2826

Civil Court

Civil Court 89-17 Sutphin Boulevard
. Jamaica, New York 11435
Civil General Information: (646) 386-5700
Civil: (718) 262-7100
Fax: (718) 262-7107
Housing General Information: (646) 386-5750

Criminal Court

125-01 Queens Boulevard
Kew Gardens, New York 11415
(212) 374-5880
Fax: (718) 520-4712

Sheriff

144-06 94th Avenue
Jamaica, New York 11435
Family Court Warrants: (718) 298-7500
Private Sector: (718) 298-7550

Rensselaer County

(Third Department, Third Judicial District)

Supreme Court

80 Second Street

Troy, New York 12180
Richard F. Reilly, Chief Clerk
(518) 285-5025
Fax: (518) 270-3714
County Clerk: (518) 270-4090

Surrogate's Court

80 Second Street
Troy, New York 12180
(518) 285-5025
Fax: (518) 272-5452

County Court

80 Second Street
Troy, New York 12180
Richard F. Reilly, Chief Clerk
(518) 285-5025
Fax: (518) 270-3714
County Clerk: (518) 270-4090

Family Court

1504 Fifth Avenue
Troy, New York 12180-4107
Patricia Beeler, Chief Clerk
(518) 270-3761
Fax: (518) 272-6573
E-mail: pbeeler@courts.state. ny.us

City Court

505 Broadway
Rensselaer, New York 12144
(518) 462-6751
Fax: (518) 462-3307

51 State Street
Troy, New York 12180
(518) 273-2434
Fax: (518) 271-2360
Criminal and Traffic
51 State Street
Troy, New York 12180
[temporary address during renovations]
(518) 271-1602

Fax: (518) 274-2816

Sheriff

4000 Main Street
P.O.Box 389
Troy, New York 12181-0389
(518) 270-5448
Fax: (518) 270-5447

Richmond County

(Second Department, Second Judicial District)

Supreme Court

18 Richmond Terrace
Staten Island, New York 10301
(718) 675-8700
Fax: (718) 390-5435
County Clerk: (718) 390-5396

Criminal Court
67 Targee Street
Staten Island, New York 10304
(212) 374-5880
Fax: (718) 390-8405

Surrogate's Court

Courthouse
18 Richmond Terrace
Staten Island, New York 10301
(718) 390-5400
Fax: (718) 390-8741

Family Court

100 Richmond Terrace
Staten Island, New York 10301
(718) 675-8800
Fax: (718) 390-5247

Civil Court

927 Castleton Avenue
Staten Island, New York 10310
Civil General Information: (646) 386-5700
Civil: (718) 390-5417

Housing General Information: (646) 386-5750
Housing: (718) 390-5420
Small Claims: (718) 390-5421
Fax: (718) 390-8108

Under Sheriff

350 Saint Marks Place
Staten Island, New York 10301
(718) 815-8407
Fax: (718) 815-8416

Rockland County

(Second Department, Ninth Judicial District)

Supreme Court

1 South Main Street
New City, New York 10956
John F. Hussey, Chief Clerk
(845) 638-5393
Fax: (845) 638-5312
County Clerk: (845) 638-5070

Surrogate's Court

1 South Main Street 2nd Floor
New City, New York 10956
Virginia Athens, Chief Clerk
Amy Miller, Deputy Chief Clerk
(845) 638-5330
Fax: (845) 638-5632

County Court

1 South Main Street
New City, New York 10956
John F. Hussey, Chief Clerk
(845) 638-5393
Fax: (845) 638-5312
County Clerk: (845) 638-5070

Family Court

1 South Main Street Suite 300
New City, New York 10956
Anna K. Osovych, Chief Clerk

Diane Gould, Deputy Clerk
(845) 638-5300
Fax: (845) 638-5319

Sheriff

55 New Hempstead Road
New City, New York 10956
(845) 638-5456
Fax: (845) 638-5460

St. Lawrence County

(Third Department, Fourth Judicial District)

Supreme Court

48 Court Street
Canton, New York 13617-1194
Mary M. Farley, Esq., Principal Law Clerk
(315) 379-2219
Fax: (315) 379-2423
County Clerk: (315) 379-2237

Surrogate's Court

48 Court Street
Canton, New York 13617
John F. Richey, Esq., Principal Law Clerk
(518) 379-2217
Fax: (315) 379-2372

County Court

48 Court Street
Canton, New York 13617-1194
Stephen J. Easter, Esq., Principal Law Clerk
(315) 379-2219
Fax: (315) 379-2423
County Clerk: (315) 379-2237

Family Court

48 Court Street
Canton, New York 13617-1194
Chrisy Q. Bass, Chief Clerk
Deborah L. Darou, Deputy Chief Clerk
(315) 379-2410

Fax: (315) 386-3197

City Court

330 Ford Street, 2nd Floor, Room 15
Ogdensburg, New York 13669
Lisa Marie Meyer, Chief Clerk
(315) 393-3941
Fax: (315) 393-6839

Sheriff

48 Court Street
Canton, New York 13617
(315) 379-2222
Fax: (315) 379-0335

Saratoga County

(Third Department, Fourth Judicial District)

Supreme Court

Municipal Center
30 McMaster Street
Ballston Spa, New York 12020
(518) 885-2224
Fax: (518) 884-4758
County Clerk: (518) 885-2213

Surrogate's Court

Municipal Center
30 McMaster Street
Ballston Spa, New York 12020
(518) 884-4722
Fax: (518) 884-4774

County Court

Municipal Center
30 McMaster Street
Ballston Spa, New York 12020
(518) 885-2224
Fax: (518) 884-4758
County Clerk: (518) 885-2213

Family Court

35 West High Street

Ballston Spa, New York 12020
(518) 884-9207
Fax: (518) 884-9094

City Court

City Hall
36 North Main Street
Mechanicville, New York 12118
(518) 664-9876
Fax: (518) 664-8606

City Hall
474 Broadway, Suite 3
Saratoga Springs, New York 12866
(518) 584-1797
Fax: (518) 584–3097

Sheriff

6010 County Farm Road
Ballston Spa, New York 12020-0600
(518) 885-6761
Civil Division: (518) 885-2469
Fax: (518) 885-2453

Schenectady County

(Third Department, Fourth Judicial District)

Supreme Court

612 State Street
Schenectady, New York 12305
(518) 285-8401
Fax: (518) 388-4520
County Clerk: (518) 388-4225

Surrogate's Court

612 State Street
Schenectady, New York 12305
(518) 285-8455
Fax: (518) 377-6378

County Court

612 State Street
Schenectady, New York 12305

(518) 285-8401
Fax: (518) 388–4520
County Clerk: (518) 388–4225

Family Court

620 State Street
Schenectady, New York 12305
Melissa Mills, Chief Clerk
(518) 285-8435
Fax: (518) 393-1565

City Court

Civil Division:
City Hall
105 Jay Street
Schenectady, New York 12305
(518) 382-5077, 8
Fax: (518) 382-5080
Criminal Division:
531 Liberty Street
Schenectady, New York 12305
(518) 382-5239
Fax: (518) 382-5241

Sheriff

Schenectady County Correctional Facility
320 Veeder Avenue
Schenectady, New York 12307
(518) 388-4596
Civil: (518) 388-4304
Fax: (518) 393-5111

Schoharie County

(Third Department, Third Judicial District)

Supreme Court

Physical Address: 290 Main Street
Schoharie, New York 12157
F. Christian Spies, Chief Clerk
Mailing Address: PO Box 669
Schoharie, New York 12157
(518) 295-8342

Fax: (518) 295-7226
County Clerk: (518) 295-8316

Surrogate's Court

Physical Address: 290 Main Street
Schoharie, New York 12157
Mailing Address: PO Box 669
Schoharie, New York 12157
(518) 295-8387
Fax: (518) 295-8451

County Court

Physical Address: 290 Main Street
Schoharie, New York 12157
F. Christian Spies, Chief Clerk
Mailing Address: PO Box 669
Schoharie, New York 12157
(518) 295-8342
Fax: (518) 295-7226
County Clerk: (518) 295-83161

Family Court

Physical Address: 290 Main Street
Schoharie, New York 12157
Mailing Address: PO Box 669
Schoharie, New York 12157
(518) 295-8383
Fax: (518) 295-8451

Sheriff

157 Depot Lane
P.O. Box 689
Schoharie, New York 12157-0089
Administration: (518) 295-7066
Civil: (518) 296-8888, (518) 295-7080
Fax: (518) 295-7094

Schuyler County

(Third Department, Sixth Judicial District)

Supreme Court

105 9th Street Unit 35

Watkins Glen, New York 14891
Karen H. Morgan, Chief Clerk
(607) 535-7760
Fax: (607) 535-4918
County Clerk: (607) 535-8133

Surrogate's Court

105 9th Street Unit 35
Watkins Glen, New York 14891
(607) 535-7144
Fax: (607) 535-4918

County Court

105 9th Street Unit 35
Watkins Glen, New York 14891
Karen H. Morgan, Chief Clerk
(607) 535-7760
Fax: (607) 535-4918
County Clerk: (607) 535-8133

Family Court

105 9th Street Unit 35
Watkins Glen, New York 14891
Lynda L. LoPresti, Chief Clerk
(607) 535-7143
Fax: (607) 535-4918

Sheriff

106 10th Street
Watkins Glen, New York 14891
(607) 535-8222
Fax: (607) 535-8216

Seneca County

(Fourth Department, Seventh Judicial District)

Supreme Court

48 West Williams Street
Waterloo, New York 13165
(315) 539-7021
Fax: (315) 539-7929
E-mail: eyoung@courts.state.ny.us

County Clerk: (315) 539-1771

Surrogate's Court

48 West Williams Street
Waterloo, New York 13165
(315) 539-7531
Fax: (315) 539-326
E-mail: rcapozzi@courts.state.ny.us

County Court

48 West Williams Street
Waterloo, New York 13165
(315) 539-7021
Fax: (315) 539-7929
E-mail: eyoung@courts.state.ny.us
County Clerk: (315) 539-1771

Family Court

48 West Williams Street
Waterloo, New York 13165
(315) 539-4917
Fax: (315) 539-4225
E-mail: cbrown@courts.state.ny.us

Sheriff

44 West Williams Street
Waterloo, New York 13165
(315) 539-9241
Fax: (315) 539-0121

Steuben County

(Fourth Department, Seventh Judicial District)

Supreme Court

3 East Pulteney Square
Bath, New York 14810
William Deninger, Chief Clerk and Commissioner of Jurors
(607) 776-7879
Fax: (607) 776-5226
E-mail: steuben-superior@courts.state.ny.us
(607) 776-9631 Ext. 3203

Surrogate's Court

3 East Pulteney Square

Bath, New York 14810
(607) 776-7126
Fax: (607) 776-4987
E-mail: pplank@courts.state.ny.us

County Court

3 East Pulteney Square
Bath, New York 14810
William Deninger, Chief Clerk and Commissioner of Jurors
(607) 776-7879
Fax: (607) 776-5226
E-mail: steuben-superior@courts.state.ny.us
County Clerk: (607) 776-9631, Ext. 3203

Family Court

3 East Pulteney Square
Bath, New York 14810
(607) 664-2136
Fax: (607) 776-7857
E-mail: Steubenfamilycourt@courts.state.ny.us

City Court

12 Civic Center Plaza
Corning, New York 14830
(607) 936-4111
Fax: (607) 936-0519

82 Main Street P.O. Box 627
Hornell, New York 14843-0627
(607) 324-7531
Fax: (607) 324-6325
E-mail: lbgriffi@courts.state.ny.us

Sheriff

Steuben County Jail
7007 Rumsey Street Extension
Bath, New York 14810
(607) 776-7009
Fax: (607) 776-7100

Suffolk County

(Second Department, Tenth Judicial District)

Supreme Court

1 Rivington Street
Riverhead, New York 11901
(631) 852-2333
Fax: (631) 852-2340

Surrogate's Court

County Center Building
320 Center Drive
Riverhead, New York 11901
(631) 852-1745
Fax: (631) 852-1777

County Court

210 Center Drive
Riverhead, New York 11901
Victor V. Rossomano, Chief Clerk
Frank Tropea, Deputy Chief Clerk
(631) 852-2121
Fax: (631) 852-2568
County Clerk: (631) 852-2000

District Court

First District Court

Civil:
3105 Veterans' Memorial Highway
Ronkonkoma, New York 11779
Len Brown, Associate Court Clerk
(631) 854-9676
Fax: (631) 854-9681
Criminal: 400 Carleton Avenue P.O. Box 9075
Central Islip, New York 11722
(631) 853-7500

Second District Court

30 East Hoffman Avenue
Lindenhurst, New York 11757
Diana Musso, Associate Court Clerk

(631) 854-1950
Fax: (631) 854-1956

Third District Court

1850 New York Avenue
Huntington Station, New York 11746
Marie Mustello, Associate Court Clerk
(631) 854-4545
Fax: (631) 854-4549

Fourth District Court

County Complex
Building C158
Veterans Memorial Highway
Hauppauge, New York 11787
Mary J. Tagarelli, Associate Court Clerk
(631) 853-5408
Fax: (631) 853-5951

Fifth District Court

Civil: 3105 Veterans Memorial Highway
Ronkonkoma, New York 11779
Elaine R. Sorkin, Associate Court Clerk
(631) 854-9676
Fax: (631) 854-9681
Criminal: 400 Carleton Avenue P.O. Box 9075
Central Islip, New York 11722
(631) 853-7500

Sixth District Court

150 West Main Street
Patchogue, New York 11772
William J. Dobbins, Associate Court Clerk
(631) 854-1440
Fax: (631) 854-1444

Family Court

400 Carleton Avenue
Central Islip, New York 11722
Patricia S. Herlihy, Chief Clerk
Linda Affourtit, Deputy Chief Clerk
Millbrook Office Campus:

899 East Main Street, Suite 308
Riverhead, New York 11901
Islip: (631) 853-4648
Fax: (631) 853-4283
Riverhead: (631) 852-3905
Ffax: (631) 852-2851

Sheriff

100 Center Drive
Riverhead, New York 11901-3389
(631) 852-2200

Sullivan County

(Third Department, Third Judicial District)

Supreme Court

414 Broadway
Monticello, New York 12701
Supreme: (845)794-9776
County: (845) 794-1248
Fax: (845) 791-6170
E-mail:elilley@courts.state.ny.us County Clerk: (845) 794-4066

Surrogate's Court

County Government Center
100 North Street Room 250
P.O. Box 5012
Monticello, New York 12701
(845) 807-0690
Fax: (845) 794-0310
E-mail: lhering@courts.state.ny.us

County Court

414 Broadway
Monticello, New York 12701
Supreme: (845) 794-9776
County:- (845) 794-1248
Fax: (845) 791-6170
E-mail:elilley@courts.state.ny.us
County Clerk: (845) 794-4066

Family Court

County Government Center

100 North Street
Monticello, New York 12701
(845) 807-0650
Fax: (845) 794-0199

Sheriff

County Jail
4 Bushnell Avenue
Monticello, New York 12701
(845) 794-7102
Fax: (845) 794-4060

Tioga County

(Third Department, Sixth Judicial District)

Supreme Court

Court Annex
20 Court Street
Owego, New York 13827
Joann Peet, Chief Clerk
(607) 687-0544
Fax: (607) 687-5680
County Clerk: (607) 687-8660

Surrogate's Court

Court Annex
20 Court Street
Owego, New York 13827
(607) 687-1303
Fax: (607) 687-3240

County Court

Court Annex
20 Court Street
Owego, New York 13827
Joann Peet, Chief Clerk
(607) 687-0544
Fax: (607) 687-5680
County Clerk: (607) 687-8660

Family Court

Court Annex

20 Court Street
Owego, New York 13827
(607) 687-1730
Fax: (607) 687-3240

Sheriff

103 Corporate Drive
Owego, New York 13827
(607) 687-1010
Fax: (607) 687-6755

Tompkins County

(Third Department, Sixth Judicial District)

Supreme Court

320 North Tioga Street
P.O. Box 70
Ithaca, New York 14851-0070
Paula M. Nicols, Chief Clerk
(607) 272-0466
Fax: (607) 256-0301
County Clerk: (607) 274-5431

Surrogate's Court

320 North Tioga Street
P.O. Box 70
Ithaca, New York 14851-0070
(607) 277-0622
Fax: (607) 256-2572

County Court

320 North Tioga Street
P.O. Box 70
Ithaca, New York 14851-0070
Paula M. Nicols, Chief Clerk
(607) 272-0466
Fax: (607) 256-0301
County Clerk: (607) 274-5431

Family Court

320 North Tioga Street
P.O. Box 70

Ithaca, New York 14851-0070
(607) 277-1517
Fax: (607) 277-5027

City Court

118 East Clinton Street
Ithaca, New York 14850
(607) 273-2263
Fax: (607) 277-3702

Sheriff

779 Warren Road
Ithaca, New York 14850
(607) 257-1345
Fax: (607) 266-5436

Ulster County

(Third Department, Third Judicial District)

Supreme Court

285 Wall Street
Kingston, New York 12401
(845) 340-3377
Fax: (845) 340-3387
County Clerk: (845) 340-3288

Surrogate's Court

240 Fair Street 3rd Floor
Kingston, New York 12401
(845) 340-3350, 3348
Fax: (845) 340-3352

County Court

285 Wall Street
Kingston, New York 12401
(845) 340-3377
Fax: (845) 340-3387
County Clerk: (845) 340-3288

Family Court

16 Lucas Avenue
Kingston, New York 12401

(845) 340-3600
Fax: (845) 340-3626

City Court

1 Garraghan Drive
Kingston, New York 12401
(845) 338-2974
Fax: (845) 338-1443

Sheriff

129 Schwenk Drive
Kingston, New York 12401-2941
(845) 340-3802
Fax: (845) 334-8125

Warren County

(Third Department, Fourth Judicial District)

Supreme Court

Warren County Municipal Center
1340 State Route 9
Lake George, New York 12845
Joseph Hughes, Jr., Chief Clerk
Pamela Waite, Deputy Chief Clerk
(518) 761-6430/6431
Fax: (518) 761-6253

Surrogate's Court

Warren County Municipal Center
1340 State Route 9
Lake George, New York 12845
Deborah Ricci, Chief Clerk
(518) 761-6514
Fax: (518) 761-6511

County Court

Warren County Municipal Center
1340 State Route 9
Lake George, New York 12845
Joseph Hughes, Jr., Chief Clerk
Pamela Waite, Deputy Chief Clerk
(518) 761-6430/6431

Fax: (518) 761-6253

Family Court

Warren County Municipal Center
1340 State Route 9
Lake George, New York 12845
AnneMarie Lavigne, Chief Clerk
(518) 761-6500
Fax: (518) 761-6230

City Court

City Hall
42 Ridge Street
Glens Falls, New York 12801
Philip Simms, Chief Clerk
(518) 798-4714
Fax: (518) 798-0137

Sheriff

Warren County Municipal Center
1340 State Route 9
Lake George, New York 12845-9803
(518) 761-6477
Fax: (518) 761-6234

Washington County

(Third Department, Fourth Judicial District)

Supreme Court

383 Broadway
Fort Edward, New York 12828
(518) 746-2521
Fax: (518) 746-2519
County Clerk: (518) 746-2170

Surrogate's Court

383 Broadway
Fort Edward, New York 12828
Phone/fax: (518) 746-2545
Fax: (518) 746-2547

County Court

383 Broadway

Fort Edward, New York 12828
(518) 746-2521
Fax: (518) 746-2519
County Clerk: (518) 746-2170

Family Court

383 Broadway
Fort Edward, New York 12828
(518) 746-2501
Fax: (518) 746-2503

Sheriff

383 Broadway
Fort Edward, New York 12828
(518) 854-9245
Main Fax: (518) 746-2483
Substation Fax: (518) 854-9720

Wayne County

(Fourth Department, Seventh Judicial District)

Supreme Court

Hall of Justice
54 Broad Street Suite 106
Lyons, New York 14489
Ellis W. Bozzolo, Chief Clerk and Commissioner of Jurors
(315) 946-5459
Fax: (315) 946-5456
County Clerk: (315) 946-7470

Surrogate's Court

Hall of Justice
54 Broad Street Suite 106
Lyons, New York 14489
(315) 946-5430
Fax: (315) 946-5433

County Court

Hall of Justice
54 Broad Street Suite 106
Lyons, New York 14489
(315) 946-5459

Fax: (315) 946-5456
County Clerk (315) 946-7470

Family Court

Hall of Justice
54 Broad Street Suite 106
Lyons, New York 14489
(315) 946-5420
Fax: (315) 946-5456

Sheriff

County Jail
7368 Route 31
Lyons, New York 14489-9107
(315) 946-9711
Fax: (315) 946-5811

Westchester County

(Second Department, Ninth Judicial District)

Supreme Court

111 Dr. Martin Luther King, Jr. Boulevard
White Plains, New York 10601
Donna Minort, Chief Clerk
Ronda Brown, Deputy Chief Clerk
Elizabeth Pace, Deputy Chief Clerk
(914) 824-5300
Fax: (914) 995-2194
County Clerk: (914) 995-3070

Surrogate's Court

111 Dr. Martin Luther King Jr. Boulevard
19th Floor
White Plains, New York 10601
Charles T. Scott, Chief Clerk
Johanna K. O'Brien, Deputy Chief Clerk
(914) 824-5656
Fax: (914) 995-3728

County Court

111 Dr. Martin Luther King, Jr. Boulevard
White Plains, New York 10601

Donna Minort, Chief Clerk
Ronda Brown, Deputy Chief Clerk
Elizabeth Pace, Deputy Chief Clerk
(914) 824-5300
Fax: (914) 995-2194
County Clerk: (914) 995-3070

Family Court

111 Dr. Martin Luther King, Jr. Boulevard
White Plains, New York 10601
James McAllister, Chief Clerk
Sonia Soto & Queenie Anderson, Deputy Chief Clerks
(914) 824-5500
Fax: (914) 995-8650
420 North Avenue
New Rochelle, New York 10801
James McAllister, Chief Clerk
Sonia Soto & Queenie Anderson, Deputy Chief Clerks
(914) 831-6590
Fax: (914) 813-5580
53 South Broadway
Yonkers, New York 10701
James McAllister, Chief Clerk
Sonia Soto & Queenie Anderson, Deputy Chief Clerks
(914) 831-6555
Fax: (914) 231-3016

City Court

Roosevelt Square
Mount Vernon, New York 10550
Lawrence Darden, Chief Clerk
Judith Hicks, Deputy Chief Clerk
Phone/fax: (914) 665-2400
Fax: (914) 699-1230

475 North Avenue
New Rochelle, New York 10801
James Generoso, Chief Clerk
Victoria Kane, Deputy Chief Clerk
(914) 654-2207
Fax: (914) 654-0344

2 Nelson Avenue

Peekskill, New York 10566
Janice Laughlin, Chief Clerk
(914) 831-6480
Fax: (914) 736-1889

21 Third Street
Rye, New York 10580
Antoinette Cipriano, Chief Clerk
(914) 831-6400
Fax: (914) 967-3308

77 South Lexington Avenue
White Plains, New York 10601
Patricia Lupi, Chief Clerk
Lynn Ward, Deputy Chief Clerk
(914) 824-5675
Fax: (914) 422-6058

100 South Broadway
Yonkers, New York 10701
Marcia Garcia, Chief Clerk
(914) 377-6326
Fax: (914) 377-6395

Sheriff

Westchester County Police
Saw Mill River Parkway
Hawthorne, New York 10532
(914) 864-7700
Fax: (914) 741-4444

Wyoming County

(Fourth Department, Eighth Judicial District)

Supreme Court

147 North Main Street
Warsaw, New York 14569
Rebecca Miller, Chief Clerk
(585) 786-2253
Fax: (585) 786-2818
Commissioner of Jurors: (585) 786-8756
Fax: (585) 786-2818
County Clerk (585) 786-8810

Court Directory

Surrogate's Court

147 North Main Street
Warsaw, New York 14569
William Beyer, Chief Clerk
Susan Scriven, Deputy Chief Clerk
E-mails: wbeyer@courts.state.ny.us
sscriven@courts.state.ny.us
(585) 786-3148
Fax: (585) 786-3800

County Court

147 North Main Street
Warsaw, New York 14569
Rebecca Miller, Chief Clerk
(585) 786-2253
Fax: (585) 786-2818
Commissioner of Jurors: (585) 786-8756
Fax: (585) 786-2818
County Clerk: (585) 786-8810

Family Court

147 North Main Street
Warsaw, New York 14569
Jacqueline Domkowski, Chief Clerk
Susan Scriven, Deputy Chief Clerk
E-mails: jdomkows@courts.state.ny.us
sscriven@courts.state.ny.us
(585) 786-3148
Fax: (585) 786-3800

Sheriff

151 North Main Street
Warsaw, New York 14569
(716) 786-8989
Fax: (716) 786-8961

Yates County

(Fourth Department, Seventh Judicial District)

Supreme Court

415 Liberty Street
Penn Yan, New York 14527

Margaret D. DiMartino, Chief Clerk
(315) 536-5126
Fax: (315) 536-5190
County Clerk: (315) 536-5120

Surrogate's Court

415 Liberty Street
Penn Yan, New York 14527
(315) 536-5130
Fax: (315) 536-5190

County Court

415 Liberty Street
Penn Yan, New York 14527
(315) 536-5126
Fax: (315) 536-5190
County Clerk: (315) 536-5120

Family Court

415 Liberty Street
Penn Yan, New York 14527
(315) 536-5127
Fax: (315) 536-5190

Sheriff

Public Safety Building
227 Main Street
Penn Yan, New York 14527
(315) 536-5182
Fax: (315) 572-4365

INDEX

[References are to the CPLR and to Uniform Rules (designated as "UR").]

A

I-1

[References are to the CPLR and to Uniform Rules (designated as "UR").]

[References are to the CPLR and to Uniform Rules (designated as "UR").]

[References are to the CPLR and to Uniform Rules (designated as "UR").]

[References are to the CPLR and to Uniform Rules (designated as "UR").]

[References are to the CPLR and to Uniform Rules (designated as "UR").]

AUCTIONS—Cont.
Money judgments, enforcement of—Cont.
Real property, sale of . . . 5236(a)

AUDIO TAPES
Disclosure . . . 3101(i)

AUTHENTICATION OF EVIDENCE
Newspapers and periodicals of general circulation, self-authentication of . . . 4532
Official record of court or government office
. . . 4540

B

BAIL
Habeas corpus proceeding . . . 7010(b)

BANKS AND BANKING
Enforcement of money judgments under CPLR (See ENFORCEMENT OF MONEY JUDGMENTS)

BATTERY
Statute of limitations period for action based on, one-year . . . 215(3)

BCL (See BUSINESS CORPORATION LAW (BCL))

BENCH TRIAL
Decision of court . . . 4213
Issues to be decided by court . . . 4211

BILL OF PARTICULARS
Amendment . . . 3042(b)
Arbitration of damages in medical, dental or podiatric malpractice actions . . . 3045
Defined . . . 3041
Demand for . . . 3042
Dental malpractice actions, arbitration of damages in . . . 3045
Failure to respond or comply with demand . . . 3042(c); 3042(d)
Improper or unduly burdensome demands, service of . . . 3042(e)
Medical malpractice actions, arbitration of damages in . . . 3045
Penalties for refusal to comply . . . 3042(d)
Personal injury actions . . . 3043
Podiatric malpractice actions, arbitration of damages in . . . 3045
Procedure for . . . 3042
Service of improper or unduly burdensome demands . . . 3042(e)

BILL OF PARTICULARS—Cont.
Supplemental without leave of court in personal injury actions . . . 3043(b)
Unduly burdensome demands, service of
. . . 3042(e)
Verification . . . 3044

BLOOD TESTS
DNA tests, admissibility of . . . 4518(d)

BONDS (See UNDERTAKINGS)

BOOKS AND RECORDS
Duces tecum subpoena to produce (See SUBPOENAS, subhead: Duces tecum subpoenas)

BRIEFS (See APPEALS)

BURDEN OF PROOF
Assumption of risk . . . 1412
Contributory negligence or assumption of risk . . . 1412
Forfeiture of proceeds of crime
Attachment, vacating or modifying
. . . 1329(2)
Requirements . . . 1311(3)
Jointly liable persons, limited liability of
. . . 1603

BUSINESS CORPORATION LAW (BCL)
Selected provisions . . . Appendix

BUSINESS RECORDS
Generally . . . 4518(a)
Certification of . . . 3122–a
Childbirth and pregnancy costs, admissibility of bills or records relating to . . . 4518(g)
DNA test, admissibility of . . . 4518(d); 4518(e)
Electronic records . . . 4518(a)
Hospital bills . . . 4518(b)
Hospital records . . . 4518
Ordinary course of business, kept in
. . . 4539
Reproduction or copy of original, admissibility of . . . 4518(a)

C

CALENDAR PRACTICE
Abandoned cases, dismissal of . . . 3404
Case management . . . UR 202.22
Dental malpractice actions (See DENTAL, MEDICAL OR PODIATRIC MALPRACTICE ACTIONS)

[References are to the CPLR and to Uniform Rules (designated as "UR").]

[References are to the CPLR and to Uniform Rules (designated as "UR").]

[References are to the CPLR and to Uniform Rules (designated as "UR").]

[References are to the CPLR and to Uniform Rules (designated as "UR").]

COMPROMISE AND SETTLEMENT—Cont.

Equal Access to Justice Act application where final judgment or settlement . . . 8602(c)

Evidence of, admissibility of . . . 4547

Forfeiture actions, filing settlement agreement in . . . 1311(11)

Incompetent, settlement by (See INCOMPETENTS AND INCOMPETENCY)

Infant, settlement by (See CHILDREN)

Malpractice actions, periodic payment of judgments in . . . 5034

Mortgage foreclosure actions
> Mandatory settlement . . . 3408
>> Uniform rules for supreme court and county court . . . UR 202.12–a

Offer to . . . 3221

Periodic payment of judgments
> Dental, medical or podiatric malpractice actions . . . 5034
> Personal injury, injury to property and wrongful death actions . . . 5047

Prompt payment following settlement . . . 5003–a

Uniform rules for supreme court and county court
> Residential mortgage foreclosure actions . . . UR 202.12–a
> Supreme court actions, applications for settlement of . . . UR 202.4

COMPROMISE OR SETTLEMENT

Workers' compensation settlements and uniform rules for supreme court and county court . . . UR 202.66

CONDEMNATION

Disclosure of appraisals for . . . 3140

Uniform rules for supreme court and county court
> Appraisal reports, exchange of . . . UR 202.61
> Award paid to other than named awardee . . . UR 202.62

CONFERENCES

Preliminary conferences . . . UR 202.12

Pre-trial (See PRE-TRIAL CONFERENCES)

CONFESSIONS

Arbitration and award by . . . 7508

Joint debtors, by . . . 3218(d)

Judgment by . . . 3218

CONFIDENTIAL COMMUNICATIONS

Attorney-client (See ATTORNEY-CLIENT PRIVILEGE)

Chiropractors . . . 4504

Clergy-penitent . . . 4505

Dentists . . . 4504

Disclosure . . . 3101(b)

Eavesdropping evidence . . . 4506

Electronic communications, privileged status of . . . 4548

Husband-wife . . . 4502(b)

Library records . . . 4509

Medical persons . . . 4504

Nurses . . . 4504

Physicians . . . 4504

Podiatrists . . . 4504

Psychologist-patient . . . 4507

Rape crisis counselor . . . 4510

Social worker . . . 4508

CONSERVATORS AND CONSERVATORSHIPS

Arbitration of controversy involving . . . 1209

Costs, liability of . . . 1205

Disposition of proceeds of claim of conservatee . . . 1206

Representation . . . 1201

Settlement of claim by
> Adverse party, preparation of papers for . . . 1208(f)
> Affidavits . . . 1208(a); 1208(b)
> Appearance before court . . . 1208(d)
> Attorney's affidavit . . . 1208(b)
> Conflict of interest . . . 1208(e)
> Hospital report . . . 1208(c)
> Medical report . . . 1208(c)
> Notice . . . 1207
> Order of settlement . . . 1207
> Papers required . . . 1208
> Procedure . . . 1208
> Special proceeding . . . 1207

Substitution of . . . 1016

Venue based on residence . . . 503(b)

CONSOLIDATION OF ACTIONS

Generally . . . 602(a)

Costs awarded to prevailing party . . . 8104

Pending cases in different courts . . . 602(b)

CONSTABLES (See SHERIFFS)

CONSTITUTION

New York State Constitution; text . . . Appendix

[References are to the CPLR and to Uniform Rules (designated as "UR").]

CONSTITUTIONAL ISSUES
CPLR; effect of unconstitutionality in part
. . . 10004
Notice to Attorney General where constitutionality in issue . . . 1012(b)

CONSUMER CREDIT TRANSACTIONS
Defined . . . 105(f)
Summons for actions based on . . . 305(a)
Venue
    Improper venue . . . 513
    Residence, based on . . . 503(f)

CONTEMPT
Enforcement of judgment by (See JUDGMENT)

CONTINUANCES
Motion for . . . 4402

CONTRACTS
Breach of contract actions, interest in
. . . 5001(a)
Election of remedies for action on
. . . 3002(c)
Installment contracts, validity of confession
of judgment before default on . . . 3201
Liquidate damages conditionally, offer to
. . . 3220
Print size and legibility, evidentiary requirements for . . . 4544
Rescission of contract . . . 3002(e)
Simplified procedure for court determination
of disputes involving contract to submit
(See SIMPLIFIED PROCEDURE FOR
COURT DETERMINATION OF DISPUTES)
Statute of limitations for action on (See
STATUTE OF LIMITATIONS)
Tender of payment to satisfy claim
. . . 3219
Venue, contractual provisions fixing
. . . 501

CONTRIBUTION
Amount of . . . 1402
Claim for . . . 1401
Indemnity right preserved . . . 1404(b)
Procedure for claiming . . . 1403
Rights of persons entitled to damages not
affected . . . 1404(a)
Subrogation right preserved . . . 1404(b)

CONTRIBUTORY NEGLIGENCE (See
NEGLIGENCE ACTIONS)

CONVERSION OF PROPERTY
Election of remedies . . . 3002(c)

CORPORATIONS
Attorney, appearing by . . . 321(a)
Business Corporation Law; selected provisions . . . Appendix
Directors and officers (See DIRECTORS
AND OFFICERS)
Dissolution of
    Proof required under uniform rules for
        supreme court and county court for
        . . . UR 202.51
    Substitution of parties upon . . . 1017
Domestic corporation defined . . . 105(h)
Foreign corporations (See FOREIGN CORPORATIONS)
Officers (See DIRECTORS AND OFFICERS)
Personal service upon . . . 311(a); 311(b)
Pleadings (See PLEADINGS)
Service upon . . . 311(a); 311(b)
Six-year statute of limitations period for corporation's action against director, officer or
stockholder . . . 213(7)
Substitution of parties upon dissolution of
corporation . . . 1017
Venue . . . 503(c)

COSTS AND FEES
Acknowledgments . . . 8009
Additional allowances (See DISBURSEMENTS AND ADDITIONAL ALLOWANCES)
Amount of costs awarded to prevailing party
(See subhead: Award of costs to prevailing
party)
Appeals
    Appellate courts, civil appeals and proceedings before . . . 8022
    Prevailing party, award of costs to
        Generally . . . 8107
            Amount of costs . . . 8203; 8204
        Taxable disbursements . . . 8301(a)
Arbitration as to fees and expenses involved
    Generally . . . 3405; 7513
    Health care arbitration (See HEALTH
        CARE ARBITRATION)
Attorneys' fees (See ATTORNEYS' FEES)
Attorney-trustee, advance payment to
. . . 8005
Award of costs to prevailing party
    Generally . . . 8101

[References are to the CPLR and to Uniform Rules (designated as "UR").]

[References are to the CPLR and to Uniform Rules (designated as "UR").]

[References are to the CPLR and to Uniform Rules (designated as "UR").]

[References are to the CPLR and to Uniform Rules (designated as "UR").]

[References are to the CPLR and to Uniform Rules (designated as "UR").]

[References are to the CPLR and to Uniform Rules (designated as "UR").]

[References are to the CPLR and to Uniform Rules (designated as "UR").]

DRL (See DOMESTIC RELATIONS LAW (DRL))

DUCES TECUM SUBPOENAS (See SUBPOENAS)

E

EARNINGS (See INCOME)

EAVESDROPPING
Admissibility as evidence . . . 4506
Suppression of evidence, motion for
. . . 4506

EDUCATION
Continuing legal education, mandatory; selected provisions . . . Appendix
Education Law; selected provisions . . . Appendix
Infant's support, allowance for . . . 1211
Tuition savings program trust fund payment monies, exemption from enforcement of money judgments against . . . 5205(j)

ELECTION LAW
Applications to Supreme Court pursuant to . . . UR 202.64

ELECTION OF REMEDIES
Agent and undisclosed principal, action against . . . 3002(b)
Contract, action on . . . 3002(c); 3002(d)
Conversion of property . . . 3002(c)
Damages, claim for . . . 3002(e)
Rescission of contract . . . 3002(e)
Several persons, action against . . . 3002(a)

ELECTRONIC TRANSMISSIONS
County court, filing papers in . . . UR 202.5–b
Depositions taken by telephone or other electronic means . . . 3113(d)
Privileged status of electronic communications . . . 4548
Service of summons and papers (See SERVICE OF SUMMONS AND PAPERS, subhead: Electronic means, by)
Supreme court, filing papers in . . . UR 202.5–b
Uniform rules for supreme court and county court . . . UR 202.5–b

EMINENT DOMAIN (See CONDEMNATION)

EMPLOYEES
Depositions . . . 3106(b); 3106(d)
Discrimination against employees and prospective employees based on wage assignment or income execution . . . 5252

ENCUMBRANCES
Statute of limitations period for commencement of action for breach of covenant of seizin or against . . . 206(c)

ENFORCEMENT OF MONEY JUDGMENTS
Generally . . . 5101; 5201
Adverse claims, proceedings to determine . . . 5239
Animal trained to assist disabled person; exemption . . . 5205(h)(2)
Appeal, release of lien or levy upon . . . 5204
Armed forces members, exemption of personal property of . . . 5205(e)
Arrest of judgment debtor . . . 5250
Auctions, public
Personal property . . . 5233(a)
Real property . . . 5236(a)
Bank accounts
Municipal corporation as judgment creditor, caption on restraining notice indicating . . . 5222–a(i)
New York State as judgment creditor, caption on restraining notice indicating . . . 5222–a(i)
Procedures for issuing restraining notice against person's . . . 5222–a
Restraining notice . . . 5222–a
Service of restraining notice . . . 5222–a(b)
Before entry of judgment . . . 5229
Commencement of proceedings . . . 5221
Compensatory damages awarded to prisoner, exemption of . . . 5205(k)
Contempt, court's power to punish for . . . 5210
Death of judgment debtor, enforcement after . . . 5208
Debts owed to judgment debtor, payment of . . . 5227
Debt subject to enforcement . . . 5201(a)
Delivery of judgment debtor's property . . . 5225
Directions to sheriff . . . 5238

[References are to the CPLR and to Uniform Rules (designated as "UR").]

[References are to the CPLR and to Uniform Rules (designated as "UR").]

[References are to the CPLR and to Uniform Rules (designated as "UR").]

ENFORCEMENT OF MONEY JUDGMENTS—Cont.
Support enforcement—Cont.
    Medical support execution
       . . . 5241(b)(2); 5241(c)(2)
    Mistake of fact, determination of
       . . . 5241(e)
    Notice
       Debtor, to . . . 5241(d)
       Restraining notice . . . 5222
    Order of support defined . . . 5241(a)
    Priority . . . 5241(h)
    Qualified medical child support order
       . . . 5241(b)(2)(i)
    Restraining notice . . . 5222
Title to real property sold, failure of
    . . . 5237
Trust exemption
    Generally . . . 5205(c)
    Tuition savings program trust fund payment monies . . . 5205(j)
Tuition savings program trust fund payment monies, exemption of . . . 5205(j)
Withholding of income . . . 5231

ENGINEERS
Dismissal motions in cases involving
    . . . 3211(h)
Statute of limitations period for action against licensed, ten-year . . . 214–d
Summary judgment motion in cases involving . . . 3212(i)

ENTERPRISE CORRUPTION
Civil actions notice . . . 1355
Civil remedies . . . 1353
Joinder of party . . . 1354

EPTL (See ESTATES, POWERS AND TRUSTS LAW (EPTL))

EQUAL ACCESS TO JUSTICE ACT
Amount of fees and expenses . . . 8602(b)
Applicability of . . . 8605
Application for fees . . . 8601(b)
Application of Article 86 . . . 8602(a)
Definitions . . . 8602
Eligibility for fees and expenses
    . . . 8602(d)
Final judgment or settlement . . . 8602(c)
Intent of Article 86 . . . 8600
Interest on award while appeal pending
    . . . 8603
Position of state defined . . . 8602(e)
Prevailing party defined . . . 8602(f)

EQUAL ACCESS TO JUSTICE ACT—Cont.
Report of awards made pursuant to
    . . . 8604
Short title . . . 8600
State defined . . . 8602(g)
When fees awarded . . . 8601(a)

ERRORS
Correction of . . . 2001
Court ruling, in . . . 2002
Depositions (See DEPOSITIONS)

ESTATES
Guardian of infant, direction as to management of estate by . . . 1210(d)

ESTATES, POWERS AND TRUSTS LAW (EPTL)
Selected provisions . . . Appendix

EVIDENCE
Acknowledged, proved or certified writing
    . . . 4538
Admission to practice . . . 9406
Agriculture Department, inspection certificate issued by . . . 4529
Arbitration . . . 7506(c)
Authentication
    Newspapers and periodicals of general circulation, self-authentication of
       . . . 4532
    Official record of court or government office . . . 4540
Burden of proof (See BURDEN OF PROOF)
Business records (See BUSINESS RECORDS)
Collateral source payment . . . 4545
Compromise or settlement, admissibility of evidence of . . . 4547
Confidential communications (See CONFIDENTIAL COMMUNICATIONS)
Contracts, requirements for print size and legibility of . . . 4544
Damages
    Joint tortfeasor, proof of payment by
       . . . 4533–b
    Prima facie proof of . . . 4533–a
Default judgment . . . 3215(f)
Depositions (See DEPOSITIONS)
Diagnostic tests, admissibility of graphic, numerical, symbolic or pictorial representations of . . . 4532–a
Disclosure (See DISCLOSURE)
Eavesdropping evidence . . . 4506

[References are to the CPLR and to Uniform Rules (designated as "UR").]

[References are to the CPLR and to Uniform Rules (designated as "UR").]

EX PARTE MOTIONS (See MOTIONS)

EXPENSES (See COSTS AND FEES)

EXPERT WITNESSES
Disclosure of . . . 3101(d)(1)
Form of expert opinion . . . 4515
Matrimonial actions, testimony of court-
  appointed witness in . . . UR 202.18

EXPRESS TRUSTS
Instrument settling account
  Filing . . . 7705; 7706
  Order or filing . . . 7706
  Recording or filing . . . 7705
Joinder and representation of persons inter-
  ested in trust property . . . 7703
Reference . . . 7704
Representation of persons interested in trust
  property . . . 7703
Special proceedings . . . 7701
Verified account accompanying petition
  . . . 7702

EXTENSIONS OF TIME
Generally . . . 2004
Appeal, for . . . 5514
Appear or plead, to . . . 3012(d)
Excusable delay or default . . . 2005
Plead, to . . . 3211(f)

F

FACSIMILE TRANSMISSION
Defined . . . 2103(f)
Summons and complaint delivery
  Attorney, transmission to
    . . . 2103(b)(5); 2103(b)(7)
  Clerk of court, to . . . 304

FAILURE TO PROSECUTE (See WANT
  OF PROSECUTION)

FALSE IMPRISONMENT
Statute of limitations period for action based
  on, one-year . . . 215(3)

FAMILY COURT PROCEEDINGS
Long-arm jurisdiction . . . 302(b)
Statute of limitations period for enforcement
  of support or maintenance, twenty-year
  . . . 211(e)

FEES (See COSTS AND FEES)

FIDUCIARIES
Award of costs against . . . 8110

FIDUCIARIES—Cont.
Premiums or undertakings by . . . 8006
Surety on undertaking of, discharge of
  . . . 2510
Undertakings
  Fees . . . 8006
  Surety on undertaking of, discharge of
    . . . 2510

FILMS
Disclosure . . . 3101(i)

FORECLOSURE ACTIONS
Settlement conference
  Mandatory . . . 3408
  Uniform rules for supreme court and
    county court . . . UR 202.12–a

FOREIGN CORPORATIONS
Corporations of pleadings . . . 3020(d)(3)
Defined . . . 105(h)
Personal service upon . . . 311(a); 311(b)
Service upon . . . 311(a); 311(b)
Venue . . . 503(c)

FOREIGN COUNTRIES
Definitions . . . 5301
Money judgments of, recognition of (See
  FOREIGN COUNTRY MONEY JUDG-
  MENTS)
Particularity of statements in pleading as to
  law of . . . 3016(e)

**FOREIGN COUNTRY MONEY JUDG-
  MENTS**
Appeal, stay in case of . . . 5306
Applicability of Article 53 . . . 5302
Citation of article . . . 5309
Definitions . . . 5301
Enforcement . . . 5303
Foreign country judgment defined
  . . . 5301(b)
Foreign state defined . . . 5301(a)
Non-recognition, grounds for . . . 5304
Personal jurisdiction . . . 5305
Recognition and enforcement of . . . 5303
Situations not covered by Article 53 provi-
  sions, recognition in . . . 5307
Stay in case of appeal . . . 5306
Uniformity of interpretation . . . 5308

FORFEITURE
Crime, proceeds of (See FORFEITURE OF
  PROCEEDS OF CRIME)
Recovery of (See PENALTY OR FORFEI-
  TURE, RECOVERY OF)

[References are to the CPLR and to Uniform Rules (designated as "UR").]

[References are to the CPLR and to Uniform Rules (designated as "UR").]

[References are to the CPLR and to Uniform Rules (designated as "UR").]

[References are to the CPLR and to Uniform Rules (designated as "UR").]

[References are to the CPLR and to Uniform Rules (designated as "UR").]

[References are to the CPLR and to Uniform Rules (designated as "UR").]

INCOME—Cont.
Sheriff's fixed fees for income
execution—Cont.
    Service upon judgment debtor
     . . . 8011(c)

**INCOMPETENTS AND INCOMPE-
TENCY**
Arbitration and incompetency of party
   . . . 1209; 7512
Conservators and conservatorships (See
   CONSERVATORS AND CONSERVA-
   TORSHIPS)
Costs of, liability of . . . 1205
Default judgment . . . 1203
Deposition, objection to competency of wit-
   ness during . . . 3115(d)
Disposition of proceeds of claim of
   . . . 1206
Guardian ad litem (See GUARDIAN AD
   LITEM)
Patients in facilities, appointments of guard-
   ians for . . . UR 202.54
Personal service upon incompetents
   . . . 309(b)
Personal transaction or communication be-
   tween witness and mentally ill person, ad-
   missibility of . . . 4519
Representation of . . . 1201
Settlement of claim by
    Adverse party, preparation of papers for
     . . . 1208(f)
    Affidavit by representative
     . . . 1208(a)
    Appearance before court . . . 1208(d)
    Attorney's affidavit . . . 1208(b)
    Conflict of interest . . . 1208(e)
    Hospital report . . . 1208(c)
    Medical report . . . 1208(c)
    Notice . . . 1207
    Order of settlement . . . 1207
    Papers required . . . 1208
    Procedure . . . 1208
    Special proceeding . . . 1207

INCONSISTENT ACTIONS OR RELIEF
(See ELECTION OF REMEDIES)

INDEMNIFICATION
Contribution and preservation of right to
   . . . 1404(b)
Prompt payment following settlement, effect
   of . . . 5003–a
Substitution of indemnitors for executing or
   attaching officer . . . 1020

INDEX NUMBER
County clerk's fees . . . 8018
County court, for action commenced in
   . . . 306–a
Supreme court, for action commenced in
   . . . 306–a
Uniform court rules for supreme court and
   county court . . . UR 202.5

INDIAN TRIBES (See NATIVE AMERI-
CANS)

INDIGENT PERSONS (See POOR PER-
SONS)

INDIVIDUAL ASSIGNMENT SYSTEM
Uniform rules for supreme court and county
   court . . . UR 202.3

INFANTS (See CHILDREN)

INJUNCTIONS
Affidavit . . . 6312(a)
Chattel, recovery of unique . . . 7109(a)
Fact, issues of . . . 6312(c)
Forfeiture of proceeds of crime (See FOR-
   FEITURE OF PROCEEDS OF CRIME)
Jurisdiction . . . 6330
Motion papers . . . 6312(a)
Obscene prints and articles . . . 6330
Preliminary injunctions (See PRELIMINARY
   INJUNCTIONS)
Temporary restraining order (See TEMPO-
   RARY RESTRAINING ORDERS)
Undertaking
    Requirements . . . 6312(b)
    Temporary restraining order
     . . . 6312(c)

IN PERSONAM JURISDICTION (See
PERSONAL JURISDICTION)

INSANITY
Statute of limitations extension . . . 208

INSTALLMENT CONTRACTS
Confession of judgment before default on,
   validity of . . . 3201

INSTALLMENT PAYMENTS
Money judgments, enforcement of . . . 5226

INSURANCE
Appeals and stay of enforcement where action defended by insurer . . . 5519(b)
Collateral source payment in, admissibility of
   . . . 4545(a)

[References are to the CPLR and to Uniform Rules (designated as "UR").]

[References are to the CPLR and to Uniform Rules (designated as "UR").]

JOINDER OF PARTIES
Enterprise corruption . . . 1354
Express trust property, persons interested in . . . 7703
Forfeiture of proceeds of crime action . . . 1338(1)
Misjoinder . . . 1003
Necessary joinder
    Generally . . . 1001
    Excusing joinder . . . 1001(b)
    Refusal of party to join . . . 1001(a)
No necessity for . . . 1004
Nonjoinder . . . 1003
Permissive joinder
    Generally . . . 1002
    Defendants . . . 1002(b)
    Plaintiffs . . . 1002(a)
    Separate trials . . . 1002(c)
Temporary receivership . . . 6401(a)
Unnecessary . . . 1004

JOINT LIABILITY
Actions against defendants . . . 1501
Defenses in subsequent action against co-obligor . . . 1502
Judgment . . . 1501
Limited liability of persons jointly liable
    Generally . . . 1601
    Application of Article 16 . . . 1602
    Burden of proof . . . 1603
    Definitions . . . 1600
    Non-economic loss defined . . . 1600
Non-economic loss defined . . . 1600
Proof of payment by joint tortfeasor . . . 4533–b
Provisional remedies in subsequent action against co-obligor . . . 1502
Service of summons . . . 1501
Surety on undertaking, liability of . . . 2511

JUDGES
Administrative judge, relief from judgment or order on application of . . . 5015(c)
County judge
    Disqualified from acting in case, effect on statute of limitations where . . . 9003
    Incapacitated, removal to supreme court where . . . 325(f)
    Motions before . . . 2213
Death, disability or incapacity of judge following verdict or decision; term of court . . . 9002

JUDGES—Cont.
Incapacity of judge
    Removal of action, as grounds for . . . 325(f); 325(g)
    Term of court . . . 9002
Jurors, judge present at examination of . . . 4107
Removal of action based on incapacity of . . . 325(f); 325(g)
Term of court
    County judge disqualified from acting in case, effect of . . . 9003
    Death, disability or incapacity of judge following verdict or decision . . . 9002
Venue for proceeding against . . . 506(b)

JUDGMENT
Accelerated judgment (See ACCELERATED JUDGMENT)
Action upon . . . 5014
Administrative judge, relief from judgment or order on application of . . . 5015(c)
Appeals (See APPEALS)
Arbitration award (See ARBITRATION)
Article 78 proceedings . . . 7806
Breach of contract actions, interest in . . . 5001(a)
Chattel, recovery of (See SEIZURE OF CHATTEL)
Class actions . . . 905
Contempt, enforcement of judgment by
    Generally . . . 5104
    Chattel, recovery of
        Generally . . . 7108
        Unique chattel . . . 7109(b)
    Money judgments . . . 5210
Content of . . . 5011
Correction of . . . 5019
County clerk's certificate and validity and correction of . . . 5019(d)
Death of party
    Entry of judgment after . . . 5016(d)
    Money judgments, enforcement of; death of judgment debtor . . . 5208
Declaratory judgment
    Granting . . . 3001
    Pleadings, demand in . . . 3017(b)
Default judgment (See DEFAULT JUDG-MENT)
Defined . . . 105(k); 5011
Dental, medical or podiatric malpractice actions; periodic payment of judgments (See DENTAL, MEDICAL OR PODIATRIC MALPRACTICE ACTIONS)

[References are to the CPLR and to Uniform Rules (designated as "UR").]

[References are to the CPLR and to Uniform Rules (designated as "UR").]

[References are to the CPLR and to Uniform Rules (designated as "UR").]

[References are to the CPLR and to Uniform Rules (designated as "UR").]

MARSHALS (See SHERIFFS)

MATRIMONIAL ACTIONS
Annulment of marriage based on fraud, three-year statute of limitations period for . . . 214(7)
Automatic orders . . . UR 202.16a
Defined . . . 105(p)
Domestic Relations Law; selected provisions . . . Appendix
Equitable distribution . . . UR 202.16
Expert witness, testimony of court-appointed . . . UR 202.18
Interrogatories . . . 3130
Long-arm jurisdiction . . . 302(b)
Particularity of statements in pleading . . . 3016(c)
Service of summons and papers (See SERVICE OF SUMMONS AND PAPERS)
Summary judgment . . . 3212(e)
Uniform court rules for supreme court and county court
    Generally . . . UR 202.16
    Alimony . . . UR 202.16
    Automatic orders . . . UR 202.16a
    Child support . . . UR 202.16
    Equitable distribution . . . UR 202.16
    Expert witness, testimony of court-appointed . . . UR 202.18
    Forms
        Financial disclosure . . . UR App A
        Proposed judgments in matrimonial actions, form of . . . UR App B
    Maintenance and support . . . UR 202.16; UR App A
    Proposed judgments in matrimonial actions, form of . . . UR 202.50; UR App B

MEDICAL MALPRACTICE ACTIONS (See DENTAL, MEDICAL OR PODIATRIC MALPRACTICE ACTIONS)

MEDICAL RECORDS
Personal injury actions, exchange of medical reports in . . . UR 202.17
Subpoena duces tecum served on municipal corporation or state
    Delivery of records to clerk . . . 2306(b)
    Transcript or reproduction of records . . . 2306(a)
Wrongful death actions, exchange of medical reports in . . . UR 202.17

MENTAL EXAMINATIONS
Disclosure . . . 3121

MENTALLY ILL PERSONS (See INCOMPETENTS AND INCOMPETENCY)

MILEAGE FEES
Sheriff . . . 8012(a); 8012(d)

MILITARY PERSONNEL
Exemption of personal property from enforcement of money judgment . . . 5205(e)
Oath or affirmation administered by officer of armed forces of U.S. . . . 2309(d)

MINORS (See CHILDREN)

MISREPRESENTATION (See FRAUD)

MISTAKES
Correction of . . . 2001
Judgment, validity or correction of . . . 5019
Law, relief against mistake of . . . 3005
Particularity of statements in pleading for action based on . . . 3016(b)
Six-year statute of limitations period for action based on . . . 213(6)
Support enforcement and determination of mistake of fact . . . 5241(e)

MISTRIAL
New trial (See NEW TRIAL)
Uniform rules . . . UR 202.45

MONEY JUDGMENTS, ENFORCEMENT OF (See ENFORCEMENT OF MONEY JUDGMENTS)

MONEY PAID INTO COURT (See PROPERTY PAID INTO COURT)

MORTGAGES
Foreclosure actions, settlement conference in residential
    Mandatory . . . 3408
    Uniform rules for supreme court and county court . . . UR 202.12–a
Redemption of property from, ten-year statute of limitations period for . . . 212(c)
Statute of limitations
    Redemption of property from mortgage, ten-year period for . . . 212(c)
    Six-year period where payment secured by mortgage . . . 213(4)

[References are to the CPLR and to Uniform Rules (designated as "UR").]

N

[References are to the CPLR and to Uniform Rules (designated as "UR").]

NEGLIGENCE ACTIONS—Cont.

Contributory negligence or assumption of risk—Cont.

Damages recoverable upon establishment of . . . 1411

Pleading, burden of . . . 1412

Personal injury actions (See PERSONAL INJURY ACTIONS)

Pleadings (See PLEADINGS)

Statute of limitations for personal injury actions (See STATUTE OF LIMITATIONS)

Wrongful death (See WRONGFUL DEATH)

NEWSPAPERS AND PERIODICALS

Fees for publication . . . 8007

Self-authentication of newspapers and periodicals of general circulation . . . 4532

NEW TRIAL

Advisory jury, new trial motion or grant relief after reference to report or verdict of . . . 4403

Appeals to court of appeals where new trial or hearing granted upon stipulation for judgment absolute . . . 5601(c)

Court of appeals

Disposition upon appeal from order granting new trial or hearing . . . 5615

Stipulation for judgment absolute, new trial or hearing granted upon . . . 5601(c)

During trial motion . . . 4402

Post-trial motion

Jury not required . . . 4404(b)

Jury required . . . 4404(a)

Uniform rules . . . UR 202.45

NEW YORK CITY CIVIL COURT ACT

Text of . . . Appendix

NONPROFIT ORGANIZATIONS

Representation by . . . 1101(e)

NOTE OF ISSUE

Generally . . . 3402

New parties . . . 3402(b)

Placing case on calendar . . . 3402(a)

Uniform rules for supreme court and county court . . . UR 202.21

Want of prosecution . . . 3216

NOTICE

Appeal, of

Generally . . . 5515

Defects in form . . . 5520(c)

NOTICE—Cont.

Appearance by defendant by serving notice of appearance . . . 320(a)

Arbitrate, intention to . . . 7503(c)

Attachment (See ATTACHMENT)

Class action . . . 904

County clerk, fees for notice to . . . 8019(c)

Default judgment . . . 3215(g)

Depositions, notice of taking (See DEPOSITIONS)

Disclosure (See DISCLOSURE)

Enterprise corruption and civil actions notice . . . 1355

Forfeiture of proceeds of crime (See FORFEITURE OF PROCEEDS OF CRIME)

Guardian ad litem, motion for appointment of . . . 1202(b)

Habeas corpus; notice before hearing . . . 7009(a)

Intervention

Constitutionality in issue, notice to Attorney General where . . . 1012(b)

Public retirement benefits in issue, notice to comptroller of New York State where . . . 1012(c)

Judgments

Full faith and credit, foreign judgment entitled to; notice of filing . . . 5403

Money judgments, enforcement of (See ENFORCEMENT OF MONEY JUDGMENTS)

Judicial notice . . . 4511

Lis pendens (See NOTICE OF PENDENCY)

Money judgments, enforcement of (See ENFORCEMENT OF MONEY JUDGMENTS)

Motions (See MOTIONS)

Pendency, of (See NOTICE OF PENDENCY)

Poor person, motion to proceed as . . . 1101(c)

Publication of notice, computation of time for . . . 2402

Referee, trial by . . . 4313

Restraining notice . . . 5222–a

Special proceedings, notice of petition in (See SPECIAL PROCEEDINGS)

Summons with, commencement of action by filing (See SUMMONS)

Taxation of cost

With notice . . . 8402

Without notice . . . 8403

[References are to the CPLR and to Uniform Rules (designated as "UR").]

OSTEOPATHS
Truth of statement, affirmation of . . . 2106

P

PAPERS
Appendices, appellant's . . . 5529
Briefs . . . 5529
Caption . . . 2101(c)
Certification by attorney . . . 2105
Confidentiality of addresses in . . . 2103–a
Copies required . . . 2101(e)
Defects in form . . . 2101(f)
Duces tecum subpoena to produce (See
    SUBPOENAS, subhead: Duces tecum sub-
    poenas)
Electronic means, service by . . . 2101(g)
English language requirement . . . 2101(b)
Filing of . . . 2102
Form of . . . 2101
Indorsement by attorney . . . 2101(d)
Language requirement . . . 2101(b)
Legibility requirement . . . 2101(a)
Quality . . . 2101(a)
Service of (See SERVICE OF SUMMONS
    AND PAPERS)
Size requirements . . . 2101(a); 8019(e)
Stipulations . . . 2104
Truth of statement; affirmation by attorney,
    physician, osteopathy or dentist . . . 2106
Uniform rules for supreme court and county
    court (See UNIFORM RULES FOR SU-
    PREME COURT AND COUNTY
    COURT)
Waiver of defects in form . . . 2101(f)

PARK DISTRICT
Personal service upon . . . 311(a)(8)

**PARTICULARITY OF STATEMENTS IN
PLEADINGS** (See PLEADINGS)

PARTIES TO ACTION
Administrative officers of unified court sys-
    tem, review of determinations by
    . . . 1026
Contribution (See CONTRIBUTION)
Impleader (See IMPLEADER)
Indemnification (See INDEMNIFICATION)
Interpleader (See INTERPLEADER)
Intervention (See INTERVENTION)
Joinder of parties (See JOINDER OF PAR-
    TIES)
Necessary joinder of parties (See JOINDER
    OF PARTIES)

PARTIES TO ACTION—Cont.
Partnerships . . . 1025
Public officers (See PUBLIC OFFICERS)
Review of determinations by administrative
    officers of unified court system . . . 1026
Service upon . . . 2103(c)
Substitution (See SUBSTITUTION OF PAR-
    TIES)
Third parties (See THIRD PARTIES)
Third-party practice (See IMPLEADER)
Unincorporated associations . . . 1025
Unknown parties, proceeding against
    . . . 1024

PARTNERSHIPS
Actions against . . . 1025
Personal service upon . . . 310–a
Venue . . . 503(d)

PENALTIES AND SANCTIONS
Bill of particulars, improper or unduly bur-
    densome . . . 3042(e)
Disclose, failure to . . . 3126
Discrimination against employees and pro-
    spective employees based on wage assign-
    ment or income execution . . . 5252
Forfeiture actions, concealment or disposition
    of property in . . . 1311(9)
Habeas corpus writ, penalty for refusal to
    issue . . . 7003(c)
Recovery of penalty or forfeiture (See PEN-
    ALTY OR FORFEITURE, RECOVERY
    OF)

**PENALTY OR FORFEITURE, RECOV-
    ERY OF**
Aggrieved person, action . . . 7202
Common informer, action by
    Generally . . . 7203
    Collusive recovery, action not barred by
        . . . 7203(c)
    Eligibility . . . 7203(a)
    Service of papers . . . 7203(b)
Good faith reliance on judicial decision de-
    fense . . . 7205
Part of penalty or forfeiture, recovery of
    . . . 7204
Recognizance, forfeiture of . . . 7201(c)
State's action for
    Generally . . . 7201
    Recognizance, forfeiture of
        . . . 7201(c)
    Statutory penalty or forfeiture
        . . . 7201(a)

PENALTY OR FORFEITURE, RECOVERY OF—Cont.
State's action for—Cont.
Treason, forfeiture on conviction for
. . . 7201(b)
Treason, forfeiture on conviction for
. . . 7201(b)

PENDING PROCEEDINGS
CPLR application to . . . 10003

PEREMPTORY CHALLENGES
Procedure . . . 4109

PERIODICALS (See NEWSPAPERS AND
PERIODICALS)

PERIODIC PAYMENT OF JUDGMENTS
(See JUDGMENT)

PERMISSIVE JOINTER OF PARTIES
(See JOINDER OF PARTIES)

PERSONAL INJURY ACTIONS
Bill of particulars . . . 3043(b)
Collateral source payment for injury, admissibility of . . . 4545(c)
Costs upon frivolous claims and counterclaims to recover damages for injury for
. . . 8303–a
Damages, demand for . . . 3017(c)
Diagnostic tests, admissibility of graphic,
numerical, symbolic or pictorial representations of . . . 4532–a
Itemized verdict . . . 4111(e); 4111(f)
Joint tortfeasor, proof of payment by
. . . 4533–b
Medical records, exchange of . . . UR
202.17
Medical tests, admissibility of graphic, numerical, symbolic or pictorial representations of . . . 4532–a
Periodic payment of judgments in (See
JUDGMENT, subhead: Periodic payment
of judgments in personal injury, injury to
property and wrongful death actions)
Pleadings
Damages, demand for . . . 3017(c)
Particularity of statements in
. . . 3016(g)
Public employer, against
Collateral source payment, admissibility
of . . . 4545(b)
Itemized verdict . . . 4111(e)
Statute of limitations (See STATUTE OF
LIMITATIONS)

PERSONAL INJURY ACTIONS—Cont.
Terminally ill plaintiff in
Preliminary conference . . . 3407
Trial preferences for . . . 3403(a)(6)
Wrongful death (See WRONGFUL DEATH)

PERSONAL JURISDICTION
Appearance by defendant, based on (See APPEARANCE BY DEFENDANT)
Foreign country money judgments . . . 5305
Long-arm jurisdiction (See LONG-ARM JURISDICTION)
Non-domiciliaries (See LONG-ARM JURISDICTION)
Service of summons (See SERVICE OF
SUMMONS AND PAPERS)

PERSONAL PROPERTY
Attachment (See ATTACHMENT)
Costs upon frivolous claims and counterclaims to recover damages for injury to
. . . 8303–a
Deposit into court (See PROPERTY PAID
INTO COURT)
Disposition of property in litigation (See
PROPERTY PAID INTO COURT)
Forfeiture actions of proceeds of crime (See
FORFEITURE OF PROCEEDS OF
CRIME)
Joint tortfeasor, proof of payment for injury
to property by . . . 4533–b
Judgment (See ENFORCEMENT OF
MONEY JUDGMENTS; JUDGMENT)
Money judgments, enforcement of (See ENFORCEMENT OF MONEY JUDGMENTS)
Periodic payment of judgments in injury to
(See JUDGMENT, subhead: Periodic payment of judgments in personal injury, injury to property and wrongful death actions)
Seizure of chattel (See SEIZURE OF CHATTEL)
Service of summons and papers without state
where no personal jurisdiction given
. . . 314(2)
Statute of limitations period abbreviated to
one year after notice for action to recovery
. . . 216(b)

PERSONAL SERVICE OF PAPERS (See
SERVICE OF SUMMONS AND PA-
PERS)

PHENOXY HERBICIDES
Statute of limitations period for action based
on personal injury caused by contact or
exposure to, two-year . . . 214–b

PHOTOGRAPHS
Disclosure
    Generally . . . 3101(i)
    Admissions . . . 3123

PHYSICAL EXAMINATIONS
Disclosure . . . 3121

PHYSICIANS
Confidential communications . . . 4504
Medical malpractice actions (See DENTAL,
MEDICAL OR PODIATRIC MALPRAC-
TICE ACTIONS)
Truth of statement, affirmation of . . . 2106

PLEADINGS
Affidavit of verification, form of . . . 3021
Amended pleading
    Generally . . . 3025
    Evidence, to conform to . . . 3025(c)
    Leave, by . . . 3025(b)
    Responses to . . . 3025(d)
    Statute of limitations period, computa-
      tion of . . . 203(f)
    Third-party defendant, plaintiff's com-
      plaint against . . . 1009
    Without leave . . . 3025(a)
Answer (See ANSWER)
Appearance, extension of time to plead or
    . . . 3012(d)
Article 78 proceedings . . . 7804(d)
Bill of particulars and (See BILL OF PAR-
TICULARS)
Commencement of action without (See SIM-
PLIFIED PROCEDURE FOR COURT
DETERMINATION OF DISPUTES)
Complaint
    Amendment of complaint by plaintiff
      . . . 1009
    Dental malpractice actions, accompa-
      nied by certificate of merit in
      . . . 3012–a
    Dismissal . . . 1010
    Impleader (See IMPLEADER)
    Medical malpractice actions, accompa-
      nied by certificate of merit in
      . . . 3012–a

PLEADINGS—Cont.
Complaint—Cont.
    Particularity of statements (See sub-
      head: Particularity of statements)
    Plain and concise statements required
      . . . 3014
    Podiatric malpractice actions, accompa-
      nied by certificate of merit in
      . . . 3012–a
    Separate trial of third-party complaint
      . . . 1010
    Service of
      Generally . . . 3012
      Demand for . . . 3012(b)
      Summons and complaint
        . . . 306–b; 3012
    Special proceedings . . . 402
    Summary judgment motion in lieu of
      . . . 3213
    Summons with, commencement of ac-
      tion by filing (See SUMMONS)
    Third-party practice (See IM-
      PLEADER)
Conditions precedent . . . 3015(a)
Confidentiality of addresses in . . . 2103–a
Construction . . . 3026
Corporate status, particularity of statement as
    to . . . 3015(b)
Corporations
    Domestic corporation, verification by
      . . . 3020(d)(1)
    Gross negligence by certain
      . . . 3016(h)
    Intentional infliction of harm by certain
      . . . 3016(h)
    Particularity of statement in pleading as
      to corporate status . . . 3015(b)
    Verification
      Domestic corporation, by
        . . . 3020(d)(1)
      Foreign corporations
        . . . 3020(d)(3)
      Nonpayment of debt, recovery of
        damages for . . . 3020(b)(2)
Correction of, motion for
    Generally . . . 3024
    Ambiguous pleadings . . . 3024(a)
    Disposition, pleading after . . . 3024(c)
    Prejudicial matter . . . 3024(b)
    Scandalous or prejudicial matter
      . . . 3024(b)
    Time limits . . . 3024(c)
    Vague or ambiguous pleadings
      . . . 3024(a)

[References are to the CPLR and to Uniform Rules (designated as "UR").]

[References are to the CPLR and to Uniform Rules (designated as "UR").]

PREVAILING PARTY, COSTS AWARDED TO (See COSTS AND FEES)

PRIESTS
Confidential communications to priest privileged . . . 4505

PRINTERS
Fees . . . 8007

PRIORITIES
Attachment orders . . . 6226
Depositions . . . 3106(a)
Forfeiture of proceeds of crime and attachment order . . . 1332
Money judgments, enforcement of (See ENFORCEMENT OF MONEY JUDGMENTS)
Trial preferences (See TRIAL PREFERENCES)

PRISONERS
Commencement of action by inmate, reduced filing fees for . . . 1101(f)
Damages awarded to
  Enforcement of money judgment, exemption from . . . 5205(k)
  Notice provisions . . . 5011
Depositions . . . 3106(c)
Escape of, one-year statute of limitations period for action against officer for . . . 215(2)
Fees reduced for inmates commencing actions . . . 1101(f)
Sheriff's fixed fees for handling . . . 8011(j)
Subpoena to produce . . . 2302(b)

PRIVACY RIGHTS
Statute of limitations period for action based on violation of, one-year . . . 215(3)

PRIVILEGED COMMUNICATIONS (See CONFIDENTIAL COMMUNICATIONS)

PRODUCTION OF DOCUMENTS (See DISCLOSURE)

PROFESSIONAL DISCIPLINARY RULES
Selected provisions . . . Appendix

PROOF OF SERVICE (See SERVICE OF SUMMONS AND PAPERS)

PROPERTY
Personal (See PERSONAL PROPERTY)
Real (See REAL PROPERTY)

PROPERTY PAID INTO COURT
Administration of property, cost of . . . 2603
Commissioner of finance of New York City, delivery of money and securities to . . . 2601(b)
County treasurer, delivery of money and securities to . . . 2601(b)
Custodian's liability . . . 2608
Delivery of money and securities to county treasurer or commissioner of finance of New York City . . . 2601(b)
Depositories, duties of . . . 2605
Discharge of party paying money into court . . . 2601(a)
Disposition of property
  Enforcement of order directing . . . 2703
  Procedure . . . 2701
  Sale of property . . . 2702
Gross sum calculation in lieu of income . . . 2604
Order for payment out of court, obtaining . . . 2606
Other than money or securities . . . 2602
Payment of . . . 2607
Referee appointed to sell property, deposit by . . . 2609
Safe deposit company, deposit with . . . 2602
Subsequent control of money or securities paid into court . . . 2601(d)
Title to funds . . . 2601(c)
Warehouse, deposit with . . . 2602

PROSECUTION, WANT OF (See WANT OF PROSECUTION)

PROSECUTORS
Private prosecutor, one-year statute of limitations period for action to enforce penalty or forfeiture given to . . . 215(4)

PROTECTIVE ORDERS
Grant of . . . 3103
Money judgments, enforcement of . . . 5240

PROVISIONAL REMEDIES
Attachment (See ATTACHMENT)
Availability of . . . 6001
Co-obligor, subsequent action against . . . 1502
Forfeiture of proceeds of crime action (See FORFEITURE OF PROCEEDS OF CRIME)
Injunctions (See INJUNCTIONS)

[References are to the CPLR and to Uniform Rules (designated as "UR").]

[References are to the CPLR and to Uniform Rules (designated as "UR").]

[References are to the CPLR and to Uniform Rules (designated as "UR").]

SANCTIONS (See PENALTIES AND SANCTIONS)

SATISFACTION-PIECE (See JUDGMENT)

SCHOOL DISTRICT
Personal service upon . . . 311(a)(7)
Venue . . . 504

SCPA (See SURROGATE'S COURT PROCEDURE ACT (SCPA))

SEALED INSTRUMENT
Six-year statute of limitations period for action based on . . . 213(3)

SEARCHES
County clerk, fees of
    Clerk of court, fees of . . . 8020(g)
    UCC, searches for papers not filed under . . . 8021(d)
Title insurance or abstract company searches as evidence . . . 4523

SECURITIES PAID INTO COURT (See PROPERTY PAID INTO COURT)

SECURITY FOR COSTS (See COSTS AND FEES)

SEIZIN
Statute of limitations period for commencement of action for breach of covenant of . . . 206(c)

SEIZURE OF CHATTEL
Additional parties . . . 7103(d)
Affidavit . . . 7102(d)
Commencement of action for . . . 7101
Contempt, judgment enforceable by
    Generally . . . 7108
    Unique chattel . . . 7109(b)
Disposition of chattel by sheriff . . . 7102(f)
Enforcement of judgment awarding possession of chattel . . . 5102
Impounding chattel . . . 7103(b)
Injunction for unique chattel . . . 7109(a)
Judgment
    Contempt, judgment enforceable by
      Generally . . . 7108
      Unique chattel . . . 7109(b)
    Enforcement of judgment awarding possession of chattel . . . 5102
    Jury's failure to fix sum . . . 7108(c)
Jury's failure to fix sum . . . 7108(c)
Less than all chattels; seizing, reclaiming or returning . . . 7104

SEIZURE OF CHATTEL—Cont.
Location of, testimony by deposition to ascertain . . . 7112
Order of seizure . . . 7102(c)
Perishable property, sale of . . . 7105
Plaintiff, on behalf of
    Generally . . . 7102
    Affidavit . . . 7102(d)
    Disposition of chattel by sheriff . . . 7102(f)
    Order of seizure . . . 7102(c)
    Service of papers . . . 7102(b)
    Undertaking . . . 7102(e)
Reclaiming chattel . . . 7103(a); 7104
Return, sheriff's . . . 7107
Returning chattel . . . 7103(c); 7104
Service of papers . . . 7102(b)
Sheriff's recovery of chattel
    Fees and expenses, payment of sheriff's . . . 7106(a); 8011(e)
    Liability of sheriff . . . 7106(b)
    Powers of sheriff . . . 7110
    Return, sheriff's . . . 7107
Substitution of indemnitors for executing or attaching officer . . . 1020
Temporary restraining order for unique chattel . . . 7109(a)
Testimony by deposition to ascertain location of . . . 7112
Three-year statute of limitations period for recovery of chattel . . . 214(3)
Undertaking . . . 7102(e); 7111
Unique chattel
    Contempt, judgment enforceable by . . . 7109(b)
    Injunction . . . 7109(a)
    Temporary restraining order . . . 7109(a)
Venue for recovery actions . . . 508

SELF-AUTHENTICATION
Newspapers and periodicals of general circulation . . . 4532

SELF-INCRIMINATION
Use of evidence . . . 4501

SEPARATE TRIALS
Joinder of claims and . . . 603
Permissive joinder of parties and . . . 1002(c)
Third-party complaint . . . 1010
Uniform rules for supreme court and county court . . . UR 202.42

[References are to the CPLR and to Uniform Rules (designated as "UR").]

[References are to the CPLR and to Uniform Rules (designated as "UR").]

[References are to the CPLR and to Uniform Rules (designated as "UR").]

SETTLEMENT (See COMPROMISE AND SETTLEMENT)

SEVERANCE
Authority for . . . 603
Costs awarded to prevailing party . . . 8104
Special proceedings, claims in . . . 407
Summary judgment . . . 3212(e)

SEWAGE DISTRICT
Personal service upon . . . 311(a)(8)

SEX OFFENSES
Rape crisis counselor, confidential communications to . . . 4510
Statute of limitations for civil claims arising out of criminal . . . 213–c; 215(8)(b)

SHERIFFS
Additional compensation . . . 8012(c)
Attachment (See ATTACHMENT)
Chattel, seizure of (See SEIZURE OF CHATTEL)
City marshals, limited powers of . . . 105(s–1)
Collection of fees on execution . . . 8014
Copies, fixed fees for . . . 8011(i)
County clerk where sheriff is party or otherwise disqualified . . . 8015
Defined . . . 105(s–1)
Enforcement of judgment (See ENFORCEMENT OF MONEY JUDGMENTS; JUDGMENT)
Fixed fees
   Generally . . . 8011
   Additional compensation . . . 8012(c)
   Attachment order . . . 8011(a)
   Chattel, recovery of . . . 7106(a); 8011(e)
   Collection of fees on execution . . . 8014
   Constables' services . . . 8011(k)
   Copies, making . . . 8011(i)
   County clerk where sheriff is party or otherwise disqualified . . . 8015
   Income execution
      Levy upon default or failure to serve judgment debtor . . . 8011(d)
      Service upon judgment debtor . . . 8011(c)
   Jurors, notification to . . . 8011(k)
   Mileage fees . . . 8012(a); 8012(d)
   Poundage fees . . . 8012(b)
   Prisoners, handling . . . 8011(j)
   Property execution . . . 8011(b)

SHERIFFS—Cont.
Fixed fees—Cont.
   Return of satisfaction . . . 8011(i)
   Sales . . . 8011(g)
   Service of summons, subpoenas and other mandates . . . 8011(h)
   Subpoenas, service of . . . 8011(h)
   Summary proceeding . . . 8011(f)
   Summons, service of . . . 8011(h)
   Undertakings . . . 8011(i)
   View, attending . . . 8011(k)
Income execution, fixed fees for
   Levy upon default or failure to serve judgment debtor . . . 8011(d)
   Service upon judgment debtor . . . 8011(c)
Jurors, notification to; fixed fees . . . 8011(k)
Mileage fees . . . 8012(a); 8012(d)
Poundage fees . . . 8012(b)
Prisoners, handling; fixed fees . . . 8011(j)
Sales, fixed fees for . . . 8011(g)
Service of papers
   Fixed fees
      Generally . . . 8011(h)
      Income execution . . . 8011(c)
   Statute of limitations (See STATUTE OF LIMITATIONS)
Statute of limitations (See STATUTE OF LIMITATIONS)
Summary proceeding, fixed fees in . . . 8011(f)
Undertakings . . . 8011(i)

SIDEWALKS
Notice of defective or dangerous condition of sidewalks to village . . . 9804
Small claims sidewalk assessment review proceedings . . . UR 202.58

SIGNATURES
Attorney, indorsement of papers by . . . 2101(d)
Depositions . . . 3116(a)
Motion, appellate court's signature on order determining . . . 2219(b)
Particularity of statements in pleading as to . . . 3015(d)
Submission of orders, judgments and decrees for: uniform rules for supreme court and county court . . . UR 202.48

[References are to the CPLR and to Uniform Rules (designated as "UR").]

[References are to the CPLR and to Uniform Rules (designated as "UR").]

[References are to the CPLR and to Uniform Rules (designated as "UR").]

[References are to the CPLR and to Uniform Rules (designated as "UR").]

[References are to the CPLR and to Uniform Rules (designated as "UR").]

STATUTE OF LIMITATIONS—Cont.
Personal injury actions—Cont.
    Chemicals—Cont.
        within three years of discovery
           . . . 214–c
        HIV, infusion of blood products result-
          ing in contraction of . . . 214–e
        Phenoxy herbicides, contact with or
          exposure to; two-year period
          . . . 214–b
        Three-year period for . . . 214(5)
        Toxic substances, injury caused by;
          commencement of action within three
          years of discovery . . . 214–c
Personal property, abbreviation of period to
    one year after notice for action to recover
    . . . 216(b)
Phenoxy herbicides, personal injury caused
    by contact or exposure to; two-year period
    . . . 214–b
Podiatric malpractice, two years and six
    months period for . . . 214–a
Privacy right violation, one-year period for
    action based on . . . 215(3)
Private prosecutor, one-year period for action
    to enforce penalty or forfeiture given to
    . . . 215(4)
Property, three-year period for recovery of
    damages for injury to . . . 214(4)
Provisional remedy, order for . . . 203(b)(3)
Public property, state's action where spolia-
    tion or misappropriation of; six-year pe-
    riod . . . 213(5)
Real property action
    Four-year period for action based on
      residential rent overcharge
      . . . 213–a
    Mortgage, redemption of property from;
      ten-year period . . . 212(c)
    Redemption of property from mortgage;
      ten-year period . . . 212(c)
    Rent overcharge, four-year period for
      action based on residential
      . . . 213–a
    Tenant's action against landlord for re-
      taliation, one-year period for
      . . . 215(7)
    Ten-year period
      Letters patent, annulment of
        . . . 212(b)
      Possession necessary to recover
        property . . . 212(a)
      Redemption of property from
        mortgage . . . 212(c)

STATUTE OF LIMITATIONS—Cont.
Real property action—Cont.
    Twenty-year period
      Grantee of state, action by
        . . . 211(d)
        State, action by . . . 211(c)
    Redemption of real property from mortgage;
      ten-year period . . . 212(c)
    Rent overcharge, four-year period for action
      based on residential . . . 213–a
    Residential rent overcharge, four-year period
      for action based on . . . 213–a
    Resident or sojourner of country at war with
      United States or allies; war tolling provi-
      sions . . . 209(c)
    Sealed instrument action, six-year period for
      . . . 213(3)
    Seizin, breach of covenant of . . . 206(c)
    Service, action commenced by . . . 203(b)
    Seven-year period for action by victim of
      criminal offense . . . 213–b
    Sex offenses, civil claims arising out of
      criminal . . . 213–c; 215(8)(b)
    Sheriff
      Delivery of summons to . . . 203(b)(5)
      Three-year period for action against
        sheriff for nonpayment of money
        collected upon execution . . . 214(1)
    Six-year period
      Generally . . . 213
      Bond or note, action on . . . 213(4)
      Contract actions . . . 213(2)
      Corporations action against director,
        officer or stockholder . . . 213(7)
      Fraud, action for . . . 213(8)
      Mistake, action based on . . . 213(6)
      Public property, state's action where
        spoliation or misappropriation of
        . . . 213(5)
      Sealed instrument action . . . 213(3)
    Slander action, one-year period for
      . . . 215(3)
    State, actions by or against
      Public property, state's action where
        spoliation or misappropriation of;
        six-year period . . . 213(5)
      Real property actions, twenty-year pe-
        riod for . . . 211(c)
Stay of commencement of action . . . 204(a)
Summons, claim interposed by filing or ser-
    vice of
    Filing, action commenced by
      . . . 203(c)

[References are to the CPLR and to Uniform Rules (designated as "UR").]

[References are to the CPLR and to Uniform Rules (designated as "UR").]

[References are to the CPLR and to Uniform Rules (designated as "UR").]

SUBPOENAS—Cont.
Hospital records—Cont.
   Transcript or reproduction of
     . . . 2306(a)
Issuance of
   Court, issuance by . . . 2302(b)
   Without court order . . . 2302(a)
Judicial subpoena, disobedience of
   . . . 2308(a)
Library of municipal corporation or state
   . . . 2307
Medical records of department or bureau of
  municipal corporation or state
   Delivery to clerk . . . 2306(b)
   Transcript or reproduction of records
     . . . 2306(a)
Modification, motion for . . . 2304
Money judgments, enforcement of (See EN-
  FORCEMENT OF MONEY JUDG-
  MENTS)
Municipal corporation or state, department or
  bureau of
   Issuance of subpoena . . . 2307
   Library, service upon . . . 2307
   Medical records of
     Delivery to clerk . . . 2306(b)
     Transcript or reproduction of
       records . . . 2306(a)
Non-judicial subpoena, disobedience of
   . . . 2308(b)
Prisoner, to produce . . . 2302(b)
Quash, motion to . . . 2304
Records, production of (See subhead: Duces
  tecum subpoenas)
Scope of . . . 2301
Service of, generally . . . 2303
State or municipal corporation, department or
  bureau of (See subhead: Municipal corpo-
  ration or state, department or bureau of)
Trial subpoenas . . . 2303–a

SUBROGATION
Contribution and preservation of right to
  . . . 1404(b)

SUBSEQUENT PROCEEDINGS
CPLR application to . . . 10003

SUBSTITUTION OF PARTIES
Appeal, presentation of . . . 1021
Committee or conservator . . . 1016
Corporation, dissolution of . . . 1017
Death, upon . . . 1015
Dismissal for failure to substitute . . . 1021
Dissolution of corporation . . . 1017

SUBSTITUTION OF PARTIES—Cont.
Extension of time for taking procedural steps
  . . . 1022
Indemnitors for executing or attaching officer
  . . . 1020
Procedure . . . 1021
Public officers . . . 1019
Receivers, in case of . . . 1017
Transfer of interest, upon . . . 1018

SUMMARY JUDGMENT
Generally . . . 3212
Architects, cases involving licensed
  . . . 3212(i)
Complaint, in lieu of . . . 3213
Dismissal motion treated as motion for
  . . . 3211(c)
Engineers, cases involving licensed
  . . . 3212(i)
Facts unavailable opposing party
  . . . 3212(f)
Grounds for . . . 3212(b)
Immediate trial . . . 3212(c)
Landscape architects, cases involving li-
  censed . . . 3212(i)
Lieu of complaint, in . . . 3213
Limitation of issues of fact for trial
  . . . 3212(g)
Matrimonial action . . . 3212(e)
Partial . . . 3212(e)
Proof requirements . . . 3212(b)
Public petition and participation, standards
  for motion in cases involving
  . . . 3212(h)
Relief to either party . . . 3212(b)
Severance . . . 3212(e)
Time for making motion . . . 3212(a)
Types of actions . . . 3212(a)

SUMMARY PROCEEDINGS
Sheriff's fixed fees . . . 8011(f)

SUMMONS
Amendment . . . 305(c)
Commencement of action without summons
  or continued after service but without
  pleadings (See SIMPLIFIED PROCE-
  DURE FOR COURT DETERMINATION
  OF DISPUTES)
Complaint and, commencement of action by
  filing
   Electronic means
     Attorney, transmission to
       . . . 2103(b)(5); 2103(b)(7)

[References are to the CPLR and to Uniform Rules (designated as "UR").]

[References are to the CPLR and to Uniform Rules (designated as "UR").]

TAXATION—Cont.

Disbursements (See subhead: Costs, disbursements and additional allowances)

Disclosure of appraisals for appropriation or review of tax assessments . . . 3140

Federal tax liens filed pursuant to lien law, county clerk's fees for services rendered in relation to . . . 8021(g)

Small claims tax assessment review proceedings . . . UR 202.58

Venue for proceeding against commissioner of taxation and finance . . . 506(b)

TEMPORARY RESTRAINING ORDERS

Generally . . . 6313(a)

Appellate division, by . . . 5518

Attachment . . . 6210

Chattel, recovery of unique . . . 7109(a)

Damages sustained by reason of, ascertaining . . . 6315

Forfeiture of proceeds of crime action (See FORFEITURE OF PROCEEDS OF CRIME)

Grounds for . . . 6301

Modification of . . . 6314

Service of . . . 6313(b)

Undertaking . . . 6313(c)

Vacation of . . . 6314

TERM OF COURT

Abatement by failure, no . . . 9001

Adjournment, no abatement by . . . 9001

Change of time or place of, no abatement by . . . 9001

County judge disqualified from acting in case, effect on statute of limitations where . . . 9003

Death, disability or incapacity of judge following verdict or decision . . . 9002

TESTIMONY (See WITNESSES)

THIRD PARTIES

Impleader (See IMPLEADER)

Summons

    Contents . . . 305(a)

    Service of . . . 306–b

TIME

Appeals, time for (See APPEALS)

Arbitration . . . 7502(b)

Extension of (See EXTENSIONS OF TIME)

Limitations (See STATUTE OF LIMITATIONS)

TOLLING OF LIMITATIONS PERIOD (See STATUTE OF LIMITATIONS)

TOWNS

Constitutionality in issue, notice to town where . . . 1012(b)

Personal service upon

    Board or commission . . . 312

    Procedure . . . 311(a)(5)

Venue . . . 504

TRANSCRIPTS

Appeals (See APPEALS)

Article 78 proceedings, filing in . . . 7804(e)

Fees for transcripts of records . . . 8001(c)

Medical records of department or bureau of municipal corporation or state, subpoena of . . . 2306(a)

Poor person's right to stenographic transcript . . . 1102(b)

Receipt stub issued with transcript of judgment; uniform rules for supreme court and county court . . . UR 202.47

Referee, trial by . . . 4317(c); 4320(b)

TRANSFER OF INTEREST

Substitution of parties upon . . . 1018

TRANSPORTATION

Carrier garnishee, additional undertaking to

    Attachment . . . 6217

    Forfeiture of proceeds of crime and . . . 1323

Printed tariff or classification subject to commissioner of transportation as evidence . . . 4540(d)

Venue for action involving New York City transit authority . . . 505

TREASON

Forfeiture on conviction for, state's action for recovery of . . . 7201(b)

TRIAL

Advisory jury (See JURY AND JURORS)

Article 78 proceedings transferred to . . . 7804(h)

Calendar practice (See CALENDAR PRACTICE)

Closing statements . . . 4016

Continuances . . . 4402

County clerks as clerks of court, fees for (See CLERK OF COURT, subhead: County clerks as, fees for)

Courthouse, trial at place other than . . . 4013

[References are to the CPLR and to Uniform Rules (designated as "UR").]

[References are to the CPLR and to Uniform Rules (designated as "UR").]

[References are to the CPLR and to Uniform Rules (designated as "UR").]

UNIFORM RULES FOR SUPREME COURT AND COUNTY COURT—Cont.

Special masters, appointment of . . . UR 202.14

Special preferences . . . UR 202.24; UR 202.25

Special proceedings . . . UR 202.9

State Division of Human Rights, judicial review of order of . . . UR 202.57

Submission of papers for trial . . . UR 202.35

Tax assessment review proceedings . . . UR 202.58 to UR 202.60

Terms of court . . . UR 202.2

Title to real property, registration of . . . UR 202.65

Transcript of judgment, issuance of receipt stub with . . . UR 202.47

Trial, submission of papers for . . . UR 202.35

Trust accounting, procedure for . . . UR 202.53

Videotape recording of deposition . . . UR 202.15

Voir dire, conduct of . . . UR 202.33; UR App E

Waiver of compliance with rules . . . UR 202.1

Workers' compensation settlements . . . UR 202.66

Wrongful death actions, exchange of medical reports in . . . UR 202.17

UNINCORPORATED ASSOCIATIONS

Actions against . . . 1025

General Associations Law; selected provisions . . . Appendix

Venue . . . 503(d)

UNIONS

Statute of limitations period for action based on union's breach of duty of fair representation, four-month . . . 217

UNKNOWN PARTIES

Proceeding against . . . 1024

V

VENUE

Arbitration . . . 7502(a)

Article 78 proceedings, filing in . . . 7804(b)

Assignees in action for sum of money . . . 503(e)

VENUE—Cont.

Change of venue

  Generally . . . 511

  Appeal . . . 511(d)

  Demand for, time for . . . 511(a)

  Grounds for . . . 510; 511

  Impartial trial, inability to have . . . 510

  Improper county as grounds . . . 510; 511(b)

  Jury, action or issue triable without . . . 512

  Motion, time for . . . 511(a)

  Order . . . 511(d)

  Stay of proceedings . . . 511(c)

  Subsequent proceedings . . . 511(d)

  Time for motion or demand . . . 511(a)

  Witness, convenience of . . . 510

Chattel, actions to recover . . . 508

Cities, action against . . . 504

Commissioner of education, proceeding against . . . 506(b)

Commissioner of taxation and finance, proceeding against . . . 506(b)

Conflicting venue provisions . . . 502

Conservator, residence of . . . 503(b)

Consumer credit transactions

  Improper venue . . . 513

  Residence, based on . . . 503(f)

Contractual provisions fixing . . . 501

Corporations . . . 503(c)

Counties, action against . . . 504

County designated, in . . . 509

Defined . . . 105(r)

District corporations . . . 504

Executors and administrators, residence of . . . 503(b)

Foreign corporations . . . 503(c)

Forfeiture actions . . . 1311(10)

Guardian, general or testamentary . . . 503(b)

Individually-owned business . . . 503(d)

Judge, proceeding against . . . 506(b)

Jury, action or issue triable without; change of place of trial . . . 512

New York City transit authority . . . 505

Officer or body, proceeding against . . . 506(b)

Partnerships . . . 503(d)

Public authorities, actions involving . . . 505

Real property actions . . . 507

Receivers, residence of . . . 503(b)

VENUE—Cont.
Residence as basis for
> Generally . . . 503(a)
> Assignees in action for sum of money
> > . . . 503(e)
> Committee . . . 503(b)
> Conservator . . . 503(b)
> Consumer credit transactions
> > . . . 503(f)
> Corporations . . . 503(c)
> Executors and administrators
> > . . . 503(b)
> Foreign corporations . . . 503(c)
> Guardian, general or testamentary
> > . . . 503(b)
> Individually-owned business
> > . . . 503(d)
> Partnerships . . . 503(d)
> Receivers . . . 503(b)
> Trustees . . . 503(b)
> Unincorporated association . . . 503(d)

School districts, action against . . . 504
Special proceedings . . . 506
Summons, designation in . . . 305(a)
Tax appeals tribunal, proceeding against
> . . . 506(b)
Towns, action against . . . 504
Trustees, residence of . . . 503(b)
Unincorporated association . . . 503(d)
Venue for proceeding against commissioner
> of education . . . 506(b)
Villages, actions against . . . 504; 9803

VERDICT
Breach of contract actions, interest in
> . . . 5001(a)
Disagreement by jury . . . 4113
Entry of . . . 4112
Entry of judgment upon . . . 5016(b)
General verdict
> Defined . . . 4111(a)
> Interrogatories, accompanied by an-
> > swers to . . . 4111(c)
> Itemized verdict . . . 4111(e); 4111(f)
Interest from . . . 5002
Interest to
> Actions in which recoverable
> > . . . 5001(a)
> Breach of contract actions, interest in
> > . . . 5001(a)
> Computation, dates used for
> > . . . 5001(b); 5001(c)
> Title, possession or enjoyment of prop-
> > erty, act interfering with
> > . . . 5001(a)

VERDICT—Cont.
Itemized verdict
> Malpractice actions . . . 4111(d)
> Personal injury actions . . . 4111(e);
> > 4111(f)
> Public employer, personal injury and
> > wrongful death action against
> > . . . 4111(e)
> Wrongful death actions . . . 4111(e);
> > 4111(f)
Malpractice actions, itemized verdict in
> . . . 4111(d)
Public employer, personal injury and wrong-
> ful death action against; itemized verdict
> . . . 4111(e)
Special verdict
> Generally . . . 4111(b)
> Defined . . . 4111(a)
> Itemized verdict . . . 4111(e); 4111(f)
Title, possession or enjoyment of property,
> act interfering with; interest to verdict
> . . . 5001(a)
Unanimous verdict not required . . . 4113(a)

VERIFICATION OF PLEADINGS (See
PLEADINGS)

VIDEO TAPES
Deposition, recording . . . UR 202.15
Disclosure . . . 3101(i)

VILLAGES
Actions against, generally . . . 9801
Constitutionality in issue, notice to village
> where . . . 1012(b)
Liability of . . . 9802
Notice of defects in certain actions
> . . . 9804
Personal service upon
> Board or commission . . . 312
> Procedure . . . 311(a)(6)
Sidewalks, notice of defective or dangerous
> condition of . . . 9804
Streets and highways, notice of defective or
> dangerous condition of . . . 9804
Venue . . . 504; 9803

VOIR DIRE (See JURY AND JURORS)

VOLUNTARY ASSOCIATIONS
Attorney, appearing by . . . 321(a)

VOLUNTARY DISCONTINUANCE
Generally . . . 3217

[References are to the CPLR and to Uniform Rules (designated as "UR").]

W